# Poetry Criticism

# Guide to Gale Literary Criticism Series

| For criticism on | Consult these Gale series |
|---|---|
| Authors now living or who died after December 31, 1999 | *CONTEMPORARY LITERARY CRITICISM (CLC)* |
| Authors who died between 1900 and 1999 | *TWENTIETH-CENTURY LITERARY CRITICISM (TCLC)* |
| Authors who died between 1800 and 1899 | *NINETEENTH-CENTURY LITERATURE CRITICISM (NCLC)* |
| Authors who died between 1400 and 1799 | *LITERATURE CRITICISM FROM 1400 TO 1800 (LC)*<br><br>*SHAKESPEAREAN CRITICISM (SC)* |
| Authors who died before 1400 | *CLASSICAL AND MEDIEVAL LITERATURE CRITICISM (CMLC)* |
| Authors of books for children and young adults | *CHILDREN'S LITERATURE REVIEW (CLR)* |
| Dramatists | *DRAMA CRITICISM (DC)* |
| Poets | *POETRY CRITICISM (PC)* |
| Short story writers | *SHORT STORY CRITICISM (SSC)* |
| Literary topics and movements | *HARLEM RENAISSANCE: A GALE CRITICAL COMPANION (HR)*<br><br>*THE BEAT GENERATION: A GALE CRITICAL COMPANION (BG)* |
| Asian American writers of the last two hundred years | *ASIAN AMERICAN LITERATURE (AAL)* |
| Black writers of the past two hundred years | *BLACK LITERATURE CRITICISM (BLC)*<br><br>*BLACK LITERATURE CRITICISM SUPPLEMENT (BLCS)* |
| Hispanic writers of the late nineteenth and twentieth centuries | *HISPANIC LITERATURE CRITICISM (HLC)*<br><br>*HISPANIC LITERATURE CRITICISM SUPPLEMENT (HLCS)* |
| Native North American writers and orators of the eighteenth, nineteenth, and twentieth centuries | *NATIVE NORTH AMERICAN LITERATURE (NNAL)* |
| Major authors from the Renaissance to the present | *WORLD LITERATURE CRITICISM, 1500 TO THE PRESENT (WLC)*<br><br>*WORLD LITERATURE CRITICISM SUPPLEMENT (WLCS)* |

ISSN 1052-4851

# Poetry Criticism

*Excerpts from Criticism of the Works of the Most Significant and Widely Studied Poets of World Literature*

## Volume 46

*David Galens*
Project Editor

GALE®

THOMSON

GALE

Detroit • New York • San Diego • San Francisco • Cleveland • New Haven, Conn. • Waterville, Maine • London • Munich

# THOMSON
™
## GALE

**Poetry Criticism, Vol. 46**

**Project Editor**
David Galens

**Editorial**
Jenny Cromie, Kathy D. Darrow, Elisabeth
Gellert, Julie Keppen, Allison Marion, Timothy
J. Sisler, Carol Ullmann

**Research**
Sarah Genik, Tamara C. Nott, Tracie A.
Richardson

**Permissions**
Margaret Chamberlain

**Imaging and Multimedia**
Dean Dauphinais, Lezlie Light, Daniel William
Newell

**Composition and Electronic Capture**
Kathy Sauer

**Manufacturing**
Stacy L. Melson

**LIBRARY OF CONGRESS CATALOG CARD NUMBER 91-118494**

ISBN 0-7876-6344-1
ISSN 1052-4851

Printed in the United States of America
10 9 8 7 6 5 4 3 2 1

# Contents

# Preface

*P*oetry Criticism (PC) presents significant criticism of the world's greatest poets and provides supplementary biographical and bibliographical material to guide the interested reader to a greater understanding of the genre and its creators. Although major poets and literary movements are covered in such Gale Literary Criticism series as *Contemporary Literary Criticism (CLC)*, *Twentieth-Century Literary Criticism (TCLC)*, *Nineteenth-Century Literature Criticism (NCLC)*, *Literature Criticism from 1400 to 1800 (LC)*, and *Classical and Medieval Literature Criticism (CMLC)*, *PC* offers more focused attention on poetry than is possible in the broader, survey-oriented entries on writers in these Gale series. Students, teachers, librarians, and researchers will find that the generous excerpts and supplementary material provided by *PC* supply them with the vital information needed to write a term paper on poetic technique, to examine a poet's most prominent themes, or to lead a poetry discussion group.

## Scope of the Series

*PC* is designed to serve as an introduction to major poets of all eras and nationalities. Since these authors have inspired a great deal of relevant critical material, *PC* is necessarily selective, and the editors have chosen the most important published criticism to aid readers and students in their research. Each author entry presents a historical survey of the critical response to that author's work. The length of an entry is intended to reflect the amount of critical attention the author has received from critics writing in English and from foreign critics in translation. Every attempt has been made to identify and include the most significant essays on each author's work. In order to provide these important critical pieces, the editors sometimes reprint essays that have appeared elsewhere in Gale's Literary Criticism Series. Such duplication, however, never exceeds twenty percent of a *PC* volume.

## Organization of the Book

Each *PC* entry consists of the following elements:

- The **Author Heading** cites the name under which the author most commonly wrote, followed by birth and death dates. Also located here are any name variations under which an author wrote, including transliterated forms for authors whose native languages use nonroman alphabets. If the author wrote consistently under a pseudonym, the pseudonym will be listed in the author heading and the author's actual name given in parenthesis on the first line of the biographical and critical introduction. Uncertain birth or death dates are indicated by question marks. Single-work entries are preceded by the title of the work and its date of publication.

- The **Introduction** contains background information that introduces the reader to the author and the critical debates surrounding his or her work.

- A **Portrait of the Author** is included when available.

- The list of **Principal Works** is ordered chronologically by date of first publication and lists the most important works by the author. The first section comprises poetry collections and book-length poems. The second section gives information on other major works by the author. For foreign authors, the editors have provided original foreign-language publication information and have selected what are considered the best and most complete English-language editions of their works.

- Reprinted **Criticism** is arranged chronologically in each entry to provide a useful perspective on changes in critical evaluation over time. All individual titles of poems and poetry collections by the author featured in the entry are printed in boldface type. The critic's name and the date of composition or publication of the critical work are given at the beginning of each piece of criticism. Unsigned criticism is preceded by the title of the source in which it appeared. Footnotes are reprinted at the end of each essay or excerpt. In the case of excerpted criticism, only those footnotes that pertain to the excerpted texts are included.

- Critical essays are prefaced by brief **Annotations** explicating each piece.

- A complete **Bibliographical Citation** of the original essay or book precedes each piece of criticism.

- An annotated bibliography of **Further Reading** appears at the end of each entry and suggests resources for additional study. In some cases, significant essays for which the editors could not obtain reprint rights are included here. Boxed material following the further reading list provides references to other biographical and critical sources on the author in series published by Gale.

## Cumulative Indexes

A **Cumulative Author Index** lists all of the authors that appear in a wide variety of reference sources published by the Gale Group, including *PC*. A complete list of these sources is found facing the first page of the Author Index. The index also includes birth and death dates and cross references between pseudonyms and actual names.

A **Cumulative Nationality Index** lists all authors featured in *PC* by nationality, followed by the number of the *PC* volume in which their entry appears.

A **Cumulative Title Index** lists in alphabetical order all individual poems, book-length poems, and collection titles contained in the *PC* series. Titles of poetry collections and separately published poems are printed in italics, while titles of individual poems are printed in roman type with quotation marks. Each title is followed by the author's last name and corresponding volume and page numbers where commentary on the work is located. English-language translations of original foreign-language titles are cross-referenced to the foreign titles so that all references to discussion of a work are combined in one listing.

## Citing *Poetry Criticism*

When writing papers, students who quote directly from any volume in the Literary Criticism Series may use the following general format to footnote reprinted criticism. The first example pertains to material drawn from periodicals, the second to material reprinted from books.

Sylvia Kasey Marks, "A Brief Glance at George Eliot's *The Spanish Gypsy*," *Victorian Poetry* 20, no. 2 (Summer 1983), 184-90; reprinted in *Poetry Criticism*, vol. 20, ed. Ellen McGeagh (Detroit: The Gale Group), 128-31.

Linden Peach, "Man, Nature and Wordsworth: American Versions," *British Influence on the Birth of American Literature*, (Macmillan Press Ltd., 1982), 29-57; reprinted in *Poetry Criticism*, vol. 20, ed. Ellen McGeagh (Detroit: The Gale Group), 37-40.

## Suggestions are Welcome

Readers who wish to suggest new features, topics, or authors to appear in future volumes, or who have other suggestions or comments are cordially invited to call, write, or fax the Project Editor:

Project Editor, Literary Criticism Series
The Gale Group
27500 Drake Road
Farmington Hills, MI 48331-3535
1-800-347-4253 (GALE)
Fax: 248-699-8054

# Acknowledgments

The editors wish to thank the copyright holders of the criticism included in this volume and the permissions managers of many book and magazine publishing companies for assisting us in securing reproduction rights. We are also grateful to the staffs of the Detroit Public Library, the Library of Congress, the University of Detroit Mercy Library, Wayne State University Purdy/Kresge Library Complex, and the University of Michigan Libraries for making their resources available to us. Following is a list of the copyright holders who have granted us permission to reproduce material in this volume of *CLC*. Every effort has been made to trace copyright, but if omissions have been made, please let us know.

## COPYRIGHTED MATERIAL IN *PC*, VOLUME 46, WAS REPRODUCED FROM THE FOLLOWING PERIODICALS:

## COPYRIGHTED MATERIAL IN *PC*, VOLUME 46, WAS REPRODUCED FROM THE FOLLOWING BOOKS:

North Carolina, 1986. Copyright © 1986 by The University of North Carolina Press. All rights reserved. Reproduced by permission.—Thieme, John. From *Derek Walcott*. Manchester University Press, 1999. Copyright © 1999 by John Thieme. All rights reserved. Reproduced by permission.—West, David. From "Horace's Poetic Technique in the *Odes*," in *Horace*. Edited by C.D.N. Costa. Routledge and Kegan Paul, 1973. Copyright © by Routledge and Kegan Paul. All rights reserved. Reproduced by permission.—West, David. From *Reading Horace*. Edinburgh University Press, 1967. Copyright © 1967 by David West. All rights reserved. Reproduced by permission.—Wieland, James. From *The Ensphering Mind: History, Myth, and Fictions in the Poetry of Allen Curnow, Nissim Ezekiel, A.D. Hope, A.M. Klien, Christopher Okigbo, and Derek Walcott*. Three Continents, 1998. Copyright © 1998 by Three Continents. All rights reserved. Reproduced by permission.

**PHOTOGRAPHS AND ILLUSTRATIONS APPEARING IN *PC*, VOLUME 46, WERE RECEIVED FROM THE FOLLOWING SOURCES:**

Carducci, Giosue, engraving. The Library of Congress.—Horace, engraving. Getty Images. Reproduced by permission.— Walcott, Derek, photograph. Liaison Agency. Reproduced by permission.

# Literary Criticism Series Advisory Board

The members of the Gale Group Literary Criticism Series Advisory Board—reference librarians and subject specialists from public, academic, and school library systems—represent a cross-section of our customer base and offer a variety of informed perspectives on both the presentation and content of our literature criticism products. Advisory board members assess and define such quality issues as the relevance, currency, and usefulness of the author coverage, critical content, and literary topics included in our series; evaluate the layout, presentation, and general quality of our printed volumes; provide feedback on the criteria used for selecting authors and topics covered in our series; provide suggestions for potential enhancements to our series; identify any gaps in our coverage of authors or literary topics, recommending authors or topics for inclusion; analyze the appropriateness of our content and presentation for various user audiences, such as high school students, undergraduates, graduate students, librarians, and educators; and offer feedback on any proposed changes/ enhancements to our series. We wish to thank the following advisors for their advice throughout the year.

# Giosue Carducci
## 1835-1907

(Also wrote under the pseudonym Enotrio Romano) Italian
poet, essayist, and critic.

## INTRODUCTION

Regarded as the finest Italian poet of the late nineteenth
century, Carducci was also a noted classicist and accomplished writer of essays and criticism. His neo-classical
ideals of reason, action, and nature evinced his strong
reaction against the predominantly romantic and sentimental mode of works written by his Italian contemporaries in
the earlier nineteenth century. Carducci also vehemently
opposed the monarchy and the Catholic Church, believing
them to be responsible for inhibiting progress towards the
unification of Italy. He employed his literary talents to
voice these controversial opinions. In his poetry, Carducci
drew from Italy's rich historical tradition in an attempt to
inspire his countrymen and restore a more heroic age. He
additionally utilized classical Greek and Latin forms and
conventions to impart his pagan ideals, perhaps most suc-
cessfully in his collection *Odi barbare* (1877; *The Barbarian Odes*.) For his exceptional poetry, Carducci was
awarded the Nobel Prize in literature in 1906.

## BIOGRAPHICAL INFORMATION

Born in 1835 in Val di Castello, Tuscany, Carducci
inherited much of his political fervor from his father, a local physician and patriotic believer in the unification of
Italy. The Carducci family moved to Tuscan Maremma
when Giosue was three. During his time there, Carducci
attended the local school and learned Latin and Italian
from his father. He also discovered his love of nature
while exploring the Tuscan countryside, a place he would
allude to frequently in his subsequent poetry. In 1848, the
family was forced to move again, this time to Florence,
when his father's political ties caused their home to be
destroyed. In Florence, Carducci began a formal education
and proved to be an excellent student, which led to his attendance at the prestigious Scuola Normale Superiore in
Pisa. After acquiring his teaching certificate and degree in
Philosophy and Philology (Classics), Carducci began
teaching Rhetoric (Latin Language and Literature) at San
Miniato al Tedesco, a local university near Florence.
Although he managed to get his first volume of poetry
published at his own expense in 1857, he lost his teaching
position due to his continued outspoken political and literary disagreements with the local press. In November of
that same year, his brother Dante committed suicide, an

event that devastated Carducci and received mention in
some of his most poignant poems. His father died less
than a year later, making Carducci the primary financial
supporter of his family. He settled in Florence editing classical texts for literary journals and teaching private lessons. In 1859, he married Elvira Menicucci. A new opportunity presented itself the following year when the
minister of education appointed him the Chair of Literature
at the renowned University of Bologna. He was a popular
teacher, which brought both financial security and the opportunity to write consistently, sometimes under the
pseudonym Enotrio Romano for more controversial works.
After the unification of Italy, Carducci's career flourished,
but his personal life suffered when his mother and his only
son died. In 1871, he turned to another woman for consolation, Carolina Priva, who was a married mother of four
children. Addressing her as Lidia or Lina in his poetry,
Carducci continued the affair for over seven years. Toward
the end of the relationship, Carducci's interest in politics
prompted him to run for and win a seat in Parliament in
1876. Unfortunately, due to a threshold on the number of

teachers permitted, he was unable to serve his term. Carolina died of tuberculosis in 1881, leaving Carducci to lean on a former acquaintance, Dafne Gargiolli, for whom he wrote many poems until she remarried in 1887. A relationship with twenty-one year old Annie Vivanti inspired poems contained in *Rime e ritmi* (1899; *The Lyrics and Rhythms*), his last collection. Illness forced him to stop teaching in 1904. In 1906, three months before his death, Carducci was awarded the Nobel Prize for Literature.

## MAJOR WORKS

Among Carducci's earliest works of verse, the provocatively titled *Inno a Satana* (1865; which may be translated as *Hymn to Satan*) praises the "pagan" principals of reason and rebellion. In the work, Carducci strongly criticized the pope, whom he believed was a major factor in preventing Italian unification. He used classical Greek and Latin metrical and verse forms to support his political views more extensively in *Giambi ed epodi* (1882; which may be translated as *Iambics and Epodes*). In a representative poem from this volume, "Ripresa: Avanti! Avanti!" (first published in 1872), galloping horses represent Carducci and his peers, and reflect the poet's disappointment and anger in seeing that his work has had little effect in stirring a hoped for revolution. This anger is much tempered in his most highly regarded poems, *Odi barbare*, (1877; translated as *Barbarian Odes*) which place contemporary Italian politics within the broadened and valorizing contexts of Roman and Italian history. Carducci's command of meter in conjunction with his ability to descriptively evoke the atmosphere of the Adriatic Sea provides the setting for tragic adventure in "Miramar," a piece from *Barbarian Odes*. In other works, Carducci applied his mastery of classical meter and unrhymed verse to more personal matters, including those he addressed to "Lina." In one of his most notable poems of this type, "Alla stazione in una mattina d'autunno" (which may be translated as "To the Station On an Autumn Morning"), Carducci says one of many farewells to his mistress, in the process revealing some of his most intimate lyrical verse. The *Rime nuove* (1887; *The New Lyrics*) marks a significant departure for Carducci in its use of Italian forms and other modern principles rather than previously preferred Greek and Latin conventions. "Nostalgia", from this collection, again offers vibrant natural imagery, but this time to suggest the idyllic countryside of his carefree youth. Furthermore, his application of contemporary forms and subjects shows Carducci broadening his literary tastes and skills. His final book, *Rime e ritmi*, demonstrates a blend of Italian and classical principles and themes.

## CRITICAL RECEPTION

Critics in the late nineteenth century were initially divided in opinion on Carducci's work. The publication of *Inno a Satana* created adversarial relationships with some. To his contemporaries, the somewhat extreme opinions contained in his works generally elicited strong reactions and exerted a greater influence on critics than the merit of his poetry. After Italian unification, acclaim was virtually unanimous, however, as Carducci became an important voice for his struggling nation. In addition, his affair with Carolina Priva brought a heightened emotional sensibility to his work, which for many made it more accessible and increasingly popular with critics. Opinions of Carducci's last work, *Rime e ritmi,* were harsh, with many criticizing the volume for its lack of progression in ideas or technique. In the twentieth century, Carducci's work began to receive notice outside of Italy, among critics from Northern Europe and the United States, where opinions ranged from acclamation to subdued indifference. Critics have since pondered whether his poetry is meaningful outside of Italy, while others have noted the difficulty in translating his work. Most scholars agree, nevertheless, that Carducci is without equal as the leading figure in Italian poetry during the late nineteenth century.

---

# PRINCIPAL WORKS

## Poetry

*Rime* 1857; revised as *Juvenilia,* 1880
*Inno a Satana* [as Enotrio Romano] 1865
*Levia gravia* 1868; revised, 1881
*Poesie: Decennalia, Levia gravia, Juvenilia* 1871
*Primavere elleniche* 1872
*Nuove poesie* [as Enotrio Romano] 1873
*Odi barbare* [*The Barbarian Odes*] 1877
*Giambi ed epodi* 1882
*Nuove odi barbare* 1882
*Ça ira* 1883
*Rime nuove* [*The New Lyrics*] 1887
*Terze odi barbare* 1889
*Rime e ritmi* [*The Lyrics and Rhythms*] 1899
*Carducci: A Selection of His Poems* 1913
*Political and Satirical Verse* 1942

## Other Major Works

*Studi letterari* (criticism) 1874
*Eterno Femminino Regale* (memoir) 1882
*Discorsi storici e letterari* (criticism) 1899

---

# CRITICISM

### Edinburgh Review (essay date April 1882)

SOURCE: "Modern Italian Poets: Cossa and Carducci." *Edinburgh Review* 155, no. 317 (April 1882): 49-60.

*[The following excerpt highlights examples of Carducci's poetry to emphasize his frank perspective and literary talents.]*

Contemporary Italian literature is comparatively so little known in England that many readers may possibly see in these pages the name of Giosué Carducci for the first time. Yet it can be said without exaggeration that in the general estimation of his countrymen he holds the first place among living Italian poets. Different from Cossa in many qualities of mind and temperament, he differs from him also in the precocious manifestation of his genius. Cossa, as we have seen, was forty years old before he produced his best work; and even his earlier poems were not written in boyhood. Carducci, on the contrary, like many another poet, scribbled verses when a mere child; and of his published poems several date from his seventeenth year. He was born in 1836, in an obscure *borghetto* called Val di Castello, in the province of Pisa, and passed his first years in Tuscany—partly in the Maremma, partly at Montamiata in the province of Siena, and partly in Pisa and Florence. It was not an indifferent circumstance for his future fame that the first accents which his ear caught and his tongue repeated were from the 'well of *Tuscan* undefiled.' Carducci's father was an honourable, industrious, and unlucky person, who migrated from one poor commune to another, filling the hard-worked and ill-paid functions of *medico di condotta*—as we should say, parish doctor. He had a very fair knowledge of the classics and his contribution to young Giosué's education consisted in teaching him Latin. They translated together Phædrus, Sallust, Ovid, Virgil, and Cicero 'De Officiis;' but the lesson was always Latin, and nothing but Latin. For his own pleasure the boy devoured whatsoever other books came in his way. He read Monti's version of the 'Iliad,' Tasso's 'Gerusalemme Liberata,' one or two French histories translated into Italian, a great number of the 'Novellieri,' something of Macchiavelli, something of Guicciardini, and the 'Promessi Sposi' of Manzoni. He himself states that his mother (who seems to have been a woman of unusual intelligence and liberality of mind) taught him to read Alfieri. He had a voracious appetite for books; and, which is not always the case, his digestion was as good as his appetite. Carducci's republican tendencies manifested themselves very early. There are amusing records of how his juvenile oratory delighted the inhabitants of a village in the Tuscan Maremma, and how he expounded to them some of the satirical poems of Giusti, at that time prohibited in Tuscany and circulated surreptitiously. The young democrat, who was about ten years old, made great friends with a little lame village tailor, of the most flaming republican principles. And in the tailor's shop, the lectures on Giusti, with critical exegesis, were held amidst universal applause. Dr. Carducci was politically Liberal, but he halted far behind his son. He admired Manzoni above all writers, inclined to the Romantic school, objected to classicism as being 'no longer suited to the times,' and seems to have held by some shreds of Catholic belief. He felt no sympathy with the fiery diatribes of the lame tailor; and unceremoniously put an end to Master Giosué's political propaganda by shutting him up in his room, and giving him only three books to read: Manzoni's 'Catholic Morality,' Silvio Pellico's 'Duties of Man,' and the 'Life of San Giuseppe Calasanzio,' by a certain Father Tosetti.

Carducci was for some time at the University of Pisa, and there devoted himself chiefly to classical studies. Afterwards in Florence he acquired a profound knowledge of the *trecentisti* and *quattrocentisti* and an enthusiastic admiration for Dante. He continued to study indefatigably, and from time to time published various critical essays, besides sundry poems, and an edition of Politian's works in the vulgar tongue. In September 1860, being then a month or two past twenty-four years of age, Carducci was appointed by Terenzio Mamiani, at that time Minister of Public Instruction, to a professorial chair at the University of Bologna. The appointment was peculiarly honourable to both, for Mamiani was an uncompromising political opponent of the young professor. But he made his selection purely in the interests of literature, and with a superiority to party rancour unfortunately too rare among his countrymen.

No more significant illustration could be found of the statements made at the beginning of this article respecting the tendency of literary thought in Italy towards classic paganism than the history of Carducci's mental growth and progress. We will give his own words on this subject taken from the preface to the third edition of his poems. After speaking of his studies in Florence, when, as he says, he 'coasted the Dead Sea of the Middle Ages,' he thus proceeds:—

> 'At the same time I studied the converse of all this— the revolutionary movement in history and literature. Gradually there manifested itself in my mind, not an innovation, but an explanation, which surprised and comforted me. How content was I with myself (forgive the word!) when I perceived that my obstinate classicism had been a just aversion to the literary and philosophic reaction of 1815; when I was able to justify it by the doctrines and the example of so many illustrious artists and thinkers; when I found that my sins of paganism had been already committed—but in how far more splendid a guise!—by many of the noblest minds and souls in Europe; and that this paganism, this worship of form, was in fact nothing else than the love of glorious nature, from which the *solitary Semitic abstraction* had so long and so ferociously divorced the spirit of man!'

These words give the key to much of that active hostility towards Christianity which marks modern Italian thought. The elevation of asceticism into a virtue, and the segregation of the religious world from the joys, toils, and sorrows of their fellow-men, are peculiarly repugnant to the gregarious and practical Italian temperament. And when, moreover, we consider that certain theories which with us remain in the region of theological or philosophical speculation are in Italy recognised as the watchwords of a political party, the hatred aroused by them becomes more comprehensible.

Carducci's genius is as distinctively lyric as Cossa's is dramatic. He asserts his own personality, and his mind is naturally protestant, and intolerant of traditional authority. Republican and democratic in politics, as an artist he has the most sovereign disdain for the opinion of the majority. And he vehemently stigmatises that tone of mind which leads a writer to follow the caprices of fashion, or the vagaries of public opinion, in his search after popularity. 'Let the poet,' he writes, 'express himself, and his own moral and artistic convictions, as clearly, sincerely and resolutely as he can. The rest does not concern him.' He is here, of course, alluding to lyric poetry, which, as being individual, will, he thinks, resist longer than any other form of poetry the 'invasion of historic realism which now pervades all departments of human thought.' But it will survive only on condition that it continue to be Art. 'If it be reduced to be a more secretion of the sensibility or sensuality of this person or that; if it give way to all the laxity and license which sensibility and sensuality permit themselves—then farewell lyric poetry.' And he quotes Théophile Gautier:—

'Point de contraintes fausses
Mais que pour marcher droit
    Tu chausses
Muse, un cothurne étroit.'

It may be observed in passing that Carducci writes admirable prose. He is the author of a variety of critical essays and studies, which, besides giving evidence of extensive and solid erudition, have the charm of an elegant, clear, and vigorous style.

The collection entitled *Poesie* is divided into three portions which the author calls respectively *Juvenilia, Levia Gravia,* and *Decennalia.* The first extends from 1850 to 1858; the second from 1857 to 1870; the third from 1860 to 1870. It will be seen that the three periods overlap each other. But the author has made the division with regard not only to chronology, but to the growth and development of his artistic convictions. He says: 'In the *Juvenilia* I am the humble shield-bearer of classicism; in the *Levia Gravia,* I keep my first vigil of arms; in the *Decennalia*—after a few somewhat uncertain lance-strokes—I enter on the career of knight-errant at my own sole risk and peril.' It is interesting to observe how the future author of the *Odi Barbare* is foreshadowed even in the earliest of the *Juvenilia.* One piece, addressed to the 'Blessed Diana Giuntini,' venerated in **'Santa Maria a Monte,'** is absolutely a sapphicode in the Horatian manner. And in connexion with this poem the following story is narrated by its author: He was passing the year 1857 between Santa Maria a Monte and San Miniato, in Tuscany, and, being already recognised as a poet, was importuned by the inhabitants to write something for the *festa* of the Blessed Diana, celebrated at Santa Maria a Monte. This Blessed Diana Giuntini is a holy patroness of her native place—'as who should say,' remarks Carducci with his calm paganism, 'a *dea indiges*'—was born in 1187, and died in the odour of sanctity in 1231. The young poet accepted the invitation and produced the ode, which appears to have delighted all

the pious folks of Santa Maria a Monte. It also—which is far more remarkable—imposed on the acuteness of a writer in the 'Unità Cattolica,' who, years afterwards, republished it to prove how Carducci had fallen away from his early faith: adding a characteristic insinuation that the poet was pious when piety was profitable and the Grand Duke reigned over Tuscany, and became impious only when the Revolution was triumphant. The fact is that Carducci, who was at the time deep in the study of Horace and the *trecentisti* (*Frigida pugnabant calidis, humentia siccis*), composed the piece to prove that it was possible to write religious poetry in classic forms. But in truth it is not merely the form which is classical here; it is also the thought. As a specimen of diversification it strikes us as being remarkable for ease and strength. Take the following strophe, which is imitated from Horace's 'Ludit herboso pecus omne campo:'—

'Disciolto il bove mormora un muggito,
Esulta il gregge nell' erboso piano,
E su l' aratro ancor dal solco attrito
    Canta il villano.'

Strongly contrasted with this is the **'Ode to Phœbus Apollo,'** also in the *Juvenilia.* It is a lover's address to the sun to hasten his declining course, and bring the evening, when he is to meet his mistress. And so far the matter is trite enough. But very far from trite is the turn the poem takes towards the end. After a fervid apostrophe to the god, full of enthusiastic Hellenism, a sense of the actual—of that 'historic realism' elsewhere alluded to—of the triumphant advance of scientific thought—comes over the poet's mood like a chill wind, and is expressed in these admirable verses:—

'Il vero inesorabile
Di fredda ombra covrio
Te, larva d' altri secoli,
Nume de' Greci, e mio.
Or dove il cocchio, e l' aurea
Giovanil chioma, e' rai?
*Tu, bruta mole, sfolgori
Di muto fuoco, e stai.*

     . . . . .

Vale, o Titano Apolline,
Re del volubil anno!
Or solitario avanzami
Amore, ultimo inganno.

'Andiam; della mia Delia
Negli atti e nel sorriso
Le Grazie a me si mostrino
Quai le mirò Cefiso
E pèra il grave secolo
Che vita mi spegnea
Che agghiaccia il canto ellenico
Nell' anima febea!'

In the *Levia Gravia* are comprised several sonnets of very great beauty and merit. There are three to Homer, of which the last is the best. After saying that the author returns with the return of each spring to delight in the songs of the divine old man whose temples are crowned with a halo of eternal youth, and invoking him to tell once more of the fair Calypso, of the Daughter of the Sun, of Nausicaa it thus concludes:—

> 'Dimmi. . . . Ah non dir! Di giudici cumei[1]
> Fatta è la terra un tribunale immondo,
> E vili i regi, e brutti son gli dei.
> E se tu ritornassi al nostro mondo,
> Novo Glauco per te non troverei:
> Niun ti darebbe un soldo, o vagabondo!'

Very fine are the last lines of the sonnet to Dante:—

> 'Son chiesa e impero una ruina mesta
> Cui sorvola il tuo canto e a 'l ciel risona:
> Muor Giove, e l' inno del poeta resta.'

Full of delicate freshness is the sonnet to Petrarch where the writer says he would fain erect an altar to the sweet singer of Laura, 'Nella verde caligine de' boschi;' but some of the finest lines of all occur in the sonnet **'To the Sonnet'** (written, as the writer states, before he had seen Wordsworth's on the same subject), wherein he enumerates some of the great poets who have delighted in that form, which he felicitously styles 'Breve ed amplissimo carme.' Alighieri, Petrarch, Camoens, and 'that new Æschylus born on Avon's shore' loved it:—

> 'Te pur vestia degli epici splendori
> Prigion Torquato; *e in aspre note e lente*
> *Ti scolpia quella man che sì potente*
> *Pugnò co' marmi a trarne vita fuori.'*

These lines not only marvellously describe Michelangelo's sonnets, they epitomise Michelangelo's genius.

But of the whole collection of poems, the one which is there placed in the division entitled ***Decennalia*** and which bears the startling inscription, **'A Satana,'** is undoubtedly that which first filled Italy with its author's name—or rather with the pseudonym Enotrio Romano, then assumed by him. It first saw the light in 1865, and was then reviewed at length in a number of the 'Ateneo Italiano.' But on December 8, 1869, the day of the opening of the Œcumenical Council, a Bolognese editor had the courage to reprint it in his newspaper, the *Popolo,* and then it raised a storm of controversy and discussion. There is something inexpressibly comic, from one point of view, in selecting that particular epoch to reproduce an Ode to Satan. And none who are not acquainted with the Italy of to-day can fully comprehend how such a flout at religion and decorum was made and accepted as being a not altogether outrageous and intolerable method of warfare. Of course the humorous side of the matter was not savoured by the champions of the Church. Nor, indeed, we incline to think, was it greatly tasted by their opponents. Both sides set to work with much vehemence to abuse or to eulogise the poem; and one natural result of this was, that everybody read it. For our part we agree, on the whole, with the author, who himself declares that, despite the benevolent judgments of some of his critics, it is 'no great

thing.' But neither is it a poor thing. Poverty is not a characteristic of Carducci under any circumstances. A good deal of ink, and some ingenuity, have been expended on the well-meant endeavour to explain, and excuse, this address to Satan. The truth is that the greater part of the quarrels arising out of it are founded—as how many other literary quarrels have been!—on a logomachy. When Carducci thus apostrophises Satan:—

> 'A te, dell' essere
> Principio immenso,
> Materia e spirito,
> Ragione e senso;

he is naturally not thinking of Martin Luther's devil with horns and hoofs, nor even of Goethe's 'Geist der stets verneint.' What he has in his mind is resumed in the concluding stanzas:—

> 'Salute, o Satana,
> O ribellione,
> O forza vindice
> Della ragione!
>
> 'Sacri a te salgano
> Gl' incensi e i voti!
> Hai vinto *il Geova*
> *De' sacerdoti.'*

Here is the word of the enigma, 'Il Geova de' Sacerdoti:' the Jehovah of the priests! And for 'the Jehovah of the priests' as understood by an Italian, neither deism nor Christianity is responsible. Still it must be distinctly admitted that Carducci is neither a Christian nor, in the ordinary acceptation of the word, a deist. His creed is a sort of philosophic pantheism, *plus* an artistic worship of Hellenism which, fortunately for ourselves and our readers, we are not here called upon to discuss. Of the other poems in the *Decennalia,* several are on political subjects, such as **'Dopo Aspromonte,' 'Per la Rivoluzione di Grecia,' 'Sicilia e la Rivoluzione,' 'To Odoardo Corazzini, killed by the French in the Campaign of Rome, 1867'** (in which occurs the tremendous stanza addressed to the Pope:—

> 'China sul pio mister che si consuma,
>     'China il tuo viso tristo:
> Di sangue, mira, il tuo calice fuma;
>     *E non è quel di Cristo'*),

**'Le Nozze del Mare,' 'Allora e Ora,'** and others. Three or four drinking-songs are scattered through the collection, which, in their form and spirit, are unique in modern Italian literature. They have the spontaneous grace, the *naïve* gaiety, the plastic perfection of a Greek bas-relief around some altar to Bacchus. And the piece entitled **'Carnival,'** supposed to be uttered by 'A Voice from the Palaces,' 'A Voice from the Hovels,' 'A 'Voice from the Garrets,' and 'A Voice from Underground,' is a powerful piece of rhetoric on the well-worn theme of the joys of the rich and the sorrows of the poor. The two last lines seem to us worth quoting, for the sake of the terrible figure which the poet sketches in with a word, and gives as a companion to the 'pallida Mors' of Horace. 'Rejoice,' he says to the great and wealthy, 'triumph and enjoy, ye powerful,' 'ye happy!'

> 'E non sognate il di ch' a l' auree porte
> *Batta la fame,* in compagnia di morte.'

A composition of Carducci's, comparatively little known, is a poem consisting of thirty stanzas, which was written in 1877 and published separately in 1878, entitled **'Il Canto dell' Amore.'** It is, however, no erotic production, but a lyric manifestation of genial, human kindness and good-will towards men, which, *pace* Giosué Carducci, we are accustomed to call Christian charity. It was suggested by the sight of the space in Perugia once occupied by the Papal fortress known as Rocca Paolina, and now planted as a garden for the townspeople. The citizens of Perugia razed the fortress to the ground in the September of 1860. There, where the huge mass darkened the earth with its shadow, 'Or ride amore, ride primavera, Ciancian le donne ed i fanciulli al sol;' and, looking across the Umbrian plain, girdled with aerial outlines of lilac mountains, illumined by the warm rays of an Italian sun, green with a promise of harvest, and dappled with human habitations, the poet feels his soul expand, his heart melt. From every village, and spire, and turret; from hamlets nestling in the dark gorges of the Appenine; from the Tyrrhene acropolis on its fertile hill; from city piazzas glorious with storied art; from vineyard, and lake, and stream, and wood, one canticle arises in a thousand songs, one hymn is sounded in a thousand prayers. And here we shall venture to depart from the original text and offer our readers a translation of the following stanzas:—

> 'Hail, human creatures, weary and oppressed!
>     Nothing is lost, nothing can perish wholly.
> Too long we've hated. Love alone is blessed.
>     Love; for the world is fair, the future holy.

> 'Who shines upon the summits with a face
>     Bright as Aurora's, in the morning ray?
> Once more along these mountains' rosy trace
>     Do meek Madonnas' footsteps deign to stray?

> 'Madonnas such as Perugino saw
>     In the pure sunset of an April sky
> Stretch wide above the Babe, in gentle awe,
>     Adoring arms, with sweet divinity?

> 'No; 'tis another goddess! From her brow
>     Justice and mercy shed effulgent splendour.
> Blessings on him who lives to serve her now!
>     Blessings on him who perished to defend her!

> 'What need I care for priest, or tyrant prince?
>     Sure their old gods are not more old than they.
> I cursed the Pope, 'tis now some ten years since;
>     I almost would make friends with him to-day.

> 'Poor aged man, perhaps his heart assailing
>     A lonely lack of love torments him sore!

> Perhaps he dreams, with fondness unavailing,
>     Of his sea-mirrored city by the shore.

> 'Let me, from out the vatican closed portal,
>     That ancient self-made captive lead; and cry
> "I drink a toast to Liberty immortal
>     Fill up a bumper, Citizen Mastai!"'

There is a certain genial pathos in these last stanzas which is delightful; and the whole poem abounds in exquisite descriptive touches, unsurpassed even among Carducci's many, and singularly vivid, descriptions of nature.

The *Odi Barbare* are an attempt to introduce into modern lyrical poetry several of the ancient metres—'to adapt to the divine foot of the Italian Muse the Alcaic Sapphic and Asclepiadean cothurnus,' as the author says, following Théophile Gautier's metaphor. Carducci calls them 'barbarous,' 'because such they would seem to the ears and the judgment of a Greek or a Roman, although composed in the metrical forms of their lyric poetry; and such, alas! they will sound to only too many Italians, although composed with the harmonies and accents of their own language.' He justifies his attempt by an appeal to the examples of Catallus and Horace who introduced Æolian metres into the Roman literature; to Dante, who enriched Tuscan poetry with Provençal *care rime;* to Chiabrera and Rinuccini who contributed to it several French strophes; and he begs that that which in those great poets and those skilled versifiers was warmly praised, to him may be at least forgiven; and finally, with a haughty humility, he asks pardon for not having despaired of the grand Italian language, and for having believed himself capable of doing in his mother tongue that which so many German poets, from Klopstock downwards, have done in theirs. The Germans, it must be said, have been among the first and most appreciative critics of the *Odi Barbare.* Some of these have had no less distinguished a translator than Mommsen who has somewhere pronounced the judgment that the Italian poet and the Italian language have succeeded in the arduous effort to reproduce the ancient metres attempted except in the Sapphic measure. In this exception, however, we cannot coincide. Other German critics have written at length about Giosué Carducci, of whom none have displayed more sympathetic appreciation, more soundness of culture, and above all, more intimate knowledge of the spirit of Italian literature, than Carl Hildebrand. The *Odi Barbare* also have given occasion to more than one important article from the pens of Italian critics. One of these, by Giuseppe Chiarini, entitled 'I Critici e la Metrica delle Odi Barbare' has been considered one of the most brilliant and erudite treatises of contemporary literature.

But it is not necessary to possess an intimate knowledge of that very intricate subject, ancient lyrical metres, in order to read the *Odi Barbare* any more than a profound study of anatomy is requisite to appreciate a figure by Raphael. Of the thirteen odes, we prefer those entitled respectively, **'Nella Piazza di San Petronio in una Sera d'Inverno,' 'Mors,' 'Alla Stazione in una Mattina** d'Autunno,' and **'Alle Fonti del Clintumno.'** Perhaps the poem called **'Alla Stazione'** displays in a more remarkable degree than any of the others the potency of Carducci's imagination and his absolute mastery of his materials. To write a description of a railway station in the dim dawn of a wet autumn morning, with all the incidents belonging to the departure of a train; to write it in a classic metre, and with classic sobriety of epithet; and so to write it as to produce an impression of the most vivid and uncompromising reality in the mind of the reader, is, it must be admitted, an achievement of no trifling difficulty; yet we believe that few readers will be disposed, after perusing this poem, to deny that Carducci has done this. The impression of reality is obtained, not by heaping one upon another a tedious catalogue of objects or epithets, but by the unerring instinct (let the word pass!) of selection, which belongs to great artists—and to great artists only. For example, this strophe, descriptive of the last moment when the lover, who has come to bid his mistress farewell, standing on the chill dreary platform of the station, all unutterably chill and dreary at that hour and season, hears and sees the final preparation for the departure of the train, is a marvel of concentrated descriptive power:

'E gli sportelli, sbattuti al chiudere,
Paiono oltraggi: scherno par l'ultimo
Appello che rapido suona;
Grossa scroscia su' vetri la pioggia.'

And again, what modern poet has surpassed the following transfiguration of a railway engine? To parallel it we must go to Turner's picture of the 'Fighting Téméraire:'—

'Già il mostro conscio di sua metallica
Anima, sbuffa, crolla, ansa; i fiammei
Occhi sbarra; immane pel buio
Gitta il fischio che sfida lo spazio.'

The same marvellous gift of seizing on what is essential and distinctive in his picture, and rendering it with that force which gives to words the glow of colour and the relief of sculpture, is displayed in the **'Ode to the Clitumnus.'** Who that has ever beheld an Umbrian landscape will not have it conjured up once more in his mind's eye on reading the following verses?

'Pensoso il padre, di caprine pelli
Ravvolto l' anche come i fauni antichi,
Regge il dipinto plaustro e la forza
De' bei giovenchi.

'De' bei giovenchi dal quadrato petto.
Erti sul capo le lunate corna
Dolci ne gli occhi, nivei che il mite
Virgilio amava.

'Oscure intanto fumano le nubi
Su l' apennino: grande, austera verde
Da le montagne digradanti in cerchio
L' Umbria guarda.'

As if to show how many and how varied chords there are to his lyre, the author adds to this collection of *Odi Barbare* a brief poem of extreme delicacy, which he calls

'Farewell,' and which he addresses 'To Rhyme'—Rhyme, 'which glitters, and sparkles, and bubbles up from the very heart of the people!'—Rhyme, which sounds the great name of Roland at Roncesvalles, which rides with the Cid, and soars with Dante to the stars!

'Cura e onor de' padri miei,
Tu mi sei
Come lor sacra e diletta.
Ave, o rima! e dammi un fiore
Per l' amore,
E per l' odio una saetta!'

Hitherto neither the flower nor the dart has been denied to him.

*Note*

1. The allusion is to a story told in a Life of Homer attributed to Herodotus, that the poet offered to the inhabitants of Cumæ to celebrate their city in his songs, on condition of being maintained at the expense of the commune; to whom a grave magistrate gravely answered that the Senate would have enough to do should it undertake to feed every blind singer who wandered about the world. Having landed at Chios, the poet was succoured by Glaucus, a goatherd.

**W. B. Wallace (essay date April 1903)**

SOURCE: Wallace, W. B. "A Tuscan Horace." *Westminster Review* 159, no. 4 (April 1903): 410-14.

[*In the following essay, Wallace finds the spirit of Carducci's writing comparable to that of Latin poet Horace.*]

It is an open secret that Italy, our good friend and faithful ally, can only maintain her present position as a Great Power at the cost of tremendous sacrifices; her history, even in our own days, has been checkered with disasters, if not humiliations; but under all these discouragements the golden shell of poesy has never fallen from her grasp, and the swans of song have never utterly forsaken the banks of her Eridanus. The genius of Greece, the most splendid development of the intellectual potentialities of humanity that the world has yet witnessed, expired with her freedom—an Englishman acknowledged and deplored the fact in the burning strophes of a hymn worthy of an Alcman or a Pindar—but even when the haughty mistress of the notions, who had inherited, appropriated, and assimilated the arts of vanquished Hellas, bowed her own proud neck at last beneath the yoke of the barbarian conquerers, she still cherished deep in her heart the inextinguishable fire of the bardic afflatus; that sacred flame she has tended through subsequent ages of trial and affliction as lovingly and vigilantly as did the Roman Vestals the red spark that shone on the hearth of their goddess. Like the live embers which the careful housewife in the Homeric simile so jealously guards and treasures for the morning's needs, the germ of song which had been dormant, not dead, since the days of Boethius, sprang up into light and glory in the *Divina Commedia* of Dante; and since that period the *aurea catena* of poets has never been broken—the fair Hesperian land has never lacked a priest to stand before the altar of Apollo.

It is, of course, a truism that in every age the *summa* of human intellect is a constant and incapable of indefinite expansion. It follows, as an obvious corollary, that when the best energies of the *fin fleur* of the races are devoted, as they are at present, to vain attempts to scale the inaccessible heights of the real—for this, whether we like to acknowledge the fact or not, is what the quest of science amounts to—the lush meads of poesy and romance must of necessity grow dry and barren for want of cultivation, just as commerce and agriculture suffer in lands where conscription is in vogue. Italy alone, burdened with taxes, handicapped with debt in her struggle for national existence, groaning beneath the weight of her armour, which is no threat to others but an indispensable guarantee of her own safety, constantly menaced as she is by intriguing and restless neighbours—Italy alone, we repeat, seems to form a glorious exception to this melancholy rule. With all her disabilities, all her poverty, she can face Europe to-day, if not as her ruler, still as her teacher, model, and guide—as *facile princeps,* not alone in science, but in the arts as well. She has a Lombroso and a Marconi; she has also a Verdi, a D'Annunzio, and a Carducci.

Giosuè Carducci, whom we have ventured to style a Tuscan Horace, bears a name which is illustrious in the artistic annals of Italy, for the Florentine brothers, Vincenzo and Bartolommeo Carducci, were painters of the seventeenth century, whose claim to be inscribed in the long list of worthies to whom the fair city of St. John has given birth has been recognised by posterity. He first saw the light at Val di Castello in 1837. Educated at Florence, his genius ripened at such an early age that he was actually appointed Professor of Italian Literature in the ancient and distinguished University of Bologna when only three-and-twenty. He had previously started, in 1858, a literary review, the *Poliziano*—named after the celebrated Politian of the fifteenth century—resembling the present *Rivista Politica e Letteraria* and the *Fanfulla*. Since then he has been a prolific writer. His principal works are: **Juvenilia, Levia Gravia,** *Commentaries on Plutarch,* **Giambi ed Epodi, Rime Nuove, Odi Barbare, Nuove Odi Barbare,** and **Terze Odi Barbare.** This last collection includes what are perhaps the most characteristic, noteworthy, and beautiful poems of the great Italian.

Carducci is frankly pagan, and, like Schopenhauer and Leopardi, æsthetically pessimistic. He might well have lived and sung under the sage and elegant Octavianus, that "present Apollo" of poets and prototype of Lorenzo de' Medici, in the Augustan age of Rome; he might have fitly consorted, a kindred soul, with Horace, Propertius, and Ovid. His muse, however, is more robust and virile than that of the two latter poets, and he has far more in com-

mon with the bard of Venusia. Like him he can sing, it is true, of love and wine, of myrtle and roses; but, like him also, he can tune his lyre, inspired by "l'ardente Clio," to loftier themes than the facile charms of a Lalage or a Cinara; he can look forth with the eyes of a seer upon the momentous epopee of the world. Amidst the laughter and ripple of the crystal fount of Bandusia, Horace could hear the expiring wail of the last daughter of the Ptolemies, who chose death rather than the degradation of figuring, as Zenobia did in later days, a captive and discrowned queen, in the pomp of a Roman triumph. The spirit of Carducci, too, arrests its majestic flight for a moment above the "white town" of the Istrian Miramare, ere it follows the course of the "fatal Novara," which bears the doomed Maximilian to Mexico—and death.

The epicurean proprietor of the Sabine farm—*parcus deorum cultor et infrequens*—and the poet-professor of Bologna, must stretch across a wide chasm of nearly two thousand years if they are to join hands; for all that, they have both dreamt the same dream, seen the same vision, and been haunted by the same mysterious triad—love and death and the world. Both are men amongst men, and for both the world is a stage whereon, amidst scenery and accessories of witching, if transitory, beauty, the tragicomedy of love is played out; for both death is the old property-man who at the appointed time extinguishes the lights and takes charge of all the tinsel splendours till they are needed by fresh actors, who assume the *rôles* of generations past and gone with the same gaiety and enthusiasm which distinguished their predecessors.

In the midst of a charming song of the spring, the season of green leaves and reviving hopes, the cheery Roman poet is abruptly subdued by the apparition of the veiled spectre who lurks so incongruously amidst the violets and the daffodils, and breathes the sad confession, "We are dust and shadow"; while the Tuscan, as he muses on Monte Mario, looking down over the Eternal City, where the vast pile of St. Peter's soars into the turquoise air like some giant shepherd keeping watch over his flock, sighs forth:

> "To-morrow we must die, as but yesterday died those whom we loved. Aye, even the brilliant ranks of future generations, who are destined to take up the torch of life which has fallen from our hands, even they must in their turn disappear into the infinite. A day will come when of all the teeming multitudes of the human race but one couple shall survive. Standing amidst the *débris* of the mountains, amidst a dead vegetation, they shall behold with glassy eyes and livid faces the sun as he sets over a boundless field of ice."

Yet again, in a spirit akin to the resignation of Horace when he says "Moriar; mors ultima linea rerum est," Carducci views the "serene image of Death" floating above the banquet, as seen in ancient days by the "divine Plato beneath the planes of Ilissus."

Amongst the **Terze Odi Barbare** are to be found compositions which in lyric splendour are not surpassed by the magnificent poems of the Fourth Book of the Odes of

Horace. There is the same sustained and lofty march of thought, the same dignity and refinement of language, the same richness of allusion and illustration. You feel at once that the writer is not alone a poet *factus ad unguem,* but a scholar as well, thoroughly imbued with classical lore, which he reproduces, not as a slavish imitator, but with an added grace and modern significance which it has acquired in the glowing crucible of his own vivid imagination. His finest effort is perhaps the **"Miramar;"** but separated from this by no great interval are **"Su Monte Mario," "Alessandria,"** and **"Presso l'Urna di Percy Bysshe Shelley."**

**"Miramar"** may be called a song of doom. Its weird majesty, its sombre and terrible imagery, its dire pursuing phantasmagoria of the raving Giovanna, the beheaded Marie Antoinette, the despoiled and murdered Montezuma, the grim Huitzilopotli, and the other vengeful Aztec divinities, remind us of the awful "Binding Hymn" of the Furies in the *Eumenides* of Æschylus. After a brief dream of wedded bliss, by the blue waters of the Adriatic, leaving his peaceful, cherished home and the quiet study, with his favourite pictures of Dante and Goethe, the master-minds who were the guides of his noble life—leaving, too, open and half-read, the chivalrous romance of the ancient Castilian writer, Maximilian, accompanied by his Charlotte, sails forth over the summer seas in the *Novara,* bound for the shores of the New World, there to expiate with his innocent blood the crimes of Spain and his ancestors. There is a distant reminiscence of Horace's

> "victorum nepotes
> Rettulit inferias Jugurthae"

in the conclusion of the poem:

> "E a la grand' alma di Guatimozino
> Regnante sotto il padiglion del sole
> Ti mando inferia, o puro, o forte, o bello
> Massimiliano."

The deep despair of **"Su Monte Mario"** and its no less deep appreciation of the Cyrenaic μονόχρονος ἡδονή, the fugitive *joie de vivre* and the captivating glamour of the transient beauties of Nature, remind us forcibly of Leopardi's famous *Ginestra* and his almost equally striking *Canto Notturno di un pastore errante dell' Asia*

As we turn to the **"Alessandria"** our thoughts insensibly revert to the warning Horatian Sapphics:

> "Pindarum quisquis studet aemulari,
> Iule, ceratis ope Dædalea
> Nititur pennis vitreo daturus
> Nomina ponto."

But Carducci, although he dares to rival the "Theban Eagle," has no cause to dread an Icarian fall. The spirited pæan which is chanted by the Macedonian soldiery as they march by the green papyrus beds of Mareotis and the banks of the mystic Nile is not unworthy of the conquering son of Philip whom it celebrates. A similar strain upon the Hellenic lyre, so ingloriously silent in those days, would as surely have elicited the gratitude and encomiums of Alexander—who was no mean judge of the beautiful—as the living bronze of Lysippus or the glowing canvas of Apelles. And then, the song ended, we can almost fancy we see the golden cuirass of the mighty founder of Alexandria flung down upon the lonely shore where in the after ages was destined to stand and flourish the great emporium of the Orient and the Occident

It is only natural that one who is pre-eminently a poet of *Italia redenta* should "love the name and revere the memory of that divine singer of the virgin brow and the Titan spirit," who was the apostle of the literary aufklärung in England and the writer of the inspired *Prometheus Unbound*—a creation as grand and unique as the Δεσμώτης of the old Athenian. And where shall we find a more glorious tribute paid by genius to genius than Carducci's **"Presso l'Urna di Percy Bysshe Shelley?"** His magic lines transport us with the celerity of an Ariosto to the resplendent Isles of Fancy, floating in distant seas—like Lucian's poetic conception of the νῆσος Μακάρων—where the heroes and the heroines of Classicalism and Romanticism wander side by side in strange but not uncongenial companionship. Siegfried and Achilles, leaning on their spears, roam together along the shores of the resounding ocean. Mary Queen of Scots and Clytemnestra, standing in the moonlight, lave their white hands in the waters; but the waves straightway become incarnadine and recede, as if in horror, from their guilty touch. Here, too, are Œdipus and Lear, Cordelia and Antigone, Helen and Iseult. To Shelley alone of modern bards, wafted hither by Sophocles from the embrace of Thesis, is it given to join the band of the elect in these newer Fortunate Isles.

The words of deepest pathos, addressed to the matchless *Cor Cordium,* with which the poem concludes may be thus paraphased:

> "O heart of hearts! above thy clay-cold urn
> Spring and her fragrant flowerets glow and burn.
>
> O heart of hearts! the sun, thy sire divine,
> Wraps thee in light—poor heart within thy shrine.
>
> Rome's pines, Rome's breezes sing of liberty!
> Where art thou, poet of a world set free?"

***Westminster Review* (essay date July 1905)**

SOURCE: "Giosue Carducci: A Character Sketch." *Westminster Review* 164, no. 1 (July 1905): 53-65.

[*In the following essay, the unsigned critic proposes that Carducci exemplified many of the ideals contained in his poetry, and examines Carducci's influence during his lifetime.*]

Italian modern literature has no greater representative than Giosue Carducci, a true-born poet of lofty ideals, to which he gave such a sublime form as to make him classic in his own times. Occasionally he was very much discussed, not for his literary merits—which were universally admitted as being unsurpassable—but owing to a fanciful interpretation given to his political writings, now by one political party, then by another. But of this we shall have something more to say in the second part of this article, as we desire to give first of all an outline of Carducci's life and character.

Giosue Carducci is now seventy years old, having been born on July 27, 1835, at Castello, near by Pietrasanta, a small Tuscan country place. His father was a doctor, and for the time being held a municipal appointment there. Both his parents were of Florentine extraction, the Carduccis being a well-known and illustrious family of Florence.

Only a few months ago an Italian paper, commenting upon the fact that the town of Volterra had given the name of Carducci to one of its new streets, explained this by making out that Carducci's mother had been born there. That was more than the poet would allow to be said about his beloved mother, and he wired at once, stating, "My mother was born in Florence." Of this Florentine origin he was very proud, and justly so considering how the name of Florence has been for ages associated with Italian literature. In Tuscany he was born and brought up, and his inner self and manly character was formed in Tuscany, and especially in the Maremme. When he was but three years old his father removed from Pietrasanta to Bolgheri, in the province of Pisa, an ancient possession of the historical family of the Counts of the Gherardesca. There our future poet lived until he was fourteen, assimilating much of the weird and almost wild nature of those inhabitants, who are in great numbers charcoal burners, hunters and herdsmen. These eleven years passed in the Maremme have left an indelible mark on the character of our poet, and much of his life and thoughts can be easily explained thereby.

Carducci's father was a Liberal, when to be such in Italy was perilous. He took some part in the Liberal revolutionary movement of 1848; and after the Austrian bayonets restored, for a very short time, the Grand Duke on the Tuscan throne, he had to give up his municipal appointment at Bolgheri, and went with his wife and three children to live in Florence. He placed his children in the schools of the "Fathers" Scolopi. This might seem to be an incongruity, yet not a few Italian patriots sent their children to study there; and, what is more marvellous, in these schools, held and conducted as they were by reactionaries, a great number of true Italian patriots, of liberal and democratic tendencies, have been educated. The only explanation one can find for this is, that there, and there only, was the study of the classics thoroughly taught; and this study was the best one could desire to enlarge the mind of the "alunni" to the higher conception of Italy's future mission. Carducci made a great impression on the "fathers," and left with them a kind remembrance of himself.

Carducci at this time taught his younger brothers much Latin and Italian from the works of Manzoni.

In 1852 Carducci ended his school days, and reached his father at Celle, where he was then again exercising his medical profession. There he continued his literary studies, and, having shown a great vocation for teaching, was sent to a higher grade school at Pisa, where future teachers were trained. There he soon won the admiration of the professors and of his schoolfellows. Before he was twenty he had graduated, and was but twenty-one when, with a splendid essay "On the Provençal Influence on the Lyric Literature of the XIII Century," he won his diploma of professor.

Soon afterwards he was appointed professor at the *Ginnasio* of San Miniato, where, however, he did not remain more than a year. The political and ecclesiastical authorities of St. Miniato did not relish the idea of having amongst their teachers a person whom they could accuse of "liberalism," and even of "hereticism." In fact, when he applied for a "chair" in the Ginnasio of Arezzo, this was the character they gave him, and, of course, his application was rejected. Whilst at San Miniato he composed and published a volume of verses, comprising twenty-five sonnets and twelve poems. This publication caused at Florence a lively discussion, carried out with much passion and little discrimination by both admirers and detractors of the new poet of Italy.

His financial means were very scanty at this time, and barely sufficed to make both ends meet. His abode was a single bedroom; his time was spent in work and studies; his only pastime was meeting some congenial friends, with whom classic authors were read and discussed.

The well-known Florentine publisher, Gaspare Barbera, was then at the outset of his prosperous career, and having decided to publish a small diamond collection of classic works, entrusted to Carducci the writing of the prefaces and notes for the same. The remuneration which he received for this work was then his only means of livelihood. About this time he lost his father. Carducci throughout his life has shown a great love for all the members of his family. From his early days he was more than a brother to his younger brothers, and when his father died he brought his mother and brothers to Florence, changing his single bed-room for a few rooms in the attics of a large house. There he proceeded with his work and study. He chose his wife from amongst the people, marrying in 1859 the daughter of a man of very liberal ideas whom he had known while he was at school, and he took his bride to the upper storey of Via Borgognissanti to share that modest abode with the rest of the family.

He went on writing for Barbera, and occasionally he sent some contributions to a literary sheet called *Il Poliziano*.

In 1860, the National Government having been established in Florence, Carducci was offered a "chair" in the Lyceum of Pistoja. He did not stay there long, he missed Florence and its libraries very much, and accordingly he applied to Signor Terenzio Mamiani, then Minister of the Educational

Department, for a "chair" in Florence. Mamiani answered by offering him a "chair" at the University of Bologna, which Carducci accepted and held until January last, that is to say for about thirty-five years.

Carducci started his professorship at Bologna in January 1861. Very few students were then studying literature at that University; Carducci, however, soon made himself known, and, as the years rolled by, the number of students of literature at "Alma Mater" greatly increased.

At Bologna Carducci continued his very unassuming life, his literary work for Barbera, and his evening literary meetings—this time with other professors of the same University, who were wont to meet in the house of Professor Rocchi, a great Latin scholar—to read and discuss Italian and Latin poetical works.

Carducci always was, and especially so at this period of his life, a very hard worker. He used to write out all his lessons in full before delivering them, and for many years he produced in great numbers Odes, Poems and literary Essays.

Up to 1866 he lived quite outside the political world, which seemed to have no interest whatever for him; but the events of that year had somewhat aggrieved him, and he identified himself with a patriotic committee formed for assisting Garibaldi in his march to Rome, which ended in the defeat of Garibaldi at Mentana. On this occasion Carducci wrote several strophes which were anything but flattering to the authorities; and the Ministry, to punish him for his bold sayings and sweeping condemnation, transferred him from the literary "chair" at Bologna to the Latin "chair" of Naples.

Carducci refused to move from Bologna, because even the Ministry had no right to transfer him to another seat of learning.

Carducci, who knew this fully well, forcibly attacked the Ministry, with the result that he was suspended from teaching, and was charged with having committed acts of rebellion.

Carducci looked upon this thunderstorm with philosophical calm, and whilst waiting for better things from Florence—where the seat of the Italian Government then was—which were not long in coming, he prepared a new edition of his works, in a volume called *Levia Gravia,* in which he collected all his poetical productions, excluding, however, therefrom the political ones. The latter, which have appeared here and there, in Journals and Reviews, were collected together later on in a volume published by Barbera in 1871.

The year 1870—most eventful for Italy—was for Carducci a year of great domestic sorrows. In that year he lost both his mother and his only son, then three years old; the joy of his life and the hope of his future. He gave peace to his

troubled mind and afflicted soul in working out some of his best poetical compositions, amongst them **"Idillio Maremmano," "On the Field of Marengo,"** and **"The Ox,"** which he published in a volume called *Nuove Poesie.* He included in it also a translation from Heine and Platen.

In 1872, as he was finishing this last-mentioned work, his youngest daughter was born, whom he christened "Liberty."

In 1870 the publisher Zanicchelli transferred his printing-office and book-store from Modena to Bologna, on a place near by where, in the eighteenth century, there was the library of Lelio Della Volpe, the meeting-place of literary men and students. Signor Zanicchelli's place soon became the rendezvous of the intellectuals. Carducci used to go there occasionally in search of books, and in a somewhat short period of time a very strong and mutual friendship was aroused between the poet and the publisher, the latter becoming in due course of time Carducci's own publisher. The first of Carducci's works published by Zanicchelli was an essay on *The Parentage of Giovanni Boccaccio,* written in 1874, and in 1875 Zanicchelli published a second edition of *Nuove Poesie.*

By this time Carducci's name and reputation was thoroughly established; he was acclaimed throughout the land as Italy's great poet. This judgment was fully confirmed and universally accepted after he published—in 1877—his famous *Odi Barbare.*

Above everything else, Carducci is a very conscientious writer. In 1875 he undertook to write the *Life of Ariosto.* With this intent he spent some time in Ferrara and Scandiano, where Ariosto was born and passed his early days; then a doubt crossed his mind whether he had at his disposal sufficient time to do full justice to his subject, and he most reluctantly decided not to carry out his work, notwithstanding that it was very dear to him.

During the General Elections of 1876, Carducci for the first and only time aspired to Parliament. He was duly elected by the constituency to whom he appealed, but he could not enter Parliament because, according to Italian law, only a certain number of teaching professors are allowed to be members of Parliament. When a greater number of professors is elected a ballot is taken, and Carducci's name was amongst those rejected.

One may say that blind fortune was then very kind to Carducci, inasmuch as he was not cut out for a political life as it is understood in the Chamber of Deputies. He, however, easily consoled himself for his parliamentary failure, and in October, at Perugia, he began his masterpiece, **"The Song of Love."**

In 1878, King Humbert and Queen Margherita paid a visit to Bologna. Carducci had but lately refused the highest honour in the power of the Italian Government to bestow, to wit, the Cross of Savoy for Civil Merit. This refusal was misconstrued by the political parties, and Carducci took this opportunity to show that he did not mean to be disrespectful to the Sovereign; he declined the honour simply on account of certain ceremonies in connection with the investiture of the same. He nevertheless went with the other professors to pay his homage to the Sovereigns, and Queen Margherita left on him an everlasting and deep impression, which he reproduced and immortalised in his *Eterno Femminino Regale*. Never was a crowned lady more fittingly praised by a great poet, and one can add that no other royal personality better deserved to be praised than Queen Margherita, who is a great worshipper of the Muses, and an admirer of their most faithful interpreters.

This work was eminently a political one, and the next work of the same kind was an ode Carducci wrote on the occasion of the hanging of William Oberdank by the Austrians. Carducci's patriotic sympathy with the Italian provinces subjected to Austria and Carducci's hatred for the latter have been emphasised in many of his works, and were even more so on this one, as Oberdank's fate deeply moved all Italy.

Strange to say, although Rome is foremost in Carducci's mind, he only visited Rome for the first time in 1874, on which occasion he only stayed a few days. He returned in 1876 for a longer stay, and since 1881—when he was appointed a member of the Educational Board—he visited Rome frequently and made special studies there. In the meantime, Carducci was appointed a member also of a Royal Commission for Historical Studies, of which in due course he became firstly the secretary and then the chairman.

In 1884 a very flattering offer was made by the Government to Carducci, the acceptance of which would have implied the abandonment of Bologna for Rome. Carducci was encouraged to accept that offer, but he refused it because, though he loved Rome very much, he loved Bologna better, where he felt at home, and where he had many friends and no masters.

In 1885 nature warned Carducci that at his age it was no longer wise to strain his nerves with much brain-work without physical exercise or proper rest. It was a terrible warning, which for a short time caused grave fears amongst his friends. Fortunately, Carducci recovered in a comparatively short space of time, and since then he has passed some months every year on the Alps.

In 1887 he was tempted to go to Rome by another offer which seemed to appeal to Carducci's most sensitive chord. The Government had created for him a special "chair" for the study of Dante, and offered it to him; he refused it because the rules were not to his liking, and that chair up to the present time is still waiting for its first occupant.

In 1888, on the occasion of the eighth centenary of the opening of the Bologna University, Carducci wrote an essay on "Learning at Bologna," which he read before a most exceptionally erudite assembly, at which the Sovereigns of Italy and the representatives of all the Universities of the world were present.

Carducci also took an active part in the municipal administration of Bologna; he was elected Town Councillor for the first time in 1869. Twenty years after, on the occasion of a General Municipal Election, Carducci's name came out at the top of the poll, which clearly shows in what high estimation our poet was held by his adopted town.

In 1890 the King nominated him a member of the Senate. This appointment was proposed to the King by the late Signor Crispi, a great admirer of Carducci, who, in his turn, admired Crispi very much.

Carducci, in his writings and speeches, held Crispi in great estimation, because he shared Crispi's political conception that it was useless to have created a United Italy if she was not to be mistress of her own destiny, or if her policy had to be guided by allies, and if she was compelled to beg for friendships granted to her only with a humiliating and protecting air. Carducci's affection for Crispi remained unshaken by the hostile demonstration he was subject to in his own University in 1891, and by the strong charges brought against Crispi by his foes in 1895 and 1896.

In February 1895 there was at Bologna a most interesting demonstration of general sympathy and admiration for Carducci on the occasion of his jubilee. From every part of Italy Carducci's pupils—now themselves already well-known professors—flocked to Bologna. Italian Universities and Corporations appointed special delegates to represent them. This demonstration ended with a most characteristic act on the part of Count Pier Desiderio Pasolini, who, having made a wreath of laurel grown on Dante's tomb at Ravenna, he crowned our poet with it.

In July, 1899, he was commissioned by the well-known publisher, Rapi, of Città di Castello, to write a preface to a new edition of Muratori's *Rerum Italicorum Scriptores*. There was to be only a few pages, but Carducci loved the subject so much that he wrote instead a fair-sized volume; but, whilst thus occupied, nature gave him another similar warning to that which it gave him in 1885. He had to rest for awhile, after which he resumed and finished the preface in question.

About this time Carducci expressed some apprehension concerning the future of his library after he had gone. Queen Margherita having heard of this, offered to pay a handsome sum for it, which offer was accepted, the library meanwhile to remain with the poet so long as he lived.

As we said at the outset, Carducci will soon be seventy years old, but he has very much aged these last few years, and, if anything, he looks older than he actually is. He does not walk easily but rather lamely, and the pen which he wielded for over fifty years and for long consecutive periods now lies almost inactive. He can now only write short things, but his mind is quite awake and as bright as ever. He passes most of his mornings with his beloved works and books, making notes with a pencil and looking after the new edition of his works begun in 1901, and of which fifteen volumes have been already published, and five more volumes are now wanting to complete the series.

As soon as it became publicly known that Carducci early in 1905 would have retired from his professorship, there was an universal demonstration of sympathy, and letters, telegrams and addresses were forwarded to the poet.

Amongst the telegrams which he received early in January there was one from King Victor Emmanuel; and the aged poet, in thanking his Majesty for his kind wishes, concluded as follows: "Your kindness to me I have always reciprocated, and will always reciprocate with sincere affection and faith."

"Carmen non dat panem" is a well-known saying, and therefore there could be no wonder that Carducci at the end of his long and honourable career should have found himself not quite well provided for in his old age.

The Italian Parliament however, faithfully echoing the national feeling, voted him an annuity of 12,000 lire, as the nation's gift to its great poet, apart from the pension due to him for his long services as professor. The Italian people expected—not altogether without reason—that the Swedish Academy would have conferred upon him (Carducci) Noebel's Prize for Literature and Poetry, and openly and feelingly spoke of this their disappointment, which, we have reason to think, will not last longer than a year.

Passing now to the second part of our article dealing with Carducci's influence on his own times, we must, for brevity's sake, forego any criticisms on his poetical works.

Much, even too much, has been said upon this matter in 1877, soon after the appearance of the first *Odi Barbare,* in which Carducci, following the example given a century before by Klopstock, and in his own times by Tennyson and Ellis, revived the ancient classic metres.

Undoubtedly form has an essential part in poetry, but by itself it does not create the grandeur of a poetical work which is substantially constituted by ideas and conceptions.

The *Odi Barbare* appeared as a striking new poetical creation, vigorous and modern, not because they were written in alcaic strophes, but because they were truly virile as opposed to a high-sounding but empty and effete poetry, as was for many years written by several Italian poets. These Odes at once fascinated and conquered the most intellectual section of the Italian public, because they were fully inspired by heroic sentiments, which seemed to have been banished by modern poets, although without it, it appears almost impossible to conceive true poetry.

Before writing these Odes Carducci had written, besides the *Rime,* published in 1857, and the *Levia Gravia,* published in 1868, *Iambics and Epods* and *Nuove Poesie.* The latter fully represented the then state of mind of our poet,—very much discontented with the political situation of Italy, which was not then such as he wished it to be. In these *Odi Barbare* all political indignation and apprehension were banished, and pure art manifested itself in all its splendour. The appearance of these Odes marked for Italian poetry the end of one artistic period and the opening of a new one, much greater, and in which Carducci for some time remained a gigantic and solitary figure, and gave forth, clearly and even rudely, the truth that was in him and as he felt it. Then, gradually, his poetical works became better understood, and the knowledge of the same more generally spread.

Carducci's telling influence was exercised on Italian literature not only as a poet, but also as a prose-writer and critic. Unsurpassable master of the Italian language, he knows how to adapt to modern exigency the beauties of the thirteenth century, and to free it from the shackles of the pedants against whom, in his younger days, he has fought many a battle.

Carducci undoubtedly is the strongest, the most forcible, and at the same time the sweetest prose-writer Italy has had for a very long time. He can with great ease be witty or invective, sarcastic or deeply serious; he can use with equal force either calm reasoning or fierce indignation, attaining, when needed, the acme of literary loftiness both in style and thoughts. With extraordinary simplicity, free from any rhetorical phrases, he knows how to move and touch the most sensible chord of human nature. He is a speaker of no mean order, though generally the words do not come to his lips so fluently as the ideas spring from his fertile brain; but occasionally, when fully inspired with his subject, he appears as one of the greatest orators Italy has ever had. As an instance, at the time of the death of Giuseppe Garibaldi, and on the occasion of the opening of the new Presidential Palace of the little Republic of San Marino, he delivered his orations so perfectly and eloquently that one must go to the classic times of Greece and Rome to find the like of them.

Upon the literature and culture of his own times Carducci has also exercised his great influence as a scholar, as a critic, and as a student of historical science. As a scholar he taught with great care and conscientiousness.

Though when he went to Bologna he found only four or five students entered for his class, this number increased soon after, and in a few years it reached and even exceeded the hundred. From his school a goodly number of professors, critics and literary men sprang who are now doing a great deal of good work throughout the land, not only by enlightening the literary world with a new light and power, but also outside it, by leading noble intellects towards neglected art. Amongst Carducci's "alunni" there are the following professors: Giovanni Pascoli, Giovanni Ferrari,

Guido Mazzoni and Severino Ferrari, all worthy disciples of so great a teacher. The first-mentioned professor was by the whole nation indicated as Carducci's probable successor, and early in June Giovanni Pascoli was duly chosen and appointed to that University chair.

Carducci is a keen and conscientious critic. All his criticism is founded in deep and careful study. He has deeply read and studied Italian and foreign literature, both modern and classic, Latin and Greek, reading also English, German and French authors in their own language. He translated Platen's lyrics and some of Heine's poems. For Shakespeare he has a great admiration, and he once wrote how he had read *Richard III.* and the *Death of Julius Cæsar* on the Alps amid the deafening noise of a roaring torrent.

With Signor Alessandro d'Ancona and Signor Adolfo Bartoli, Carducci has renewed in Italy historical criticism as applied to Belles Lettres, and he became the centre and mainspring of a new form of criticism.

Carducci's geniality and versatility are fully manifested in his investigations of art in every age, from the origin of the Provençal and Italian lyrics up to Parini, Manzoni and Gabrielle Rossetti. His wide knowledge and culture, the acumen and keenness of his mind, his profound erudition and his exquisite taste, have made of him a powerful critic of great modernity and merit. In a poetry with which he became inspired during a visit he paid to the tomb of Percy Bysshe Shelley, he showed in its fulness the mighty power of his analytic and, at the same time, synthetic criticism.

In the study of history he has shown a great love and devotion since his early school days. These historical studies have formed so to say, the substratum of his vast culture and learning. He read into history with a searching and open mind, and no doubt this has served to give our poet his most admirable uprightness of character and judgment.

Professor Chiarini, Carducci's intimate friend and biographer, has written that our poet, even outside poetry, has not been the man of his times, but rather a severe, and occasionally a pitiless judge and censor of the same. His severity and sternness greatly influenced the writings and thoughts of his contemporaries. Occasionally in the past he has been very much hated by a small and noisy party for his alleged political changes, but now a better and juster judgment is passed on him, even in connection with his political manifestations, as the present generation of Italians are more able to compare the same with the political events of Italy from 1865 to 1870, during which period Carducci identified himself with the most advanced parties. Rome was the magic word that moved and ruled the minds and hearts of Italian patriots. Every patriotic aspiration had for its aims the liberation of Rome from the Papal yoke. Any act of the Government which did not fully correspond to this national aspiration was fiercely denounced; and Carducci, who in 1860 had greeted King Victor Emmanuel II as the Liberator of Italy, in the years 1865-1870

sided with the Republicans. But when, in due time, the King of Italy marched to Rome and freed the Eternal City once and for ever from the rule of the Popes, Carducci's Republicanism, like that of many other great Italian patriots, came to its natural and logical death. And when, in 1876, King Victor Emmanuel summoned to power the leaders of the Liberal party, Carducci came forward, as we have said, as a Liberal Parliamentary candidate.

It so happened that in the sixties the Republican party claimed him as their own, and, accordingly, he was loved by them and despised by the opposite party. In the eighties the Monarchical party had much reason to be pleased with him, and they openly showed their satisfaction and admiration, whilst the Republicans cried out that he had gone over to the "enemy." He was very much misunderstood by both. Carducci never was of this or that party, though some of his writings might have occasionally favoured one or the other political tendency; but he was throughout his long and glorious life a patriot in the truest meaning of the expression, both in his severe rebukes and his warm praises. His political ideas and principles—as shown in all his poems and writings—have been consistent. At times he wrote, it is true, most feelingly against this or that measure or policy, against this or that Ministry, but always keeping foremost the ideals of an Italy free, great, strong, and a guide to less fortunate nations in the paths of liberal national government. Never a word did he utter against the supreme ruler of the country. For King Humbert he cherished a strong affection, and when he was murdered he sent a most touching telegram to the bereaved Queen Margherita. The devotion of the poet to the Queen, and the Queen's admiration for the poet, are of very long standing, dating from the first year of the late King Humbert's reign.

Carducci himself, in pages which will accompany his name into posterity, has most brilliantly, and with great sincerity, fully described that striking period of his eventful life, putting forth most convincing reasons in explanation of his political evolution. Yet these were not accepted by the younger section of the Republican party—then rather strong in Bologna and the neighbouring provinces—and our poet in his own seat of learning was subject to hostile demonstrations. Once he was fiercely attacked by a mob of students, and was left by the University authorities to defend himself as best he could. He faced the music in a manly way. Lamps were smashed, the chair torn to pieces amidst a great uproar. The mob were shouting, "Down with Carducci!" "Down with the author of the poetry to the Queen!" "Down with the admirer of Crispi!" Carducci stood wonderfully calm, and addressing that adverse assembly, said: "It is useless for you to shout down with me, as nature has placed me on a lofty stage." He waited patiently until the hostile demonstration had exhausted itself. The students one by one left the hall, and when the last one had turned on his heels, Carducci also left. As he was entering a cab to return home, one student, personally known to Carducci, tried to strike him on the head with a big key. He was prevented from carrying out his design by a policeman, who arrested him. Brought before the magistrate, Carducci's assailant was condemned to a fine; he would have been more severely dealt with had not Carducci, in his great generosity and magnanimity declared that he had not noticed anything.

This disgraceful demonstration was universally condemned, the students themselves felt ashamed of it, and on the morrow they tried to justify their actions by saying that their demonstrations were not against the poet and the literary man, but they merely wished to hoot and hiss the "Deserter of the Flag." Any excuse is better than none, but we are afraid that this one was very poor indeed inasmuch as Carducci has had but one Flag, "the country's flag"; but one programme, the country's greatness and welfare. All his writings clearly show this. With them he did not aim at writing books to be handed over to a publisher to make money, but he composed them to teach others how to love the country, art, and beauty; how to fight against injustice, oppression, and vulgarity, and whereby to prepare worthier citizens to the nation. This is now recognised by every one, and Carducci in leaving his "chair," which he so much honoured, saw, as it were, all the nation prostrate before his greatness, and the partisan demonstrations of many years ago fall into insignificance at the sight of the universal apotheosis of last January.

In Carducci we find a most striking harmony between the man and the poet, the lofty ideals of the latter not being omitted in the former, but rather the actions of the man seem to integrate and complete the thoughts of the poet. His whole life has been a continual tribute of love and duty to the country, to the family and to the school, upholding at all hazards truth and uprightness.

No one could be more democratic than he in the simplicity of private life and in the aversion for any form of prejudices and conventionalities; and, *vice versa,* no one could be more aristocratic than he in the appreciation of beautiful, great, strong and generous actions and things. His good and bad qualities are derived from the same source; his shortcomings are not the result of any weak point in his character, but they are due to the great exuberance of his passion and love. With the same abundance of feeling he loves what is beautiful, noble, and great; he hates what is ugly, ignoble, and low. Mankind has not a greater lover than he; any reform tending to improve social conditions, or to bring about a better understanding between man and man, and between nation and nation has always commanded and obtained his influential support. Italian Socialism has utterly misunderstood him: perhaps the loftiness of his ideal was much above its reach, especially so when he preached that: "A nation's ideal must have as its standing ground a gradual levelling up of the lower classes, and an ordained development of its economical resources, accompanied by all the political and social safeguards as suggested by Italian national traditions."

A poet's influence on his own times greatly depends upon his personal character. Carducci for some time enjoyed a reputation which he did not deserve, namely, of being a

wild person, almost unapproachable, full of hatred for everything he disliked; while, as a matter of fact, he is loving-kindness itself, and ready to forgive injuries he received and to forget them; and on more than one occasion he has utterly humiliated with his kindness some of his detractors—who had received at his hands courteous help and assistance—instead of crushing them with the strong rebuke which they fully desérved. Much more could be said upon this feature of the character of our poet, and from the several volumes written on Carducci it would be very easy to cull many instances of Carducci's love for his foes and adversaries, and narrate striking examples of democratic love expressed with aristocratic grace and nobility; but we have to close our paper.

Carducci's career as a poet and teacher is ended, sooner, perhaps, than his faithful admirers had foreseen. As a critic some more work is expected from him. As a citizen he will no doubt continue, in his old age and well-deserved rest, to honour the nation he belongs to and which he loved so much, and to be to others a living model of honesty, goodness, and virtue.

In concluding, we venture to express the hope that these few pages, in which we have striven to condense many things gathered from the poet himself and from some of his intimate friends, may serve to give the English public a just and truthful appreciation of the poet and of the man in whom Italy, art, and literature are equally exalted and honoured.

### *Living Age* (essay date 16 March 1907)

SOURCE: "Giosuè Carducci." *Living Age* 34, no. 3271 (16 March 1907): 698-700.

[*The following essay pays tribute to Carducci shortly after his death.*]

In Carducci rather than in any other Italian modern Italy seems to be summed up and expressed; he is the father as it were of the new generation, and his work in his art, like theirs in politics, is a struggle first for liberty and then for unity; his praise is that he achieved both and restored Poetry to Italy.

Born in 1836 in Valdicastello, near Pietrasanta, in the very garden of Tuscany, he came of an old family that had given a Gonfaloniere to Florence but was poor, his father being a doctor in the Pisan Maremma, that desert where for centuries nothing has broken the silence. There, in the midst of that marvellous and tragic country, the young Giosuè grew up, turning in the long evenings with his father his first pages of Virgil, of Horace, of Dante, of Tasso, the poets of his land: and wandering amid all that mysterious desolation he would shout the hexameters of Homer to the mountains and the sea dreaming of Ulysses, of Brutus, of the Gracchi, of Scipio Africanus who flung back Hannibal and saved Rome. Thus the classics early came to be for him no mere school books, but the very expression of life. His father, however, was not his only teacher, for it was his mother who taught him to love Alfieri when even a second-hand book seems to have been hard to come by and Chiarini tells us that when he got Ugo Foscolo's work he made her kneel and kiss it.

His father, an ardent Italian in the days when to be an Italian was to be anti-clerical, doubtless brought him up to hate the Church, and as a punishment made him learn Manzoni's "Morale Cattolica" by heart; but when he was thirteen the family went to Florence and Carducci was sent to the friars to the Scuole Pie. They certainly treated the classics less as poetry than as school books, and after the freedom of his life in Maremma it is not surprising if his dislike of the priests was aggravated by the discipline of school. In 1853 he was sent to the Normal School of Pisa, of which he speaks so bitterly: "Here you will find a chattering professor who will merely tire you with his dates, copied from all sorts of books, then he will tell you with a grand air, without any explanation or reasoning, things which children of the second elementary school know, things hashed and rehashed by all the academicians in all academies of all time. Thus you will pass three years in studying Latin literature and lose your days in learning mere dates. As for Greek, you will have two professors who know Greek and pass their time in heated and angry arguments on the value of an aorist. . . ." Later he went to the Ginnasio di S. Miniato al Tedesco in Val d'Arno. His father was doctor at Pian Castagnaio when the cholera epidemic broke out, and we find the young Carducci giving up his literary work, for already he was a poet, to nurse the sick. Then he went to Florence, really to earn his living by teaching and by writing, living in a tiny attic, and it was here that the news of his brother's death reached him, and no long time after of his father's, which left him with his mother, his young brother, his cousin and future wife entirely dependent on him, for there were but two lire left in the house after the funeral. "How we lived I can't now tell," he writes later, "but the impression remains that one can exist on next to nothing." It was in 1857 that he published his first book of verses **Rime,** and out of it, though it can have brought him but little money and less outside fame, sprang the society Gli Amici Pedanti. Carducci at this time certainly hated Romanticism; it was as much a political hatred as a literary, for Romanticism as he understood it was foreign, "an irreverence" as he said, "to our classical writers": only the wise Nencioni seems to have dissented. It was the work of the Renaissance that he sought to continue, and to make this clearer the journal of Gli Pedanti was called "Il Poliziano." Meanwhile in 1859, though he could not volunteer to serve either with Garibaldi or in the army—and this he speaks of as the second of his great trials in life—he addressed Vittorio Emmanuele in a magnificent ode, for at that time he seems to have looked to him as the saviour of Italy, while he heard the battle cries of Milan, of Brescia, of Venice, and the rattle of the Austrian rifles in Piazza della Signoria.

Italy was really free and united at last, when in 1861, just after the death of Cavour, Mamiani appointed Carducci to the chair of Literature in the University of Bologna. His advent there was a sort of challenge: his lectures were crowded, he was known for his vigorous eloquence, his satire and his rationalism. Just before this began to appear those editions and texts of the classics that are even to-day the best we have, the poetry of Lorenzo Magnifico, of Alfieri, Giusti and the rest, edited with the rarest scholarship and learning, founding a tradition that was under his direction to bear such splendid fruit later in the work of Casini, Straccali and others.

He hated, as we know, all priests, and at last, in 1865, he published at Pistoja, under the name of Enotrio Romano, the famous **"Inno a Satana,"** written in 1863, in which, like our own Milton, but without his splendor or self-deception, he took the supreme rebel for his hero. That poem has been more than overpraised; it has been used to support every stupidity of which the Liberal cause is capable. It is his punishment that of all his verses it is the best known, while the beautiful lines **"Presso l' urna di Shelley"** and **"Alle fonti del Clitumno"** are for the most part ignored; and indeed the least pleasing spectacle in his life is concerned with this hymn. He had married in 1866, and in 1870 his mother died, only just before his adored child at the age of three years. "He was beautiful," says Carducci simply, "and a real miracle for his age, he used to recite 'Salute O Satana o ribellione' in his clear voice, striking the table with his little hand and stamping the floor." It is difficult to forgive Carducci for that.

It is in 1877 that the first *Odi Barbari*—Barbari because they would have been so to Greeks and Romans—were published. With this new rhythm, rhyme became useless and Carducci gladly rejected it not without bidding it good-bye. Here at last he has returned to his first love, that pagan sentiment and antique form which with him was altogether sincere and natural. He was content that the form which he loved should limit, as form always and rightly must do, his imagination while lending him in an ode like that to Eugenio Napoleone, as has been well said, something of the largeness of Sophocles. But in the second *Odi Barbari* something personal has already come into his work and in the third he knows that "the poetry of our time is no longer an element of national life nor a need of society . . . it is an individual expression." Thus his work was completed; he had expressed himself at last. We are not concerned with his political career, nor to tell the manifold stories of his integrity, vigor and splendid common-sense. For him Queen Margherita imitated Cosimo di Medici, buying Carducci's library as Cosimo bought Niccoli's. He is dead, his verse remains and will remain the glory of his awakened and immortal country. In thinking of this man, inevitably involved in hatred as well as love, it is with gladness one remembers those last verses, written just ten years ago:

> Ave Maria! Quando su l' aure corre l' umil saluto, i piccioli mortali scovrono il capo curvano la fronte
>
> Dante ed Aroldo.

and, who knows, Carducci too. the third among the poets of Italy.

**J. Slingsby Roberts (essay date April 1908)**

SOURCE: Roberts, J. Slingsby. "Giosue Carducci." *Quarterly Review* 208, no. 415 (April 1908): 293-321.

[*In the following essay, Roberts analyzes the accessibility of Carducci's work, particularly to non-Italians.*]

There are certain writers whose privilege it seems to give to the contemporary genius of their country an adequate expression in literature. They neither follow public opinion nor lead it, for their minds are so constituted that they are almost certain to find themselves in accord with their countrymen. Tennyson is an instance in England, and in France Victor Hugo. Tennyson united the gifts of an incomparable literary artist with the convictions of an average Englishman under Queen Victoria. In boyhood he rang the church bells to celebrate the first Reform Act, and he lived long enough to become an ardent Imperialist. Victor Hugo, even while he denounced the *bourgeois*, was never really out of touch with the French middle class. Brought up as a Catholic and Legitimist, he lived to be a zealous champion of republicanism and free thought. In less tangible matters also than religious and political opinion, in that general outlook on life in which differences and likenesses elude classification, these men were inwardly at one with their fellow-citizens. The very moderation of Tennyson is national; so is the vehemence of Victor Hugo. Such authors may be regarded from two main standpoints—firstly, as literary artists, a quality that can be properly estimated only by men whose language is theirs; secondly, as interpreters of their age, an aspect which tends to become the most prominent to historians and foreigners. Italy has recently lost a man of this representative type in Giosue Carducci, who was born in 1836, and died in 1907.

Yet, while fully representing the Italian genius in many ways, Carducci was almost free from that quality in it which tends more than any other to repel the taste of northerners, the quality which the Italians themselves praise under the name of *morbidezza*. From the time of the Catholic revival, and even earlier, this melting mood seems to cling about the atmosphere of Italy. Already traceable in the later artists of the Renaissance, in Correggio, in Luini, in Andrea del Sarto, it becomes unbearably cloying in the devotional paintings of the Bolognese school, and in the insipid pastorals of Marini. When the Romantic movement revitalised the literature of Europe an unwholesome tinge of self-pity tainted its Italian exponents. Absent from the fiery Alfieri, it appears strongly both in Manzoni and in Leopardi. The great Italian novelist of reaction lacked the manliness of Walter Scott; and the virtue of 'I Promessi Sposi' is pathetic resignation, not the strong self-reliance of Henry Morton or Jeanie Deans. Great poet as he was, Leopardi was not untouched by the national malady. Scepticism in the Italian Shelley took a shape quite as unhealthy as piety in Manzoni. The title of one of his poems, 'Amore e Morte,' might well describe the whole work of his later years, when ill-health and political embit-

terment had deepened his inborn pessimism. Indeed Goethe's well-known saying, that classic art is healthy art, romantic art is sickly art, is perhaps truer of Italian literature than of any other. For in Italy the Romantic movement failed to permeate, as in Germany and France, the inmost being of the nation. It found neither, as in Germany, a fallow soil unencumbered by classical tradition, nor, as in France, a national consciousness palpitating with mighty cataclysms and achievements, with the upheaval of the Revolution and the epic campaigns of the First Empire. Being the outcome of foreign influences, it only affected isolated men of letters, as Carducci himself contended in an interesting essay on the 'Renewal of the National Literature.'

Like Matthew Arnold, Carducci was a historian and teacher of literature as well as a poet; and this didactic side of his career has an important bearing on his poetry. His appreciations and studies have the twofold interest that always belongs to those of a creative artist; we read them as much for the light they reflect on the critic as for that which they throw on the subject of his criticism. As is natural in an Italian, the touchstone of his literary sympathies and insight is best found in his apprehension of Dante. On the one hand, as a southerner and a poet, he was in touch with aspects of Dante's mind which have perplexed Teutonic professors. To him there is no contradiction between the ethereal platonism of the 'Vita Nuova' and the fiery purgation on the threshold of the Earthly Paradise; for, to the more analytic, as well as more impulsive, southern temperament, the juxtaposition of one love purely of the intellect with many loves wholly of the senses scarcely offers a problem. On the other hand, when he says that the object of Dante's love is not the living woman, Beatrice Portinari, but an idea, surely the modern critic is severing the two elements, human and divine, actual and ideal, which it was the genius of the medieval poet to unite. Of course, like every one endowed with a feeling for literary art, Carducci, a literary artist to the backbone, admired the manner of Dante, the *dolce stil nuovo*, which reinaugurated literature in Europe after its eclipse in the dark ages; in Dante's subject-matter what aroused his enthusiasm was the love for Italy rather than the love for Beatrice. With what was allegorical, mystical, distinctively medieval, in Dante he is never in emotional, as distinct from intellectual, contact. When he repeats, more than once, that Dante should be regarded, not so much as the poet of Florence, but rather as the supreme exponent of the mind of medieval Christendom, we feel that he speaks from the brain, not from the heart. His inmost soul was with Dante, the Italian patriot; it was not with Dante, the cosmopolitan mystic.

This partial, not to say unsound, view of Dante was largely determined by Carducci's attitude to the political and religious controversies of his own day. From the outset he was an extreme partisan in both. He grew up during the prolonged struggle for Italian unity and freedom, at a time when political feeling, exasperated by alternations of armed revolt and savage repression, rose to a height almost inconceivable by those accustomed, as we are, to purely civil and parliamentary differences. Moreover, it has been the misfortune of modern Italy that political and religious parties became inextricably interwoven. The head of the national worship was also the ally of the nation's foreign foes; and hostility to alien and despotic rule came to involve hostility to the Catholic Church, almost to Christianity itself, for Italians of all parties have always tended to look on religion rather as an institution than as a personal influence.

Carducci was thoroughly Italian in his blend of anti-clerical with republican enthusiasm; and it is no wonder that a political and religious bias so marked as his should have somewhat warped his literary and artistic judgment. Most men have the defects of their qualities; and with Carducci an exquisite sense of what was ancient and pagan was balanced by a certain insensibility to what was medieval and Christian. This insensibility sometimes led him to odd critical pronouncements. For example, he calls Petrarch's eighth *canzone* the finest hymn ever addressed by a Catholic to the Virgin. Had he forgotten Villon's immortal *ballade*—in his wide reading he must have come across it—or did he deliberately postpone its throbbing directness to the semi-pagan artistry of Petrarch? He was out of touch, not only with devotional poetry, but with other features of medieval literature tainted, in his eyes, by Catholic and feudal associations. His treatment of chivalry was never satisfactory; and allegory so repelled him that he could see no merit in that charming allegorical poet, Guillaume de Lorris. This aversion from the medieval spirit in its own day naturally applied far more strongly to its attempted revival in modern times. The Gothic proclivities of the leading Romantics aroused in his mind a violent dislike to the whole school.

Accordingly, his earliest volume of poems, *Juvenilia,* opens with a repudiation of the Romantic movement in all its phases, Catholic and Satanic—a beginning that certainly suggests the student rather than the poet—though categoric avowals of literary faith are less repugnant to the spirit of Italian poetry than to that of ours. The trend of the Latin mind to classification and analysis asserts itself in literature as elsewhere. Poetry with the Latin nations is more gregarious, more a product of schools and fraternities, less of isolated inspiration, than with us. Quite genuine French and Italian poets often set out to advocate and exemplify definite poetic theories. Still the formality of the repudiation betrays the professor, just as its motives betray the partisan. They are political rather than strictly literary.

Romanticism is transalpine in origin and essentially anti-national. Tuscan by birth, Carducci will seek sounder traditions, the classic Roman poets and the Florentines of the fourteenth century. From the first there can be no doubt which of these two influences is to be really vital with him. When he writes sonnets in Petrarch's manner on Petrarch's subjects of love and exile, we feel that he is thinking of Petrarch, not of the lady to whom they are ad-

dressed; exquisite in dreamy music, they are far too imitative to convince. So soon as he expresses genuine feeling the only influence is that of the ancients, as in the sonnets on the death of his elder brother. One of these especially unites perfect sincerity with literary reminiscence, and reaches the famous valediction of Catullus by a path as direct and natural, though wholly diverse. The Horatian Odes that follow, though, from their subjects, without this tragic intensity, all have the same genuine ring, whether the poet is upbraiding his degenerate countrymen or celebrating the genialities of friendship and wine. In his **'Canto di Primavera'** a sensuous joy at the return of pleasant weather blends quite naturally with a more complex wistfulness in presence of the year's renewal. It is Horace indeed still, but Horace in his most modern mood, the Horace of that 'inhorruit veris adventus,' the modernity in which shocked the scholarly instincts of Bentley. The breezes of the old Horatian spring seem interfused with the more languorous airs of Botticelli.

Of these early Odes, none, strange as it may seem, is more truly Horatian in spirit than that addressed to 'La beata Diana Giuntini, venerata in Santa Maria a Monte.' Carducci appeals to the saint by that which, after all, can alone make supernatural being real to us—her kinship to ourselves. She lived, it is true, in the age of faith.

> 'Quando pie voglie e be' costumi onesti
> Erano in pregio e cortesia fioriva
> Le tósche terre, qui l' uman traesti
> Tuo giorno, o diva.'

Yet, though a *diva* (is it saint or goddess?) now, her day was human, and she had human, not to say feminine, weaknesses to overcome.

> 'E ti fûr vanto gli amorosi affanni,
> Onde nutristi a Dio la nova etate,
> E fredda e sola ne l'ardor de gli anni
> Virginitate:
>
> Pur risplendeva oltre il mortal costume
> La dia bellezza nel sereno viso,
> E dolce ardea di giovinezza il lume
> Nel tuo sorriso.
>
> Te in luce aperta qui l' eteree menti
> Consolâr prima di letizia arcana,
> Poi te beata salutâr le genti,
> Alma Diana.
>
> Onde a te, dotta de l' uman dolore,
> Il nostro canto e prece d' inni ascende,
> E, pieno l'anno, di votivo onore
> L' ara ti splende.'

When pious wishes and good honest customs were rightly valued and courtesy blossomed in the Tuscan lands, here didst thou spend thy human day, O holy one. Thou didst turn to glory the yearnings of love, whence thou didst foster Godward the spring of thy years, and thy maidenhood was cold and lonely in the heyday of youth. Yet, beyond mortal wont, a godlike beauty shone in thy tranquil visage, and the light of youth glowed soft in thy smile. Here in the light of day the empyrean spirits first consoled thee with mystic gladness, then the nations hailed thee as blessed, gentle Diana. Wherefore to thee, taught by human sorrow, arise our praises and our prayers in hymns, and, when the year is full, thine altar is decked with votive honour.

The poet then beseeches this patroness of the hamlet to rain blessings on the fields and homesteads of her worshippers, and, be it added, to help them to practise the more homely virtues. The whole ode renders to perfection the holiday religion of Italy, the decorated altars and shrines, the processions of flower-laden children. At the end we are left wondering whether this tutelary *diva,* who smiles from her cloudless heaven, is really a saint or only a heathen goddess after all. Viewed thus, indeed, the worship of local saints in Italy is little more than a continuation of the old anthropomorphic cults. For anything distinctively Christian about her, the 'alma Diana' might almost be her maiden namesake of the 'Carmen Sæculare.'

Such thorough interpenetration of ancient with modern feeling is in strong contrast with most northern imitations of Roman literature. We do not here speak of felicitous Latinisms of phrase, for we all remember many such in Milton and Tennyson, but of elaborate efforts to recapture the Roman outlook. Whenever these efforts aspire beyond mere *vers de société,* the outcome is almost always a lifeless literary exercise, such as the mythological poems of Leconte de Lisle or of Théodore de Banville. This is not true of the Italians to anything like the same degree. The Renaissance itself with them was, after all, the reawakening of a culture largely indigenous; and humanism was more able to bear its weight of learning like a flower, because the flower was of native, not exotic, growth. So with more recent imitation of the ancient classics, especially the Roman. The northerner is imitating a literature produced in a foreign climate by a civilisation which even the French have imperfectly assimilated; when the Italian imitates Latin poetry he is merely treading in the footsteps of his own forefathers. The landscape of the Latin poets is his own Italian landscape. The vines and olives that gladdened the heart of Horace still clothe the Umbrian and Sabine hills, the sunshine still glows that ripened them in Horace's day. The Roman glories too are his. The strife with Hannibal is his own repulse of a foreign invader; and the names of the great consuls stir patriotic as well as literary memories. Hence no violent mental transposition was needed for Carducci to place himself at the Horatian standpoint. Horace's mood of genial enjoyment, crossed by flashes of patriotic pride, came to him unsought.

In the main, Carducci's poetic gift was strong enough to absorb his classical and his historical learning and convert them to its own use; it had a harder task with his political and religious partisanship, a task indeed that it sometimes failed to accomplish. For politics are even more conspicuous in his poetry than in his criticism. Already, in one of his early sonnets, he announces that he will devote himself

to rekindling patriotic ardour in his countrymen; and in his later career he became the unofficial laureate of the Risorgimento—a position that has probably contributed more than any other cause to restrict his reputation abroad and also to enhance it, for the time being, in his own country. Everywhere verses on national topics make a wider immediate appeal than those of more intimate inspiration; and in Italy Carducci, by giving them prominence, only carried forward a national tradition which dates from the Romans. For the Romans, less meditative and less imaginative than the Greeks, brought into public life almost all the emotional intensity of which they were capable. Virgil's line about the elder Brutus, 'Vincit amor patrie laudumque immensa cupido,' might be the watchword of the whole Roman people. From Ennius to Claudian, nearly every Roman poet wrote on public topics, and often wrote his best on them. Horace is at his happiest when celebrating Roman glory; Ovid is patriotic in the 'Fasti'; even the tender Propertius is fired by the tidings of Actium. The greatest of Latin poems has nothing greater than Æneas' vision of the mighty Romans sweeping past him toward the upper world, and the address to the genius of Rome that follows. Patriotism is again conspicuous in the later poetry of Italy. The first and greatest poet in her modern tongue was also a statesman; and a passionate love of Florence burns in the 'Divine Comedy.' The exiled Petrarch felt keenly the woes of his native land, and became the friend and upholder of Rienzi. In more recent times there is as much patriotic as dramatic fervour in the eloquence of Alfieri. Even the decadent Leopardi was at his finest in the 'Canzone all' Italia' and the 'Monumento di Dante'; the best known verses of the romantic Manzoni, 'Il Cinque Maggio,' were written on the death of Napoleon. The Roman tradition in this respect, as in others, extended to French poetry also. Victor Hugo was seldom more poetic than in 'Les deux Îles' or 'Le Chasseur Noir.'

There is a wide gulf here between the literature of the Latin races and that of the Teutonic, especially our own. In the nineteenth century, at least, the genius of English poetry has been mainly lyrical and personal, not public or rhetorical. Our poets have either held aloof from public questions, like Keats, or been at their worst when referring to them, like Shelley. So far as the the poet's interest has been with the world and not absorbed in his own soul, his concern has been with individuals, not with generalities. When Browning and Rossetti wrote on this very theme of the Italian Risorgimento they produced 'The Italian in England' and 'A Last Confession,' not an ode to Italy or an invective against Austrian tyranny. Our conception of the poetic temperament is that described by Wordsworth as his own at the time of his visit to Orleans in 1791:

'. . . to acts
Of nations and their passing interests,
If with unworldly ends and aims compared,
Almost indifferent, even the historian's tale
Prizing but little otherwise than I prized

Tales of the poets, as it made the heart
Beat high, and filled the fancy with fair forms,
Old heroes and their sufferings and their deeds.'

Enquiry into the probable causes of this difference between the Latin literatures and our own raises curious problems of national temperament and history. From the nature of the case the two influences cannot be sharply distinguished. National history is the outcome of national temperament and reacts upon it in a way that baffles analysis, while national literature is the outcome of both, as reflected and manifested in certain minds of distinction. By temperament we are more meditative and imaginative than the Latin peoples, more reserved and self-centred than they. We tend to brood over emotion rather than to give it instant utterance. Hence, as a nation, we are bad public speakers; and it is curious to note how many of our prominent preachers and orators have been of Celtic or Jewish origin. History has combined with temperament to induce in the typical Englishman a rational, rather than an emotional, treatment of public questions. Our marriage with freedom is a *mariage de raison;* our love of freedom is that love which Tennyson admired in Arthur Hallam:

'Of freedom in her regal seat
Of England; not the schoolboy heat,
The blind hysterics of the Celt.'

And Tennyson, certainly not an unpoetic nature, probably regarded most French and Italian political verse rather in that light.

The temperament indeed of our leading poets has been in this respect at one with that of the nation at large, and has kept our poetry further from rhetoric than that of our neighbours. Chateaubriand, Lamartine, Victor Hugo, were all famous as orators. Wordsworth confesses himself—we may well believe with truth—'little graced with power of eloquence' and 'all unfit for tumult and intrigue.' The very notion of Keats or Shelley making a speech has something incongruous. Although Tennyson was greatly interested in public questions, and often refers to them in his poems, we can scarcely fancy him a successful debater in a popular assembly. When, indeed, our poets—and it happens far more seldom than with those of France or Italy—do enter on political themes, they do so in a less rhetorical spirit. Wordsworth is philosophic and contemplative. Both in the books of the Prelude concerning the French Revolution and in the 'Sonnets dedicated to National Independence and Liberty' he is too preoccupied in analysing the processes within his own mind to have much leisure for eloquence about outside events. Mr Swinburne, with all his wonderful command of sonorous metre, is, like all the Pre-Raphaelites, primarily pictorial. His rhythm moves swiftly enough, but what is in his mind is form and colour rather than movement. The only leading English poet of a rhetorical turn is Byron; and this is probably one of the chief reasons why his popularity is greater on the Continent than in England. With us, when a poet's work is recognised as akin to rhetoric, it is classed by that kinship as second-rate.

Apart, moreover, from any prepossession we may feel against political and rhetorical verse in general, Carducci's poems of this kind already suffer in England, as they must suffer everywhere outside his own country, from the further disadvantage that many of them refer to incidents only known to students of recent history. While Wordsworth describes his feelings as he watched the vicissitudes of the French Revolution, we can understand that the fate of mankind was at stake; when Victor Hugo utters his sonorous periods about the downfall of the first Napoleon, that titanic personality dominates our imagination. In Carducci foreign readers are perplexed, if not exasperated, by panegyrics on heroes and elegies on martyrs of whom they never heard, by pæans over victories and dirges over defeats which led to no lasting or widespread outcome. The Italian Risorgimento is now too far off to give us the thrill of contemporary excitement; on the other hand, it is still too recent to have won the halo of a romantic past. Perhaps no events in which England was not directly concerned ever stirred Englishmen more deeply at the time they happened; certainly none, not even the insurrections in Poland, are so often mentioned in English poetry. To-day the successful achievement of Italian unity, and the quite unromantic processes by which that unity was at length attained, have relegated the whole movement into the region of prose. Most educated English people travel in Italy, and the new régime suffers in their eyes from the vandalism, partly inevitable, which has followed in its wake. Heroes like Garibaldi, statesmen like Victor Emmanuel and Cavour, are vulgarised by the hideous statues put up to them and the 'long, unlovely streets' that bear their names. Again, those travellers who also read the Italian newspapers get a doubtless exaggerated impression of the jobbery and financial scandals amid which these pretentious eyesores were reared, while the corruption and iniquities of preceding governments are now forgotten.

Once this drawback is overcome a comparison of Carducci's poems on contemporary events with those of Victor Hugo is rather to the advantage of Carducci. Even in his earlier, contentious period the attack is more on institutions, less on individuals, than in 'Les Châtiments,' and sinks less often into abuse. Yet Carducci also could be vehement at times, and with success, as in his poems on the raid into the Papal States in 1867; in one he effectively uses the customary exposition of the Host for twenty-four hours before capital punishments to bring out the incompatability of the Two Swords; in another the point that, if Pius IX sees blood in the chalice, it will not be that of Christ, is clinched in Victor Hugo's most telling manner. After the abolition of the temporal power the tone grows far less combative. Advancing years brought to Carducci, as to most broad-minded men, a more tolerant and philosophic temper. Events also tended to chasten enthusiasm. The freedom and unity of Italy were not achieved in the way that patriots, especially republican patriots, had dreamt. The victors, not the vanquished, of Aspromonte entered Rome by the Porta Pia; Mazzini died an amnestied rebel; Garibaldi was repudiated to conciliate Prussia. It seemed to many that Italian freedom had been sacrificed to Italian unity.

Yet Carducci, a democrat by temperament and abstract conviction, felt nevertheless obliged to accept the monarchy. It would be a superficial view to regard his conversion as brought about by the beauty and affability of Queen Margherita, his verses to whom were interpreted by both sides as a formal retractation of republican principles. In truth he saw, as Crispi saw, that the house of Savoy could hold Italy together, while a republic would divide her. Still, he felt keenly the decline in her ideals, the mediocrity of her political and intellectual leaders. Giants had perished in the strife and left pygmies to enjoy the triumph. Disappointment at the victors made Carducci more tolerant towards opponents now finally overcome. As he sits in the public garden at Perugia, where the papal stronghold of Rocca Paolina once had stood, he reflects that in the fine spring weather the pontiff must be growing weary of his self-imprisonment, and jocularly invites 'Citizen Mastai' to come out of the Vatican and drink a health to Liberty, for which he had been so eager in his youth.

Quite apart, however, from Carducci's militant hostility to the Catholic Church, a hostility almost wholly due to transitory causes, there lay deep in his temperament an elective kinship with paganism. His Vicinese contemporary, Fogazzaro, while sharing his political views as an Italianissimo, remained an 'anima naturaliter Christiana'; Carducci, on the other hand, was an 'anima naturaliter pagana.' But his paganism is natural in every sense of the word, the genial worship of nature in a land of sunshine and vintage, quite different from the artificial paganism of the North, where paganism is an exotic, like the rest of classical culture. The northern pagan is a decadent; his dominant tone is a rebellion against moral limitations, against 'creeds that refuse and restrain.' Even the academic Leconte de Lisle spells 'Désir' with a capital letter, and in his 'Chant Alterné' treats Aphrodite Pandemos as the representative goddess of Athens. Landor is perhaps the only English pagan quite free from decadence or morbid hedonism. Most of our pagans are but melancholy Cyrenaics. Their unhealthy yearnings after Hellenism bring them nothing of Hellenic blitheness; the wine of Circe is to them a cup that inebriates but does not cheer. If we take two typical pagan poems of Mr Swinburne, 'Laus Veneris' and 'Proserpina,' the former describes an irresistible dominion of the senses, the latter is a hymn to a chthonic deity. The paganism of Carducci is of quite another tinge. There is nothing decadent or anti-social about it; and the only ethical defiance is against asceticism. When Carducci seeks to recover the Hellenic outlook he is not trying to get behind morality, but merely to get back to a more fundamental form of it. Indeed paganism would almost seem with him to resume its etymological meaning of village religion, a religion which rests on man's unsophisticated instincts. He appeals from the teaching of St Paul to that of Homer and Aristophanes, from a moral code based on personal holiness and self-denial to a moral sense of social ties and the human sanctities of the family.

This is the standpoint that Carducci sets forth in his **'Nozze,'** an imitation of the well-known hymeneal song of Catullus. Like his forerunner, the modern poet gives his ode to alternating choruses of youths and maidens, and thus, by retaining the framework of ancient marriage poetry, leads us at first to believe that he will attempt to render ancient feeling on a subject whereon it differs perhaps more subtly from our own than on any other. So, to some extent, he does; but his aim is even bolder, namely, to apply such feeling to the life of our own day. Accordingly a chorus of youths contrasts the several ideals of womanhood upheld by Dante, Michael Angelo, and Raphael; and a chorus of girls awards the palm to the last. So daring a transfer of marriage customs essentially ancient into modern times is a historical solecism rather hard to defend; once, however, it is admitted, the opinions it serves to put forward have much inward historical truth. The award quite correctly renders the classical view. As between the serene motherhood of Raphael's Holy Families and any form of purely spiritual intensity, whether as etherealised by Dante or as embodied in titanic muscularity by Michael Angelo, there is no doubt which would have appealed to the ancient mind, with its strong dislike of morbidity and maidenhood. Nature, as Renan once pointed out, cares nothing for chastity; and the ancients were nearer to nature than we are in this respect, as in many others. A modern author could scarcely let a body of maidens avow a preference for wedded over platonic love elsewhere than in a classical setting, for the intervening centuries that worshipped virginity have made impossible such frankness as that of Antigone to the Theban elders. Indeed in one respect the conception of propriety has become precisely reversed. In Hellas a girl might express a general wish for marriage, not a wish to marry a certain man; with us she may admit her love for a certain man, not her general inclination to marriage. At the end of Carducci's poem the choruses unite to upbraid the unwillingness of the modern woman to bear children and to suckle them if she does. Here, again, we are in the full tide of contemporary life, quite classically treated, however; for, although Jean-Jacques Rousseau and M. Gaston Brieux have uttered such warnings in prose, any of the Latin satirists might well have done so in verse; even the bachelor Horace spoke rather like this in his serious moods.

It is a spirit of intellectual and political, not of moral, defiance that inspired the famous **'Inno a Satana,'** which is as far removed as possible from the unwholesome decadence of Baudelaire's 'Litanies de Satan.' The Satan here glorified is not Baudelaire's unclean patron of orgies, not even Goethe's spirit that ever denies, not even Milton's leader of a cosmic opposition; he simply personifies the recreative forces of nature. Carducci assumes himself the standpoint he ascribes in one of his essays to the Middle Ages: 'Nature, the world, society, is Satan.' The love-deity, who is one of his avatars, is the benign worldwide power sung by Lucretius, worshipped under many names round the shores of the Mediterranean.

> 'A te, Agramainio,
> Adone, Astarte,
> E marmi vissero
> E tele e carte,
>
> Quando le ioniche
> Aure serene
> Beò la Venere
> Anadiomene.
>
> A te del Libano
> Fremean le piante,
> De l' alma Cipride
> Risorto amante:
>
> A te ferveano
> Le danze e i cori,
> A te i virginei
> Candidi amori,
>
> Tra le odorifere
> Palme d' Idume,
> Dove biancheggiano
> Le ciprie spume.'

To thee, Agramainius, Adonis, Astarte, lived marbles and canvas and parchments, when Venus Anadyomene made happy the calm breezes of Ionia. To thee the cedars of Lebanon quivered, re-arisen lover of the Cyprian goddess. To thee the dances and choruses exulted. To thee yearned the unsullied loves of the maidens, among the scented palms of Idumea or where whitens the Cyprian spray.

It is true that Venus is the first of the old heathen gods to awaken in the soul of Abelardus after the long slumber through the dark ages.

> 'O dal tuo tramite
> Alma divisa,
> Benigno è Satana:
> Ecco Eloisa.
>
> In van ti maceri
> Ne l' aspro sacco;
> Il verso ei mormora
> Di Maro e Flacco.'

O soul sundered from thy path, Satan is kindly; behold Eloise! In vain dost thou macerate thyself in the harsh sackcloth: he murmurs the verses of Virgil and Horace.

Strenuous, as well as sensuous, forms surge upward from the ancient world in the wake of Satan.

> 'Ei, da le pagine
> Di Livio, ardenti
> Tribuni, consoli,
> Turbe frementi
>
> Sveglia; e, fantastico
> D' italo orgoglio,
> Te spinge, o monaco,
> Su 'l Campidoglio.'

He from the pages of Livy awakens the ardent tribunes, the consuls, the eager throngs, and urges thee toward the Capitol, O monk distraught with the pride of Italy.

Satan not only restores the old Roman self-reverence; he is also the spirit of intellectual freedom; in the words of the essay, he is 'happiness, dignity, liberty.' His reawakening is the Renaissance 'in its noblest aspect, as a resurrection of ideal naturalism.'

> 'E già già tremano
> Mitre e corone:
> Dal chiostro brontola
> La ribellione,
>
> E pugna e prèdica
> Sotto la stola
> Di fra' Girolamo
> Savonarola.
>
> Gittò la tonaca
> Martin Lutero:
> Gitta i tuoi vincoli.
> Uman pensiero,
>
> E splendi e folgora
> Di fiamme cinto;
> Materia, inalzati
> Satana ha vinto.'

Already mitres and crowns are tottering; rebellion growls from the cloister, and fights and preaches beneath the cowl of Fra Girolamo Savonarola. Martin Luther throws off the hood; throw off thy fetters, thought of man; shine and glister, girt with flame; matter, raise thyself; Satan has won.

Even when Satan is thus sublimated, it is rather startling to find the religious reformers among his vanguard; and Carducci seems here strangely at one with their extreme adversaries and his. Savonarola, who made a holocaust of ancient manuscripts at Florence, and Luther, who put forward justification by faith alone, rather depart from their historical setting in becoming advocates of free thought. They make dignified figures, no doubt, in the pageant of the human intellect, 'mais ils ont diablement changé en route.' On reflection, however, we are inclined to think that their ghostly foe has met them more than half-way. There is, indeed, no longer anything very fiendish about him, and we begin to share the hopes of Origen and Tillotson for his ultimate salvation. Nor can anything very like devil-worship be left in a religion, which is not only, like that of Flaubert's liberal-minded chemist in 'Madame Bovary,' 'celle de Socrate, de Franklin, de Voltaire, et de Béranger,' but also that of Luther and of Savonarola. Indeed Carducci's association of the revolted archangel with the Reformers, in some ways slightly comic, sheds a strong light on his own outlook. His quarrel is with social institutions, not with society itself. His dissatisfaction is finite, not the divine discontent of Werther or Obermann, too disgusted with mankind to wish to better them. It was largely this freedom from personal antinomianism that threw Carducci's literary preferences on the side of order, that of the classics.

The only strong romantic and non-classical influence on Carducci—for with him the influence of Dante was scarcely non-classical—was that of Heine. It seems strange that this influence should come to him from beyond the Alps, from the Germany he so hated; but Heine, Semitic by descent and French by sympathies, could not be suspected of the social and political medievalism which had made things German so hateful to Italian patriots. What, indeed, first attracted Carducci to Heine seems to have been the contrast in this respect between him and most of his brethren and followers of the Romantic school. At least this contrast is brought out both in the essay on the mock-heroic Atta Troll, and also in the verses 'A un Heiniano d'Italia.' Very inferior as inspired criticism to Arnold's 'Heine's Grave,' these lines also dwell on a quite different aspect of the poet's career, that which he himself expressed by telling his friends to lay on his grave a sword, as a brave soldier in the liberation-war of humanity. Still, in his method of warfare, the humorist who called Luther 'the lover of truth and of Catherine von Borna,' had little in common with the orator of the **'Inno a Satana'**; and to Carducci, as to many others, Heine's irony proved somewhat of a snare. Such moods as that of the meditations at Trent in the 'Reisebilder,' or of 'Mir träumte wieder der alte Traum,' are not to be imitated. Only perfect sincerity can excuse in art a systematic exposure of emotional reactions. If we once suspect exaggeration or, worse still, artificial exacerbation, such exposure becomes offensive; and Carducci, in his **'Brindisi funebre'** and parts of his **'Intermezzo'** treads perilously near the verge. It is quite otherwise with the shorter lyrics. Such lines as **'Tedio Invernale'** have not merely Heine's technical perfection, far easier to achieve in so musical a tongue as Italian, but also that ironic sadness which seems peculiar to the North. For the time it becomes to Carducci a second nature. A second nature, however, it remains, and one that cannot long displace the first. Such a sentiment as this in **'Ballata Dolorosa,'**

> 'Cimitero m' è il mondo allor che il sole
> Ne la serenità di maggio splende,'

> The world is a graveyard to me when the sun shines in
> the serenity of May.

is inspired by a chequered northern spring, not by the serene Maytime of Italy. We need only contrast the next poem, **'Davanti ad una Cattedrale.'** Here we are back in the South once more, not on the dew-drenched lawn of a Gothic minster, but in front of an Italian duomo, on a piazza deep in sand and baked by the noonday sun. Suddenly, from the darkness within the doorway, an unsightly corpse glides into the yellow light. Again, in his vivid **'Rimembranze di Scuola,'** Carducci describes how the thought of the cold stillness of the grave smote him with an icy thrill, as from his schoolroom he watched the birds and bees and butterflies shimmering in the warm summer without; thus again and again, he says, in later years the

foreboding of death has come and gone. How unlike are these gusts of sadness to the enigmatic presence that visited the boyhood of Musset in the December night and abode with him until the morning. Into the joyous Mediterranean sunshine 'Death, the crowned phantom, may leap with the flashing of cataracts'; he is not, and cannot become, the haunting terror of northern melancholy. He may leer as a macabre anatomy from a tomb; he cannot, as with Holbein, dance beside his victim through all the winding labyrinth of life. Such besetting nightmares, like the witches and fire-drakes of Carducci's **'Carnia,'** may come southwards from Germany in the twilight of dawn; offspring of savagery and gloom, they vanish at the rising of the sun and the singing of Homer.

On the whole, Carducci's early distrust of the Romantics had been a sound instinct. Now once more he compares the classic spirit to the sun, that ripens the wheat and the grapes; the romantic spirit to the moon, that glimmers on dank graveyards and forsaken ruins. Again, romantic beauty is the beauty of autumn, doomed to fade away; classic beauty is the beauty of spring, fertile and full of hope. In the *Primavere Elleniche* the note of regret is there, but it is not persistent, as in northern *nostalgies de paganisme*. In the lands of their birth the gods of Hellas never die; they only slumber, awaiting the spring, in stream and flower and tree.

> 'Muoiono gli altri dèi; di Grecia i numi
> Non sanno occaso; ei dormon ne' materni
> Tronchi e ne' fiori, sopra i monti, i fiumi,
> I mari, eterni.'

> Other godheads die; the gods of Hellas know no setting; they sleep in the trees that gave them birth, the flowers, the hills, the streams, the seas, everlastingly.

In the *Odi Barbare,* where Carducci's classicism at length finds perfect expression, what first strikes us is the novelty of the metre. Hitherto, although skilful and varied in his verse, he had never been an innovator. In theory he repudiated metrical elaborations as a veil to conceal poverty of poetic content, and in practice seldom experimented in them. His only conspicuous *tour de force* is his **'Notte di Maggio,'** which is written in the most difficult of all strict metres, at all events, of all western metres, the sestina; it will bear comparison with the finest examples of Dante and Petrarch, or the exquisite lines of Mr Swinburne, 'I saw my soul at rest upon a day.' In the main, Carducci had used the lyric methods of his contemporaries; and his only unrhymed metre had been the narrative blank verse, often employed by Leopardi and others. When, in the *Odi Barbare,* he attempts the unrhymed lyrics of the ancients, the lines he prefixes from Platen, and his own 'Odio l' usata poesia,' show that he fully appreciated the difficulties. So far as a foreigner may presume to judge, he has solved them.

It is not by their metre only that the *Odi Barbare* attach themselves to what was best in the poetry of ancient Rome. They have much also of that wistful melancholy with which Virgil watched his native land, composed at length, after manifold tumults, in the golden mediocrity of Augustan peace. As the modern poet also listens to the murmur of the perennial stream and watches in the Umbrian valley the quiet life of tilth and meadow, the same to-day as two thousand years ago, he feels the poetry latent in the daily toil of country life, a feeling especially present at all times to the Latin races, and one that gives a vaguely Virgilian solemnity to the peasants and landscapes of Jean François Millet. In Virgil's own land his Georgics make an appeal scarcely understood by those only familiar with the rougher field-work of the North; and on this homelier aspect of his genius Carducci dwelt with peculiar fondness at the dedication of the monument to him in his native Mantua. Of this, too, he is reminded now as he watches the yeomen guide the plough and the 'forza de' bei giovenchi' (a wilfully Virgilian locution)—

> 'de' bei giovenchi dal quadrato petto,
> erti su 'l capo le lunate corna,
> dolci ne gli occhi, nivei, che il mite
> Virgilio amava,'

and feels the old spirit of Italy kindle within him—

> 'Sento in cuor l' antica
> patria e aleggiarmi su l' accesa fronte
> gl' itali iddii.'

He thinks, too, as Virgil thought, of the glories of Rome, of her standards planted proudly on the surrounding hills, of her steadfastness in defeat, of her magnanimity in victory; how her former foes answered her call to arms after Thrasymene, how the Carthaginians poured in headlong flight from the walls of Spoleto. The source and soul of all this greatness, in arms and in song, lay in the open-air life of the ancients:

> 'A piè de i monti e de le querce a l' ombra
> co' fiumi, o Italia, è de' tuoi carmi il fonte.
> Visser le ninfe, vissero: e un divino
> talamo è questo.'

Now all is silence:

> 'Tutto ora tace, o vedovo Clitumno,
> tutto: de' vaghi tuoi delubri un solo
> t' avanza, e dentro, pretestato nume,
> tu non vi siedi.

> Non più perfusi del tuo fiume sacro
> menano i tori, vittime orgogliose,
> trofei romani a i templi aviti: Roma
> più non trionfa.'

The comely, square-chested oxen, their moon-shaped horns curving up above their heads, mild-eyed, snow-white, that the gentle Virgil loved. . . . I feel in my heart my ancient fatherland and the gods of Italy brush my kindled forehead with their wings. . . . At the foot of the mountains and under the shade of the oaks, as of thy streams, O Italy, so of thy songs is the fount. The nymphs lived, they lived indeed, and this is a bridal

chamber of gods. . . . All now is silent, O widowed Clitumnus, all; of thy pleasant shrines one alone is left thee, and, within, O god robed in senatorial garb, thou sittest no longer. No longer the bulls, proud victims laved in thy hallowed stream, draw Roman trophies to the ancestral shrines: Rome triumphs no more. . . .

Rome triumphs no more; and the poet's wrath is kindled against the faith that overthrew her. As he watches the devotional processions crossing the Forum Romanum the sense of historic drama that fascinated Gibbon is merged in patriotic anger. The tutelary gods of Italy fled,

> 'quando una strana compagnia, tra i bianchi
> templi spogliati e i colonnati infranti,
> procedé lenta, in neri sacchi avvolta,
> litanïando,

> e sovra i campi, del lavoro umano
> sonanti, e i clivi, memori d' impero,
> fece deserto, ed il deserto disse
> regno di Dio.'

Far more truly than the Roman legions, a band of celibate ascetics have made a wilderness and called it peace. They have substituted the abortive ecstasies of mysticism for the sanctities of family life and the fruitful labour of the harvest:

> 'Maledicenti a l' opre de la vita
> e de l' amore, ei deliraro atroci
> congiugnimenti di dolor con Dio
> su rupi e in grotte:

> discesero ebri di dissolvimento
> a le cittadi, e in ridde paurose
> al crocefisso supplicarono, empi,
> d' essere abietti.'

When a strange company, between the ravaged white temples and broken colonnades, slowly paced, wrapped in dark sackcloth, singing litanies, and over the plain, that rang with human toil and the heights mindful of imperial sway, they made a desert and called that desert the kingdom of God. . . . Cursing the works of life and of love, they held frenzied communion of grief with God on rocks and in caves. They came down mad for annihilation to the cities, and, in affrighted chorus, impiously besought the crucified godhead that they might be abject.

Whereas north of the Alps one of the most usual reproaches against Catholicism is that it is too Italian, Carducci, as an Italian, blames it as not Italian enough. To him it appears as a morbid orientalism overspreading the healthier instincts of the Latin race, one among the many religions of the East that sapped the life of the Roman Empire. In **'Alexandria'** he even represents the victory of the Church as Egypt's revenge on Rome for Augustus' triumph over 'her bleating gods.'

His meditations, **'In una chiesa gotica,'** lead by a more personal road to a somewhat similar conclusion. His purpose, he says, is not worship, but a meeting with his mistress, a meeting which he compares to that of Dante with Beatrice. His mood perhaps reminds us rather more of Léon Dupuy, as he waited for Madame Bovary in Rouen Cathedral. Yet somehow an assignation in a church, which even Musset, certainly no pietist, condemned, does not seem very profane in Italy. Here at least there is no trace of the æsthetic decadent's search after emotional reactions, not even any ostentations defiance of the Christian standpoint; the poet simply records, not very regretfully, that it has passed him by. He expresses, quite naturally, the impatience of a southern temper in the gloom of twilight and self-denial and its eagerness to get outside into sunshine and enjoyment:

> 'Non io le angeliche glorie né i démoni,
> io veggo un fievole baglior, che tremola
> per l' umid' aere: freddo crepuscolo
> fascia di tedio l' anima.
>
> Addio, semitico nume! Continua
> ne' tuoi misteri la morte domina.
> O inacessibile re de gli spiriti,
> tuoi templi il sole escludono.'

I see not the angelic glories nor the demons, but a feeble gleam through the dank air; chill twilight swathes my soul in gloom. Farewell, Semitic godhead! Death rules continuous in thy mysteries. O inaccessible king of spirits, thy shrines shut out the sun.

A poem even more suggestive than this of prose fiction, both in mood and incident, is that called **'A la Stazione in una Mattina d'Autunno,'** which describes the parting of a lover from his mistress at a railway station. At first sight this introduction into poetry of what to most of us is least poetic in modern life, its mechanism, seems a defiantly hazardous experiment. Hazardous of course it is, yet with less of deliberate defiance than would at first appear, far less than there would be in a like experiment by an English poet, although there are plenty of allusions to mechanical invention in English poetry. Tennyson, in the opening, afterwards cancelled, to his 'Dream of Fair Women,' describes the view from a balloon. James Thomson wrote some pretty lines about a return by train from Hampstead Heath; and Mr Henley, in his 'Song of Speed,' attempted to turn the motor-car to poetic uses. Nevertheless, efforts to treat in verse what is most modern in modern life always savour in English of the *tour de force*. A railway does not seem a natural object in a poem, any more than—in spite of Turner's 'Rain, Steam, and Speed'—it seems so in a picture. Such things are part of life's prose; and it is in the genius of our literature that prose and verse should stand apart. If they do not necessarily treat different subjects, they look at these subjects from a widely different standpoint. In English, when modern life is looked at from the poetic standpoint—the standpoint we expect in a writer of verse—what is distinctively modern in it drops out of the field of vision. If it appears, we feel it has been dragged in through some eccentric literary theory, or, worse still, from a wish to attract attention by a deliberate defiance of criticism. It would not present itself of its own accord.

There is not the same gulf between prose and verse among the Latin nations. With them there is usually little difference of subject, often none at all of standpoint; prose and verse are merely two ways of saying the same thing. It is therefore not strange that Carducci's subject, and his treatment of it, should remind us more of scenes in contemporary French novels than of any parallel in poetry. The opening description suggests impressionism, because impressionists alone have depicted such things, but there is nothing impressionist in the manner of describing:

> 'Oh quei fanali, come s' inseguono
> accidïosi là dietro gli alberi,
> tra i rami stillanti di pioggia
> sbadigliando la luce su 'l fango!
>
> Flebile, acuta, stridula fischia
> la vaporiera da presso. Plumbeo
> il cielo e il mattino d' autunno,
> come un grande fantasma, n' è intorno.'

Nor is there anything forced or unnatural in the lines that follow:

> 'Tu pur pensosa, Lidia, la tessera
> al secco taglio dài de la guardia,
> e al tempo incalzante i begli anui
> dài gl' istanti gioiti e i ricordi.
>
> Van lungo il nero convoglio e vengono
> incappucciati di nero i vigili,
> com' ómbre; una fioca lanterna
> hanno, e mazze di ferro: ed i ferrei
>
> freni tentati rendono un lugubre
> rintòcco lungo: di fondo a l' anima
> un' eco di tedio risponde
> doloroso, che spasimo pare.
>
> E gli sportelli sbattuti al chiudere
> paion oltraggi: scherno par l' ultimo
> appello che rapido suona:
> grossa scroscia su' vetri la pioggia.'

O those lanterns, how they follow each other, lazily yonder behind the trees, between the branches, dripping with rain, casting a chequered light on the mud. Mournful, piercing, and strident, the steam-engine whistles close by. The sky is leaden, and the autumn morning, like a huge phantasm, is around us. . . . Thoughtful, Lydia, you give the ticket to the hard clip of the guard, and to time you give, as he treads down your years of beauty, the moments of gladness and the memories. Like phantoms, the watchmen, hooded in black, pass up and down along the dark carriages; they hold a glimmering lantern and hammers of iron, and the iron couplings as they are tested, give forth a mournful reverberation, long-drawn-out; from the depths of my soul an echo of weariness answers sorrowfully and seems an agony. And the doors slammed at shutting seem insults; the last call, that whistles sharply, seems a taunt; the rain in coarse drops bickers against the panes.

Examined from the standpoint of academic criticism these comparisons verge on the grotesque; viewed psychologically they seem quite likely to suggest themselves to an imaginative temperament in an exasperated nervous condition. What is grotesque in them is quite true to life; yet the ideas would only have occurred to a most penetrative insight, while only a supreme artist would have dared to use them.

Treatment such as this of individual incident or feeling is, however, the exception in the *Odi Barbare* as always with Carducci. What chiefly raises these Odi above his former work is their impressive amplitude of historic recollection, perhaps only possible in a land so rich as Italy in manifold memories. Everywhere the thought of the mighty dead is with him as he drifts down the full-fed stream of the Adda, past the ruined ramparts of Lodi, past 'battlefields that nature has long since reconciled to herself with the sweet oblivion of flowers'; as he muses before the Gothic citadel of Verona, or at Bologna, his adopted home, before her towers and monasteries; as he sits by the still waters of Sirmio, where Catullus yet seems to contemplate his absent Lesbia, mirrored in the quiet shimmerings of the lake.

> 'Dolce tra i vini udir lontane istorie
> D' atavi, mentre il divo sol precipita,
> E le pie stelle sopra noi viaggiano,
> E tra l' onde e le fronde l' aura mormora.'

'Tis sweet among the vines to listen to far-off tales of our forefathers, while the godlike sun is setting and the gracious stars are voyaging over us, and across the waters and among the leaves the breeze is soughing.

In this sunset glow of thronging recollections patriotic pride is sobered into a sense of the continuity in national tradition. On the death of Mazzini he had hailed him the spiritual heir of Gracchus and Dante and Columbus. Now, when Garibaldi visits Rome for the first time since the Italian occupation, he welcomes the modern dictator as one of Livy's men, worthy to take his place by the side of Romulus and Camillus. The old political and religious hatreds too are softened. The note of reconciliation, still slightly ironic in the lines at Rocca Paolina, takes a more solemn tone. The 'pie stelle,' that voyage over the head of the poet at Desenzano, are no longer lucid shapes fulfilling their destiny without heed to mankind, as in one of the early sonnets; they are become Virgil's 'conscia fati sidera.' Indeed, although in this epithet of 'pie,' recurring again and again after the ancient manner, lingers no doubt the ancient suggestion of natural duties accomplished, yet it bears also its present Italian meaning of clement, pitiful, the old Virgilian *pietas* passing into that modern pitifulness of which Virgil had such strange foreshadowings. As Carducci muses at the castle of Miramar, whence Maximilian sailed for Mexico, the republican indignation of the sonnets on the expedition, and the resentment against the house of Austria that vents itself in the 'Cradle-song of Charles V,' are hushed. A solemn awe, as in the presence of mysterious forces of retribution, raises this poem to the level of tragedy. It has the grand manner of the ancients in handling contemporary events, the manner of Æschylus in the 'Persæ.'

The strongest poems in Carducci's last volume, *Rime e Ritmi,* are those that continue this historical vein, the most congenial to his peculiar quality. Lines entitled 'Alle Valchirie,' on the murder of the Austrian Empress, recall 'Miramar,' though certainly inferior to it. Altogether there is a falling-off since the *Odi Barbare* in strength and spontaneity, in the higher kind of imagination, a falling-off that leaves the besetting weaknesses more evident. A still larger proportion of the poems are on political and occasional topics, and everywhere the philosophic observer of public events tends more and more to override the poet. So does the historian and critic of literature. Like most literary poets in this age of criticism, Carducci at all times of his career wrote much in verse about other poets, sometimes by way of panegyric, sometimes in order to reconstruct a historical setting, sometimes to study the mood that a poem induced in himself.

Among his pieces of this kind the most interesting to English readers are probably those on English poets. He shared the general admiration of the Latin peoples for Byron, to whom there is a fine sonnet in the *Rime e Ritmi,* and the *Odi Barbare* include poems written 'Beside the Urn of Shelley' and 'On Reading Christopher Marlowe.' His sense of these poets is not quite that of Englishmen to-day. He greets Byron as the champion of Hellenic freedom, and disclaims his pessimism and satire. Shelley is welcomed to the islands of the blessed by the epic and tragic heroes and heroines, and hailed as 'poeta del liberato mondo'; surroundings and titles alike suggest 'Prometheus' and 'The Cenci,' perhaps even 'The Revolt of Islam,' rather than the lyrics which are now Shelley's chief glory in his own country. As Carducci reads Marlowe on a sultry journey by the seashore of the Campagna, the malarial landscape leads him to dwell on what seems unwholesome and mephitic in the playwright, his fondness for lurid crimes and barbaric excesses. What may be called the romantic side of the Renaissance, its love of strangeness, its lawless assertion of the prerogative of personality, was uncongenial to Carducci; to his essentially classical temperament the Renaissance appealed as a return from the superstitious frenzy of the Middle Ages to the ordered sanity of the ancients. As he grew older his poetic imagination lost the ardour needed to fuse his literary and historical learning into poetry. One need only compare the sonnets to Nicola Pisano in his last volume with the ode to La Beata Diana Giuntini in his first. Each renders the blending of paganism with the Catholic faith; in the ode it is suggested with the intuition of poetic fancy; in the sonnets it is set out with the precision of a philosophic history of Tuscan art.

Carducci's strong sense of local colour also now sometimes betrayed him. Many of his poems with topographical titles degenerate into mere enumeration of places and their characteristics, as in 'Piemonte.' In others the limitations of his historical sympathy still handicap him. Even in the Church of Polenta the Gothic capitals seem grotesque intruders from the northern gloom into a land hallowed by Hellenic memories. Yet, while the poet sits and muses where Dante may once have knelt and beheld the face of God, as he wept for his 'bel San Giovanni,' dislike of Catholicism is overcome by a sense of the historic function of religion as the great consoler. He summons the Italian people, 'l' Itala gente da le molte vite,' to answer the call of the angelus to prayer and closes with lines not unworthy to be set beneath Millet's picture:

'Una di flauti lenta melodia
passa invisibil fra la terra e il cielo:
spiriti forse che furon, che sono
          e che saranno?

Un oblio lene de la faticosa
vita, un pensoso sospirar quïete,
una soave volontà di pianto
          l' anime invade.

Taccion le fiere e gli uomini e le cose,
roseo 'l tramonto ne l'azzurro sfuma,
mormoran gli alti vertici ondeggianti
          Ave Maria.'

A soft melody of flutes passes unseen between earth and heaven; spirits perhaps that were, that are, and are to be. A soft forgetfulness of wearisome life, a thoughtful sighing after rest, a gentle yearning for tears, steals over the soul. Men and beasts and things are silent, the sun sets in rose-coloured vapours, and the lofty waving heights murmur 'Ave Maria.'

An overpowering sense of such things—the vaguest word is the best—is the unmistakable token of the poetic temperament; and a power like this to express that sense in an artistic form would alone mark Carducci as a genuine poet.

We venture to doubt, however, whether, outside Italy, he will ever acquire widespread poetic fame. The exceptional difficulty of his Italian is not an insuperable hindrance; Dante, most obscure of Italian poets, is also the most widely read. Still, this difficulty is a hindrance to many English people, even to such as have a working knowledge of the language. These may be advised to begin on a translation of selected poems, with the Italian on the opposite page, lately brought out by Mrs Francis Holland. Mrs Holland has hampered herself by a resolution to adhere to the original metres, and, perhaps for that reason, her renderings will hardly give the English reader much idea of the beauty of Carducci's work. But they will be a useful help to those who know a little Italian and wish to make acquaintance with Carducci. For her book, which opens with a short introductory study, includes several of the poet's finest pieces. And indeed it is a good illustration of the wealth of really striking work he produced that Mrs Holland's selections scarcely anywhere overlap the quotations here given. There are, however, other causes besides the difficulty of his language which have hampered his reputation abroad and also suggest misgivings as to its permanence at home, at least in its present extent. Everywhere the average reader of poetry reads it for the matter, not for the manner; and Carducci will cease in time to give that reader what he seeks, the reflection and

interpretation of his own feelings. In pure literature what makes for lasting popularity is individual human interest. 'Maud' is read for the hero's love story, not for the author's opinions on the Crimean war and the Manchester school in economics; the emotional crises in the life of Jean Valjean make us bear with the political disquisitions in 'Les Misérables.' Now this human interest, present in Tennyson and Victor Hugo, is absent from Carducci. He never attempted the creation of character; and his own feelings expressed in verse are seldom of lyric intensity or such that all mankind can share them. His own reference in his **'Intermezzo'** to

'Questo cuor, che amor mai non richiese,
     Se non forse a le idee,'

This heart which no love ever claimed, save perhaps for ideas.

is rather too suggestive of Goethe's saying about Platen, that he had every other gift but wanted love. To enjoy what is best in the *Odi Barbare* requires historic imagination and the knowledge that alone gives that imagination scope. In the marmoreal ode **'Sul' Adda,'** for instance, there is an impressive reverie over departed conquerors not unworthy of Omar Khayyam; there is no throb of human passion as in Browning's 'Love among the Ruins.'

Carducci's fame will endure, but with the few, not with the many. His appeal in the future will be to those endowed with historic imagination and the still rarer literary perception needed to appreciate his mastery of poetic form. For readers so gifted, nowhere very numerous, the *Odi Barbare* will become a classic in the truest sense, and Carducci will continue to be what Signor d' Annunzio has called him, in the 'Greeting to the Master' that closes the 'Laus Vitæ,' 'the mediator between two worlds,' that of ancient Rome and that of modern Italy.

**Beulah B. Amram (essay date January 1916)**

SOURCE: Amram, Beulah B. "Swinburne and Carducci." *Yale Review* 5, no. 2 (January 1916): 365-81.

[*In the following essay, Amran compares the life and poetry of Carducci to that of English Victorian poet Algernon Swinburne.*]

The first decade of the twentieth century saw two giant branches lopped off the tree of European literature. When Algernon Charles Swinburne died in 1909 at the age of seventy-two, England lost the last of her great Victorian poets. When Giosuè Carducci died in 1907 at the age of seventy-one, Italy lost her one incontestably great poet, her greatest literary figure since Leopardi. There is much interesting comparison to be drawn between these two representative geniuses of two closely related literatures.

In Swinburne and Carducci we have two supremely great poets of almost coterminous lives: the first a profound student of classical, continental, and English literatures, who used a magnificent but overloaded style as the medium for brilliant but uncertain criticism; the second one of the greatest contributors to that enormous mass of Dante criticism that in Italy is a criterion of scholarship, a student of foreign literatures, a great teacher, philologist, pamphleteer, satirist, and orator, who used to their utmost capacity the marvellous cadences of Italian prose. Both poets were distinguished as writers of vitriolic attacks on Christianity, on priesthood and kingcraft. Both were professed pagans, exalting the spirit of man and the conquest of human thought, rebelling against Christian asceticism and aspiring towards the serene beauty of antiquity. Both men were classicists, with faith in Homer as the father of poets, claiming kinship, Swinburne with Catullus, Carducci with Horace. Both excelled in their adaptations to new uses of classical metres, Swinburne striving most to master the difficulties of the Pindaric ode, Carducci of the Alcaic and the Sapphic stanza. Both, because of their natural command over the musical resources of their native languages, augmented by their studies in prosody, exercised a profound influence over versification, giving freedom and variety in place of metrical monotony and conventionality. Through their apotheosis of revolt both influenced the youth of their day, Swinburne being the fountain-head of the so-called "decadent school," Carducci, as the leader of the classical school, inspiring high ideals of scholarship and patriotism. Both confessed great debt to Victor Hugo and worshipped him as the embodiment of virility and creative energy. Both adored Italy and sang their noblest songs in her behalf. Both loved Giuseppe Mazzini as the lofty idealist, the austere republican, Giuseppe Garibaldi as the great hero, the pure patriot.

After having published academic poems of limited influence, both poets achieved national fame in their early thirties through *succès de scandale*. The shock of Swinburne's "Poems and Ballads" in 1866 on a society devoted to Tennyson was much the same as the shock of Carducci's **"Hymn to Satan"** in 1865 on a society devoted to Manzoni. In both cases, this early fame was a not unmixed blessing, for Swinburne was always associated with a sensuality that he soon outgrew, and into Carducci's fiery verse was read an active political creed, subsequent secession from which was called treachery to republican principles. Both were intellectual aristocrats, free from the prejudices of their class, writing from themselves unto themselves, superbly disdainful of the judgments of Philistia. Carducci, however, in accord with his temperament and the custom of Italian polemics, assailed his critics with the fiercest invective, *senza guanti*.

In their style there is little likeness. Swinburne's style is decadent in the sense that he opens his page to every idea, breaking up the unity of the whole to develop the part. His difficulties are not, as is too often said, due to vagueness of thought. Each separate sentence means exactly what it says. It is not confusion of thought but profusion of detail. Where other men saw one image, Swinburne saw a dozen, and his intellectual habit did not lend itself to controlling the torrent of ideas that tumbled in upon his sensitive

mind from the wide resources of his culture. Even under the influence of classicism, Swinburne shows the prodigality, the exuberant energy of the Elizabethans, little of that sobriety, order, and proportion that we call classical. On the other hand, Carducci is as precise as Swinburne is loose. His art is the restrained, concentrated art of the Latins. His most profound poem has the architectonic simplicity of a basilica. There is nothing decorative in him, nothing of the luxurious detail that gives to so much of Swinburne the effect of mediaeval tapestry. Carducci's difficulties are those flowing out of profound scholarship. His thought feeds on deep springs of learning, and the wealth of his allusions confuses the less erudite mind. Carducci's unity of construction gave him opportunity for a lifting of tone, a convincing climax that we rarely find in Swinburne, whose long poems to Victor Hugo and Walter Savage Landor, for example, can end almost anywhere without impairing the effect. Compare for form their odes on the proclamation of the French Republic, both written September 1870, their poems to Victor Hugo, on the anniversary of the Battle of Mentana, on the death of Giovanni Cairoli—the last of the four sons of Signora Cairoli to die for Italy. Compare their memorial poems. Of the many poems that Swinburne wrote in memory of dead friends, none starts the sympathetic tear, except the exquisite sequence of sonnets to Philip Bourke Marston, the blind poet who died at the age of thirty-five, and the reason is that here he has written with directness and simplicity, restraining the involutions, the conceits that cloud so much of his work.

There is little similarity between the external life of the polished English aristocrat, a northern child of earth and sea, living a sequestered life among admiring and sympathetic friends, knowing of struggle only the bitter-sweet memory of literary antagonisms, and the life of the rugged provincial Italian, gray with the fight against poverty, enmity, jealousy, who for more than forty years as teacher at the University of Bologna, gave of his best to the youth of Italy. There is little similarity between the temper of the passionate youth who in **"Hesperia,"** weary of the dead sea-fruit of the senses, could write

> I have loved over-much in my life; when the live bud
>   bursts with the blossom
> Bitter as ashes or tears is the fruit, and the wine thereof
>   shame.
>
>             . . . . .
>
> Too soon did I love and lost love's rose and I cared
>   not for glory's,
> Only the blossoms of sleep and of pleasure were mixt
>   with my hair;—

and of the austere young patriot who could with profound sincerity say in his heroic **"Avanti! Avanti!"**

> Ahi, da' primi anni, o gloria, nascosi del mio cuore
> Ne' superbi silenxi il tuo superbo amore.
>
>             . . . . .
>
> Ed obliai le vergini danzanti al sol di maggio
> E i lampi de' bianchi omeri sotto le chiome d'òr.

> Ah, from my first years, O Glory, I hid thy proud love
> in the proud silences of my heart. . . . And I forgot
> the maidens dancing in the sun of May and the shining
> of their white shoulders under the tresses of gold.

Still less of similarity is there in their relation to their own countries. Conservative England had never recovered from the shock of Swinburne's attack on cherished ecclesiastical and state institutions and refused burial in Westminster Abbey to the apostle of a hedonistic paganism that meant hatred of the established religion and destruction of the established morality. The truth is that Swinburne never spoke for the nation. His sympathies were with France, with Greece, with Italy. His very excellencies, his facile mastery of new forms of verse, annoyed the English, who are repelled by an aesthetic pre-occupation with form, preferring the security of didactic poetry to the most perfect roundel that was ever wrought. His classicism could by the very nature of things have but a limited appeal, being essentially intellectual and exotic. His odes were too literary, his plays too scholarly. Swinburne was to England always a poet for poets, always an undisciplined boy, eternally young, eternally rash and unreliable. I am inclined to think that the solemn words that he addressed to the nation in his later years fell on deaf ears. Sober Albion did not look for help to the passionate singer of Dolores and Cypris.

Carducci, on the other hand, died the adored of a nation, truly a national figure, the heir to the laurels of Foscolo and Leopardi. He stood in a relation to his country that is granted only to the greatest, speaking her language to interpret her soul. His works had the weight that comes from participation and interest in national politics. His desk was an altar, his poems oracles. His material is Italian, its spirit and form Italian, born of her ancient hills and streams, animated by her ideals, nurtured by her history. Carducci is a remarkable example of the persistence of a national type. For after twenty centuries, he represents in its original strength the genius of Latium, the Etruscan-Roman spirit of the Maremma. His is the thoughtful, satirical, caustic Latin spirit, capable of impressive eulogy, of national enthusiasm, of savage invective. His is the Latin *virtù,* the martial spirit, the large manner, the moral authority. He is the spiritual descendant of Juvenal—"Horace with an active political conscience."

I find no indication in either poet of mutual acquaintance. Yet Swinburne, who in 1858 took the Taylorian prize for French and Italian, must have known Carducci. Carducci, whose disciple Nencioni introduced Victorian literature into Italy, must have known the work of the inspired singer of "Atlanta in Calydon." Swinburne, who worshipped the leonine independence and the rugged vigor of Hugo and Landor, who himself represented the immortal spirit of youthful revolt, would have loved all of Carducci, his wholesome paganism, his zeal for classical poetry, his fiery sincerity, the capacity for love and hate of the disdainful soul, who felt himself "a fish out of water in majorities," who even as a youth acknowledged himself "dispre-

giator, ch 'altro non posso, eterno" (eternal despiser, because I cannot be otherwise). But Carducci's austere soul would have had little sympathy with Swinburne's "dead lute-players that in dead years had done delicious things." Carducci's robust paganism did not include an interest in the scarlet and secret sins of Greece and the Renaissance. And I am sure that he would have saved the choicest epithets of his rich vocabulary of invective for the Aholibahs, the Faustinas, the Semiramises, whose loves fill so large a space in Swinburne's first volume. That Carducci could be frank to a degree that exceeded the limits of what we are pleased to call good taste, no one can deny who has read **"Meminisse Horret."** His savage wrath never calls a spade by any other name. But against sensuality he set his face. Dead and famous courtesans interested him no more than living and vulgar ones. In the words of Nencioni, "La musa Carducciana fu casta." He came with pure hands and spotless vestments to the altar of Phoebus Apollo.

But Carducci would have taken to his heart the Swinburne of "A Song of Italy," which more than any of Swinburne's long poems maintains throughout its superb inspiration. He would have loved the singer of the passionate laments and chants and paeans of "Songs before Sunrise," to whom Mazzini was the symbol of ideality, the theme of most beautiful lines of dedication and tribute. Carducci would have had unbounded sympathy with the Swinburne whose paganism meant not only the revel of the senses but the freedom of the soul that was destroyed by Christianity when

> Fire for light and hell for heaven and psalms for
>    paeans
> Filled the clearest eyes and lips most sweet of song,
> When for chant of Greeks the wail of Galileans
> Made the whole world moan with hymns of wrath and
>    wrong.

Swinburne's "Hymn to Proserpine," written as of the year of the proclamation in Rome of the Christian faith—the "death-song of spiritual decadence,"—his "Hymn to Man"—"the birth-song of spiritual renaissance,"—"The Last Oracle," "Before a Crucifix," "The Altar of Righteousness,"—all thunder out his wrath at the failure of Christianity to establish its lofty claim and his hatred of the cult of the "pale Galilean" at whose breath the world grew pale. How they answer Carducci's own words in his masterpiece, **"Alle Fonti del Clitumno" ("At the Sources of the Clitumnus"),** of the "Galileo di rosse chiome"!

> Quando una strana compagnia, tra i bianchi
> Templi spogliati e i colonnati infranti,
> Procedè lenta, in neri sacchi avvolta,
> Litaniando,
>
> E sovra i campi del lavoro umano
> Sonanti e i clivi memori d'impero
> Fece deserto, et il deserto disse
> Regno di Dio.

A strange company wrapped in sack-cloth went slowly among the despoiled white temples and the broken columns, singing hymns, making a desert of the fields sounding with human labor and the hills with their memories of empire—and this desert they called the Kingdom of God.

The spirit of Swinburne's "The Last Oracle" is the spirit of Carducci's **"In Una Chiesa Gotica" ("In a Gothic Church")**—the true expression of the sensuous side of paganism, its blitheness, its love of art, music, nature, love. Both men saw in Pauline Christianity, as in all creeds that "refuse and restrain," the enemy of life, restraining the senses in their rightful enjoyment of the fresh beauty of the world—the fair face of nature, the fairer faces of the daughters of men,—refusing the claim of the human mind to exercise itself free from the check of dogmatic theology with its traditional standpoint on the problems of life and death. It is these two external elements of joy in life and faith in reason that make paganism the deathless enemy of a church that lives in contemplation of the spiritual and the subjection of the individual opinion. Asceticism that sees sin everywhere, that curses what the sun blesses, meant to both men the denial of the eternal laws of nature. To the social-minded Carducci, it was doubly hateful as being uncivil as well as unnatural.

For the Son of Man, Swinburne would substitute the Holy Spirit of Man, who should free the world from the thrall of fear laid upon it by a false priesthood. From the tyranny of the gods of gloom, "i foschi di," Carducci appeals to the human soul that lived serene by the Ilyssus, upright and whole by the banks of the Tiber.

> Glory to Man in the highest! For Man is the master of
>    things

says Swinburne, and again

> God, if God there be, is the substance of men which
>    is Man.

Swinburne, whose generous soul lived by adoration of human greatness, exalting Hugo, Landor, Mazzini, Shakespeare, Marlowe, Aurelio Saffi, Louis Blanc, saw holiness not in an anthropomorphic God of wrath and thundering vengeance but in the limitless capacity of the human mind, believing with Blake that "the worship of God is: Honoring his gifts in other men, each according to his genius and loving the greatest men best; those who envy or calumniate great men hate God; for there is no other God."

> A creed is a rod,
> And a crown is of night;
> But this thing is God,
> To be man with thy might,
> To grow straight in the strength of thy spirit,
>    and live out thy life as the light.

This is but another phase of Carducci's Satan, that robust first cousin of Lucifer, son of the morning, "forza vindice de la ragione," (the avenging force of reason), "thought that flies, science that experiments," the spirit of revolt against dogmatic, feudal, dynastic authority, the spirit suc-

cessively of naturalism, pantheism, polytheism, art, history, science, sociology,—that brooding sculptured Satan of Antokolski that he wanted to call the nineteenth century.

The dominant note in European arts and politics since 1815, when Napoleon tried to destroy all national spirit, has been the note of nationality. Why do we crown the work of Carducci, Mistral, Selma Lagerlöf, Heyse, Tagore, Yeats? Because each, with the voice of art that speaks to all hearts, has shown the soul of a people in the form developed by that people. The nineteenth century, that in the wake of the Napoleonic *débâcle* saw so many national revivals—Gaelic, Celtic, Russian, Provençal, Hebrew,—that saw renewed interest in national music, dances, folklore, epics, lyrics,—received its greatest inspiration from the discovery that for the artist, greatness lies not in an unattainable cosmopolitanism, but in a faith in national tradition, national form, free from artificiality and imitation, true to its sacred origin. For wherever found, all origins are sacred. Time purges the stain, leaving only the aspiration, and the tradition becomes holy through association with austere virtues. How then shall an Italian of a new-born Italy be most national, an Italian to whom the word *antica* has none of our sense of distant, dead, but is instinct with reverence and patriotism? How save by a return to the forms of Latin literature? The modern Italian has no merely intellectual or aesthetic love for classical lore. With the scholar's appreciation of the ethnic and philological affinities of Latin and Italian, he mingles the desire of the poet and the hope of the patriot for the quickening through every medium of national memories. He sees eye to eye with Horace and Virgil, brother not only of the spirit but of the blood. Carducci accomplished what Italian and continental classicists since the fifteenth century had attempted to do and had failed in doing, because, free from the "literary servitude" that Mazzini hated in the classicism of lifeless imitation, he filled the ancient cups with the new wine of solid, sincere, modern thought, discarding the age-worn classical material and allowing himself perfect freedom in his choice of subject.

It is this national inspiration behind Carducci's classicism and his use of the classical metres that distinguishes it from the similar attempt of Swinburne. Thought, scholarship, and taste can produce such literary masterpieces as "Atalanta in Calydon" and "Erechtheus," rich in exquisite lyrics and noble choruses, showing Swinburne's mastery of form, the magic of his music, the wonder of his rhymes, the richness of his knowledge; but we shall look in vain in "Atalanta" for that profound feeling that communicates itself spontaneously to the sympathetic reader. This is not the place to discuss at length the success of attempts to reintroduce the metres of Greek and Latin poetry. Classicists there have always been, men who would revive the fair spirit of Greece through the renewal of her prosodical forms. But such attempts have always smelt of the lamp. The Sapphics and choriambics and heptameters of Swinburne, like the galliambics and Alcaics of Meredith and Tennyson—what are they at best but interesting metrical exercises? Swinburne like other English poets learned music, variety, depth from his classical models, but his influence on English versification was due not to his classical experiments but to his wonderful manipulation of English metres.

This then is the essential difference between the classicism of Swinburne and Carducci. Moreover, Swinburne's enthusiasm was for Greece, Carducci's for Rome. Swinburne, though he calls Catullus brother, sings the songs of Pindar and Sappho, of Sophocles and Aeschylus. Carducci, it is true, was surpassed by none in his love for Greece. The divine countenance of Homer ("la diva sembianza d' Omero") that smiled upon him as a boy was the light of his whole life. And in his beautiful lines **"Near a Monastery" ("Presso Una Certosa")** with which his poems end, the aspiration of his closing life is still for that smile, that light:

> A me, prima che l'inverno stringa pur l'anima mia
> Il tuo riso, o sacra luce, o divina poesia!
> Il tuo canto, o padre Omero,
> Pria che l'ombra avvolgami!

> For me, before winter seizes my soul, thy smile, O sacred light, O divine poetry! Thy song, Father Homer, before the shadow envelops me.

Like Landor, Carducci looks past Rome,

>         . . . sees beyond
> Into more glorious Hellas.

But he loves Hellas not only as "the nurse of Gods and God-like men" but as the mother of Rome, the tutor of her civilization and her literature. His are the trumpets of Rome, not the flutes of Greece. His Alcaics and Sapphics are based less on the Greek originals than on the forms made Latin by the painstaking experiments of Horace. Even his odes show nothing of the Pindaric form with its elaborate and formal structure of strophe, antistrophe, and epode, but reflect the fact that the Roman poets made little attempt to imitate Pindar and Bacchylides, preferring the personal lyric ode to the choric voice.

Swinburne like many another prodigy has suffered from his early fame. The chords of passion struck so boldly by the youth of twenty-three soon died away. After the first volume of "Poems and Ballads," we hear little of the fames and sins of forgotten and none too respectable goddesses, earthly and divine—Astarte and Isis and Venus, Phaedra and Helen and Sappho, Faustine and Félise and Dolores. The mature poet never forgot the gods of his youth, Hugo, Mazzini, Landor, the poets of republicanism, freedom, revolt. His practised hand strikes with ever growing vigor the note of liberty, of enfranchisement from political and intellectual slavery. The singer of Venus has become definitely the votary of the Delphic Apollo,—the lover of song, the greatest gift to man, the lover of the sun, the symbol of life and universality, the lover of the sea, the symbol with its wide horizon and unyoked energy of largeness of purpose, greatness of soul. In his preface to his collected poems, inscribed to Watts-Dunton, Swinburne

refused to recant, proclaiming each early poem of dalliance the result of a mood justified by its sincerity and spontaneity. But it is quite evident from the "Hesperia" and the dedication of the first series of "Poems and Ballads," when he had "fled and escaped from the rage of her reign" who was sweet to him once, that he did not consider his early loves fit company for the austere patriots, the poets, and the children to whom he gave his ripened allegiance. Carducci's development was more even. His poems are the poems to be expected of the son of a conspirator, who as a boy drank in the deeds of 1823 and 1847, who dreamed over Homer and was reared on Alfieri. But Carducci, who lived to see *Italia risorta,* modified his fiery antagonisms. His acceptance of the monarchy, which by the republicans was denounced as treasonable inconsistency, was an indication not only of the evolution of the times but of the man. There is in one of the last poems of this pagan and anti-Catholic a realization of the human value of prayer and the function of the church during the Middle Ages. And fierce contempt for the Galilean, the "Galileo di rosse chiome," softened into something like sympathy for the human martyr who suffered mortal pain and discouragement.

Swinburne was essentially the literary poet, Carducci the social poet, the man of action, who frequently felt a great distaste for the whole business of poetry, "di tutta questa rimaria italiana." Indeed it was the tragedy of his life that circumstances prevented him from easing in action the passion that consumed him. Swinburne's was the aesthetic, Carducci's the social and moral view of art. Swinburne's genius inclined him to search all fields and to experiment with every form. Even the sonnet he made harder by limiting himself to two sets of rhymes for all the fourteen lines. His proficiency bewildered by its very cleverness and adaptability and inconsistency. His interest in form prevents that interpenetration of the artist and the man that gives the note of sincerity. The clever critics dismissed his transcript of actual experience as mere dramatic imaginings and scolded him for autobiographical confessions that were really dramatic studies.

With Carducci such confusion was impossible. The unfinished "Canzone di Legnano" is his only attempt at telling a story. The opinions in his poems are the views not of dramatic characters but of the passionate lyrist who felt them with his magnificent capacity for passion. He felt the influence of the great European figures. Indeed it was a conscious part of the new national Italian programme to cultivate European literature so that Italy might thereby be again identified with that Europe from which she had been too long isolated. Hugo, Heine, Goethe tread with no uncertain step through his pages, but their form is rarely imitated. It may seem strange to say it of one whose fame is so closely associated with the revival of old metrical forms, but Carducci's interest in prosody was as much spiritual and political as artistic. The artist in him felt the charm, the freedom, the beauty of classical measures, but the patriot, the nationalist, the political thinker saw in them salvation from romantic artificiality, puerility, and unwholesomeness. Swinburne might say that "a poet's business is presumably to write good verse and by no means to redeem the age and re-mould society. It is not his or any other artist's business to warn against evil." With Carducci, "every strophe is a slap at something." Like Mazzini he saw in poetry a powerful means to aid his conscious effort to re-make Italy morally, intellectually, artistically. With undying fidelity to national ideality, Carducci looked forward to the building up of a healthy nation, "una robusta prole," redeemed to new industry, to new thought, to the old ideals, purified and made new by justice and liberty. For this he studied the past, lifting up in a white light the great republicans and liberators, Arnold of Brescia, Cola di Rienzi, Burlamacchi, praising Dante not only as the great poet but as the patriot, the first to believe in the unity of the Italian tongue. For this he gave his whole soul to his teaching at Bologna, so that his pupils should go out as so many centres of elevating influence, to an Italy that should be the vindicator to the nations of eternal law and liberty.

The predominance in either poet of the aesthetic or the social ideal shows itself again in their treatment of nature. Swinburne sang with unmatched passion and energy and variety of the sea that holds

> . . . in her spirit strong
> The spirit of all imaginable song.

Carducci sang of the fecundating forces of the streams and the hills. Swinburne was the poet of the sun, who is God, the "father of all of us," the source of song. Carducci was likewise the poet of the sun, of the benignant, triumphal sun blessing the happy labor of free men in the field. Swinburne loved nature for herself as companion and consoler. Carducci, like Meredith, loved her for her laws that are a guide to men. Swinburne's landscapes and seascapes are objective studies inexhaustibly rich in beautiful images and phrases. Carducci's landscapes are wide luminous backgrounds for men and human affairs. Here is no idyllic meditative retreat from the strepitous city but a scene of virile action—fields sounding with human labor, vibrating with human energy. The smiling Umbrian valley—the mysterious arcanum of lost civilizations, the spiritual centre, the home of St. Francis and Perugino, with its circle of watchful vineclad hills and its fertile plains gay with happy women and children where once the dreaded papal fortress of Paul the Third burdened the earth,—sings a grand antiphonal chant to the poet's hymn of praise for a restored Italy.

This same contrast of ideals explains their differing attitude towards romanticism and mediaevaldom. Swinburne could be at the same time classical and romantic, antique and mediaeval. He sang with equal enjoyment of the Venus of the Horsel and of the Venus Anadyomene. It was the secret of Carducci's antagonisms, on the other hand, that things in themselves base became no less base under the veiling glamour of art and history. The ignorance and cruelty and superstition of the Middle Ages were as hate-

ful to him as the archaic affectation that exalted them under the forms of simplicity and faith. There are no dulcimers and shawms in Carducci, nor the shepherd's pipes of an equally false Arcadian classicism. Inasmuch as romanticism meant the spontaneous expression of personal emotion, Carducci sympathized with it, but he had little taste for romanticism that meant grotesqueness, supernaturalism, the malevolent power of beauty and its ascetic reaction. Romanticism that sought its inspiration in the Middle Ages was hateful to him as to Goethe, like the sterile moon that plays over ruins, and the artist could not extol what the thinker despised. Though he felt the rich artistry of the middle centuries, he hated the feudalism that despised the husbandman, that, shutting men out from the soil, shut them out from the virtue that comes from the tradition of the earth.

Strange as it may sound, neither poet wrote love poems. Even the gravest of Swinburne's early poems are but dalliance with passing loves. That Swinburne had an appreciation of other than the voluptuous aspects of woman is shown by his poems to George Eliot, to Christina Rossetti, to Grace Darling, to Mrs. Lynn Lyndon—the daughter of Walter Savage Landor,—and the beautiful "Study from Memory." But his women are either sinuous panthers or middle-aged gentlewomen. His lines to them show no trace of the love that fills Browning and Meredith. Carducci too wrote no love poems. His early years of struggle and political stress left little time for the play of personal emotion, and his austerity kept him free from the sensuality of Stecchetti, who led the other branch of the reaction against Manzonian romanticism. There are women in Carducci, but they have none of the romantic splendor of the Middle Ages. They are sturdy peasants fit for large burdens, with broad shoulders bent over the harvest, with strong arms to guide the beautiful white oxen, with clear eyes to watch the looms, superb peasants fit to bear healthy children, the backbone of a nation. And there are other women, Lydias and Lalages and Linas,—types of deep-eyed women whose candid brows and tender glances hold a refuge for tired souls, offering the solace of beauty and of peace.

Swinburne wrote many poems to pictures and to music. Carducci, surrounded by the countless art treasures of Italy, wrote nothing of pictures. His one poem **"La Madre,"** to a sculptured group by Adriano Cecioni of a mother and baby, shows again the supremacy of the social over the aesthetic ideal. For in that strong woman whose hair and face are colored by Tuscan sunsets, who but yesterday was admired by the farmers as she walked barefoot over the sweet-scented hay or singing at mid-day defied the raucous crickets on the hills,—in that sturdy mother who prattles sweetly with her little one, while around her smile the signs of her domestic labor, the tremulous blades on the green hills, the lowing cattle,—from such a group he sees a comfort for the soul, a lofty hope for the centuries of an age when labor shall be happy, when love shall be secure, when a strong free people shall say, looking at the sun, "Shine not on sloth and on wars against tyrants, but on the pious justice of labor."

Quando il lavoro sarà lieto?
Quando securo sarà l'amore?
Quando una forte plebe di liberi
Dirà guardando ne 'l sole: Illumina
Non ozi e guerre a i tiranni
Ma la giustizia pia del lavoro?

"The pious justice of labor." Surely a memorable phrase: "pious," not in our sense connoting religious uses but with the piety that has always been associated with the sowing of the fields, the tending of the kine and the flocks, the ripening corn, the laden orchards and hillsides; "justice," the right of willing hands to labor and enjoy the fruits of labor.

Who is there to take the place of these tremendous figures? How puerile, now that England needs them, sound the voices of her poets! Not the sum of all of them can compass the passion of but one of Swinburne's odes. Perhaps that mould is broken. Perhaps the times will re-make it. For not yet has that day come, that day so profoundly hoped for, when the sun shall shine no more on the wars of tyrants. Before the crisis of a world at war, reason staggers, yet believes that when, with the loss of much that men hold dear, shall come the destruction of falsehood and the ghastly mockeries that men call religion, the builders of that purer epoch shall work on the foundations of liberty and justice laid by you, great-souled and lofty-minded poets.

## Ruth Shepard Phelps (essay date 1924)

SOURCE: Phelps, Ruth Shepard. "Giosuè Carducci." In *Italian Silhouettes*, pp. 11-32. New York: Alfred A. Knopf, 1924.

[*In the following essay, Phelps studies Carducci's political, religious, and emotional roots. In the second section, Phelps observes that Carducci brought new and sometimes radical ideas to the Italian public by using forms and meters of the classical tradition.*]

I

It is a commonplace to say that the nations of the North have seen in Italy from the first the home of romance, the pleasure-place of the imagination. And they have always delighted to heighten her effects. From Chaucer to Walter Pater she has ever been the land of mystery and tragedy, of soft lascivious manners and gorgeous crimes, of a deep magical melancholy which has laid a spell upon the Northern mind—a spell, however, which that mind itself and its tastes have created. The deep racial differences have fascinated the Teutonic imagination, which in turn has exaggerated them; and they have done for the Italian temperament in our fancy what the Tuscan cypress does for the grave Italian landscape, given it that touch of strangeness added to beauty which for Pater's mind constituted the romantic. But to think thus of Italy is to

deal in a kind of pathetic fallacy. Italy is not romantic in her own view; in her own view she is classic, wholly and unescapably. Her mystic landscape is the same that Virgil and Horace celebrated without a hint of mysticism; Pliny had a villa on Lake Como, Catullus one at Garda; everywhere the antique world underlies the Middle Ages and the Renaissance. Italy was classic before ever romanticism was invented, and classic she remains.

Not that the Italians are the Romans, or think they are. They went through the Middle Ages with the rest of Europe, though with a difference. But their classical heritage is in their memories. Even the greatest mediæval and Christian poem in the world betrays the classic instinct in its magnificent framework, its structure and its pattern. Petrarch's sonnets are romantic in their personal note of self-revelation; but his hope of fame, we must remember, he based upon Latin works executed as far as he knew how in the classic spirit, and it would have seemed to him an irony that his "Song-Book," a mere lover's diary, should be the thing of his to take the fancy of a romanticizing posterity. With the Renaissance came the complete recovery of Italy's inheritance from antiquity, and a recognition of the true lineage of native inspiration; and Italian literature—even when romantic in subject, as in Ariosto and Tasso—has been classic in method ever since.

So the Romantic Movement was never at home on Italian soil. It was but one more invasion by the barbarians. It came in by the door of political thought, with the ideas of the French Revolution, and when Italy's own conflict was over, her brief attack of the romantic fever left her. Leopardi's romantic pessimism of mood was deeply rooted in the classical tradition of form, and when Italy's other great nineteenth-century poet came to be born (in the very decade which had begun with the publication of *Hernani*), he was born a classic; and as we see Carducci discarding the foreign romantic wear in literature at the very moment when Italy was repudiating foreign political domination, we seem to feel that classicism—native and traditional as it is—fits as closely the new idea of unity and integrity as romanticism earlier had fitted the time of struggle.

The birth of Giosuè Carducci, which met the need of a robuster spirit in Italian poetry to match the renewal of national hope, occurred in 1835. He witnessed the whole of the struggle for independence, and lived nearly forty years under the free tricolour. When he was born, Silvio Pellico had been five years out of his Austrian prison, and Charles Albert on his throne for four; when Carducci was thirteen the first Italian army took the field against Austria, and he saw its initial successes and its speedy defeat at Custoza; a year later, a boy of fourteen, he sorrowed over the disaster of Novara. He was twenty-five when Victor Emmanuel came to the throne and Cavour to the ministry, and thirty-five when the King at last entered Rome.

His birthplace was a little village named Valdicastello in the garden of Tuscany. His father was a physician, an ardent patriot and anti-clerical, who brought the boy up to love his country and hate the Church. Besides the medical library, there was a precious collection of what Lamb would have admitted as *biblia* on the shelves of the bare little house where poetry and poverty dwelt together. This village doctor read and cherished his scanty library, and nourished his son upon Virgil and Horace, Dante and Tasso, and two works of history whose titles are significant—Rollin's "Rome," and Thiers's "History of the French Revolution." The perusal of Thiers and Rollin, added to conversations overheard in which the father proclaimed his own liberal principles, fired the boy with a passion for republican government, a passion which he translated into action by organizing republic after little republic with his brothers and their young companions—a republic with archons, with tribunes, with consuls, it mattered little which, he says, so long as each was inaugurated with a revolution. The revolutions were conducted with stone-throwing and debate, and after one too-violent Jacobin demonstration his father imprisoned him for some time with Manzoni's "Christian Morals" and Silvio Pellico's "Duties of Man." One cannot help tracing some of Carducci's later dislike of all moralizing, sentiment, romanticism, and Christianity, to this early incarceration in the undesired company of saints. Parental discipline likewise drew the first poetry out of him. He had three cherished pets which he delighted to fondle—an owl, a falcon, and a young wolf—but one day his father, out of patience with these singular tastes, slew the birds and gave the beast away. Carducci, like many another broken-hearted lover, assuaged his grief with song, and his first verses were those thus wrung from him by sorrow. Wordsworth's phrase comes to mind at this picture of a madcap little boy all activity and emotion. The whole future man can be discerned here in him—the revolutionist, the inveterate decrier of Manzoni, and the poet.

There came an end to the days at Valdicastello, and he was sent first to a clerical school where he was as out of his element as might be expected, and then to the normal school in Pisa, which he felt was conducted by pedants. In spite of the scorn which he entertained for the methods of education practised upon him, he was an eager and untiring student from the first, as several of his schoolmates, who have grown up to be men of letters, testify. One of them says the boy was as economical of his time as a miser of his purse, and that as the long and frequent religious exercises irked him as so much time lost, he used to carry with him instead of his prayer-book some classic of similar binding and dimensions, and read it voraciously during the service. A poem reminiscent of these years, called **"A Recollection of Schooldays,"** shows us how little we can guess what is going on in small heads that bend above school-books. He recalls a day in mid-June, when, the conjugation of *amo* suddenly beginning to dance before his eyes upon the yellow page of his grammar, and the droning voice of the black-frocked priest, his teacher, to grow faint, his thoughts fly out of the window where a cherry-bough red with fruit is beckoning to him. Beyond, he can see a mountain-top and a strip of sky and a patch of the blue Ligurian sea, and hear the hum of bees and the song of birds. Then suddenly across his mind, thus occupied with growing live things, strikes the sharp thought of death, the knowledge that he must some day lie insensible to all these outdoor solicitations while the birds go on singing, not for him. And the little boy's heart is shaken with fear.

He received his doctorate from Pisa, at the age of twenty-one, and thus describes the ordeal of his examination in literature in a letter to Giuseppe Chiarini, the friend who was to become his biographer, the "Caro Beppe" to whom many of the letters are addressed:

> "Yesterday I had my examination, or rather discussed the theme in Italian literature which I had chosen, and the result was more than gratifying. From the beginning, contrary to custom, I had my audience—famous white-haired men in doctors' gowns—silent and all attention for an hour. (And I was supposed to have spoken a half-hour.) There was one, a little professor of rational philosophy, who pronounced himself awestruck at my citations from memory!

> "I could not complete my discourse, and came off ten minutes short because the Provost said to me at last, seeing there was no end to it: 'I must announce to Dr. Carducci, to my regret, that the time allotted to him by law has already been exceeded by thirty minutes,' and then rang his little bell. . . . Then came congratulations, embraces and kisses, from all the most distinguished and the least distinguished, and the whole roomful pressed around me.

> "It all ended in a great lark; for in the evening, on the Lungarno, accompanied by Pelosini, Tribolati, and others, I declaimed extempore an epic poem to Father Arno, an Etruscan deity with sea-green locks, who refused to countenance electric light, gas, or steam. Tarquin, Lars Porsena, the virgin Camilla and Turnus were in it, and went about extinguishing all the gasjets, and unearthing ancient lamps from the sepulchre of Tarquinia and the Etruscan tombs. The hero of the piece, whose part I half sang and half declaimed, was an Etruscan vase, which broke into the shops, smashing cups, tumblers, and all such modern trash. The others laughed tremendously, as I went on chanting, now in blank verse and now in *ottava rima*, while the general public passed by in the distance, intimidated. All this I did in my dress-suit, with my best waistcoat on, and an enormous white cravat around my neck."

It is a pity that more of the letters of Carducci's later years do not exhibit him in this vein of extravagant humour; but the first volume of them to be published is largely taken up with business notes to publishers, and the hasty letters to friends are oftenest concerned with questions of literary or textual criticism.

Soon after his examination, with its triumphant issue, there came a family tragedy. His brother Dante, in a fit of melancholy, killed himself at the breakfast-table before his parents' horror-stricken eyes. His father's death followed hard upon this disaster, and on Carducci fell the support of his mother, his young brother, his cousin, and his cousin's wife. They had moved to Florence by this time, and were living in a modest house near the Porta Romana, which to-day wears a tablet. A year or so later, in 1857, appeared the first little book of verses, entitled **Rhymes,** published rather reluctantly in the single hope of eking out expenses, a hope naturally destined to disappointment. At the same time he was engaged with some other ambitious young men in founding a little society to take the field against the romanticists. They called themselves *Gli amici pedanti* ("Pedant Friends") and fought their foe chiefly on patriotic grounds, alleging romanticism to be "an irreverence done our great classical writers."

Meanwhile, in order to live, he was teaching school, first at San Miniato del Tedesco, and then, when newly married in 1859, at Pistoia. His marriage brought him children, a beautiful little son who died at the age of three, named Dante for the dead brother, and three daughters who lived to grow up. His wife seems to have left not the smallest impress on his letters or his poetry, but his little son's death and his daughter's marriage inspired beautiful poems. In 1860, when he was but twenty-five, there came a welcome bolt from the blue, his appointment to the chair of literature at Bologna, a post he continued to fill until just a few years before his death in 1907. His activities as professor were many. He edited a great many texts, besides teaching, lecturing, and writing poetry and criticism; and his personal influence was inspiring to his students. He had small patience, however, with their premature literary aspirations, and was a stern critic of their first attempts. He used to say that he was going to introduce an Education Bill, of which Article XXXIX should read: "Any professor whose students shall be found publishing prose or verse within three years of graduation, shall be deprived of his chair; and any professor whose students shall be found publishing prose or verse while still in college, shall be beaten with rods." William Roscoe Thayer says of Carducci's professorship: "He was a scholar of the best German type, familiar with the apparatus of the philologian, a stickler for perfection in line and word and comma. Yet this was but the beginning. Since Schiller taught at Jena, no such poet had sat in a professor's chair, while Carducci was what Schiller was not, a profound and careful scholar as well." His capacity for work was enormous. He could put in eight or ten hours on end, with one off for the mental refreshment of proof-reading. During his first year at Bologna he says that he rose at three even in January, to prepare his lectures on Petrarch. Here are some sentences from a letter written that same year:

> "I am studying and reading constantly, incessantly; I make no acquaintances, I go nowhere, not even to the café. I write nearly all day, and besides writing, read Latin and study Greek. In the last two weeks I have devoured the *Electra* of Sophocles and six books of Virgil, corrected the *Stanze* [a work of Politian's that he was editing], and written the commentary on fifty-six of them. You see I am at work. I don't know when I shall get back to poetry, but should like to write a poem on the monument to Leopardi, finish my ode to Liberty, write a song in *terza rima* to Rome, and an ode to the people. But I greatly fear I shall write no more verses."

When those words were penned, the **Nuove rime** and the **Odi barbare** were still unwritten!

It is necessary to touch upon Carducci's political opinions. He had begun, as will be readily guessed, a red Republican, but as he saw the heroes of the *Risorgimento* pass and leave the stage to lesser men, he came to agree with the wise Cavour that Italy was not ripe for democratic government, and to acquiesce in a kingdom under the house of Savoy. He even served a term as senator under the new régime. His change of front, however, laid him open to misconstruction and at one time to something like persecution from his hotheaded young students at Bologna. It has been ascribed, and French critics characteristically accept this view, to his great admiration for the gracious Queen Margherita, whose long friendship for him was published when, a few years before his death, she purchased his library to preserve it from being scattered. But his sincerity and patriotism are as unquestionable as his courage—courage in the face of poverty, grief, misrepresentation. All who write of his character find the same word for it—leonine. In him we are in touch with a personality of power, with some elements of true greatness. Wayward and wilful, to be sure, hot-tempered and quick to tears, proud as Lucifer and unselfconscious as a child, a mixture of hero and *enfant terrible,* generous, laborious, and brave, he answers to the sociologist's definition of genius, he is the eternal adolescent. He suggests, somewhat, Walter Savage Landor, so exquisitely polished an artist, yet a personality so burly, and might almost as well have sat for the caricaturing portrait of Boythorn. In friendship he was ardent and self-devoted, but whimsical. The child of village folk, in drawing-rooms he was ever unwieldy. In humour he was somewhat lacking, save in Ben Jonson's sense, and good spirits seem not to have accompanied him very far upon the highway of our life. In an early letter he describes himself as not very well fitted to live upon this globe, not so much by reason of circumstances as because of the temper of his mind. And he exhorts "Caro Beppe" somewhere: "Write, write—and forget this life, which is a vain thing." Vivacity in his letter-writing is called out only by his dislikes; he says himself: "I was ever more ready to hate evil than to love good," but the truth is rather that he enjoyed himself more in the expression of his antipathies.

Of all the anecdotes and reminiscences which it is tempting to quote, we must content ourselves with one, the chapter of recollections contributed by Annie Vivanti (Mrs. Chartres). The young poetess was his great friend and pet. No one else has such characteristic incidents to recount of him. Mrs. Chartres recalls driving over the border from Switzerland into Italy with him once, when two Germans had begged the privilege of riding in his carriage that they might have the experience of seeing Italy first in the company of her greatest poet. As they reached the line, a group of the too-familiar beggars rose up at the side of the road to clamour for *un soldo,* which the Germans, delighted at their picturesqueness, gladly gave them. But Carducci was cut to the heart at this exhibition of his countrymen's weakness; standing up in his carriage, he thunderously commanded the unoffending Germans to descend and leave him, and forbade Annie Vivanti to speak a word, while he sat brooding in silence over his humiliation.

> "This small impersonal incident," she says, "wounded him far more than any personal slight ever could. When in 1895, after he had renounced Republicanism, his students in Bologna turned against him with insults and violence, hissing him, and even in one instance striking him, he was unmoved and calm. When they cried: 'Down with Carducci!' he shook his leonine head gravely and said: 'No, never down with me! God has set me on high!' On the day after these events he came to see us in Genoa, and we were horrified to see his hand, the strong small hand which has penned some of the most beautiful poetry Italy has produced, wounded and bruised. One of his students had struck him with a large key. Carducci smiled indulgently, almost tenderly. 'They are good boys, I love them,' he said. 'They think they are in the right, so they are right.'
>
> "'Why did you leave them?' I asked. 'Why turn back?'
>
> "'My child,' he answered, 'easy it was and a joy to lead a band of eager youths to the ringing words 'Republic' and 'Freedom.' All young Italy followed with shouts and cheers. But should I have been worthy of their trust if, when I saw that we had struck the wrong path, I had not turned round and told them so? Indeed, it takes courage to face the sorrow and mistrust of all those young hearts. I am grieved for their grief. But they will understand one day that Italy is not ready for a republic.'"

On another occasion Carducci took his favourite to see the composer Verdi, then an old man, in his villa by the sea.

> "On arrival, Carducci went out on the marble terrace overlooking the shimmering Mediterranean, and sat there without speaking a word. Verdi, calling to me, sat down at his piano and, easily as the wind blows, played rambling and beautiful music as though he were talking to me. Then he rose and stepped through the open window to the terrace, where Carducci still sat motionless staring at the sea. We sat down beside him and nobody spoke for a long time. . . . Carducci said suddenly: 'I believe in God,' and Verdi nodded his white head."

Here is an anecdote in different vein. "His hatred of all forms of adulation," Mrs. Chartres says, "was profound. *'Buon giorno, Poeta!'* exclaimed a beautiful young man at Madesimo one day, saluting him with a wide sweep of his hat. Carducci stopped and stared at the stranger. 'Poet,' he said. 'Who Poet? I am not Poet to you. To you I am Signor Carducci.' And he strode angrily on." On another occasion they were in the street together when a ragged journalist stopped them, asking help for his sick wife and unluckily adding that it was he who had written an article in appreciation of Carducci which had appeared the week before. Carducci, in anger that anyone should think he could be won with praise, struck the man with his cane. But then sent the wife a hundred-franc note the same evening!

And here is Mrs. Chartres's personal tribute:

> "Since the day of our first meeting, he has been a friend to me and mine. Carducci's friendship! No one who does not know him well can understand what that means. . . . To all the world he is a great poet, historian, scholar; and a noble man, stern, rugged, severe, uncompromising, splendid in his austere serenity. But those whose hand he has held in friendship, who have seen him day by day in his simplicity and goodness, his kindliness and strength . . . those fortunate ones to whom the full purity and humility of his great soul have been revealed, speak his name with tender breath, and write of him with halting hand, as I do; with eyes, perhaps, as mine, brimming over with tears."

## II

Carducci's poetic work fills a thousand pages, a thousand pages of short poems. Not one above six pages, and those of such length few; not one narrative poem, not one long elegy or meditative work, not a closet drama; a thousand pages of lyric poetry by a poet who hated subjectivity. The "lyric cry" we think to recognize in the personal note, and he is seldom personal. When he is, it is not his feelings but his opinions that he usually expresses. Love and *Weltschmerz,* the burden of most lyric poetry, are absent. We might say, to be sure, that to express prejudices and predilections is to strike as intimate a note as to sing of passion and despair, yet even this so much drier and less exuberant kind of personal expression is lacking in his latest, greatest volume.

The first two hundred and fifty pages of the collected poems contain the **Juvenilia,** poems written between the ages of fifteen and twenty-five. They are the verses of an angry young man, angry with almost equal heat against the enemies of Italy, bad poetry, his own base and cowardly generation—"vile little Christianizing century," as he calls it—and Alessandro Manzoni. His lifelong rage against that gentle and revered poet, already full of years and honours by the time Carducci was grown, has something droll in its exaggeration. Carducci used Manzoni's name to conjure up a whole set of detested associations, very much as the romanticists were accustomed to revile classicism, artificiality, and the eighteenth century under the name of Pope; though it is only fair to say that Carducci the critic did larger justice to Manzoni and the whole Romantic Movement in Italy than did the poet or the letter-writer; but, as a French critic aptly puts it: "In his prose he says what he knows, in his poetry what he thinks."

In the verses of this young man, moreover, there are almost no love poems, and he repents of only two or three as heartily as did Petrarch of his whole "Song-Book." His repentance seems to have been lifelong. There is hardly a love poem in the whole collection. We can find one or two to shadowy ladies with classical names—Lydia or Lalage—but only one to a real woman, the lovely **"Idyl of the Maremma."** This celebrates *bionda Maria,* strong and beautiful daughter of the fields, beloved in his youth; it is somewhat in the temper of Landor's "Fiesolan Idyl," and so beautiful that we can only wish there were more.

The next twenty years of professorship at Bologna, during which he wrote so many lectures and volumes of criticism, are yet the most fruitful of poetry. In the volumes known as *Levia Gravia* and *Iambs and Epodes,* the poems are mostly occasional tributes to friendship or comment upon political events, since in Italy, more than elsewhere in Europe, poetry has always been a friend to politics. They include the celebrated **"Hymn to Satan,"** published in 1865, which called such a storm about his ears; the young secessionists of letters applauded, while the clergy shuddered, and his name immediately became common property from one end to the other of the peninsula.

The *New Rhymes* (*Nuove rime*) are scattered along over these same years between twenty-five and fifty. The only romantic influence Carducci ever underwent was Heine's, and here in the *Nuove rime* is his one small oblation to the romantic spirit of his time. Besides several translations from Heine and other German ballad-writers, there are a precious scant half-dozen of purely personal lyrics. Here are the heart-breaking songs over the little son so long dead, and a few upon the tedium and heaviness of life; here are the **"Idyl of the Maremma"** and the **"Remembrance of Schooldays."** These poems, with their homelike note of northern melancholy, together with many of the *Barbaric Odes*—descriptive and historical, divorced from his earlier didacticism—these are the ones, I dare be sure, that the English reader will oftenest go back to.

The *Odi barbare* are his greatest work. They are unrhymed, and written in the classic metres of the Latin poets—alcaics, sapphics, hexameters—and called barbaric, not because their novelty of form owes anything to the northern barbarian, but because they would have sounded so to Virgil and Horace. The Italians are an exceedingly sensitive literary people by whom all novelty in language or form is speedily punished, so the *Odi barbare* provoked a tempest which kept their author on the defensive for years. It passed in time, leaving the odes securely placed in Italian literature, which they are now recognized to have greatly enriched. Their unrhymed melody the foreigner probably never fully appreciates, but he can see that in them Carducci has attained his ideal of a pure objective beauty, expressed, as all Italian critics are now prompt to tell us, with a kind of helpless perfection of style.

This volume is full of beauty and full of ideas, but few individual poems can be conceded to contain both. His principal ideas are three: first, patriotism, with a passionate love of liberty and democracy; second, an aversion to romanticism and all its works; third, a dislike of Christianity. He was a pagan, a classicist, and a democrat. It may be objected that these things—patriotism, love, aversion, dislike—are feelings, not ideas. We can only say that in Carducci his feelings were his ideas, and if an idea which

is a feeling is best described as a prejudice, it could be no one's intention to exonerate Carducci from that. He was prejudiced; but, at any rate, his ideas, feelings, prejudices, whatever we may agree to call them, were compelling in him. They had reality, and coloured all his work. The belief in democracy seems a singular third with the other two; for Christianity is democratic, yet he is anti-Christian, romanticism is democratic, yet Carducci was a classicist. This antagonism was reconciled by his national feeling. It was part of his patriotism to repulse foreign ideas as well as foreign troops; he longed to see Italy develop and unify from within, intellectually as well as politically. If he had been reminded that democracy also was a foreign idea, born of the French Revolution and the English constitution, he would have pointed backward to the Roman Republic and the free Italian communes of the Middle Ages. For the sense of continuity was strong in him, the line of tradition in his imagination ran unbroken from Cincinnatus to Garibaldi; that event from which the Western world reckons forward and backward did not divide the stream of history for him.

But Christianity and romanticism were both clearly foreign. And as we have seen him and his young pedant friends combating romanticism as an irreverence done the great Italian classics, so it is perhaps not too fanciful to conceive him as rejecting Christianity partly as an irreverence to the local pagan divinities, whom, if he could not believe in, he loved and understood. "The other divinities perish," he says in a poem entitled **"Hellenic Spring"**; "the gods of Greece have known no setting." He seems to have been, like John Stuart Mill, naturally non-Christian, without the pain of severing an allegiance he had never sworn. *Anima naturaliter pagana.* "Nature he loved, and next to Nature, Art."

But Carducci's quarrel with Christianity and romanticism was not only because they were foreign; to his mind both were sentimental, sickly. And the foreign and the morbid made a combination in the highest degree obnoxious to him. His corrective for them was Nature and Reason, the classic spirit. There are two poems of his which illustrate his attitude towards Christianity better than any discussion can, **"The Springs of Clitumnus"** and the **"Hymn to Satan."** **"The Springs of Clitumnus"** shows his opposition to Christian asceticism and glorification of sorrow, and his sense that Christianity has been an unwelcome interruption from without, an obstacle in the path of man's natural development, while the **"Hymn to Satan"** provides the corrective. This demoniac canticle, or what seemed such to churchly imaginations, celebrates a divinity that has nothing in common either with Milton's disdainful hero or with the Prince of Darkness of Christian theology, but is a kind of compound of Phœbus Apollo and the great god Pan, with a touch of Prometheus.

On the Romantic Movement Carducci looked with vision equally astigmatic. Just as he saw in Christianity not a spiritual discipline and an attitude towards life, but merely clericalism and asceticism, so he conceived of romanticism as just *Weltschmerz* and sentimentality. Of all the definitions which it has vexed the critics to make, Goethe's must have pleased him best: "Classicism is health, romanticism a disease." "After all," to quote his own words, "when all is said, Leopardi sends folk to the hospital, Manzoni to the confessional, and Byron to the galleys." Carducci missed entirely that aspect of romanticism which was inspired by the liberating spirit, the spirit of revolt (the very spirit, in fact, of his Satan), and for this reason: Romanticism he conceived as the cult of the Middle Ages, and the Middle Ages as they affected the North of Europe. Now the two great mediæval institutions of the North were feudalism and monasticism; the one enslaved men's bodies, the other their minds. No intellectual movement which drew its inspiration from such a period could influence Carducci.

If the pagan world as compared with the Christian seemed to him as sunlight to darkness, classicism beside romanticism was as sunlight to moonlight. There is a poem of his that, read without its title, would be just a beautiful objective description of the two planets that light our earth by night and by day, but he has ironically named it *Classicismo e romanticismo,* and given us the clue. We know, as we follow his descriptions, that *classicismo* is the sun, *romanticismo* the moon. The sun, he says, glistens on the ploughshare in the furrow, smiles upon fertility and man's labour, yellows the grain, reddens the grape and gladdens the windows of the poor; but the moon, pale, infecund ghost, loves best to embellish ruins and graveyards and adorn our melancholy, to waken the poor man at night to remember his griefs, to befriend wastrel poets and lawless lovers—she ripens neither flower nor fruit.

Looking at Carducci's poetry as a whole, we perceive that he and his ideas present a double paradox. In political ideas a modern, in his artistic and intellectual sympathies we find him among the ancients; whilst his form and content contradict one another, since he is a lyric poet almost devoid of lyricism. It would be as presumptuous as idle to attempt to estimate his ultimate significance, but we can suggest that it will be different for Europe and for Italy. For Italy it is his ideas that count; the austerity of his literary taste and his intolerance of what is facile must act like a tonic upon the literature of a language so fatally full of rhymes and a people so fatally gifted at improvisation as the Italian, while his idealism, courage, single-mindedness, and his belief in the destiny of his country, will kindle the Italian heart to noble resolution.

But outside of Italy it is not for his ideas that he will live and be beloved. They inspired too many local poems, too many merely political, too many merely angry. And save for the belief in democracy, they are not the ideas of his time. His prejudices keep him from being an intellectual power, his inability to understand Christianity puts him out of touch with his world; he is a thankless child to the Romantic Movement which helped produce him, and his bright impersonalism too often declines the poet's duty of baring his own heart in order to reveal to us our own. In all these ways he fails to be to the Northern peoples *simpatico.* It must be by sheer beauty that he can prevail, but of sheer beauty there is enough.

Something of it, possibly, may show through this version of the sonnet on the death of the poet's little son Dante. The poem is addressed to Carducci's brother Dante, dead in their youth by his own hand.

### "Funere mersit acerbo"

O thou among the Tuscan hills asleep,
    Laid with our father in one grassy bed,
      Faintly, through the green sod above thy head,
Hast thou not heard a plaintive child's voice weep?
It is my little son; at thy dark keep
    He knocketh, he who bore thy name, thy dread
      And sacred name—he too this life hath fled
Whose ways, my brother, thou didst find so steep.

Among the flower-borders as he played,
    By sunny childish visions smiled upon,
      The Shadow caught him to that world how other—
Thy world long since. So now to that chill shade
    Oh, welcome him! as backward toward the sun
      He turns his head to look and call his mother.

## Mario Praz (essay date 1935)

SOURCE: Praz, Mario. "Giosue Carducci As a Romantic." *University of Toronto Quarterly* 5 (1935): 176-96.

[*In the following article, Praz maintains that though Carducci scorned romanticism, his poetry shows romantic tendencies.*]

Giosue Carducci was born at Valdicastello, in the district of Pietrasanta in Versilia, on July 27, 1835. The poet's centenary has been celebrated in Italy with speeches and articles, and has seen the publication of the first volumes of the National Edition of his works. The year 1935 was indeed an *anno carducciano* for Italy, and such it was thanks to one aspect, certainly the most typical of this poet, which makes him popular in Italy's present hour.

This aspect may be summed up in two words: the *romanità* and the sanity of Carducci. I have had the opportunity of listening to several commemorations by Italians of different ages, and whether they were senior academicians such as Ugo Ojetti,[1] or public figures of the Fascist era such as Arturo Marpicati,[2] or young students, stress was laid over and over again on those two characteristics: the *romanità* and the sanity of Carducci. Side by side with the public celebrations, tending to emphasize one sole aspect of Carducci, the "out-and-out Italian who made no concessions to any kind of exoticism"—as Marpicati puts it—, it may be enlightening to quote from an article by Professor Attilio Momigliano, published in the *Corriere della Sera* of June 6, 1935, with the title "Sanità di Carducci." This article, by an academic critic, is not written for a rhetorical effect like the speeches mentioned above: it aims at being an unimpassioned survey of Carducci's art. "After having scornfully censured romantic poetry," Momigliano says, "Carducci found, through a slow process of liberation from models, rhetorical effects, and attitudes, the kind of poetry which flashed across his mind as a contrast to the formlessness, sentimentality, and morbidity of romanticism." He goes on specifying: "It is significant that among so much historical poetry, there is never in Carducci the theme of ruins and silence as a note of melancholy and neglect." He gives instances from **"Dinanzi alle terme di Caracalla,"** etc., makes a comparison with D'Annunzio, the romantic singer of the Cities of Silence, and concludes: "Carducci has been able to sing the Communes and pagan Rome; he could not have sung Ravenna, a harbour whence the soul sails forth towards the realms of contemplation and death, nor the Venice of the forsaken canals, dripping with melancholy like a sonata of Chopin or a picture by Böcklin."

This allusion to Böcklin, who was after all a mediocre painter, recalls to my mind the essay of another professor, Cesare De Lollis, who in the now very distant 1912, in contrasting a famous passage from **"Alle fonti del Clitunno"** with Leopardi's "Già di candide Ninfe i rivi albergo . . ." ("Streams, once the abode of white Nymphs," from "Alla Primavera o Delle Favole Antiche"), remarked[3] that the whole stanza of Leopardi "is a miraculous selection of themes of the mythico-pastoral world interpreted with the concreteness which Böcklin brought to the interpretation of that world;" whereas in Carducci's lines,

Egli dal cielo, autoctona virago
ella . . .

("From heaven he, she an autochthonous heroine . . ."), "there is nothing either seen by the poet or to be seen by the reader." For Momigliano, therefore, Böcklin stands for "the formlessness and morbidity of romanticism;" for De Lollis, on the contrary, he signifies romantic "concreteness" as opposed to the abstractions of academic poetry. If two professors of this century, when romanticism has been so thoroughly explored, cannot see eye to eye upon the subject, Carducci may well be excused for having formed no clear idea of it by the middle of the last century, for having defined as classical certain aspirations we would rather call romantic, for having kept confused, sometimes in a hardly extricable manner, an authentic classical inspiration, from Horace, with a pseudo-classical, or rather romantic, Parnassian one.

Modern Italians who, like Marpicati, isolate the first of these inspirations, and connect it with Fascism, act legitimately; the same cannot be said, in my opinion, of Momigliano's confusing of the two tendencies, and labelling them: *sanità di Carducci.*

And since Böcklin's name has been mentioned, his art, bearing an unmistakable stamp of pagan romanticism, may be conveniently used to describe the pseudo-classicism that throve in the second half of the nineteenth century, of which we find so many instances in Carducci. Whoever compares the mythological subjects of the painters of the Premier Empire, such as Prud'hon, Guérin, Gérard, with Böcklin's mythological subjects, will at once notice the difference between the striving of the first to render as real presences such forms as embody a metaphysical idea of beauty, and the attempt of the second to steep in a dreamland atmosphere forms partaking of common humanity. Böcklin's "concreteness" is, however, only apparent: his fleshy nymphs, his wild tritons and centaurs are realistically treated precisely in order to emphasize that wistful yearning, that *Sehnsucht* which emanates from the whole scene, from the skies either impossibly blue or stormy, from the bewitched waters, from the trees now throbbing with the sap of a rank springtide, now gilded by the touch of a preternatural sunset. Böcklin's painting is indeed a painting of *Sehnsucht,* of conscious yearning after a *fata morgana,* which hovers—a shifting enchantment—on the verge of nothingness. It is a painting of desire and regret, not of pure contemplation.

How different the attitude of the painters of the Premier Empire towards mythology! They aimed at establishing canons, not at dreaming visions. Theirs was still the Roman classicism, an actual presence. Mythology was a part of everyday experience, the ancient world came to life again in fashion, in dress, in furnishing, in politics; Napoleon was one of the Caesars, *Alexander redivivus;* heroes could be seen walking about the streets, the battlefields of Europe were a match for the fights beneath the walls of Troy, and whoever compared the fair mistresses or wives of the brave with the heroines and goddesses of antiquity, did nothing but show the survival of the past in the present. This may well be called a masquerade of heroes; but fantasy found, in putting it into practice, a fulfilment untroubled by nostalgia. Fantasy idolized a present, did not hearken back to an irretrievable past. In other words, the classicism of the Premier Empire is, it may be said, academic, but not exotic.

Quite another thing is the Hellenism, or rather the Hellenic dream that haunted Europe by the middle of the last century. This, by way of contrast, I propose to call *Hellenism, Second Empire:* Second Empire, a period no longer heroic like the Napoleonic one, but democratic, bourgeois, where no antique masquerade was possible in practical life. Rather, everyday life seemed such a shabby affair in that first, gloomy phase of the industrial era, controlled by steam (in comparison with which the modern phase, controlled by power, looks so bright), that the souls of the artists sought refuge and forgetfulness in a dream-world of their minds: forgetfulness from the disappointments of political revolutions, 1830 and 1848, refuge from the growing squalor of towns, from the growing meanness of familiar and social life. Instead of a classical masquerade, they had a classical opium den: *le rêve hellénique.*[4] This did not hark back to the Alexandrian tradition (for in the Alexandrian is implied also the Roman), but rather to the tradition of the great German romantics, Goethe, Schiller, for whom the Mediterranean was a dream, the South a *fata morgana,* mythology an exotic thing, the whole seasoned by the yearning to see of people who are in darkness: *Sehnsucht.* Böcklin signifies such exoticism placed within reach of all: opium made cheap, the wistful vision of a vanished world made easy to conjure up by the thousand Madame Bovarys of a gray, industrial, and democratic era. "La beauté sereine et tranquille de l'art grec paraissait exprimer merveilleusement les nouveaux besoins d'apaisement"—according to the formula of one of the most penetrating students of Neo-Hellenism, René Canat.[5]

I have chosen instances from the painters, but the contrast between *classicism, Premier Empire,* and *pseudoclassic romanticism, Second Empire,* may well be illustrated by two quotations from Italian poets, the first from Ugo Foscolo's famous Ode to Luigia Pallavicini, the second from Carducci's **"Primavera Dorica."**

When Foscolo says to the fair lady,

> I balsami beati
>> Per te le Grazie apprestino,
>> Per te i lini odorati
>> Che a Citerea porgeano
>> Quando profano spino
>> Le punse il piè divino,
>
> Or te piangon gli Amori,
>> Te fra le dive liguri
>> Regina e diva! e fiori
>> Votivi all'ara portano
>> D'onde il grand'arco suona
>> Del figlio di Latona . . . ;[6]

when Foscolo evokes these Graces and Loves to minister to the fair patient, he does not strike any nostalgic note. In order to understand fully the note of actuality which is in these lines, one needs only remember that Graces and Loves were familiar presences no less in the rooms of a lady of the Premier Empire than in those of a Roman or Pompeian lady: they were in the *appliques* of the furniture designed after classical models, they were the candle-bearing Cupids and the Graces supporting a clock or running in a fair frieze round the crown of a chandelier. The images of the poet came natural in a period when the night-table was called *somno,* the cheval-glass *psyché,* the arm-chair an *agrippine,* the incense-burner and the wash-stand *athénienne,* a period when the bed imitated an altar surmounted by a temple-shaped baldaquin.

But read side by side with Foscolo's lines a similar evocation of mythological beings made by Carducci for a fair lady:

> Ti rapirò nel verso; e tra i sereni
>> Ozi de le campagne a mezzo il giorno,
>> Tacendo e rifulgendo in tutti i seni
>>> Ciel, mare, intorno,

> Io per te sveglierò da i colli aprichi
>> Le Driadi bionde sovra il piè leggero
>> E ammiranti a le tue forme gli antichi
>>> Numi d'Omero.

> Muoiono gli altri dèi: di Grecia i numi
>> Non sanno occaso; ei dormon ne' materni
>> Tronchi e ne' fiori, sopra i monti i fiumi
>>> I mari eterni.

> A Cristo in faccia irrigidì ne i marmi
>> Il puro fior di lor bellezze ignude:
>> Ne i carmi, o Lina, spira sol ne i carmi
>>> Lor gioventude;

> E se gli evòca d'una bella il viso
>> Innamorato o d'un poeta il core,
>> Da la santa natura ei con un riso
>>> Lampeggian fuore. . . .[7]

Whereas Foscolo's evocation was thoroughly urban and Alexandrian, and Graces and Loves appeared as familiar ministering presences, we notice at once that in Carducci nymphs and deities are conceived as spirits of a natural scene, and that scene is a romantic one; it is the Holy Nature of Rousseau and his numberless followers, the holy pagan Nature which the Parnassians represented as cursed by Christianity.

> Da la santa natura ei con un riso
> Lampeggian fuore. . . .

This sudden laughter of deities surging from the serene idleness of the noonday fields, while the sky and sea silently glow in all their quarters, with a silence and a glow which the music of the verse conveys to us as immense, this surging laughter of deities which wants to be so thundering and is so pathetically distant and hollow, is exactly the laughter of Böcklin's nymphs, tritons, and centaurs; these Greek gods of Carducci, who know of no setting, are indeed *die Götter Griechenlands* of Schiller, *schöne Wesen aus dem Fabelland,* conjured up by the German poet with many a sigh and *Ach!* of yearning:

> Schöne Welt, wo bist du? Kehre wieder,
> Holdes Blüthenalter der Natur!
> Ach, nur in dem Feenland der Lieder
> Lebt noch deine fabelhafte Spur.
> Ausgestorben trauert das Gefilde,
> Keine Gottheit zeigt sich meinem Blick;
> Ach, von jenem lebenwarmen Bilde
> Blieb der Schatten nur zurück.[8]

The contrast between the mirth of the pagan world, and the gloom of the Christian, is already in Schiller:

> Finstrer Ernst und trauriges Entsagen
> War aus eurem heitern Dienst verbannt. . . .
>
> Damals trat kein grässliches Gerippe
> Vor das Bett des Sterbenden. . . .[9]

And if Schiller pined with many an *Ach!* for this vanished fairyland, Carducci did not spare his *Ahi!* This longing

*Ahi!* of *Sehnsucht* we find at the end of a phantasmagoria of Nature suggesting Böcklin. The Oreads—visions of an opium dream—speak thus to the poet's friend:

> Poi nosco ti addurrem ne le fulgenti
> De l'ametista grotte e del cristallo,
> Ove eterno le forme e gli elementi
>      Temprano un ballo.
>
> T'immergerem ne i fiumi ove il concento
> De' cigni i cori de le Naidi aduna:
> Su l'acque i fianchi tremolan d'argento
>      Come la luna.[10]

The poet concludes:

> Ahi, da che tramontò la vostra etate
> Vola il dolor su le terrene culle![11]

Let us look again at the landscape: in the lines quoted above we have seen serene idleness of noonday fields, silent glow of sea and sky, sunlit hills; now we see grottoes bright with amethyst and crystal, where the elements and fair shapes move in an eternal dance, rivers melodious with swans, on whose waters the limbs of the nymphs glisten silver-like; from the same poem we may quote similar visions of enchantment, such as a fair island kissed by the fragrant kisses of the waves, Dorian forums into which Bacchantes break with lyres and flowers, a solitary valley crowned with tall pine-woods, a lonely promontory facing the Sicilian sea, towards which white lambs flock. . . . It is, in a word, the romantic Greece, or rather Hellas, of the Parnassians, fixed once for all in the prose and verse of Théophile Gautier, Louis Ménard, Leconte de Lisle.[12]

The picture of the serene Hellenic world recurs in Carducci's **"Fantasia"** (1875), which is to be studied side by side with Baudelaire's "Parfum exotique," the poem with a significantly romantic title, which has inspired it:[13]

> Tu parli; e, de la voce a la molle aura
> lenta cedendo, si abbandona l'anima
> del tuo parlar su l'onde carezzevoli,
> e a strane plaghe naviga.
>
> Naviga in un tepor di sole occiduo
> ridente a le cerulee solitudini. . . .[14]

The start is the same as in Baudelaire's sonnet: a sensuous stimulus (more so in Baudelaire, being a perfume) coming from the beloved, carries the poet away to a dream-landscape:

> Quand, les deux yeux fermés, en un soir chaud
>      d'automne,
> Je respire l'odeur de ton sein chaleureux,
> Je vois se dérouler les rivages heureux
>      Qu'éblouissent les feux d'un soleil monotone. . . .

In the poem which immediately follows in "Les Fleurs du Mal, La Chevelure," the poet, dealing with the same theme of exotic vision, says:

> Comme d'autres esprits voguent sur la musique,
> Le mien, ô mon amour! nage sur ton parfum.

Carducci classifies himself among the spirits of the first kind, those who float on a stream of music; this more intellectual stimulus does not conjure up, as in Baudelaire, *la langoureuse Asie et la brûlante Afrique,* nor

> Une île paresseuse où la nature donne
> Des arbres singuliers et des fruits savoureux,

but the isles of Greece, the Hellas of Goethe, Schiller, Ménard, Leconte de Lisle: a soothing vision which allows the soul to forget the present in recollections of the ancient days—in fact, the first title of **"Fantasia"** was "Rimembranze antiche": ancient memories. Baudelaire seeks for a deeper languor in his surrender to the flesh; Carducci, a romantic but not a decadent, knows of no such surrender; he, too, seeks oblivion, but the conventional picture of Greece suffices for his exotic aspiration:

> tra cielo e mar candidi augelli volano,
> isole verdi passano,
>
> e i templi su le cime ardui lampeggiano
> di candor pario ne l'occaso roseo,
> ed i cipressi de la riva fremono,
> e i mirti densi odorano.[15]

White birds, white temples gleaming from the summits: unavoidable elements of such landscape, *cignes blancs, acropoles blanches* of Ménard and his school.

Baudelaire goes on:

> Guidé par ton odeur vers de charmants climats,
> Je vois un port rempli de voiles et de mâts
> Encor tout fatigués par la vague marine,
>
> Pendant que le parfum des verts tamariniers,
> Qui circule dans l'air et m'enfle la narine,
> Se mêle dans mon âme au chant des mariniers.

And Carducci:

> Erra lungi l'odor su le salse aure
> e si mesce al cantar lento de' nauti,
> mentre una nave in vista al porto ammaina
> le rosse vele placida.[16]

*Guidé par ton odeur,* Baudelaire had said, who derives the whole picture from the perfume of the beloved. But, in imitating this link in *Erra lungi l'odor,* Carducci has had to resort to a makeshift: in his poem, the scent is that of the myrtles which the poet imagines he sees. The passage reads like an interpolation, and Carducci's verse, at this point, falls much below Baudelaire's unity of inspiration. If the perfume of the fair bosom naturally evoked for Baudelaire

> des femmes dont l'oeil par sa franchise étonne,

where the languorous appeal of the perfume takes shape, Carducci, after having confined to a parenthesis the theme of the perfume he has utilized so awkwardly, adds, too, a vision of women, but his vision is one of the commonplaces of the conventionalized Hellas:

> Veggo fanciulle scender da l'acropoli
> in ordin lungo; ed han bei pepli candidi,
> serti hanno al capo, e in man rami di lauro,
> tendon le braccia e cantano.[17]

Nor happier proves the amplification of the Baudelairian line:

> Des hommes dont le corps est mince et vigoureux

in this conventional figure of a Greek warrior:

> Piantata l'asta in su l'arena patria,
> a terra salta un uom ne l'armi splendido:
> è forse Alceo da le battaglie reduce
> a le vergini lesbie?[18]

The new element Baudelaire has introduced into Carducci's vision of a classical world of serenity and oblivion beyond reach, is woman as a medium, an intercessor. In **"Primavera Dorica,"** as we have seen, the poet led the way himself: "Ti rapirò nel verso . . . io per te sveglierò da i colli aprichi. . . ." The poet's verse is the "open Sesame" of the dream-world, according to Schiller's recipe ("nur in dem Feenland der Lieder . . ."), which ultimately goes back to Horace.[19] Baudelaire teaches Carducci a more sensuous and Natural manner of evocation (I write Natural with a capital N with reference to the worship of the romantics for Nature): a charm which emanates from the beloved carries the poet away to the land of his heart's desire. Woman, a dispenser of oblivion, imparts also that supreme form of forgetfulness which is the exotic ecstasy. Woman is for the poet the priestess of the divine Hellenic mysteries. Again, a comparison with Foscolo proves illuminating. In the "Ode all'amica risanata" we read:

> E quella, a cui di sacro
>   Mirto te veggo cingere
>   Devota il simulacro
>   Che presiede marmoreo
>   Agli arcani tuoi lari,
>   Ove a me sol sacerdotessa appari,
> Regina fu: Citera
>   E Cipro, ove perpetua
>   Odora primavera,
>   Regnò beata. . . .[20]

In these lines the beloved is Venus' priestess, intercedes for the poet at the shrine of the goddess with a rite which is felt as an ancient one, in the same way as the marble image of Venus is the reincarnation of a Greek masterpiece due to Canova or another classical sculptor. All these things were concrete and actual; they were not mere phantoms of the mind. Compare with this attitude that of Carducci, so pierced with *Sehnsucht:*

> Tu parli; e de la voce a la molle aura
> lenta cedendo, si abbandona l'anima

> del tuo parlar su l'onde carezzevoli,
> e a strane plaghe naviga.

Here the voice of the beloved acts as a spell; elsewhere, the spell is wrought by her eyes. Thus in a short occasional poem to Delia,[21] "O Delia, dei laghi lombardi . . . ," and in the better known ode **"Su l'Adda"**:

> . . . perdermi lungi da gli uomini
> amo or di Lidia nel guardo languido,
> ove nuotano ignoti
> desiderii e misterii.[22]

Exotic desires, to be sure, elusive dreams, "the vain longing after ancient beauty." And romantic mysteries, like the one recorded in the **"Vendette della luna,"** a poem admittedly modelled on one of Baudelaire's *Petits poèmes en prose, Les Bienfaits de la lune;* where the poet drinks "a strange, unspeakable sweetness" from the eyes of the beloved,

> Com'uom che va sotto la luna estiva. . . .
> Ed ei sente un desio d'ignoti amori
> Una lenta dolcezza al cuor gravare,
> E perdersi vorria tra i muti albori
>   E dileguare.[23]

If the classical allusions of **"Fantasia"** could still cloak the romantic character of Carducci's inspiration, no one is likely to be mistaken about it in seeing the precise, conventional, Hellenic landscape make place for "unknown desires and mysteries," "a desire for unknown loves," or that for an "unknown strange shore" (*il desio d'un ignoto estraneo lito*) of the sonnet **"Mattutino e notturno."** For the "desire for an unknown strange shore" is nothing less than the *ulterius ripae amor,* the exotic nostalgia which forms the very essence of romanticism. And if this is not the "formlessness, sentimentality and morbidity of romanticism," from which Professor Momigliano, in the article quoted above, proclaimed Carducci exempt, one wonders what he means by them. Moreover, is Momigliano right in saying that "there is never in Carducci the theme of ruins and silence as a note of melancholy and neglect"? Let us take the central theme of the ode **"Alle Fonti del Clitunno,"** apropos of which Momigliano writes: "The sylvan, idyllic, moonlit silences of Clitumnus are filled with a war-cry which is repeated from mountain to mountain, and with a rout of warriors and horses." One might point out to Momigliano that the war-cry precedes, and that "Tutto ora tace" ("All is silence now") follows, and introduces the funeral elegy of the departed nymphs, driven away by the red-haired Galilean, according to the formula of romantic Neo-Hellenism (Schiller, Ménard). True, that "Tutto ora tace" is not to be interpreted in too romantic a light. To De Lollis[24] it recalled Byron's "Far other scene is Trasimene now;" however, certain lines of Propertius,[25] which can hardly be defined pre-romantic, are just as apposite:

> heu Vei veteres! et vos tum regna fuistis,
>   et vestro posita est aurea sella foro:
> nunc intra muros pastoris bucina lenti

cantat, et in vestris ossibus arva metunt.

While undoubtedly Carducci in the last part of his ode swings over to the genuinely classical, Horatian, manner, with his apostrophe to the "Itala madre," there is little doubt that the central part of the poem, with its complaint "Visser le ninfe, vissero," is typical of Neo-Hellenism, Second Empire. Indeed, it is curious to see how the poet, who misses on the banks of Clitumnus classical ilexes and cypresses, and deprecates the weeping willow, seems not to be aware that he himself is planting on those banks, through his elegy, the most melancholy weeping willow that a Böcklin might have imagined. Now, already Leopardi's canzone "Alla Primavera o Delle Favole antiche" was an elegy for the departed nymphs,

Vivi, tu, vivi, o santa
Natura? . . .
Già di candide Ninfe i rivi albergo . . . ;[26]

a canzone whose theme, that

. . . la sciagura e l'atra
Face del ver consunse
Innanzi tempo

(sorrow and the gloomy torch of Truth destroyed too soon) the glorious age of the joyous fables of old, Carducci had taken up in a mediocre juvenile poem to Phoebus Apollo:[27]

Il vero inesorabile
Di fredda ombra coprio
Te larva d'almi secoli
Nume de' greci e mio.[28]

Carducci went on:

E pèra il grave secolo
Che vita mi spegnea,
Che agghiaccia il canto ellenico
Nell' anima febèa.[29]

Such lines, insignificant as poetry, are nevertheless significant in so far as they help us to understand why Carducci, when he discovered the foreign Neo-Hellenism, mistook it for genuine classicism. The *grave secolo* was the time in which young Carducci lived, *i.e.,* the Italian romantic period which bore the imprint of Manzoni's Christianity. The naïve, false idea Carducci formed in those juvenile years of the character of romanticism, was responsible for the misunderstanding which brought about, in his mature poetry, the odd contamination of genuine classicism by pseudo-classicism, *i.e.,* romantic exoticism. To Carducci the Neo-Guelph movement (Gioberti in politics, Manzoni in literature) appeared in those years almost as the philosophical background of the feeble mediaeval and sentimental strain of Giovanni Prati and the other provincial disciples of foreign romanticism who then held the field. Here is the definition of the romantic school Carducci gave in the essay "Di alcune condizioni della presente letteratura in Italia" (1867):

Faith is the principle and foundation of this school; *i.e.,* in philosophy proper it returns to the Holy Fathers, in political philosophy to the Holy Fathers as well, in particular to the ideas of Saint Augustine and Bossuet; in poetry it returned to the Middle Ages and meant to draw from reality, but soon went astray from reality, soon degenerated into mysticism and sentimentality, which are distortions of intellect and feeling that go well together.

When Carducci wrote these words, he had just begun to make a direct acquaintance of the great foreign romantic writers. Of these masters whom Carducci took as models, forgetting his juvenile plea for an out-and-out native (*paesana*) art, Victor Hugo and Heinrich Heine came first. But what Carducci saw in them were not the more deeply romantic aspects, but rather a rhetoric of contrasts and antitheses, of strained and violent images, which are no more romantic than baroque; such flashes of style as: "Laissez passer Caïn! il appartient à Dieu!", "Non, Liberté! non, peuple! Il ne faut pas qu'il meure,"

Ich trage im Herzen viel Schlangen
Und dich, Geliebte mein.

No, Carducci's romanticism did not begin with the polemic and ironical verse written in imitation of Barbier, Hugo, Heine: his actual romanticism began when his soul found itself in the condition of receiving that form of the *mal du siècle* whose formula is, as we have seen: "La beauté sereine et tranquille de l'art grec paraissait exprimer merveilleusement les nouveaux besoins d'apaisement."

Carducci found himself in this state of mind after 1870, when that kind of craven politics which had succeeded to the fertile passions of the Risorgimento, prompted him to seek refuge from nauseating reality in a world of pure contemplation. The Neo-Hellenic exoticism of the Parnassians seemed designed to satisfy the *besoin d'apaisement* of the ancient worshipper of the classics, Carducci. Just at the time of the **Primavere elleniche,** which are the first fruits of Carducci's exotic dream, the poet wrote to a friend: "From time to time one must grant me these returns to the serene, almost idolatrous contemplation of the aesthetic forms of naturally divine Greece: from time to time I must be allowed to seek some rest in this labour of craftsmanship, to take my mind off reality, which otherwise would stifle me with indignation and disgust." *La Grecia naturalmente divina:* the Parnassian opium den where Carducci sought oblivion, down to the Baudelairian *cupio dissolvi* in the woman-landscape of dreamland. The romantic Hugo and Heine had supplied Carducci only with a store of baroque metaphors and epigrammatic conceits; but this Carducci still had a firm grip upon reality, upon the present, kept upon it a steadfast gaze in order to warn and inveigh. It was the "classical" craftsmen, the polished Gautier and Platen, who transformed Carducci into a thorough romantic; while hammering his verse, he might well have imagined he was imitating his ancient master Horace; actually his face was turned away from reality, the Parnassian syren murmured:

L'ora presente è in vano, non fa che percuotere e
  fugge;
    sol nel passato è il bello, sol ne la morte è il vero.[30]

The Carducci of these lines, contrary to what Momigliano
imagines in his article on "Sanità di Carducci," might have
sung Ravenna, the city made beautiful by death; this Carducci is not he who, in Marpicati's words, "made no
concessions to any kind of exoticism:" it is not to this Carducci, who couched in classical rhythms a romantic
inspiration, in the footsteps of Platen,[31] that the Italians of
to-day pay their tribute. They live in the present; they see
Truth and Beauty only in the present life of the dynamic
Italy of Mussolini. Their Carducci is the poet of
**"Nell'Annuale della fondazione di Roma,"** that *carmes
saeculare* of Rome, the eternal and ever new.

## Notes

1. Commemoration held at Bologna on June 25, 1935,
   reproduced in part in the *Corriere della Sera* as *La
   romanità e la fede di Giosue Carducci,* and printed
   in its entirety in *Pan* (July, 1935) as *Carducci e noi.*

2. Inaugural lecture at the University of Rome on the
   theme *La passione politica di G. Carducci,* partly
   reprinted in the *Corriere della Sera,* March 9, 1935.

3. *Appunti sulla lingua poetica del Carducci,* in *Saggi
   sulla forma poetica italiana dell' Ottocento,* Bari,
   1929.

4. Of the drug-like nature of this pseudo-classicism
   Carducci himself seems to warn us in the poem
   which introduces the *Odi barbare, Ideale:* "Since a
   soothing vapour of ambrosia, shed from thy cup, has
   enwrapped me, O Hebe, smilingly vanished with a
   goddess' step, I no longer feel on my head the
   shadow of Time or of cold Care; I feel, O Hebe, hellenic life flow tranquil through my veins." One
   notices in these lines the elusive, romantic image,
   typical of an opium dream, of "smilingly vanished"
   Hebe.

5. *Une Forme du Mal du Siècle, Du sentiment de la
   solitude morale chez les Romantiques et les Parnass-
   iens,* Paris, 1907 (conclusion).

6. "Let the Graces prepare for thee the blessed balsams,
   for thee the scented linen they spread for Cytherea
   when a sacrilegious thorn pricked her divine
   foot. . . . Now Loves weep for thee, thou queen and
   goddess among Ligurian deities! and they bring votive flowers to the altar whence thunders the mighty
   bow of Latona's son."

7. "I will carry thee away on the wings of poetry; and
   among the serene idleness of the noonday fields,
   while the sky and sea around silently glow in all
   their quarters, I will awake for thee from the sunlit
   hills the fair-haired Dryads light of foot, and the
   ancient Homeric gods enraptured by thy form. The
   other deities die: those of Greece know of no setting;
   they sleep in the maternal trees and flowers, on the
   mountains, streams, and seas eternal. In the face of
   Christ there froze in the marble the pure bloom of
   their naked beauties: only in songs, O Lina, only in
   songs breathes their youth; and if the face of a
   woman in love or the heart of a poet evokes them,
   they flash with a laughter out from holy nature."

8. "O lovely world, where art thou? Come back,
   splendid prime of Nature! Alas, thy legendary imprint
   lives on only in the fairyland of song. The stricken
   countryside saddens; no divinity shows itself to my
   eyes. Alas, of that life-warm vision only the shadow
   was left behind."

9. "Gloomy sternness and sad renunciation were
   banished from your blithe service. . . . Then no
   fearful skeleton came before the death-bed." Schiller's conception passes on to Leconte de Lisle
   (*Hypatie*), Swinburne (*Hymn to Proserpine, Dolores*),
   *etc.* Leconte de Lisle's lines on the pagan virgin
   martyr:

   Dors, ô blanche victime, en notre âme pro-
     fonde, . . .
   Dors! l'impure laideur est la reine du monde,
   Et nous avons perdu le chemin de Paros.
   Les Dieux sont en poussière et la terre est muette:
   Rien ne parlera plus dans ton ciel déserté.
   Dors! mais, vivante en lui, chante au coeur du
     poète
   L'hymne mélodieux de la sainte beauté.—

   and Swinburne's lines on the pagan arch-prostitute,
   Dolores,

   (What ailed us, O gods, to desert you
   For creeds that refuse and restrain? . . .
   Cry aloud; for the old world is broken:
   Cry out; for the Phrygian is priest. . . .)

   are informed with the same *Sehnsucht.*

10. "Then we will lead thee to the grottoes bright with
    amethyst and crystal, where the elements and fair
    shapes move in an eternal dance. We will dip thee
    into the streams where the music of the swans sum-
    mons the choirs of the Naiads: on the waters their
    limbs glisten silvery like the moon."

11. "Alas, since your age has set, sorrow hovers on the
    earthly cradles."

12. See for all *Rèveries d'un paien mistique: Euforion,
    La Grèce; Hellas,* by Ménard, on whose Hellenism
    *l'esthétique parnassienne repose,* according to Mau-
    rice Barrès.

13. The relation between Carducci and Baudelaire has
    been dealt with by Professor P. P. Trompeo in two
    lectures, delivered in April, 1935, before the Arcadia,
    in Rome.

14. "Thou speakest; my soul, softly yielding to the
    languid cadence of thy voice, abandons itself on the
    caressing waves of thy speech, and sails to strange
    shores. It sails in a warmth of setting sun, smiling at
    the azure solitudes."

15. "White birds fly between the sky and the sea; green islands drift, and the temples, high on the summits, gleam with Parian sheen in the rosy sunset, and the cypresses on the shore quiver, and the thick myrtles send forth their perfume."

16. "The perfume is scattered abroad on the salty breezes, and mingles with the slow singing of the mariners, while a ship in sight of the harbour peacefully lowers its red sails."

17. "I see maidens descending from the acropolis in a long file; they wear the comely white peplos, garlands on their heads, and laurel branches in their hands; they stretch out their arms and sing."

18. "Having fixed his spear on his native land, a man shining in armour leaps ashore: is he perchance Alceus coming back from the battlefield to the Lesbian virgins?"

19. Odes to Lollius (IV, ix) and to Melpomene (III, xxx); the theme of immortality secured by verse was taken over by the poets of the Pléiade and by Shakespeare, Schiller, Gautier

> (Les dieux eux-mêmes meurent,
> Mais les vers souverains
>                     demeurent
> Plus forts que les airains),

Carducci ("Muor Giove, l'inno del poeta resta").

20. "And she, whose image I see thee garlanding with sacred myrtle, the marble image which holds sway over thy innermost home, where thou appearest priestess to me alone, she was a queen: she ruled in her blessedness over Cythera and Cyprus, where is the scent of a perpetual spring."

21. Delia was the Greek name of a Junoesque actress, Adele May, who in the circle of the *Cronaca Bizantina* in Rome played a part not unlike that of Madame Sabatier, Gautier's Apollonie, in the Parnassian *milieux* in Paris.

22. "Now I love to lose myself, far from mankind, in Lydia's languid eyes, where unknown desires and mysteries float."

23. "Like a man who wanders beneath the summer moon . . . and feels a desire of unknown loves weigh on his heart with a lazy sweetness, and would wish to lose himself in the mute glimmer and fade away."

24. *Appunti sulla lingua poetica del Carducci,* p. 131.

25. Propertius' lines are to be read in the light of *Elegies,* IV, i: "Hoc quodcumque vides, hospes . . . ," and IV, iv: "Quid tum Roma fuit . . . ," where the situation is reversed.

26. "Dost thou live, dost thou live, O holy nature? . . . The streams, once the dwelling-place of white nymphs. . . ."

27. Edizione Nazionale, I, p. 79.

28. "Inexorable Truth cast a cold shadow over thee, a phantom from glorious centuries, deity of the Greeks and mine."

29. "May the stern century perish, which stifled my life and freezes the Hellenic song in the Phoebean soul."

30. "The present hour is in vain, it does nothing but strike and fly away; Beauty is only in the past, Truth is in death only" ("Presso l'urna di Percy Bysshe Shelley").

31. The relation of Carducci to Platen has been studied by various critics (M. Azzolini, *G. Carducci und die deutsche Litteratur,* Tübingen, 1910; F. Sternberg, *La poesia neo-classica tedesca e le Odi barbare di G. Carducci,* Trieste, 1910; F. Hunziker, *Carducci und Deutschland,* Aarau, 1927). But these critics seem to have overlooked the derivation of the ode *Per la morte di Napoleone Eugenio* (which offers an excellent instance of romantic inspiration) from Platen's *Die Wiege des Königs von Rom.* In both poems is the same nostalgic vision of a heroic past beyond recall, the same fearful sense of mysterious forebodings:

> Aber ach! Kein Wiegengesang der Liebe,
> Waffenlärm schlug hart an das Ohr des Säuglings:
> Eine Welt, schon lagert sie sich um seine
>                     Tragische Kindheit.

Compare with:

> Vittoria e pace da Sebastopoli
> sopian co'l rombo de l'ali candide
> il piccolo: Europa ammirava. . . .
> Ma di dicembre, ma di brumaio
> cruento è il fango, *etc.*

There is a clear parallelism between the figures of Platen's Maria Louisa and Carducci's Laetitia; both figures strike the same romantic note: *Weh, alles nusonst! . . . Alles so tief liegt!* The conclusion of Carducci's ode, as a critic (Azzolini p. 35) has noticed, seems to echo the conclusion of Schiller's *Der Taucher:*

> Es kommen, es kommen die Wasser all,
> Sie rauschen herauf, sie rauschen nieder—
> Den Jüngling bringt keines wieder.

The connection between Platen's ode on the young son of Napoleon who lost his crown, and Schiller's ballad on the youth who dives into the depths in order to recover the cup which the king has thrown there, may have been brought about by a fanciful analogy between the two destinies, as well as by such verbal singularities as that between Platen's last phrase: "Alles so tief liegt!" and the opening of Schiller's ballad:

> Wer wagt es . . .
> Zu tauchen in diesen Schlund? . . .
> Wer ist der Beherzte, ich frage wieder,
> Zu tauchen in diese Tiefe nieder?

## Eugenio Donadoni (essay date 1969)

SOURCE: Donadoni, Eugenio. "Giosuè Carducci." In *A History of Italian Literature,* pp. 455-87. New York: New York University, 1969.

[*In the following essay, Donadoni follows Carducci's career path and classifies Carducci's poems chronologically into groupings of landscape, introspection, political poetry, and lyrics that combined these characteristics.*]

Writing within a prevailingly Romanticist or Manzonian generation, the figure of Giosuè Carducci was that of a restorer of the classical tradition. His style and language, as though reverting to the somewhat solemn modes of Foscolo, departed from the "spoken" character of Manzonian prose and recovered a native literary flavor. Drawn more from the wellspring of writers than from the ordinary popular language, they raised even the speech of the people to the special tone of the more distinctly literary tradition. In so doing, there was no contriving or willful capriciousness, because such was the spontaneous tendency of the poet.

Furthermore, a large part of Carducci's poetry touched on themes which seemed to depart from the atmosphere of the Romantic nineteenth century. It carried human nostalgia back, not towards the Middle Ages, but towards Hellenism and the Roman spirit. Nonetheless Carducci was a poet, and poetry is incompatible with polemical schemes and principles. While on the one hand he was in accord with the Classicists of the pre-Manzonian and pre-Romantic tradition, on the other hand he brought to his poetry and even to his prose the affections and the ways and the forms of a more intense Romanticism.

As always happens with true poets, he had at one and the same time the visage of tradition and that of innovation. D'Annunzio and Pascoli later were to take their treatment of the poetic image from his example, and from him D'Annunzio derived the form of his prose phraseology, although directing it to other ends.

Carducci was born on July 27, 1835 in Val di Castello, a hamlet of Pietrasanta in Versilia, Lunigiana (near Viareggio), to Dr. Michele and his wife Ildegonda Celli. His father was among those affected by the great patriotic aspirations that resulted in the Italian Risorgimento, and because of his ideas he had been confined for a year in Volterra.

In 1838 young Giosuè followed his father to Bólgheri, a hamlet of Castagneto in the Maremma region. It was in that place that the world of his affections and imagination was formed. We might say that the nostalgic foundation of Carducci's poetry, that which nourished the melancholy of his great odes came from this experience directly, because in poetry it brought him recollections of that land, and also indirectly, because the first movement of his meditations upon the "enormous mystery of the universe," upon the change of forms in the immutability of life, was always joined to an image of that sunny and funereal land which was an illustrious burial place of the Etruscans and revealed some of their abandoned ruins. Thereafter, in whatever place he happened to be, he always silently compared the landscape with that of the Maremma in which he spent his childhood.

From Alfieri he received his first images of poetry and his first civic affections, and it was with Alfieri's tragedies that his mother taught him to read. The emotional force of the Carduccian style, in its best virtues and also in its defects, would sometimes seem the natural result of such teaching. He learned Latin from his father, and it was by that path that the heroic myths of classical antiquity entered his mind. Homer and Vergil attracted him far more than Manzoni, whom his father, a "fervent Manzonian," never succeeded in making him truly like. He read Roman history and was passionately drawn to the French Revolution.

In 1848, the year when the movement for independence seemed close to victory and then was miserably disappointed, Dr. Michele, opposed by the reactionaries and even struck by peasants, was obliged to abandon that inhospitable country and move, first to Laiatico and later to Florence. The boy went to finish his studies in the humanities and rhetoric with the padres of the *Scuole Pie* [religious schools] and stayed there until 1852. His teacher of rhetoric was Father Geremia Barsottini, to whom the poet rendered homage for his prose translation of all the odes of Horace and to whom he always remained devoted.

These studies revealed to him the greatness of poetry. In awaiting Italian unification, his feeling drew from the liberalism of his father and his favorite authors, such as Mazzini and Foscolo. Because of the privations of his impoverished home, the mind of the adolescent was tempered in lofty passions including the supreme passion of poetry, and there too was formed that difficult, disdainful character which often made difficulties for him in social encounters.

When he had completed his secondary education, he went for a year to Celle on Monte Amiata, following his father's peregrinations, but towards the end of 1853 he won a competition for a resident scholarship in the Normal School of Pisa. In 1856 he received his doctor's degree and the degree for teaching.

In that year, with his friends Gargani, Targioni and Chiarini, he founded the literary society of the *Amici Pedanti* [Pedantic Friends]. This was an anti-Romantic and pagan movement, which quickly aroused violent arguments, as may be seen in the writing which Carducci published in December, *Giunta alla derrata.* Meanwhile, in October, he had begun teaching rhetoric in the secondary school of San Miniato al Tedesco.

In July, 1857, the first book of poems by Giosuè Carducci appeared, the *Rime.* It contained twenty-five sonnets, twelve cantos, and three lyrics entitled **"Saggi di un canto** alle Muse" ["**Essays of a Song to the Muses**"]. The poet had repudiated any poems which testified to a romantic immediacy, and here he soberly published what best represented him. He was still far from his great poetry, but already, in certain places, the particular accent of the poet was discernible, that accent which was to sound purer and higher in the *Rime Nuove* and in the *Odi Barbare.*

In that same year, he was the winner in a competition for the chair of Greek in the secondary school of Arezzo, but his appointment was not approved by the granducal government. Thereupon he went to Florence, where he existed in dignified poverty by giving some lessons. Meanwhile, he was studying and reading.

In November of that year his brother Dante took his own life, casting the darkest sorrow into the heart of Carducci, who penned heartbroken lines to his dead brother. And a new misfortune struck the poet the following year, the death of his father; he found now himself the head of the ruined family. In August of 1858, he took his mother and his brother Walfredo to a very poor house in the Borg'Ognisanti section of Florence and set to work to earn a living by giving private lessons and editing the texts of the Bibliotechina Diamante of the publisher Gaspare Barbèra. In March, 1859, he married young Elvira Menicucci.

On April 27 of that year, the union of Tuscany to Italy became a fact; times were changing, and the free spirits of the Risorgimento felt that their hour had struck.

Toward the end of the year the poet went to take the chair of Greek in the secondary school of Pistoia and remained there until November, 1860. Terenzio Mamiani, the minister of education, appointed him to the chair of Italian eloquence in the University of Bologna. On the 27th of that month, the poet gave his inaugural lecture. At first he felt uncomfortable; he felt the conflict between his own poetry and the obligations of philology. But while he fortified his knowledge of the classics at Bologna, he also turned his attention to the poetry and prose of other nations.

The political life of Italy, only just emerging from the great travail of the Risorgimento, was pressing everywhere and urgently with all its passions. Many hopes seemed to be disappointed, because the highest-minded men always found that everything that was accomplished was inferior to their great dream. Hence, criticism and discontentment were born.

Carducci had been a monarchist, and now, after the tragic event of Aspromonte in Calabria (where Garibaldi was wounded and captured by government troops, August 29, 1862), he felt himself a republican. For a man of Carducci's stature, however, being a monarchist or a republican did not mean shutting oneself up within a party; it meant rather having a feeling for whichever party might seem best fitted to further the development of Italy. Faithful to this important truth, in his riper years Carducci could look toward the monarchy with new sympathy without being unfaithful to his principles.

So now Carducci was a republican, and an impatient one. His nature was too impetuous for him to realize what a great effort the men coming after the heroic period were making to weld a unity so recently achieved. He felt too much urgency, and his language was impregnated with that sense of urgency, losing expressive force in proportion to its increase in violence; just as when a man falls prey to rage, his voice changes to strangled, inarticulate sound. Many of his poems of this period bear in their lines the aggressive impetuosity which he could not give vent to in political action.

Then, under the pseudonym of Enotrio Romano, he wrote his polemical poems, those which would be called *Giambi* [*Iambi*], the name which one of his books of collected poems later bore. In 1863 he wrote his famous "**Inno a Satana**" ["**Hymn to Satan**"].

In 1868 the volume *Levia Gravia* appeared; then in 1871 the volume of *Poesie,* which, in addition to the preceding collections, contained the *Giambi ed Epodi* and is divided into three parts: *Decennali* (1860-1870); *Levia Gravia* (1857-1860); and the *Nuove Poesie* (1872).

Having suffered so many trials, the poet finally freed himself of that sort of fieriness which sometimes kept him from being poetical. By now, more than one of the poems that were to form the *Rime Nuove* (Eng. tr., 1916, *New Rhymes*), in which is found the best of Carducci's art, had been composed. In 1873 the poet began the *Odi barbare,* of which the first series appeared in July, 1877.

With the *Odi barbare* the poet intended to depart from the old meters: "I hate the outworn poetry," he wrote. This was a momentary hate, but it is certain that he felt an urge for new melodic forms, which would give to the Italian language the swirls and spirals of the ancient meters: the hexameter and the pentameter, the Alcaic, the Asclepiad and the Sapphic. The result was an amplification of his own melodic ability. Even when Carducci turned back to the usual meters of Italian poetry, he bore the musical experience that he had acquired in the *Odi barbare* and reached a more inward and original melodiousness.

From 1881 Carducci's fame, especially with the younger generation, grew stronger and more assured. It was helped by new literary periodicals, such as the *Fanfulla della Domenica,* the *Cronaca Bizantina,* and the *Domenica Letteraria.* His poems were awaited by his followers with an anticipation of beauty that was never disappointed. His words as a teacher and a great Italian brought light to their minds and encouraged them.

The *Nuove Odi barbare* appeared in 1882, and in that year he delivered his famous speech "On the Death of Giuseppe Garibaldi," a full-voiced oration in which, with epical accent, the legend of the hero in the years to come is foretold. In 1883 the sonnets of the *Ça ira* appeared. Then in 1887 the *Rime Nuove,* followed in 1889 by the third series of *Odi barbare.*

The last volume of Carducci's poetry, ***Rime e Ritmi***, appeared in 1899. Then the poet collected all his poetic work from 1850 to 1900, and in farewell set the famous lines:

> Fior tricolor,
> Tramontano le stelle in mezzo al mare
> E si spengono i canti entro il mio core.
> . . . . .
> [Three-colored flower,
> The stars set in the sea
> And in my heart the songs die away.]

He had written them one joyous evening, with other *stornelli* [ditties] in the office of the *Cronaca Bizantina* in Rome. He detached them and included them with a different meaning in that collection.

The last years of his life were sad. Illness had already set in by 1885. Then in 1899 hemiplegia deprived him of the use of one hand and made speech difficult. Nevertheless, he kept on working, but in 1904 he had to resign from teaching. He had been made a senator in 1890, and the Italian Parliament decreed him a pension. The poet answered: "Who am I that a national pension should be given me? What have I done, except love the fatherland, this poor and great and lovely Italy, even when I seemed most provoked with her! I have done this and nothing more. But it is little." In 1906 he was awarded the Nobel Prize in literature, but that prize came to a man exhausted and almost destroyed by illness. On February 16, 1907, Giosuè Carducci died in his modest house in Bologna.

In various ways the critics have indicated certain ideal stages in the development of Carducci's poetry, grouping the various compositions according to their spontaneous affinity. This is a matter of chronological, not inward phases. In this study we shall make use of this expedient, arranging the various moods of inspiration in groupings which best serve interpretation of that poetry.

A first stage is the landscape: the vision of nature; yet in which human history is present, for there is no fragment of earth where the memory of man is not alive. But the poet's mind clings closer to the vision of nature than to the appeal of human history, or to a need to retire into himself and to resolve the landscape into an inner meditation. The heights to which this Carduccian poetry of the elementary landscape can reach are shown in the verses of **"San Martino"** or of **"Mezzogiorno alpino."** (I say "elementary" to distinguish it from the landscape on which the imprint of human history is stronger than nature.)

In **"San Martino,"** that rough land, that sea howling and lashed to whiteness under the mistral, and the mist, the odor of the wine, the first crackling under the spit, and the hunter who whistles and watches the migration of the flights of birds black as "exiled thoughts," make up in sharp focus, a simple town, which has the same the enchantment of a *fata morgana* (of a mirage).

Even more inward is **"Mezzogiorno alpino"** [**"Alpine Noontime"**], which was written on August 27, 1895, at Courmayeur. The silence of "the great circle of the Alps" is expressed with solemn quietness in eight lines, in which even the rhyme of the fourth and the last lines, accented and broken off, contribute to the creation of a new musicality as a prelude to more modern styles:

> Nel gran cerchio de l'alpi, su'l granito
> Squallido e scialbo, su' ghiacciai candenti,
> Regna sereno intenso ed infinito
> Nel suo grande silenzio il mezzodi.
>
> Pini ed abeti senza aura di venti
> Si drizzano nel sol che gli penètra,
> Sola garrisce in picciol suon di cetra
> L'acqua che tenue tra i sassi fluì.
> . . . . .
> [In that great circle of the Alps, on the granite
> Bleak and pale, above shining glaciers,
> Intense and infinite in its great silence
> Serenely reigns midday.
>
> Pines and firs in the still air
> Stand in the sun which pierces them,
> Only the water with faint sound of lyre
> Murmurs softly as between the stones its flows.]

But sometimes landscapes are partly real, partly of desire, as in a sonnet from ***Iuvenilia:***

> Candidi soli e riso di tramonti
> Mormoreggiar di selve brune a' venti
> Con sussurio de fredde acque cadenti
> Giú per li verdi tramiti de' monti . . .
> . . . . .
> [Bright suns and laughter of sunsets,
> Murmuring of dark woods in the winds,
> With whispering of icy waters falling
> Down, beside green pathways in the mountains . . .]

In these landscapes of desire ("and bright moonlight which whitens the silent paths"), there is often a thought of woman ("And the cherished appearance of my lady"), and sometimes recollections of history, but not such that taking them unto himself the poet creates a personal, almost autobiographical lyric, as he does at other times.

In **"Mattutino e Notturno"** [**"Matinal and Nocturne"**], thought of a woman is linked with a landscape: in the morning purified by rain, the poet's thought wings back to a woman "like the trill of an ascending lark": in the moonlit night, "he admires the moon glimpsed from the lone hillocks . . ." The same is true also in **"Sol e Amore"** [**"Sun and Love"**]; **"Primavera classica"** [**"Classical Spring"**]; **"Autunno romantico,"** and so on.

**"Vendette della Luna"** [**"Moon's Revenge"**] is a lunar landscape seen above a moon-white girl, and in it are visual touches of rare lightness, "a green night of April," and a sweet and gentle ending:

> Com'uom che va sotto la luna estiva
> Tra verdi susurranti alberi al piano
> Che in fantastica luce arde la riva
> Presso e lontano,

Ed ei sente un desio d'ignoti amori
Una lenta dolcezza al cuor gravare,
E perdersi vorria tra muti albori
E dilaguare.

. . . . .

[As one who to the plain goes through green trees
Rustling beneath the summer moon
Which bathes in wond'rous light the shore,
Both near and far,

And feels desire of unknown loves
Etch slow a sweetness on his heart,
And gladly mid the silent trees would lose himself
And vanish.]

Then there is the **"Notte di Maggio"** [**"May Night"**], a Petrarchan sonnet, elegant in its purely melodic play of rhymes and echoes: *notte, stelle, onde, verde, colli, luna.* It is a nostalgic landscape, but one where the remembrance is something still fleeting and tenuous: "Alas! how much of my early youth I saw again at the top of the shining hills." There is something of a diffused, pale moonlight in the lines. For no matter how Carducci vituperated the moon, and in spite of lines like "I hate your stupid round face" (*Classicismo e Romanticism),* the moon is still an essential part of much of his poetry.

**"La Madre"** is landscape, and one of the finest in Carducci. The sight of the sculptured group in which Adriano Cecioni had shaped a mother and her child, creates in the poet's mind a landscape over which questioning and hopes arise concerning the "pious justice of work." The dawn saw this woman who is now tossing her little one in the air: "watched her as with rapid bare feet she passed through the dewy odor of the hay" (where one must admire that dexterous juxtaposition, that *callida junctura* of the *roridi odori* "dewy odors" still more daring than the "green silence" which was so much discussed). The landscape takes sharper focus in the luminous lines that follow. "As she bent her broad back at noon over the blond furrows, the elms white with dust heard her humming defiance of the raucous crickets on the hillocks."

At another time, this landscape will be that of **"Il Bove"** [**"The Ox"**] where all the images that depict the "pious ox" create around him the broad atmosphere of the countryside, that *divin del piano silenzio verde* [divine silence of the green plain], which is one of the boldest and most charming expressions of the poet.

Even the ideal image of a poet will, for Carducci, resolve itself into a landscape, as in the sonnet **"Virgilio."** An extended melody evokes lyrical reminiscences of Vergil: the "compassionate moon," which over the "parched fields" "diffuses the impending summer coolness," the river bank, the "hidden nightingale," and the vast serenity. Here Carducci has composed a landscape in words which will close with a line taken from Vergil, and before Carducci, was translated by Tasso: *Tale il tuo verso a me, divin poeta.* [So is thy verse to me, divine poet].

In this poetry of landscapes, not yet affected by the inspiration of history, the sonnet **"Momento epico"** has a place. The epos rises to the poet's mind from the vision of "rich Bologna," passing on to "epic Ferrara," and in his heart "once more the sun kindles the immortal fantasies"—a sonnet of grave and powerful beauty. Here too is the place of the pathos of the sonnet **"Santa Maria degli Angeli"** in which the poet invokes Fra Francesco as an image of that landscape. Also the poem **"Fiesole":**

Su le mura, dal rotto etrusco sasso,
La lucertola figge la pupilla,
E un bosco di cipressi a i venti lasso
Ulula, e il vespro solitario brilla.

. . . . .

[On the walls, from the crumbled Etruscan rock,
the lizard stares,
And a weary wood of cypresses wails in the wind,
and the lonely evening shines].

**"Courmayeur"** is a vast landscape in which the view suggests this introspective movement. "The soul strays in slow wandering, coming from its regretted memories, and reaches eternal hopes."

This sense of landscape will touch still more tenuous, ghostly, and dreamlike forms, as in **"Visione,"** which ends: "Without memories, without sorrow, yet like an island, green, afar, in a pale serenity."

The vignette, or sketch, also has some relation to landscape; for example, those lines which Carducci himself named **"Vignetta,"** in which he sketches a girl in a "tender forest," and in that sketch entitled **"Egle."** Sometimes the landscape is a recollection, as in the beautiful hexameters of **"Un Sera in San Pietro"** [**"An Evening in Saint Peter's"**].

Although dominated by his sense of landscape, the poet voiced an invective against "old Nature" in **"Idillio di Maggio."** "Oh, how shabby is this masquerade of roses and violets! This vaulted sky, how closed! How wan thou art, O Sun!" But it is a pose; the first impulse of Carducci's heart is to cling to Mother Earth, not to the old but to eternal Nature.

Whereas in this first stage of the Carduccian lyric, the landscape, external nature, prevails over the inward affections of the poet and over history made by men. In the second stage the poet contemplates his own heart, his own joys and sorrows, and questions himself, binding those feelings to the landscape and at times attaining the highest nostalgia.

*Levia Gravia,* the book in which there is already more apt gracefulness of images and rhythms than in his polemical poems, opens with the **"Farewell"** which, as it announces "the new hymns," sings:

Addio, serena etate,
Che di forme e di suoni il cor s'appaga;
O primavera de la vita, addio!
Ad altri le beate
Visioni e la gloria, e a l'ombra vaga
De' boschetti posare appresso il rio

E co 'l queto desio
Far di sé specchio queto al mondo intero:
Noi per aspro sentiero
Amore e odio incalza austero e pio,
A noi fra i tormentati or convien ire
Tesoreggiando le vendette e l'ire.

. . . . .

[Farewell, serene age
Which appeases the heart with forms and sounds,
O springtime of life, farewell!
For others the blessed visions,
And the glory and, in the pleasant shade
Of woods to rest at water's edge
And, moved by calm desire,
To serve as quiet mirror of all the world:
We must needs tread the rough harsh path,
By love and hate pursued, stern and devout,
Our lot 'tis now to mingle with tormented men,
Treasuring the vengeance and the wraths.]

The fact is that that "springtime of life" in the poetry of Carducci is an ideal time that acts as a "quiet mirror of all the world." It is a moment which he is going to find in every epoch of his life: in th[at] of *Juvenilia* and *Giambi* ["Iambuses"] as well in that of *Rime nuove* and of *Odi barbare.*

One of the first and clearest examples of this introspective poetry is the **"Ripresa"** [**"Resumption"**] between Books I and II of *Giambi ed Epodi: Avanti! avanti!* [**"Forward!"**] of October, 1872. Here attention to word and rhythm is greater than in previous compositions. The invocation to glory, with that withdrawal of the poet within himself, has with a certain expressive ease the marks of high poetry: the words to Mameli are intimately pure.

The lines to the author of *Il Mago* are part of this introspective poetry: "O Severino [Ferrari], the dwelling of thy songs, the haunt of thy dreams, I know it well." The sonnet **"Francesco Petrarca,"** in *Levia Gravia,* is an idyllic desire of the world to raise an altar to the poet of Laura "in the green darkness of the woods," "with a nightingale singing 'mid the fronds."

Then there are the poems which might be called "songs of Maremma nostalgia." Such a nostalgic song is **"Colli Toscani"** [**"Tuscan Hills"**]. Another is fittingly called **"Nostalgia"** and contains these rough, unforgettable lines:

Dove raro ombreggia il bosco
Le maligne crete, e al pian
Di rei sugheri irto e fosco
I cavalli errando van,

Là in Maremma ove fiorio
La mia triste primavera,
Là rivola il pensier mio
Con i tuoni e la bufera.

. . . . .

[Where the scarce woods shade
The evil clays, and on the plain
Bristling and dark with cork oaks
The horses go awandering,

There in Maremma, where flowered
The sad springtime of my youth,
There on the wings of the gale
With the thunder flies my thought.]

The poem entitled **"Davanti San Guido"** [**"Before San Guido"**] is famous, almost popular. As he rides by on the train, the poet sees again the great cypress-lined road that leads from San Guido to Bólgheri, where he had spent his childhood. The beloved earth calls to him, and everything thereabouts has a part in the life and griefs of the poet, who had learned the myths of the past there, and had dreamed of the future. Even the dead call to him, and in his memory his grandmother Lucia appears, she who was sleeping in "the lonely cemetery up there." Even the cypress trees speak to him as though they had divined his hidden sorrow: "You can tell your human sadness and your grief to the oaks and to us." They recall to him the vital sense of holy Nature; they bring to mind the cherished illusions of the countryside. "And eternal Pan, who goes on the solitary heights at that hour and on the lonely plains, alone, will sink the discord of thy cares, O mortal, in the divine harmony."

In **"Traversando la Maremma Toscana"** [**"Crossing the Tuscan Maremma"**], the poet finds a promise of peace in the land of his childhood: "Oh, that which I loved, that which I dreamed, was all in vain; and always I ran and never reached the end; and tomorrow I shall fall. But from afar your hills say, peace, to the heart, with their dissolving mists and the green plain laughing in the morning rains."

The **"Idillio maremmano"** [**"Maremma Idyll"**], another song of pungent nostalgia, is also famous and rightly committed to memory. It is a poem in which the poet compares his literary life with that of the people who work the Maremma land, as he saw in childhood: "Oh how cold thereafter was my life, how obscure and disagreeable it has been!" He says it would have been better to remain there in the fields, to be a peasant of the Maremma, to marry blond Maria, and to forget himself in labor: "Better to forget, while working, without inquiring, this huge mystery of the universe." Here the nostalgia for the Maremma gives rise to a deep meditation and a discouragement with life. And who will forget the gentle sweetness of that **"Sogno d'estate"** [**"Dream of Summer"**] from the *Odi barbare?* "I dreamt, quiet things of my childhood dreamt."

With this poetry of evocative themes can be included **"Tedio invernale"** [**"Winter Boredom"**]; **"Maggiolata"** [**"May Song"**]; and even **"Dipartita"** [**"Departure"**]; **"Disperata"** [**"Song of Despair"**]; **"Serenata"** [**"Evening Song"**]; and **"Mattinata"** [**"Morning Song"**], where the poet reveals in himself a sort of popular vein of ancient knowledge. Here is where almost all Carducci's love poetry should be placed, whether as in **"Ruit hora"** [**"Time is Fleeting"**] where he is singing of wine and love to Lidia in the "yearned-for green solitude"; or as in the sorrowful lines of **"Alla Stazione in una Mattina d'Autunno"** ["**At the Railroad Station on an Autumn Morning"**], by which he sketches the feeling of the season and the monstrous life of the train: "Oh what a fall of leaves, icy, mute, heavy, upon the soul!" The same kind of poetry is found in the **"Elegia del monte Spluga"** ["**Elegy to Mount Spluga"**: Swiss, Splügen], a love elegy of the mature poet; and in that winged song for the birthday of M. G. entitled **"Sabato santo"** ["**Holy Saturday"**]: "the bells are singing with waves and flights of sounds from the cities on hillocks distantly green."

There are songs of domestic sorrow, the verses for his dead brother and his dead son. In **"Funere mersit acerbo,"** he entrusts his brother Dante, a suicide, with his little son who bore the same name and who is dead too: "It is my little boy who is knocking on your lonely door. . . ." In **"Pianto antico"** ["**Ancient Lament"**], the most felicitous poem that Carducci ever wrote in short lines, a serene sorrow makes him compare the green pomegranate tree, which is flowering again, with the little boy who stretched out toward that tree *la pargoletta mano* [his little hand] and now is dead, and never again will flower.

At another time he may meditate on death. He does so in **"Colloqui con gli alberi"** ["**Conversations with Trees"**], which in places recalls one of Zanelli's poems that Carducci greatly admired, *Egoismo e Carità* [*Selfishness and Charity*]. He no longer admires the "thoughtful oak" or craves the "unprolific laurel"; now he loves the vine: ". . . compassionate of me, thou ripenest the wise forgetfulness of life." But he honors the fir most: "he, between four planks, a simple coffin, finally closes the obscure tumults and the vain desiring of my thought." And in **"Nevicata"** ["**Snowfall"**] he pronounces a gentle chant of farewell to the world: "Soon, O dear ones, soon—be calm, unconquered heart—down into the silence I shall go, in the shade I shall rest."

Another stage is that of the civil poetry, from which, in celebrating heroes and memorable deeds, he passes on to the calm contemplation of history, to the epos.

The first style of Carducci's civil or political poetry is more a fine oration from the platform than a form of lyric poetry, but little by little it is purified, losing the violence of the direct polemic. In *Juvenilia* a fierce hymn **"Alla Libertà rileggendo le opere di Vittorio Alfieri"** ["**To Liberty, On Rereading the Works of Vittorio Alfieri"**] is found, and one day he would exclaim: "Would that I had lived to exterminate tyrants, with you, Rome and Athens. . . ." And he develops a long ode **"Agli Italiani"** ["**To the Italians"**] to remind them of the great examples, and he sings a hymn **"Alla Croce di Savoia"** ["**To the Cross of Savoy"**]. He invokes Victor Emanuel, "a new Marius" for the redemption of Italy. He sings of Garibaldi, and he evokes the battles of the liberation: Montebello, Palestro, and so on. He sings **"Sicilia e Rivoluzione."** Then in the second book of *Levia Gravia*, he chants **"Per la Proclamazione del Regno d'Italia"** ["**For the Procla-**

mation of the Kingdom of Italy"]; and **"In Morte di G. B. Niccolini"** ["**On the Death of G. B. Niccolini"**]; **"Roma o morte;"** **"Dopo Aspromonte"** ["**After Aspromonte"**]; **"Carnevale;"** **"Per la Rivoluzione di Grecia"** ["**The Greek Revolution"**]; **"Per il Trasporto delle Reliquie di Ugo Foscolo in Santa Croce"** ["**Transfer of the Remains of Ugo Foscolo to Santa Croce"**]; all political and heroic poems.

From Pieve Santo Stefano, on August 23, 1867, he sent out the violent and nostalgic quatrains **"Agli Amici della Valle Tiberina"** ["**To Our Friends of the Tiber Valley"**] where the landscape with its memories runs to the *fatal prora d'Enea* [the fated prow of Aeneas]. And there is the polemical shout "Death to the tyrants" and the violent close: "And flames instead of water to unworthy Rome, to the cowardly Capitol, I will send."

For January 19, 1868, he readied the poem **"Per Eduardo Corrazzini,"** who died of wounds received in the Roman campaign of 1867. A violent invective against the Pope closes these burning lines. Then, for November 30, 1868, he composed the epode **"Per Giuseppe Monti e Gaetano Tognetti,"** martyrs to Italian efforts to claim Rome, a poem in which, among other things, as a contrast to the violent words spoken against Pope Pius IX occur the fine quatrains on the Messiah which end thus: "The little ones smiled their profound sky-blue smile at the humble prophet; He weeping caressed their blond curls with pure and slender hand." The poem **"In morte di Giovanni Cairoli"** ["**On the Death of Giovanni Cairoli"**] is dated January, 1870, and begins in the style of the musical ariosa: "O Villagloria, from Crèmera, when the moon mantles the hills . . ." (Villa Glóri was a vineyard outside the Porta del Popolo of Rome where, on October 23, 1867, Enrico and Giovanni Cairoli and sixty-eight comrades heroically resisted the papal troops in desperate battle).

As was remarked above, Carducci often wrote violent polemics rather than poetry, but already in the lines **"A certi Censori"** ["**To Certain Censors"**], which bear the date December 19, 1871, he was transmuting his activity as a political poet into beautiful strophes: "When I ascend the mountain of the centuries sad-faced and alone, like falcons the strophes rise and flutter around my brow." Then the strophes assume the substance of mythical nymphs:

> Al passar de le aerëe fanciulle
> Fremon per tutti i campi
> L'ossa de' morti, e i tumoli a le culle
> Mandan saluti e lampi.
>                 . . . . .
> [As the airy maidens pass,
> In all the fields
> The bones of the dead quiver, and the tombs to the
>     cradles
> Send greetings and lightnings.]

Therefore he can say to them: "Fight against every evil power, against all tyrants."

Closer to poetry and often completely poetical are the praises of artists, poets, and saints: **"Niccolò Pisano," "Carlo Goldoni," "Dante," "Petrarca," "Ariosto,"** and other Italian poets, as well as Homer [**"Omero"**], **"Virgilio,"** and even **"Jaufré Rudel"** in the famous *novenari* (verse lines of nine syllables), which relate the romantic love and the romantic death of the troubadour, and even **"Martino Lutero"** [**"Martin Luther"**], in a sonnet which closes with a lofty, so very human, prayer: "Yet, looking behind him, he sighed: Lord, call me to Thee: weary am I; pray I cannot without cursing." We can even include **"San Giorgio di Donatello"** [**"Donatello's Statue of Saint George"**], a poem in which the voice of the prophet is heard: "Worthy, Saint George (oh that I might see it with these weary eyes), that a conquering people of heroes under arms should pass before you in review." Finally, the sonnet to Giuseppe Mazzini, of February, 1872, has lines of high poetry: "And a dead people formed ranks behind him. Ancient exile, to a sky mild and stern raise now thy countenance that never smiled, 'Thou alone,' thinking, 'O ideal, art true.'"

The ode to Victor Hugo is beautiful and songlike: "From the mountains smiling in the morning sun, descends the epic of Homer, which like a divine river peopled with swans goes flowing across the green Asian plain." And the expectancy of the close is clear and wholesome in that ode: "Sing to the new progeny, O divine old man, the age-old song of the Latin people; sing to the expectant world: 'Justice and Liberty.'"

There are lyrics inspired by a deed or by a historical figure, such as **"La Sacra di Enrico Quinto"** [**"The Consecration of Henry V"**]; with the pace of a romantic ballad, full of skulls and bones, it is a hearty thing. So too are **"La Leggenda di Teodorico,"** which is even more delightful, and **"Nina Nanna di Carlo V"** [**"The Lullaby of Charles V"**].

As the years passed, the praises grew purer and more calmly expressed. The poet reached the time of the odes entitled **"Alla Regina d'Italia"** [**"To the Queen of Italy"**], **"Il Liuto e la Lira"** [**"The Lute and the Lyre"**], **"A Giuseppe Garibaldi," "Scoglio di Quarto"** [the little port from which Garibaldi and his Thousand set forth on the conquest of Sicily, May 6, 1860], **"Saluto Italico," "Per la Morte di Eugenio Napoleone," "Alla Vittoria"** [**"To Victory"**], **"Sirmione"** [birthplace of Quintus Valerius Catullus], **"Miramar"** [Adriatic castle near Trieste, from which Maximilian departed to become Emperor of Mexico]. In these poems, every image transfigures the vehemence of his passion. The sonnets of the *Ça ira* are violent and explosive, but beautiful just the same and harmonious with great self-possession.

Then come the odes of serene, historical contemplation, which were to culminate in the epos, the stupendous preface to which is the inspired ode **"Ad Alessandro d'Ancona"** with its strophe of lyrical pride: "Slothful terrors of the Middle Ages, black progeny of barbarism and mystery, pale swarms, away! The sun is rising, and Homer sings."

Already in *Juvenilia,* songs of love, landscapes, nostalgia, there is the call to Greece, to "free human genius," to "Mother Rome," to "thou, enigmatic Rome of our people," and the poets also sings hymns to Phoebus Apollo and Diana Trivia. Then he composed in great strophes the passion for the Roman spirit which he nourished within his bosom. "And everything in the world which is civilized, great, august, it is Roman still," he sang in the ode bearing the title **"Nell'annuale della Fondazione di Roma"** [**"On the Anniversary of the Founding of Rome"**]. And in the ode entitled **"Roma,"** he said: "I do not come to thee curious about little things: Who looks for butterflies under the Arch of Titus?" But he gave a still more austere, almost religious feeling of the Roman spirit in the ode **"Dinanzi alle terme di Caracalla"** [**"Before the Baths of Caracalla"**] with that severe landscape: "Between the Celio and the Aventine the clouds run darkly: the wind blows damp from the dreary plain: in the background stand the Alban Hills, white with snow." He describes the place in solemn, awe-struck lines, and in contrast to the present time which those Baths recall. He also invokes Fever, calling on that goddess to repulse "the new men" and "their trifling affairs; this horror is religious: here sleeps the goddess Rome." Here the Roman spirit is represented as a sacred sentiment in the form of high melancholy.

Indeed, this religious emotion that arose when he looked at history was to inspire the Carducci of maturity and old age. A limpid strength, softened by a calm melancholy, generated the poet's new odes, such as the one entitled **"Furi alla Certosa di Bologna"** [**"Outside the Monastery of Bologna"**]: "Here at the foot of the hill sleep the Umbrian forebears who first, with sound of axes, broke thy sacred silences, O Appennine: sleep the Etruscans descended with the horn [*lituus*], with the spear, with eyes fixed aloft on the green mysterious slopes, and the great, ruddy, red-haired Celts running to wash away the slaughter in the cold Alpine waters which they hailed as Reno, and the noble race of Rome, and the long-haired Lombard, who was last to camp on the wooded peaks."

There are praises of a people, or of a district, such as the odes **"Piemonte," "Cadore," "Alla città di Ferrara," "Bicocca San Giacomo," "Le due Torri"** [**"The Two Towers"**], **"La Moglie del Gigante"** [**"The Giants's Wife"**], **"Davanti il castel vecchio di Verona"** [**"Before the Old Castle of Verona"**], **"A una Bottiglia di Valtellina del 1848"** [**"A Bottle of 1848 Vintage Valtellina"**]. In each of these poems there are passages of high beauty; for example, the opening of **"Piemonte,"** which begins like a majestic dance, or the beginning of the second part of the ode to Ferrara: "O pensive land fading out to sea in the lowering sullen air, between gray sands and motionless pools of water, now shaded only by a few oaks, where rarely the wild boar roots," and so on.

**"L'Antica Poesia Toscana"** [**"Ancient Tuscan Poetry"**] or **"I Poeti di Parte Bianca"** [**"The Poets of the White Faction of Dante's Florence"**] bring us again to historical evocations. The lines that begin: *Era un giorno di festa e* *luglio ardea* ["It was a holiday and July was waxing hot"], take us back to the joy of seeing again in imagination an old, old story.

**"La Canzone di Legnano,"** epically serene and sorrowful, sketches in whole hendecasyllables almost without syntactical breaks, the victory of the Lombard over Barbarossa, and the figure of Alberto di Giussano stands out in masculine greatness: "And his voice like thunder in May."

Among the newest and most inward historical odes of Carducci—and among the most beautiful of modern poetry—are the odes entitled **"Sui Campi di Marengo"** ["On the Fields of Marengo"], **"Faida di Commune"** ["A Communal Feud"], and **"Il Comune rustico"** ["The Rustic Commune"]. The first of these has fitted the Alexandrine verse, which in Italian poetry almost always has a facile and slovenly musicality, to a sustained and elegant rhythm which permits strophes such as the one which depicts the emperor:

> Solo, a piedi, nel mezzo del campo, al corridore
> Suo presso, riguardava nel ciel l'imperatore:
> Passavano le stelle su'l grigio capo; nera
> Dietro garria co'l vento l'imperial bandiera."
>
> . . . . .
>
> [Standing alone in mid-field, hard by his passageway,
> The emperor was looking up at the heavens:
> The stars passed above his gray head;
> Black behind him the imperial banner fluttered in the wind].

In **"Faida di Comune,"** history takes concrete shape in lyrical poetry without any residue. It is all infused with an ineffable love for that Tuscan landscape which played such an important role in the heart of Giosuè Carducci. There are the fertile hillocks where

> . . . lieti
> Ne l'april svarian gli ulivi!
> Bacchian li uomini le rame,
> Le fanciulle fan corona,
> E di canti la collina
> E di canti il pian risona,
> Mentre pregni d'abbondanza
> Ispumeggian i frantoi
> Scricchiolando.
>
> . . . . .
>
> [. . . joyous
> In April the olive trees in their changes!
> The men knock the olives from the branches
> as the girls form a circle,
> and with songs, the hill
> With songs the plain resounds,
> While, rich in abundance,
> The olive-crushers foam,
> Creaking.]

There are also the rough stubble of the fields, all silvery with frost," the "languid olive groves," and the "stripped grapevines." Together with the historical incident which brought the Pisans and the Lucchese face to face, there is the airy and storied feeling of an ancient legend:

> Bel castello è Avane, e corte
> Fu de i re d'Italia un giorno.
> Vi si sente a mezza notte
> Pe' querceti un suon di corno.
> Vi si sente a mezza notte
> La real caccia stormire,
> Dietro ad una lepre nera
> Un caval nero annitrire.
>
> . . . . .
>
> [Avane is a fine castle,
> And once upon a time it was the court of the Italian kings.
> At midnight there, a sound of horns
> Is heard through the oak groves;
> There, is heard at midnight
> The royal hunt thundering by,
> Hard after a black hare,
> And a black horse neighing.]

The **"Comune rustico"** is a landscape out of ancient history, sketched with a purity of images and of language that induce in the heart that Olympian melancholy which constitutes the effect of the loftiest poetry. "And the red heifers on the meadow / Beheld the little senate passing by, / As the light of noon shone down upon the fir trees." This last line tells the meaning of that sun at highpoint in the heavens which shines on the fields and stills the air of high noon. Carducci rarely reached such an intense and hidden understanding in the music of his verse.

It might be said that the ultimate stage of Carducci's poetry gathers together all these motifs into a cosmic vision in which objective history, landscape, and memories arrange themselves so as to express the high meaning of life, the supreme melancholy of living. In such moments Carducci, reaching a new serenity, feels "the Hellenic life flowing tranquilly in his veins." His poetry might be compared to the serene Hebe whom he extols in a landscape, like the one which surrounds "the gentle daughter of Jesse, all enwrapped in golden sparks," and she "contemplates, ethereal," villas, fields, rivers, harvests, and "the snows radiant upon the Alps," and smiles amid the clouds "at the flowering dawns of May, at the sad sunsets of November."

Examples of this Carduccian poetry are to be found in all the volumes of Carducci, without regard to chronological consideration. The stages of Carducci's poetry, which have been seen in landscape, in subjective, as well as nostalgic moments, in civil praise and political celebration and in history, and finally, in moments more complex and yet spontaneous in which all the others are mingled and fused, are ideal stages and therefore belong to any period of the poet.

In this last stage, the **"Canto dell 'Amore"** should also be included, although it has passages in which eloquence forces the lyrical quality somewhat. Here a historical recollection sets fire to his imagination: the Paolina fortress, which once stood in the very place from which the poet now is contemplating the valley, was destroyed by the people in September, 1860—it was a symbol of tyranny. But now the poet, overcome by the beauty of springtime, raises his eyes above the human struggles and feels the song of love rising within him: ". . . but like sapphire I feel every thought of mine shining." Now he no longer cares about the priests and the tyrants whom he detested; he would become reconciled with the pope: "Open up the Vatican. I want to embrace him who is his own old prisoner. Come, I drink a toast to liberty. Citizen Mastai [Count Giovanni Mastai Feretti, Pope Pius IX], drink a glass!" And the whole composition is just a bit intoxicated with this last glass of wine so that sometimes it seems just too plebeian, but it is wholesome, and even amusing in certain benign sarcasms. There are unhackneyed lines of real poetical worth: "Do madonnas still walk the rose-colored pathway of these mountains? The madonnas seen by Perugino descending in the pure sunsets of April, with their arms opened in adoration over the child with such gentle divinity?"

**"In una Chiesa Gotica"** [**"In a Gothic Church"**] expresses a sentiment of pagan life (while he has amorous Lydia sitting beside him) against the Semitic god. It is the same impulse that would inspire him to pen the invective against the Galilean with the red locks. Now, however, the Carduccian form has lost the quite physical vehemence of certain epodes, and here, as in the ode **"Alle Fonti del Clitunno"** [**"The Sources of the Clitumnus"**], his protest against Christianity has the tone of poetry. But poets' songs are fleeting, universal sentiments; it was not much later that Carducci was to welcome even Christian poetry, and in the **"Chiesa di Polenta"** [a church of the eighth century], which is one of the great odes of *Rime e Ritmi*, he would feel the religious fascination of the Ave Maria.

The ode **"Alle Fonti del Clitunno"** is famous, and justly so: the initial landscape in itself would suffice to make it so, with its stern energy and its verdant freshness; here the reminiscence of the classical images naturally brightens into a genuine sensation.

Next to these odes should be placed the *Primavere elleniche* [*Hellenic Springs*] to which Carducci gave such an eminent position in his work; **"La Moglie del Gigante"** [**"The Wife of the Giant"**]; or **"I due Titani,"** which is more mature in feeling and in form, and in which Prometheus and Atlas curse the tyrant Jove in a sort of new hymn to Satan.

**"Su l'Adda"** [**"On the River Adda"**] is mainly love poetry; nevertheless, the presence of Lydia does not destroy the voice of history that the landscape evokes in the poet's heart; in vain he has exclaimed: "Adieu, history of man."

In **"Presso l'Urna di P. B. Shelley"** [**"Close by Shelley's Grave"**], however, the loving woman stands before the poet as a cherished being to whom he addresses a serene yet sorrowful discourse: "Lalage, I know what dream wells up from the bottom of thy heart." The presence of the woman infuses the words of the poet with tenderness: "The present hour is in vain; it but strikes and flees; only in the past is beauty, only in death is truth."

The thought of death inspired in him the powerful couplets with the title of **"Mors"**:

> Quando a le nostre case la diva severa discende,
> da lungi il rombo de la volante s'ode,
> e l'ombra de l'ala che gelida gelida avanza
> diffonde intorno lugubre silenzïo.
> Sotto la veniente ripiegano gli uomini il capo,
> ma i sen feminei rompono in aneliti.
> Tale de gli alti boschi, se luglio il turbine addensa,
> non corre un fremito per le virenti cime:
> immobili quasi per brivido gli alberi stanno,
> e solo il rivo roco s'ode gemere
>
> . . . . .
>
> [When to our abodes the stern goddess descends,
> From afar is heard the roar of her flight,
> And the shadow of the wing that advances coldly,
>   coldly,
> Spreads all about a mournful silence.
> Beneath the goddess who comes, men lower their
>   heads,
> But feminine breasts burst into sobs.
> So from the high woods, if July condenses the whirl-
>   ing storm,
> Not a quiver runs along the verdant peaks:
> Motionless as though gripped by horror stand the trees,
> No sound is heard but the moaning of the stream.]

In the verses **"All'Aurora"** [**"To the Dawn"**], he fuses in a new melody the ancient myth of Aurora and her daily birth upon the world of today. He tells of her beauty and the bondage of those whom she awakens. He lifts the heart to a lofty new religious myth: "Carry me," he says, "Aurora, on thy steed of flame! Into the fields of stars, carry me, whence I may see the earth, all smiling once again in thy rosy light."

A deep melancholy converts the words of the ode entitled **"Nella Piazza di San Petronio"** into the purest of sounds; for example, he describes a sunset: "It is the soft sweet hour when the sun about to die hails thy towers and thy temple, holy Petronius." In that sunset, it seems as though the sun "reawakens the soul of the centuries . . . and a sad desire through the stern air awakens, a desire of red Mays, of hot, fragrant evenings, when the pagan women danced in the square, and the consuls were returning with defeated kings."

In **"Su Monte Mario"** [**"On Mount Marius"**], there is a sorrowful and pagan vision of a dying world. The poet says, "Pour out, atop the luminous hill, pour, friends, the blond wine, and let the sun be refracted in it. Smile, lovely women: tomorrow we shall die." Rarely has his poetry reached the heights of these following lines:

> Addio, tu madre del pensier mio breve,
> terra, e de l'alma fuggitiva! quanta
> d'intorno al sole aggirerai perenne
> gloria e dolore!
> fin che ristretta sotto l'equatore
> dietro i richiami del calor fuggente
> l'estenuata prole abbia una sola
> femina, un uomo,

che ritti in mezzo a' ruderi de' monti,
tra i morti boschi, lividi, con gli occhi
vitrei te veggan su l'immane ghiaccia,
sole, calare.

          . . . . .

[Adieu, earth, thou mother of my brief thought
And of my fugitive soul!
How much glory, and sorrow,
Wilt thou whirl around the everlasting sun,
Until, forced beneath the equator
In search of waning warmth,
thy exhausted progeny shall number
One woman only, one man,
Who standing among the ruins of the mountains,
amid the dead woods, livid and with glassy eyes
Shall over the vast cruel ice see thee,
Sun, set!]

The power of this vision that pictures the ultimate catastrophe of the world has few equals in modern European poetry.

But against this sadness of the death of the earth, Carducci could set the joyous song of love: "Everything passes and nothing can die." That prodigious **"Canto di Marzo"** [**"March Song"**], transcribes even more clearly the sentiment previously expressed in the **"Canto d'Amore."** Here the art of Carducci is in its moment of grace, and this March, this spring, without any symbolical meaning, becomes naturally the myth of the eternal change and renewal of the world. Here are the enchanting lines on "the forest which puts on its first throbs," or those which describe how ". . . the shadow of the clouds passes in splashes over the green as the sun pales and brightens," or the others which paint a vivid country scene: "Here comes the rush of rain and the grumble of thunder; the calf pokes its head out of the wet cowshed, the hen, shaking her wings, makes a din, deep in the orchard the cuckoo sighs, and on the threshing floor the children jump."

Such was the poetry of Giosuè Carducci. Beside it must be set the best part and the spirit of the Carduccian prose, which fills several volumes: *Discorsi storici e letterari* [*Historical and Literary Lectures*], which include "Lo Studio di Bologna, Dello Svolgimento della letteratura nazionale" ["Development of the National Literature"], **L'Opera di Dante** ["The Works of Dante"], "Per la Morte di Giuseppe Garibaldi," and writings on Vergil, Petrarch, Boccaccio, and so on; *Archeologica Poetica*, essays on Petrarch, Matteo Frescobaldi, and on the Italian popular lyric of the thirteenth and fourteenth centuries; *Studi letterari,* on the poems and varying fortune of Dante, and on music and poetry in the fourteenth century, and so forth; *Cavalleria e Umanesimo* [*Chivalry and Humanism*], in which are found, among others, an essay on poetry and Italy in the Fourth Crusade, and a long essay on Poliziano; *Studi su L. Ariosto e T. Tasso; Melica e Lirica del Settecento* [*Melic and Lyrical Poetry in the Eighteenth Century*]; *Il Parini Maggiore* [*The Greater Works of Parini*]; and *Il Parini minore.* There are also various essays in the volumes *Primi Saggi, Studi Saggi e Discorsi, Bozzetti e Scherme* [*Sketches and Polemics*], *Poesia e Storia, Confessioni e Battaglie,* as

well as in *Ceneri e faville* [*Ashes and Sparks*]. The poet also personally chose and brought together in one volume his most representative prose writings.

In so many pages of prose, what really strikes the reader is the poetical power of the style, though supported in part by ideas that he drew from the culture of his time and even from *De Sanctis,* the criticism of Carducci is above all useful for an understanding of the strength of his own style. That does not mean that the Carduccian studies of literary history do not have great importance. There is in them the soundness and the experience of a man of taste, and the authority of a man who felt poetry and who also wrote it. His remarks on the structure of a canto, of an expression, and of a poetical line serve to explain the essence of a poet: even the use of the schemata of the literary genres is redeemed in him by the way he groups them historically to grasp affinities, influences, and sources. From all his prose works it is possible to extract a Carduccian history of Italian literature; but, nevertheless, the real interest of Carducci's prose is not in the value of the criticism and history.

Carducci's prose always has a tendency to become poetry. And he worked on it as one would poetry: attentive within each phrase to the music in the accents, pauses, and contractions of the diphthongs; attentive to the creation of an imaginative and decorative substance around each idea, imparting to the very impetus of an invective the grave mischievous composure which redeems its passion. It is necessary to say that in prose polemics Carducci preserved a sense of limit, which, on the contrary, he seemed to lose in certain overly vigorous verses. Truly, the poetical prose of which Leopardi had spoken in connection with the *Operette Morali* is here displayed in full bloom.

The language that Carducci draws from the noblest literary tradition is enlivened by the new warmth with which he infuses the words, especially because of the poetical tendency that impregnates their rhythm and imagery; for example, the beginning of the five lectures on the development of the national literature (*Dello svolgimento della letteratura nazionale*) where he describes the men at the start of the year one thousand, and his pages on the *ottava rima* of Lodovico Ariosto, or the prose *Eterno femminino regale,* or the polemic for *Ça ira.*

Carducci's literary expression always seeks a poetic aura; and this is the great novelty of the prose of his time.

**Christopher Cairns (essay date 1977)**

SOURCE: Cairns, Christopher. "Giosuè Carducci." In *Italian Literature: The Dominant Themes,* pp. 68-70. Devon, U.K.: David & Charles Limited, 1977.

[*In the following essay, Cairns examines historical, patriotic, and political themes in Carducci's poetry.*]

Carducci's life had the unification of Italy at its centre, as can be seen from his dates, 1835-1907. He was not without companion poets—such as Mameli, Mercantini, Prati and Aleardi—to chronicle the *Risorgimento* political conscience, but Carducci came to be looked on as the official poet of the new Italy, and his poems survive the test of time better than many by his contemporaries. Thus Carducci became the true heir of Alfieri, Foscolo and Leopardi.

His father had been politically active in the revolution of 1848 and Carducci lived through the thick of the political ferment from which the new nation emerged. He grew old in the idealism of university teaching and translated the image of the poet-patriot into the more modern poet-professor. His work is characterised by an uncompromising and fiery liberalism in its rejection of the insipidities of romanticism in literature, and of the Catholic Church in politics. He reacted against the more recent writers of his own century in favour of a return to classical models; he celebrated several moments in the political progress towards Italian unity in his poetry, became an impassioned republican and supporter of Mazzini, and attacked vehemently what he thought was the obstruction by the Vatican of Italy's logical destiny. Carducci was never content to remain on the political sidelines. He identified himself closely with a variety of dissident groups, being lucky, in 1869, to escape the severe consequences of conspiracy. He occupied various university chairs, the most important being the Chair of Eloquence at the University of Bologna. After a long and eventful life, in which amorous as well as political escapades drew strong reactions from his critics, Carducci was awarded the Nobel Prize for Literature in 1906, the year before his death.

Like many of his contemporaries, Carducci was convinced of the appropriateness of history in poetry, a principle we have seen in the novels of the Italian political conscience in his generation. The examples are legion, but **"Piemonte"** will serve as an example. This poem, which was an ode to the state which started the movement towards Italian unity, is typical of Carducci's fusion of historical, patriotic and sentimental values. The countryside of the region, with all the abrupt contrasts of its mountainous terrain, is bathed in the light of antique glory; the king, Charles Albert, is seen as the hero of that first military intervention and the poet Alfieri, a native of the region, symbolises the coming together of the themes of Piedmont and One Italy in his prophecy. The whole is written in impassioned, emotionally charged and high-sounding terms and raises the achievement of the *Risorgimento* to epic proportions. Alfieri announced the coming of liberty in his Piedmontese Israel, and Charles Albert fulfilled this glorious prophecy. The result is a poem which exults in the patriotism of Italians in those years and transposes incident and event into epic. Many of the major events of the 'trauma' can be read into the poem, but they are built into

a close-knit complex of spiritual and political values. **"Piemonte"** is a poem which, like its author, is full of minor imperfections, but seems to express the charged atmosphere and the political conscience of Italians of Carducci's generation. Hardly corresponding entirely with today's taste, it none the less gives a vivid impression of political enthusiasm.

If **"Piemonte"** was a poem of reflection on the *Risorgimento,* Carducci also wrote political and patriotic poems of occasion. **"Alla Croce di Savoia"** of 1859 celebrated the voluntary annexation of Tuscany to Piedmont. Several later poems like **"Il Plebiscito"** and **"Sicilia e la rivoluzione,"** as well as those addressed to Garibaldi, expressed similar transitory moments in the progress towards unity, fixing the enthusiasm and euphoria of Italians into a poetic mould, but not significantly outliving their historical popularity. The **"Inno a Satana"** of 1865 was perhaps the climax of Carducci's anticlericalism, but is less satanic than it sounds, representing the progressive spirit of man in his struggle with tradition and superstition rather than the antithesis of Christianity.

Carducci was constantly the rebel and the agitator, combining poetry with pamphleteering, speechmaking and protesting, according to very modern handbooks of political activity, but he was not insensitive to other poetic currents in his century; in that turbulent epoch, mood and feeling produced some fine poetry, particularly in the more personal and reflective *Rime nuove.* In the lyrically personal **"Pianto antico,"** the identification of the sadness of a lost son with associations of the changing seasons, and in poems like **"San Martino"** or the **"Idillio Maremmano"** one finds a more enduring Carducci; and it is possibly Carducci's train in **"Alla Stazione in una mattina d'autunno,"** with its echoes of that other side of the nineteenth century, the industrial revolution, that remains with the young student approaching Carducci from the distance of the twentieth century. With Carducci's train we are reminded of D'Annunzio's torpedo-boat in another more brutal celebration of the poetry of steel, but the Carducci of **"Pianto antico"** leads straight to Pascoli.

*Works Cited*

Poems: *Oxford Book of Italian Verse* (1952); *Penguin . . .* (1960)

*Le tre corone, poesie e prose: Carducci/Pascoli/D'Annunzio,* ed Augusto Vicinelli (Mondadori, 1969)

Rosario Contarino and Rosa Maria Monastra. *Carducci e il tramonto del classicismo* (Lett Ital Laterza), 53

**Silvano Garofalo (essay date 1979)**

SOURCE: Garofalo, Silvano. "Giosuè Carducci." In *Dictionary of Italian Literature,* pp. 100-03. Westport, Conn.: Greenwood Press, Inc., 1979.

*[In the following essay, Garofolo discusses themes of nature and Roman history in Carducci's works.]*

Carducci, Giosuè (1835-1907), poet, critic, and scholar. Son of a doctor and the oldest of three children, Carducci spent most of his childhood in Bolgheri, south of Livorno, the setting of two of his finer poems, **"Davanti San Guido"** (**"Before San Guido"**) and **"Idillio Maremmano"** (**"The Idyll of Maremma"**). His republican political views gave way to acceptance of the monarchy with the annexation of Rome to the Italian kingdom. In 1860, he was appointed professor of Italian literature at the University of Bologna and held this position until 1904, when he retired because of failing health. His accomplishments as a leading poet of the new Italy were recognized by the government, which made him senator for life in 1890. In 1906, he was awarded the Nobel Prize and thus received international recognition.

For nearly forty years, Carducci dominated the Italian literary scene with collections of poems, critical studies, and polemical essays on literary and political subjects. His writings are collected in fifty-two volumes in the Edizione Nazionale. Although his reputation has waned considerably upon the national and international scene, he remains the most important Italian poet of the second half of the nineteenth century. His perceptive scholarship constitutes a significant advance in the field of criticism. The studies on Cino da Pistoia, Dante, Petrarch, Lorenzo il Magnifico, Poliziano, Ariosto, Tasso, Parini, and the erotic poets of the eighteenth century retain their value for the contemporary student of Italian literature. Carducci is part of that group of critics who, along with Alessandro D'Ancona (1835-1914), Adolfo Bartoli (1833-1894), and Domenico Comparetti (1835-1927), adhered to the historical approach to a text.

His youthful polemic against the late romantics and romanticism in general stemmed from his distaste for what he considered alien to the Italian tradition and a distraction from the study of classical writers. To be sure, he did not remain immune to romantic precepts. That he was affected by them is evident in his concept of poetry as a representation of life and its values, his belief in historic progress, and his awareness of the contrast between reality and ideals. Over the years, his views on modern foreign writers were modified, and he came to appreciate them. Carducci, who came to be known as the civic and moral poet of the new Italy, valued literature on strictly utilitarian grounds, i.e., as a means of education and inspiration to noble deeds. His **"Inno a Satana"** (1863, **"Hymn to Satan"**), of pantheistic inspiration, is a hymn to the active life, to the exaltation of rationalism over Christian theology, and to the affirmation of the individual as a free agent over his destiny.

Carducci sought to develop a consciousness in the citizens of the newly formed kingdom of Italy which would make them keenly aware of their cultural past. For him this past had its roots in the remote pagan world of Roman antiquity. This link with the past was reinforced by a language and style which refuted the simple and spoken forms advocated by Manzoni in favor of a native literary flavor. In *Odi barbare* (1877-89, *The Barbarian Odes*), he attempted to recapture the spirit of antiquity by reproducing the rhythmic structure of Greek and Latin verses through concentration on accents rather than syllabic length; hence the title "barbarian." These poems, which are for the most part historical, along with *Rime nuove* (1861-87, *The New Lyrics*) which are of a personal nature, represent his finest poetry. Here his poetic voice achieved its own authentic form. In these two books, the poet has completely freed himself from the classical models, which in varying degrees can be noted in his first three collections: *Juvenilia* (1850-60, *Youthful Writings*), *Levia gravia* (1861-71, *Light and Serious Poems*), and *Giambi ed epodi* (1867-79, *Iambics and Epodes*). A decline in quality characterizes his last collection *Rime e ritmi* (1898, *The Lyrics and Rhythms*), because of a certain mannerism which permeates many of the poems.

Carducci's concept of life is reminiscent of Foscolo's in the sense that he too sought to overcome the frailty of the human individual through the evocation of exemplary episodes of the past. In a world where the purpose of creation seems to be that of destruction, there is a need for ideals which would assert life over death. Carducci, however, did not go back to the Greeks, but to the Romans and to episodes from medieval and contemporary history. The ancient world takes concrete shape and acquires meaning for the modern reader with **"Alle fonti del Clitumno"** (**"By the Sources of the Clitumnus"**), **"Dinanzi alle Terme di Caracalla"** (**"Before the Baths of Caracalla"**), and **"Nell'annuale della fondazione di Roma"** (**"On the Anniversary of the Founding of Rome"**). Here the ancients' concept of nature is fused with the immediacy of contemporary painting. In vivid colors, he presents the virile magnanimity of the Roman spirit as opposed to the weak, stagnant life of the new Italians. The obvious didactic lesson is the emulation of the ancient Romans. Carducci, who saw a direct link between the Roman spirit, on the one hand, and the Italian Communes and the Renaissance on the other, believed that this bond should extend to the new Italy. An austere morality and an intrepid love for freedom guides the lives of the people of the Communes in poems such as **"Su i campi di Marengo"** (**"On the Fields of Marengo"**), **"Comune rustico"** (**"The Rustic Commune"**), and **"Faida di comune"** (**"A Communal Feud"**).

On the personal level, Carducci revealed the depth of his humanity with **"Funere mersit acerbo"** (**"Plunged in Bitter Death"**) and **"Pianto antico"** (**"Ancient Lament"**), where the desolation of the poet over the sudden death of his three-year-old son reaches moving pathos. The grief which is so intimate and personal becomes universal, as the poet recognizes death as a constant threat against life. As the title of one of the poems indicates, it is an "ancient lament," a grief that has been part of the life process since the beginnings of the human race. Death always destroys regardless of human sentiments.

Nature is a fundamental theme in Carducci's poetry. The emotions which spur the poet at a particular moment of his poetic creation are fused with the natural scene. In **"Before San Guido,"** nature assumes a soothing quality as it reminds the poet of his carefree childhood in the midst of a bucolic countryside. In **"Traversando la Maremma Toscana" ("Crossing the Tuscan Maremma"),** the tortuous lines of the landscape seem to reflect the tormented soul of the poet. Now that his youthful dreams have failed miserably, the memory of the natural scene where he had spent his childhood inspires peace and tranquility. The autumnal panorama of **"San Martino"** so vividly captures the scene following grape-gathering that one can nearly smell the fermentation of the wine and feel the chill of that foggy, misty November weather so typical of central and northern Italy. The poems in which the landscape plays a dominant role, regardless of the themes treated within, represent some of Carducci's most beautiful and enduring work.

### Bibliography

*Edizione nazionale delle opere di Giosuè Carducci* (Bologna: Zanichelli, 1935-40); *A Selection of His Poems,* trans. G. L. Bickersteth (London: Longmans, Green, 1913); *From the Poems of Giosuè Carducci,* trans. Romilda Rendel (London: Kegan Paul, Trench, Trubner, 1929); *Poems of Giosuè Carducci,* trans. Frank Sewall (New York: Dodd Mead, 1892); *A Selection from the Poems,* trans. Emily A. Tribe (London: Longmans, 1921); Anne Paolucci, "Moments of the Creative Process in the Literary Criticism of Giosuè Carducci," *Italica* 33 (1956), 110-20; S. E. Scalia, *Carducci: His Critics and Translators in England and America 1881-1932* (New York: Vanni, 1937); Orlo Williams, *Giosuè Carducci* (London: Houghton, 1914).

## Nicolas J. Perella (essay date 1979)

SOURCE: Perella, Nicolas J. "Giosuè Carducci." In *Midday in Italian Literature,* pp. 98-107. Princeton, N.J.: Princeton University Press, 1979.

[*In the following essay, Perella explores Carducci's recurring use of midday in his poetry.*]

For the most part we are far from such negative noontide violence in the writings of Giosue Carducci, where it is rather the splendor and glory of the midday sun that illuminate more than one scene. In considering the role of midday in Carducci, we may begin with the idyllic and nostalgic evocation of **"Idillio maremmano" ("Idyll of the Maremma").** Here, at the center of the world-weary poet's vision of a simple and healthy life in communion with nature, which might have been his, is the figure of a young woman who strides "alta e ridente" along the furrows of fields of wheat. Carducci's "bionda Maria" may remind us somewhat of Zanella's Ruth at midday, except that Maria is clearly a pagan poet's vision of a nature god-

dess of health and fertility, a nostalgic but vigorous nympholepsy. The nigh-noon sun of midsummer with its heat and light bathes her in glory as in an act of homage, and she moves Juno-like in it as in her natural element:

> . . . e a te d'avante
>
> La grande estate, e intorno, fiammeggiava;
> Sparso tra' verdi rami il sol ridea
> Del melogran, che rosso scintillava.
>
> Al tuo passar, siccome a la sua dea,
> Il bel pavon l'occhiuta coda apria
> Guardando, e un rauco grido a te mettea.[1]
>
>> (24-30)
>
> . . . and before you,
>
> And all around, the great summer blazed.
> The sun was laughing scattered through the green
> Boughs of the pomegranate tree that sparkled red.
>
> When you passed by, the beautiful peacock, as though
> Looking at its goddess, opened its eye-splendored tail
> And hailed you with a strident cry

An even more openly paganizing classical midday scene is at the center of the second of the three odes of ***Primavere elleniche*** **("Spring in Hellas").** In this hymn to love the poet invites his beloved to an imaginary voyage to a Theocritean Sicily "where the shepherd Daphnis sang divine songs amid the fountains" (27-28). There, with the magic of his verse he will enrapture her, and in the midst of the noontide calm and leisure, at that hour when light and silence pervade all of nature, he will evoke the presence of the swift-footed sylvan nymphs:

> Ti rapirò nel verso; e tra i sereni
> Ozi de le campagne a mezzo il giorno,
> Tacendo e refulgendo in tutti i seni
> Ciel, mare, intorno,
>
> Io per te sveglierò da i colli aprichi
> Le Driadi bionde sovra il piè leggero.[2]
>
>> (41-46)
>
> I will steal you away with my verse; and midst
> The placid indolence of the fields at noon,
> Silently shining in all breasts
> The sky and sea, around,
>
> For you I will summon from the sun-bathed hills
> The blond dryads fleet of foot.

How emblematic of refuge into a world of calm, happiness, and harmony with nature this theme of midday nympholepsy was for Carducci is evidenced by the fact that the same invitation and evocation are at the center of what still remains his best-known poem—**"Davanti San Guido" ("Passing by San Guido").** As in **"Idillio maremmano"** here too the theme is that of the pastoral opposition between the simple rural life close to nature and the active, care-filled life demanded by the city. As the poet returns by train to the city and his obligations as a man of the world, the cypress trees familiar to him from his childhood seem to invite him to stay, offering the promise of innocent pleasures and repose. It has become fashionable of late among critics to belittle this poem, but there can be no doubt that the three stanzas containing the nympholeptic evocation are among Carducci's finest poetic achievements. It is a vision of pagan bliss invoked in one sentence that carries over three quatrains, syntactically one of the most amply constructed sentences of Italian poetry in the second half of the nineteenth century:

> Rimanti; e noi, dimani, a mezzo il giorno
> Che de le grandi querce a l'ombra stan
> Ammusando i cavalli e intorno intorno
> Tutto è silenzio ne l'ardente pian,
>
> Ti canteremo noi cipressi i cori
> Che vanno eterni fra la terra e il cielo:
> Da quegli olmi le ninfe usciran fuori
> Te ventilando co 'l lor bianco velo;
>
> E Pan l'eterno che su l'erme alture
> A quell'ora e ne i pian solingo va
> Il dissidio, o mortal, de le tue cure
> Ne la diva armonia sommergerà.[3]
>
> (53-64)

Stay: and tomorrow at noon
When in the shade of the great oaks
The horses stand muzzle to muzzle and all around
Everything is silent in the burning plain,

We cypresses will sing to you the chorus
That wafts eternal between earth and sky:
From those elms the nymphs will come forth
Fanning you with their white veils;

And Pan the Eternal who goes along the solitary
    heights
At that hour and all alone over the plains,
Will submerge the anguish of your cares,
Oh mortal, in the divine harmony.

First we have the evocation of the midday hour as a time of stillness and fierce heat over a vast expanse in which arcane sentiments and voices seem to float, then the sylvan nymphs who fan the poet. Finally there is Pan, not asleep at noontide and not the *daimon* causing terror, but Pan the Eternal, personification of a pantheistic concept of the universal harmony of nature that is revealed in the sacred hour of midday and into which the care-worn individual can sweetly merge.

There are other midday references in Carducci. **"Elegia del Monte Spluga"** (1898) once again evokes, as in an atmosphere between dream and reality (cf. Leopardi, Foscolo, Chenier, Mallarmé), a classically nympholeptic midday in which, however, a Nordic Lorelei also appears (1-12). And leaving the classical and paganizing world, the solemn evocation of the medieval Alpine commune in **"Il comune rustico"** (**"The Rustic Commune"**) acquires a quality of fixity and stunning intensity by virtue of the poem's final image in which we learn that the midday sun has illuminated the scene:

> A man levata il popol dicea Sì.
> E le rosse giovenche di su 'l prato
> Vedean passare il piccolo senato,
> Brillando su gli abeti il mezzodì.[4]
>
> (33-36)

With hand raised high, the people said "Yes."
And the red heifers from the meadow
Saw the small senate pass by,
As midday shone brightly on the fir trees.

In **"Fuori alla certosa di Bologna"** (**"Outside the Charterhouse of Bologna"**), the sun at its zenith figures as the symbol of the joy and intensity of life in opposition to the symbols of death (as extinction of the self) represented by the tombs of the Carthusian cemetery the poet has just visited. Under that blazing midday sun flooding the earth with a "kiss" of light, the cicadas' "song" is not an irritant but a paean to summer, and even the dead, in the poet's mind, seem to invite the living to love one another. The noonday sun is here equated with the eternal splendor of love. In this vein, however, Carducci's most exalted paean to the midsummer midday sun and to the sense of a rich immersion of the self in nature at the hour of Pan occurs at the beginning of one of his best-known prose compositions, *Le risorse di San Miniato al Tedesco* (*The Resources of San Miniato al Tedesco*). And here the poet's cue is taken from the ubiquitous and (for him) much maligned cicadas whose persistent shrill filling the air is interpreted as the audible voice of the irrepressible energy and joy of all of nature, eternally young and drunk with the light and heat of the sun:

> Come strillavano le cicale giù per la china meridiana del colle di San Miniato al Tedesco nel luglio del 1857. . . . Io non ho mai capito perché i poeti di razza latina odiino e oltraggino tanto le cicale. . . . Poi tutto un gran coro [di cicale] che aumenta d'intonazione e d'intensità co 'l calore e co 'l luglio, e canta, canta, canta. . . . Nelle fiere solitudini del solleone, pare che tutta la pianura canti, e tutti i monti cantino, e tutti i boschi cantino: pare che essa la terra dalla perenne gioventù del suo seno espanda in un inno immenso il giubilo de' suoi sempre nuovi amori co 'l sole.[5]

How the cicadas stridulated down along the slope of the hill of San Miniato al Tedesco under the midday sun in July 1857. . . . I have never understood why poets of Latin descent so greatly hate and insult the cicada. . . . Then a whole large chorus [of cicadas] that increases in intonation and intensity with the heat of July, and sing, sing, sing. . . . In the fierce solitude of the midsummer sun it seems as though the whole plain sings, and that all the mountains sing, and all the forests sing: it seems that from the perennial youth of its bosom the very earth expands into an immense hymn the celebration of its ever new love with the sun.

In this pantheistic nirvana—the metaphor of nirvana is Carducci's own—of light and exultation, which is in fact the sensation of an intense life, Carducci "drowns" in a willing surrender of the self's identity and its cares in order to become at one with the pulsating life of the All of nature, and the very body of the poet seems to be of the essence of the cicadas' wild song:

A me in quel nirvana di splendori e di suoni avviene e
piace di annegare la coscienza di uomo, e confondermi
alla gioia della mia madre Terra: mi pare che tutte le
mie fibre e tutti i miei sensi fremano, esultino, cantino
in amoroso tumulto, come altrettante cicale.[6]

In that nirvana of splendor and sounds I have the
pleasurable experience of drowning my human consciousness and of merging with the joy of my mother
earth: I feel that all my nerves and all my senses quiver,
exult, sing in an amorous tumult like so many cicadas.

It would be difficult to find a more extreme contrast than
that between the noontide vision and sensations recounted
by Carducci in this passage and the *meriggio* of Leopardi's "Vita solitaria." In a strict sense, to be sure, the term
*nirvana* does not apply to either noon piece, but as a
metaphor it is more suited to characterize the earlier poet's
experience. Leopardi, we saw, is released from sentiency
and the consciousness of self into a metaphysical nothingness emblematized by the perfect stasis of his noonscape.
On the other hand, Carducci's senses are literally thrilled
and set to vibrating by an exuberance that throbs in the
very heart of hot midday's fierce silence—"Nelle fiere
solitudini del solleone." In a moment of Panic inebriation
and expansion, Carducci is "released" precisely from the
anguish of the thought of the nothingness that follows
death, an anguish symbolized by the image—frequent in
this writer—of the cold silence of the tomb: "Non è vero
che io sia serbato ai freddi silenzi del sepolcro! io vivrò e
canterò, atomo e parte della mia madre immortale."[7] (It is
not true that I am destined for the cold silence of the
tomb! I will live and sing, particle and part of my immortal mother.)

It is quite possible that Carducci's use of the metaphor of
drowning to speak of the surrender of the self may be an
echo from Leopardi's "L'infinito," although it is a common enough image in the writings of religious mystics.
Again, however, where Leopardi drowns voluptuously in a
sea of infinite silence—"E il naufragar m'è dolce in questo
mare"—Carducci drowns in a sea (or "nirvana," as he puts
it) of luminosity and sounds—"nirvana di splendori e
suoni." These meridian "sounds" are first of all the actual
chirring of the cicadas, but also, it should be noted, the
metaphorical yet exultant "singing" of all of nature—fields,
mountains, and forests. What may be involved here is the
acoustical impression that the very absoluteness of midday's silence seems at times to arouse in an absorbed
spectator. It is a psycho-aural phenomenon that we have
referred to already, and we shall soon meet with it again.

But the experience of the midday sun as an ambiguous
and even negative demonic power of nature was not
unknown to Carducci. This is most evident in the short
lyric **"Davanti una cattedrale"** (**"In Front of a
Cathedral"**), as sardonic a poem as any written by the
*Scapigliati* (i.e., Italy's *poètes maudits*) contemporary with
him. Here the images of the sun and tombs, normally used
by the poet as terms of an opposition between life and
extinction, appear in an ambivalent relationship:

Trionfa il sole, e inonda
La terra a lui devota:
Ignea ne l'aria immota
L'estate immensa sta.

Laghi di fiamma sotto
I domi azzurri inerte
Paiono le deserte
Piazze de la città.

Là spunta una sudata
Fronte, ed è orribil cosa:
La luce vaporosa
La ingialla di pallor.

Dite: Fa fresco a l'ombra
De le navate oscure,
Ne l'urne bianche e pure,
O teschi de i maggior?[8]

. . . . .

The sun triumphs, and floods
The earth that is devoted to it:
Afire in the motionless air
Summer hovers immense.

The abandoned and inert
Squares of the city
Seem lakes of flames
Beneath blue domes.

There, suddenly a sweaty
Forehead emerges, and it is a horrible sight:
The misty light
Gives it a yellow pallor.

Say: Is it cool in the shadow
Of the dark naves,
Within the pure white urns
Oh skulls of our ancestors?

A fiercely triumphant summer sun vanquishes the earth
and fixes everything in a broiling immobility. Already in
the first stanza an ambiguity or irony is suggested by the
attitude of devotion that the earth is said to have toward
the sun, for in point of fact the earth has succumbed to the
sun. The second stanza makes it clear that this is specifically an urban noonscape (itself a rarity), and the deserted
squares of the city (a sure sign it is noontide) appear as
lakes of motionless fire beneath a deep blue sky. In the
third stanza the sense of noontide oppression is heightened
by the sudden appearance of a solitary perspiring figure.
We may take this figure to be the poet himself who is approaching the cathedral in the square. He is rendered
grotesque and yellowish in a deathlike pallor by the light
that seems to deform and disintegrate all objects. Finally,
the last stanza brings a macabre twist to the motif of the
midday retreat to a shady refuge. The cathedral before
which the poet stands contains cool shade but also the
tombs of the dead. It is a place of darkness and so, in a
Carduccian view, a place where life is absent. But the
derisive, Baudelairean guise in which he poses his question to the dead interred in the cathedral may also be self-
mockery. For in this case, at least, the midday sun in which
he stands is experienced as the destructive Gorgon.

But let us take leave of Carducci on a more truly solar note. The following Alpine midday in the poem by that title (**"Mezzogiorno alpino"**) is, for all its brevity, among the most highly suggestive evocations of the special sense of timelessness that noontide seems so often to arouse:

> Nel gran cerchio de l'alpi, su 'l granito
> Squallido e scialbo, su' ghiacciai candenti,
> Regna sereno intenso ed infinito
> Nel suo grande silenzio il mezzodì.
>
> Pini ed abeti senza aura di venti
> Si drizzano nel sol che gli penètra.
> Sola garrisce in picciol suon di cetra
> L'acqua che tenue tra i sassi fluì.[9]

. . . . .

> In the great circle of the Alps, on the granite rock
> Bleak and pale, on the shining glaciers,
> Serene, intense and infinite
> Midday reigns in its majestic silence.
>
> Pines and firs in the windless air
> Rise in the sun that penetrates them.
> Alone, like a faint sound of a lyre, chirps
> The water that has flowed tenuously through the rocks.

One must revert to the category of the sublime in considering this poem which presents the grandiose spectacle of the Alps in the absolute silence and light of midday. In part there is gray granite whose barrenness seems to be the more exposed in the totality of light, in part, the peaks and patches of ice and snow glistening with a dazzling radiance. Sole protagonist here is midday "reigning" over all things in majestic immobility, imparting a light and silence that are the same phenomenon. The adverbial adjective *intenso* refers not to the sun's heat, but to the quality of fixity and absoluteness of the light and silence, just as *sereno* bespeaks their purity while denoting a vision of a cloudless sky, and *infinito* conveys the impression of their timelessness. Below these highest regions, forests of pines and firs stand tall and motionless in the windless air and seem now to be of the substance of the luminous silence that has penetrated and possessed them. The one sound is that of a vein of water playing steadily like a musical instrument. But it is not a wild or intense sound like that of the cicadas. Significantly, the acoustic sensation suggested by *garrisce* is immediately attenuated by the qualifying notation of *in picciol suon,* and like the soft rustling of the wind through the foliage in Leopardi's "L'infinito," its effect is not to break a surrounding preternatural silence but rather to throw that silence (and the majestic setting to which it is attached) into a greater relief, to deepen it, as it were.[10] This effect is heightened by the daring use of the past absolute tense of the important verb *fluì*. The idea or impression that this creates is that the water, even as it flows through and by the stones and rocks, seems continually to have already passed by. The flow of water is an archetypal image of the fluidity of time, and here it signifies the present moment that is continually transforming itself into the past, becoming lost or nullified in the stillness and timelessness (as opposed to never-ending time) experienced in the deep midday stasis.

Here then time is recognized less in Plato's sense of a moving image of eternity than as an illusion that vainly seeks to conceal the reality of eternity.[11]

The final word in each of the two stanzas of Carducci's poem has extraordinary value in contributing to the quality of the evocation. The key word *mezzodì* (midday) occurs precisely at the midway point of the poem, at the very end of the first stanza. The word, of course, also refers to the subject of the poem, and as the subject of the sentence occupying the whole stanza, it has been postponed to the very end by the syntactical inversion. With its strong accent on the last syllable, it creates a sense of suspension (the midday pause) and fixes the entire vision of the first part of the poem in a zone of indeterminacy, wonder, and expectation. Likewise *fluì*, the last word of the poem, echoes the acoustic effect of *mezzodì* with its accented last vowel (which creates the illusion of a rhyme) and thereby keeps us suspended in the midday impression of indeterminacy and timelessness.[12] Thus the word *fluì* has an enormously important role in the poem. It functions on one level—the visual—to indicate motion, whereas on another level—the acoustical—it suggests immobility. Such an impression of motion in immobility, or energy in stasis, is one of the ambiguities, perhaps the most important one, that contribute to the mystery of midday.

*Notes*

1. *Poesie di Giosue Carducci 1850-1900,* 24th ed. (Bologna, 1957), p. 678. The peacock, we may recall, was sacred to Juno.

2. Ibid., p. 659.

3. Ibid., p. 688.

4. Ibid., p. 709. In the poem the image of the midday sun already occurs at lines 26-27: "e de gli eletti / In su le fronti il sol grande feriva." The poem opens with references to the Alpine landscape seen in the morning and in the setting sun, the place being dear to the poet at both moments. But the evocation of the commune itself and of its inhabitants is set in the brilliant light of noon.

5. *Prose di Giosue Carducci 1859-1903* (Bologna, 1957), pp. 943-945.

6. Ibid., p. 945.

7. Ibid.

8. *Poesie di Carducci,* p. 640.

9. Ibid., p. 1,045.

10. This sensation will be readily recognized as true by the reader, but I offer another poetic testimony to it in the following lines from Wordsworth's "Airey-Force Valley":

> _____ Not a breath of air
> Ruffles the bosom of this leafy glen.
> From the brook's margin, wide around, the trees
> Are steadfast as the rocks; the brook itself,

Old as the hills that feed it from afar,
Doth rather deepen than disturb the calm
Where all things else are still and motionless.

(1-7)

11. This too must necessarily bring to mind Leopardi's "L'infinito" where the wind's rustling is an image of the flow of time, of the present "age" that is "flowing" into the infinite "sea" of silence. Lines 3-4 of Carducci's poem also recall Leopardi's poem. The flow of water as an archetypal image of the flow of time, passing and "disappearing" amid rocks and stones, recurs in the poem "Crisalide" by E. Montale, a poet who will receive much attention later in this study: ". . . ecco precipita / Il tempo, spare con risucchi rapidi / Tra i sassi, ogni ricordo è spento." Also in Montale we find the phrase: "il gocciare / Del tempo inesorabile" ("Mediterraneo," 3, in *Ossi di seppia*) and, in a late poem by the poet, there occurs the clear statement that "I grandi fiumi sono l'immagine del tempo / Crudele e inesorabile" ("L'Arno a Rovezzano," in the volume *Satura*). This is existential time, that is time experienced as *Angst*— the awareness of one's finitude and the dread of being swept along into nonbeing.

12. There is a fine commentary on Carducci's poem by Cesare Federico Goffis. Concerning the last line of the first stanza he writes: "Il quarto verso con la tronca segna un distacco vivace nel ritmo, una sincope che pare sospendere indeterminatamente l'impressione." So too on the poem's second stanza he notes: "È colto un istante di pace che il verbo al passato dell'ultimo verso sembra sospendere, dissolvendolo in armonia musicale." In *La poesia di Giosue Carducci* (Genoa, 1972), II, p. 120. And on the use of the past definite *fluì* he has the following excellent observation: "L'uso del perfetto con valore continuativo che indica il fluire dell'acqua ('*fluì*') sembra proprio voler rimuovere ogni senso di tempo dall'animo del poeta, che si stacca dalla vita e s'immerge non nella gioia panica del meriggio di *Davanti San Guido,* ma nel regno immutabile ('sereno intenso ed infinito') dell'ora solare." Ibid., p. 119.

## Remo Catani (essay date 1993)

SOURCE: Catani, Remo. "The Mixed Blessings of Tradition: An Examination of Carducci's 'Idillio maremmano.'" In *Italian Lyric Tradition: Essays in Honour of F. J. Jones* pp. 73-90. Cardiff, U.K.: University of Wales Press, 1993.

[*In the following essay, Catani uses "Il maremmano" to showcase Carducci using the classical form to avoid rather than temper emotion.*]

When, after long gestation, Giosue Carducci eventually came to compose **'Idillio maremmano'** in September 1872, he was Professor of Italian Literature at Bologna and an established poet, patriot and public figure.[1] Much to the annoyance of his wife Elvira Menicucci, he had for some time been pouring his heart out for an erudite, coquettish, sophisticated lady from Milan, Carolina Cristofori Piva, who was to figure as the Lidia of the *Odi barbare.* In all their years together he had barely given Elvira an affectionate mention, and now, in **'Idillio maremmano',** he suddenly wrote what on the surface seems to be a love poem for a blond, buxom country lass imaginatively plucked from his idealized childhood and early adolescence in the Maremma of well over twenty years before. He cries: 'Meglio era sposar te, bionda Maria!' (32) It has already been suggested that Elvira is unlikely to have been overjoyed at this latest utterance from her famous husband.[2]

Nor has it gone unnoticed that Carducci moves uncomfortably in the mainstream of the traditional Italian love lyric. Often forcefully formulated or skilfully adorned, his declarations of love remain unconvincing. Carducci is, for Thovez, fundamentally literary and non-poetic: he has no true awareness of love, and his women are 'motivi verbali, eleganti manichini letterarii vestiti di incerti paludamenti classici'.[3] Croce's more perceptive and sympathetic evaluation finds a voluptuous appeal in the love poems, but recognizes that, though simple and sensuous, they are subordinate in significance, providing only 'qualche istante di abbandono e di sogno' to a poet who is clearly categorized as heroic rather than amorous.[4] Even if Luigi Russo has insisted more recently on the importance of the role played by Giosue's relationship with Carolina, his only true love, in his poetic development, it is Thovez's thesis that has persisted in critics such as Renato Serra who writes: 'Le sue passioni e i suoi tormenti erano tutti letterari . . . Egli non ha mai scritto un verso d'amore, altro che per reminiscenza o esercitazione letteraria'.[5]

Nowhere does Carducci show greater stylistic unease in the expression of love, or does his considerable literary inheritance contribute more to the creation of that unease, than in the poem ostensibly inspired by the memory of his fair-haired Maria. This re-examination of the famous idyll aims to throw light on two vexed questions in Carduccian criticism: that of the composition's stylistic coherence, and, by extension, the more fundamental question of the efficacy of Carducci's often over-academic literary borrowings. In doing so, it will also direct attention to an important dimension of the theme central to this volume: the ambivalence of the lyric tradition which is shown to be capable of impeding renewal by stifling, under the weight of its own influence, the originality essential to the poetic process itself.

Maria's precise identity, if indeed she ever existed, is manifestly of no consequence.[6] But the *rapprochement* made with Carolina Piva has an undoubted relevance. Russo finds himself better able to comprehend the great poet's predilection for a simple rustic girl in the light of the following words written to Lina (Carolina) not long before the poem was composed: 'Io, democratico in tutto, in amore sono aristocratico: odio le cameriere, aborro le figure borghesi: quell'ideale di bellezza alta, svelta, languida, come un tronco di palma, tenera e fina, voluttuosa e spiritosa, ridente e altera a un tempo, quell'armonia di grazia di piacere e di decoro . . . mi rapiscono.'[7] The association, however, of such an aristocratic figure with 'il fianco baldanzoso ed il restio / Seno' (10-11) of Carducci's 'giovinetta', even when she is presented walking in classical adornment through the cornfield (16-30), is not obvious. Giosue's love poems and letters are always more about himself than about literature or the women who are the object of his love. The link between Lina and Maria can be made more convincingly earlier in the same letter of 23 April 1872, on a more subjective level:

> Mi par di essere tornato a venti anni! E non avrei mai creduto di dover più amare! parte gli studi aridi e lunghi e solitari a cui mi abbandonai perdutamente negli anni che seguirono il mio venticinquesimo, parte il disprezzo e lo sdegno che ho della società moderna . . . parte l'oblio e l'odio degli uomini, mi avevan dovuto fare al cuore come uno smalto . . . e in vece io amo, deliro, come a venti anni; e vorrei, o Lina, soffocarti di baci.[8]

The spontaneous, unadulterated sentiment of youth clashes with a burning disdain for the stultifying effects of academic and civic pursuits; just as it does in **'Idillio maremmano'** (40-5). Is it permissible then for us to equate the languid society lady with the peasant girl? After all, Lina too has brought him back to his youthful reveries. In another letter, written just ten days earlier, he writes: 'Superba regina, tu hai richiamato ai sospiri e ai sogni di un giorno il poeta degli epòdi, oh via, non mi par vero!'[9] Certainly, the numerous letters addressed to Lina, so attentively read by Russo, can be seen as an expression of an unspecified need for love, love seen as solace, as forgetfulness.[10] On 24 April he writes: 'Oh potessi, un momento, un solo momento, obliar tutto su'l tuo cuore, e di lì passare al seno della terra antica, solo riposo per me!'[11] And in **'Idillio maremmano'** he writes: 'E il cuor che t'obliò, dopo tant'ora / Di tumulti ozïosi in te riposa . . .' (4-5).

Both the poet's childhood in the Tuscan countryside and a classical world which assumes personal, intimate significance serve distinctly and at varying moments as a haven far from the cruel blows of fate and from the disenchantment and apparent futility of public endeavour. At other moments, they merge into a single concept, a single symbol of love, warmth and comfort, a single elegiac myth. There is an ambivalence in his 'Seno della terra antica'. Against Thovez's condemnation of Carducci as an exterior, academic poet lacking in depth of feeling and subjectivity, Croce and others in his wake have highlighted these twin currents in Giosue's sad poetic flow. Sad because his one sincere note is, as De Lollis puts it, 'la nota elegiaca dell'irremediabilmente svanito'. Carducci is more than the renowned *poeta-vate* of the heroic moment: he is also the 'poeta del rimpianto' who, despite his attacks on Romantic excess, reveals a Romantic need for the illusion of beauty in the fleeting moments of the past and in a remote yet personalized antiquity.[12]

Carducci's erudition and profound belief in tradition assure an abundance of literary sources and echoes in his works. 'Idillio maremmano' is no exception: scholars have cited numerous authors of widely varying style and stature, from Petrarch to Poliziano, Parini and Prati, to the more obscure Mazza, Zanella, Savioli and Scalvini.[13] Unmistakable in Giosue's idyll is the voice of Leopardi in **'Sogno', 'Le ricordanze'** and **'A Silvia'.**[14] Yet the Renaissance, with its love of antiquity, was an age with which Carducci was more in tune than with his own century, even in the guise of the greatest and most classically imbued of all its Italian poets. Insufficient weight has been given to Poliziano's influence in the composition of **'Idillio maremmano'**, despite the mention of possible borrowings from the first book of the *Stanze per la giostra*.[15] It is not difficult to link specific words, phrases and images in the idyll with others in the fifteenth-century poem. Carducci bemoans the loss of his young country girl, but his mind is on carefree, invigorating hunting trips in the Maremma:

> Meglio era sposar te, bionda Maria!
> Meglio ir tracciando per la sconsolata
> Boscaglia al pian il bufolo disperso,
> Che salta fra la macchia e sosta e guata . . .
>
> (33-6)

It is to this same dream that he returns with regret at the close of the poem:

> Oh miglior gloria, ai figliuoletti intenti
> Narrar le forti prove e le sudate
> Cacce ed i perigliosi avvolgimenti
> Ed a dito segnar le profondate
> Oblique piaghe nel cignal supino . . .
>
> (55-9)

Simple, country pursuits without doubt, but in Carducci's mind not disconsonant with those that delight Poliziano's 'bel Iulio', engaged Hippolytus-like in the hunt, 'dando sovente a fere agro martiro' (St. IX, 4), protagonist in an idealized golden age:

> Quanto è più dolce, quanto è più sicuro
> Seguir le fere fuggitive in caccia
> Fra boschi antichi fuor di fossa o muro,
> E spïar lor covil per lunga traccia!
>
> (St. XVII, 1-4)

A classical dream? Certainly, but one that embraces the same honest, liberating endeavour that Carducci longs for:

> Ah quanto a mirar Iulio è fera cosa!
> Rompe la via dove più il bosco è folto
> Per trar di macchia la bestia crucciosa,
> Con verde ramo intorno al capo avvolto,
> Con la chioma arruffata e polverosa,
> E d'onesto sudor bagnato il volto.
>
> (St. XXXIII, 1-6)

The gentler touch that depicts the young Iulio protecting his face from the sun with a green branch echoes an earlier description: 'E 'l volto difendea dal solar raggio / Con ghirlanda di pino o verde faggio' (St. X, 7-8), but it also brings to mind Carducci's description of a Juno-like Maria walking majestically through the cornfield: 'Sparso tra' verdi rami il sol ridea / Del melogran, che rosso scintillava' (26-7). Indeed, Poliziano's celebrated description of the nymph Simonetta in the first book of the *Stanze* (XLII-L) was also in all probability in Carducci's mind in his idealization of Maria who, like Simonetta, is presented in divine form: 'Al tuo passar, siccome a la sua dea, / Il bel pavon l'occhiuta coda apria / Guardando, e un rauco grido e te mettea' (28-30). The nymph in Iulio's vision subdues and placates all around her with a calm, burning glance:

> Volta la ninfa al suon delle parole,
> Lampeggiò d'un sì dolce e vago riso
> Che i monti avre' fatto ir, restare il sole.

(St. L, 1-3)

The peasant girl of Carducci's dream is made to assume the same role:

> Alta e ridente, e sotto i cigli vivi
> Di selvatico fuoco lampeggiante
> Grande e profondo l'occhio azzurro aprivi!

(19-21)

But, rather than in a disempassioned listing of literary correspondences, Poliziano's presence is better perceived in the continuance of the same envious affinity that led Carducci to edit and borrow from him many years before he wrote **'Idillio maremmano'**. As early as October 1857 Carducci proposed to the Florentine publisher Gaspero Barbera an edition of all Poliziano's Italian works to be ready by the following June.[16] In the long canzone, from his period of classical apprenticeship, **'Alla memoria di D.C.'** (**Juvenilia**), written a month after the tragic suicide of his brother Dante in November 1857, the influence of Poliziano's Iulio is already very clear.[17] With a group of friends in Florence, Carducci founded a literary review entitled *Il Poliziano* in 1859.[18] His research into the manuscripts was scholarly and painstaking, but it was a labour of love.[19] In reviewing Carducci's edition for *La Nazione* in December 1863, Teza highlights the attraction exerted by Poliziano, 'lo scrittore elegante che contempera le tradizioni latine agli eccitamenti della musa di popolo'.[20] Of particular interest is Carducci's long essay on Poliziano's poetry in the vernacular, composed in October 1863 as an introduction to his edition.[21] The exceptional, relaxed achievement of the earlier poet, produced by the natural conjunction of the classical and the rustic is what impresses Carducci and leaves him envious.[22] In Simonetta he admires 'la dignità restituita alla materia, alla carne, alla forma'.[23] Above all, Carducci is envious of Poliziano because he happily combines consummate classical learning with popularity and accessibility:

> E qui sta la meraviglia; come non ostante i classicissimi studi dei quali sa pur pompeggiarsi, il Poliziano riuscisse poeta popolare a' suoi giorni, e di fama popolare siano tuttora le *Stanze;* delle quali come di parecchie ballate la grazia e la bellezza nativa è palese a tutti i leggitori senza bisogno di dissertazioni che insegnino a gustarle.[24]

For Poliziano, Leopardi and Carducci alike the origins of the Italian lyric tradition lie in the ancient world. Poliziano and Leopardi however impart their classicism with an ease that Carducci fails to attain. It is consonant with the natural elements they directly observe and record in their poetry, whereas in Carducci the classical and literary are all too often, as in **'Idillio maremmano'**, ill-attuned to the rustic and popular. The irony is that such a dissonance was abhorrent to Carducci himself. 'I letterati ritoccano, ripuliscono, riordinano: quando son grandi, ricreano la creazione popolare, quando son piccoli, la scimiotteggiano.'[25] He distinguishes 'quel classicismo tecnico che è quasi uno spogliatoio teatrale' from 'quel classicismo eterno che è l'armonia più intima del concetto col fantasma e della contenenza con la forma'.[26] He is averse to jarring academism and strives towards a practical linguistic syncretism that shuns the abstract, towards a 'ritorno alle origini' in which the classical and popular coincide.[27]

Carducci's efforts are not always successful, but there are several compositions of clear classical inspiration that are successful. **'Alessandrina'** (*Rime nuove,* May 1872), third of the *Primavere elleniche,* describes his loved one in an Elysian setting far removed from the Maremma. It lacks raw, rustic vigour but combines the classical and sensual well to produce a *voluptas* that, even if perceived as stylized, has the merit of avoiding artificiality and maintaining a unified tone. Elsewhere, we have already noted, the return to Rome and Greece transcends the parameters of civic thought and literary classicism to become an ideal source of refuge and solace. **'Fantasia'** (*Odi barbare,* April 1875) is such a poem. His loved one speaks and the sweet harmony of her voice transports his soul on a fantastic journey that not only aspires towards a remote, serene age but adds an intimate dimension in its description of personal ecstasy and abandon. **'Fantasia's'** debt to Baudelaire's 'Parfum exotique' has not gone unnoticed, and indeed in the metrical experimentation of the *Odi barbare* Carducci manages to achieve effects that communicate the *enivrement* or the *ennui* of the modern psyche.[28] Even in the most emotive poems of personal tragedy in *Rime nuove* Carducci turns, openly or unthinkingly, to his classicism, and throughout his entire poetic production he experiences little difficulty in placing it convincingly at the service of the widest range of expression.[29]

The extent to which he succeeded in imparting the popular or the rustic with equally relaxed conviction is more debatable. The intention and deep-felt desire to do so are not in doubt. In **'Idillio maremmano'**, Maria is quickly transformed from an apparition of tender, long-forgotten love to the 'espressione . . . della forte e sana e libera esistenza campagnuola' perceived by Getto, the 'robusta donna a capo nudo' seen by Baldini.[30] Critics from Croce onwards have been struck by the similarity between Carducci's idyll and his Alcaic ode **'La madre'** (*Odi barbare,* April 1880).[31] In the idyll he writes:

> Ché il fianco baldanzoso, ed il restio
> Seno a i fren del vel promettean troppa

Gioia d'amplessi al marital desio.
Forti figli pendean da la tua poppa
Certo, ed or baldi un tuo sguardo cercando
Al mal domo caval saltano in groppa

(10-15)

And in the ode:

Or forte madre palleggia il pargolo
forte; da i nudi seni già sazio
palleggialo alto, e ciancia dolce
con lui che a' lucidi occhi materni
intende gli occhi fissi . . .

(13-17)

A similar vignette emerges from the opening quatrains of **'Alle fonti del Clitumno'** (*Odi barbare*, June 1876), and in **'Canto di marzo'** (*Odi barbare*, March 1884) he exhorts: 'Chinatevi al lavoro, o validi omeri . . . schiudetevi a gli amori, o cuori giovani' (26-7). Was Maria then not an early love after all, but no more than an earth-mother to be admired dangling babies from her breast and revelling in **'La giustizia pia del lavoro'** (**'La madre,'** 36)? As Getto observes, these descriptions 'vogliono creare un clima non meramente fisico ma di sano significato morale'.[32] Although such sentiments and the sculptural figures that embody them have in the past been praised by eminent critics, it is more difficult to see their appeal in our present disabused age. The Fascist era has intervened; bitterness and derision have followed in its wake. A. S. Novaro wrote in 'A Mussolini' (1935): 'E le madri alla gonfia / Mamella appesero ancora / I poppanti come gioielli'; in 1947, Baldini found the image 'sardanapalesco'.[33] *Romanità* and *sanità* were of course eminently laudable in Carducci's eyes. In **'Congedo'** (*Rime nuove*, August 1873) the poet himself is presented as a blacksmith or craftsman ('grande artiere') who produces songs to incite men to civic endeavour and hymns that celebrate beauty, friendship and other wholesome virtues.

The impression changes, however, when these rustic figures are allied to the sad, personal association with his beloved Maremma. They are then able to recapture the intimacy and depth of feeling which assure an apparently authentic and spontaneous poetic quality more acceptable to our modern ear. The association with the Maremma is sad because he knows that his idealized past which contrasts so sharply and painfully with present reality has gone for ever. None the less, the dream is a fount of solace. A ray of sunlight or the advent of April can trigger off visions that warm his soul, only to leave it cold and dark again when they vanish. But the Maremma's primary role is to console by allowing the poet to escape to a happy past that remains eternal. In **'Sogno d'estate'** (*Odi barbare*, July 1880) his own personal rustic Elysium takes its place alongside his classical ones. His heart returns to his 'cari selvaggi colli che il giovane april rifioria' (8) and he sees himself in the company of his brother Dante walking with their radiant young mother in a colourful rustic setting:

. . . su 'l rio passeggiava mia madre
florida ancor ne gli anni, traendosi un pargolo a mano
cui per le spalle bianche splendevano i riccioli d'oro.
Andava il fanciulletto con piccolo passo di gloria,
superbo de l'amore materno . . .

(10-14)

The comparison with Maria is easy to make.[34] A similarity can even be seen in the haunting figure of his grandmother in **'Davanti San Guido'** (*Rime nuove*, December 1874) where the sentiment often runs parallel to that in **'Idillio maremmano'**. The equally famous sonnet **'Traversando la Maremma toscana'** (*Rime nuove*, April 1885) contains no mother-figures, but it does encapsulate the ambivalence towards the Maremma which seems to pervade his most successful compositions: 'Ben riconosco in te le usate forme / Con gli occhi incerti tra 'l sorriso e il pianto' (5-6). Occasionally the smile fades completely and a full awareness of his tragic loss prevails, as in **'Nostalgia'** (*Rime nuove*, September 1874) where memory leads to controlled desperation rather than illusory comfort.[35]

What then of **'Idillio maremmano'**? Is it to be taken as flawed in its hesitation, in its lack of resolution and uniformity? If so, the indecision should not be ascribed to Maria's ambivalence in itself, which can be accepted as the poetic representation of an inner vacillation, a confluence of emotions. It is Carducci's stylistic uncertainty in the idyll that is less acceptable. But this too is a point at issue: critics have disagreed across the years, alternating in the acceptance or rejection of controversial *terzine*. Croce sees an authentic rustic unity that renews the traditional theme of the pastoral by harmoniously conveying a directly experienced reality.[36] De Lollis shifts the emphasis to the elegiac theme of regret, but challenges Croce's perception above all through an awareness of the poem's stylistic unevenness. For him, Maria's 'fianco baldanzoso' and 'restio seno' clash with the preceding Leopardian echoes in 7-8 ('Ove sei? senza nozze e sospirosa / Non passasti già tu'), just as the 'striscia di sobrio paesaggio leopardiano' of 50-1 ('E verdi quindi i colli e quindi il mare / Sparso di vele') is at odds with the Juno-like portrayal of Maria in 16-30. It is this crucial portrayal that provokes De Lollis's principal charge against Carducci of ornate Arcadian artificiality.[37] Baldini's exhaustive literary references only serve to draw attention to stylistic fluctuations and incongruities, yet he faithfully follows the Crocean line in considering the idyll a 'poesia di sodo fondo rusticano' and firmly rebutting De Lollis's accusation.[38] The impression of excessive pastoral decoration however has persisted alongside the prevalent rustic interpretation. The divergence of critical opinion in the years immediately following Carducci's death is mirrored fifty years after the event in the variance between Giovanni Getto and Luigi Russo.[39] Getto views the composition as an 'idillio campestre' and Maria as an embodiment of healthy country living. His carefully considered analysis marks a progression in the presentation of the rustic viewpoint: he senses a tension between the idyll's deeply autobiographical inspiration and the literary nature of its formal expression, and he feels the need for a reasoned rather than peremptory riposte to those who perceive a stylistic dichotomy in this tension. He identifies three distinct tonal areas: the vigorous 'rilievo possente' of the earth-mother (8-15); the long *rimpianto* in conclusion (31-61) with its 'duplice registro delle voci forti e di quelle delicate'; and the ornate vision of Maria as a demi-goddess (16-30), which is, in Getto's opinion, a necessary interposition intended to attenuate the poem's initial forceful style and avoid an unacceptable clash between the opening and closing sections. Russo, on the other hand, does not shrink from drawing our attention to a 'dissidio formale': 'vorrebbe essere un componimento di carattere popolaresco-realistico, e saltano fuori molte formule classicheggianti'; or from expressing, like De Lollis before him, his aversion to the apparition of Maria in the cornfield. He takes particular exception to her 'chioma flava' (23), to the 'serto di fiori' (18) she carries in her hand, to the 'cíano seren' (22) with which her eyes are compared. He avoids a confusion of Carducci's intention with the result: 'Si tratterebbe d'un amore rusticano, e la rusticità dell'ispirazione avrebbe dovuto salvare il poeta da certe stonature classicistiche.'

Giosue did try to avoid the dissonance. Nowhere is this more apparent than in the reworked manuscript draft of the first twenty-one lines, where he is seen striving to convey robust vigour and wholesome sensuality unadorned by literary refinement.[40] 'Certo il natio / Villaggio adorni ancor florida sposa' in the first draft becomes 'certo il natio / Borgo ti accoglie lieta madre e sposa' (8-9). The 'fianco baldanzoso' of 10 is a revision of 'fianco giovinetto'. Lines 13-15 in the original draft read:

> I figli che pendean da la tua poppa
> Certo già innanzi agli occhi tuoi scherzando
> Al mal domo destrier saltano in groppa.

The sons become 'forti' and 'baldi'; 'scherzando' is deemed inappropriate; the literary 'destrier', reminiscent of Poliziano, gives way to a matter-of-fact 'caval'. In its final version, the vision of Maria in the cornfield begins:

> Com'eri bella, o giovinetta, quando
> Tra l'ondeggiar de' lunghi solchi uscivi
> Un tuo serto di fiori in man recando,
> Alta e ridente.

> (16-19)

The first draft reads:

> Com'eri bella, o fanciulletta, quando
> Tra l'ondeggiar dei solchi biondi uscivi
> Un tuo mazzo di fiori in man recando,
> Bionda tu stessa.

The changes add force and a touch of down-to-earth sensuality, with the exception of the substitution of 'serto' for 'mazzo', which takes the opposite, pastoral path that De Lollis and Russo find so jarring. Even more florid lines are to come:

> Come 'l cíano seren tra 'l biondeggiante
> Or de le spiche, tra la chioma flava

> Fioria quell'occhio azzurro; e a te d'avante
> La grande estate, e intorno, fiammeggiava.

> (22-5)

The first draft is unfortunately unknown to us. It would have been interesting to see if he had initially considered the simple 'fiordaliso' and 'capelli biondi'. In any case, the revision to 'serto' introduces a clear change of direction: in these pivotal lines (16-30), Carducci opts unequivocally in his final version for a classical, literary style that stands in stark contrast to the one he is at pains to sustain in the preceding lines.

It may well be then, as Getto would have it, that this classical adornment has a conscious functional role, that it is intended to temper an over-robust tone in preparation for the final *rimpianto*. But what in that case of the discord between the rustic and classical heard by De Lollis and Russo, and indeed, as his revisions show, by Carducci himself? In the final analysis, Getto's attempt at patching up stylistic uncertainty and tonal inconsistency is unconvincing, not only in his presentation of the 'delicatezze' of 16-30 as 'immagini familiari alla fantasia del Carducci', but also in his description of unfortunate moments of empty sublimity (37 and 39-45) and irascibility (60-1) as minor blemishes. De Lollis and Russo are of course correct in seeing a dichotomy of style. But in dismissing classical adornment one should remain aware that it was Carducci's literary soul that drove him to emulate Poliziano's crisp, magical combination of the rustic and classical, whereas Giosue's penchant in fact was towards a more forceful depiction often associated with an idealized Maremma. There is a further reason for Carducci's vacillation in **'Idillio maremmano'**: neither style is an adequate vehicle for the expression of personal grief; neither can easily sustain an ensuing *rimpianto*. Poliziano's natural world, for all its realism, is a classical dream far from individual travail, just as Carducci's vital, sun-drenched countryside is an illusory source of comfort in the past that is the diametric opposite of present loss and suffering. When this essentially consoling function is recognized, it combines happily with the present reality. To take just one example, this is illustrated in the closing lines of **'Sogno d'estate'**: when the radiant vision passes, Carducci returns content to his comfortable life in Bologna with his own children:

> Passâr le care imagini, disparvero lievi co'l sonno.
> Lauretta empieva intanto di gioia canora le stanze,
> Bice china al telaio seguia cheta l'opra de l'ago.

> (35-7)

The stylistic defect of **'Idillio maremmano'** is not just that Poliziano's envied combination of the popular and classical is not achieved, or even that such a combination, however successful, is in its own turn badly conjoined to the vigorously rustic. In whichever manner it is presented, nature in Carducci cannot in stylistic terms, as it can in Leopardi, bear the superimposition of painful personal loss. Thovez uses Leopardi as a yardstick for measuring

Carducci's failure. He writes: 'il Leopardi aveva scrostato la forma da ogni eleganza di scuola e si era ridotto a una nudità sublime: il Carducci l'arricchí di nuovi adornamenti.'[41] The use of such a comparison to impute artistic regression has been amply refuted by Croce.[42] As a straightforward comment on Carducci's stylistic shortcomings, however, it should be dismissed with caution.

In his refutation, Croce writes: 'ogni poeta ricomincia da capo il viaggio.'[43] But each poet sets out with the ambivalent legacy of the lyric tradition at his disposal, and is free to draw on it as he chooses. It is certainly true that forced, academic borrowing makes for compositions that are hybrid and stilted, militating against the renewal of tradition. By the same token it is possible to bring the renewal about by directing attention to the shortcomings rather than the achievements of the past through ironical rather than admirative imitation. It was no doubt Carducci's conviction that he too in his turn would leave a literary legacy. Some successors, even in spite of themselves, echoed him with serious intent.[44] Others not so. Baldini cites a possible parody in Gozzano.[45] A much more irreverent one is to be found in Govoni's 'Sul fiume':

> Dove sei, bionda Lilly, molle giunco
> del mio fiume? Già vecchia,
> sfiancata dai bestiali parti,
> decrepita, due peli incanutiti
> la chioma al vento come orifiamma . . .
> I grandi occhi fulminei, grinze pietre;
> la bocca senza denti che fu un giorno
> un bocciuolo di rosa offerto al sole
> come il nodo di rughe innominabile
> dove ha l'uovo cantato la gallina;
> le mani di velluto così pronte
> a difenderti a oltranza, forse ad arte,
> da ogni carezza troppo ardita,
> per ritirarsi poi vinte in disparte,
> due patte di schifosa tartaruga:
> è questo il tuo ritratto odioso, o Lilly,
> Gesú! Gesú!, mio dolce molle giunco
> di fiume . . .

(124-41).[46]

Would Giosue Carducci, the respected Senator and Nobel prizewinner, have approved? How could a poet who strove throughout his life with such single-minded dedication for an awareness of the past and for the continuing revitalization of the Italian lyric tradition possibly have objected?

### *Notes*

1. The autograph MS of the first twenty-one lines of IM bears the note: 'Pensata aprile 1867; scritta settembre 1872.' Cf. *Poesie di G. C. nei loro autografi*, ed. by A. Sorbelli (Bologna, 1935), tav. IX. A. Baldini, '"IM" (vv. 1-21)', in *Fine Ottocento* (Florence, 1947), 242.

2. Cf. P. P. Trompeo, *Carducci e D'Annunzio* (Rome, 1943), 69.

3. Cf. E. Thovez, *Il pastore, il gregge e la zampogna* (Naples, 1910), 71: 'nemmeno il più acceso degli

erotomani può credere che le Lidie, le Lalagi, le Dafni, le Line carducciane siano donne di carne ed ossa.'

4. B. Croce, *G. Carducci: studio critico* (Bari, 1961, 6th edn.), 48, 153-4. See too 'Poesia d'amore e poesia eroica', in *Poesia antica e moderna* (Bari, 1950, 3rd edn.), 177-84.

5. Cf. L. Russo, *Carducci senza retorica* (Bari, 1957), 243-57; R. Serra, *Scritti*, ed. G. De Robertis and A. Grilli (Florence, 1958, 2nd edn.), II, 444-5.

6. The attempts to identify 'bionda Maria' during the poet's lifetime were hardly literary in intent. Leopoldo Barboni, supposedly an eye-witness, recounts a meeting that took place in October 1885 in a café in Castagneto when an old country-woman was brought along to meet the illustrious bard, who of course failed to recognize her. The association of the idyll's source of inspiration with a certain Maria Bianchini was made in an article in the 'Resto del Carlino' of 27 November 1901 which provoked a denial in a letter to the editor from Carducci: 'Vago e delizioso il racconto della Bionda Maria accolto da Lei nel foglio di questa mattina: ma non ha parola che rassomigli a verità' (*Edizione Nazionale delle opere di G. C.*, XXVII, 328). Barboni's description of the old woman, quoted by Trompeo (*Carducci e D'Annunzio*, 70-1), is amusing: 'mezzo risolente e spaventata, i capelli brizzolati, rinfronzolita alla meglio lì per lì per la circostanza solenne e un viso un po' avariato'. Cf. Baldini, '"IM"', 242, and G. C., *Rime nuove*, ed. P. P. Trompeo and G. Salinari (Bologna, 1961), 261.

7. *Ed. naz.*, VII, 147. Cf. Russo, *Carducci*, 365.

8. *Ed. naz.*, VII, 146.

9. Ibid., 130.

10. It appears to have gone unnoticed that Russo, attentive though he was, is in fact mistaken in the month of composition of 'IM': '. . . fu scritta nell'aprile del 1872, proprio alla vigilia dell'innamoramento del poeta per la Lina Piva. Si direbbe che già nella sua fantasia tumultuassero questi desideri di amore' (*Carducci*, 364). By September Carducci's love is in full flight: the majority of letters written in this month (*Ed. Naz.*, VII, 307-51; letters 1439-58) are impassioned love letters to Lina. This error only partly invalidates Russo's argument. Maria could now be seen as an expression during the period of sad separation of his love for Lina in another guise, rather than of a hopeful anticipation of that love. On 22 September he writes: 'Abbi pietà della mia solitudine, e rivelatimi sotto tutte le forme che il tuo angelico spirito può assumere.' (ibid., 338).

11. Ibid., 149. Cf. Russo, *Carducci*, 365.

12. Cf. C. de Lollis, 'Appunti sulla lingua poetica del C.', in *Saggi sulla forma poetica italiana dell'Ottocento* (Bari, 1929) 126-7.

13. Minutiose glosses, occasionally of doubtful relevance, can be found in Baldini, '"IM"', 242-50. See too Trompeo, *Carducci e D'Annunzio*, 73-8, where the possibility of a foreign influence in Sainte-Beuve is rejected, and G. C., *Rime nuove* (1961), 261-5, where Carducci's ironical reaction to an alleged source of Maria's 'restio seno' (10-11) is cited (p. 262: 'Ora sapete voi donde ho disegnato quel seno? Da un verso del Foscolo nelle *Grazie* . . . Ve ne sareste accorti voi? No? Né men io, né, credo, nessuno' (*Critica ed arte, Ed. Naz.*, XXIV, 259)). On the other hand, he is said to have confided to Guido Mazzoni, 'Il troppo ascoltare, ammirando e imitando, i bei suoni altrui, mi ha scemato talvolta l'inspirazione' (cf. Baldini, '"IM"', 246).

14. The 'raggio de l'april nuovo' of line 1 recalls the ray of sunlight at the beginning and end of 'Sogno'. 'Ove sei?' (7) is a clear echo of the call to Nerina in 'Le ricordanze' (144-5), just as 'passasti' of the following line can be recognized in no less than four lines of the same poem by Leopardi (149, 152, 169, 170), as well as in 'A Silvia' (53) which has other clear echoes in 16 (IM 56-7), 25 (IM, 50) and 45 (IM, 23).

15. Cf. Baldini, '"IM"', 247; also N. Busetto, *G. C.* (Padua, 1958) 181.

16. Cf. Guido Mazzoni's introduction to *Le Stanze, l'Orfeo e le rime'*, edited by G. C. (Bologna, 1912, 2nd edn.), vii-viii. The edition, without the prose writings, did not in fact appear until October 1863. It is interesting to note that Carducci chose to send a copy of his edition with his first deferent letter to Sainte-Beuve of 1 April 1867, the alleged moment of conception of IM; cf. *Ed. Naz.*, V, 103-4.

17. Cf. 'Qual fu a vederlo con ardor virile / Ruotare in breve giro agil destriero / E disserrarlo per l'aperto campo! / Gli occhi suoi mesti allor mettean un lampo, / Correa co'freschi venti il suo pensiero / De l'anno e de l'età nel dolce aprile' (12-17).

18. Cf. Mazzoni's introduction: 'Nel nome del grande umanista e insieme popolaresco toscano avevano il Carducci e gli altri voluto richiamare la nuova Italia alla riverenza e gratitudine per la grecità e la romanità' (*Le Stanze* (1912), xiii).

19. In a letter written to Chiarini on 10 August 1860 he writes: 'Oh i codici, i codici del Poliziano e dei poeti antichi in Ricciardiana! Io li veggo: io li veggo; io li rivoglio!' (*Ed. Naz.*, II, 125).

20. *Le Stanze*, (1912), xxiv.

21. Ibid., 3-244.

22. Cf. ibid., 242, and *Ed. Naz.*, XII, 373-4: 'Lo spirito del Poliziano . . . rimase segnatamente in quel che è pregio principalissimo, la congiunzione dell'eleganza antica alla vivezza paesana.' Also *Le Stanze*, (1912), 67, and *Ed. Naz.* XII, 200-1: 'Nelle lodi della vita campestre . . . sentirai da principio l'eco dell'epòdo d'Orazio e della Georgica; ma nel bel mezzo un paesaggio toscano ritratto al naturale . . . cancella la prima sensazione.' See too *Le Stanze* (1912), 201-2, and *Ed. Naz.*, XII, 333.

23. *Ed. Naz.*, XII, 203.

24. Ibid., 243.

25. *Ed. Naz.*, VIII, 408. Cf. G. Paparelli, *Carducci e il Novecento* (Naples, 1953), 38-9.

26. *Ed. Naz.*, VII, 407. Cf. Paparelli, *Carducci*, 18-19.

27. Cf. Paparelli, *Carducci*, 40.

28. Cf. M. Praz, *Gusto neoclassico* (Florence, 1940), 283-6. See too, for example, 'Alla stazione' (*Odi barbare*, June 1875).

29. The two well-known short poems on the death of his infant son Dante, 'Funere mersit acerbo' (*Rime nuove*, 1870) and 'Pianto antico' (*Rime nuove*, 1871), are a case in point. Carducci's classicism is evident in the hemistich from the *Aeneid* that constitutes the title of the first; but the ambivalent title of the second is equally indicative.

30. Cf. G. Getto, *Carducci e Pascoli* (Naples, 1965), 45 (the essay on Carducci was first published by Zanichelli in 1957); Baldini, '"IM"', 248.

31. Cf. Croce, *Carducci*, 90; also Baldini, '"IM"', 247, and Getto, *Carducci e Pascoli*, 43.

32. Getto, *Carducci e Pascoli*, 43.

33. Baldini, '"IM"', 247.

34. The month of April assumes a special function in such re-evocations. In 'Ripresa' (*Giambi ed epodi*) written the month after 'IM', he cries: 'E a noi rida l'april, / L'april de' colli italici vaghi di messi e fiori, / L'april santo de l'anima piena di nuovi amori, / L'april del pensier' (126-9). Cf. 'Alla memoria di D. C.', 17. It is interesting to note that 'La madre' and 'Traversando la Maremma toscana' were both written in April. Baldini ('"IM"', 243) also quotes 'Alla Regina d'Italia', 'Vignetta' and the first of four sonnets to Nicola Pisano.

35. Cf. 'Là in Maremma ove fiorio / La mia triste primavera / Là rivola il pensier mio / Con i tuoni e la bufera: / Là nel ciel nero vibrarmi / La mia patria a riguardar, / Poi co'l tuon vo' spronfondarmi / Tra quei colli ed in quel mar (25-32). On G. C.'s poems dealing with the Maremma, see too G. De Robertis, *Saggi con una noterella* (Florence, 1953), 118-20.

36. Croce, *Carducci*, 81.

37. De Lollis, 'Appunti', 125-7.

38. Baldini, '"IM"', 246 and 248: 'No, Maria la bionda apparizione nuova . . . è la donna che Giovanni Fattori e Silvestro Lega impostavano più di gusto sulle

loro tele' (248). Eight years before, in 1939, Trompeo had admired the 'ritratto macchiaiolo di Maria' (*Carducci e D'Annunzio*, 70).

39. Cf. Getto, *Carducci e Pascoli*, 44-6; Russo, *Carducci*, 364-6.

40. Sorbelli (ed.), *Poesie di G. C.*, tav. IX.

41. Thovez, *Il pastore*, 55.

42. Cf. Croce, *Carducci*, 19-23.

43. Ibid., 22.

44. On Carducci's haunting influence on d'Annunzio, see Ivanos Ciani, 'D'Annunzio e Carducci (o di una lunga infedelissima fedeltà)', in *Carducci poeta: Atti del Convegno Pietrasanta e Pisa, 26-28 settembre 1985* (Pisa, 1987), 215-43.

45. Baldini, "'IM'", 250.

46. Corrado Govoni, *Poesie (1903-1959)*, ed. G. Ravegnani (Milan, 1961), 1224-5.

**David H. Higgins (essay date 1994)**

SOURCE: Higgins, David H. "Commentaries & Notes." In *Giosue Carducci: Selected Verse*, pp. 227-63. Warminster, U.K.: Aris & Phillips Ltd., 1994.

*[In the following commentary, Higgins provides extensive background information to some of Carducci's best works.]*

A SATANA

Written in September 1863 (although not completed until its publication two years later), the poem was recited first at a dinner-party amongst friends as a toast (*brindisi*). **'To Satan'** sums up pungently and colourfully Carducci's progressive principles (what he later called his 'razionalismo radicale'). It is, in effect, a challenging manifesto of his most deeply felt convictions and cherished beliefs, which he occasionally modified, but never really abandoned over the following forty years. Here 'Satan' stands for 'le due divinità . . . la natura e la ragione,' which represent for Carducci all those worthwhile things which the Church, in the Italy of his day, seemed to him to belittle, oppose or denounce: physical love, beauty in nature and art, confidence in man's ability to transform the material world, freedom of thought and expression, unprejudiced intellectual enquiry, industrial and social progress. **'A Satana'** was published provocatively, a second time, in December 1869 in Bologna's radical newspaper, *Il Popolo*, under Carducci's *nom de plume* Enotrio Romano. Not by chance, it appeared on the same day as the formal opening of the 20th Vatican Ecumenical Council, and provoked furious polemics, both from the Church, and even from moderate, progressive journals

such as the *Indipendente,* whose editor pronounced it 'anti-Mazzinian'. Indeed, the aging Mazzini was said never to have really acknowledged Carducci because of these verses.

As with other examples of the genre of *brindisi* (see **Juvenilia** II.29, VI.94; *Rime nuove* III.57 **'Brindisi funebre'**), Carducci employs stanzas of four short, emphatic lines. Here the lines are of five syllables (*quinari*), where the second and fourth are rhymed *versi piani* (i.e. where the accent of the rhyme-word falls on the penultimate syllable), whilst the first and third lines are unrhymed, but respond to each other as *versi sdruccioli* (i.e. where the accent of the final word in the line falls on the prepenultimate syllable). The metre appears to echo the insistent rhythm of a locomotive speeding over its tracks. Indeed, in the end, 'Satan' is seen precisely as a railway-engine, a beneficent iron 'monster', whose progress (fortunately for the human race) is unstoppable.

25-27    reference is to the spiritual sword of St. Michael the Archangel, who led the army of faithful angels against the dismayed forces of the rebel Lucifer (Satan) and his angels.

28-41    Carducci (playfully or blasphemously) subverts the account of the Fall of Satan in the Bible. Satan is left victorious in the realm of the material world (37-41), having witnessed the 'rusting' of Michael's sword, the impotence of the Creator, and the fall of the faithful angels.

42-64    Satan's authority (1.42 'impero') can be perceived wherever the life-force is in evidence: in the flashing eye of a woman in a state of arousal, in the bubbles of a restorative glass of wine, and in Carducci's own polemical verses.

61-62    Both popes and kings—the heads of authoritarian regimes—were anathema to the republican Carducci.

65    Arimanus: Ahriman or Angra Mainyu, Persian god of darkness.

66    Adonis: the lover of Venus, was Phoenician in origin (see below 73-6); Astarte: Phoenician goddess of fertility.

72    Anadyomene: i.e. 'emergent': Venus, born from the foam of the seas around Cyprus, represents the blessings of Greek civilisation.

73-76    Adonis, in love with Venus ('holy Cyprian'), was killed by a wild boar, but resurrected by Jupiter at Venus's urgent request.

77-84    Carducci understands the Greek festivals of Adonis as having originated along the Syrian coast and its hinterland (Idumaea)—the region of ancient Phoenicia.

85f    Carducci sees the destruction by early Christianity of the temples and sacred statues of the clas-

-sical world from the pagan viewpoint: as a uni-versal and impious act of vandalism by religious fanatics. Moreover, it proved a pointless enormity, since the essence of this pantheism (or 'Satanism', which Carducci arbitrarily equates with the exaltation of physical joy, material good, rationalism and freedom of enquiry) survived 'underground' to reemerge at different times and at crucial turning-points in the human story: and not least in twelfth-century rationalism, in fifteenth-century Humanism, the Reformation, and in the nineteenth century, age of revolutions, applied science, and industrialisation.

97-      Carducci sees the origins of modern medicine in
112      the maligned witch-craft of the early centuries, and the beginnings of science in the essentially rationalist pursuits of alchemy and sorcery.

113      The Theban desert of middle Egypt was favoured by early Christian (Coptic) hermits, before the arrival of Islam.

117-20   Carducci addresses Abelard, the Thirteenth-century Franciscan monk whose rational philo-sophical method disturbed the School of Theol-ogy in Paris and elsewhere. His affair with Héloise ended in castration and exile, but his love for her on an intellectual plane persisted throughout his life: 'compensation' from a benign Satan.

124      Maro and Flaccus: the Augustan poets Virgil and Horace.

131-2    Mistresses of classical poets: Licoris, mistress of Cornelius Gallus (mentioned by Virgil), and Glycera admired by Horace.

136-44   The monastic cell of such as Abelard is populated, through the imagination, with yet other scenes of the secular world: orators and crowds, from the political history of Rome (Livy, 138), and figures from more recent history of Italy: the rebel monk Arnold of Brescia (143), who, inspired by Abelard's rationalism, advocated the radical reform of the Church, and a republican constitu-tion for Rome (144, the Campidoglio or Capitol).

148      John Wycliffe and Jan Huss, early reformers and martyrs of the late Thirteenth and early Four-teenth centuries.

159      Savonarola: Dominican monk who preached self-abnegation, asceticism and radical ecclesiastical reform in Medicean Florence. He was burned at the stake in 1499.

160-2    The list of rebels against authority finds its climax with Martin Luther, the spiritual father of the protestant Reformation in Europe, who divested himself of his monk's habit in 1524, to marry a

former nun. The choice of Luther as the epitome of intellectual protest against authority says as much about Carducci's anticlericalism as his libertarianism. With Luther, the human mind is definitively liberated, initiating a new age in the progress of the human spirit. He might have ad-duced here Descartes, or Voltaire, or any other major figure of the Enlightenment. That he taunts the Catholic Church with the name of Luther reveals the depth of his distaste for the Church's hampering involvement in the secular destiny of Italy.

187-88   The steam-engine is a fitting symbol of Carduc-ci's Satan, as a contrivance devised by man from his unprejudiced investigation of the laws of mat-ter. Relatively new to Italy, the train brought with it exciting suggestions of the industrial revolution of Northern Europe. Progressing apace there, new industry was retarded in Italy, because, in Car-ducci's view, of centuries of political division, religious obscurantism, and intellectual sloth.

199-     In this new age of industry, Satan has conquered
200      the Jehovah of the priests. But what Satan, and what Jehovah? Both images must be understood in the light of this final stanza. 'Satan' is not strictly that of the theologians, but as Carducci chooses to portray him, with special polemical significance, a symbol of free intellectual activ-ity—just as 'Jehovah' is arbitrarily limited in Carducci's presentation of Him to the stifling at-titudes of the Church in matters of politics, education, science and social progress. The whole tone of the poem is taunting, goading, triumphal-ist—less a serious theological statement than a political nose-thumbing from a boisterous, over-gifted and impertinent adversary.

AGLI AMICI DELLA VALLE TIBERINA (GE.I.1)

Dated 25 August 1867, this iambic ode (four-line stanzas of hendecasyllables, alternating *rime piane* and *rime tronche*) was written as an affectionate valediction to the Corazzini family, fervent republicans, whom Carducci had visited in their home at Pieve S. Stefano in the upper Tiber Valley. The poem is animated by the sadness of departure, a historic feeling for the natural scenery, and a passionate antipathy towards the papacy which, for Carducci, had long obstructed the legitimate aspirations of the Italians for national unity.

6        Bulciano: on the right bank of the Tiber, near Pieve S. Stefano, twenty kilometres or so from the river's source. The castle ruins are now gone, its moat and bailey given over to pasture and woodland.

9       Cerbaiolo: a peak in the high Apennines (Alpe di Luna), overlooking Pieve, which Carducci here personifies as a giant, impatient to begin hunting.

27-8    the wholesome sounds of productive industry have now replaced sounds associated with the superstitious fears of religion.

29-30   reference is to the legend that St. Francis struck the mountain-side to produce a stream near the monastery of La Verna, some distance from Pieve.

35-6    In 1867 the Tiber had not been finally 'liberated' in its course through Rome from Papal slavery. This was to occur late in 1870, when General Cadorna breached the Porta Pia and took the city.

41-2    Tarcon: mythical priest-king of Etruria (Tuscany).

47      the golden shield: a gift to Aeneas from his mother Juno.

49      Furius Camillus saved Rome from the invading Gauls in 390 B.C. Caius Marius (d. 186 BC), of a country family (hence 'ploughman') near Arpino, defended Rome against the dictatorial ambitions of Sulla.

51      The Temple of Jupiter was on the Capitoline Hill in Rome, where important victories were celebrated.

54      The Tiber rises in Tuscany, in a humble pastoral setting. Better its beginnings, therefore, Carducci states, than its end in the marble splendours of Rome governed still by the Papacy under Pius IX.

64      Milvian Bridge: the most historic bridge of Rome, marking the old northern boundaries of the city, where Constantine, the future Christian Emperor of Rome, defeated his rival Maxentius in 312 AD.

68      The Aventine Hill in Rome was the rallying-point of the Roman populace in times of conflict with the ruling patriciate. Carducci's republican sympathies are evident here.

71-2    reference is to the Garibaldian volunteers of Tuscany and Umbria, in their advance against papal and French forces in Rome.

75      i.e. the people of Rome, who still delay their rebellion against their papal and French oppressors.

### 'Meminisse horret' (GE.I.2)

This epode (four-line stanzas of double *senari* with alternate *rime piane* and *rime tronche*), dated November 1867, is typical of the form produced by Carducci. Polemical and sarcastic in tone, it was written in the wake of Garibaldi's failure to capture Rome in that year, and his defeat at Mentana on 3 November by a French expeditionary force sent by Napoleon III. Garibaldi's defeat was followed by his humiliating arrest ordered by King Victor Emmanuel II, to the chagrin of such as Carducci.

The epode is the record of a nightmarish dream, in which Carducci witnesses some of the great figures of Florentine history humiliate themselves before their adversaries or in public. The poem explores the extremes of irony and sarcasm, and consciously aims to shock the Italian people into action by its final obscenities. As he writes, close to the events of Mentana, Carducci's soul 'shudders at the recall' ('meminisse horret', *Aeneid* II.12) of this frightful incubus.

4       yellow: the traditional colour of evil, but prominent also in the Papal standard in the golden keys of St. Peter.

8       Piero Capponi: 1446-1496, People's Magistrate ('Gonfaloniere della Giustizia') in Florence, who opposed the entry of the French king, Charles VIII, into Italy in 1494. Charles' invasion had been instigated by Lodovico 'il Moro' Visconti.

9       struggle: the siege of Florence, 1529-30, by the forces of Emperor Charles V and Pope Clement VII.

10      reference is to the thunder of cannon upon the blond heads of Charles V's mercenary troops from Germany.

13      Francesco Ferrucci, heroic defender of Florence in the imperial siege, was killed by the Spanish mercenaries of the Calabrian Fabrizio Maramaldo in 1530, whilst uttering the famous words 'Tu dai a un uomo morto' ('You are striking down a dead man').

15      Gian della Bella promoted the political reforms of the 'Ordinances of Justice' in Florence in 1293, in favour of the common people against the power of Magnates such as Berto Frescobaldi.

18      Dante is seen as a common guide (*cicerone*) to tourists in the Duomo di Santa Croce, where such as Michelangelo, Machiavelli, Galileo and Foscolo are buried.

25      Machiavello: disparaging reference (singular for patrician plural) to the shade of Machiavelli, acting as procurer for his 'mother' Italy. Italy as 'mother' is found in Petrarch's famous canzone 'Italia mia', and used later by Carducci, without the irony employed here, in 'Alle fonti del Clitumno'.

### Versaglia (GE.II.21)

Dated 21 September 1871, this iambic ode (for metre see notes to **'Agli amici della Valle Tiberina',** . . .) celebrates the 79th anniversary of the founding of the French Republic on 20 September 1792. At the same time it exalts the efforts of the Parisian Communards, who from March to May 1871, unsuccessfully attempted, by a popular rising, to re-establish the French Republic under the noses of the French National Assembly. The latter, largely royalist in persuasion, was seeking the restoration of the monarchy and the restitution of Church property and power. The National Assembly met in the sumptuous Palace of Versailles, with its memories of the absolutism of Louis XIV—a monarchy which the Assembly (in Carducci's eyes) was treacherously committed to restoring. The poem, which addresses Versailles, attacks the corruption of absolute monarchy in the career of Louis XIV. But the ode also offers an attractive side: its ironic humour, pungent wit, and the sincerity of its political passion. These were from a poet who, disappointed republican that he was, consistently targeted the absolutism of the Papacy and the prerogatives of the Italian monarchy in the early years of Unification.

1 Versailles: the royal palace near Paris, built by Louis XIV, which remained the centre of French political and cultural life until the Revolution of 1789. It was later the meeting-place of the National Assembly, which in 1871 suppressed the Parisian Commune. King Louis XIV (1638-1715), the 'Sun King' (cf. l.27), was a proponent of monarchical absolutism. In his reign France also aspired to the cultural and political leadership of Europe.

4 the conspiracy of monarchy and church to suppress the people's legitimate aspirations is here suggested as a fraud perpetrated in the name of God.

13-16 reference is to the servile surrender by the French courtiers of their integrity, and to the degradation of the peasantry in their slavish labour to provide leisure facilities for their 'Christian' monarch (here the construction of the royal lodge of the Deer Park).

28 Carducci here emphasises the impersonal cultural influence of a self-authenticating, insensitive monarchy, exercised upon an incoherent, subject people.

30 influential preachers such as Bossuet kept Louis assiduously away from the paths of religious reform and tolerance. A notable instance of intolerance was Louis' revoking of the Edict of Nantes in 1685, which so far had guaranteed official Catholic tolerance of the French protestants (the Huguenots). Appalling consequences of genocide followed in the mountains of the Cévennes in south-east France (l.31), where the Huguenots had fled in disbelief at Bourdaloue's promises of safe-conduct. Bourdaloue (l.32) was the king's Confessor.

33-44 three stanzas in which Carducci lingers over Louis' adulteries, actively tolerated by a materialistic Church. The king's three notorious mistresses determined, in Carducci's eyes, the low moral tone of the 'Sun King's' reign.

33 Ox-eye: the 'Oeuil-de-boeuf', anteroom to Louis' bed-chamber, in which he entertained his mistresses: the unmarried Louise-Françoise de la Vallière (l.38), the married Mme de Montespan (l.40), and the widowed Mme de Maintenon (l.42).

36 golden dome: the Heavens, as represented in the ceiling fresco of the anteroom, in which God appeared to be blessing the immoral activities below.

41 Engedi: the place of origin of the lilies mentioned in The Song of Songs (l.14). The irony of the sexual innuendo is not to be missed.

43-44 Louis cynically raised any of his subservient clergy ('faithful Aaron'), who were tolerant of his sexual misdemeanours, from obscurity to ecclesiastical honours (from the humble black of parish priests to the 'purple' of the cardinalate).

45-48 kings and capitalists ('court and city') in pre-Revolutionary days lent their names to historical periods according to the rise and fall of fashions, whilst the common people measured time from the incidence of famine and other scourges. Then, when the people rose up in revolution, they characterised their history according to the death of princes.

49 that day: the 'Day of the People', the French Revolution of 14 July 1789.

49-52 Carducci sees the French Revolution as deriving from the people's search for truth from different approaches, so that the idols of authority came crashing down. Kant, in his *Critique of Pure Reason,* and Robespierre in his political activities, dethroned both God and the King (Louis XVI) respectively.

53 ff. the two dead (also 'the two carcasses' of l.57): Carducci refers to the Church and the Monarchy, whose claims for reinstatement the National Assembly of 1871, meeting at Versailles, were debating. In the end, the claims of the Republicans were vindicated. However, in Carducci's eyes, the purer, revolutionary republican cause had already been tragically lost by the Parisian Communards in the same year. The 'monument' of Church and Monarchy is the tomb.

54 The 'skulls' are those of the victims of Church and Monarchy, held guiltily in the hands of the two sculpted figures who, kneeling in an abject plea for mercy, symbolise the two institutions.

60 The Communards set fire to the Palace of the Tuileries in their unsuccessful attempt to unseat the National Assembly and restore the Republic by revolutionary means.

## GIUSEPPE MAZZINI (GE.II.23)

Composed 11 February 1872, this sonnet was written when Mazzini had withdrawn from public life, to reconsider the revolutionary republican ideals which had sustained him in his struggle for Italian independence and unity. These the Italian people had finally rejected in the plebiscite of 1860, which had produced votes in favour of a monarchy. For Carducci, both Christopher Columbus and Mazzini, who were Genoese by birth, had contemplated distant ideals: Columbus new worlds; Mazzini a free, united, democratic (republican) Italy. In this poem, Carducci displays his strong sympathies with Mazzini, the man and his cause. Both Mazzini and Carducci had been driven by political notions which in the end proved unattainable dreams. Carducci's regret at unachieved goals—personal, cultural and (here) political—tinge several of his more intimate lyrics in the *Rime nuove* and the *Odi barbare.*

3     Mazzini was born in Genoa in 1805, at a time of national misfortune for Italy under Austrian and Napoleonic rule.

8     Graccus: Caius Graccus, as Tribune of the People, laid down his life in defence of the rights of the common Roman people, the plebs, in 121 B.C. Dante Alighieri (1265-1321), author of the Divine Comedy, was seen by leaders of the Risorgimento, including Mazzini, as the prophet of an Italian nation.

10-11     Mazzini, founder of the patriotic society 'La Giovane Italia' (Young Italy), inspired Italians to struggle by force of arms for the independence, unity and democracy of their country. Although the outcome in 1861, an Italian Kingdom, was not agreeable to someone of Mazzini's convictions, he nevertheless clung to his ideals despite all. Lamartine (d.1869), the French poet, had despaired of Italy's ever gaining its independence, and dubbed her 'la terre des morts', a charge to which Carducci alludes ironically here.

14     i.e. the ideal, existing platonically beyond space and time, is indestructible, therefore alone 'true'. It is man's nature ever to entertain ideals as incentives to action, even though in themselves necessarily unattainable. The line appears to be based on Victor Hugo: 'O toi! o idéal! toi seul existes!' (*Les Misérables* I.1.10).

### A UN HEINIANO D'ITALIA (GE.II.25)

In this epode (four-line stanzas of alternate rhyming hendecasyllabics and heptasyllabics), written in 1872, Carducci vehemently satirises a contemporary poet Bernardino Zendrini, who had had the temerity to translate into Italian some of the poetry of Carducci's idol Heinrich Heine (1797-1856). Carducci considered Heine (whom he too translated) a model of the sublime, rebellious, anti-authoritarian poet, and Zendrini the model of the effete, arcadian, sentimentalist poetaster.

4-5     Heine's poetry and prose-works express his often violent anti-clerical, iconoclastic thought, and his left-wing ideals.

15     Thor: the Germanic god of war is depicted hanging on Heine's every word, ready for action at the poet's nod.

17-24     the 'Songs' of Heine are like a gale bending the 'forests' of innumerable Gothic spires, nests of clerical obscurantism and reaction since the time of Charlemagne (1.23), who is depicted cowering in his winding-sheet in the Cathedral of Aachen. Charlemagne was the first emperor of the Holy Roman Empire, crowned in 800, and symbolises for Carducci the sinister conspiracy between the ecclesiastical and secular powers of Europe.

25     the subject of the apostrophe is Bernardino Zendrini (1839-1879) whom the robust realist Carducci characterises as 'tubercular' ('weedy'), his standard description of introspective late-Romantic or 'Arcadian' poets (cf. *Intermezzo*, ll.121-4, not included in this volume, attacking Zendrini and the Scapligliati).

27     reference is to the salons of the neo-Arcadian academicians, whom Carducci berates here.

37     flowers traditionally associated with sentimental poetry.

40     cauliflowers: an ironic image used again in 'Congedo'/'Envoi', p.140, l.16.

42     shepherd-boys: ironic reference to the misguided patrons and admirers of Zendrini's arcadian effusions, stimulated by his poetry to engage in frivolous, sexless affairs (1.44) with their 'shepherdess' mistresses (Chloe, 1.47, one such).

### IL CANTO DELL'AMORE (GE.II.30)

This poem was conceived, as Carducci himself records, during his official visit to Perugia over the summer examination period of the 'licenza liceale' in 1877, and elaborated in the following year: 'in Perugia nella piazza ove già sorgeva la Rocca Paolina'. It begins by recalling the historical origins and fate of the papal fortress, then passes to a sensitive observation of the beauty of the countryside around, from which emanates a mystical force of universal love that dissolves the tensions, quarrels and hate in the poet's own heart and potentially in the hearts of all men. Even Carducci's distaste for Pope Pius IX is mitigated, whom the poet now sees as less a tyrant than a poor, wretched prisoner in his own Vatican.

The penultimate poem of *Iambics and Epodes,* this iambic ode of four-line stanzas of hendecasyllables, with *rime piane alternate* (except for every third stanza with *rime tronche* in the second and fourth lines) loses therefore the contentious note of its species, and instead exalts love as a reconciling force not only in the cosmos, but also in the hearts of men everywhere—even in his political antagonists. And it is this love which, in Carducci's mind, moves the universe towards an ineluctably brighter future for man whoever or wherever he may be. The poem thus balances the polemics of the opening iambic ode of the book, **'Agli amici della Valle Tiberina'/'To friends in the Tiber Valley',** and reflects the more dispassionate and mature political attitudes of the later *Odi barbare.*

1.     Rocca Paolina: the fortress of Perugia built by the architect Sangallo (l.14), but conceived by Pope Paul III c.1540 following the defeat of the city by his forces after a long resistance. It was violently destroyed by the citizens of Perugia in September 1860, when the city became part of the new kingdom of Italy upon the collapse of papal rule. The site of the Rocca is now a public square, with only the foundations and subterranean passages surviving.

4.     Paul III (d. 1549) is shown as torn between his religious and humanistic inclinations, symbolised by the Latin of the Missal and the elegant Latin prose of the literary and linguistic works of his protegé Cardinal Bembo (d. 1547).

9.     *Coelo tonantem:* the opening words of the ode (III.5) by the Latin poet Horace, which refers to the popular belief that thunder signified the anger, and therefore existence of the gods. Pope Paul's wide classical scholarship is suggested by Carducci, as also his hypocrisy and cynical abuse of spiritual authority.

12     Engedi and Sharon are pastoral localities mentioned in the Song of Songs (1.14, 2.1) of the Old Testament, famed for their flora, especially roses and lilies.

21-24  The poet Francesco Maria Molza (d. 1544) wrote in praise of Perugia's new fortress, whilst the Pope himself was inspired to bless the citizens with the 'spiritual gifts' of an artillery bombardment.

33-44  The razed fortress has become a municipal square with gardens, enjoying a broad vista of the countryside, from the placid Umbrian mountains, over the Tiber valley, to (Carducci affirms) the distant snow-capped peaks of the Abruzzi. The mature art of Carducci's landscape poetry is already in evidence in the atmospheric description of lines 41-44, where the light plays tantalisingly and creatively over a vast panorama.

45-60  The sensitive notes of the observed scene are transmuted into the colder delineations of a 'classical' personification: the mountains and plains of the landscape became the recumbent female form of 'Italy', upon whom the sun, her lover, presses in the heat of his passion. The sighs of this cosmic love-making (1.51) are sensed in the blood by Carducci (1.54), whose

response, determined by the scene, is one of reciprocal love(1.56). The somewhat dispassionate expression of the conventional prosopopoea leads thus paradoxically to an impassioned, quasi-mystical impulse to love generously. But Carducci admits that his poetry, though inspired, must fall short of the ecstatic experience of participation in the endless, epic 'poem' of lovemaking in the created universe (59-60).

61-96  Enraptured by this mystical experience, Carducci seems to hear the mute hymn of petition voiced by the Italian people, rising from numberless locations in the landscape. The plea, in harmony with the mysterious act of love in the universe, is for the exercise of love and reconciliation between the discordant elements and factions in Italian national life. Life itself is an eternal transmutation (1.94)—let it be reconstructed therefore according to notions of beauty and sanctity (1.96) for the benefit of mankind crushed hitherto by hate and suffering (1.95).

97-120 Carducci's hearing mystical truths is now superseded by visions of a female figure new to the landscape of Umbria: not one of Perugino's rapt and adoring madonnas, but the personification of Liberty, for whom modern Italians have fought, suffered and died. Again the poetic feeling is perhaps inhibited by the artifice (97-108), and Carducci only just retrieves the situation with a personal statement of reconciliation directed towards the aging and pathetic figure of the reigning pope Pius IX, whose loveless isolation in the Vatican, seven years after his enforced surrender of Rome to Italy, provokes Carducci's pity. If pity really is the stuff of poetry, Carducci attempts it here, but the truer poetic note, perhaps, is in ll.115-16, where the landscape of the Pope's native Senigallia is briefly and nostalgically evoked. Across this assumed common feature of their emotional lives, Carducci's triumphalism is abated, and his fellow-feeling for the aged and lonely pontiff is vigorously expressed.

ALLA RIMA (RN.I.1)

Written in 1877, this, the first poem of the **Rime nuove,** like the last (**'Congedo',** . . .), treats the subject of poetry. In six-line stanzas of eight and four syllables (rhyme scheme AaBCcB), Carducci produces a brisk outline of the origins and development of poetry as he perceives it. Following Dante in the *De Vulgari Eloquentia,* he descries the three capital subjects of poetry as warfare, love and morality (Dante's *rectitudo*). Poetry originated, to the democratic mind of Carducci, in the rural culture of the peoples of pre-classical times, and (it is implied) is destined for the people. Yet in the centuries between Dante's masterpiece and his own times, Carducci implies a lacuna which he proposes to fill, restoring once more to the service of the queen-empress Poetry the pure passions of love and hate (ll.65-66), emotions that had been conspicuously lacking in the intervening centuries before his providential appearance.

7ff.   Carducci sees poetry as having originated in the peasant dance (stanza 2) and rituals (stanza 3) of harvest celebration in pagan times, its earliest rhythms deriving from the triple beat (*tripudium*) of the harvesters' feet on the ground, awakening the spirit of the earth.

19-36   The first of the legitimate uses of poetry is discerned in the epic battle-poems of the Middle Ages (chansons de geste) such as the *Song of Roland* and the *Poem of My Cid.*

25-27   Roland, nephew of Charlemagne, was entrusted with the rear-guard of the Frankish army as it retreated through the pass of Roncevaux (Pyrenees) into France. Ambushed, Roland gave the alarm on his horn the Oliphant (l.28), but was overwhelmed by the Moors before Charlemagne could come to his aid. Poetry recorded the event in the *Song of Roland* (11th century), thus 'filling the valley' again with the sound of Roland's 'great name'.

33   Babieca: the horn of the Spanish warrior El Cid (1040-1199), hammer of the Moors, and Spanish national hero.

37-48   The second traditional role of poetry is to express the experiences of love. European love-poetry began in the 11th century in Provence, through which the Rhone (l.37) flows.

37-42   Poetry is personified as a female figure, her hair dusty from her long journey from the Spain of El Cid to the banks of the Rhone in Provence.

43-48   Carducci cites the poetry of Jaufré Rudel (12th century) as typical of the tradition of troubadour verse. His poems, expressive of an 'amor de lonh', were written for Melisenda of Tripoli (Syria) whom he knew only by repute. He set out to find her, only to die in her arms on his arrival.

49-54   Poetry's third proper subject is, following Dante, *rectitudo;* unsurprisingly, the Divine Comedy is referred to in its three parts: Hell, Purgatory and Paradise.

55f.   Carducci resumes the apostrophe to Poetry, now seen as 'empress' of the arts, and 'queen' of Romance ('Latin') literatures.

59   Poetry of Carducci's own times is seen by him as 'embattled': under assault from inferior versifiers. He would have had in mind the poets of theneo-Arcadian school (such as Zendrini) and the'Scapigliatura milanese' (such as Boito and

Tarchetti). See 'A un hieniano d'Italia', . . . and'Intermezzo' of *Giambi ed Epodi* (not included in this volume).

61-63   Carducci expresses his religious love and respect for poetry, the sort of affection in which it was held
by his illustrious antecedents, and by which they gained honour as poets.

65-66   The poem ends on a challenging, polemical note, announcing the two prime, virile emotions that will drive his poetry, whatever its subject-matter: love and hate.

### IL SONETTO (RN.II.3)

Book II of the **Rime nuove** is composed of 34 sonnets on a variety of subjects, including this piece, the second of two poems on the sonnet form, written in 1870. Here Carducci enumerates outstanding exponents of the sonnet in the history of Italian literature, from Dante to Foscolo, epitomising their chief characteristics in a series of symbolic associations.

2   blue and gold are the colours favoured by Gothic artists and illuminators of manuscripts.

5-8   Torquato Tasso (1544-1595), whose favourite classical poets were Virgil (born near Mantua) and Horace (born in Venusia, Apulia), drew inspiration from his solitary walks in the Tivoli gardens (hence 'Tiburtan'), in whose vicinity he owned a villa. The tragedian Vittorio Alfieri (1749-1803) wrote against tyranny in an Italy oppressed beneath the yoke of France and Austria.

9   Ugo: Ugo Foscolo (1778-1827), poet of the sonnet sequence *Le Grazie,* which Carducci revered for its classical features, was born on the Greek island of Zante—hence references here to Greek ('Ionian') cypresses and to the acanthus plant, the distinctive motif of Greek (Corinthian) architecture.

12   'not sixth': in Inferno IV.102, Dante had boldly claimed for himself sixth place in the line of immortal poets after Homer, Virgil, Horace, Ovid and Lucan. Carducci puts himself in last place, behind Foscolo—a falsely modest claim, which, at this stage of his career, would have been thought wholly presumptuous.

### IL BOVE (RN.II.9)

First published in 1873 under the title **'Contemplazione della bellezza'** (**'Contemplation of Beauty'**), this sonnet epitomises in symbolic form Carducci's profound veneration of the Roman virtue of *pietas* (dutifulness to gods and man). Inspired by Virgil's Georgic poetry, the sonnet eulogises the principal working-animal of Roman and Italian farms through the millennia—the ox. Patient, powerful, and unremitting in its obedience and toil in the service of man, the ox, by virtue of its employment also in sacrifices and religious festivals in the Roman world, is seen here as unconscious mediator between the world of Nature and the world of man.

### VIRGILIO (RN.II.10)

Written in 1862, revised several times and perfected four years later, this sonnet expresses, through a series of evocative analogies, the *impression* on Carducci's mind and emotions of Virgil's poetry. The setting, a moonlit scene in the countryside, is rich in thematic associations, and evinces emotions from awe to grief. But if the overriding feeling is one of melancholy, induced doubtless by the Virgilian sense of 'lacrimae rerum', it is a sadness assuaged by the feeling of a numinous presence in the natural scene.

### 'FUNERE MERSIT ACERBO' (RN.II.11)

The title of this threnody is taken from Virgil's *Aeneid* VI.429, alluding to the bitterness and grief afforded by the premature death of infants. The sonnet was written a few days after the sudden death, at the age of three years, of Carducci's only son Dante, on 9 November 1870. In the poem, which turns on the contrast between the light of day and (classically) the shadows of the shores of the dead, Carducci refers also to the suicide of his brother Dante in 1857 ('O thou . . .), and to the death of his father Michele, which occurred within a few months of each other. Their graves lie side by side in the cemetery of S. Maria al Monte, Tuscany. The mood of tragic calm and the controlling classicism of this piece were replaced within a few months by the more direct expression of emotion in **'Pianto antico'** (**'Ancient Grief'**, . . .).

### FIESOLE (RN.II.13)

This sonnet appears at first sight merely a celebration of the antiquity of Fiesole (Tuscany), continuous in its history from Etruscan to modern times, with, in the final tercet, a reminder of its contribution to Italian art. It is, however, more complex than this in its themes. Written one evening in 1886 on the *rocca* of Fiesole, the town which had overlooked the Arno before even the foundation of Florence, the poem sees Carducci pondering more deeply the civilising effects of rational, humanistic belief over superstition. Symbol of the rational ideal is the bell-tower of the cathedral of Fiesole. The slim *campanile* which dominates the scene dates from the 11th century, when Italy (as the poem reminds us) finally shook itself free from the superstitious terrors of the millennium, through a recovered faith in the natural world (witnessed in the Quattrocento art of Mino da Fiesole referred to in the final tercet). What followed were the great Italian city-communes (Florence one such), cradles, for Carducci, of European democracy. The articulation of the poem's moods is part of its message. It moves from melancholy induced by the tolling of bells, by the sight of Franciscan friars walking slowly to vespers, and the moaning of the wind in the cypresses, to a contrasting mood of incipient joy. The change of mood is marked by the symbolic asser-

tion of the bell-tower over the countryside and the poet's recollection of the cathedral's triptych painted by Mino da Fiesole, which celebrates inspiration drawn from the natural world in the development of early Renaissance art (datable, in fact, from L. B. Alberti's treatise *On Painting,* of 1435). The sonnet's major theme emerges, arguably, as the vindication of a rational, humanistic faith in the natural order, over debased religious superstition and asceticism, the latter ever a subject of Carducci's detestation (see **'A Satana',** . . . and **'Alle fonti del Clitumno',** . . .). It is significant also, in the development of Carducci's attitude to the church, that the positive symbols of Italian humanism in the poem are ecclesiastical (cathedral bell-tower and altar-piece). The sonnet is one in this respect with **'Il Comune rustico',** written a year before . . ., in its acknowledgment of the part played by the Christian faith in the progress of Italian civilisation: a late 'conversion' on the part of Carducci, but nonetheless a position consistently held afterwards (see **'La chiesa di Polenta'** of 1897, in *Rime e ritmi,* . . .).

2       Sulla: according to early histories, Florence was founded by veterans of the army of the dictator, Lucius Cornelius Sulla, in the 1st century B.C.

11      The approach of the year 1000 A.D., the 'millennium', induced the fear throughout medieval Europe that the end of history and the Last Judgement were imminent. Once this superstitious terror had subsided, Italy regained her confidence: the foundations of the city-communes were laid, trade revived, and a new era of civilisation dawned in which Italy was pre-eminent.

### SANTA MARIA DEGLI ANGELI (RN.II.15)

In the Umbrian countryside, not far from Assisi, rises the church of Santa Maria degli Angeli, a 16th century edifice built around the 'Porziuncola', the tiny chapel in which St Francis died in 1226. In this sonnet of 1877 (perfected in 1886), Carducci's gaze is drawn from this embracing monument and its impressive dome to the countryside under a July sun, alive with the work and song of labourers, in whose very fields St Francis had lived, worked and preached. Carducci records here his longing to emulate the saint in his command of poetic vernacular language, and in a moment of incipient rapture, yearns to see and hear him, with his arms uplifted, praising God in the words of his *Cantico Creaturarum*.

2       the dome is now known to have been the work of the architect Galeazzo Alessi (1512-1572), rather than that of Jacopo Barozzi 'Il Vignola'.

13-14   'Laudato sia. . . .': adapted from l.27 of St Francis' canticle.

### DANTE (RN.II.16)

In this sonnet of probably 1867, Carducci assesses his precise debt to Dante: it is not Dante's religious or political convictions that he extols (indeed, Carducci's *credo* was entirely alien both to Dante's religious and political persuasions). What Carducci venerates is the immortal poetry which Dante nonetheless extracted from his convictions, especially the Divine Comedy, which had gloriously survived the collapse of universal Church and Holy Roman Empire upon which Italy's greatest poet had built his hopes.

2      Carducci's portrait-bust of Dante is still kept in his study in Bologna.

5      St Lucy of Syracuse, Dante's patron saint.

6-7    Matelda: Dante's guide in Earthly Paradise on Mount Purgatory, who baptised him in the waters of two sacred streams before his ascent with Beatrice to Paradise proper.

11     Frederick I (Barbarossa) of Swabia, Emperor of the Holy Roman Empire, was defeated by the League of Lombard towns and their Veronese allies at the battle of Legnano in the Val d'Olona, on 29 May, 1176.

### 'QUI REGNA AMORE' (RN.II.23)

This sonnet, composed in 1872, takes its title from a line in Petrarch's canzone for Laura, 'Chiare, fresche e dolci acque' (c.126.52), and exploits a range of *topoi,* lexis and phrases found there. In the poem Carducci assumes that wherever Lydia (Carolina Cristofari-Piva) may be in the countryside, perhaps bathing in some water (in biographical probability, the sea), she will experience sights and sensations to which his passion for her, by its very power, will have contributed.

### VISIONE (RN.II.24)

Written in 1872, following a letter from Carolina describing a moonlit scene in her garden in Milan, this sonnet, by an extended simile, raises Carducci's relationship with her above the mundane level of a liaison to the realm of myth. Its theme rests on the legend of Endymion, the beautiful shepherd of Mount Latmos in Caria, with whom the moon-goddess Selene fell in love and whom she cast into deep sleep each night in order to visit and contemplate him. Just so on that moonlit night in Spring, the season of love, the moonlight sought out and illumined the brow of Carolina-Lydia. The equation is more complex than this, however; for if Lydia is Endymion, then Carducci, by an artful reversal of sexual roles, is Selene. The implication of a chaste love affair between minds thus emerges, endorsed by the traditional notion of the chastity of Selene (Diana), and also by the fact that it is Lydia's forehead, the seat of the intellect, that is illumined by the moon (Selene-Carducci).

### MOMENTO EPICO (RN.II.30)

Sketched out in 1878 on a train journey from Bologna to Venice, via Ferrara, the poem was completed four years later. Ferrara is the subject of the sonnet, depicted here in the symbolic golden light of sunset, and extolled as the seat of the Renaissance princes of the D'Este family,

patrons of the poets of romantic epic: Boiardo (*Orlando Innamorato*), Ariosto (*Orlando Furioso*) and Tasso (*Gerusalemme Liberata*).

10     The Heliads were the daughters of the sun-god Helios (Apollo). They were transformed into poplars through their excessive grief over the death of their brother Phaethon, whose reckless driving of his
        father's sun-chariot was brought to a drastic end by Zeus, alarmed at the prospect of the scorching of the earth. Phaethon ended his mad career in the river Po, whose banks are lined with poplars, exuding still their tear-like drops of amber.

### TRAVERSANDO LA MAREMMA TOSCANA (RN.II.34)

Conceived whilst crossing the Maremma by train, one early morning in the Spring of 1885, the sonnet recalls the years of Carducci's childhood spent in the region between 1838 and 1849 (mostly in Bolgheri, a short time in Castagneto). It is an affectionate, nostalgic tribute to the wild, windswept countryside which, he claims, formed both his robust, independent character and his poetic temperament. In sight once more of the remembered hills around Castagneto, his spirits rise and he finds solace and peace of mind from the tribulations of his failed affections and unachieved ideals. The piece is a notable example of Carducci's handling of landscape, full of reminiscence (here autobiographical), but in which atmosphere and the play of light (see ll.13-14) suffuse the whole with tender subjectivity.

### PRIMAVERA CLASSICA (RN.III.39)

Written in March 1873, and loosely based on Horace *Odes* IV.7 'Diffugere Nives', this anacreontic ode (quatrains of heptasyllabics *sdrucciolo, piano, piano, tronco:* abbc, deec) surveys a burgeoning countryside where the poet, however, seeks the 'true' sun not in the cool, blue skies of springtime, but in the cool, blue eyes of his beloved. Classical then in its form (despite the partial rhyme), and in the pagan sun-symbolism dear to Carducci. Classical too in its debt to the Horatian model, with its pastoral setting, its sense of the inevitable passage of the seasons, of the brevity and uncertainty of life, and the need to seize the fleeting moment. Romantic at the same time in its expression of committed passion to a woman of unusual beauty and charisma.

### AUTUNNO ROMANTICO (RN.III.40)

A companion piece to the preceding ode **'Primavera classica',** but written a year before, this poem in sapphic meter (quatrains of three hendecasyllabics plus one heptasyllabic line, alternately rhymed) rehearses the poet's contrasting feelings at the fall of the year, the season associated especially with romantic sensibility (cf. Keats' *Ode to Autumn*). In the late autumn landscape Carducci perceives analogies both with the features of Iole (her eyes and dress) and with his own state of mind, one of regret and a growing sense of inertia and loss: a 'romantic' melancholy which at other times Carducci would have despised. The sun, therefore, in this autumnal scene, is bereft of its normal Carduccian associations (life, vigour, optimism: see **'Primavera classica'** above, and **'Classicismo e romanticismo'**, . . .): it shines but lends no warmth, seeming to signal the definitive end of his love-affair.

15      Iole: classical pseudonym of Maria Torriani, Milanese poetess, whom Carducci held in some regard and for whom these verses were written. Through Maria, Carducci first made the acquaintance of Carolina Cristofari-Piva (Lina, Lydia).

### PIANTO ANTICO (RN.III.42)

Written in June 1871, seven months after the death of his little son Dante (see also **'Funere mersit acerbo'**, . . .), this short ode in anacreontic stanzas (quatrains of heptasyllabics rhymed abbc, deec) explores the contrast between the renewed vitality of nature in springtime (the blossoming of the pomegranate tree in Carducci's garden in Bologna) and the mortification in his heart 'withered' by his only male child's death. The poignancy of the poem—a more starkly subjective statement than the allusive **'Funere mersit acerbo'**—is increased by the nevertheless classical employment of apostrophe and anaphora in the final pair of stanzas, which brings it closer in form and spirit to the ancient Greek *threnos* upon which it is distantly based. The solemn brevity of the final truncated syllable, in each fourth line (*verso tronco*), also works its stark tonal effect.

### TEDIO INVERNALE (RN.III.44)

In anacreontic ode form (see notes to **'Pianto antico'** above), this brief poem was written in the last phases of the long winter of 1875. It conveys well the brittleness of Carducci's temperament, whose mood and morale depended much on the presence of sunlight. Hence the frequency of the sun in his poetry as a whole, a Carduccian *leitmotif* which expresses the joy and confidence of ancient pantheism, and a faith in the secular values of 'youth, glory, beauty, faith, virtue and love', qualities which in this poem Carducci pronounces long gone, and which the prolonged absence of the sun in that gloomy season seems to confirm.

10      Homer: major poet of the Greek heroic epic; Valmic: the ancient Hindu epic poet of the *Ramayana*.

### ANACREONTICA ROMANTICA (RN.III.49)

Written in 1873, during the early years of his liaison with Carolina Cristofori-Piva, this ode aptly fulfils the terms of its title. It resembles the verses of Anacreon (6th century B.C.) in its theme (the repudiation of love by means of wine and spite), in its playful treatment, as well as as in its anacreontic metre (here rendered by Carducci in quatrains of heptasyllabics with alternately rhymed *versi piani* and *tronchi*). It is 'romantic' in its mood and imagery: the poet

confesses to an all-consuming passion, whilst his mistress is vampire-like in her dominance of his thoughts during the night-time hours (the references are to the then fashionable legend of Dracula and vampirism, the subject of a dissertation by G. Davanzari of Naples in 1789, and popularised by such late nineteenth-century writers, as Z. Zanetti in Itlay and Bram Stoker in England).

### SAN MARTINO (RN.III.58)

Saint Martin's day falls on 11 November, the traditional day for the *svinatura,* the drawing of the wine from the vats for bottling. This is the subject of this anacreontic ode (for metre see notes to **'Pianto antico'**, . . .), written in 1883, which conveys impressionistically the sights, sounds and smells of an autumnal village scene, probably in the Tuscan Maremma, against the backdrop of a stormy sea: a rural *quadretto* of the type which Giovanni Pascoli, Carducci's pupil, would later extensively employ in his poetry. The objectivity and social realism of the representation is artfully broken, however, by the simile of the penultimate line, to establish the poet's subjective presence in the scene.

### PRIMAVERE ELLENICHE II. DORICA (RN.IV.63)

The second of a suite of three 'Hellenic' poems, composed in 1872 at the untarnished dawn of Carducci's love for Carolina Cristofari-Piva, this sapphic ode (quatrains of three hendecasyllabics and one five-syllable line, with alternate rhyme) invites his lady Lina into an imaginary Sicily in the period of its early Greek colonisers, the Dorians. It offers her a landscape of unspoilt beauty: woods, springs and hills over which shepherds herd their white flocks, scattered with the gleaming Dorian architecture of the early settlements. It is a landscape alive too with the nymphs, dryads and oreads of mythology as recorded in the pastoral poetry of Theocritus (lines 29-36 are a rendering of some of his verses). Safely transported by Carducci's buoyant imagination into this archaic Sicilian world, Lina becomes the object of the demigods' admiration, who promise her apotheosis, as in the final lines the poet himself offers to her his uninhibited passion. It is a *tour de force* of Carducci's hellenism, close in inspiration to Goethe's poem 'Mignon', and remarkable for its sustained notes of rapture and enthusiasm, despite the brief intrusion of anti-Christian polemic (ll.53-4). Notwithstanding this jarring note, Carducci wrote to Carolina:

Questa è la più nobile, la più pura, la più greca poesia che io abbia mai fatta per donna; ed è tua. Di più, oso dire, che una poesia come questa non la poteva fare che Ugo Foscolo, il Foscolo delle *Grazie*.

(This is the noblest, purest, most Grecian poem that I have ever composed for woman; and it is yours. Moreover, I am confident enough that a poem like this could only have been equalled by Ugo Foscolo—Foscolo of *The Graces*.)

1       Cf. the first line of Goethe's poem *Mignon:* 'Kennst du das Land, wo die Zitronen blühn'.

| 3-4 | Galatea, the nymph for whom the Cyclops Polyphemus lusted, was in love with Acis. Polyphemus attempted to crush Acis beneath a rock, but Galatea transformed him into the river which bears his name (river Aci, near Catania, Sicily). |

| 5 | Pelasgian: lit. 'sea-people', the Pelasgians were the aboriginal inhabitants of Sicily. Mount Eryx (now Monte Giuliano, Erice, near Trapani in N.W. Sicily) was the centre of the cult of Venus Aphrodite. |

| 10 | the Ennean maid: Persephone (Proserpina), daughter of Zeus and Demeter, was carried off by Pluto to the Underworld as she gathered flowers in the meadows of Enna in Sicily. Persephone's annual return to the upper world brings springtime to the continents. |

| 13-15 | Alpheus, the Grecian river-god, fell in love with Arethusa when she bathed in his waters. She fled from him to Ortygia in Sicily, where she was transformed by Artemis into a fountain. But Alpheus, flowing under the sea, was finally reunited with her. The river Alpheus, one of the largest rivers in Greece, rises in Arcadia. The Arethusa spring is on the island of Ortygia in Syracuse harbour. The mingling of Alpheus and Arethusa thus symbolises the uniting of Greek poetry and Italic themes in the works of such as Pindar and Theocritus. |

| 19 | Bacchus (Dionysus): the god of transformations, thus of harvest and wine, whose rites were accompanied by orgies. |

| 23 | Theban hymn: the grand, courtly odes in Dorian dialect of Pindar (d. 438 B.C.), born in Thebes, whose patron was Hieron I of Syracuse. |

| 25 | Nebrodian mountains: in N.E. Sicily. |

| 27 | Daphnis: mythical shepherd and poet, who is to be equated here with Theocritus of Syracuse (d. 260 B.C.), creator of the pastoral idyll. |

| 29-36 | Lines translated from Theocritus *Idylls* VIII.53-56. |

| 29 | throne of Pelops: Greece; Pelops was the mythical conqueror of part of Greece. |

| 39-40 | i.e. Lina, devotee of Greek literature and endowed with the bodily beauty of Dante's Beatrice. |

| 41f. | Carducci's poem now develops a theme similar to Heine's *Lyrisches Intermezzo* 'Auf Flügeln des Gesanges' ('On the wings of song . . .'), but it is to Doric Sicily, not to the banks of Heine's Ganges, that he proposes to transport Lina. |

| 46 | dryads: nymphs of trees and woodland. |

| 49-60 | lines uttered with the fervour of Carducci's poetic faith. Hellenism for him was not simply a |

question of neoclassical aesthetics, but of beliefin the power of poetry to recreate and sustain the illusion of an ideal, pantheistic present continuous with the ancient past.

| 53-4 | an expression of Carducci's anti-Christian sentiment. For Carducci, the beauty and mystery of the ancient pagan beliefs and civilisation had been ruthlessly suppressed by the fanaticism of the early Church (see also 'A Satana', . . . and 'Alle fonti del Clitumno', . . .). |

| 61 | oreads: nymphs of the mountainsides. |

| 69 | Helen: wife of King Menelaus, whose abduction by Paris was the cause of the Trojan War. |

| 70 | nepenthe: an anodyne to subdue the fear of pain, prepared by Helen. |

| 71 | Gaea: mythical earth-goddess. |

| 75 | Amphitrite: wife of the sea-god Poseidon (Neptune), sister to Galatea. |

| 83-4 | the camelia, 'sister' to the rose. |

| 90 | naiads: water nymphs. |

| 93-6 | references are to Mount Olympus, dwelling of the gods. |

| 98 | Hylas: handsome member of Jason's Argonauts, sent to collect water on the shores of Mysia, was presumed drowned in the springs, but saved by the enamoured naiads, and transported to the courts of the gods. |

| 101 | i.e. the age of pagan cults before the coming of Christianity. For Carducci, the ancient pantheistic religions had provided the world with the consolations of a natural, life-enhancing relationship with the vital forces of the cosmos. |

| 104 | i.e. the dryads and oreads (see ll.61f.) who wish to transport Lina to the the home of the gods on Mount Olympus, as the naiads who in ancient time had conveyed Hylas. |

| 106 | Ascrean honey: i.e. poetry. Ascra was a city at the foot of Mount Helicon, sacred to Apollo god of poetry and to the Muses; the home also of Hesiod, an early Greek poet. |

| 107 | Theban lyre: lyric poetry in the mode of Pindar of Thebes (see note to l.23). |

| 108 | Alcaeus: one of the earliest lyric poets of Greece (7th/6th century B.C.). |

| 112 | immortal flower: the hyacinth. |

### IDILLIO MAREMMANO (Rn.V.68)

In form a 'capitolo' (a composition in *terza rima* based originally on the divisions of Petrarch's *Trionfi*), this idyll is one of the most intimate confessional pieces in Carducci's work, related closely to **'Davanti San Guido'** . . . in theme, if not in treatment. The poem presents, at its core, an idealised picture of what his life might have been had Carducci remained in the Maremma of his childhood and youth (1838-1849), instead of vainly pursuing ephemeral glory as intellectual, patriot and poet. That neglected life might have been one as small landowner and farmer, married to his youthful (probably fictitious, certainly idealised) love Maria, a country girl of fine physique and glowing health, potential mother of sturdy children: a life lived in avoidance of the siren snares of philosophical speculation, but dedicated the rather to salubrious activity, honest toil, prolific paternity, close to nature according to the ancient Roman ideal. The poem's especial force and poignancy derive in part from its mixed genesis: conceived, as Carducci pointed out, in April 1867, and written up in September 1872. Conceived, that is, at the time of the full flood of his Roman (republican) fervour as Garibaldi made preparation for his move on Rome (did Carducci smell here a successful end to the struggle for Italian unity, and anticipate his retirement from the political arena, like Cincinnatus, to a rural existence?); written five years later when all the turmoil over Italy's painful acquisition of its capital had died down, when he had released the bile of his immediate political disillusionment in the *Giambi ed Epodi,* and had exorcised his grief over the premature death of his son; and before his playful interest in Carolina Cristofari-Piva had become an overwhelming passion. **'Idillio maremmano'** is thus at once nostalgic and melancholy, ruminating and declamatory, evasive and realistic. It is also a fine example of Carducci's iconographic classicism (the Junoesque features of Maria), as well as of his sensitive treatment of Italian landscape (here, that of the coastal plain of the Maremma).

28    peacocks were sacred to Juno, the consort of Jupiter, king of the gods, and the goddess of woman-kind and maternity. Carducci endows Maria with the statuesque beauty of Juno in lines of unusual (for Carduccci) sensual description (10-12).

37-45  lines of deeply-felt personal disappointment over his (claimed) failed role as poet, intellectual and republican propagandist: all Italy had been deaf to his cries in the wilderness.

62    The final line is a shaft directed at the special objects of Carducci's contempt: firstly, the compromising politicians of Third Italy who had betrayed the democratic (republican) ideals of such as Mazzini and Garibaldi; and secondly, the spineless intellectuals of 'official Italy' who filled the key appointments in education and culture, and were betraying, it is implied, the highest standards of art and thought, to be found, Carducci believed, only in the hard challenges of classicism. Trissotin, in Molière's *Les Femmes Savantes,* is to be understood as archetype of the materialistic literary poseur.

### CLASSICISMO E ROMANTICISMO (RN.V.69)

Dialectical in tone, this iambic ode (quatrains of alternating rhymed hendecasyllabic and heptasyllabic lines) rehearses the poet's sentiments on the subject, dear to his heart, of what constitutes the essence of classicism and romanticism. Carducci is emphatically in favour of the former (see also the antithetical pair **'Primavera classica'**, . . . and **'Autunno romantico'**, . . .). The symbol of classicism is (as usual in Carducci) the sun: a powerful, constant, life-giving force, inspiring virile morality and art amongst 'the people' (for Carducci, for the most part country-dwellers). The symbol of romanticism is the moon: pallid, changeable, infertile, enticing poets to introspection and morbidity, encouraging isolation and decadent individualism with no moral appeal or example for 'the people'. The poem is also a political statement: the squalor of the urban proletariat and 'romantic' individualism are virtually equated here, while with the moon are also associated, for good measure, Gothic architecture (hence ecclesiastical obscurantism and asceticism), infecundity, disintegration of the social fabric, exploitation of the people. With the sun again, on the other hand, are linked nature's 'architecture' in the countryside, healthy toil in the fields, harvest, wine, wealth, the sense of community and solidarity in peasant life, all expressed in the authentic art of the popular songs of field-workers, whence poetry originated in antiquity (see **'Alla rima'**, . . .).

### DAVANTI SAN GUIDO (RN.V.72)

First laid down in December 1874, and brought to its final form in August 1886, **'Davanti San Guido'** has been considered the major confessional poem of Carducci's maturity, to be ranked with **'Idillio maremmano'** . . . and **'Traversando la Maremma Toscana'**. . . . This ode of hendecasyllabic quatrains with alternate rhymed *versi piani* and *tronchi* (cf. **'Agli amici della Valle Tiberina'**, . . .) was conceived by the poet on a train journey from Rome to Bologna, whilst pausing at the railway halt of San Guido. Here, adjacent to the small oratory-chapel of that name, begins the straight, mile-long avenue of cypresses leading to Bolgheri. These are the trees which, in the poem, vainly invite Carducci to stay and pick up the threads of his happy childhood and adolescence. The offer is debated at length by Carducci, but declined: it is too late. Despite his fame, or because of it, he is an unfulfilled man beyond any easy redemption. Although here, close to nature, the ultimate truths may perhaps be found, and life, as far as it is able, could bring satisfaction, the attempt to recreate that life would be to risk further futility, a further confirmation of his failure. This is a deeply sincere statement of the disillusionment which afflicted Carducci even at the apogee of his career: a comment on the deceptions of ambition, and on the insignificance of the individual in the order of things. In terms of its technique, the poem has been praised by Italian critics as the finest example of Carducci's 'polytonality' (A. Momigliano). It does, indeed, cover a wide range of invention, image and tone (whether too wide, the reader must judge): animated and vocal cypresses, a vision of the long dead 'nonna Lucia', the god Pan and his retinue of nymphs, a snatch of fable, even linguistic commentary; the whole rounded-off, in the imagery, by ponies, a donkey, and the train itself, all bearing deeper meanings. Serious in its intent, poignant in its intellectual honesty and existential pain, occasionally sentimental, the poem is perhaps coherent in its incoherency, presenting a complexity of subject and mood which is in many ways a true reflection of the complex personality which lay beneath the confident façade of Carducci's reconstructed classicism.

65     i.e in Bologna, in whose university Carducci held the Chair of Italian Literature.

66     Libertà, Carducci's two year-old daughter.

70     'Manzonian' writers commanded instant popularity and financial reward for their safe, traditional works in imitation of Italy's greatest exponent of the novel, Alessandro Manzoni.

74     the poet's paternal grandmother, Lucia Santini, died in 1843 and was buried in Bolgheri, when Carducci was eight.

81-4     Carducci alludes to the naturalness and vigour of a true Tuscan dialect (here, of the Versilia), in contrast to its awkward and exaggerated imitation by undescriminating followers of Manzoni's linguistic doctrine. This proposed that the cultivated, literary form of the Italian language should be based on spoken Florentine (the major dialect of Tuscany). Stenterello was a masked clown in the tradition of the Florentine *commedia dell'arte,* who spoke a coarse, uneducated form of the city's language.

86     Versilia: coastal region of N.W. Tuscany between the Apuan Alps and the sea.

87     *sirvente:* medieval poetic form, Provençal in origin, on religious, social or political issues.

93-100     a retelling of the popular fable *Re porco,* concerning a girl who suffered immeasurable hardship in the search for her lover, whom she finally found in perpetual sleep: i.e. a tale of the apparently successful search for a good which proves illusory—the story, Carducci claims, of his own life.

109     the train symbolises the ineluctable force of Carducci's personal destiny.

111-16     the graceful, wild ponies of the Maremma here signify the untamed flights of fancy of Carducci's youth—dreams, no doubt, of literary, scholarly and political success. The donkey, on the other hand, content with thistles, symbolises a realistic, undeceived sense of this world and its attractive snares (although even a donkey may dream dreams: see 'A un asino' / 'To a Donkey', II. 27 of *Rime nuove,* not included in this volume).

### Il Comune rustico (Rn.VI.77)

Composed in August 1885 whilst Carducci was on vacation in Piano d'Arta, in the Carnic Alps (Friuli-Venezia Giulia), this historical idyll, in sextets of rhymed hendecasyllabic lines, is in effect an extended *envoi* addressed to that region. In an imaginative excursus, Carducci evokes a scene of crisis in the life of an early commune of the 11th century, situated on the N.E. borders of Italy, as it prepares its defences, following Mass, against invasion by marauding Huns and Slavs. The poem therefore proposes Christianity's positive role in the forging of Italian civilisation, identity and purpose, in contrast to the earlier anti-Catholic sentiment in such poems as **'A Satana'** (1863) or **'Alle fonti del Clitumno'** (1876). Carducci lends his early commune the features of both Roman political pragmatism and Christian transcendentalism: Roman still in the forms of its administration (consul and senate), Christian in its spirit (Mass and the veneration of the Madonna)—its tiny population buoyed up by the blended ideals of Roman *virtus* and Christian hope. It is therefore one with the Christian accommodation of the sonnet **'Fiesole'** . . . written a year later, both poems preparing the way to the major poem of reconciliation **'La chiesa di Polenta'** (1897) of *Rime e ritmi.* . . . The poem also had contemporary political significance, as in the late 19th century the question of Italy's N.E. borders was still not settled. Venezia-Giulia and Istria were subject still to the modern 'Huns and Slavs' of Austro-Hungary.

### Congedo (Rn.IX.105)

Known also under its earlier title **'Il poeta'** (**'The Poet'**), **'Congedo'** concludes the poems of the *Rime nuove,* answering at the same time to the book's opening piece **'Alla rima'** (**'To Poetry'**, . . .), which is written in the same metre. This complementary pair comprises in effect Carducci's poetic manifesto, as **'A Satana'** . . . epitomises his intellectual stance. The three opening stanzas of **'Congedo'** confirm anaphorically and polemically (the targets are deviant contemporary poetry and mistaken notions of the role of the poet) what the poet is not: he is neither an entertainer nor a plagiarist, neither a parasitic social commentator nor a vague mystic, neither a utilitarian didact nor a fashionable scribbler. The poet is first and foremost a scrupulous craftsman (cf. the Dantean *fabbro* of *Purgatorio* XXVI.117); his themes (reflecting Dante's threefold classification in the *De Vulgari Eloquentia:* love, war and morality) are love, patriotism (entailing inevitably war) and reason (the basis of Carducci's moral outlook); his inspirations are ideals of freedom, glory and beauty; his vision is at once retrospective (embracing Italy's classical past) and progressive (envisaging a new Italian spirit and purpose based on that past). Carducci's aim is therefore to restore to the role of poet the severe intellectual and moral commitment of a Dante, Italy's 'miglior fabbro' and conscience of the nation. Carducci's emphasis on technique recalls also the recent formulations of the Parnassian School of French poetry, particularly that of Gautier's *L'Art* of 1852:

> Oui, l'oeuvre sort plus belle
> d'une forme au travail rebelle . . .

The poem also, for all its classical reminiscences (the forge of Vulcan, the cult of *lares* and *penates*), carries unmistakable overtones of Wagner, whom Carducci admired (the heroic defiance of the poet in the final image is high Wagnerian romanticism), and inevitably of Nietzsche (the poet as Superman). In the end, however, the poem's subtext is political as much as aesthetic, and integrates with Carducci's wider philosophy. It addresses the people of Italy, reminding them both of their classical heritage and their recent past in the heroic phases of the Risorgimento ('the record and the glory of their fathers and their race'), an ideological platform upon which to build a more solid future in the uncertain years following the country's unification.

## Nell'annuale della fondazione di Roma (Ob.I.3)

Composed in late April 1877, this alcaic ode (quatrains of 11,11,9,10 syllable lines, unrhymed) was conceived in celebration of the founding of Rome (official date 21 April, 753 B.C.). The vigour of the poem is due in no small measure to the fact that the anniversary fell during Carducci's first visit to Rome at the age of 42. Rome, the actual capital of Third Italy, was only achieved in 1870 after a long and painful struggle, to which Carducci had been a frustrated witness. It was also for him the spiritual capital of Western civilisation, as well as his own spiritual *patria* and inspiration of his new classical poetry. The ode combines patriotic enthusiasm with political polemics, objective historicism with autobiographical subjectivity, and observed landscape with imagined topography, rising to a crescendo of unreserved optimism over Italy's future, its national destiny as reborn leader amongst the free nations of Europe.

2-3   according to legend, Romulus founded Rome on the Palatine hill, first tracing the square plan of its walls with oxen and plough.

8   Flora: the name for Rome used in religious rites and ceremonies, recalling the flowered hillside of its origins (see 1.1).

9-10   Rome's citadel was built on the adjacent Capitoline hill (the Campidoglio, now seat of modern government buildings), which the High Priest (Pontiff) and the senior Vestal Virgin (of the order of Priestesses of Rome) would ascend, to sacrifice at the temple of Juno Moneta on important occasions of state (see Horace *Odes* III.30, 'Exegi monumentum', 1.7).

11   the Via Sacra, passing by the foot of the Palatine, traversed the Forum to the foot of the Capitoline, and was the principal route for religious processions and military triumphs in ancient Rome.

## Dinanzi alle Terme di Caracalla (Ob.I.4)

This sapphic ode (quatrains of three hendecasyllabics and one five-syllable line, unrhymed), composed in April 1877 during Carducci's first visit to Rome, is a vigorous statement of the poet's deep veneration for the capital of Italy, its classical past and its legacy to the modern world. In contrast to the triumphant tones of the previous poem, **'Nell'annuale della fondazione di Roma'**, it is shot

through with a brooding melancholy and jealous defensiveness, as the poet contemplates the imposing ruins of Caracalla's baths standing gaunt, stripped of their marble cladding, in their continued defiance of the centuries; but now the object, it seems, only of the bookish attentions of tourists, or else vilely ignored by the uncouth peasantry from the adjacent *campagna*. The modern age is simply unworthy of such a legacy, and Carducci petitions Febris, primitive deity of the city, to drive out its unworthy modern inhabitants and their works, allowing the goddess Rome to slumber on until a generation worthy of her (it is implied) restores to her the respect and love she deserves. For Carducci these ruins are no empty 'marble wilderness' such as Byron had seen them, dear also to generations of viewpainters, archaeologists and tourists. For him they were imbued with a vital power, ready for rebirth as the informing spirit of a modern Italian nation, in a new age of social progress, industry and invention (cf. the final stanzas of **'Alle fonti del Clitumno'**, written the year before . . .).

1   two of the seven hills of Rome, the Caelian to the S.E., the Aventine to the S. of the Forum.

15   close to the Baths are situated the Lateran Palace and the Basilica of St John Lateran, the former the site of the papal residence from the early years of Christianity to the exile of the papacy in Avignon, in 1309.

17   the *Ciociari* were peasant shepherds of the Roman Campagna, so-called from their heavy sandals (*cioci*).

19   Febris, propitiated as goddess of malarial fever, was one of the earliest divinities of Rome.

26f.   In early Roman times, the Tiber, later diverted, flowed at the foot of the Palatine, between that hill and the Aventine to the south.

27   According to legend, Evander, a Greek, had settled a colony of his fellow Arcadians on the future site of Rome, before the arrival of Romulus, using the Palatine hill as his citadel (see Virgil, *Aeneid* VIII).

29   Quirites: the name by which the earliest soldier-citizens of Rome were known.

30   Saturnian: archaic Latin verse, accentual and alliterative, was known later by this name to suggest its ancient origins. Saturn was reputed the earliest King of Rome, a god also of agriculture, whose reign was considered the Age of Gold. His temple, in which were stored the records of Rome, stood below the Capitoline hill.

39   the Porta Capena, near the Baths, opens on to the Via Appia Antica, the first of the great Roman roads, leading through Capua to Brindisi.

## Alle fonti del Clitumno (Ob.I.6)

For the genesis and general significance of this sapphic ode of 1876, similar in metre to **'Dinanzi alle Terme di**

**Caracalla'** above, see Introduction. . . . **'Alle fonti del Clitumno'** is arguably Carducci's 'pastoral symphony', conceived as a sequence of movements:

Stanzas 1-6:   a stately introduction, in which Carducci observes features of the contemporary pastoral setting of the pools that are continuous with the ancient past of Umbria.

7   Virgil in the *Georgics* (II.145f.) and Propertius in the *Elegies* (II.19f.) refer to the practice of dipping livestock in the sacred pools of the Clitumnus, in order to bleach fleece or hide. Such included the bulls which, with their snow white hides, had long been favoured for use in religious ceremonies and sacrifices in Rome.

17   Columella in *De Re Rustica* (IV.1) describes the powerful flanks of the bull-calves in similar terms.

18   Horace in his *Odes* (IV.2) so describes the crescent curve of the bull-calves' horns.

Stanzas 7-10:   opening with an apostrophe to the river Clitumnus, Carducci develops a polemical parenthesis: the ages have declined since the fall of Rome, and contemporary cultural values, identified with romanticism, are corrupt.

29f.   the weeping willow, a late import into Europe from Asia Minor, symbolises the decadent ethos of romanticism, despised by the classicist Carducci; whereas holm-oaks and cypresses are the hardy, native trees of Italy, with a long tradition of use in its literature from classical times onwards.

Stanzas 11-19   an evocation of the glorious past of the region, significant in the history of the three Italic races: Umbrians, Etruscans and Romans.

43   velites: Etruscan light infantry armed with javelins.

43-4   translated from Virgil's *Georgics* II.533: 'Sic fortis Etruria crevit'.

45   the confederation of twelve Etruscan cities.

46   Mount Cimino, near Viterbo, marked the boundary between Latium and Etruria.

47   Gradivus: Mars, Roman god of war.

52f.   near Lake Trasimeno, the Carthaginians under Hannibal, in the Second Punic War (217 B.C.), defeated the Romans under Flaminius for the third time.

55   Mevania: modern Bevagna.

58   Nar: modern river Nera, tributary of the Tiber.

68   cf. Horace *Odes* II.12: 'dirum Hannibalem'.

72   at the siege of Spoleto, before Rome's fourth defeat at Cannae, Hannibal was repulsed with considerable losses.

73   the Moors (Mauretanians) and Numidians were the mercenary shock-troops of the Carthaginians.

Stanzas 20-22:   in contrast to the region's heroic and bloody past, the present scene is one of pastoral tranquillity.

77   'Tutto ora tace' is the dominant refrain of the ode, introducing a dialectical 'variation' (cf. 11. 105-140).

Stanzas 23-26: an evocation of the religious (pantheistic) past of Umbria.

94-5   naiads: nymphs of rivers, pools and streams; their 'tawny sisters' the oreads, nymphs of the mountainsides.

99-100   Janus, the earliest mentioned god of Italy ('god of gods'), with the nymph Camesena, engendered the Italic peoples before the arrival of Aeneas, forebear of Romulus and the Roman race.

Stanzas 27-35:   in contrast to the region's vital religious past, the present age has witnessed the destruction of Rome, its civilisation and religion, by the (for Carducci) fanatical breed of Christian converts in the succeeding centuries.

105   see note to 1.77: here the 'variation' is highly polemical (and controversial), in the tones of Carducci's earlier diatribes in 'A Satana'. . . .

113-14   Christ, the 'red-haired Galilean', is referred to here. The Campidoglio is the ancient Capitolium, seat of Rome's authority and government.

117-20   three types of nymph in Italic animism: naiads, dryads and oreads.

121-40:   a savage (and factually suspect) reference to the ascetic Christian movements of the Middle Ages (Flagellants, Patarines, Insaccati, Fraticelli), reminiscent of the colourful hyperbole of Jules Michelet in his 16 volumes of *L'Histoire de France,* which struck a sympathetic chord in the anticlerical Carducci.

Stanzas 36-39:   the peroration or 'finale', introduced by an apostrophe of greeting and encouragement to the human spirit, downtrodden now, but heir always to Greek rational thought as well as to Roman moral integrity; and a greeting also to Italy in its ancient role as civilising force and legislator in the affairs of mankind. The poem's final appeal is therefore to Italians to arise and shake off the yoke of their repressive religion, and claim for themselves once more the spirit of the classical world: its positive attitude to life, its faith in rational endeavour, its veneration of human freedom. For ancient Rome and modern Italy are, ideally, indivisibly one; they are divided only in practice by the historic intrusions of clerical and foreign tyrannies. A modern era of industry, science and human progress, symbolised by the railway engine in the final stanza, awaits Italy if it is ready to defy its old masters of church and state, and reassert its ancient moral hegemony amongst the modern nations.

141     Ilissos: the river which descends through Attica in Greece, to the S. and S.E. of Athens.

142     Tiber: the major river of Italy, which flows through Umbria for much of its course, hence to Rome and the sea. The river Clitumno (Maroggia) joins the Topino and finally the Tiber along its course through Umbria.

151-2   these lines reflect Carducci's complete confidence that the Roman values of ancient Italy were exactly those required in the new era of the country's restored unity in the Third Italy, to invigorate, inspire and teach contemporary Italians, fitting them for the modern world.

## Nella piazza di San Petronio (Ob.I.10)

Written in February 1877 in Bologna, in appropriate elegiac couplets (unrhymed hexameter and pentameter lines), this ode evokes a legendary Middle Ages of courtesy, valour and chivalry, whilst at the same time lamenting its passing. The frankly romantic historicism of the piece contrasts sharply with the dismissive spirit displayed by Carducci in his usual treatment of the Middle Ages (represented as a period of suffocating religious conformity, superstition and obscurantism: see **'A Satana'** . . . and **'Alle fonti del Clitumno'** . . .). Yet it is consistent with his view of the medieval commune (Bologna one such) as Italy's unique contribution to European democracy and civilisation: see the later pieces **'Fiesole'** . . ., **'Il Comune rustico'** . . ., and **'La chiesa di Polenta'**. . . .

2       the hill is San Michele in Bosco, to the S. of Bologna.

4       the 'temple' is the Basilica di San Petronio, the vast brick-built Gothic church of 1390, which dominates the central square (Piazza Maggiore) of Bologna.

18      reference is to the capture of the son of Emperor Frederick II, Enzo, at the battle of Fossalta (1249). This occurred in the struggle between the renewed alliance of autonomous northern Italian cities and an imperial army from Modena, led by Enzo, bent on their subjugation to imperial authority. 'Re Enzo' was kept a close prisoner until his death in a wing of Bologna's Palazzo del Podestà, which still bears his name.

## Fuori alla Certosa di Bologna (Ob.I.12)

For the genesis and general significance of this elegiac ode of 1879, written in the same metre as **'Nella piazza di San Petronio'** above, see Introduction. . . .

1-2     the Certosa is Bologna's municipal cemetery a former Carthusian monastery (Charterhouse), where Carducci's mother lay and where he himself would be buried.

8       reference is to the river Reno.

11      the Colle della Guardia, which overlooks the Certosa, is crowned by the Sanctuary of the Madonna di San Luca.

17      Adele Bergamini (1845-1925) was a poetess and minor dramatist of Rome. . . .

21      *lituus:* either a bugle, or the curved wand carried by Etruscan priests.

## Su l'Adda (Ob.I.13)

For a general appraisal, see Introduction. . . . Composed in December 1873, **'Su l'Adda'** is written in asclepiadean stanzas (quatrains of 11,11,7,7 syllabic lines, unrhymed), and is the first of Carducci's attempts at his 'barbarous' adaptations of classical poetic forms.

2       Addua: the Latin name of the river Adda.

5       the bridge at Lodi witnessed Napoleon's defeat of the Austrians in 1797 during his first Italian campaign, and the retreat of the Austrians in June 1859 during the Second War of Italian Independence.

13-14   reference is to the battle in 476 A.D. between the barbarian army of Odovacar and Romulus Augustulus, the last Roman Emperor of the West, marking the final collapse of the Roman Empire.

13      Mars was the Roman god of war: a metonymic allusion to the army of Rome.

15-16   following the battle of Legnano in 1176, the Milanese and their allies of the Lombard League destroyed Lodi, which had inopportunely joined the invading army of Emperor Frederick I Barbarossa.

17      the Larius: Lake Como; Eridanus: the Po.

22      the pale Corsican: Napoleon Bonaparte.

25      Celtic: i.e. the French; Teuton: i.e. Austrian.

33      Pompey as Consul granted Lodi its Roman rights in 89 A.D.

34      reference is to Emperor Frederick I's red beard (hence Barbarossa) and his kindom of Swabia.

## Per la morte di Napoleone Eugenio (Ob.I.17)

Written in 1879, the year of Eugène Napoleon's untimely death, this alcaic ode (for metre see notes to **'Nell' annuale della fondazione di Roma'**, . . .) marks an important stage in Carducci's evolving political outlook as we find it in his poetry. The previous seven years had witnessed the deaths of notable figures—protagonists and antagonists—caught up in the history of the Risorgimento and Italian unification: Mazzini in 1872, the deposed Napoleon III in 1873, both Pope Pius IX (pontiff through the earlier years of the Risorgimento from 1846) and Victor Emmanuel II (first monarch of united Italy) in 1878. That latter year also brought to the throne a new king, Umberto I, confirming, against republicanism, the monarchical solution to the rule of Italy. It was also the year of the visit of Umberto and his queen Margherita to Bologna and its university, when Carducci was wooed into submission by the queen who so admired his poetry. With the disappearance of so much of the old order, and his reconciliation with the Italian monarchy, the scot of republican bile which Carducci still nourished was released instead on to more distant targets, and from a more universal standpoint. Already in 1878, a visit with Carolina Cristofari-Piva to the Habsburg castle of Miramare, near Trieste, had prompted thoughts on the notion of cosmic justice, the 'nemesis' which stalked the guilty often through their offspring, and which the violent death of Maximilian of Habsbug in Mexico in 1867 had seemed to confirm (see **'Miramar'** below). Now the equally violent and unpredictable death of Eugène Napoleon by a Zulu assegai, in 1879, appeared as further corroboration of the god's punishment of *hybris*. In 1879 news reached European capitals of the death of the 23 year-old Eugène, the only son of the late Emperor of France, Napoleon III (emperor 1852-1870). Napoleon III, one of Carducci's favourite political targets, had first achieved power in 1851 in a coup d'état which swept away the freedoms of the second French Republic. He had also played, as far as Carducci was concerned, a devious game in the last years of the Risorgimento: an untrustworthy broker, seemingly Italy's ally, but stealing from her Nice and Savoy, and artfully delaying the annexation of Rome as Italy's capital. Justice—delayed but inexorable—had finally been done on the Emperor by visiting his punishment upon his only male descendant. It was a justice indeed that had already been partially exacted upon the whole Napoleonic clan with the death, which the poem also records, of Joseph-François-Charles (Napoleon II), the son of the first Emperor Napoleon Bonaparte. The latter's great crime against liberty had been the coup d'état of 1799, which had brought to an end the glorious achievements (for Carducci) of the great French Revolution of 1789 together with its First Republic, imposing instead upon the luckless French the tyranny of an imperial dynasty (First Empire 1804-1814).

1    Eugène Napoleon (born 1856), only son of Napoleon III (Emperor of France 1852-1870), was educated at the Royal Military Academy, Woolwich. His mother Empress Eugénie had taken refuge in England after the fall of the Second Empire. Eugène was killed in a British expedition against the Zulus in South Africa in 1879.

3    the 'fancied visions' were born from his aspirations of glory, in emulation of the achievements of hisfather, Napoleon III, and his great-uncle, Napoleon Bonaparte (Emperor Napoleon I).

5    Joseph-François-Charles Napoleon (the uncrowned Napoleon II), titular King of Rome, only son of Napoleon Bonaparte and Princess Marie-Louise of Austria, was held a virtual prisoner at the Austrian court in Vienna after his father's exile in 1814. He died there aged 21 of tuberculosis brought on (it was alleged) by an extravagant and immoral life.

17   Napoleon III was the son of Louis Napoleon (King of Holland and brother of Napoleon I) by Hortense de Beauharnais (daughter of Napoleon I by his marriage to Josephine).

20   From 1854 to 1856 the army of Napoleon III fought as allies of the British in the Crimea, a war which ended with the victory of Sebastopol.

24   The victory column in the Place de Vendôme, Paris, was erected by Napoleon I to celebrate his defeat of Russia and Austria at the battle of Austerlitz in 1805. It was constructed from the bronze of his enemies' cannons.

25   a hostile allusion to the coups d'états of 1799 and 1851 which had brought Napoleon Bonaparte and Napoleon III respectively to power, on the ruins of the First and Second Republics. Both of these events, which Carducci considered betrayals of human freedom, took place in Brumaire (November/December) of the years in question.

29   Napoleon Bonaparte, first Emperor of France, was born in Ajaccio, Corsica.

33   Letizia Ramolino (1750-1836), mother of Napoleon Bonaparte.

39   Napoleon Bonaparte, after the coup of 1799, established the Consulate, with himself as First Consul. France remained a republic in name, however, until 1804, when Napoleon was crowned first Emperor of France.

42   Caesar: *per antonomasia,* Emperor Napoleon I.

46   Letizia Bonaparte's daughters, Elisa, Pauline and Caroline, married into the Italian or Bonapartist aristocracies, and died far from their native Corsica.

49   Niobe: a symbol of maternal bereavement. Wife of Amphion, she had fourteen children and boasted of them to the goddess Latona, who had only two. The latter, Apollo and Diana, slew all fourteen to avenge the slight.

53   Letizia's youngest son, Jerome, was created King of Westphalia. His son by his first marriage

(dissolved) to Elizabeth Paterson of Baltimore, also named Jerome, died in America in 1847.

54    references are to Napoleon III, who spent much time in England after the fall of the Second Empire (1870), and to his son Eugène (see note 1).

### Miramar (Ob.I.22)

The Archduke Maximilian of Habsburg, last Austrian Governor of Lombardy-Venetia, whose death this sapphic ode records (for metre see notes to **'Dinanzi alle Terme di Caracalla',** . . .), built the neogothic castle of Miramare as a love-nest for his wife, Charlotte of the Belgians, on a rocky promontory overlooking the Gulf of Trieste. Created Emperor of Mexico in 1864 by Napoleon III, Maximilian was captured and executed three years later by Mexican rebels under Benito Juarez, later the first President of Mexico. The Empress Charlotte (d.1927) was driven to insanity by the tragedy. In this poem of 1878 (perfected 1889), following a visit to Miramare with Carolina Cristofari-Piva, Carducci reconstructs the events surrounding Maximilian's death, proposing that it was orchestrated by an implacable nemesis as quittance for the oppression of the Aztecs of Mexico by his distant ancestor Emperor Charles V, in the sixteenth century. (See also Introduction . . .).

11    towns on the Istrian coast. Egida is modern Capodistria.

17    Nabresina (modern Aurisina) lies near the coast N.W. of Miramare.

33-40    references are to two large paintings, one depicting the apotheosis of Maximilian and the other an allegory of the reign of Emperor Charles V; also referred to are the twenty Latin inscriptions, and, in the library, the busts of famous writers, and an open volume of Castillian romantic epics; lastly, overlooking the small harbour, a statue of the sphinx.

43    Spain of the Aztecs: Mexico, conquered by Hernán Cortés, and renamed by him New Spain.

45    off Cape Salvore in 1178, the imperial fleet of Frederick I Barbarossa, commanded by his son Otto, was defeated by the combined fleets of Venice and Istria. The Venetian and Istrian dead here seek vengeance on their Teutonic enemies.

48    the vengeful sprites of Istrian folklore.

50    *Novara:* the Piedmontese, under their king Charles Albert, were defeated by the Austrians at Novara in 1849, in the First War of Italian Independence. The name of the ship suggests, therefore, the Habsburgs' arrogance and treachery against Italians, and the revenge of the Italian dead through the fate of Maximilian.

53f.    the sphinx assumes the sinister features of Habsburgs who suffered tragic destinies, or those of

their victims seeking vengeance: Joanna of Aragon, wife of Philip (Habsburg) of Castille, and mother of Emperor Charles V, went mad; Marie Antoinette, the Habsburg wife of Louis XVI, was guillotined in 1793 during the Great Terror of the French Revolution; Montezuma, emperor of the Aztecs, was killed by the Spanish *conquistadores,* who were acting with the authority of Charles V, in 1520.

66    Huitzilopochtli: Aztec sun-god and warrior.

77    Guatimozin: last of the Aztec kings, who was tortured to death by the Spanish invaders of Mexico in 1524.

### Fantasia (Ob.II.27)

The voice of his beloved Lydia (Carolina Cristofari-Piva) is the catalyst that releases Carducci's imagination into an ancient Mediterranean landscape of ideal order and harmony. The scene appears specifically focussed on the Aegean island of Lesbos, in the 6th century B.C., as the warrior-poet Alcaeus returns to Mytilene from distant wars against Athenian imperialism or against other, more local, tyrannies. Written in April 1875, this asclepiadean ode (quatrains of 11,11,11,7 syllabic lines, unrhymed) follows the lines of the longer hellenic journey poems of *Primavere elleniche* (see II. **'Dorica'**, . . .), written three or four years earlier. The tradition of Carducci's art at evidence here is close to the neoclassical spirit of Winkelman, Goethe and Schiller in Germany, or Chénier and Leconte de Lisle in France. It is reflected also in the 19th century tastes of contemporary painters in Victorian England, Lord Leighton and Alma Tadema. But as Cesare de Lollis pointed out, the inspiration is as much to be found, perhaps, in the 17th century neoclassicism of Claude Lorraine, for example in *Harbour at Sunset,* or *Débarquement de Cythère.*

### 'Ruit hora' (Ob.II.28)

Written in 1875, a few months after **'Fantasia'** (see above), this iambic ode (quatrains of 11,7,11,7 syllabic lines, unrhymed) records all the sensuality of Carducci's passion for Carolina Cristofari-Piva, which the elegant classical allusions intensify here, rather than (as in other poems, for example **'Visione'**, . . .) disperse or mitigate. **'Ruit hora'** (**'Time flies'**), the common inscription on sundials, is translated in 1.29, although with an implied shift in the tense.

6    Lyaeus: Bacchus (Dionysus), the god of transformations, hence of harvest and wine.

28    Hyperion: Titan and sun-god, dethroned by Phoebus-Apollo.

### Alla stazione in una mattina d'autunno (Ob.II.29)

For the genesis and general significance of this alcaic ode, which was composed in December 1876 and is similar in metre to **'Nell' annuale della fondazione di Roma'**, above, see Introduction. . . .

### EGLE (OB.II.37)

The elegiac couplets of this piece (for metre see notes to **'Nella piazza di San Petronio'**, . . .) were written for Dafne Gargiolli in February or March 1889, recording a walk in her company along the Via Appia Antica, in Rome. Egle was the fairest of the Naiads, upon whom Apollo fathered the three Graces. In this poem, Dafne, as Egle, is a portent of springtime. In her presence the ancient tombs along the Appian Way appear to lose all the historical significance usually associated with ruins in Carducci's landscape poetry.

### 'PRIMO VERE' (OB.II.38)

Begun in the same circumstances as the previous poem **'Egle',** this asclepiadean ode, similar in metre to **'Fantasia'** above, was written for Dafne Gargiolli as Lalage, and records the first intimations of Spring (hence the poem's title) in 1889. Its completion in September of the same year marks it as the last poem for Dafne, with whom Spring is normally associated in Carducci's poetry. The event therefore accounts for the tears of sadness in the 'smile' of the season, referred to in the last stanza.

### SALUTO D'AUTUNNO (OB.II.41)

Composed in June 1881 at the country villa of Carlo and Dafne Gargiolli in San Leonardo near Verona, this alcaic ode (for metre see notes to **'Nell' annuale della fondazione di Roma'**, . . .) was written in reply to some melancholy verses by Dafne inspired by a recent bereavement. It is also, in some ways, addressed to the poet himself, still unreconciled to the death of Carolina Cristofari-Piva in the February of the same year. See also Introduction. . . .

3    Delia: the pseudonym normally of Adele Bergamini, but here clearly appropriated for Dafne Gargiolli.

12   Hebe: daughter of Zeus and Hera, goddess of perpetual youth.

### SU MONTE MARIO (OB.II.42)

For the origins and general significance of this sapphic ode, written in 1882, see Introduction. . . . For the metre employed, see notes to **'Dinanzi alle Terme di Caracalla'.** . . .

1    Monte Mario lies to the north of Rome on the right bank of the Tiber, from which, in Carducci's day, before modern urban development, the whole of Rome could be seen.

13   Lalage: pseudonym here of the poetess Adele Bergamini.

### PRESSO L'URNA DI PERCY BYSSHE SHELLEY (OB.II.48)

For the genesis and general significance of this elegiac ode of December 1884, similar in metre to **'Nella Piazza di San Petronio'** above, see Introduction. . . . The poem had earlier borne the alternative title **'Antiverismo',** in vindication of the imaginative and mythopoetic faculties of poets against the claims of current realist trends in Italian literature (the *verismo* of such as Capuana and Verga). However this alternative title was later dropped by Carducci, together with two polemical couplets on the matter (see *Lettere* XV.72 to Chiarini).

1    Lalage: Dafne Gargiolli, with whom Carducci visited the Protestant Cemetery in Rome where the ashes of Shelley are enshrined. Carducci deeply admired Shelley's poetry, particularly his *Prometheus Unbound* of 1820, which he saw as a manifesto of human liberty, and which he defined as 'the greatest poem of the century'.

5    Clio: Muse of epic poetry.

13   Siegfried: hero of Germanic legend (*Niebelungenlied*); Achilles: Greek hero of Homer's *Iliad*.

15   Ophelia: the ill-fated lover of Hamlet in Shakespeare's tragedy.

16   Iphigenia: Agamemnon's daughter, sacrificed by him to the goddess Diana in order to provide the wind which would allow the departure of the Greek fleet from Aulis.

17   Roland: paladin of Charlemagne, whose heroic defence of the rearguard of the Frankish army at Roncevaux against the Moors (778) is recorded in the *Chanson de Roland;* Hector: Trojan hero slain by Achilles at the siege of Troy (*Iliad*).

18   Durendal: Roland's sword.

19   Andromache: Hector's wife (see note 17 above).

20   Aude: Roland's betrothed, Olivier's sister (see note 17 above).

21   Lear: see Shakespeare's *King Lear;* Oedipus: tragic hero of Sophocles' *Oedipus Rex* and *Oedipus at Colonnus*.

23   Cordelia: the deposed King Lear's one faithful daughter; Antigone: faithful daughter of the blind King Oedipus in his wanderings after the loss of Thebes.

25   Helen: abducted by Paris and brought to Troy, Helen was the cause of the Trojan War against the Greeks (*Iliad*); Isolde (Iseult): King Mark of Cornwall's wife, who fell in love with Tristan, Mark's friend and bravest warrior (see Arthurian legend).

29-30  the Scottish queen: Lady Macbeth, who drove her husband to regicide (see Shakespeare's *Macbeth*); Clytemnestra: wife of King Agamemnon, whom she murdered to gain the love of Aegisthus (see Aeschylus's trilogy *Oresteia*).

39   Richard Wagner, contemporary composer of operas, whom Carducci admired.

43      Tethys: consort of Oceanus, god of seas and rivers. Carducci proposes that the spirit of Sophocles, the greatest of the Greek tragedians, saved Shelley from drowning ('Tethys's deadly grasp') to transport him to this island of heroes and heroines.

45      the reference is to the inscription on Shelley's tomb: 'Cor Cordium' ('Heart of Hearts').

50      the allusion is to Shelley's *Prometheus Unbound,* where Prometheus is the unyielding champion of mankind, provider of fire and the arts and skills of man, to whom even Jupiter succumbs (in intentional contrast to the events of *Prometheus Bound* of Aeschylus).

### MEZZOGIORNO ALPINO (RR.16)

Composed, as the **'Esequie della guida E.R.'** below, in Courmayeur (Aosta) in August 1895, this *quadretto* (short descriptive poem) of two quatrains, in largely unrhymed hendecasyllabic lines, captures with economy of means and Parnassian objectivity the imposing silence of a high Alpine location.

### L'OSTESSA DI GABY (RR.17)

Written in the Alpine village of Gaby (Val de Gressoney), in August 1895, this *quadretto* in elegiac couplets (for metre see notes to **'Nella piazza di San Petronio,'** . . .) depicts an early morning scene in which the pastoral realism of the first three couplets gives way to a nostalgic, literary reminiscence of the epic scenery of such chivalrous romances as Ariosto's *Orlando Furioso.*

### ESEQUIE DELLA GUIDA E.R. (RR.18)

The first draft of this minor ode, in terza rima (tercets of hendecasyllabic lines rhymed ABA,BCB,CDC etc.), was written on 25 August 1895 in Courmayeur (Aosta), and perfected three years later. As landscape poetry, it reflects the later, mature style of Carducci's art in its unadorned topographical detail and the realism of its social observation. The poem records the precise moment of the funeral of the alpine guide Émile Rey, who, in these early years of mountaineering, was killed in a climbing accident on Mont Blanc. A concession to romantic feeling is nevertheless made in the concluding lines, as the 'Dente del Gigante' ('Aiguille Noire'), a minor peak in the Mont Blanc massif, visible from Courmayeur, appears in a rent in the clouds, a sublime and indifferent witness to the mournful event beneath. Within the vast arena of unforgiving natural forces, unmoved by heroism or prayer, the world of man has little lasting significance.

4    La Saxe: the hamlet adjoining Courmayeur, where Émile Rey lived.

### LA CHIESA DI POLENTA (RR.22)

The subject of this sapphic ode of 1897 (for metre see notes to **'Dinanzi alle Terme di Caracalla',** . . .), is the 8th century romanesque church of Polenta, near Cesena, which was in the process of restoration as a national monument, and which Carducci visited in the June of that year with the Contessa Silvia Pasolini. The poem is Carducci's contribution to the public appeal for the restoration funds (see 11. 105-112). The church was famous for its associations with the da Polenta family (whose castle lies close to the church), and thus with Dante whose last patron was Guido Novello da Polenta, Lord of Ravenna, and nephew of the ill-starred Francesca da Rimini recalled in *Inferno* V. References to Dante and the Polenta clan memorably occupy the first ten stanzas, but this idyllic opening gives way in the following stanzas to the by now standard thematics of Carducci's mature patriotic verse: the formation of Italy as a nation, and the question of the place of Christianity in this historical process. **'La chiesa di Polenta'** is the last of Carducci's major poetry on these themes (and indeed aroused something of the old polemics between his supporters and detractors). Carducci's stance here is quite consistent, however, with the broad lines of his developing views on the question through the years: the poem restates his unchanged opinion that the early Middle Ages in Italy was an era of national debasement—the Church contributing to the deterioration of the moral fibre of Italians through its encouragement of superstition and its insistence on guilt and penitence, whilst foreign invaders took full advantage of this to enslave the passive population (see **'A Satana'** . . . and **'Alle fonti del Clitumno',** . . .). In the High Middle Ages after the year 1000 (see **'Fiesole',** . . .), the Church offered (despite its theocratic absolutism, always detested by Carducci) something positive and essential in its role as reconciler of its ethnically mixed peoples, and hence as moulder of modern Italians and Italy (see 11. 85-92). This view of the Church as an instrument of good in the making of Italians was signalled unequivocally as early as 1885 in the poem **'Il Comune rustico'** . . . reflecting a crucial moment in Carducci's developing views, and which bears on this poem. In that poem of the *Rime nuove* the spirit of resistance to Slav and Hunnish invaders derives from two precise things: the survival of Roman notions of political order, however rudimentary (senate and consul), and the spiritual solidarity of the people provided by a simple faith in the efficacy of the Church's rites (the symbols of the Mass). This combination of the political pragmatism of Rome and the spiritual realism provided by the Christian faith was now for Carducci the essential ingredient which gave rise to the *Comune* of the title, the autonomous, democratic city of the Italian Middle Ages, proposed as Italy's great contribution to European civilisation and freedom. This great creation of the Italians is extolled again here in **'La chiesa di Polenta',** whilst its founding spirit is seen to derive more explicitly from the parallel endeavours of Queen Theodolinda (who in the 7th century converted her Langobards from Arianisim to orthodox Catholicism), and pope Gregory the Great (who strenuously opposed the Langobard invaders of Italy in the name of Christianity and its Latin civilisation): an ideal cooperation between State and Church, Roman power and Christian love (see 11. 85-100). It is a proposition that the Carducci of **'A Satana'** would have derisively refuted.

The last part of **'La chiesa di Polenta'** (11.101-128) returns to the idyllic mood of the opening stanzas, in what is at once a celebration, vindication and encouragement of a new era of Italian consciousness. This is seen as having been nourished rather than retarded by the spiritual teaching of the Church, the latter epitomised in the refrain 'Ave Maria'. Whatever implications this may have for our understanding of Carducci's personal spiritual condition towards the end of his life (the debate continues: is this Carducci's confession of a tardy conversion to Christianity, or not?), the historic religious sense of Italians is certainly recognised and encouraged. There are no jarring notes: Caducci's antagonism towards contemporary Catholicism appears dormant, if not dead, and, at the least, agnosticism rather than atheism is alive. The stanzas roll to their conclusion in a mood of Christian piety, if not strictly faith. The feelings which determine the mood, however, perhaps owe more to the evening meditations of Byron's *Don Juan* than to *Purgatorio* VIII from which this derives—to which (as also to Dante) there is an allusion in 1.116. There is certainly, in this long finale, a sense of the transcendental, of a spiritual dimension in things (see the penultimate stanza), but is this all more pronounced or very different from the exalted mood of **'Il canto dell' amore'** (11. 49-108) of *Giambe ed Epodi,* written 1877-78? The final 'Ave Maria' murmured by the swaying treetops, despite the Christian message, arguably derives as much from Carducci's residual animism as from the Gospels.

3    the allusion is to the illicit passion of Francesca da Rimini, of the house of da Polenta, for her brother-in-law Paolo Malatesta, recorded by Dante in *Inferno* V.

12   Guido Vecchio da Polenta, founder of the dynasty, took a black eagle as his heraldic device.

13-20   a restatement of an old position adopted by Carducci: only ideals are eternal (see 'Giuseppe Mazzini', . . . and 'Il canto dell' amore', . . .), whilst the beauty of woman and the works of man are ephemeral things.

26   Dante's *Paradiso* ends with the record of his vision of God 'face to face'.

28   San Giovanni: the ancient Baptistry of Florence, in which Dante was baptised, and which symbolised all the good that Florence meant to him in his exile (see *Inferno* XIX.17 and *Paradiso* XVI.25).

35-6   *In exitu:* the opening line of Psalm 113 (Vulgate), which Dante proposes the redeemed sing on their arrival in Purgatory (*Purgatorio* II).

61f.   references are to the ravaging of the Italian coastline by the Vandals under Genseric in the 5th century A.D.

65   Odin: god of war of the barbarian (Teutonic) races.

67   Poseidon: god of the seas and earthquakes (hence Carducci's 'Enosigeon': lit. 'earth-shaker').

70   the armies of Attila the Hun invaded Italy in 452 A.D.

77   the Langobards (otherwise 'Vinili') invaded and occupied Italy in the 7th to 8th centuries A.D.

96   Queen Theodolinda (d. 628 A.D.), wife of King Agilulf of the Langobards, led the conversion of her people from their Arian heresy to orthodox Catholicism.

97   Pope Gregory the Great (d. 604) vigorously opposed the barbarian invaders of Italy, and by his preaching and example encouraged their conversion to orthodoxy as well as their adoption of the Latin language and civilisation.

112   'Ave Maria': the archangel Gabriel's greeting to the Virgin Mary at the Annunciation ('Hail Mary, full of grace, the Lord is with thee; blessed art thou amongst women': Luke 1.28).

116   allusions are to Dante's description of dusk on Mount Purgatory (*Purgatorio* VIII.1-6), and to that by Byron (here 'Harold', recalling his *Childe Harold's Pilgrimage*) in *Don Juan* III, stanzas 102-3, of 1818, which draws from Dante. The significance seems to be that great poets are sensitive to the immanent mysteries of dusk, both Christian poets (Dante) and sceptics with a mystical leaning (Byron in the first instance, but by now arguably Carducci also).

ELEGIA DEL MONTE SPLUGA (RR.25)

This elegiac ode (for metre see notes to **'Nella piazza di San Petronio',** . . .) was written by Carducci following an excursion with Annie Vivanti, in August 1898, into the mountainous upper reaches of the Val de Gressoney (Italian Alps). Besides an essay in landscape poetry, the ode is also a tribute to Annie and those aspects of her that so charmed him in his old age (Carducci was 63): her foreignness, her somewhat naïve imagination and enthusiasm, and finally her daring and affectionate teasing of him, the major literary figure of Italy. The poem explores one landscape, in two moods: the first rapturous (11.1-32), in which the imagination reigns supreme and brings to life the nymphs and fays of Italian and Germanic myth (a syncretism reflecting the romantic harmony between the Italian Carducci and the German-educated Annie). The second mood (11.33-40) is one of nostalgia and loss, as Carducci contemplates the same scene alone, bereft of her stimulating presence. It is now an existential world of concrete reality, unrelieved by the vivid colours of the imagination. In the bare realism of this final passage's contours and detail, Carducci's new approach to landscape, signalled in **'Esequie della guida E.R.'** (1895), is confirmed.

4    Thetis: sea-maiden, daughter of Nereus and sister to Galatea, who rose from the sea to Olympus in order to elicit Jove's protection of her son Achilles (*Iliad* I).

10   Lorelei: the nymph of Germanic legend, who from the rocky island in the Rhine named after her, drew sailors siren-like to their destruction (cf. Heine's poem 'Lorelei').

17   monster: lit. 'orc', the sea monster who preyed on human flesh, especially of maidens (see Ariosto, *Orlando Furioso* VIII). It was the nickname for Carducci used affectionately by Annie in their relationship.

35   reference is to the Piano della Dogana (now Piano di Spluga), which in Carducci's day was pitted with small lakes, but is now partially submerged beneath a reservoir.

38   the 'idle river' is the Liro.

39   monkshood: *aconitum napellus,* well-known in high damp woodland for its blue or purple flowers and poisonous sap.

---

# FURTHER READING

## Biography

Higgins, David H. Introduction to *Giosue Carducci: Selected Verse,* pp. 1-32. Warminster, U.K.: Aris & Phillips Ltd., 1994.

Provides extensive biographical information on Carducci's life.

## Criticism

"The poetry of Carducci." *Edinburgh Review* 209, no. 428 (April 1909): 338-62.

Thorough examination of Carducci's best works, including *Odi barbare.*

Garnett, Richard. "Carducci." In *A History of Italian Literature,* pp. 396-402. New York: D. Appleton and Company, 1898.

Analyzes specific elements that made Carducci the leading voice of his nation and time.

"Italian Poets of Today." *Living Age* 17, no. 3045 (15 November 1902): 385-403.

Considers differences between Carducci and other leading poets of late nineteenth century. *Portraits and Elegies.*

Wilkins, Ernest Hatch. "Carducci and Other Poets." In *A History of Italian Literature,* pp. 436-44. Cambridge, Mass.: Harvard University Press, 1974.

Overview of Carducci's poetry, along with a brief synopsis of his other literary works.

Additional coverage of Carducci's life and career is contained in the following sources published by the Gale Group: *Contemporary Authors,* Vol. 163; *European Writers,* Vol. 7; *Reference Guide to World Literature,* Eds. 2, 3; and *Twentieth-Century Literary Criticism,* Vol. 32.

# Horace
## 65 B.C.-8 B.C.

(Full name Quintus Horatius Flaccus) Roman satirist, lyric poet, literary critic, and essayist.

## INTRODUCTION

Most well known for his *Odes, Epistles, Epodes,* and *Satires,* Horace is thought to be one of the most accomplished lyric poets to have written in Latin. His poetry is important because it provides a glimpse of peacetime in the Roman empire after years of civil war. Horace's poetry is known for its wit, and his *Ars Poetica* became a style manual for poets of the sixteenth and seventeenth centuries and was required reading in British schools.

## BIOGRAPHICAL INFORMATION

Horace was born Quintus Horatius Flaccus in southern Italy in 65 B.C., the son of a freedman. Thanks to a father who recognized his talent early, Horace was educated in Rome, studying under Orbilius (a grammarian), and later in Athens where he encountered the Greek poets who profoundly influenced his work.

On the heels of Julius Caesar's assassination in 44 B.C., Horace joined Brutus's forces, traveling to Asia Minor and rising to the rank of tribune despite his humble background. His military exploits were short-lived, however, and he returned to Rome after Brutus's defeat at Philippi in November 42 B.C. Although the move to Rome garnered him a position in the Roman treasury, this was more importantly the time during which he began to write poetry.

The poetry written during this period impressed Virgil and other Roman poets, who eventually introduced Horace to Maecenas, with whom he formed a lasting friendship. Between 35 and 30 B.C., Maecenas is thought to have given Horace a small estate in the Sabine Hills. The area is often mentioned in his poetry and he remained there (and in Rome) until his death in November 8 B.C.

## MAJOR WORKS

Horace's life, and hence his works, cover a crucial historical period; his poetry reflects the changing conditions and moods of those times and their events. These works include *Satires* Books I and II (c. 35 and 30 B.C.), *Epodes*

(c. 29 B.C.), *Odes* Book I-III and Book IV (c. 23 and 13 B.C.), *Epistles* Books I and II (c. 20 and 15 B.C.), the *Ars Poetica* (c. 19 B.C.), and *Carmen Saeculare* (c. 17 B.C.).

The *Odes* and *Epodes* are most indebted to the Greek poets, especially those of the sixth and seventh centuries and those of the Hellenistic period, including Archilochus, Hipponax, Alcaeus, and Pindar. The *Odes* Books I-III include eighty-eight poems in Greek meter and concern philosophy and personal relationships.

The *Epistles,* excellent examples of Horace's casual, conversational approach, deal with the poet's concerns with respect to living a moral life. *Epistles* Book I includes twenty poems and gives the reader a window on Horace the man. One sees the change—a more melancholy mood—that took hold of the poet after the *Satires.* He is more concerned with finding answers to personal spiritual and moral questions and the ethos is decidedly philosophical. *Epistles* Book II, although it includes only three poems, is more intricate than *Epistles* Book I. It is a montage of examples, anecdotes, and vivid imagery that further the reader's understanding of the poet as a man.

The *Ars Poetica* is perhaps the poet's best-known work. Structured as a conversational collection of thoughts on a number of literary matters, it became a significant influence on a diverse group of authors including Ben Johnson, Dante, St. Augustine, and Alexander Pope.

## CRITICAL RECEPTION

Horace's work has gone through periods of interest and neglect. During his lifetime his work was honored and studied at academies, followed by a period of critical neglect and a rebirth of interest during the Renaissance and continuing through the nineteenth century. Current interest unfortunately lies primarily in the academic and scholarly communities, a result of the decrease in Latin courses offered in recent times.

Critical study of Horace has included Horace's use of Greek meter, Horace as a man, comparisons of his work with other poets, studies of his influence on other poets and the poets who influenced his work, his ability to interpret the events of his times, and specific, detailed analysis of his style and technique.

Thayer and Showerman discuss Horace the man—the information we can glean from his writings, his skill at interpreting and reporting the historical events of his life, his commonsense philosophy, and his skill as an observer. Thayer goes on to name several poets who have been influenced by Horace, including Browning, Tennyson, Keats, and Shelley but cautions that "there is no one who is to English letters what Horace is to Roman—nay, to all letters. He is unlike all others." As a further window on Horace's life, Bowditch investigates the socioeconomic conditions that influenced Horace's work: "social relations of exchange provided more than a context for the production of verse; they also informed a shared system of rhetorical figures through which poets negotiated both their own interests and those of their varied audiences."

Herrick and Russell address the *Ars Poetica.* Herrick's basis is that the growth of formal literary criticism began with the principles of Horace's *Ars Poetica* and Aristotle's *Poetics.* The author traces translations of these works into other languages and provides evidence of sixteenth- and seventeenth-century discussions of these principles and their significant influence on writers of these times. Russell offers an in-depth study of the *Ars* as "the last of the great innovator's creations."

Reckford discusses the "Trip to Brunisium," from the *Satires,* focusing on three aspects: "the theme of *amicitia,* private and public; the *agon,* or insult-match between Sarmentus the *scurra* and Messius Cicurrus; and the 'wet dream' and 'failed miracle' sequences toward the end." Reckford sets the stage for his analysis by developing a hypothetical involving Horace's creation, first reading to friends, and first publication of this work.

In the area of analysis, West offers some basic principles for reading Horace, and is particularly concerned with the need to accurately translate the Latin and that the works be viewed with an open mind, unencumbered by prejudices of the reader's time: "So modern tastes do not like blood running in water. This is neither here nor there. What is important is that the Romans were familiar with the notion of sacrificing animals into fountains. . . . The critic must shed his local prejudices." West also provides analysis of the *Odes,* focusing on certain poetic techniques. Williams, Santirocco, and Pucci also provide insight on the *Odes.* Williams offers ideas as to the Greek poets who may have influenced Horace and discusses the hymn and symposium poem forms and the themes of this collection. Santirocco considers the arrangement of the poems of *Odes* Books I-III, and Pucci examines Augustine's allusion to *Odes* 1.3 in his *Confessions* 4.6 and how the two texts can be compared with respect to the dilemma of writing. Ancona discusses the use of the temporal adverb and Horace's manipulation of time in *Odes* 1.25, 2.5, and 3.7. Lee considers the use and arrangement of words in Horace's works including the oxymoron, hendiadys, and word association.

---

# PRINCIPAL WORKS

## Poetry

*Satires* Book I c. 35 b.c.

*Satires* Book II c. 30 b.c.

*Epodes* c. 29 b.c.

*Odes* Books I-III c. 23 b.c.

*Epistles* Book I c. 20 b.c.

*Ars Poetica* [*On the Art of Poetry*] c. 19 b.c.

*Carmen Saeculare* [*Secular Hymn*] c. 17 b.c.

*Epistles* Book II c. 15 b.c.

*Odes* Book IV c. 13 b.c.

## Principle English Translations

*Odes and Epodes of Horace* (translated by Joseph P. Clancy) 1960

*Satires and Epistles of Horace* (translated by Smith Palmer Bovie) 1962

*Third Book of Horace's Odes* (translated by Gordon Williams) 1969

*The Odes and Epodes* (translated by C. E Bennett) 1991

*Satires I* (translated by P. Michael Brown) 1993

*Epodes* (translated by David Mankin) 1995

*The Odes of Horace* (translated by David Ferry) 1998

*The Complete Odes and Satires of Horace* (translated by Sidney Alexander) 1999

*The Epistles of Horace* (translated by David Ferry) 2001
*The Satires of Horace* (translated by William Matthews)
  2002

---

# CRITICISM

## Mary Rebecca Thayer (essay date 1916)

SOURCE: Thayer, Mary Rebecca. Introduction to *The
Influence of Horace on the Chief English Poets of the
Nineteenth Century,* pp. 11-51. New Haven, Conn.: Yale
University Press, 1916.

[*In the following essay, Thayer begins by discussing what
Horace shares of himself and his work through his poetry,
and how he was viewed by his contemporaries. She goes
on to suggest poets with whom we might reasonably
compare Horace, choosing Wordsworth, Coleridge, Tennyson, and Browning among others.*]

In order properly to discuss the influence of one writer
upon another, it is necessary to determine as nearly as may
be for what each of them stands; for the measure of real
influence is, after all, the amount of sympathy which exists between the two. Therefore, prior to taking up the
relation of Horace to nineteenth-century English poetry,
we must endeavor to obtain a true idea of him as he shows
himself to us.

The attempt to discover a man in his poems is always
fascinating, but also to a greater or less extent dangerous.
The reason for this is twofold: first, most poets have the
faculty of merging their own identity from time to time in
the imaginary men and women of whom they write, so
that it is indeed Oedipus, or Francesca, or Lady Macbeth,
or Paracelsus, whom we hear speaking; secondly, the eager
interpreter is all too apt to forget the 'infinite variety'
which goes to make up every human being, and, dwelling
on certain poems, while disregarding others, to construct
therefrom a caricature which the poet himself would be
the last to recognize as his portrait.

From the first of these dangers Horace is not so likely to
suffer; for it is true that some poets commit more of
themselves to their verse than do others, and he belongs to
the former class. So careful a student as the late Professor
Sellar finds him one of the most self-revealing of poets;
and Professor J. Wight Duff, the able historian of Latin
literature, says of him: 'No Roman author except Cicero
has left anything like so complete a self-revelation as
Horace.'[1]

It is well for us that this is true, since there is no record of
him except the brief life by Suetonius, which furnishes a
mere biographical outline, but not the vastly more

important details of the poet's personality. Concerning
Horace there has come down to us none of the contemporary appreciation which helps us to realize even so
inscrutable a figure as 'gentle Shakespeare.' It is from
Horace alone that we may hope to know Horace—the
friend of Virgil, the favorite of Maecenas, the protégé of
Augustus, the poet of us all.

From the second danger, however, Horace suffers much.
Critic after critic has taken the lighter odes, the *vers de société* which the poet could write so charmingly, and with
them for background has painted a picture of an amiable
trifler, feeling deeply on no subject except perhaps when
the ugly thought of inevitable death obtrudes itself; a
finished workman, caring far more for the polishing and
setting than for the gem itself. Thus we find Keble saying:[2]

> 'I reluctantly confess myself hitherto unable to discover
> any peculiar and dominating spring of Horace's poetry.
> In fact, I suspect his light touch of all subjects betrays
> to us that he dwelt with no serious regard on any one
> of them. He professes at times a notable enthusiasm for
> the country and rural life: yet one always feels that his
> interest was rather after the manner of those who
> merely seek recreation there than of the country-folk
> themselves; that Rome was all the time in his thoughts;
> that he cherished his little farm and his homely belong-
> ings, less for their own sake than for their restful
> repose, their elegant hospitalities, and whatsoever other
> like attractions they offered. In brief: he enrolled
> himself . . . without misgiving in the ranks of the
> Epicureans; setting before him as his sole rule of life
> the hope of grasping the gifts of the passing hour,
> whatever they might chance to be. . . . We see, then,
> in him a genial gentleman, one too nearly in sympathy
> with the crowd, who indulge their own bent, to be
> deeply influenced by any tender regard for things far
> away.'

This criticism contains an element of truth. Horace *was* an
Epicurean; he *was* a genial gentleman. But, for the rest,
we surely will not acknowledge that *carpe diem* was his
'sole rule of life,' when we recall (to take a familiar
instance) the golden mean upon which he time and again
insists; we cannot agree that he took no active interest in
country life when we read such passages as the following:

> Vivere naturae si convenienter oportet,
> Ponendaeque domo quaerenda est area primum,
> Novistine locum potiorem rure beato?
> Est ubi plus tepeant hiemes? . . .
> Est ubi divellat somnos minus invida cura?
> Deterius Libycis olet aut nitet herba lapillis?
> Purior in vicis aqua tendit rumpere plumbum,
> Quam quae per pronum trepidat cum murmure rivum?
> Nempe inter varias nutritur silva columnas,
> Laudaturque domus longos quae prospicit agros.
> Naturam expelles furca, tamen usque recurret;[3]

and if we carefully consider the entire body of Horace's
work, we must refuse to admit that he touched all subjects
lightly. Rather we may accept the judgment of Sellar:[4]

> 'He is at once the lyrical poet, with heart and imagina-
> tion responsive to the deeper meaning and lighter

amusements of life, and the satirist, the moralist, and the literary critic of the age.'

CHARACTERISTICS OF HORACE

The safe method, then, is to discover, if we can, for ourselves what Horace reveals of himself in his works; not, be it understood, such facts of his life as that his father was a freedman, and that he once narrowly escaped being struck by a falling tree, but the characteristics of the man as his poetry discloses them. And for a first descriptive epithet we may echo one of Keble's—'genial.'

Geniality, indeed, is the key-note of Horace's work. We see it in the epistles, which, though addressed to dead and gone Romans, are really, we feel, for us all; yet are not impersonal 'open letters,' but rather a delightful admission of the interested to his confidence. We see it even in his most sharply satirical passages; for virtually all students of Horace the satirist have noticed that he almost never loses his good humor—that he laughs at follies instead of railing at them. We see it in many of his lyrics, such as *Vides ut alta . . . Soracte, Integer vitae,* and *Septimi Gadis aditure mecum.* It is everywhere apparent, so that we find ourselves feeling that here is a man whom it would have been a pleasure to know and to talk with.

Yet, though nearly always good-humored, Horace is far from being always happy. There is, indeed, a sombre strain in him that frequently shows itself when we least expect.

> Diffugere nives, redeunt iam gramina campis,

he sings,

> Arboribusque comae;
>
> . . . . .
>
> Gratia cum Nymphis geminisque sororibus audet
>     Ducere nuda choros.

And then he adds abruptly:

> Immortalia ne speres, monet annus et almum
>     Quae rapit hora diem.
>
> . . . . .
>
> Damna tamen celeres reparant caelestia lunae:
>     Nos ubi decidimus
> Quo pius Aeneas, quo dives Tullus et Ancus,
>     Pulvis et umbra sumus.[5]

Or again:

> Solvitur acris hiems grata vice veris et Favoni.
>
> . . . . .
>
> Nunc decet aut viridi nitidum caput impedire myrto
>     Aut flore terrae quem ferunt solutae;
> Nunc et in umbrosis Fauno decet immolare lucis,
>     Seu poscat agna sive malit haedo.
> Pallida mors aequo pulsat pede pauperum tabernas

> Regumque turris. O beate Sesti,
> Vitae summa brevis spem nos vetat incohare longam.[6]

It is in this feeling of the inevitableness of death that the melancholy of Horace usually shows itself.

> The glories of our blood and state
>     Are shadows, not substantial things;
> There is no armor against fate;
>     Death lays his icy hand on kings—

the thought runs throughout his poetry; and from this naturally enough follows the desire to get out of life all it has to offer.

> Carpe diem, quam minimum credula postero,[7]

he again and again advises, though in varying words. Yet that this desire for instant happiness is with him no mere unregulated impulse is evident to any reader; for perhaps the chief element of the Horatian philosophy is moderation. The golden mean is the standard which the poet sets before himself and those who care to listen to him, and he despises alike the avarice of the miser and the extravagance of the spendthrift. The happiness he wishes for his brief life is, then, carefully planned, and dependent upon the scrupulous balancing of desire with desire. He carries this doctrine to its logical conclusion, and tells us: *Virtus est medium vitiorum.* The fact that this advice to be moderate is so often reiterated in his work goes to show that the poet was sincere in giving it. It is no passing fancy, but an integral part of his conduct of life.

Thus we should expect to find Horace a man of simple tastes; and so he professes to be.

> Persicos odi . . . apparatus,[8]

he cries; and though the particular ode is light in tone, the theme is sounded again and again in more serious moments.

> Vile potabis modicis Sabinum
> Cantharis,

he warns no less a person than Maecenas;

>         mea nec Falernae
> Temperant vites neque Formiani
>     Pocula colles.[9]

> Me pascunt olivae,

he says elsewhere,

> Me cichorea levesque malvae.[10]

Many similar expressions may be found:

> Non ebur neque aureum
>     Mea renidet in domo lacunar.
>
> . . . . .
>
>         Nihil supra

Deos lacesso nec potentem amicum
Largiora flagito,
　　Satis beatus unicis Sabinis.[11]

Purae rivus aquae silvaque iugerum
Paucorum et segetis certa fides meae
　　Fulgentem imperio fertilis Africae
　　　　Fallit sorte beatior.[12]

And so on. A part of this may be, as many scholars would have us believe, a pose; all of it can hardly be.

It naturally follows that Horace is content with his own lot.

Si natura iuberet,

says he,

A certis annis aevum remeare peractum
Atque alios legere, ad fastum quoscumque parentis
Optaret sibi quisque, meis contentus honestos
Fascibus et sellis nollem mihi sumere.[13]

Hoc erat in votis: modus agri non ita magnus,
Hortus ubi et tecto vicinus iugis aquae fons
Et paulum silvae super his foret. Auctius atque
Di melius fecere. Bene est. Nil amplius oro,
Maia nate, nisi ut propria haec mihi munera faxis.[14]

Me . . .
. . . quid credis, amice, precari?
Sit mihi quod nunc est, etiam minus.[15]

Examples could be multiplied.

From all this we should surmise that Horace was responsive to the charm of external nature; for the person whose tastes are simple rarely fails to admire the beauties which he sees in the undisturbed world about him. And we cannot deny this habit of mind to the Roman poet. It is almost impossible to feel that he was insincere in his many protestations of his preference for the country over the town. The Sabine farm, mentioned so often as his chief treasure, is described in *Epist.* 1. 16 as none but a true lover of nature could describe it. We see the mountain-range broken only by the dark valley; the oaks and ilex-trees with their grateful shade; the stream (*rivo dare nomen idoneum*), as cool and pure as Hebrus. The entire picture is given us in a dozen lines, yet it is perfectly distinct. This, in fact, is the principal merit of the descriptions of external nature in Horace—the creation of a vivid impression by the use of exactly the right word or phrase. What lover of the *Odes* does not know *amoenum Lucretilem* and *Albuneam resonantem* and *praecipitem Anienem?* We see with Thaliarchus

　　ut alta stet nive candidum
Soracte;[16]

and the country round about Tibur is familiar ground to us. What though archaeologists cannot identify all these places? They are not the less real to the inward eye of the imagination.

Especially does Horace seem to have delighted in groves and streams. Over and over again he describes himself, or another, stretched at ease beside rippling water, under a shade-giving tree. He nearly always names his trees, and his favorites are many: the arbutus, the ilex, the plane, and the more familiar oak, pine, and poplar. And wherever Horace is known, there also is known the *fons Bandusiae, splendidior vitro*. The poet's promise,

Fies nobilium tu quoque fontium,
Me dicente,[17]

has come true.

So marked is this predilection for waters and trees that we are tempted to apply to him his own words:

Quae Tibur aquae fertile praefluunt,
Et spissae nemorum comae
　　Fingent Aeolio carmine nobilem.[18]

Yet let no one make the mistake of deeming Horace a recluse; for his paramount interest is always *human* nature. He loves the country, but also, notwithstanding temporary periods of distaste, he loves busy Rome with its crowded streets—yes, even with its 'smoke and riches and noise.' His keen eye observes all the people he meets, and his ready mind reproduces them for us, so that we see again the singer Tigellius, and the dinner-giver Nasidienus, and the bore who met him on the Via Sacra, and a host of others, both named and nameless.

Horace was interested not only in the inhabitants of Rome, but in the city itself, then at the height of its glory. Though born in Venusia, he was a true Roman, with all a Roman's pride in the mistress of the world. His patriotism manifests itself in two ways. The first is the obvious one of recounting the triumphs, past and present, of her whom he proudly calls *domina Roma*. We feel that he delights in merely rehearsing the names of the city's great men—

Romulum . . . an quietem
Pompili regnum . . . an superbos
Tarquini fascis . . . an Catonis
　　Nobile letum;[19]

and in lofty verse he sings the illustrious achievements of the heroes of old:

Quid debeas, O Roma, Neronibus,
Testis Metaurum flumen et Hasdrubal
　　Devictus et pulcher fugatis
　　　　Ille dies Latio tenebris,

Qui primus alma risit adorea,
Dirus per urbis Afer ut Italas
　　Ceu flamma per taedas vel Eurus
　　　　Per Siculas equitavit undas.

　　　　　. . . . .

Gens quae cremato fortis ab Ilio
Iactata Tuscis aequoribus sacra

Natosque maturosque patres
Pertulit Ausonias ad urbis,

Duris ut ilex tonsa bipennibus
Nigrae feraci frondis in Algido,
Per damna, per caedis, ab ipso
Ducit opes animumque ferro.[20]

Nor do the present glories of Rome less excite his pride. He writes concerning the 'golden age' of Augustus:

Iam mari terraque manus potentis
Medus Albanasque timet securis,
Iam Scythae responsa petunt superbi
Nuper, et Indi.

Iam Fides et Pax et Honor Pudorque
Priscus et neglecta redire Virtus
Audet, adparetque beata pleno
Copia cornu.[21]

His second method of showing patriotism is very different; for here he appears as the censor, who sees and deplores the evils that threaten his beloved city. The old Roman virtues are no more, he says:

Di multa neglecti dederunt
Hesperiae mala luctuosae.
Iam bis Monaeses et Pacori manus
Non auspicatos contudit impetus
Nostros et adiecisse praedam
Torquibus exiguis renidet.

Paene occupatam seditionibus
Delevit Urbem Dacus et Aethiops.

. . . . .

Fecunda culpae saecula nuptias
Primum inquinavere et genus et domos:
Hoc fonte derivata clades
In patriam populumque fluxit.

. . . . .

Non his iuventus orta parentibus
Infecit aequor sanguine Punico
Pyrrhumque et ingentem cecidit
Antiochum Hannibalemque dirum.[22]

Not once, but many times, does he sound this note. He foresaw only too well whither the growing luxury and laxity of the empire were tending, and did his best to warn his fellow countrymen. His patriotism, then, was not superficial, but a real part of him, serious and concerned for the future.

The friends of Horace were many, and we may judge from his poems that friendship was no meaningless word to him.

Amicum
Qui non defendit alio culpante, . . .

. . . . .

. . . hic niger est, hunc tu, Romane, caveto,[23]

he tells us; and again:

At pater ut gnati, sic nos debemus amici
Siquod sit vitium non fastidire.[24]

His own greatest friend is the powerful minister, Maecenas; and though possibly much of Horace's adulation of him is due to the memory of benefits conferred, and also to a natural enough pleasure in showing himself to be upon terms of intimacy with so influential a man, we need not deny all sincerity to his protestations of affection for his patron. The beautiful lines,

Non ego perfidum
Dixi sacramentum: ibimus, ibimus,
Utcumque praecedes, supremum
Carpere iter comites parati,[25]

ring true. And there are humbler friends—humbler, that is, at the time, though nowadays one of them at least is ranked above Augustus himself. This is Virgil, in whose honor Horace wrote his fine *proempticon*, two lines of which serve to express the esteem in which the younger poet held the elder:

Reddas incolumem precor
Et serves animae dimidium meae.[26]

Then there are Pompeius, whom our poet addresses as *meorum prime sodalium*, and Septimius, *Godis aditure mecum*, and a score or more of others, many of them only names to us, but to Horace dear and intimate friends.

No portrait of Horace would be complete without some mention of his delightful sense of humor. It shows itself again and again—now in the description of his brief military experience, now in his account of his meeting with the bore, now in the inimitable bit of dialogue between Lydia and her lover. The humor is generally delicate; yet we cannot use a popular figure and compare it to a rapier-thrust, for it is almost always good-natured. Rarely does Horace approach sarcasm; when he does, it is as likely to be directed against himself as another, for he possesses the happy faculty of laughing at himself.

Here, then, is the Roman poet as he shows himself to us—a genial man and of a kindly disposition, moderate in his life, simple in his tastes, with an artist's eye and feeling for the beauties of external nature, and an artist's interest in humanity; a lover of his country and of his friends; at times giving himself over to mirth and enjoyment, at other times yielding to melancholy; serious withal, and sincerely concerned about what he deemed the great things of life; indeed, a figure to command affection and admiration.

### Characteristics of Horace's Poetry

When we turn to Horace the artist, we find that all critics, whatever may be their feeling about the matter of his poetry, agree that he is a master-craftsman. It is evident to the merest novice that his advice about the use of the file was drawn from his own practice. As a result, whatever he has to say is said in so felicitous a manner as to make us feel it could be altered only for the worse. Especially is this true of the **Odes,** where almost every sentence is an exquisitely cut gem. He has an astonishing power of compression—the faculty of making one or two words imply a dozen ideas. This is what makes it absolutely impossible to translate Horace adequately; yet, by a curious sort of irony, it is perhaps this very perfection that attracts so many would-be translators—men so diverse as Milton and Eugene Field, Cowper and Gladstone. The poet himself evidently realized his own mastery of technique. He speaks of his work as *operosa.*

> Parios ego primus iambos,

he boasts;

> Ostendi Latio, numeros animosque secutus
> Archilochi;[27]

and even in the lofty *Exegi monumentum* he rests his chief claim to renown on the fact that he was the first to adapt Aeolian verse to Italian measures.

But, as Horace realizes, and as he more than once tells us, poetry consists not alone in technical skill.

> Non satis est,

he says,

>                puris versum perscribere verbis,
> Quem si dissolvas, quivis stomachetur eodem
> Quo personatus pacto pater.[28]

> Ingenium cui sit, cui mens divinior atque os
> Magna sonaturum, des nominis [poetae] huius honorem.[29]

In his **Satires** and **Epistles,** accordingly, he disclaims the honor:

>            Neque, siqui scribat uti nos
> Sermoni propiora, putes hunc esse poetam.[30]

We prefer to take his valuation of himself in the **Odes:**

> Non omnis moriar. . . .
> . . . Mihi Delphica
> Lauro cinge volens, Melpomene, comam.[31]

The poetry of Horace is far from being the superficial, trivial verse that some critics would have us believe. It is true that he wrote many odes upon conventional themes, treating these themes in such fashion as to make them memorable; it is true that he wrote delicately-finished bits of verse on trifles—*Quis multa gracilis, Persicos odi, Vides ut alta,* and many others; it is also true that he wrote noble poems, such as **Caelo tonantem, Ne forte credas,** and the triumphant **Exegi monumentum,** the first few lines of which are among the finest utterances on the immortality conferred on a poet by his work.

As must be the case with every real artist, Horace rated his calling high. In his opinion, as we have seen (p. 17), the poet must possess *ingenium, mens divinior, os magna sonaturum.* When we find him speaking in a slighting way of poetry, it always proves to be the work of the uninspired, untrained poetaster that he has in mind; for he believed that the poet must be made as well as born. The **Ars Poetica** is a witness to the value he set on his vocation.

> Quod si me lyricis vatibus inseris,

he tells us in a well-known ode,

> Sublimi feriam sidera vertice.[32]

Throughout his works we find evidence of his high esteem for his instrument—perhaps none more satisfying than that in **Carm.** 4. 8:

> Non incisa notis marmora publicis,
> Per quae spiritus et vita redit bonis
> Post mortem ducibus, . . .
> . . . clarius indicant
> Laudes quam Calabrae Pierides; neque
> Si chartae sileant quod bene feceris
> Mercedem tuleris.[33]

And for his own writings his prophecy is true: Maecenas the statesman is a shadow; Maecenas the friend and patron of Horace is known to every lover of the poet.

In Horace, then, to borrow the happy phrase of De Quincey, 'the exquisite skill co-operated with the exquisite nature'; and the result is one of the world's treasures. And that the world has treasured his work is abundantly clear. Of all his words none has proved more truly prophetic than

>              Postera
> Crescam laude recens.[34]

He has been called the most popular of poets; possibly no other classical writer is so often quoted. This is partly due to the fact that his conciseness makes his verses lend themselves to quotation; yet there is another reason, which is well expressed by Sellar:[35]

> 'Among all ancient poets he suits the greatest variety of modern tastes. . . . He has an attraction not merely of early association for educated men whose lives are cast in other spheres than that of literature; while to those who seek in the study of great poets to gain some temporary admission within the circle of some of the better thoughts, the finer fancies, the happier and more pathetic experiences of our race, he is able to afford this access. To each successive age or century, he seems to express its own familiar wisdom and experience. . . . He is one of the few ancient writers who unite all the cultivated nations of modern times in a common admiration. They each seem to claim him as especially their own.'

Let it be added that, as has often been noticed, Horace makes an appeal to both young and old. We are told, indeed, that it takes the weight of years to bring a man to a full appreciation of him; for his work, small in quantity though it is, covers his whole life, and he shows us himself at each period, so that there is something for all.

## HORACE AS SEEN BY HIS CONTEMPORARIES

It has been pointed out above (p. 7) that contemporary records of Horace are of the scantiest. That his work was admired we may gather from the fact that Augustus more than once called his Muse into requisition, and also from the patronage with which Maecenas favored him; but Ovid (*Tristia* 4. 10. 49-50) seems to be the only writer of the times who mentions him:

> Et tenuit nostras numerosus Horatius aures;
> Dum ferit Ausonia carmina culta lyra.[36]

The adjective here applied to the poems of Horace is worthy of note; Ovid evidently appreciated his compatriot's mastery of technique. Yet the praise is mild, and its force is diminished by the fact that Horace is only one in a list of writers mentioned by the other poet, some of them of very doubtful merit. Horace himself, if we may judge at all from his own writings, would seem frequently to imply that he was considered inferior to epic poets such as Virgil, Varius, and Jullus.

> Ego apis Matinae,

he says,

> More modoque
> . . . operosa parvus
> Carmina fingo.[37]

## HORACE IN THE MIDDLE AGES

Yet, as the centuries passed, and many of the classic writers fell into oblivion, Horace was not forgotten. From the ninth century to the thirteenth,[38] every cycle shows a considerable number of Horatian quotations in every important literature; and the Middle Ages produced more than one Horatian specialist such as Conrad von Mure. It was the didactic works of the Roman poet, however, that attracted most attention; the lyrics fell more and more into the background, and in 1280 Hugo of Trimberg wrote:

> Sequitur Horatius, prudens et discretus,
> Vitiorum emulus, firmus et mansuetus;
> Qui tres libros etiam fecit principales,
> Duosque dictaverat minus usuales;
> Epodon videlicet, et librum odarum,
> Quos nostris temporibus credo valere parum.
> Hinc poetrie veteris titulum ponamus,
> Sermones cum epistolis dehinc adiciamus.[39]

Notwithstanding this neglect of what we now consider the flower of his work, Horace was placed upon a lofty pedestal by the men of the Middle Ages. We at once think of Dante's selection of him as one of the five great poets of antiquity, in *Inferno* 4. 89—where he figures as 'Orazio *Satiro.*' Long before this, Alcuin, in the literary circle which he organized at the court of Charlemagne, assumed the name of 'Horatius Flaccus.'

## HORACE AND CHAUCER

When we come nearer home, and regard the first great figure in English literature, we find only a few traces of Horace in Chaucer; and these few, Professor Skeat thinks, show only a second-hand knowledge.[40] 'It is obvious,' he says, 'that Chaucer never saw Horace's works in the complete state; if he had done so, he would have found a writer after his own heart, and he would have quoted him even more freely than he has quoted Ovid.' It is worth noting, however, that the few quotations or paraphrases which we do find are all from the didactic works—a fact which corroborates the statement made above of the superior popularity of these poems.

## HORACE AMONG THE ELIZABETHANS

But by 'the spacious times of great Elizabeth' the *Odes* had once more come to their own. We find them translated and paraphrased by the poets of the day; quoted by the writers of prose; and even set down piecemeal in schoolbooks. We remember how Chiron, in *Titus Andronicus,* says of *Integer vitae:*

> O! 'tis a verse in Horace; I know it well:
> I read it in the grammar long ago.

In fact, most of the Elizabethans must have been familiar with Horace from early youth. We are told[41] that 'the afternoon lessons of the boys at Rotherham School [a typical grammar school of the period] in Shakespeare's time were "two days in Horace, and two days in Seneca's Tragedies; both which they translated into English."' Ever since, let it be added, Horace has served as a text-book for English schoolboys; thus the fate against which he humorously inveighed has come upon him:

> Hoc quoque te [meum librum] manet, ut pueros el-
> ementa docentem
> Occupet extremis in vicis balba senectus.[42]

That this dislike of having his poems used as texts for schoolboys was not without reason we shall see when we take up the opinions of several of the most illustrious of these students; yet there is much to be said for a system which puts Horace at the end of a man's tongue.

It is still a question whether the greatest poet among the Elizabethans knew Horace. Since he attended Stratford Grammar School, it is likely that he did; moreover, it seems that his works contain internal evidence of such a knowledge. However that may be, there is no doubt that Ben Jonson was saturated with Horace, even going so far as to call himself by the Roman poet's name in his *Poetaster;* and many other writers of that prolific age show a strong Horatian influence.

## Horace and the Cavalier Poets

As we come down through the cavalier poets, we find the vigorous influence of Horace no whit abated. Herrick, perhaps, echoes him oftener than do any of the others; but all feel his attraction.

## Horace and Milton

Milton, as great a contrast to these as could well be imagined, has many reminiscences of Horace. And so it goes until we arrive at the so-called 'classic period,' when most of the Roman poets were at the high tide of popularity in England, with Horace as one of the leaders.

## Horace in the Eighteenth Century

Throughout the eighteenth century our poet holds his own; when a writer wished to do a bit of elegant translating, or when he stood in need of an apt quotation, more often than not he turned to Horace. But about the beginning of the nineteenth century there was a considerable change in English literature. Poets deliberately turned away from the traditions of the 'classic school,' and began to seek new paths for themselves, or to reopen neglected ones. It might be supposed that Horace, the favorite of the old school, would be discarded by the new; whether or not this was the case, the following pages will attempt to show.

## Divisions of Horace's Work

But before separately taking up the great poets of the age, we shall do well to pause for a short time at the two principal divisions of Horace's verse. These have been already referred to as the didactic and the lyric. It remains to see what each group includes, and what influence each has exerted.

The didactic poems comprise the *Satires*, the *Epistles*, and the *Ars Poetica*. They are all written in dactylic hexameter, and they deal with a variety of subjects in a pleasing conversational way—*sermoni propiora,* as Horace himself puts it. Some are merely narratives of events in the poet's daily life, such as the journey to Brundisium; others rebuke the follies of the time—not after the manner of a Juvenal or a Swift, but in a gentler way which would correct without stinging. 'Come, let us reason together,' these poems seem to say. 'Let us look impartially at this or that, and see how foolish and harmful it is.' Others treat of philosophy—the poet's philosophy of life, which he has worked out for himself. Some, again, discuss literary matters; many are autobiographical. All are precious, not only for their inherent charm, but as a record of the opinions and actions of a poet; they might almost be entitled, as was *The Prelude* of Wordsworth, 'the growth of a poet's mind.' But to none of them would Horace himself have given the name poetry. As he says in the *Satires,*

> Primum ego me illorum, dederim quibus esse poetas,
> Excerpam numero.[43]

And at the beginning of his first epistle he laments:

> Non eadem est aetas, non mens . . .
> Nunc itaque et versus et cetera ludicra pono.[44]

When we come to the lyrics, however, the case is different. Their bulk is small—four books of *Odes,* one of *Epodes,* and the *Carmen Saeculare;* but, as we have seen, they contain 'songs for man or woman, of all sizes.' They range in tone 'from grave to gay, from lively to severe,' and each style is fittingly handled.

We have already noticed that during the Middle Ages the didactic works of Horace were in the foreground, the lyrics almost forgotten. The Renaissance brought a change; and throughout the latter half of the sixteenth and the first half of the seventeenth century the *Odes* seem to have exerted the greater influence. This was natural; for the poets of those days were in the main essentially singers, caring but little for ethical teachings, and interested in musical language and metres, as well as in the material suitable to lyric treatment. The pendulum swung the other way in the 'classic period,' and the didactic poems came again to the front. The insistence of Horace on polish and finish—an insistence chiefly to be marked in his *Satires* and *Epistles*—could not fail to attract such lovers of elegance as the writers of the age of Anne; his hexameters suited ears which preferred the heroic couplet to any other form of verse. Moreover, Horace was a satirist; and the times were rich in satire, with him as one of the models. Therefore literary epistles in verse and imitations of Horace—always of the didactic Horace—ran riot, while the *Ars Poetica* was accepted as the gospel of good taste in writing. An age which, with all its merits, was usually so unnatural in its treatment of external nature, and so little interested in the subjectivity which is the essence of the lyric, could hardly be expected fully to appreciate the *Odes* of Horace.

With the return of the subjective to poetry—in the period with which this thesis deals—the lyrics of Horace were once again the most popular part of his work, though the *Satires* and *Epistles* were not forgotten. Even now one occasionally hears an elderly person speak of 'Horace the satirist,' although probably for one reader of the didactic poems there are six of the *Odes*. This is unfortunate: we cannot properly know the poet without seeing him from all sides.

## With Whom May We Compare Horace?

But, in spite of the popularity which Horace has enjoyed among our men of letters, we are perplexed when we look about for some writer with whom to compare him. Is there any one who may claim the honor of being his English analogue? Not Ben Jonson, for all his own confidence in his similarity to the Roman poet whom he so admired. Indeed, we can hardly imagine two great writers temperamentally farther apart than the genial Augustan and the often ungenial Elizabethan. Horace may now and again have been moved to 'strip the ragged follies of the time naked as at their birth,' but his was no 'armed and resolved hand,' no 'whip of steel.' Rather did he believe:

Ridiculum acri
Fortius et melius magnas plerumque secat res.[45]

Points of close resemblance we may find between the nature of Horace as revealed in his writings and the natures of a score or more of authors prominent in our literature. Addison's admirers, moved, we must suppose, by the gentle satire of the *Spectator* papers, have hailed him as the English Horace. Stevenson, perhaps through his inherent Epicureanism, often strongly reminds us of Horace in his **Epistles** and **Satires.** More Horatian than either of these is Thackeray, who, moreover, has so rare a knowledge of the Roman poet as always to be ready, so it seems, with an apt quotation. None of these men, however, can for a moment compare with Horace in his first and preferred capacity—that of writer of lofty and beautiful poetry. We turn to Herrick, who has his supporters; and, indeed, he does at times recall to us the singer of Lydia and Chloë, Lalage and Leuconoë. But that which is high and serious in Horace—the often neglected side—finds no parallel in Herrick, whose flights are seldom above the roof of his parsonage, despite his own claim that he sings 'of heaven.' Many of our greater poets from time to time remind us of this lofty Horace—the attempt of the following pages will be in part to show this; but none is so near to him as to challenge comparison in all respects.

Is this to say that Horace is greater than any English writer? Not at all: the giants of our literature are as far beyond him as is Homer, and he would be the first to admit it. But, notwithstanding this fact, there is no one who is to English letters what Horace is to Roman—nay, to all—letters. He is unlike all others.

Bearing this in mind, we may now go on to investigate just what sort of influence Horace exerted on each of the foremost poets of the nineteenth century. And the first we meet is Wordsworth, whose *Lyrical Ballads,* published in 1798, mark the beginning of nineteenth-century poetry.

WORDSWORTH

The opinion has somehow become prevalent that Wordsworth as a writer was almost uninfluenced by the classics, or, indeed, by any books—that he was a poet largely dependent upon his 'spark of nature's fire.' There could hardly be a greater mistake. Many of the poet's utterances which go to disprove this have been preserved, would people but look for them. One is particularly relevant to the present inquiry: 'First read the ancient classical authors; *then* come to *us;* and you will be able to judge for yourself which of us is worth reading.'[46]

Wordsworth was himself well-read in at least the Roman half of classical literature. The reader of his poems who is also a student of Latin hardly needs the statement which the poet makes in a letter to Walter Savage Landor (April 20, 1822):

'My acquaintance with Virgil, Horace, Lucretius, and Catullus is intimate.'

He adds, indeed, that he 'never read them with a critical view to composition'; but it is certain that their thoughts, and often their language, entered into the texture of his verse, on some occasions, as we shall see, becoming so closely interwoven with his own thought that it is difficult to separate warp from woof.

In the passage just quoted, Horace shares the honors with three great compatriots; but other testimony places him above any of them in Wordsworth's favor. Bishop Wordsworth[47] tells us that his uncle said:

'How graceful is Horace's modesty in his "Ego *apis* Matinae more modoque," as contrasted with the Dircaean Swan! Horace is my great favorite: I love him dearly.'

Again Wordsworth says, in his *Letter to a Friend of Robert Burns:*

'It is delightful to read what, in the happy exercise of his own genius, Horace chooses to communicate of himself and his friends.'

We may add to this the evidence of two of Wordsworth's friends. The Reverend Perceval Graves says of the poet:

'He was a very great admirer of Virgil. . . . From him, and Horace who was an especial favorite, and Lucretius, he used to quote much.'[48]

And De Quincey tells us, in his *Literary and Lake Reminiscences:*

'Wordsworth finally became a very sufficient master of the Latin language, and read certain favorite authors, especially Horace, with a critical nicety, and with a feeling for the felicities of his composition.'[49]

It is De Quincey, too, who writes, in connection with Coleridge's Latinity (in *Coleridge and Opium-Eating*):

'It is remarkable that Wordsworth, educated most negligently at Hawkshead School, subsequently, by reading the lyric poetry of Horace, simply for his own delight as a student of composition, made himself a master of Latinity in its most difficult form.'[50]

The reason given for Wordsworth's reading of Horace is evidently a mistake, since it contradicts the poet's own words; but with regard to the knowledge itself, De Quincey is doubtless an able judge.

I have been able to find but one dissenting voice on this question, and that is recorded in a letter from Charles Lloyd the younger to his father (1809), with reference to the latter's translations of Horace:

'Both Coleridge, Wordsworth, and Southey profess to admire thy translation of Homer very much, and often voluntarily introduce the subject in order to express their commendations; but, as a reason for omitting to obey thy injunction which applies equally to all three, I must inform thee that I know they have next to a contempt for Horace; and the best translations that could possibly be conceived of his verses would not, I believe, give them any pleasure.'

Lloyd then goes on to enumerate particular reasons for his not showing the translations to the three in question. Wordsworth 'is so much occupied . . . with a pamphlet which he has in the press on the Portuguese Convention'; Coleridge is 'miserable in mind and body'; Southey has 'an invincible dislike to Horace.' Of him alone is this said individually; and when we recall that Wordsworth's pamphlet bears on its title-page a long quotation from Horace, we are not inclined to attach great importance to Lloyd's inclusive statement.

But what in Horace especially appeals to Wordsworth? Why should the later poet speak of the earlier as 'my great favorite'? The full appreciation of poetry must be based upon a sympathy existing between author and reader. It remains to discover wherein lies this sympathy between the Roman and the English bards.

Wordsworth himself gives us the key to his preference when, in praising Horace, he speaks of his 'graceful modesty,' and of 'what he chooses to communicate of himself and his friends.' A further testimony is found in the poem called *Liberty* (ll. 96-110):

> Let easy mirth his social hours inspire,
> And fiction animate his sportive lyre,
> Attuned to verse that, crowning light Distress,
> With garlands, cheats her into happiness;
> Give *me* the humblest note of those sad strains
> Drawn forth by pressure of his gilded chains,
> As a chance-sunbeam from his memory fell
> Upon the Sabine farm he loved so well;
> Or when the prattle of Bandusia's spring
> Haunted his ear—he only listening—
> He proud to please, above all rivals, fit
> To win the palm of gaiety and wit;
> He, doubt not, with involuntary dread,
> Shrinking from each new favor to be shed,
> By the world's Ruler, on his honored head!

Here, then, is the Horace whom Wordsworth 'loved dearly'—not the humorist, nor the singer who strove to forget or cover up gloomy thoughts; not particularly, it would seem, the patriot deeply concerned for his country's welfare, nor the apostle of moderation and contentment, though in both interests the Roman poet and Wordsworth had much in common; but, above all, the lover of external nature, the bard who modestly considered his genius *tenuis grandia,* the conversational recorder of little daily happenings. Horace resting at ease beneath ilex or arbutus, listening to 'the prattle of Bandusia's spring' and resolving to immortalize it, or Horace watching the sun fall below the 'continuous mountains' which protected his farm, would have a peculiar attraction for the poet who sympathetically scrutinized celandine and daffodil, cuckoo and green linnet; and Horace spending a pleasant evening by his modest fireside, while out of doors the snow fell so deep that *nec iam sustineant onus silvae laborantes,* must seem near akin to the man who loved to sit

> In the loved presence of my cottage-fire,
> And listen to the flapping of the flame,
> Or kettle whispering its faint undersong.

One who says of himself,

> The moving accident is not my trade;
> To freeze the blood I have no ready arts:
> 'Tis my delight, alone in summer shade,
> To pipe a simple song for thinking hearts,

would be sure to admire the 'graceful modesty' of Horace as shown in the famous passage about the 'Matine bee,' and elsewhere. And above all, the things that Horace 'chooses to communicate of himself and his friends' would be appreciated by one who knew so well as Wordsworth the value of companionable friendship. This aspect of the English poet is often neglected; but we have only to read the letters of the Wordsworth family to realize that the circle of acquaintances which had its centre at Grasmere was held to this centre by ties unusually close. Just as Horace had for friends Maecenas, Virgil, Aristius Fuscus, so Wordsworth had the Beaumonts, Coleridge, Henry Crabb Robinson, and others. Moreover, the man who could write *The Prelude,* as well as other autobiographical poems (for Wordsworth also is very self-revealing), could not fail to enjoy the confidences of Horace about himself.

In view of all this, it is not surprising that we find Wordsworth the most Horatian of all the poets considered in this study. Others may quote more frequently; but it is he who appears most thoroughly to have assimilated the spirit of Horace. At times he seems actually to reproduce that spirit—or rather, the part of it which he especially admired.

## COLERIDGE

Very different is the case of Wordsworth's fellow-poet and friend, Coleridge. De Quincey points out (and doubtless truly enough, since his testimony is corroborated by what we know of the training afforded by Christ's Hospital) that the early linguistic studies of Coleridge were necessarily thorough and far-reaching; but he goes on to say:[51]

> 'Latin, from his regular scholastic training, naturally he read with a scholar's fluency; and indeed he read constantly in authors such as Petrarch, Erasmus, Calvin, etc., whose *prose* works he could not then have found in translations. But Coleridge had not cultivated an acquaintance with the delicacies of classic Latinity.'

In Coleridge's own high praise of his schoolmaster, the Reverend James Boyer, he makes no mention of having studied Horace at Christ's Hospital, save for an inclusive 'those [poets] of the Augustan era'; and indeed his only reference, so far as I have been able to discover, to his having used our poet as a text-book occurs in a letter, written to his brother from Cambridge (January 24, 1792), regarding a scholarship examination:

> 'The examination for my year is "the last book of Homer, and Horace's *De Arte Poetica*."'

Evidently any early acquaintance with Horace which he might have had made no deep impression on his mind, although three early poems—*Easter Holidays, Dura Navis,* and *Nil Pejus est Caelibe Vita,* all written in 1787—show traces of Horatian influence. But neither then nor later do we find evidence of any real fondness; in *Table Talk,* collected by Coleridge's nephew during the last years of the poet's life, virtually every well-known Latin author except Horace is discussed.

There are, however, in Coleridge's prose writings a few expressions of admiration for this poet. The most enthusiastic is from *A Lay Sermon:*

'I will refer you to the darling of the polished court of Augustus, to the man whose works have been in all ages deemed the models of good sense, and are still the pocket companions of those who pride themselves on uniting the scholar with the gentleman. This accomplished man of the world has given an account of the subjects of conversation between the illustrious statesmen who governed and the brightest luminaries who then adorned the empire of the civilized world.'[52]

The quotation from the **Satires** which follows leaves no room for doubt as to who is meant by 'this accomplished man of the world.' As for the qualities which Coleridge praises in Horace, they are the very ones which Wordsworth tells us did not appeal to him. Yet, generous as this praise is, there is something about it that does not ring true. It is as if the writer accepted the fact of Horace's excellence because it had been agreed upon by 'all ages,' but at the same time did not himself feel any of the things he was saying.

More spontaneous is a sentence from a letter to Thomas Poole (January 28, 1810):

'Read, for instance, Milton's prose tracts, and only *try* to conceive them translated into the style of *The Spectator,* or the finest part of Wordsworth's pamphlet. It would be less absurd to wish that the serious **Odes** of Horace had been written in the same style as his **Satires** and **Epistles.**'

We see from this that Coleridge realized that Horace had written serious poems—a fact which, as we know, many readers miss; and the implication is that he admired them, and considered their style suited to their subjects.

Again, we find Horace mentioned in Coleridge's notes on Luther's *Table Talk:*

'"Fulgentius [says Luther] is the best poet, and far above Horace both with sentences, fair speeches, and good actions; he is well worthy to be ranked and numbered with and among the poets."

'*Der Teufel!* Surely the epithets should be reversed. . . . The *super*-Horatian effulgence of Master Foolgentius! O Swan! thy critical cygnets are but goslings.'[53]

In criticizing Wordsworth's theory of poetic diction, Coleridge writes with reference to irrelevant particularization in composition:

'Nothing but biography can justify this. If it be admissible even in a *novel,* it must be one in the manner of De Foe's, that were meant to pass for histories, not in the manner of Fielding's. . . . Much less, then, can it be legitimately introduced in a *poem,* the characters of which, amid the strongest individualization, must still remain representative. The precepts of Horace on this point are grounded on the nature both of poetry and of the human mind. They are not more peremptory than wise and prudent.'[54]

This raises an interesting point. Coleridge the poet, as we shall further observe, seems not to have been particularly drawn to Horace the poet; but Coleridge the literary critic would not fail to be impressed by the value of Horace's criticism. This is also shown by another quotation from the *Biographia Literaria:*

'But it was as little objected by others as dreamt of by the poet [Southey] himself that he *preferred* careless and prosaic lines on rule and of forethought, or indeed that he pretended to any other art or theory of poetic diction besides that which we may all learn from Horace, Quintilian, the admirable dialogue *De Causis Corruptae Eloquentiae,* or Strada's *Prolusions.*'[55]

Here, then, is all the direct testimony that we have about Coleridge's feeling for Horace; for we can attach no importance to the statement of Charles Lloyd (see p. 26). When we turn to the indirect evidence afforded by the traces of Horace discernible in Coleridge's writings, two points are at once noticeable. First, these traces are nearly all quotations, and for the most part are found in the prose writings. Now Coleridge, like other Englishmen educated in public schools, liked to scatter fragments of Latin throughout his prose; and all the important Roman authors were grist for his mill. The second point is a corollary of the first: the influence of Horace on Coleridge's poetry is almost negligible. This is more truly the case with him than with any other poet we shall study, Keats alone excepted. It is not that Coleridge did not know Horace, but simply that he was not affected by him. The two men, in the capacity of poet, are utterly unlike. Coleridge, with his taste for the intricacies of German metaphysics, could hardly agree with Horace's Epicurean philosophy and his precepts for right living; and Coleridge's subjects for poetry are not those of Horace. Who can imagine the latter treating such material as that of *Christabel* or *The Rime of the Ancient Mariner?* Temperamentally the two were different; and accordingly the one did not to any appreciable extent react on the other. To Coleridge, Horace was 'the darling of the polished court of Augustus,' and little more.

### Byron

When we turn to Byron, we find that most of those who know anything of his opinions about Horace know them by only one line:

Then farewell, Horace—whom I hated so.[56]

Thus the poet receives an undeserved reputation for absolute scorn of Horace—a reputation which would never be his if his detractors would read no more than the context of the line. I quote here the three stanzas which contain the complete thought:

> These hills seem things of lesser dignity;
>    All, save the lone Soracte's height, displayed
> Not *now* in snow, which asks the lyric Roman's aid
>
> For our remembrance, and from out the plain
>    Heaves like a long-swept wave about to break,
>    And on the curl hangs pausing: not in vain
> May he who will his recollections rake,
>    And quote in classic raptures, and awake
> The hills with Latin echoes—I abhorred
>    Too much to conquer for the Poet's sake
> The drilled dull lesson, forced down word by word
> In my repugnant youth, with pleasure to record
>
>    Aught that recalls the daily drug which turned
>       My sickening memory; and, though Time hath taught
>    My mind to meditate what then it learned,
>       Yet such the fixed inveteracy wrought
>       By the impatience of my early thought,
>    That, with the freshness wearing out before
>       My mind could relish what it might have sought,
> If free to choose, I cannot now restore
> Its health—but what it then detested, still abhor.
>
>    Then farewell, Horace—whom I hated so,
>    Not for thy faults, but mine: it is a curse
>    To understand, not feel thy lyric flow,
>    To comprehend, but never love thy verse;
>    Although no deeper Moralist rehearse
>    Our little life, nor Bard prescribe his art,
>    Nor livelier Satirist the conscience pierce,
>    Awakening without wounding the touched heart,
>    Yet fare thee well—upon Soracte's ridge we part.

This serves to explain any positive dislike that Byron manifests for Horace; it lies rooted in the memory of school-days, when studying Latin was a required task. Years afterward we find Tennyson making the same complaint; but Tennyson outgrew his distaste, while Byron, it would seem, never did. Moore says:

> 'It was not till released from the duty of reading Virgil as a task that Gray could feel himself capable of enjoying the beauties of that poet; and Lord Byron was, to the last, unable to vanquish a similar prepossession with which the same sort of school association had inoculated him against Horace.'[57]

Yet it is dangerous to accept the statement without qualification. It is never safe to judge a man on partial evidence; and it is doubly unsafe in the case of Byron, who wrote impulsively, and whose opinions were so changeful that after reading his most positive assertions we find ourselves asking: 'Will he have the same feeling the next day?' To take a single instance, we find him writing to Murray, after the publication of Keats' *Hyperion*:

> 'Here are [*sic*] Johnny Keats' . . . poetry. . . . Pray send me *no more* poetry but what is rare and decidedly

good. There is such a trash of Keats and the like upon my tables that I am ashamed to look at them. . . . No more Keats, I entreat:—flay him alive; if you don't, I must skin him myself: there is no bearing the drivelling idiotism of the Manikin.'

A year later he writes:

> 'My indignation at Mr. Keats' depreciation of Pope has hardly permitted me to do justice to his own genius, which, *malgré* all the fantastic fopperies of his style, was undoubtedly of great promise. His fragment of *Hyperion* seems actually inspired by the Titans, and is as sublime as Aeschylus. He is a loss to our literature.'

Nevertheless, though it is difficult to say anything definite about the opinions of a man who was so unstable, it is probably true that Byron never greatly cared for Horace, and this despite the fact that he quotes him copiously. As we have seen, the English poet was forced into a close acquaintance with Latin at Harrow; and that 'almost preternatural' memory of his, of which Mary Shelley speaks, permanently recorded these early impressions, though often, let us add, inexactly. It is not strange, then, that we find him writing on the fly-leaf of his *Scriptores Graeci*,[58] where were inscribed the names of some old friends at school:

> Eheu fugaces, Postume, Postume,
> Labuntur anni;

and he scattered phrases from Horace through his correspondence. Occasionally he gives the reference for his quotation, showing that he did not always disdain verifying, despite his youthful vaunt in his *List of Historical Writers whose Works I Have Perused in Different Languages* (1807): 'Greek and Latin without number;—these last I shall give up in future.'[59]

Notwithstanding these frequent quotations, Byron seems always to speak of Horace in a rather patronizing manner. 'The great little poet,' he calls him in *Don Juan* (14. 77); and in spite of the regret expressed in the passage from *Childe Harold* (above, pp. 31-32), we cannot help feeling that the 'curse' is one to which Byron willingly submits, indeed taking some pride in his idiosyncrasy. The 'lyric flow' of Horace he never attains, even at his best, and therefore it was inevitable, considering the kind of man he was, that he should underrate it. It is characteristic of Byron to be careless in his use of language, both as regards sound and sense. He wrote easily and rapidly—*in hora saepe ducentos versus dictabat stans pede in uno*, as Horace says of Lucilius; and he could not appreciate the exquisite skill and pains with which the other molded his verse. He would rather scorn such care for detail; and although he could paraphrase the **Ars Poetica,** he could not benefit by all its precepts.

All this bears upon Horace as a lyric poet. When we come to the second division of his work, there is another story to tell. It is significant that the praise given in *Childe*

*Harold* is to Horace the 'moralist,' the 'satirist,' and the 'prescriber of his art.' In other words, Byron cared most for the **Epistles,** the **Satires,** and the **Ars Poetica.**

Byron himself was a satirist of extraordinary power. *Don Juan,* generally conceded to be his greatest work, is mainly satirical; and many of his other poems belong to this *genre.* We are at once led to ask whether these satires show the spirit of Horace—that spirit which, as we have seen, preferred argument to invective. But the answer to such a question must be negative. Byron could comment admiringly on Horace's power of 'awakening without wounding the touched heart'; but when he himself came to deal with the things in the universe to which he objected, he was usually as savage as Juvenal or Persius. Either he adopted a cynical attitude towards the follies of mankind, or he loosed himself from all restraint, and launched forth into bitterness which a century after makes us wince. Horace nearly always refers to the poets of his time with great generosity, and when he finds fault does it without leaving a sting; we cannot imagine him uttering the insults which Byron heaped upon Wordsworth, upon Keats, and above all upon Southey—but indeed, upon almost all contemporary men of letters.

We now come to the closest approach of Byron to Horace—the *Hints from Horace,* a paraphrase of the **Ars Poetica.** Byron took a greater interest in this than in any of his other works. 'I look upon it and my Pulci as by far the best things of my doing,' he writes to Murray in 1821, ten years after making the paraphrase; and he shows unwonted eagerness about the proof-sheets of it. Moore, too, mentions this 'preference of the Horatian Paraphrase.'[60]

It seems strange enough that so negligent an artist as Byron should choose to work with a theory of poetry; but it becomes less strange when we read the *Hints.* In the precepts for writing, Byron in general merely translates Horace, making good his boast, found in a letter to Murray, of his fidelity to the original. He substitutes names, but not ideas; he is simply transcribing precepts which he himself usually honors in the breach. But frequently he uses the Horatian maxims to introduce digressions of his own, and these are pure Byronic satire. The interpolations constitute a large part of the poem, and make it rather a piece of bitter satirical verse than an epistle about literature, with only an incidental element of mild satire, as is the original. The *Hints from Horace,* therefore, so far from being really Horatian in tone, rather serves to accentuate Byron's lack of sympathy with Horace.

That, indeed, there was a lack we cannot doubt. Byron knew Horace widely, but superficially. He never realized the true value of the Roman poet in the world's literature. He was proud of paraphrasing the **Ars Poetica,** because he considered it 'the most difficult poem in the language';[61] but he looked upon it rather as a vehicle for personal satire than a treatise to be studied and followed. And aside from it and an indifferent early translation of part of the famous ode **Iustum et tenacem,** the many traces of Horace

found in his poems are nearly all chance phrases, quoted either in Latin or in English. They are, on the whole, external embellishments, not real elements of the poet's work; in perhaps every case they are consciously and deliberately used. We cannot refuse to believe Byron when he tells us that he could never love the verse of Horace; we may doubt the other part of the statement—that he comprehended it, in the sense in which he uses the word. Yet, as I have tried to show, we are mistaken if we take the 'hated so' as literal and abiding.

## SHELLEY

If we should attempt—and the attempt has been made—to divide English poets into two classes, calling one class Greeks, and the other Romans, according to their characteristics and the influences to which they have responded, we should unhesitatingly put Byron among the Romans; and just as unhesitatingly we should place the poet whose name is oftenest associated with his—Shelley—with the Greeks. Nor should we make a mistake in this: Shelley's work is decidedly more Greek than Latin, and to him the literature and ideals of Greece meant more than those of any other nation. 'You see how ill I follow the maxim of Horace,' he writes to Thomas Love Peacock (January 26, 1819), 'at least in its literal sense: *nil admirari*—which I should say, *prope res est una*—to prevent there ever being anything admirable in the world.' And then rashly, 'Fortunately Plato is of my opinion; and I had rather err with Plato than be right with Horace.' And in the preface to *Hellas* he says:

> 'We are all Greeks. Our laws, our literature, our religion, our arts have their root in Greece. But for Greece, Rome, the instructor, the conqueror, or the metropolis of our ancestors, would have spread no illumination with her arms, and we might still have been savages and idolaters.'

Yet we must not forget that Shelley for a great part, if not all, of his life knew Latin much better than Greek, and that his early training, like that of all Englishmen educated in the public schools of his day, placed far greater emphasis on the language and literature of the Romans. We are told that early in his married life, 'whilst reading Greek classics with the help of "cribs," he [was] teaching Harriet Latin so as to give her a general notion of Horace's **Odes** and Ovid's *Metamorphoses.*'[62] And though he later became so expert in Greek as to make many fine translations, he never forgot Latin in his preference for the other tongue. He writes in the preface to *The Revolt of Islam:*

> 'The poetry of ancient Greece and Rome and modern Italy and our own country has been to me, like external nature, a passion and an enjoyment.'

That he knew Horace well there is abundant evidence; and we also learn that his acquaintance with the Roman poet was not confined to his school-days. We have already seen that he read the **Odes** with Harriet. In later years Horace appears in the list of books which were at once his study and pleasure, along with Aeschylus, Aristophanes, Theocritus, Xenophon, Herodotus, Lucian, and Virgil.[63] It is true that he never ranks Horace with the great names of Greek literature; in the *Defense of Poetry* he says that 'Horace, Catullus, Ovid, and generally the other great writers of the Virgilian age saw man and nature in the mirror of Greece.' Yet that he does give him a high place in literature is implied by a paragraph in the preface to *Prometheus Unbound*:

> 'Poets . . . are, in one sense, the creators, and, in another, the creations, of their age. From this subjection the loftiest do not escape. There is a similarity between Homer and Hesiod, between Aeschylus and Euripides, between Virgil and Horace, between Dante and Petrarch, between Shakespeare and Fletcher, between Dryden and Pope.'

And again, in the *Defense of Poetry:*

> 'Let us for a moment stoop to the arbitration of popular breath, and . . . let us decide without trial, testimony, or form, that certain of those who are "there sitting where we dare not soar" are reprehensible. Let us assume that Homer was a drunkard, that Virgil was a flatterer, that Horace was a coward. . . . Posterity has done ample justice to the great names now referred to.'

This placing of Horace among the greatest men in literature is doing him greater justice than ever came from Byron or Coleridge. Indeed, it was inevitable that Shelley, with his wonderful lyric gift, should appreciate the felicity of expression, the melody of language and cadence, of his Roman predecessor. It is noteworthy that he always considers Horace in the capacity of lyric poet. In the preface to *The Revolt of Islam* he says:

> 'Poetry and the art which professes to regulate and limit its powers cannot subsist together. Longinus could not have been the contemporary of Homer, nor Boileau of Horace.'

He here deliberately disregards Horace as a literary critic, although on occasion he quotes the **Ars Poetica**. Most of his citations, however, are from the **Odes;** and in nearly every echo of Horace other than quotation which we find in Shelley's works the influence comes from the lyric poetry. It is unnecessary to remark that to such echoes we must look for a real accord between two poets. Quotation is a more or less artificial thing; we all quote the writers with whom we happen to be most familiar, rather than those for whom we care most—though often, of course, the two classes coincide. But when one poet incorporates the thoughts or expressions of another into his own work, making them a part of himself, so to speak, we may be sure that the two possess some bond of fellowship.

Now this is just what Shelley does, to a limited extent, with the lyrics of Horace. Fundamentally the two men were very different. Shelley would never, after fighting on the side of Brutus at Philippi, have settled down in Rome and enjoyed the patronage of Augustus; Horace would never have attempted to excite the Irish by throwing handbills out of the windows to them. Horace was naturally an Epicurean; Shelley was steeped in Platonic and neo-Platonic doctrines. But since both were lyric poets, Shelley could appreciate Horace's gift of expression. He probably could not appreciate it so fully as could a more careful artist like Tennyson; but his poetic feeling showed him something of its beauty, and to that extent he was influenced by Horace more truly than was the case with Byron.

KEATS

The traces of Horace in the works of Keats are so slight as to be virtually negligible. In the entire body of his poetry I have been able to find no certain proof of an acquaintance with the Roman poet; and the two or three chance phrases in his letters might have been picked up from various sources. Fortunately there is a sentence from a letter to John Hamilton Reynolds (February, 1820) which proves that Keats had read for himself at least a part of Horace:

> 'If I were well enough, I would paraphrase an ode of Horace's for you, on your embarking in the seventy years ago style. The packet will bear a comparison with a Roman galley, at any rate.'

This paraphrase of Horace's *proempticon* was probably never made; but the reference to the ode (1. 3) shows that Keats knew it. Whether he, like most of the other poets included in the present study, made his first acquaintance with Horace in his school-days is doubtful, for his early education was not thorough. It is probable that he never read Latin with much ease. 'When I have done this language [Italian] so as to be able to read it tolerably well,' he writes to his brother George in September, 1819, 'I shall set myself to get complete in Latin, and there my learning must stop. . . . I would not go so far if I were not persuaded of the power the language gives me.' It was his life which stopped rather than his learning, and he probably was unable to carry out his intention of 'getting complete' in Latin. Yet among the books that he left was a copy of *Auctores Mythographi Latini* which showed signs of having been used—and in one place, at least, misunderstood.[64]

But we cannot ascribe Keats' freedom from Horatian influence altogether to his incomplete knowledge of Latin; for, although he knew no Greek at all, his work was greatly influenced by translations from that language. As truly as Shelley, though in a different way, he was a 'Greek'; perhaps this is one reason why Latin literature did not especially attract him. 'I have loved the principle of beauty in all things,' he wrote to Fanny Brawne—a sentence which manifests the Hellenic spirit as we now regard it. It is the principle on which all his best poetry is founded, and it is not distinctively Roman.

Then, too, Keats consciously endeavored to avoid foreign influence. To his brother George he wrote (September, 1819):

'I shall never become attached to a foreign idiom so as to put it into my writings. The *Paradise Lost,* though so fine in itself, is a corruption of our language. . . . Miltonic verse cannot be written, but is the verse of art. I wish to devote myself to another verse alone.'

It is idle to speculate whether Keats would have outgrown these youthful notions—whether he would really have perfected himself in Latin, and thus have come to a fuller appreciation of the worth of its literature. The time he longed for was denied him; he died, leaving work of great value and of still greater promise.

We may say, then, that Keats' knowledge of Latin was probably insufficient to let him appreciate the quality in Horace that attracted Shelley—beautiful diction and rhythm; and that, for the rest, Keats was too remote in temperament from the other to enjoy him greatly. The things he cared for were not those for which Horace cared; hence we find no Horatian element in his poetry.

### TENNYSON

In 1850, when Wordsworth died, the last as well as the first of that generation of poets, the office of Poet Laureate was conferred upon Tennyson; and by an interesting coincidence, the second Laureate among our seven poets stands immediately after the first in point of the influence exerted upon him by Horace.

There are several reasons for this. In the first place, Tennyson received the customary classical education of the sons of English gentlemen, but, unlike many boys so educated, responded well to it, so that his works show a wide knowledge of all the great Latin poets. It is significant that the author in whom he was most thoroughly grounded in his boyhood was Horace. Then, too, among all English writers none is more careful in the use of his medium than Tennyson. He worked over his verses with the care of a scholar joined to the sensibility of an artist, always striving for felicity of expression and beauty of diction; he suppressed poems when he came to feel that they did not do him justice, until one can hardly make sure that one has studied the entire body even of his published work. It was inevitable that so painstaking a workman should admire the skill of the greatest Latin master of poetical technique; indeed, we shall find him frequently expressing his admiration for the art of Horace. Furthermore, the two poets have many characteristics in common. Though Tennyson's philosophy of life is loftier than that of Horace, he, too, believes in moderation and simplicity. He, too, loved external nature—not, as did Keats, for its sheer sensuous beauty, nor as did Shelley, for the spirit which he felt to be incorporated in it, but rather as did Horace, and, usually, Wordsworth—for the calm comfort and enjoyment which he received from it. And he, too, shows in his poetry a vein of melancholy, which is not relieved, however, by so genial a strain of humor as is the Roman poet's.

Tennyson's first acquaintance with Horace did not promise any great future liking. 'My father,' writes Hallam Tennyson, 'said that he himself received a good but not a regular classical education. At any rate he became an accurate scholar, the author "thoroughly drummed" into him being Horace; whom he disliked in proportion. He would lament: "They use *me* as a lesson-book at schools, and they will call me 'that horrible Tennyson.' It was not till many years after boyhood that I could like Horace. Byron expressed what I felt: 'Then farewell, Horace, whom I hated so.' Indeed I was so overdosed with Horace that I hardly do him justice even now that I am old."'[65]

If it was an overdose, it nevertheless was productive of good results, as the event showed. Had we only this single expression from Tennyson about Horace, we should know that he came to appreciate the Latin poet. For a man's words, which are but the record of passing moods, are not of so much account as his actions; and no student of Horace can read Tennyson without realizing that the later poet cared much for the earlier.

That his fondness, however, came comparatively late in life is again made clear by his son, who quotes the poet as saying:

> "'X—has said that Tennyson told him that Horace and Keats were his two masters. X—must have misunderstood,'" and adds: 'He did not care for Horace at all until after he was thirty. He had said "Horace and Keats are masters."'[66]

William Allingham corroborates this. He tells us that Tennyson said to him: 'I never appreciated Horace until I was forty.'[67]

There is abundant evidence of Tennyson's admiration of some of Horace's metres. Palgrave, in his recollections of Tennyson, records that 'he [was] deeply moved by the Roman dignity which Horace has imparted to the Sapphic in the *Non enim gazae; . . .* although,' he adds, 'in general Tennyson did not admire the Horatian treatment of that metre, which he would audaciously define, alluding to the Adonic fourth line, as "like a pig with its tail tightly curled."'[68]

But for the Alcaics of Horace he has only praise. In his own note to *The Daisy* he says: 'In a metre which I invented, representing in some measure the grandest of metres, the Horatian Alcaic.' His son also refers to this: 'He was proud of the metre of *The Daisy,* which he called a far-off echo of the Horatian Alcaic.'[69]

The poet makes the following note to his own *Alcaics:*

> 'My Alcaics are not intended for Horatian Alcaics, nor are Horace's Alcaics the Greek Alcaics, nor are his Sapphics, which are vastly inferior to Sappho's, the Greek Sapphics. The Horatian Alcaic is perhaps the stateliest metre in the world except the Virgillian hexameter at its best. . . . I did once begin an Horatian Alcaic Ode to a great painter, of which I only recollect one line:

> Munificently rewarded Artist.'

Hallam Tennyson, in his journal for March 17, 1890, writes of his father:

> 'He had all but recovered from his influenza, and sat in the sun in front of the study window, and read Jebb's *Homer;* quoted *Virtus repulsae nescia sordidae,* and dwelt on the stateliness imparted by Horace to the Alcaic stanza.'[70]

This quoting from Horace in conversation would seem to have been no infrequent thing. For instance, Hallam Tennyson notes (April 10, 1892):

> 'My father and Warren walked in the ball-room. My father quoted the line of Horace,
>
> Nec satis est pulchra esse poemata, dulcia sunto,
>
and asked Warren to explain it.'[71]

It is evident that Tennyson's early and thorough grounding in Horace did not give him, in his own opinion, a sufficient knowledge to last through life; for Hallam Tennyson says, in describing the journey to Italy in 1851:

> 'He took with him his usual traveling companions, Shakespeare, Milton, Homer, Virgil, Horace, Pindar, Theocritus, and probably the *Divina Commedia* and Goethe's *Gedichte.*'[72]

Truly an illustrious group of travelers! It is pleasant to fancy Tennyson reading Horace on the soil of that Italy dearer to the Latin poet than

> claram Rhodon aut Mytilenen
> Aut Epheson bimarisve Corinthi
> Moenia vel Baccho Thebas vel Apolline Delphos
> Insignis aut Thessala Tempe.[73]

Nor did Tennyson's early training cause him to refrain from teaching Horace to his own sons while they were children. 'The first Latin I learnt from him,' writes his son Hallam, 'was Horace's *O fons Bandusiae.*'[74]

There are other witnesses to Tennyson's admiration for Horace. Allingham says that Tennyson remarked to him: 'Catullus, Horace, and the others gave only their best.'[75]

In Palgrave's personal recollections of Tennyson we read: 'Much as he loved Horace, he rose above the epigrammatic narrowness of his brilliant *Non di, non homines.*'[76]

And Palgrave records another allusion to Horace by the poet:

> '"The poet's work is his life, and no one has a right to ask for more," he would always say; reaching once even the barbarity, as I could not help calling it, that if Horace had left an autobiography, and the single manuscript were in his hands, he would throw it into the fire.'[77]

This, let us observe, is different from the well-known attitude of Browning. The latter discountenances any expectation by the public that a poet will reveal his own personality through his works; Tennyson's objection is to inquiries about the poet *outside* of his works. But that his objection was not absolute is proved by his having consented to the writing of his memoir by his son.

We must now observe an utterance of Tennyson which would seem at first thought to be in opposition to an inquiry like the present. The poet says, in his introductory notes to *The Princess:*

> 'There is, I fear, a prosaic set growing up among us, editors of booklets, book-worms, index-hunters, or men of great memories and no imagination, who *impute themselves* to the poet, and so believe that *he,* too, has no imagination, but is for ever poking his nose between the pages of some old volume in order to see what he can appropriate. They will not allow one . . . even to use such a simple expression as the ocean "roars," without finding out the precise verse in Homer or Horace from which we have plagiarized it.'

The same example is given by Hallam Tennyson:

> 'He himself had been "most absurdly accused of plagiarizing," e.g., "The moanings of the homeless sea," "moanings" from Horace, "homeless" from Shelley. "As if no one else had heard the sea moan except Horace."'[78]

Evidently this particular charge had made an unpleasant impression on Tennyson. Yet that his objection would have extended to a study such as the present I cannot believe. Indeed, he himself leans to the contrary position when he says, a few lines above the passage first quoted:

> 'Far indeed am I from asserting that books as well as Nature are not, and ought not to be, suggestive to the poet. I am sure that I myself, and many others, find a peculiar charm in those passages of such great masters as Virgil or Milton where they adopt the creation of a bygone poet, and reclothe it, more or less, according to their own fancy.'

Now with just such instances as these the present study aims to deal. It was not undertaken with the purpose of picking out trivial chance resemblances between Horace and other poets, in order to substantiate a charge of plagiarism; the purpose is rather to find the 'reclothings' of which Tennyson speaks, and from them to infer the influence of Horace upon a great epoch of English poetry. 'My paraphrases of certain Latin and Greek lines seem too obvious to be mentioned,' says Tennyson in the brief prefatory notes to his collected works. No one would accuse him of plagiarism on account of such paraphrases; yet from them can be gleaned material of value about his tastes in literature. According to his own statement, a poet should be known by his works.

Such characteristics as Horace and Tennyson have in common have frequently been noticed by others. C. S. Calverley[79] calls attention to one group:

> 'Between Horace, especially, and the modern poet there exist, we think, in point of style and workmanship, many similarities. A stanza of *In Memoriam* is a thing

compact, *teres atque rotundus,* as is a stanza in a Horatian ode. Both writers are equally intolerant of any but the right word, and both have the gift of making it fit into its place apparently by a happy accident. The condensed phraseology, the abruptness, the ease (attained probably *per laborem plurimum,* until art became a second nature) which characterize the *Odes* of Horace characterize the cantos, so to call them, of *In Memoriam.* Even Mr. Tennyson's compound epithets are paralleled, and more than paralleled, in Horace.'

To turn from similarities of technique to similarities of temperament, we find Andrew Lang[80] saying of Tennyson: 'He constantly reminds us of Virgil, Homer, Theocritus, and even Persius and Horace.'

And though the coupling of Horace with Persius would indicate that Lang had Horace the satirist in mind, the truth is that Tennyson even more often reminds us of Horace the lyrist. As Palgrave, says:[81]

> 'It was, indeed, more than most poets that Tennyson (as justly has been remarked about Horace) felt the two impulses described by M. Arnold, one driving the poet "to the world without" and "one to solitude"; although the happier circumstances of Tennyson's life allowed him less of Rome and more of Tibur and the Sabine farm than fell to the lot of the great Italian.'

But more convincing than any of these statements, I venture to hope, will be an examination of the actual resemblances found between the poetry of Horace and that of Tennyson, since they are so many, and so much a part of the latter's work.

### BROWNING

Browning, the son of cultivated and talented parents, had every opportunity to form an early acquaintance with Horace. His father, we are told, 'knew by heart . . . all the *Odes* of Horace,'[82] and he could hardly have failed to make his son familiar with a favorite author. When the poet was twelve years old, his uncle, Reuben Browning, presented him with Christopher Smart's translation of Horace[83]—a version which, though not always felicitous, has the advantage of being in prose, and is fairly accurate. Browning may have been thinking of this gift when, more than sixty years later, in his *Parleyings with Certain People of Importance* (*Parleyings with Christopher Smart*), he mentioned as an 'unsightly bough':

> Smart's who translated Horace.

But it is unlikely that the poet did not know something of Horace long before he was twelve—and that, too, in no translation, but in the original Latin. His biographer, William Sharp, says (though I have not been able to find other authority for the statement) that Browning at the age of eight 'began to translate the simpler odes of Horace.'[84] These early translations, as well as the Horatian ode which Sharp in the same paragraph tells us the ten-year-old Browning wrote in honor of his first sweetheart, have

disappeared, with the rest of the poet's juvenile efforts. The only translation of any considerable portion of Horace found in Browning's extant works (the version of part of *Carm.* 1. 3 in *Fifine at the Fair*) is literal and accurate.

For better evidence of Browning's knowledge of Horace we turn to his own poetry, where on occasion he quotes the Roman with a fluency and readiness equalled by few. We are almost inclined to attribute to him his father's extraordinary acquaintance with our poet, so easily do the phrases come to him—and phrases not always the most familiar. Yet mark that it is 'on occasion.' In large proportion, the numerous citations from Horace in Browning's poems are found in the ninth and tenth books of *The Ring and the Book*[85]—comprising the briefs of the two advocates. The poet, able to quote to an unlimited extent when he so desires, is equally able to suppress any trace of Horace for hundreds of pages.

There is an explanation for this. Browning is one of those authors who are little given to self-revelation; he disapproves of a poet's 'unlocking his heart' to a curious world—'if so, the less Shakespeare he!' As for himself, he seldom speaks *in propria persona* in his poems. In fact, although Browning's finest work is not found in his plays, his genius is essentially dramatic so far as regards treatment of character. The poet has the faculty of altogether identifying himself, Robert Browning, with Fra Lippo Lippi, or with the duke who exhibits his dead wife's picture, or with the dying bishop. We do not even know the names of many of his personages; but we do know the persons, and the workings of their minds and souls, as we do not know their creator. Generalities, of course, we can determine; as the fact that Browning was more interested in the inner nature of human beings than in anything else in the universe. But what were his own thoughts and feelings about many subjects on which he writes must remain a blank to us. So it is that when he is impersonating Dominus Hyacinthus de Archangelis, or Juris Doctor Johannes-Baptista Bottinius, he quotes a great deal of Horace because it seems appropriate that these advocates steeped in Latin should be for ever showing their classical erudition; whereas, when he turns to other characters, he endows them with other knowledge, or with none at all, to suit his purpose.

We must allow, then, that the large amount of Horace found in Browning is for the most part not a characteristic element in his work. Indeed, Browning was really little influenced by any one. Sources he often had and used, of course; but of genuine influence upon his poetry, such as that of Milton upon Wordsworth, or of Spenser upon Keats, there is almost none. Browning—though it may sound rather paradoxical after all that has been said—is emphatically himself; rarely can a line of his poetry be mistaken for the work of any one else. In his letters, where, if anywhere, we look for the real Robert Browning, he seldom quotes; it is as if he had so much of his own to say that what others have said does not occur to him. The same reason explains the rapidity with which he wrote—a rapidity which sometimes lends support to the charge of obscurity, and which certainly is foreign to Horace. Unlike Horace, too, are the self-concealment which we have noticed, and the buoyant optimism which recurs so constantly that we can safely point to it as one of Browning's characteristics. Though at first thought we might say the two poets were alike in their deep interest in human nature, we soon see that even here their attitudes are different: Horace is interested in what he sees the men about him doing; Browning cares for their deeds only in so far as they reveal their thoughts and help him to understand their souls. With him, in very truth, ''tis not what man does that exalts him, but what man would do.'

With Browning we reach the last of the great English poets of the nineteenth century. Many lesser singers there were, but none who could rank with the seven here discussed. Nor are these all of equal merit; yet each plays a considerable part in the literature of his country, and for the present, at least, demands our attention. No one can predict what the judgment of succeeding ages may be. Horace's place in the world's culture is secure; but these others 'abide our question.' Not all of them, as we have seen, cared for Horace or understood him; but all knew him, and almost all used him. His manysidedness, which after all is his chief claim to distinction, makes it virtually impossible for any one person to appreciate him fully. Yet it also gives nearly every one something in common with him, and ensures the permanence of his fame, which has indeed been *aere perennius*.

### DETAILS CONCERNING THIS STUDY

The following pages record the resemblances I have found between Horace and the seven poets. In making this record I have, except in cases where there are other obvious traces, disregarded such commonplaces as 'the golden mean,' 'the man of fixed and virtuous will,' the immortality conferred by poetry, and so on, since these have been so often used as to be no longer the property of Horace, but of the world. I have also refrained from citing chance Horace-like phrases in the prose of Byron and Coleridge; these two were so prone to scatter fragments of Latin—often only a word or two—throughout their writings that we cannot justly ascribe every such occurrence to the influence of a particular Latin author. The habit merely shows a facile memory providing a familiar catchword. All the important citations in their prose I have noted; and, of course, every one, no matter how slight, in their poetry. Finally, I have normalized the spelling and punctuation of all quotations throughout the thesis, except where the poets themselves quote Horace inexactly; in all such cases I have noted the deviation from the accepted text.

### Notes

1. *A Literary History of Rome,* p. 496.

2. *Lectures on Poetry,* tr. E. K. Francis, 2. 467 ff.

3. If we are to live in accordance with nature, and first of all are to hunt for a spot to build a house, do you know a place preferable to the prosperous country? Is there any place where the winters are milder? Is there any place where carking care less disturbs our sleep? Does grass smell less sweet or look less beautiful than pavements? Is water which tries to burst its pipes in the streets purer than that which hurries murmuring down its channel? Why, even among columns of variegated marble trees are tended, and a house which has a view of far-away fields is praised. You may drive out nature with a pitchfork, but she will ever return. (*Epist.* 1. 10. 12-24.)

4. *Horace and the Elegiac Poets,* p. 3.

5. The snow has fled away, grass now returns to the fields, and leaves to the trees. The Grace, with the Nymphs and her own twin sisters, ventures unrobed to lead the choric dance. 'Do not hope for immortality,' is the warning of the year and the hour which snatches from us the cheerful day. Swift-changing moons repair their wanings; but when we have once departed to where pious Aeneas and rich Tullus and Ancus have gone before, we are but dust and shadow. (*Carm.* 4. 7. 1-16.)

6. Sharp winter is driven away by the grateful coming of spring and the soft breeze. Now is the time to wreathe shining heads with myrtle or flowers borne by the freed earth; now is the time in shady groves to make offering to Faunus of a lamb if he ask it, or if he like better, of a kid. Pale death strikes with impartial foot the huts of poor men and the palaces of kings. The brief span of life forbids us, happy Sestius, to lay the foundation of a long hope. (*Carm.* 1. 4. 1-15.)

7. Lay hold upon to-day, trusting nothing to to-morrow. (*Carm.* 1. 11. 8.)

8. I hate the pomp and circumstance of the Persians. (*Carm.* 1. 38. 1.)

9. You will drink cheap Sabine wine from modest measures. The Falernian vines and the slopes of Formiae do not flavor my cups. (*Carm.* 1. 20. 1-12.)

10. Olives are my food, and chicory and wholesome mallows. (*Carm.* 1. 31. 15-16.)

11. Not ivory nor golden ceiling shines resplendent in my house. I ask nothing more of the gods, nor do I importune further my powerful friend, happy enough with just my Sabine farm. (*Carm.* 2. 18. 1-14.)

12. A stream of pure water and a wood of a few acres and a sure reliance on my crops is a truer happiness than the brilliant lot of the lord of fertile Africa, unconscious of it though he be. (*Carm.* 3. 16. 29-32.)

13. If nature commanded us to go back from a certain time over our lives again, and to choose whatever other parents each of us would wish for himself according to his pride, I, content with my own, would not want to select new ones honored with state offices. (*Serm.* 1. 6. 93-97.)

14. This was my prayer: a piece of ground not too large, where there was a garden and a spring of ever-flowing water near the house, and, besides, a little woodland. The gods have done better and more abundantly than this. It is well. I ask nothing more, O son of Maia, except that thou make these gifts permanently mine. (*Serm.* 2. 6. 1-5.)

15. What do you think, my friend, that I pray? That I may have what now is mine, or even less. (*Epist.* 1. 18. 104-107.)

16. How Soracte stands white with deep snow. (*Carm.* 1. 9. 1-2.)

17. Thou also shalt become one of the renowned founts through my singing. (*Carm.* 3. 13. 13-14.)

18. The waters flowing through fertile Tibur and the tangled foliage of the groves shall make him renowned for Aeolian song. (*Carm.* 4. 3. 10-12.)

19. Romulus, or the peaceful reign of Pompilius, or the proud emblems of Tarquin, or Cato's noble death. (*Carm.* 1. 12. 33-36.)

20. What thou owest, O Rome, to the house of Nero the river Metaurus bears witness, and the vanquished Hasdrubal, and the day made beautiful by the driving of darkness from Latium, the first day that smiled with sweet victory since the dread African rode through the cities of Italy as fire goes through pitch-pine or the east wind through the Sicilian waves. The race which bravely bore from the ashes of Ilium to the Ausonian cities its shrines, storm-tossed on Tuscan waters, and its children and old fathers, like an ilex-tree shorn of its branches by cruel axes in Algidus the bearer of dark leaves, draws strength and courage, through losses and wounds, from the sword itself. (*Carm.* 4. 4. 37-60.)

21. Now on sea and land the Mede fears our powerful bands and our Alban axes; now the Scythians, but lately so arrogant, and the Indians, beg to know our wishes. Now Faith and Peace and Honor and old-time Modesty and neglected Virtue dare to return, and happy Plenty appears with full horn. (*Carm. Saec.* 53-60.)

22. The neglected gods have showered many evils upon sorrowful Italy. Already Monaeses and the band of Pacorus have twice crushed our unlucky attacks, and rejoice in having added to their slender necklaces our booty. The Dacian and the Ethiop have nearly destroyed our city racked by rebellion. The age, steeped in guilt, has first polluted wedlock and the race and the home. Calamity, sprung from this source, has overflowed the country and the people. It was not a young manhood born of parents like these that dyed the sea with the blood of Carthage and killed Pyrrhus and great Antiochus and dread Hannibal. (*Carm.* 3. 6. 7-36.)

23. He who does not defend his friend against another's blame is evil; beware of him, Roman. (*Serm.* 1. 4. 81-85.)

24. Just as in the case of a father and his son, we ought not to despise a friend because he has some fault. (*Serm.* 1. 3. 43-44.)

25. I have sworn no false oath: we shall go, whenever you lead the way, we shall go ready to take our last journey as comrades. (*Carm.* 2. 17. 9-12.)

26. Return him safe, I pray, and preserve the half of my soul. (*Carm.* 1. 3. 7-8.)

27. I was the first to import Parian iambics into Italy, imitating the numbers and the spirit of Archilochus. (*Epist.* 1. 19. 23-25.)

28. It is not enough to write a verse in correct language, when if you take it to pieces you find that anybody might storm like the father in the play. (*Serm.* 1. 4. 54-56.)

29. To him who has genius, to him who has a more god-like mind and a tongue made to speak lofty things, give the honor of this name [poet]. (*Serm.* 1. 4. 43-44.)

30. If anybody writes, as I do, things more like ordinary talk, don't think he is a poet. (*Serm.* 1. 4. 41-42.)

31. I shall not wholly die. Gladly, Melpomene, wreathe my locks with the Delphic laurel. (*Carm.* 3. 30. 6-16.)

32. But if you rank me with the lyric poets, with my proud head I shall strike the stars. (*Carm.* 1. 1. 35-36.)

33. Not marbles graven with deeds of public renown, by which breath and life come back to worthy captains after death, show forth praises more clearly than do the Muses of Calabria; and if the written word were stilled you would not bear away the guerdon of what you have done. (*Carm.* 4. 8. 13-22.)

34. In after days I shall ever increase in fame. (*Carm.* 3. 30. 7-8.)

35. *Horace and the Elegiac Poets,* p. 4.

36. And tuneful Horace has held our ears, when he strikes well-wrought songs from his Ausonian lyre.

37. I, after the custom and manner of the Matine bee, fashion in my small way my studied songs. (*Carm.* 4. 2. 27-32.)

38. A large part of my data for this paragraph comes from Dr. Edward Moore's *Studies in Dante* (first series), pp. 197 ff. This, in turn, derives some of its material from Dr. Manitius' *Analekten zur Geschichte des Horaz im Mittelalter,* which I have consulted.

39. Next comes Horace, prudent and discreet, jealous of faults, firm and kindly. He wrote three principal books and composed two that are less familiar; namely, a book of epodes and one of odes, which in our times are, I think, of little value. Hence let us set

down the title of his *Ancient Poetry* [the *Ars Poetica*], adding also his satires and epistles. (*Registrum Multorum Auctorum*, ll. 66-73.)

40. *The Works of Geoffrey Chaucer,* ed. Skeat, 2. lii.

41. J. W. Cunliffe, *The Influence of Seneca on Elizabethan Tragedy,* p. 12.

42. This also awaits you [my book], that faltering old age shall seize upon you, when in the suburban schools you shall teach boys their beginner's tasks. (*Epist.* 1. 20. 17-18.)

43. I omit myself first of all from the number of those whom I would allow to be poets. (*Serm.* 1. 4. 39-40.)

44. My age is not the same, nor my mind; so now I lay aside my verses and the rest of my playthings. (*Epist.* 1. 1. 4-10.)

45. Ridicule very often decides things of importance better and more effectually than severity. (*Serm.* 1. 10. 14-15.)

46. Christopher Wordsworth, *Memoirs of Wordsworth* 2. 477.

47. *Memoirs of Wordsworth* 2. 479.

48. See Knight's *Life of Wordsworth* 2. 328.

49. *Works,* ed. Masson, 2. 265.

50. *Works,* ed. Masson, 5. 204.

51. *Coleridge and Opium-Eating, Works,* ed. Masson, 5. 204.

52. *Works,* ed. Shedd, 1. 435-436.

53. *Works,* ed. Shedd, 5. 298.

54. *Biographia Literaria,* ed. Shawcross, 2.106-107.

55. *Biographia Literaria,* ed. Shawcross, 1. 40.

56. *Childe Harold's Pilgrimage* 4. 77.

57. *Life of Byron* 1. 98

58. See Moore's *Life of Byron* 1. 91.

59. Moore, *Life of Byron* 1. 143.

60. *Life of Byron* 2. 18.

61. See letter to R. C. Dallas, September 4, 1811.

62. Jeaffreson, *The Real Shelley* 2. 140.

63. See Dowden, *Life of Shelley* 2. 215.

64. Starick. *Die Belesenheit von John Keats,* p. 70.

65. Hallam Tennyson, *Alfred Lord Tennyson* 1. 16.

66. Hallam Tennyson, *Alfred Lord Tennyson* 2. 386.

67. Allingham and Radford, *William Allingham: a Diary,* p. 350.

68. *Alfred Lord Tennyson* 2. 500.

69. *Ibid.* 2. 341.

70. *Ibid.* 2. 377.

71. *Alfred Lord Tennyson* 2. 403.

72. *Ibid.* 1. 341.

73. Far-famed Rhodes, or Mytilene, or Ephesus, or the walls of Corinth with its two seas, or Thebes renowned for Bacchus, or Delphi for Apollo, or Thessalian Tempe. (*Carm.* 1. 7. 1-4.)

74. *Alfred Lord Tennyson* 1. 370.

75. Allingham and Radford, *William Allingham: a Diary,* p. 294.

76. Hallam Tennyson, *Alfred Lord Tennyson* 2. 506.

77. *Ibid.* 2. 484.

78. *Alfred Lord Tennyson* 2. 385.

79. *Works,* London, 1901, pp. 508-509.

80. *Alfred Tennyson* (*Modern English Writers*), p. 223.

81. See Hallam Tennyson, *Alfred Lord Tennyson* 2. 489.

82. Mrs. Sutherland Orr, *Robert Browning* 1. 16.

83. Griffin and Minchin, *Life of Robert Browning,* p. 6.

84. *Life of Robert Browning,* p. 26.

85. Lest it should be thought that the quotations from Horace occur in Browning's original, I may note here that I have examined *The Old Yellow Book,* and find no trace of Horace in the lawyers' papers.

*Bibliography*

Allingham, H., and Radford D. (editors). *William Allingham: A Diary.* London, 1907.

Byron, Lord. *Letters and Journals* (ed. Prothero). London, 1898-1901.

Calverley, Charles Stuart. *Works.* London, 1901.

Coleridge, Samuel Taylor. *Biographia Literaria* (ed. Shawcross). Oxford, 1907.

Coleridge, Samuel Taylor. *Complete Works* (ed. Shedd). New York, 1853.

Cunliffe, John William. *The Influence of Seneca on Elizabethan Tragedy.* London, 1893.

De Quincey, Thomas. *Works* (ed. Masson). Edinburgh, 1889-1890.

Dowden, Edward. *Life of Percy Bysshe Shelley.* London, 1886.

Duff, John Wight. *Literary History of Rome.* New York, 1909.

Griffin, W. Hall, and Minchin, H. C. *Life of Robert Browning.* London, 1910.

Hodell, Charles Wesley. *The Old Yellow Book*. Washington, 1908.

Jeaffreson, John Cordy. *The Real Shelley*. London, 1885.

Keble, John. *Lectures on Poetry* (tr. Francis). Oxford, 1912.

Lang, Andrew. *Alfred Tennyson*. Edinburgh, 1901.

Manitius, M. *Analekten zur Geschichte des Horaz im Mittelalter*. Göttingen, 1892.

Moore, Edward. *Studies in Dante* (first series). Oxford, 1896.

Moore, Thomas. *Life of Byron*. London, 1832.

Orr, Mrs. Sutherland. *Life and Letters of Robert Browning*. Boston, 1891.

Sellar, William Young. *Horace and the Elegiac Poets*. Oxford, 1892.

Skeat, Walter William. Introduction to Vol. 2 of *Works* of Geoffrey Chaucer, Oxford, 1894.

Starick, Paul. *Die Belesenheit von John Keats und die Grundzüge seiner literarischen Kritik*. Berlin, 1910.

Tennyson, Hallam. *Alfred Lord Tennyson: A Memoir*. New York, 1897.

Wordsworth, Christopher. *Memoirs of William Wordsworth* (ed. Reed). Boston, 1851.

## Grant Showerman (essay date 1927)

SOURCE: Showerman, Grant. "Horace Interpreted." In *Horace and His Influence*, pp. 3-68. New York: Longmans, Green and Co., 1927.

[*In the following essay, Showerman begins by exploring the poet as a man, the times in which he lived, and his work as an "interpreter" of his own times, popular wisdom, religion, and philosophy.*]

I. HORACE INTERPRETED

*THE APPEAL OF HORACE*

In estimating the effect of Horace upon his own and later times, we must take into account two aspects of his work. These are, the forms in which he expressed himself, and the substance of which they are the garment. We shall find him distinguished in both; but in the substance of his message we shall find him distinguished by a quality which sets him apart from other poets ancient and modern.

This distinctive quality lies neither in the originality nor in the novelty of the Horatian message, which, as a matter of fact, is surprisingly familiar, and perhaps even commonplace. It lies rather in the appealing manner and mood of its communication. It is a message living and vibrant.

The reason for this is that in Horace we have, above all, a person. No poet speaks from the page with greater directness, no poet establishes so easily and so completely the personal relation with the reader, no poet is remembered so much as if he were a friend in the flesh. In this respect, Horace among poets is a parallel to Thackeray in the field of the novel. What the letters of Cicero are to the intrigue and turmoil of politics, war, and the minor joys and sorrows of private and social life in the last days of the Republic, the lyrics and "Conversations" of Horace are to the mood of the philosophic mind of the early Empire. Both are lights which afford us a clear view of interiors otherwise but faintly illuminated. They are priceless interpreters of their times. In modern times, we make environment interpret the poet. We understand a Tennyson, a Milton, or even a Shakespeare, from our knowledge of the world in which he lived. In the case of antiquity, the process is reversed. We reconstruct the times of Caesar and Augustus from fortunate acquaintance with two of the most representative men who ever possessed the gift of literary genius.

It is because Horace's appeal depends so largely upon his qualities as a person that our interpretation of him must center about his personal traits. We shall re-present to the imagination his personal appearance. We shall account for the personal qualities which contributed to the poetic gift that set him apart as the interpreter of the age to his own and succeeding generations. We shall observe the natural sympathy with men and things by reason of which he reflects with peculiar faithfulness the life of city and country. We shall become acquainted with the thoughts and the moods of a mind and heart that were nicely sensitive to sight and sound and personal contact. We shall hear what the poet has to say of himself not only as a member of the human family, but as the user of the pen.

This interpretation of Horace as person and poet will be best attempted from his own work, and best expressed in his own phrase. The pages which follow are a manner of Horatian mosaic. They contain little not said or suggested by the poet himself.

*1. Horace the Person*

Horace was of slight stature among even a slight-statured race. At the period when we like him best, when he was growing mellower and better with advancing years, his black hair was more than evenly mingled with grey. The naturally dark and probably not too finely-textured skin of face and expansive forehead was deepened by the friendly breezes of both city and country to the vigorous golden brown of the Italian. Feature and eye held the mirror up to a spirit quick to anger but plenteous in good-nature. Altogether, Horace was a short, rotund man, smiling but serious, of nothing very remarkable either in appearance or in manner, and with a look of the plain citizen. Of all the ancients who have left no material likeness, he is the least difficult to know in person.

We see him in a carriage or at the shows with Maecenas, the Emperor's fastidious counsellor. We have charming glimpses of him enjoying in company the hospitable shade of huge pine and white poplar on the grassy terrace of some rose-perfumed Italian garden with noisy fountain and hurrying stream. He loiters, with eyes bent on the pavement, along the winding Sacred Way that leads to the Forum, or on his way home struggles against the crowd as it pushes its way down town amid the dust and din of the busy city. He shrugs his shoulders in good-humored despair as the sirocco brings lassitude and irritation from beyond the Mediterranean, or he sits huddled up in some village by the sea, shivering with the winds from the Alps, reading, and waiting for the first swallow to herald the spring.

We see him at a mild game of tennis in the broad grounds of the Campus Martius. We see him of an evening vagabonding among the nameless common folk of Rome, engaging in small talk with dealers in small merchandise. He may look in upon a party of carousing friends, with banter that is not without reproof. We find him lionized in the homes of the first men of the city in peace and war, where he mystifies the not too intellectual fair guests with graceful and provokingly passionless gallantry. He sits at ease with greater enjoyment under the opaque vine and trellis of his own garden. He appears in the midst of his household as it bustles with preparation for the birthday feast of a friend, or he welcomes at a less formal board and with more unrestrained joy the beloved comrade-in-arms of Philippi, prolonging the genial intercourse

> "Till Phoebus the red East unbars
> And puts to rout the trembling stars."

Or we see him bestride an indifferent nag, cantering down the Appian Way, with its border of tombs, toward the towering dark-green summits of the Alban Mount, twenty miles away, or climbing the winding white road to Tivoli where it reclines on the nearest slope of the Sabines, and pursuing the way beyond it along the banks of headlong Anio where it rushes from the mountains to join the Tiber. We see him finally arrived at his Sabine farm, the gift of Maecenas, standing in tunic-sleeves at his doorway in the morning sun, and contemplating with thankful heart valley and hill-side opposite, and the cold stream of Digentia in the valley-bottom below. We see him rambling about the wooded uplands of his little estate, and resting in the shade of a decaying rustic temple to indite a letter to the friend whose not being present is all that keeps him from perfect happiness. He participates with the near-by villagers in the joys of the rural holiday. He mingles homely philosophy and fiction with country neighbors before his own hearth in the big living-room of the farm-house.

Horace's place is not among the dim and uncertain figures of a hoary antiquity. Only give him modern shoes, an Italian cloak, and a walking-stick, instead of sandals and toga, and he may be seen on the streets of Rome today. Nor is he less modern in character and bearing than in appearance. We discern in his composition the same strange and seemingly contradictory blend of the grave and gay, the lively and severe, the constant and the mercurial, the austere and the trivial, the dignified and the careless, that is so baffling to the observer of Italian character and conduct today.

## 2. Horace the Poet

To understand how Horace came to be a great poet as well as an engaging person, it is necessary to look beneath this somewhat commonplace exterior, and to discern the spiritual man.

The foundations of literature are laid in life. For the production of great poetry two conditions are necessary. There must be, first, an age pregnant with the celestial fires of deep emotion. Second, there must be in its midst one of the rare men whom we call inspired. He must be of such sensitive spiritual fiber as to vibrate to every breeze of the national passion, of such spiritual capacity as to assimilate the common thoughts and moods of the time, of such fine perception and of such sureness of command over word, phrase, and rhythm, as to give crowning expression to what his soul has made its own.

For abundance of stirring and fertilizing experience, history presents few equals of the times when Horace lived. His lifetime fell in an age which was in continual travail with great and uncertain movement. Never has Fortune taken greater delight in her bitter and insolent game, never displayed a greater pertinacity in the derision of men. In the period from Horace's birth at Venusia in southeastern Italy, on December 8, B.C. 65, to November 27, B.C. 8, when

> "Mourned of men and Muses nine,
> They laid him on the Esquiline,"

there occurred the series of great events, to men in their midst incomprehensible, bewildering, and disheartening, which after times could readily interpret as the inevitable change from the ancient and decaying Republic to the better knit if less free life of the Empire.

We are at an immense distance, and the differences have long since been composed. The menacing murmur of trumpets is no longer audible, and the seas are no longer red with blood. The picture is old, and faded, and darkened, and leaves us cold, until we illuminate it with the light of imagination. Then first we see, or rather feel, the magnitude of the time: its hatreds and its selfishness; its differences of opinion, sometimes honest and sometimes disingenuous, but always maintained with the heat of passion; its divisions of friends and families; its lawlessness and violence; its terrifying uncertainties and adventurous plunges; its tragedies of confiscation, murder, fire, proscription, feud, insurrection, riot, war; the dramatic exits of the leading actors in the great play,—of Catiline at Pistoria, of Crassus in the eastern deserts, of Clodius at Bovillae within sight of the gates of Rome, of Pompey in Egypt, of Cato in Africa, of Caesar, Servius Sulpicius, Marcellus, Trebonius and Dolabella, Hirtius and Pansa, Decimus Brutus, the Ciceros, Marcus Brutus and Cassius, Sextus the son of Pompey, Antony and Cleopatra,—as one after another

"Strutted and fretted his hour upon the stage,
And then was heard no more."

It is in relief against a background such as this that Horace's works should be read,—the *Satires,* published in 35 and 30, which the poet himself calls *Sermones,* "Conversations," "Talks," or *Causeries;* the collection of lyrics called *Epodes,* in 29; three books of *Odes* in 23; a book of *Epistles,* or further *Causeries,* in 20; the *Secular Hymn* in 17; a second book of *Epistles* in 14; a fourth book of *Odes* in 13; and a final *Epistle, On the Art of Poetry,* at a later and uncertain date.

It is above all against such a background that Horace's invocation to Fortune should be read:

Goddess, at lovely Antium is thy shrine:
Ready art thou to raise with grace divine
Our mortal frame from lowliest dust of earth,
Or turn triumph to funeral for thy mirth;

or that other expression of the inscrutable uncertainty of the human lot:

Fortune, whose joy is e'er our woe and shame,
With hard persistence plays her mocking game;
Bestowing favors all inconstantly,
Kindly to others now, and now to me.
With me, I praise her; if her wings she lift
To leave me, I resign her every gift,
And, cloaked about in my own virtue's pride,
Wed honest poverty, the dowerless bride.

Horace is not here the idle singer of an empty day. His utterance may be a universal, but in the light of history it is no commonplace. It is the eloquent record of the life of Rome in an age which for intensity is unparalleled in the annals of the ancient world.

And yet men may live a longer span of years than fell to the lot of Horace, and in times no less pregnant with event, and still fail to come into really close contact with life. Horace's experience was comprehensive, and touched the life of his generation at many points. He was born in a little country town in a province distant from the capital. His father, at one time a slave, and always of humble calling, was a man of independent spirit, robust sense, and excellent character, whose constant and intimate companionship left everlasting gratitude in the heart of the son. He provided for the little Horace's education at first among the sons of the "great" centurions who constituted the society of the garrison-town of Venusia, afterwards ambitiously took him to Rome to acquire even the accomplishments usual among the sons of senators, and finally sent him to Athens, garner of wisdom of the ages, where the learning of the past was constantly made to live again by masters with the quick Athenian spirit of telling or hearing new things.

The intellectual experience of Horace's younger days was thus of the broadest character. Into it there entered and were blended the shrewd practical understanding of the Italian provincial; the ornamental accomplishments of the upper classes; the inspiration of Rome's history, with the long line of heroic figures that appear in the twelfth **"Ode"** of the first book like a gallery of magnificent portraits; first-hand knowledge of prominent men of action and letters; unceasing discussion of questions of the day which could be avoided by none; and, finally, humanizing contact on their own soil with Greek philosophy and poetry, Greek monuments and history, and teachers of racial as well as intellectual descent from the greatest people of the past.

But Horace's experience assumed still greater proportions. He passed from the university of Athens to the larger university of life. The news of Caesar's death at the hands of the "Liberators," which reached him as a student there at the age of twenty-one, and the arrival of Brutus some months after, stirred his young blood. As an officer in the army of Brutus, he underwent the hardships of the long campaign, enriching life with new friendships formed in circumstances that have always tightened the friendly bond. He saw the disastrous day of Philippi, narrowly escaped death by shipwreck, and on his return to Italy and Rome found himself without father or fortune.

Nor was the return to Rome the end of his education. In the interval which followed, Horace's mind, always of philosophic bent, was no doubt busy with reflection upon the disparity between the ideals of the liberators and the practical results of their actions, upon the difference between the disorganized, anarchical Rome of the civil war and the gradually knitting Rome of Augustus, and upon the futility of presuming to judge the righteousness either of motives or means in a world where men, to say nothing of understanding each other, could not understand themselves. In the end, he accepted what was not to be avoided. He went farther than acquiescence. The growing conviction among thoughtful men that Augustus was the hope of Rome found lodgment also in his mind. He gravitated from negative to positive. His value as an educated man was recognized, and he found himself at twenty-four in possession of the always coveted boon of the young Italian, a place in the government employ. A clerkship in the treasury gave him salary, safety, respectability, a considerable dignity, and a degree of leisure.

Of the leisure he made wise use. Still in the afterglow of his Athenian experience, he began to write. He attracted the attention of a limited circle of associates. The personal qualities which made him a favorite with the leaders of the Republican army again served him well. He won the recognition and the favor of men who had the ear of the ruling few. In about 33, when he was thirty-two years old, Maecenas, the appreciative counsellor, prompted by Augustus, the politic ruler, who recognized the value of talent in every field for his plans of reconstruction, made him independent of money-getting, and gave him currency among the foremost literary men of the city. He triumphed over the social prejudice against the son of a freedman, disarmed the jealousy of literary rivals, and was assured of fame as well as favor.

Nor was even this the end of Horace's experience with the world of action. It may be that his actual participation in affairs did cease with Maecenas's gift of the Sabine farm, and it is true that he never pretended to live on their own ground the life of the high-born and rich, but he nevertheless associated on sympathetic terms with men through whom he felt all the activities and ideals of the class most representative of the national life, and past experiences and natural adaptability enabled him to assimilate their thoughts and emotions.

Thanks to the glowing personal nature of Horace's works, we know who many of these friends and patrons were who so enlarged his vision and deepened his inspiration. Almost without exception his poems are addressed or dedicated to men with whom he was on terms of more than ordinary friendship. They were rare men,—fit audience, though few; men of experience in affairs at home and in the field, men of natural taste and real cultivation, of broad and sane outlook, of warm heart and deep sympathies. There was Virgil, whom he calls the half of his own being. There was Plotius, and there was Varius, bird of Maeonian song, whom he ranks with the singer of the *Aeneid* himself as the most luminously pure of souls on earth. There was Quintilius, whose death was bewailed by many good men;—when would incorruptible Faith and Truth find his equal? There was Maecenas, well-bred and worldly-wise, the pillar and ornament of his fortunes. There was Septimius, the hoped-for companion of his mellow old age in the little corner of earth that smiled on him beyond all others. There was Iccius, procurator of Agrippa's estates in Sicily, sharing Horace's delight in philosophy. There was Agrippa himself, son-in-law of Augustus, grave hero of battles and diplomacy. There was elderly Trebatius, sometime friend of Cicero and Caesar, with dry legal humor early seasoned in the wilds of Gaul. There were Pompeius and Corvinus, old-soldier friends with whom he exchanged reminiscences of the hard campaign. There was Messalla, a fellow-student at Athens, and Pollio, soldier, orator, and poet. There were Julius Florus and other members of the ambitious literary cohort in the train of Tiberius. There was Aristius Fuscus, the watch of whose wit was ever wound and ready to strike. There was Augustus himself, busy administrator of a world, who still found time for letters.

It is through the medium of personalities like these that Horace's message was delivered to the world of his time and to later generations. How far the finished elegance of his expression is due to their discriminating taste, and how much of the breadth and sanity of his content is due to their vigor of character and cosmopolitan culture, we may only conjecture. Literature is not the product of a single individual. The responsive and stimulating audience is hardly less needful than the poet's inspiration.

Such were the variety and abundance of Horace's experience. It was large and human. He had touched life high and low, bond and free, public and private, military and civil, provincial and urban, Hellenic, Asiatic, and Italian,

urban and rustic, ideal and practical, at the cultured court and among the ignorant, but not always unwise, common people.

And yet, numbers of men possessed of experience as abundant have died without being poets, or even wise men. Their experience was held in solution, so to speak, and failed to precipitate. Horace's experience did precipitate. Nature gave him the warm and responsive soul by reason of which he became a part of all he met. Unlike most of his associates among the upper classes to which he rose, his sympathies could include the freedman, the peasant, and the common soldier. Unlike most of the multitude from which he sprang, he could extend his sympathies to the careworn rich and the troubled statesman. He had learned from his own lot and from observation that no life was wholly happy, that the cares of the so-called fortunate were only different from, not less real than, those of the ordinary man, that every human heart had its chamber furnished for the entertainment of Black Care, and that the chamber was never without its guest.

But not even the precipitate of experience called wisdom will alone make the poet. Horace was again endowed by nature with another and rarer and equally necessary gift,—the sense of artistic expression. It would be waste of time to debate how much he owed to native genius, how much to his own laborious patience, and how much to the good fortune of generous human contact. He is surely to be classed among examples of what for want of a better term we call inspiration. The poet *is* born. We may account for the inspiration of Horace by supposing him of Greek descent (as if Italy had never begotten poets of her own), but the mystery remains. In the case of any poet, after everything has been said of the usual influences, there is always something left to be accounted for only on the ground of genius. It was the possession of this that set Horace apart from other men of similar experience.

The poet, however, is not the mere accident of birth. Horace is aware of a power not himself that makes for poetic righteousness, and realizes the mystery of inspiration. The Muse cast upon him at birth her placid glance. He expects glory neither on the field nor in the course, but looks to song for his triumphs. To Apollo,

> "Lord of the enchanting shell,
> Parent of sweet and solemn-breathing airs,"

who can give power of song even unto the mute, he owes all his power and all his fame. It is the gift of Heaven that he is pointed out by the finger of the passer-by as the minstrel of the Roman lyre, that he breathes the divine fire and pleases men. But he is as perfectly appreciative of the fact that poets are born and also made, and condemns the folly of depending upon inspiration unsupported by effort. He calls himself the bee of Matinum, industriously flitting with honeyed thigh about the banks of humid Tibur. What nature begins, cultivation must develop. Neither training without the rich vein of native endowment, nor natural talent without cultivation, will suffice; both must be friendly conspirators in the process of forming the poet. Wisdom is the beginning and source of writing well. He who would run with success the race that is set before him must endure from boyhood the hardships of heat and cold, and abstain from women and wine. The gift of God must be made perfect by the use of the file, by long waiting, and by conscious intellectual discipline.

### 3. *Horace the Interpreter of His Times*

#### HORACE THE DUALITY

Varied as were Horace's experiences, they were mainly of two kinds, and there are two Horaces who reflect them. There is a more natural Horace, simple and direct, of ordinary Italian manners and ideals, and a less natural Horace, finished in the culture of Greece and the artificialities of life in the capital. They might be called the unconventional and the conventional Horace.

This duality is only the reflection of the two-fold experience of Horace as the provincial village boy and as the successful literary man of the city. The impressions received from Venusia and its simple population of hard-working, plain-speaking folk, from the roaring Aufidus and the landscape of Apulia, from the freedman father's common-sense instruction as he walked about in affectionate companionship with his son, never faded from Horace's mind. The ways of the city were superimposed upon the ways of the country, but never displaced nor even covered them. They were a garment put on and off, sometimes partly hiding, but never for long, the original cloak of simplicity. It is not necessary to think its wearer insincere when, constrained by social circumstance, he put it on. As in most dualities not consciously assumed, both Horaces were genuine. When Davus the slave reproaches his master for longing, while at Rome, to be back in the country, and for praising the attractions of the city, while in the country, it is not mere discontent or inconsistency in Horace which he is attacking. Horace loved both city and country.

And yet, whatever the appeal of the city and its artificialities, Horace's real nature called for the country and its simple ways. It is the Horace of Venusia and the Sabines who is the more genuine of the two. The more formal poems addressed to Augustus and his household sometimes sound the note of affectation, but the most exacting critic will hesitate to bring a like charge against the odes which celebrate the fields and hamlets of Italy and the prowess of her citizen-soldiers of time gone by, or against the mellow epistles and lyrics in which the poet philosophizes upon the spectacle of human life.

#### I. THE INTERPRETER OF ITALIAN LANDSCAPE

The real Horace is to be found first of all as the interpreter of the beauty and fruitfulness of Italy. It is no land of mere literary imagination which he makes us see with such clear-cut distinctness. It is not an Italy in Theocritean

colors, like the Italy of Virgil's *Bucolics,* but the Italy of Horace's own time, the Italy of his own birth and experience, and the Italy of today. Horace is not a descriptive poet. The reader will look in vain for nature-poems in the modern sense. With a word or a phrase only, he flashes upon our vision the beautiful, the significant, the permanent in the scenery of Italy. The features which he loved best, or which for other reasons caught his eye, are those that we still see. There are the oak and the opaque ilex, the pine and the poplar, the dark, funereal cypress, the bright flower of the too-short-lived rose, and the sweet-scented bed of violets. There are the olive groves of Venafrum. Most lovely of sights and most beautiful of figures, there is the purple-clustered vine of vari-colored autumn wedded to the elm. There is the bachelor plane-tree. There are the long-horned, grey-flanked, dark-muzzled, liquid-eyed cattle, grazing under the peaceful skies of the Campagna or enjoying in the meadow their holiday freedom from the plow; the same cattle that Carducci sings—

> "In the grave sweetness of whose tranquil eyes
> Of emerald, broad and still reflected, dwells
> All the divine green silence of the plain."

We are made to see the sterile rust on the corn, and to feel the blazing heat of dog-days, when not a breath stirs as the languid shepherd leads his flock to the banks of the stream. The sunny pastures of Calabria lie spread before us, we see the yellow Tiber at flood, the rushing Anio, the deep eddyings of Liris' taciturn stream, the secluded valleys of the Apennines, the leaves flying before the wind at the coming of winter, the snow-covered uplands of the Alban hills, the mead sparkling with hoar-frost at the approach of spring, autumn rearing from the fields her head decorous with mellow fruits, and golden abundance pouring forth from a full horn her treasures upon the land. It is real Italy which Horace cuts on his cameos,—real landscape, real flowers and fruits, real men.

> "What joy there is in these songs!"

writes Andrew Lang, in *Letters to Dead Authors,* "what delight of life, what an exquisite Hellenic grace of art, what a manly nature to endure, what tenderness and constancy of friendship, what a sense of all that is fair in the glittering stream, the music of the waterfall, the hum of bees, the silvery gray of the olive woods on the hillside! How human are all your verses, Horace! What a pleasure is yours in the straining poplars, swaying in the wind! What gladness you gain from the white crest of Soracte, beheld through the fluttering snowflakes while the logs are being piled higher on the hearth! . . . None of the Latin poets your fellows, or none but Virgil, seem to me to have known as well as you, Horace, how happy and fortunate a thing it was to be born in Italy. You do not say so, like your Virgil, in one splendid passage, numbering the glories of the land as a lover might count the perfections of his mistress. But the sentiment is ever in your heart, and often on your lips. 'Me neither resolute Sparta nor the rich Larissaean plain so enraptures as the fane of echoing Albunea, the headlong Anio, the grove of Tibur, the orchards watered by the wandering rills.' So a poet should speak, and to every singer his own land should be dearest. Beautiful is Italy, with the grave and delicate outlines of her sacred hills, her dark groves, her little cities perched like eyries on the crags, her rivers gliding under ancient walls: beautiful is Italy, her seas and her suns."

## II. THE INTERPRETER OF ITALIAN LIVING

Again, in its visualization of the life of Italy, Horace's art is no less clear than in the presentation of her scenery. Where else may be seen so many vivid incidental pictures of men at their daily occupations of work or play? In *Satire* and *Epistle* this is to be expected, though there are satirists and writers of letters who never transfer the colors of life to their canvas; but the lyrics, too, are kaleidoscopic with scenes from the daily round of human life. We are given fleeting but vivid glimpses into the career of merchant and sailor. We see the sportsman in chase of the boar, the rustic setting snares for the greedy thrush, the serenader under the casement, the plowman at his ingleside, the anxious mother at the window on the cliff, never taking her eyes from the curved shore, the husbandman passing industrious days on his own hillside, tilling his own acres with his own oxen, and training the vine to the unwedded tree, the young men of the hill-towns carrying bundles of fagots along rocky slopes, the rural holiday and its festivities, the sunbrowned wife making ready the evening meal against the coming of the tired peasant. We are shown all the quaint and quiet life of the countryside.

The page is often golden with homely precept or tale of the sort which for all time has been natural to farmer folk. There is the story of the country mouse and the town mouse, the fox and the greedy weasel that ate until he could not pass through the crack by which he came, the rustic who sat and waited for the river to get by, the horse that called man to aid him against the stag, and received the bit forever. The most formal and dignified of the *Odes* are not without the mellow charm of Italian landscape and the genial warmth of Italian life. Even in the first six *Odes* of the third book, often called the *Inaugural Odes,* we get such glimpses as the vineyard and the hailstorm, the Campus Martius on election day, the soldier knowing no fear, cheerful amid hardships under the open sky, the restless Adriatic, the Bantine headlands and the low-lying Forentum of the poet's infancy, the babe in the wood of Voltur, the Latin hill-towns, the craven soldier of Crassus, and the stern patriotism of Regulus. Without these the *Inaugurals* would be but barren and cold, to say nothing of the splendid outburst against the domestic degradation of the time, so full of color and heat and picturesqueness:

'Twas not the sons of parents such as these
That tinged with Punic blood the rolling seas,
Laid low the cruel Hannibal, and brought
Great Pyrrhus and Antiochus to naught;

But the manly brood of rustic soldier folk,
Taught, when the mother or the father spoke
The word austere, obediently to wield
The heavy mattock in the Sabine field,

Or cut and bear home fagots from the height,
As mountain shadows deepened into night,
And the sun's car, departing down the west,
Brought to the wearied steer the friendly rest.

## III. THE INTERPRETER OF ROMAN RELIGION

Still farther, Horace is an eloquent interpreter of the religion of the countryside. He knows, of course, the gods of Greece and the East,—Venus of Cythera and Paphos, of Eryx and Cnidus, Mercury, deity of gain and benefactor of men, Diana, Lady of the mountain and the glade, Delian Apollo, who bathes his unbound locks in the pure waters of Castalia, and Juno, sister and consort of fulminating Jove. He is impressed by the glittering pomp of religious processions winding their way to the summit of the Capitol. In all this, and even in the emperor-worship, now in its first stages at Rome and more political than religious, he acquiesces, though he may himself be a sparing frequenter of the abodes of worship. For him, as for Cicero, religion is one of the social and civic proprieties, a necessary part of the national mechanism.

But the great Olympic deities do not really stir Horace's enthusiasm, or even evoke his warm sympathy. The only **"Ode"** in which he prays to one of them with really fervent heart stands alone among all the odes to the national gods. He petitions the great deity of healing and poetry for what we know is most precious to him:

"When, kneeling at Apollo's shrine,
    The bard from silver goblet pours
Libations due of votive wine,
    What seeks he, what implores?

"Not harvests from Sardinia's shore;
    Not grateful herds that crop the lea
In hot Calabria; not a store
    Of gold, and ivory;

"Not those fair lands where slow and deep
    Thro' meadows rich and pastures gay
Thy silent waters, Liris, creep,
    Eating the marge away.

"Let him to whom the gods award
    Calenian vineyards prune the vine;
The merchant sell his balms and nard,
    And drain the precious wine

"From cups of gold—to Fortune dear
    Because his laden argosy
Crosses, unshattered, thrice a year
    The storm-vexed Midland sea.

"Ripe berries from the olive bough,
    Mallows and endives, be my fare.
Son of Latona, hear my vow!
    Apollo, grant my prayer!

"Health to enjoy the blessings sent
    From heaven; a mind unclouded, strong;
A cheerful heart; a wise content;
    An honored age; and song."

This is not the prayer of the city-bred formalist. It reflects the heart of humble breeding and sympathies. For the faith which really sets the poet aglow we must go into the fields and hamlets of Italy, among the householders who were the descendants of the long line of Italian forefathers that had worshiped from time immemorial the same gods at the same altars in the same way. They were not the gods of yesterday, imported from Greece and Egypt, and splendid with display, but the simple gods of farm and fold native to the soil of Italy. Whatever his conception of the logic of it all, Horace felt a powerful appeal as he contemplated the picturesqueness of the worship and the simplicity of the worshiper, and reflected upon its genuineness and purity as contrasted with what his worldly wisdom told him of the heart of the urban worshiper.

Horace may entertain a well-bred skepticism of Jupiter's thunderbolt, and he may pass the jest on the indifference of the Epicurean gods to the affairs of men. When he does so, it is with the gods of mythology and literature he is dealing, not with really religious gods. For the old-fashioned faith of the country he entertains only the kindliest regard. The images that rise in his mind at the mention of religion pure and undefiled are not the gaudy spectacles to be seen in the marbled streets of the capital. They are images of incense rising in autumn from the ancient altar on the homestead, of the feast of the Terminalia with its slain lamb, of libations of ruddy wine and offerings of bright flowers on the clear waters of some ancestral spring, of the simple hearth of the farmhouse, of the family table resplendent with the silver *salinum,* heirloom of generations, from which the grave paterfamilias makes the pious offering of crackling salt and meal to little gods crowned with rosemary and myrtle, of the altar beneath the pine to the Virgin goddess, of Faunus the shepherd-god, in the humor of wooing, roaming the sunny farmfields in quest of retreating wood-nymphs, of Priapus the garden-god, and Silvanus, guardian of boundaries, and, most of all, and typifying all, of the faith of rustic Phidyle, with clean hands and a pure heart raising palms to heaven at the new of the moon, and praying for the full-hanging vine, thrifty fields of corn, and unblemished lambs. Of the religious life represented by these, Horace is no more tempted to make light than he is tempted to delineate the Italian rustic as De Maupassant does the French,—as an amusing animal, with just enough of the human in his composition to make him ludicrous.

IV. THE INTERPRETER OF THE POPULAR WISDOM

Finally, in the homely, unconventional wisdom which fills *Satire* and *Epistle* and sparkles from the *Odes,* Horace is again the national interpreter. The masses of Rome or Italy had little consciously to do with either Stoicism or Epicureanism. Their philosophy was vigorous common sense, and was learned from living, not from conning books. Horace, too, for all his having been a student of formal philosophy in Athens, for all his professed faith in philosophy as a boon for rich and poor and old and young, and for all his inclination to yield to the natural human

impulse toward system and adopt the philosophy of one of the Schools, is a consistent follower of neither Stoic nor Epicurean. Both systems attracted him by their virtues, and both repelled him because of their weaknesses. His half-humorous confession of wavering allegiance is only a reflection of the shiftings of a mind open to the appeal of both:

> And, lest you inquire under what guide or to what hearth I look for safety, I will tell you that I am sworn to obedience in no master's formula, but am a guest in whatever haven the tempest sweeps me to. Now I am full of action and deep in the waves of civic life, an unswerving follower and guardian of the true virtue, now I secretly backslide to the precepts of Aristippus, and try to bend circumstance to myself, not myself to circumstance.

Horace is either Stoic or Epicurean, or neither, or both. The character of philosophy depends upon definition of terms, and Epicureanism with Horace's definitions of pleasure and duty differed little in practical working from Stoicism. In profession, he was more of the Epicurean; in practice, more of the Stoic. His philosophy occupies ground between both, or, rather, ground common to both. It admits of no name. It is not a system. It owes its resemblances to either of the Schools more to his own nature than to his familiarity with them, great as that was.

The foundations of Horace's philosophy were laid before he ever heard of the Schools. Its basis was a habit of mind acquired by association with his father and the people of Venusia, and with the ordinary people of Rome. Under the influence of reading, study, and social converse at Athens, under the stress of experience in the field, and from long contemplation of life in the large in the capital of an empire, it crystallized into a philosophy of life. The term "philosophy" is misleading in Horace's case. It suggests books and formulae and externals. What Horace read in books did not all remain for him the dead philosophy of ink and paper; what was in tune with his nature he assimilated, to become philosophy in action, philosophy which really was the guide of life. His faith in it is unfeigned:

> Thus does the time move slowly and ungraciously which hinders me from the active realization of what, neglected, is a harm to young and old alike. . . . The envious man, the ill-tempered, the indolent, the wine-bibber, the too free lover,—no mortal, in short, is so crude that his nature cannot be made more gentle if only he will lend a willing ear to cultivation.

The occasional phraseology of the Schools which Horace employs should not mislead. It is for the most part the convenient dress for truth discovered for himself through experience; or it may be literary ornament. The humorous and not unsatiric lines to his poet-friend Albius Tibullus,— "when you want a good laugh, come and see me; you will find me fat and sleek and my skin well cared for, a pig from the sty of Epicurus,"—are as easily the jest of a Stoic as the confession of an Epicurean. Horace's philosophy is individual and natural, and representative of Roman common sense rather than any School.

HORACE AND HELLENISM

A word should be said here regarding the frequent use of the word "Hellenic" in connection with Horace's genius. Among the results of his higher education, it is natural that none should be more prominent to the eye than the influence of Greek letters upon his work; but to call Horace Greek is to be blinded to the essential by the presence in his poems of Greek form and Greek allusion. It would be as little reasonable to call a Roman triumphal arch Greek because it displays column, architrave, or a facing of marble from Greece. What makes Roman architecture stand is not ornament, but Roman concrete and the Roman vault. Horace is Greek as Milton is Hebraic or Roman, or as Shakespeare is Italian.

*4. Horace the Philosopher of Life*

HORACE THE SPECTATOR AND ESSAYIST

A great source of the richness of personality which constitutes Horace's principal charm is to be found in his contemplative disposition. His attitude toward the universal drama is that of the onlooker. As we shall see, he is not without keen interest in the piece, but his prevailing mood is that of mild amusement. In time past, he has himself assumed more than one of the rôles, and has known personally many of the actors. He knows perfectly well that there is a great deal of the mask and buskin on the stage of life, and that each man in his time plays many parts. Experience has begotten reflection, and reflection has contributed in turn to experience, until contemplation has passed from diversion to habit.

Horace is another Spectator, except that his "meddling with any practical part in life" has not been so slight:

> Thus I live in the world rather as a Spectator of mankind than as one of the species, by which means I have made myself a speculative statesman, soldier, merchant, and artisan, without ever meddling with any practical part in life. I am very well versed in the theory of a husband, or a father, and can discern the errors in the economy, business, and diversion of others, better than those who are engaged in them: as standers-by discover blots which are apt to escape those who are in the game.

He looks down from his post upon the life of men with as clear vision as Lucretius, whom he admires:

> Nothing is sweeter than to dwell in the lofty citadels secure in the wisdom of the sages, thence to look down upon the rest of mankind blindly wandering in mistaken paths in the search for the way of life, striving one with another in the contest of wits, emulous in distinction of birth, night and day straining with supreme effort at length to arrive at the heights of power and become lords of the world.

Farther, Horace is not merely the stander-by contemplating the game in which objective mankind is engaged. He is also a spectator of himself. Horace the poet-philosopher contemplates Horace the man with the same quiet amusement with which he surveys the human family of which he is an inseparable yet detachable part. It is the universal aspect of Horace which is the object of his contemplation,—Horace playing a part together with the rest of mankind in the infinitely diverting *comédie humaine.* He uses himself, so to speak, for illustrative purposes,—to point the moral of the genuine; to demonstrate the indispensability of hard work as well as genius; to afford concrete proof of the possibility of happiness without wealth. He is almost as objective to himself as the landscape of the Sabine farm. Horace the spectator sees Horace the man against the background of human life just as he sees snow-mantled Soracte, or the cold Digentia, or the restless Adriatic, or leafy Tarentum, or snowy Algidus, or green Venafrum. The clear-cut elegance of his miniatures of Italian scenery is not due to their individual interest, but to their connection with the universal life of man. Description for its own sake is hardly to be found in Horace. In the same way, the vivid glimpses he affords of his own life, person, and character almost never prompt the thought of egotism. The most personal of poets, his expression of self nowhere becomes selfish expression.

But there are spectators who are mere spectators. Horace is more; he is a critic and an interpreter. He looks forth upon life with a keen vision for comparative values, and gives sane and distinct expression to what he sees.

Horace must not be thought of, however, as a censorious or carping critic. His attitude is judicial, and the verdict is seldom other than lenient and kindly. He is not a wasp of Twickenham, not a Juvenal furiously laying about him with a heavy lash, not a Lucilius with the axes of Scipionic patrons to grind, having at the leaders of the people and the people themselves. He is in as little degree an Ennius, composing merely to gratify the taste for entertainment. There are some, as a matter of fact, to whom in satire he seems to go beyond the limit of good-nature. At vice in pronounced form, at all forms of unmanliness, he does indeed strike out, like Lucilius the knight of Campania, his predecessor and pattern, gracious only to virtue and to the friends of virtue; but those whose hands are clean and whose hearts are pure need fear nothing. Even those who are guilty of the ordinary frailties of human kind need fear nothing worse than being good-humoredly laughed at. The objects of Horace's smiling condemnation are not the trifling faults of the individual or the class, but the universal grosser stupidities which poison the sources of life.

The Horace of the *Satires* and *Epistles* is better called an essayist. That he is a satirist at all is less by virtue of intention than because of the mere fact that he is a spectator. To look upon life with the eye of understanding is to see men the prey to passions and delusions,—the very comment on which can be nothing else than satire.

And now, what is it that Horace sees as he sits in philosophic detachment on the serene heights of contemplation; and what are his reflections?

The great factor in the character of Horace is his philosophy of life. To define it is to give the meaning of the word Horatian as far as content is concerned, and to trace the thread which more than any other makes his works a unity.

### I. THE VANITY OF HUMAN WISHES

Horace looks forth upon a world of discontented and restless humanity. The soldier, the lawyer, the farmer, the trader, swept over the earth in the passion for gain, like dust in the whirlwind,—all are dissatisfied. Choose anyone you will from the midst of the throng; either with greed for money or with miserable ambition for power, his soul is in travail. Some are dazzled by fine silver, some lose their senses over bronze. Some are ever straining after the prizes of public life. There are many who love not wisely, but too well. Most are engaged in a mad race for money, whether to assure themselves of retirement and ease in old age, or out of the sportsman's desire to outstrip their rivals in the course. As many as are mortal men, so many are the objects of their pursuit.

And, over and about all men, by reason of their bondage to avarice, ambition, appetite, and passion, hovers Black Care. It flits above their sleepless eyes in the panelled ceiling of the darkened palace, it sits behind them on the courser as they rush into battle, it dogs them as they are at the pleasures of the bronze-trimmed yacht. It pursues them everywhere, swifter than the deer, swifter than the wind that drives before it the storm-cloud. Not even those who are most happy are entirely so. No lot is wholly blest. Perfect happiness is unattainable. Tithonus, with the gift of everlasting life, wasted away in undying old age. Achilles, with every charm of youthful strength and gallantry, was doomed to early death. Not even the richest are content. Something is always lacking in the midst of abundance, and desire more than keeps pace with satisfaction.

Nor are the multitude less enslaved to their desires than the few. Glory drags bound to her glittering chariot-wheels the nameless as well as the nobly-born. The poor are as inconstant as the rich. What of the man who is not rich? You may well smile. He changes from garret to garret, from bed to bed, from bath to bath and barber to barber, and is just as seasick in a hired boat as the wealthy man on board his private yacht.

And not only are all men the victims of insatiable desire, but all are alike subject to the uncertainties of fate. Insolent Fortune without notice flutters her swift wings and leaves them. Friends prove faithless, once the cask is drained to the lees. Death, unforeseen and unexpected, lurks in ambush for them in a thousand places. Some are swallowed up by the greedy sea. Some the Furies give to destruction in the grim spectacle of war. Without respect of age or person, the ways of death are thronged with young and old. Cruel Proserpina passes no man by.

Even they who for the time escape the object of their dread must at last face the inevitable. Invoked or not invoked, Death comes to release the lowly from toil, and

to strip the proud of power. The same night awaits all; everyone must tread once for all the path of death. The summons is delivered impartially at the hovels of the poor and the turreted palaces of the rich. The dark stream must be crossed by prince and peasant alike. Eternal exile is the lot of all, whether nameless and poor, or sprung of the line of Inachus:

> Alas! my Postumus, alas! how speed
> The passing years: nor can devotion's deed
> Stay wrinkled age one moment on its way,
> Nor stay one moment death's appointed day;
>
> Not though with thrice a hundred oxen slain
> Each day thou prayest Pluto to refrain,
> The unmoved by tears, who threefold Geryon drave,
> And Tityus, beneath the darkening wave.
>
> The wave we all must one day surely sail
> Who live and breathe within this mortal vale,
> Whether our lot with princely rich to fare,
> Whether the peasant's lowly life to share.
>
> In vain for us from murderous Mars to flee,
> In vain to shun the storms of Hadria's sea,
> In vain to fear the poison-laden breath
> Of Autumn's sultry south-wind, fraught with death;
>
> Adown the wandering stream we all must go,
> Adown Cocytus' waters, black and slow;
> The ill-famed race of Danaus all must see,
> And Sisyphus, from labors never free.
>
> All must be left,—lands, home, beloved wife,—
> All left behind when we have done with life;
> One tree alone, of all thou holdest dear,
> Shall follow thee,—the cypress, o'er thy bier!
>
> Thy wiser heir will soon drain to their lees
> The casks now kept beneath a hundred keys;
> The proud old Caecuban will stain the floor,
> More fit at pontiffs' solemn feasts to pour.

Nor is there a beyond filled with brightness for the victim of fate to look to. Orcus is unpitying. Mercury's flock of souls is of sable hue, and Proserpina's realm is the hue of the dusk. Black Care clings to poor souls even beyond the grave. Dull and persistent, it is the only substantial feature of the insubstantial world of shades. Sappho still sighs there for love of her maiden companions, the plectrum of Alcaeus sounds its chords only to songs of earthly hardships by land and sea, Prometheus and Tantalus find no surcease from the pangs of torture, Sisyphus ever rolls the returning stone, and the Danaids fill the everemptying jars.

### II. THE PLEASURES OF THIS WORLD

The picture is dark with shadow, and must be relieved with light and color. The hasty conclusion should not be drawn that this is the philosophy of gloom. The tone of Horace is neither that of the cheerless skeptic nor that of the despairing pessimist. He does not rise from his contemplation with the words or the feeling of Lucretius:

O miserable minds of men, O blind hearts! In what obscurity and in what dangers is passed this uncertain little existence of yours!

He would have agreed with the philosophy of pessimism that life contains striving and pain, but he would not have shared in the gloom of a Schopenhauer, who in all will sees action, in all action want, in all want pain, who looks upon pain as the essential condition of will, and sees no end of suffering except in the surrender of the will to live. The vanity of human wishes is no secret to Horace, but life is not to him "a soap-bubble which we blow out as long and as large as possible, though each of us knows perfectly well it must sooner or later burst."

No, life may have its inevitable pains and its inevitable end, but it is far more substantial in composition than a bubble. For those who possess the secret of detecting and enjoying them, it contains solid goods in abundance.

What is the secret?

The first step toward enjoyment of the human lot is acquiescence. Of course existence has its evils and bitter end, but these are minimized for the man who frankly faces them, and recognizes the futility of struggling against the fact. How much better to endure whatever our lot shall impose. Quintilius is dead: it is hard; but patience makes lighter the ill that fate will not suffer us to correct.

And then, when we have once yielded, and have ceased to look upon perfect happiness as a possibility, or upon any measure of happiness as a right to be demanded, we are in position to take the second step; namely, to make wise use of life's advantages:

> Mid all thy hopes and all thy cares, mid all thy
>     wraths and fears,
> Think every shining day that dawns the period to
>     thy years.
> The hour that comes unlooked for is the hour that
>     doubly cheers.

Because there are many things to make life a pleasure. There is the solace of literature; Black Care is lessened by song. There are the riches of philosophy, there is the diversion of moving among men. There are the delights of the country and the town. Above all, there are friends with whom to share the joy of mere living in Italy. For what purpose, if not to enjoy, are the rose, the pine, and the poplar, the gushing fountain, the generous wine of Formian hill and Massic slope, the villa by the Tiber, the peaceful and healthful seclusion of the Sabines, the pleasing change from the sharp winter to the soft zephyrs of spring, the apple-bearing autumn,—"season of mists and mellow fruitfulness"? What need to be unhappy in the midst of such a world?

And the man who is wise will not only recognize the abounding possibilities about him, but will seize upon them before they vanish. Who knows whether the gods above will add a tomorrow to the to-day? Be glad, and lay hand upon the gifts of the passing hour! Take advantage of the day, and have no silly faith in the morrow. It is as if Omar were translating Horace:

> "Waste not your Hour, nor in the vain pursuit
> Of This and That endeavor and dispute;
>     Better be jocund with the fruitful Grape
> Than sadden after none, or bitter, Fruit.

> "Ah! fill the Cup: what boots it to repeat
> How Time is slipping underneath our Feet:
>     Unborn TOMORROW, and dead YESTERDAY,
> Why fret about them if TODAY be sweet!"

The goods of existence must be enjoyed here and now, or never, for all must be left behind. What once is enjoyed is forever our very own. Happy is the man who can say, at each day's close, "I have lived!" The day is his, and cannot be recalled. Let Jove overcast with black cloud the heavens of to-morrow, or let him make it bright with clear sunshine,—as he pleases; what the flying hour of to-day has already given us he never can revoke. Life is a stream, now gliding peacefully onward in mid-channel to the Tuscan sea, now tumbling upon its swirling bosom the wreckage of flood and storm. The pitiful human being on its banks, ever looking with greedy expectation up the stream, or with vain regret at what is past, is left at last with nothing at all. The part of wisdom and of happiness is to keep eyes on that part of the stream directly before us, the only part which is ever really seen.

> You see how, deep with gleaming snow,
> Soracte stands, and, bending low,
>     Yon branches droop beneath their burden,
>         And streams o'erfrozen have ceased their flow.

> Away with cold! the hearth pile high
> With blazing logs; the goblet ply
>     With cheering Sabine, Thaliarchus;
>         Draw from the cask of long years gone by.

> All else the gods entrust to keep,
> Whose nod can lull the winds to sleep,
>     Vexing the ash and cypress agèd,
>         Or battling over the boiling deep.

> Seek not to pierce the morrow's haze,
> But for the moment render praise;
>     Nor spurn the dance, nor love's sweet passion,
>         Ere age draws on with its joyless days.

> Now should the campus be your joy,
> And whispered loves your lips employ,
>     What time the twilight shadows gather,
>         And tryst you keep with the maiden coy.

> From near-by nook her laugh makes plain
> Where she had meant to hide, in vain!
>     How arch her struggles o'er the token
>         From yielding which she can scarce refrain!

### III. LIFE AND MORALITY

But Horace's Epicureanism never goes to the length of Omar's. He would have shrunk from the Persian as extreme:

> "YESTERDAY This Day's Madness did prepare,
> TOMORROW's Silence, Triumph, or Despair,
>   Drink! for you know not whence you came,
>   nor why:
> Drink! for you know not why you go, nor where."

The Epicureanism of Horace is more nearly that of Epicurus himself, the saintly recluse who taught that "to whom little is not enough, nothing is enough," and who regarded plain living as at the same time a duty and a happiness. The lives of too liberal disciples have been a slander on the name of Epicurus. Horace is not among them. With degenerate Epicureans, whose philosophy permitted them "To roll with pleasure in a sensual sty," he had little in common. The extraction from life of the honey of enjoyment was indeed the highest purpose, but the purpose could never be realized without the exercise of discrimination, moderation, and a measure of spiritual culture. Life was an art, symmetrical, unified, reposeful,—like the poem of perfect art, or the statue, or the temple. In actual conduct, the hedonist of the better type differed little from the Stoic himself.

The gracious touch and quiet humor with which Horace treats even the most serious themes are often misleading. This effect is the more possible by reason of the presence among his works of passages, not many and for the most part youthful, in which he is guilty of too great freedom.

Horace is really a serious person. He is even something of a preacher, a praiser of the time when he was a boy, a censor and corrector of his youngers. So far as popular definitions of Stoic and Epicurean are concerned, he is much more the former than the latter.

For Horace's counsel is always for moderation, and sometimes for austerity. He is not a wine-bibber, and he is not a total abstainer. To be the latter on principle would never have occurred to him. The vine was the gift of God. Prefer nothing to it for planting in the mellow soil of Tibur, Varus; it is one of the compensations of life:

> "Its magic power of wit can spread
> The halo round a dullard's head,
> Can make the sage forget his care,
> His bosom's inmost thoughts unbare,
> And drown his solemn-faced pretense
> Beneath its blithesome influence.
> Bright hope it brings and vigor back
> To minds outworn upon the rack,
> And puts such courage in the brain
> As makes the poor be men again,
> Whom neither tyrants' wrath affrights,
> Nor all their bristling satellites."

When wine is a curse, it is not so because of itself, but because of excess in its use. The cup was made for purposes of pleasure, but to quarrel over it,—leave that to

barbarians! Take warning by the Thracians, and the Centaurs and Lapiths, never to overstep the bounds of moderation. Pleasure with after-taste of bitterness is not real pleasure. Pleasure purchased with pain is an evil.

Upon women he looks with the same philosophic calm as upon wine. Love, too, was to be regarded as one of the contributions to life's pleasure. To dally with golden-haired Pyrrha, with Lyce, or with Glycera, the beauty more brilliant than Parian marble, was not in his eyes to be blamed in itself. What he felt no hesitation in committing to his poems for friends and the Emperor to read, they on their part felt as little hesitation in confessing to him. The fault of love lay not in itself, but in abuse. This is not said of adultery, which was always an offense because it disturbed the institution of marriage and rotted the foundation of society.

There is thus no inconsistency in the Horace of the love poems and the Horace of the *Secular Hymn* who petitions Our Lady Juno to prosper the decrees of the Senate encouraging the marriage relation and the rearing of families. Of the illicit love that looked to Roman women in the home, he emphatically declares his innocence, and against it directs the last and most powerful of the six *Inaugural Odes;* for this touched the family, and, through the family, the State. This, with neglect of religion, he classes together as the two great causes of national decay.

Horace is not an Ovid, with no sense of the limits of either indulgence or expression. He is not a Catullus, tormented by the furies of youthful passion. The flame never really burned him. We search his pages in vain for evidence of sincere and absorbing passion, whether of the flesh or of the spirit. He was guilty of no breach of the morals of his time, and it is likely also, in spite of Suetonius, that he was guilty of no excess. He was a supporter in good faith of the Emperor in his attempts at the moral improvement of the State. If Virgil in the writing of the *Georgics* or the *Aeneid* was conscious of a purpose to second the project of Augustus, it is just as likely that his intimate friend Horace also wrote with conscious moral intent. Nothing is more in keeping with his conception of the end and effect of literature:

> It shapes the tender and hesitating speech of the child; it straight removes his ear from shameless communication; presently with friendly precepts it moulds his inner self; it is a corrector of harshness and envy and anger; it sets forth the righteous deed; it instructs the rising generations with the familiar example; it is a solace to the helpless and the sick at heart.

### IV. LIFE AND PURPOSE

Horace's philosophy of life is thus based upon something deeper than the principle of seizing upon pleasure. His definition of pleasure is not without austerity; he preaches the positive virtues of performance as well as the negative virtue of moderation. He could be an unswerving follower and guardian of true virtue, and could bend self to circumstance.

He stands for domestic purity, and for patriotic devotion. *Dulce et decorum est pro patria mori,*—to die for country is a privilege and a glory. His hero is Regulus, returning steadfastly through the ranks of protesting friends to keep faith with the pitiless executioners of Carthage. Regulus, and the Scauri, and Paulus, who poured out his great spirit on the disastrous field of Cannae, and Fabricius, of simple heart and absolute integrity, he holds up as examples to his generation. In praise of the sturdy Roman qualities of courage and steadfastness he writes his most inspired lines:

> The righteous man of unswerving purpose is shaken in his solid will neither by the unworthy demands of inflamed citizens, nor by the frowning face of the threatening tyrant, nor by the East-wind, turbid ruler of the restless Adriatic, nor by the great hand of fulminating Jove himself. If the heavens should fall asunder, the crashing fragments would descend upon him unterrified.

He preaches the gospel of faithfulness not only to family, country, and purpose, but to religion. He will shun the man who violates the secrets of the mysteries. The curse of the gods is upon all such, and pursues them to the day of doom.

Faithfulness to friendship stands out with no less distinctness. While Horace is in his right mind, he will value nothing so highly as a delightful friend. He is ready, whenever fate calls, to enter with Maecenas even upon the last journey. Among the blest is he who is unafraid to die for dear friends or native land.

Honor, too,—the fine spirit of old Roman times, that refused bribes, that would not take advantage of an enemy's weakness, that asked no questions save the question of what was right, that never turned its back upon duty, that swore to its own hurt and changed not; the same lofty spirit the recording of whose manifestations never fails to bring the glow to Livy's cheek and the gleam to his eye,—honor is also first and foremost in Horace's esteem. Regulus, the self-sacrificing; Curius, despising the Samnite gold; Camillus, yielding private grievance to come to his country's aid; Cato, dying for his convictions after Thapsus, are his inspirations. The hero of his ideal fears disgrace worse than death. The diadem and the laurel are for him only who can pass on without the backward glance upon stores of treasure.

Finally, not least among the qualities which enter into the ideal of Horace is the simplicity of the olden time, when the armies of Rome were made up of citizen-soldiers, and the eye of every Roman was single to the glory of the State, and the selfishness of luxury was yet unknown.

> Scant were their private means, the public, great;
>    'Twas still a commonwealth, that State;
> No portico, surveyed with private rule,
>    Assured one man the shady cool.
>
> The laws approved the house of humble sods;
>    'Twas only to the homes of gods,

> The structures reared with earnings of the nation,
>    They gave rich marble decoration.

The healthful repose of heart which comes from unity of purpose and simple devotion to plain duty, he sees existing still, even in his own less strenuous age, in the remote and peaceful countryside. Blessed is the man far from the busy life of affairs, like the primeval race of mortals, who tills with his own oxen the acres of his fathers! Horace covets the gift earnestly for himself, because his calm vision assures him that it, of all the virtues, lies next to happy living.

### V. THE SOURCES OF HAPPINESS

Here we have arrived at the kernel of Horace's philosophy, the key which unlocks the casket containing his message to all men of every generation. In actual life, at least, mankind storms the citadel of happiness, as if it were something material and external, to be taken by violent hands. Horace locates the citadels of happiness in his own breast. It is the heart which is the source of all joy and all sorrow, of all wealth and all poverty. Happiness is to be sought, not outside, but within. Man does not create his world; he *is* his world.

Men are madly chasing after peace of heart in a thousand wrong ways, all the while overlooking the right way, which is nearest at hand. To observe their feverish eagerness, the spectator might be led to think happiness identical with possession. And yet wealth and happiness are neither the same nor equivalent. They may have nothing to do one with the other. Money, indeed, is not an evil in itself, but it is not essential except so far as it is a mere means of life. Poor men may be happy, and the wealthy may be poor in the midst of their riches. A man's wealth consisteth not in the abundance of the things he possesseth. More justly does he lay claim to the name of rich man who knows how to use the blessings of the gods wisely, who is bred to endurance of hard want, and who fears the disgraceful action worse than he fears death.

Real happiness consists in peace of mind and heart. Everyone desires it, and everyone prays for it,—the sailor caught in the storms of the Aegean, the mad Thracian, the Mede with quiver at his back. But peace is not to be purchased. Neither gems nor purple nor gold will buy it, nor favor. Not all the externals in the world can help the man who depends upon them alone.

> Not treasure trove nor consul's stately train
> Drives wretched tumult from the troubled brain;
> Swarming with cares that draw unceasing sighs,
> The fretted ceiling hangs o'er sleepless eyes.

Nor is peace to be pursued and laid hold of, or discovered in some other clime. Of what avail to fly to lands warmed by other suns? What exile ever escaped himself? It is the soul that is at fault, that never can be freed from its own bonds. The sky is all he changes:

The heavens, not themselves, they change
    Who haste to cross the seas.

The happiness men seek for is in themselves, to be found
at little Ulubrae in the Latin marshes as easily as in great
cities, if only they have the proper attitude of mind and
heart.

But how insure this peace of mind?

At the very beginning, and through to the end, the searcher
after happiness must recognize that unhappiness is the
result of slavery of some sort, and that slavery in turn is
begotten of desire. The man who is overfond of anything
will be unwilling to let go his hold upon it. Desire will
curb his freedom. The only safety lies in refusing the rein
to passion of any kind. "To gaze upon nothing to lust after
it, Numicius, is the simple way of winning and of keeping
happiness." He who lives in either desire or fear can never
enjoy his possessions. He who desires will also fear; and
he who fears can never be a free man. The wise man will
not allow his desires to become tyrants over him. Money
will be his servant, not his master. He will attain to wealth
by curbing his wants. You will be monarch over broader
realms by dominating your spirit than by adding Libya to
far-off Gades.

The poor man, in spite of poverty, may enjoy life more
than the rich. It is possible under a humble roof to excel in
happiness kings and the friends of kings. Wealth depends
upon what men want, not upon what men have. The more
a man denies himself, the greater are the gifts of the gods
to him. One may hold riches in contempt, and thus be a
more splendid lord of wealth than the great landowner of
Apulia. By contracting his desires he may extend his
revenues until they are more than those of the gorgeous
East. Many wants attend those who have many ambitions.
Happy is the man to whom God has given barely enough.
Let him to whom fate, fortune, or his own effort has given
this enough, desire no more. If the liquid stream of Fortune
should gild him, it would make his happiness nothing
greater, because money cannot change his nature. To the
man who has good digestion and good lungs and is free
from gout, the riches of a king could add nothing. What
difference does it make to him who lives within the limits
of nature whether he plow a hundred acres or a thousand?

As with the passion of greed, so with anger, love, ambition for power, and all the other forms of desire which
lodge in the human heart. Make them your slaves, or they
will make you theirs. Like wrath, they are all forms of
madness. The man who becomes avaricious has thrown
away the armor of life, has abandoned the post of virtue.
Once let a man submit to desire of an unworthy kind, and
he will find himself in the case of the horse that called a
rider to help him drive the stag from their common
feeding-ground, and received the bit and rein forever.

So Horace will enter into no entangling alliances with
ambition for power, wealth, or position, or with the more
personal passions. By some of them he has not been

altogether untouched, and he has no regret; but to continue,
at forty-five, would not do. He will be content with just
his home in the Sabine hills. This is what he always prayed
for, a patch of ground, not so very large, with a spring of
ever-flowing water, a garden, and a little timberland. He
asks for nothing more, except that a kindly fate will make
these beloved possessions forever his own. He will go to
the ant, for she is an example, and consider her ways and
be wise, and be content with what he has as soon as it is
enough. He will not enter the field of public life, because
it would mean the sacrifice of peace. He would have to
keep open house, submit to the attentions of a bodyguard
of servants, keep horses and carriage and a coachman, and
be the target for shafts of envy and malice; in a word, lose
his freedom and become the slave of wretched and burdensome ambition.

The price is too great, the privilege not to his liking. Horace's prayer is rather to be freed from the cares of empty
ambition, from the fear of death and the passion of anger,
to laugh at superstition, to enjoy the happy return of his
birthday, to be forgiving of his friends, to grow more gentle
and better as old age draws on, to recognize the proper
limit in all things:

> "Health to enjoy the blessings sent
>     From heaven; a mind unclouded, strong;
> A cheerful heart; a wise content;
>     An honored age; and song."

## Marvin T. Herrick (essay date 1946)

SOURCE: Herrick, Marvin T. Introduction to *The Fusion
of Horatian and Aristotelian Literary Criticism, 1531-
1555,* pp. 1-6. Urbana: University of Illinois Press, 1946.

[*In the following essay, Herrick states that literary criticism in western Europe is based on the principles of
Horace and Aristotle, respectively from the* Ars Poetica
*and* Poetics, *citing commentaries on the* Ars Poetica *from
the sixteenth and seventeenth centuries.*]

It is well known that formal literary criticism in western
Europe stems from Horace and Aristotle. As Spingarn and
others have pointed out, the beginnings of formal criticism
in Italy, France, and England fairly coincided with the first
translations of Horace's *Ars Poetica* into the vernacular:
Dolce's Italian version in 1535, Pelletier's French version
in 1545, and Drant's English version in 1567.

Translations of Aristotle's *Poetics* into the vernacular
lagged behind translations of the *Ars Poetica.* Bernardo
Segni's *Rettorica et Poetica d'Aristotile* appeared in 1549,
but there were no French or English translations for more
than a century later. Nevertheless, Latin versions of the
Greek *Poetics* served to introduce Aristotle's theory of
poetry to readers in the sixteenth century. Paccius' Latin
version, first published in 1536, has been especially
influential. So far as I can make out, Georgio Valla's Latin

translation, which appeared in 1498, has had relatively little influence; it is occasionally mentioned by Aristotelian commentators, but rarely followed. Paccius' Latin version, however, has been reprinted many times; together with the Greek, it constitutes the text of the important commentaries by Robortellus (1548) and Madius (1550), and it has been used by many scholars and critics during and after the sixteenth century.

Translations of the *Ars Poetica* into Italian, French, and English, then, more or less coincided with the dissemination of Paccius' edition of the *Poetics*. The critical activity stimulated by an increasing popular knowledge of Horace's theory of poetry more or less coincided with a growing knowledge of the Aristotelian theory of poetry, and Renaissance theories of poetry were based on joint studies of Horace and Aristotle. Consequently, Aristotelian and Horatian features in Renaissance critical theory were almost inextricably mingled. The reader of an Elizabethan work like Sir Philip Sidney's *Defense of Poesy,* for example, finds it impossible to determine whether Aristotle or Horace is ultimately responsible for many of the author's observations; he can only be sure that both Aristotelian and Horatian theories, as interpreted by the sixteenth-century commentators and critics, shaped Sidney's criticism.

The commentators and critics of the sixteenth century were largely responsible for the formulation of the Renaissance theories of poetry in Italy, France, and England. Julius Caesar Scaliger, Castelvetro, and Minturno have received the major share of credit for formulating and propagating these theories, and it is true that these critics, especially Scaliger, long enjoyed great prestige in western Europe. Castelvetro's influence was mainly Aristotelian, for Castelvetro was not an admirer of Horace. The critical doctrines of Minturno and Scaliger, however, are primarily Horatian and then Aristotelian. Minturno's treatise *De Poeta* appeared in 1559, his *L'Arte Poetica* in 1564; Scaliger's *Poetices* in 1561; Castelvetro's edition of the *Poetics,* with Italian translation and commentary, in 1570. Some years before these important publications, however, the harmonizing, or blending, of Horace with Aristotle had been done by the commentators on the *Ars Poetica* and on the *Poetics;* some of these, like Robortellus and Madius, left commentaries on both treatises.

Robortellus' commentary (1548) on the *Poetics* has not been neglected by the literary historians, but his Latin *Paraphrase* (1548) of the *Ars Poetica* is seldom mentioned. Yet the two works go together, as the author doubtless intended. Robortellus repeatedly refers to the *Poetics* in his *Paraphrase,* and in his commentary on the *Poetics,* he repeatedly quotes from, and refers to, the *Ars Poetica.* The same method was followed, in greater detail, by Madius, whose commentaries (1550) were not only bound together but paged continuously. Robortellus and Madius contributed most, I believe, to the amalgam of Horace and Aristotle that characterizes Renaissance literary criticism, but they were not the only or even the earliest contributors.

Franciscus Philippus' commentary (1546) on the *Ars Poetica,* so far as I know, has never been even mentioned in any account of sixteenth-century literary criticism. Yet this commentary anticipates the method practiced by Robortellus and Madius. Philippus was familiar with the *Poetics,* in the Greek-Latin edition by Paccius, and he made good use of Aristotle in his interpretations of Horace. Philippus anticipated many critical observations of Robortellus and Madius, who, in turn, anticipated much of the critical theory and practice that Scaliger, Minturno, and Castelvetro popularized throughout western Europe.

Although modern scholarship[1] finds no direct connection between the *Ars Poetica* and the *Poetics,* sixteenth-century scholars agreed that Horace was following Aristotle's theories as formulated in the *Poetics* and *Rhetoric.* Parrhasius (1531), for example, believed that Horace had imitated Neoptolemus and Aristotle.[2] Madius believed that the Horatian epistle is a stream flowing from the Aristotelian spring of the *Poetics;* and the main purpose of his commentary on the *Ars Poetica* was to make clear Horace's "obscure and subtle imitation."[3] Therefore Madius tried to find parallels in the *Poetics* for nearly every statement in the *Ars Poetica,* never doubting, apparently, the direct connection between the Greek and the Roman arts of poetry. Madius and his fellow commentators in the sixteenth century were not the only ones who accepted the *Ars Poetica* as a Horatian adaptation of the *Poetics.* For many years after 1555 literary men thought of Horace as the interpreter of Aristotle's criticism. Dryden's statement in his *Essay of Dramatic Poesy* (1668) is typical: "Of that book which Aristotle has left us, περὶ τῆς Ποιητικῆς, Horace his *Art of Poetry* is an excellent comment."[4]

No one questions the established fact that Horace and Aristotle were the leading authorities for the makers of literary criticism in western Europe during the sixteenth, seventeenth, and eighteenth centuries. One may question, however, the ways and means by which this compound of literary theory, usually labeled Aristotelian, sometimes labeled Horatian, but more accurately to be labeled Aristotelian-Horatian or Horatian-Aristotelian, was fashioned. So far as I know, no literary historian has yet given a detailed description of the process. In this study, I propose to examine in some detail several English translation of the *Poetics,* which I use for all the numerous quotations from that treatise. It is true that both Bywater's text and translation are sometimes at odds with sixteenth-century interpretations, but I have found that Bywater usually gives a meaning that agrees tolerably well with what Robortellus, Madius, and others evolved. Where Bywater's reading seriously disagrees with the reading of Paccius, I call attention to the disagreement. For the English sense of the Renaissance Latin used by all the Horatian commentators, I have relied upon a sixteenth-century Latin-English dictionary, Thomas Cooper's *Thesaurus* (1565), and upon Littleton's *Latin Dictionary* (1723), which is based on Cooper.

*Notes*

1. There is no certain evidence in the *Ars Poetica* that Horace was familiar with either Aristotle's *Rhetoric* or *Poetics*. The most reasonable conjecture is that some Alexandrian critical treatises have come between Aristotle and Horace. Yet there is no questioning an Aristotelian influence on the *Ars Poetica*. Roy Kenneth Hack has gone so far as to say that Horace's "whole poem is a spiritual quotation of the *Poetics*." See *Harvard Studies in Classical Philology* 27 (1916).61.

2. "Scripserunt de ea ex iis, qui ad nostram peruenere memoriam, Neoptolemus, Aristoteles, et utrunque imitatus est. Q. Horatius Flaccus, qui eminentissima quaeque breui sed pretioso libello comprehendit" (p. 4v).

3. "Quoniam uero partes illae duae libelli huius, quas praecipuas esse diximus, totae fere ad Poetices Aristotelis imitationem conscriptae sunt: non inutile futurum existimaui, si postquam ea, quae ad Aristotelis Poeticam attinebant, explicauimus; cuius ratione omnis mihi fuerat susceptus labor; quae hic ab Horatio habentur, in Aristotele, uelut in fonte demonstrarem, a quo uelut riuulum, librum hunc deduxit. . . . Erit igitur huius nostri scripti institutum, occultam atque artificiosam hanc Horatii imitationem patefacere" (p. 328).

4. *Essays* [Selected and edited by W. P. Ker. Oxford, 1926] 1.38. Cf. John Dennis, *Critical Works* [Edited by Edward Niles Hooker. 2 vols. Baltimore, 1939-1943] 2.286.

**David West (essay date 1967)**

SOURCE: West, David. "Some General Principles." In *Reading Horace,* pp. 125-41. Edinburgh: Edinburgh University Press, 1967.

[*In the following essay, West proposes some general principles for the reading of Horace, including the need to be as true as possible to the Latin in translation and the need to view the text within the framework in which it was written, discarding contemporary prejudices.*]

> 'Then farewell, Horace, whom I hated so,
> Not for thy faults, but mine: It is a curse
> To understand, not feel, thy lyric flow,
> To comprehend, but never love thy verse.'

Lord Byron Childe Harold's Pilgrimage

In analysing these few *Odes,* I have attempted to convey some impression of the quality of Horace's lyric poetry: his sense of humour, his sympathetic response to life in its many aspects, his profound debt to many previous Greek writers. Pindar is only one of the great poets whose work Horace absorbed and imitated. This we have seen in some

of the most characteristically Horatian features of the *Odes:* their complex structure, their contrived transitions and their oracular language. But most striking is the wide variety of tone, topic, and technique which make it difficult to organise our impressions into a general picture of Horace's lyric poetry. Instead, this last chapter will develop some points which may be of some use to those proposing to read Horace.

First, it is essential to know the language well, and to care for the details of it. This is true of the reading of any poetry. For example, the first fragment of Archilochus reads '. . . for the waves of the roaring sea have overwhelmed so many' (of our fellow-citizens), 'and our lungs are swollen with grief'. The translation, by Bonnard, in Lasserre's Budé edition has 'la plainte gonfle nos cœurs.' Hearts here instead of lungs is a rejection of the poetry.

But it is not simply a question of seeing the sustained image:

> Soluitur acris hiems grata uice ueris et Fauoni
>     trahuntque siccas machinae carinas,
> ac neque iam stabulis gaudet pecus aut arator igni
>     nec prata canis albicant pruinis.

Odes 1 4 1-4

Here Commager writes (***The Odes of Horace*** 268): '*Ships move* from the *dry prison* of the land, flocks *emerge* from their stables, the *farmer leaves* the *confines* of his *cottage*'. Every word which I have italicised is false to the Latin. In the first picture ships are not moving from a dry prison, winches are hauling them down to the water after they have spent the winter ashore upside down to let their bottoms dry out. In four words Horace vividly evokes the scene in a busy little Italian harbour in the springtime. He was just the sort of man who would enjoy watching people working:

> . . . quacumque libido est,
>     incedo solus, percontor quanti holus ac far,
> fallacem circum uespertinumque pererro
>     saepe forum, adsisto diuinis;

Satires 1 6 111-14

*'I go for my solitary walk wherever the fancy takes me, asking all about the price of vegetables and flour, wandering round all the rogues in the circus, and strolling through the forum every evening, dropping in at religious services.'*

Similarly, in the third line there is nothing about flocks emerging or farmers leaving. The Latin says that the flock is no longer enjoying its stables, or the ploughman his fire. This firmly evokes the comfortable warmth of stabled cattle, and the countryman who had been yarning round the fire, probably the blacksmith's,[1] all winter and was now out with the plough. In fairness to Commager, it must be noted that he is paraphrasing, not translating, and that it is not ignorance of Latin that has led him into these omissions, inaccuracies, extraneous metaphors, and this triple insistence on the moment of emergence. It is rather a desire to make the Horace more 'poetic'. But it is not easy to see how this could be consistent with a proper understanding of the poem.

The second suggestion I should like to make in this chapter is equally obvious. In reading and responding to a poem by Horace or by anybody else, we must at first arrest any mental patterns of our own which are clearly different from the patterns of our poet and his contemporary readers. Campbell's criticism of the **Bandusia Ode** (3 13) is a clear example of this egocentricity.

O fons Bandusiae, splendidior vitro,
dulci digne mero non sine floribus,
   cras donaberis haedo,
      cui frons turgida cornibus

primis et uenerem et proelia destinat—5
frustra, nam gelidos inficiet tibi
   rubro sanguine riuos
      lasciui suboles gregis.

te flagrantis atrox hora Caniculae
nescit tangere, tu frigus amabile 10
   fessis uomere tauris
      praebes et pecori uago.

fies nobilium tu quoque fontium
me dicente cauis inpositam ilicem
   saxis, unde loquaces 15
      lymphae desiliunt tuae.

*O fountain of Bandusia, sparkling like crystal,*
*you well deserve your offering of sweet pure wine and*
*   flowers.*
*      Tomorrow you will receive a kid,*
*      the first horns*

*swelling on its forehead, marking it out for love and*
*war.*
*In vain, for it will stain your cold current*
*   with its red blood,*
*      this lusty young goat.*

*The pitiless hour of the scorching dog-star*
*makes no difference to you; you offer welcome cool-*
*   ness*
*      to bulls weary of the plough*
*      and to the grazing² flocks.*

*You too will be one of the famous fountains,*
*for I am singing of the oak growing in the hollow*
*   of the stones from which your water*
*      leaps down chattering.*

Suppose it actually *were* the dog-days; that you were tired and hot and thirsty, and no drink available; but, suppose, at the same time, that you had a pocket Horace; in the search for *some* refreshment, you might naturally turn to that. Any purely beautiful poem might be expected to serve you as in some measure a restorative; but if your eye then chanced to fall on the beginning of this very ode, it would seem welcome not

alone as poetry but as poetry on an appropriate theme. "O fountain of Bandusia, more glittering than glass, worthy of sweet wine, not without flowers"—so far, all well. But now what follows? "To-morrow thou shalt be presented with a kid, whose brow, now swelling with his sprouting horns, gives promise of his loves and battles. Vain promise! for he shall"—to-morrow, that is—"stain thy cool waters with his red blood—he, the offspring of the wanton flock."

Who wants a drink out of the fountain of Bandusia after that?

You would return your Horace to your pocket, and bear up again as best you could.'

A. Y. Campbell *Horace* 1-2

So modern taste does not like blood in running water. This is neither here nor there. What is important is that the Romans were familiar with the notion of sacrificing animals to fountains (e.g. *fonti rex Numa mactat ouem,* Ovid *Fasti* 3 300). The critic must shed his local prejudices. The day is hot, the spring is cool and clear. When you cut a kid's throat over the water the spurts of thick warm blood are instantly diluted, as the colour spreads through the running water:

gelidos inficiet tibi rubro sanguine riuos.

The language has a density and vividness rare in any poetry, and what is described is a complex stimulus, the life blood spurting from an animal's jugular, an ancient religious observance of your race, the promise of a good supper, good wine and good company, perhaps with some music and love, and the canonisation of this little Italian spring for all time along with the great poetic fountains of Greece, Hippocrene, Castalia, and Arethusa (cf. page 112). The sensory precision of this and also its rich emotional overtones help to make a great Horatian poem, and it is a pity to have it spoilt by critics who are unwilling to let Horace be different from themselves.

This plea for the understanding of Horace first of all in his context, leads us to the political element in his poetry. His political career was varied. In his early twenties after the assassination of Caesar, he joined the tyrannicides, the republicans, and fought against Octavian in the battle of Philippi, 42 BC. By the time of Actium, 31 BC, he is reconciled to Octavian and has accepted his place in the new regime. So when Horace writes in praise of Octavian at the end of his second ode, Nisbet (*CE* 213), comments 'As for Horace's talk about the avenger of Caesar, one can only ask him, "What were you doing at Philippi?"'

Horace's political record is easy to sympathise with. As a young man he followed the republican flag, but he soon realised that his own future and the future of his war-torn country lay with Octavian. As Augustus entrenched himself more and more securely as the redeemer of Rome from her sins and the wars which they had occasioned, and as the guarantor of peace, prosperity, and settled government, Horace's enthusiasm and gratitude increased too. He became friendly with Octavian but never his tool. He persists in offering serious advice to the princeps, in the Roman Odes, for instance. On the other hand he never dissembles or rejects his republican past,[3] and *Odes* 2 7 shows how he was prepared to honour it:

O saepe mecum tempus in ultimum
deducte Bruto militiae duce,
   quis te redonauit Quiritem
      dis patriis Italoque caelo,

Pompei, meorum prime sodalium, 5
cum quo morantem saepe diem mero
   fregi coronatus nitentis
      malobathro Syrio capillos?

tecum Philippos et celerem fugam
sensi relicta non bene parmula, 10
   cum fracta uirtus et minaces
      turpe solum tetigere mento:

sed me per hostis Mercurius celer
denso pauentem sustulit aere,
   te rursus in bellum resorbens 15
      unda fretis tulit aestuosis.

ergo obligatam redde Iovi dapem
longaque fessum militia latus
   depone sub lauru mea nec
      parce cadis tibi destinatis. 20

obliuioso leuia Massico
ciboria exple, funde capacibus
   unguenta de conchis. quis udo
      deproperare apio coronas

curatue myrto? quem Venus arbitrum 25
dicet bibendi? non ego sanius
   bacchabor Edonis: recepto
      dulce mihi furere est amico.

                    *Odes* 2 7

*You and I, Pompeius, have often been led
to the edge of hell on campaign with Brutus.
   Who has given you back as a Roman citizen
   to your ancestral gods and the skies of Italy?*

*O Pompeius, first of my friends, many's the time
we have worn out the lingering day with wine undiluted,
   with garlands on our heads, and our hair
   sleek with Syrian ointment.*

*With you I went through Philippi throwing away my
   shield,
I'm ashamed to say, and taking to my heels,
   when our virtue was broken and after all our threats
   our chins rubbed the dust in defeat.*

*Terrified, I was snatched from my foes by Mercury,
and whisked away in a dense mist.
   But you were sucked back into the swirling currents
   and borne off again to war.*

*So then pay to Jupiter the feast you owe him,
and under my laurel lay down your body*

*worn out by long campaigning
and don't spare the cask I have reserved for you.*

*Massic wine brings oblivion, fill up the shining
   Egyptian cups
with it, pour the ointments from huge conches.
   Who is responsible for hurrying up the garlands
   of parsley and myrtle?*

*The throw of the dice will decide who is to see to the
   wine.
I intend to rave like a Bacchante.
   Now that I've got my friend back,
   I'm all for an orgy.*

This poem provides a sharp insight into Horace's political situation. Octavian declared a general amnesty in 29 BC, so the question in the third line is an oblique compliment to him. Similarly the second stanza hints that the two men who espoused the cause of Brutus in 42 BC were young and irresponsible. So again, when Horace has to express the intractable fact that Pompeius fought against Octavian for a dozen years, he suggests that Pompeius was carried away by a current too turbulent to resist. All this makes it quite clear that Horace's republican phase is over. He is welcoming back a friend who fought with him against Octavian. But it is Octavian's peace that has made this possible. Horace is now on the other side, and never leaves any room for doubt about that. Nevertheless, he is not thinking solely of his own interests.

This approval of Octavian, quietly and firmly offered in this *Ode,* is doing no harm to Pompeius' prospects. The poem is full of understanding and consideration for his less fortunate friend. There is the lightness and irony with which he refers to Pompeius' flight at Philippi, emphasising his own share in the débâcle by saying that he threw away his shield, as Archilochus, Alcaeus, and probably Anacreon had done before him, and was whisked off the battlefield in a mist like a Homeric hero. There is the great warmth and affection of Horace's welcome to his old friend. It is typical of Horace to understand that the first thing you think of when you meet an old friend is the sufferings you have shared, and then pretty soon, any drinking you've done together:

Tam lo'ed him like a very brither;
They had been fou for weeks thegither.

                   Robert Burns *Tam o' Shanter*

Lines 3 and 4 are as densely suggestive as anything in Horace, glowing with pleasure at the thought of Pompeius' demobilisation and rehabilitation and his return to the Italian skies. Only an Italian could move properly to that phrase; these dead paraphrases are a dismal substitute for the living Latin. In the third last stanza almost every word helps to deepen the expression of affection so that the whole sentence rings with friendship carried to the point of genius; *obliuioso* in the second last stanza gently advises

Pompeius to make a fresh start and allows Horace to modulate at the end of the Ode towards the ordinary things he loved so much. But he doesn't quite contain himself for his normal quiet close here. *sanius bacchabor Edonis . . . furere* comprise a rousing sustained image.

When a man is capable of such humanity, subtlety, and maturity in a political situation, his critics should surely try to show some of the same qualities.

There is no love poetry in Latin more rich and sensitive than Horace's, and none more persistently maligned, presumably because commonsense is not a quality highly regarded by readers of erotic verse. The old notion that these poems can be used as evidence to reconstruct Horace's private life has fallen out of fashion, but in rejecting this documentary fallacy some important modern scholars have swung to the opposite naïveté and now believe that 'the erotic themes of these poems have nothing to do with real life'. This position, which may best be studied in the writings of R. G. M. Nisbet and G. Williams,[4] depends upon three main propositions. The first is that if a passage in Horace is an imitation of Greek, then it has nothing to do with real life. The second is that if such a passage contains inconsistencies or improbabilities, then it has nothing to do with real life. The third is that if a poem is not some sort of account of what the poet actually did, then it is an inferior poem. The first and third of these propositions are clearly false and the second falls to the ground because so few of these poems do contain inconsistencies or improbabilities. The conclusion may be valid for these few, but there is no warrant to extend it to the other poems.

The truth here is simple. The poems are no evidence for Horace's private life, nor is there any evidence that what they say about his private life is false. We all reject the documentary fallacy nowadays, and I do not see how we can accept this 'unreality' fallacy. We just do not know how Horace lived; whether he ever dreamt about a young boy as he most vividly and particularly says that he did in

    nocturnis ego somniis
      iam captum teneo, iam uolucrem sequor
    te per gramina Martii
      Campi, te per aquas, dure, uolubiles.

                        **Odes** 4 1 37-40

*In my dreams sometimes I catch and hold you, sometimes I pursue you as you run over the grass of the Campus, or swim through the rolling waters of the Tiber paying no attention to me.*

Nor do we know, when Horace issues his moving invitation to Phyllis, whether there ever was such an invitation, or such a woman:

      age iam, meorum
    finis amorum,
    —non enim posthac alia calebo
    femina—

                        **Odes** 4 11 31-4

*Come then, last of my loves, for you are the last woman who will ever warm my heart . . .*

Williams believes that this is not a real invitation, nor even conceivably real (41); I believe that we don't know anything about this. This difference is slight, so slight that I think Williams sometimes seems to conflate the two views, as on page 42, 'The erotic themes of these poems have nothing to do with Horace's real life. Horace may have been the greatest rake imaginable: but his odes have no bearing on the question one way or the other.' But the distinction is worth being very careful about, since the one view leads to adverse criticism of the poems for their artificiality, whereas I insist that, since this sort of thing went on in Rome, Horace may well have done it himself, or understood it very well from the outside, and am therefore under no temptation to pass any pejorative judgment on the poetry.

But this may be rather a high-handed and uncomprehending simplification of a difficult argument, and it would be only fair if I went over the ground again more explicitly, starting with an invitation poem which is not a love poem, because it offers a brief and vivid demonstration of this type of criticism.

                    ***Odes*** 1 20

    Vile potabis modicis Sabinum
    cantharis, Graeca quod ego ipse testa
    conditum leui, datus in theatro
      cum tibi plausus,

    care Maecenas eques, ut paterni (5)
    fluminis ripae simul et iocosa
    redderet laudes tibi Vaticani
      montis imago.

    Caecubum et prelo domitam Caleno
    tu bibes uuam: mea nec Falernae (10)
    temperant uites neque Formiani
      pocula colles.

*You will drink from modest cups
the cheap Sabine wine which I laid down
with my own hands and sealed in a Greek jar
the day the theatre rose to you,*

*a Roman knight, my dear Maecenas,
when the banks of Father Tiber
and the Vatican Hill tossed back together
the echoes of your praises.*

*You will drink Caecuban and the grape
tamed in the Calenian presses, but the harshness
of my wines is not moderated by Falernian grapes
or the Formian hills.*

Here Nisbet comments on page 188 'When the modest poet contrasts his *vin du pays* with the cellar of his patron, the touch seems agreeably Horatian: yet Philodemus had said much the same when inviting L. Piso to his frugal supper (*Palatine Anthology* 11 44).' In this paragraph Nisbet is arguing that in such poems 'the element of reality is negligible', and it is an obvious *non sequitur*. If Philodemus apologised for his wine, this does not mean that Horace didn't.

Nisbet reinforced this in his lecture to the Joint Meeting of the Greek and Roman Societies in Oxford in August 1965, by an attempt to find improbabilities in this Ode: first, that it is very odd of Horace to offer cheap Sabine to his patron when he frequently drank expensive wines himself; second, that the whole situation is impossible, because it requires us to suppose that on the day of Maecenas' first public appearance after his illness, either a messenger rode posthaste from the theatre at Rome and prompted Horace to begin his commemorative bottling, or that Horace had been in the theatre, and had leapt on a horse immediately the applause began and rode hard to his Sabine farm to get down to work before dusk fell.

But a little imagination shows what a fine poem this is. Horace has been bottling. A couple of days pass and he hears about Maecenas' great reception. He realises that at that very moment he had been bottling, or rather jarring, his own wine, and thinks, 'Splendid, I'll mark that, and the next time Maecenas comes I'll give him some. It's just a blowpipe wine of course, in comparison with what he normally drinks, but in its way it's not at all bad.' The facts are suitably doctored. The poem takes shape, and is full of marvellous intimacies. Anybody who has ever grown anything can't wait to inflict it on his friends, complete with apologies, and quietly stressing that it is all his own work (*ipse . . . conditum leui*). If Philodemus expressed a quarter of this in his poem to Piso, this does not make it a whit less Horatian. And it is all linked with Horace's pleasure at his friend's recovery, and at the public acclaim he enjoyed. The only helpful comment on this is the famous phrase in Maecenas' will where he asks Augustus to look after Horace as though he were himself. *Horati Flacci ut mei esto memor.*

This consideration of an invitation poem leads us to one of Williams' most destructive arguments. He observes (41) that generally when Horace mentions distinguished Romans in connection with drinking parties girls are not present, and when he mentions girls, no distinguished Roman is invited. Now it is generally agreed that such parties did take place in Rome but were regarded as not wholly respectable (Williams 41 and cf. 36: 'however complacently these liaisons were regarded in real life'), and the obvious explanation of Williams' observation is that Horace is exercising a little commonsense in not naming any public figures in this connection, yet by an astounding twist of the argument Williams concludes that such parties were not real nor even conceivably real, unless Horace ties them to a Roman occasion, names a distinguished Roman, and does not mention girls.

This seems to me to go beyond the evidence. But many readers of Horace feel an atmosphere of unreality about these poems, an impression of artificiality, a lack of sincer-ity. When they establish genuine inconsistencies or improbabilities in a poem, then our evaluation of that single poem will be affected, but normally we are dealing with alleged improbabilities which vanish after a moment's charitable thought, with alleged imitations which seem to us to be frigidly derivative only because they refer to a way of life the Romans shared with the Hellenistic Greeks but not with us. Of course Horace imitated Hellenistic poets, but all this talk of Horace's fantasy world of Greek and Roman forgets that Rome was a Mediterranean city, and a Hellenistic city, teeming with Greek importations. So many people make easy jokes about implausibilities, about literary furniture, about flute girls, nard, wine, and garlands of *apium,* that we must dig in our heels and insist that Romans did wear perfume and garlands of celery, they even drank wine in great quantities and spent evenings with girls, from time to time listening to their music. We do not. But there is nothing funny about it, nor implausible. There is no reason to believe that Horace did not sometimes do this sort of thing.

But from the point of view of the poetry all this controversy is irrelevant. There is no need to believe that Horace did any such thing. Should subsequent research reveal that these poems were written by a Vestal Virgin, their quality would remain unaffected. Was there in fact any real historical connection between Maecenas' recovery and work on the wine on Horace's farm? When Horace penned the invitation to Phyllis, did he have a real Phyllis in mind who looked like being his last love? We do not know and never can know and it does not matter. The point is not what Horace did, but what he wrote, and it is still quite respectable to feel that some of these poems are great poems. Those who believe that Horace did not live like this have not made their case, and if they had the poems would be none the worse. They would still be wise, witty, sensitive, suggestive and deeply understanding, and moving, and there is nothing implausible in them.

In odes 1 19, for instance, the last poem we shall look at, the first half shrewdly fits our own observation of life. We smile when Horace makes Venus come down on him like a thunderclap (cf. *Odes* 1 16 12). We are amused by the difficulty he finds in writing political verse. And at the end we warm again to this rightminded lover, whose reserve can say so much. This is not a defence against love, or a flight from it. Horace has decided to have an intimate supper party and do the thing graciously.

### *Odes* 1 19

Mater saeua Cupidinum
    Thebanaeque iubet me Semelae puer
et lasciua Licentia
    finitis animum reddere amoribus.

urit me Glycerae nitor (5)
    splendentis Pario marmore purius,
urit grata proteruitas
    et uoltus nimium lubricus adspici.

in me tota ruens Venus
  Cyprum deseruit nec patitur Scythas (10)
et uersis animosum equis
  Parthum dicere nec quae nihil attinet.

hic uiuum mihi caespitem, hic
  uerbenas, pueri, ponite turaque
bimi cum patera meri: (15)
  mactata ueniet lenior hostia.

*Merciless Venus, mother of Desires,*
  *and the god of wine, son of Theban Semele,*
*and the weakness of my flesh*
  *bid me call a dead passion back to life.*

*I am in love with Glycera,*
  *with the sheen of her skin, a purer white than the*
  *Parian marble,*
*with her delicious sexuality*
  *and her face fatal to look at.*

*Venus has abandoned Cyprus*
  *and come rushing down on me with all her power. I*
  *cannot speak*
*of Scythians, or Parthians aggressive in retreat,*
  *or anything else bar love.*

*Put down here, boy, by me a piece of living turf*
  *and sacrificial branches and incense*
*with a goblet of two-year-old wine undiluted.*
  *If I kill a victim, the visitation of Venus will be less*
  *violent.*

This somewhat polemical chapter may make a depressingly negative end to this little book. But it is not purely negative. A poem is a stone thrown into the pool of the mind. We can establish that certain ripples are historically necessary, or historically impossible, but apart from these each pool (if it has any water in it at all) has a different depth, a different fringe of vegetation, a different colour, different lighting (if any) and a different bottom; so after the critics have done with the poem, there will remain innumerable patterns evanescent and elusive, neither necessary nor refutable, the valid personal impact of the poem on the man who reads it. Through the haze of two millennia we have to repress all our contemporary preconceptions, to deploy an exhaustive philological and historical learning and still be able to feel like human beings.

Clearly the task is impossible. But to those who attempt it, the *Epistles* of Horace, as we have seen, offer any amount of good sense and good humour, an endearing persona genially and cunningly revealed, a wide range of interesting observation, thought, and emotion, and something very like the kind of delight which great poetry gives. The *Odes* it would be stupid to attempt to characterise in this fashion. We must just read and be ready for anything.

*Notes*

1. Hesiod *Works and Days* 493.

2. J. Henry *Aeneidea* on Virgil *Aeneid* 5 560, quoted by C. J. Fordyce on Catullus 64 271.

3. Cf. *Epistles* 1 20 23. But there is a very shady reference at the end of *Odes* 3 2. Can this be Horace washing his hands of some Murena (executed for conspiracy 22 BC), or some Gallus (driven to suicide 26 BC perhaps amongst other things for defaming Augustus?). On *Odes* 2 7 see the careful analysis by Collinge *The Structure of Horace's Odes* 128-49. On the political bearing of the *Odes* contrast Williams *JRS* [*Journal of Russian Studies*] 52 (1962) 28-46 and Fraenkel *Horace*, e.g. 273.

4. Nisbet *CE* [*Critical Essays in Roman Literature, Elegy and Lyric*, edited by J. P. Sullivan] 181-218, Williams 35-46. My quotation is from page 42.

## M. Owen Lee (essay date 1969)

SOURCE: Lee, M. Owen. "Words." In *Word, Sound, and Image in the Odes of Horace*, pp. 7-28. Ann Arbor: University of Michigan Press, 1969.

[*In the following essay, Lee examines Horace's use and arrangement of words, including the use of the transferred epithet, hendiadys, word association, and oxymoron.*]

"Beauty of form has made him immortal, and fully half that beauty lies in the order of his words."

—GILBERT MURRAY

Poems Are Made from words. But not quite as walls are made from bricks. Bricks are durable and insensitive. They are, moreover, made for building. But words—some simply do not look right on the printed page; others are not suited to the metrical scheme; others are too lofty or too lowly for the poet's purpose:

audebit, quaecumque parum splendoris habebunt et sine pondere erunt et honore indigna ferentur, verba movere loco, quamvis invita recedant

(*Epistles* 2.2.111-13).

(The poet) will have the courage to strike out all such words as have not the requisite beauty, gravity or dignity, though they may not want to give place.[1]

If nothing else will do, picturesque archaisms will have to be called forth from retirement:

obscurata diu populo bonus eruet atque proferet in lucem speciosa vocabula rerum, quae priscis memorata Catonibus atque Cethegis nunc situs informis premit et deserta vetustas

(115-19).

Words long buried in darkness the good poet will unearth and bring to light—those picturesque phrases which were once mouthed by old Cato and Cethegus and the rest, but which have grown old and ugly and are now covered over with the rust of neglect.

Occasionally, and with great care, new words can be forged:

> si forte necesse est indiciis monstrare recentibus abdita rerum, fingere cinctutis non exaudita Cethegis continget, dabiturque licentia sumpta pudenter

> (*AP* [*Ars Poetica*] 48-51).

If it so happens that you need new terms to explain some abstruse subject, then you have a proper occasion to coin words never heard by the straight-laced Cethegi; the right will be yours, if you use it with restraint.

But a careful and sensitive poet will not need to resort to extreme measures often. He will use old words and give them new luster by juxtaposition:

> in verbis etiam tenuis cautusque serendis dixeris egregie notum si callida verbum reddiderit iunctura novum

> (46-48).

Be sensitive, too, and careful in combining words. You will have spoken especially well, if some clever juxtaposition has made a familiar word new.

In this last department Horace has set a standard still unequalled by the world's poets. The *callida iunctura* is his specialty. Of all the accolades accorded it, Nietzsche's, the most quoted, is still the most apt:

> This mosaic of words, in which every word, by sound, by position and by meaning, diffuses its influence to right and left and over the whole.[2]

The reader may think "every word" at least a slight exaggeration,[3] but there are poets who will not think it so. T. S. Eliot sees in poetry a "perpetual slight alteration of language, words perpetually juxtaposed in new and sudden combinations."[4] In a poem, as in a sentence,

> every word is at home,
> Taking its place to support the others,
> The word neither diffident nor ostentatious,
> An easy commerce of the old and the new,
> The common word exact without vulgarity,
> The formal word precise but not pedantic,
> The complete consort dancing together.[5]

On the simplest level, Horace is unequalled in the placing of words for eye-catching effect in the stanza. And while Nietzsche may see them as tiny pieces of a mosaic, blocks or hewn stones might be a more apt description for the words as structured in almost any of Horace's Sapphic stanzas:

> rebus angustis animosus atque
> fortis appare; sapienter idem
> contrahes vento nimium secundo
>   turgida vela

> (2.10.21-24).

Here is a metrical scheme modeled on the light stanza of a Greek poetess but reworked[6] so as to give maximum effect to great resounding Latin words built into some sort of lapidary statement. The words seem to fall by their own weight into place, leaving at the close a single dactyl and spondee, visually isolated and musically resounding, lodged in the memory.

Another stanza from the same poem will show how the ode's theme—the Golden Mean—is emphasized by the placing of the key word, the double-weighted *mediocritatem,* above the neatly substructured phrases *caret obsoleti* and *caret invidenda:*

> auream quisquis mediocritatem
> diligit, tutus caret obsoleti
> sordibus tecti, caret invidenda
>   sobrius aula

> (5-8).

If the eye is allowed to move vertically through the stanza, the reader sees as well as hears the echoes: *quisquis . . . tutus . . . tecti; sordibus . . . sobrius.* Part of the credit for these effects must go to the Latin language, which dispenses with the article, auxiliary verbs, and many prepositions—smaller words which might tend to clutter the line. (The necessary monosyllables, *si* and *non* and the rest, can be worked into a line of poetry unobtrusively: in the poem from which we have quoted, all but two of these are concentrated in a single stanza.) But most of the credit must go to Horace, who strives to give each word an importance, a visual, almost tactile role in the structure of the stanza.

Because Latin is an inflected language, the endings of the words will establish the necessary grammatical relationships, and there is no need, as in modern languages, to place the words in an order demanded by the sense. Words can be rearranged almost at will, and to striking effect. In the first ode of Horace, a Marsian boar is, on the printed page, within the supple nets:

> teretes Marsus aper plagas

> (1.1.28),

a hind is sighted, and surrounded, by faithful hounds:

> catulis cerva fidelibus

> (27),

and a peaceful gentleman's limbs are quite visually shaded by a green arbutus:

> viridi membra sub arbuto

> (21).

Similarly, Horace illustrates how sea-monsters fill the teeming ocean:

> scatentem / beluis pontum

> (3.27.26-27),

how Bandusia's oak is set amid hollow rocks:

> cavis impositam ilicem / saxis

> (3.13.14-15),

how, within the thick cloud which rescued him from Philippi, he did the trembling, Mercury the lifting:

> denso paventem sustulit aëre
>
> (2.7.14).

There are examples of this by the hundred, but the *locus
classicus* for such word-placing is the fifth ode in the first
book. The lady addressed is embraced by a handsome boy:

> gracilis te puer,

and the two are surrounded by roses:

> multa gracilis te puer in rosa
>
> (1.5.1).

It seems the lady, Pyrrha, lies within a pleasure cave:

> grato, Pyrrha, sub antro
>
> (3)

by the side of a sea tossed by black winds:

> nigris aequora ventis
>
> (7).

The boy and girl embrace: . . .

while Horace, thankful for his escape from this siren, puts
up a votive plaque on a chapel wall, with his dripping gar-
ments as testimonial, to the powerful sea-god who effected
his rescue—and the nouns and adjectives, arranged in
interlocking pairs before and after the main verb, form a
checkerwork as intricate as the plaque-covered chapel wall
itself: . . .

This effect has only recently been marked by writers on
Horace[7]—though one suspects that the schoolboy, numbering the words in order in his text, saw it long ago.

### TRADITIONAL PATTERNS

A word-pattern favored by ancient grammarians is *chiasmus,* wherein corresponding pairs of words are arranged
so as to form the letter chi (x) if one pair is written above
the other: . . .

Horace does not make extensive use of this somewhat
rhetorical device. But more than two dozen times in the
*Odes* we find the so-called Golden Verse, defined by Dryden as "two substantives and two adjectives with a verb
betwixt to keep the peace."[8] In Horace the two adjectives
almost invariably come first, and the resulting arrangement
is sometimes chiastic:

> fragilem truci / commisit pelago ratem
>
> (1.3.10-11),

sometimes achiastic, or interlocking:

> superiecto pavidae natarunt / aequore dammae
>
> (1.2.11-12).[9]

The effect is to afford the reader a glimpse first of the
detail, descriptive or emotional, leaving subject matter
undefined until the verb has, as it were, brought the picture
to life, e.g.:

> a fragile—to the savage—he entrusted—to the sea—
>                                                     a skiff,

and:

> in the overwhelming—trembling—they swam—
> in the water—deer.

### SHARED EPITHET

Often Horace intends a single adjective to qualify two
nouns, and accordingly places it between the two (though
it is conjoined only to the second). Thus the lad making
love to Pyrrha will often bewail her (broken) promise and
the fickle gods:

> fidem / mutatosque deos flebit
>
> (1.5.5-6).

Both the horses and the chariot of the sky-god are winged:

> equos volucremque currum
>
> (1.34.8).

Both senate and traditional values are subverted by the
defection of Crassus' soldiers:

> pro curia inversique mores
>
> (3.5.7).[10]

Similarly, a well placed adjective can serve adverbially to
qualify two verbs. Both Horace and his serving boy are
*sedulus:*

> nihil allabores / sedulus curo
>
> (1.38.5-6).
>
> I earnestly ask that you add
> nothing, in your earnestness.

### TRANSFERRED EPITHET

Horace is fond of the figure of speech known as hypallage
or transferred epithet: an adjective appearing in a context
with two substantives seems to have been transferred from
the one to which it belongs in sense, and made to agree
grammatically with the other. The reader is jolted,
recognizes the figure, pauses to transfer the epithet back to
its proper substantive, while marking that, in a secondary
sense at least, it does somehow qualify the word it is made
to modify. So Queen Cleopatra is said to prepare "mad
ruin" for the Capitol:

> regina dementes ruinas
>
> (1.37.7).

Surely, one thinks, the *dementes* should be *demens,* modifying *regina:* she is spoken of as maddened and deranged throughout the first half of the poem, and transferring the epithet gives the passage a neat parallelism—"the mad queen was plotting ruin for the Capitol and destruction for the empire." But as the words stand the effect is richer: *dementes* between the two similar-sounding nouns goes in sense with *regina* and grammatically (and in a secondary sense, and with graphic effect) with *ruinas.*

When he uses this figure, Horace usually contrives to juxtapose the epithet and the word with which it goes in sense. So we do not allow angry Jove to lay aside his (angry) thunderbolts:

> iracunda Iovem ponere fulmina
>
> (1.3.40),

and glistening Minos passes (glistening) judgment:

> splendida Minos / fecerit arbitria
>
> (4.7.21-22),

and the poet came close to seeing the dusky realms of (dusky) Proserpine:

> furvae regna Proserpinae
>
> (2.13.21).[11]

Richer and more startling still are the instances of *double* hypallage. In Horace's opening poem, the peaceful man is said to recline at times at the gentle source of some sacred stream:

> ad aquae lene caput sacrae
>
> (1.1.22).

But, we reflect, the guardian nymph dwells at the *source* of the stream: *sacrae* should modify *caput.* And the stream would hardly be one to rest by unless its *waters* were gently rippling: *lene* should modify *aquae.* The complex, magical phrase is usually translated with both epithets transferred, "at the sacred source of some gentle stream," but any translation must lose fully half of the original. And again, Horace's placing of the words has helped.

Another fine example of double hypallage is in the ode to Pyrrha:

> aspera / nigris aequora ventis
>
> (1.5.6-7).

Does this mean "the sea roughened by dark winds" or "the sea darkened by rough winds"? To the reader's delight and the translator's despair, it means both.

Double hypallage is the best solution to the riddle posed by Horace's famous boast:

> princeps Aeolium carmen ad Italos
> deduxisse modos
>
> (3.30.13-14).

Surely, the puzzled reader objects, this is not right; Horace brought Latin song to Greek meters, not vice versa. But when both epithets are transferred,[12] the boast is well founded: Horace was the first to bring Latin song to Greek (at least, if we except three poems by Catullus, to Aeolian) meters. Then, knowing Horace's way with hypallage, we pause to look into the secondary sense, and note that the expression is, even as it stands, quite true, and a part of Horace's glorious claim: his Latin *carmen* has a Greek delicacy and finish, and the *modi* originated by Greeks will ever after be thought of as Latin—indeed, as Horatian.

## HENDIADYS

On an equal level of invention is Horace's use of hendiadys—the expression of a single idea by two connected nouns. Invariably the second of the two qualifies the first, adding the personal, the graphic, the limiting detail. So when Horace reminds Pompeius how they experienced the swift rout at Philippi:

> Philippos et celerem fugam
>
> (2.7.9),

what he says in effect is "with you I experienced Philippi—(not the glory of it, but) the unceremonious retreat." So an enormous troop of impious Titans:

> impios / Titanas immanemque turbam
>
> (3.4.42-43)

is, more properly, "impious Titans—a great swarm of them." And mists and bad weather:

> nebulae malusque / Iuppiter
>
> (1.22.19-20)

are "mists—the kind Jupiter sends when he is in a bad mood."

There is a pair of such expressions (and another *celerem fugam*) in 2.13.17-19:

> miles sagittas et celerem fugam
> Parthi, catenas Parthus et Italum
> robur . . .

The full implication here is that the (Roman) soldier fears arrows—(not just any arrows, but) those the Parthians shoot on their swift retreat-maneuver, while the Parthian fears imprisonment—(not at home, but) in the Roman strong-place in the Mamertine.

## OXYMORON

The ancient species of paradox known as oxymoron is only a sophisticated use of word-placing, and Horace is the prime exponent of this sort of literary jolt. Hypermnestra, who alone of Danaus' fifty daughters disobeyed paternal orders and spared her husband on that fatal wedding night, is gloriously deceitful (*splendide mendax* 3.11.35); Juba's land is dry, but it nurses lions (*leonum / arida nutrix* 1.22.15-16); the wine jug wrests secrets from the tippler, so it may be called a gentle sort of rack (*lene tormentum* 3.21.13). Less famous than these examples, but worth noting, are the reference to the mad wisdom of Epicurean thought (*insanientis . . . sapientiae* 1.34.2— usually overlooked in the discussion of Lucretius' reported madness), and that egregious pun—Regulus hastening forth to exile an *egregius . . . exsul* (3.5.48), i.e., not only glorious but, in exile, standing out from the *grex*.

Most of the punning in Horace's **Odes** owes at least as much to word-placing as it does to verbal similarities. Mercury is *lyrae parentem* (1.10.6), though in the context we are reminded that he was a *puer* (actually not a full day old) when he fathered the lyre; the Argonauts looked undismayed at the terrors of the sea, but as the words and their placing have it, they looked with dry eyes at swimming monsters:

> siccis oculis monstra natantia
>
> (1.3.18).

At times, the juxtaposition of proper name and qualifying pun is wit of the subtlest variety, defying translation:

> *Parca non mendax*
>
> (2.16.39)
>
> the sparing goddess, true to her name
>
> *immitis Glycerae*
>
> (1.33.2)
>
> your embittered Sweetheart
>
> *Lalagen . . . dulce loquentem*
>
> (1.22.23-24)
>
> my sweet-talking Chatterbox
>
> *Bibuli consulis amphoram*
>
> (3.28.8)
>
> a wine jar from Bibulus' consulship.

### ASSOCIATION

As words carry the weight of associations, a strategically placed word can call up the memory of a separate context. Thus, memories of Homer may be evoked by such brief phrases as *densentur funera* (1.28.19—cf. Homer's αἰεὶ δὲ πυραὶ νεκύων καίοντο θαμειαι in *Iliad* 1.52), and *iuga demeret / bobus* (3.6.42-43—cf. Homer's recurrent βουλυτόνδε), and *quicumque terrae munere vescimur* (2.14.10—cf. Homer's βροτῶν, οἳ ἀρούρης καρπὸν ἔδουσιν in *Iliad* 6.142, and ὅσσοι νῦν βροτοί εἰσιν ἐπὶ

χθονὶ σῖτον ἔδοντες in *Odyssey* 8.222). But Horace's personal experience is bound up less with Homer than with the lyric poets of Greece:

> *non, si priores Maeonius tenet*
> *sedes Homerus, Pindaricae latent*
> *Ceaeque et Alcaei minaces*
> *Stesichorive graves Camenae;*
>
> *nec, si quid olim lusit Anacreon,*
> *delevit aetas; spirat adhuc amor*
> *vivuntque commissi calores*
> *Aeoliae fidibus puellae*
>
> (4.9.5-12).

Even though Maeonian Homer holds first place, the other muses do not hide their faces—not Pindar's, or Simonides', or Alcaeus' warlike maid, or the stately muse of Stesichorus;

nor has time destroyed all that Anacreon wrote in sport; and that love still breathes, those passions still live that were confided to the harp-strings of the Aeolian maid.

Horace borrowed themes as well as meters from these predecessors, particularly from Alcaeus. The devotion of Roman disciple to Greek master is revealed twice, in the touching 1.32 and the semi-humorous 2.13. At least a few of the **Odes** are free and imaginative adaptations of Alcaean poems: the hymn to Mercury, 1.10, may be compared with fragment 308 LP, and the "ship of state" ode, 1.14, with fragment 326 LP.

Adaptations, however, were not Horace's real purpose. He rather employs quotations from the Greek lyricists as motifs in the **Odes**—a not inappropriate device for a poet who was apprenticed to these writers, and almost obsessively desirous of joining their ranks. Latinized bits of *Lyra Graeca* thread their way through the **Odes,** charged no doubt with personal associations for Horace himself, imbuing his poems with a romantic, centuries-old atmosphere, and challenging the educated reader to intellectual as well as emotional response. Though we cannot hope to trace all of Horace's allusive borrowings from the now fragmentary writings of Alcaeus, we can see, for example, that the opening of the Cleopatra ode (*Nunc est bibendum,* 1.37) is a Latinized quote from Alcaeus' celebration of the fall of the Lesbian tyrant Myrsilus (332 LP), that 1.9 (the Soracte ode), 1.18, and 3.12 all take their opening "mottoes" from once-familiar lyrics of Alcaeus (338, 342, and 10 LP) and then veer off on new poetic tangents; that Simonides is probably the source of the famous *innumerabilis / annorum series et fuga temporum* (3.30.4-5); that there are echoes of Anacreon in 1.23, the ode to Chloë as fawn (408 P), in 1.27, the brawl over the drinking cups (356 P), in 1.25, 2.5, and 3.11; that 1.12 begins with a Pindaric "motto" and is reminiscent throughout of the second Olympian; that 1.15 is modeled on Bacchylides. As Pasquali[13] is at pains to point out, this is not *imitatio*. It is an allusive and very personal use of literature and its associations. One is reminded of T. S. Eliot's elaborate deployment of passages from the many writers who people his subconscious.[14]

To a lesser extent, Latin poets are quoted for effect. When Horace writes an ode for Virgil, he pays him the compliment of using words Virgil has charged with meaning. The third ode in the first book, addressed to the ship bearing Virgil on a perilous voyage, contains a number of references to and words from the sea-scenes in the early books of the *Aeneid.* Aeolus and his prison of the winds, Africus, Notus, Aquilo, and the Hyades are all transferred from Aeneas' Mediterranean to the sea which Virgil must cross and which is for Horace almost symbolic of destruction, the Adriatic. A Virgilian line:

> *et mulcere dedit fluctus et tollere vento*
>
> (1.66)
>
> and gave the power to soothe the waves, and lift
>     them with the wind

prompts the Horatian:

> *tollere seu ponere volt freta*
>
> (1.3.16)
>
> whether he choose to lift or lull the
>     sea.

But most notable in both poets is the use of *incubo.* Properly the word means "lie upon," but in the sea passages of the first books of the *Aeneid*[15] Virgil gives it an ominous, sinister force; it comes to mean "brood over, settle upon." So when the word appears in Horace's ode on Virgil's sea voyage:

> *et nova febrium*
> *terris incubuit cohors*
>
> (1.3.30-31)
>
> and a legion of strange diseases
> settled upon the earth,

we think of the *febres* as malevolent powers settling like birds of ill omen upon their victim.

The spirit of Catullus is invoked in 1.22, which virtually quotes both of the earlier poet's efforts in the Sapphic meter: *iter . . . facturus* (1.22.5-6) with attendant travelogue is close to the opening of Catullus 11, while *dulce ridentem* (1.22.23) is an unmistakable quotation from Catullus 51. Also reminiscent of Catullus 11 is Horace 2.6: though the earlier poem is full of half-smothered sarcasm and the latter is genial and sentimental, both begin with a *vademecum* and end with unexpected poignancy; Horace even recalls Catullus' best adonic (*tunditur unda*) with his similarly placed *aestuat unda.* Then Horace's Lydia is much like Catullus' Lesbia: she causes the poet's senses to quiver and quake (compare Catullus 51 and Horace 1.13); she enters into amoebean discourse with him (compare Catullus 45 and Horace 3.9); and Lydia, it is forecast, will end her days as Catullus says

Lesbia did, a tramp in a narrow alleyway, *in solo levis angiportu* (Horace 1.25.10—compare Catullus 58 and the use of *levis* in 72.6). Finally Horace begins the last of his spring songs with a tribute to Catullus: *iam veris comites* (Horace 4.12.1—compare Catullus 46.1, 9), and then writes a variant of Catullus 13: Virgil is invited to dinner but must bring his own ointment. In each case it is the carefully chosen, carefully placed word which brings the association of the previous context to bear on the present one. Catullus himself is never mentioned.

Nor is Lucretius, but similar compliments are nonetheless paid him, particularly in the odes of Book II, with its predominantly Epicurean tone.[16] Lucretius' line

> *iam iam non domus accipiet te laeta, neque uxor*
>
> (3.894)
>
> no more, no more will your happy home welcome
>     you, nor your wife

is the source of Horace's

> *linquenda tellus et domus et placens / uxor*
>
> (2.14.21-22).
>
> you must leave your land and home and lov-
>     ing wife.[17]

The opening stanzas of 2.16 (*Otium divos*) may recall Catullus' Sapphic stanza on *otium,* but there is a distinct echo of Lucretius as well in the lines:

> *patriae quis exsul*
> *se quoque fugit?*
>
> (19-20)
>
> what man, exiled from his country,
> escapes himself as well?

Lucretius has *hoc se quoque modo fugit* (3.1068), and similarly in a section where he describes the vain attempts of men to escape anxieties that gnaw from within. Finally, in the loveliest of the spring songs, Horace begins with a stanza which may call to mind the opening of Lucretius' poem:

> *Diffugere nives, redeunt iam gramina campis*
> *    arboribusque comae;*
> *mutat terra vices, et decrescentia ripas*
> *    flumina praetereunt*
>
> (4.7.1-4).
>
> The snows have fled. So soon the grass is come
> back to the fields, the leaves to the trees.
> The earth is changing its seasons, and sub-
>     siding
> rivers are flowing past their banks.[18]

The third stanza seems a reworking of Lucretius' parade of the seasons in Book V:

> *frigora mitescunt Zephyris, ver proterit aestas*
> *    interitura simul*

*pomifer autumnus fruges effuderit, et mox
bruma recurrit iners*

(9-12).

Winter gives way to Spring's breath, Summer
drives away Spring, only to perish itself as
soon as apple-bearing Autumn has poured
forth its fruits. And soon Winter stumbles
back, all-but-dead.[19]

With Horace's next stanza, the echoes are surer and
remarkably varied:

*damna tamen celeres reparant caelestia lunae:
nos, ubi decidimus
quo pater Aeneas, quo Tullus dives et Ancus,
pulvis et umbra sumus*

(13-16).

Yet the swift-changing moon repairs its heavenly losses. We, when once we have descended
whither father Aeneas and king Tullus and
Ancus have gone, we are dust and shadow.

Line 15 is reminiscent of Virgil (*pater Aeneas*), of Horace's *Epistles* (1.6.27), of Lucretius:

*lumina sis oculis etiam bonus Ancus reliquit*

(3.1025)

even good Ancus closed his eyes to the light
of day,

and of the passage Lucretius was using from Ennius
(*Annals* 149). And the evocative line is set in a paraphrase
of Catullus'

*soles occidere et redire possunt:
nobis, cum semel occidit brevis lux,
nox est perpetua una dormienda*

(5.4-6).

The sun can set and rise again.
But for us, when once our brief light
has set,
there is but one everlasting night to
sleep through.

*nobis, cum semel occidit:: nos, ubi decidimus*—Horace's
words have special poignancy when we set them against
those of the earlier poet. The theme has changed from
major to minor: Catullus' *soles* become *lunae* in Horace;
peaceful, everlasting night has turned to dust and shadow;
Catullus' regular hendecasyllables are part of a vigorous
affirmation of life, while Horace's uneven distichs are
resigned and melancholy—every second line is halted,
almost hushed.

As for associative use of his own work, Horace sometimes
refashions whole odes (1.4 and 4.7 are variations on the
same theme, as are 2.3 and 2.14), but usually it is only a
slight touch, a combination of words, that calls to mind an
association elsewhere. Why is the last stanza of the ode to
the *fons Bandusiae* so charming? If those melodious lines:

*fies nobilium tu quoque fontium,
me dicente cavis impositam ilicem*

*saxis, unde loquaces
lymphae desiliunt tuae*

(3.13.13-16),

You too will become one of those glorious
fountains, as I sing of the oak tree
perched on hollow rocks, whence your
speaking waters leap down,

are compared with a couplet from the *Epodes*:

*mella cava manant ex ilice, montibus altis
levis crepante lympha desilit pede*

(16.47-48),

Honey flows from the hollow oak tree, and from
the steep hills gentle water leaps down with
splashing step,

it will be seen that not only the phrase *lymphae desiliunt*
but *cavis . . . ilicem* as well carries liquid association for
Horace, and for the reader who is alert to the word-placing.

### CALLIDA IUNCTURA

We have mentioned thus far word-placing of various types
for various effects, but have yet to touch upon the heart of
the matter—what Horace himself styled *callida iunctura*,
and Gilbert Murray described as "juxtaposition of those
words which specially affect or explain or intensify one
another, and so, without altering the intellectual meaning
of the sentence, invest it with depths and shades of feeling, and knit it into a whole, like Aristotle's 'live
animal.'"[20] It is largely because commentators and critics,
even the best of them, were insensitive to Horace's *iunc-
turae* that some of the famous odes have been slighted as
incoherent, "sad stuff" or "poor" or "vile" or "trash."[21]

First, it should be said again (and Horace never tires of
saying it in his critical writings)[22] that words have a life of
their own; they have ancestors, a place of birth (which can
often be traced), and as they live out their lifespans they
take on associations more or less personal to themselves.
The poet specializes in these associations—the overtones,
the connotations, the suggestive power in words. In poetry,
as Cleanth Brooks puts it, "the connotations play as great
a part as the denotations."[23] Therein lies the difference
between the scientist and the poet in their use of language:
science uses the denotations, restricting the meanings of
words to their dictionary definitions; poetry cannot ignore
the denotations, but must also be sensitive to the connotations of words. Indeed, in so doing, it sometimes expands
and explodes the dictionary meanings. Why do we need
art at all if not for this? Art expresses what science, with
its self-imposed principles of investigation, never can.
Think of the sea as a chemical formula or as the subject of
the science of oceanography—and then think what it
means to Conrad, Turner, and Debussy. Think of sorrow as
a psychological phenomenon or as a physical disturbance—
and then think how Mozart expressed it in his G Minor
symphony. Art seems to exist to give expression to vast

areas of non-conceptual knowledge, feeling and association which the more reasoned, impersonal fields of philosophy and science cannot express.

Was Horace sensitive to the overtones in words? Let us look again at that passage from the *Ars Poetica.*

> in verbis etiam tenuis cautusque serendis
> dixeris egregie notum si callida verbum
> reddiderit iunctura novum
>
> (46-48).

*Callida iunctura*—two well-worn words carefully juxtaposed can take on new meanings. Each word, to quote Brooks again, "has to be conceived of, not as a discrete particle of meaning, but as a potential of meaning, a nexus or cluster of meanings."[24]

The most striking single instance[25] of this in Horace's *Odes* (striking in itself and also because it has enabled "new critics" to defend the poem from its attackers) is the two-word phrase lodged in the middle of the seemingly disjointed Soracte ode:

> virenti canities
>
> (1.9.17).

The lexicon meanings of the two words are "vigorous" and "a whitish-grey color." But when the two words are juxtaposed, *virenti* (vigorous) reminds the reader that *canities* can also stand for "old age," and *canities* (white) in turn colors *virenti:* we recall that it can legitimately mean "green." Here, at least, Nietzsche was right. Each word "diffuses its influence to the right and left," so that the other takes on an additional meaning. But more astonishing is how their influence extends "over the whole":

> *Vides ut alta stet nive candidum*
> *Soracte, nec iam sustineant onus*
> *silvae laborantes, geluque*
> *flumina constiterint acuto.*
>
> *dissolve frigus ligna super foco*
> *large reponens atque benignius*
> *deprome quadrimum Sabina,*
> *o Thaliarche, merum diota.*
>
> *permitte divis cetera, qui simul*
> *stravere ventos aequore fervido*
> *deproeliantes, nec cupressi*
> *nec veteres agitantur orni.*
>
> *quid sit futurum cras fuge quaerere et*
> *quem Fors dierum cumque dabit lucro*
> *appone, nec dulces amores*
> *sperne puer neque tu choreas,*
>
> *donec virenti canities abest*
> *morosa. nunc et campus et areae*
> *lenesque sub noctem susurri*
> *composita repetantur hora,*
>
> *nunc et latentis proditor intimo*
> *gratus puellae risus ab angulo*

> *pignusque dereptum lacertis*
> *aut digito male pertinaci.*

You see how Soracte stands shimmering in deep snow, how the straining woods no longer support their burden, how the rivers are halted by the sharp ice.

Take the chill off, pile the logs high on the hearth, Thaliarchus, and draw more generous draughts of four-year wine from the Sabine jar.

Leave the rest to the gods, for once they have laid to rest the winds that clash in battle on the raging sea, no cypress, no venerable ash tree stirs.

Ask not what the morrow will bring. Put down as gain each day that fate grants you. And spurn not the delights of love and the dance, my boy,

As long as hoary old age lingers afar from your green youth. Now is the time to seek out the Campus Martius and the city squares, and soft whispering in the night at the trysting hour.

Now is the time for happy laughter from some secret corner (betraying the lass hiding there), and a token wrested from an arm or finger that scarcely resists at all.

Until recently, this poem has been criticized[26] as lacking that very unity Horace insists on in the *Ars Poetica:*

> *denique sit quodvis, simplex dumtaxat et unum*
>
> (23).
>
> So then, let your work be what you like, but at least let it be simple and unified.

Horace begins the ode in sight of a wintry landscape, and ends it with the command to make love now, while green springtime is at hand. But we are only apt to think the poem ill thought out or disjointed if we limit the words in *iunctura* to their dictionary meanings. It may be questionable etymology to pass from *virens* and *vir* and *viridis* to *ver*, but there is in the combination *virenti canities* (the green bloom of youth / the white hair of old age) a clear suggestion of spring / winter—enough to indicate that the poem need not be taken as a monologue spoken against realistic backdrops (though the backdrops are there and winter's at least is fully detailed). The poem seems rather a meditation in which, as so often in Horace, the landscapes are intended to mirror the seasons of man's life. The ratio

| *virenti* | *canities* |
|-----------|------------|
| youth | old age |
| green | white |
| spring | winter |

reminds us that, in the poem, Thaliarchus is a *puer* while the Horace of the *Odes* is approaching middle age; that the warring winds of the third stanza may stand for passionate youth which gives way, when the gods so ordain, to old age (*veteres . . . orni*) and death (*cupressi*); that the opening stanza (the mountain covered with snow, the trees bent under their burden, the rivers halted by the ice) is as much a description of *canities* in all its associations as the closing stanzas (playing fields, whispers, and lovemaking) are of *virenti*.[27]

Each of the two words has a specific meaning, but within the structure of the poem it refuses to so limit itself; casting influence "to right and left and over the whole" it points to larger possibilities of interpretation. The associations the two words carry are what gives the poem its meaning.

If we think of the *Odes* of Horace as simple prose statements—if like some interlinear translator, we mentally rearrange the component words in prose order—we are likely to find ourselves saying, with Tyrrell, that Horace "did not much trouble himself whether the train of ideas was consecutive, or indeed whether there was any regular march of thought at all."[28] Worse, we may join the insensitive objectors who dismiss Horace because he forever mouths the same Epicurean platitudes and never says anything original or important. Such judgments are based on the false assumption that the meaning of a poem can be reduced to a prose summary, a paraphrase. Poetry is not made to communicate such meanings. In an ode of Horace every word plays a part. Any poet worth his salt will tell you that is the way it must be.

"Why do you want to write poetry?" W. H. Auden asks a hopeful beginner. "If the young man answers: 'I have important things to say,' then he is not a poet. If he answers: 'I like hanging around words listening to what they say,' then maybe he is going to be a poet."[29]

### Notes

1. In the *Ars Poetica* and other literary epistles, Horace writes as critic, not as practitioner revealing the secrets of the trade. It is, however, reasonable to suppose he would expect his dicta to apply to his own lyric poetry, even *mutatis mutandis* those dicta which strictly apply to epic and drama.

2. *Götzendämmerung:* Was ich den Alten Verdanke, 1.

3. See, for example, N. E. Collinge, *The Structure of Horace's Odes* (Oxford, 1961), p. 2.

4. Quoted in Cleanth Brooks, *The Well Wrought Urn* (New York, 1947), p. 9.

5. From the last of the *Four Quartets*.

6. See p. 38 [of this text].

7. See, for example, L. P. Wilkinson, *Golden Latin Artistry* (Cambridge, 1963), p. 220, and Ernest A. Fredricksmeyer, "Horace's Ode to Pyrrha," *CP* 60 (1965), p. 183.

8. From the preface to *Sylvae.*

9. H. D. Naylor (*Horace, Odes and Epodes* [Cambridge, 1922], pp. xiv-xv, § 7) lists 12 instances of the chiastic, 15 of the achiastic type.

10. For further examples, see Naylor, *op. cit.,* p. xxii, § 33.

11. For a fairly complete list, see Naylor, *op. cit.,* p. xxx, § 52.

12. This was first suggested by Collinge, *op. cit.,* p. 32.

13. Giorgio Pasquali, *Orazio Lirico* (Florence, 1918).

14. Several other odes of Horace show no discernible borrowing, but are very much in the style of Pindar (1.7 and 4.4), Stesichorus (1.16), the dithyrambic poets (2.19 and 3.25), and the Hellenistic epigrammatists (1.30 and 3.22). Tenney Frank (*Catullus and Horace* [New York, 1928], pp. 232-39) suggests that Horace used the mottoes to help the literate Roman identify the meter.

15. Cf. *ponto nox incubat atra* (1.89) and, from the related *incumbo, incubuere mari* (1.84) and *angues / incumbunt pelago* (2.205). Though the odes were published four years before the *Aeneid,* 1.3 could easily have followed the composition of the first books of the *Aeneid,* which was ten years in the writing. Indeed there is a strong tradition for placing 1.3 among the latest of the odes; see Wickham's edition (Oxford, 1877), *ad loc.* For Virgilian echoes in 1.24 see *infra,* Part II, chapter 4; on 4.12, see C. M. Bowra, "Horace, *Odes* IV, 12," *CR.* 42 (1928), pp. 165-67.

16. Parts of the introduction to Book II of Lucretius are refashioned in Book II of the *Odes.* Cf. Lucr. 2.27 and Horace 2.18.1-2; Lucr. 2.28 and Horace 2.16.11-12; Lucr. 2.29-33 and Horace 2.3.4-12. These Lucretian themes are forcefully restated in Horace 3.1.13-24.

17. Kenneth Quinn (*Latin Explorations* [London, 1963], pp. 99-108) sees the Lucretian echo as a clue to the form of the ode: a dramatic monologue, table-talk such as Lucretius mentions in 3.912-15. Thomas Gray also remembered Lucretius in the sixth stanza of the *Elegy:*

> For them no more the blazing hearth shall burn,
> Or busy housewife ply her evening care.

18. Compare Lucretius 1.6-15; *te fugiunt venti . . . tibi suavis daedala tellus / summittit flores . . . species patefactast verna diei . . . rapidos tranant amnis.*

19. Compare Lucretius 5.737-47. But note too that the startlingly placed *et mox* also occurs in *Odes* 1.4.20, balanced by *-et nox* in line 16 there. One thinks of the *-et nox* in Catullus 7.7 and the use of *lux / nox* in Catullus 5.5-6.

20. *The Classical Tradition in Poetry* (rep. New York, 1957), p. 151.

21. Marginal glosses made by Walter Savage Landor, quoted in A. Y. Campbell, *Horace, A New Interpretation* (London, 1924), p. 8.

22. See *Epistles* 2.2.115-19 and *Ars Poetica* 60-72.

23. *Op. cit.,* p. 8.

24. *Ibid.,* p. 210.

25. Other notable instances are *pinus ingens albaque populus* (2.3.9), *gelidos . . . rubro sanguine rivos* (3.13.6-7), and another passage in the Soracte ode (1.9.21-22), which has received a glowing tribute from Murray, *op. cit.,* p. 150. Petronius' two-word summary of Horace's style, *curiosa felicitas,* is itself an instance of *callida iunctura.* So too Quintilian's verdict, *verbis felicissime audax.*

26. See A. Y. Campbell, *op. cit.,* p. 224, and Eduard Fraenkel, *Horace,* pp. 176-77. The defense, led by L. P. Wilkinson (*Horace and His Lyric Poetry* [Cambridge, 1945], pp. 129-31), crested in the late 1950's: H. C. Toll, "Unity in the *Odes* of Horace," *Phoenix* 9 (1955), esp. pp. 162-63; M. P. Cunningham, "*Enarratio* of Horace *Odes* 1.9," *CP* 52 (1957), pp. 98-102; M. G. Shields, "*Odes* 1.9: A Study in Imaginative Unity," *Phoenix* 12 (1958), pp. 166-73; E. M. Blaiklock, "The Dying Storm," *Greece and Rome* 6 (1959), esp. pp. 208-9; N. Rudd, "Patterns in Horatian Lyric," *AJP* 81 (1960), pp. 373-92.

27. In Epode 13.4-5 *virent genua,* contrasted with *senectus,* indicates a similar pattern. In 2.11.6-8 *levis iuventas* is contrasted with *arida canitie.*

28. *Latin Poetry* (London, 1895), p. 206.

29. "Squares and Oblongs," in *Poets at Work* (New York, 1948), p. 171.

## D. A. Russell (essay date 1973)

SOURCE: Russell, D. A. "*Ars Poetica.*" In *Horace,* edited by C. D. N. Costa, pp. 113-34. London: Routledge and Kegan Paul, 1973.

[*In the following essay, Russell provides an in-depth examination of the* Ars Poetica, *Horace's poem on poetics.*]

Quintilian[1] alludes to this poem as **ars poetica** or **liber de arte poetica.** The manuscript tradition, instead of associating it with the **Epistles,** gives it a separate place, in company with the **Odes** and **Epodes.** Its differences from the **Epistles** are in fact more significant for its understanding than its resemblances to them. It is very much 'a treatise with *Dear so-and-so* at the beginning'.[2] Its length, its didactic formulae, the recurrent addresses to the Pisones in the manner of Lucretius' to Memmius, and especially its very technical content, mark it out as an experiment. Perhaps it was the last of the great innovator's new creations; for, though the arguments about its date[3] are indecisive, there is much to be said for a late one, after the last book of the **Odes.** Porphyrio's identification of the Piso father with the future *praefectus urbi*[4] (48 B.C.-A.D. 32) may be right after all: he could well have had, by his late thirties, two sons old enough to be thought interested in poetry.

What Horace is attempting is, to put it as briefly as possible, a poem on poetics. Both halves of this description, however, need to be clarified. Despite *nil scribens ipse* (306), where Horace speaks as the non-practising theorist, the **Ars,** like the **Epistles** and **Satires,** is composed on poetical principles. Transitions and movements of thought depend on verbal association and emotional tone rather than on logical or rhetorical arrangement. The choice of topics and the degree of elaboration accorded to them is determined, as in Lucretius or the *Georgics,* more by the poetical potential or viability of the theme than by the need to give a certain weight to a certain matter because of its place in an overall pattern of argument or precept. Second, the subject of this eccentric didactic poem—as far removed from the norm of the *Georgics* as Ovid's *Ars* was to be—is not poetry, but poetics: the body of theory formulated, largely out of earlier insights, by Aristotle and his successors, and current in Hellenistic times in a variety of handbooks and summaries.

Porphyrio, of course, informs us that Horace drew specially on one such handbook:

congessit praecepta Neoptolemi τοῦ Παριανοῦ de arte poetica, non quidem omnia sed eminentissima.

We naturally view this with scepticism, mindful of the exaggeration with which ancient scholarship was wont to proclaim discoveries of derivation and plagiarism. We do not believe Servius when he tells us that *Aeneid* IV comes *paene totus* from Apollonius' *Argonautica,* because we can check the facts. Why then should we believe Porphyrio here? A fair analogy; but even Servius does not lie, he only exaggerates. Porphyrio should be given the credit of a right, or at least plausible, diagnosis. What little we know in other ways of Neoptolemus supports the case. But suppose we had Neoptolemus *in extenso*: is it likely that this would further our understanding of the **Ars** more than, say, Varro's *De re rustica* furthers our understanding of the *Georgics?*[5] The poem before us does not after all look at all like a versified treatise. Nor, on all the analogies that ancient literature affords, was it written to make poets of us or the Pisones. Its aim surely was to please us and compliment them.

Yet (l. 343)

Omne tulit punctum qui miscuit utile dulci.

Is not Horace trying to do this too? Of course; but in a way that needs defining. Peripatetic treatises on poetics tended to have a certain layout, resting on general theory: basically, it would seem, the principle of Aristotle's *Rheto-*

ric (not to be found in the *Poetics*) that content and argument should be discussed independently of form and language. This simple division into 'what is to be said' and 'how it is to be said' goes back anyway to Plato, for we find it in the moral critique of poetry which he makes in *Republic* II and III.[6] It exists in more sophisticated forms in the Hellenistic critics: the famous ποίημα/ποίησις distinction in Neoptolemus is one of these, for ποίησις (the act of composing a whole poem) deals with the entire business of plot, and ποίημα (the work of making verses, or the verses so made) involves the entire topic of the linguistic medium.[7] Now Horace does indeed recognize this *res/verba* division (40 ff.). And he naturally discusses vocabulary at some length in some places, and plot at some length in others. But he does not submit his exposition to it as a principle of division of the material, as a textbook writer would. Even if one supposes (and there is plausibility in this) a shift from form to content at l. 118, it is heavily overlaid: simplicity and variety, with which the poem begins, are topics of content; vocabulary and metre, matters of form, recur often enough in the latter part, from l. 232 onwards. The most significant point of technical arrangement in the poem is the simple one, often observed, that the whole of the last part (from about l. 295) is devoted, not to the poet's works, but to his person and function in society. The caricature at the end is of the mad, disorganized poet; the caricature at the beginning, which it seems to balance, is of the chaotic, disorganized work of art. Now we know that Philodemus criticized in Neoptolemus the tripartite division of the subject ποίημα/ποίησις/ποιητής.[8] It is an obvious and captious point, not untypical of much ancient polemic, that a poet is not a species of poetry. But however unfair Philodemus' argument, we need scarcely doubt that this is how Neoptolemus divided the matter. In following him, Horace not only reproduced a textbook order of things, but (far more important) opened his own way to satire and moral interest.

I shall return to this point. In all other respects, the process of turning poetics into poetry manifestly did not depend on a given articulation of the subject. What was far more important to Horace was the richness of the topics built into the system. These we may group in two sets of three. The first set consists of certain ideas which were of basic importance in Aristotelian theory and its Hellenistic developments: unity, propriety (*decorum*), the historical development of the *genres* and in particular of drama. The second comprises themes to which Horace seems to have devoted more space than we might have expected: the importance of *ars* compared with *ingenium*—a presupposition of anyone who writes an *ars;*[9] the commitment of the poet not only to conscientious workmanship but to socially valuable moral principles; and the difference between Roman attitudes and Greek. These latter points arise mainly in the last part of the poem; they represent the most serious lesson it has to teach. For towards the end the 'poem on poetics' seems to become more hortatory. It is not indeed a protreptic to poetry. The Pisones might well find it rather a warning off (372-3):

> Mediocribus esse poetis
> non homines, non di, non concessere columnae.

It is difficult to write a sentence about the *Ars,* especially one which claims to paraphrase it, without acute diffidence. Problems posed, solved or dissolved by four centuries of scholarship have resulted in a neurotic confusion unexcelled even in classical studies. It is easy to see how this has happened. Here is a poem the content of which has seemed peculiarly important in every age when European literature has looked back to its classical roots. It is also a poem of great delicacy and allusiveness. There is a sort of printing in two tones which reveals different legends as you turn it towards or away from the light. A lot of the *Ars* is like that. Lines and sections read quite differently according to what you hold in mind from the context, and whether you look forwards or back. Analysis is therefore almost always controversial. Anyone who undertakes to guide a party round the poem is likely to be pointing out things that are not there, and missing things that are. Nevertheless, some sort of paraphrase is the only help worth having. So I attempt one.

'While he teacheth the art, he goeth unartificially to work, even in the very beginning'[10] wrote a seventeenth-century critic, following Scaliger's damning phrase, *ars sine arte tradita.* But the caricature of the Scylla-like monster with which the poem opens is in fact not without art. An introductory comparison, often quite bizarre, is a common exordium, for example, in works of popular philosophy like Plutarch's. It attracts attention, and relates the subject to something outside it—a good move to excite interest. Here, by relating poetry to painting, Horace makes a special point: both are forms of imitation, traditionally paired together. Painting, said Simonides, is silent poetry.[11]

When unity and disunity are in question, Horace thinks particularly of epic: so here, so also below in ll. 136-52. A grand enterprise is spoilt by a superfluous description (*ecphrasis*), however pretty it may be. A 'purple patch', in fact, involves a breach not only of unity but of *decorum,* since this implies the consistent maintenance of a single tone of discourse. But the main point in all this paragraph is unity: it is emphasized by two more parallels, from painting and pottery (19-22), and by the analogy of other literary vices.

These last lines (24-31) deserve a closer look. The general principle they convey is that the effort to achieve some good quality often leads us into a bad one: brevity into obscurity, smoothness into flabbiness, grandeur into bombast, caution into dullness—and variety into absurdity. This is standard literary theory, based ultimately on the Aristotelian doctrine of 'mean' and 'extremes'.[12] The way out of the danger is afforded by *ars;* this alone enables us to distinguish success from failure. Horace's economy is noteworthy: in a few lines, he reminds us of the traditional 'three styles'—grand, slight and smooth—as well of the traditional justification of *ars* and the relation of the question of unity to the more general one of technique. At the same time he elaborates on his theme with charm and humour: on the *ecphrasis* (17-19), on the unsuccessful sculptor in bronze (32-5), on beautiful black eyes and hair (37).

Alternation between fullness and brevity is a feature of the poem, one of its chief techniques of variety. This is perhaps to be regarded as a Hesiodic inheritance, for the *Works and Days,* a much-studied model for the Alexandrians, is like this: brief gnomic wisdom alternates with set pieces of description. Nowhere is this technique clearer than in the next part of the *Ars.* First, a fundamental *praeceptum:* choose your subject within your powers (38-40). This is elaborated only to the extent of being said twice over, with a certain amount of metaphor (*umeri*) and anaphora (*quid . . . quid . . .*). From competent choice of subject will follow both style and arrangement (40-1). These two are taken up in reverse order: arrangement of material briefly (42-5),[13] vocabulary at length. Characteristically Augustan is the emphasis laid on ingenious word-combination (*iunctura,* σύνθεσις) as the road to distinction and novelty. It could be a veiled compliment to Virgil, whose detractors turned this notion on its head to speak of the insidious affectation (*cacozelia*) inherent in his use of common words.[14] The theory of poetic vocabulary involved various topics: foreign words or 'glosses,' metaphors and neologisms. Horace chooses only the last. It has no doubt a special relevance to Latin, where the conscious expansion of vocabulary on Greek lines was an active issue. More important, it leads to a general topic with a moral aspect: the dependence of vocabulary on usage (*usus*) and the consequent mortality of words. The conventional exemplification of *debemur morti nos nostraque* (61) takes us for a while away from the critic's lecture to the world outside.

At l. 73 comes a sharp break. The entertaining survey of metres in relation to genres looks wholly forward, to the *discriptas . . . vices operumque colores* of l. 86. Metre is the principal *differentia* of genre. But ll. 86-8 seem at first sight to look both ways: not only back to the metres but on to ll. 89-98, to the differentiation of tragedy from comedy by language, and the circumstances in which each may sometimes usurp the other's manner. It is a question of some importance whether this apparent double face is really there. The passage on metre is incomplete without ll. 86-7. It is the same sort of economical incorporation of background theory that we saw in ll. 25-8, and like that passage is futile without its conclusion. On the other hand, the passage 89-98 has a completeness in itself. It does not need the generalization, though it may be held to illustrate it. We should, I think, be careful not to seek connections where they are not. Hesiod reminds us that chains of *gnomai* often have loose or broken links. A reading of the ancient technical treatises—notably Demetrius, *On Style*—should warn us further that even these works are often lacking in logical order. In interpreting this passage, we should allow for some deliberate disjointedness: paragraph not (as some editors) at l. 85, but at ll. 88, 91, 92, 98.

All this is about drama. Epic has slipped from sight, the other genres appear only incidentally as examples of the diverse *colores.* This concentration is typical of Peripatetic criticism. It becomes more and more pronounced as the *Ars* proceeds. From now on, the whole of the poem (up to l. 295) is concerned with drama, except for ll. 131-52, an encomium of Homer which is an evident digression. It is a natural and proper conclusion from this that the scope of the poem is something different from a critique of the contemporary Augustan literary scene. However important those lost masterpieces, Varius' *Thyestes* and Ovid's *Medea,* may have been, they were marginal to the Augustan achievement. Strange if Horace did not know this too. The literary scene, which is his subject for example in the *Letter to Augustus* (*Epist.,* II.1), is not the topic here: here it is the theory that he takes as his material.

Diction, said the textbooks,[15] should be appropriate to emotion, character and circumstance. Horace follows this pattern: emotion (99-111), circumstance (112-13), character (114-18)—in the usual technical sense of the determinate *ēthos* of a particular sort of person. Much of the detail of this discussion is known to be part of the technical tradition. With ll. 114-17, we rightly compare the censure of Aristophanes in Plutarch:[16] 'You could not tell whether it is a son talking or a father or a farmer or a god or an old woman or a hero.' What remains puzzling is probably traditional also: the mysterious Colchian, Assyrian, Theban and Argive (118) will also have a history in lost books of poetics.

Line 119 comes in abruptly:

> aut famam sequere aut sibi convenientia finge.

Read without context, this advice has a more general application than to features of character. Indeed, as we read on, it proves to include plot. But at the moment Horace disguises the shift. He exemplifies his maxim from the field of which he has just been speaking. Just as farmer, nurse and hero had to have appropriate language, because their character is a datum, so the known heroes of mythology must be represented in their accepted colours. A non-traditional character, on the other hand, has merely to obey the law of internal consistency. Now non-traditional *stories*—here is the shift of subject, masked by the common element of breach with tradition—are in fact the clothing of general statements about action and personality in particular forms. *Proprie communia dicere* (128), much disputed, is a more philosophical way of expressing the process more superficially seen by Aristotle as 'adding names'.[17] This is a difficult matter. Better therefore to use traditional stories—but make them your own by distinctive treatment. To illustrate this Horace turns to epic, and gives us an encomium of Homer, in just those respects which most attracted Hellenistic craftsmen—or for that matter Virgil: his sense of how to begin, the plunge *in medias res,* the limitation of the subject, the selection of the poetically viable, the grasp of overall unity. The last point (152) brings us back to the theme of Horace's own exordium. The recollection gives emphasis and a sense of pause, as at the completion of a movement. But the whole passage is, of course, something of a digression. It is a virtuoso piece too: everyone remembers its highlights, the proverbial mouse (139), the alliterative *cum Cyclope Charybdim* (145), the *in medias res* (148).

So back to the stage, to an audience willing to endure to the epilogue (153-5). And back also to the portrayal of character. We seem to be in the situation of ll. 125-8; we are now to hear in more detail how the dramatic *persona* should be maintained. As a teaching example, Horace chooses the Ages of Man. He gives us four:[18] but he bases himself a good deal on the three Ages described from the orator's point of view by Aristotle.[19] Thus Aristotle says of the young:

> They are full of desire and liable to do what they desire. Among bodily desires they are most inclined to follow that of sex, in which they have no self-control. They are changeable and fickle in their desires, which they form quickly and give up quickly.

All this comes to half a line:

> cupidusque et amata relinquere pernix
>
> (165)

At the same time, there is much in Aristotle for which Horace finds no place: the confidence and hopefulness of the young, their mercifulness, bashfulness, and freedom from disillusion. It is partly of course that these qualities are of interest to the orator, who needs to know how to influence such characters, more than to the poet who has just to represent them; but it is noticeable also that Horace's description has a more satiric tinge, at once vivid and censorious. His timid and grumbling old men, too, show something of this, though the basic features of their character are already in Aristotle. In all this, the poeticizing of the subject involves not only selection but a marked change of tone from the clinical to the satiric.

This connected development is followed, for contrast, by a series of *praecepta* on points of dramatic art. Deliberately not linked, these *praecepta* are varied by the mock-heroic summaries of legends in ll. 185-7, and by the expansive account of the moral attitudes appropriate to a chorus in ll. 196-201.

A taste of such material evidently suffices. If we look ahead, we glimpse a motive for it: the overpowering importance of techniques and observance of the proprieties, which is shortly to be illustrated in a very striking way.

But no signs yet of what is coming. Only a quite natural transition from the chorus to the accompanying music (202). But not the music as it is now: a historical perspective unexpectedly appears. It is a moralist's view of things, Platonic rather than Aristotelian, associating prosperity with luxury and, in some sense, decadence. Aristotle,[20] it is true, had noted that pipe-playing was introduced into education after the Persian wars; and also that changes in musical taste were liable to come from the demands of an uneducated audience. But there is an element in Horace's account of the theory that moral decline and luxury were associated: the audience of the later period was no longer *frugi castusque* (207). It is reasonable therefore to think of Plato, of the 'vile theatrocracy' condemned in the *Laws*.[21]

Horace had handled this topic of fifth- and fourth-century cultural history elsewhere, in the Letter to Augustus.[22] Here he divorces it from its historical setting. At the same time he touches it with a master hand: *vino diurno* (209), the matching of oracular style with sense in ll. 218-19. It is yet another set piece; but not complete in itself, since it is essential logical preparation for what follows.

The licentious audience of post-war Greece needed special titillation at the end of the day;[23] satyr-plays, performed at the end of sets of tragedies, provided it. This is to choose one of two rival accounts of the development of drama: not Aristotle's,[24] according to which tragedy grew as a refined form of the satyr-play, which is seen as something more primitive; but a later and commoner one[25] in which Pratinas, a successor of Thespis, invented satyr-plays as a new variety. Horace's choice—which may also be Neoptolemus'—is poetically apt, and it is more important to see this than to wonder about the historical judgment behind it. The story of prosperity and moral laxity leads up to the new discovery, and the new discovery leads to what is evidently the end-point of the whole development: namely, advice on how to write this peculiar genre.

Now there may of course be circumstances which, if known to us, would reduce our astonishment at this move. The Pisones may have burned with ambition to conquer even this literary corner for Rome. Horace may have thought that this was a desirable step in the progress of Augustan literature. Alexandrian satyr-plays, such as the *Lityerses* of Sositheos, may have been notable in themselves or have attracted the attention of the theorists whom Horace follows. It is in this last point, I am inclined to say, that the heart of the matter lies. Satyr-drama aroused special theoretical interest. In its classical form, it was burlesque in content, but tragic in language and metre. This intermediate status called for definition, for a close analysis of metre and style in terms of decorum. It is the consequent rather complicated play with critical concepts that Horace here turns into thirty lines of poetry.

It is a study in balance and the Aristotelian mean. The serious and the humorous must be blended in such a way that heroic characters, already introduced in the serious plays, neither disgrace themselves nor soar above human ken. Satyr-drama is tragedy on holiday, as it were; it is not comedy, for its characters, after all, are divine. It will not eschew metaphor, but it will depend for its distinction on arrangement rather than on unfamiliar language (240-4). This last point is a little strange: it is not true of classical satyr-drama, which has a good deal of exaggerated diction. But Horace is presumably legislating for a refined form of the genre. Finally, the humour must steer clear of the erotic and the indecent. We aim at a respectable audience (248-50).

It would be wrong to suppose that just because this topic occupies a comparatively large space, it is proportionately important in the thematic structure of the poem. We could not after all make a case for this for the Ages of Man. But it would be wrong too to regard the satyr-section as a mere episode. It is too central for that—and not only in position, though it may well be significant that it comes plumb in the middle of the poem. As an illustration of the vital importance of knowledge and technique, it touches the heart of the poem's subject. Moreover, it seems to close a distinct phase in the argument. Little has been said so far to refer us specifically to the Roman situation: ll. 49-58, on vocabulary, seems the only significant exception. With the halfway mark passed, and the satyr-section out of the way, this is to change. Roman problems are dominant in ll. 251-94, prominent also in the rest of the poem.

The organization of ll. 251-94 is not easily missed, and it is important to recognize it. The tongue-in-cheek beginning, as if we did not all know what an iambus was, may mislead for a moment; but it soon becomes obvious that its function is solely to prepare for the point that traditional Roman metrical technique has a crudity and heaviness which are nowadays unforgivable. Modern taste should not accept a Plautine standard of metre—any more than a Plautine standard of humour. Where Rome has done well is in enterprise: not only has she followed Greeks in the successive inventions of tragedy and comedy (275-84), but ventured outside Greek range into historical and Italian plays. Where she fails is in technique: *limae labor et mora.* This alone, apparently, prevents Rome from achieving the traditional praise of the Greeks. Other considerations to come may modify this; but for the moment, the argument seems complete, and the formal address to the Pisones (291-4) both emphasizes the importance of what is said here and signals the end of the main part of the poem.

But even this break, though the most meaningful in the whole composition, is not complete. There is a bridge. Technical perfection in the work has had its emphasis. In what follows, Horace examines the balance of the poet's make-up, and the relation of *ars* to *ingenium* in him. The last part of the poem thus parallels and complements the earlier parts in various ways. None the less it has its independence: it is certainly *de poeta,* and the common comparison with the account of the perfect orator with which Quintilian closes the *Institutio* is an illuminating one. Two features, of very different kinds, give an air of separateness. One is the element of caricature. A welcome butt has presented himself: the poet who relies on his 'genius'. This unpleasing eccentric now keeps cropping up: ll. 295-302, 379-84, 416-18, and especially ll. 453-476. He brings with him a more satirical tone, evident notably in the 'friend and flatterer' development of ll. 422-52. But, second, we have for the first time in the poem an apparent formal division of the material (307-8):

> (i) Unde parentur opes, quid alat formetque poetam, (ii) quid deceat, quid non, (iii) quo virtus, quo ferat error.

The most influential person to take this seriously was Eduard Norden.[26] His identification of (i) with ll. 309-32, (ii) with ll. 333-46, (iii) with l. 347 - end, has been much disputed. But it grows on one; and it, or something like it, must be right.

(i) There is certainly truth in the first part. Here there are three interconnected themes: the practical need of the poet—especially the dramatist—for a knowledge of ethics, and particularly the detailed, preceptive ethics which comes, for example, in treatises *de officiis;* the triumph of a piece that gets character and moral sentiments right over one that is technically competent but trivial; and the supporting instance of Greece, whose immortal literature is grounded on a moral character free from all greed save greed for fame. This, I think, is the point of the brilliant classroom scene of ll. 325 ff.; Horace is answering an objection which he imagines, but does not spell out: the objection that the emphasis on *mores* in ll. 319-22 seems to conflict with the admiration for Greek technique which is axiomatic in the poem. His answer is that what has been said needs some supplementing: the Greek miracle did not really depend solely on technique, but also on moral qualities, on a generosity and unworldliness not natural to dour, money-grubbing Rome. That meanness is inimical to the growth of literature is a common enough thought: we may compare the last chapter of *De Sublimitate,*[27] where the link between avarice (φιλοχρηματία) and the loss of true standards of excellence is worked out in some detail.

(ii) The reconciliation of the aims of pleasure and utility (333-46) attaches loosely to what precedes: *prodesse* relates to the effect of the *speciosa locis . . . fabula, delectare* to that of the melodious nonsense. But this section has its own coherence. It is a neat, spare little exercise in balances and antitheses: ll. 335-7 take up *prodesse;* ll. 338-40 *delectare;* ll. 341 and 342 repeat the pair; l. 343 states the solution and l. 344 repeats once again: a bland compromise reconciles ψυχαγωγία and διδασκαλία as it does *ingenium* and *ars.*

(iii) But at l. 346 comes a more decided break. We find a string of propositions: (a) small faults are venial; (b) some poetry bears careful and repeated inspection; (c) it's no use being a mediocre poet, though it may be some use being a mediocre lawyer; (d) keep your work eight years before publishing. At first sight, there are contradictions in this, if one takes it all as a recipe for good writing. But it is a whole, and a familiar one. 'Longinus', with different emphasis, combines similar elements: small errors are venial (33-6); great writing sustains repeated study (7); no one would wish to be Apollonius rather than Homer (33).

The appeal to Piso (366), taken up in l. 385, seems to add emphasis to an attitude which, despite the disavowal of obsessive perfectionism, remains somewhat discouraging. Poetry is here a luxury art, and can be compared with the accessories of a good dinner (374-6); we therefore exact a higher standard of perfection than we would in something one might be obliged to do, like speaking in public in a lawsuit. Consequently, if the well-born Roman attempts it, he should put his efforts aside, submit them to rigorous and friendly critics, and only publish them after long reflection and revision. There may be examples of amateurs who rush in (384-5); these are much to be deprecated.

Piso might surely ask: Why then should I bother to write at all? The answer to this, and the counter as it were to all this discouraging perfectionism, appears in ll. 390-407. The connection here, once again, is a suppressed question, a matter of an imaginary debate, not a textbook sequence of headings. The answer is that the reason for not feeling ashamed of taking endless trouble is that poetry is a very grand thing—a great civilizing force in human history. This is a splendid section: precise, delicate, urbane, steering clear both of the banal and of the pompous. Horace begins with an allegorical version of two myths: Orpheus' taming the savage beasts represents his suppression of cannibalism—or rather, perhaps, of meat-eating; Amphion's miraculous building of Thebes represents (presumably) the power of music to produce order in minds and in society. Lawgiving was thus the first achievement of the ancient *vates;* martial excitement, moral advice, flattery and entertainment followed—in that order.[28]

The ideal poet begins to take shape. A scrupulous but unpedantic craftsman, a balanced moralist and a shrewd observer, he takes his trade seriously because he understands its place in human history. But, by the terms of the poem, he is also a Piso. It is part of the transposition of 'poetics' which the composition of the *Ars* involved that the perfect poet should have the special features of a young Roman nobleman. As the portrait proceeds, this becomes clearer. He must beware of flatterers. Here (419-52) follows a standard topic of ethics, the distinction of flatterer and friend,[29] with a standard Hellenistic illustration.[30] Individuality is given by the reminiscence of Quintilius, the transposition of Aristarchus' obelizing procedures to the critic-friend, and especially by the important *sententia* at the end (451-2):

> hae nugae seria ducent
> in mala . . .

What makes poetry important to a Piso is that his hobby may make him ridiculous. The critic-friend must do his duty.[31]

The final episode of the poem is pure caricature: the enemy is mercilessly traduced; he is not worth keeping alive; goodness knows what impiety has damned him to writing verses; he is a dangerous lunatic—and his recitations spell death.

Set this conclusion side by side with the exordium, and it prompts an observation which may help to bring out the unity of the whole. We began with a monstrous poem; we end with the pseudo-poet who might write it. The *Ars*, with its many facets, the shimmering surface that catches so many different lights, admits of course many observations on this level. But this one is worth more than a moment's pause. It brings out two essentials of the process that turned poetics into this sort of poetry. It reminds us that the *poiēma,* the thing made, could never be material for a poem without the maker, without his emotions and morals, his credibility, his honesty. Only by bringing in the artist could the 'art' be made to live. And second, this particular sort of poem, like the *Satires* and *Epistles,* needs something to laugh about, and, perhaps more important, someone to laugh at. It is the madman who sticks in our mind most, it is the caricature that brings the complicated and allusive artfulness of the whole poem most vividly to life.

The *Ars* is one of those *aurei libelli* treasured in medieval and Renaissance education as containing a particularly potent distillation of the wisdom of antiquity. That it is, in its own right, a subtle, bold and, on the whole, successful poem matters far less historically than its doctrinal content and its apparent utility as a model of a kind of humorous didactic piece. It was for long the most accessible source of the basic tenets of classical criticism: the doctrines of propriety and genre, and the underlying assumption that the poet, like the orator, sets himself a particular task of persuasion and is to be judged by his success in bringing it off. The history of its influence is therefore long and complex; all I can do here, by way of appendix, is to indicate a few points of entry and give a few illustrative extracts from some of the less accessible places.[32]

From the early middle ages, Horace was a curriculum author, and no part of him was more studied than the *Ars,* with its valuable literary lore and its impeccable morality. Medieval poetics, very much an art of the schoolroom, was inevitably much influenced by it: poetical *artes* sprang up which, however different in content, owed their being in the last resort to Horace.[33] In the Renaissance, imitation took a different road. Girolamo Vida's *Poeticorum Libri III* (1527)[34] is a notable landmark. It was the most famous and successful didactic of the age. Formally, nothing could be much less like the *Ars.* Vida's model is the *Georgics,* his ideal poet is Virgil. There is nothing of Horace's play with theory. Vida's concern is straightforwardly didactic—to teach Virgilian composition, by precept and still more by example. But there are passages of Horatian inspiration, and the basic assumptions of the *Ars* are there. Here, for example, is how Vida handles what is in effect Horace's advice on epic prooemia (II.18-21, 30-9):

> Vestibulum ante ipsum primoque in limine semper
> prudentes leviter rerum fastigia summa
> libant et parcis attingunt omnia dictis
> quae canere statuere: simul caelestia divum
> auxilia implorant, propriis nil viribus ausi . . .
> incipiens odium fugito, facilesque legentum
> nil tumidus demulce animos, nec grandia iam tum
> convenit aut nimium cultum ostentantia fari,
> omnia sed nudis prope erit fas promere verbis:
> ne, si magna sones, cum nondum ad proelia ventum,
> deficias medio irrisus certamine, cum res

postulat ingentes animos viresque valentes.
principiis potius semper maiora sequantur:
protinus illectas succende cupidine mentes
et studium lectorum animis innecte legendi.

(Before the courtyard, on the very threshold [*Aeneid,*
II.469!], the wise always dip lightly into the essentials
of the story, and touch on everything they have resolved
to sing with a few, sparing words. At the same time,
they beg the heavenly help of the gods, for they venture
nothing by their own strength. . . . When you begin,
avoid causing disgust; have no bombast about you, but
soothe your readers' willing ears. At this point it is out
of place to talk grandly or in a way that displays too
much polish. It will be quite proper to set out everything, almost, in the barest words; if you sound a loud
note now, when you have not yet reached the battle,
you may well fail ridiculously in the middle of the
encounter, when the story demands great courage and
powerful strength. Let what follows always be greater
than the beginning. Forthwith inflame the captive mind,
with eagerness, and bind the zeal to read upon your
readers' hearts.)

Neologisms are another Horatian theme (III.267-84):

Nos etiam quaedam idcirco nova condere nulla
religio vetat indictasque effundere voces.
ne vero haec penitus fuerint ignota suumque
agnoscant genus et cognatam ostendere gentem
possint, ac stirpis nitantur origine certae.
usque adeo patriae tibi si penuria vocis
obstabit, fas Graiugenum felicibus oris
devehere informem massam, quam incude Latina
informans patrium iubeas dediscere morem.
sic quondam Ausoniae succrevit copia linguae:
sic auctum Latium, quo plurima transtulit Argis
usus et exhaustis Itali potiuntur Athenis.
nonne vides mediis ut multa erepta Mycenis,
Graia genus, fulgent nostris immixta, nec ullum
apparet discrimen? eunt insignibus aequis
undique per Latios et civis et advena tractus.
iamdudum nostri cessit sermonis egestas:
raro uber patriae tibi, raro opulentia deerit.

(No scruple therefore forbids us to invent some new
words, and utter sounds unspoken before. But let them
not be altogether unknown: let them acknowledge their
ancestry, be able to show their relationships, and rely
on an origin in some certain race. If the poverty of our
native vocabulary obstructs you very much, it is right
to import from the happy shores of Greece some shape-
less mass which you can mould on a Latin anvil and
command to unlearn its native ways. This is how the
resources of the tongue of Ausonia grew of old. This is
how Latium was developed. Use transferred many
things there from Argos; Italians won the plunder of an
exhausted Athens. Do you not see how many words,
stolen from the heart of Mycenae, Greek in origin,
gleam amid our own? They show no difference; in like
uniform, citizen and stranger move through the realms
of Latium. Our language's poverty has long since
yielded; rarely will the rich soil of your country, rarely
its wealth fail you.)

But the best parts of Vida are perhaps the most independent. The long development on sound and sense towards

the end of Book III begins with a reminiscence of Horace,
but soon moves away into a sensitive lesson in Virgilian
artistry (III.365-76):

Haud satis est illis utcumque claudere versum,
et res verborum propria vi reddere claras:
omnia sed numeris vocum concordibus aptant,
atque sono quaecumque canunt imitantur, et apta
verborum facie, et quaesito carminis ore.
nam diversa opus est veluti dare versibus ora
diversosque habitus, ne qualis primus et alter,
talis et inde alter, vultuque incedat eodem.
hic melior motuque pedum et pernicibus alis
molle viam tacito lapsu per levia radit:
ille autem membris ac mole ignavius ingens
incedit tardo molimine subsidendo.

(It is not enough for them to round off the line anyhow
and to make the subject clear by the correct force of
the words. They suit everything to harmonious verbal
rhythms and imitate the subjects of their song in
sounds, with apt shapes of words and a poetical expression diligently sought. For one has as it were to give
the lines different expressions and different guises, so
that the first is not followed by another and then another
of the same kind, moving along with the same look on
its face. One is speedier of foot and wing and gently
glides over its smooth away with silent motion: another,
of mighty limbs and mass, moves more sluggishly,
pausing in its slow effort.)

Vida, for all his limitations and pedagogic tone, deserves
more attention than he gets. With his concern for practice
rather than theory, he follows in a sense in the line of the
medieval *artes;* but his Virgilianism and his skill in
mimicry are new. Writing in the 1520s, he was still
comparatively unaffected by the more profound and
speculative poetics that developed from the renewed study
of Aristotle.

It was inevitable that, as a source for theory, Horace should
take a back seat once the *Poetics* became familiar. He is
very much a subsidiary source to the great theorists, a
Minturno or a Castelvetro. But he did of course remain
popular, and at a somewhat humbler level we see much of
his influence in the latter part of the century. G. Fabricius
(*De Re Poetica,* 1560) drew up a list of forty-one propositions derived from the *Ars,* with some from the *Epistles*
and *Satires.* This proved a popular compendium: William
Webbe's *Of English Poetry* (1586) reproduces it.[35] Two of
the great literary manifestos of the age also clearly owe a
good deal to Horace: du Bellay's *Deffence et Illustration
de la langue françoise* (1549) and Sidney's *Apology for
Poetry* (1583).[36] But in the field of scholastic poetics,
Scaliger's negative judgment was important (*Poetics,* 1561,
preface):

Horatius Artem quam inscripsit adeo sine ulla docet
arte ut Satyrae propius totum opus illud esse videatur.

And he made himself little use of the *Ars.* Explicitly, or
more often tacitly, he criticizes its viewpoints on various
matters. His rhetorical prescriptions for the appropriate

portrayal of different national characteristics (3.17)[37] and of the Ages of Man (3.15) rest on other sources. For the latter topic, he returns conspicuously to the chapters of Aristotle's *Rhetoric* from which Horace departed.

It is probably broadly true that in the seventeenth century the *Ars* was more important as a poetic model than as a source of critical theory. In England, it attracted Ben Jonson both as commentator (the commentary is lost) and as translator.[38] In France, it served as the model of the most Horatian and most famous of its imitations—Boileau's *Art Poétique* (1674). Boileau's Horatianism is not primarily a matter of the direct allusions, numerous and interesting as these are.[39] It is far more that his insistence on correctness and technique overlaps a good deal, though not completely, with Horace's doctrine of the relation of *ars* and *ingenium;* and that his particular brand of urbanity found the model of the Horatian satire congenial and reasonably well within grasp. There is a difference of tone: more courtliness, less vigour; less conciseness; more obvious order in the layout. But essential Horatian qualities remain, as they do also in Pope's *Essay on Criticism,* where a new slant is given to the traditional material (Vida's as well as Horace's) by concentrating on the function and person of the critic—now not just a friendly and frank Quintilius, but a new sort of professional man.

Horace, we may suspect, would have enjoyed the parodies of himself, or at least some of them, that were a vogue in the eighteenth century. They presuppose the close familiarity with the *Ars* that its use in education so long assured. I quote two excerpts from William King's *Art of Cookery* (1709).[40] First, the Ages of Man (214 ff.):

> If you all sorts of persons would engage,
> Suit well your eatables to ev'ry age.
>     The fav'rite child, that just begins to prattle,
> And throws away his silver bells and rattle,
> Is very humoursome, and makes great clutter
> Till he has windows[41] on his bread and butter;
> He for repeated suppermeat will cry,
> But won't tell mammy what he'd have or why.
>     The smooth fac'd youth that has new guardians
>    chose,
> From playhouse, steps to supper at The Rose,
> Where he a main or two at random throws:
> Squandering of wealth, impatient of advice,
> His eating must be little, costly, nice.
>     Maturer Age, to this delight grown strange,
> Each night frequents his club behind the 'Change,
> Expecting there frugality and health
> And honor, rising from a Sheriff's wealth . . .
>     But then, old age, by still intruding years,
> Torments the feeble heart with anxious fears:
> Morose, perverse in humor, diffident,
> The more he still abounds, the less content;
> His larder and his kitchen too observes,
> And now, lest he should want hereafter, starves;
> Thinks scorn of all the present age can give,
> And none, these threescore years, know how to live.

And this is what King (331 ff.) makes of *Ars,* ll. 270-84:

> Our fathers most admir'd their sauces sweet
> And often ask'd for sugar with their meat;
> They butter'd currants on fat veal bestow'd
> And rumps of beef with virgin-honey strow'd.
> Inspid taste, old Friend, to them who Paris know
> Where rocambole, shalot, and the rank garlic grow.
>     Tom Bold did first begin the strolling mart
> And drove about his turnips in a cart;
> Sometimes his wife the citizens would please
> And from the same machine sell pecks of pease:
> Then pippins did in wheelbarrows abound,
> And oranges in whimsey-boards went round.
> Bess Hoy first found it troublesome to bawl
> And therefore plac'd her cherries on a stall;
> Her currants there and gooseberries were spread
> With the enticing gold of gingerbread:
> But flounders, sprats and cucumbers were cry'd
> And ev'ry sound and ev'ry voice was try'd.
> At last the law this hideous din supprest,
> And order'd that the Sunday should have rest,
> And that no nymph her noisy food should sell
> Except it were new milk or mackerel.

These *jeux d'esprit* are a proof of the familiarity of the *Ars* to the educated. There is another proof too, perhaps more striking and still with us—the number of phrases of the work that have penetrated our ordinary speech: 'purple patch' (15), *sub iudice* (78), *in medias res* (149), *laudator temporis acti* (173), the mountain giving birth to the mouse (139), Homer nodding (359). All Horace's works have earned this kind of testimony: the *Ars* has it to a rather special degree.

### Notes

The literature on the *Ars* is vast. Most recent, and much the most useful guide, is C. O. Brink's *Horace on Poetry* (vol. i, *Prolegomena,* Cambridge, 1963; vol. ii, *Commentary,* 1971). This chapter was written in the main before Brink's *Commentary* was available: I have not made any substantial changes in the light of it. See also G. W. Williams's review of Brink's first volume, *JRS,* 54 (1964), 186-96; and P. Grimal, *Horace: Art Poétique,* Les cours de Sorbonne, 1966. My attempt at a prose translation is in D. A. Russell and M. Winterbottom, *Ancient Literary Criticism,* Oxford, 1971, pp. 279-91.

1. Praef, 2, 8.3.60.

2. Cf. Demetrius, 228: συγγράμματα τὸ χαίρειν ἔχοντα προςγεγραμμένον.

3. For recent discussion see R. Syme, *JRS,* 1960, 12-20.

4. Tacitus, *Ann.,* vi.10.

5. Varro indeed is better placed to help us, for he tells us facts of ancient rural life which we need to know. The theorist Neoptolemus unlocks no such stores of otherwise unattainable knowledge.

6. *Rep.,* 392.

7. See esp. Brink, op. cit., pp. 59 ff.

8. Ibid., p. 58.

9. Cf. 'Longinus' 2.

10. H. Peacham, *The Compleat Gentleman* (1622).

11. Plutarch, *Moralia,* 346 F.

12. See, e.g. 'Longinus' 3, Demetrius, 114, [Cicero] *ad Herennium* IV, for 'adjacent faults' of various kinds.

13. Or to 44, if Bentley's transposition of *hoc amet, hoc spernat . . .* to follow *in verbis . . . serendis* is right, as (e.g.) Vahlen, Kiessling-Heinze, and Brink maintain.

14. Donatus, *vita,* 44: 'novae cacozeliae repertorem, non tumidae nec exilis [i.e. not arising from the common perversions of the grand and simple styles] sed ex communibus verbis atque ideo latentis.'

15. Cf. Aristotle, *Rhetoric,* 3.7.

16. *Moralia,* 853D. The parallel confirms the reading *divus* in 114.

17. *Poetics,* 1451b10.

18. Cf. in general F. Boll, *Die Lebensalter, Neue Jahrbücher* XXXI, 89-146 (1913), reprinted in *Kleine Schriften zur Sternkunde des Altertums,* Leipzig, 1950.

19. *Rhetoric,* 2.12-14.

20. *Politics,* 1341$^a$ 28, $^b$15.

21. 700 A-701 B. But see Cicero, *De Legibus,* 2.38.

22. *Epist.,* II.1. 93 ff.

23. Cf. ll. 154-5 for the idea of 'keeping' the audience till the end of the performance.

24. *Poetics,* 1449$^a$ 20, if this is the right interpretation of ἐκ ϲατυρικοῦ ϲεταβαλεῖν. Cf. also Dioscorides, *Anth. Pal.,* VII.37.1-6.

25. *Suda,* s.v. 'Pratinas'.

26. *Hermes,* 40 (1905), 481-525.

27. 'Longinus' 44.6-7.

28. A verbal—but hardly significant—contradiction of l. 377: *animis natum . . . poema iuuandis.*

29. See especially Plutarch's *De adulatore et amico.*

30. Diodorus, 20.63.1

31. Not to do so would be to yield to a pernicious inhibition, what Greek moralists called δυϲωπία: cf. *pudens prave* (l. 88.)

32. See, besides the standard general histories of criticism: J. E. Spingarn, *A History of Literary Criticism in the Renaissance,* New York, 1908; B. Weinberg, *History of Literary Criticism in the Italian Renaissance,* Chicago, 1961; M. T. Herrick, *The Fusion of Horatian and Aristotelian Literary Criticism, 1531-1555,* New York, 1946.

33. On Matthew of Vendôme's *Ars versificatoria* and Geoffrey of Vinsauf's *Poetria nova,* see F. J. E. Raby, *Secular Latin Poetry,* ii, 30, 122; E. Faral, *Les arts poétique du XII$^e$ and XIII$^e$ siècle,* Paris, 1923; J. de Ghellinck, *L'essor de la littérature latine au XII$^e$ siècle,* Brussels, 1946, ii, 243 ff.

34. Many editions down to the eighteenth century. An excellent English verse translation was made by Christopher Pitt (1725).

35. Text in G. Gregory Smith, *Elizabethan Critical Essays,* vol. i (1904), Oxford, 290 ff. (English), 417 ff. (Latin).

36. The standard editions give the necessary information: Sidney is in Gregory Smith, op. cit., i, 148 ff., for du Bellay see the edn of H. Chamard, Paris, 1945. In du Bellay, note especially: 2.4. Ly donques et rely premierement . . . feuillete de main nocturne et journelle les exemplaires grecs et latins: 2.4 te fourniront de matière les louanges des Dieux et des hommes vertueux, le discours fatal des choses mondaines, la solicitude des jeunes hommes, comme l'amour: les vins libres, et toute bonne chere: 2.6 ne crains donques . . . d'innover quelques termes . . . avecques modestie toutefois . . . Du Bellay's Latinisms were severely attacked in a pamphlet published in 1550, 'le Quintil Horatian', which takes its title from Horace's critic-friend.

37. Cf. *AP,* l. 118. Only *Assyrii* occur of Horace's examples. It is tempting to cite some of the rest:

    Germani fortes, simplices, animarum prodigi, veri amici, verique hostes. Suetii, Noruegii, Gruntlandii, Gotti, beluae. Scoti non minus. Angli perfidi, inflati, feri, contemptores, stolidi, amentes, inertes, inhospitales, immanes . . .

38. *Works,* ed Herford and Simpson, viii, 303 ff.

39. E.g. 1.11 (*AP,* 38); 1.64 (*AP,* 31); 1.77 (*AP,* 343); 1.190 (*AP,* 424); 3.61 ff. (origin of tragedy); 3.124 (*AP,* 125); 3.269 ff. (*AP,* 136 ff.); 3.375 ff. (ages of man—omits childhood); 4.26 (*AP* 372); 4.71 ff. (the good critic); 4.135 ff. (civilizing effect of poetry).

40. For the author's character, see Johnson's *Life.*

41. I.e. patterns made with sugar on the bread.


**David West (essay date 1973)**

SOURCE: West, David. "Horace's Poetic Technique in the *Odes.*" In *Horace,* edited by C. D. N. Costa, pp. 29-58. London: Routledge and Kegan Paul, 1973.

[*In the following essay, West examines the* Odes, *focusing on a particular, frequently used poetic technique and giving examples to clarify the reader's understanding of the passages where it is used.*]

The English-reading student in 1973 is well-placed to study Horace's poetic technique. He might start with the work of Gordon Williams,[1] particularly helpful on Horace's originality and the organization of the **Odes.** He should then move to Nisbet and Hubbard's[2] massive commentary on the first book, which raises and solves a vast range of problems and abundantly deploys the common store on which Horace drew. This chapter will enter the still exhaustless mine of contemplation by a different shaft, narrow and hazardous. We shall start from a small point of technique and show that it is frequent and important in the **Odes;** then study some apparent examples of this technique in the hope of improving our understanding of the passages where it occurs or seems to occur; then gather our observations to present a general picture of Horace's poetic technique in the **Odes.**

Aeneas is *blazing* as he sinks his sword in Turnus' breast, but the limbs of Turnus are loosened with *cold* (*Aeneid,* XII.951):

> feruidus; ast illi soluuntur frigore membra.

Norden[3] is astounded at this last ornament by contrast in the *Aeneid.* It is the last of many. Collinge[4] examines such contrasts in Horace's **Odes** in his stimulating first chapter and shows that 'the setting off of A against B is the major motif of Horatian verbal composition'.

It takes many forms: oxymoron (*audaces agnos,* III.18, *inaudax raptor,* III.20, *palluit audax,* III.27); antitheses (*hac Dorium illis barbarum,* **Epodes,** 9.6), often of some complexity (III.12.10-12):

> catus idem per apertum fugientis agitato
> grege ceruos iaculari et celer arto latitantem
>     fruticeto excipere aprum.

> (He is shrewd at spearing stags when the herd of deer / is alarmed and flying over the open plain, and swift / to receive the boar hiding in the undergrowth.)

The symmetry of this formidable quintuple antithesis is relieved by minute variations: *celer* is the precise counterpoise to *catus,* but *per apertum* is different in form from *arto fruticeto; agitato grege* is an extra in the first colon but similar in form to *arto fruticeto* in the second; *fugientis* comes after *per apertum,* but *latitantem,* its counterpoise, is cunningly contained within *arto fruticeto;* in a final flourish 'the stags to spear' is set in chiasmus against 'to meet the boar'. After this fanfare we may look back and wonder why cunning is prized in the chase and speed in the ambush.

Sometimes these symmetrical structures contribute so much to the poetry that commentators can fairly be faulted for ignoring them. In I.13 the antithesis is triple (I.13.1-4):

> cum tu, Lydia, Telephi
>     ceruicem roseam, cerea Telephi
> laudas bracchia, uae meum
>     feruens difficili bile tumet iecur.

> (When you Lydia, praise Telephus's / rosy neck, and Telephus's / waxen arms, oh my liver boils / and swells with bile it can't contain.)

There the counterpoint between the line endings and the shape of the antitheses leads us towards the balancing items: the derisive repeat of *Telephi;* the colour contrast highlighted by the juxtaposition of *roseam* and *cerea;* and, most important of all for the sense of the poem, the placing of *tu* and *meum,* amounting to a dramatic direction to the reader.

Antithesis in this essay, like *contentio* in *Rhetorica ad Herennium* and in Quintilian, is taken to mean balanced contrast. Contrast without balance is more difficult to name (Schuster[5] calls it 'Nebeneinanderstellunggegensätzlicher Begriffe'), but even more frequent in the **Odes.** For example, contrasting terms are juxtaposed in each of the first four **Odes**—*partem solido, aequore dammae, fragilem truci, soluitur acris:* the hedonist spends part of his whole day at his pleasures; the deer are at sea; the boat is fragile, the sea is grim; winter was frosty, now it is thawing. But often the trick goes deeper, as in I.15.1-2:

> pastor cum traheret per freta nauibus
> Idaeis Helenen perfidus hospitam

where treachery clashes with the hostess; where the shepherd betrays his calling by plundering, and is out of his element at sea on board ship; where *Idaeis Helenen* offers the standard contrast of nationalities which we have already seen in **Epodes,** 9.6 and which Horace so often uses in describing his own achievement in setting Latin poetry to Greek metres. *Dic Latinum, barbite, carmen* (I.32) and *Aeolium carmen ad Italos* (III.30) are the same device and the same claim.

Polar tension is often relevant to the argument of a poem. The first ode of the second book is concerned with Pollio and his history of the civil wars until the last stanza (II.1.37-40):

> sed ne relictis, Musa procax, iocis
> Ceae retractes munera neniae;
>     mecum Dionaeo sub antro
>     quaere modos leuiore plectro.

> (But O my immoral Muse, don't give up your fun, / don't take to the task of producing dirges like Simonides: / come with me to the cave of Venus / and look for tunes that suit a lighter plectrum.)

'The horrors of the past', writes Fraenkel,[6] 'seem to have faded away; in the gentle finale we are watching a scene of sheltered peace.' We are watching also a point-by-point refusal to write like Pollio. Pollio's Muse of severe tragedy is briefly to desert the theatre (*paulum seuerae Musa tragoediae desit theatris,* 9-10); Horace's immoral Muse is not to abandon her frolics; she is to be with him in the grotto of Venus; not in the tragic theatre, and not coping with sterner divinities (*Iuno et deorum quisquis amicior Afris,* 25-6); Pollio is engaged in matters of weight and substance; but *grauis* (3), *plenum* (6) and *grande* (11) are answered by *leuiore;* so *tractas* (7) by *retractes;* *coturno* (12) the tragic boot, by *plectro;* the *munus* of tragedy (11) by the *munera* of Simonides; *repetes* (12) by *quaere;* Pollio is concerned with *ludum Fortunae* (3); Horace's Muse is not to give up her *iocis;* Pollio is concerned with *belli modos* (2); Horace's Muse with a different kind of *modos.* If *Dionaeo* and *Ceae* could be held to be counters to *Cecropio* (12), every word in the last stanza (except *sub*) is in polar tension with at least one word in the body of the ode. 'Better without', wrote Landor in his margin opposite this stanza, and without this stanza Horace would have written a nobler poem, but nobility is only one of Horace's targets. This student might find six such points of contrast in the last two lines of III.1, and many too at the end of II.16 and II.17, and in other modest disavowals by this poet.[7]

But similar contrasts occur in many different contexts (II.14):

Eheu *fugaces,* Postume, Postume,
labuntur anni nec pietas *moram*
    rugis et *instanti* senectae
      adferet *indomitaeque* morti,
non si trecenis quotquot eunt dies,
amice, *places inlacrimabilem*
    Plutona tauris, qui ter *amplum*
      Geryonen Tityonque tristi
*conpescit unda,* scilicet omnibus,
quicumque *terrae* munere uescimur,
    enauiganda, siue *reges*
      siue *inopes* erimus *coloni.*
frustra *cruento* Marte carebimus
fractisque *rauci* fluctibus Hadriae,
    frustra per autumnos nocentem
      corporibus metuemus Austrum.
*uisendus ater* flumine *languido*
Cocytos errans et Danai genus
    *infame* damnatusque *longi*
      Sisyphus Aeolides laboris.
*linquenda* tellus et domus et *placens*
uxor, neque harum, quas colis, arborum
    te praeter *inuisas* cupressos
      ulla *breuem* dominum sequetur.
*absumet* heres Caecuba dignior
*seruata* centum clauibus et mero
    tinguet *pauimentum superbo,*
      pontificum potiore cenis.

(Alas Postumus, Postumus, the gliding years are in flight / and devotion cannot block the pursuit / of wrinkles, old age and irresistible death:—/ no my friend, not if you sacrificed three hundred bulls a day / to appease this pitiless god of the underworld, / who confines the triple-vast Geryon / and Tityos / within the river which we know must be crossed / by all who feed upon the bounty / of earth, kings / and poor tenant-farmers alike. / In vain we shall avoid the bloody god of battle / and the roaring breakers of the Adriatic, / in vain in the autumn we shall worry / about unhealthy winds from the South; / we must all go to the dark, sluggish, winding river / of Cocytus, to the notorious daughters / of Danaus, to Sisyphus son of Aeolus, / condemned to his long labour. / You must leave behind

your land and your home / and the wife you love, and none of your trees / will follow their short-lived owner / bar the cypress which you hate. / Your heir, a better man than you, will go through / the Caecuban you have locked behind a hundred keys / and the proud vintage, too good for a priest's banquet, / will dirty the marble paving.)

'The first half of this poem', according to Nisbet,[8] 'falls short of greatness, for though the words are solemn and sonorous, they make no clear picture.' Williams[9] is equally in the dark with the ticking away of time and the approach of death. There is a perfectly clear picture in this stanza and there are no approaches or clocks. Polar tension is often a useful key to the force of a metaphor, and not only in Horace. A simple example will demonstrate the method. 'Ac per hos dies libentissime otium meum in litteris colloco quos alii otiosissimis occupationibus perdunt', writes Pliny (*Epistles,* IX.6)—'During these days with immense satisfaction I invested my idle time in literature while others were squandering theirs in utterly idle occupations.' For *colloco* the translators offer 'devote' or 'fill' and the commentators have nothing. But in this heavily antithetic author, *colloco* balancing *perdunt* must have a financial connotation. By a similar *e sequentibus praecedentia,*[10] *fugaces* in *Odes,* II.14 is to be understood in the light of *moram* and each of these words in the light of the two contrasting words that follow, *instanti* and *indomitae.* The years are on the run, old age and wrinkles are pressing them hard, death is invincible, devotion cannot stop any of the three of them. The picture is clear. It is a battle scene, a rout, vivid and precise.

In the second stanza, *places* and *inlacrimabilem* are in tension, 'placate the pitiless'. So *ter amplum* and *compescit,* 'confine the triply vast'.[11] *Terrae* speaks to *unda,* 'all who feed upon the earth must cross the wave'. The *coloni* are *inopes* as opposed to the *reges.* Stanzas 4-6 comprise a triple triad. Three things we shall avoid in vain (*frustra . . . frustra*). Three things we must visit (*uisendus* first in the stanza). Three things you must leave behind you (*linquenda* first in the stanza). Mars is bloody, but Cocytus is black. The breakers of the Adriatic are noisy, but Cocytus is winding and languid, and both form a counterpoise to the land you must leave behind. The daughters of Danaus are infamous because they murdered their husbands on the wedding night. How different from the wife who pleases you, and she again from the cypresses you hate. Sisyphus is condemned to long labour in the underworld. The owner of the trees is short lived. In the last stanza, the Caecuban is laid down behind a hundred locks, but your heir will drink it all. As a last juxtaposition of opposites *pauimentum superbo* vividly suggests that the highest pride will be laid low.[12]

Is polar tension too frequent in this ode? Is it a sign of routine work? Certainly not. Rather the varied contrasts between so many details lend a characteristically Horation density to the thought. Collinge[13] says that the ode 'almost looks like a *cento* of Horation commonplaces . . . The four stanzas simply say that death has no regard for (1) character, (2) offerings, (3) status, (4) evasive action.' Our study of the contrasts, which are only a tiny part of what is in the ode, suggests that such paraphrases have the same use as the man in the foreground of the photograph of the Eiffel Tower.

The italics in the text of II.14 show at a glance that in this ode at least, 'the setting off of A against B is the major motif of Horatian verbal composition.' One last example may illustrate the convenience of this pattern of thought (III.4.13-16):

> . . . mirum quod foret omnibus,
> quicumque *celsae* nidum Aceruntiae
> *saltusque* Bantinos et *aruum*
> pingue tenent *humilis* Forenti,

(. . . a miracle to all who live / in the lofty nest of Aceruntia, / the pastures of Bantia and the rich tilth / of low-lying Forentum,)

*Celsae Aceruntiae* is in explicit contrast to *humilis Forenti*, and between these two *saltus Bantinos* provides a further diversification: Aceruntia (833 metres above sea-level), a bird's nest on its hill-top (Cicero had already used the image, *De Orat.*, I.196); and from crag to pasture, Bantia (570 metres) high among its grassy valleys; and from pasture to arable, *aruum pingue humilis Forenti* suggesting in this context an alluvial plain, although Nissen[14] has to resort to assumptions to bring it down to 462 metres. When Horace is looking for three villages from his own part of the world to canonize in Aeolian verse, his main criterion of choice and the main characteristics celebrated are contrasting contours and contrasting land use. This tells us something about his technique and about his imagination. It is confirmed seven lines later when we read *arduos Sabinos* and *Tibur supinum*. This motif is so frequent that it might be called a formula for the provision of ornamental epithets. Poets using this formula would be in constant danger of falling into a mechanical reproduction of vacuous patterns. Not so Horace, or not often so. If we observe such contrasts in the *Odes,* we are led to a keener sense of the genius responsible for them. They demonstrate rather the richness of his dramatic sense, his visualization, his imagery and his tone of voice.

CONTRASTS AND DRAMATIC SENSE

*Neu uiuax apium neu breue lilium* (*Odes,* 1.36) may look like slack writing. Celery keeps fresh for some time; lilies wilt. *Ergo* two epithets from the machine, *uiuax* and *breue*. But this is not a generous view of the line. We are at a banquet of lovers. The contrast in expectation of life of the two vegetables is adding a dimension to the talk of love. The antithesis broadens the dramatic purchase of the poetry; it is not just a rhetorical carbuncle. There is however another passage where the drama does seem to labour (IV.9.19-28):

> . . . non pugnauit *ingens*
> Idomeneus Sthenelusue solus
> dicenda Musis proelia, non *ferox*

> Hector uel *acer* Deiphobus *grauis*
> excepit ictus pro pudicis
> coniugibus puerisque primus.
> uixere *fortes* ante Agamemnona
> multi; sed omnes inlacrimabiles
> urgentur *ignotique* longa
> nocte, carent quia uate sacro.

(. . . Neither huge Idomeneus nor Sthenelus has been alone / in fighting battles worthy of the voice / of the Muses; neither fierce Hector / nor deadly Deiphobus has been the first / to suffer heavy blows in the defence / of their children and chaste wives. / Brave men have lived before Agamemnon in great numbers, but all of them unwept / and unknown are crushed in endless night / because they have no divinely inspired poet.)

*ingens, ferox, acer, grauis,* the intensives roll on a little too repetitively, until the poem is saved by its great climax in *fortes* and the annulling contrast *ignoti*. If this fails, it fails because of an abuse not of contrast, but of hyperbole, the besetting failure of the *Aeneid*.[15]

There are other passages in the fourth book of the *Odes,* where poetry is degenerating into rhetoric.

'There is hardly anything in the *Odes* that can be called ornamentation: *Ode* III.16.1-8 is most unusual in that every noun has an adjective (most of them merely ornamental) which is placed next to it.' So says Williams, and he finds these adjectives 'the one serious weakness of the composition'.[16]

> *Inclusam* Danaen turris *aenea*
> *robustaeque* fores et *uigilum* canum
> *tristes* excubiae *munierant* satis
> nocturnis ab adulteris,
> *si non* Acrisium uirginis *abditae*
> custodem *pauidum* Iupiter et Venus
> risissent: fore enim *tutum* iter et *patens*
> conuerso in pretium deo.

(Shut in her tower of bronze, Danae / had been well enough secured from night callers / by stout doors, / by savage and unsleeping watch dogs / if Jupiter and Venus had not made a mockery / of her nervous guardian Acrisius. / They knew a safe and open road—/ turn the god into his fee.)

Far from being a weakness of this composition, the accumulation of epithets gives it its dramatic force. *Inclusam* vigorously states the theme and each of the next four adjectives increases the apparent security of Danae, *aenea, robustae, uigilum, tristes;* and *munierant* contributes the finality of the indicative mood—'they actually had protected her',—all forming a great enceinte breached with absurd ease by the two little words at the beginning of the next stanza—*si non. Abditae* and *pauidum* then characterize the nervous precautions taken by Acrisius to preserve his daughter's chastity. *Tutum* makes nonsense of the second, *patens* of the first, a splendidly satirical lead-in for the shock in the crowning epigram, where Jupiter is turned, not as expected into a shower of gold, but into payment for services rendered. This paraphrase is meant to show that nine of the epithets in this extract are in polar tension and that all go to shape a nicely judged dramatic movement. The tone is sardonic. Fraenkel's 'frigid allegory'[17] and Williams' 'poetic mystery'[18] are equally wide of the mark.

CONTRAST AND VISUALIZATION

The clash of colours is a stock device of Latin verse. Norden collects more than a dozen examples from the sixth book of the *Aeneid* in his note on ll. 9-10, and Virgil offers many other examples, some of them, like his description of the Nile, as weird as the temperature contrast with which this chapter began (*Georgics*, IV.293-1):

> usque *coloratis* amnis deuexus ab Indis,
> et *uiridem* Aegyptum *nigra* fecundat harena

> (the river flowing down from the coloured Indians, /
> and fertilizes green Egypt with its black sand)

Such devices are equally common in the *Odes* of Horace. Enough to cite III.27.19-20 with *ater* and *albus* at the end of succeeding lines and I.7.15-21, where two examples occur in one sentence ('albus *ut* obscuro' and '*seu* fulgentia *castra tenent seu* densa *tenebit* umbra'). This casts a glimmer of light on the famous epigram (III.1.38-40):

> neque
> decedit *aerata* triremi et
> post equitem sedet *atra* Cura.

We have all seen the dark figure seated behind the horseman. But a brass-plated ship will sparkle in the Mediterranean sun. *Aerata* is in tension with *atra*. We must see also the dark figure against the glittering trireme.[19] And if this is how Horace works we must look again at (II.16.21-2):

> scandit *aeratas uitiosa* nauis
> Cura nec turmas equitum relinquit

> (Tarnished Care boards the ships of brass / and cleaves
> to the cavalry squadrons).

The brass plating on a rich man's ship is a manifestation of power, and *uitiosa* obviously suggests the corruption which attends upon it. But apart from this moral observation, we are led also to a material visualization. The panoply gleams in the sun and *uitium* is the tarnishing of the brass.

It may support this suggestion to notice that Horace often uses the word *sordidus* in the *Odes* with a contrast between the dull and the brilliant. In II.1, after the flashing armour, Horace imagines the great leaders soiled but not disgraced by dust ('fulgor *armorum, non indecoro puluere* sordidos'). In II.16 the family salt-cellar gleams on the table and sordid lust doesn't carry off light sleep ('splendet *salinum nec levis somnos cupido* sordidus *aufert*'). In III.2 virtue knows nothing of the squalor of electoral defeat but shines with honours unsullied ('repulsae *nescia* sordidae *intaminatis* fulget honoribus'). In IV.11.11 the flames are spinning the

dirty smoke ('sordidum *fumum*', ll. 10-11) as opposed to the smiling of the silver ('ridet *argento domus*') and the brilliant beauty of Phyllis, (ll. 5-6).[20]

Another visualization is clearly indicated by a multiple antithesis (I.35.21-6):

> te Spes et albo rara Fides colit
> uelata panno nec comitem abnegat,
>     utcumque mutata potentis
>         ueste domos inimica linquis,
> at uolgus infidum et meretrix retro
> periura cedit

> (Hope and that rare visitant Honesty, / draped in holy
> white, attend you, / and stay with you when you change
> your dress / and leave the rich man's house in
> displeasure. / But the mob breaks its pledge and the
> fickle whore / falls back)

In this incomprehensible address to Fortune, there is contrast, as Nisbet and Hubbard see, between *rara* and *uolgus*, *Fides* and *infidum*, *nec comitem abnegat* and *retro cedit*. *Fides* also makes a clear counterpoise to *meretrix periura*. Since this is so, and since *Fides* is draped in white, a strong invitation is issued to our visual imagination to see against the white of *Fides* the contrasting gaudiness of the prostitute. Such is the characteristic difference between married woman and *meretrix* (*Epistles*, I.18.3-4):

> ut matrona meretrici dispar erit atque
> discolor.

A simile is an invitation to visualize resemblances (IV.2.25-32):

> *multa Dircaeum leuat* aura *cycnum,*
> tendit, Antoni, quotiens in *altos*
> *nubium* tractus: ego *apis Matinae*
>     more modoque,
> grata carpentis *thyma per laborem*
> *plurimum*, circa nemus uuidique
> Tiburis *ripas operosa paruos*
>     carmina fingo.

> (Antonius, a great wind lifts the swan of Dirce /
> whenever it soars into the lofty tracts / of the clouds: I
> am like a bee / from the Matine hill / harvesting the
> lovely thyme with enormous / labour. Along the dripping banks / of wooded Tibur, in my own small way / I
> mould laborious songs.)

This is a 'dissimile', an invitation to visualize contrasts. The breeze lifts the swan; Horace, like a bee, has no such extraneous assistance (*per laborem plurimum, operosa*); Pindar is the swan of Dirce, the famous fountain of Thebes which resounds through Greek lyric poetry; Horace is the bee of a mountain or promontory or plain (we still do not know what Matinum was and it is not mentioned in extant poetry before Horace). In the first book of the *Odes* also it appears in a belittling context (I.28.1-4):

> Te *maris et terrae numeroque carentis* harenae
>     mensorem cohibent, *Archyta,*

*pulueris exigui* prope litus *parua Matinum*
  munera.

(You have measured the sea, Archytas, the earth / and
the unnumbered sand. You are now confined / near the
Matine shore by the tiny tribute / of a little dust.)

The swan flies high *in altos nubium tractus;* the bee works
the river bank, and thyme is a creeper. So much for
bilateral contrasts; but the wealth of this poetry depends
also upon unilateral contrasts, where only one member of
the pair is mentioned. The swan is proverbial for the sweetness of its singing; we are left to imagine the buzzing of
the bee. *Multa aura* is all very well for swans; but not for
bees, as all readers of Virgil knew ('principio sedes apibus
statioque petenda, / quo neque sit uentis aditus', *Georgics,*
IV.8-9). The river bank and the trees are other requisites of
bees which lend poetic strength to this metaphor and they
too are stressed early in the fourth *Georgic* (18-24). So too
*fingo* is a bee word (*Georgics,* IV.57 and 179). And the
minuteness of the bees is a motif of Virgil's masterpiece,
exploited by Horace as are all the other bee references
noted in this stanza in a similar context in *Epistles,* I.3.[21]

### CONTRAST AND METAPHOR

There are many passages in Horace where we can see the
characteristic Horatian contrast if we see the literal force
of the words (I.16.17-20):

  irae Thyesten exitio *graui*
  *strauere* et *altis* urbibus ultimae
      *stetere* causae, cur perirent
          *funditus inprimeretque* muris . . .

(Anger laid Thyestes low in a heavy doom, / and stands
revealed as the primary reason / for the destruction of
lofty cities to their foundations / and the razing of their
walls . . .)

Nisbet and Hubbard comment upon *stetere,* 'anger is the
appointed or determined cause', and they write that *altis*
means 'great and proud' rather than 'high'. But there is
more to it than that. Surely in this context *stetere* and *altis*
are set against *graui, strauere* and *inprimeret?* This is not
to argue for my translation 'standing' *rather* than
'appointed', for 'high' *rather* than 'proud'. The translation
is offered to isolate the point. The words do mean what
Nisbet and Hubbard say they mean. They have at the same
time another function.

The contrasts are more elaborate, but they also lead to the
literal force of the words in (II.4.9-12):

  barbarae postquam cecidere turmae
  *Thessalo uictore* et *ademptus Hector*
  tradidit *fessis leuiora tolli*
      *Pergama Grais.*

(After the barbarian squadrons fell / to the Thessalian
conqueror and the removal of Hector / made the taking
of Troy / a lighter task for the weary Greeks.)

The last line presents the standard contrast of nations at its
barest. The second line has a similar confrontation but
with variation in shape and content, the Thessalian victor

and the removed Hector. But more important for the poetry
is the relationship between *leuiora* and *tolli.* Of course this
means that Troy was easier to capture, but it presents the
reader with an extra picture. If the removal of Hector
makes Troy *leuiora tolli,* we are driven to see the literal
sense of *ademptus,* and of *leuiora,* and of *tolli.* Horace
plays the same trick in III.4.44, 'immanemque turbam fulmine sustulerit caduco'—'he destroyed (and caught *up*)
the monstrous horde with his *falling* thunderbolt'.[22]

Sometimes contrast leads to the literal meaning of the
word and this exposes a pun (IV.11.25-8):

  terret ambustus Phaethon auaras
  spes et exemplum *graue* praebet *ales*
  *Pegasus terrenum equitem grauatus*
      Bellerophontem,

(The burning of Phaethon frightens our greedy hopes. /
Winged Pegasus, throwing off the weight / of his
earthly rider Bellerophon, provides / a weighty
example,)

'There is a half comic irony', observes Wickham in his
commentary, 'in the array of mythological instances of the
folly of misplaced ambition.' There is also a pun, and
carefully disposed contrasts to lead us to it. *ales Pegasus
terrenum equitem* is the usual tooling and *grauatus Belle-
rophontem* completes the pattern: Pegasus and Bellerophon; winged and earthly; the tossing of the rider. In this
setting when *Pegasus grauatus exemplum graue praebet,*
the example is weighty, not sharp. *graue grauatus* is not a
slovenly repeat, but a pointed polyptoton. There are two
passages in Lucretius which may have sparked off this
pattern of thought: one, his pun on *grauis* where downy
seed-heads find it no light task to fall (*qui nimia leuitate
cadunt plerumque grauatim,* III.387); two, where Lucretius
is taking the credulous to task for their belief that lightning
is the weapon of the gods, and asks in a cataract of rhetorical questions why they strike the innocent as well as the
guilty (VI.390-2):

  cur quibus incautum scelus auersabile cumquest
  non faciunt icti flammas ut fulguris halent
  pectore perfixo, documen mortalibus acre?

(Why do they not so ordain that men guilty of loathsome crimes / should be struck by lightning and made
to exhale its flames / through their riven breasts? That
would be a sharp lesson for mortals.)

Sharp indeed, not to say acrid, since lightning burns with
the smell of sulphur: (*grauis halantes sulpuris auras,*
VI.221).

A clear example may now lead us to something more
elusive (II.3.1-2):

  *aequam* memento rebus in *arduis*
  seruare mentem

(Try to stay level-headed when the going / is rough.)

The word *arduis* is used seven times in the *Odes,*[23] and
always with its literal sense of 'steep', as in the triple
contrast *arduis pronos relabi* (I.29). As the commentators

see, opposition between *aequam* and *arduis* framing the first line of II.3 above, guarantees here too the presence of the literal force. This assists our understanding of I.3:

> expertus uacuum Daedalus aera
> pinnis non homini datis;
> perrupit Acheronta Herculeus labor.
> nil mortalibus ardui est:
> caelum ipsum petimus stultitia neque
> per nostrum patimur scelus
> iracunda Iouem ponere fulmina.

(I.3.34-40)

(Daedalus tried the empty air / with superhuman wings. / The labour of Hercules / burst through the underworld. No path is too steep for mortals: / we scale the sky itself in our foolishness / and by our sin we prevent Jupiter / from laying aside his anger, and his lightning.)

Commentators sometimes condemn this ode without mentioning the two main sources of poetic power at the end of it: one, the allusion to the Civil Wars as a divine judgment on contemporary Rome; two, the visualization. Three offences are listed: man's first flight, the descent into the underworld, the scaling of Olympus (*per arduum*, II.19.21). All of these offenders went by a steep road, and *ardui* in its literal sense links them all and gives the passage a sensory vitality. The word is often interpreted simply as 'difficult' and the line explained as a reflection of Greek commonplaces. This is half the story. The commonplaces cited have not the serious topical relevance of Horace. Nor his visualization.

Our last cluster of contrasts and metaphors is a virtuoso piece (III.28.1-8):

> Festos quid potius die
> Neptuni faciam? *prome reconditum,*
> Lyde, *strenua* Caecubum
> *munitaeque adhibe uim* sapientiae.
> *inclinare* meridiem
> sentis et, ueluti *stet uolucris* dies,
> *parcis deripere* horreo
> *cessantem Bibuli* consulis amphoram?

(What better is there for me to do / on Neptune's day? Up with you, Lyde. / Draw out the long-stored Caecuban / and mount an attack on the citadel of wisdom. / You see the midday giving way, and yet / as though the flying day were standing fast / do you spare the shirking jar of Bibulus the consul, / and hesitate to tear it out from its cellar?)

Once again the oppositions force us to appreciate the metaphors. *Strenuitas* is a cardinal military virtue, guaranteed by *munitae* and *adhibe uim*. But if Lyde is asked *strenua* to bring out the *cessantem amphoram*, the jar is not just delaying, it is shirking battle.[24] This alerts us to *parcis* which must in such a context flick at its military sense. And *cessantem* is opposed not only to *strenua* but also to *deripere*. The jar is lingering, so it should be hustled out of the cellar. *Cessantem* and *Bibuli* are in discord and at the same time in harmony: in discord, because a man

with the name of Bibulus should be ready to tipple and therefore anything but hesitant; in harmony, because Bibulus was famous for his procrastination during the consulship of Julius Caesar.

There is another conspicuous contrast. Lyde sees the midday sun *departing* from the vertical, and yet she temporizes as though the fleeting day were *standing* still. *Inclinare* and *stet,* in this astronomical sense, are in polar tension. But we have seen a clearly marked military metaphor in ll. 3 and 4 and 7 and 8. *Inclinare* and *stare* in ll. 5 and 6 may also be playing with a military sense. *Inclinare* is a technical military term for the buckling of a line of battle (e.g. *inclinatur acies,* Livy, I.12.3) and *stare* is its opposite. If this opposition is felt to be part of the military allusion, the logic of the metaphor is under strain. Who are the contestants in this battle? Lyde is attacking the barricades of wisdom. The *amphora* of wine is shirking and Lyde is 'sparing to drag it out', so it seems to be a potential ally. But already the metaphor is strained. Normally it is an enemy that would be spared, not an ally. And how are the forces of time aligned? There is no need to ask. The allusion may be an enlargement and complication rather than a precise analogy. Horace is playing with contrasts and images, not model-building.

### CONTRAST AND TONE OF VOICE

> adduxere sitim tempora, Vergili.
> sed *pressum* Calibus ducere *Liberum*
> si gestis, iuuenum nobilium cliens,
> nardo uina merebere.
> *nardi paruus onyx eliciet cadum,*
> qui nunc Sulpiciis *accubat* horreis,
> *spes donare nouas largus amaraque*
> curarum eluere efficax.
> ad quae si *properas* gaudia, cum tua
> *uelox merce* ueni: non ego te meis
> *inmunem* meditor *tingere* poculis,
> plena diues ut in domo.
> uerum pone *moras* et studium lucri . . .

(IV.12.13-25)

(These are thirsty times Virgil, but if / you fancy a draught of vintage from the presses / of Cales, you client of the young nobility, / you must pay for your wine with nard. / A small box of nard will tempt out the jar of wine / now reclining in the cellars of Sulpicius. / It will grant you new hopes in abundance / and effectively wash away the bitterness of sorrow. / If you are in a hurry to taste these joys, come quickly / with your barter: I do not intend to let you dip / in my cups scot-free, as though I were / a rich man in a full house. / But throw aside delay and your eagerness for profit . . .)

This essay has freely hypothesized puns and word-play, but there are limits. The last phrase of the first book, *arta sub uite bibentem,* leaves Horace drinking under the dense foliage of a vine, not as M. O. Lee[25] believes, thinking of *uita uiuentem,* not at all; and not at all thinking that the phrase echoes *sera morietur,* which Lee conjures out of *sera moretur* in the previous stanza. Nor should *Bacchus*

(*Liber*) leap to the mind as we read *nunc est bibendum nunc pede libero* (I.37.1), as Commager proposes.[26] True the play on these two meanings occurs in Plautus (*Captiui*, 577; *Cistellaria*, 127), but *pede Libero* makes no sense. *Pressum ducere Liberum* (IV.12.14) is slightly more tempting because of the standard polarity of the expression, 'to lead free what had been pressed' (cf. *Satires*, II.4.69, 'pressa *Venafranae quod baca* remisit *oliuae*').

A small box of nard is set against the abundant hopes, the onyx box perhaps against the earthenware jar, the coaxing out against the reclining in the cellars, freshness against bitterness, hopes against cares, giving against washing away,[27] with goods as opposed to empty-handed, haste as opposed to delay. Less obvious is the interplay between the washing away and the dipping, but not less characteristic. Wine effectively washes away bitterness, but Virgil is not going to be allowed to dip in it. Another possible crosscurrent is the interaction of *efficax* and *immunem* after *Liberum*, both adjectives being used elsewhere by Horace in religious contexts (*Epodes*, 3.17; 17.1; *Odes*, III.23.17).

Virgil has been dead for half-a-dozen years and here is Horace calling him 'a client of the young nobility' and teasing him for his desire to make money. 'If we find anything offensive in these phrases as applied to the poet Virgil it is surely only because for us Virgil is not, as he was for Horace, the friend with whom we have joked and drunk wine on the road to Brindisi.' So argues L. A. Moritz,[28] and explains the commercial references as a private joke between the two. Perhaps a straw of support for this contention may be found in the only two other passages in the *Odes* where Horace mentions Virgil's name.

The first of these is addressed to the ship on which Virgil is sailing to Greece (I.3.5-8):

> nauis quae tibi *creditum*
> 　　*debes* Virgilium: finibus Atticis
> *reddas* incolumem precor
> 　　et serues animae dimidium meae.

(You are the ship to whom Virgil has been entrusted. / You owe him. Pay him intact I beg you / to the land of Attica, / and keep safe the half of my life.)

'One is meant to think', according to Nisbet and Hubbard, 'of a valuable object deposited with a friend for safe keeping.' Yes. But, in fact, *creditum*, *debes* and *reddas* could cover a wide range of commercial or financial transactions and *dimidium* suggests rather the deposit or loan of a sum of money.[29] The second reference is similar (I.24.9-12):

> multis ille bonis flebilis occidit,
> nulli flebilior quam tibi, Vergili.
> tu frustra pius, heu, non ita *creditum*
> 　　*poscis* Quintilium deos.

(Now he is dead and many good men will weep for him, / but none more than you Virgil. You pray the gods / with useless devotion, to give back Quintilius. / He was not entrusted to us on those terms.)

The three references to the name of Virgil in the *Odes* of Horace are all associated with commercial or financial allusions. Coincidence? Aided by the fact that these motifs occur in other *propemptica* and *consolationes*?[30] Perhaps. But 'Horace is the poet, above all, of human relationships', and commentators amply demonstrate his penchant for banter.[31] This is *ad hominem* poetry. Its allusions are often lost irretrievably. Its tone was for the ears of a small circle of friends. Virgil was Horace's friend, and generally thought to be the greatest of the Roman poets. Horace twice mentions his name in mercantile contexts, and now, so soon after his death, speaks of him as a mercenary social climber. It is just conceivable that this was some private joke between the two. It is not conceivable that the tone of IV.12 could be malicious. The coarseness directed towards Horace in the letters of Augustus preserved by Suetonius shows that this coterie enjoyed offensive endearments. The tone of this ode must be affectionate.

In this study of contrasts in the *Odes*, certain points of technique have been seen to recur. We shall gather these together by studying one whole poem (II.10):

> Rectius uiues, Licini, neque altum (1)
> semper urgendo neque, dum procellas
> cautus horrescis, nimium premendo
> 　　litus iniquum.
> auream quisquis mediocritatem (5)
> diligit, tutus caret obsoleti
> sordibus tecti, caret inuidenda
> 　　sobrius aula.
> saeuius uentis agitatur ingens (9)
> pinus et celsae grauiore casu
> decidunt turres feriuntque summos
> 　　fulgura montis.
> sperat infestis, metuit secundis (13)
> alteram sortem bene praeparatum
> pectus: informis hiemes reducit (15)
> 　　Iuppiter, idem
> submouet; non, si male nunc, et olim (17)
> sic erit: quondam cithara tacentem (18)
> suscitat Musam neque semper arcum
> 　　tendit Apollo.
> rebus angustis animosus atque (21)
> fortis adpare, sapiensque idem
> contrahes uento nimium secundo
> 　　turgida uela.

(You will live better Licinius, if you don't always go straining over the high seas, nor should you worry about storms and hug the rocky coast too close.
Whoever loves the Golden Mean is safe, without the squalor of a filthy garret, and moderate, without a mansion for men to envy.
The huge pine tree is tossed more violently by winds, the high towers come down with a heavier fall, the lightning strikes the top of the mountains.
The well-prepared heart hopes in adversity for a change in fortune, and fears in prosperity a change in fortune.
　　Jupiter brings back ugly winters and Jupiter

removes them.
If life is bad now, it won't
    always be bad.
sometimes Apollo rouses
the silent Muse with his lyre. It's not always
his bow he stretches.
    When things are tight show spirit
and courage. When the wind is too strong
at your back, be sensible, shorten
the bulging sail.)

The gaps in the translation show that this poem is a series of eight antitheses (ten if we count the third stanza as three). Each appears to express some aspect of the Golden Mean. This may therefore be viewed as a string of ten examples of the same rhetorical figure devoted to the same ethical commonplace. Unpromising raw material. How does Horace make poetry out of it?

First, the disposition of the antitheses. As the line numbers show, the first three stanzas are coextensive with the first three antitheses. Then the even divisions cease. The next three antitheses progressively decrease in length, each ending in the middle of a line, one of them striding over a stanza. The next increases again, and even division is restored in the last stanza, all forming a kind of ring composition. Counterpoint between sense and line and stanza is difficult to expound, but easy and live to hear, and part of the dramatic pacing of the poem.

Horace varies not only the length of the antitheses but also their shape. Lines 6-8 run A*BC*D *BC*AD, with BC representing the close response of *caret inuidenda* to *caret obsoleti* at the end of successive lines. In the third stanza huge trees are tossed more violently, tall towers fall more heavily, and lightning strikes the top of the mountains. In each colon the phrasing is varied, the word order is tellingly disposed in counterpoint to the line endings, and the opposites are left to our imagination. Line 13 is ABAB; ll. 15-17 ABBA; ll. 17-18, *non si male nunc et olim sic erit,* not if AB, BA, the starkest possible expression of the transitoriness of bad fortune; ll. 18-20 defy formulae, but none the less they present three pairs of interacting elements (sometimes, not always; the lyre and the bow; the rousing and the stretching, an irregular ABC ABC).

The manipulation of metaphor is vital to this poem. Ring composition is visible again, the relationship between the navigational metaphor in the first stanza and the nautical metaphor in the last. Within each of these the details are precise and active in the poem, like *semper* and *iniquum.* It would be foolhardy *always* to cut across the open sea. Equally it is dangerous to hug a coast too close if it is *rocky.* The full force of some of the metaphors is grasped only after we apprehend the contrasts round about them. *urgere altum* for instance, is an intensive variation of the normal phrase *tenere altum,* to steer across the high seas, suggesting *inter alia* the impatience of the sailor; but the force of *altum semper urgendo* depends upon its audible correspondence with *nimium premendo litus.* Similarly, it

is the context which illumines the Golden Mean. This dazzling oxymoron has been too successful. We are too familiar with it to realize how provocative it is, and how it fits the argument. Mediocrity is drab. In calling it golden, Horace is differentiating it from the squalor of poverty (*obsoleti sordibus tecti*), and also from the rich man's palace (*inuidenda aula*).[32] It is the mean that is truly golden, not the golden gewgaws of the wealthy (cf. Lucretius, II.24-8). In the second last stanza, again the antithesis leads to a keener apprehension of the image. Apollo sometimes rouses the Muse with his lyre; he does not always stretch the bow. This invites us to visualize Apollo stretching the strings of the lyre. And finally, in the nautical metaphor, the contrasts again stimulate the senses. When things are tight (*rebus angustis*) you don't tighten your bulging sails (*contrahes turgida uela*); when the favouring wind is too strong (*uento nimium secundo*) you don't show yourself to be high-spirited (*animosus*). It is reasonable in reading this poet to be led by the carefully tooled contrast to think of the application of the word *animosus* to winds (*animosi Euri,* Virgil, *Georgics,* II.441).

The argument of the poem is well constructed. Aristotle's treatment of virtue as a mean provides a useful comparison. 'In the section confined to the feelings inspired by danger you will observe that the mean state is "courage". Of those who go to extremes in one direction or the other the man who shows an excess of fearlessness has no name to describe him, the man who exceeds in confidence or daring is called "rash" or "foolhardy", the man who shows an excess of fear and a deficiency of confidence is called a "coward".'[33] And so Aristotle moves systematically through the same sort of material as Horace from the mean of courage with an extreme on each side of it, to the mean as applied to the giving and acquiring of money, to ambition, to man's attitudes to the fortunes of neighbours. Horace's argument is less clearly signposted than Aristotle's, but no less valid and dynamic. The first three stanzas hang together. Always taking risks is one extreme and it is contrasted with a nervous excess of precautions. *iniquo* is anything but a vacuous epithet. Horace is making the interesting point that an excess of caution leads to danger. The next two stanzas apply the doctrine of the mean to wealth and to eminence. The fourth stanza propounds a new but related thesis, that the man whose mind is well-prepared is ready for a reversal of fortune. This reversability of fortune is then asserted three times, beginning with Jupiter, then in the barest possible terms which cannot but speak directly to Licinius' predicament ('non si male nunc et olim / sic erit'), then with reference to Apollo. The final stanza pulls together the two topics of the mean of courage and the reversability of fortune, and relates them: when Fortune is adverse, be brave; be cautious when she is favourable. This ode is not a repetitive string of clichés. The final thesis has not previously been propounded. It is the conclusion of the argument. Characteristic of the Pindaric style of Horace are the 'abrupt admonitions' and 'portentous maxims paratactically introduced.' But the absence of connectives does not mean the absence of connection. Equally characteristic of Horace are the shaping and movement of the argument. This is an intelligent rumination on two generalizations culminating in a combination of them.

Williams[34] suggests that much of the life and tension of moralizing poetry depends upon the movement from particular to general. In this poem this movement is vividly manifested in the syntax. The first stanza is addressed to Licinius and his name appears in the vocative with a verb in the second person jussive future. The poem then moves from the personal to the universal with *quisquis* in l. 5, and gives a series of generalizations mounting to Jupiter and Apollo. In the last stanza it returns to the second person with an imperative and another jussive future, completing yet another ring composition.

And the personal element is vital. This is *ad hominem* poetry, and expounded as such by Hanslik.[35] Aulus Terentius Varro Murena (formerly Licinius Murena) was consul in 23 B.C. He was removed from office by Augustus in the summer of 23. This ode was then written. In the next year he defended M. Primus on a charge of *maiestas,* joined the conspiracy of Fannius Caepio and was executed. 'Every word in Horace's Ode corresponds to the situation,' writes Hanslik. 'The cares of his friend were his own and he was trying not only to please Murena but also to improve him and help him.' This claim appears to be near the truth. The third stanza, for instance, is less abstract than it appears to be. If it was written immediately after Murena's removal from office, it takes on a tone at once complimentary and consolatory. 'You reached the pinnacle of political ambition. You must not be surprised if you were in an exposed position.' The first stanza is also topical, striking a judicious balance between foolhardiness and over-caution; the last (and the difference is useful and thoughtful) strikes the balance between courage and over-confidence. In electing to defend Primus, Murena missed both of these golden means.

But Hanslik claims too much. After three articles in *Historia*[36] in recent years it is still not possible to be certain of the precise dating of Murena's career and therefore of the precise application of the words of Horace's ode. Equally it may be an over-simplification to talk of 'advice'. Sometimes he gives the impression that he is advising the great to do what he knows they have already decided to do. This is eulogy rather than admiration. But the essential point stands. The poem has a purchase in real life. It spoke thoughtfully and directly to a man who had to contend with a problem which was to bring him to his death. This we should allow for, as we read the apparently abstract moralizing. 'Horace is the poet, above all, of human relationships.'

APPENDIX 1 SUSTAINED IMAGES

When a *single* word is used in Latin in a metaphorical sense it is difficult to be sure whether its literal sense is felt. It would be rash to insist upon any notion of flowering or heat in *adhuc florente iuuenta feruidus,* still hot in

the flower of youth (*Ars Poetica,* 115-16); and foolish to think of fertility when Mercury delivers the souls of the dead to their joyous abodes (*tu pias laetis animas reponis sedibus, Odes,* I.10.17), or of nursing when time snatches along the kindly day (*almum quae rapit hora diem,* IV.7.7).

When *two* or *more* words appear to be involved in the metaphor it is safer initially to assume that the metaphor is alive. The notion of nursing is not absent from *alit* alongside *nutrix* (I.22.14-16); *feruens* with *tumet* (I.13.4) suggests boiling; *laetas florere* in Lucretius (I.255) suggests that identity of human and vegetable growth which is fundamental to the argument of the whole passage.

But even with two or more terms there is room for doubt. Sometimes the literal sense of the words does not fit closely enough. *generat* for instance between *alit* and *nutrix* just cited (I.22) confuses the functions of the sexes. Similarly *rectius* in the navigational metaphor at the beginning of II.10 could well in theory introduce the notion of a straight course but that does not fit the navigational context. Sometimes the literal sense is not frequently enough attested. This may tell against any literal force in *animosus* (II.10.21). Sometimes the metaphor itself is ill suited. The argument requires 'spirited' at that point, not 'windy'. Sometimes coincidence or mechanical word association may have brought together words which do not work together. So perhaps *inclinare* and *stare* (III.28) and *pressum Liberum* (IV.12) noted above.

There *is* an area for disagreement. But scepticism has gone too far. Some views are just wrong. To question the vegetative image in *laetas florere* (Lucretius, I.255) because Cicero frequently uses *florere* without any reference to flowers; or to question another image because if it were felt, it would end in the middle of a sentence; or to question the application of a simile to the surrounding argument because the simile is comprehensible without recourse to that argument—this is bad method.[37] Nisbet and Hubbard are also cautious, but at a different level, in their general assessment of Horace. 'By and large he avoids alliteration, onomatopoeia, and haunting vowel sounds: he does not evoke more than he says. His metaphors are sparse and trite.'[38] The first colon of the assessment could be refuted by reference to almost anything that L. P. Wilkinson has written on Horace, and to any reader whose ear has ever been haunted by a phrase from the *Odes.* The rest of it is annulled by the alert apprehension of allusions and images in their own great commentary, for example the legal flavour of *fruitur credulus aurea qui semper vacuam* (I.5) and the shepherding in *compulerit Mercurius gregi* after *uirga* (I.24). Their extremity of caution (*nimium premendo litus iniquum*) is perhaps to be explained as an over-reaction to some of the work on imagery being done at the moment in the United States (*altum semper urgendo*). It is not easy to remain temperate on reading for example that in the third stanza of II.10 '*celsae* implies the expansiveness of life; *graviore* the confining oppression of death',[39] or that in I.5 Pyrrha is 'like a Siren on a Siren's rock' and also 'like the living-dead golden bough' and also 'akin to the *nitentes Cycladas*', and on the next page that she 'becomes a beacon fire that lures ignorant seafarers to their destruction' and also 'the pyre on which they suffer the *ardor* not of love but of death'.[40] These promiscuous associations do not touch the poem. But they sully the critic. It is worse than useless to posit a meaningful interaction between words in widely separate contexts in obvious defiance of the apprehension of any normal reader or listener, and of the obvious statistics of language. When a word or image recurs in a Latin poet, we do not always have to believe that he is passing an arcane comment upon its occurrence 500 lines before.

Horace is not a brilliant excogitator of new similitudes. In his imagery he often falls short of the euphony and passion of Virgil. But in other respects he is superior. He lifts the old metaphor up to the light and turns it round and sees new facets and colours in it and relates these in new ways to each other and to the reality he is trying to illustrate, always with a wide range of subtly differentiated emotional tone, often with humour. It is enough to compare the simple metaphor of Anacreon with the virtuosic complexities of Horace's adaptation in II.5, to see that this is an important element in his technique.

APPENDIX 2 SURREALISM IN HORACE

When Horace writes *fulmine sustulerit caduco* (III.4.44) he means primarily that Jupiter destroyed the Titans with his falling thunderbolt. The purpose of this appendix is to ask whether he means also to exploit the clash between *caduco,* and the primary meaning of *sustulerit,* 'lifted'. Is Horace teasing us by suggesting that something can be lifted by something which is falling?

The question may be reset in a more extreme form. When he writes *deprome quadrimum Sabina . . . merum diota* (I.9), is he saying simply, 'draw off the four-year-old wine from its two-eared Sabine jar', or is he flashing a triple conceit before his readers? Common sense rejects the triple conceit. Against common sense can be urged some facts of Horatian language.

The national contrast has been noted so often in this chapter that there is no need to argue for a calculated interplay between *Sabina* and *diota* in I.9, but it is worth mentioning that the Sabine and the Sabellan are never mentioned in the **Odes** except in conscious and telling contrast to the foreign. *Sabinum cantharis* (I.20), where Nisbet and Hubbard shed new light, is a close parallel to our passage. So is *Latinum barbite* (I.32) mentioned at the beginning of this chapter.

Second, Horace has a tendency to juxtapose numerals which do not belong together arithmetically. Hecate is *triple*-formed and hears when called *three* times (ter *uocata—diua* triformis (III.22.3-4); *twice* a day the boys will pound the earth *three* times (bis *pueri die—*ter *quatient humum* IV.1.25-8); we shall more than *once* cry out 'Io Triumphe' (Io Tri*umphe non* semel *dicemus, io* Tri*umphe*

III.2.49-50) and he calls it *twice; four-*horse chariots are set in antithesis with *double*-dyed after a *hundred* flocks (te greges centum—*tibi—apta* quadrigis *equa, te* bis—*murice tinctae lanae* II.16.33-6). In view of all these there is surely a play between 'second' and 'third' in (IV.14.37-8)

> Fortuna lustro prospera tertio
> belli secundos reddidit exitus,

And it is no accident that *four-*year-old wine is kept in a *two-*eared jar.

The third relevant fact of Horace's language is his tendency to achieve weird effects by juxtaposing parts of the body. Once again Virgil provides examples of similar technique put to different work, for example when Palinurus clutched with his hands at the heads of the mountain ('prensantemque uncis *manibus capita* aspera montis', *Aeneid,* VI.360). Similarly in the account of the wounds of love sustained by Dido, we read that there was sticking in her, piercing her breast—and expect the subject to be some weapon—it is a face: 'Haerent infixi *pectore uoltus /* uerbaque' (*Aeneid,* IV.4-5).

Horace shows that he realizes that this trick can misfire by beginning his **Ars Poetica** by making fun of painters who depict animals with human heads and horses' necks, and other such Chimaeras dire ('humano *capiti ceruicem* pictor equinam iungere si uelit . . .'). When he writes about Orpheus drawing with his lute the eared oak trees (*auritas ducere quercus,* I.12.11-12), he is flamboyantly courting a similar disaster. This is not pomposity or ineptitude, but a humorous delight in mythology taken to its logical conclusion, and he often evinces this delight. So with the conjunction of foot and thumb in IV.6.35-6 where *pedem* means a metrical foot. So when the crowd in the underworld is packed shoulder to shoulder drinking in with their ears (*densum umeris bibit aure uolgus,* II.13.32). Here the quasi-chiastic structure alerts the mind to the relationship between the parts so symmetrically ordered. To mould this symmetry the strange expression, *densum umeris,* dense with the shoulders, is excogitated to balance *aure uolgus.* Further, in a language as sensitive as Latin to the literal sense of words, to drink with the ear is something of a feat. And why many shoulders, but a single ear? The answer is at one level metrical, at another it is an intellectual provocation.

Horace is enjoying the same kind of nonsense in (II.19.1-4):

> Bacchum in remotis carmina rupibus
> uidi docentem, credite posteri,
>  Nymphasque discentis et auris
>  capripedum Satyrorum acutas.

(I have seen, believe me all you generations to come, / Bacchus teaching among the remote crags / and the Nymphs learning and the ears / of the goatfooted Satyrs cocked to listen.)

Bacchus is teaching, the Nymphs learning, so when we are told that the ears of the Satyrs are sharp, the formal antithesis forces us to realize that the sharpness is not just an anatomical description.[41] So much is unmistakable. But within this conceit about the Satyrs there is embedded a contrast, *auras capripedum,* 'the ears of the goatfooted.' The result of this jugglery is to heighten the weird and wonderful effect of the scene. This harmonizes with the plea, *credite posteri,* 'believe me, future generations,' which, according to Williams,[42] 'strikes a note which is characteristic of the style of rather lighthearted, cynical, Hellenistic poetry'. Juxtaposition of different parts of the body is combined with a numerical play in (II.13.33-5):

> quid mirum, ubi illis carminibus stupens
> demittit atras belua centiceps
>     auris . . .

(Little wonder when the hundred-headed beast / is struck dumb by these songs and its ears / drop . . .)

All two hundred of them we calculate, seeing the characteristic collocation, *centiceps auris.* There is another example of anatomical number play when Cerberus licks the feet and legs of Bacchus with his triple-tongued mouth (II.19.31-2):

> recedentis trilingui
> ore pedes tetigitque crura

After we disentangle the anatomy and the language which expresses it, we may, with Horace, lose sight of common sense and be ready to entertain the possibility that in *quadrimum Sabina merum diota* we are to savour a triple conceit, the Sabine against the Greek, the four against the two, and the numeration of the ears.[43]

If so, we should catch a similar conceit flickering in *sustulerit caduco,* and in many other examples of surrealism and παρὰ προςδοκίαν in this strange poet. In **Ars Poetica,** 47-8 Horace argues that poetic excellence is a matter of making the old word new by placing it in a cunning setting. The very form of this utterance from *notum* to *nouum,* AB AC BA ('notum *si callida uerbum / reddiderit iunctura* nouum') gives a hint that whatever else *callida iunctura* means, it includes this sort of word order. And if this kind of placing makes words new, it sometimes does so by interactions like those posited in this chapter.

### Notes

1. G. Williams, *Tradition and Originality in Roman Poetry,* Oxford, 1968; *The Third Book of Horace's Odes,* Oxford, 1969.

2. R. G. M. Nisbet and M. Hubbard, *A Commentary on Horace Odes, Book I,* Oxford, 1970.

3. E. Norden, *P Vergilius Maro Aeneis Buch VI,* Darmstadt, 1957 on line 321.

4. N. E. Collinge, *The Structure of Horace's Odes,* London, 1961. The quotation is from p. 36. Further examples are given by E. Stemplinger, *RE,* 8 (1912), 2384 s.v. 'Horatius'. See also F. Bücheler, Index Scholarum Hib. Bonnae, 1878-9; *Kleine Schriften,*

Leipzig and Berlin, 1915-30, 2.318-19, 'huiusmodi oxymora cum multis Romanis placuerunt tum maxime Horatio cui fatendum erit grammatici quam poetici ingenii benigniorem fuisse venam.'

5. M. Schuster, *RE,* 2.7 (1948) 2388 s.v. 'Valerius'.

6. E. Fraenkel, *Horace,* Oxford, 1957, 239.

7. These contrasts confirm the comma after *procax* and not before it. She is *procax,* immoral, as opposed to *severae;* not *procax* in the sense of exceeding her proper function by writing dirges. For more general studies of such poems see H. J. Mette, *Museum Helveticum,* 18 (1961), 136-9; and P. L. Smith, *AJP,* 89 (1968), 56-65.

8. R. G. M. Nisbet, *Critical Essays on Roman Literature: Elegy and Lyric,* ed., J. P. Sullivan, London, 1962, 192.

9. Williams, *Tradition,* 114.

10. See *Lucan,* I, ed. R. J. Getty, Cambridge, 1940, lv.

11. *Compescere* is used spatially with *fluentis ramos* (Virgil, *Georgics,* II. 370) and *spatiantia bracchia* (Ovid, *Metamorphoses,* XIV, 630).

12. For other etymological plays see *superbos* pointed by *imo,* I.35, and by *occidit,* IV.4.701 *Glycera* by *immitis,* I.33; *Lyaeo* by *retegis,* III.21 and *solvere, Epode* IX.38; *duram* by *callet,* IV.9.49. For studies of II.14 see N. Rudd, *AJP,* 81 (1960), 376-9 and A. J. Woodman, *Latomus,* 26 (1967), 377-400. For other analyses which bring out contrasts in Horatian odes see H. Womble, *TAPA,* 92 (1961), 537-49 and S. Commager, *The Odes of Horace,* New Haven and London, 1962, 79-85.

13. Collinge, op. cit., 87-8.

14. These three heights are taken from H. Nissen, *Italische Landeskunde,* Berlin, 1902, 2, 908, 907 and 831.

15. See J. Henry, *Aeneidea,* Dublin, 1873-89, on *ingens* in *Aeneid* V.118.

16. *The Third Book of Horace's Odes,* 20 and Williams, *Tradition,* 600.

17. Fraenkel, op. cit., 229.

18. Williams, *Tradition,* 600.

19. On triremes see M. J. McGann, *Studies in Horace's First Book of Epistles,* Brussels, 1969, 22.

20. For other such contrasts see IV.2.23, 4.39-40, 7.21-5.

21. *Paruos* is in irrational tension with *multa.* The minuteness of bees and its implications are examined by Fraenkel, 437, and the other bee references by D. West, *Reading Horace,* Edinburgh, 1967, 30-9.

22. For a developed metaphor from the balance see *Satires,* I.3.70-2. On *sustulerit caduco* see Appendix 1 and the pun on *tolli* at Velleius, 2.62.6.

23. i.3.37, 29.10; ii.3.1, 19.21; iii.4.21, 24.44, 29.10.

24. For the antithesis see 'quodsi cessas aut strenuous anteis', *Epistles,* i.2.70; for the military force of *cessare* see 'cessantis ad arma concitet', *Odes* i.35, and compare Cicero, *De Senectute,* 18.

25. M. O. Lee, *AJP,* 86 (1965), 280.

26. Commager, op. cit., 91.

27. For *amara* in a liquid metaphor cf. ii.16.26. For *eluere* of washing out a dye see Lucretius 6.1077.

28. L. A. Moritz, *GR,* 16 (1969), 174-6, 187-93, and *CQ,* 18 (1968), 119.

29. For *incolumis* of a sum of money see Plautus, *Persa,* 324, and compare Livy, vi.15.5.

30. On life as a loan see Pseudo-Plato, *Axiochus* 367B, and H. A. Khan, *Latomus* 26 (1967), 112-14.

31. For one example of banter see Nisbet and Hubbard on i.29. The quotation is from Williams, *Tradition,* 83.

32. C. J. Reagan, *RSC,* 18 (1970), 182.

33. Aristotle, *Nichomachean Ethics,* 2.7, ed. J. A. K. Thomson.

34. Williams, *Tradition,* ch. 9.

35. R. Hanslik, *Rh. Mus,* 96 (1953), 282-7.

36. See Nisbet and Hubbard, op. cit., xxxvii, and *Oxford Classical Dictionary* (1970)² 1108.

37. M. L. Clarke, *CR,* 21 (1971), 41-3.

38. Nisbet and Hubbard, op. cit., xxii.

39. Reagan, op. cit., 183.

40. M. C. J. Putnam, *CP,* 65 (1970), 252-3.

41. 'et ad audiendum et ad ipsarum aurium figuram' Pseudoacron ad loc.

42. Williams, *Tradition,* 69.

43. Compare K. J. Reckford, *Hermes,* 90 (1962), 476-83.

**Matthew S. Santirocco (essay date 1986)**

SOURCE: Santirocco, Matthew S. "Horace's *Odes* and the Ancient Poetry Book." In *Unity and Design in Horace's "Odes,"* pp. 3-13. Chapel Hill: University of North Carolina, 1986.

[*In the following essay, Santirocco considers the arrangement of the poetry in the* Odes, *Books I through III.*]

ONE

One of the most important achievements of recent Horatian criticism has been the rediscovery of structure—not the mechanical dissection of poems into component parts, but an awareness of how form is inseparable from content and how unity proceeds from design.[1] Although the individual ode has by now received sufficient critical attention, the structure of the first lyric collection, the three books of **Odes** published together in 23 B.C., remains problematic. This is not to say that it has been neglected. The initial observations of von Christ and Kiessling a century ago inspired continental scholars to search for the one principle according to which all the odes were arranged.[2] Suggestions were usually numerological and spatial: applying the criteria of metrical, thematic, and verbal reminiscence, they described triads, pentads, enneads, and decads, with the poems in each group and the groups themselves disposed in an abstract pattern such as concentric framing or chiasmus.[3] By the turn of the century an investigator could justly complain that not a single possibility had been left untried.[4]

Detailed refutation is unnecessary as such grand schemes have ceased to convince most people, if they ever did so. They were possible only because their adherents isolated meter from content and were very selective in their handling of evidence, ignoring more obvious, not to say ostentatious, signs of order. Methodology aside, very elaborate patterns also raise the question of probability. One is reminded of the reviewer who discovered that the sections of Duckworth's book on the *Aeneid* were inadvertently related to each other in the same Golden Ratio that Duckworth detected in the *Aeneid.*[5] Finally, there is a further and more fundamental problem with any approach that sacrifices texture for architecture and that reads poetry only in terms of visual effects and not also in terms of music. As Charles Segal reminds us: "The danger is that such schemes, in their abstractional purity, lead us farther and farther away from the primary experience of the work as poetry. . . . These analytic patterns and numerologies, if developed beyond a certain point, lack any connection with either our fictions or our lives."[6]

It is not surprising that a reaction has set in. Though interest in structural study is running high, most current applications of the approach to Horace are less ambitious,[7] offering only an overview of the problem or focusing on isolated phenomena.[8] One scholar, for instance, speaks of "any stray principle" and another of "a little window dressing."[9] Recently there has been a further retreat from the large-scale schematizations of the past. In their commentary on the **Odes** Nisbet and Hubbard characterize studies of order as "such trivialities,"[10] and Gordon Williams, who omits the entire subject from his *Tradition and Originality,* mentions it elsewhere only to dismiss it: "While some plausible reasons for particular collocations may be guessed at, it is a waste of time to speculate on a matter of which the poet himself probably had no clear idea and which, in any case, has minimal literary relevance."[11]

Although understandable as a reaction to past excesses, this degree of skepticism is itself excessive for several reasons. First, several considerations suggest that Horace had at least some concern for design. These include the well-documented interest in poetry books among Hellenistic and Roman writers (discussed in sections two to four below); the aesthetic implications of the book roll, the physical format of which necessitates sequential reading; the existence of certain undisputed signs of arrangement in *Odes 1-3,* such as the frame of C. 1.1 and 3.30 or the grouping of Parade Odes (C. 1.1-9) and Roman Odes (C. 3.1-6); and, finally, the relatively restricted thematic repertoire that facilitates the discovery of connections among odes by poet and reader alike. It is not a priori unlikely, then, that the *Odes* should reveal signs of larger order.[12] In addition, the extremely skeptical position is based on two unwarranted preconceptions: first, that the whole inquiry is by nature too subjective, and second, that external arrangement has no real bearing on literary appreciation. But controls on subjectivity can be applied to this as to all other literary study (see section five below), and the critical relevance of the subject, if not yet apparent, is nonetheless precisely what remains to be tested. Ultimately, though, the skeptical position is unsatisfactory for the same reason that earlier imaginative schemes failed: both misrepresent the special nature of the collection, its heterogeneity. That this is unique to the *Odes* becomes apparent from consideration of the parallels and precedents available to Horace.

Two

Most discussions of the order of the *Odes* cite as parallels the earlier Augustan poetry books, the works of the young Vergil, Tibullus, and Propertius,[13] and even of the young Horace himself.[14] For all these publications it is possible to demonstrate some sort of elaborate design even though scholars disagree on what the precise design is, or what bearing it has on interpretation.[15] And yet, to consider the *Odes* in light of these earlier poetry books is to set up false and misleading expectations. Although they are certainly precedents, these earlier collections, including Horace's own first book of *Sermones,* are not truly parallel to the *Odes,* for they enjoy what the *Odes* lack, namely a built-in coherence, both formal and thematic, apart from any coherence that conscious artistic arrangement might later impose. The *Bucolics* are all hexameters, so too are the *Sermones,* and elegies are composed in the couplet that gives its name to the genre. Similarly, a general affinity of subject matter unifies each collection: the *Bucolics* are largely pastoral, the *Sermones* satiric (in Horace's sense of the word, not ours), and the elegies erotic.

The first three books of *Odes,* on the other hand, are a very heterogeneous collection. Formally, they comprise eighty-eight poems in twelve different meters, an achievement that Horace repeatedly vaunted. In tone and topic, too, they range equally widely. Thus, whereas a unified plan may lie behind the other Augustan poetry books, the *Odes* are less likely to be structured in so coherent a fashion. For them, true parallels are to be found not in the homogeneous collections of the other Augustans but rather in the heterogeneous collections of earlier writers. The

common misinterpretation that the ordered poetry book originated in the Augustan Age[16] and the fragmentary nature of literary survivals from other periods have obscured the relevance of Hellenistic and Roman republican practice.

Three

The poetry book seems to be a Hellenistic phenomenon. Before that time (and even to some extent afterward) literature arose out of a specific social context, either ritual, agonistic, or sympotic, and was intended for performance within that social setting rather than for individual reading. It was in the fifth century that books began to be circulated, owing perhaps to the popularity of tragedy and the teaching methods of the sophists. However, we are totally ignorant about the principles of arrangement, if any, operative in these books, and, in any case, it was not until the Hellenistic Age that a truly "bookish" society emerged.[17]

The standard reconstruction of the origin and development of the poetry book during and after this period was offered by Kroll over fifty years ago.[18] Since then, however, impressive papyrus discoveries and literary analyses have made a new account necessary. Kroll, for example, maintained that the editions of the older poets which the Hellenistic scholars produced were used by the Hellenistic poets as models for the creation of new poetry books. Though the interaction between literature and scholarship was very great at Alexandria, this genealogy is nonetheless dubious because the Hellenistic editions of the classical authors and the books in which the Hellenistic poets published their own works were structured along very different lines. Basically, they arose out of two very different impulses which, for convenience, may be termed the editorial and the aesthetic.

The former is represented by the standard Alexandrian edition of the lyric poets in which Horace surely read his models.[19] For several of the authors contained therein, very general features of arrangement can be discerned. An epigram (*A.P.*7.17) by Cicero's freedman, Tullius Laurea, alludes to a division of Sappho's works into nine books,[20] and the assignable fragments suggest that the first books were metrically homogeneous, with a shift to arrangement by subject matter in the last book, the Epithalamians.[21] Within the individual books no principle of ordering can be safely adduced despite Lobel's suggestion of alphabetization.[22] In the arrangement of Pindar, Bacchylides, and Simonides, on the other hand, meter played no discernible role as poems were grouped by *eidē* or types into hymns, paeans, epinicians, and the like. Again, there is no evidence as to how poems were arranged within these large categories, except for alleged alphabetization in the British Museum papyrus of Bacchylides's *Dithyrambs*[23] and for the fact that Pindar's epinicians are classed by festival[24] whereas those of Simonides were named after the type of event commemorated.[25]

From this brief and necessarily tentative reconstruction, it is nonetheless clear that the Hellenistic scholar's interest in the arrangement of earlier poets was a corollary of his larger scholarly activity, the classification and editing of texts. An arrangement based on meter, *eidē,* and perhaps alphabetization is editorial rather than aesthetic; that is, it exists for convenience of classification rather than to enhance meaning or create effect.[26] For this reason, the Hellenistic editions of the classical poets are far less significant than the collections the Hellenistic writers made of their own works. Here, for the first time, aesthetic design rather than editorial decision plays the major role in arrangement.

Basic to this type of collection is *variatio* as the Latins call it, or *poikilia* in Greek, the exact opposite of the editors' method of grouping poems by categories.[27] Diversification is now the key as meter, theme, and even dialect vary, with poems disposed to make the most of this variation. And yet, *variatio* has been overemphasized by Kroll and others. Ultimately it is a negative approach to arrangement, the avoidance of certain obvious groupings and collocations. But there are also more positive types of design.

In this, as in many other literary innovations, Callimachus seems to have led the way. His *Iambs,* for example, display most of the techniques available to the Hellenistic poet. There is, first of all, the framing of the collection by a programmatic prologue (1) and epilogue (13). Within this frame there is some grouping on the basis of affinity or contrast. Thus, on metrical grounds, two groups of stichic poems (1-4, 8-13) surround a group of epodes (5-7). On thematic grounds, 7 to 11 are placed together since all offer aetiologies, whereas 11 and 12 are set side by side to juxtapose their forms, an epitaph and a *genethliacon.* There is even greater formalization in the pairing of alternate poems and the creation of a midpoint break in the collection (i.e. *Iamb* 6 balances 12 in that both are personal poems at the end of varied half dozens).[28] The *Aetia* shares the same techniques. After the polemical apology (fr. 1 Pf.),[29] the second fragment and the last (fr. 112 Pf.) frame the work with references to the Muses and their initiation of Hesiod on Mount Helicon (cf. *Theog.* 22 ff.). There is also a break in the middle as the fiction of a conversation with the Muses, which provides the narrative structure of Books 1 and 2, seems to have been dropped in Books 3 and 4.[30] Finally, a new technique is now added to the poet's repertoire, a sort of cross-reference or connecting of works within a larger oeuvre. Thus, when Callimachus in the last fragment of the *Aetia* bids farewell to the Muses and announces that he will pass on to those goddesses' more prosaic pasture, Μουϲέων πεζὸν . . . νομόν (fr. 112.9 Pf.), he seems to be looking ahead to the *Iambs.*[31]

Not all the Hellenistic poets display Callimachus's interest in design. For example, Lawall's suggestion that the first seven *Idylls* of Theocritus and the eight *Mimiamboi* of Herodas were arranged as poetry books[32] not only lacks any testimonial evidence but also seems contradicted by the manuscripts, the dissension among the three Theocritean families regarding the sequence of *Idylls,*[33] and the fragments of a ninth mime contained in the British Museum papyrus of Herodas.[34] One last category of Hel-

lenistic poetry, however, is relevant to arrangement: the epigram. A revival of interest in this old genre led to the creation of new epigrams, either fictitious dedications and epitaphs or else new noninscriptional forms of erotic and sympotic content.[35]

The first book of such epigrams may be the *Soros* mentioned in the scholia to the *Iliad* (Schol. Ven. A to *Il.* 11.101). Because the *Soros* is there said to contain poems by Posidippus, and because Asclepiades, Posidippus, and Hedylus not only occur in a single couplet in Meleager's preface (*AP* 4.1.45-46 = 3970-71 G.-P.) but also share joint attributions in the *Anthology,* Reitzenstein concluded that the *Soros* contained works by all three poets.[36] The Homeric scholiast, however, does not indicate anyone other than Posidippus, and such literary collaboration is otherwise unknown from antiquity. Moreover, if the poem identified by Lloyd-Jones as the *sphragis* of Posidippus was originally attached to the *Soros,* it is too personal a signature for a joint collection.[37] Reitzenstein's hypothesis, then, remains unsubstantiated and the *Soros* may well have contained just poems by Posidippus. In any case, the title, which means a heap of grain, is very suggestive. First, it may suggest winnowing, i.e. the removal of chaff, and thus affirm Alexandrian standards of polish and labor.[38] And second, a heap or pile implies perhaps some degree of diversity or *poikilia.*[39] Thus, it is at least likely that this publication of epigrams shared with the other Hellenistic poetry books a commitment to Alexandrian aesthetic refinement in all areas, including its arrangement.

More relevant to Horace on account of its variety, size, and date is the *Garland* of Meleager. Although no longer extant, its principles of arrangement can be reconstructed from uncontaminated Meleagrian stretches in the *Anthology.* Alan Cameron has suggested that the *Garland* was divided into four books on the basis of subject matter.[40] This is an editorial mode of arrangement resulting from the special nature of the *Garland* as an anthology of many works on many subjects by many hands. But the framing by prologue (*AP* 4.1 = 3926 ff. G.-P.) and epilogue (*AP* 12.257 = 4722 G.-P.) and the variation worked out in topic, expression, and even author sequence (the rhythmical alternation of poems by the four major *Hauptdichter*)[41] are aesthetic devices. Meleager signals this when, in his opening poem, he calls his work a πάγϗαπον ἀοιδάν, "a many-blossomed song" (*AP* 4.1.1 = 3926 G.-P.). Gow and Page object that "ἀοιδάν is a little odd of a book the miscellaneous contents of which are emphasized by the adjective."[42] But the singular noun indicates that the *Garland* was conceived not as a mere anthology editorially arranged, but rather as an aesthetic whole, a poetry book.

FOUR

From republican Rome, as from Alexandria, much relevant literature is again either mutilated or missing. In the absence of much of Lucilius[43] and almost all of Laevius, Horace's unacknowledged predecessor in lyric, it is the Catullan corpus that most closely resembles Horace's *Odes* in being a miscellany of meters and subjects.[44] Although the verbal and thematic influence of Catullus on Horace has been amply documented,[45] no one has seriously explored the possibility that the two collections might be structured along similar lines, much as Horace in his first book of *Sermones* and Tibullus in his first book of elegies might have looked to Vergil's *Bucolics* as a model of arrangement.[46] The investigation, however, is complicated by the difficulty of determining the principles of arrangement employed by Catullus himself. Some sort of authorial organization is indicated by the mention of a *libellus* in the first poem and by references in Pliny (*Epist.* 1.16.5)[47] and Martial (4.14.4, 11.6.16) to a body of poems, the latter suggesting the title *Passer*. But despite the magisterial authority of Wilamowitz—"Catullus devoted the most careful thought to the arrangement of his book of poems. If there's anyone who can't see that, so much the worse for him"[48]—there is no real agreement concerning the extent of the original *libellus* and its relation to the present corpus.

Thus, the most obvious principle of arrangement, the tripartite division into *polymetra* (1-60), long *neoterica* (61-68, with 65 marking a permanent shift to the elegiac meter), and short, non-neoteric epigrams (69-116),[49] can afford a parallel to Horace's distribution of his *Odes* over three books only if several recent scholars are correct in maintaining that the entire Catullan corpus as it stands was arranged by the poet.[50] But this thesis is rendered problematic by the sad state of the text and by the fact that the total number of lines, over 2,300, far exceeds the known capacity of ancient books[51] and also violates Callimachean strictures against length. Thus, it is easier to follow Clausen in locating the original *libellus* among the *polymetra*,[52] and it is here, and not in the overall disposition of the corpus, that parallels to the order of the *Odes* can be found.

First of all, the *variatio* familiar from Hellenistic poetry books is here carried to such an extreme that interlocking and interrupting poems complicate whatever cycles or patterns have been discerned.[53] Hellenistic framing is perhaps also operative in that the *polymetra* nearly open (2-3) and nearly close (58) with poems on Lesbia, initially positive but at the end bitterly invective. Then there are certain recurrent techniques of grouping such as the separation of two related poems by a third to form an A-B-A pattern,[54] or the use of transitions either on the surface or at some deeper level,[55] to move the reader from one poem to the next. Although examples of all these techniques can be found in Horace's *Odes,* the most striking parallelism, perhaps, is the way in which both collections open. Building on Barwick's study of the first Lesbia poems, Charles Segal has shown that Catullus 2-11 are a cycle, tracing the progression of the love affair from its beginning (2-3), through its fruition (5, 7) to its bitter end (8, 11), and integrating it with other central themes.[56] If these poems stood at the head of the original corpus, they may have

influenced Horace to open his book too with a cycle, the Parade Odes, which, as we shall see, introduce most of the meters and many of the themes and personalities prominent in his poetry.

FIVE

To sum up thus far: the origin and development of the pre-Augustan poetry book can only be reconstructed. Not only are we missing potentially relevant works such as the lyrics of Callimachus and Laevius, but also of those works that do survive, some, like the *Iambs* of Callimachus, are fragmentary, and others, such as the poems of Theocritus, Herodas, and to a lesser degree Catullus, do not reveal with any certainty the extent to which they were arranged by their authors. Nonetheless, a survey of the extant literature indicates that certain common assumptions about the poetry book are inaccurate. It did not, for example, arise in Augustan Rome but in Alexandria. Similarly, to locate its source in the scholarly edition ignores the very great distinction between an editorial response to a classic text and the more aesthetic designs a poet can work out in the publication of his own verse. Of these, *variatio,* though important, has been overemphasized. There were other, more positive, principles of arrangement, and, though the pre-Augustan poetry book was not coherently structured around any one of them, all were operative.

It has been necessary to dwell at some length on this background, for it has important critical implications for the study of Horace's *Odes.* First, the extensive prior history of the poetry book renders it very likely that Horace too had some concern for the larger unity and design of his lyric collection. Second, this concern appears to be yet another of his unacknowledged debts to Alexandria,[57] for a true parallel to *Odes* 1-3 is to be found not in the other Augustan poetry books which are relatively homogeneous, but in the Hellenistic collections which were formally and thematically varied. Finally, appreciation of this special characteristic of the *Odes* enables us to avoid the excesses of much previous scholarship, which has either ignored their heterogeneity by searching for a single principle of arrangement or made too much of their heterogeneity by denying any extensive ordering. As befits Horace, the champion of *aurea mediocritas,* the truth lies somewhere in between.

What we expect, and what we shall actually find, is that Horace shares the Hellenistic poet's familiarity with many methods of arrangement and that he relies on no one of them exclusively. Thus, the reader must be constantly alert to a wide variety of possibilities—to relationships based on contrast as well as similarity, to dynamic movements as well as static patterns, to groupings of contiguous poems and linkages among poems widely separated in the collection. Most importantly, the reader must be attuned to the various and ever-shifting criteria on which these larger designs are founded—not just meter, theme, and addressee, but internal structure, imagery, and that vague but crucial quality, tone.

Although it must be admitted that such an investigation might seem rather subjective, there are controls that can be applied to this as to all other literary study. Obviously, when a number of criteria converge—as, for example, in the Roman Odes—we can be sure of the poet's intent. We must not insist on such certainties, however, for many of the most interesting and suggestive relationships among poems exist at only one of these many levels. But that does not mean that they are fortuitous. Faced with the formidable task of arranging so many and varied poems, Horace would have had to exploit connections, random or planned, at whatever level they appeared.[58] Fortunately, a second control is provided by sequential reading. As a methodology, the consideration of the poems in their published order not only reproduces their effect on the ancient audience, for whom the physical format of the papyrus roll necessitated such a sequential reading, but it also respects the intention of their author, who is reasonably assumed (in the absence of evidence to the contrary) to have put them in this order in the first place. Finally, and most importantly, we can control subjectivity by pursuing arrangement not as an end in itself but as part of the larger interpretative enterprise. In other words, a perception of design, in order to be plausible and meaningful, must accord with an interpretation of the individual odes that is self-consistent. Recent studies of other lyric traditions—of the modern poetic sequence by M. L. Rosenthal and Sally Gall, or of Keats's odes by Helen Vendler—suggest the fruitfulness of such an approach, which places the individual poem within the larger context provided by the other poems.[59] Something similar is needed for Horace's *Odes*—not another study of arrangement but a new critical reading of the poetry which recognizes that the ensemble is itself one important context for understanding and appreciation.

*Notes*

1. This chapter derives from my article in *Arethusa* 13 (1980). I have taken this opportunity not only to update it but also to discuss methodology more fully and to revise (esp. in the notes) some of my earlier views.

2. Von Christ, "Uber die Verskunsi," pp. 1-44; Kiessling, "Horatius I," pp. 48-75.

3. A roughly chronological survey of such theories with some refutation was provided by Raiz, "Die Frage nach der Anordnung," pp. 43-56; see also Simon, *Zur Anordnung der Oden;* Häusser, Review of Raiz and Simon, pp. 362-66. When meter was abandoned as the sole criterion for order in favor of verbal or thematic links, the results were equally fanciful; see Simon, ibid.; Verrall, *Studies Literary and Historical,* pp. 90-120 and passim; Belling, *Studien über die Liederbücher des Horaz.* Many of these studies, however, at least had the advantage of noting verbal echoes, for which see now Huber, *Wortwiederholungen in den Oden des Horaz.*

4. See Draheim, "Die Anordnung der Gedichte," col. 1268.

5. Duckworth, *Structural Patterns and Proportions;* Dalzell, Review of Duckworth, pp. 314-316. For general remarks on numerology see Wilkinson, *Georgics of Virgil,* pp. 316-22.

6. Segal, "Ancient Texts," p. 13. The entire article is interesting, and on the larger questions it raises see also Wilkinson, "Ancient Literature," pp. 13-26.

7. A remarkable exception is Dettmer, *Horace: A Study in Structure.* In a complicated exposition illustrated over 150 charts and diagrams, Dettmer attempts to show all 88 odes are arranged by theme in a ring composition which is occasionally interrupted at parallel intervals by smaller groups that may not be themselves symmetrically arranged. Utilizing a complex terminology that distinguishes between "outer-ring" and "inner-ring" poems, and between "structural" and "non-structural" ones, Dettmer searches for verbal, numerological, and metrical "clues" that the poet furnished to point up his complicated "thematic concatenation." Such ring composition, finally, is alleged to be the "predominant organizational pattern" not just of *Odes*1-3 but of all the Augustan poetry books as well as of the Catullan corpus. A strange throwback, this approach suffers in general from the same deficiencies as the earlier scholarship discussed above, namely problems of methodology, probability, and conception. For a more specific critique of this, see p. 210, n. 2, below; see also the review of Dettmer by Syndikus, pp.11-15. Because our ways of reading are so fundamentally opposed, I have for the most part chosen to engage in a dialogue with Horace rather than with Dettmer, whose argument the reader may evaluate independently. I have, however, cited Dettmer on points of agreement or information.

8. Apart from Dettmer, *Horace: A Study in Structure,* the only other comprehensive and systematic study of the collection was published sixty years ago by Port who, more judiciously, espoused no monolithic theory ("Die Anordnung," pp. 280-308, 427-68). For a briefer account of the Augustan poetry book that omits Horace and stresses ring composition, see Michelfeit, "Das augusteische Gedichtbuch," pp. .347-70. Other, briefer overviews include Stemplinger, "Horatius," col. 2372; Schanz and Hosius, *Geschichte der römischen Literatur* 2:126-27; Wickham, Works of Horace 1:25-30; Perret, Horace, pp. 80-84; M. Schmidt, "Die Anordnung der Oden," pp. 207-16; Giardina, "Sulla struttura delle odi," pp. 44-55; Silk, "On Theme and Design," pp. 47-54; Collinge, *Structure of Horace's Odes,* pp. 36-55 (with the review by Ludwig, pp. 171-77). I regret that it has not been possible for me to obtain the thesis of Fontaine, *Enchaînement et groupement,* which is mentioned by Collinge, ibid., p. 36 n. 2. More common than overviews, finally, are useful observations on specific groupings and collocations, especially in the introductions to individual poems by Kiessling and Heinze, *Oden und Epoden;* in random remarks

in Wili's *Horaz und die augusteische Kultur;* and in the periodical literature. All of these will be cited where appropriate in the notes below.

9. Wilkinson, *Horace and His Lyric Poetry,* p. 15; Dawson, "The Iambi of Callimachus," p. 140.

10. Nisbet and Hubbard, *Horace: Odes, Book I,* p. xxiii; see also ibid., p. xxiv: "It is only too easy to imagine some subtle principle either of similarity or difference in every juxtaposition, not to mention more complicated sequences and cycles. Most of these suggestions seem completely fanciful, and equally ingenious reasons could be adduced to justify any arrangement." The same authors' later commentary on Book 2 is somewhat more moderate: "The book contains 20 odes . . . and as usual is arranged with a measure of design. . . . The organization is most apparent in the first half, particularly in the formal aspect of metre; otherwise Horace may have noticed some superficial resemblances, which may or may not now be divined, but even then he was likely to have been left with a few poems that did not fit any scheme precisely. After all he was not composing a cycle of odes, but in ancient terminology 'arranging a garland'" (Horace: *Odes,* Book II, pp. 5-6).

11. G. Williams, *Third Book of Horace's Odes,* p. 23; see also his Horace, p. 35: "The arrangement of the odes has attracted increasing attention—to little purpose." For the inadequacies of the treatment of arrangement generally in Williams's *Tradition and Originality,* see the review by Otis, pp. 316-30.

12. It should perhaps be noted at this point that there is no good reason to doubt that the order of the *Odes* as we have it is the poet's own. Whereas the position of the lyrics with relation to Horace's other works varies in the manuscripts, there is unanimity regarding the placement of individual lyrics, with only occasional dissension about poem divisions. Testimonia concur in this numeration. Finally, Horace may himself allude to a presentation copy of this work in *Epistle* 1.13, where the description of the contents as *carmina* (17) and the references to plural volumes (*volumina,* 2; *libellis,* 4; *chartae,* 6) would suit *Odes* 1-3 very well.

13. A convenient survey of theories on the *Bucolics* may be found in Rudd, *Lines of Enquiry,* pp. 119-44; to this should now be added Van Sickle, *Design of Virgil's Bucolics;* Dettmer, *Horace: A Study in Structure,* pp. 2-14. For Tibullus, see the listing in Harrauer, *Bibliography to Tibullus,* pp. 45-46; to this should be added Powell, "The Ordering of Tibullus Book I," pp. 107-112; Leach; "Poetics and Poetic Design," pp. 79-96; Dettmer, ibid., pp. 14-22; Mutschler, *Die poetische Kunst Tibulls,* pp. 157-200, 279-302. For Propertius, studies of arrangement are complicated by the textual transmission—see Ullman, "The Book Division of Propertius," pp. 45-52; and, more recently, the novel suggestion of Butrica, "The Prop-

ertian Corpus," p. 6. The extensive literature is listed in Harrauer, *Bibliography to Propertius,* pp. 101-2; to this should be added Barsby, "Composition and Publication," pp. 128-37; King, "Propertius' Programmatic Poetry," pp. 108-24; Putnam, "Propertius' Third Book," pp. 97-113; Dettmer, ibid., pp. 22-32; Hutchinson, "Propertius and the Unity of the Book," pp. 99-106; Stahl, *Propertius,* passim.

14. On the *Iambi* see Carrubba, *Epodes of Horace.* On the *Sermones* see Ludwig, "Komposition der beiden Satirenbücher," pp. 304-25; Jensen, "Secret Art," pp. 208-15; Rambaux, "Composition d'ensemble du livre I," pp. 179-204; Dettmer, *Horace: A Study of Structure,* pp. 32-35; and the series of lengthy articles by van Rooy under the general title "Arrangement and Structure of *Satires,"* listed in the bibliography.

15. Although we are concerned with the precedents available to Horace, it should be noted that interest in arrangement persists in later books: see, for example, Ludwig, "Anordnung des vierten Horazischen Odenbuches," pp. 1-10; Putnam, *Artifices of Eternity;* McGann, *Studies in Horace's First Book of Epistles,* pp. 33-87; Buchheit, *Studien zur Corpus Priapeorum,* pp. 43-53; Buchheit, *Studien zur Corpus Priapeorum,* pp. 43-53; Loercher, *Aufbau der drei Bücher von Ovids Amores;* Evans, *Publica Carmina,* passim; Jacobson, *Ovid's Heroides,* passim; Newmyer, *Silvae of Statius,* pp. 45-58, 122-30. Not unrelated to the poetry book is the disposition of episodes in the *Kollektivgedicht:* see, for example, Ludwig, *Struktur und Einheit der Metamorphosen Ovids;* Otis, *Ovid as an Epic Poet,* pp. 45-90; Galinsky, *Ovid's Metamorphoses,* pp. 79-109.

16. E.g. Otis, Review of G. Williams's *Tradition and Originality,* p. 326: "So far as we can tell, this sort of collection or poetical context was Roman and not Greek. There is, for example, no indication that Hellenistic poetry books were constructed in this way"; Otis, "Propertius' Single Book," P. 38 n. 8; Ross, *Backgrounds to Augustan Poetry,* p. 49, who seems to suggest that Gallus came up with the idea.

17. For a general account of the transition in Greek culture from the oral to the written word, see Havelock, *Literate Revolution in Greece;* Pfeiffer, *History of Classical Scholarship,* pp. 16 ff.; Davison, *From Archilochus to Pindar,* pp. 86-128. It should be noted that, even after the rise of the book, reading was largely done aloud: see Balogh, "Voces Paginarum," pp. 84-109, 202-40, with supplements by Hendrickson, "Ancient Reading," pp. 182-96, and correctives by Knox, "Silent Reading," pp. 421-35.

18. Kroll, *Studien zum Verständnis,* pp. 225-46.

19. For a description of this edition see Wilamowitz-Moellendorff, *Textgeschichte der griechischen Lyriker.* That Horace used it is likely because his placement of *C.* 1.2, which ends with Mercury as political savior, seems to recall the Alcaeus edition in which

the second position was also occupied by Hermes: see below, pp. 21-22, with p. 187, n. 27. It should be noted, however, that not every poet's text might have achieved such fixity in antiquity. For instance, the common assumption that the Ambrosian list of Pindar's seventeen books reproduces the order of a standard Alexandrian edition is called into question by the existence of other dissenting lists: see Race, "*POxy* 2438 and the Order of Pindar's Works," p. 106.

20. On the remote possibility that the division of Sappho's work is older than the Alexandrian edition because the sticho-metrical subscript of POxy 1231 is in Attic notation rather than the Milesian in use in Egypt at the time, see Lobel, Σαπφοῦς Μέλη, pp. xii-xvii.

21. See Page, *Sappho and Alcaeus,* p. 126, for the principles behind the disposition of the Epithalamians.

22. See Lobel, Σαπφοῦς Μέλη, pp. xv-xvi; see also Daly, *Contributions to a History of Alphabetization,* p. 23 n. 3.

23. See Daly, ibid., p. 23, with literature there cited.

24. This does not mean that other factors could not also have been operative. *Olympian* 1, for example, may owe its prominent placement to its popularity in antiquity (Lucian, *Gallus* 7), the centrality of its myth to the Olympic Games, and the importance of its occasion. But an editor's occasional appreciation of such niceties is not the same as a poet's truly aesthetic design.

25. There is no evidence to suggest that the distinction between choral lyric and monody (Plato, *Laws* 6.764d-e) or between monostrophic and triadic systems (*Schol. Epimetr. Pind.* III, p. 310.27 Dr.) played any part in arrangement: see Harvey, "Classification of Greek Lyric Poetry," pp. 157-75.

26. This conclusion seems valid not only for the lyric poets whom we have been considering, but also for the other early writers from whose works one occasionally receives the impression of organization. For instance, the elegiacs attributed to Theognis are clearly by several hands, and their collection and arrangement was the work of a later editor: see M. L. West, *Studies in Greek Elegy and Iambos,* pp. 40-64. For Mimnermus's *Nanno* also there is no evidence of aesthetic design because the fragments are very varied in content, and the idea that the poet's love for the girl provided a thematic unity may well be a Hellenistic invention on analogy with Antimachus's *Lyde:* see West, ibid., pp. 74-76. Finally, though the Attic *scolia* (Ath. 15.693-5) may have constituted a book from which uninventive guests could select a poem to recite at the symposium (see Wilamowitz-Moellendorff*Aristoteles und Athen,* 2:316-22), the variety of social and political constituencies repre-

sented by the poems preludes any real aesthetic unity, and such grouping as has been observed seems editorial: see Bowra, *Greek Lyric Poetry,* pp. 375-76; Cuartero, "Estudios sobre el escolio ático," pp. 5-38.

27. For a general discussion of *poikilia/variatio* as a larger feature of all aspects of composition, see Deubner, "Ein Stilprinzip hellenistischer Dichtkunst," pp. 361-78; Schulze, "Über das Princip der Variatio," pp. 857-78. It should perhaps be noted here that structural studies often use familiar technical terms in new or more specific meanings. Thus, *voratio* is used to refer to the diversification of poems that are placed together and not just to the practice of "theme and variation." Similarly, "ring composition," which usually refers to the archaic Greek style whereby the beginning and the end of a poem are temporally linked, can also refer to the disposition of poems in concentric frames.

28. See Dawson, "The Iambi of Callimachus," pp. 1-168; Clayman, *Callimachus' Iambi.*

29. It is commonly assumed with little real authority that this prologue headed a second, collected edition of Callimuchus's *Aetia* and other works: see Pfeiffer, "Ein neues Altersgedicht," pp. 339-41, and his *Callimachus,* 2: xxxvi-vii. For an alternative view, however, see Eichgrün, *Kallimachos und Apollonios Rhodios,* pp. 64 ff., where the idea of consequential publication is rejected. The entire question is reexamined and Pfeiffer's theory is rejected by Alan Cameron in a forthcoming monograph, *Callimachus and His Critics.*

30. According to the new reconstruction of the *Aetia* by Parsons, "Callimachus: Victoria Berenices," pp. 1-50, the last two books were also framed, by poems in honor of Berenice.

31. This does not mean that there was a collected edition in which the *Iambi* followed the *Aetia* as they do in *POxy* 1011 and in the Milan Diegesis: see above n. 29. On the meaning of πεζὸν . . . νομόν, see Van Sickle, *Design of Virgil's Bucolics,* pp. 104-5.

32. Lawall, *Theocritus' Coan Pastorals.* While Lawall's arguments do not prove the existence of poetry books by Theocritus or Herodas, the interconnections he observes among poems are very illuminating and have great interpretive value in other respects.

33. For an account of the MSS see Gow, *Theorcitus,* 1: xxx ff. A detailed critique of the presuppositions underlying Lawall's interpretation is provided in the review by Giangrande, pp. 170-73. For an alternative sense in which the poems constitute a *libellus,* see Segal, "Thematic Coherence and Levels of Style,"

34. See Cunningham, *Herodas: Mimiamboi,* p. 160; on the possibility of pairing see Cunningham, "Herodas 6 and 7," pp. 32-35.

35. On the history of the epigram see Fraser, *Ptolemaic Alexandria,* 1: 553-617 and 2:791-869, with literature abundantly cited. For a list of papyrus anthologies of

epigrams from the Hellenistic period see Pack, *Greek and Latin Literary Texts,* p. 92. To this should now be added *PKöln* 204 which contains the remains of six epigrams by Mnasalkes which are arranged into pairs by theme. Dating to the middle of the second century B.C., this is the earliest extant collected edition of an epigrammatist. For more detailed discussion of this and other collections, see Cameron, *The Greek Anthology.*

36. Reitzenstein, *Epigramm und Skolion,* pp. 94 ff.

37. Lloyed-Jones, "The Seal of Posidippus," pp. 75-99.

38. See Webster, *Hellenistic Poetry and Art,* p. 45, who argues for this meaning by citing as a parallel the use of the word Theocritus 7.155, a literary harvest, see also Gow, *Theocritus,* 2:169. It should at least be noted, however, that, while the notion of winnowing can be supplied from the Theocritean context, the word ϛωρός usually conveys only the undifferentiated quality of a heap.

39. A third-century B.C. papyrus appears to be the beginning of a collection of Posidippus (the *Soros?*): see Lasserre, "Aux origines de l'Anthologie, I," pp. 222-47. The MS bears the title *Symmeikta Epigrammata,* which may carry literary critical implications parallel to those detected in the title *Soros;* see Webster, *Hellenistic Poetry and Art,* p. 46.: "*Symmeikta* seems from its uses elsewhere to mean 'mixed' rather than 'blended'; it emphasizes the variety of the contents rather than the choice of each epigram to suit its neighbor."

40. Cameron, "Garlands of Meleager and Philip," pp. 323-49.

41. These principles were discovered by Radinger, *Meleagros von Gadara,* pp. 88-107, and Weisshäupl, "Zur den Quellen der Anthologia," pp. 184-88.

42. Gow and Page, *The Greek Anthology,* 2:597.

43. On metrical *voratio* in Lucilius see Puelma-Piwonka, *Lucilius and Kallimachos,* pp. 364-67.

44. The publication of prose letters would seem initially to offer another parallel. Pliny, for example, tells us (*Epis.* 1.1) that his letters are not chronologically arranged but occur as they came into his hands, which suggests conscious *voratio* and which calls to mind his insistence on variety in his lyric poetry (*Epis.* 4.14.3, 8.21.4). Futhermore, though elaborate schemes are not convincing, there is evidence that "[in] each book Pliny sought to include a representative collection of the major themes, but he did not bind himself to an arithmetical proportion" (Sherwin-White, *Letters of Pliny,* p. 50; and see the full discussion of distribution on pp. 20-56). But Pliny is much later than Horace. The earlier letters of Cicero are not relevant either, for they seem to have been published posthumously and their organization displays no real aesthetic design: see Shackleton Bailey, *Cicero's Letters to Atticus,* 1:59-76, and his *Cicero: Epistulae ad Familiares,* 1:2-24.

45. See, for example, Ferguson, "Catullus and Horace," pp. 1-19; van der Paardt, "Catullus en Horatius," pp. 287-96; Lee, "Catullus in the *Odes* of Horace," pp. 33-48.

46. It is interesting that Vergil's *Bucolics,* Horace's *Sermones* 1, and Tibullus 1 all contain ten poems, and that Horace's *Iambi* divide after the first ten poems, which are all in the same meter. In this concern for the number ten, as in other respects, Vergil may have influenced his fellow poets: see van Rooy, "'Imitatio' of Vergil," pp. 69-88; Leach, "Vergil, Horace, Tibullus: Three Collections of Ten," pp. 79-105.

47. Pliny compares a dead friend, Pompeius, to Catullus who is said to have placed harsh poems among light ones (*inseit sane . . . mollibus levibusque duriusculos quosdam*). Whether or not this accurately describes Catullus's methods and although it does not indicated which poems are involved, it does imply some sort of organized collection.

48. Wilamowitz-Moellendorff, *Sappho and Simonides,* p. 292, translated by Quinn, *Catullus: An Interpretation,* p. 11.

49. On the distinction between neoteric and non-neoteric see Ross, *Style and Tradition in Catullus.*

50. See, for example, E. A. Schmidt, "Catullus Anordnung," pp. 215-42; Wiseman, *Catullus: An Interpretation;* Skinner, *Catullus' Passer;* Most, "On the Arrangement of Catullus' Carmina Maiora," pp. 109-25. Those who support the view that the entire corpus was arranged by the poet may find support in Macleod, "Catullus 116," pp. 304-9, reprinted in his *Collected Essays,* pp. 181-86, where the last poem is treated as suitable Callimachean epilogue; see also Van Sickle, "Poetics of Opening and Closure," pp. 65-75.

51. Of course, the papyrus roll and the literary book are not to be equated: the physical capacity of the former could exceed the length arbitrarily fixed for the latter. For full discussion see Van Sickle, "The Book Roll," pp. 5-42, with literature there cited.

52. See Clausen, "Catulli Veronensis Liber," pp. 37-43.

53. Ellis, *Commentary on Catullus,* pp. xlviii-ix, uses this very fact to cast doubt on the discovery of conscious design in Catullus. On the other hand, Quinn, *Catullus: An Interpretation,* p. 16, draws a very different conclusion: "Indeed, I think it likely that the illusion of a work unfinished, of a collection made up in large part of fragments of poems which are too short, too abrupt in the way they begin or end to be felt as complete poems, but which plainly belong together—snatches of conversation, as it were, in an easily imagined context—was one of the principles adopted by Catullus in putting his collection together. Rather as a modern painter or sculptor leaves his painting or bust at a stage where it is, by normal standards, unfinished (the likeness just emerg-

ing from the marble, say) because it is finished for him; or because to finish it off means robbing it of life."

54. E.g. 5/7 (*basia*), 21/23 and 24/26 (Furius and Aurelius), 37/39 (Egnatius). Such separated pairs also occur outside the *polymetra* (e.g. the famous Lesbia poems, 70/72) where they may be taken as traces of the poet's own conscious design, now lost, or as the work of a perceptive editor.

55. An example of a surface glide occurs early in the *polymetra:* poem 9, on Veranius's return from Spain as a member of Piso's cohort, leads into 10 which alludes to Catullus's own experiences in the Bithynian cohort of Memmius, and thus introduces 11 which opens with a travelogue (see Kinsey, Catullus 11, pp. 537-44; Ferrero, *Interpretazione di Catullo,* p. 221). An example of a less superficial sequence occurs at the end of the *polymetra:* poem 50, an account of the *otiosi* Catullus and Calvus, is followed by 51, the last strophe of which condemns *otium,* and thus prepares for 52-54, a return to the *negotium* of politics (See Wiseman, *Catullan Questions,* p. 15). As was the case with A-B-A patterns, sequences of contiguous poems also occur after the *polymetra* (e.g. 88-91, on Gellius, the longest run of contiguous poems on a single individual) and may be viewed either as the work of an editor or (in some cases at least) as traces of a now lost original design by the poet. For useful lists of such clusters throughout the corpus see Ellis, *Commentary on Catullus,* pp. xlv-l; Kroll, *C. Valerius Catullus,* p. x.

56. Barwick, "Zyklen bei Martial," pp. 284-318; Segal, "Order of Catullus, Poems 2-11," pp. 305-21.

57. The Alexandrian influence was first explored in great detail by Pasquali, *Orazio lirico,* pp. 141-641.

58. The question naturally arises at this point of whether the *Odes* were written to occupy their positions in the collection or whether placement was a subsequent activity. For certain collections like Vergil's *Bucolics* and the other homogeneous books of ten, it is possible that some elements of overall design preexisted the composition of individual poems. The *Odes,* however, are so numerous and varied that it is probably safer to assume that, in most cases, arrangement came later. Thus, the poems of even the most cohesive cycle, the Roman Odes, give evidence of having been composed at different times. That disposition followed composition, however, does not mean that it was an afterthought, an unrelated or less important creative activity (as we shall see). Also, we need not exclude the possibility that at least a few poems might have been reworked to suit their context in the collection, and that a few might even have been written with an eye on their placement. This hypothesis certainly suits *C.* 1.1 and 3.30 and perhaps also pairs like *C.* 1.31 and 32, which read as if they were a single poem (see the discussion on pp.

69-72). Such pairs certainly exist in Ovid (e.g. *Amores* 1.11-12) and Propertius (e.g. 3.4-5). On the whole question see now Hutchinson, "Propertius and the Unity of the Book," pp. 99-106.

59. Rosenthal and Gall, *Modern Poetic Sequence;* Vendler, *Odes of John Keats.*

**Joseph Pucci (essay date fall 1991)**

SOURCE: Pucci, Joseph. "The Dilemma of Writing: Augustine, *Confessions* 4.6 and Horace, *Odes* 1.3.¹" In *Arethusa* 24, no. 2 (fall 1991): 257-79.

[*In the following essay, Pucci considers Augustine's allusion to Horace's* Odes *1.3 in his* Confessions *4.6, beginning with a reading of* Odes *1.3, a comparison with Augustine, and an examination of how the texts illustrate the dilemma of writing.*]

> Mirabar enim ceteros mortales vivere, quia ille, quem quasi non moriturum dilexeram, mortuus erat, et me magis quia ille alter eram, vivere illo mortuo mirabar. Bene quidam dixit de amico suo: dimidium animae meae.²
>
> (*Conf.* 4.6.27-28)

For I wondered that other mortals were living, because he whom I had loved as if he would not ever die had indeed died, and I wondered more that I was living rather than he, because I was his other self. Well Horace put it of Virgil: "the other half of my soul."

> Sic te diva potens Cypri,
> sic fratres Helenae, lucida sidera,
>   ventorumque regat pater
> obstrictis aliis praeter Iapyga,
>   navis, quae tibi creditum
> debes Vergilium; finibus Atticis
>   reddas incolumem, precor,
> et serves animae dimidium meae.
>
> (*Odes* 1.3.1-8)

Let the powerful goddess of Cyprus, let the brothers of Helen (bright stars), let the father of winds (by which all things are bound before Iapyx) rule you, ship, who owe Virgil entrusted to you; to Attic shores may you bring him unharmed, I pray, and preserve the half of my soul.³

Augustine's attitudes toward classical literature have normally been cast by scholars in the archetypal terms drawn from *Confessions* 1.13, where Augustine describes his reading of Virgil's *Aeneid.* In this justly famous recollection, Augustine offers that his excursions in the *Aeneid* were nothing more than an enchanting dream, futile, empty, worthy of avoidance, and much—perhaps too much—has been made of this episode and of its wider implications for Augustine as a reader of classical poetry. One overlooked aspect of this recollection, for instance, with fundamental implications about Augustine's attitudes toward classical poetry, is the fact that in the telling of his story, with all its attendant antipathy and doubt about Virgil and classical poetry, Augustine inserts a Virgilian half-line (*atque ipsius umbra Creusae, Aen.* 2.772), seemingly contaminating his own work with a pagan tag, but also linking his own spiritual state to the figure of Creusa who, like Augustine, is lost, dead to the world, a phantom.

There are other moments in the *Confessions* where Augustine will allow a classical text to intrude into his own story in this way. These episodes normally are flagged by Augustine, as here by the use of meter, in order to make the reader notice them. Invariably they deepen and enrich the context of his own spiritual history when they are made to function coherently in his own narrative. Unfortunately, such moments have yet to be examined in even a cursory way in Augustinian studies.[4] Indeed, the literary element of Augustine's creative work in general awaits substantive treatment.[5] While one paper cannot fill the lacuna represented by such an omission in Augustinian scholarship, a more modest goal can be advanced: to make good on this error of omission in one instance by examining an episode similar to the allusion to Creusa.

Such an episode, an allusion at *Confessions* 4.6 to Horace *Odes* 1.3, is the topic of the present essay. It will be analyzed in two parts. In section one, a reading of *Odes* 1.3 is ventured. Then, section two considers the ways such a reading is corroborated by *Confessions* 4.6 before going on to determine the ways in which the two texts form a composite meaning, a meditation on the dilemma posed by the act of writing and the morality of mimesis.

### 1. HORACE READS VIRGIL: *ODES* 1.3

*Odes* 1.3, the so-called *propempticon* for Virgil, has long embarrassed commentators, who have not known very well what to do with it.[6] Some have suggested that it is two poems.[7] Others have held that its *tono scherzoso* makes it a humorous extravaganza.[8] It has often been viewed as a genuine *propempticon,* but this aspect of the ode has also been rightly questioned on several grounds. Scholarly contention aside, however, there can be little doubt that the poem is about crafting, writing, and the morality of textual mimesis, and if most commentators have not stated the central issue of this ode in language quite this frank, then they nevertheless have sensed this truth regardless of how they chose ultimately to present it. The presence of Virgil in a Horatian ode makes this general statement of meaning more or less indubitable.

Indeed, the presence of Virgil in 1.3 would seem to be the fundamental interpretive datum of the poem. The problem in the literature has been to determine the tone of the ode relative to its famous addressee and in going about this task, commentators have roamed far and wide, as we shall see presently, in attempting to make Horace and Virgil the best and greatest of friends. The diversity of scholarly opinion[9] over this ode has also been a result of the inherent tensions between the form (genre) Horace has chosen in 1.3, the *propempticon,* and the content of the ode, which

seems to subvert that genre.[10] There are two fundamentally opposed ideas at play in this ode: there is the idea, implicit within the *form* of the ode itself, of *propempticon,* which functions by definition to offer a prayer for a safe return of a loved one;[11] and opposed to this formal idea is the contextual idea that men have no business boldly travelling over the water, challenging nature and the gods themselves. *Odes* 1.3 is a classic example wherein form challenges content (and vice-versa).[12]

Much of the work done on this ode has stood aloof from the problems inherent in such a challenge. Because Virgil would seen to play a prominent role in this ode, readers have been particularly hesitant to read much that is negative in its lines, since such a view would of necessity impinge upon Horace's estimation of Virgil.[13] As a result, the inherent tension between form and content has often meant that scholars have chosen to privilege either the ode's form or content.[14] Many have been content, for example, to read the ode generically as a *propempticon,* in which case the negative characterization of travellers as *audax* has usually been viewed as ironic or playful, or, in the worst cases, entirely ignored.[15] Those who have sensed the fundamental negativity of the ode toward the image of the *audax* traveller, those who have viewed travellers as symbols of human volition and of the evil of human progress, have generally downplayed the connection of such a negative view to Virgil and have read the ode instead as so much philosophical lecturing[16]—or have opted to read a positive tone into the negativity found here.[17]

While evidence in the poem supports all of these interpretations to a certain degree, any reading that hopes to achieve the virtue of coherency within the confines of what the text itself says must take into account three variables that heretofore have tended to be analyzed separately, as if they had little to do with each other. First, the presence of Virgil in this ode must be acknowledged as central, not ancillary to some desire on Horace's part to lecture about formal philosophy via a whimsical reference to his greatest competitor for poetic fame.[18] Then, the meaning and implications of the phrase *animae dimidium meae*[19] must be tackled, a task that explicitly will involve an analysis of the figure of Virgil in the ode. Then, finally, the function assigned by Horace to the adjective *audax* must be more specifically determined. The phrase *animae dimidium meae* is important because it is used to describe how Horace seemingly feels toward Virgil; *audax* is important because it is used generically to describe every figure introduced in the ode after Virgil; and the figure of Virgil himself is important because nothing in the ode makes very good sense without his presence as a model of poetic mimesis of a specific kind.

The opposition between form and content inherent in this ode is mirrored initially in its opening lines, where various mythological figures are named periphrastically. Venus, for example, is *diva potens Cypri* (v. 1); Castor and Pollux are *fratres Helenae* (v. 2); Aeolus is *ventorumque pater* (v. 3).

The mental process required to translate the periphrasis of these names in order to determine the identities involved highlights the larger disjunction between form and content upon which the ode is predicated. Horace's opening language, in other words, points to one thing but means another, a posture the ode in general will assume toward Virgil and his poetry. Moreover, the diction and tone of these lines is curiously liminal, as if to highlight the clash between what is said and what is meant through the addition of epic diction to lyric verse.[20] Venus, after all, is called after her epic title here, *diva potens,* while *lucida sidera* would seem to imply not only St. Elmo's fire but also, and more importantly, the serene images of epic night.[21] Even the phrase *fratres Helenae* suggests not only Helen herself, so imposing an epic figure, but also the image of the Dioscuri in their single, epic, aspect and this image has special resonances for the ode.[22] The Dioscuri are twins, presumably the closest relationship possible in human terms. But the details of their mythology highlight not the closeness presumed to animate their relationship but rather the division, the separation of the twins. Though Pollux was inconsolable at Castor's death, one version of their story has it that they were allowed to be together for half of the time, while another version holds that Castor was allowed to live again, but only at the expense of the life of Pollux, so that they lived on alternate days. In both myths, the twins live, but always separate and divided from each other. The symbology of the Dioscuri, then, in addition to highlighting the dissonance of epic diction amidst lyric verse, also points to a disjunctive relationship in which two brothers, once inseparable, now live only by virtue of their separation.

The opposition between form and content is specified further in the opening lines of the ode in the all-important phrase *animae dimidium meae.* This phrase participates in such oppositions because it follows on the heels of the periphrastic namings that sensitize the reader to the oppositions possible between form and content and which include the joining of epic and lyric language. The phrase is used to describe Virgil and the *opinio communis* has it that such a phrase is evocative, warm, tender.[23] Yet, given its proximity to the liminal language of the opening lines— especially the image of the Dioscuri separated from each other—it is not possible to read this phrase as only positive. This very well may be a positive statement, but it may also imply a negative sentiment. Given its position, it is simply too early in the ode to judge the tone of the phrase except to note that it is vague.

An examination of comparable phrases in the poetry of Horace is helpful in order to determine the tone of this key phrase, and *meae . . . partem animae* from *Odes* 2.17.5 is exemplary in this regard. There can be no doubt as to the warm emotion and tender devotion of this phrase, used by Horace to describe Maecenas, to commend the friendship he shares with him, and to affirm Horace's own resolve to die with Maecenas rather than live without him. 2.17 is surely not the only ode that suggests the intimacy and devotion of Horace and Maecenas,[24] yet if there is

doubt about the positive qualities of *animae dimidium meae,* the indubitable devotion implied in *meae partem animae* is a nearly perfect phrase with which to front a comparison.

The rationale for choosing one phrase to apply to Virgil in 1.3, and another to apply to Maecenas in 2.17, can be situated in a clear historical context retrievable from the *oeuvre* of Horace, the details of which affirm Horace's tone relative to Virgil in *Odes* 1.3. That context is grounded in the solid fact that Horace and Virgil knew each other. Generally it has been assumed that they were friends— even good friends.[25] Evidence for their "friendship," however, comes mainly from the *Satires.* For example, there is no evidence in the *Odes* (as there is in the case of Horace and Maecenas), to suggest that they were close spiritually and emotionally during the 20s B.C., when both poets were working hard on their respective masterpieces, the *Odes* and the *Aeneid.* The passage of choice is *Sat.* 1.5.39 ff., where Horace is effusive in his praise, mentioning his friends Plotius and Varius in the same breath as Virgil, and describing them all as . . . *animae qualis neque candidiores / terra tulit,* before going on in the next several lines to render them in warm and intimate terms.

Yet, the evidence in the *Satires* is, at best, inadequate to the present task because of chronology. *Satires* 1.5, for example, written sometime before 35 B.C. (the date of the publication of Book 1 of the *Satires*) represents Horace at about age thirty, a man whose views on friends, poetry, and the craft of writing are bound to be "younger," less mature, than those expressed in the *Odes.* Moreover, the Virgil recalled in the *Satires* is not the poet of the *Aeneid* (as he is in *Odes* 1.3), but is rather the pastoral poet of the *Eclogues* (published in 38 B.C.) who, at *Sat.* 1.10.44 ff., is explicitly praised as such in no uncertain terms: . . . *molle atque facetum / Vergilio adnuerunt gaudentes rure Camenae* (cf. 1.10.81 f.).

This specification of the role and function of the Virgil that Horace finds praiseworthy in the *Satires* demonstrates that Horace's view of (and praise of) Virgil in the *Satires* is a praise of a specific kind of Virgilian mimesis found in the *Eclogues.* And that praise must be considered in the context of Horace's own immaturity, for he is by any accounting a different sort of man at this point, still questioning and formulating his concepts about poetry. In fact, he goes so far in *Satires* 1.4 as to disclaim the title of *poeta* altogether, while granting it to Virgil (*me illorum [poetarum] . . . / excerpam numero, Sat.* 1.4.39-40; cf. vv. 41 ff., also).

In charting the evidence by which the relationship of Virgil and Horace might be more profitably gauged relative to *Odes* 1.3, chronology is important. *Odes* 1.3, written no later that 23 B.C., that is, as much as a decade after the *Satires,* and conjuring up images of the *Aeneid*—not the *Eclogues*—deals with an older Virgil, a Virgil with a different vision. Horace, by the same token, is older, too. He has become the *poeta* he said he was not in the *Satires,* the author of the *Odes* contemplating the author of the *Aeneid*. The historical situation of the two authors offers one way to begin to think about the difference implied between the phrases *animae dimidium meae* and *partem animae meae:* there must be a good reason why Horace does not use the word *pars* in describing Virgil but chooses instead *dimidium*. Attention to the etymology of *pars* and *dimidium* suggests a further difference that goes a long way toward corroborating the idea that their early friendship did not endure on the same terms, that Horace, as he matured, came to question Virgilian epic mimesis.

*Dimidium* is related to *dimidio,* meaning "to divide into two equal parts, to halve."[26] *Pars* is much more intriguing etymologically. Lewis and Short offer no verbal root in Latin, but the Latin noun *portio,* a word which means "a share, a part, a portion,"[27] is listed as kindred to *pars,* and the Greek *poro,* "to furnish, to offer, to give,"[28] is listed as kindred to both these nouns. The implications of "halving" and "sharing" implied in the words *dimidium* and *pars* make good sense in the context of *Odes* 1.3. The etymology of *pars,* for example, corroborates what the history of Horace's *Odes* already tells us about the friendship of Horace and Maecenas. *Pars* is a more inclusive word than *dimidium* and does not imply separation in the way *dimidium* does. Based on etymological data that imply sharing or a relation of one thing to another,[29] it is possible to view *pars* as denoting quite a different idea than *dimidium*.[30] This does not mean that the phrase of 2.17 is wholly positive and the phrase of 1.3 is entirely negative; but it does mean that the tenderness, the idea of one soul that is shared by two, the implications of a relationship that is based on a joining of selves, in short, the images and ideas suggested etymologically and historically by the word *pars* as used by Horace in 2.17, do not obtain in 1.3.

There, the use of *dimidium* implies a starker image, one based in cutting, in the division of something into two separate things, the halving of something.[31] This image is quite apart from the inclusiveness suggested by *pars*. The key implication of *dimidium* would seem to be the idea of halving, which implies a former unity that is now changed, a wholeness cut asunder. This idea well symbolizes the relationship of Horace and Virgil in 1.3. Their souls, once joined, are now—for reasons that will become clearer as the ode progresses—halved into two separate but equal parts. The image of the Dioscuri found in the opening verses of the ode comes to mind now again, for the mythology of these twins represents an intimacy that is transformed by circumstance into situations of separation and division, precisely what seems to be suggested here by Horace in the phrase *dimidium animae meae*.

The extrapolation to poetry writing and textual mimesis is not difficult to make at this point, and the historical context offered by the *Satires* corroborates what the later evidence in the *Odes* suggests. Virgil and Horace were once of a kind, twin souls, as it were, like the Dioscuri themselves, but they have been separated by the different paths down which their talents have drawn them. Virgil is the "other

half" of Horace's soul in the sense that he, Virgil, writes poetry of a completely different kind than Horace. And he is the "other half" in a personal sense since, as Fraenkel has noted, there was a wide disparity in the temperament of these two great Augustan poets.[32] Ultimately, this becomes an aesthetic statement: Horace is not a Virgilian poet. He prefers a different kind of craft. As a human being, Horace understands Virgil's epic and tragic vision, but as a poet who has struggled long and hard for his own vision he cannot abide such a vision (if he ever could) because it is not his (and can never be).

The use of periphrasis in the opening lines of the ode is important not only because it suggests a disjunction of form and content as specified in the phrase *animae dimidium meae,* but also because it sensitizes readers to the first mention of Virgil who, in stark contrast to Venus, Aeolus, and Castor and Pollux, is called simply by his *nomen*. Such a naming, in addition to calling attention to itself in its clarity and precision, suggests on the part of Horace veneration, respect, understanding, but also an urge to isolate, fix, and wag his finger at the poet of the *Aeneid,* to control him at least textually and lecture him about the topic of good and bad poetry and moral and immoral mimesis by refusing to envelope him in anything other than clear language. Here clarity implies control so that something important might be said about mimesis and the contours of the lecture that will follow are implied in the division implicit within the word *dimidium*.

The lecture that follows consists of two blocks of material identical in length, vv. 9-24 and vv. 25-40.[33] In the first block, Horace worries over the "trip" Virgil is about to undertake by thinking about the hypothetical "first traveller" of the seas, but here again form and content collide, for Horace refuses the typical inclusion of a *schetliasmos,*[34] choosing, instead of cursing the inventor, to praise the "first traveller," of ships:

>        illi robur et aes triplex
> circa pectus erat, qui fragilem truci (10)
>        commisit pelago ratem
> primus. . . .

to him was oak and three times bronze encircling his chest, who committed his fragile boat to the savage sea before anyone else. . . .

*Ratis* is especially noteworthy, for although it functions here in the context of fragility, it will eventually come to represent something much more negative. After framing Virgil in the context of a first traveller, a context that certainly has a literary analogue in Virgil's pathbreaking travels through Latin letters, Horace offers this catalogue:[35]

> . . . nec timuit praecipitem Africum
>        decertantem Aquilonibus
> nec tristis Hyadas nec rabiem Noti
>        quo non arbiter Hadriae (15)
> maior, tollere seu ponere vult freta.
>        quem mortis timuit gradum,
> qui siccis oculis monstra natantia,

> qui vidit mare turbidum et
> infamis scopulos Acroceraunia? (20)
> nequiquam deus abscidit
> prudens Oceano dissociabili
> terras, si tamen impiae
> non tangenda rates transiliunt vada.

. . . he feared not the rushing Southwest wind fighting with the North wind, nor the gloomy Hyades, nor the rage of the South wind (no judge to the Adriatic greater) whether desiring to excite or to quiet the seas. What approach of death feared he, who, with thirsty eyes, saw monsters floundering, seas troubled, and the infamous promontories of Acroceraunia? Pointlessly God chopped off in his wisdom the lands from the incompatible ocean, if perverse boats still cross the seas that ought to remain untouched.

This catalogue is hardly written to make the prospective traveller feel more comfortable. It is filled with storms, winds, monsters, promontories, and evil tidings. It suggests in its negative view of nature and of travel a literary analogue since it well describes the *Aeneid* itself, so full of monsters, storms, wanderings, and evil places. But there can be little doubt that the language of these lines is hardly credible as a formal *propempticon,* especially when taken in the context of the second block of material.

That block begins with a severe questioning of the *ratis,* the vessel used by the traveller in this ode and metaphorically the means by which Virgil travels through and in language. Virgil is the first traveller of Latin letters, riding out a great epic storm, but his *ratis* of a sudden becomes *impia* at v. 23 and he himself as the traveller of this ode becomes *audax* at v. 25. Now the disjunctions and liminalities of the opening lines of the ode are transformed. Horace crosses the threshold and begins a reasoned lecture on Virgilian epic mimesis:

> audax omnia perpeti (25)
> gens humana ruit per vetitum nefas.
> audax Iapeti genus
> ignem fraude mala gentibus intulit.
> post ignem aetheria domo
> subductum macies et nova febrium (30)
> terris incubuit cohors,
> semotique prius tarda necessitas
> leti corripuit gradum.
> expertus vacuum Daedalus aëra
> pinnis non homini datis; (35)
> perrupit Acheronta Herculeus labor.
> nil mortalibus ardui est;
> caelum ipsum petimus stultitia, neque
> per nostrum patimur scelus
> iracunda Iovem ponere fulmina. (40)

Bold to allow all things, humankind runs, despite prohibition, to crime. The bold son of Iapetus brought forth fire by means of a fraud evil to all men, for after fire had been pilfered from its heavenly home, poverty and a new company of ills lied upon earth, and remote once and slow, the necessity of death rushed its pace. Daedalus tried the free air with wings not given to men; Herculean effort broke the way through to Acheron. Nothing for mortals is too steep; heaven itself

we seek foolishly, nor through our sin do we suffer Jove to lay aside resentful bolts of thunder.

The transformation of *ratis,* from *fragilis* (vv. 10-11) to *impia* at vv. 23-24 is fundamental to the lecture Horace offers here. When Horace writes *si tamen impiae / non tangenda rates transiliunt vada,* it seems hard to defend such an image as somehow appropriate to the purposes of a serious *propempticon.* If the means by which journeys are undertaken are condemned, then the prayer for safekeeping is undermined.[36] When such a destabilization occurs, *ratis,* as a metaphor, becomes a key symbol by which Horace questions the kinds of literary journeys Virgil had undertaken (in the *Aeneid*). Such journeys are themselves metaphorized in the figures of Prometheus, Daedalus, and Hercules. Beyond their appropriateness as epic heroes, figures who "did it all"—or tried to—is their shared arrogance. Each was, in his own way, supremely bold in doing what he did and their *audacia* was in due course punished. But since *nil mortalibus ardui est* (v. 37), Jupiter can scarcely afford to rest the *fulmen,* the mechanism of punishment.

If Horace is less than convinced that Jupiter's thunderbolt will come crashing down on Virgil's head, then he clearly believes nevertheless that there are problems that exist for those who are *audax* and special problems for literary *audacia* of the kind represented by Virgil as an epic poet.[37] To be sure, Horace does not excuse himself from the company of those who try to do bold things with language. He makes the final verbs of the poem first person plural (*petimus, patimur,* vv. 38, 39) for just this reason.

But beyond that inclusion lurks the problem of degree. Poetry is written by degree, ranging the spectrum from the purely personal singing of lyric to the comprehensive song of epic. Epic is not lyric. The song of self embodied in lyric is not the same as the song of epic, always seeking a grander purview and vision, indeed always seeking *caelum ipsum.* To sing lyric is not to compete with the master poet Homer, either, and if Horace ever admitted to himself that he was in fact competing in his lyrics with Pindar it must be carefully noted that he always goes out of his way to say that he was not—and could not be—a Pindaric singer.[38]

Horace seems to say that Virgil had tried too much in the same way that Daedalus, Prometheus, and Hercules had tried too much. The *audacia* involved in epic journeying of a Virgilian kind is fundamentally to challenge the gods at their own game, to try to recreate "everything" in the epic genre as if the poet were a god of creation himself. The desire to achieve this kind of mimesis is akin to the desire to move about the world over the water or to give fire to men or to try to fly. To attempt such acts invites, if not divine punishment, then surely psychological punishment: in beginning to feel as if he has conquered nature, for example, man can begin to substitute himself for nature, or for God(s), can begin to think that he can control nature more fully or completely simply because he has controlled it in one instance. Such a substitution is dangerous ultimately because it can lead to a sense of invulnerability which is always, as the histories of Daedalus, Hercules, or Prometheus demonstrate, associated with punishment or death or both.

*Audax* is the key word of the second block of material (vv. 25-40), the quality Horace challenges most strongly. It is a special word in his vocabulary, most often used in his poetry to describe figures who seek great accomplishments, with the idea that these accomplishments should not be sought in the first place. In *Epistle* 2.1.182, for example, it is used to describe a kind of poet (*poeta audax*) who is showy, who writes only to gain the attention and approbation of the audience. Although Horace claims the highest respect for such a poet, there is a sense of irony in this epistle, addressed, after all, to the emperor Augustus and prominently mentioning as it does another *audax poeta,* Virgil himself. At *Odes* 4.2.10 *audax* is also used of the would-be Pindaric poet, the poet whom Horace says he cannot be. In *Odes* 1.12.21, *audax* is used of Athena in a poem that emphasizes—while it seems to close—the gap that remains between what humanity can do and what it wants or seeks to do.[39]

The linkage of these supreme examples of *audacia* and the figure of Virgil is stark. The special connotations of *audax,* when coupled with the stylistic features of the opening of 1.3 and the ways in which the ode as a *propempticon* fails to do what it is supposed to do, suggests that this ode is anything but a *propempticon* written by one poet-friend to another. In attempting to replicate in text a comprehensive and fundamentally negative view of the world, Virgil had achieved only a vision of evil and doom that highlights mankind's inability to know his world entirely or even clearly. Virgil, in a poetic sense, as an artist, had sought heaven itself, and the consequences, so Horace suggests in this ode, do not bode well for mankind in general or for Virgil in particular as a poet.

Strategic transformations and symmetries manifest and exploit the disjunction of form and content as the ode comes to a close. The opening prayer is transformed into the harsh image of Jupiter hurling his thunderbolt, so that Venus, the goddess of love (and Aeneas' mother) becomes Jupiter himself, the harsh father doling out punishment. The genre of the ode is transformed also before readers' eyes, so that the *propempticon* ultimately does exactly what it is not supposed to do. Virgil is also transformed, along with the craft upon which he sails, from *animae dimidium meae* who travels upon a *fragilis ratis,* to Prometheus, Daedalus, Hercules, challenging nature like the *impia ratis* of vv. 23-24. We begin then with prayer, fragile boats, a neutral vision of Virgil, and we end with condemnation, impious boats, and a questioning of textual mimesis as practiced by Virgil in the *Aeneid.*

## 2. AUGUSTINE READS HORACE (READING VIRGIL): *CONFESSIONS* 4.6

Horace's *Odes* 1.3 supplies a sublime distance, the allusive background against which Augustine composed the details of *Confessions* 4.6, one of the more poignant recol-

lections of his autobiography. Augustine's text is, on one level, a controlled but emotionally charged memoir of the death of his youthful best friend. Increasingly, however, as the play of allusion occurs, the emotion of this memoir is transformed into a meditation on the morality of textual mimesis that mirrors Horace's apprehensions in 1.3. The same tension between form and content found in *Odes* 1.3 is found at *Confessions* 4.6.

The text opens with a deceptively touching and simple recollection, in which Augustine recalls what was surely a keenly felt loss within the context of the friendship of Pylades and Orestes. Such a recollection makes good sense and seems natural, at least initially. More than simply suggesting an appropriate context in which to frame the loss that he feels, the presence of figures from classical lore suggests that Augustine is describing the event historically, that is, as he remembers it happening in the past. It seems not at all contrived, as one reads *Confessions* 4.6, to think of Augustine recalling one of classical literature's great friendships, and the reverberation of that friendship in the *Confessions* lends a depth and subtle grace that the story otherwise would lack. Moreover, it is not hard to believe that Augustine thought of this prototypical friendship as his friend lay dead, nor is it difficult to imagine Augustine considering this friendship in such a context earlier, while his friend lived.

A few lines after this recollection, however, Augustine alludes to *Odes* 1.3 in a rather obvious manner (*bene quidam dixit de amico suo . . .*) as if desiring to draw close attention to the passage. When focused on these lines, such attention occasions an important shift in tone, transforming the memoir from seriousness to irreverence and mimicking the ways in which the tone of *Odes* 1.3 moves from seeming seriousness to something else altogether. *Confessions* 4.6, after all, is about a leave-taking distinguishable from Virgil's only in permanence: Virgil is travelling east in *Odes* 1.3 while Augustine describes in 4.6 the death of his best friend. The allusion initially strikes, then, all the wrong chords and makes Augustine seem to be about to lose control of his memoir.

Beyond irreverence, however, the allusion transforms what had been a tender recollection into a contrived literary reflection, and this contrivance sets up the textual mechanism by which Augustine continues to command his classical material as we would like. Part of the contrivance inheres in Augustine's advertisement that he is alluding in the first place (*bene quidam dixit . . .*). Beyond this, the transformation is achieved stylistically through the intrusion of the allusive material itself, since the allusion is inappropriate to the tone of the text at this point. It is asking too much of any reader to believe that Augustine would have thought of *Odes* 1.3 at the time of his friend's death. The line he recalls in and of itself is touching enough, but Augustine knows the entire ode, as would any audience responding to this allusion, and Horace's third ode of Book 1 is not an emotional nor even a very lyrical moment in his work.

Moreover, the Horatian allusion calls attention to the fact that the narrative, heretofore operating as if it were an historical account, is actually a contrived recollection of a past event from the purview of the present. Instead, the allusion highlights the literary quality that intrudes into the text at this point, accentuating the act of writing itself, not the memory being recalled. The recollection of these lines, in other words, moves from historical accuracy as found in the example of Pylades and Orestes (this is what happened at the time that it happened, as I remember it), to literary contrivance (this is what I am thinking about in the present, as I write about a past event). The distinction is crucial in any attempt to understand 4.6, since the movement across time implies an ongoing dialectical process wherein the historical act of recollection is questioned and examined in the literary act of writing.

Beyond this implication, however, one must consider the reason Augustine would allude at this point to *Odes* 1.3 at all. Under what circumstances might this allusion offer insight into his own situation of discourse? In addition to transforming the narrative pattern at this point in the text, the allusion draws attention to Augustine as a literary reader. Yet given that, why should this sensitive and prolific reader of classical texts pick this particular moment in Horace to use in the *Confessions*? Certainly he could have chosen other, more lyrical, moments; why did he not choose *Odes* 2.17, for example, and the particularly apt phrase discussed above, *meae partem animae*? Given the context of 4.6, the phrase from 2.17 is certainly just as apt as the phrase from 1.3 that Augustine ultimately did choose, and even more so.

If, on the other hand, Augustine means to suggest certain ideas about the rectitude of writing in general and of the kinds of writing he is pursuing in particular, then this allusion, after the fashion of a Chinese landscape,[40] offers a sublime distance against which the details of the text of the *Confessions* takes shape. A warm recollection of youthful friendship is cast in the wider context of the rectitude of Christian mimesis in general: just as Virgil had attempted too much in 1.3, so Augustine suggests that he himself has attempted too much in talking to God. Such a reading is particularly apt since the linkage between *Confessions* 4.6 and *Odes* 1.3 is grounded in the phrase *dimidium animae meae*,[41] which accentuates not simply the ties between the two "friends," but also the particular kind of "ties" implied in 1.3. The word *dimidium* is central to the meaning of *Confessions* 4.6, then, since through this key word Augustine frames his portrayal of youthful friendship.

The spiritual implications of 4.6 are such that *dimidium* makes sense in a way that *pars* never could. Ultimately, 4.6 is not about spiritual unity or close friendship as much as it is about error. Augustine's text is filled with questions grounded in moral outrage and spiritual horror. He cannot quite get over the fact that he loved his friend more than anything else. This error is compounded with the realization that, being so blind, yet he was somehow able to

extricate himself from the spiritual morass that such an unfounded love implied. The death of his friend comes to symbolize an essentially evil soul, longing after a life that it knows imperfectly, fearing the death that can offer it eternal salvation, mired in this world, yet unaware of its condition. The initial question of this chapter is exemplary: *quid autem ista loquor* ("why do I even talk of such things?").

The implications of that question are rhetorical and moral. Rhetorically, the question represents Augustine's attempt at self-incrimination, a way for him to suggest boldly that he has little if any business saying anything at all in text, especially of topics about which he clearly knows little. On another level, this question represents the proper moral severity necessary in a text that recounts youthful indiscretion and sin. Augustine was leading a life wholly insufficient and inadequate in Christian terms, and his response to the death of his dead friend is but one example of the exaggerated and "worldly" response to temptation. In this light, the use of *dimidium* well suggests the halving of his soul implicit in the act of Augustine's conversion, his separation, as it were, from a prior spiritual state. Superficially lending a tender feeling to the recollection, the word also subtly suggests the more permanent separation or "halving" that occurred between his friend and himself by virtue of Augustine's conversion. In remembering the death of his friend, Augustine could also see a severe choice being made; like Horace, Augustine had chosen one path while his friend—through death—had taken another. And like Horace, the starkness of the former path seems at once formidable and harrowing, all the more since it was part of his former soul that has since been saved.

Read with the Horatian allusion more specifically in mind, however, the question, like the text in which it is imbedded, is transferred from the rhetorical to the moral realm. The halving in Horace that is poetic is transferred to the spiritual realm in Augustine, but the separation and distance implied in the phrase *animae dimidium meae* are stark and real. The impropriety of Virgil seeking *caelum ipsum* certainly carries over here into Augustine's language, forming the moral context in which he contemplates this loaded question. More than simply shaking his head and lamenting at oats wildly sown, Augustine here wonders at the moral implications of what he is doing as a literary artist while in the very process of doing it.

This is a broad and severe questioning with several important aspects, all of which are specified in the Horatian context brought forward allusively in Augustine's text. On the one hand Augustine would seem to imply a nagging sense that to inscribe in text youthful indiscretion—even in the name of deploring it—is somehow morally to perpetrate it, to fix it and modulate it for all to see. This would seem to be one of the key problems with Virgilian epic poetry in Horace's view, which is filled with gloom, monsters, death, and larger than life evils that are somehow made real, fixed, modulated, in their inscription in language and text. Of what use is such a vision? Are there not inherent dangers involved in such a vision? For a Christian, of course, the moral implications of such a problem are cast in quite different though no less profound terms than for a pagan, but the sensitivity of the discreet and nebulous powers of language is unmistakable and tantalizing in either work.

On a larger scale, the questioning of language in a Horation context devolves ultimately onto the figure of God, with implications about the very ways in which we conceive of and talk about Him. In this sense the Horatian allusion highlights the absolute sublimity (and so the absolute absurdity) involved in the detailed writing to God about one's (God-given) life as if He were a confessor-priest. Augustine, in doing this, seeks *caelum ipsum,* seeks to talk to God and, more than this, succeeds in "textualizing" Him, limiting Him and constraining Him in text, modulating and fixing Him for all to see in the process.

This act, which might on one level seem ultimately submissive, is, in a larger sense, the height of *audacia* for a Christian, the boldest act he or she might attempt—bolder even than the *audacia* of Hercules, Prometheus, or Daedalus. But such a realization, as horrible and as terrorizing as it must have been for Augustine, also must have held out the real possibility of delight, else why would Augustine have dared to write the *Confessions* at all. Such a delight might in fact be considered a kind of temptation. To acknowledge such a fundamentally skeptical view of language, after all, would not be the same as acting upon such a view. To succumb to the overwhelming oblivion to which the imperfection of human truth leads would be to succumb to the temptation to doubt the efficacy of faith itself. But to challenge such a skepticism would be to affirm faith in a perfect God even if it were an affirmation imperfectly cast in human terms.

Such a discordancy is perfectly mirrored in the texture of the Horatian allusion, for it offers a most effective way of meditating on this problem at a distance, allusively, without being subsumed by it. As such, Augustine is able to suggest both the dilemma and the delight of the issue. Horace's presence at this point in the *Confessions* seems precisely the evidence that allows readers to gauge the extent of Augustine's sensitivity to the fundamental moral dilemma involved in writing. And the finely tuned literary sensibility employed to express such a dilemma shows Augustine to be caught in—and to be aware of—the paradoxical horror and delight of the twisting, imperfect, lanes of language.[42] His sensitivity to this issue surely would have suggested to him that to write the *Confessions* was supremely *audax,* in the same sense that Prometheus or Daedalus, or even Virgil, were supremely bold.

Beginnings and endings are always important in the *Confessions.* Augustine begins chapter 6 with a frank question of the propriety of his talking (writing), the details of which concern the death of his youthful friend. The Horatian allusion there, lingering at a distance in the allusive

play of these texts, seems calculated to confirm that question and widen its scope in a Christian context significantly. We share with Augustine the grief and tenderness of a moment in his life, but looming from beyond the humanity of this moment is a huge question concerning the morality of writing about such events in the first place (the distance of the landscape). Always in Augustine's view, to write was to fail.[43] To write of such topics as if God were one's confessor was to stretch human understanding of God beyond reason, to stand the concept of God on its head, to compete with God as supreme *auctor,* molding and shaping experience to one's own ends. For one so immersed in Christianity, the thought of writing to God might seem at first to be wonderfully attractive, but for a Christian such as Augustine only the prospect, not the reality, would have been inviting.

*Notes*

1. I owe thanks to my teachers, W. R. Johnson, Winthrop Wetherbee, and Frantisek Svejkovský, who helped to formulate at an early stage some of the ideas presented here; to E. A. Schmidt, who read the penultimate version with incomparable erudition, for which I am wholly grateful; to Louis J. Swift, who read earlier and lengthier versions several times amidst heavy burdens of his own; and, finally, to my students at Brown in several courses over the past two years on late antique poetry and rhetoric, for their avid interest, many corrections, fresh enthusiasms.

2. My edition of the *Confessions* is Skutella, Solignac, Trehorel, Bouissou 1962.

3. The translations of the Latin, which are my own, attempt to preserve the Latin word order while communicating (in the case of Horace) the fundamental negativity for which my reading of his ode argues.

4. The moments I analyze here represent my own personal interests. There are countless other moments in the *Confessions,* none of which have been studied. Relative to Horace, one might also analyze 9.1.9 ff. where *Odes* 1.18.4 is normative or 6.10.38 where *Epodes* 2.3 is normative. Horace exists in other places in the *Confessions* and a lengthy study could be devoted to them. For a partial list, see the *Index Scriptores Profani* in Skutella 1969.378-379. Skutella's list is far from complete. A more complete survey of the Horatian material in Augustine, something computer technology might hasten, is a present need. The last work to attempt such a survey was Keseling 1931.1278-1280.

5. Marrou 1958 is the basic work in this area; Courcelle 1963 is standard for the context in which the *Confessions* was written. In general, however, work on the literary content of the *Confessions* does not exist apart from the other more prominent concerns of Augustinian scholars. So, for example, one finds all sorts of aesthetic discussions in O'Connell 1969 but no specific discussion of literary issues. There are a

few exceptions. Arthur 1941 is a very large discussion of art that includes, as one would expect, literary concerns along the way. Burke 1970 discusses the forms and functions of language in Augustine, the logical beginning point for literary studies. O'Meara 1963.252-260 treats Augustine's relationship with a classical poet. Cf. Hagendahl 1967. O'Donnell 1980.144-175 is a recent exception to the tendency not to impute much importance to literary reading in Augustine. Spence 1988 offers an up-to-date bibliography in this regard with important readings of her own relative to Christian rhetoric. There are other works that could be mentioned; the point is that there is a need for specific studies dealing with Augustine's use of the classical *poetae* in a literary way. There is no study that treats Augustine and Horace exclusively in any language to my knowledge.

6. The characterization is from Commager 1962.118. By way of example, Nisbet and Hubbard 1970.44-45 say this about 1.3: "[it] is an accomplished piece of versification, but little more. The poet . . . shows none of his usual tact and charm; there is not a hint of Virgil's poetry [sic, this is just plain wrong], and it is wrong to argue . . . that the ode's sombre and religious tone is directed specifically towards the recipient. The second part of the poem is equally unsatisfactory; . . . here the trite and unseasonable moralizing seems out of place in a poem of friendship. . . . Nor is the flatness of the thought redeemed by any special excellence in the writing . . . we miss the Horatian virtues of brevity and incisiveness." Williams 1968.159 makes much the same comment, calling the ode "undistinguished," and concluding that there is not "the slightest sense of a personal relationship in the greater part of the poem."

7. So argues Prodinger 1907.165 and, with equal vigor, Verrall 1884.120 who asserts, as always with enormous erudition and persuasion, that the first eight verses of the ode are a true *propempticon* simply added to vv. 9 ff., which were written earlier and not as a *propempticon*. Most recently, Carrubba 1984.166-173 has argued for the coherency and structural integrity of this ode.

8. See Hahn 1945.xxxii-iii, who would see comedy at work in this ode.

9. For a complete bibliography, see Elder 1952.140-159, for works up to 1952, and Basto 1982.30-43, for the bibliography since then.

10. On the genre relative to Horace's use and abuse of it see now Basto 1982.30-31 and nn. 1-5.

11. Although Horace does not do this; instead, he prays for a safe passage. Cf. below, n. 36.

12. I do not hold to the view that genres in classical poetry are immutable, fixed like Platonic "forms," but surely to change accepted norms of a genre—however fluid they may be—is to invite attention to that change. Such attention may occasion, as here, the discovery of something novel in the (newly configured) genre.

13. Thus Moore 1902.63 f. calls Horace "tactless" in linking Virgil to the idea of *audacia*.

14. Thus Lockyer 1967.41-45 reads vv. 9 ff. for their "positive" tone "which," he goes on to add, "when read negatively, have often led critics astray" (p. 43). I believe we must be led astray in this way in order to make this ode coherent.

15. So Hendrickson 1907-1908.100-104 tried to explain away the tension by arguing that the first eight lines were all that Horace intended Virgil to hear (thus establishing Horace in his view as following Menander in the form of the *propempticon*), and that the rest of the poem was out of Virgil's earshot. Even so, how does that mitigate the negativity of what is to follow in the ode?

16. So Delatte 1935.309-336 argues that the ode condemns, under Cynic influence, the study of theology, astrology, and cosmology, not Virgilian mimesis.

17. Thus Elder 1952.140-159 is followed by Lockyer 1967.41-45 in reading this ode as a positive symbol for the poetry of Virgil. Basto 1982 follows this line of argument most recently.

18. I do not believe Horace and Virgil were enemies, but both men were enormously gifted and it seems to me indubitable that either would have felt rivalry toward the other. Cf. Duckworth 1956.281-316, and below, p. 265 f. on the developing relationship of these two poets as evidenced in the *Odes* and *Satires*.

19. The idea has an ancient provenance, possibly appearing as early as Plato (*Symp.* 189C ff.), and recurring in Callimachus (*Epigram* 41.1), Meleager and others. Yet the idea of someone being an *alter idem* should not be brought to bear here (cf. Aristotle, *Nic. Eth.* 1168b6 f., e.g.), since Horace does not say *alter idem* here and we owe it to him to pay attention to what he does say, not what his language suggests by way of commonly accepted cultural tags. See Nisbet and Hubbard 1970.48 and the bibliography found here.

20. I follow Basto 1982.31 here.

21. Ibid.

22. Ibid.

23. See generally Nisbet and Hubbard 1970.48.

24. See Pucci 1988.75-80.

25. Fraenkel 1957.409 is coy in noting, in a wholly ambiguous phrase, that there was a "wide difference in the constitution and temperament of the two friends. . . ." Just how friendly can we suppose two people of widely differing constitution and temperament to be? Just how friendly could they have been in maturity, regardless of an earlier, more youthful, connection?

26. Thus Lewis and Short 1879.581, s.v. *dimidio.*

27. Lewis and Short 1879.1401, s.v. *portio.*

28. Technically, *poro* is presumed to be the present form of the aorist active *eporon,* on which see Liddell and Scott 1940.1452, s.v. *poro.*

29. On this specifically see Lewis and Short 1879.1401, s.v. *portio,* II.

30. In fact, I would suggest that reliance upon what seems to be a Greek prototype has led to a misinterpretation of the function of this phrase. Some commentators, such as Villeneuve 1944, have felt that the phrase was too obvious to warrant comment. The *opinio communis* has invariably held that *dimidium* is to be read as a tender word. Shorey 1899.153 reads *dimidium* as explicitly synonymous with *pars* in 2.17 (cf. p. 283). Kiessling 1930.21 is not as bold in asserting the similitude but generally sees the phrase as comparable to that found in 2.17. Page 1962.142 gives a fuller history of the references to Virgil in Horace's poetry. Smith 1904.14, following earlier commentaries, notes that the phrase is "borrowed" from an old Greek definition of friendship and Diogenes Laertius 5.1.20 is seen to be exemplary: *miá psuchě dúo sōmata enoikoûsa.* Here is where the misinterpretation might lie, since Horace's Latin is not a translation of the Greek. It is one thing to rely verbally on a phrase from a prior text (i.e., to allude), and another thing simply to use a common idea that is part of a culture. Horace is doing the latter here and it cannot be denied that he creates a new phrase that stands out noticeably within his *oeuvre* and works to other than positive purposes in the meaning of this ode.

31. See Lewis and Short 1879.581, s.v. *dimidius,* III A.

32. Fraenkel 1957.408-410.

33. Nisbet and Hubbard 1970.40 offer a tripartite division as does Collinge 1961.83. Kiessling 1930.19 offers a four part division. I arrived independently at the same kind of division as that offered by Carrubba 1984.168-169 and agree with the ways he would see the ode structured.

34. See Basto 1982.40 n. 5.

35. There is nothing new in reading the language of the ode in this way; see, for example, Kidd 1977.97-103. Reading the negativity that follows the introduction of this metaphor as part and parcel of the metaphor itself is, however, new and something that I think must be done here.

36. It should be noted that even in this regard Horace deviates from the norm. A *propempticon* should pray for a safe return. Horace prays here for a safe passage, thus highlighting again the disjunction of form to content. This does imply a metaphorical, poetic level at which the poem must be read, but does it not

also imply that the poet may not be returning from his travels, just as Hercules, Prometheus, and Daedalus did not, a position with which Ovid would seem to agree in his own meditations on Virgilian epic.

37. On the issue of priority and dating, I follow Basto 1982.36-37. Virgil died only four years after Horace published *Odes* 1-3 and, although the date of 1.3 is uncertain, it is clearly not, as some have held, one of the earlier odes of the collection. By 23 B.C., in any case, the first two-thirds of the Aeneid would have been in presentable form (all of the allusions, incidentally, to Virgil in Horace come from books 1-7), so that Horace would have a very good idea of what the Aeneid was—in his view—about.

38. The would-be Pindaric poet is specified, not coincidentally, at *Odes* 4.2.10 as an *audax poeta.* Cf. the opening images of this ode also.

39. *Odes* 3.4.56, 3.18.13, 3.27.28; *Epistles* 2.2.51; *Satires* 1.1.30, 2.3.165, 2.5.29, 1.10.76; *Ars Poetica,* v. 237.

40. The metaphor is used by Brown 1967.76 to describe the literary artistry of the *Confessions.*

41. Augustine has changed the word order for purposes of stylistics, since Horace's phrase had to fit into an asclepiad in 1.3.

42. The phrase is Augustine's in *De Catechizandis rudibus* 10.15.

43. See, for example, *De Magistro* 5.14, 8.22 ff., or *De Catechizandis rudibus* 10.15 among other examples.

**Ronnie Ancona (essay date 1994)**

SOURCE: Ancona, Ronnie. "'The Temporal Adverb." In *Time and the Erotic in Horace's "Odes,"* pp. 22-43. Durham, N.C.: Duke University Press, 1994.

[*In the following essay, Ancona examines the use of the temporal adverb in Odes 1.25, 2.5, and 3.7, and the manner in which Horace causes time to control the erotic situations in his work.*]

My discussion of the temporality of love begins at the level of the word, specifically, the temporal adverb. In each of the following poems—***Odes*** 1.25, ***Odes*** 2.5, and ***Odes*** 3.7—there is a key temporal adverb that plays a central role in establishing the dominance of the theme of temporality in the particular love situation. In the first two poems, the key temporal adverb begins the poem and helps to set up certain expectations from that point on; in the third, it occurs two-thirds of the way through the poem and makes us rethink what has come before. While these are not the only love odes with what I call key temporal adverbs (cf., for example, *donec* in ***Odes*** 3.9, *nuper* in ***Odes*** 3.26, and *diu* in ***Odes*** 4.1—all of which signal the importance of temporality from the poem's first line), they do show especially well how such an adverb, reinforced by other indicators of temporality, can function as one device by which Horace makes time dominate the erotic situation. Further, as we shall see, this dominance of temporality has consequences for our understanding of the positions of the lover and the beloved.

In *Odes* 1.25 and 2.5, the lover seeks to draw a distinction between himself and the beloved by pointing to how the beloved's experience is determined by time, and this distinction is itself the basis of the lover's effort to control the beloved. Where these poems clearly delineate the roles of male lover and female beloved by distinguishing between the lover's position outside of time and the beloved's temporality, *Odes* 3.7 instead points to a temporal predicament in which lover and beloved seem equally enmeshed. However their differing relationships to time will reveal yet another example of the hierarchical and gendered distinctions between male lover and female beloved.

### ODES 1.25

Parcius iunctas quatiunt fenestras
iactibus crebris iuvenes protervi,
nec tibi somnos adimunt amatque
    ianua limen,
quae prius multum facilis movebat (5)
cardines. audis minus et minus iam
"me tuo longas pereunte noctes,
    Lydia, dormis?"
invicem moechos anus arrogantis
flebis in solo levis angiportu, (10)
Thracio bacchante magis sub inter-
    lunia vento,
cum tibi flagrans amor et libido,
quae solet matres furiare equorum,
saeviet circa iecur ulcerosum, (15)
    non sine questu
laeta quod pubes hedera virenti
gaudeat pulla magis atque myrto
aridas frondes hiemis sodali
    dedicet Hebro. (20)

More sparingly do bold young men shake your joined windows with frequent hurling of stones, and they do not take away your sleep, and the door loves its threshold—the door which earlier moved so much its easy hinges. You hear less and less now "while I, your love, am perishing through long nights, do you sleep, Lydia?" In turn, an inconsequential old woman, you will weep over haughty adulterers in the lonely alleyway, while the Thracian wind rages like a bacchant even more under the moonless sky, when for you blazing love and desire, the sort that maddens the mothers of horses, will rage around your wounded heart, not without complaint that, happy, the youth rejoice in green ivy more than gray myrtle, and dedicate dry leaves to Hebrus, companion of winter.

*Parcius,* the first word of *Odes* 1.25, establishes a temporal perspective that influences the reading of the entire poem.[1] It sets up a contrast between the erotic successes of Lydia's past, and her present decline, which will only

continue. The influence of *parcius* is particularly direct in the first eight lines of the poem. Although all but one of the finite verbs in these lines are in the present tense, there is nevertheless an overwhelming impression of the past.[2] In the first two lines Horace achieves this effect through the choice and placement of the initial comparative adverb. The tense of *quatiunt,* the main verb of lines 1-2, is present. *Parcius,* though, which modifies *quatiunt,* changes the effect of the present tense. Implicit in the comparative degree of *parcius* is the question "more sparingly than when?" This inherent duality challenges *quatiunt* and, read in conjunction with the present tense of the main verb, causes us to be simultaneously aware of both past and present.

The phrase *iuvenes protervi,* highlighted through its postponement to the end of its clause, continues the focus on time by foreshadowing the contrast between youth and age, which becomes more pronounced later in the poem. In the future Lydia will be an old woman (*anus* 9) ignored by the *pubes* (17). The meaning of *protervi* (insolent, bold) underscores the disruptive activity expressed by *quatiunt,*[3] while the prefix *pro-*, combined with the final position of *protervi,* additionally specifies a dimension of urgent, forward movement. The iterative meaning of *crebris* further reinforces the aggressive quality of *iuvenes protervi,* while it contrasts with the controlling temporal adverb, *parcius.* The image created in the first two lines— the picture of the closed windows, the repeated hurling of stones, the violence of the stones hitting the windows, the potential threat to the person inside—is a powerful one, yet having previously absorbed the force of the comparative adverb *parcius,* we know that the activity described is happening less often now, and that the lovemaking that is the goal of this activity belongs increasingly to the past.

The control of *parcius,* though, even in these first two lines, is still more complicated, for *parcius* secondarily modifies the perfect passive participle *iunctas* as well. When *parcius* is seen to affect *iunctas* as well as *quatiunt,* the entire phrase *parcius iunctas . . . fenestras* suggests that Lydia's windows are perhaps not quite as resolutely closed as they appear. Back in the days of Lydia's sexual prime we can imagine that her windows stayed shut. One as sought after as Lydia might not have needed to show her eagerness for love by standing at the window. By qualifying *iunctas* (joined, closed), Horace may be suggesting that while lovers seek out Lydia less often, she is more "open" to their advances. Perhaps we should picture the present-day Lydia degraded by peeking out her window for lovers who now rarely appear. This hint in *parcius iunctas . . . fenestras* of Lydia's movement toward taking the initiative in the love situation becomes fully developed later in the poem when Lydia no longer looks longingly out her windows, but roams the streets filled with a lust that finds no takers. In addition, because of the erotic potential of *iungo* as the "joining" of sexual intercourse, *parcius iunctas* ("joined" less often) links the temporal with the erotic, thus neatly revealing in the poem's first two words the theme of diminishing eroticism.[4]

Despite the violence implicit in impudent youths pelting Lydia's windows with stones, this activity, which belongs increasingly to the past, at least had the positive quality of showing Lydia as an object worthy of erotic attention. Its decline shows that Lydia is no longer as desirable as she once was.

In the first two lines of the poem, then, Lydia's sexual decline is characterized through her status as a less frequent object of aggressive erotic attention. This characterization begins with the phrase *parcius iunctas,* which signals the poem's theme of diminishing sexual attraction. Lydia is established as the former recipient (cf. the passive voice of *iunctas*) of erotic attention. Her sexuality is defined as arising not from within her, as desire, but rather in terms of her desirability. Thus, the sign that she was once desirable is that she was pestered and disturbed by young men, whereas now, her becoming too old for love is signaled through the absence of such attention. In each case, what is constant is her status as an *object* of desire for young men, while her own condition is determined temporally. Who she is in the present is determined by the change from the past, which the present manifests. But that change is itself finally significant only because of the differing reactions that young men (themselves apparently unchanging) have to her; her own despair at this situation is itself the consequence of how her temporality is understood by others.

The blending of past and present continues in *nec tibi somnos adimunt.* Although this statement has its main verb in the present tense, by negating it Horace reveals, as he did through *parcius iunctas quatiunt,* at least as much about Lydia's past as her present. While being deprived of sleep might under other circumstances be viewed as undesirable, in this erotic context it is not. What appears on the surface as potentially pleasant, that rowdy youths are not disturbing Lydia so that presumably now she can sleep, is in fact an indication that she is being ignored.[5] Later in the poem Lydia, kept sleepless not by noisy young men but by her own unsatisfied lust, will resort to wandering the streets at night.

The poem's first seemingly simple statement about present time devoid of any modifier or negative, *amatque / ianua limen,* in fact contains a negative meaning for Lydia. In her situation a closed door implies that no one any longer wants to enter her house. And further, although the personification of the door is a common motif in erotic contexts in Latin poetry,[6] the use of an inanimate subject for the verb *amare,* while not unprecedented in Horace, is striking in this context.[7] While Nisbet and Hubbard miss the full erotic potential of *amatque* and the phrase in which it appears,[8] other commentators have noted the sexually suggestive nature of Horace's language. Catlow points out that Horace is "mockingly transferring to her surroundings the sexually suggestive words which no longer apply to Lydia herself (*iunctas, amatque, facilis*),"[9] while Copley finds the phrase sarcastic, an "unkind reminder to Lydia of her earlier popularity, when she could choose at will

among her many lovers those for whom her door would open at a touch, and those to whom it would remain stubbornly closed."[10] To Boyle, the door hugging the threshold is ironic,[11] while Collinge sees wit: "the only hugging at Lydia's house will be between door and threshold."[12]

We may conclude that the door "loving the threshold" certainly suggests hostility on the part of the speaker toward the fulfillment of Lydia's desire and underscores the lack of loving in her present life (*parcius iunctas*). *Amatque / ianua limen* creates a closed circle of loving inhabited only by personified objects and excluding Lydia from the roles of both lover and beloved—of both subject and object of desire. Indeed there is something almost masturbatory about this description of loving—the door loving a part of itself—which further heightens Lydia's exclusion. The door's easy movement of the past, *quae prius multum facilis movebat / cardines,* contrasts with the static image of the door's present. *Prius,* which recalls the opening *parcius,* shifts the temporal perspective from the present time of *amat* to some unspecified time in the past. The imperfect aspect of *movebat* prevents us from focusing on a fixed moment in time and suggests, rather, the duration of Lydia's sexually active past.

Whether *multum* in the phrase *quae prius multum facilis movebat / cardines* should be construed grammatically with *facilis* or *movebat* has occasioned discussion among commentators. Against taking *multum* with *movebat,* Nisbet and Hubbard argue as follows: "Porphyrio takes multum with *movebat* ('often moved'), and he has been followed by some modern editors. It could be argued that on this interpretation the contrast with *parcius* is expressed more clearly. On the other hand it is infelicitous to have two adverbs, *prius* and *multum,* both modifying *movebat.*"[13] It is surprising that Nisbet and Hubbard find this "infelicitous" when in the very next line of the poem *audis* is modified by both *minus et minus* and *iam.* There is no reason why *multum* cannot play double duty here as *parcius* does earlier in the poem. But regardless of how one resolves this issue, the temporal effect of *multum* is undeniable. It echoes the iterative meaning of *crebris* and provides additional contrast with *parcius.* Once again, it is by contrast with the past that the poet creates the present.

With *audis* we seem to return to the present. However, *audis* is immediately qualified by *minus et minus iam* which further splits our attention between past and present. The comparative degree of *minus,* which shifts us away from the present, echoes the temporal control *parcius* has exerted since the beginning of the poem. The repetition of *minus,* combined with the reinforcement of the present tense by *iam* strengthens the impression of mixed past and present. The contrast between *audis minus et minus iam* and *me tuo longas pereunte noctes, / Lydia, dormis?* brings to a climax the juxtaposition of past and present in lines 1-8. By directly quoting the words of the shut-out lover, and at the same time undercutting their immediacy by all but relegating them to the past, Horace dramatically illustrates once again the contrast between Lydia's former and present lives. Both the immediacy of the direct address to Lydia (albeit as part of a quotation) and the word order of *me tuo* point to the intimacy sought by the lover. However Horace makes it clear that such desirability is all but a thing of the past for Lydia. *Pereunte,* a common word in amatory vocabulary, ironically foreshadows Lydia's future when, with roles reversed, she will be "dying" not only from lust, but from old age.[14]

The initial antithesis of past and present becomes in the second part of the poem one half of a new antithesis: of then and now (lines 1-8) with future time (lines 9-20).[15] *Invicem* is the pivotal word, which alerts us to a shift both from what has immediately preceded (the shut-out lover's lament) and from the opening temporal distinctions.[16] With *invicem . . . flebis* the poet suddenly unleashes his harsh prediction of Lydia's future, which takes the form of one long sentence filled with language that both echoes and contrasts with that of the first eight lines of the poem. Lydia, having become an old woman (*anus*), will haunt the lonely alleyways,[17] and weep over men who now refuse her.

The future is made more immediately present through the suddenness of *anus* and the placement of *flebis* before the dependent (explanatory) clause *cum . . . saeviet,* which in turn is reinforced by the present participle *bacchante.* Lydia's age (as now projected by the speaker)[18] contrasts with that of her former suitors (*iuvenes*), and the loneliness of the streets is a reminder that the days of her frequent visitors are over (*parcius . . .*).

Lydia now becomes like her former suitors. She is the one seeking companions and lamenting those who are unresponsive (*moechos . . . arrogantis*). Her forays at night (*sub inter- / lunia*) recall the long nights spent by the shut-out lover in front of her closed door (*longas pereunte noctes*). In addition, both the shut-out lover and Lydia lament their lack of success in gaining access to the one(s) they desire. The aggressiveness of Lydia's new actions (her taking on the role of pursuer) is not unlike that of the *invenes protervi.* Their implied threat of violence earlier in the poem (1-2) foreshadows the wildness that the poet attributes at first to the wind (*Thracio bacchante magis sub inter- / lunia vento*) but then to Lydia as well (cf. *flagrans, furiare, saeviet, iecur ulcerosum*). The comparative adverb *magis* (11) increases the storminess of the picture and contrasts with *parcius,* which had a controlling effect on the activity implicit in the first two lines of the poem.

While the passage of time creates some similarities between Lydia's situation and that of her former suitors, it ultimately serves to separate Lydia both from her former self and from her past and potential lovers. While her former suitors are described as *protervi* (bold), Lydia is now *levis* (light). The meaning "fickle" may have applied to Lydia in the past, but now the word clearly looks forward to the end of the poem where Lydia's "inconsequentiality" will make her easy to ignore and discard. Another way in which Lydia's situation echoes that of her

former lovers is the time at which love (or attempted love) takes place—the night. However, while the *longas noctes* (7) of the shut-out lover's vigil are recalled by *inter- / lunia* (11-12), Lydia's interlunar night has an eerie, displacing quality absent from the shut-out lover's situation.[19] Lydia is not only spatially dislocated to the lonely and dark outdoors; she is located temporally in an in-between time (*inter-lunia*), which further serves to isolate her not only from humanity but at least momentarily from the world of nature (the natural cycles of the moon) as well.

*Matres . . . equorum*—not, as Nisbet and Hubbard suggest,[20] merely poetic diction for "mares"—continues the emphasis on things temporal. It further develops the impression of Lydia's advancing age (mother versus daughter) and thus underscores the untimeliness of her desire. The attribution to Lydia, a human being, of a *flagrans amor et libido* possessed by mares in heat creates a repulsive picture of Lydia's transformed sexuality as wild and animal-like. From Vergil's comment (*Georgics* 3.266-83) on the proverbially excessive lust of mares (*scilicet ante omnis furor est insignis equarum . . .*) we see that Lydia's comparison to a mare in heat signals not only an animal-like desire, but, more specifically, a desire known for its extremity. The repugnant image of Lydia as mare-in-heat represents the culmination of Lydia's indecorous movement toward desire and away from desirability. A virtually failed object of desire, she becomes a subject of overwhelming desire.

Lydia, however, while possessing the mare's lust, is not even the mare's equal in other important respects. Lydia's likely infertility due to her advanced age contrasts unfavorably with the mare's procreative abilities. In addition, the notion popular in antiquity that mares were sexually stimulated by the wind and could become pregnant by it without mating suggests the mare's further superiority to Lydia; having been aroused, the mare could often become pregnant without unions (*saepe sine ullis / coniugiis, Georgics* 3.274-75), while Lydia cannot even find mates (*moechos . . . arrogantis* 9).[21]

The placement of *laeta* before the *quod* of the clause to which it belongs, creates not only the *callida iunctura* of *questu / laeta* but also a momentary ambiguity about what *laeta* modifies; until the reader hears *pubes,* Lydia (the "you" of *flebis*) is what *laeta* ironically seems to modify. This hyperbaton abruptly juxtaposes Lydia's unhappiness and the happiness of the current-day youth. Their enjoyment of fresh ivy rather than somber myrtle (and by extension, young women to aging ones) recalls the increasingly rare visits to Lydia by the *iuvenes* at the poem's outset.[22]

Lydia's devastation becomes complete in the last two lines of the poem where she is casually, but thoroughly, repudiated, a dry leaf tossed to the water, winter's companion. The image of the leaf strips Lydia not only of her power to attract but of her desire as well. The dryness of leaves replaces the wetness of the aroused state (cf. *hippomanes* and *lentum virus, Georgics* 3.280-81). The emphasis on temporality throughout the poem and specifically on Lydia's aging is highlighted a final time by the association of Lydia with winter. Yet even here where a union (and thus at least a sort of love) with death might have been anticipated, Lydia is still kept at a distance from love, for she is dedicated by the youth to the Hebrus, which *in turn* is the companion of winter.[23] Lydia's ultimate isolation, a result of her diminishing sexual attraction, concludes the process begun by *parcius*.

But how are we to respond to this isolation? An obvious possibility is simply to replicate the disgust, as in Collinge's claim that *Odes* 1.25 is "the crudest and nastiest poem in Horace's lyrics."[24] However, if we choose not to succumb to such hysteria, a more sober strategy might be to see in the poem a self-evident truth about the unseemly quality of love and desire beyond the proper time for love.[25] Such criticism would thus see in the male perspective of the poet/lover a "human" perspective—that is, to suppose that we could just as easily substitute a male for Lydia (or a female for Horace, for that matter) without any substantive change in perspective. However, such sobriety fails to recognize how specifically it is *Lydia's* temporality that occasions the disgust. What is evoked by *parcius* is a notion of the beloved as firmly situated within the poet/lover's own idea of what the proper relationship should be between gender and time. Lydia's temporality occasions disgust because it stands outside of what is proper for a woman, but what is crucial to recognize is that such disgust is itself the consequence of a privileging of the male poet/lover's belief that temporality and eroticism cannot be joined. There is no reason that we must share such privileging.

*ODES* 2.5

Nondum subacta ferre iugum valet
cervice, nondum munia comparis
    aequare nec tauri ruentis
        in venerem tolerare pondus.
circa virentis est animus tuae 5
campos iuvencae, nunc fluviis gravem
    solantis aestum, nunc in udo
        ludere cum vitulis salicto
praegestientis. tolle cupidinem
immitis uvae. iam tibi lividos 10
    distinguet autumnus racemos
        purpureo varius colore,
iam te sequetur; currit enim ferox
aetas et illi quos tibi dempserit
    apponet annos. iam proterva 15
        fronte petet Lalage maritum,
dilecta quantum non Pholoe fugax,
non Chloris albo sic umero nitens
    ut pura nocturno renidet
        luna mari, Cnidiusve Gyges; 20
quem si puellarum insereres choro,
mire sagaces falleret hospites
    discrimen obscurum solutis
        crinibus ambiguoque vultu.

Not yet can she bear the yoke with neck subdued, not yet equal the duties of her mate, nor endure the weight of the bull rushing into love. Amid the green fields is

the mind of your heifer, now relieving the oppressive heat with river streams, now very eager to play in the damp willows with the calves. Take away your desire for the unripe grape. Soon for you autumn, varied in its purple color, will set off bluish clusters of grapes. Soon she will follow you; for cruel time runs on and will add to her the years it will have subtracted from you. Soon with forward brow Lalage will seek a mate, loved as was not fleeing Pholoe, not Chloris, shining with her white shoulders just as the bright moon gleams upon the night sea, or Cnidian Gyges, who, if you placed him in a troop of girls, would wonderfully deceive shrewd strangers, difficult to distinguish, with his loosened hair and androgynous face.

*Odes* 2.5, like *Odes* 1.25, deals with the effect on love and sexuality of time's passing, although here the focus is shifted from temporality that destroys the beloved's desirability to that which the would-be lover hopes will tame the beloved. Here, temporality appears to hold open the possibility that the beloved's elusiveness in the present will be transformed as she ages, but this hope for fulfilled desire will be defeated by the impossibility of controlling temporality itself. This theme of temporality as that which escapes the lover's control is expressed through the poem's dominant motif, "the inevitable cycle of time."[26] The time sequence *nondum . . . nondum . . . nunc . . . nunc . . . iam . . . iam . . . iam . . .* supports the construction of this motif.

Kiessling-Heinze sees the theme of the poem expressed already in its first word, *nondum;*[27] for Nisbet and Hubbard "in its emphatic position it [*nondum*] sums up the message of the poem."[28] This temporal adverb, which denies something up to and including the present, holds out the possibility of change in the future. The ambiguity of the poem's narrative outcome—that is, whether the addressee will finally be united with the beloved[29]—is anticipated by the open-ended quality of the future suggested by *nondum*. The poem's first word, like *parcius* in *Odes* 1.25, gives us a temporal perspective as soon as the poem begins.

We saw in *Odes* 1.25.1-8 that a combination of comparative adverbs and a negative found in conjunction with the present tense had the effect of creating a temporal perspective broader than the present. Horace's use of *nondum,* a temporal adverb that itself contains a negative, has a similar effect in *Odes* 2.5. Like *parcius,* it has an impact on the verb tenses and the images that follow. Just as *parcius* by its position modified both the participle *iunctas* (which followed it directly) and *quatiunt,* the main verb, so *nondum* influences both *subacta* and *valet*. *Nondum subacta* suggests that there will be a time when the "subduing" will have been completed, just as *nondum valet* denies a present state but suggests its future reversal. These three words—*nondum, subacta,* and *valet*—in combination open up a vista of past, present, and future in the poem's first line.

The metaphor for mating suggested by *subacta, ferre iugum,* and *munia*[30] becomes overt in the picture of the bull rushing into sexual intercourse: *nec tauri ruentis / in ve-*

*nerem tolerare pondus* (3-4). While some have called it gratuitously "crude,"[31] there is a point to the language.[32] It gives graphic expression to sexual desire and fulfillment, while at the same time, through the control of *nondum* and *nec,* postponing its satisfaction. It provides us with a statement about the impossibility of sexual intercourse in the present, along with the image or fantasy of its attainment.[33]

This tension between what Horace says and what he shows, between literal sense and the impression he makes with words, is a common feature of his poetry. We saw the same contrast between literal meaning and impression in *Odes* 1.25.1-8 where despite the predominance of the present tense, our vision was also of the past. Commager has written of the conflict between Horace's formal attitude and his emotional sympathies: "just as it is the Egyptian queen who steals that poem (1.37), so it is the haunting sound of *rosa quo locorum sera moretur* (1.38.3-4) that beguiles our imagination now. The rose lingers in our memory longer than Horace's renunciation of it."[34] So, in *Odes* 2.5.3-4 (. . . *nec tauri ruentis / in venerem tolerare pondus*) the image of desired intercourse outlasts its denial.

The erotic language in the poem continues, but with a shift in focus to the heifer and her activities (lines 5-9) from which the would-be lover is excluded. The youthfulness of the heifer is mirrored by the object of her interest (*virentis . . . campos* 5-6). The young heifer is interested in the correspondingly young/green fields. While *virentis,* through its appearance before the noun with which it agrees, opens up the idea of youth or greenness in a generalized way, the specific identification between the youth or "greenness" of the heifer and the object of her interest is strengthened by the interlocked word order in lines 5-6: . . . *virentis . . . tuae / campos iuvencae.*

The use of the word *gravem* (6), commonly used in reference to passion,[35] to describe the heifer's heat (*aestum* 7) reinforces the sexual potential of *aestum.* The heifer's ability to relieve her own heat (*fluviis . . . / solantis aestum* 6-7) contrasts with the would-be lover's unsatisfied desire. In addition, the sexual connotations of her intense eagerness[36] to frolic with the young calves in wet thickets (*in udo / ludere cum vitulis salicto / praegestientis* 7-9) once again excludes the would-be lover. The repeated *nunc . . . nunc* (6, 7), although specifically suggesting alternatives (now this, now that), by recalling *nondum . . . nondum* (1, 2), underlines the disparity between the heifer/girl's current activities and those for which her potential lover is eager. In addition, the alternation of relief or rest (*solantis*) and play (*ludere . . . praegestientis*) the heifer experiences shows a satisfaction on her part, which escapes the would-be lover.

The injunction to eliminate desire for the unripe grape, *tolle cupidinem / immitis uvae* (9-10), at first appears to cut off all hope for the potential lover based on the heifer's lack of readiness. (It should be noted that the word *immitis*—which in reference to fruit primarily means "harsh" or

"bitter," and in reference to people, "harsh" or "unkind"[37]— suggests lack of interest as another possible reason besides lack of readiness for the separation between the girl and the would-be lover.) The mention of autumn, with its ability to ripen grapes, introduces a possible hope that time will bring her closer to the desiring lover. Yet while autumn is endowing the grapes with their purple/bluish color (*purpureo . . . colore* 12, by transference, and *lividos* 10 modifying *racemos*), suggesting ripeness, the word *lividos* with its connotations of "bruising, envy, and malice" make the picture less pleasant. Reckford has pointed out that "the ironies explored in the fourth stanza may be traced back to the single focal image, *Autumnus,* for autumn, the giver of ripeness . . . is also the twilight season of fading, of oncoming death."[38] *Iam* (10), while initially hopeful for the poet (as a contrast to *nondum*), may ironically mean "all too soon."

Autumn's arrival (*iam tibi . . . colore* 10-12) holds out less hope than it initially seems to; such is the case as well with *iam te sequetur* (13). Nisbet and Hubbard have called *iam te sequetur* "a clear imitation of one of the most famous lines in ancient love-poetry, Sappho 1.21 (καὶ γὰρ αἰ φεύγει, ταχέως διώξει [for if she flees, she will quickly pursue])."[39] However, it is significant that Horace is imitating Sappho with a new twist, for the ambiguity of *sequetur* in Latin ("follow," i.e., "come later than" / "pursue") is not present in the Greek διώξει, which does not have the temporal sense of "follow." Therefore *iam te sequetur* prepares for the ironic explanation (*enim* 13) that time will give to the girl what it takes from the would-be lover. As Reckford observes: "The conceit, that time will add to the girl the years it 'takes from' her lover, shows the fallacy of wishful thinking, for the two will never meet, the one ripening, the other growing younger, in an ideal balance. There will instead be a new and worse disparity. Venus can be very funny—and very cruel."[40] Time's cruelty (*ferox aetas* 13-14), which recalls the negative personification of time suggested by *lividos . . . racemos,* is proven by the lack of evidence that the husband Lalage will boldly seek (*iam proterva / fronte petet Lalage maritum* 15-16) will be the would-be lover.[41] The hurried movement toward an imminent future (*iam . . . distinguet* 10-11, *iam . . . sequetur* 13, and *iam petet* 15-16[42]) with its triple use of *iam* (as compared with *nondum, nondum, nec* and *nunc, nunc*) recedes into memories of the past (*dilecta* 17-24), which bring not fulfillment but merely the dissipation or distancing of desire.[43]

The insistent time sequence begun by the poem's first word, *nondum,* switches in the final two strophes to a reverie on past time, which spins out from the perfect passive participle *dilecta,* modifying Lalage. The pressing movement toward the future is lost as well as the certainties of the indicative mood. Lalage is left behind with questions unanswered. There is no ablative of personal agent with *dilecta,* which leaves unstated by whom Lalage will have been loved. Is it the would-be lover? Is it someone other than the would-be lover? Will she be loved by the would-be lover while she seeks a different mate?

Former loves should logically recede in comparison to La-lage, loved more than they were (*dilecta quantum non . . .*). However, while there is a remote quality to these former loves—Pholoe's shyness (*fugax*), Chloris' almost statue-like white beauty, and Gyges' lack of gender-specific features—the expanding tricolon of Pholoe described by one word (*fugax*), Chloris by ten, and Gyges by more than a strophe, makes these past loves the focus of the present. Further, the surprising lack of distinction between Gyges and a girl creates a sense of uncertainty about the very object of desire, miming the uncertainty about whom Lalage will love and for whom she will be the object of desire. While the opening of the poem held out the possibility that the inevitability of time might eventually allow Lalage to be tamed and controlled (she is *nondum* [not yet] available to his desire), the end of the poem shows that the would-be lover, by wanting Lalage's desire to be temporally determined, is placed as well within the uncertainties of time. Not only does time make it impossible to be certain whom Lalage will love; it equally leaves uncertain what will be the focus of the would-be lover's erotic attention.

The many indications of uncertainty—the subjunctive mood in the present contrary-to-fact condition, the use of *fallo* (deceive), and the appearance of *ambiguo*—in the poem's final strophe all contribute to an open-ended conclusion for the poem. The excitation of the poem's beginning and the postponement of fulfilled desire (*nondum*) are curiously gone by the end of the poem. The possibilities about the future opened up by *nondum* are never neatly resolved. Thus, while in *Odes* 1.25 it appeared as if temporality condemned the beloved to be nothing more than an object of lovers who themselves stood mysteriously outside of time, here instead it is temporality that places the beloved in a realm that defeats the would-be lover's own attempt to control time.

### ODES 3.7

Quid fles, Asterie, quem tibi candidi
primo restituent vere Favonii
    Thyna merce beatum,
        constantis iuvenem fide,
Gygen? ille Notis actus ad Oricum (5)
post insana Caprae sidera frigidas
    noctes non sine multis
        insomnis lacrimis agit.
atqui sollicitae nuntius hospitae,
suspirare Chloen et miseram tuis (10)
    dicens ignibus uri,
        temptat mille vafer modis.
ut Proetum mulier perfida credulum
falsis impulerit criminibus nimis
    casto Bellerophontae 15
        maturare necem refert;
narrat paene datum Pelea Tartaro
Magnessam Hippolyten dum fugit abstinens;
    et peccare docentis
        fallax historias movet, (20)
frustra. nam scopulis surdior Icari
voces audit adhuc integer. at tibi
    ne vicinus Enipeus

plus iusto placeat cave,
quamvis non alius flectere equum sciens (25)
aeque conspicitur gramine Martio,
    nec quisquam citus aeque
        Tusco denatat alveo.
prima nocte domum claude neque in vias
sub cantu querulae despice tibiae, (30)
    et te saepe vocanti
        duram difficilis mane.

Why do you weep, Asterie, for Gyges, a youth of constant faith, whom the bright Favonian winds will restore to you at the beginning of spring, rich with Bithynian goods? He, driven to Oricum by the South wind after the rising of Capra's wild stars, spends cold nights sleepless not without many tears. But a messenger from his excited host, Chloe, saying that she is sighing and burning unhappily for your lover, crafty, tests him in a thousand ways. He recounts how Proetus' treacherous wife drove him, credulous, with false accusations to hasten death for too chaste Bellerophon; he tells of Peleus almost given to Tartarus while fleeing, without touching her, from Magnesian Hippolyte, and, tricky, promotes stories teaching him to stray, in vain. For more deaf than the rocks of Icarus he hears the words, faithful up to now. But lest your neighbor Enipeus please you more than is right, beware, although no other equally good at controlling a horse is seen on the grass of Mars' field, nor anyone equally swift swims down the Tuscan river. When night comes, close up your house and do not look down into the street at the song of the plaintive flute, and to him always calling you hard-hearted, stay hard to get.

In our discussions of *Odes* 1.25 and *Odes* 2.5 we saw how attending to the implications of an initial temporal adverb revealed both a desire for temporality not to be extended beyond the experience of the beloved to that of the lover, and the impossibility of such a desire being achieved. In each of these poems, a temporal adverb—*parcius* in *Odes* 1.25 and *nondum* in *Odes* 2.5—helped to establish a temporal perspective that affected how both lover and beloved are understood in the entire poem. In *Odes* 3.7 we look once again at a significant temporal adverb. This time, though, it makes its appearance not at the beginning, but two-thirds of the way through the poem. Despite this placement, it plays a role as important as that played by the two initial temporal adverbs already discussed. What we find in this case is that the temporal adverb subtly prepares us for the surprising realization that both lover and beloved are enmeshed in temporality. Thus, while the first two poems struggle to limit temporality to a condition of the beloved, here instead temporality is acknowledged as a predicament involving both lover and beloved. We shall see, though, that even when the lover's relation to temporality is acknowledged along with that of the beloved, she is seen both as more vulnerable than he to the vicissitudes of time and as responsible for ensuring her lover's continuing fidelity.

In *Odes* 3.7 the speaker asks Asterie why she is weeping for her lover Gyges who, unhappily detained on his journey home, will be restored to her at the beginning of spring. Gyges, firm in his loyalty, passes cold, sleepless nights. Although a go-between from his host tells him stories designed to compromise his fidelity, Gyges remains faithful (*adhuc integer* 22).

*Adhuc* is the first indication that anything might alter Gyges' faithfulness. Whether one interprets *adhuc* as "still" or "so far," its appearance with *integer* adds a temporal potential to our perception of Gyges' fidelity by suggesting that his defenses might someday be broken down. *Adhuc,* which affirms something starting in the past and proceeding up to the present, functions as the opposite of *nondum* (discussed above in *Odes* 2.5), which denies something starting in the past and proceeding up to the present. In both cases, though, a tension is opened up about whether the future will confirm the hopes of the present—in the first case for a fulfillment of the potential lover's desire, and in the second for a continuation of Gyges's fidelity.

The importance of *adhuc* has gone unrecognized by most recent Horatian scholars.[44] Williams, for example, in his commentary on and translation of Book 3 of the *Odes,* makes no mention of *adhuc;* indeed, he even fails to translate it. The remarks of Pasquali, written in 1920, have been largely ignored by later scholars. Having noticed the sense of "evil prophecy" (*cattivo augurio*) introduced by *adhuc,* he questions how long Gyges will remain faithful.[45] The oxymoron *surdior . . . / voces audit* (21-22) with its play on deafness and hearing, positioned directly before *adhuc integer,* prepares the way for an ironic use of *adhuc* with *integer.*

Two previous uses of the word *integer* in the *Odes* provide a further suggestion that we should not take *adhuc integer* at face value. The final strophe of *Odes* 2.4 suggests an ironic interpretation of *integer* in that poem:

> bracchia et vultum teretesque suras
> integer laudo; fuge suspicari
> cuius octavum trepidavit aetas
>     claudere lustrum.

(21-24)

Uninvolved I praise her arms and face and smooth calves; stop being suspicious of one whose age has hurried to complete forty years.

In these lines the speaker seems to say "I praise this girl impartially. Don't worry about me—I'm too old for love." However, that he chooses to linger over the details of the girl's beauty, part by part, using the sensuous-sounding word *teretesque* with its "tactile" dimension, leads one to believe that *integer* as "uninvolved," "innocent," or literally "untouched," is other than straightforward. If the speaker were convincingly beyond suspicion because of age, he would not make such an issue of it. The placement of *Odes* 2.5 immediately after these lines continues the theme of the problematic relationship between aging and sexuality. The irony of Horace's use of *integer* in *Odes* 2.4 suggests that we read his use of it here suspiciously. Of course, *integer* appears very prominently as the first word of *Odes* 1.22 (*Integer vitae*), where its meaning must be revised in the context of the poem.[46]

In *Odes* 3.7, then, if Gyges' future fidelity cannot be taken for granted, we must reevaluate the speaker's reassurances to Asterie about Gyges' return (1-6). The definitive quality of the future tense *restituent* (2) is called into question. The description of Gyges as a young man of steadfast loyalty (*constantis iuvenem fide* 4) sounds less believable. Williams remarks that "the archaic form of the genitive *fide . . .* adds an impressiveness of tone to the assertion of his constancy."[47] This may be, but the "impressiveness" becomes mockserious when read in light of the description of Gyges as *adhuc integer.*[48]

There is another Gyges in classical literature, who may be significant to our understanding of the Gyges in this ode: that of Herodotus *Histories* 1.8-12 and Plato *Republic* 2.359d.[49] Gyges also appears in Archilochus, fragment 19 West, and Herodotus states that his Gyges is the same as that of Archilochus. In Horace, Gyges is described as *Thyna merce beatum* (3), "rich with Bithynian goods." In the Archilochus fragment the focus is on Gyges' wealth (πολύχρυσος, of much gold) and power, while in Herodotus (*Histories* 1.14), Gyges sends gold and silver gifts to Delphi. Finally, in Plato, Gyges has a gold ring. The notion of wealth, then, is the first connection with the Gyges of Greek literature. Perhaps more important, though, the stories of Gyges in the *Histories* and the *Republic,* while varying because of the different purposes they fulfill in each work, contain the same basic love plot with negative resonance for the Horatian Gyges, that of the man who kills the king with the help of the queen and takes over the kingdom.[50]

In Plato's version, Gyges, in possession of a magic ring that can render him invisible at his will, seduces the wife of the king and with her help kills him and takes over the kingdom. In Herodotus' story, Gyges is forced by Candaules, the king of Lydia, to do something against his principles, namely, to see the queen naked. (Candaules, possessed of a passion for his wife, thinks she is the most beautiful of women and demands that Gyges see her to confirm this.) Gyges is caught by the queen and given the choice of either being killed or killing the king and marrying her. He chooses the latter course of action.

At the beginning of Herodotus' account, Gyges is portrayed as one of the most loyal men in the kingdom and as a close friend of the king. He is an innocent man (*integer*?) who, to save his own life, kills the king, obedience to whom had earlier required him to do wrong (see the queen naked). In Plato's version of the story, Gyges is not "innocent." He is a man who acts purely from self-interest without any sense of justice. In fact the desire exhibited by Plato's Gyges to possess queen and kingdom is reminiscent of the possessiveness shown not by Gyges, but by Candaules, in Herodotus. (As one critic has noted, Candaules' treatment of his wife as an object to be seen by another man violates the customs of the marriage bond.)[51] Herodotus' Gyges, although initially innocent and loyal to his king, when threatened, accedes to the queen in order to save his own life; unlike Peleus and Bellerophon

(13-18), who both reject the advances of their hosts' wives, he does give in to a powerful woman.

In using the name Gyges, Horace calls to mind a well-known figure from the Greek tradition whose acquisition of another's wife (albeit with different motives in the two versions) cannot help but influence our perception of the situation of the Gyges of *Odes* 3.7. The recollection of these two versions of the Gyges story prevents us from having complete confidence in the ability of Asterie's Gyges to resist temptation, the persuasiveness of others, or unjust acts. While it is the Herodotean Gyges whose initial innocence is particularly recalled by *integer* in *Odes* 3.7, the Gyges of Plato is, significantly, set up by Glaucon, who narrates the story, as an example of what both the unjust and the just man would do given no societal constraints. Recollection of these two Gygeses—the one given no real choice but to take up with the queen, the other acting solely out of his own acquisitive interests—clearly reinforces the ironic sense of *adhuc integer* in *Odes* 3.7 and undermines confidence in Gyges' fidelity.

*Adhuc integer* has another effect besides making us doubt what we have heard so far in the poem. It subtly prepares us for the *para prosdokian* which immediately follows: the speaker's warning to Asterie, who we suddenly discover is a serious candidate for infidelity herself. He warns Asterie not to find Enipeus too pleasing, although there is no better horseman or faster swimmer. He tells her to close up her home as soon as evening comes, to ignore the flute music serenading her from the streets, and to remain "hard to get" (*difficilis*) though she is often called hard-hearted (*duram*).

The speaker's warning to Asterie is not only surprising, but gently humorous. By cataloguing Enipeus' "manly virtues" (riding and swimming), and by claiming that in these he has no equal (*non alius . . . aeque . . . nec quisquam . . . aeque* 25-27), the speaker makes Enipeus quite an attractive figure.[52] Indeed the verb "is seen" (*conspicitur* 26) and the adjective "neighboring" (*vicinus* 23) specifically point to Enipeus' visual appeal and his physical proximity. His frequent contact (albeit verbal) with Asterie (*te saepe vocanti / duram* 31-32), reminiscent of the thousand methods of persuasion (*mille . . . modis* 12) and the words (*voces* 22) used on Gyges by the clever go-between, emphasizes the persistence of Enipeus' courting. Pasquali has rightly noticed that Horace is using language in such a way as to tempt Asterie.[53] The speaker indirectly entices Asterie with his description, while literally telling her to ignore Enipeus' advances. This strategy is reminiscent of the ironic final strophe of *Odes* 2.4 (mentioned above), where the poet's literal message that he praises Phyllis "uninvolved" (*integer*) because of his age is countered by the sensuousness of the language used to describe her.

The go-between in *Odes* 3.7 is described as *vafer* (12) and *fallax* (20) for testing Gyges and for promoting stories teaching him to stray: *et peccare docentis / fallax historias*

*movet* (19-20). The parallel here to the speaker's own role in counseling Asterie suggests that the speaker is himself another deceiver, and that Asterie, perhaps like Proetus, who believes his wife's false accusations of attempted seduction on the part of Bellerophon, is too trusting of false reports (*Proetum . . . credulum* 13). There seems no way to explain how the speaker can know what is happening to Gyges on Oricum, and thus his story seems to exist merely to scare Asterie into believing that Gyges might not remain faithful.[54] Indeed, the statement of Gyges' faithfulness "to this point" (*adhuc integer*) seems a pointed warning to Asterie that somehow her fidelity is required for Gyges to remain faithful.

The assurances Horace offered to Asterie in the beginning of the poem are thrown into doubt. And even if Gyges remains faithful, perhaps Asterie would really prefer Enipeus. Perhaps this is why she is weeping. The simple question that begins the poem—*Quid fles, Asterie?*—is by the end of the poem no longer simple. The situation Horace has constructed creates more questions than it answers, and the primary function of such questions is to cast doubt on whether desire can itself be removed from the uncertainties of time. Indeed, the attempt at closure in the conclusion of the poem confirms the uncertain temporality lurking within the speaker's pledge of Gyges' faithfulness. The final advice to Asterie—*difficilis mane* ("stay hard to get")—while ostensibly paralleling the claim that Gyges is *adhuc integer,* casts doubt on the very possibility of a faithfulness or integrity that stands outside of time. The move from *integer* to *difficilis* encapsulates the impossibility of denying time: while Gyges is said to possess an *integritas* that presumably no temporality would threaten, the uncertain nature of such integrity is revealed by the temporal adverb to which it is attached. In contrast, the advice to Asterie that she remain *difficilis* acknowledges temporality even as it seeks to deny it. By being *difficilis,* by situating her resolve in relation to the demands of others, Asterie would open herself to the temporality and contingency that *integritas* seeks (impossibly) to deny.

Finally, we must note that while Gyges and Asterie both participate in the predicament of temporality, their relation to it is not identical. The male lover is portrayed as resisting temptation alone, while Asterie needs the speaker of the poem to dissuade her from infidelity. Still further, Asterie is expected to function, as her name ("starry one") would suggest, as a beacon for Gyges on his voyage home. Thus her fidelity, rather than having any intrinsic value, is instrumental for ensuring the faithfulness of Gyges. By tempting Asterie to look at him (cf. "do not look down" *neque . . . despice* 29-30), Enipeus threatens to disrupt Asterie's status as subservient to Gyges. We realize, then, that the danger presented to the erotic by temporality is not shared equally by Gyges and Asterie. It is the female beloved who is seen as both more vulnerable to temptation and as responsible for maintaining both her own and her lover's fidelity.

*Notes*

1. For an expanded version of the following discussion of *Odes* 1.25, which interprets further the identification of Lydia with nature, see my article "Horace *Odes* 1.25: Temporality, Gender, and Desire."

   While not "strictly" a temporal adverb, *parcius* (more sparingly) functions as such in this ode.

   Syndikus (*Die Lyrik des Horaz: Eine Interpretation der Oden Band 1,* 248) points out the words, including *parcius,* that signal time's inevitable passing: "'Seltener,' 'und nicht,' 'früher,' 'schon immer weniger' sind die Leitworte, die das unabwendbare Weitergehen der Zeit rücksichtslos aufzeigen" ['More seldom,' 'and not,' 'formerly,' 'already less and less,' are the chief expressions that ruthlessly show the inevitable continuing of time]. See also La Penna ("Tre Poesie Espressionistiche di Orazio," 191), who notes the comparative *parcius* at the beginning of the ode and the return of the comparative with *prius, minus et minus,* and *magis.*

2. Most commentators have recognized the combination of past and present in lines 1-8. Boyle ("Edict of Venus," 176) sees strophes 1-2 as a distinct temporal unit concerned with the past and present. Pöschl speaks of the present and the remembrance of the past ("Horaz C. 1,25" 188-89). Catlow ("Horace *Odes* I,25 and IV,13: A Reinterpretation," 815) aptly states that "the first two stanzas imply a whole history and define the poem's immediate context." Kiessling-Heinze's temporal description of strophes 1-2 indicates an awareness of the opposition between past and present: "Die beiden ersten Strophen schildern das Jetzt und zugleich den Gegensatz des Einst" [Both of the first two strophes describe the present and, at the same time, the contrast of the past] (*Q. Horatius Flaccus: Oden und Epoden,* 109). Collinge (*The Structure of Horace's Odes,* 114), however, defines lines 1-8 as "the present—Lydia's fading powers of attraction," thus missing the careful mingling of past and present in these lines.

3. A further sense of violence may be latent in *protervi* through the influence upon it of *protero* (trample down). See Ernout and Meillet, *Dictionnaire Étymologique de la Langue Latine,* under *protervus.* For the connecting of *proterve* with *protero* as well as a meaning for the verb denoting what a bull does *in appetitu coitus feminarum* [in his desire for sexual union with females], see Donatus on Terence *Hecyra* 503, as quoted by Maltby, *A Lexicon of Ancient Latin Etymologies,* under *protervus.*

4. For *iungo* as a term used to denote the "joining" of sexual intercourse, see Glare, *The Oxford Latin Dictionary,* under *iungo* 3b, "to unite sexually"; and Adams, *The Latin Sexual Vocabulary,* 179. For another example of this sense of *iungo* in Horace, cf. *Odes* 1.33.8 (*iungentur capreae lupis*). Cf. also *iugum* of the sexual bond (at least metaphorically) in *Odes*

2.5.1 (*ferre iugum*) and *Odes* 3.9.18 (*Venus / diductosque iugo cogit aeneo*).

5. Porter ("Horace, *Carmina,* IV,12," 77) points out that the unbroken sleep of Lydia in *Odes* 1.25.3 and 7-8 contrasts ironically with the *perpetuus sopor* of Quintilius in the preceding ode (1.24.5).

6. Cf., e.g., Plautus *Curculio* 147-55 (*pessuli, heus pessuli, vos saluto lubens . . .*). On the personification of the door in the *exclusus amator* motif in Latin love poetry, see Copley, *Exclusus Amator: A Study in Latin Love Poetry,* 28-42; for the representation of the door in terms more appropriate for a woman, see also Hallett, "*Ianua iucunda:* The Characterization of the Door in Catullus 67." Pucci, "Lingering on the Threshold," discusses the significance in Propertian elegy of the *limen* as that which is to be transgressed.

7. For the erotic overtones of Horace's use of *amare* with an inanimate subject elsewhere in the *Odes,* cf. *Odes* 2.3.9-11: *quo pinus ingens albaque populus / umbram hospitalem consociare amant / ramis?;* and *Odes* 3.16.9-11: *aurum per medios ire satellites / et perrumpere amat saxa potentius / ictu fulmineo.*

8. Nisbet and Hubbard (*Odes Book 1,* 293) translate *amatque* as "keeps to," saying "Horace uses an expression appropriate to a chaste woman."

9. Catlow, "Horace *Odes* I,25 and IV,13: A Reinterpretation," 815 (hereafter "Horace *Odes* I,25 and IV,13").

10. Copley, *Exclusus Amator: A Study in Latin Love Poetry,* 59.

11. Boyle, "Edict of Venus," 177.

12. Collinge, *The Structure of Horace's Odes,* 52.

13. Nisbet and Hubbard, *Odes Book 1,* 294.

14. See under *perire* in Pichon, *Index Verborum Amatoriorum,* 230-31.

15. I follow the bipartite division of the poem (1-8 and 9-20) made by Collinge (*The Structure of Horace's Odes,* 114) and Boyle ("Edict of Venus," 176). Others divide it into three parts: 1-8, 9-16, and 17-20, as, e.g., Kiessling-Heinze (*Q. Horatius Flaccus: Oden und Epoden,* 109); Syndikus (*Die Lyrik des Horaz: Eine Interpretation der Oden Band 1,* 250), who nevertheless acknowledges that the sentence structure divides the poem in two; and Pöschl ("Horaz C. 1,25," 188-89).

16. Boyle ("Edict of Venus," 176) sees *invicem* as the key word in the ode, "with its overt promulgation of the inevitability of change." He also recognizes its structural importance as the word that divides the two parts of the poem. In my view, *parcius,* with its initial position in the poem and its comparative degree, is even more important than *invicem,* for it sets up a temporal perspective that affects the entire poem. The effectiveness of *invicem* is due in part to the preparation *parcius* provides.

17. Here, as earlier in the poem, emotional content is carried by words that reflect on Lydia's condition but are grammatically construed with her surroundings (*in solo . . . angiportu*).

18. Catlow rightly remarks ("Horace *Odes* I,25 and IV,13," 814) that Horace is projecting his desires for Lydia into the future rather than reacting to "an accomplished fact."

19. Cf. the disquieting effect of *imminente luna* in *Odes* 1.4.5.

20. Nisbet and Hubbard, *Odes Book 1,* 297.

21. Catlow's point is well taken that *matres equorum* implies procreative value to the horse's sexuality, something presumably no longer available to Lydia at her advanced age ("Horace *Odes* I,25 and IV,13," 816).

22. Fresh ivy, gray myrtle, and dry leaves parallel three stages of life: youth, maturity, old age. Cf. Strato *Palatine Anthology* 12.215 for these periods represented by spring, summer, and the stubble (of old age). The *pubes* prefer ivy, which is evergreen, even to myrtle, which is associated with Venus (cf., e.g., Vergil *Georgics* 1.28). For dry leaves (old women) they have no use at all. In *Odes* 1.25 Horace shows Lydia's progression from youth (in the past) to maturity (in the present) to old age (in the future). In the dramatic time of the poem (the present), Lydia is already at the "myrtle" stage; by the end (which lies in the future), she will have reached old age.

  I take *atque* (18) as "than," not "and." For discussion of this issue, see Nisbet and Hubbard, *Odes Book 1,* 298.

23. I think my interpretation of the poem works with either reading (*Hebro* or *Euro*), however, following Lee, "Horace, *Odes* 1.25: The Wind and the River," I see no need for the emendation to *Euro.*

24. Collinge, *The Structure of Horace's Odes,* 52. For a critique of the sort of approach to a text that focuses on what is represented in the text to the exclusion of the literary purpose or function of that representation, see Suleiman's comments on Andrea Dworkin's criticism of Bataille's *Histoire de l'oeil* in "Pornography, Transgression, and the Avant-Garde: Bataille's *Story of the Eye.*" Suleiman's own strategy is summed up as follows: "a feminist reading of Bataille's and other modern male writers' pornographic fictions must seek to avoid both the blindness of the textual reading, which sees nothing but *écriture,* and the blindness of the ultrathematic reading which sees nothing but the scene and its characters" (129-30).

25. See, e.g., Commager, *The Odes of Horace: A Critical Study,* 247-49 (hereafter *Odes of Horace*), and Boyle, "Edict of Venus," 174-78. Boyle, while acknowledging Lydia's specificity ("the poet's . . . presentation of the terrible consequences of time's passing upon one specific, and especially vulnerable, human individual"), concludes that "Horace's concern in I.25 is not so much with vituperation (although the mode of presentation is vituperative) as with change and the human consequences of change—hence the explicit nature symbolism of the final stanza, which places the personal devastation to be suffered by Lydia within the context of a universal law of nature" (176, 177). It is this leap of Horace's to the universal which, while aptly described by Boyle, remains unexamined. Catlow ("Horace, *Odes* I,25 and IV,13") recognizes the speaker's personal stake in the situation of the poem, which undercuts his own (and most commentators') attempts at universalizing his and Lydia's situation: "To interpret this poem, with Commager, as a moral statement about the unseemly futility of defying the decorum of nature and change is to ignore its mood, structure and the assumptions with which we are clearly intended to approach it, for it is vital to remember that Horace is not disgusted with an accomplished fact but himself wills this moral and physical depravity on a woman who, we are to understand, has formerly rejected him. The development of this poem sheds as much light on the emotional state of a rejected lover as on the moral disaster wrought b[y] untimely sexuality" (814). For a critique of Boyle's alliance with Horace's universalizing, see chapter 1 (pp. 10-12).

26. Boyle, "The Edict of Venus," 180.

27. Kiessling-Heinze, *Q. Horatius Flaccus: Oden und Epoden,* 180.

28. Nisbet and Hubbard, *A Commentary on Horace: Odes Book 2,* 80 (hereafter *Odes Book 2*).

29. There are two distinct but related issues concerning *Odes* 2.5 that have attracted scholarly attention. First is the issue of whether *Odes* 2.5 is addressed to Horace himself or to someone else who remains unnamed. (See Nisbet and Hubbard, *Odes Book 2,* 77, who state that "the primary problem of this poem was already posed by pseudo-Acronian scholia: '*incertum est quem adloquatur hac ode, utrum amicorum aliquem an semet ipsum*'" [It is uncertain whom he addresses in this ode—one of his friends or himself].) The second concerns the poem's outcome, specifically, whether the would-be lover finally gets together with the girl. I am inclined toward taking the poem as a soliloquy, that is, as the poet addressing himself. Boyle ("Edict of Venus") points out in support of this view the fact that *Odes* 2.5 "is the only amatory ode in which the name of the addressee is not mentioned" (179). However to preserve the ambiguity about the addressee, I have chosen to refer to the "would-be lover" or the "potential lover" rather than the poet/lover. As for the poem's outcome, I agree once again with Boyle, who finds the outcome intentionally unresolved: "[The] realization of the unbridgeable gulf between Lalage and himself

produces the ambiguous final statement (15-16), in which *maritum* ('spouse') is purposefully vague; it is no longer obvious, as was implied in the first supporting statement (10-12), that Lalage's husband will be himself" (180). This view and the view that completely rejects an outcome of union between Lalage and the would-be lover depend in large part upon not taking *tibi* (10) as a dative of advantage, allowing for the ambiguity of *sequetur* (13), not interpreting the statement about time in lines 14-16 as favorable to Horace, and not assuming that *maritum* (16) refers to Horace.

A different approach to the poem has been taken by Quinn (*Horace: The Odes*, 205-8), who takes the poem as addressed to a husband who, married to quite a young girl, must be patient until she is sexually more mature; and by Fantham ("The Mating of Lalage: Horace *Odes* 2.5"), who takes the poem as "addressed to a man betrothed or contemplating marriage, and concerned not with the readiness of the girl for sexual congress, but with her maturity for breeding" (48).

30. For discussion of these expressions as erotic, see Adams, *The Latin Sexual Vocabulary*, 155-56 and 207 on *subigo*, 207-8 on *ferre iugum*, and 164 on *munus*; cf. also Nisbet and Hubbard, *Odes Book 2*, 80-81. On *iugum*, see also the discussion above of *iunctas* in *Odes* 1.25.1, and *iugo . . . aeneo* (*Odes* 3.9.18). There is an echo of *Nondum subacta ferre iugum . . .* (2.5.1) in line 2 of the ode that immediately follows (*Cantabrum indoctum iuga ferre nostra . . .*); in 2.6, however, the context has switched from sexual to political.

31. See Nisbet and Hubbard, *Odes Book 2*, 81 on *ruentis in venerem*.

32. Minadeo ("Sexual Symbolism in Horace's Love Odes," 410), points out the use of *ruo* in *Odes* 1.19.9, where the poet is (figuratively speaking) the object of Venus' sexual assault (*in me tota ruens Venus*).

33. For other examples of the imaging of the fulfillment of desire in the context of its denial, see my discussion of *Odes* 1.23 below.

34. Commager, *Odes of Horace*, 117-18.

35. Cf., e.g., Horace *Epodes* 11.2: *amore percussum gravi*.

36. On *praegestientis,* Minadeo ("Sexual Symbolism in Horace's Love Odes," 402) points out both the intensive aspect of *prae-* and its temporal suggestion of "beforehand."

37. See Jones, "Horace, Four Girls and the Other Man," 34; see also Glare, *The Oxford Latin Dictionary*, under *immitis*.

38. Reckford, "Some Studies in Horace's Odes on Love," 28.

39. Nisbet and Hubbard, *Odes Book 2*, 86.

40. Reckford, *Horace*, 104.

41. Nisbet and Hubbard assume the husband will be the addressee: "Though the mate is unspecified, *te* must be implied" (*Odes Book 2*, 89), as does Cairns (*Generic Composition in Greek and Roman Poetry*, 86), who sees *Odes* 2.5 as a particular variant on the "threat-prophecy" in which "the speaker can say that the addressee will grow to an age to feel the same sentiments as the speaker but with happy outcome." See note 29 above, for further discussion of this issue.

42. The manuscripts are divided on the reading; either *petet* or *petit* works well. *Petet* continues the pattern of *iam* plus the future tense; *iam . . . petit* suggests that "the future has already arrived."

43. Cf. the end of *Odes* 1.25 where Lydia's desire is forgotten by the *pubes* and the end of *Odes* 4.1 where fulfillment is found only in dreams.

44. However, Porter (*Horace's Poetic Journey: A Reading of Odes 1-3*, 175) acknowledges that *adhuc* (and *difficilis*) "seem not to rule out entirely the possibility of passing flirtations"; and Quinn (*The Odes*, 260) suggests that *adhuc integer* "[d]oesn't so much imply that he may yet give in to Chloe, but that this is Gyges' first port of call and further temptations can be counted on to follow." Owens ("*Nuntius Vafer et Fallax:* An Alternate Reading of Horace, C 3.7," 163) cites Pseudo-Acro on the possibly ominous implications of *adhuc:* "adhuc integer: adhuc continens tamquam eum demonstret trahi posse in posterum, si diutius moretur" [as if "holding back to this point" shows that he could be led astray for the future, if he were to delay longer].

45. Pasquali, *Orazio Lirico*, 466.

46. See my discussion of *Odes* 1.22 below.

47. Williams, *The Third Book of Horace's Odes*, 69.

48. Boyle's comments ("Edict of Venus," 185-86) on the "comic morality-play aspect" of lines 5-22 indirectly support the idea that *adhuc integer* cannot be taken at face value.

49. Kiessling refers to the wealthy Gyges of Archilochus in the second edition of his commentary (1890), a reference later deleted by Heinze. Cf. Harrison, "Horace, *Odes* 3.7: An Erotic *Odyssey*?" 186, and Mutschler, "Eine Interpretation der Horazode '*Quid fles Asterie*,'" 127, note 9. See also Mutschler, 128, note 19, on the relevance of the Herodotean Gyges.

The other appearances in the *Odes* of the name Gyges—2.5.20, discussed above (page 35), and 2.17.14 and 3.4.69 (both references to the mythological giant *centimanus Gyges*)—do not seem relevant to this poem.

50. For discussion of the Gyges story in Herodotus, see Dewald, "Women and Culture in Herodotus' *Histo-*

ries," 107-09, and Konstan, "The Stories in Herodotus' *Histories* Book I," 11-13.

51. Konstan, "The Stories in Herodotus' *Histories* Book I," 13.

52. The significance for the poem, if any, of the name Enipeus is not obvious. There may be an intended recollection of the attractive river-god Enipeus with whom Tyro is in love; cf. Homer *Odyssey* 11.235-59. Cf. also, Propertius *Elegies* 3.19.13-14 (*testis Thessalico flagrans Salmonis Enipeo, / quae voluit liquido tota subire deo.*), where Enipeus is the object of great lust.

53. Most commentators have missed the tongue-in-cheek nature of Horace's warning to Asterie. Copley, *Exclusus Amator: A Study in Latin Love Poetry,* sees Horace throughout the poem in the role of "interested bystander, the old family friend" presenting the "claims of the accepted moral code" (66). Although Bradshaw in "Horace and the Therapeutic Myth: *Odes* 3.7; 3,11, and 3,27," recognizes the "sensual image" of Enipeus, he maintains that Horace "adopts the tone of a stern uncle in addressing Asterie" (159, 156). Cairns, *Generic Composition in Greek and Roman Poetry,* defines *Odes* 3.7 as an inverse komos because, in his opinion, the poet is working against the interests of Enipeus, the excluded lover (208-11). At least two commentators, though, have noticed the seductive (and therefore somewhat ironic) undercurrent of Horace's warning to Asterie. Owens, in a paper entitled "The Go-Between: An Interpretation of Horace, Ode 3.7," sees the poet as an agent, like the clever slave in New Comedy, sent from Enipeus to seduce Asterie. (An expanded version of this thesis appears in Owens's "*Nuntius Vafer et Fallax:* An Alternate Reading of Horace, C 3.7.") Of particular interest is his suggestion that the end of the poem can be read as an injunction for Asterie to not look down on, i.e., reject, Enipeus (*despice*), but (with a comma placed between *difficilis* and *mane*) to wait (*mane*) and hear him out ("*Nuntius Vafer et Fallax,*" 166-67). Pasquali (*Orazio Lirico,* 466-67) has noted several examples of how Horace admonishes Asterie to be faithful, but with words that seem intended to emphasize more than necessary the degree of temptation ("ma con parole che sembrano studiarsi di mettere in rilievo anche piu del necessario quanto forte sia la tentazione" [467]). Concerning the poet's advice not to find Enipeus pleasing *plus iusto* (more than is right), he asks "qual é il iustum? [what is the right amount?]" (467). He sees the poet helping Enipeus to victory both through the *quamvis* clause enumerating his virtues and, at the end of the poem, by mischievously eliciting sympathy for him from Asterie.

54. Bradshaw's view in "Horace and the Therapeutic Myth: *Odes* 3,7; 3,11, and 3,27" is that the poet, through the use of mythological stories, attempts not to reassure Asterie, but to scare her into maintaining the proper behavior befitting a Roman wife, i.e., being faithful. He calls this kind of persuasion (which he also sees in *Odes* 3.11 and 3.27) the "therapeutic use of myth."

*Bibliography*

Adams, J. N. *The Latin Sexual Vocabulary.* Baltimore, 1982.

Boyle, A. J. "The Edict of Venus: An Interpretive Essay on Horace's Amatory Odes." *Ramus* 2 (1973): 163-88.

Bradshaw, A. "Horace and the Therapeutic Myth: Odes 3, 7; 3, 11; and 3, 27." *Hermes* 106 (1978): 156-76.

Cairns, Francis. *Generic Composition in Greek and Roman Poetry.* Edinburgh, 1972.

Catlow, L. W. "Horace, *Odes* I, 25, and IV, 13: A Reinterpretation." *Latomus* 35 (1976): 813-21.

Collinge, N. E. *The Structure of Horace's Odes.* London, 1961.

Commager, Steele. *The Odes of Horace: A Critical Study.* New Haven and London, 1962.

Copely, Frank. *Exclusus Amator: A Study in Latin Love Poetry.* Baltimore, 1956.

Dewald, Carolyn. "Women and Culture in Herodotus' *Histories.*" *Women's Studies* 8 (1981): 93-127.

Ernout, A., and A. Meillet. *Dictionnaire Étymologique de la Langue Latine.* 3d edition. Paris, 1951.

Fantham, Elaine. "The Mating of Lalage: Horace, *Odes* 2.5." *Liverpool Classical Monthly* 4 (1979): 47-52.

Glare, P. G. W., ed. *The Oxford Latin Dictionary.* Oxford, 1982.

Hallett, Judith P. "*Ianua iucunda:* The Characterization of the Door in Catullus 67." *Collection Latomus: Studies in Latin Literature and Roman History* 2, edited by C. Deroux, 106-22. Brussels, 1980.

Jones, F. "Horace, Four Girls and the Other Men." *Liverpool Classical Monthly* 8.3 (1983): 34-37.

Kiessling, A. *Q. Horatious Flaccus: Oden und Epoden.* 11th ed., revised by R. Heinze, afterword and bibliography by E. Burck. Zurich and Berlin, 1964.

Konstan, David. "The Stories in Herodotus' *Histories* Book I." *Helios* 10 (1983): 1-22.

La Penna, Antonio. "Tre Poesie Espressionistiche di Orazio." *Belfagor* 18 (1963): 181-93.

Lee, M. Owen. "Horace, *Odes* 1.25: The Wind and the River." *The Augustan Age* 4 (1985): 39-44.

Maltby, Robert. *A Lexicon of Ancient Latin Etymologies.* Leeds, England, 1991.

Minadeo, R. "Sexual Symbolism in Horace's Love Odes." *Latomus* 34 (1975): 392-424.

Mutschler, Fritz-Heiner. "Eine Interpretation der Horazode 'Quid fles Asterie.'" *Symbolae Osloenses* 53 (1978): 111-31.

Nisbet, R. G. M., and Margaret Hubbard. *A Commentary on Horace: Odes Book 1*. Oxford, 1970.

————. *A Commentary on Horace: Odes Book 2*. Oxford, 1978.

Owens, William M. "The Go-Between: An Interpretation of Horace, 'Ode 3.7.'" Paper delivered at the AIA-APA Annual Meetings 1982, abstract in American Philological Association Abstracts: Annual Meeting 1982.

————. "*Nuntius Vafer et Fallax:* An Alternate Reading of Horace, *C.* 3.7." *Classical World* 85 (1992): 161-71.

Pasquali, Giorgio. *Orazio Lirico*. Firenze, 1920.

Pichon, René. *Index Verborum Amatorium*. Hildesheim, Germany, 1966.

Porter, David H. "Horace, *Carmina*, IV, 12." *Latomus* 31 (1972): 71-87.

————. *Horace's Poetic Journey: A Reading of Odes 1-3*. Princeton, 1987.

Pöschl, Victor. "Horaz C. 1,25." In *Dialogos für Harald Patzer,* edited by J. Cobet, R. Leimbach, and A. Neschke-Hentschke, 187-92. Wiesbaden, 1975.

Quinn, Kenneth. *Horace: The Odes*. London, 1980.

Reckford, Kenneth. *Horace*. New York, 1969.

Suleiman, Susan Rubin. "Pornography, Transgression, and the Avant-Garde: Bataille's *Store of the Eye*." In *The Poetics of Gender,* edited by Nancy K. Miller, 117-36. New York, 1986.

Syndikus, H. P. *Die Lyrik des Horaz: Eine Interpretation der Oden Band 1*. Darmstadt, Germany, 1972.

Williams, Gordon. *The Third Book of Horace's Odes*. Oxford, 1969.

**Kenneth J. Reckford (essay date 1999)**

SOURCE: Reckford, Kenneth J. "Only a Wet Dream? Hope and Skepticism in Horace, *Satire* 1.5." *American Journal of Philology* 120, no. 4 (1999): 525-54.

[*In the following essay, Reckford considers Horace's Satires 1.5, the "Trip to Brundisium," focusing on the theme of* amicitia, *the* agon *between Sarmentus and Messius Cicirrus, and the "failed miracle sequences" at the end of the work.*]

Long enjoyed as an entertainment piece, Horace's **"Trip to Brundisium"** has continued to baffle its readers by recounting trivialities while ignoring politics. A brief, tactful hint at great affairs is quickly abandoned:

huc venturus erat Maecenas optimus atque
Cocceius, missi magnis de rebus uterque
legati, aversos soliti componere amicos.
hic oculis ego nigra meis collyria lippus
illinere. interea Maecenas advenit . . .

(*S.* [*Satire*] 1.5.27-31)

In his first *hic ego* (7), Horace missed dinner because of stomach trouble. In the second (30), he misses Maecenas' arrival—and its meaning—because of eye trouble. Is he unable to see what is going on around him?[1]

Horace's persona in **Satires** 1.5 is well crafted: the naive, good-humored traveling companion, concerned primarily with his own intrusive comforts and discomforts. He likes good food, drink, and sleep, good health and good company, and he especially enjoys his friends: *nil ego contulerim iucundo sanus amico* (44). He was taken along, it would appear, rather passively from the first (*egressum magna me accepit Aricia Roma*), on a mission that had something to do with "reconciling friends" who had fallen out. That is all he knows, and all he needs to know.[2]

We may well suspect that Horace was keeping a diplomatic silence, that Maecenas confided in him, here and elsewhere, precisely because he did not have a "leaky ear."[3] He would be teasing, then: teasing prospective readers who would suspect that he was withholding privileged information with intent to annoy, and (rather beyond his intent?) teasing modern scholars who cannot even take the satire's date for granted, let alone follow the diplomatic maneuvers of Octavian and Antony in 38-37 B.C.[4] If we follow Horace's lead, all those amusing particulars that render the political picture so opaque convey us insistently into the "little world" of poetry, friendship, and simple human satisfactions. It is tempting to confine our attention to this "little world," accepting Horace at face value as an amiable entertainer, with brief excursions, perhaps, into comparing the esthetics of his narrative with the reconstructed narrative of the casually autobiographical Lucilius—an attempt that, from insufficient evidence, must also end in frustration. But there is more. I propose here that the poem is both more public and more private than it seems. Reading between the lines, though without abusing allegory, we find Horace deeply implicated in issues of war and peace. Through the distorting lens of the satiric and comic imagination he portrays how a sensitive and thoughtful person might waver between hope for a peaceful, even "friendly" resolution of conflict and skeptical awareness of the gap between personal wish-fulfillment (the "wet dream" of my title) and political reality. Yet this same wavering, and Horace's consequent, very human vacillation between emotional involvement with Rome and Epicurean disengagement, are the stuff of which genuine poetry—and, consistently over time and through different genres, Horatian poetry—is made.

My argument focuses on three aspects of **Satire** 1.5: the theme of *amicitia,* private and public; the *agon,* or insult-match between Sarmentus the *scurra* and Messius Cicirrus; and the "wet dream" and "failed miracle" sequences toward the end. But first, because Horace's satires are in part exploratory, like all good poetry, and because meanings notoriously shift as a work progresses in time and is made available to different audiences or circles of readers, I begin with a hypothetical framework consisting of (1) the occasion and first plan, (2) the sketching-out and refining of the satire, (3) its first reading(s) to friends, and (4) its first publication in book form. Further questions of reader reception and the organization of the *libellus* are deferred until the close of the essay.

HYPOTHETICAL STAGES OF COMPOSITION AND
RECEPTION

(1) *The poem is conceived.* We begin with the happy conjunction of two opportunities (*kairoi*), Roman and Horatian. The larger *kairos* involves the diplomatic mission of 37, a renewed attempt to prevent (or postpone) conflict between Octavian and Antony, to settle their differences, and to provide for their mutual assistance against Sextus Pompey. All this was accomplished at Tarentum— for the time being. With Symeian hindsight we can see the conference as a major diplomatic victory for Octavian. He was still a junior Caesarian, short of ships, and inexperienced in warfare; Antony might still have joined with Sextus and the senatorial republicans to crush Caesar's revolutionary heir.[5] As seen in retrospect, Octavian was playing for time, borrowing ships, building up his strength toward Actium. In 37, however, people might still reasonably have hoped for a durable peace agreement, for there was world enough to divide between Antony and Octavian, and no great necessity to fight, and the Caesarian legions were weary of fighting, uncertain whom to support.[6] In the short run, everyone except Sextus gained from reconciliation. And in the long run? Many war-weary Romans must have practiced denial, preferring, despite history's lessons, to indulge in hope.

And Horace? Was he brought along for comic relief? (Maecenas must have been feeling the pressure.) Or to write up the journey, setting its events in a pleasant, harmless, and politically correct light? It is hard to say. But for Horace, the invitation must have signaled his further belonging, not long after his first acceptance by Maecenas "in the company of his friends" (*amicorum in numero, S.* 1.6.60-62; cf. *S.* 2.6.40-42). It also gave him the chance to follow literally and figuratively in the tracks of Lucilius:[7] their journeys to Sicily and Brundisium would coincide as far as Capua and then diverge, a fine living metaphor for the creative and critical work of Horatian *aemulatio.*[8]

(2) *Horace begins the journey.* As he travels, he takes notes, sketches out ideas for his poem, develops a plan. Again we are frustrated: there are no journal entries with which the final version can be compared. Contrast the happy situation of students of eighteenth-century British literature, who not only can compare Johnson's moral and aesthetic choices as shown in his finished *Journey to the Western Isles of Scotland* (1775) with Boswell's very different choices in his *Journal of a Tour to the Hebrides* (1785) but also can discover from Johnson's preserved letters to Hester Thrale what personal details he chose to omit from his more abstract, scientific, and proper *Journey;* or again, from Boswell's earlier manuscript, what details he too very properly (and sometimes self-servingly) omitted from his final *Tour.* Later, too, we may compare Hester Lynch Piozzi's *Observations and Reflections Made in the Course of a Journey through France, Italy, and Germany* (1789) with her journal entries in *Thraliana* for 1786-87. The improvements are not merely artistic. Piozzi changed details, changed descriptions of her feelings of (for example) irritation, indignation, and fear, to convey the consistent persona of a calm, reasonable, good-humored traveler who could take vicissitudes in her stride and appreciate peoples and cultures very unlike her own.[9]

Similarly, Horace must have omitted or played down personal complaints and anxieties, sometimes refining them into a general, good-humored account of the group's collective experience (what was annoying, what was enjoyed) and sometimes using them, I suggest, to hint at larger matters. As he warns a youthful acquaintance many years later, "If you're taken along to Brundisium or lovely Surrentum," you'd better not complain about one thing after another—the dirt, the cold, the rain, the ransacked luggage—or you'll lose your credibility pretty fast (*Ep.* 1.17.52-57).[10] A cynical twist here—and a recollection of how Horace played the good sport about travel back in 37?

Along the way Horace must have noted details he could use, episodes he would describe. In the (?) final version, probably written back at Rome after several un-Lucilian revisions, certain episodes are highlighted (the canal trip, the insult-match) while others are drastically curtailed. The journey is articulated subtly into balancing sections and subsections.[11] The pace of narrative varies, as though following the actual journey, but despite its apparent casualness it achieves an overall speed and concision that must have made Lucilius seem wordy, careless, and rambling by comparison.[12] It may be that Lucilius meant his account to be serviceable to future travelers, like an early Michelin or Fodor's Guide giving directions, distances in miles, road conditions, and other useful advice about food and drink, inns and innkeepers, places to stay or to avoid.[13] Horace mentions these things too, dutifully and perhaps somewhat parodically, especially as his poem hastens to its weary end, but he is (it would appear) less scientific than Lucilius, more concerned with the emotional vagaries of human beings and the ways in which these may be caught momentarily in art. We may imagine Horace's satisfaction in completing his satire, shaped and reshaped to modern standards (Callimachean, Neoteric, pre-Augustan) and ready to be presented to a discriminating audience of friends and fellow writers.[14]

(3) *Horace reads and shows his work to friends.* The practice is attested negatively in *Satire* 1.4, where he emphasizes the non-publicity, hence the non-dangerousness of his satire-writing:

nec recito cuiquam nisi amicis, idque coactus,
non ubivis coramque quibuslibet.

(*S.* 1.4.73-74)

Whether such "private readings by request" might still
have constituted a first "publication" of satire, whether
"slanderous" comments might quickly circulate in Rome,
is not discussed here.[15] Satire is more aggressive and more
dangerous than its ironical master lets on. My point, for
now, is that Horace not only writes for a select readership
of educated people and friends, several of whom he finally
names in *Satire* 1.10, but enjoys that same in-group,

Plotius et Varius, Maecenas Vergiliusque,

(1.10.81)

together with (perhaps) Valgius, Octavius, Aristius Fuscus,
and the Visci, as a living audience whose criticism,
encouragement, and sheer pleasure in his performance of
satire need not be deferred until the *libellus* is complete
and published.

May we go further and imagine Horace performing his
"Journey" for Maecenas and his friends as a special after-
dinner entertainment several weeks after the event?[16] Not
only would Horace's actual audience coincide momentarily
with the ideal implied audience for whom he wrote;[17] it
would include figures central to the narrative,

Plotius et Varius Sinuessae Vergiliusque . . . ,

(1.5.40)

for whom Horace evokes the shared pleasures, and also
the shared discomforts and frustrations, which they now
laugh to recall. We must imagine the varying tonalities of
such a performance, over which Horace still has control:
the voices assumed, especially for the insult-match; the
smiles and laughs and grimaces; and the occasional, carefully controlled comic gesture—for Horace cannot afford
to let himself be confused with a mime, let alone with the
parasite and clown who provide the comic play within his
play. The pleasure of the performance, for poet and audience alike, must have been memorable.

In performance, too, the satire enacts an aesthetic and
social agenda. Even as he displays his literary and dramatic
skill in competition with Lucilius, Horace confirms his assured position within Maecenas' circle by making himself
a spokesman for the aesthetic and moral values, and
especially the bond of friendship (*amicitia*), that hold the
group together. He demonstrates, that is, not only his intelligence and wit (always a two-edged sword) but also, with
it, the same moral ethos of the *liber amicus* that is prepared
in *Satire* 1.3, proclaimed in 1.4, and reaffirmed in 1.6 and
1.9. Horace's friends will enjoy seeing through the "naive"
persona. Maecenas will be pleased by Horace's discretion
in not even hinting at whatever confidences they may have
shared. In less than a year Horace's position *amicorum in
numero* has become, not just secure, but centrally creative
of the little world it purports to describe.

(4) *Horace works steadily toward the publication of* Satires
*book 1 around 35* B.C. Let us for the moment defer discussion of how 1.5 was placed and integrated within the *libellus,* and how this placement may affect our reading.[18] For
now, I want only to stress the importance of relative dating to interpretation. In a way, the publication of around
35 B.C. comes closer to our own nonprivileged reading
today than to that hypothetical in-group performance of 37
B.C., for we are ignorant of so much relevant data that
Horace's first audience knew at first hand and took for
granted. Again, the politics of 35 must have looked and
felt very different from those of 37, when the satire was
conceived and written. By 35 Sextus had been beaten, Octavian's position strengthened; Antony had distanced
himself from the reconciling figure of Octavia; and from
various signs, both military and propagandistic, an all-out
clash will have seemed more inevitable than before. And
Horace's fine balancing act between hope and skepticism,
engagement and disengagement, might not, in the later
year, have been achieved so nicely.

### AMICITIA

Although accounts of the conference at Tarentum in Plutarch, Appian, and Dio are scattered and even contradictory, some elements seem reliable, going back perhaps via
Livy to Asinius Pollio. We hear, for example, that when
they finally met, Octavian and Antony gave public
demonstrations of mutual trust; that skilled intermediaries,
notably Cocceius and (unofficially but centrally) Octavia,
worked hard for concord; and that the armies rejoiced
heartily when the agreement was completed.[19] Again we
can say in retrospect that the displays of friendship,
especially on Octavian's part, were "play-acting" and fiction. Appian (5.94) puts it realistically: "Thus their
behavior constantly swung between suspicion, arising from
their desire for power, and trust, arising from their current
needs" (trans. John Carter). In the long run, the suspicions
proved themselves justified, or created their own reality.
("All's true that is mistrusted," says Othello.) In the short
run, trust may have seized its chance, and Horace's naive
endorsement of the spirit of reconciliation (*aversos soliti
componere amicos,* 1.5.29), may have reflected a widespread popular sentiment, not just triumviral propaganda.

Differently, *Satire* 1.5 privatizes *amicitia,* taking us from
the euphemistic description of the widening breach
between Antony and Octavian as a friends' quarrel needing reconciliation (29), through the description of Fonteius
Capito as Antony's special friend (33), to Horace's expression of delight at being reunited with his own dear friends:

postera lux oritur multo gratissima; namque
Plotius et Varius Sinuessae Vergiliusque
occurrunt, animae qualis neque candidiores
terra tulit neque quis me sit devinctior alter.
o qui complexus et gaudia quanta fuerunt!
nil ego contulerim iucundo sanus amico.[20]

(1.5.39-44)

Happiness lies in bringing friends together, sadness in
their separation (cf. Varius' departure, 93); and the poet
who realizes the incomparable value of friendship (*nil ego*

*contulerim,* 44) knows also the value of reconciliation (*aversos . . . componere amicos,* 29). Can a bridge be built, as Horace's insistent repetition of *amicus* suggests, between the easy friendship of Horace, Virgil, Varius, and Plotius, and the very uneasy alliance of Antony and Octavian?

As Horace describes it, the first, more private *amicitia* has strong Epicurean overtones. Epicurus had praised, taught, and exemplified the value of friendship as a reliable source of pleasure and security, both private and public. Virgil, Varius, and Plotius may have studied at Naples with the Epicurean Siro, and they knew Philodemus, who lived nearby in Piso's villa at Herculaneum and who wrote, among other things, treatises on flattery (*peri kolakeias*), a perversion of friendship; and on correcting friends' errors honestly but considerately (*peri parrhēsias*).[21] These are Horace's *animae candidae.* If (to anticipate) we read **Satire** 1.5 as it comes in the published *libellus,* after 1.3 and 1.4—the former a vindication of friendship and tolerance, somewhat on Epicurean grounds, against absolutizing Stoic demands; the latter refurbishing Horace's self-image as *liber amicus,* a good, honest person and friend—then Horace may be presenting himself as a proven connoisseur of friendship as well as poetry, one who may represent and proclaim the group's high human values on the satiric stage. But can these shared private experiments in pleasure and value reach out, as with widening ripples of health (*nil ego contulerim iucundo sanus amico,* 44), to help heal the ailing commonwealth?[22] Or is this an idle dream? I give two versions of Horace's answer, two equally possible readings of 1.5.

In the positive view, *amicitia* spreads infectiously from private to public along a happy continuum. Virgil's little group of friends, poets, and critics belongs also to Maecenas' circle, which Horace, with some self-irony at the expense of his naive persona, yet represents quite seriously in **Satires** 1.6 and 1.9 as a charmed sphere of mutual consideration, forbearance, gratitude, and support. Of course, his words help create the reality of which they speak. Although Maecenas was always the "greater friend," whose status and dignity required a certain respectful distance, it seems that Horace and he succeeded admirably in reviving the genuine *amicus*-quality in a relationship of *amicitia* that might so easily, with others, have sunk into mutual exploitation.[23] As for politics: Horace will eventually follow Maecenas, who follows Octavian (**Epode** 1, in 31 B.C.), but before 35 (**Satire** 1.10) he proudly claims friends in both camps, *ambitione relegata* (84). Why, then, shouldn't the poet-friends contribute to the mood of reconciliation in 37? Why shouldn't the brittle, formal *amicitia* of Octavian and Antony be reanimated by the spirit of genuine friendship that Horace knew and loved so well?

Lucretius began *De Rerum Natura* with a similar hope. He prayed to Venus—love goddess, mother and patroness of Rome, the creative force of *philia* that unites, governs, and sustains the living universe—first, to endow his scientific poem with erotic attractiveness, and second, by (the

sympathetic magic of) her erotic subjugation of Mars, to grant peace throughout the Roman world:

> nam neque nos agere hoc patriai tempore iniquo
> possumus aequo animo nec Memmi clara propago
> talibus in rebus communi desse saluti.

*(DRN 1.41-43)*

The mental equilibrium that Epicurus so insistently preached is threatened here by Roman dissension and war. Even a good Epicurean must become involved. Yet Memmius is invited to be more Epicurean, not less. When Lucretius writes

> sed tua me virtus tamen et sperata voluptas
> suavis amicitiae quemvis efferre laborem
> suadet et inducit noctes vigilare serenas . . . ,

*(1.140-42)*

he is not, I think, simply complimenting a patron or would-be patron. As a better Epicurean, Memmius would be a better friend and ally, would help extend Venus' realm against that of Mars. Although Epicurus urged retreat from public life into the philosophical tranquility of the Garden, his elite Roman followers must sometimes have felt, or wanted to feel, that their private practice of Epicurean quietude and restraint could help to heal a *res publica* battered by competition and strife.[24] Cicero thought otherwise, and even Lucretius must have had his doubts; but still, the hope was there.

So too, I suggest, Horace's **"Trip to Brundisium"** implies a deep-set wish, and even a hope, that the life forces may win out this time, surging outward from the joys of private friendship to revitalize the greater alliances and bind up the commonwealth's wounds. But there is also (as in Lucretius) a counter-movement of skepticism and fear, enforcing a more negative reading. Say that the great world of *Realpolitik* is not amenable to the charms of Horace's "little world" of friendship and poetry. Say that *amicitia* proves deceptive, that Antony and Octavian must inevitably clash, that more Roman blood must be shed by Romans in a tragically unending cycle.[25] What then can a sensitive person do but seek refuge from the storm in the seclusion of private life? Epicureanism would then be an escape hatch, not a bridge. Did everyone, Horace included, know that from the start?

The wish to escape from political necessities, as from thoughts of death, recurs throughout Horace's poetry. The early **Epode** 16 ends despairingly with a call to flight (*fuga,* both literal and imaginative flight) from the recurring turmoil of civil war and from the vice that is said to pervade the Age of Iron. Although Horace's personal situation improved drastically, and Rome's (however we judge Octavian/Augustus) at least stabilized, that wish to escape remains a notable feature of his poetry, one side of a continuing, almost programmatic vacillation between engagement and disengagement, emotional involvement in Rome's great affairs (*nunc desiderium curaque non levis,*

*O.* [*Odes*] 1.14.18) and emotional flight into a happier because more readily controlled world of wine, women, and song—and friends. I give two contrasting later examples.

*Ode* 2.1 voices appreciation of Pollio's dangerous history writing, his skillful recreation of the civil wars:

> Motum ex Metello consule civicum
> bellique causas et vitia et modos
>    ludumque Fortunae *gravisque*
>      *principum amicitias* et arma
>
> nondum expiatis uncta cruoribus. . . .

(O. 2.1-5)

Horace here catches the historian's thought and exposition: the sequence of events; the "causes, faults, and modes" that characterize, and partly explain, the outbreak, escalation, and further course of war; the governing "play" of chance; and, more particularly, the "damaging friendships of princes."[26] The alliance of Pompey and Caesar did harm; still more, its dissolution. (Can the reader think of another such alliance?) That is the stuff of history as conveyed by an accurate and honest writer. After Horace plunges sympathetically into reenvisioning and emotionally reliving the horrors of civil war, his mind finally recoils; and his command to the lyric Muse to return to her proper (and safer) world of lovemaking (*sed ne relictis . . .*) is at once a tribute to Pollio's integrity and skill, a subtle comment on Horace's lyric transmutation of epic material, and an expression of his severe discomfort with renewed emotional involvement, actual or imaginative, in high Roman affairs. He tries it, briefly though programmatically, and he flees.

*Ode* 3.1, like the Roman Odes (3.1-6) taken together, is more ambivalent. Here Horace builds on earlier odes (2.16, 2.18) and, through them, on Lucretius to proclaim the moral necessity of accepting human limits. He implies that his own hard-won contentment, set against troubling desires and fears (and, not least, the fear of death), might serve as a good example to the commonweal; accordingly, the praise of simplicity and contentment in 3.1 heralds other, more difficult virtues in 3.2-6. Yet the assertion of his personal choice at the poem's end rings ambivalently. If riches and luxuries can't diminish pain—so far, Epicurus and Lucretius—"why should I exchange my Sabine valley for more burdensome riches?" A good example, yes: but also a retreat (and not the last) from the overwhelming complexities and demands of public life. The ode's tone is strongly Epicurean and, in the end, it looks both ways.

So too, I suggest, does the friendship theme earlier in *Satire* 1.5. It is hopeful to a point, though it keeps the escape hatch always in view. The *agon* passage to which I now turn is also ambivalent, as an implicit demonstration of poetry's civilized and civilizing play, but also as a veiled reminder of unresolved conflict and the threat of war.

## THE AGON

Can violence be contained? This is the subtext of *Satire* 1.5. War and the threat of war are hinted at, early on, by Horace's mock-heroic *ventri indico bellum* (7-8); aggressiveness is deployed, also comically, in the exchange of reproaches between slaves and sailors (*convicia ingerere*, 11-12) and the comic beating of the sluggish mule and sailor who have delayed the canal trip (22-23). At the satire's literal center is the "fight" at Cocceius' comfortable villa, introduced in a significantly brief, mock-Homeric invocation:

>        nunc mihi paucis
> Sarmenti scurrae pugnam Messique Cicirri,
> Musa, velim memores, et quo patre natus uterque
> contulerit litis.

(1.5.51-54)

This episode, for which I borrow the term *agon* from Aristophanic comedy, is pointedly extensive (20 lines out of 104), a careful revision of a Lucilian entertainment scene. Has it any bearing on the questions of war and peace that Horace is so carefully not reporting?

Some have thought so, have taken this *agon* as alluding to the clashes of Roman generals in the civil wars.[27] The improbability of any one precise reference—for example, to Sextus Pompey and Octavian!—does not exclude the general likelihood of travesty, if indeed the threatened combat of the great generals, based on ambition and the drive for honor and power, is transformed comically into the insult-match of Messius Cicirrus, the low Oscan clown, and Sarmentus, the parasite and ex-slave. Such travesty always subverts the order of established hierarchies and beliefs, as in Aristophanes' *Acharnians* and *Knights* or in Plautus' *Miles Gloriosus* and *Amphitruo*, or, for that matter, in the Marx Brothers' film *Duck Soup*, where the escalating conflict between the peanut seller (Harpo) and the lemonade seller parodies the "normal" course of events leading to war. At the same time, it provides a substitute for history's actual violence, a demonstration of how aggressive impulses threatening the social order may be played out harmlessly, exorcized by the artist's civilizing imagination. Just so, as Johan Huizinga argued in his *Homo Ludens: The Play Element in Culture,* societies have substituted the verbal duel, the sports contest, and the legal altercation for the unbounded warfare and bloodshed that preceded them.[28]

It would be worth asking how far Huizinga's theories might be corroborated by the history of gladiatorial contests at Rome, in all their murderous violence, or by the developed procedures of the law courts, whose oratorical duels, including insult-exchanges, defined the great Republican game in which riches, power, and political influence were daily won and lost. Lucilius' satires reenact such contests as secondhand entertainment. Book 4 included a mock-heroic version of a notable, though one-sided gladiatorial contest involving the famous Pacideianus.[29] In book 2 Lucilius travestied a legal contest between Albucius and Mucius Scaevola notable (at least in the retelling) for the vehemence of its insult-exchanges and ending with a practical joke that, according to Scaevola, accounted for Albucius' personal hostility (*inimicitia*) toward him.[30] Similarly, and perhaps in deliberate imitation of Lucilius, Horace's *Satire* 1.7 gives a comic account of a legal altercation judged by Brutus in 43, when he was propraetor of Asia. It ends with a bad joke (and a dangerous one) on Rupilius Rex: *cur non hunc Regem iugulas?* Let Brutus show himself worthy of his ancestry by slaughtering/condemning *this* King. The joke, indeed the entire satire, pays a backhanded tribute both to the older Lucilian satire with its privileged *libertas* of abuse, and to the free-spirited competition of the pre-Caesarian law courts (which Cicero recalled so nostalgically in his *Brutus*). A few years later, and these rough Republican games have become strangely obsolete, a thing of the almost distant past, like Brutus himself.

But Horace was not simply nostalgic for that Republican *libertas*, either in politics or in poetry. Rather, in *Satire* 1.4 and later, he redefines satire's aesthetic and moral aims away from casual lampooning, toward more careful artistry and better, more sociable humor. As scholars from Hendrickson to Freudenburg have argued, Horace's theory of the development of satire, and of his own role in that ongoing development, owed much to Aristotle's version of the development of Greek comedy from casual improvisation to ordered plot and from unbridled aggressiveness, license, and attacks on individuals to the more general, restrained, civilized, and truly "liberal" humor of social comedy, best realized in the post-Aristophanic comedy of Aristotle's own time (and, for later Peripatetic theorists, by Menander).[31] One oxymoron says it all: good comedy is *pepaideumenē hybris,* "educated insolence."[32] And so, in Horace's version of the prehistory of modern (comedy or) satire: the aggressiveness of popular, holiday funmaking got out of hand, attacking people indiscriminately (like a rabid dog), and had to be controlled by law. Aesthetically, too, like all Latin verse, it had to be civilized and shaped to the standard of the best Greek models, and thereby brought into conformity with generic as well as social "laws."[33] Had fate somehow thrust Lucilius into our own age, says Horace (building ironically on Lucilius' own critical pronouncements about poetry and drama), he would not have written such rambling verses, or attacked his "enemies" so indiscriminately. Rather, he would have written (like Horace) with more art, and with better manners, and might even have contributed (as Horace intends) to making the world a more decent and friendly place in which to live.

As it presently stands in the *libellus,* *Satire* 1.5 gives a practical demonstration of the aesthetic and moral principles enunciated, however ironically, in 1.4, and of Horace's own very civilized competition (*aemulatio*) with Lucilius, in whose footsteps he literally and figuratively follows—up to a point. Unfortunately, we cannot make detailed comparisons. The *agon* should be a test case:

similarities of subject matter, as in the use of "likenings" (Greek *eikasmoi*) by both Lucilius and Horace, probably revealed subtle differences of art and taste.[34] Lucilius' best insult, *non peperit, verum postica parte profudit* (119M), has found no echo in Horace. What we observe rather, and may reasonably suspect was lacking in Lucilius, is the careful artistry, the narrative speed and conciseness (as in the Hellenistic *iambos* or literary mime) with which the combatants are presented, the combat played out. What is described as a delicious, prolonged entertainment of Cocceius' travel-weary guests has been rendered in twenty hexameter lines (mock-heroic grandeur, comic mimesis, and all), in programmatic contrast to a contest in Lucilius that may have been, like the journey as a whole, some three times as long. *Nunc mihi paucis,* indeed!

Significantly, too, Horace has taken the kind of reported *agon* that constituted the whole of *Satire* 1.7 and Lucilius' book 2, and has framed it within the larger structure of *Satire* 1.5. Our answer(s) to that earlier question "Can violence be contained?" will depend on how we read the relation between the insult-match inset and the larger poetic and diplomatic journey.

Although the contest between Messius and Sarmentus does not end even in arbitrary victory for either combatant, as *Satire* 1.7 does, and as Lucilius' Albucius/Scaevola *agon* did, its framing here suggests a kind of closure. The clown conflict enhances the dinner party but has no continued existence outside it. Again, as suggested earlier, the distinction of "Horace" the privileged narrator outside the frame from Sarmentus the player within it may point to another desirable distinction, between Horace the *liber amicus* and full participant in Maecenas' circle, and Sarmentus the mere professional entertainer, who might almost be Horace's shadow self.[35] On a different, metasatirical level, the framed *agon* enacts Horace's larger competition with Lucilius and his *fautores* for control of the world of satire; and Horace's clear victory in this larger literary *agon* also implies a victory of those civilized and civilizing values, at once aesthetic and moral, for which he stands.

Can violence be contained? Within the aesthetic realm here represented by satire, it can; for Horace's satire, by subduing contentiousness to art more than twice over, suggests that the poet can be a public educator, as Lucilius (for all his virtues) was not. For Lucilius pursued private and political feuds with various *inimici,* while representing himself as Virtue's stalwart champion: witness the great *Virtus* fragment and Horace's backhanded compliment,

scilicet uni aequus virtuti atque eius amicis.[36]

(*S.* 2.1.70)

Differently, Horace's satire journeys outward from the "little," protected world of friendship and poetry making into a larger, more dangerous Roman world where, more than ever before, "friends" must be "brought together" and their potentially murderous competition rendered harmless for the common good. Might even a sheltered poet contribute to this end through the civilizing power of play and art, as also through the contagious practice of friendship?

That is one way of reading the inset. But there is another, more subversive and troubling reading. If the little *agon* is a microcosm of the larger satire, then we may become alerted to the truth that *satire is itself a game,* a most civilized and civilizing game, to be sure, yet in the end only a game, played out within the bounds of a (for now) protected literary and social playground. But outside, in the unmapped larger world of politics and war, can any limits hold? Virgil asks similar questions in his *Eclogues.* His sheltered, hypercivilized world of pastoral, and of poetry and friendship, has an almost Orphic power to transform nature, yet is finally vulnerable to the invasive passions of love and war and the displacements of history. So too with satire. Can Horace's game, however well played, really exorcize the forces of aggressiveness and violence? How long can his mild satiric laughter, his "educated mockery," keep them at bay? Maybe only for a brief, happy moment on the journey, which will continue through difficulties, frustrations, and (comic) disappointments: the "wet dream," the failed miracle at Gnatia, the inconclusive "arrival" at Brundisium.

## Wet Dream, Failed Miracle

Among later difficulties Horace recounts what may, for quite extraneous reasons, have become the best-remembered event of his journey:

> hic ego mendacem stultissimus usque puellam
> ad mediam noctem exspecto: somnus tamen aufert
> intentum Veneri; tum immundo somnia visu
> nocturnam vestem maculant ventremque supinum.

(1.5.82-85)

It is well told. He waits, expectantly and obscenely "intent on Venus," but in place of the promised assignation he only gets, after finally and wearily falling asleep, a wet dream. It is all very humiliating. "The man who doesn't get laid" is, of course, a familiar figure in comedy, from Cinesias in Aristophanes' *Lysistrata* to Sceparnio in Plautus' *Rudens,* who, after almost assaulting Ampelisca earlier, must stand onstage like a gaping idiot, holding the "sacred urn of Venus," until he realizes that she won't show up after all. (It isn't her fault, but that doesn't affect the joke.) Differently, Horace's episode may owe something to Lucretius' description in book 4 of the deceptive power of dreams, climaxing in (a) the children who dream that they are urinating outdoors at the latrine, but in reality soak the beautiful bedcovers; and then (b) the adolescent youths tricked by gorgeous sexual images:

> qui ciet irritans loca turgida semine multo,
> et quasi transactis saepe omnibu' rebu' profundant
> fluminis ingentis fluctus vestemque cruentant.

(DRN 4.1034-36)

Lucretius' account joins disparate elements: the scientist's clinical account of sexuality, sympathetic evocation of the youth's sensuous yearnings, and a perhaps personal memory of the disturbing violence of (male) sexuality, whose earliest manifestations can sometimes be traumatic. All this, especially the deceptiveness, provides an easy transition to Lucretius' climactic attack on the passion of love that concludes book 4.[37] It may be significant that Horace treats his wet dream more lightly, as a good joke on himself. Has it any bearing on larger issues?

Scholars have generally ignored this episode, written it off as "embarrassing," or diverted their attention to Horace's possible imitation of a similar scene in Lucilius, in which case the "wet dream" might have been as much a generic fiction as the shield that Horace threw away at Philippi. Unfortunately, Lucilius' wet dream seems itself to be a useful fiction, arising from a circular argument from Horace to reconstructed Lucilius and back again to Horace.[38] If indeed Lucilius described a sexual encounter with a *caupona* in book 3, it was probably successful. To judge from surviving fragments, his usual persona was that of a man who enjoyed sex and who kept control of the situation, much as "Archilochus" did before him in the Cologne Epode. Once, to be sure, he has recourse to masturbation, perhaps after an erotic disappointment like Horace's; but still, those "tears" of frustration were easily "wiped away."[39]

I venture to guess (a) that the wet dream really happened,[40] and (b) that Horace welcomed its literary possibilities. Perhaps he contrasted his own sexual failure with Lucilius' success. That would suit the general impotence of his "Flaccus" persona, the rather passive, quiet-loving fellow whom other, more aggressive types would walk over, given half the chance. But I would go further and argue that Horace's deceiving dream is connected with the prospects, for good or bad, of the diplomatic mission of 37. Hence the title of this essay.

Most simply, Horace may be suggesting that hopes for a settled agreement and a lasting peace are illusory, "only a wet dream." The negotiations, that is, may produce only a deceptive (and politically correct) image of *amicitia,* not the real thing. The treaty of Brundisium in 40 fell short of its promise (partly celebrated by Virgil in Eclogue 4); there might even be a hint in Horace's episode of how Antony was "stood up" by Octavian in 38 when he sailed to Brundisium and was not met there. A cynical reading of the "wet dream" seems inviting. It may be, however, that Horace is tempering genuine hopefulness about peace with a caution familiar from fable and proverb, introducing an indecent and very funny version of "Don't count your chickens before they're hatched!" Or, differently, he might be offering up his personal humiliation as a kind of apotropaic magic, a substitute frustration to ward off the gods' envy and forestall the greater disappointment of failed peace negotiations. Obscenity is often apotropaic. We might compare frustration scenes from Aristophanes' *Acharnians* and *Lysistrata,* and especially *Peace,* where hope and skepticism, a sense of the gods' gifts and a sense of the urgency of human effort, are kept in comic balance. So too, in Horace's satire, there may be a delicate, carefully negotiated balance between the three possible attitudes just now suggested.

A second episode highlighted by Horace, the failed "miracle" at Gnatia, tilts the satire more decisively toward skepticism:

> dein Gnatia lymphis
> iratis exstructa dedit risusque iocosque,
> dum flamma sine tura liquescere limine sacro
> persuadere cupit. Credat Iudaeus Apella,
> non ego: namque deos didici securum agere aevum,
> nec si quid miri faciat natura, deos id
> tristis ex alto caeli demittere tecto.

> (1.5.97-103)

Horace speaks here as one who has memorized his Epicurean catechism, word for word. Lucretius had warned his readers that unless they thoroughly accepted the principle that every event in nature, however miraculous-seeming, can and must be explained in terms of natural causation and scientific law—a principle carefully illustrated, after Epicurus, in the various but complementary accounts of thunder, lightning, and the thunderbolt in book 6—they may "be swept back" into the old religious beliefs and practices through impulses of wonder or terror:

> nam bene qui *didicere deos securum agere aevum*,
> *si* tamen interea *mirantur* . . .

> (*DRN* 5.82-83 = 6.58-59)

"Not me," says Horace. Perhaps he, or his now pseudo-sophisticated persona, protests too much. But perhaps, too, he takes some pride in distinguishing himself from the superstitious throng, much as he distinguished himself earlier from the ordinary run of clowns, parasites, and mere entertainers. He may laugh a little at the doctrinaire followers of Epicurus, much as he does in *Satire* 1.3 (99-112), where he gives a hilarious "instant" version of Lucretius' account (over many lines, and countless years) of the slow, gradual development of society, language, law, and civilization. Yet there, despite the parody, Horace clearly sees Epicurean (or Democritean) anthropology as reinforcing humane practices of friendship against Stoic absolutism. And so here, despite the touch of parody and self-irony, Horace's disbelief in miracles may go deep, and its placement just before the arrival at Brundisium may be pointed. "It will be a miracle if things work out—and I don't believe in miracles!"

The point is supported by a second, less obvious Lucretian echo from a passage about the creation of human beings, who were not "let down from heaven by a golden rope,"

> haud, ut opinor, enim mortalia saecla superne
> aurea de *caelo demisit* funis in arva,[41]

> (*DRN* 2.1153-54)

which Horace conflates with Virgil's "Messianic" line

> iam nova progenies *caelo demittitur alto*

> (*E.* 4.7)

to produce his own

> tristis ex *alto caeli demittere* tecto.

> (*S.* 1.5.103)

Virgil's high prophecy in Eclogue 4 included a deliberate undoing of Lucretius' denial, a playful remythologizing of the old Golden Age picture of human happiness and ease, now to be regained as the world winds backward through various mystic stages, through and away from struggle and war. By contrast, Horace returns to Lucretian orthodoxy. Miracles just don't happen. If things turn out well, it won't be by divine intervention, but rather by human effort, perseverance, and sheer muddling through. Which may be what this journey is finally about.

The satire ends abruptly, as Horace comes to the end of poem and journey alike:

> Brundisium longae finis chartaeque viaeque est.

> (1.5.104)

He has completed the twofold job of traveling with the embassy and writing up the trip. The abrupt ending works like a punch line elsewhere, or a blackout. In the "little world" of poetry and friendship, of literary endeavor in the competitive field of satire and promotion of good humor within the (allegedly) noncompetitive circle of Maecenas and his friends, Horace's ending marks a definite achievement, a modestly implied fulfillment. In the "greater world" of politics and history, closure might seem arbitrary, not least (as will be seen in retrospect) when it befalls at Brundisium; for in fact, Maecenas and his fellow diplomats went on to Tarentum, where Octavian and Antony (temporarily) settled their business about ships, legions, and Sextus Pompey.[42] Was Horace left behind at Brundisium? Are poets only useful, or entertaining, up to a point? Are the great events of history carried on, beyond their understanding or control, for good or ill? That is not clear. The near-miracles of honest friendship, good humor, and good poetry carry us to Brundisium and no farther. Horace's satire might be called "Making It to Brundisium." Its task has been well accomplished. It will find a decent resting place at last in the published *libellus* of 35. For the diplomats doing Rome's business and, differently, for Horace as he conducts his own shuttle diplomacy between public and private, between emotional involvement in Rome's affairs and emotional disengagement or flight back into the pleasures and accomplishments of private life, the journey—at once of poetry and of life—will continue.

## THE PUBLISHED SATIRE

I suggested earlier that however *Satire* 1.5 might have been heard in 37 B.C., its personal and historical meanings will have shifted by 35: partly because it was read now by strangers, not heard by friends and fellow travelers, and partly because history had moved on, the balance of power was shifting, a final conflict (Actium) may have seemed more inevitable than before; so that, seen in retrospect, skepticism about the negotiations of 37 must have overbalanced hope. Horace's earlier feelings and intentions, which I have tried here to reconstruct, now become less relevant, not to say less authoritative; for, as he himself knew and pointed out humorously in *Epistle* 1.20, the published book escapes its master's control.[43] Let me turn to a related, more limited question. Why did Horace give *Satire* 1.5 that particular placement in the *libellus?* What new meaning(s) might it have adopted while still in the author's controlling hands, in that carefully arranged sequence?

By most accounts, Horace's first book of satires (a) has a tripartite arrangement with a coda (1-3, 4-6, 7-9; 10), and/or (b) falls into two halves (1-5, 6-10).[44] The overall structure comes remarkably close to Virgil's book of ten eclogues in its overall plan and detailed contrasts. In both, the fifth poem stands out, whether as a climax of the first half, before a significantly new beginning, or as the centerpiece of the central group of poems. How, then, should *Satire* 1.5 be read in relation to satires placed before and after?

In *Satires* 1.1-3 (to follow the tripartite structure), Horace experiments with diatribe satire on ethical themes: most simply and effectively in 1.1, on avarice; with more self-mocking incoherence in 1.2, on sex; and turning against satire itself and the usual persona of the aggressively critical satirist in 1.3, on friendship and tolerance. This gives an easy transition to the more personal *Satires* 1.4-6, where he plays out his choices in literature and in life, redefining the aesthetic and moral aims of satire, as against Lucilius, and reinventing his own satiric persona, if not also (as I would argue) himself, as *liber amicus,* an honest man and a good friend. *Satires* 1.7-9 are simpler, perhaps earlier and more Lucilian entertainment pieces; and 1.10 reaffirms Horace's debt to his precursor even as he proclaims his adherence to the best literary standards of his own time, in close company with Virgil, Varius, and his other friends and primary readers.

Thematically, then, 1.5 builds on 1.3 and 1.4. Most obviously, its *aemulatio* of Lucilius tests out the redefinition of satire heralded, though with strong self-irony and -contradiction, in 1.4 I have argued that competition with Lucilius is an important subtext of 1.5, especially as mirrored in the *agon*. But 1.5 builds also on Horace's cumulative exploration of *amicitia* in 1.3 and 1.4. He has turned satire against the inhuman Stoic standards that so easily destroy friendship because of minor offenses that someone has committed (the "censorious" critic being unaware of his own, often greater failings); and his satire writing has distanced itself more than ironically from the *character Lucilianus,* the aggressive spirit with which Lucilius, and satire generally, have become identified. All this prepares the reader for 1.5, where, if we read between the lines, Horace is taken along not merely as an entertainer, but as a *liber amicus* and an expert though unofficial adviser, precisely, in the business of maintaining and restoring friendship, *aversos solit(us) componere amicos.*

Horace's "Journey to Brundisium" may be read, then, as the high point of *Satires* book 1, corresponding roughly to Virgil's Eclogue 5, the Daphnis poem and center of the visionary Eclogues 4-6.[45] This is Horace's furthest venture into public affairs, a high-water mark of his involvement with Rome's great affairs, or his attempted involvement—for politics and history are, in the end, frighteningly beyond his grasp. It seems all the more significant, then, that in 1.6, the concluding poem of 1.4-6 and the new beginning of 1.6-10, Horace moves inward, away from the world of Roman politics in which he no longer has a place, into Maecenas' accepting circle; and, more inward still, into his almost pastoral enjoyment of *otium* even in great Rome. In the "little world" of poetry, friendship, and self-reflection, he can (for the time being) feel content.

Let me return briefly to the parallel with Virgil's *libellus.* Leach has argued that poem 10 in both collections summarizes the poet's literary achievement but also the limits of that achievement: for Virgil, both in personal life, for the passion of love cannot be calmed, let alone contained, by the ease of pastoral; and in history, for (as Putnam too has argued, not least in his dark reading of Eclogue 9) the achievement of poetry depends finally on peaceful surroundings, quietness of spirit, and the gifts or favor of the "gods."[46]

Horace's epilogue, *Satire* 1.10, seems brighter and more confident than Virgil's. It affirms Horace's pride in his satiric achievement, even as it places that achievement securely within the sphere of Virgil and Varius, of good modern poetry. Horace surely knows, with Virgil, that the pleasures of friendship and poetry in the "little world" are vulnerable to events in the "great world" beyond their control. Although Virgil's singers possess an Orphic power to re-create nature, their voice can still, in bad times, be silenced. No more can the apotropaic magic of Horace's *Satires* and *Epodes* ward off external dangers. Still, Horace feels his powers, in *Satire* 1.10 as in 1.5; the journey has been exciting and, in many ways, successful; and the retreat in 1.6 into private life may yet prove, as its placement suggests, both an end and a beginning. Over time, Horace's poetic variations on the dance theme of advance and retreat will stamp his experiments in different poetic genres with the continuing impression of his special personality and genius.[47]

### Notes

1. The literal malady can be treated with ointment, but figuratively, Horace sees more clearly than he pretends (or better, sees through the comic mask of *nigra collyria*); cf. *S.* 1.3.25-26 earlier, on forgiving friends, a theme highly relevant to the present satire: *cum tua pervideas oculis mala lippus inunctis, / cur in amicorum vitiis tam cernis acutum?* Differently, Stahl (1974, 31) sees Horace as restoring his sense of priorities, "nachdem sie durch politisches Übergewicht gefährdet war."

2. DuQuesnay (1984, 41) calls this "a masterpiece of understatement which minimizes the tension and makes inevitable the successful outcome of the

negotiations." The poem, he argues, "justifies the propaganda of the Triumvirs, who advertised their continuing friendship after Tarentum" (40).

3. Cf. *S.* 2.6.46, *et quae rimosa bene deponuntur in aure,* with the popular reaction, 53-54 ("*ut tu . . . semper eris derisor*") and 57-58 (his allegedly superhuman silence). He is, of course, a mocker; *S.* 2.6.42-43 (*quem tollere raeda . . . vellet iter faciens*) may recall the Journey to Brundisium; and later, in *O.* 3.2.25-26, Horace's longtime *fidele silentium* may implicitly entitle him to some honor in the world of heroic attainment. On the dangers of loose talk cf. *S.* 1.3.94-95 and, in later retrospect, *Ep.* 1.18.37-38, 67-71.

4. On dating see Pelling 1988, 214 (37 more likely, but perhaps 38; cf. Rudd 1966, 280-81), and Pelling 1996, 25-27, on the conference at Tarentum and its political background (with n. 112, "a July-August date is most likely"). The main sources, none of them altogether reliable, are Plut. *Ant.* 35, App. *BC* 5.93.386-95.398, Dio Cass. 48.54.3; we badly miss Pollio. For the historical use of the term *kairos* cf. *Ant.* 30.5 on the opportunity for peace before Brundisium made possible by Fulvia's death.

5. Syme 1939, 213 (Octavian's need and fear), 226 (the aftermath): "Antonius had lost the better part of two years, sacrificing ambition, interest and power."

6. Christopher Pelling kindly reviewed with me the hard facts behind the peace negotiations, including the war-weariness and uncertain loyalty of the legions in 37. Cf. Pelling 1988, 201, on Brundisium earlier.

7. For the remains of Lucilius' journey-satire in book 3 see Marx 1904, 9-12 (text), and 1905, 46-71 (commentary); also Cichorius [1908] 1964, 251-61 (mostly following Marx, with a few modifications), and Krenkel 1970, 140-59 (text, translation, commentary). Lucilius probably went to Sicily after the Servile War in Sicily, so between 120 and 116 B.C.: to inspect his property and see to a sick *bubulcus* (105M), and perhaps to deal with a severe crisis involving hardship and conflict (Marx 1905, 46-48). We might well compare passages from book 3 with stories and anecdotes from the Numantine campaign, dedicated to Scipio as a sort of *Commentarii de Bello Numantino* (cf. Puelma 1978, 77). Scipio might have brought Lucilius along to celebrate his military deeds in verse, but what emerged were Stories from the Front (154-57).

8. Lucilius' journey took him to Capua, then either by land on the Via Popilia as fat as Valentia or, more likely, by sea from Puteoli (Marx 1905, 45). Horace reaches Capua at line 47, nearly halfway through his satire, and then diverges from Lucilius' route. Radke (1989) gives a finely detailed account of his probable itinerary, taking the Via Minucia to Brundisium. Significantly, the "road not taken," the Via Appia, went to Brundisium via Venusia (Horace's birthplace) and Tarentum.

9. Johnson and Boswell: Rogers 1993. Johnson's letters to Hester Thrale: Redford 1993, 51-119. Boswell's earlier manuscript: Pottle and Bennett 1967. Sherman (1996, 185-222) brilliantly analyzes this "diurnal dialectic in the Western Islands" against the long, gradual development of the travel diary and narrative; his account is suggestive for Horace's hypothetical improvements on Lucilius. Cf. Harrison 1987, 44-45, on Horace's impression of Lucilius' published poems "as a versified diary or notebook," inartistic and indiscreet. For Piozzi see Marrs 1997, esp. ch. 3, "Mrs. Piozzi, the Good-Natured Traveler."

10. Although the weather has changed, some details remain suggestive:

    Brundisium comes aut Surrentum ductus amoenum,
    qui queritur salebras et acerbum frigus et imbris,
    aut cistam effractam et subducta viatica plorat. . . .

    *(Ep.* 1.17.52-54)

    Cf. also *Ep.* 1.18.20 for a closely related reminiscence: *Brundisium Minuci melius via ducat an Appi.* Differently, Leach (1978, 90) sees Satire 1.5 as marking Horace's personal success: "how far the man of humble country origins has come as a sophisticated city dweller keenly sensitive to the incommodities of provincial accommodation."

11. For structural and narrative technique see Sallmann 1974, 186-97, with a nice appreciation of Horace's "virtuoses Wechseln zwischen Nah- und Fernperspektive, mit dem das persönliche Beteiligtsein des Erzählers am Reiseverlauf in sinnvoller Abstufung gekoppelt ist" (197). Cf. also Freudenburg 1993, 201-2, and the perceptive comments of Gowers (1993) on Horace's "diversions" in journey and poem (51) and his changes and variations of pace (53, 56-58), concluding that "the journey poem is a chart full of circumscriptions, suggesting all the constraints that have led modern satire to be rerouted" (60).

12. Horace's criticisms of Lucilius in *Satires* 1.4, 1.10, and 2.1 are well known and often cited, although we may miss elements of humor and caricature; cf. Harrison 1987. What we fail, for lack of evidence, to imagine is Lucilius' creative originality in his journey poem, as elsewhere, and the kinds of incentive it provided for Horace's *aemulatio.*

13. Most probably, Lucilius wrote for a friend who had missed the trip but might well take another. Cichorius ([1908] 1964, 256-59) suggested that book 3 included at least two separate poems: one a *propemptikon,* another on Lucilius' journey.

14. This would be the "provisional clean text" posited by Quinn (1982, 170), to be submitted, both orally and in writing, to trusted friends and critics. Horace might make further revisions (a) following their advice and (b) later on, when preparing the *libellus* for publication.

15. Horace's warning against publishing prematurely or leaving unpublished drafts around, *nescit vox missa reverti* (*AP* 390), might also apply to verses read aloud at some point and circulated around town.

16. Both Quinn (1982, 158) and Fantham (1996, 70-71) suggest that the more formal public *recitatio* introduced by Asinius Pollio grew naturally from after-dinner recitations. The convivial setting may also be mirrored in *S*. 2.6.70-117 (Cervius' fable as edifying postprandial entertainment); perhaps also in *S*. 2.2.1-7 if, as I suspect, Horace is asking his fellow dinner guests, comfortably wined and dined, to imagine themselves as ascetic would-be philosophers: *verum hic impransi mecum disquirite* (7).

17. See Muecke 1990, esp. 34-35, on Horace's fictive and actual audiences.

18. I am assuming, given no evidence to the contrary, that revisions of 1.5 between the years 37 and 35 were minimal.

19. Plut. *Ant.* 35.3; App. *BC* 5.94; Dio Cass. 48.54.3-5; also the fragments of Livy, book 127 (a bit garbled, but the armies' happiness in joining together, *cum magna laetitia,* may go back to Pollio).

20. Thus Classen (1973) sees friendship as a dominant theme of 1.5: strong, reliable private friendships are contrasted with "eine Freundschaft zwischen den Grossen, die erzwungen werden soll, um politischen Zwecken zu dienen" (250).

21. As Long and Sedley point out (1987, II no. 22, 134-39), Epicurean friendship created and still maintains the social fabric, together with law and justice; cf. *DRN* 5.1019 (*amicitiem coeperunt iungere*), 1145-46 (*nam genus humanum, defessum vi colere aevum / ex inimicitiis languebat*). "It is not surprising, then, that Lucretius links sentimental and prudential considerations in his account of the origin of friendships between neighbors, or that his account of its motivation is the social contract that defines justice" (137). For Philodemus' connection with the Latin poets in Siro's school (Virgil, Varius, Plotius, Quintilius) and, less directly, with Horace see Tait 1941; Gigante 1984, 67-92; Gigante and Capasso 1989; Gigante 1990, 29-36, 56-60; also, on Philodemus and Horace, Oberhelman and Armstrong 1995. Gigante argues suggestively for the practical, not just theoretical influence of "il grande messaggio di civiltà epicurea nella sintesi di *parrhesia, philia, charis, eunoia* che presentava in modo esemplare la comunità epicurea" (1990, 35).

22. Cf. Anderson 1982, 21, on Horace's high valuation here of the simple pleasures of life as against political competition and travail, and Van Rooy 1965, 51-52, 57-59, on the thematic uses of the *sanus/insanus* contrast (among other striking connections) in 1.4 and 1.5.

23. So Konstan argues (1995), following Brunt (1965), that *amicus* is not just synonymous with client or patron. "There was . . . a tense dialectic between *amicitia* and clientship. But the rhetorical tendency to assimilate the two ideas could be disrupted by irony or satire just because they remained implicitly distinct" (341). Even in politics "it was a personal bond that was able to survive disagreement and conflicting ambitions in the public sphere" (335 n. 28). Again, Konstan argues (1997, 122-48) for *amicitia* at Rome as a continuum from close, intimate relations to respectful public connections; but we see it most clearly in the private sphere, in "a relationship of mutual fondness and commitment" transcending inequality, like that of Horace and Maecenas (137).

24. For Lucretius' (not entirely negative) attitude toward political life see Fowler 1989. Epicureanism may sometimes have lent itself to practical mediation and compromise: cf. Syme 1939, 135-36, on L. Piso.

25. For deceptive "friendship" cf. Tacitus' damning anti-Augustus summary in *Ann.* 1.10.3: *sed Pompeium imagine pacis, sed Lepidum specie amicitiae deceptos; post Antonium, Tarentino Brundisinoque foedere et nuptiis sororis inlectum, subdolae adfinitatis poenas morte exsolvisse.* Tacitus puts Tarentum first in this hendiadys of treachery in order to build to the greater deception of the marriage alliance.

26. Cf. Lyne 1995, 92 and n. 26: "Horace uses *amicitia* here in its cynical, political sense" (with several examples); also the fine analysis of complexity and vision in "Ode 2.1" by Lowrie (1997, 175-86): "Pollio's history has drawn Horace more into the topic than he would wish, into narration, into epic and history. . . . All the distance that kept the trauma safely in the past, in someone else's history, vanishes" (185).

27. See Rudd 1966, 57, and Sallmann 1974, 185-86, on attempts to find political allegory in 1.5.

28. Huizinga 1955, esp. "Play and Law" (76-88) and "Play and War" (89-104).

29. Lucil. 149-58M. Marx suggests (1905, 73) that the gladiatorial combat described in book 4 was preceded by verbal skirmishing and insult-exchange like that in book 3, 117-22. Horace may draw on both episodes: note the rhinoceros at 159M, attributed to book 4, not 3.

30. See Gruen 1992, 289-91: Lucilius "had a field day with both protagonists" (290). However, we cannot tell how much coloring he added to the actual trial.

31. Freudenburg 1993, 52-108.

32. On Aristotle's "shrewd oxymoron" in *Rhet.* 1289b10-12 see Halliwell 1991, 292; also 284: "wit, he adds, is a form of educated/cultured hybris—behaviour, that is, which would be offensive and insulting if it were not transmuted (by verbal form and social context) into an admissible strain of mutually pleasurable communication."

33. *Ep.* 2.1.142-55 (festive comedy); cf. the complex joke about satire and the law at *S*. 2.1.79-86.

34. Marx (1905, 55) sees the *agon* in Lucilius book 3 as an insult-contest between *scurrae* or, more likely, gladiators; there may be overlap, or confusion, between books 3 and 4. Cichorius ([1908] 1964, 253) doubts that an actual gladiatorial contest occurred in book 3. His reasons are unconvincing, but he may be right, following Lachmann, to posit a contest between two *scurrae* that parodied a gladiatorial combat—cf. Horace's mutual-admiration contest at *Ep.* 2.2.95-101! Terzaghi (1934, 297-98) suggests the burlesque performance of an Atellana, with insults followed by blows. Fiske (1971, 308) follows Cichorius. He also suggests (n. 217) that Messius played Cicirrus, the Cock, an Atellane role.

35. Damon (1997, 109-12) places Sarmentus, with other *scurrae,* in the parasite tradition. He will resurface in Juv. 5.3-4 as a type who will put up with (almost) anything: cf. Braund 1996, 276-77. Although Horace has established himself in Satire 1.4 as a *liber amicus* (cf. Hunter 1985, 480-85), Sarmentus, the freedman, may be one of those shadow selves, like the *ineptus* of 1.9, that Horatian satire (vainly?) attempts to expel. See now Oliensis 1998, 29: "The other point about this satiric entertainment [in addition to its not drawing blood] is that it is not Horace who provides it. For the benefit of those detractors who imagine him to play the buffoon for the amusement of his social superiors, Horace takes care to locate himself very definitely in the audience, far above the satiric boxing ring. The men who take his place in the ring are men without face."

36. Horace's comment, that Lucilius was only "a match for / fair to" Virtue and her friends, may recall Lucilius' specific boast in the great *Virtus* fragment (1326-38M),

    > hostem esse atque inimicum hominum morumque malorum,
    > contra defensorem hominum morumque bonorum, hos magni facere, his bene velle, his vivere amicum,

                                                    (1334-36)

    as well as his political partisanship elsewhere and his zestful participation in political and personal feuds.

37. Thus Brown 1987, 199: *cruentant* (4.1036) looks forward to the blow, wound, and spurting of blood at 1049-57. I would add that it also conveys something of the male adolescent's psychological experience of shock and injury (*crede perito*) when his first nocturnal emission comes. Brown also points out (68-76) that although the wet dream may be understood physiologically as a simple release of tension, the mix of effluences (*simulacra*) and illusion is programmatic for the subsequent account of *amor* and its dangers: *sic in amore Venus simulacris ludit amantis* (4.1101).

38. The modest suggestion of Marx (1905, 140) that Lucilius might have been waiting for a faithless girl

with "the pains of Tantalus" (fr. 140-41), and his tentative comparison of fr. 1248, *permixi lectum, imposui pede pellibus labes,* was carried further by subsequent scholars who wanted more definitely to transfer fr. 1248 to book 3, interpreting Lucilius from Horace—and Horace, in a circular argument here and elsewhere, from Lucilius. Rudd (1966, 55) is more cautious. (He also points out that the *poenae* of Tantalus at fr. 140-41 may have manifested themselves in stomach trouble, not sex.)

39. Fr. 307M, *at laeva lacrimas muttoni absterget amica:* a man substitutes his ready left hand (*laeva*) for an unavailable mistress (*amica*). Krenkel (1970) compares, for this interpretation, Mart. 9.41, 11.73.4. There may be a similar sexual reference at 206M, *absterge lacrimas.*

40. Thus Rudd (1966, 54-56) warns against overskepticism: we have no right to infer from (hypothetical) literary borrowings that any one episode is fictitious. La Penna puts it well: "molte volte noi (e un autore antico più di noi) trasceliamo dalla nostra vita vissuta ciò che acquista senso alla luce delle reminiscenze letterarie" (1993, 45-46).

41. Although *aurea* primarily modifies *funis,* with an Iliadic golden rope as precedent, it may be taken secondarily with *saecla,* recalling Hesiod's "golden race."

42. According to Plutarch (*Ant.* 35.1), Antony with three hundred ships was refused entry to Brundisium, so sailed to Tarentum instead; and Octavia and others, including Maecenas and Agrippa, persuaded Octavian to meet there peaceably with Antony. Appian ignores Antony's hostile feelings and his rejection by the suspicious men of Brundisium: "for him the meeting was peaceable, and it seems that it was always *planned* for Tarentum" (Pelling 1988, 213). "If Maecenas had earlier travelled to Brundisium with Horace . . . , he presumably doubled back to join [Octavian]'s main retinue" (214). The sequence of events and their causes eludes scholars today and may not have been much clearer to Horace, or even to Maecenas, at the time.

43. Loss of control: Oliensis 1995, esp. 211-13; dealing with conflicting aims (elite readership/popularity and fame), 215-16.

44. Cf. Van Rooy 1965; Leach 1978; Zetzel 1980; Parker 1986; Freudenburg 1993, 198-211.

45. Leach 1978, 82-83.

46. Leach 1978, 96-97; Putnam 1970, 293-341. Leach more optimistically emphasizes "the achievement of an artistic identity through the completion of a poetic book" as marked in each epilogue (96); but on the same page, she admits that "to these damaging encroachments of the real world that art cannot control there is no answer save reassertion of the poet's faith in artistic order for its own sake."

47. I am grateful to Susanna Braund and David Konstan for their advice and encouragement; to our departmental brown bag luncheon group, who heard and responded to a short version of this essay; and to the thoughtful advice of an unnamed referee who, inter alia, suggested further comparisons with Virgil and Tibullus that seemed promising but might have seduced me too far beyond my chosen bounds.

### Bibliography

Anderson, William S. 1982. *Essays on Roman Satire.* Princeton: Princeton University Press.

Braund, Susanna Morton, ed. 1996. *Juvenal: Satires Book I.* Cambridge: Cambridge University Press.

Brown, Robert D. 1987. *Lucretius on Love and Sex.* Leiden: Brill.

Brunt, P. A. 1965. "'Amicitia' in the Late Roman Republic." *PCPS* 11: 1-20.

Cichorius, Conrad. [1908] 1964. *Untersuchungen zu Lucilius.* Berlin: Weidmann.

Classen, Carl Joachim. 1973. "Eine unsatirische Satire des Horaz?" *Gymnasium* 80:235-50.

Damon, Cynthia. 1997. *The Mask of the Parasite: A Pathology of Roman Patronage.* Ann Arbor: University of Michigan Press.

DuQuesnay, I. M. Le M. 1984. "Horace and Maecenas." In *Poetry and Politics in the Age of Augustus,* edited by Tony Woodman and David West, 19-58. Cambridge: Cambridge University Press.

Ehlers, Wido-Wolfgang. 1985. "Das 'Iter Brundisinum' des Horaz (Serm. 1.5)." *Hermes* 113:69-83.

Fantham, Elaine. 1996. *Roman Literary Culture: From Cicero to Apuleius.* Baltimore and London: The Johns Hopkins University Press.

Fiske, George C. [1920] 1971. *Lucilius and Horace: A Study in the Classical Theory of Imitation.* Westport, Conn.: Greenwood Press.

Fowler, D. P. 1989. "Lucretius and Politics." In *Philosophia Togata: Essays on Philosophy and Roman Society,* edited by Miriam Griffin and Jonathan Barnes, 120-50. Oxford: Clarendon Press.

Freudenburg, Kirk. 1993. *The Walking Muse: Horace on the Theory of Satire.* Princeton: Princeton University Press.

Gigante, Marcello. 1984. *Virgilio e la Campania.* Naples: Giannini.

———. 1990. *Filodemo in Italia.* Florence: Le Monnier.

Gigante, Marcello, and Mario Capasso. 1989. "Il ritorno di Virgilio a Ercolano." *SIFC* 7:3-6.

Gowers, Emily. 1993. "Horace, *Satires* 1.5: An Inconsequential Journey." *PCPS* 13: 48-66.

Gruen, Erich S. 1992. *Culture and National Identity in Republican Rome.* Ithaca: Cornell University Press.

Halliwell, F. S. 1991. "The Uses of Laughter in Greek Culture." *CQ* 41: 279-96.

Harrison, Geoffrey. 1987. "The Confessions of Lucilius (Horace *Sat.* 2.1.30-34): A Defense of Autobiographical Satire?" *CA* 6: 38-52.

Huizinga, Johan. 1955. *Homo Ludens: A Study of the Play Element in Culture.* Boston: Beacon Paperback.

Hunter, R. L. 1985. "Horace on Friendship and Free Speech." *Hermes* 113: 480-90.

Konstan, David. 1995. "Patrons and Friends." *CP* 90: 328-42.

———. 1997. *Friendship in the Classical World.* Cambridge: Cambridge University Press.

Krenkel, Werner, ed. 1970. *Lucilius: Satiren I, II.* Leiden: Brill.

La Penna, Antonio. 1993. *Saggie e studi su Orazio.* Florence: Sansoni.

Leach, Eleanor W. 1978. "Vergil, Horace, Tibullus: Three Collections of Ten." *Ramus* 7: 79-105.

Long, A. A., and D. N. Sedley. 1987. *The Hellenistic Philosophers.* Vol. I, *Translations of the Principal Sources with Philosophical Commentary.* Vol. II, *Greek and Latin Texts with Notes and Bibliography.* Cambridge: Cambridge University Press.

Lowrie, Michele. 1997. *Horace's Narrative Odes.* Oxford: Clarendon Press.

Lyne, R. O. A. M. 1995. *Horace: Behind the Public Poetry.* New Haven and London: Yale University Press.

Marrs, Lu Ann. 1997. *Hester Piozzi and the Art of Travel.* Diss. University of North Carolina, Chapel Hill.

Marx, Fridericus, ed. 1904-5. *C. Lucilii Carminum Reliquiae I, II.* Leipzig: Teubner.

Muecke, Frances. 1990. "The Audience of/in Horace's *Satires.*" *AUMLA* 74: 34-47.

Oberhelman, Steven, and David Armstrong. 1995. "Satire as Poetry and the Impossibility of Metathesis in Horace's *Satires.*" In *Philodemus and Poetry: Poetic Theory and Practice in Lucretius, Philodemus, and Horace,* edited by Dirk Obbink, 233-54. New York and Oxford: Oxford University Press.

Oliensis, Ellen. 1995. "Life after Publication: Horace *Epistles* 1.20." *Arethusa* 28: 209-24.

———. 1998. *Horace and the Rhetoric of Authority.* Cambridge: Cambridge University Press.

Parker, Alison. 1986. *Comic Theory in the Satires of Horace.* Diss. University of North Carolina, Chapel Hill.

Pelling, C. B. R. 1996. "The Triumviral Period." In *The Cambridge Ancient History* X 1-69.

———, ed. 1988. *Plutarch: Life of Antony.* Cambridge: Cambridge University Press.

Pottle, Frederick A., and Charles H. Bennett, eds. 1961. *Boswell's Journal of a Tour to the Hebrides with Samuel Johnson 1773.* New York, Toronto, and London: McGraw-Hill.

Puelma Piwonka, Mario. [1949] 1978. *Lucilius und Kallimachos.* New York and London: Garland.

Putnam, Michael C. J. 1970. *Virgil's Pastoral Art.* Princeton: Princeton University Press.

Quinn, K. 1982. "The Poet and His Audience in the Augustan Age." *ANRW* XXX.1 75-180.

Radke, Gerhard. 1989. "Topographische Betrachtungen zum *Iter Brundisinum* des Horaz." *RhM* 132: 54-72.

Redford, Bruce, ed. 1993. *The Letters of Samuel Johnson.* Vol. II, *1773-1776.* Princeton: Princeton University Press.

Rogers, Pat, ed. 1993. *Johnson and Boswell in Scotland: A Journey to the Hebrides.* New Haven and London: Yale University Press.

Rudd, Niall. 1966. *The Satires of Horace.* Cambridge: Cambridge University Press.

Sallmann, Klaus. 1974. "Die Seltsame Reise nach Brundisium: Aufbau und Deutung der Horaz Satire 1.5." In *Musa Iocosa,* edited by Udo Reinhardt and Klaus Sallmann, 179-206. Hildesheim and New York: Olms.

Sherman, Stuart. 1996. *Telling Time: Clocks, Diaries, and English Diurnal Form, 1660-1785.* Chicago and London: University of Chicago Press.

Stahl, Hans-Peter. 1974. "Peinliche Erfahrung eines kleines Gottes: Horaz in seinen Satiren." *Antike und Abendland* 20: 25-53.

Syme, Ronald. 1939. *The Roman Revolution.* Oxford: Oxford University Press.

Tait, J. I. M. 1941. *Philodemus' Influence on the Roman Poets.* Diss. Bryn Mawr.

Terzaghi, Nicola. 1934. *Lucilio.* Turin: L'Erma di Bretschneider.

Van Rooy, C. A. 1965. *Studies in Classical Satire and Related Literary Theory.* Leiden: Brill.

Zetzel, J. E. G. 1980. "Horace's *Liber Sermonum:* The Structure of Ambiguity." *Arethusa* 13: 59-77.

**Phebe Lowell Bowditch (essay date 2001)**

SOURCE: Bowditch, Phebe Lowell. "Gladiatorial Imagery: The Rhetoric of Expenditure." In *Horace and the Gift Economy of Patronage,* pp. 1-29. Berkeley: University of California Press, 2001.

[*In the following essay, Bowditch draws on principles of cultural anthropology to propose that Horace functioned in a "gift economy," and that to some extent his poetry allowed him to resist the patronage that supported him*]

"The gladiator: crude, loathsome, doomed, lost (*importunus, obscaenus, damnatus, perditus*) was, throughout the Roman tradition, a man utterly debased by fortune, a slave, a man altogether without worth and dignity (*dignitas*), almost without humanity" (Barton 1993, 12). No wonder that so many scholars of Horace, confronted with his image as a retired gladiator at the beginning of *Epistles* 1.1, either make little comment or smile wryly at the irony of the speaker's rhetoric and dismiss the trope as humorously extreme in its depiction of patronal relations as well as public performance.[1] Tired of beseeching the crowd, already presented with the wooden foil symbolizing discharge, the speaker complains that Maecenas, his patron, wishes to confine him again to his old school and sport (*quaeris / . . . antiquo me includere ludo*).[2] Such highly figurative language has been read—and rightly, to a degree—as ironic metaphor: in complying with a patron, Horace was certainly no slave; and though perhaps his odes were not as well received as he might have wished, he never presumed to please the Roman masses. Thus, the opening of the poem is generally considered an elaborate conceit to justify the poet's decision to abandon lyric and embark instead on the new genre of the verse epistle.[3]

But what if this figurative image of a *ludus* (gladiatorial school) and the shows (*munera*) for which such training prepared, compounded by the gladiatorial reference at the end of *Epistles* 1.19, were given a more "literal" reading—one that privileges the terms of the metaphor rather than its referent—and were placed within the context of a larger cultural practice?[4] What if these images were understood not only as ironic figures for Horace's compromised freedom but also within the context of imperial patronage as a form of public expenditure dependent on spectacle? As Paul Veyne remarks, "'Giving gladiators' became the best way to make oneself popular," so that although the practice began as a funeral *largesse,* during the late Republic and early Empire it turned into *euergesia* "pure and simple," a form of electoral corruption (1990, 222).[5] Both Suetonius and Augustus himself record the emperor's lavish spending on such gladiatorial games, mock sea battles (*naumachiae*), athletic competitions, beast hunts, and theatrical performances (Augustus, *Res Gestae* 22-23; Suet. *Aug.* 43). Although originally brokered through Maecenas as a middleman, might not the regime's expenditure on Horace as a public poet be reflected in this image of a *munus,* "gladiatorial display," ultimately directed at a public, however difficult to define, whose loyalty and adherence the emperor desired? That is, perhaps we should view the poetic rhetoric of Horace's vision of patronal relations here as embedded in a greater cultural practice of expenditure that also functions rhetorically in its aim to control and to persuade.[6]

Over the past few decades it has become increasingly clear in literary studies that a text can be interpreted as neither an isolated document nor a simple reflection of its historical backdrop. Socioeconomic practices account for the conditions of any work's production as well as for many of the "symbol systems" by which a text communicates meaning to an audience. This is particularly true for Augustan literary patronage: social relations of exchange provided more than a context for the production of verse; they also informed a shared system of rhetorical figures through which poets negotiated both their own interests and those of their varied audiences. My study of Horace explores these rhetorical negotiations but argues that they are embedded within, and partly determined by, material and discursive practices outside of the literary text. The triangular relationship of poet, patron, and "public" audience must be interpreted in the social context of ancient Rome, where the exchange of goods and services provided for the ideological cohesion of a community. Poetry, as one such good exchanged, not only distinguishes a benefactor, providing the important boons of status and immortality, but it also speaks to a wider audience and, as Horace's gladiatorial image suggests, constitutes a form of gift or public *munus* to the community at large. The language of *munera*—"gifts," "games," "funereal offerings," or "political office," to name the major definitions—along with related socioeconomic diction, appears in several contexts in Horace's poems. Focusing on the trajectory of Horace's work during the early years of the Augustan Principate (31-12 B.C.E.), I argue that the cultural practices behind such contexts— social benefaction, political euergetism, and religious sacrifice—inform the relationship between a discourse of sacrificial expiation in Horace's *Odes* and the rhetorical gestures of autonomy displayed by the speaker of the *Epistles.*

Drawing on scholarship in cultural anthropology on gift economies, I interrogate in several Horatian poems the rhetoric that suggests the following related concepts. First, the public service (or *munus*) that the poet performs by writing his political poems constitutes a form of sacrificial expenditure, and ultimately a sacrifice of self, that the philosophically oriented first book of *Epistles* reclaims: as a priest of the Muses, or *sacerdos Musarum,* Horace's political poems provide the "gift" of purification for a people corrupted by the civil wars. Second, though many of the poems serve to reinforce a certain ideology of voluntarism in Augustan literary patronage, they also expose its contradictions. Just as gift-exchange societies conceal economic interests behind the concept of the disinterested gift, so the rhetorical language concerned with benefaction similarly occludes but may also reveal calculation in regard to the return gift of verse. Horace deploys different registers of imagery to expose the conflict between the "philosophy" of voluntary benefaction and the often-distorted reciprocity ethic by which the practice in fact operated in the upper echelons of Roman society. And third, Horatian poetic rhetoric often draws on larger cultural practices of expenditure in a way that produces an ideological effect sympathetic to his patrons even as it simultaneously provides the ground for the poet's gestures

of autonomy. At the risk of simplification, my inquiry may be summed up by this question: if the gifts of patronage symbolically expropriate the poet's self, obligating him to make the return gift of poetry as the embodied or "reified" form of his labor, then in what ways and to what degree does the figurative language concerned with this exchange permit resistance to that same patronal discourse?

During the 20s B.C.E. the Augustan regime solidified its power by transforming political structures and by communicating a coherent—if negotiable and evolving— ideological vision.[7] Although no mere propaganda, Horace's political poems contribute to, and arguably constitute, aspects of that vision: in particular, the sequence of poems called the Roman Odes presents a construction of history that both accounts for civil decline and lays the moral foundations for social and spiritual renewal. Recent criticism has tended to downplay the propagandistic character of these poems and, perhaps as a consequence, resists viewing them in a socioeconomic context of exchange relations.[8] However, any discussion of Horace's political poems must not only acknowledge a context of patronal benefaction but must also consider the degree to which that context intersects with other discourses of exchange and expenditure. Not much prior to 32-31 B.C.E., the literary evidence suggests that Maecenas, perhaps the figure then closest to Augustus (still called Octavian), gave Horace his celebrated "Sabine farm."[9] The political poetry of Horace's *Odes* 1-3 was written over the course of the next decade and published in 23 B.C.E., the very same years that decisively established Augustus in power. Rather than view the gift of land as an isolated act in the Horatian biography, or even as simply an example of the gifts presented by the elite to their friends, we should consider it both in the context of the massive land expropriation and redistribution that marked the 40s and 30s and in relation to sacrificial practices implied by the Horatian posture of the *sacerdos Musarum,* or "priest of the Muses."

Land grants, since the time of Sulla and even before, were both an incentive held out to prospective soldiers and, arguably, a means of securing loyalty—a political strategy that enabled a general to maintain relations with his veterans, once released from service, and thus to move from the sphere of military to political power. In the context of literary patronage, the gift of land by figures close to the center of political power must similarly be considered as a strategy to aid the benefactors. In Horace's case, I argue that the probable grant of his estate in the early 30s puts into circulation a form of capital that is further circulated in terms of a symbolic discourse of sacrificial expenditure in his poems. For example, the appearance of the estate in a discourse of Epicurean quietude in the first Roman Ode has often led critics to find the "public" nature of these poems problematic, since the call to public service found in many of the odes' gnomic statements sits oddly with the poet's foregrounding of his own withdrawal from the sphere of political action (e.g., Lyne 1995, 158-63). However, I suggest that the estate figures here partly as an indication of the *munus,* or gift, that leads to the assumption of the role of priest, or *sacerdos,* whose poetry constitutes an act of expiatory sacrifice for the sake of a "public" audience. Sacrificial practice in ancient Rome, as Richard Gordon has recently analyzed, "could be made into aesthetic action, action for itself, free of self interest"; and "formulaic religious action represented the pure accumulation of 'symbolic capital[,]' . . . the most durable form of wealth" (1990a, 193-94). As I discuss at greater length in chapter 1, "symbolic capital" exercises power in the form of gratitude and obligation, and it is precisely this form of capital or wealth that the regime initially creates with grants of land—and that Horace perpetuates through his invocation of a sacerdotal motif. Not only does the priestly role accord with these odes' ideological production of Roman imperialism in terms of destiny, piety, and proper religious observance, but it also serves to "veil" the exchange of land for poetry by presenting them as voluntary expenditures on the part of both benefactor and poet.[10]

Though the evidence for the benefaction of the estate is admittedly tenuous, deriving from the poems themselves with reinforcement from the scholiasts and Suetonius, scholarly literature has fostered a vision of Maecenas's gift as both indisputable fact and canonical myth. Whereas the mythic stature of the estate quietly reinforces the assumption of fact regarding its provenance, the illusion of empiricism in turn reifies the poet's relationship with his patron as one indissolubly linked with this act of benefaction. Rather than get caught in this circle of assumptions regarding historical events that elude empirical recovery, I choose to view Horace's estate as a symbol of benefaction that is variously constructed in his poetry and multiply implicated in cultural discourses and practices of the Augustan period: in addition to sacerdotal practice and hierarchical patronage, we see land expropriation and redistribution, Epicurean withdrawal from public life, upper-class "friendship," and the intellectual pursuits of villa society, as well as market economics, slavery, and the material production of a livelihood. Indeed, I believe that the very ubiquity of the farm's implied presence in so many poems, coupled with the frequent absence of extended reference, lends the implicit image its discursive power.

In keeping with the excessively stratified nature of Roman society, and the biography of "freedman's son" that Horace presents for himself in his verse, representations of the estate reveal it particularly as a source of anxiety concerning the poet's status: Does the gift convert the freeborn poet too completely into a client, entailing too many obligations to those clearly superior in terms of political as well as socioeconomic status; or does it constitute a symbol of the poet's elite landholding rank, a gift in the spirit of voluntary and affective friendship? And, if the latter, do the estate's associations with aristocratic *otium* belie or create fissures in the poet's creed of modest living and rustic simplicity—an attitude at once propagandistic or "Augustan" and self-interested? The answer to all these questions is, of course, affirmative, but which affirmative

dominates is always determined in relation to the identity of the particular audience whose interests the speaker has in mind (and frequently identifies with).

To determine the actual lineaments of Horace's audience and the literate population in ancient Rome under the Principate is by no means easy, or even possible; the effort has occupied much recent scholarship.[11] The difficulty is compounded by the numerous ways in which literature might be experienced—at a "public" performance, at a private recitation for a small circle, listening to a slave employed as reader, or, finally, reading—though probably vocalizing aloud—to oneself. Hence, there may very well have been those who "heard" poetry in the most public of contexts but who were not in fact literate themselves. Superimposed on this issue of the actual audience, as determined by the specific context in which a work was either heard or read, is the variety of audiences notionally implicated in the text itself. Thus, a single ode or epistle of Horace's has at least four different levels of audience, to whom it speaks regardless of the actual site of consumption: the addressee or the pronominal "you" of the lyric or epistolary form, Horace's patrons—Maecenas and Augustus—to whom individual poems or whole collections are addressed, the greater readership of Rome (for example, the public to whom Horace's epistolary collection is "set free" in *Epistles* 1.20), and posterity.[12] In spite of the frequency with which these several audiences may overlap, the generic transition from the *Odes* to the *Epistles* accentuates the distinction between "public" and "private" and actively reconfigures the relations between poet, patron, and audience, as Horace retreats from the public position of lyric priest, offering a gift of symbolic sacrifice, into the didactic role of the philosopher in his epistolary garden.

The concept of the "gift," I suggest, brings into focus this particular dynamic by which the social relations defining Horace's experience of literary patronage at once determine and are reflexively modified by his poems. The idea of a gift economy as a hermeneutic lens or methodological tool for interpreting this reciprocal dynamic is by no means unprecedented. In his monumental exploration of imperial *euergetism* in the Greco-Roman world, *Bread and Circuses* (1990), Veyne shows the strong influence of Marcel Mauss's essay *The Gift* (1990 [1950]) and the subsequent work in cultural anthropology that it promoted. Moreover, scholars of personal or "social" patronage, such as Richard Saller (1982) and Suzanne Dixon (1993), as well as of the Roman economy, such as Keith Hopkins (1983b), also offer interpretations informed by anthropological studies of the gift. Only Dixon's study, however, draws explicit parallels between the character of "primitive" economies and the meaning of gifts and debt in the Roman elite. Moreover, although the work of scholars such as Leslie Kurke (1991), among others, has demonstrated the relevance of anthropology to the interpretation of Greek literature, such scholarship has not, for the most part, been undertaken in Roman literary studies. Because anthropological studies have been invoked in discussions of the

Roman economy and social relations, but rarely examined in detail as comparative paradigms and then not in the context of interpreting Latin literature, my first chapter attempts to be as explicit as possible about the relevant areas of comparison and the usefulness of anthropology as a hermeneutic point of departure.

Indeed, as Mauss's speculations suggest, the early history of Roman contract law may have reflected social attitudes toward material transactions that resemble those of the gift economies of Polynesia, Melanesia, and the native peoples of the Pacific Northwest—the societies on which he based his case studies (1990 [1950], 47-53). In his analysis of the rituals and language of Roman legal transactions Mauss, followed by Emile Benveniste and Pierre Bourdieu, observed that the ideas of "gift" and "contract" were originally compressed into a single vocabulary that later split into two (Benveniste 1973, 66-82; Bourdieu 1977, 172). In line with Mauss's observations, we find that the *Epistles* present a vision of Horace's "past" lyric self that evokes the idea of the *nexum,* a form of debt-bondage in archaic Rome incurred when a loan was paid off through the recipient's physical labor:[13] the body of the debtor was quite literally owned by the lender until the loan was made good. In his discussion of the archaic economy, Mauss views the *nexum* as a kind of transitional state between primitive gift exchange and Roman contract law (1990 [1950], 49). Though patronage was not legally a contractual relationship, Horace's literary treatment of benefaction—particularly in the seventh epistle—evokes the trace of contract law's "prehistory."

In addition, the mytho-historical past that Rome constructed for itself—the hybrid world of the Homeric era—displays social gift exchange in the rituals attending *xenia,* or guest-host friendship. Horace's own reference to *xenia* and the aristocratic gift exchange by which it functioned, again in *Epistles* 1.7, points up the degree to which such former social stages, whether mythical or historical, could provide a way of conceptualizing the obligations and expectations entailed in patronage. Traces of older economic systems inhabit the culture of the late first century B.C.E. as the "ideological fallout" of previous periods.[14] To what effect does Horace invoke these older systems and figure patronage in terms of a specifically *contractual* reciprocity? And what effect does such figuration have on the maintenance or reappropriation of poetic autonomy? That is, though Horace may present his debt as "paid off," in what ways does he still need to reclaim authority? It is questions such as these that the chapters on *Epistles* 1 treat.

Insofar as I introduce the conclusions drawn by cultural anthropologists about strictly "primitive" nonmonetary cultures, my paradigm of a gift economy may appear an inexact fit for Roman literary patronage in some particulars. However, as Charles Martindale has pointed out in his book on hermeneutics and classical scholarship, *Redeeming the Text,* a particular hermeneutic lens or methodology enables us to "perceive" phenomena that otherwise we

might not see (1993, 2). Because critical access to the institution of patronage is mediated, for the most part, through textual sources, it is never free of the ideology inherent in language.[15] This problem of getting behind the language that a society uses to describe its own functions is of course compounded when so much of the documentary evidence available is literature. Hence, the gap between the interpretive lens—the paradigm of a "gift economy"—and its object of study allows me "to take [a] stand outside the Roman value system in order to understand it" (Wallace-Hadrill 1989, 4). Such a stance would seem inevitable for the twenty-first-century American critic, but the spirit of historical empiricism in which much philological study has been conducted assumes not only the complete objectivity of the critic but also a corollary: that a society's self-conception accurately describes the way that society functions. The task of the empiricist is thus to gather together the evidence and let it "speak for itself," a procedure that assumes a one-to-one correspondence between language and reality or takes language to be, in Simon Goldhill's phrase, "a transparent illustration of thought" (1986, 111).[16] However, anthropologists have long noted the discrepancies between the claims that a society makes and "the unrecognized system of ideas and organization of attitudes giving rise to the express statements of significance" (Goldhill 1986, 112). And though the dangers of distortion afflict any act of interpretation, a hermeneutic lens focused on the possible distortions and ideological veils in a society's own self-conception may in fact clarify rather than obscure.

Nonetheless, I emphasize that my reading of Horace in the following chapters is an interpretation, and all interpretations are, for better or worse, translations into meaning: that is, by rendering the inaccessibility and opacity and refractoriness of a foreign culture into terms that are meaningfully productive for us, an interpretive reading necessarily performs a kind of translation. As Peter Rose points out in his defense of the relevance of a Marxist approach to classical antiquity, the intelligibility of our answers depends on the terms in which they are cast.[17] The type of reading practices that fall under the rubric "Marxist" in fact share a certain ground with anthropological approaches. Both note the presence of ideological distortions in a culture's self-conceptions; but whereas anthropology tends to emphasize the functional element of ideology and symbolic systems, Marxism focuses more on the potential antagonism between interest groups lying beneath an ideology that serves to maintain the position of those with economic power.[18] My interpretations of the social relations of patronage are informed overall by the writings of Mauss, Marshall Sahlins, Karl Polanyi, and Bourdieu, but I have eschewed a dogmatic or fundamentalist application of any single theoretical paradigm, preferring rather to make use of a range of insights drawn from different disciplines or schools of thought when the literary rhetoric of the poems is profitably addressed by such means. Hence, my discussion of the gaps or fissures in the patronal system's "ideology of voluntarism," particularly in regard to poems that figure Horace's estate, owes much to reading practices that fall loosely under the critical aegis of "Marxist aesthetics." This approach usefully highlights, for example, how the contrary figurings of patronal experience that seem to intersect at the site of the estate derive from more than the essential anxiety about status that benefaction, as a practice, often mobilizes. Such representations reinforce the ideology or interests of the elite even as they reveal the exploitation that the system of benefaction might enable. In addition to insights informed by anthropological and Marxist approaches, readers will also encounter concepts drawn from linguistics, the writings of Michel Foucault, and deconstruction. Though some will no doubt question this apparent theoretical eclecticism, my varied recourse to different writers is always taken to illuminate the text and make it possible for us to "perceive" phenomena that otherwise we might not see.

### RECENT STUDIES OF HORACE AND LITERARY PATRONAGE

The need for critical distance is all the more imperative in the case of Horace. Even a half century after the lessons of the New Critics have taught the reader to beware the postures of autobiographical personae, to distinguish between the historical self and the artifice it assumes on the page, the Horatian speaker continues to project a seductive believability. Two of the most recent full-length books on Horace (Johnson 1993; Lyne 1995), for all their authors' negotiations between irrecoverable history and the mimetic illusions of poetry, clearly (and willingly) rest their interpretations on reconstructed versions of a "historical" Horace.[19] This recourse to historical background is a literary approach more characteristic of "conventional" than of "new" historicism, insofar as it attempts to reconstruct the thoughts and intentions of the poet. However, it also indicates the overall critical trend away from the purely formalist concerns of New Criticism and a renewed interest in the context—social, historical, economic, and political—of any literary work's production. In some ways, the change of orientation is more noticeable in studies of genres or periods in which the literary texts are not as apparently suffused in the momentous political changes of the time as are the works of Augustan Rome. The subject matter, explicit or otherwise, of much Augustan literature—empire and its discontents—makes a dismissal of context nearly impossible.

Thus, it may be precisely because Horace the "propagandist" has always been an issue in Augustan criticism that there have been few, if any, full-length New Historical treatments of his poems. The "return" to history for which such an approach calls may seem not new enough, too dangerously capable of collapsing the cultural discourses shaping poetic rhetoric into the biographical referentiality of the "old" historicism.[20] Ellen Oliensis (1998), for example, reads Horace's poems as gestures of deference and authority, appealing to and manipulating a variety of historical audiences; yet her interest focuses more on the poems as performative speech acts than on their embed-

dedness in culture.[21] Other theoretical approaches to Horace tend to limit the context of inquiry to the verse itself, either exploring modes of rhetorical persuasion (Davis 1991), uncovering the constructions of gender implicit in such rhetoric (Ancona 1994), or, finally, analyzing the ultimately deconstructive tendencies of figurative language (Fowler 1995; Lowrie 1997). Ironically, these recent deconstructionist approaches to Horace point up the degree to which certain critical issues will always be at stake in his poems. On the one hand, as Don Fowler remarks, the debate over whether Horace or Ovid was "pro-" or "anti-" Augustan has yielded to such question as "What is the relation that we construct between Horatian or Ovidian discourse and that of other contemporary systems?" (1995, 250). On the other hand, despite the terms of Fowler's argument, which examines whether the rhetoric of Epicureanism, allied with Callimachean aesthetics, could even permit valid or "authentic" panegyric, his conclusion—that such poetic emperor worship unravels as a result of contradictions and tensions in the lyric discourse—ultimately rescues the poet from sycophancy. In other words, the claim of failed unity and the desire to shift the inquiry from the level of sincerity to that of the discursive strands of the lyric fabric itself may in fact conceal a romantic desire to safeguard Horace from the charge of compliant toadyism and thus protect a form of "agency" external to the text.

In whatever terms the issue of panegyric is posed, it suggests that the socioeconomic practice of imperial patronage looms as the inescapable backdrop to Horatian poetic discourse. Scholarship on literary patronage has evolved considerably since the early views of Sir Ronald Syme, which held that Augustus, via Maecenas, orchestrated a unified program of poetic propaganda to influence public opinion (1960 [1939], 459-75). On one end of the spectrum are the literary critics such as James Zetzel (1982), Matthew Santirocco (1986, 1995), or R. O. A. M. Lyne (1995), whose attention (variously directed) to the conventions and rhetorical representation of patronage either disassociates the text from historical causality, reveals the poet as creating his own agenda, or problematizes any full-fledged endorsement of the regime. At the other extreme are historians such as Peter White (1993), whose meticulous and valuable examination of the historical evidence leads him to conclude that poets celebrated Augustus out of a spontaneous attraction to, and fascination with, the emperor's potent image and the social changes that he effected. Writing from a perspective both historical and literary-critical, Barbara Gold (1987) essentially sees patronage for the Augustan writers as "subject matter in itself" and a "literary phenomenon" in which the "desires of patrons seem to have influenced the writers . . . only in indirect and nonspecific ways" (1987, 66).[22] Similar assumptions also underlie the work of Michael Putnam (1986), whose readings of Horace's fourth book of *Odes*—poetry notoriously "requested" by Augustus—encourage a rejection of toadyism in order to preserve the poet's aesthetic integrity. By no means ignoring and often emphasizing Horatian irony and its subversive potential, scholars of Horace (with some exceptions, of course) tend to endorse a view of the poet's *libertas* that accords with what I have dubbed "an ideology of voluntarism" in the literature on benefaction.[23] To be sure, this endorsement of the poet's creative independence fully acknowledges the practice of reciprocity in Roman social relations; but it tends to downplay the psychology of debt in a gift economy—how the persuasive coercions of *gratia,* or gratitude toward a patron, may affect the ideological content of the poetry itself.

I believe that this investment in Horatian "agency" issues from two basic sources. On the one hand, Horace's situation involves the plight of human liberty, and though the historical modalities of this concept clearly change over time, the desire for freedom—whether from social roles or government interference, whether circumscribed or infinite—remains with us. On the other hand, as Ernst Doblhofer (1966) early acknowledged, critics often respond to the political climate of their own countries, displaying biases that reflect their own historical situation.[24] And thus, just as Syme's dark view expressed in his *Roman Revolution* must be seen in the light of Nazi totalitarianism, so critics who adhere to a vision of the unconstrained autonomy of the artist in their assessment of Horace may reflect the premium that they, often tenured scholars of the ivory tower and citizens of liberal democracies, place on their own academic freedom and political liberties.

As I have outlined, my discussion of Horatian verse seeks to frame the issue of patronal pressure in new terms, employing the concept of a gift economy as a hermeneutic lens that brings into focus the contradictions inherent in literary patronage and in the rhetorical language by which it is figured. For example, those who argue for the voluntary nature of poetry in support of Augustus sometimes give a material justification, claiming that all the Augustan poets were *equites* before any imperial benefactions were made and thus had no actual need of material support. This statistic appears to support the poets' "uncompromised" position: not in need of the regime's help, they offer a voluntary celebration, neither the obliged response to specific requests nor the return issuing from actual debt.[25] Peter White, who makes this argument, acknowledges that poets derived substantial benefits— "Gifts of cash, estates, emoluments, and dowries"—from their powerful "friends," but he insists that such gifts, "once conferred . . . were valuable also in the sense that they left the recipient relatively independent of the giver" and that "support was not directly keyed to literary output" (1993, 17). White's treatment of the evidence is both impressive and persuasive on many counts, but I nonetheless believe that an examination of the poetic rhetoric by which Horace figured his experience of patronage, when considered in relation to Rome's cultural practices of exchange and expenditure, suggests a greater degree of debt and obligation than the phrase "relatively independent" would imply.

For as I discuss at length in chapter 1, the gift economy operates by displacing the economics of debt into the sphere of courtesy, so that obligation is concealed beneath the decorum of disinterested giving. This decorum, an ideology of voluntarism, appears in such Horatian rhetorical motifs as the *cornucopia,* the spontaneous fertility of the golden age, or the posture of the *sacerdos* sacrificing for the public at large. These poetic figures suggest the dynamics of what the cultural anthropologist Pierre Bourdieu identifies as the social misrecognition of the economics of gift exchange—in this case, a reconstrual of calculated transactions in terms of friendship, generosity, or imperial euergetism (expenditure for the public good) (Bourdieu 1977, 171; Harker, Mahar, and Wilkes 1990, 19). However, in Horace these rhetorical motifs are often undercut by their context or by allusive echoes in later poems that unmask such images as complicitous with the ideology of voluntarism. Horace's epistolary poems to Maecenas, for example, look back to the sacrificial rhetoric of the Roman Odes from the perspective of contractual exchange.

By going to social and cultural anthropology, I am by no means ignoring the extensive writing by the ancients on the theory or philosophy of benefaction, liberality, and social exchange. Rather, as chapter 1 demonstrates, I wish to illuminate this material from an anthropological angle, and I analyze the Horatian representation of patronage from both perspectives. Such an approach owes much to the field of "cultural studies." On the one hand, like other contemporary critics, I am to bring the insights of other disciplines to bear on the study of antiquity. Thus, to take a clearly interdisciplinary example, recent work on Catullus makes use of feminist film theory and the concept of the "gaze" as a means of understanding the sensual relationship between the reader and the visual pleasures offered by Ariadne, and the golden age, in Catullus 64 (Fitzgerald 1995, 140-68). On the other hand, those engaged in cultural studies acknowledge the tenuous and even artificial boundary between "literary" and "nonliterary" texts and seek to understand the reciprocal relations between the two, recognizing that cultural practices often constitute discursive or semiotic systems in their own right. As Dennis Feeney remarks in his discussion of the interpenetration of literary and religious discourse in ancient Rome, "Rather than asking how religion is transmuted into literature, . . . we should instead be thinking in terms of a range of cultural practices, interacting, competing, and defining each other in the process" (1998, 1).[26] Similarly, in addition to employing the insights of anthropology, I wish to view the literary representation of patronage in relation to a range of discursive and material practices involving exchange and expenditure—one of which is social benefaction itself.

### AUTONOMY AND THE DISCURSIVE CONVENTIONS OF PATRONAGE

For a study that interrogates the poetic rhetoric of literary patronage, the "nonliterary" texts of Aristotle's *Nicomachean Ethics,* Cicero's *On Duties,* and Seneca's *On Benefits* all contain material pertinent to the practice and psychology of ancient social relations considered in "economic" terms. But to restrict an inquiry to just these sources as a conceptual lens through which to view the Horatian poetic subject in his relation to patronal discourse poses a few problems. First, these ancient texts, particularly Cicero and Seneca, deal with the broader social phenomenon of liberality or benefaction, of which literary patronage is really a subset with its own unique characteristics. Second, these works are prescriptive rather than descriptive, presenting the ideology of benefactions analyzed by those in the society itself, who have no critical distance on their own historical context. Third, as many have noted, philosophers and poets alike avoid the language of patronage, and the corresponding diction of *clientela* or "clientship," when describing relations between those of elite social status.[27] Literary patronage, as I discuss in more detail below, was referred to almost exclusively in terms of *amicitia* or friendship.

Nonetheless, these social discourses of benefaction clarify the problem of Horatian autonomy or agency in relation to discursive conventions. As Seneca and Cicero so repeatedly display, codes and conventions governed the behavior of those giving and receiving benefactions; the ideal prescriptions contained in *On Duties* (*De officiis*) and *On Benefits* (*De beneficiis*) suggest the degree to which patronage, friendship, and the practice of benefaction were discursive practices in the Foucauldian sense—social modes of interaction that could achieve greater or lesser degrees of ideal stylization in their own right. Given this discursive element within the actual practice of patronage, the stylized treatment of its conventions in verse would be simply a higher order of representation: poetry and philosophical treatise are drawing on, and reciprocally informing, many of the same cultural codes. From this point of view, the problem of Horatian autonomy becomes the issue of the freedom of the Horatian subject. If, as I discuss further in chapter 4, the Horatian subject is an effect of language, a composite of social discourses invoked and activated by the speaking "I" of lyric and epistolary forms, then autonomy becomes a matter for language as well. On the one hand, the production of poetry as a gift involved in the exchanges of poet and patron takes place within the conventions of actual patronage; on the other hand, the invocation of the discourse of *amicitia* (friendship, patronage among the elite), together with all the related concepts of *gratia* (gratitude, favor, influence), *beneficium* (benefit, favor, kindness), *officium* (duty, favor), *munus* (gift, favor, duty, public show), and so on, as a "culture pattern" that informs the rhetorical figures of poetry, puts the issue of the poet's autonomy on that same level—that is, the level of poetic representation.

The problem of autonomy in relation to subjectivity regularly besets New Historical interpretations: where is a freely choosing self if linguistic consciousness is simply a culturally determined effect of social discourses?[28] For Horace, I argue, the question of liberty should be posed in terms not so much of freedom from the patron as of freedom within the overlapping discourses of patronage, friendship, and "literary benefaction." In this regard, the discursive or semiotic aspect of actual material practices should be kept somewhat distinct from the ideological lens or prescriptive discourse through which they were conducted. Taking as my starting point that literary patronage as a material practice operates as a system of gift exchange or gift economy, I argue that Horace experienced all the constraint and obligation—the sense of debt, gratitude, and compulsion to return—that such an economy would impose on him. The "context" of a gift economy, then, inevitably informs the text beyond conventions such as the dedication to a patron or the *recusatio*—the "refusal" poem in which a poet declines to write political panegyric even as the gesture toward praise is duly made. The poems themselves, in addition, constitute objects in which the labor and subjecthood of the poet have been reified. As we shall see in the discussion of the ***Epistles*** as they look back to, and comment on, the lyric poems, Horace's epistolary self draws attention to such "reification" of the self as a potential consequence of the patronal system. Ultimately, however, these references constitute one of many discursive systems or registers of imagery on the level of poetic representation; once he has revealed literary patronage as potentially exploitative, the poet renegotiates his relations by rhetorically inscribing himself in the ranks of the elite.

Reified selves occur as a result of systems of exchange, when the "subject" status of a person becomes implicated in the exchanges of objects and has a value determined by such exchangeability. Though we are accustomed to think of reification as the result of capitalism, Sahlins points out that in primitive reciprocity there is a "mystic alienation of the donor" in the gift that parallels Marx's notion of alienated human social labor in commodity production (1972, 181).[29] This mystic presence of the donor in the gift is what ensures reciprocity, causing the one who receives an object to be given over to, or temporarily bought by, the one who gives it, until a compensatory return has been made (Mauss 1990 [1950], 50). Though not "primitive," the system of Roman patronage operates by such reciprocity; and the seemingly voluntary gift may be said to reify or alienate its donor and its recipient when the context foregrounds the various values, the economic or symbolic capital, into which the benefaction may be translated. For example, if the context reveals calculation on the part of the giver regarding some kind of return, or if the recipient perceives or represents his "gratitude" in the reified terms of an obligatory "payback" in which the emphasis on commensuration outweighs the libidinal feeling of thankfulness, then a form of reification, however loosely defined, has entered the process.

But though such calculation with its open expectation of reciprocity is sometimes visible in the letters of Cicero and Pliny, members of the elite who publicly advertised their own participation in the practice of benefaction, it is clearly presented as problematic in the philosophical literature on the topic. When Seneca, for example, distinguishes between a voluntary return of gratitude (*referre gratiam*) and repayment in a monetary context (where the verb *reddere* would be employed), he points up an ideological discomfort with the calculation or manipulation of benefits and services to which the system potentially was inclined.[30] Indeed, as I discuss in more depth in the next chapter, one of the most distinctive features of the discourse of benefaction is the libidinal or emotive language in which the practice of gift giving was conducted. And so when we examine the discourse of patronage and friendship in Cicero's letters, the reciprocity ethic—though taken for granted—is generally couched in terms of the emotions of friendship and esteem. Thus, in a letter of Plancus to Cicero, Plancus concludes by professing both his strong affection and his desire, through the performance of reciprocating services, to make Cicero's previous favors or benefactions "more pleasing" (*iucundiora*) to him as benefactor (*Fam.* 10.23.7).[31] And in a recommendation letter that Cicero writes to Caesar, seeking to attach the young Trebatius Testa to Caesar's retinue on his Gallic campaign, Cicero invokes the language of friendship as a preface to his request: "Observe how I take it for granted that I have in you a second self (*te me esse alterum*), not only in what concerns me personally, but also in what concerns my friends. . . . I am beginning to wish that whatever Trebatius had hoped for from me, he should expect to get from you" (*Fam.* 7.5.1).[32]

And yet, as also appears in the literature, the libidinal and affective context of the transactions may yield to a pure emphasis on reciprocal obligation, revealing the bonds of friendship as a more contractual relationship. Not surprisingly, this emphasis is most evident when a relationship other than that between the letter writer and the recipient is being discussed. In a letter rebuking Trebatius for his formerly mercenary attitude toward his post in Caesar's retinue in Gaul, Cicero writes: "For you were in a hurry to snatch the money and return home, just as if what you had brought the commander-in-chief was not a letter of recommendation, but a bill of exchange [*syngrapham*]" (*Fam.* 7.17.1).[33] Here, we may note that Trebatius is figured as attempting to convert Cicero's "influence" or *gratia* with Caesar into its cash equivalent. Such conversion of "symbolic" into "material" capital, as chapter 1 demonstrates, is a characteristic operation of the gift economy. This very attempt to profit from the debt imposed by benefactions reveals an economic interestedness that belies the libidinal language of friendship. Thus Caelius in a letter to Cicero complains that Appius, having refused a loan of money, "is beginning to hate me, because he is indebted to me for great kindnesses; and miser that he is, being unable to enforce upon himself the discharge of that debt, he has declared a secret war against me" (*Fam.* 8.12.1). Resentment of this kind constitutes the negative extreme to which the sense of debt could lead, but it is important to register such emotion as a response to the benefactor's open efforts to call in the debts created by his benefactions.

For all their tact, affection, and humor, Horace's two epistolary refusal poems, 1.1 and 1.7 to Maecenas, suggest the background scenario of a benefactor wishing to call in old debts. However, as I argue, even as the poet reveals his relationship with the regime as having an underlying contractual component, he also manipulates the discourse of libidinal voluntarism as a means of reconfiguring his social relationships. To fully understand such manipulation, we must review briefly the two major questions besetting discussions of Augustan literary patronage. First, does the language of *amicitia* allow us to speak of patronage? And second, to what degree does the relationship resemble its social counterpart, and in what ways does it constitute a unique phenomenon?

## LITERARY AMICITIA

One of the difficulties with making assertions about literary patronage in the Augustan period, and about Horace's experience in particular, is that so much of the evidence (with the exception of Suetonius's biographies) comes from the poetry itself. Another related problem is the ambiguous nature of the language used to describe the relationship. As I mention above, the terms *patronus* and *cliens* were rarely used to refer to the relations between a benefactor and his protégé, whether social or literary, in the aristocratic elite.[34] As a passage from Cicero's *De officiis* claims, Romans of some social standing thought it "like death to be called clients or to benefit from patronage" (*patrocinio vero se usos aut clientes appellari mortis instar putant,* 2.69).[35] Consequently, the more circumspect if possibly misleading terms *amicitia* and *amici*, most straightforwardly translated as "friendship" and "friends," were used to describe relations of a frequently utilitarian—if not an economically dependent—nature between those whose status is clearly different.[36] Such terms are confusing for the modern scholar because we are accustomed to associate a certain nonutilitarian parity with the concept of friendship.[37] To add to the confusion, the intimacy of shared interests and values that such parity implies did characterize the more philosophical conceptions of *amicitia* in Roman intellectual thought.[38] Moreover, in the case of Horace and Maecenas, as the numerous allusions to the high regard and affection between them testify, personal feelings of real friendship transcended their initial social or economic disparities.[39] Finally, in addition to the wide range of meanings covered by *amicitia,* Horace's own poetic exploitation of the connotative ambiguities of the term contributes to the difficulty of determining its sense in any particular context. His frequently adopted Epicurean attitudes, for example, often complicate his exploration of *amicitia* understood in patronal terms.[40]

It is precisely this language of friendship that contributes to White's view that "literary patronage" is a misnomer when applied to the relationship that the Augustan poets had with their benefactors. For not only does the term "literary patronage" imply regular material support, it also suggests "a more or less deliberate policy of encouraging literature and art" (P. White 1978, 79). A scrupulous and judicious examination of the primary historical and poetic texts provides no evidence, for White, of either consistent material benefits or of a conscious will, by either the government or simply powerful friends, to shape the literary output of poets in their orbit (1993, 110-55). Consequently, White interprets *amicitia* as an example of "the affect-laden language" that marks the discourse of friendship among the Roman elite and suggests that it "is probably to be interpreted as an effort by both parties to neutralize those status differences which do still stand between them" (14).[41] Finally, although he argues that the literary relationship is embedded in Roman social practices, he downplays the significance of even sporadic material benefactions in comparison to other "goods and services" that a more powerful *amicus* could give his dependent.[42] In particular, as I have already noted, he emphasizes that the Augustan poets all enjoyed the status of *equites,* and thus the economic wherewithal of such standing, before any material benefactions were made by their powerful friends. Hence, White claims that the connotation of economic dependency implied by the term "patronage" is misleading. This argument clearly aims to restore historical particularity to the language of *amicitia,* and to reconstruct the milieu in which poets, their friends and benefactors, and the larger public interacted, but I believe it does not sufficiently acknowledge the psychology of debt, created in the form of *gratia,* that drives a gift economy.

In Horace's case we find the most evidence of what the modern critic would call "literary patronage": not only do the poetry and the biography point to concrete, material benefactions—the grant of the Sabine estate, in particular—but the panegyric and patriotic content of the fourth book of *Odes* and the *Carmen saeculare* corroborate Suetonius's information that Augustus requested the one and commissioned the other.[43] Although my focus is not on the openly encomiastic verse of Horace's later period, my analysis nonetheless tends to justify the use of the term: for insofar as I view Horace as needing to recover, or poetically negotiate for himself, a compromised autonomy, I incline to the opinion that Horace received benefactions from a regime more than a little interested in his poetic support. As I argue in chapter 4, Horace's epistles to Maecenas suggest as much and coyly flirt with demystifying their past relationship as one of patron-client exchange rather than friendship.

On one level, the debate over whether "patronage" is an appropriate term for Horace is a matter of translation and reflects the cultural baggage that inevitably attends the particular scholar setting the level and perspective of inquiry. As Andrew Wallace-Hadrill writes concerning patronage in general: "Is it a pattern of relationships that exists objectively in certain societies whether or not the participants themselves acknowledge or approve it, or is it a way in which the actors perceive and formulate the relationships in which they are engaged? That is to say, are we talking about a structure or an ideology?" (1989, 65). His answer to this question—that both structure and ideology are involved in our inquiry—suggests additional reasons for the connotative ambiguities of the term *amicitia:* not only does it protect the self-image of the person of lower status, as Cicero's comment implies, but its philosophical implications of ideal parity and genuine affection for another make ideologically palatable the objective constituents of the actual structure as one in which each party profits. That is, a desire to maintain the appearance of disinterested giving—to establish a certain distance from a crude expectation or exploitation of the reciprocity ethic—by espousing an ideology of voluntarism may partially determine this preference for the language of emotive relationship.[44]

In his frequently invoked definition of personal patronage, or social *amicitia,* Saller lists three necessary criteria and emphasizes the role of exchange as paramount in the relationship: "First, it involves the reciprocal exchange of goods and services. Secondly, to distinguish it from a commercial transaction in the marketplace, the relationship must be a personal one of some duration. Thirdly, it must be asymmetrical, in the sense that the two parties are of unequal status and offer different kinds of goods and services in the exchange—a quality which sets patronage off from friendship between equals" (1982, 1). Cicero's discussion of such ideal friendship recognizes the component of utility in the relationship, but sees it as the *result* of a spiritual feeling of fellowship.[45] In contrast, patronage may be said to dominate as the meaning of *amicitia* when the relationship is defined primarily by the exchange of goods and services otherwise unavailable— that is, when utility precedes sentiment. If one accepts Saller's criteria, examples of the language of friendship applied to utilitarian fellowship are ready to hand. The letters of Cicero, Pliny, and Fronto all display this "affect-laden" terminology when referring to relationships both useful and hierarchically differentiated.[46] Horace's own *Epistles* offer several instances: in his letter to Iccius, for example, the poet presents an aristocrat, or man of "some social standing," living on and enjoying the fruits of Marcus Agrippa's estate in Sicily. The ostensible occasion for the letter is to encourage Iccius to "make use" (*utere*) of Grosphus, a wealthy landowner also in Sicily, whose friendship may be acquired "inexpensively" through the provision of modest services: "If he will ask for anything, oblige him willingly; Grosphus will seek nothing but what is just and fair. The going rate of friends is cheap (*vilis amicorum est annona*) when good men are in need" (1.12.22-24). Here, despite the obvious difference in status between Iccius and Grosphus (Cicero reminds us that land-ownership was the paramount indication of social standing),[47] their prospective relationship is called one of *amici.* To be sure, Horace's emphasis on the more utilitarian nuances of *amicitia* verges on ironic exaggeration, and he perhaps pointedly invokes such praxis only to oppose Cicero's ideal views.[48] Nonetheless, we should recognize that exchange, inequality of station, and the implicit projection of their "friendship" into the future—Saller's three criteria for patronage—are all here.

My own recourse to a scholar of social—and personal— patronage to identify the problems posed by the Latin terminology points up the second question with which we began: to what degree was the literary relationship unique and to what degree was it merely another form of *amicitia* in which one of the parties happened to be a poet? Certainly Saller's three criteria are present in literary *amicitia* if we consider "inequality" of station as reflecting not exclusively differences in wealth or the social status of *eques* or senator that such money conferred but also proximity to political power. For example, several months after Horace first meets Maecenas, he is said to be included *in numero amicorum* ("in his group of friends" or "in the category of those called friends"; *Sat.* 1.6.62), a phrase that at face value points simply to a distinction between those who are "in" and those who are "out," and inadvertently suggests what Dixon calls the "ideology of internal egalitarianism" within the elite (1993, 453).[49] However, this inclusion is simultaneously seen in terms of gradations of power, of proximity to the ultimate source of benefactions: Horace is now closer to the "gods" than is the average man on the street. This phrase is uttered by a passerby whom the poet encounters in *Satires* 2.6 as he hurries off to pay his morning call to Maecenas. While the passerby inquires about the place of settlement for veteran soldiers—information to which the poet is presumed to have access because he is now "close" to power—the main thrust of the poem concerns a different "resource" from which the poet's *amicitia* with Maecenas has profited: the grant of land that has given Horace his escape from the irritations of city living. It is significant that the satire connects these two resources—land and information—in an almost overdetermined way: even as the poet is presumed to have *knowledge about* land grants because he is close to the gods, the beginning of the poem shows the poet *actually having* land because he enjoys such divine proximity.[50] One might go further and say that he is now presumed to have knowledge because gifts from the powerful have distinguished him as one in the know. Thus, as the street encounter emphasizes, Horace's status is relational; previously no different, perhaps, from the veteran soldiers who receive land as a means of ensuring their continuing loyalty, he is then ranked somewhere between his *potens amicus* ("powerful friend" or "patron" among the elite) whom he visits and the man seeking information.

Finally, we should also note that although Horace shrewdly avoids displaying himself as "in attendance" on his patron,[51] the morning *salutatio* as a client's obligation—and the public visibility of such an *officium,* or duty—points up the degree to which the reciprocity ethic that marked both friendship and patronage was more "visible" and publicly "revealed" as exchange in an openly patron-client relationship.[52] The tension between such open exchange and the moral and affective discourse of friendship is what earns Trebatius Testa a reproof from Cicero for his mercenary attitude toward Caesar: in that case, the relationship between the young man and the general to whose retinue he attaches himself is marked as an example of elite patronage not only by the discrepancy of power between the two but also by the openness with which Trebatius views it as an opportunity to profit.

When we turn from questions concerning the ambiguity of the term *amicitia* to those actual goods and services exchanged between a poet and his benefactor, the relationship displays characteristics that are decidedly sui generis. Because this material has been so well covered by critics such as Gold and White, I offer only the briefest summary here. To be sure, as the poems of Horace, Juvenal, and Martial evidence, poets often perform the duties expected in the purely social context of *amicitia* or patronage among the elite—greeting their patron in the morning *salutatio,* providing companionship on a journey or at a dinner, or listening to the literary efforts of their superiors. In return, the greater *amicus* of a poet may provide the services of social visibility, literary endorsement, and often a concrete place or venue for reciting works (P. White 1978, 85; 1993, 14-27; Gold 1987, 1-2). A benefactor might give lump sums of cash and, as in the case of Vergil and Horace, the important boon of land. While endorsements and the like clearly distinguish this relationship as one specifically pertaining to literature and its audience, it is qualitatively set off from social or personal *amicitia* by the poetry itself, as the most significant "good" exchanged. The nature and circumstances of literary production in antiquity even encouraged the objectification of poetry as a concrete good. The use of papyrus rolled up into a scroll made a collection of poems a tangible gift; and the elegists present images of their poems—histrionic missives of self-representation—sent to their mistresses through the streets of Rome, etched on tablets.[53] As I discuss in chapter 5, Horace's thirteenth epistle conceives of *Odes* 1-3 in just such terms: an object of "reified labor" exchanged in his relationship with Augustus.

But embedded in the poems as concrete offerings are the varied conventions, topoi, and generic categories that literary patronage structures as a form of gift: the dedication, the *recusatio,* the invitation poem, the literary epistle of advice or recommendation, and the full-blown panegyric all display the socioeconomic roots of the relationship as a potentially motivating force for the verse.[54] In particular, it is the status conferred on their recipient by political panegyric or dedications that constitutes a substantive gift in the exchanges of literary *amicitia.* Moreover, the public acknowledgment implied in this status is complex: on the one hand, it refers to the standing of the recipient in the eyes of his contemporaries—an issue that, as we shall see in chapter 1, gets into questions of ideology; on the other, good poetry also confers the even more prestigious status of immortality—public recognition that transcends temporal boundaries.

Here, it is important to note with Joseph Hellegouarc'h (1963, 203) that the Latin word for "gratitude," *gratia,* originally meant a form of "praise" (*laus*), so that the "return" implied in phrases such as *referre gratiam*—"to render thanks"—consisted quite simply in the praise of a patron's generosity. Indeed, we see the similar phrase *gratus referam camena,* "I gratefully celebrate in song," employed by Horace in *Odes* 1.12.39, where the sacrifices of distinguished Romans of the past—Regulus, the Scauri, and L. Aemilius Paullus—have earned Horace's gratitude. As a poem that begins with the speaker's rhetorical query as to whose praises he should sing, "what man, or hero . . . what god," and whose prominent parade of figures from these three categories ends with Caesar second only to Jove, this rather stiff encomium alludes to the dynamics of imperial patronage and the gratitude of praise through their displacement onto the figures of the past.

Using a different form of metonymic displacement, Horace simultaneously accords with the demands of gratitude and creates a discursive site that resists obligations. For if patronal *munera* have created debts that require various expressions of acknowledgment in the form of dedications, encomia, and ideological endorsement of the Augustan regime, then one can display gratitude by showing the pleasure that these gifts have occasioned. By representing his Sabine estate in its "pleasing" aspect, as the passive sense of *gratus* denotes, Horace may express his gratitude at the same time that he removes his *res,* or property, from the discourse of implicit exchange by valuing it for its aesthetic character.[55] That is, rather than remain in perpetual debt to his patrons, a debt symbolized by allusions to the "exchange value" of gifts from the regime, the poet endows the ultimate symbol of that beneficence—the representation of his Sabine "farm"—with properties that stress its character as a *locus amoenus,* thus making it a symbol of aesthetic production. Although it is a *munus* that requires reciprocation, the farm is conceived as *a-moenus,* as something outside the realm of political office, profit, and negotiation. This conception involves simultaneously appropriating the discourse of libidinal voluntarism (the affective language of friendship) and displacing it onto the estate. By discursively fashioning the farm as a place of pleasure—property, or *res,* valued for its aesthetic sensuousness—the poet aligns himself with the values of elite *otium* rather than with the material dependency and debt of a subordinate "client," and he thereby lays rhetorical claim to the aristocratic status of the landholding elite.

Whether his poetry is understood as public ritual or as private epistles, then, Horace's literary "gifts" target and implicate an audience beyond his immediate patrons. To understand fully the role of this third party in the patronal gift economy, we must turn to the writings of anthropology and their relevance to Horace. This is the subject of chapter 1, which follows a brief synopsis of the book.

. . . . .

After a discussion of the economic diction in Horace's letter to Augustus, chapter 1 makes explicit in what ways cultural anthropology illuminates contradictions in the Roman discourse of benefaction and its relevance to Augustan literary patronage. Drawing on the work of Moses Finley (1973, 1974), Keith Hopkins (1983a), Veyne (1990), and Dixon (1993), authors who have made use of the anthropological literature on the gift, I first discuss the view of the ancient economy as embedded. Acknowledging the presence of coin and cash transactions in ancient

Rome, I explore the degree to which the views of Cicero and Seneca on benefaction resemble the "functionalist" ideas about exchange held by Mauss (1990 [1950]), Sahlins (1972), Bronislaw Malinowski (1961 [1922]), and Lewis Hyde (1979). I then discuss benefaction in light of Bourdieu's (1977) ideas of "symbolic capital": here, gift exchange conceals economic self-interest and serves to reproduce social relations of domination. Finally, I consider certain key events in the received "biography" of Horace in light of this conflict between the ideology of voluntarism (and its model of social cohesion) and the presence of economic interest, symbolic capital, and exploitation.

In keeping with the functionalist view of a gift economy, chapter 2 explores odes in which I perceive the public *munus* of Horatian verse as a "voluntary" sacrificial expenditure that is intended to promote social cohesion. Drawing on René Girard (1977), a literary critic much influenced by anthropology, I contend that both the Pollio ode and *Odes* 3.1-6, as lyric invocations of tragedy, perform a symbolic sacrifice—and gift—of expiation for the crimes of the civil wars. From one perspective, tragedy serves as a mimesis of the public ritual of sacrifice and, in Girard's view, as a genre that reestablishes cultural differentiation. Assuming the role of *sacerdos Musarum,* Horace performs a metaphorical sacrifice for the Roman public by offering political lyric that, like tragedy, seeks to restore distinctions and the capacity to make them in a society where civil war has threatened to erase all difference. This gift of sacrifice, moreover, is embedded in political and social forms of exchange. By assuming the role of public priest, Horace deflects attention from the regime as the political source for his sacrificial expenditure on behalf of the people: although appearing "voluntary," Horace's *munus* of expiation is in part a reciprocating gift that responds to his own debt for receiving patronage from the state.

In the anthropological terms of a gift economy, the acceptance of gifts or property, *res,* symbolically expropriates the spirit and labor of the recipient. Rhetorical imagery that runs throughout the Horatian corpus suggests that if the Roman Odes constitute the embodiment of the poet's sacrificial labor, then it is the gift of the Sabine estate that lays a claim to such expenditure of self. Chapter 3 therefore examines representations of land or property in light of a rhetorical tension between an ideology of voluntarism and the contractual connotations of the gift. Drawing on concepts of Marxist aesthetics that address the ideological work of literature, I first discuss Vergil's *Eclogues* in regard to its historical backdrop of land expropriation and redistribution during the civil wars, and then the function of Vergilian allusions in Horace's depictions of the Sabine farm in the *Satires* and *Odes.* The *Eclogues,* I argue, assimilate a discourse of benefaction—as exemplified by land grants—to the conventions of the pastoral landscape. Horace, in turn, appropriates topoi associated with the golden age, or pastoral more generally, in a way that both confirms the model of social cohesion to which patronage aspires and reveals a certain calculated self-interest behind such aspirations. Such a "double hermeneutic" appears in different guises in *Satires* 2.6 and *Odes* 1.17. Moreover, it is in these two poems, particularly in the image of the *cornucopia* of 1.17, that we perceive the rhetorical strategies that later govern the epistolary speaker's treatment of patronage in his verse letters. By converting his estate into a *locus amoenus,* he simultaneously creates a *locus* of signifying excess that enables the aesthetic subversion of the patronal discourse, which expects his *gratia* to be expressed in particular forms.

Chapter 4 argues that Horace exploits this signifying multiplicity of the Sabine farm to refashion his relationship with Maecenas over the course of *Epistles* 1. Though the estate incurs an ongoing obligation in the discourse—or cultural practice—of patronage, it simultaneously provides the ground of independence from which the poet speaks in an egalitarian relationship of *amicitia:* the farm constitutes both the benefaction that the poet promises to return in *Epistles* 1.7, should it continue to oblige him, *and* the symbolic *rus* (country) from which he makes this gesture. What I emphasize in this chapter is how Horace dramatizes this ambiguity, incorporating gestures of refusal and independence into a poetics of socioeconomic exchange. Images of currency and exchange suggest that the "coin" of the speaker's language has value depending on his audience. By employing two types of *ainoi,* or illustrative stories, that appeal to different levels of status in his simultaneously public and private audiences, the speaker both reveals the economic self-interest that drives the implicit, if distorted, contract behind patronage and reinscribes himself in a relationship of aristocratic and egalitarian *amicitia* distinguished by an ideology of decorous and voluntary giving.

Chapter 5 focuses on the epistolary representations of Horace's estate in regard to the "contractual" understanding of patronage and the symbolic implication that the speaker's self has been expended as "reified labor" in the poetry of the *Satires* and the *Odes.* As a preface to my discussion of the Horatian poems, I analyze the dynamic of privation, song, and plenitude in Vergil's second eclogue. I then provide close readings of *Epistles* 1.14 and 1.16, letters to Horace's bailiff and to Quinctius, arguing that the poet represents his self as "reappropriated" through the epistolary process and the construction of the estate as a *locus amoenus.* By invoking details from either a golden age *topos* or the more inclusive generic frame of pastoral, the speaker identifies with an Epicurean vision of plenitude. Such plenitude and the capacity of the farm to render aesthetic and philosophical returns derive from what I call an "economy of *otium,*" a concept introduced in chapter 3.

By making a distinction between the farm's role in producing real goods in a market economy and its role as source of aesthetics and Epicurean *ataraxia, Epistles* 1.14 and 1.16 reveal the poet's social anxiety and ambivalent claims to the aristocratic elite. Thus, despite taking an egalitarian

tone, the speaker rhetorically exploits his bailiff by setting him up to compete in a philosophical agon concerning the problem of desire. By displaying the bailiff as an "enslaved" soul, the speaker naturalizes what are in fact social and economic disparities, confirming his own entitlement to the philosophical pursuits enabled by *otium* and shoring up the boundaries of elite affiliation and aristocratic status.

In the conclusion, I discuss the epistolary speaker's "gift relations" with his reader: by invoking the textual image of a *locus amoenus* the speaker not only restores himself through the philosophical praxis of writing these letters; he simultaneously emits, or gives, a pleasurable icon of himself that appeals to his readers in a way consonant with Bernard Frischer's (1982) understanding of Epicurean motivation and conversion.

This reading explores the rhetoric of Horace's poems as both shaped by, and participating within, the cultural discourses of religious expenditure (sacrifice), imperial expenditure (the *munera* of games, public buildings, etc.), and the social expenditure of private liberality or benefaction. Such a hermeneutic lens enables me to understand the particular relationship between the discourse of religious expiation informing the Roman Odes and the socioeconomic rhetoric of refusal informing the speaker's posture to his patron in the *Epistles.* These gestures of independence are revealed as participating within a larger patronal discourse of debt and expenditure that informs the speaker's representations of self, "public" and private audience, time, his Sabine property, and the verse itself as reified object of exchange.

### Notes

1. Cf. Kiessling and Heinze 1960, ad loc., on the technical aspects of the image; G. Williams 1968, 4: "humor and parody"; Kilpatrick 1986, 2: "ironic comparisons." Acknowledging the darker side of the image, Johnson (1993, 12) pinpoints the problem: "Horace is not like the gladiator Veianius, and writing poetry is not like being condemned to hack one's way out of the theater of death."

2. For a full quotation of the passage, see chapter 4.

3. Becker (1963, 38) makes no comment on the the gladiatorial imagery and merely claims that in contrast to philosophy, "das Dichten . . . als bloßes Spiel und Getändel erscheint." This figurative reading is eased by the play on *ludus,* a word also used to connote poetry. Hence, even critics who emphasize the seriousness beneath the irony subordinate the metaphor—the gladiatorial imagery—to its referent, Horace's generic choice. See Macleod 1983, 286, and Hirth 1985, 114-15. I discuss this image further in chapter 4.

4. On such a "literal" reading, see de Man 1979a, 3-19; Dunn 1995, 165-69; Hinds 1998, 10-16. This reading involves taking the rhetorical figure seriously so that, in the case of metaphor, the terms of the vehicle as a mode of persuasion are privileged over the tenor or referent.

5. On gladiators, see too chapter 4 [of this text], nn. 24 and 25.

6. See Dunn 1995, 171, for such an approach to the pronouns of lyric.

7. See Syme 1960 [1939], 387-475; Raaflaub and Toher 1990 for a reevaluation of Syme and more current views of the Augustan Principate. Zanker (1988) addresses the evolution of "ideology" in the plastic arts; see, too, Galinsky (1996) and the essays in Powell (1992). Critics of the past decade no longer see Augustus in the Orwellian terms of Syme, but increasingly take the position of Feeney (1992, 3) that ideologies of the period were a "product of contestation and dialogue" and that "'Augustanism' was not a dogma conceived by a small band and handed down to a receptive, passive audience." On the "politics" of the terms "Augustan" and "anti-Augustan" in criticism of the period, see D. Kennedy 1992.

8. See chapter 2 [in this book], n. 67, and my discussion later in the introduction.

9. Fraenkel (1957, 15) gives 31 B.C.E. as the *terminus ante quem* for the gift of the Sabine farm. The evidence for both gift and date derives from the comments of Porphyrio and PseudoAcro on *Epodes* 1.31 and *Odes* 2.18.12-14, and the implications of *Satires* 2.6. See chapter 3 [in this book], n. 6, for further and more recent bibliography on Horace's estate.

10. I borrow the term "ideological veil" from Gordon (1990a, 192), who, himself quoting from Merquior (1979, 24-34), writes that "ideology acts as an 'unconscious veil distorting the image of social reality within [a] class and sublimating its interest basis.'"

11. For discussions of the multiple audiences of Horatian verse, see Oliensis 1998, 6, and Gold 1992, 162-63. For levels of audience in relation to public readings or performance in particular, see Quinn 1982, 140-64. See Harris 1989, 222-29, for a quick overview of literacy and "book production" in the late Republic and early Empire. Both Quinn and Harris emphasize that literature was most often an aural experience, citing the common use of readers by the upper classes.

12. Oliensis (1998, 6-7) places Maecenas and Augustus, when not the addressees, in the category of "over-readers"—an audience implicated in, but not directly addressed by, a poem.

13. For discussions of the *nexum* and problems with the evidence, see Watson 1975, 111-24. See too the bibliography of Mauss 1990 [1950], 137 n. 5.

14. Turner (1974, 14) claims: "The culture of any society at any moment is more like the debris, or 'fall-out,' of past ideological systems." Cf. Kurke 1991, 88, for the relevance of this idea to archaic and classical Greece.

15. See D. Kennedy 1992 on the problem of language and ideology for the critic of the Augustan period.

16. See Habinek 1998, 8, for reading practices that challenge the notion of the transparency of the linguistic sign. On "historical empiricism" as a philological method that denies its hermeneutic status, see Galinsky 1992b, 1-40, and Peradotto 1983, 22.

17. Rose 1992, 22 n. 39: "for any answers about a different society to be intelligible to us, they must at least be cast in terms that are analytically productive for us."

18. See Saller 1982, 37-38, on these two views regarding patronage.

19. While Johnson is conversant with the innovations introduced by poststructuralist theory to classical criticism over the past twenty years, his "psycho-biographical" (and fascinating) reading of the *Epistles* betrays a willingness to fall under the spell of Horace's seeming accessibility if not candor. My own argument is, no doubt, similarly vulnerable.

20. For the distinction between "new" and traditional or positivist historicism, see Preminger and Brogan 1993, s.v. "historicism." See too the collection of essays in Veeser 1989. Greenblatt 1980 is the seminal text for New Historicism. Goff (1995b, 1-37) provides a very lucid discussion of the status and history of literary theory, and New Historicism in particular, in relation to classics as a discipline.

21. Because Ellen Oliensis's book came out at the time that my manuscript was under review, I was unable to profit as much as I would have liked from her insights into Horace's poems. As I acknowledge in chapter 3, n. 58, her work on Horace's *Satires* is an exception to this.

22. See, too, Gold's statement that "men like Virgil and Horace . . . were independent and free to choose when they wrote and what they wrote, or even if they wrote" (1987, 14).

23. Notable exceptions to this tendency include G. Williams (1990) and Horsfall (1981).

24. For discussion of Doblhofer, see Fowler 1995, 248-66.

25. On the equestrian status of many Republican and Augustan writers, see Nicolet 1966, 441-56; Taylor 1968; P. White 1993.5-14, 211-22. In addition to an appendix on the financial, and hence social, status of the major writers of the period, White includes one on the contexts in which the verb *iubeo* appears in relation to requests for poetry. The apparent lack of any real exercise of power in the situations he cites leads him to ascribe use of the verb to mere convention, further support for his case for voluntarism in the Augustan poets. For an interpretation that acknowledges the implications of actual power in such language, see Santirocco 1995, 236.

26. Feeney also quotes the relevant observation of Conte that "'real life' is itself 'the locus of cultural images and models, symbolic choices, communicative and perceptual codes'" (1998, 1).

27. Moreover, Nicols (1995, 11) stresses that the Romans, in fact, made a distinction between formal "patronage" and "benefaction": "That is, to the modern 'patronage' is indeed created by a benefaction, while to the Roman formal *patrocinium* may not have been."

28. For the problem of the autonomous subject in New Historicism, see Lentricchia 1989, 241: "The central commitment of historicists, old and new, is to the self as product of forces over which we exercise no control—the self as effect, not origin. . . . The central, unacknowledged, and perhaps unacknowledgeable desire of historicism—it is not part of their officially stated position on the self—is to avoid the consequences of that central commitment, to find a space of freedom and so free us from a world in which we are forced to become what we do not wish to become."

29. See Appadurai 1986, 11-16, for a more expanded notion of the "commodity" that applies, in certain instances, to primitive gift exchange.

30. Sen. *Ep.* 81.9: *Sic certe solemus loqui: "ille illi gratiam rettulit." Referre est ultro, quod debeas, adferre. Non dicimus "gratiam reddidit," reddunt enim et qui reposcuntur et qui inviti et qui ubilibet et qui per alium.*

31. All translations of Cic. *Fam.* are from the Loeb edition, W. Williams 1929, unless otherwise noted.

32. For the language of friendship in terms of "another self," see Cic. *Amic.* 6.22-24. For critical commentary on this series of letters, see Shackleton Bailey 1977, vol. 1, letters 26-39.

33. Shackleton Bailey 1977, ad loc., defines *syngrapham* as "A recognition of debt in the form of a contract signed by both parties."

34. By the time of the late Republic, the term *patronus* appears in three specific contexts: it can refer to an orator defending someone in court, to a person who takes an interest in the welfare of a community or a civic or corporate body, or, finally, to a master who has freed his slave. See Saller 1982, 9; P. White 1993, 30. Significantly, Horace uses both *patronus* and *cliens* to describe the disastrous patronal relationship initiated by the lawyer Philippus in *Epistles* 1.7, a striking example of usage that fits none of the above three contexts (the client, Volteius Mena, is not a beneficiary of Philippus in the courtroom).

35. My translation. Saller (1989, 52) adduces Sen. *Ben.* 2.23 and *Brev. vitae* 19.3 as evidence that this attitude continued into the Empire.

36. Saller 1982, 15. Saller (1989) clarifies that the social behavior and conventions required of an aspiring junior aristocrat—or *amicus inferior*—in regard to

his *potens amicus* were those typical of the more humble and openly labeled *cliens:* e.g., the morning *salutatio* by which a client pays his respects to a patron. Horsfall (1981) inclines to Saller's view that the language of *amicitia* encompasses patron-dependent relations among the elite. I will generally refer to Maecenas as Horace's benefactor or "patron," although, as I argue in chapter 4, the poet discursively refashions his relationship with him into a more egalitarian relation that merits the translation "friendship." I refer to Horace as "protégé," "dependent," or "client," depending on my reading of the connotations of the context.

37. P. White (1993, 13-14) claims that it is the sympathy of cultural interests and pursuits that creates parity between figures like Maecenas and Horace, despite the evident difference in their social status.

38. Cicero's *De amicitia* is just one example of the Roman adoption and synthesis of Greek theories of friendship, which furnished part of the cultural backdrop of the late Republic. Parity is an important component of Aristotle's view of friendship in books 8 and 9 of the *Nicomachean Ethics.* For an overview of friendship in the classical world that argues against the functionalist view held by many critics, in particular those influenced by anthropology, see Konstan 1997. See Brunt 1965 for a discussion of *amicitia* that separates it from an easy equation with party politics and restores its philosophical nuances even in the public and social contexts of the late Republic.

39. Cf. the claim of Suet. *Poet. Vita Horati,* that Maecenas in his will requested Augustus to be as mindful of Horace as of himself: *Horati Flacci ut mei esto memor.* For a good overview of the trajectory of Horace's relationship with Maecenas, see Gold 1987, 115-41. For the aesthetic development of the relationship over the course of *Odes* 1-3, see Santirocco 1986, 150-68, which charts an evolution from the poet's initial dependency on Maecenas to his creative independence from, and even spiritual patronage of, his benefactor.

40. *Epistles* 1.18 provides a good example of the tension between the philosophical and the sociopolitical connotations of Roman *amicitia.*

41. P. White adds: "In any society the category of 'friend' often functions in opposition to ascriptive categories, contrasting self-selected relationships with those given by kinship or other institutional identities" (1993, 14). Konstan (1997, 21; 1995, 329) essentially agrees with White's position and argues that when the language of *amicitia* is used by poets to refer to their benefactors, the diction was intended to mean what it said. In an earlier article on poets in early Imperial Rome, White (1978, 81) cites the common practice of distinguishing persons of higher status with such titles as *potens amicus, magnus amicus,* or *dives amicus,* not as polite and euphemistic refer-

ences to a "patronal" relationship, but rather as examples of the particularly Roman consciousness of nuances of status. Perhaps this position can be reconciled with his later claim that the language of *amicitia* was intended to neutralize status differences by saying that phrases like *potens amicus* functioned as compromise formations or negotiations that both acknowledged the distinction in status *and* attempted to soften it.

42. P. White 1993, 18: "Important as material goods were, however, they did not outweigh the more intangible but everyday rewards which the leaders of society were in a position to bestow."

43. P. White nonetheless concludes that "It would be perverse to read the *Secular Hymn* as a composition written to glorify Augustus, to articulate his ideology, or to summarize his administrative program" (1993, 127). This statement strikes me as too extreme in its wish to deny encomiastic intent. I agree, however, that "ideology" is not a prepackaged set of beliefs able to be summed up in a poem.

44. For example, when Porphyry comments that Horace should use the terms *patronus* or *cliens* rather than *amicus* in *Epode* 1, his objection points to the difficulty of conceiving Horace's relationship with Maecenas, at this early stage, as a "friendship"— particularly when the poem emphasizes Horace's gratitude for the benefactions he has received: *satis superque me benignitas tua / ditavit* (31).

45. Cic. *Amic.* 8.26-9.32, esp. 9.30: *Sed quamquam utilitates multae et magnae consecutae sunt, non sunt tamen ab earum spe causae diligendi profectae.* See Brunt 1965, 1-2, for further discussion.

46. Wallace-Hadrill (1989, 77) refers to Cotton (1981) for documentary examples.

47. Cic. *Off.* 1.151. See the discussion in d'Arms 1981, 6, and Finley 1973, 42-44.

48. Dilke 1965, ad loc., and others refer Horace's statement to a saying of Socrates, the ironist par excellence: "Economists say one should buy when something of great value is going cheap: as business is now, good friends are for sale very cheap" (Xen. *Mem.* 2.10.4).

49. On the phrase *in amicorum numero,* Horsfall (1981, 5) speculates: "by the late second century B.C. there were even, in the manner of the Ptolemaic court, classes of 'friends' at the *salutatio* (Gelzer, 104f.); the existence of a written register of clients cannot, I think, be proved, but the work of the *nomenclator,* or, worse still, of the imperial *officium admissionis,* will have been unimaginable without some semi-formalised register. Horace was now on the *numerus,* and should have had no problems with the *nomenclator.*"

50. The concentric structure of knowledge and resources in relation to a central locus of power, staged by this encounter, conforms to Wallace-Hadrill's understanding of patronage in terms of social integration (1989, 63-87).

51. On the motives for Horace's exclusion of this scene, see Oliensis 1998, 48.

52. See too chapter 4 [of this text], n. 60.

53. Catull. 1.1, *Cui dono lepidum novum libellum,* conflates the "abstract" gift of the dedication with the materiality of the scroll itself. See Gold 1987, 2-3, on the objectification of poetry; Habinek 1998, 112-13, on the uses of papyrus as a sign of elite prestige and hegemonic control.

54. Generic conventions thus are to be distinguished from the theme of patronage in verse: conventions, rather than "themes," display the "material trace" of the socioeconomic world. For the invitation poem as a form of gift, see Pavlock 1982. Also see Edmunds 1982, 184-88.

55. See Benveniste 1973, 161, and Moussy 1966, 161-80, for the semantic range of *gratus* as "pleasing" or bringing pleasure.

*References*

Ancona, R. 1994. *Time and the Erotic in Horace's Odes.* Durham, N.C.

Appadurai, A. 1988. *The Social Life of Things: Commodities in Cultural Perspective.* Cambridge.

Bailey, S. 1982. *Profile of Horace.* Cambridge, Mass.

Barton, C. 1993. *The Sorrows of the Ancient Romans: The Gladiator and the Monster.* Princeton.

Becker, C. 1963. *Das Spätwerk des Horaz.* Göttingen.

Benveniste, E. 1973. *Indo-European Language and Society.* Trans. E. Palmer. Coral Gables, Fla.

Bourdieu, P. 1977. *Outline of a Theory of Practice.* Trans. R. Nice. Cambridge.

Brunt, P. A. 1965. "*Amicitia* in the Late Roman Republic." *Proceedings of the Cambridge Philological Society* 191, n.s. 2: 1-20

Cotton, H. 1981. *Documentary Letters of Recommendation in Latin from the Roman Empire.* Beiträge zur klassischen Philologie, vol. 132. Konigstein/Ts.

D'Arms, J. 1981. *Commerce and Social Standing in Ancient Rome.* Cambridge, Mass.

Davis, G. 1991. *Polyhymnia: The Rhetoric of Horatian Lyric Discourse.* Berkeley.

de Man, P. 1979a. *Allegories of Reading.* New Haven.

Dilke, O. A. W., ed. 1965. *Horace: Epistles Book I.* 3rd ed. London.

Dixon, S. 1993. "The Meaning of Gift and Debt in the Roman Elite." *Echos du Monde Classique/Classical Views* 37: 451-64

Doblhofer, E. 1966. *Die Augustuspanegyrik des Horaz in formalhistorischer Sicht.* Heidelberg.

Dunn, F. 1995. "Rhetorical Approaches to Horace's *Odes.*" *Arethusa* 28.2-3: 165-76.

Edmunds, L. 1982. "The Latin Invitation-Poem: What Is It? Where Did It Come From?" *American Journal of Philology* 103: 184-88.

Feeney, D. C. 1992. "*Si licet et fas est:* Ovid's *Fasti* and the Problem of Free Speech under the Principate." In A. Powell, ed. *Roman Poetry and Propaganda in the Age of Augustus,* 1-25. London.

———. 1998. *Literature and Religion at Rome.* Cambridge.

Finley, M. I. 1973. *The Ancient Economy.* Berkeley.

Fitzgerald, W. 1995. *Catullan Provocations: Lyric Poetry and the Drama of Position.* Berkeley.

Fowler, D. 1995. "Horace and the Aesthetics of Politics." In S. J. Harrison, ed., *Homage to Horace: A Bimillenary Celebration,* 248-66. Oxford.

Fraenkel, E. 1957. *Horace.* London.

Frischer, B. 1982. *The Sculpted Word: Epicureanism and Philosophical Recruitment in Ancient Greece.* Berkeley.

Galinsky, K. ed. 1992b. *The Interpretation of Roman Poetry: Empiricism or Hermeneutics?* Frankfurt.

———. 1996. *Augustan Culture: An Interpretive Introduction.* Princeton.

Girard, R. 1977. *Violence and the Sacred.* Trans. P. Gregory. Baltimore.

Goff, B. 1995b. Introduction. In B. Goff, ed., *History, Tragedy, Theory: Dialogues on Athenian Drama,* 1-37. Austin. Tex.

Gold, B. K. 1987. *Literary Patronage in Greece and Rome.* Chapel Hill, N.C.

———. 1992. "Openings in Horace's *Satires* and *Odes:* Poet, Patron, and Audience." In F. M. Dunn and T. Cole, eds., *Beginnings in Classical Literature. Yale Classical Studies* 29: 161-86.

Goldhill, S. 1986. *Reading Greek Tragedy.* Cambridge.

Gordon, R. 1990a. "From Republic to Principate: Priesthood, Religion, and Ideology." In M. Beard and J. North, eds., *Pagan Priests: Religion and Power in the Ancient World,* 177-98. Ithaca.

Greenblatt, S. 1980. *Renaissance Self-Fashioning.* Chicago.

Habinek, T. 1998. *The Politics of Latin Literature.* Princeton.

Harker, R., C. Mahar, and C. Wilkes, eds. 1990. *An Introduction to the Work of Pierre Bourdieu: The Practice of Theory.* London.

Harris, W. V. 1989. *Ancient Literacy.* Cambridge.

Hellegouarc'h, J. 1963. *Le vocabulaire latin des relations et des partis politiques sous la république.* Paris.

Hinds, S. 1998. *Allusion and Intertext: Dynamics of Appropriation in Roman Poetry.* Cambridge.

Hirth, H-J. 1985. *Horaz, der Dichter der Briefe: Rus und urbs—die Valenz der Briefform am Beispiel der ersten Epistel an Maecenas.* Hildesheim.

Hopkins, K. 1983b. Introduction to P. Garnsey, K. Hopkins, and C. R. Whittaker, eds., *Trade in the Ancient Economy,* viii-xxv. Berkeley.

Horsfall, N. 1981. "Poets and Patron: Maecenas, Horace, and the *Georgics,* Once More." *Publications of the Maquaries Ancient History Association* 1981.3:1-24.

Hyde, L. 1979. *The Gift: Imagination and the Erotic Life of Property.* New York.

Johnson, W. R. 1993. *Horace and the Dialectic of Freedom: Readings in "Epistles" I.* Cornell.

Kennedy, D. 1992. "'Augustan' and 'Anti-Augustan'" Reflections on Terms of Reference." In A. Powell, ed., *Roman Poetry and Propaganda in the Age of Augustus,* 26-58. London.

Kiessling, A., and R. Heinze, eds. 1960. *Q. Horatius Flaccus: Oden und Epoden.* 10th ed. Berlin.

Kilpatrick, R. 1986. *The Poetry of Friendship.* Edmonton.

Konstan, D. 1995. "Patrons and Friends." *Classical Philology* 90: 328-42.

———. 1997. *Friendship in the Classical World.* Cambridge.

Kurke, L. 1991. *The Traffic in Praise: Pindar and the Poetics of Social Economy.* Ithaca.

Lentricchia, F. 1989. "Foucault's Legacy: A New Historicism?" In H. A. Veeser, ed., *The New Historicism,* 231-42. New York.

Lowrie, M. 1997. *Horace's Narrative Odes.* Oxford.

Lyne, R. O. A. M. 1995. *Horace: Behind the Public Poetry.* New Haven.

Macleod, C. 1983. "The Poetry of Ethics: Horace, *Epistles* I." In *Collected Essays,* 280-91. Oxford.

Malinowski, B. 1961 [1922]. *Argonauts of the Western Pacific.* New York.

Martindale, C. 1993. *Redeeming the Text.* Cambridge.

Mauss, M. 1990 [1950]. *The Gift: The Form and Reason for Exchange in Archaic Societies.* Trans. W. D. Halls. New York.

Merquior, J. G. 1979. *The Veil and the Mask: Essays on Culture and Ideology.* London.

Moussy, C. 1966. *Gratia et sa famille.* Paris.

Nicolet, C. 1966. *L'Ordre équestre à l'époque républic-aine.* Paris.

Nicols, J. 1995. "Civic Patronage in Ancient Rome." Department of History, University of Oregon. Typescript.

Oliensis, E. 1998. *Horace and the Rhetoric of Authority.* Cambridge.

Pavlock, B. 1982. "Horace's Invitation Poems to Maecenas: Gifts to a Patron." *Ramus* 11:70-98.

Peradotto, J. 1983. "Texts and Unrefracted Facts: Philology, Hermeneutics, and Semiotics." *Arethusa* 16.1-2: 15-34.

Powell, A. 1992. *Roman Poetry and Propaganda in the Age of Augustus.* London.

Preminger, A., and T. V. F. Brogan, eds. 1993. *New Princeton Encyclopedia of Poetry and Poetics.* Princeton.

Putnam, M. C. J. 1986. *Artifices of Eternity. Horace's Fourth Book of Odes.* Ithaca.

Quinn, K. 1982. "The Poet and His Audience in the Augustan Age." *Aufstieg und Niedergang der römischen Welt (ANRW)* 2.30.1: 76-180. Berlin.

Raaflaub, K., and M. Toher, eds. 1990. *Between Republic and Empire: Interpretations of Augustus and His Principate.* Berkeley.

Rose, P. 1992. *Sons of the Gods; Children of Earth: Ideology and Literary Form in Ancient Greece.* Ithaca.

Sahlins, M. 1972. *Stone Age Economics.* New York.

Saller, R. P. 1982. *Personal Patronage under the Early Empire.* Cambridge.

———. 1989. "Patronage and Friendship in Early Imperial Rome: Drawing the Distinction." In A. Wallace-Hadrill, ed., *Patronage in Ancient Society,* 49-62. New York.

Santirocco, M. 1986. *Unity and Design in Horace's Odes.* Chapel Hill, N.C.

———. 1995. "Horace and Augustan Ideology." *Arethusa* 2.3: 225-43.

Syme, R. 1960 [1939]. *The Roman Revolution.* London.

Taylor, L. R. 1968. "Republican and Augustan Writers Enrolled in the Equestrian Centuries." *Transactions of the American Philological Association* 99: 469-86.

Turner, V. 1974. *Dramas, Fields, and Metaphors: Symbolic Action in Human Society.* Ithaca.

Veeser, H. A., ed. 1989. *The New Historicism.* New York.

Veyne, P. 1990. *Bread and Circuses: Historical Sociology and Political Pluralism.* Trans. B. Pearce. London.

Wallace-Hadrill, A. 1989. "Patronage in Roman Society: from Republic to Empire." In A. Wallace-Hadrill, ed., *Patronage in Ancient Society,* 63-88. New York.

Watson, A. 1975. *Rome of the XII Tables.* Princeton.

White, P. 1978. "Amicitia and the Profession of Poetry in Early Imperial Rome." *Journal of Roman Studies* 68: 74-92.

———. 1993. *Promised Verse: Poets in the Society of Augustan Rome.* Harvard.

Williams, G. 1968. *Tradition and Originality.* London.

———. 1990. "Did Maecenas 'Fall from Favor'?" In K. A. Raaflaub and M. Toher, eds., *Between Republic and Empire: Interpretations of Augustus and His Principate,* 258-75. Berkeley.

Williams, W. G., trans. 1929. *Cicero: The Letters to His Friends.* 3 vols. Loeb Classical Library. Cambridge, Mass.

Zanker, P. 1988. *The Power of Images in the Age of Augustus.* Ann Arbor, Mich.

Zetzel, J. E. G. 1982. "The Poetics of Patronage in the Late First Century B.C." In B. Gold, ed., *Literary and Artistic Patronage in Ancient Rome,* 87-102. Austin, Tex.

### Randall L. B. McNeill (essay date 2001)

SOURCE: McNeill, Randall L. B. "The Horaces of Horace." In *Horace: Image, Identity, and Audience,* pp. 1-9. Baltimore, Md.: Johns Hopkins University Press, 2001.

[*In the following essay, McNeill examines the history of critical debate on Horace, the man. Although there has been considerable contention in the past with respect to whether the Horace in the poetry is or is not the result of careful self-presentation, McNeill (and other critics cited by him) now focus on the depictions in the poetry rather than the poet.*]

Although many ancient authors have suffered through long periods of disfavor and neglect, their literary stars rising and falling according to the vagaries of changing tastes, Quintus Horatius Flaccus has remained consistently popular through the centuries. He has stood as a cornerstone of classical education for countless generations of students; poets from Pope to Hölderlin to Brodsky have read and admired his works; ancient commentators, humanists of the Renaissance, and scholars from the Enlightenment to the present day have written prolifically on the man and his texts. Some two thousand years after his death, he continues to challenge, astonish, and fascinate his readers, whether they encounter him for the first time or discover him anew.

Much of Horace's appeal, of course, derives from the sheer impact of the lively and engaging personality that springs forth for anyone who undertakes even the most cursory perusal of his poems. Horace does not simply make frequent use of himself as a character in his works, describing his personal triumphs and travails as he goes through life. He seems to speak directly to us throughout his poetry; he talks openly about his private thoughts and experiences, inviting our scrutiny and our response. "Here I am," he seems to say, "here are my inner feelings and quirks of personality, my strengths and weaknesses, my friendships and love affairs, my views and my ideals." As David Armstrong has noted, "It is commonplace to say about Horace that [his work] gives us a self-portrait of a striking individuality and apparent frankness not easily paralleled in classical literature, certainly not in classical poetry. We can read at vastly greater length [the correspondence of Cicero or Pliny the Younger] without getting any such illusion that we know perfectly the person who is speaking, and could . . . continue the conversation without difficulty if Horace walked into our presence now."[1] Horace himself comes across as being so likable—so genial and witty, so thoughtful and sensitive, and capable of such strikingly beautiful and sophisticated verse—that it is all too easy to assume that he is being completely open and honest with us in this presentation. The poet lives in his poetry, often dazzling his readers into a wholehearted embrace of the vital and charismatic figure he cuts for himself.[2]

But is this really the picture of Horace we should have? He says a great deal about himself, to be sure; but is he telling the truth? It is, after all, misleading and even dangerous to think of there being a single "Horace" in Horace's poetry. He may present what at first appears to be a persuasive and believable self-portrait, but elsewhere he continually contradicts or alters this picture. There seem, in fact, to be many Horaces on display, or else separate images that have been given Horace's name and features. Each is vivid, powerful, and highly attractive in its way, but is caught up with very different themes and concerns not easily reconciled with the others. What is more, this variance transcends those differences of self-presentation that might have been necessitated by the requirements and limitations of the literary genres within which Horace works. In every case, the poet has made his projected personality so compelling that the reader is almost inexorably drawn to accept each particular portrait as being the true one—at the time of its presentation.[3]

Here is Horace the client, attending and entertaining his powerful patron in return for material support and encouragement; there is Horace the lofty public speaker, exhorting the Roman people to shun the horrors of civil war and embrace their destiny as the rulers of a new Golden Age. Horace the genial moralist offers us comfortable philosophical commonplaces and amusing social commentary, while Horace the anxious *arriviste* of obscure origin fends off sneers and attacks as he struggles to hold his hard-won place among the highest circles of Roman society. Horace the unlucky lover is routinely humiliated by unsuccessful assignations or difficult mistresses, but Horace the political operative smoothly manages the complex large-scale organization of public opinion on behalf of the emperor himself. These images may be facets of a persona or entirely different personae, but together they do not constitute a single, readily encompassable personality. Thus, when people speak of liking Horace's character or believing what he tells us, we must ask to which "Horace" in particular they refer.

Failure to pose this crucial question has undoubtedly contributed much to the intractability of the once furious scholarly debate over whether what we see in his poetry is Horace's own face or a mask with Horace's features. In years past, this particular offshoot of the "Personal Heresy" controversy (as articulated in a well-known exchange between E. M. W. Tillyard and C. S. Lewis) attracted the attention of many classicists, including W. S. Anderson, Niall Rudd, and Jasper Griffin, among others.[4] In essence, the choice was long either to believe that Horace's poems offer us a reasonably accurate record of his life[5] (or a reliable index to the plausible reconstruction of his historical experience); or to treat his texts solely as self-conscious and artificial literary works, more the products of craft than of earnest self-revelation. Until quite recently, all Horatian scholars continued to make this choice, taking up positions on one side or the other of the essential fault line between what might be termed the biographical and the rhetorical interpretations of Horace's self-image.[6] Thus, in 1993 Kirk Freudenburg advocated a rhetorical approach when he identified "Horace" as he appears in the *Satires* as being a wholly invented mask—one self-consciously projected by the author, based on literary and moral philosophical precedents, and not necessarily bearing any resemblance to the historical Horace.[7] By contrast, Oliver Lyne argued in 1995 that the "real" Horace's shifts in his public and political commitments can be reconstructed through examination of his poetry and that an array of societal and political considerations directly prompted Horace to make changes in his public image over time.[8]

Open debate on this subject has largely been suspended of late, with most Horatian scholars now in agreement that any appearance of openness and genuine personal revelation in the poet's work should be recognized as the result of an artful and carefully managed process of self-presentation, which must be scrutinized by the reader with equal care. However, no true consensus has been reached. The past few years have instead witnessed a general retreat from the whole issue, as scholars increasingly turn toward treating Horace's poems *strictly* as literary documents. According to current thinking, it should be obvious that there is no reliable way of getting past Horace's enticing array of images to arrive at a clear picture of his "true" self. We can never be absolutely sure of what is true and what is false in his self-presentation, and as such it becomes the wrong question to be asking.[9] Much of the latest work done on Horace thus tends to follow the path laid out by Ellen Oliensis in her book *Horace and the Rhetoric of Authority*. For Oliensis, "Horace's poetry is itself a performance venue"—hence her emphasis upon its most overtly rhetorical aspects. Indeed, this conviction leads her to treat Horace as an object of consideration specifically and solely as he appears within the poetry itself: "I make no clear, hard-and-fast distinction between the author and the character 'Horace.' Horace is present in his personae, that is, not because these personae are authentic and accurate impressions of his true self, but because they effectively construct that self . . . [there is a] de facto fusion of mask and self."[10]

Oliensis stands as one of the foremost advocates of the view that Horace is indistinguishable from the text, since the text is all we have. Other scholars have subsequently given implicit endorsement to this line. In a recent analysis of the generic considerations that lie behind two of Horace's seemingly most forthright and personal poems, for example, Catherine Schlegel moves beyond reaffirming the extent to which Horace's "autobiographical" persona has been shaped by its poetic context, to argue that the literary requirements of this persona have a priori shaped Horace's poetry—in effect, that Horace's art has shaped his life, not (as has long been thought) the other way around.[11]

Much vital work has recently been done through pursuit of this critical approach. Indeed, by leaving aside the whole problematic issue of Horace's "true self" to focus instead on his rhetorical and generic manipulations, we have immeasurably heightened our understanding of the intricacy and multifaceted character of the poet's sophisticated literary technique. There is an inherent risk, however, in turning away from a lingering problem before it has been thoroughly investigated to the satisfaction of all concerned. We may have gone too far in rejecting or bypassing any consideration of Horace's poems as evidence for the direct and personal experiences of this unusual historical individual. At the very least, the suspicion commonly directed nowadays toward all forms of biographical literary criticism—and toward the author as an object worthy of attention and careful study—does a disservice to those who would understand the nature of Horace's art. For Horace encourages and even demands that we as readers experience the sensation described earlier of coming to "know" him intimately. Horace's indirect and subtle methods of self-presentation force us to struggle with the mysterious and protean nature of his portrayed image, rather than either accept blithely what he tells us without question or take it all as pure invention and turn our minds to other issues. Questions of what is real and what is invented lie at the very heart of Horace's poetry. We cannot simply dismiss the "real" Horace from our considerations but must instead confront his existence, and his poetic function, head-on.

In meeting this challenge, we might draw inspiration from an appealing suggestion made years ago by Gilbert Highet: Horace's self-image reflects the man, being neither a wholly artificial creation nor an entirely truthful revelation.

> The pose of naiveté and ignorance of diplomatic affairs which Horace adopts in his *Sermones* may perhaps be called a *persona:* but not a *persona* to be separated and distinguished from Q. Horatius Flaccus. It is a pose: it is one of the faces which the real Horace wished to present to the world . . . In his poetry Horace appears

in many different guises—as vengeful lampoonist in the *Epodes,* in some of the *Odes* as inspired *vates* and in some as gay amorist, in the Sermones as critic of others and as critic of self; but each is Horace—or one part of Horace.[12]

And yet even this balanced formulation does not completely solve the basic problem; for although Highet alludes to the multiplicity of Horace's self-images, he does not attempt to explain their sheer number and variety, nor to define their strangely fluid coexistence within single works and individual poems. He recognizes but does not resolve the difficulty scholars have generally had in fitting the totality of Horace's self-presentations into a single interpretive framework without resorting to untested assumptions and preconceived notions of what is "important" in Horace's poetry. Indeed, regardless of the specific critical viewpoint or interpretation adopted, there is invariably a vibrant and fully realized image of Horace somewhere in his corpus that cannot be made to fit.[13]

Whether or not the Horace of the poems is an accurate rendering of "the real Horace," any sense we get of being able to *know* this "real Horace" in some deeply intimate way is certainly deceptive. Horace as he appears is a carefully developed characterization, representing solely those aspects of a projected personality that he wanted us to see and believe in, in a variety of specific contexts. This is perhaps not so unusual; to some degree we all consciously or unconsciously monitor the way we come across in our interactions with those around us, as we manage our words and actions to suit our personal circumstances. But Horace directs every aspect of this process with a remarkable facility that is almost unique among ancient poets. The Horaces of Horace are *personae,* as Highest suggests; yet the poet focuses attention not on their self-contained existence as separate characters but rather on the social settings and relationships within which they are presented.[14] He does more than shape the way he presents himself; he shapes the way others (including ourselves) respond to these self-presentations by tailoring his remarks and addresses to the specific interests, tastes, and expectations of a surprisingly wide array of readers and audiences.

In this context we recall the thoughtful comments made by Barbara Gold in her 1992 study of the dedicatory poems of Horace's *Satires* and *Odes.*[15] Gold identifies the presence of multiple audiences within these works, noting that "from each of his audiences Horace expects to elicit different responses, and [that] it is through attention to these audiences that Horace's reader perceives all the various dimensions of his work." Pursuit of this idea leads her to adopt the schema of layers of audience presented by Victoria Pedrick and Nancy Rabinowitz as an integral aspect of audience-oriented criticism.[16] But the difficulty experienced even by so accomplished and sensitive a reader as Frances Muecke in attempting to fit the *Satires* into their proposed format illustrates the comparative unwieldiness of this complicated approach when it is applied to the poetry of Horace.[17] Gold herself concludes that Horace's audiences must be constantly shifting in relative importance, even trading places with one another; for "if we posit several audiences (as we must for all of Horace's works), how can Horace be speaking *directly* to all of them at once?"[18] And yet this is precisely what Horace often manages to do. What is needed is a revised interpretive model, one that offers a simpler arrangement of categories and makes clearer the extent to which Horace is able to anticipate and handle simultaneously the different reactions of these audiences.

This book thus shares with the work of Oliensis a basic operating premise—namely, that when one examines the poetry of Horace, the main subject of discussion must be Horace's depiction of his relationships with those whom he addresses. Beyond this common point of departure, however, we diverge markedly in our aims and methodologies, the organization and specific arguments of our studies, and in our fundamental difference of opinion and approach regarding the nature and significance of Horace's self-presentation. Oliensis acknowledges that she has introduced discussion of Horace's life, his surrounding social milieus, and his shifting place in society only insofar as such issues are relevant to her reading of Horace's rhetorical technique: "I am interested not in the light Horace's poetry can shed on his extrapoetic life but in the life that happens in his poetry . . . My focus in this study is on Horace's poems, not on his life or his times or his culture."[19] By contrast, I take an approach that is in many ways guided specifically by those ideals and goals that Oliensis puts aside, for I find Horace's poems worth studying precisely because of what they can reveal to us about the society and culture in which he purports to have operated. I embrace the idea that there exists a sharp and very real distinction between the personae on view in the poems and the poet who created them; and that, moreover, the distinction is identifiable in the very act of their presentation. But in taking as my focus this discernible gap between the poet and his poetry, I maintain that careful scrutiny of the inner workings of the poet's self-portrayal enables us to identify the basic conditions and characteristics of his actual personal and social situation—as he wished them to be understood.

I do not, therefore, advocate any return to the old and strictly biographical interpretation, with its underlying conviction that Horace as he appears in his poetry is automatically the true and historical Horace. Instead, my intention is to offer a reconciliation of once irreconcilable positions: to suggest that the biographical and the rhetorical are by design inextricably linked in Horace's self-portrayal, with both elements constantly being deployed in the other's service. In effect, I propose that we approach Horace's texts as tools of detection: first, as a means of exploring further the poet's employment of created self-images in order to shape the perceptions of those around him, and second, as a basis for reconstructing the larger surrounding social, political, and "professional" artistic situations in which these poems were written and first received. For Horace's extraordinarily self-conscious portrayal is not simply marked by his preternatural aware-

ness of a large number of separate audiences, each with different responses to his work; it is further enhanced by his total control and constant manipulation of these same audiences toward acceptance of the specific impressions he wishes to convey.[20]

To identify the general patterns and techniques of Horatian self-presentation and their function within the poet's immediate situation as it can be reconstructed, we must take the entire sweep of the poet's literary corpus into consideration: the *Epodes, Satires, Odes, Carmen saeculare,* and the *Epistles* (including the *Ars poetica*). Although the discussion is focused mainly on the *Satires* and *Epistles,* passages from each of the works are analyzed throughout so as to demonstrate the extent to which the same issues (and similar methods of response) occupied his creative attention from genre to genre across much of his career.[21] As noted above, Horace's techniques of self-presentation essentially depend on the self-conscious depiction of his social interactions with those around him. Therefore, individual chapters examine his portrayal of his disparate, idiosyncratic, and constantly fluctuating relationships with his patron Maecenas, his audience as a whole, his fellow poets, and the Augustan Principate.

The first two chapters are designed to show that we can best understand Horace's contemporary readership as consisting of a series of concentric rings, based not so much on the relative authority or absolute social standing of each of Horace's readers as on their varying levels of intimacy and direct personal contact with the poet. I then broaden my focus in the later chapters to consider how this mechanism of concentric rings shapes Horace's treatment of himself as an author and as a participant in Augustus's program of political and cultural renewal. In each case, the evidence suggests that Horace uses his self-images primarily to comment on the social pressures and uncertainties of these relationships.[22] Thus, Horace's representation of his interaction with each "ring of audience" holds significant implications for our understanding of crucial aspects of Roman society and social culture. In effect, we may employ Horace's portrayed relationships as lenses through which to glimpse the several cultural frameworks within which the "real-life" historical models for such portrayals were originally developed.

By giving powerful expression to the social, political, and artistic pressures that he claims to have endured throughout his life, Horace both articulates and shapes his relationship with the people and audiences around him. The poet presents a vast surrounding web of social interactions: a vivid and engaging world of dinner parties and country estates, love affairs and close friendships, patrons, fellow citizens, and potential readers. He creates his rich and complicated self-portraits as a part of this picture, infusing them with the liveliness and humanity that make them so compelling. Horace's genius lies in his remarkable ability to project himself precisely as circumstances—and the specific interests of particular readers—demand. Directed toward so many different audiences and covering such a wide variety of themes, his multifaceted self-presentation serves to illustrate the complexity and interconnectedness of his experience and the intricacies of the world in which he purports to have actually lived.[23] In the end, therefore, Horace's poetic self-image remains precisely that: an image created by the poet, not an unguarded insight into himself. Nevertheless, this image does possess the poet's actual features, even if it has been distorted by the transmitting medium of his poetry. When we encounter Horace in his works, we do not gaze directly on his actual face, nor are we looking at a wholly artificial mask whose features have been identified with his. Instead, we see the real Horace—obliquely, through the polished lens of his poetry, as one would see a reflection in a mirror.[24] In scrutinizing this reflected image, we may be able to catch fleeting but direct glimpses of the poet and, over his shoulder, the character and features of his long-vanished world.

## Notes

1. D. Armstrong, *Horace* (New Haven, 1989), 2.

2. Indeed, there survives among scholars a strong tendency to accept Horace's account of himself at face value even in this more guarded and cautious age; see D. Levy, *Horace: A Life* (New York, 1997), for a recent manifestation of this impulse. On the dangers of being seduced by the force of Horace's self-portraiture, however, see, e.g., R. Ancona, *Time and the Erotic in Horace's* Odes (Durham, N.C., 1994), 147-50, nn. 20, 28.

3. For an astute analysis of the intergeneric links between poems, one very much in sympathy with the position I advocate here, see M. C. J. Putnam, "From Lyric to Letter: Iccius in Horace *Odes* 1.29 and *Epistles* 1.12," *Arethusa* 28 (1995): 193-207, esp. 206.

4. C. S. Lewis and E. M. W. Tillyard, *The Personal Heresy* (Oxford, 1939); see also, e.g., N. Rudd, "The Style and the Man," *Phoenix* 18 (1964): 216-31; W. S. Anderson, "Roman Satirists and Literary Criticism," *Bucknell Review* 12 (1964): 106-13, and "Autobiography and Art in Horace," in *Perspectives of Roman Poetry,* ed. K. Galinsky (Austin, 1974), 35-56, both reprinted in W. S. Anderson, *Essays on Roman Satire* (Princeton, 1982); J. Griffin, *Latin Poets and Roman Life* (London, 1986).

5. As typified by the staunchly biographical approach of Eduard Fraenkel in his seminal work on the poet, *Horace* (Oxford, 1957). Fraenkel's famous declaration that "Horace . . . never lies" (260) neatly captures his unyielding belief in the factuality of the Horace on view in certain poems of the Horatian corpus (as chosen by Fraenkel himself; see Charles Martindale's introduction to C. Martindale and D. Hopkins, eds., *Horace Made New* [Cambridge, 1993], esp. 11-13).

6. Individual views on this central question are not always openly declared; scholars often indicate their leanings only indirectly, by emphasizing certain aspects of Horace's self-image and omitting others in their reading and analysis of his works. For further discussion of this phenomenon, see Martindale, introduction to *Horace Made New,* 2-13.

7. See K. Freudenburg, *The Walking Muse* (Princeton, 1993), esp. 1-7, for his opening statement of this view.

8. R. O. A. M. Lyne, *Horace: Behind the Public Poetry* (New Haven, 1995); Lyne's fundamental assumptions are implicit even in the title of his book. Cf. P. White, *Promised Verse* (Cambridge, Mass., 1993), who argues that the external personal relationships and responsibilities of the Augustan poets affected but did not control their poetry. It is worth noting that despite this basic difference of opinion, White too takes an inherently "biographical" approach in his attempt to use the poets' works to reconstruct the nature and conditions of their historical existence.

9. See D. West, *Reading Horace* (Edinburgh, 1967), for an earlier consideration of this point.

10. E. Oliensis, *Horace and the Rhetoric of Authority* (Cambridge, 1998), 1-2.

11. C. Schlegel, "Horace and His Fathers: *Satires* 1.4 and 1.6," *American Journal of Philology* (AJP) 121 (2000): 93-119. Schlegel makes the suggestion that Horace praises the moral training he received from his "biological father" in order to distance himself and his work from his "literary fathers": Lucilius, his predecessor in the genre of satire, and Maecenas, his patron. This is persuasive; but her conclusion—that Horace breaks away from these literary fathers by making his biological father "the prior poetic cause" in a paradoxical act of "subtle rebellion" (117)—seems overextended.

12. G. Highet, "Masks and Faces in Satire," *Hermes* 102 (1974): 321-37.

13. Thus, as Martindale (introduction to *Horace Made New,* 11-12) points out, Fraenkel's vision of a kindly, avuncular Horace depends on an outright dismissal of the fierce and erotic Horace found in other poems. Similarly, the learned literary theorist portrayed by Freudenburg (and at far greater length by C. O. Brink, *Horace on Poetry* [Cambridge, 1963]) misses altogether the lively and vivid personality that the poet himself takes such pains to project. Can these discrepancies be put down simply to considerations of genre? Inasmuch as Horace worked within many different literary forms, the respective strengths and limitations of each genre are, of course, extremely important for determining the specifics of his self-presentation. However, we shall demonstrate that there exists a remarkable similarity of self-presentation techniques throughout Horace's works, across genres and even generic groups; much the same images and tactics are employed in the *Satires, Epistles, Epodes,* and *Odes* alike. As such, this issue demands further accommodation and analysis beyond the recognition of variations based solely on genre.

14. For a detailed analysis of the way in which Horace addresses readers from many different social levels in his poetry, see M. Citroni, *Poesia e lettori in Roma antica* (Rome, 1995), 208-9, 241-42, although Citroni is interested in showing that Horace and the other Augustan poets were aiming for a general public circulation rather than limiting themselves to the narrow upper-class focus of recent generations of authors, and as such he does not fully explore the personal dimension of the poet's representations.

15. B. K. Gold, "Openings in Horace's *Satires* and *Odes*: Poet, Patron, and Audience," *Yale Classical Studies* (*YCS*) 29 (1992): 161-85; the quotation is taken from 185.

16. V. Pedrick and N. Rabinowitz, "Audience-Oriented Criticism and the Classics," *Arethusa* 19 (1986): 105-14; see also P. Rabinowitz, "Shifting Stands, Shifting Standards: Reading, Interpretation, and Literary Judgment," in the same issue (115-34). The proposed audiences here consist of the *actual* audience (the person or people who are reading the text at any given moment), the *authorial* audience (the hypothetical audience the author originally had in mind at the moment of composition), and the *narrative* audience (the audience that is implied in the text, to whom the narrator thinks he is speaking). The last of these three concepts is the least useful for understanding Horace, since his "authorial" and "narrative" audiences so often overlap (or are identical). As a result, Gold presents a different framework of audiences (see the original text of Gold, "Openings"): (1) the *primary* (the dedicatee, who appears infrequently and is given only brief though prominent mention); (2) the *internal* (an implied naïf whom Horace has contrived to play the "straight man," to pose as the interlocutor for his rhetorical questions, and to misunderstand the ironies of the satire); (3) the *authorial*, the first-century B.C. Roman upper-class writers and politicians to whose experience and values Horace appeals and who could be counted on to understand the full effect of Horace's mixed signals and ironic tone; and (4) the *actual* (as above).

17. See F. Muecke, "The Audience of/in Horace's *Satires*," *Journal of the Australian Universities Language and Literature Association* (*AUMLA*) 74 (1990): 34-47, esp. 39-40, 44-45,.

18. Gold, "Openings," 164-70, 173-75; the quotation is taken from 166.

19. Oliensis, *Rhetoric of Authority*, 3, 13.

20. Like all authors, Horace primarily wrote for his contemporaries (despite his evident anticipation of his own glorious *Nachleben,* as manifested in *Odes* 3.30 and elsewhere). Thus, he necessarily placed his accounts of his life in a world that would be recognizable to them—both in his references to specific contemporary events and individuals (and, where appropriate, to his experiences), and elsewhere in conjuring up invented scenes and figures who nevertheless required an essential plausibility to have an impact. For this reason, it is insufficient simply to identify Horace's use of a particular image or episode as a literary *topos* (even one with a long-established pedigree). Why did Horace choose to adapt a particular literary *topos* in any given instance? His choices clearly stemmed not from mere antiquarianism but because in some way the themes and motifs he included had a direct cultural resonance for some segment of his contemporary readership.

21. In most cases I have followed H. W. Garrod's edition of the *Oxford Classical Text* of Wickham (1901); all translations are my own unless otherwise noted.

22. It should be noted that Lyne, *Behind the Public Poetry,* also acknowledges that there were pressures placed on Horace by virtue of his position in society and as a poet. But Lyne envisions only one Horace—the real Horace—responding to these pressures in his poetry. I would assert instead that multiple, consciously invented self-images are at work within Horace's self-presentation. Even when these images operate simultaneously they nevertheless remain separate creations, aimed at different sections of Horace's audience. In any event, contrary to Lyne, I would say that Horace's allusions to his pressures and difficulties are undertaken as a means of calling attention to various aspects of his contemporary world rather than necessarily as a means of overtly defending himself against them.

Lyne holds, as I do, that Horace remained under considerable social and political pressure throughout his literary career. However, he attempts to identify a single, monolithic *persona* that Horace constructed in order to alleviate these pressures. Oliensis, *Rhetoric of Authority,* similarly points to an evolution over time of Horace's distinctive "face" and strategy of face-maintenance, contending that Horace's successful career garners him increasing authority and "symbolic capital," and allows him to adopt new strategies of self-defense and promotion. I am in fundamental disagreement with Lyne and Oliensis on these points; for Horace employs a multiplicity of self-images, with glaring mutual and internal contradictions, and separate functions within a variety of specific contexts. The social and professional pressures Horace purports to face remain substantially the same throughout his career, as do the audience-directed techniques of self-presentation that he develops in response. Structural divisions based on genre and chronology are therefore potentially misleading and comparatively less important to the discussion (though questions of genre naturally remain contributing factors). Rather than search for a gradual evolution in Horace's self-presentations, one should focus on the particular personal and social context in each case. My organizing principle is therefore to examine separately Horace's several audiences and his relationships with them; Horace himself becomes, in effect, the lens through which to view these audiences.

23. My critical position on Horace differs from the interpretive strategies of various modern schools of literary criticism (neatly summarized by Martindale, introduction to *Horace Made New*) and yet shares certain elements with each school. Like the New Critics, I hold that "Horace," as he appears, represents a set of created images (I prefer to avoid the loaded term *mask* or *persona*) adopted by Q. Horatius Flaccus to establish a particular rhetorical stance or series of stances. But I also agree with the New Historicist position that Horace employed techniques of self-fashioning (or "self-positioning") partly to construct an advantageous position for himself in society, although this self-fashioning plays an important role *within* his poetry as well. A "real" Horace had to select and project these images, and is theoretically distinguishable from what is presented. However, I do not support the Derridean deconstructionists' claim that this "real" Horace lies entirely outside the text and is therefore irrelevant to our understanding of it. My assertion that the overall impact of Horace's poetry depends on his simultaneous address of different audiences bears some similarity to a basic tenet of reader-response criticism, but I diverge from this school in suggesting that Horace, as author, controls and directs the responses of each of his audiences (where reader-response tends to focus solely on the perspective of modern or "actual" readers). One might attempt a synthesis of different critical approaches rather than wholeheartedly accept or reject any single one, inasmuch as each is applicable and effective within a different area of Horace's *oeuvre* and, as such, might fruitfully be combined into a single interpretive framework.

24. The metaphor of the mirror was also recently invoked in a sensitive (if notably traditional) treatment of Horace by the historian V. G. Kiernan (*Horace: Poetics and Politics* [New York, 1999]); in describing Horace at the outset of his literary career, a newcomer to the city of Rome, Kiernan writes, "[Horace] would have to hold up the mirror to society, and at the same time to himself, a self still only half formed, not much better known to him perhaps than the Rome he now contemplated" (26). Kiernan paints an interesting picture of Horace as a perpetual outsider in the world he described, one who admired Rome and its empire without ever becoming immersed in it, "a natural partisan of a genuine middle class, if he could have found one" (40). Although Kiernan oversimplifies by ignoring the heightened self-consciousness of Horace's writing (and by anachronistically applying the concept of a middle class to Augustan Rome), his essential portrait of Horace's independence of thought and perspective is compelling.

# FURTHER READING

## Biography

Sedgwick, Henry Dwight. *Horace: A Biography*. New York: Russell and Russell, 1947, 182 p.
　　Biography of "the poet of civilized man."

## Criticism

Bonavia-Hunt, Noel A. *Horace the Minstrel: A Practical and Aesthetic Study of His Aeolic Verse*. Kineton, Great Britain: Roundwood Press, 1991, 268 p.
　　Bonavia-Hunt proposes that Horace was an accomplished musician who played the lyre, that the instrument's qualities affected his work, and that he wrote at least some of his verses to be sung rather than read.

Commager, Steele. "The World of Nature: Time and Change." In *The Odes of Horace: A Critical Study*, pp. 235-306. Bloomington: Indiana University Press, 1982.
　　Discusses Horace's treatment of nature in the *Odes*.

Davis, Gregson. Polyhymnia: The Rhetoric of Horatian Lyric Discourse. Berkeley: University of California Press, 1991, 282 p.
　　Studies Horace in the following division: modes of assimilation, of authentication, of consolation, and of praise and dispraise.

Green, Roger. "Horace's *Odes* in the Psalm Paraphrases of Buchanan." In *Acta Conventus Neo-Latini Guelpherbytani: Proceedings of the Sixth International Congress of Neo-Latin Studies,* pp. 71-9. Binghamton, N.Y.: Center for Medieval and Early Renaissance Studies, 1985.
　　Discusses Buchanan's use of Horace's principles.

Haight, Elizabeth Hazelton. "The Making of a Poet." In *Horace and His Art of Enjoyment*, pp. 5-45. New York: E. P. Dutton and Company, 1925.
　　Haight provides significant background on Horace's early life, the influence of his father, the times in which he lived, and how these factors influenced his work.

Lowrie, Michèle. Spleen and the *Momentum*: Memory in Horace and Baudelaire." *Comparative Literature* 49, no. 1 (winter 1997): 42-58.
　　Lowrie argues that Baudelaire's second *Spleen* poem reflects Horace's *Odes* 3.30, the epilogue to his first lyric collection, displaying what Lowrie calls "poetic memory."

Minadeo, Richard. "The Love Odes." In *The Golden Plectrum: Sexual Symbolism in Horace's "Odes,"* pp. 15-64. Amsterdam: Rodopi, 1982.
　　Minadeo addresses the love odes, their sexual symbolism, and compares them to the work of other poets.

Porter, William Malin. "Milton and Horace: The Post-Bellum Muse." *Comparative Literature* 35, no. 4 (fall 1983): 351-61.

> Discusses Milton's use of a quote from one of Horace's odes at the opening of *Paradise Lost.*

Putnam, Michael C. J. "Ode Fifteen." In *Artifices of Eternity: Horace's Fourth Book of Odes,* pp. 262-306. Ithaca, N.Y.: Cornell University Press, 1986.

> Provides an in-depth examination of Ode fifteen, Horace's last ode.

Rudd, Niall. *Horace 2000: A Celebration: Essays for the Bimillenium.* Ann Arbor: University of Michigan Press, 1993, 150 p.

Collection of essays on Horace and his work.

Stapleton, M. L. "'*He* Nothing Common Did or Mean': Marvell's Charles I and Horace's *Non Humilis Mulier. English Language Notes* 30, no. 3 (March 1993): 31-40.

> Stapleton draws parallels between Horace's *Non Humilis Mulier* and Andrew Marvell's "An Horantian Ode upon Cromwell's Return from Ireland."

Williams, Gordon. "*Odes* I-III." In *Horace.* Oxford: Clarendon Press, 1972, pp. 21-35.

> Williams discusses the *Odes,* the Greek poets who may have influenced Horace's writing of them, they hymn and symposium poem forms used in the *Odes,* and their subject matter and themes.

**Additional coverage of Horace's life and career is contained in the following sources published by the Gale Group:** *Ancient Writers,* Vol. 2; *Classical and Medieval Literature Criticism,* Vol. 39; *Concise Dictionary of World Literary Biography,* Vol. 1; *Dictionary of Literary Biography,* Vol. 211; *Literature Resource Center;* **and** *Reference Guide to World Literature,* Ed. 2.

# Derek Walcott
## 1930-

(Full name Derek Alton Walcott) West Indian poet and playwright.

## INTRODUCTION

A Nobel laureate and prominent West Indian literary figure, Walcott is known for writing poetry and drama that transcends traditional boundaries of race, geography, and language while exploring themes of cross-cultural ethnicity, political chauvinism, and postcolonial Caribbean history.

## BIOGRAPHICAL INFORMATION

Walcott was born on January 2, 1930, in Castries—the capital city of Saint Lucia, a small Caribbean island that was once a British colony in the Lesser Antilles. His father, who died during Walcott's early life, was British; his mother was West Indian. Both were teachers who valued education, cultural enrichment, and creative expression. Encouraged by their mother, Walcott and his twin brother Roderick were active with a local theater group as children and young adults. Walcott displayed an early talent for poetry, publishing his first work at fourteen and his first book, *25 Poems* (1948), at eighteen. At twenty he wrote and staged *Henri Christophe* (1950) and cofounded the Santa Lucia Arts Guild with his brother, who also became a playwright.

In 1953 Walcott received a bachelor's degree in English, French, and Latin at the University College of the West Indies in Jamaica. Soon thereafter, he began to teach in West Indian schools, while continuing to write and produce plays. In 1958 he accepted a Rockefeller fellowship to study drama in New York City. The next year, he moved to Trinidad, where he established the Little Carib Theatre Workshop, which would later become the Trinidad Theatre Workshop.

Although he also continued to create and produce plays, during the next decade Walcott turned his attention once again to poetry. His 1962 volume, *In a Green Night,* garnered positive reviews in the English-speaking world and brought his name to the forefront of emerging nontraditional poets. In 1971 Walcott's play *Dream on Monkey Mountain* (1967) received an Obie award. This marked Walcott's first major notice as an internationally recognized playwright.

Walcott received a Guggenheim fellowship in 1977; in 1979 he was named an honorary member of the American Academy of Arts and Letters. During the early 1980s, Walcott began teaching at several universities in the United States, including Columbia, Howard, and Boston University. He divided his time between residences in the Caribbean and in the United States. In 1992 Walcott became the first native Caribbean to receive the Nobel prize for literature.

## MAJOR WORKS

The central theme of Walcott's poetry focuses on dichotomy of Caribbean and Western civilization as seen through the prisms of postcolonial race relations and cross-cultural identity issues. His first significant collection, *In a Green Night* (1962), established several of the themes that would appear in subsequent verse. His 1969 volume, *The Gulf and Other Poems,* is notable for stylistically diverse poems that are unified through a repeated thematic examination of separation and loss. Also among his early volumes of poetry is *Another Life* (1973), an autobiographical book-length work.

Walcott's primary poetic output is considered by some observers to be that which was published between 1976 and 1987, including *Sea Grapes* (1976), *The Star-Apple Kingdom* (1979), *The Fortunate Traveller* (1981), *Midsummer* (1984), and *The Arkansas Testament* (1987). In 1989, Walcott published his epic poem *Omeros,* which was based on the themes and portrayals of odyssey and identity found in Homer's classic *The Iliad.*

Later works of poetry include *The Bounty,* which was published in 1997, and *Tiepolo's Hound* (2000), a book-length poem illustrated with the author's own paintings.

## CRITICAL RECEPTION

Although his dramatic works are also highly regarded, Walcott's literary reputation is based most securely on his poetry. He has been widely lauded as an accomplished poet known for masterful explorations of racial, cultural, and historical consciousness that incorporate both classical and Afro-Caribbean themes and experience. Among Walcott's poetry, *In a Green Night, Another Life,* and *Omeros* have been particularly well-received by literary critics.

Despite—or perhaps because of—his prominence as an accomplished English language wordsmith, some critics have charged that Walcott's written expression is so refined and technically intricate that it can obscure or overshadow his meaning. Walcott's self-defined position as a cross-cultural artist and commentator has also invited criticism from both sides of an often contentious cultural divide: he has been called too Western by some Afrocentric critics and too Afro-Caribbean by some Eurocentric critics. This type of criticism has softened somewhat as his international literary status has grown. Walcott has earned a literary reputation that, by many accounts, places him among some of the greatest contemporary writers.

## PRINCIPAL WORKS

### Poetry

*25 Poems* 1948
*Epitaph for the Young: XII Cantos* 1949
*Poems* 1951
*In a Green Night: Poems, 1948-1960* 1962
*Selected Poems* 1964
*The Castaway and Other Poems* 1965
*The Gulf and Other Poems* 1969
*Another Life* 1973
*Sea Grapes* 1976

*Selected Verse* 1976
*The Star-Apple Kingdom* 1979
*The Fortunate Traveller* 1981
*Midsummer* 1984
*Collected Poems, 1948-1984* 1986
*The Arkansas Testament* 1987
*Omeros* 1989
*Poems, 1965-1980* 1992
*Derek Walcott: Selected Poems* 1993
*The Bounty* 1997
*Tiepolo's Hound* (poetry, plays, and essay) 2000

### Other Major Works

*Dream on Monkey Mountain* (play) 1967
*Dream on Monkey Mountain and Other Plays* (plays and essays) 1970
*The Joker of Seville* [with music by Galt MacDermot] (play) 1974
*O Babylon!* [with music by Galt MacDermot] (play) 1976
*Remembrance* (play) 1977
*Pantomime* (play) 1978
*Beef, No Chicken* (play) 1982
*A Branch of the Blue Nile* (play) 1986
*The Capeman: A Musical* [with Paul Simon] (play) 1997
*What the Twilight Says: Essays* (essays) 1998
*Walker and Ghost Dance* (plays) 2002

## CRITICISM

### Lloyd W. Brown (essay date 1976)

SOURCE: Brown, Lloyd W. "Caribbean Castaway New World Odyssey: Derek Walcott's Poetry." *Journal of Commonwealth Literature* 11, no. 2 (1976): 149-59.

[*In the following essay, Brown offers an overview of Walcott's poetry, tracing the theme of "the New World" that appears throughout his work.*]

In the poem **'Elegy'** Derek Walcott offers a bleak image of the American Dream as New World nightmare:

> Our hammock swung between Americas
> we miss you, Liberty. Che's
> bullet-riddled body falls,
> and those who cried the Republic must first die
> to be reborn are dead.[1]

This elegy on the democratic ideal in the New World as a whole is interwoven with an exposé of the essential falsities that have always been inherent in the rhetoric of idealism within the United States:

Still, every body wants to go to bed
with Miss America. And, if there's no bread,
let them eat cherry pie . . .
Some splintered arrowhead lodged in her brain
sets the black singer howling . . .
and yearly lilacs in her dooryards bloom,
and the cherry orchard's surf
blinds Washington and whispers
to the assassin in his furnished room
of our ideal American, whose flickering screens
show, in slow herds, the ghosts of the Cheyennes
scuffling across the staked and wired plains.

(***The Gulf***, p. 31)

This poem deserves to be cited in some detail, because it provides a useful introduction to some of the typical emphases in Walcott's poetry, specifically, his interest in a New World experience that is concentrated in a Caribbean consciousness and symbolized by United States history. In turn, this interest is rooted in a sense of crisis regarding the myths and institutions of moral idealism. On the one hand, the idea of a New World conjures up the image of new beginnings, the promise of a re-created order of things; and this new order is fraught with new epistemological possibilities—with new ways of perceiving and describing (or naming) things. On the other hand, there is a brooding suspicion that the new possibilities have been betrayed in that historical process which destroyed the dreams of a Che, and before him, groups like the Cheyennes. (It is dramatically appropriate that Che's name represents the first three letters of 'Cheyennes'.) The orthographic coincidence points up a telling historical analogy: it is the same analogy which links the oppressed Black (by way of the arrowhead metaphor) with the dispossessed Indian, or (ironically) the bullet-riddled Che with the victim (John Kennedy, presumably) of a presidential assassin. Moreover, the geographical image of the West Indian archipelago ('our hammock') unobtrusively links the tragedy of dispossession in North America with the destruction of the hammock-weaving Arawaks of the pre-Colombian Caribbean. The cultural and geographical divisions of the New World have been deliberately obscured in Walcott's vision of betrayed ideals and corrupted institutions in the New World as a whole.

The poet subjects the mythic traditions of the New World to similar juxtapositions. In one sense the mythological process is creative and vitalizing: it both represents and facilitates the human need to articulate the perceived truths of experience and those dream ideals which transform reality. Walcott's Che is, thus, the poet's mythic apotheosis of social justice and reform. But, in another sense, myth is not a transforming truth but a mere falsehood decked out in the transparent images of specious innocence. Hence the all-American sex code is a feigned but profitable puritanism ('every body wants to go to bed / with Miss America'). Having demolished the wholesome image of the innocent all-American, the poet establishes a highly suspect image of that perennial symbol of American innocence—the cherry pie. Thus the cherry tree invokes not only the legendary honesty of George Washington (that

pre-eminently 'ideal' American), but also suspicions about Washington's possible contributions to the falsehoods of America's 'innocence', falsehoods that are palpable in the fates of the Cheyennes and the Blacks. The echoes of Marie Antoinette's Old World decadence ('let them eat cherry pie') are, therefore, shocking precisely because they are unexpected in the 'innocent' ambience of the New World. Finally, the poem offers a self-conscious view of the artist's role in it all. Walcott associates his own analysis of the New World with the works of those writers whose insights and techniques are pertinent to his themes. Hence the theme of death and re-birth, which mocks the history of promise and disillusionment in New World democracy, echoes T. S. Eliot's vision of life and death in *The Waste Land*. The image of 'yearly lilacs' recalls Eliot's grasp of the paradox of life co-existing, even dependent upon, death;[2] and it also reflects Walcott's awareness of the old corruptions which have destroyed the early promises of the New World, as well as his continuing optimism that there can be a genuinely new order that is intrinsic to the New World although rooted in the old waste land. In a similar vein, the cherry orchard reference recalls Chekov's vision, in *The Cherry Orchard*, of the possibilities of rebirth-in-death.

On the whole, this theme of new beginnings assumes the dimensions of an odyssey in Walcott's poetry. In a general sense, he envisages the odyssey of the artist (Eliot or Chekov, for example) as the search for, or a re-assertion of, stable values in a moral and social waste land. Hence the grim moral landscape of the Americans in **'Elegy'** is counterbalanced by the kind of moral energy that is evoked by the implied references to the insights of *The Waste Land* and *The Cherry Orchard*. Chekov and Eliot assume outsider identities because their moral idealism contrasts so strongly with the false or aborted ideals with which they are surrounded in Walcott's America. The artist's identity as outsider, or castaway (to anticipate a typical Walcott archetype), emphasizes his lonely odyssey for renewal in an environment of decaying values. In more specifically West Indian terms, Walcott's artist is the outsider archetype, not only in the traditional sense of the alienated artist, but also as an example of the West Indian as ethno-cultural castaway from Europe and Africa. And for this West Indian artist-castaway the quest for moral meaning is also a special odyssey for that new sense of being, that renewal of human possibilities, which Walcott derives from the geo-cultural symbolism of his New World ambience.

What we have in **'Elegy'**, then, is an overview of the cultural and moral malaise which prompts the odyssey of the castaway figures in his poetry as a whole. It is the kind of malaise that he describes repeatedly in the first three volumes of poems (***In a Green Night, The Castaway,*** and ***The Gulf***). In **'Goats and Monkeys'** the racial and sexual tensions of Shakespeare's *Othello* represent the divisiveness of a world in which love has failed. The 'innocent' Desdemona and the 'malevolent' Moor are equally the victims of that failure:

Virgin and ape, maid and malevolent Moor,
their immoral coupling still halves our world.
He is your sacrificial beast, bellowing, goaded,
a black bull snarled in ribbons of its blood.

(The Castaway, p. 27)

As the allusive quality of **'Elegy'** has already demonstrated, Walcott's vision of the waste land habitually invokes the insights of his literary predecessors, and the Shakespearean themes of **'Goats and Monkeys'** are typical instances. So is **'The Prince',** for here the intellectual figure contemplating moral corruption is represented by Hamlet, brooding over his mother's 'lechery' and the murder of his father (*The Castaway,*) p. 29).

In both these poems Walcott intensifies his vision of the failure of love and idealism by locating that failure, as did Shakespeare, in the family—in Othello's marriage and in the corrupted family ties of Hamlet's world. However, the failures symbolized here by the family are extended more explicitly to society as a whole in other poems. **'The Gulf'** envisions the Gulf of Mexico as a symbol of human division (*The Gulf,* p. 27-30). The lift-off of a jet airliner over the Gulf enacts an emotional and moral separation, or detachment, that is essentially destructive: 'the divine soul detaches / itself from created things'; and human separateness is a foreboding of some punitive withdrawal by a Divine force. In the process, this kind of separation has transformed the United States from the symbol of New World beginnings into a three-fold paradigm—of individual alienation ('we leave [Dallas'] Love / Field'), of the violence of presidential assassination, and of the betrayal of old ideals ('the divine union / of these detached, divided States, whose slaughter darkens each summer now'). The prospects for the future are not re-assuring: 'The Gulf, your gulf, is daily widening.' The prophetic warning to the 'divided' States is grimly ambiguous: since the United States is, after all, a symbol of the human condition, the word 'states' extends the American experience to all nations and to all states of being; and finally, 'your gulf' not only addresses the American with a wry reminder of America's hemispheric possessiveness: it also unceremoniously yanks Walcott's collective readership from the role of detached spectator by involving us all in the pervasive effects of conflict and separation. Indeed, the ubiquitous gulf is manifest in all areas of our lives, and ironically, it is most in evidence where we are ostensibly engaged in intimate communication or close feelings. Thus in **'Blues'** a Central Park mugging by a Black youth gang negates the rhetoric of Black unity and racial brotherhood (*The Gulf,* p. 35). Marriage is a yawning 'chasm' between 'twin bed / and boredom' in **'Goodnight Ladies, Goodnight Sweet Ladies'** (*The Gulf,* p. 57). And in **'A Careful Passion'** sexual 'intimacy' actually turns out to be a kind of mutual alienation: the appearance of intimacy merely camouflages the 'original curse' of Cain's children—the curse of loneliness and isolation. According to Walcott's lover-persona, 'the self-seeking heart / So desperate for some mirror to believe / Finds in strange eyes the old original curse' (*In a Green Night,* p. 44).

As **'Elegy'** demonstrates, this kind of isolation motif is crucial in Walcott's work as a whole. In poems like **'The Gulf'** and **'Careful Passion'** isolation is the effect of emotional and moral failure. But viewed in the light of other poems, the isolation theme is significantly ambiguous in Walcott's work as a whole. Isolation is not mere flight and non-communication, but may also be a process of identification rather than self-denial. In this latter sense, it encourages that intense introspection which leads to the discovery of self, and ultimately, to a re-definition of moral meanings and cultural values. Or, in the words of Walcott's favourite castaway figure (Robinson Crusoe) in the poem, **'The Castaway'**:

> Pleasures of an old man:
> Morning, contemplative evacuation; considering
> The dried leaf, nature's plan.

The contemplation of 'nature's plan' leads to the scrutiny of the individual's role in that plan: 'We end in earth, from earth began. / In our own entrails, genesis.' And, in turn, this awareness of humanity-in-nature brings us to his self-consciousness as artist-creator:

> If I listen I can hear the polyp build,
> The silence thwanged by two waves of the sea,
> Cracking a sea-louse I make thunder split.

Moreover, the isolated self-consciousness of the artist is really an example of the creative self-knowledge of all castaway, introspective selves:

> Godlike, annihilating godhead, art
> And self, I abandon
> Dead metaphors like the almond's leaf-shaped heart.

(The Castaway, p. 9-10)

In ethnic terms, the White Robinson Crusoe, colonial overlord of Friday, has, ironically, become the symbol of West Indians whose self-identification is bound up with their history as castaways from Africa, Asia, and Europe. The multiple roles of Walcott's isolato archetype (universal isolation, the alienated artist, the castaway West Indian) underscore the limitations of the view that Walcott's castaway is simply the artist in isolation.[3] The image also demonstrates the complex nature of the isolated self in contemplation—the intensity and the insight which enable the isolated personality to perceive itself, simultaneously, as the paradigm of the artist, the castaway West Indian, and all alienated, isolated beings. In short, Walcott's image explores one of the paradoxes that are characteristic of the contemplative isolato: in **'Castaway'** the experience of *isolation* initiates and intensifies an awareness of *connections*—connections within nature, between the individual and nature, and between the self and its own consciousness. Thus in the act of contemplative evacuation Crusoe traces links between excrement and soil, thus invoking the cycle of perennial creation, death, and re-creation ('We end in earth, from earth began'). Finally, the biological analogy of an eternal cosmos gives way to the image of the eternal, god-like creativity of mind which creates and populates worlds in its isolation. The contemplative isolato discovers not only his own selfhood, but also the links between that self and its universe.

Ironically, the discovery of a crowded, inter-connected universe takes place in solitude: one senses the infinity of things within the finite worlds of self and island. Or, in metaphorical terms, the 'eye' of the perceptive isolato sees infinity in the horizon even as the beholder stands within the symbolic enclosure of the beach and sand:

> The starved eye devours the seascape for the morsel
> Of a sail.
> The horizon threads it infinitely.

> *(The Castaway,* p. 9)

Moreover, the isolation which has generated the self-discovery and the knowledge of others has also encouraged a 'devouring' need to communicate one's perception to a newly discovered universe. But the very modes of perception which he owes to isolation separate the castaway from others. Hence not only does isolation engender perception, but, in turn, perception intensifies one's aloneness. On an ethnic level this means that the castaway imagination of the West Indian artist separates him from the very conditions and groups with which he yearns to communicate. In **'Crusoe's Island'**, for example, the poet tries to bridge the gulf between himself and little church-goers ('Friday's progeny, / The brood of Crusoe's slave'). But:

> . . . nothing I can learn
> From art or loneliness
> Can bless them as the bell's
> Transfixing tongue can bless

> *(The Castaway,* p. 57)

His failure, however, has the paradoxical effect of reinforcing that transcendental self-awareness which initially inspired the longing to communicate. So that although there is none of that easy communication which Gerald Moore, for one, attributes to the castaway's situation, neither are Cameron King and Louis James quite justified in assuming that non-communication is itself a liability or a sign of inadequacy.[4] On the contrary, the poem celebrates the poet's isolation as a kind of transcendental triumph over the colonial culture which has 'transfixed' (i.e. hypnotized and/or impaled) the human psyche.

For West Indians in general and the West Indian artist in particular, the historical experience of New World isolation has been especially ironic in its ambiguity. 'Mundo Nuevo', to borrow the phrase from **'Crusoe's Journal'**, has historically negated the promise of New World beginnings through the fragmenting effects of slavery and colonialism. Yet the heirs to this negative tradition have created a history and a culture out of the very experience of being African-European castaways in the New World. Hence the colonial Fridays have transformed Crusoe's imperial tools into their own instruments: 'good Fridays

. . . we make his language ours.' And in the process they have adopted the 'hermetic skill' with which Crusoe created things (e.g. his journal) out of the very essence of his isolation. In other words, Crusoe's imperial language, and its literary traditions, now serve the special needs of Friday's new perspectives and new, anti-colonial self-definitions:

> So from this house
> that faces nothing but the sea, his journals
>    assume a household use,
> We learn to shape from them, where nothing was
>    the language of a race . . .
> drunks, castaways, beachcombers, all of us
>    yearns for those fantasies
> of innocence, for our faith's arrested phase.

> *(The Castaway,* pp. 52-53)

The new Friday-Crusoe-castaway is Adamic, bestowing on the New World names which mean 'nothing' (i.e. have no intelligible meaning) in their borrowed European tongues, but which impose new meanings and identities on what has hitherto been a history of nothingness (cultural destruction and moral chaos): 'Adam speaks that prose / which, blessing some sea-rock, startles itself / with poetry's surprise' *(The Castaway,* p. 51). Thus when the old sailor is asked what 'La Guaira means' (in **'Nearing La Guaira'**), 'he grins / Says it means nothing'; and, as the poet muses, 'nothing' encompasses green water, sun, moon, La Guaira itself *(In a Green Night,* p. 21). The very act of describing and evaluating his history and environment enables this New World Adam to claim new meaning and identity from an Old World heritage of colonial 'nothings'.

Finally, this quest for meaning and identity endows the composite archetype of West Indian Adam-Crusoe-Friday with yet another dimension, that of the Odysseus archetype. The Caribbean is both a geographical symbol and an historical allegory of that mythic process through which cultures search out and describe the patterned significance ('embroidery') of their 'histories'. Hence in **'A Sea-Chantey'** the islands are

> Refracted embroidery
> In feverish waters
> Of the sea-farer's islands,
> Their shorn, leaning palms,
> Shaft of Odysseus,
> Cyclopic volcanoes,
> Creak their own histories

> *(In A Green Night,* p. 64)

Moreover, such an odyssey aims at that sense of cultural unity and purpose which could replace petty insularity. In **'A Map of the Antilles'**, this odyssey could counterbalance that failure of love which dominates so much of Walcott's other poetry:

> And so an emerald sea, wild as this one
> Seemed to Odysseus a destructive ocean,

Even as he lingered in Circean seas;
Since in no magic port was there such peace
As where his love remained. This is a brief
Ignored by our first parliaments, to chart
The dangerous currents of dividing grief
That make our union a mockery of the heart.

(***In a Green Night,*** p. 55)

This odyssey motif pervades the mood and themes of ***Another Life,*** Walcott's fourth volume of poetry. It opens with an emphasis on movement which captures a sense of search; and, in turn, this questing emphasis replaces a sense of atrophy or stasis with the possibilities of change. Thus the second chapter starts out with the moon-symbol of change, the life-death cycle of birth, christening, marriage, and burial. The pejorative view of the West Indian as a person without history is rebutted with the poet's image of his culture in time-as-movement, movement-as-change, change-as-history:

The sheets of Monday
are fluttering from the yard
The week sets sail

(***Another Life,*** p. 11)

The structure of Walcott's image is itself a precise analogy of the historical experiences and modes of perception which he is describing here. The 'Monday' (moon day) reference invokes the sense of change which is dramatized by the movements that constitute the image. And that movement imagery juxtaposes the past and present through the ambiguity of 'sheets' and 'yard': laundry day in the twentieth-century Caribbean suggests the sights and sounds, as well as movements, through which the Middle Passage of the past forged West Indian history. But this juxtaposition reinforces, rather than contradicts, the poet's insistence on West Indian history as change and creation; for, by implication, the imaginative perception (e.g. the poet's) which facilitates such a juxtaposition is in itself the most crucial evidence of the insights and experiences that have been created out of the 'nothing' of the Caribbean past. Later in the poem Walcott is much more explicit on this point:

that child who puts the shell's howl to his ear,
hears nothing, hears everything
that the historian cannot hear, the howls
of all the races that crossed the water,
the howls of grandfathers drowned
in that intricately swivelled Babel,
hears the fellaheen, the Madrasi, the Mandingo, the
    Ashanti

(***Another Life,*** p. 143)

In effect, 'nothing' not only confirms the destructiveness and nihilism of the Caribbean past, but is also a rebuttal of the view of West Indian history as complete non-achievement.[5] And this rebuttal takes the form of a celebration of that cultural imagination through which the West Indian has transformed castaway beginnings into the creative quest of a cultural odyssey: to hear the destructive

nothingness of the past and to accept what one hears as part of a larger evolutionary process *is* to hear everything. It is to re-define 'history' from a narrow notion of building [monuments and empires] into the self-redeeming 'story' of one's ultimate significance in the universal order of things. In keeping with these psycho-mythic transformations, the Middle Passage of death has become an odyssey of life. Accordingly, Walcott envisages his islanders, 'the stars of my mythology', as Homeric heroes—from the Back-to-Africa Garveyite and his African odyssey to Auguste the sailor whose occupation makes him the perpetually 'lone Odysseus' (***Another Life,*** pp. 16-22). Simultaneously, the collective Caribbean odyssey is exemplified in its most intense and revealing form by the insights and role of the artist. One cannot help noticing that so many of Walcott's archetypes are associated, implicitly or otherwise, with art, especially literary art. Eliot and Chekov, Defoe, and the Old Testament Adam now join the gallery of writers in the odyssey tradition in ***Another Life.*** Odysseus's Homer is everywhere. The Roman odyssey of Vergil's Aeneas is recalled in the Vergilian motto of Walcott's native St. Lucia, 'Statio haud malefidia carinis' (p. 30). And more recent literary history is suggested by that 'lone Odysseus', Captain Auguste, who is also a Joycean Bloom/Ulysses, complete with a St. Lucian Molly Bloom, whose infidelities represent that gulf which Walcott's odyssey motif seeks to negate: 'when he ulysseed, she bloomed again, / the bat-swift transients returned' (p. 31).

Altogether, both the West Indian artist and the collective West Indian consciousness are presented through literary and mythological perspectives which have the effect of simultaneously establishing Caribbean history as a paradigm of a larger experience in fragmentation and isolation, and presenting the West Indian artist as a symbol of the artistic experience generally, but also as a microcosm of the West Indian's odyssey for a sense of cultural wholeness and creativity. Finally, then, the West Indian artist as castaway-isolato is really the quintessence of, rather than exception to, a collective West Indian psyche; and his/her odyssey in art is the microcosm of a common West Indian quest which, in turn, encapsulates what the New World experience can and should be. Hence Walcott's recollection of the fellow artists of his youth really describes the odyssey of the castaway West Indian, the Caribbean's Adam-Crusoe-Friday:

we were the light of the world
We were blest with a virginal unpainted world
with Adam's task of giving things their names.

(***Another Life,*** p. 152)

*Notes*

1. References to Walcott's poetry are to the following editions: *In a Green Night: Poems 1948-1960,* Cape (Cape Poetry Paperback edn.), 1969; *The Castaway and Other Poems,* Cape (Cape Poetry Paperback edn.), 1969; *The Gulf and Other Poems,* Cape, 1969; *Another Life,* Cape, 1973.

2.     April is the cruellest month, breeding
       Lilacs out of the dead land, mixing
       Memory and desire.

                              (*The Waste Land,* ll. 1-3)

3.  C. King and L. James, 'In Solitude for Company:
    The Poetry of Derek Walcott', *The Islands in
    Between: Essays on West Indian Literature,* ed. L.
    James, O.U.P., 1968, p. 98.

4.  G. Moore, *The Chosen Tongue: English Writing in
    the Tropical World,* Harper & Row, New York, 1970,
    pp. 21, 25-6; and King and James, op. cit., pp. 98-9.

5.  For example, V. S. Naipaul's famous remark: 'His-
    tory is built around achievement and creation, and
    nothing was created in the West Indies.' (*The Middle
    Passage,* Macmillan, New York, 1963, p. 29.).

**Valerie Trueblood (essay date May-June 1978)**

SOURCE: Trueblood, Valerie. "Valerie Trueblood on
Derek Walcott." *American Poetry Review* 7, no. 3 (May-
June 1978): 7-10.

[*In the following essay, Trueblood discusses poems from
multiple volumes of Walcott's poetry, including* In a Green
Night, The Castaway and Other Poems, The Gulf, Another
Life, *and* Sea Grapes.]

The West Indian poet Derek Walcott published his first
book of poetry in 1949, when he was still in his teens. His
second, **In a Green Night,** came out in 1962, and since
that time he has given us five more (as well as numerous
plays) and a world. "World" has lost its punch from being
applied to the districts of too many writers; I wish it could
be reclaimed for Walcott's poetry, which keeps an axis and
has size, and sometimes has a grand, planetary movement
carrying the movement on its surface. When I read **The
Gulf** I thought of the three-year-old next door who called
the white end-papers of his book "sky". This very largeness, of subject and of feeling, has seemed a flaw to some
critics, and it is true that Walcott's poems run the risk of
the impersonal and the rhetorical. It seems to me they
defeat these enemies and in doing so many of them move
up and away from the common run of poems and close to
the best ones.

Of course, affinity with the best can be seen as a flaw,
when much poetry is code, or tender hallooing to the self.
Walcott is a balanced, meditative poet; he regards, thinks,
looks for resolution, blames angrily but specifically, and
does not single himself out as the last sane man in bedlam,
nor yet as the most burdened, the prisoner or the victim.
First and last he praises. He makes his reader work, but
what we find out is something more than how complex he
is. He isn't the poet-mailman, getting the stuff to us
through sleet and storm and who knows what-all intolerable conditions. Sometimes the "private" poetry being

written now reminds me of somebody doing Kung-Fu:
face frozen, movements fluid, that odd mixture of the bale-
ful and the ridiculous. It is hard to link it with any normal
experience ("Experience isn't *normal* nowadays!"). On the
other side we have a poetry of relentless normality (i.e.
pattern) insofar as we have asked poets to be naturalists
and they have obligingly botanized, some with wonderful
results and some without, or we have liked catalogues, and
the feeling of picking our way through many objects, and
they have written poems in which everything is plural
including the author and the whole is unsortable. These
methods can give richness, and Walcott himself uses them
for that end. But when he looks at Nature it doesn't come
apart into components, it enlarges, and includes him. The
heat of the "unsubtle, unequivocal sun" comes down on all
confusion and sometimes "the wind smells of salt / and a
certain breeze lifts / the sprigs of the coralita / as if, like
us, / lifting our heads, at our happiest, / it too smells the
freshness of life." In **"Sainte Lucie",** the long poem at the
center of *Sea Grapes,* the secret "for which the dolphins
kept diving / that should have rounded the day" seems to
be reality, the "something always being missed" that eludes
him until he finds it by means of the poem.

*Sea Grapes* starts on an island and goes everywhere,
always coming back, as Walcott has done, to islands. Many
of his themes sound in the title poem (which almost steals
the show): the wanderer, home, "the ancient war between
obsession and responsibility", the possible consolation of
art.

> That sail which leans on light,
> tired of islands,
> a schooner beating up the Caribbean
>
> for home, could be Odysseus,

but "This brings nobody peace" and the book starts on its
own journey to find out why not.

Peace is what we require and refuse; **"The Bright Field"**
is one of several poems about a conscious attempt not to
refuse it. In this romantic poem the speaker, angry in the
press of London crowds, is moved to see the people heading for home after a workday as "walking sheaves of
harvest" "conveyed to one end by the loud belt of the
street": the subject is death and the unity of the ones bound
for death. Birds are flying over the city of a people who
once held slaves and, in his memory, over the bays where
their slaves' descendants live. The mixture in Walcott of
worldly irritability and this simplifying, calming vision is
one of the things that gives his work its strength. He closes
the poem by telling us directly that he is speaking of "The
vision that brought Samuel Palmer peace" and that the
"involuntary bell" of compassion tolls "for everything,
even in London, / heart of our history, original sin". The
question of open statement in poetry won't be solved
except in individual poems, and I think this one succeeds
as a record of a mind persuaded from anger to mystical
resignation and delight. But he has his own doubts about
this Wordsworthian mood; in an older poem he snarled
about "That fabled, occupational / Compassion, suppos-

edly inherited with the gift / Of poetry", and in another called peace something you "contract" when dead.

He has absorbed so many influences that picking them out of his poetry is like saying aha, baking powder! when you taste a cake. If the image of people as harvest in **"The Bright Field"** "derives" from Auden's "As I Walked out one Evening" it also derives from the Bible and from collective perception. How risky is it to write an unironic poem using such materials? The danger for a poet is in adopting an attitude not quite his own. Attitude can be like the teeth of Berenice, that tempted the lover into his crime: whole schools of poets have thought if they got to possess Moore's or Williams' they'd be saved, when the thing was privately owned and it had to grow in, too. Walcott's attitude is his own and has been growing in since he started with poems like **"A Far Cry from Africa"** and **"Return to D'Ennery; Rain"**. His alternating anger and pacifism have their roots in Caribbean life and in the traits and gifts that make him a poet. His struggle with his history and circumstances is part of the struggle to be truthful as well as to be ready for signal moments like the one in **"The Bright Field"**, of release from history.

The circumstances include what George Lamming called "the debt of vocabulary" owed to England. Lamming felt it most strongly when he got off the plane in Accra and heard black people speaking Fanti and Ga, not tied as he was by "debt" to an oppressor. Walcott called it "that first indenture / to her Word". This and the "massive pliability" (his term) that brought about the slaves' conversion to Christianity are inescapable pieces of his history and part of the obsession in his "ancient war between obsession and responsibility". But his is not interested in "a poetry of revenge"; he says, "The slave converted himself, changed weapons, adapted the masters' language, purified the soiled cult". His interest is in what is possible—and what must be made possible—in Caribbean culture now. The adapted language is what he has, and it too is pliable for what he wants, "the new naming of things".

His political poems are notable for their lack of satisfaction and their sense of responsibility. There is no poet sitting in them with all the right ideas. Still, some of them have such authority that it seems there must be self-righteousness too, lurking somewhere; there isn't:

> Here he comes now, here he comes!
> Papa! Papa! with his crowd,
> the sleek, waddling seals of his Cabinet,
> trundling up to the dais,
> as the wind puts its tail between
> the cleft of the mountain, and a wave
> coughs once, abruptly.
> Who will name this silence
> respect? Those forced, hoarse hosannas
> awe? That tin-ringing tune
> from the pumping, circling horns
> the New World? Find a name
> for that look on the faces
> of the electorate. Tell me

> how it all happened, and why
> I said nothing.

> **("Parades, Parades")**

For some reason it is easy for critics, albeit on the left, to take Third World writers to task for not being radical enough. (It is especially odd for North American critics to do this.) "Radical" means several things when applied to writing. Usually we mean by it something a little bit vague, not the writer's politics so much as his or her rebelliousness. Certainly in the Caribbean countries it means more than experimental and audacious—it takes more than that to speak for the dispossessed. So Walcott has been criticized at home for not making the break with the great tradition of English literature and writing in "the language of the tribe". He has written and talked about this subject; he knows the times "a bush would turn in the wind / with a toothless giggle, / and certain roots refused English". His way is to find what we didn't know was there in English, while keeping its excellences.

Because his mood is often one of deep chagrin, even despair, it may be his readers have been waiting for the mood to turn to rage, and for the language to become unbeautiful. The rage was there all along for the looking; it is tougher now, in poems like **"The Lost Federation"** and **"Parades, Parades",** and the language has been pared down but it still has its abundance:

> Don't you remember the hustings by the beach
> with their sulphurous lanterns,
> and your lies in the throat of the sea?

> **("The Lost Federation")**

After "You should get your arse baked till your back / is an old map of blisters" comes "and come back with a sieve for your heart".

> . . . Listen, you

> could still come with me again,
> to watch the rain coming from far
> like rain, not like votes,

> like the ocean, like the wind,
> not like an overwhelming majority,
> you, who served the people a dung cake of maggots

is followed by an offering, "the processional flambeaux of the poui, / the immortelles; feel it with me." This language has gotten Walcott treated as a sort of homegrown Lafayette, when there seems to me to be no poem in *Breaklight,* Andrew Salkey's anthology of vanguard Caribbean work, more direct and ferocious than **"The Lost Federation"**, or one Salkey printed, **"Negatives"**.

**"Negatives",** from *The Gulf,* opens with a television scene of the invasion of Biafra, corpses "sprawled on the white glare entering what's its name— / the central city?" A white newscaster "illuminates the news behind the news, /

his eyes flash with, perhaps, pity". In the middle verse the sensible tone of the first changes into an outcry, and the rhythm changes to a short, broken one:

> I never knew you Christopher Okigbo
> I saw you when an actor screamed "The ttribes!
> The tribes!" I catch
> the guttering, flare-lit
> faces of Ibos,
> stuttering, bug-eyed
> prisoners of some drumhead tribunal.

where the halting uh-sounds intensify the abruptness and distress. He imagines Okigbo's body "on the white road / entering . . . the tribes, the tribes, their shame— / that central city, Christ, what is its name?"

The emotion in this poem, with its shrill long i's, its scene experienced as a photographic negative, is, first, the uncomfortable pity of the TV watcher looking at desperate people elsewhere. It is also the sorrow of one poet speaking to another—a political and visionary one, young, dead (killed fighting for Biafran independence)—who was often accused not being "native" enough in his verse. Finally it is the anguish of a particular man, a West Indian descendant of Africans, who does not take the deaths in the poem impersonally. Sooner or later somebody reading this poem is bound to charge it with "flourish", or the opposite, "earnestness" (the same way we like to call religious feeling either cerebral or simple—to satisfy us completely the Third World poet would have to be a revolutionary who kept mum). But there is a force behind the poem that is what Roethke meant when he required that poetry reveal "a disciplined mind and a truly passionate heart". What does it demand of us (and of its author)? That we remember the name of the city, and thus know what happened. And once we know what happened? Perhaps a U.S. reader connects her grocery bill with a war in which people were killed over food. And then . . . Walcott does not prescribe. Asking a poet for manifestoes, to prove he is not of the Devil's party, is like the marriage license application in my state which has the betrothed "depose" that they are not imbecile, nor common drunkards. Poetry is one place doubt should be sheltered, and Walcott's subjects are the "large things, where one *may* doubt" that Thoreau reserved the conscience for.

The long autobiographical poem *Another Life* followed the lonely, fiery work of *The Gulf,* and in it Walcott explored his past and his culture, trying to "begin again, from what we have always known, nothing". That "nothing" is humble indeed, coming at the end of a book that has longed so hard to know, and known so much. The heightened language of *Another Life* gives it a gravity like that of Schwartz's *Genesis:* both use a lifting, uncovering, working language, the language of strong explanation. Both take the reader trustingly into a childhood where the poet is undergoing the magical trials that made him the poet. There the resemblance ends; where Schwartz is filled with a wretched mirth by the story of his origins and still bleeds at the touch of his relatives, Walcott is calmer, his

eye is not on the worst contingencies of domesticity. The island where his childhood took place is a character in this book and unlike relatives it can endlessly absorb a poet's love and rancor. The distance between Walcott and the child and youth of *Another Life* is implied in the title, yet he is re-established (on another island, Trinidad) in the world he left, and a sense of the power he has drawn from his home pervades his work.

Where Schwartz gloriously, heavily wallows in irony, Walcott mistrusts the irony of his own people and steers clear of it. The wryness of Naipaul, the stinging, comical irony of Lamming, say, describing the war coming to Barbados in his childhood, are missing from this poem, which attempts something different, the evocation of a paradise. But all is not sweetness: the child's innocence is mixed with presentiments of treachery, and his street in paradise contains an "alphabet of the emaciated" including an old garbage-hauling horse named Ajax, a Midas,

> Monsieur Auguste Manoir,
> pillar of business and the Church
> rising to watch the sunlight work for him,
> gilding the wharf's warehouses with his name.

"Vaughan, / battling his itch, waits for the rumshop's / New Jerusalem", and Weekes, the black grocer going toward his shop is

> propelled in his tranced passage by one star:
> Garvey's imperial emblem of Africa United,
> felt slippers muttering in Barbadian brogue,
> and, entering his shop,
> is mantled like a cleric
> in a soutane of onion smells, saltfish and garlic,
> saltflake Newfoundland cod hacked by a cleaver
> on a scarred counter where a bent half-penny
> shows Edward VII, Defender of the Faith, Emperor of
>   India,
> next to a Lincoln penny, IN GOD WE TRUST
> "and in God one, b'Christ," thinks Mr. Weekes,
> opening his Bible near the paradise plums,
> arm crooked all day over a window open
> at the New Jerusalem, for Coloured People Only.
> At Exodus.

This alphabet may be too "made", clever in a disconcerting way—Walcott undercuts it himself later: "Provincialism loves the pseudo-epic". I hesitated at the line about the felt slippers and the brogue, doubted the two pennies so representative, but the plums and the cleaver and the window with the elbow on it are *there,* fully themselves. If these passages can give a hint of the companies of smells, sights, characters, moral problems and emotions—the sheer goods of life—set before the reader in *Another Life,* it is only a hint. Yet the poem is never a catalogue or a travelogue, it is unified, a Story. The burning of the city of Castries in 1948 is in it; an education, a first—and still reverberating—love affair, a deep friendship with a painter, whose paintings are also in it; leavetakings ("forgive our desertions, you islands") and homecomings; and the coal-carrying women, the shacks, the diseases of the poor ("We cure it," / said the young research scientist, / "and multiply the unemployment problem"), the sea.

Walcott is known as a poet of finish and control, one so controlled that he can dispense with the convention for understatement. Yet one of the interesting things about his poetry is its occasional abandon, when he is suddenly speaking up very emotionally or with a particular guileless susceptibility. You don't expect, after the first ten pages of *Sea Grapes,* to arrive at **"The Cloud"**, which is about Eden. In it a cloud is passing over the first couple after their lovemaking, and the last line is "and, as it moved, he named it Tenderness". This kind of line, with its capital letter and its woozy hopefulness, is an example of the passivity that can sometimes come over Walcott. It has a funny charm. There are examples of it throughout his work, and sometimes a whole poem is conducted in this mood—a kind of innocence. In **"Frederiksted Nights"**, the poet wanders over to the La Cuenca (the corner) Cafe in what sounds more like pique than sorrow over someone's departure, and kicks things, or feels like it, and pities himself, and goes on in a resentful defeatist tone using words like "abhor". It seems to be a poem that started off serious, became petulant, and then had a serious second thought—"My life has no corners to turn". But even this line has a sort of innocence and disbelief to it, before the speaker gets himself in hand as a poet and turns to the "rain-hazed horizon". However he also turns to "the corpses of poems"—a somber thought to poets, maybe more somber than parting. It is as if his metaphor released a worry that released a portent. Even his surroundings have gone through several changes, from a beginning which included submarines, electric guitars, whores and bullets, to a white street with gates, oleanders, library, and back to the pier and the horizon, with a couple of stops at the La Cuenca Cafe. I go on at such length about this poem because it is carefully organized in space, ranging over a surprising amount of ground and expanding to include the moon and the sea and all sorts of activities in the port of Fredericksted, but its organization is almost beside the point. It is basically populated by only three, the poet, the one who has left, and the proprietor of the cafe, who is also gone. This is where the issue of control comes in: the poem is about loneliness; we hear it in the softly dignified r-filled lines "your radiance also turned off / by your own hand". But it is touching because it has been all over the place—like many an improvised poem without Walcott's control—and found the answering tone in everything, as the Romantics do, and not been helped. Frederiksted at the end of the season, with its cafes closed and its "short-circuited" nightlife, and the abandoned middle-aged speaker are in the same boat. This pairing, of course, the poem set out to do. It is the *mood* that escapes discipline, especially in the fourth verse where the speaker complains distractedly. It is an odd poem, sort of a stray, with a stray's wistfulness.

**"Oddjob, a Bull Terrier"** might not have been allowed in by a younger poet. It is in a special English tradition of animal poems; we think of Hardy's poem to his cat. Wal-cott has placed the poem near the end of the book, a "serious" position, among the more personal poems that seem to signal the going-deeper and clearing-away of a new period. We have a thriving animal-poetry now, much of it wishing a wild animal would appear or remembering when one unaccountably did (usually to be run over). Few treat the domestic animals and fewer still concede mystery to them. **"Oddjob"** is an elegy. The dog's silence is one of its mysteries—and its death that leaves more silence. The poet looks for a reason for his disproportionate grief and finds only that "You prepare for one sorrow / but another comes", and that love can't be put anywhere safe from this silence: "it is the one love, it is the same, / and it is blest / deepest by loss".

Walcott's poems are inhabited by birds, which are what snow was for Delmore Schwartz. When they appear everything pauses. Pigeons, hawks, geese, herons, crows, pelicans—large homely birds without much song that do one thing, fly. When they fly over we should look down, at what they are leaving. Sometimes they officiate, blessing something going on below, or they compensate, rising to counteract the earthward pull of the human events, or like "the owls leaving earth's load" in **"Sea Canes"** or the pelican going to the rock of Soledad in **"At Last"** or the ibises coming out of the rushes in **"A Far Cry from Africa"** they simply lift off and fly and that is their comment. (They are seldom used as metaphors, although some bishops and ministers are "buzzards" and "corbeaux" and the U.S.A. (I think) is a hawk in one poem.) Their presence above him seems to be consoling, as trees are also. "Holy is Rampanalgas and its high-circling hawks, / holy are the rusted, tortured, rust-caked, blind almond trees": these lines from *Another Life* contain his emblems.

His pleasure in the emblematic results in one odd kind of personal poem: the shy one. He likes to show a feeling or an idea for a minute and then move it out of the way before we're tired of it, sometimes before we're sure what it is. **"The Fist"** and **"Endings"** in *Sea Grapes* do this; it is interesting that these are two of the shortest poems in the book, and the most abstract. They each contain a feeling that he half disclaims by making it an axiom (in **"Endings"**, "Things do not explode, / they fail, they fade") or a figure, in **"The Fist"**, or **"Dark August"** (or **"Star"**, in *The Gulf*). They have a peculiar modesty, a withholding quality. An idea is there but the stuffing is left out and the idea has a meek distracted look despite its largeness. The poems almost say "You should see the part that got away," but they are too discreet. We are hard put to react to **"The Fist's"** "Hold hard, then, heart" because we don't address our own hearts this way and suspect that the poet doesn't his except in extreme cases; even the least voyeuristic reader must want details. To pick on this little poem one more time, "And I gasp / Brightness" is current and falls short of the more traditional "I gasp at her sane brightness" in **"The Morning Moon"**, and "plunging howling into the abyss" makes the reader shy too. With the modest claim of **"The Harvest"** we simply disagree: it seems he is asking us to see his poems as violets, "the coarsest,

commonest, toughest, nondescript, resilient" flower—
which they are not.

But if every agent produces an effect like itself Walcott
must be wonderful; read the poems that contain "O earth,
the number of friends you keep / exceeds those left to be
loved", and "Still haunted by the cycle of the moon / rac-
ing full sail / past the crouched whale's back of Morne
Coco Mountain", and "The classics can console. But not
enough." He is not always lyrical. Sometimes he sees in
"some grey monochrome, much like this metre". Or the
lyrical must be fought down: "Haven't you sworn off such
poems for this year, / and no more on the moon?" In
**"Spring Street in '58",** the funniest poem I've seen of
his, he reminisces about a "poetic" past in New York:

> . . . the cheap cocktail bars
> by which I homed,
> their neon flickered like Mars,
> then, we could still write "The moon . . ."

> \* \* \*

> and one caught style from others like a cold.

He is prey to melancholy:

> pray for us, pray for this house, borrow your neigh-
>   bor's
> faith, pray for this brain that tires,
> and loses faith in the great books it reads;
> after a day spent prone, haemorrhaging poems

> ("The Walk")

**"Nearing Forty"**—"nearer the day when I may judge my
work / by the bleak modesty of middle age"—ends with
rain doing its work "even when it seems to weep".
Throughout the later books there is a struggle with time.
**"The Morning Moon"** and **"To Return to the Trees"**
take the unexpected position that "fine sprigs of white" in
the beard are a happiness and that "grey has grown strong
to me, / it's no longer neutral", though he slyly wonders
"Or am I lying". How *likable* is the poet who says "when
to have written 'heart' / was to know a particular spasm",
and

>           . . . but now pain comes
> where I least expect it:
> in the hissing of bicycle tires on drizzled asphalt,
> in the ambush of little infinities
> as supple with longing as the word "horizon."
> Sad is the felon's love for the scratched wall,
> beautiful the exhaustion of old towels,
> and the patience of dented saucepans
> seems mortally comic.

This is from **"Guyana"** *(The Gulf),* which grows with
every reading.

His descriptive language is sometimes an old one. "The
wind, wave-muscled, kept its steady mowing" could come
out of Virgil, but "so there are little wires of music / some

marron up in the hills, by Aux Lyons, / some christening"
could only have come from this island poet, with "cande-
labra of cocoa" and "the lost, lost valleys / of sugar, the
busrides", and "when the morning sunlight / shivered with
malaria, / and the night sea grew tepid/with weeds, like a
bush-bath". Or this:

> . . . follow the path
> of the caked piglet through
> the sea-village's midden,
> past the repeated
> detonations of spray,
> where the death-rattle
> gargles in the shale,
> and the crab,
> like a letter, slides
> into its crevice"

> (*Another Life,* chapter 21)

Just when you are thinking a particular poem is the best
you reread the elegy **"The Wind in the Dooryard",** or
the age-poems, or **"The Bridge",** or the deceptively
slumbrous **"Midsummer, England"** with its Shakespearean "prodigious summer" spreading out for a people
chilled by their fear of "the imperial blood corrupted, the
dark tide" of immigration; or this passage from **"Natural
History"**:

>           . . . History
> is natural—famine, genocide,
> as natural as moonlight—
> and man is great who rises at this cost;
> like the Bikini turtles, who, after the holocaust,
> swam deeper into sand, their history reversed
> from nature, or the mad birds
> that burrowed into earth, while ocean,
> a god once, rages, at a loss for words.

**"Volcano",** with its homage to Conrad, is one of the finest
poems in *Sea Grapes.*

> One could abandon writing
> for the slow-burning signals
> of the great, to be, instead,
> their ideal reader, ruminative,
> voracious, making the love of masterpieces
> superior to attempting
> to repeat or outdo them
> and be the greatest reader in the world.
> At least it requires awe
> which has been lost to our time

But awe is alive in these poems.

When you come to the end of **"Sainte Lucie",** the central
poem of *Sea Grapes,* you turn back to the beginning to
see how you arrived at the feeling of grace that closes it.
The poem opens in the island's "sun-bleached villages"
"with crabs crawling under the house-shadow / where the
children played house" and the poet reaching for the secret
of his own childhood and of the island. Part 2 is a sinuous
column of island names, snatches of speech, and a parade

of creatures, products, crops, colors, "small rivers / with important names". In the middle of all this is an invocation to the language that enshrines the liveliness:

> Come back to me
> my language.
> Come back
> cacao,
> grigri,
> solitaire,
> ciseau
> the scissor-bird
>
> * * *
>
> jardins
> en montagnes
> en haut betassion
> the wet leather reek
> of the hill donkey

Here Walcott receives the true island language, in the names of its properties. Then comes a Creole song he says he heard on the back of a truck, and last a beautiful section entitled **"For the Altarpiece of the Roseau Valley Church, Saint Lucia"**: this is where you are taken to the center of the island, turned around three times, and shown the secret. First the chapel altarpiece where two "earth-brown labourers / dance the botay" at the center of the valley "fat with things"—bananas, "leaf-crowded mountains, / rainbellied clouds, / in haze, in iron heat". Then the curse of the valley, "the broken mules, the swollen children, / . . . the dried women, their gap-toothed men", then two real lovers, oblivious of curse, though a snake is present, sliding into "a chalice of leaves". It would be possible to argue about likening the serpent to the host, but this is Walcott's Eden, where the snake may be heavenly too, and the faith spoken of is nearly pantheism, close in spirit to Whitman's "And will never be any more perfection than there is now". And finally the two dancers of the altarpiece again, where steeped in silence and afternoon light "one might see/if one were there, and not there, / looking in at the windows / the real faces of angels".

## Andrew Salkey (essay date winter 1982)

SOURCE: Salkey, Andrew. "Inconsolable Songs of Our America: The Poetry of Derek Walcott." *World Literature Today: A Literary Quarterly of the University of Oklahoma* 56, no. 1 (winter 1982): 51-53.

[*In the following essay, Salkey discusses recurring themes of light, harmony, and completeness in Walcott's poetry.*]

Rather like the generalized implication that there is a whole unified scene going for all of us in the New World, in the geographical, historical and political concept of José Martí's *nuestra américa,* anything anyone says about the poetry of Derek Walcott can be argued as true. His is a

new voice redolent with traceries of the elitist elegance of the Old World. His poetry, or at least much of it, is also a radical truth-saying in "other words," in our time, an old report brought forward with sensitive alterations from "another country" to *nuestra américa.* And further, it is the Anglophone Caribbean bringing the salt of her history and received language to bear on the comparatively recent seasoning of our hemisphere's newness.

But more than anything else, it is Walcott's territorial and ontological promise in **"Islands,"** from **In a Green Night,** that makes me know where I am in relation to and what I am to expect from his contribution to *nuestra américa.*

> I seek
> As climate seeks its style, to write
> Verse crisp as sand, clear as sunlight,
> Cold as the curled wave, ordinary
> As a tumbler of island water. . . .

But first, how about that "island"? How about those islands which are the centrality of our Caribbean input into the hemisphere? Walcott's timely warning in that direction is one of the finest in Caribbean poetry that I know and one seldom ever reckoned with when his work is written about in the United States and Britain. His warning also comes from "islands," and I personally take it seriously; for after all, deep down we all do know that "islands can only exist / If we have loved in them." That is to say, in effect, that Walcott is our greatest living love poet and that his profoundly important contribution to *nuestra américa* is his poetry of island love, archipelago love, sea love, ocean love and his loving recollection of the formation of *nuestra américa.* It is from that view of volume after volume of his crystalline poems that I see Walcott's significance and impact in our problematical New World.

If **In a Green Night** announces his territorial and historical perspective of love, then the **Selected Poems** further enhances it and deepens his announcement into a personal declaration. **The Castaway** is another collection that carries forward the statement of New World caring in those two earlier books. Here Walcott reminds us that Crusoe is adrift on Caribbean islands, cut off from the outside world, and consequently must learn to expect little of it. Indeed, **"Crusoe's Journal,"** one of the memorable poems in **The Castaway,** has for its epigraph a quotation from *Robinson Crusoe* which ends with Abraham's words to Dives: "Between me and thee is a great gulf fixed." In a sense **The Castaway** heralded Walcott's next book, **The Gulf.** And there is a line in **"Miramar"** which more than hints that "There is nowhere to go." Yet at the same time, Walcott's commitment to hope, as the first step toward gaining the necessary courage to approach and break through the inherited gloom of Caribbean underdevelopment and pessimism, urges him to complete the line as follows: "There is nowhere to go. You'd better go."

In 1969, when I read **The Gulf** in the Jonathan Cape edition, I mistook the central emphasis of the poems as suggesting that the loneliness of islands, their abject isolation, causes all islanders (hence *all* people so isolated) to strive inordinately for a protective identity, and especially for a quick, hard-edged, materialistic one at that. And, of course, there was more than enough textual evidence to endorse the mistake of that reading. Rereading **The Gulf** later on in 1975 and again in 1981 for this article, I discovered that there was just as much corroborative evidence to suggest that the metaphorical loneliness of islands (together with their "lack of identity" in the outside world's false reckoning) could also be interpreted as the inaccessible quality of love as it becomes enisled. In other words, my later readings yielded Walcott's poetic theory of isolation and namelessness as a paradigm of the death of love.

And so, even in the most literal, surface reading of *Another Life,* Walcott's autobiographical long poem of over 4,000 lines, his specific recollections of love, misconstrued and reappraised, connect fairly readily.

> Maman,
> only on Sundays was the Singer silent,
> then,
> tobacco smelt stronger, was more masculine.
> Sundays
> the parlour smelt of uncles,
> the lamppoles rang,
> the drizzle shivered its maracas,
> like mandolins the tightening wires of rain,
> then
> from striped picnic buses, *jour marron,*
> gold bangles tinkled like good-morning in Guinea
> and a whore's laughter opened like sliced fruit.

Here again, the poet speaks lovingly to his mother, his very own St. Lucian **"Maman,"** but also to mine in Jamaica and to the mother of us all, everywhere throughout the Area, the ever-present Caribbean Sea, the old, loving shelter.

> Old house, old woman, old room
> old planes, old buckling membranes of the womb,
> translucent walls,
> breathe through your timbers; gasp
> arthritic, curling beams,
> cough in old air
> shining with motes, stair
> polished and repolished by the hands of strangers,
> die with defiance flecking your grey eyes,
> motes of a sunlit air,
> your timbers humming with constellations of carci-
>   noma,
> your bed frames glowing with radium,
> cold iron dilating the fever of your body,
> while the galvanised iron snaps in spasms of pain,
> but a house gives no outcry,
> it bears the depth of forest, of ocean and mother.
> Each consuming the other
> with memory and unuse.

And similarly in the objects of the old house, the ones handled by Maman, the same ones recollected by the poet, in pained tranquillity, those that help frame the anguished questions:

> . . . when did the tightened scream
> of that bedspring finally snap,
> when did that unsilvering mirror finally
> surrender her vanity,
> and, in turn, these objects assess us,
> that yellow paper flower with the eyes of a cat,
> that stain, familiar as warts or some birthmark,
> as the badge of some loved defect. . . .

*Another Life,* apart from being a "self-inquiry and cultural assessment in the context of a Caribbean life" and the dismantling and redefining of a former colonial poet's "cultural apparatus of . . . imperialist tutelage," as George Lamming, the distinguished Barbadian novelist and poet, correctly put it, is also an affecting heroic narrative of historical and contemporary defects lovingly owned up to and accepted, in spite of their harrowing memories, lingering scars and half-healed wounds. Walcott's recall of the inconsolable burden of innocence and experience of a people breaking out of the aching silence of colonial defects, cracking the solitude of underdevelopment and neo-colonialism, is the most truly remarkable personal cri de coeur so far published by any Caribbean writer I know.

When I think of the stinging truth of the following lines, I'm acutely aware of how deep Walcott has dredged our psychic loss and caused our current pain to surface—and especially so in the tellingly chosen poetic diction and metaphorical usage of his imaginative report.

> Skin wrinkles like paint,
> the forearm of a balustrade freckles,
> crows' feet radiate
> from the shut eyes of windows,
> and the door, mouth clamped, reveals nothing,
> for there is no secret,
> there is no other secret
> but a pain so alive that
> to touch every ledge of that house edges a scream
> from the burning wires, the nerves
> with their constellation of cancer,
> the beams with their star-seed of lice,
> pain shrinking every room,
> pain shining in every womb,
> while the blind, dumb
> termites, with jaws of the crabcells consume,
> in silent thunder,
> to the last of all Sundays,
> consume.

And he continues by daring us to touch those closed windows, the ledge of that house, the burning wires, those nerves, to touch the terror of death in life, if only to prove our capacity for loving a world we can't hope to move or embrace with our love.

> Finger each object, lift it
> from its place, and it screams again
> to be put down
> in its ring of dust, like the marriage finger
> frantic without its ring;
> I can no more move you from your true alignment,
> mother, than we can move objects in paintings.

Equally haunting reflections on love (ones which when lifted off the page, up to memory and recall, seem to scream to be put back instantly), together with their concomitant sense of loss and actuality of present pain, also appear in many of the poems in Walcott's latest book, *Sea Grapes.* Take this one on love turned round and badly used as a suction-trap for the unsuspecting: in part five of **"Sainte Lucie," "For the Altarpiece of the Roseau Valley Church, Saint Lucia,"** the poet's ironic lunge at the power of the ever-loving church in underdevelopment comes first, I suspect, from his personal detestation of the betrayal of the poor and, secondly, from his quiet, political appraisal of that betrayal. In fact, the dream-laden altarpiece sucks everything toward it, rather like a reverential art work that gobbles the faith of worshipers and distantly trusting spectators; and so the Valley Church is simply another institutional hungry maw that swallows whole the labor of the people, the goodness of the land, the dreams of the hopeful.

> This is a cursed valley,
> ask the broken mules, the swollen children,
> ask the dried women, their gap-toothed men,
> ask the parish priest, who, in the altarpiece,
> carries a replica of the church,
> ask the two who could be Eve and Adam dancing.

Of course, there's no sentimental regret here concerning the death of our own Edenic Caribbean or indeed our own Edenic New World. That is not Walcott's point at all. What I believe he truly regrets is the death of harmony, the death of love. And Walcott's is a telling, quiet regret. It matches the tone and quality of the many glimpses of love he evokes and makes poems out of in *Sea Grapes.* Both his regret and the love that it laments are understated and true, for Walcott well knows that

> Things do not explode,
> they fail, they fade,
>
> as sunlight fades from the flesh,
> as the foam drains quick in the sand,
>
> even love's lightning flash
> has no thunderous end,
>
> it dies with the sound
> of flowers fading like the flesh. . . .

And, by the way, those lines from **"Endings"** are reflected elsewhere in *Sea Grapes,* particularly in the title poem and in others like **"Sunday Lemons," "The Cloud," "Ohio Winter"** and **"The Wind in the Dooryard."**

One or two of Walcott's myopic critics accuse him of moving narrowly from the elegiac to the barely concealed sentimental, of having two main voices only. I can't agree. His poetic range of expression is as wide as his human concerns and as all-of-a-piece as his sense of harmony and his preoccupation with the nature of love. As a matter of fact, some of Walcott's most memorable poems include cameos of irony, humor, satire, invective, vernacular wit,

St. Lucian patois and classical pastiche. Yet for all that, in a poet so harmonious in sound and sense,

> . . . the silence is all:
> it is deeper than the readiness,
> it is sea-deep,
> earth-deep,
> love-deep,

as he affirms in **"Oddjob, a Bull Terrier."** And notice where he places love! Qualitatively, it is the most profoundly silent. For Walcott, love is *the* true silence, a condition of the unspoken will to connect, an absence of utterance stronger than thunder.

> . . . it becomes unutterable
> and must be said,
> in a whimper,
> in tears,
> in the drizzle that comes to our eyes
> not uttering the loved thing's name,
> the silence of the dead,
> the silence of the deepest buried love is
> the one silence,
> and whether we bear it for beast,
> for child, for woman, or friend,
> it is the one love, it is the same,
> and it is blest
> deepest by loss. . . .

Though he writes again and again of love as lost when it is enisled, as fading into nothingness when isolated, he does imagine it nevertheless as a force, as rain which will hammer the grass blades into the ground. In **"Force"** he names it for what it can also be: "love is iron." And in **"Winding Up"**: "Love is a stone / that settled on the sea-bed / under grey water."

*Sea Grapes* is Derek Walcott's sixth book of poems. There are other publications, brought out earlier in the Caribbean, which make rewarding reading today. I like looking back on those books and learning about his way forward from the clear trajectory of his burgeoning talent and unfolding confidence and control. He is a poet I respect and admire greatly. His work is accomplished and resonant in a concerned, people-centered way which I regard highly. And in that particular alone, *Sea Grapes,* along with *Another Life,* must be considered his most outstanding achievement so far.

Clarity and light, harmony and completeness in his finest poems are Walcott's gifts to all of us. Let him continue to reveal *nuestra américa* as he goes. Let us listen and look carefully as he redraws the old map with his songs of love and hope. I, for one, a wanderer far from home, a willful exile, a drifter-believer (the kind of runner Walcott himself has refused to become, staying rootedly in the Caribbean as he has all his writing years), will always listen to his acutely clear-sighted songs of love and hope and look at them again and again.

**Robert Bensen (essay date spring 1986)**

SOURCE: Bensen, Robert. "The Painter as Poet: Derek Walcott's *Midsummer*." *Literary Review: An International Journal of Contemporary Writing* 29, no. 3 (spring 1986): 259-68.

[*In the following essay, Bensen examines the centrality of painting and imagery in Walcott's* Midsummer.]

An island of obsessive beauty, a people impoverished but rich in their cultural heritage from Africa and Europe, and a lifetime to celebrate them in art: these gifts had been given the young Derek Walcott, who swore with his friend Dunstan St. Omer not to leave St. Lucia before they had put the island on canvas and in words—every ravine, inlet, mangrove swamp and hill track.[1]

Walcott had been drawn to art early by being "more deeply moved by the sight of works of art than by that of the things which they portray," as Malraux wrote of Giotto. Walcott used Malraux's anecdote as an epigraph in *Another Life,* in which he wrote of his discovering art as if he were Saul, blinded with revelation of the true religion (*AL,* p. 1). His will alone could "transfigure" the mountain shacks of the poor into a "cinquecento fragment in gilt frame" (*AL,* p. 4). He felt the power of art to recreate the world, to transcend the poverty of those shacks, to redeem his dispossessed people and their history. The task was as immense as that of Adam standing before his unnamed world, though Walcott had this advantage: in the books of his father's library, he had inherited the work of centuries of European masters.

The West Indian reverence for ancestors became for Walcott a need to assimilate tradition, to assume its features, to make it part of his visual vocabulary. He believed that his knowledge of tradition would augment his treatment of the island's watercolor seas, its vegetation ripe for oils. But where St. Omer painted "with the linear elation of an eel," Walcott's own hand was "crabbed by that style, / this epoch, that school / or the next" (*AL,* p. 59). Tradition proved too powerful a master; he was its sunstruck Caliban.

His gift emerged instead in the multiple facets of metaphor, in language as physical as what it described. Horace's critical observation, *ut pictura poesis,* Walcott made into a conduit for painting to nourish his poetry, in the character of his imagemaking, his visual imagination, as well as in his sense of line and composition. Painting pervades his use of metaphor, as in this imagistic Moebius strip in which art and life imitate each other endlessly: "The hills stippled with violet, as if they had seen Pissarro," or in this rendering of a seascape as still life: "A peel of yellow sand / curled like a lemon rind across the sea's blue dish" (*AL* p. 74; pp. 66-7).

The connection between poet and painter in Walcott lies deeper than eye-level, being rooted in his early, most basic experience of the world. *Another Life* is the autobiography of his life as a young artist, an intimate odyssey in which he first experiences the primal facts of life and death through art. He undertakes the conventional epic journey to the underworld, the land of the dead, which he finds in books of paintings by the European masters:

I learnt their strict necrology of dead kings,
bones freckling the rushes of damp tombs,
the light-furred luminous world of Claude,
their ruined temples, and in drizzling twilights, Turner.

         —*AL,* p. 44

Among the relics of art, he recognizes his father, who is not his natural father (also a painter, but who had died young) and not the liturgical Our-Father-who-art-in-heaven, but "Our father, / who floated in the vaults of Michelangelo" (*AL,* p. 44). His spiritual father could be accessible only through art, wherein Walcott collects his true heritage and recognizes his future.

It was then
    that he fell in love, having no care
for truth,
    that he could enter the doorway of a triptych,
that he believed
    those three stiff horsemen cantered past a rock,
    towards jewelled cities on a cracked horizon,
    that the lances of Uccello shivered him,
    like Saul, unhorsed,
that he fell in love with art,
    and life began.

         —*AL,* p. 44

If European art was a reliquary, it was also a revelation. He fell in love with its power over him and with the power it places in the hands of the very few.

*Ars longa, vita brevis.* Those chosen by the Muse must devote their lives to the practice of her art; there is no other way. In Walcott's Caribbean, the artist, the story-teller, the poet, the *raconteur, houngan,* or priest; all exercise power over domains beyond the ken of the uninitiated—the past, the future, the dead, the fortunes and misfortunes of the living. The monumental certainty of vocation in Walcott's poetry comes out of a selfhood that is forged in a culture rather more distant from that of the United States than has been generally recognized in this country. Certainly the magnitude of his appropriation of European traditions in art and literature for his life-long effort to make poetry and painting "cohere" and ultimately "ignite" suggests the primal role of the artist as a tribal, and Promethean, fire-starter, on whom the survival of his people depends (*AL,* pp. 58-9).

Painting has always been at the heart of Walcott's poetry, as central as St. Omer's altarpiece is to the Roseau Valley in **"St. Lucie,"** in which the painting reflects the life of the valley that surrounds it.[2] The preoccupation with painting in the autobiographic mode of *Another Life* moves toward self-portraiture in *Midsummer.*[3] In the former volume, painting is the occasion for the high drama of self-discovery, as the author recounts his enthusiasm and disappointment as a young painter. After thirty years of devotion to both arts, the episodic narrative of the young painter continues in *Midsummer* in poems frequently conceived and composed as verbal paintings—portraits, landscapes, seascapes, studies and sketches. Painting informs many of the poems directly as subject ("**Gauguin**" XIX and "**Watteau**" XX), as a source of imagery, in the handling of qualities of light and color, and in the range of themes. Painting prompts his intense scrutiny of his motives for art, of large historical questions about the relationship between art and power, and of the value of art in the confrontation of human mortality.

I

*Midsummer* is the poet's sketchbook, the artist's diary, running the course of one year from summer to summer. It is less a recording or a chronology than it is a clearing of vision, an arrangement of things in their true significance, which is what both painter and poet mean by composition:

> Through the stunned afternoon, when it's too hot to think
> and the muse of this inland ocean still waits for a name,
> and from the salt, dark room, the tight horizon line
> catches nothing, I wait. Chairs sweat. Paper crumples the floor.
> A lizard gasps on the wall. The sea glares like zinc.
> Then, in the door light: not Nike loosening her sandal,
> but a girl slapping sand from her foot, one hand on the frame.
>
> —XXV

Light, its movements and textures and intensities and absence, is all. It glazes the brilliant seascape and shades the room, both of which the poet has carefully prepared as ground for the figure of one of his daughters, or the nameless muse herself, coming in from the beach. She is also the artist's model, her silhouette balanced momentarily in one long line that is backlit by the previous line. Her image is both painterly and sculptural, classical and modern. She is not Nike, but she assumes her pose *à la* Degas, which Walcott alters both toward the Baroque by her hand's bracing against the frame, and toward a sly Post-Modernist pun, as the frame itself is framed within the poetic image. The loving portrait is in part the work of a bored father with nothing to do but wait for his daughter and her everyday grace. It is also the work of a poet with a painter's eye for nuances of light and composition, for the suggestion of the figure's weight, balance and form in the girl's gesture. Her very being, in its simplicity, answers the poet's masked self-portrait which begins the poem ("The sun has fired my face to terra-cotta") and the Faustian promise of the surf that he

> shall see transparent Helen pass like a candle
> flame in sunlight, weightless as woodsmoke that hazes
> the sand with no shadow.

The girl is neither mask nor spirit. She is just what the poet had been fishing for with the horizon line, a well-

made pun on his own poetic line. Until she enters, his lines have caught nothing of moment, merely the momentary, the static objects at hand which, lacking her presence, fail to cohere into composition. The setting needs her, the poetic line needs her, the artist needs her—indeed, her coming allows time, which had nearly ceased in the poet's torpor, to resume. She is no more than a sketch, but those quick, bold strokes of the pen bear the emotional weight of the poem.

Where the young painter in *Another Life* wanted to surround his island's shacks with a gilt frame, the seasoned master in *Midsummer* concludes that "the frame of human happiness is time," knowing that the frame of time is art. At the beginning of *Another Life,* line after line calls back the moment when light failed and his drawing was done, and his future as a painter seemed assured. The poet stitches his lines into a verbal net that pulls the moment back and holds it, briefly: "I begin here again, / begin until this ocean's / a shut book. . . . / Begin with twilight . . ." (*AL,* p. 3).

In *Midsummer,* time has entered the very lines, extending their duration, becoming part of the artist's gesture. The apparent ease with which the girl in the doorway is fixed in portraiture lies in the grace of the poetic line swelling beyond the surface tension of iambic pentameter, the measure most conformable to English phrasing and rhythm. Walcott uses that meter elsewhere in poetry and verse plays with Elizabethan richness and Jacobean wit. But in *Midsummer* he takes deep draughts of the warm Caribbean air and his line lengthens with the amplitude of his West Indian English. It lengthens as the fecund Caribbean crowds into his field of vision. The poems press toward the white margin like a sea of words at high tide. And because time moves slowly in the tropics, the line takes longer to ripen, all motion slows but that of the mind and the mind's eye:

> Something primal in our spine makes the child swing
> from the gnarled trapeze of a sea-almond branch.
> I have been comparing the sea-almond's shapes to the suffering
> in Van Gogh's orchards. And that, too, is primal. A bunch
> of sea grapes hangs over the calm sea.
>
> —XXVIII

Here is the poet at ease, on holiday with his daughters, getting a few lines down in his sketchbook, perhaps for *Midsummer's* cover painting of the sea-almond tree, as well as for the poem. The long lines might read as prose, did not the end-rhymes staple the aural canvas taut for the internal Pointillism of vowels and consonants, which register on the ear as a patterned aura around the shape of the child. The long vowels in *primal, spine,* and *child* establish a declarative line that anchors the precarious *swing* as firmly as the baroque branch anchors the child in the second line, with its clustered consonants twisting around the darker *e*'s and *a*'s. The initial long *i*'s, the firm open tones of the poet's meditative mind-set, prepare the ear for the stroke of the ideogrammatic *I*, the body's slender stalk from which the poem's speculative intelligence will branch.

Comparing the sea-almond's shape to that of Van Gogh's olive trees is neither pretentious nor an idle exercise of Postcolonial wit. Rather, he is asserting the validity of his experience and culture in that island which is "known . . . for making nothing" (I). In his youth, he had imagined the landscape transformed into fourteenth century pastoral in a gilt frame, but now the frame is gone, the European manner is gone, and the tree itself as an image of suffering is at issue. And the issue is resolved instantly and certainly.

The poet resumes his composition of the landscape by noticing the bunch of sea grapes. He outlines the arrangement of things on the beach and out on the reef, a still ground against which the most minute movements register on the surveying eye, as in a painting so lifelike the viewer thinks something moved:

>      . . . Noon
> jerks toward its rigid, inert center.
> Sunbathers broil on their grid. . . .
> In the thatched beach bar, a clock tests its stiff elbow
> every minute and, outside, an even older iguana
> climbs hand over claw, as unloved as Quasimodo,
> into his belfry of shade, swaying there.

The day's heat brings the human figures, the lizard and clock all near the melting point of Daliesque surrealism, but Walcott has them all hold their poses timelessly on a day as infinitely repeatable as any other in the tropics.

But the poet is not to be self-hypnotized by his own idyll.

>      . . . When a
> cloud darkens, my terror caused it. Lizzie and Anna
> lie idling on different rafts, their shadows under them.
> The curled swell has the clarity of lime.
> In two more days my daughters will go home.
> The frame of human happiness is time,
> the child's swing slackens to a metronome.
> Happiness sparkles on the sea like soda.

Isolate the last line, and it's pure corn, tacked onto a perfectly good final quatrain, and a violation of Pound's dictum not to turn abstractions into symbols such as "dim lands of peace." But it is also the perfect grace note to the sombre intimation of mortality in the beat of the child's swing, a serendipitous dance on the graver, epigrammatic, "The frame of human happiness is time." The line effervesces just as the poet almost submits to Time and Fate; it freshens like a late afternoon breeze; it gently declines to fret; it insists that for the moment at least, the poet of exile and rootlessness look no further.

## II

But the sparkle dissipates, the sun declines a few degrees, the moment with its tranquility passes, and the sequence resumes on the next page. Walcott's calm is the eye of the

hurricane, the moment before "that thundercloud breaks from its hawser" (XXVI), or the morning after "a storm has wrecked the island" (XLIX). The West Indian poet must either master or submit to the extremes of his region's nature as well as its history. Walcott's powers are always sustained by the immediate, the local, firmly grounded as a lightning rod driven into the earth to pull divine flame from the sky:

> Christ, my craft, and the long time it is taking!
> Sometimes a flash is seen, a sudden exultation
> of lightning fixing earth in its place; the asphalt's skin
> smells freshly of childhood in the drying rain.
>
>           —XIII

Art is long, life short: the labor continues, work accumulates, the lines increase stroke by stroke their store of reality. His work bears nothing of the self-cancelling exercises in syntax that are the other side of modernism. *Midsummer* is studded with brief self-portraits of the poet as laborer, working his physical and metaphoric lines:

> My palms have been sliced by the twine
> of the craft I have pulled at for more than forty
>   years. . . .
> The lines I love have all their knots left in.
>
>           —XXV

The West Indian sailor-fisherman must keep his nets mended or he catches nothing. The knots give a sure grip on the experience that is the object of the poet's handiwork. Walcott's line can thin out to a watercolor wash, or thicken into impasto, to such density that the nouns stuck in the verbiage pull the syntax to a halt: "Mud. Clods. The sucking heel of the rain-flinger" (XXXV). Halfway between Homer and Heaney, the thick, clotted monosyllables ballast the agile feminine ending: from dull earth springs the mythic god. His lines have a muscular energy that confirms the self-portraits of the poet as Herculean laborer, doomed to pull the full weight of his memory in his wake:

> I drag, as on a chain behind me, laterite landscapes—
>       . . . I pull the voices
> of children behind me.

Or, as a tailor, an important occupation in the Caribbean, remembering his mother treadling at her Singer:

> I stitch her lines to mine now with the same machine.
>
>           —XVII

Or, as the painter at once glorifying his subject and laboring to provide through art an antidote to the destruction of history:

> A radiant summer so fierce it turns yellow
> like the haze before a holocaust. Like a general,
> I arrange lines that must increase its radiance, work
> that will ripen with peace, like a gold-framed meadow
> in Breughel or Pissarro.
>
>           —VIII

Yeat's conception of things falling apart from a failing center pervades *Midsummer*—the island wrecked by storm, clouds as "pages in a damp culture that come apart," the poet's exile from his family—though in the West Indies that may all be business as usual. The fisherman and tailor keep mending, and the poet, like the painter, composes his lines to harness the sun and harvest the parched, intractable fields.

### III

> I can sense it coming from far, too, Maman, the tide
> since day has passed its turn, but I still note
> that as a white gull flashes over the sea, its underside
> catches the green, and I promise to use it later.

—XV

Sensing the approach of death, the poet persists in recording the minute truths of his experience, storing his sensory impressions to use later in a painting. There is no diminishing of ambition, just the recognition that of the thousands, perhaps millions of seagulls he has surely seen, he is just now noticing how its belly reflects the ocean. In *Another Life,* the young artist was awakened through painting to the power of death. His tropical paradise admits death, breeds it as rapidly as life, awaits its stroke as the poet and his mother anticipate the inevitable tide. Death gives meaning to his life's work, though such a tidy consolation seems remote in *Midsummer.* Momentarily one can cherish the memory of "clean, scoured things that . . . / the sea has whitened, chaste":

> A yard, an old brown man with a mustache
> like a general's, a boy drawing castor-oil leaves in
> great detail, hoping to be another Albrecht Durer.
> I have cherished these better than coherence
> as the same tide for us both, Maman, comes
> nearer. . . .

But the emotional tide of the poetic sequence will not settle into nostalgia, as, in the following poem, the poet looks beyond the individual death toward the massive symmetries of metropolis and necropolis, and asks, "So what shall we do for the dead . . . ?" (XVI). The imagination that returns the things of this life is futile in supposing that the dead "share the immense, inaudible pulse of the clock-shaped earth." Our treasured memorabilia they cannot see, and natural beauty means nothing to those suspended outside of time, neither grim nor beatific, who on the shore "wait neither to end' nor begin." The echo of Milton's "They also serve who only stand and wait" (Sonnet XIX) focusses the problem in both poems: the value of human effort in the face of death. Walcott asks, "What use is any labor we / accept?" He does not, like Hercules, gain life thereby, or like Milton, an afterlife in paradise. It is the question the artist asks of his vocation, and while it is not answered as a theologian or philosopher might, neither is it dismissed. It broods above the progress of *Midsummer* from the moment the clouds part in the first poem. If we are incapable of imagining our end, what use is the imagination? What use is the life devoted to it,

and why spend years in its cultivation? Why labor only to grow, as the poet laments, "more skillful and more dissatisfied?" (IX).

The issue of the efficacy of art is enlarged by the sense of the artist's diminishing power to affect the outcome of humanity's large struggles. Walcott's helplessness in the face of tyranny, poverty, and high-tech weaponry is fixed in an emblematic triptych:

> The stalled cars are as frozen
> as the faces of cloaked queues on a Warsaw street,
> or the faces of black derelicts flexing over a fire-
> barrel under the El; above, the punctured sky
> is needled by rockets that keep both Empires high.

—XLII

The imperial power-junkies rule both skies with absolute despair. It may be too late, certainly too late to establish even a lopsided equation between the potential for absolute destruction and the value of art. The poem ends with a vision of a city bombed back almost to the Stone Age. For the origin of such despair, Walcott turns back to the beginnings of modern warfare and modern art in the late nineteenth century.

Impressionism, the beginning of modernity in art, accomplished by isolating the momentary effects of light, made possible the fragmentation of space and obliteration of form that was to come, and the meaning of art increasingly lay in its surface, its superficiality:

> Art was *une tranche de vie,* cheese or home-baked
>   bread—
> light, in their view, was the best that time offered.
> They eye was the only truth, and whatever traverses
> the retina fades when it darkens; the depth of *nature
>   morte*
> was that death itself is only another surface
> like the canvas, since painting cannot capture thought.

—XVIII

The Impressionist surface is lovely, capable of *joie de vivre* and nostalgia, but death arrived on a much grander scale than the painters of "bustled skirts, boating parties, zinc-white strokes on water" could handle, and they retreated into abstraction.

> Then, like dried-up tubes, the coiled soldiers
> piled up on the Somme, and Verdun. And the dead
> less real than a spray burst of chrysanthemums,
> the identical carmine for still life and for the slaughter
> of youth. They were right—everything becomes
> its idea to the painter with easel rifled on his shoulders.

The image of the painter is borrowed from the more confident days of *Another Life,* when painting was a disciplined act of love:

> Gregorias, the easel rifled on his shoulder, marching
> towards an Atlantic flashing tinfoil,
> singing 'O Paradiso'

till the Western breakers laboured to that music,
his canvas crucified against a tree.

—*AL,* p. 52

Gregorias is marching off to his Passion, his holy war. In *Midsummer,* the painter retains the posture, but the soldiering is ambivalent, a mimicking of the real soldier going off to nearly certain death, and the pure motive of art for art's sake is sullied by the carnage it can represent, but not prevent, with generous amounts of carmine.

The bitterly sardonic tone of "They were right," about coolly abstracting from harsh reality its Platonic idea, updates Auden's famous line, "About suffering they were never wrong, / The Old Masters."[4] The farmer plows and the galleon sails while Icarus drowns unnoticed by all except by the artist, who sees all and understands all and tells all. But Walcott's artist is also right: art is abstraction. To create art=to paint pictures=to write poems. Between infinitive and object, between the making and the made, the triggering subject cannot intrude, merely follow appended by a preposition: to paint a picture *of,* to write poems *about.* The artist is removed from his subject by the very act of creating. The challenge is to connect himself to his subject through the art, even if the subject is oneself: "I cannot connect these lines with the lines on my face" (VI). How much more difficult then it must be to connect with matters of conscience. His bitter acknowledgement of the rectitude of those for whom death "is only another surface / like the canvas" underscores his deepest doubts about his vocation, which he had begun with the greatest exuberance: "I felt that/the gift of poetry had made me one of the chosen, / that all experience was kindling to the Muse" (XLI). To be one on whom nothing is lost is almost to lose oneself to that Apollonian as well as Hebraic flame. The burning of the chosen one is of course double-edged in a poem about Hitler's death camps. The ultimate question in that poem parallels Walcott's earlier question in XVI about the value of labor in the face of death.

> But had I known then
> that the fronds of my island were harrows, its sand the
>   ash
> of the distant camps, would I have broken my pen
> because this century's pastorals were being written
> by the chimneys of Dachau, of Auschwitz, of Sachse-
>   hausen?

The rhyme of the last, prolific camp with *pen* and *written* tightens the sense of complicity of the artist, now self-accused. The syllables mount like the dreaded piles of human kindling.

IV

Where Auden's subject in "Musee des Beaux Arts" was the single tragedy that fails to touch the common lives of men, Walcott reverses the proportion: how mass suffering fails to touch the artist absorbed in his work. We expect the artist to be a seismograph of his culture and register its shock. According to Pasternak, "The more self-contained the individuality from which the life derives, the more collective . . . is its story. In a genius the domain of the subconscious . . . is composed of all that is happening to his readers."[5] If what is happening in the world is unprecedented destruction, and if the scale of threatened destruction multiplies astronomically over half a century, the artist's imagination can no longer draw vitally from the collective life and his choice of subject becomes amoral: whether to paint the casualty or the chrysanthemum makes no difference to the dead.

Randall Jarrell diagnosed the malady afflicting modern poets who "no longer have the heart to write about what is most terrible in the world of the present: the bombs waiting beside the rockets, the hundreds of millions staring into the temporary shelter of their television sets."[6] Today the bombs are clustered atop the rockets and the Doomsday scenario is a prime-time television movie starring the people of Lawrence, Kansas. More and more, there is no place to hide.

The paralysis of the artist is perhaps an accurate reflection of a world trapped by its own defense systems. The artist, if we take *Midsummer* at face value, needs to confront the terror, to risk incinerating the will and drowning out the muse's call. In the poem about the death camps, though forty years after the fact, their impact raises the question of whether the poet would have continued to write had he known of their horror.

The question is not rhetorical, even if it comes late, because it is really a question of faith and sustenance. That the poem has been written is the answer to its own question. Art turns out to be not for its own sake but for the sake of the artist, turns out to be his way of sustaining faith that there is more to life than dying, the faith that allows him to move into the unknown territory of his work.

Those, like Rimbaud, who lose that faith, quit and go on living in spiritual if not physical exile, or quit living altogether. In the last poem of *Midsummer* Walcott writes of the boyhood "faith I betrayed, or the faith that betrayed me" (LIV), the "distracting signs" of which rise before him out of the landscape. He wonders where is "the heaven I worship with no faith in heaven," and in that paradox is the strength to persevere, to create what he began by celebrating. The portrait of the poet and painter as the ambivalent, troubled, yet titanic creator is completed in the final lines of the book. As he had in the first poems of the book, he addresses the Russian poet Joseph Brodsky, who epitomizes the artist exiled from the land that sustains his art:

> Ah, Joseph, though no man ever dies in his own
>   country,
> the grateful grass will grow thick from his heart.

The poet's metaphorical recreation of his world is not complete until his body physically joins its nature to that larger nature, which in life it could never completely align with.

Art is the way to explore that misalignment, to draw the figure it makes upon the human spirit. That is where painting and poetry meet in Walcott's work. A line is made by a point of no dimension moving in one unchanging direction. That ideal line can scarcely exist in painting, and not merely because the point of a brush is at least as thick as one sable hair. The painter works in areas of paint, and the line is defined by their misalignment, becoming a record of their disjuncture. Walcott's poetic line is similarly shaped as a record of the disjointedness of his experience in the world. The true artist is the maker—poet or painter—whose line is the seam joining the world together, composing it as fast as our collective despair keeps letting it fall from our grasp.

### Notes

1. Derek Walcott, *Another Life* (New York: Farrar, Straus and Giroux, 1973), p. 52. Cited as *AL*. Walcott has frequently written of the West Indian writer's need to resist the tendency to sentimentalize poverty and lapse into the romantic cliche that the beauty of the Caribbean can inspire. Nevertheless his elemental response to that beauty is awe: "The beauty is overwhelming, it really is. It's not a used beauty, there are no houses; it's not a known beauty, and so the privilege of just looking at these places and seeing their totally uncorrupted existence remains an Adamic experience" ["An Interview with Derek Walcott," conducted by Edward Hirsch, *Contemporary Literature* XX:3 (1979), 283].

2. *Sea Grapes* (New York: Farrar, Straus and Giroux, 1976), p. 46. "The chapel, as the pivot of this valley, / round which whatever is rooted loosely turns . . . / draws all to it, to the altar / and the massive altarpiece. . . ."

3. *Midsummer* (New York: Farrar, Straus and Giroux, 1984). Poems from *Midsummer* are cited in the text by their Roman numeral.

4. *Collected Poems* (New York: Random House, 1976), p. 146.

5. Boris Pasternak, *Safe Conduct,* trans. Beatrice Scott (New York: New Directions, 1958), pp. 26-7.

6. "Fifty Years of American Poetry," *The Third Book of Criticism* (New York: Farrar, Straus and Giroux, 1969), pp. 332-3.

### David Mason (essay date spring 1986)

SOURCE: Mason, David. "Derek Walcott: Poet of the New World." I *Literary Review: An International Journal of Contemporary Writing* 29, no. 3 (spring 1986): 269-75.

[*In the following essay, Mason explores the geographic expansion of Walcott's "literary territory" from the Caribbean roots of his earliest writings to North American and Mediterranean settings.*]

Although Helen Vendler has called Derek Walcott a "Poet of Two Worlds,"[1] it may be more accurate to call him a poet of the New World, a world which has absorbed the old and is still faced with its own lack of definition. His formal proclivities help him bridge old and new writing styles, and, increasingly, his work is shaped by a history of self-exile and divorce, a continuous breaking down of the structures in which complacency breeds. He is one of a handful of modern poets who root themselves in tradition, yet become reliable witnesses to modern life.

In the marketplace of Castries, the capital of St. Lucia, where Derek Walcott was born, the audible mixtures of English and patois remind one of the voices in Walcott's poems: the English and French with their Anglo-Saxon and Latin heritage, the vestiges of African dialects that survive in a few inflections or turns of phrase. Walcott has mastered the speech of former rulers and former slaves, which gives him a special right to speak of "The leprosy of Empire."[2] Like Ovid at the fringes of Roman domination, Walcott has observed imperial power, but he has also witnessed life in a New World of which Ovid never dreamed. As both poet and playwright, he has set himself an ambitious schedule of assimilation. His literary territory, which began as the Caribbean basin, has expanded to include North America and Europe (particularly England, Greece, Rome and, via Brodsky and Mandelstam, Russia). Perhaps because his vision is of Whitmanesque proportions, the work itself has been uneven. He has produced a few gems among his poems, and a great many rougher stones which still repay examination.

"The emotional attitudes of Walcott's early verse were authentic," Vendler writes, "but shallowly and melodramatically phrased."[3] It is true that a certain Latin grandiosity creeps into his style, creating moments of unjustified inflation. But Vendler also emphasizes Walcott's unique point of view:

> Walcott's agenda gradually shaped itself. He would not give up the paternal island patois; he would not give up patois to write only in formal English. He would not give up his topic—his geographical place, his historical time, and his mixed blood; neither would he give up aesthetic balance, "the rightness of placed things," he was in all things "a divided child," loyal to both "the stuffed dark nightingale of Keats" and "the virginal unpainted world" of the islands . . .[4]

Unlike most poets, Walcott was born with a subject; he had something to say, in large part because he was born in a place that embodies so many diverse elements of the modern world, and he was gifted with an ear for its languages. This tenacity, this refusal to let his purpose be diminished, is precisely what has always given Walcott the potential for a kind of greatness.

Inheritance and imitation, coupled with fresh experience, resulted in complex ambitions, illuminated by Walcott himself in his memoir, "What the Twilight Says":

> In that simple schizophrenic boyhood one could lead two lives: the interior life of poetry, the outward life of action and dialect. Yet the writers of my generation

were natural assimilators. We knew the literature of Empires, Greek, Roman, British, through their essential classics; and both the patois of the street and the language of the classroom hid the elation of discovery. If there was nothing, there was everything to be made. With this prodigious ambition one began.[5]

It is ambition as great as Joyce's, as great as Whitman's, and even to identify it is quite an accomplishment. Though it is difficult to tell at this point whether Walcott's poetry will ever completely defeat the clamor of influences, he has his own mature style supple enough to be recognizable in *vers libre* as well as closed forms and blank verse. There is practically no verse technique in which he has not, at some point, worked well.

Throughout his career, Walcott has "caught style from others like a cold,"[6] but this is not necessariy indicative of a dire condition. His very ambition and assimilation have demanded imitation of others, to which he has always added a Walcott presence, more definable with each new volume. In *Selected Poems,* which gathers work completed earlier than 1964, Walcott's indebtedness to the seventeenth-century poets is evident on nearly every page. The title of his first significant volume (or at least the first published in the "imperial" capital, London) was *In a Green Night,* a phrase from Andrew Marvell's "Bermudas." In his title poem Walcott borrows Marvell's imagery, but recasts it into tetrameter quatrains that convey doubts of the poet's role in an Edenic landscape. Marvell's is not the only seventeenth-century influence found in *Selected Poems.* "Orient and Immortal Wheat" takes its title and epigraph from the Third Century of Thomas Traherne's *Centuries of Meditations,* and bits and quotations from other poets of the period are sprinkled throughout. *The Fortunate Traveller,* Walcott's sixth book of poems (depending on how you count), gets its title, playfully, from Thomas Nashe, who died at the opening of the seventeenth century.

The same volume illustrates Walcott's experimentation with a very different tradition, island patois, to evoke characters of Caribbean folk tradition. In the dialect poem, "The Spoiler's Return," Walcott, although lapsing into English poetic diction, produces long passages that work splendidly. None of his earlier attempts at dialect poetry works quite so well. With "The Spoiler's Return," Walcott is not so much creating the character of the Spoiler for us as he is playing with the voice to produce sophisticated local satire. Except for the poem's mock-dialect, it could be compared to many of the verse satires of the seventeenth-century, from Jonson to Suckling to Marvell, as well as their Augustan successors.

In all them project, all them Five-Year Plan,
what happen to the Brotherhood of Man?
Around the time I dead it wasn't so,
we sang the Commonwealth of Caiso,
we was in chains, but chains made us unite,
now who have, good for them, and who blight, blight;
my bread is bitterness, my wine is gall,
my chorus is the same: "I want to fall."

. . . . .

. . . as for the Creoles, check their house, and look,
you bust your brain before you find a book,
when Spoiler see all this, ain't he must bawl,
"area of darkness," with V. S. Nightfall?

The personal reference to Walcott's favorite whipping boy, V. S. Naipaul, is straight out of English satirical tradition, and perhaps, too, the tradition of the Calypso taunt. Clearly Walcott is having literary fun, and does not expect us to believe, in street-life terms, that his dialect is accurate.

Like Ben Jonson, Walcott can turn his "ventriloquism" (Vendler's word) to good use when it comes to paying compliments. His poem, "Beachhead," written for Anthony Hecht, suggests the imagery of war remembered in some of Hecht's best poems. Though its measure is shorter than that which Hecht has most often used, his voice is still suggested:

A sepia lagoon
bobbing with coconuts—
helmets from the platoon
of some Marine unit—

whose channel links those years
of boyhood photographs
in *Life* and *Collier's*
to dim Pacific surf.

An earlier poem, "R.T.S.L.," written in memory of Robert Lowell, takes on Lowell's *Life Studies* voice convincingly:

. . . there was the startle of wings
breaking from the closing cage
of your body, your fist unclenching
these pigeons circling serenely
over the page. . . .

Walcott's own mature voice is most evident in poems like "Hurucan," "The Hotel Normandie Pool," and in the momentary transcendence of "The Season of Phantasmal Peace." "Hurucan" derives its strength from description:

When the power station's blackout
grows frightening as amnesia,
and the luxury resorts
revert to the spear-tips of candles,
and the swimming pools in their marsh light
multiply with hysterical lilies
like the beaks of fledglings uttering your name,
when lightning fizzles out
in the wireless, we can see and hear
the streaming black locks of clouds.

The seventh line of this passage contains an image that isn't quite clear, but the rest of it is stunning writing. In "The Hotel Normandie Pool" Walcott takes up the familiar theme of exile. He is not, like his friend, Joseph Brodsky, a political exile barred from returning to his native country. Yet, for Walcott, the pain and responsibilities of adulthood are themselves a kind of exile, and childhood is a landscape to which he can never return; the Castries of his childhood was long ago gutted by a fire. The personal and political exile of other poets before him seems a haunting presence; Constantine Cavafy and George Seferis play important roles in *The Fortunate Traveller.* Cavafy visited Athens only a few times; Seferis lost his Smyrna early, and Greece itself during the German occupation. "Suddenly you discover you'll spend your entire life in disorder," Seferis wrote. "It's all that you have; you must learn to live with it."[7] The same sense of moodiness infects Walcott's **"The Hotel Normandie Pool"**:

> Then Ovid said, "When I was first exiled,
> I missed my language as your tongue needs salt,
> in every watery shape I saw my child,
> no bench would tell my shadow, 'Here's your place';
> bridges, canals, willow-fanned waterways
> turned from my parting gaze like an insult,
> till, on a tablet smooth as the pool's skin,
> I made reflections that, in many ways,
> were even stronger than their origin.

He begins with an image of the poet sitting down to write in what would seem a second-class hotel:

> I choose one of nine
> cast-iron umbrellas set in iron tables
> for work and coffee. The first cigarette
> triggers the usual fusillade of coughs.

The poet's solitude is exile, however self-willed, and in the end Ovid taunts him with his own activity: "Because to make my image flatters you." It is a graceful and moving poem about delusion and diligence, and its final note is struck with real precision.

As early as *Selected Poems* there are pieces that only Walcott could have written. In **"A Sea-Chanty,"** he composes a good portion of his poem out of Caribbean place names and indigenous nouns. Like Adam or Whitman, he becomes the New World figure pointing and naming, a tendency he continued in his 1969 book, *The Gulf*:

> I loved them all, the names
> of shingled, rusting towns, whose dawn
> touches like metal. . . .

He makes an effort not only to absorb his culture, but to define it for others. This goal explains why a novelist like V. S. Naipaul, who seems to hold no hope for the region, becomes emblematic of a despised pessimism. Naipaul may very well be the "winter-bitten novelist" of the poem, **"Hic Jacet,"** who is "praised for his accuracy of phlegm" (*The Gulf*). In *Sea Grapes* (1976), a poem called **"At Last,"** subtitled "To the exiled novelists," begins:

> You spit on your people,
> your people applaud,
> your former oppressors
> laurel you.

Walcott has his own dark, brooding side, his pessimism about the potential of black power movements, politicians, tourism, Rastafarianism; but usually he is less concerned

with judgment than with vision and meaning. Naipaul's fastidiousness and tone of disgust—at least in *The Mimic Men* and *Guerrillas*—would be perceived by Walcott as unhelpful, out of place, and even ignorant. Walcott is more of a sensualist than Naipaul; he may dislike what corrupt governments do to human life in his "tourist archipelagoes,"[8] but he can still see positive vitality and culture in the population.

This social stance—an attitude of commitment which is the converse to his attitude in poems about self-exile and historical solitide—is best expressed in Walcott's plays. Like the poems, they are uneven. His musical, *O Babylon!,* is about the sufferings of a small band of Rastafarians in Jamaica. In his efforts to express the full range of Caribbean life, Walcott must have found the subculture of Rastafarianism fascinating.[9] He has adapted their unique language for the stage, trying to avoid the betrayal of a complete English translation. In the end he creates a celebration of reggae among motley shanties on a Jamaican beach.

Like America's hippies, Walcott's Rastas greet each other with, "Peace and Love," and like so many spiritual movements before them, the Rastafari have been pushed aside to make room for economic development. Thus, Walcott has found in his community a microcosm for the strange mutations of political oppression.

He probably founded the Trinidad Theatre Workshop (in 1959) with a great sense of idealistic purpose. His plays have been experimental, mythological and poetic—in fact, he must be one of the few successful writers of theatrical verse in this century, although his best play, *Pantomime,* is written in prose. Writing for the theater has sometimes allowed Walcott to be playful, less rigorous, and to liberate lines that might be difficult in a poem:

> Thy kingdom come, condominium—

But occasionally the poet overwhelms the dramatist, and actors are asked to deliver lines unthinkable for their characters, even given Walcott's elevated stage poetry.

Apparently Walcott's dreams of a catalytic theater responsible for social change or at least social identity have been disappointed, but his theatrical contribution has nevertheless been a substantial public service, developed from the same impulses that motivate his poetry:

> . . . my first poems and plays expressed this yearning to be adopted, as the bastard longs for his father's household. I saw myself legitimately prolonging the mighty line of Marlowe, or Milton, but my sense of inheritance was stronger because it came from estrangement.[10]

There is a question as to whether Walcott, in his recent work, has abandoned his social mission for a more personal art. His satirical pot-shots continue unabated, and he has apparently not abandoned the stage, where he may continue to have a brilliant career. But the scale of his work in both genres appears to be more personal and focussed. That he learns and grows from every encounter—if his art is any indication—should be encouraging. One wonders how an island so small and (seemingly) simple could have produced a poet with the knowledge and ambition of Derek Walcott. But of course it wasn't the smallness of the place that mattered so much as the language and the twin needs: to be adopted by the larger world and to speak of his origins. One is left with an image of Walcott on one of his visits south, perhaps to Trinidad, barefoot on the sand, gazing out at a "sail which leans on light," and uttering what may be the best pentameter line he has ever written:

> The classics can console. But not enough.

*Notes*

1. Helen Vendler, "Poet of Two Worlds" *The New York Review of Books,* March 4, 1982, pp. 23-27.

2. Derek Walcott, *Selected Poems* (New York: Farrar, Straus and Company, 1964), p. 5.

3. Vendler, p. 23.

4. Ibid.

5. Walcott, *Dream on Monkey Mountain and Other Plays* (New York: Farrar, Straus and Giroux, 1970), p. 4.

6. Walcott, *Sea Grapes* (New York: Farrar, Straus and Giroux, 1976) p. 52.

7. George Seferis, *A Poet's Journal* translated by Athan Anagnostopoulos (Cambridge: The Belknap Press, 1974), p. 53.

8. Walcott, *The Star-Apple Kingdom* (New York: Farrar, Straus and Giroux), p. 40.

9. The Rasta lifestyle is a growing and, apparently, positive force in black culture, but its "true" members represent a way of life diametrically opposed to the white Englishman's and the white North American's. As the English travel writer, Patrick Leigh Fermor, wrote in 1950, "What a curious, dreamy and lotus-eating life they lead! Their existence consists exclusively of dodging the police, singing songs in praise of a monarch who knows nothing about them, planning the downfall of the white world, drinking rum, throwing dice and smoking reefers." Rastafarians are a minority with strong and basically peaceful beliefs (violent Rasta crime is said to be committed only by those who are not "true believers") and their own language. For a more thorough discussion of Rastafarianism, see *The Caribbean Review,* volume XIV, no. 1.

10. Walcott, *Dream on Monkey Mountain and Other Plays,* p. 31.

## Derek Walcott and Rebekah Presson (interview date 1992)

SOURCE: Walcott, Derek, and Rebekah Presson. "The Man Who Keeps the English Language Alive: An Interview with Derek Walcott." *New Letters* 59, no. 1 (1992): 8-15.

*[The following interview focuses on Walcott's epic poem,* Omeros.*]*

*[Presson]: The last time we talked you made much of what* **Omeros** *is not, and so what would you say it is?*

[Walcott]: It's long. I don't know. In the reviews that have been coming out, they've been using the word "epic" a lot. I just reread it again, and I suppose in terms of the scale of it—as an undertaking—it's large and does cover a lot of geographic elements, historical ground. I think that's the word. I think the reason why I hesitate about calling it that is I think any work in which the narrator is almost central is not really an epic. It's not like a heroic epic. I guess that's what I think of it, that since I am in the book, I certainly don't see myself as a hero of an epic, when an epic generally has a hero of action and decision and destiny.

*The hero, I guess, is the whole village.*

There are different characters in the book who have elements of the heroic in them. I think even a character like the retired English sergeant major is a heroic figure, even if he's slightly ridiculous.

*Is that because he's at least making an effort to record what's happening?*

Well, no. He was in the war; he was in World War II. World War II was probably the last war that had a sort of moral reason, in a way. He served and retired and was wounded and has a memory of a wound. So in action he was heroic, not more than anyone else, but certainly in terms of the fact that he served in a war. The endeavors of Achille, the day-to-day fisherman, are heroic. I don't put myself in that company, that's all.

*So the story in* **Omeros** *starts out with a picture of this village and of these fishermen and their canoe that they fish from, which has the name "In God We Troust"—sort of a variation on trust.*

There's an actual canoe like that that I saw spelled like that—T-R-O-U-S-T—and I thought, this is very touching, because the ordinary thing, "In God We Trust," you would have just passed by, but the error was interesting; I mean the spelling was interesting and personal, and perhaps more devout than the regular spelling.

*Your poem* **Omeros** *follows the form of an epic in some ways. It's written in hexameter, but it seems to me that you pull out your other writing tricks, too. There's actual dialogue, as in a play, and needless to say, you are a* *prolific playwright, and you vary the passages between lyric passages and dialogue passages and action passages. Is this a pull-out-the-stops kind of thing?*

No. I didn't know what I was going to encounter as the poem proceeded. I was aware in the beginning that there would be voices; I didn't know about the dramatic encounters that would happen. But also, I had been working on film scripts as well, and I think that there's an element of a scenario of a film script in there, certainly in terms of the width of the thing and the possibility of a cinematic version of some aspects of it. In a large poem, though, the writing is like a novel, and as in a novel, everything is in there—geographic description, the weather, the characters, and the action, and so on. So, what was exhilirating was to widen yourself to such an extent that you could just bring in everything that you wanted to do.

*It is interesting that you'd been working on a film script, because another cinematic aspect is that you cut quickly between times and places. Achille is in his journey to Africa and suddenly you cut to Helen, or cut back to St. Lucia, or cut to a different time.*

That kind of editing keeps the story going, because about four or five of them going at the same time help the propulsion of the narrative, as you edit and jump and cut back to another and continuous story. It's the same technique as film, right?

*Some of your plays have a fairly large cast, but it seems like there are a lot of balls in the air here, a lot of people to keep track of. How much of a challenge was that?*

I don't think there are that many. There are certainly the principle characters, and their lives, and so on. Sometimes I wish I'd gone into the lives of one or two of them a little more deeply, but then the narrative goes on, and it pulls people along with it. But each domestic situation has its own drama, as in life, so that Achille and Helen and Hector is one kind of play or drama or story, and then Major Plunkett and his wife is another story, and Philoctete with his wound, and so on. So it was exciting to live one life one day, and go to another life another day, and connect them. But I didn't have a plot design as such, saying, today I'll do this; tomorrow I'll do that. Whatever seemed to be needed, I would do. Then, when it needed to be arranged in a kind of a sequence that would build the momentum, I sometimes drafted the chapters in a line and then needed spaces to connect. It would make a mural, in a sense.

*Do you feel like you were writing a novel?*

Not a novel, but I have felt for a long time that poetry has surrendered too much of what it used to do. The novel used to be an epic poem, and it's sort of withering and withdrawing into small, personal, diaristic considerations that a lot of lyric poetry has. Everybody has an ego, and nobody's ego is interesting, none. Art is interesting, but not the person who makes it, really.

*What is your obsession as a writer? Are you primarily concerned with giving a clear and accurate picture of life in the Caribbean?*

That's certainly what I had in mind. It is a votive act. I feel grateful for the kind of life that's down there. It's simple. The rhythm of life there, the beauty and simplicity of the people. All of it sounds patronizing and sort of wrong, but those values are there. Certainly the values are there in the beauty of the islands.

*And I suppose what all this leads to is the middle passage of the book in which Achille has a sunstroke and takes an imaginary, spiritual journey to the Africa of his preslavery ancestors.*

In this section, Achille the fisherman, for a moment that contains all of history, staggers and has a sunstroke. Within that moment he goes back to Africa, and time is concentrated in that. I mean, it's longer than just a second; it does go beyond that. When he gets on this imaginary journey, which is led by a sea swift up the river, from across the ocean, he sees someone whom he recognizes as his father, because the man walks like him, looks like him; and he stops and searches in the face of the man for the features of his father and it is his father, from generations back.

*The segment in which the protagonist, Achille, meets up with his preslavery ancestor is the pivotal scene in Achille's growth as a character. Could you talk about what it means to Achille to question finally what his name means, and who he is?*

I think the condition of colonialism, or of any first migration of people who were given another language, means the erosion of identity and the desperation to preserve their identity, which can sometimes be punished or banned. But even deeper than that, in adjusting names, somebody from Europe comes over here and changes his name. Something goes into that, in the process of adapting to the name that you've been given, because as an immigrant it's better to call yourself Smith than some unpronounceable, apparently Czechoslovak name, or something. What happens in the process of that naming? If someone is called Achille, what is he? You have to go through a whole process of becoming a name that you have been given. It's the process and technique of removing identity and altering identity so you can rule or can dominate. There must be a moment in a woman's life when she changes her name, like in marriage—if women are supposed to change their names—when that person becomes Mrs. X. Yet, who is Mrs. X?

*I'm talking about Achille himself, his personal decision. His decision is that he is Achille the fisherman from St. Lucia, he is not an African, because he's not happy in Africa.*

Who's happy going back to that scene? That's not his home. That's another point in the book. You talk to a third-generation American, and you say, Why aren't you

Russian; why aren't you Japanese; why aren't you Czech? And the person says, well, I'm American. The whole idea of America, and the whole idea of everything on this side of the world, barring the Native American Indian, is imported; we're all imported, black, Spanish. When one says one is American, that's the experience of being American—that transference of whatever color, or name, or place. The difficult part is the realization that one is part of the whole idea of colonization. Because the easiest thing to do about colonialism is to refer to history in terms of guilt or punishment or revenge, or whatever. Whereas the rare thing is the resolution of being where one is and doing something positive about that reality. And this would be true of the Caribbean, where all the races of the world are central, are collected, like in Trinidad, for instance. Syrian, Indian, Chinese—they're all there. Of course, it's wonderful to keep the heritage and even the distinction of identities in terms of culture, but when it's ultimately said, that is the composite nature of Trinidad. It has all these various things. That is what it means to be Trinidadian. If I lived in Trinidad thoroughly, I would have to understand Chinese culture; I would have to understand Indian culture, African culture, Middle-eastern culture, as well, because those realities are there.

*You anticipated my question. I was going to ask you what all this means to Derek Walcott, because you don't fit in one world. Achille has a niche in the world, but you fit in many worlds.*

Not really, I don't think.

*You're a professor at Boston University.*

All the time I'm teaching I want to be on the beach swimming. That's what I want to do. But, I know what you mean; one can adapt to situations, and you can have a function. My ideal is not simply to be on the beach swimming. I would really prefer to be working and writing and painting in the Caribbean; so I know exactly where I want to be.

## Derek Walcott and Rose Styron (interview date May-June 1997)

SOURCE: Walcott, Derek, and Rose Styron. "Derek Walcott: An Interview by Rose Styron." *American Poetry Review* 26 (May-June 1997): 41-46.

[*In the following interview, conducted in January 1995 with poet and journalist Rose Styron, Walcott discusses the influences of multiculturalism on the creation and appreciation of literature.*]

[*Styron*]: *So let's start at the beginning: tell me a bit about your early childhood on St. Lucia—your first memories, or your parents in this multi-racial, multi-cultural group of islands—where you went to school, and how you started writing poetry.*

[Walcott]: I was born here, not far from where I am now, near the sea, up at Becune Point. I was born in the very small town of Castries, which is the capital of St. Lucia. My mother was a school teacher and a widow. I have a twin brother and a sister.

I think my mother's encouragement obviously, and because of the fact that my father was a painter and an amateur writer and evidently a director of theatricals as well—was very encouraging in terms of our writing. So I owe her that. I mean she was not one who discouraged it, in a place like this where it, you know, conceptually it seemed to be crazy to want to be a writer, and particularly a poet, and for her that was perfectly okay, and she is the one who physically, practically, helped me, by giving me some money to have my first book printed in Trinidad. I owe my mother for that kind of encouragement.

And of course teachers who were splendid young men who felt that it was perfectly okay to want to be a poet. That's not a common thing, in any country.

*It's a very uncommon thing, from the poets that I have had conversations with—on this program and everywhere else. So you did not feel alienated, or different, as they did; you were in effect in the mainstream, in your family, if not in school?*

I'm saying it was never much trouble at any point for me to consider that I was making some choice that would not be to my or to other people's benefit. That I am very grateful for.

*Were you always aware of and concerned with the multiculturalism, with the many races and backgrounds in the Antilles as you seem to be now? It seems to me to be almost your grand theme—in your Nobel lecture on the Antilles, for instance, you speak of St. Jean Perse in Guadaloupe, of his "the swaying palm trees recite by heart"—Perse was the former Nobelist from this area—and you say the fragrant and privileged poetry that Perse composed to celebrate his white childhood, and the Indian music behind the graceful young brown archers whom you speak of in Trinidad, in Felicity, as they were recreating the Ramayana there—Trinidad has the same cabbage palms, set against the same sky, and you say, "They pierce me equally." So is the source of your poetry, and of your love for the Antilles, partly its multi-cultural background?*

No, I think I arrived at that, and I think we, in the Antilles, arrived at that too, politically, because basically the Caribbean, from Cuba down—Cuba of course a little earlier—is basically a feudal setup—it was pyramidal, hierarchical, and frankly feudal, because it meant in terms of the land that there were fewer white owners with large estates, on which, in the smaller Caribbean, in the lesser Antilles, the working population were principally African—and it's only when I went to Trinidad I think that I became fully aware—certainly absolutely more aware—of the complexity and variety of races. In Trinidad, and for us, in a passage that I myself have gone through—which would be the equivalent in terms of, if I were dividing my life into political sections, I would say—the childhood would be colonialism, the adolescence might have been adult suffrage, the maturity would be independence, and then perhaps the independence would be chaos, I don't know—the way you feel when you get to my age.

But anyway, that's a political parallel. So that if a multicultural society wasn't there early, I think the explosion of races that I encountered, the mute explosion of different faces that were there in Trinidad, is tremendously exciting, and remains that way to me. It is happening more and more in the Caribbean. For instance there are more Syrians here now, there are certainly a few more Indians, and so on, so that, you know, the mosaic, and the mural, of different faces—that you see around you in the Caribbean—wasn't that rich and complicated—it was very simple at the beginning.

I think the sense of multiplicity came to me when I got to Trinidad, and that became a tremendous heritage, because it meant that I was perfectly entitled to study Chinese literature, because there were Chinese in Trinidad. And they are West Indian, and you know, Arabic, and—English obviously, and Spanish, and African—all of those things existed, and they are as much my heritage as, say, the African heritage is.

*I know you say that—at least you say one way or another, that "the ideal city is a writer's heaven"—I think you spoke about Trinidad in relation to cities—and cities are also a source of culture. So what for you would be the ideal city? Is it the city you found in Trinidad? Or have you found cities in other parts of the world that give you that same feeling?*

I remain a small island boy, no matter where I go. And I don't know Europe, so every city I go to in Europe comes as a total shock of experience in a sense, so that's not an experience that I know, and one that I'm still, in a sense, afraid of. Like I'm scared of Italy because it might be too overwhelming; I might want to stay there. I was scared of Spain, and now I'm not cowed by Spain, and love it very much.

But in terms of the proportions of a city, what I meant was—Auden had a wonderful line that he wrote in his middle period about lakes, and he said, a lake allows the average father, walking slowly, to circumvent it in an afternoon. I think the same thing said by Auden about lakes may be true about a city, that I think that a city's got to be basically, for a certain distance, ambulatory; I think we should be able to walk, almost around the circumference. Now—perhaps you can do that in some cities, but you really can't, ultimately. I think the width, and sense of dissipation, of identity, that can happen in a city, is not something that I personally am excited about. I think the proportions of cities, and certain historical peaks of great literature, or painting, for example, all have a neighborli-

ness, a familiarity, even a provinciality, to them. And perhaps when that provinciality goes out of a metropolis, then what it creates is very small pockets, that don't cohere. You know, inner cities, or sections for the rich, or another kind of section—whereas I think certainly in a West Indian city there's a kind of coherence and rhythm that is affable, and, you know, penetrable, and so on—at least for me. So I find that in Port of Spain—not that I walk that much, in fact I never walk, but—so there's a lie there, but I mean—I'm talking about the sense of circumference that is there in a city. That's what I feel. And if that city can contain all these races and there's an affability that is possible in the idea of the neighbor, the next-door neighbor, who may be Chinese, or African, or Syrian, as is the case in Port of Spain, then that's to me an ideal thing.

*Can you see a dark time when tourism, or political conflict, or overcrowding would cause Port of Spain, or any of the island cities, to become like New York, like Washington, where races clash, where the ethnic neighborhoods are set against each other—or like Belfast, where religious groups fight each other?*

No, I think—for instance in Trinidad there are Muslims and Hindus—if someone tried to exploit the religious differences that exist between them—you know, if you're smart enough you can always exploit anger or resentment or jealousy or whatever, but I think that it would be hard to do that in Trinidad. Even if it were attempted that should certainly be stopped—eradicated—quelled—whatever. I don't think that the idea of exploiting, the idea of racial hatred, is out of the question—I think it could happen for instance in Trinidad, where there is, you know, a lot of tension in a sense between the Indian and the African politicians, still, and it could happen in Guayana, and so on. This is not such a threat, though. I think that after awhile the rejection and absurdity of it would strike the Trinidadian—particularly the Trinidadian—as being a waste of time and stupid and not practical.

And that's what I like about the temperament of Trinidad and the Caribbean. But I think the threat, the danger is the expansion that can happen with tourism—that you could have like many Miamis, all along the Antilles. Especially in the flat islands, in which, you know, the growing and the spread of malls and marinas and shops and hotels and so forth, can suddenly transform a place into a large shopping mall with a beach. I think the responsibility of that control rests with the politicians. You can't blame them. If our politicians, and they do do that, encourage things like, you know, drug lords, or encourage land sales, or hotel developments in which they make some deals—we have to examine the corruption of our politics before we accuse people from abroad of, say, corrupting our life style. Self-examination is more important than blaming Americans for corrupting the Caribbean.

*When you talk about the blessed obscurity of your island, you also talk about the fact that there can be a virtue in deprivation, because it can save you from what you call "a cascade of high mediocrity." Do you think there's more danger in high mediocrity invading your island than anything else?*

Well, I think it's a world-wide threat, I think the tide, you know, sort of that mass tide of not-quite-good, or okay, you know, not a masterpiece, but tolerable. You know, the fat paperback with the silver and gold-raised things that you find in airports—it's hard to define what it is, because it sort of looks elegant and is *terrible*—that's the seepage that I think is dangerous. What I meant by that is not to say that, you know, there are qualities and virtues in poverty; I'm just saying that what I remember of my boyhood is that a library had to choose the best because of the budget that it had; there were no second-rate novels in the library in Castries—they couldn't afford them—so what you had to have is Dickens and you had to have Scott—even occasional novels were quality novels. It might be O'Hara, it might be Hemingway, or English writers, like Waugh and so on. So that's what I meant—in terms of the rigidity or astringency of a particular budget, if you equate that with poverty, the kind of education that one had was a part of that kind of deprivation. A lot of the writers of the Caribbean, who were quite brilliantly educated in many respects, had to look for themselves and create their own idea of what writing could be. I think now—I think that there's so much tolerable trash out, you know, that for us it is dangerous because we don't have the alternatives. If you live in New York you can say, I don't want to watch any more television, I'm sick of MTV, and then you get something else—then you can go to a movie that you really want to go to, or a play or something—when you don't have that recourse, and you're flooded with stuff that is okay, you know—it doesn't hurt anybody—but if that's the only thing you have, then that's a terrible thing that I think is happening in the Caribbean. And what one has to fight against and preserve.

*As a child then, in a library with good taste—what inspired you? What literature did you read that made you want to become a writer? Or was it just spontaneous knowledge rather than other reading?*

No—there's no point pretending—I think if one asks oneself why do you become a writer, I think you have to answer quite simply, quite humbly, and quite gratefully, that you were gifted. And that's what my answer is, and it's quite acceptable for me to say that about myself. I don't think of it as something that separates me from anyone else, I just think of it as a reality. I knew that I had this gift, that I wanted to develop it and so on. So I knew that early.

In terms of how one felt about reading other writers, I think that happens to every writer; I think you lose your originality like your virginity, you know—at the beginning you're original. The most original period of any writer's life is when that writer begins to write. Thomas Traherne says "I learned the dirty devices of the world." I think the

dirty devices of syntax, about how to be a writer, can corrupt a writer in a sense. I think for instance a writer like Blake, trying to get back to an inner sense of syntax—you can only have one writer like that. Then—to take an example of supreme magnificent decadence, you'd have to say Milton, or aspects of Shakespeare. But it's magnificent, right? What I mean is, that clarity and inner sense that is there in the beginning writer—that goes. And then the writer learns how to write, from other writers.

What I think that I feel was very exciting for writers of my generation, given the apparent constrictions of where we were, is—this is what was happening. You would go to school, on a hot day—you would have to wear a blazer, you'd have to wear a pork helmet, you'd have to wear long pants, gray flannel—I mean this was like murder, and to go home in those clothes. However, that was a discipline imposed on the equivalent of an English schoolboy. Of course it was mimicry but that was the discipline. The mimicry was good, I think, because although it created an elite, it made you aware that you were going to a particular place to do something. And there you would go and you would be studying Latin, and you would be studying French poetry, in a tropical climate, very hot and so on—now I think the danger is for people to teach that as being incongruous. *That is* dangerous. The other thing is not dangerous. The other thing is not what you would call white-washing, or colonializing. I think *that* is stupid. The width of encountering, say, Latin writers, or Shakespeare, or French writers—it wasn't Baudelaire, too early to do that—but to have that kind of experience, that is wider. I remember being in the library, in the Carnegie Library, and reading Wilson's *Axel's Castle*. Now I was a much older person, maybe at sixteen or seventeen—I remember the tremendous kick—I mean it's physical—it was like a heart thudding, reading—you know, reading the criticism of Wilson on Joyce, and the same that happened a little later in Eliot's criticism of the Jacobean playwrights.

Now here you are in the tropics, sitting down, you know, wherever you are, and outside there's a fierce, oven-like heat, and black people out there, walking, continuing their lives; how do you connect that with what's happening outside? For a while you can live with that and simply file it as a kind of separation and division. And then you realize as you get older, there's no division. There's no separation. Because the person who's outside there, the woman who's walking with her basket, wants her son to be where you are. And why would you deny her son, you know, because she's black or poor, the place where you are, because you have been given a scholarship or something? So there's no incongruity, to me, of having gone through that. And I think it's a kind of experience that created the sharpness, the acuity, and the depth, of writers like C. L. James, who's written brilliantly about it in *Beyond the Boundary,* and writers like Naipaul, and other writers like Hearn, and Wilson, Harris, have had that experience. That sense of almost being disconnected with the world outside, but knowing that one has to push further on and make that connection.

*Before you decided to push further on and meet the world outside, whether it was in the Antilles or the States, or—I don't know how much time you spent in Greece—*

I've never been to Greece—no—I think if I'd been to Greece I wouldn't have written the book.

*It's such a remarkable evocation of the islands in* **Omeros**—*so you were acquainted with Homer through reading rather than through—*

Well I should confess—I've never read Homer—I've read fragments of Homer—this is terrible, but—the Homer I read was mainly like reading Hemingway—I mean the physical Homer, the geographic Homer. The Homer of myth and the gods and so on I found very hard to absorb. As reality.

*Was myth, or religion of any kind, a reality for you when you were a boy?*

Oh, certainly in terms of super—if you want to call it superstition—but it's really religion, in terms of African religion, African pantheism, and story-telling and music and so on. Definite influence, and I put it in my plays.

*Was theater as attractive to you as poetry early on? Did you know that you would write plays and found a theater?*

My brother and I did that—we did it a little later, but—he put me on to writing plays—but my mother used to perform, you see, she used to recite a lot of Shakespeare, and evidently my father had staged it—there's a man I knew who played Shylock and my mother played Portia, and it must have been young people just doing fragments of Shakespeare. So that theatrical thing that was there in my mother, through my father's encouragement. I have a strong belief in heredity, you know, through environment. Absolutely.

*Did you act as a child? Did you act as a young man?*

No no no. I gave up acting when I was on stage once and I had to say a line like, "Roger's coming now," and Roger didn't come so I got very angry—I was furious, and then I quit.

*Was that right here in St. Lucia?*

That's right. That's the end of the career, right. So then I started to punish people by writing plays.

*Did you also direct—when you were in Trinidad?*

Yes, I direct, sure, yes.

*Does that still appeal to you, or not?*

Definitely.

*You've directed your own—*

Yes.

*Have you allowed other people to direct them too?*

Yeah, I have—it's very difficult if you form your own company, which I have. The companies are now thirty-five years old, you know, and I've always premiered the plays with them, and I know the actors and I write for them—it can be very painful unless you find a director who understands exactly what you want. And even then a minimal gesture, a little thing that's, you know, out of alignment with what you meant, can be distracting. But generally, when I have been lucky, as I have been recently with a young director from England, then you can see a lot of things that you never thought were possible, coming out of the actors, and the staging. But yes, I really enjoy working with the company.

*Was this young director from England directing your plays here, or in the States?*

No; well, he did the *Odyssey* at the Royal Shakespeare Company, at the Barbican, then he came out and did a stage reading and also directed another play called *A Joke of Seville,* which we took to Boston. So the company love him and he's a terrific young guy, and it's nice to work with him. Sometimes, though, particularly I think in the American theater, there's so much self-torture about motivation, tragically.

*When we were swimming the other day, right near here, you and Carlos Fuentes were talking about production of plays, particularly with the American Repertory Theater.*

Be careful here now—

*Okay—*

But go ahead—

*I just wondered if you had another director there, or did you direct your own?*

No—I think the thing that happened with that play—if I have to make a lot of excuses, which I think I need to—is that a musical is a very complicated, long process which requires—there's so many aspects to it that it requires a lot of time to get right. And in that particular case, whatever the book was, it needed a lot of work, and the music—it was just too short, and the conditions were—this is a particular example of what I was saying—and since I write a lot of musicals, the hours and length of time it would take to get one right, I would think we should be steadily working on for at least six months or a year.

*How long have you been working with Paul Simon?*

About a year and a half now.

*And how much longer do you think you'll be working on it?*

He might be listening, I can't talk—but it's going very well.

*So you work together daily on the music and the book?*

Well, not daily, because he's in New York and I'm here sometimes, and sometimes I'm in Boston, and you know, we have to get a little closer together now, because we're getting close to the end.

*Do you see yourself in the future doing more theater than poetry, or more epic poetry or lyric poetry, or do you play it by ear day by day?*

Well, I have a lot of work now—I have a couple of films—scripts—that are required, that I have to do, and then there are a couple of musicals—there's a lot—and there's a new book of poems, and then there's supposed to be a book of essays—plenty to do.

*That's exciting for all of us—*

It's terrifying. It's frightening.

*It's wonderful for us. Were you a great seer of films all of your life?*

Um—Yeah, certainly in St. Lucia. Absolutely. And in Trinidad to some degree. Not so much in the States now, because, you know, everybody gets so busy doing their own work, you hardly have time to go to the movies—I haven't been for a while. When you don't go it's always a thrill to go and find out how exciting a good film could be.

I think the—I'm trying to think very carefully here. I was wondering this morning, for instance, whether you get the same kind of echo, inner reverberations, that you get from a book, as you might from a movie. And probably not—but I think the films that you do want to see again, that have a classic symmetry to them—some of the obvious ones—their refrain is almost like a line of poetry, it's beautifully done, it manages to have a reason—it all adds up to a sound—the sound of itself.

I think for instance of *My Darling Clementine* by Ford. It's a movie I keep seeing, over and over, and admire every shot in it, and so on. Obviously Kurosawa. And *Treasure of Sierra Madre* I think is a great film that you can look at over and over. I don't know how many movies you can do that with, though—all the names I think are by obvious artists, like Fellini, Kurosawa and so forth.

*I know that one of my favorites is Kurosawa's* Dreams.

I haven't seen that. I think *Seven Samurai* is—well everybody says probably the greatest movie—but it's one of the great—absolutely one of the great movies, I think. The full *Seven Samurai*—the complete thing.

*I wonder if you've seen* The Treasure of the Sierra Madre *as many times as my husband has.*

It's an amazing film.

*He and Peter Matthieson can quote great passages of it.*

I think what's astonishing in a director like Huston, and for every writer, especially a playwright, is how short these movies are. In essence—short in terms of content, and the volume, the width of the movie—see today, I think people—if you're going to do a movie like *Treasure of the Sierra Madre*, it's going to be two and a half hours long, and—conceptually, I don't think they can do it any more. I don't think they have that fantastic sense of economy, that Ford and Huston, for instance, had. When you think of the content of *Treasure . . .* and the amount that happens—it's astonishing.

*Seven Samurai is long—and* Lawrence of Arabia *is long. It's when they're long and empty—I think that's the thing, you know.*

*Let's get to poetry a little bit, since we've talked about everything else—*

How can you interrupt John Huston for poetry?

*Well I don't know—since you're a poet I'm going to force you to—your poetry is made so vivid, I guess by the movies you've seen, and whatever you've read, but especially by natural observation, and the echoes of music, and the intensity of your memory. Could you say how you most often begin a poem? Is it sort of a sudden psyching of one of your swifts crossing the water, or the curlew, or the scarlet ibis? Or is it the feel of the trade winds, or the beat or melody of the surf, or an old song, or a vision of a painting? Which of your senses do you start through? Or is it through an idea, or a phrase, or an event you've experienced? An emotional crisis?*

This is the point at which all poets get very pompous. And they give these enigmatic answers and say, well, you know, generally it comes this way and so forth—I don't really have an answer, so I'm going to cut down on the pomposity. But I would say—if it were explainable, then it might disappear. It's not explicable. I think perhaps to a musician a phrase might come and then it can develop, and develop into a huge thing. And I think—like music it may come in some notes whose equivalent is words, you know? And those words may be a phrase that just comes out of the air. Not necessarily out of the immediate experience, you know? And then out of that I think the thing begins to develop.

And Graves said he thinks that every poem begins with half a line and then the next half of a line. That the sound of it is that. And I think that that's pretty true. That what you hear is the second half of the same line. Not the beginning. I think the beginning is prose. I think if you go one two three four, and you get the first line right away, then it might be pretty good, pretty competent, but not a really inspired thing. I think what can happen, is that maybe that phrase, that's the half-phrase, is continued, and I think that margin on the right gives a structure for the left. This is Grave's theory, and I think—I'm not saying this only applies to me or to everyone else—there are all sorts of theories—but you can't say that it comes out of something related to an object that you're looking at or an experience that you have—it may just be something that you don't quite know the meaning of, and that's the pompous and mysterious part of it.

But it is—I mean I do think that when it does come, it comes—as Keats said, you know, it comes like leaves come to a tree, you know? Either it comes that way or it doesn't come at all. So what may appear to be leaves on a tree, are really like artificial leaves on an artificial tree. But you know that when it does happen. And when it does happen the poem seems to go right through and finish itself down to its roots. I don't think it starts from the roots, but like it starts in air and gets down to roots. Or something. A lot of this is nonsense in a sense, but it just—we're trying to explain something. So I don't have an argument or a reason for saying this; I think if you have an occasional poem, a poem aimed at a subject, yes, you can do that, because that's your craft, and you can make it happen. As to when it can happen, and when it does happen, I think it's just the continous practice of verse that creates poetry.

*A real labor of the imagination.*

Yes—I guess the craft—I mean working at the craft—creates I think for young writers, what they must do every day, is just write—they don't have to write on a subject—when I teach my class I tell them, don't try to finish a poem, just go as far as you feel is honest and then abandon it. But there's this desperation to complete things that the young have, you know?

*So when you start a poem you don't necessarily know where it's going, or have a vision of the end, even if you can't hear it—*

Well I think one of the reasons why I use rhyme, is because rhyme takes over, right? There's one kind of reason—there's a reason, which I think is a prosaic reason, which says, this is the subject, and stick to it, you know? And this is the prose reason. Whereas if you use a rhyme—let's say you're heading toward the end of a line, then you find a rhyme—whatever the design of it—it could be far down, but—I think all poems are based on the concept of rhyme. Every poem is based on that idea. It's used or it's not used, but the instinct is that. So if you are using rhyme, when it does happen, when you're heading towards those last couple of syllables, and you're desperate, and you don't know what it's going to be, and if it does happen—it can alter meaning. It can absolutely lift meaning in a certain direction or in another direction, and what you then do is you have to follow what the subterranean thing that

has suddenly emerged dominates in your direction. And you keep following that, and you're still trying to maintain direction, some original direction, but you're discovering what you're writing, as you write it, you know? And that's when it becomes magical. But that's not common. That's not often.

*That's beautifully said. I rhyme more often than not rhyme, and a number of poets I've recently talked with seem to be against rhyme, feel that they have left rhyme behind, and that contemporary poets should. And I never thought—*

I'll tell you something—let me interrupt here for a second, because this always infuriates me. For one—American arrogance can be astounding. American arrogance about esthetics. America believes a lot of things—it also believes—I'm talking about the worst aspect of arrogance of American esthetics—for instance the idea that they invented breathing—right? That the American pulse is somehow different from the Victorian pulse. And that it works in free verse. The American pulse is free verse, and you don't breathe in and out, but there's some other kind of rhythm—I don't know what's between breathing—inhaling and exhaling, but a lot of people who—when you say this thing about saying we have gone beyond rhyme and we have gone beyond X or Y—I have had too many maimed students, I think, crippled students, who have come to me from certain classes from somewhere, in which they have been told not to use rhyme, there is too much melody. Someone has said to me, once I was told—try to avoid music. This is the only culture in the history of the world that has ever said that about verse. Absolutely. This is ridiculous—it's absurd. The apocalypse. Armageddon.

*Americans say, and I've heard it a lot recently, from platforms from classrooms—that Whitman is the father of American poetry, and Dickinson is the mother. Some advocate moving, today, in the father's direction.*

Oh, but—we need two hours—Dickinson is the greatest American poet. Okay? She is wider and deeper than Whitman. She is more terrifying than Whitman. There is no terror in Whitman. There is no fear in Whitman. There is an elegaic kind of fear. I'm not criticizing Whitman. If you think, if one thinks that because Whitman wrote in a line that basically was based on Italian opera, not on inventing American rhythm. And the Bible. Which are old books. I don't mean opera—but I mean it's a form from another thing. People misunderstand Whitman when they say, when they quote him and he says, cross out his over-due accounts. He's not saying that you don't have any debt to Greece and to Rome, he's just saying, you know, we've paid it; it's okay. That's what he's saying. People misinterpret it to mean, you should not acknowledge a debt to Greece and Rome. That is ridiculous. How can—Whitman would not allow someone to speak to him that way.

When you learn finally to come to Dickinson and realize that here in a box-shape, you know, very tight stanzas, that are like little prisms of things—all this experience is contained, and that the half-lines are staggering—Astonishing. Frightening—that that little box contains more in it that the loud, amplified line of Whitman, then you are a mature person. Then you have grown up.

*Then the box is a prism, not a prison.*

Exactly.

*What do you have your students read, in the way of poetry?*

Well I tend to—I let them do a lot of Auden—and by heart, too—because I think that Auden is a great twentieth-century poet; I think for intelligence, for wit, and the courage of his forms, for instance, that he's astonishing, more so than Eliot or Pound, so I do a lot of that—then I do Hardy, because very few people discover Hardy. I do a lot of George Meredith—a discovery to a lot of people—I do *Modern Love,* which is a great poem. And Larkin and so forth. So I tend to do writers who are, if you want to use the jargon, which I detest, formal, and so on. And sometimes you should give them exercises. You see one of the crippling things that has happened I think to the young American writer, is if you give them a simple exercise, like a composition, a pentametrical composition, right?—what you see is terrifying. Because [what] you generally see is somebody who, like a horse galloping, collapses, or breaks his leg, when it comes to the Caesura. The rhythm goes off. They can go so far—they can go for five syllables. The second half—especially if it's going to rhyme—goes into an alarming banality. And you can judge from the second half of the pentameter if that person is gifted. Because, it's okay to write, you know, to splice the verse down the line and do it, you know, for so many beats, and not do it in verse. But when you give them a simple thing to do—and you hear that happening, and something has gone off, there's no point in arguing about saying, you know, the American ear is different to the English ear, or whatever, you know? But that's not a test—it's one of the things that you see happening. So sometimes the exercises I do, I tend to do, is not to force the pentameter on them, but to point out that if they can't do it, then they've got a problem. They have a problem.

*Do you give them any poetry in translation? Russian, or German?*

Oh yeah, sure—*anything* is good—I do Adam's poems: "Going to Lvov" is a great poem. I do it all the time.

*That's Adam Zagajewski.*

I do different people—I make it international if I can—I do Lorca—

*I would have guessed that. Rilke?*

I'm beginning to think Rilke is kind of dangerous for people at a certain age. Like liquor. Booze. Drugs. Metaphysical booze, in a way. Just whiskey, in a way. I think—*The Duino Elegies*—maybe toward the end of a course, but not before. Not too early.

*How about contemporary Russians like Ahkmatova or Mandelstam?*

I tell them to read—they don't always have to take it up in class, but I ask them to read, sure. And other Spaniards apart from Lorca—Aleixandre, and Latin American poets—early Vallejo is superb—Borges—again Neruda I think is someone you want to keep, because I think it gets—pretty flagellant—I mean as an influence, you know what I mean? A rhetorical thing can happen.

*Before we run out of time I think I'd like to ask you to do some reading. And then if we have time we can come back and talk some more.*

Okay—

*Do you want to read, or recite? . . . Before you start, just let me ask you how you know so much about ornithology, and sailing, and sea battles, which seem to me to dominate* **Omeros** *in a way.*

Well if you ask Stephen Crane, how do you know so much about the Civil War, he would have said, books. I mean it's right out there, you know—the sea is out there—the one thing I don't feel that I am is a scholar, really—I don't think of myself that way—academically. So I don't think that if one looked at it hard that the history that's in the books is anything serious or anything profound; I think it—I think part of the superficiality of the knowledge of history here is part of the experience of being Caribbean, but it shouldn't go too deep. Because if it goes too deep you tend to think "dispossessed," that the history belongs to somebody else, and it's not yours. And since there is no chronicle here—that's a whole subject that necessarily one needs to go deeply into—I don't believe in the expression, Those who don't know history are condemned to repeat it, because look at how many know history and are repeating it anyhow, you know?

All right, this is a section from **Omeros** about coming home to an island that is changing—coming to the south of the island and driving north towards Castries and noticing what's been happening. In it there's a reference to a taxi driver who has died hurrying to make a lot of money with the tourist trade.

> Drivers leant over the rail. One seized my luggage
> off the porter's cart. The rest burst into patois,
> with gestures of despair at the lost privilege
>
> of driving me, then turned to other customers.
> In the evening pastures horses grazed, their hides wet
> with light that shot its lances over the combers.
>
> I had the transport all to myself.
>                     "You all set?
> Good. A good pal of mine died in that chariot
> of his called the Comet."
>                     He turned in the front seat,
>
> spinning the air with his free hand. I sat, sprawled out

in the back, discouraging talk, with my crossed feet.
"You never know when, eh? I was at the airport

that day. I see him take off like a rocket.
I always said that thing have too much horsepower.
And so said, so done. The same hotel, chief, correct?"

I saw the coastal villages receding as
the highway's tongue translated bush into forest,
the wild savannah into moderate pastures,

that other life going in its *"change for the best,"*
its peace paralyzed in a postcard, a concrete
future ahead of it all, in the cinder-blocks

of hotel development with the obsolete
craft of the carpenter, as I sensed, in the neat
marinas, the fisherman's phantom. Old oarlocks

and rusting fretsaw. My craft required the same
crouching care, the same crabbed, natural devotion
of the hand that stenciled a flowered window-frame

or planed an elegant canoe; its time was gone
with the spirit in the wood, as wood grew obsolete
and plasterers smoothed the blank page of white
    concrete.

I watched the afternoon sea. Didn't I want the poor
to stay in the same light so that I could transfix
them in amber, the afterglow of an empire,

preferring a shed of palm-thatch with tilted sticks
to that blue bus stop? Didn't I prefer a road
from which tracks climbed into the thickening syntax

of colonial travelers, the measured prose I read
as a schoolboy? That cove, with its brown shallows
there, Praslin? That heron? Had they waited for me

to develop my craft? Why hallow that pretence
of preserving what they left, the hypocrisy
of loving them from hotels, a biscuit-tin fence

smothered in love-vines, scenes to which I was at-
    tached
as blindly as Plunkett with his remorseful research?
Art is History's nostalgia, it prefers a thatched

roof to a concrete factory, and the huge church
above a bleached village. The gap between the driver
and me increased when he said:
                "The place changing, eh?"

where an old rumshop had gone, but not that river
with its clogged shadows. That would make me a
    stranger.
"All to the good," he said. I said, "All to the good,"

then, "whoever they are," to myself. I caught his eyes
in the mirror. We were climbing out of Micoud.
Hadn't I made their poverty my paradise?

That enough?

*No, I think you should definitely read another. Obviously
your mode is loving the world, so I'm sure there's another
piece of the world you'd like to read about. I love the fact
that you say you're impatient for sunrise. That the morning is your time, and you want to transfix the light in
amber.*

All that Greek manure under the green bananas,
under the indigo hills, the rain-rutted road,
the galvanized village, the myth of rustic manners,

glazed by the transparent page of what I had read.
What I had read and re-written till literature
was guilty as History. When would the sails drop

from my eyes, when would I not hear the Trojan War
in two fishermen cursing in Ma Kilman's shop?
When would my head shake off its echoes like a horse

shaking off a wreath of flies? When would it stop,
the echo in the throat, insisting, "Omeros";
when would I enter that light beyond the metaphor?

But it was mine to make what I wanted of it, or
what I thought was wanted. A cool wood off the road,
a hut closed like a wound, and the sound of a river

coming through the trees on a country Saturday,
with no one in the dry front yard, the still leaves,
the yard, the shade of a breadfruit tree on the door,

then the track from which a man's figure emerges,
then a girl carrying laundry, the road-smell like loaves,
the yellow-dressed butterflies in the grass marges.

*That's beautiful, and evokes the character of Helen in*
**Omeros** *with her beautiful yellow frock—perhaps because
I'm a woman and it's such a romantic image.*

*Well, I think I've taken enough of your time, and I thank
you. If there's anything from your new work you would
like to read I would love to hear it, or if you have a stanza
or a few lines in your head that you'd like to end with,
that would be very nice.*

Well, I'm working on a new book, so I might read
something that's new.

"Oedipus at Colonus" [published as **"After the plague, the
city-wall caked with flies, the smoke's amnesia"** in *The
Bounty*]

After the plague, the city-wall caked with flies, the
    smoke's amnesia,
learn, wanderer, to go nowhere like the stones since
your nose and eyes are now your daughter's hand;
go where the repetition of the breakers grows easier
to bear, no father to kill, no citizens to convince,
and no longer force your memory to understand
whether the dead elect their own government
under the jurisdiction of the sea-almonds;
certain provisions of conduct seal them to a silence
none dare break, and one noun made them transpar-
    ent,

where they live beyond the conjugations of tense
in their own white city. How easily they disown us,
and everything else here that undermines our toil.
Sit on your plinth in the last light of Colonus,
let your knuckled toes root deep in their own soil.
A butterfly quietly alights on a tyrant's knee;
sit among the sea-eaten boulders and
let the night wind sweep the terraces of the sea.
This is the right light, this pewter shine on the water,
not the carnage of clouds, not the expected wonder
of self-igniting truth and oracular rains,
but these shallows as gentle as the voice of your
     daughter,
while the gods fade like thunder in the rattling
     mountains.

*Well. Anything I say now would be anticlimactic. Thank
you for reading from "Oedipus." Not many writers are
willing to share a work-in-progress. I can see, looking
over your shoulder, that the page is still in your handwrit-
ing.*

*I guess we covered a bit of everything except the mischief
of your poems—all the witticisms, the humor, the significant
spelling, the diverse voices and dialects you do, differentiating the tone as superbly as the psychology of the
speaker. You make me laugh, often, as I read. Do you
laugh when you're writing, ever?*

Yes!


**Edward Hirsch (essay date autumn 1997)**

SOURCE: Hirsch, Edward. "Poetry: Derek Walcott." *Wilson Quarterly* 21 (autumn 1997): 109-11.

[*In the following essay, Hirsch offers a positive assessment
of Walcott's career as a poet and playwright.*]

There is a force of exultation, a celebration of luck, when
a writer finds himself a witness to the early morning of a
culture that is defining itself, branch by branch, leaf by
leaf, in that self-defining dawn," Derek Walcott said in his
Nobel Prize lecture for 1992. That force of exultation and
celebration of luck, along with a sense of benediction and
obligation, a continuous effort of memory and excavation,
and a "frightening duty" to "a fresh language and a fresh
people," have defined Walcott's work for the past 50 years.
He has always been a poet of great verbal resources and
skills engaged in a complex struggle to render his native
Caribbean culture: the New World—not Eden but a successor to Eden, a polyglot place, an archipelago determined
to survive—a world he calls "a ferment without a history,
like heaven . . . a writer's heaven."

Derek Walcott is the greatest poet and playwright writing
in English that the West Indies has produced. His *Collected Poems* (1986) is itself a massive achievement, bringing together work from 10 previous books written between
1948 and 1984. It moves from his first privately printed
pamphlet, *25 Poems,* to his Lowellian sequence, *Midsummer.* It includes early work from *The Castaway* and *The
Gulf,* and his major autobiographical poem *Another Life*
(which is his Portrait of the Artist as a Young Man); and
later work from *Sea Grapes, The Star-Apple Kingdom,*
and *The Fortunate Traveller.* Since *The Collected Poems,*
he has published *The Arkansas Testament* (1987), *Omeros*
(1990), which is a booklength reprise to *The Odyssey* that
parallels Greek and Antillean experience, and *The Bounty*
(1997). The themes of Walcott's poems are echoed and
counterpointed by the ritual action and vernacular language
of his major plays, from *Dream on Monkey Mountain* to
*Remembrance and Pantomine* and on to *Beef, No Chicken,
The Last Carnival,*and *A Branch of the Blue Nile.* Reading
through Walcott's lifework, one is always aware of the
covenant he has made with a people and a place.

Walcott has one of the finest ears of any poet writing in
English since Hart Crane or Dylan Thomas. His descriptive powers are, as Joseph Brodsky pointed out, truly epic.
He has repeatedly sought to give voice to the inlets and
beaches, the hills, promontories, and mountains of his native country. The sea is an inescapable presence in his
work and has fundamentally affected his sense of being an
islander. ("The sea was my privilege / and a fresh people,"
he writes in *Omeros.*) He exults so much in the salty tang
of words themselves that at times it feels as if the vowels
and consonants of his three-language vocabulary (English,
English patois, and French patois) have been saturated by
the sea itself. Each phrase seems "soaked in salt.".

Here is the beginning of his early lyric **"A Sea-Chantey"**:

Anguilla, Adina, Antigua, Canelles, Andreuille, all the
     I's, Voyelles, of the liquid Antilles . . .

There is a quality of earthly prayer in the way Walcott
luxuriates in sounds and savors letters, turning over the
words, holding up the names. A sacred sense of vocation
informs his high eloquence and powerful commitment to
articulating his native realm, calling out "the litany of
islands, / The rosary of archipelagoes" and "the amen of
calm waters."

Walcott was born in 1930 in Castries, the capital of St.
Lucia. He entered the province of poetry empowered by
the feeling that he was speaking not just out of his own
experience but for everything he saw around him, naming
a world thus far undefined:

Forty years gone, in my island childhood, I felt that the
gift of poetry had made me one of the chosen, that all
experience was kindling to the fire of the Muse.

                                        (*Midsummer*)

Walcott's early Adamic pact with his island was also balanced by a sense of self-division and estrangement. He
grew up as a "divided child"—a Methodist in an over-
whelmingly Catholic country, a developing artist with a
middle-class background and a mixed African, English,
and Dutch ancestry coming of age in a mostly black world,

a backwater of poverty. Some of the dramatic tension in his work comes from the gap he has always had to cross to describe the people with whom he shares an island. So, too, a great deal of rage sometimes breaks loose in his work as a fury against racism: against those who have typed the poet as neither black nor white enough; against those who still view the Caribbean people as illegitimate and rootless; against the legacies of slavery and colonialism.

Walcott has called himself "a mulatto of style," and increasingly has given voice to the contending languages and cultures operating inside him. The Odyssean figure of Shabine undoubtedly speaks for his creator when he uses the demotic and turns the language of colonial scorn into a source of pride:

> I'm just a red nigger who love the sea,
> I had a sound colonial education,
> I have Dutch, nigger, and English in me,
> and either I'm nobody, or I'm a nation.

("The Schooner Flight")

Homer has become Walcott's tutelary spirit, and he mimics *The Odyssey* here by echoing that moment when Odysseus slyly deceives the Cyclops by calling himself "nobody." He is also asserting that this "nobody" is the culture's representative figure, "a nation." Walcott's Caribbean reworking of *The Odyssey, Omeros,* suggests that the task of the Homeric bard is to unearth lost lives and shattered histories, but also to sing of a new people and a new hope.

Walcott is ultimately a poet of affirmations, a writer who believes that the task of art is to transcend history and rename the world. As he says in **"The Antilles: Fragments of Epic Memory,"** "For every poet it is always morning the world. History a forgotten, insomniac night; History and elemental awe are always our early beginning, because the fate of poetry is to fall in love with the world, in spite of History." The poet's enterprise is a redemptive one, a joyous calling. Derek Walcott's lifework is a grand testament to the visionary powers of language and to the freshening wonders of a world that is always starting over again despite History, a world that is always startling and new.

## Robert D. Hamner (essay date 1997)

SOURCE: Hamner, Robert D. "Philoctete's Wound." In *Epic of the Dispossessed: Derek Walcott's* Omeros, pp. 33-58. Columbia: University of Missouri Press, 1997.

[*In the following essay, Hamner offers a critical analysis of Walcott's epic poem* Omeros, *focusing particular attention on the role of the character Philoctetes.*]

Despite the explicit parallels and allusions linking *Omeros* with its numerous epic predecessors, Walcott insists on more than one occasion that he deliberately resists writing

a traditional "heroic poem." This position may be traced at least as far back as "What the Twilight Says," his introduction to *Dream on Monkey Mountain and Other Plays,* wherein he asserts, "The last thing which the poor needed was the idealization of their poverty." Walcott is too traditional to undertake an anti-epic, yet his authorial intrusions and variations on conventional epic devices in *Omeros* interrogate conventional expectations. Anticipating publication early in 1990, Walcott informs interviewer J. P. White that regardless of his "Homeric line and Dantesque design," *Omeros* captures not the epic machinery of gods and endless battles but the "names of things and people in their own context. . . . Its the origin of the real Caribbean nouns that I'm after." Far from rewriting the *Odyssey* or the *Aeneid,* he confesses to White that he has read no more than excerpts from these two classics. A few months later he reiterates to D. J. R. Bruckner that while his poem may have one central battle (the Battle of the Saints) it lacks the requisite great wars and warriors of epic tradition. Another disclaimer leads off an interview with Rebekah Presson in 1992. "I think any work in which the narrator is almost central is not really an epic. It's not like a heroic epic. I guess . . . since I am in the book, I certainly don't see myself as a hero of an epic, when an epic generally has a hero of action and decision and destiny."[1] These cumulative reservations tend to focus on the ancient formula without allowing for innovations beginning as early as Dante, who first inserted himself as narrator into *The Divine Comedy.*

Nevertheless, Walcott concedes to Presson that there are characters in *Omeros* who possess heroic elements. As a matter of fact, in conversation with Bruckner, Walcott emphasizes the debt he owes to the neglected peasantry of his native St. Lucia.

> The whole book is an act of gratitude. It is a fantastic privilege to be in a place in which limbs, features, smells, the lineaments and presence of the people are so powerful. . . . And there is no history for the place. . . . One reason I don't like talking about an epic is that I think it is wrong to try to ennoble people, . . . And just to write history is wrong. History makes similes of people, but these people are their own nouns. . . . A noun is not a name you give something. It is something you watch becoming itself, and you have to have the patience to find out what it is. In the Caribbean, people come from everywhere, from Africa and Europe and the Mediterranean and the Middle East and the Orient. . . . There is a restless identity in the New World. The New World needs an identity without guilt or blame.

Walcott reveals in these lines not only the basis of his inspiration but also two of his fundamental themes. The islands await a historical treatment on their own terms, and his people deserve to be reified within their authentic context. This means that Walcott must walk a thin line between the immediacy of personal experience and the artificiality of literary form. In keeping with his respect for humble islanders, Walcott chooses to emulate the act of a man, "Homer the poet of the seven seas," rather than the valorized tradition that has accumulated around his work for more than two thousand years.[2] The distinction is significant enough that Walcott incorporates his image of a blind, outcast Omeros in a variety of guises throughout the poem. At the same time, he subverts nearly all of the conventional epic paraphernalia.

It is not as though there were no heroic material available to Walcott. In spite of the general opinion that nothing worthy of note had ever occurred in the West Indies, Walcott could have taken a cue from that imperial advocate James Anthony Froude and glorified European exploits in the New World. In the late 1800s Froude had predicted,

> If ever the naval exploits of this country [Britain] are done into an epic poem—and since the *Iliad* there has been no subject better fitted for such treatment or better deserving it—the West Indies will be the scene of the most brilliant cantos. . . . At the supreme crisis in our history when America had revolted and Ireland was defiant, when the great powers of Europe had coalesced to crush us . . . Rodney struck a blow in the West Indies which sounded over the world and saved for Britain her ocean scepter.[3]

Although Walcott does include cantos on the justly famous Battle of the Saints, he lays claim to another subject that is "better fitted for such treatment and more deserving it" in the newly enfranchised citizens of that receding empire. Rather than contribute another chapter to the European saga of discovery and conquest, Walcott chooses to undertake a new legend: the tale of his own sojourn, the struggle of his tribe.

Structurally, *Omeros* converts linear narrative development into incremental loops of self-reflexive exposition. No matter how far the leading characters may wander literally or imaginatively, their lives continually revolve around each other; and much as they learn, they inevitably return to their point of origin. Ironically, Walcott cites the examples of prose writers Rudyard Kipling, Joseph Conrad, and Ernest Hemingway as major influences on the poetry of *Omeros.* "I learned a lot in writing this poem," he tells Bruckner:

> I did not realize how much great prose I had absorbed into my nervous verse system. When I began to write in hexameter lines and in stanzas, well the structure is there in the architecture of the best turn-of-the-century prose, in Conrad and Kipling. And you find in them the wit of the paragraph; mentally, it keeps the rhythm up. . . .
>
> . . . When I was writing this book, you might say I was thinking of the two great Caribbean artists, Hemingway and Homer. . . .
>
> . . . It is a book for people, not a conundrum for scholars. It was as if I was learning to read Homer when I was writing it.

The result is a layered and essentially reciprocal complex of interrelated narrative lines that uncannily approximates the subversive type of postcolonial fiction described in Arun Mukherjee's *Towards an Aesthetic of Opposition.*

The new Commonwealth novelists, then, have had to build structures which allow them to capture the spider-web of relationships which constitute community life in the developing countries. These structures may seem loose or episodic to the western critic, yet they have a coherence if judged in accordance with the forms of experience they set out to explore. These structures are political choices on the part of the new Commonwealth writers, a declaration that the metropolitan forms do not fit their needs. . . . Their use of parabolic structures, indigenous story telling conventions, folk tales, parodies of western and indigenous forms and rituals have not attracted adequate attention due to the critics' obsession with western categories.[4]

Due to the heavily narrative structure of the epic genre itself and Walcott's admitted reliance on prose models, *Omeros* exhibits many of the episodic, communal qualities enumerated by Mukherjee.

Natural and linguistic reciprocity emerge on every level throughout *Omeros.* The process is often subtle and follows the geographic subdivisions of the text. As I shall argue, although the book is thoroughly integrated as a whole, there are discernible movements within the developing story that lend themselves to separate treatment. Books one and two establish the St. Lucian foundation by introducing characters and themes that will be continually augmented. Books three through five retrace the Middle Passage first to Africa, then to North America and Europe before returning to the West Indies. Books six and seven round off the action back in St. Lucia without suggesting a definitive conclusion. After all, self-discovery for an individual as well as a people obviates stasis; it is an ongoing creative act of becoming. From the outset, Walcott prepares for such an open conclusion. It can be anticipated, for example, from both the initial scene of book one and the foreshadowing vision that simultaneously ends book two and prepares the stage for book three. It is ensured by the flexible, shifting perspectives of a series of narrative voices.

Rather than begin with the pronouncement of a grand theme, invocation of the muse, or even the introduction of his protagonist, Walcott launches *Omeros* in medias res with the minor character Philoctete. As is the case with his classical Greek namesake, Philoctete once sustained a painful, festering wound that was offensive to everyone who came near. With just a hint at antecedent information about a magical cure (that might be disclosed for a price), Philoctete introduces the first narrative voice to be heard in *Omeros.* Willing enough to provoke curiosity by displaying the unsightly scar, he entertains tourists with a description of native fishermen felling the trees that will be hewn into seagoing canoes. Folklore permeates the scene as Philoctete, Hector, Achille, and their mates pay homage to the spirits of the trees they must violate in order to secure their livelihoods. Air, earth, fire, and water coalesce in Philoctete's poignant imagery. Not only does the wind stirring the undergrowth evoke the sound and swell of the restless ocean, but "the logs gathered that thirst / for the sea which their own vined bodies were born with" (7). This is but the first suggestion of nature's reciprocity; in this case we are reminded of the water cycle that inextricably binds all the elements. Heat from the sun initiates evaporation and provides the lifeblood of the trees in the first place. Then shipwrights use fire to transform solid logs into the shells of canoes that hereafter float in the element that once permeated their every fiber in the mountains.

In what may be no more than a salve to his conscience, Philoctete projects into the logs the feeling that they do not feel "death inside them, but use— / to roof the sea, to be hulls" (7). The spirituality of these earthy peasants is underscored by their empathy with the natural environment and the raw materials of their humble trades. The animistic flavor of their Africanized Catholicism makes them respect not only living creatures but also the ancestral ghosts of Aruac and Carib tribesmen who first called their island "'Iounalao,' 'Where the iguana is found'" (4). Significantly, when Achille (pronounced "A-sheel" with only two syllables), the first of the key protagonists, is introduced, his attention is drawn to the torn canopy where the recently cut trees have created an opening to the sky. As Achille gazes heavenward, a sea-swift crossing the gap elicits from him "a swift sign of the cross" (6). Never one to overlook a pun or visual and verbal correspondences, Walcott waits only a few stanzas to exploit the connection between the sign of the cross and the image of the swift's outspread shape among the clouds. Thus at the dedication of the new pirogues, Achille notices that the priest makes "the swift's sign" of consecration.

The ceremony sets the occasion for one further semantic ploy. When the priest sees humor in the misspelled name of Achille's canoe, *In God We Troust,* Achille insists "Leave it! Is God' spelling and mine" (8). There is more to Walcott's emphasis on a picturesque orthographic lapse here than the fact of his actually having discovered this hand-painted epithet on a local fisherman's pirogue. While Achille's slip in literacy might elicit a condescending smile, Walcott has come to view such misprision as cause for celebration. In his 1992 interview with Rebekah Presson, he confides that when he chanced upon the misspelled "Troust," it struck him as "interesting and personal, and perhaps more devout than the regular spelling." At a conference in Jamaica in 1988, he asserts the value of error in the creative process. In preparing his address for this audience, he confesses he accidentally typed "love" into his "Caligula's Horse" manuscript where he intended "life." Although he corrected himself, he editorialized, "to discover, through a typographical error, what is accidental but also true . . . That is one part of the poetic process, accident as illumination, error as truth, typographical mistakes as revelation."[5] Even if Walcott had not made his position explicit, other characters within *Omeros* react to Achille's misspelling, and the appellation is repeated often enough to acquire a life of its own. Epithets on these indispensable pirogues reflect faith, as in *Praise Him,* or love of their homeland, as in *St. Lucia* and *Light of My*

*Eyes* (the latter of which commemorates simultaneously the island and the blind saint for which it is named). Similar connotations are embedded in the descriptive terminology as well. When the newly launched vessels are first drawn upon the shore, Walcott refers to them ambiguously as staring like "myrmidons hauled up by the heels" (10). Were "Myrmidons" capitalized, the trope would be an apposite allusion to the Thessalian followers of Achilles against Troy. In the actual lower-case form, they are just as suitably cast as proficient instruments of their master's will. Inconsequential as many such details may appear to be at first reading, nearly all of them assume cumulative significance as they are woven into the rest of the poem: Philoctete's wound, the swift, *In God We Troust,* and the sea become motifs with thematic overtones.

Having established the setting and cultural atmosphere by the end of the opening chapter, the perspective shifts unobtrusively from Philoctete to a disembodied observer. At the same time, the narrative takes up the antecedent action of the first of three primary, interlocking plots. In the days when Philoctete's shin was still putrid from the cut of a rusty anchor, trouble arose between Achille and Hector. The first blows appear to be struck over a worthless tin can Achille took from Hector to bail out his canoe, but we learn that the real source of conflict runs much deeper: "The duel of these fishermen / was over a shadow and its name was Helen" (17). Associating these three classical names as he does, Walcott obviously invites comparison with the *Iliad.* While there may be irony in drawing parallels between superhuman warriors and these poor fishermen, Walcott adds more than a literary dimension to his work. Since slaveholders often borrowed names for their slaves from mythical and biblical sources, heroic names are perpetuated in contemporary West Indian society. The names already at hand, it remains only for Walcott to provide motive for his earthy characters to strive toward fulfillment of their more restricted dreams and aspirations. That motivation builds throughout the intricately sustained subplots of *Omeros.*

Walcott's lifelong commitment to drama is unmistakable in his distribution of conflicts. Undergirding the rising dramatic interest at all stages is the urge toward reconciliation and redemption in one form or another. For this reason the context of the struggle between Achille and Hector is as important as the contention itself. Multidimensional troubles radiate outward, affecting not only other characters but eliciting self-reflexive responses from the author as well. On the same fateful morning that Achille and Hector draw cutlasses over a bailing tin, we are introduced to blind old St. Omere, "Seven Seas," who is Walcott's embodiment of the Homer figure. In an apostrophe that comes as close to an invocation of the muse as Walcott ever gets in *Omeros,* the modern poet acknowledges his indebtedness to the ancient master.

> O open this day with the conch's moan, Omeros,
> as you did in my boyhood, when I was a noun
> gently exhaled from the palate of the sunrise.
>         . . . . .

> . . . Only in you, across centuries
> of the sea's parchment atlas, can I catch the noise
> of the surf lines wandering like the shambling fleece
>
> of the lighthouse's flock, that Cyclops whose blind
>   eye
> shut from the sunlight. Then the canoes were galleys
> over which a frigate sawed its scythed wings slowly.

Combined in these tercets are an invocation and a metaphorical confiscation of imagery. Just as Homer is superimposed on St. Omere, Odysseus's Cyclops (the shepherd Polyphemus in the *Odyssey*) becomes a one-eyed lighthouse overlooking the white fleece of Caribbean surf; Greek galleys become local fishermen's canoes; but the rhythms of waves, of the frigate bird's flight and of poetry remain as they were thousands of years ago for the poet of the Mediterranean.

From the beginning, some of Walcott's key images are protean in their application and in their transmutations. Over the course of the epic the blindness of Homer, of Seven Seas/Omeros, and of St. Lucia's patron saint herself is symbolic of inner enlightenment as opposed to limited physical vision. Eyes in turn are not only mentioned in connection with individual characters, but are metaphorically elicited in association with cameras, marble busts, statues, fish, drowned men, cyclones, lighthouses, telescopes, birds, the novelist James Joyce, self-centered poets, and the sun. Perhaps even more ubiquitous is the repetition of "O," which is not only the first letter of **Omeros** but also the sound emitted from the blown conch shell and by the dove. At one time or another, the figure is the oval shape of a mouth, a throat, a vase, a cave, an island, and a circular journey.

In addition to the imagery, larger periods of time, scenes, and levels of consciousness intermingle even further as Walcott's own persona emerges from the page: "A wind turns the harbour's pages back to the voice / that hummed in the vase of a girl's throat: 'Omeros'" (13). The ensuing stanzas of chapter two are devoted to a brief interlude. In it the author recounts a scene wherein a Greek sculptress teaches him the correct pronunciation of "O-meros" and he pronounces its connotative etymology.[6]

> . . . I said, "Omeros,"
>
> and *O* was the conch-shell's invocation, *mer* was
> both mother and sea in our Antillean patois,
> *os,* a grey bone, and the white surf as it crashes
>
> and spreads its sibilant collar on a lace shore.
> Omeros was the crunch of dry leaves, and the washes
> that echoed from a cave-mouth when the tide has
>   ebbed.
>
> (14)

Under the influence of this woman he calls Antigone, he moves from the vibrations of a throat to other encircling enclosures (with all their Freudian implications)—conch shells, cave mouths, vases, the parted lips of a Homeric

bust—and to the affective syllables of his own poetic title. The interlude fades, as effortlessly as it begins, into the uproar surrounding Hector and Achille fighting on the beach.

In addition to the physical altercation, Walcott makes clear that jealous rage and shame have destroyed a brotherly closeness that tears at their hearts. Ever-widening extensions of their spiritual malaise touch Philoctete and Seven Seas as well, who spend their days isolated from normal human activities because of their afflictions. While other tradesmen go about their work, these two outcasts seek the cool shade of Ma Kilman's No Pain Cafe. Ma Kilman provides yet another perspective and new insights into the growing cast of characters. As the narrative detours through her mind, we learn that St. Omere's sotto voce monologues are so unintelligible as to be "Greek to her. Or old African babble" (18). The irony of juxtaposing Greek and African tongues as equally alien may be hidden from her, but the reader must weigh its implicit commentary on her uprooted existence. That necessity is underscored as Ma Kilman commiserates with Philoctete in his suffering. He interprets his wound as a racial affliction,

> He believed the swelling came from the chained
>   ankles
> of his grandfathers. Or else why was there no cure?
> That the cross he carried was not only the anchor's
>
> but that of his race, for a village black and poor
> as the pigs that rooted in its burning garbage,
> then were hooked on the anchors of the abattoir.

At the same time, Ma Kilman searches her memory for an herbal remedy her African grandmother could have prepared to draw out the poison.

> It have a flower somewhere, a medicine, and ways
> my grandmother would boil it. I used to watch ants
> climbing her white flower-pot. But, God, in which
>   place?
>
> Where was this root? What senna, what tepid tisanes,
> could clean the branched river of his corrupted blood,
> whose sap was a wounded cedar's? . . .
>
> (19)

From this point, the symbolic ramifications of Philoctete's wound become paramount, and Ma Kilman's quest must be to reestablish a connection with her ancestors in order to help him.

Although Ma Kilman casually alludes to ants in passing, these insects soon join the swift both as symbols and as potent links with the healing forces of the natural world. The ants and the swift are on Philoctete's mind as he limps from the No Pain Cafe to tend his yam patch in the mountains. Passing the overturned ruins of an abandoned sugar plantation on the way, he reflects bitterly that this is the only history left his black people, if their detritus may be considered historical. As he sees it, they

. . . set out to found no cities; they were the found,
who were bound for no victories; they were the bound,
who levelled nothing before them; they were the
ground.

(22)

With these passing thoughts, Philoctete summarizes the historical vacuum that leaves his people rootless and downtrodden. At the same time they reveal the fissures, the fault lines in heroic tradition, that provide Walcott the opening needed to experiment with the epic form. Neither the poet nor his unassuming characters urge the necessity of recognizing their human worth. That burden rests with the reader in experiencing the evolving story. Much as we may appreciate Philoctete's righteous indignation as he meditates on injustices of the past and present, for his own peace of mind, he resolves to emulate a patient horse and endure his afflictions calmly.

On that contemplative note—Philoctete waiting, the conflict between Hector and Achille on hold, the new element of social concern simmering beneath the surface—Walcott abruptly shifts the narrative for the first time away from the indigenous population of the island to introduce an expatriate couple among his cast of characters: retired Major Dennis Plunkett and his wife Maud. The Plunketts broaden the cultural spectrum, but only slightly, having lived in St. Lucia, breeding pigs and orchids, since the end of World War II. Despite their European origins (Dennis is English, Maud Irish) and a longing especially on Maud's part to see the old country again, they have adopted the island as their home. As a matter of fact, offended by the "phony pukka tones" of their fellow expatriates, they long ago turned their backs on the "middle-clarse farts" of the Victoria Club (25). The traces of a Homeric parallel are hardly sufficient to warrant extensive exploration; however, as a pig farmer existing on the outer fringes of empire, the Major does resemble Odysseus's faithful swineherd, Eumaios. Whereas Homer's swineherd is a generous host and indispensable assistant in Odysseus's assault on Penelope's unwanted suitors, Walcott derives even greater service out of the Major as a participating narrator.

The Plunketts' story complements the plot already underway. The Major's military career gives him firsthand experience on the frontier of a waning empire and underlies his poignant regard for the annual ceremonies of Remembrance Day (30).[7] Their background, the antecedent circumstances that shape their perspective, includes Dennis's head-wound, suffered in the British Eighth Army's Egyptian campaign (25-26); Maud's nursing him to recovery (27); their marriage; and the dream of a new Eden unspoiled by history, which led them to St. Lucia (28). The vital force that links the Plunketts with Achille and Hector is Helen, who until recently served as their housemaid. They reluctantly dismissed her when she began making them feel like interlopers in their own home. It was as though Helen had usurped their place, blithely going through Maud's clothes and jewelry as she pleased. As ubiquitous as her yellow dress becomes through Walcott's

repeated references to it, the Major never seems to settle finally within his own mind whether Helen stole or was given the frock by Maud (64).

Using a strategy that helps to extract the maximum impact from Helen as a person and as an image, Walcott suspends her actual entrance until the final line of chapter four. By then, our acquaintance with the men whose lives she dominates has prepared the way for her influence. Achille and Hector long for her physically; the Major just as passionately wishes to possess her as the veritable essence of the island itself. It is through the author's persona, however, that we first glimpse her effect on all observers. Her regal carriage evokes the image of a panther, or a mirage in a madras head-tie,

but the head proud, although it was looking for work.
I felt like standing in homage to a beauty

that left, like a ship, widening eyes in its wake.
"Who the hell is that?" a tourist near my table
asked a waitress. The waitress said, "She? She too
proud!"

As the carved lids of the unimaginable
ebony mask unwrapped from its cotton-wool cloud,
the waitress sneered, "Helen." And all the rest followed.

(23-24)

"All the rest" that follows may be taken quite literally. If Walcott risks thematic diffusion by scattering the narrative perspective, sharing the protagonist's role among a succession of voices and expanding the geographical and chronological boundaries to include distant continents and ancient Greece, the cohesive center of *Omeros* remains this figure of Helen.

Not only do separate characters reflect Helen's influence, but Walcott ensures that the reader must also step back and contemplate the terms of her existence. The first time he takes the reader into explicit confidence is shortly after introducing Dennis Plunkett.

This wound I have stitched into Plunkett's character.
He has to be wounded, affliction is one theme
of this work, this fiction, since every "I" is a

fiction finally. Phantom narrator, resume.

(28)

When the "phantom" resumes, we find the Major committing himself to a grand scheme that will give purpose to his own life and immortalize Helen. Plunkett's affliction that Walcott underscores for the poem as a whole, like that of Philoctete, runs much deeper than its physical manifestation. The Plunketts' union has proved to be barren, and the Major is not able to accept the fact that his life will terminate without issue. At the same time, it occurs to him that while he lacks personal immortality, Helen's existence takes place in a historical void.

In one epiphanic flash he realizes that Helen needs a history and that the subject is worthy of his complete dedication. The idea impresses him in terms of historic and mythic hallucinations because of its overt Ithacan connotations. Not only is she named Helen, but her island is often referred to as "Helen," the "Gibraltar of the Caribbean," because of the European powers who fought over her until she was finally ceded to England by France through the 1814 Treaty of Paris. However, the Major insists he must tell "Not his, but her story." He sees her village as another Troy, the island's Pitons as her breasts, the Battle of the Saints as her Homeric conflict (30-31). These people have no Parthenon, and Latin is replaced by native dialect, but he can envision their athletic contests as Olympiads. Thus Hector and Achille run marathons and wrestle not for victory's laurels or shields but to win Helen.

Extending the Major's train of thought, Walcott's narrative cuts away to Helen inquiring among the women for openings at the beach restaurant. Pregnant and unsure of who is the father of her unborn child, she must find a job. Despite the paucity of available work and her predicament, she remains so much at peace with her situation that she can be heard softly murmuring the Beatles's "Yesterday, all my troubles seem so far away" (34), dialectically eliminating the past-tense marker from the verb "seemed." Then as she passes through a cloud of smoke from burning leaves, a second wave of classical associations arises, this time drawing a sharp distinction between the Greek and this contemporary Helen. In the moment of historical change, "white Helen died," and "her shadow ambles, filly of Menelaus / while black piglets root the midden of Gros Îlet" (34). The fact that this shadow is the darker impression of an original design is clear enough in these lines. What is less apparent but perhaps even more relevant than Walcott himself intended is the appearance of the piglets. Of course their blackness is an obvious foil for the Greek's whiteness; but they can be taken for much more than that. Not only are these rooting animals as lowly as the inhabitants of Gros Îlet, but it is also worth noting that the supernatural sign given to Aeneas, letting him know where he is to found his promised kingdom, is a white sow and her thirty offspring.[8]

Whatever Walcott's assorted reasons for mentioning these piglets (he may have intended no epic allusions), they conform to a pattern. Dennis Plunkett is associated with these animals because of the herd he maintains on his farm. Moreover, in a subsequent chapter we overhear the Major argue that the people of the island are not "resigned / to living with garbage" despite the fact that "Empires were swinish," and "History was Circe" with power to convert men to swine (63-64). Meanwhile as the Major is imagining the transformation of this black Helen, his new "filly of Menelaus" is suddenly joined by a stallion galloping down the smoke-shrouded beach. In one of Walcott's most elusively amorphous scenes, he builds on the lyrics of the Beatles' song we have just heard Helen singing. We are reminded that "yesterday" the horse was wooden, his thundering hooves were battle sounds, and

this village was ravaged Troy, on the banks of Scamander (35). Once again, in the New World this time, Helen's troubles which "seem so far away" echo those of the heralded past, and her travail becomes our present story. What is most frustrating, however, in coming to that story is the fact that it can be told from such antithetical perspectives. The Major/narrator is so caught up in his classical atlas that Helen suddenly vanishes from his sight.

Helen's physical disappearance into the smoke of burning leaves signals a flashback that confronts us with yet another among the poem's myriad starting places. The next scene recreates the wrenching moment that drives Helen from Achille into Hector's arms. The demeaning incident involves nothing more significant than whether Helen or Achille should carry their basket of purchases home from the market. In the midst of the crowded produce stalls they exchange harsh words, then a flurry of blows. An embarrassed Achille is left to pick up the scattered fruit while Helen escapes in Hector's transport van. Hector is no Trojan Paris, yet he has just as effectively stolen Helen, and this new wound is opened. After Achille returns to his empty cottage, he relives the first painful moment when he began to doubt Helen. He had been diving illegally for conch shells, trying to make extra money, when there on the redoubt above the bay was Helen in her unmistakable yellow dress, meeting Hector. Looking back on the event, he sleeps only to dream fitfully of their love-making in happier days. Imperceptibly, the dream merges into the author's reverie about an Adamic paradise before corruption, "before it gaped into a wound, like Philoctete" (42).

Although Walcott's intrusion into Achille's libido is not as explicit as his earlier claim to the Major's perspective, it is nonetheless evident that he not only is present in *Omeros* in his own right as author but also is never far beneath the surface of each of his invented characters. This unavoidable feature of the narrative exposition should come as no surprise to anyone who has become familiar with the autobiographical strain that is endemic to Walcott's poetry and drama. He has drawn from his island background for numerous characters. For example, forerunners of Achille, Hector, and Philoctete are discernible in the resilient fisherman Afa from *The Sea at Dauphin,* the misanthropic Chantal from *Malcochon,* and the visionary charbonnier Makak in *Dream on Monkey Mountain.* Major Plunkett's quest to identify himself with the island is prefigured by the crude machinations of the title character in the unpublished *Franklin,* the ineffectual Harry Trewe in *Pantomime,* and Clodia De La Fontaine in *The Last Carnival.* Each of these earlier works contains indigenous villagers or colonists who struggle to define their colonial roots. Walcott's personal attachment to the islands is never far from the surface of the poetry as well. When asked about the autobiographical facets of *Another Life,* he replied that "it would be hard for one to leave out the details of a person's life in a book of that kind. It is a particular experience. But in a sense it is a biography of an 'intelligence,' a West Indian intelligence."[9]

Among all the figures in *Omeros,* however, it is Helen herself who emerges most directly from a sequence of informing sources. The name alone is almost unavoidable since, as Walcott has pointed out, St. Lucia has been called the Helen of the Caribbean. In the poetry the beauty of the island and women are both frequently couched in terms of their power to seduce. Although she bears little resemblance to Achille's Helen in *Omeros,* one of her first manifestations serves as a classical comparison for a prostitute in *Another Life.*

> Helen?
> Janie, the town's one clear-complexioned whore,
> with two tow-headed children in her tow,
> she sleeps with sailors only, her black
> hair electrical
> as all that trouble over Troy,
> rolling broad-beamed she leaves
> a plump and pumping vacancy.

By 1987 in *The Arkansas Testament,* her image is equally sensual but far richer in its multifaceted applications through **"The Villa Restaurant," "The Light of the World,"** and **"Menelaus."** The terra-cotta waitress described in **"The Villa Restaurant"** is not named; however, her slate irises and feminine curvature lead the poet to prefer her shapely "living vase" to sculpted stone, whether carved or fired. The message derived from his choice of the warm flesh over the cold marble is that "Your sea has its own *Iliads;*" therefore, she becomes his artistic ideal.

> the cracked ground in Mantegna
> is hers, the golden apple;
> the blue gesso behind her
> head is my Sistine Chapel.

Against a background of Renaissance masterpieces and the prize of Helen won by Paris in awarding the golden apple to Aphrodite, the poet admires this waitress dutifully tending her station:

> her beauty not her fault as
> her palm smooths the flaws
> of linen laid like altars
> with crumbs and today's flowers.

She remains anonymous when she appears again in **"The Light of the World,"** the poem Walcott mentions to J. P. White as containing Elena, his prototype for the heroine of *Omeros* (35). Here he anticipates his feline imagery for Helen, as "a still panther." Under her spell, he wishes he could enter her home, lie beside her,

> tell her in silence
> that her hair was like a hill forest at night,
> that a trickle of rivers was in her armpits,
> that I would buy her Benin if she wanted it,
> and never leave her on earth. But the others, too.

To do this, of course, he would have to become Achille. Yet his heart is in the right place. Impossible as it is to become one with her among the villagers of Gros Îlet, or

to "buy her Benin," he captures the moment by creating for them all "The Light of the World." When it comes to **"Menelaus"** near the end of *The Arkansas Testament,* the mood is less accommodating. We encounter a disillusioned Menelaus who now sees Helen of Troy as white trash, who contemplates his "Ten years. Wasted in quarrel / for sea-grey eyes. A whore's."[10] Were this the final word, all we should have is the melancholy tragedy of the past. Obviously, this confined view is inadequate for Walcott. Three years later in *Omeros,* he determines to reclaim Helen as the centerpiece of a New World epic of survival. Discarding traditional forms of imperial heroism, he turns his attention to the equally vital if less spectacular saga of the dispossessed.

Chapter eight of the first book of *Omeros* departs briefly from Achille's painful loss of Helen to introduce the legend attached to an artifact in the island's small museum. It is a bottle encrusted with fool's gold that is said variously to be lost from a storm-driven galleon out of Cartagena or from the French flagship in the Battle of the Saints, the *Ville de Paris.* Local myth prefers to believe it spilled from the *Ville de Paris,* now an illusive wreck said to be guarded by an octopus-cyclops. The dream of sunken treasure that might win Helen back lures Achille to illegal diving along the reef. All he gets for his trouble is a startling vision of a hollow relic under the relentless gaze of a moon-eyed creature. When it occurs to him that it will be necessary to abandon all hope of ever locating the haunted wreck, he interprets it as a sign that he must also accept the fact that he may never get Helen back (46). The loss of Helen has a second dimension that is brought out by Philoctete. In spite of the bad blood between Hector and Achille, Philoctete undertakes the restoration of their severed friendship, arguing that their shared occupation as fishermen is enough to guarantee their fundamental brotherhood (47).

In the structural arrangement of the first two books, the low point of the narrative arrives during hurricane season. The inclement weather that drives fishermen to land also forces the Plunketts to sedentary pursuits in their study. Walcott uses the contrast between inner and outer weather to consolidate the status of his main characters before branching out in pursuit of three complementary subplots. Achille temporarily abandons his pirogue for the concrete feeding trough of Major Plunkett's farm. To Achille, who cowers alone in his shack, elements of the raging storm are personified as African and Greek deities. Shango, Erzulie, Ogun, Damballa, and Neptune are

> holding a hurricane-party in their cloud-house,
> and what brings the gods close is the thunderous
>    weather,
> where Ogun can fire one with his partner Zeus.

(53)

While Achille imagines that Hector is safely comforted in Helen's arms, his nemesis is engaged in a futile battle to save his canoe (51). His anchor torn away, he is forced to dive into the raging sea and escape to the beach. The lost anchor has thematic consequences beyond the moment, virtually leaving him adrift for the rest of his life. Having lost his pirogue, Hector abandons his calling as a fisherman to pursue the career of a taxi driver.

In the Plunkett household, Maud, preferring the seasonal regularity of her Irish homeland to this tropical deluge (48), takes up the embroidery of a tapestry representing all the birds of the Caribbean. Depressed by the foul weather, the Major senses that Maud is slipping away, not just transported melodiously by her *Airs from Erin,* but out of life.[11] Light does break through the clouds, however, and in the aftermath of the baptismal rain the world is refreshed. Achille gratefully bails out his canoe (54), while the Plunketts set out in their Land Rover to tour the coastal mountains (57).

At the beginning of their drive, the Major returns to his interest in history. For the first time the term "History" is capitalized in the middle of a sentence, apparently in order to signify the imprimatur of official authority. As the Major applies the capitalized version, he reacts against Eurocentric marginalization. Preparing to write his own record of Helen's island ("Not his, but her story," 30) Plunkett develops the practice of using the lower-case "history" to designate his newly generated rendition of events. The Land Rover trip provides more than an opportunity for epic cataloging of place names—La Sorcière, Cul-de-Sac valley, Roseau, Anse La Raye, Canaries (58-59). We learn that the folk name for the volcanic island's La Sorcière is the same as that of the proprietress of the No Pain Cafe, Ma Kilman, "because the village was darkened by their belief / in her as a *gardeuse,* sybil, obeah-woman" (58). The open wounds of the sulfuric "Malebolge" beneath the Pitons near Soufrière remind the Major of putrid Auschwitz (59). Nearby, the imperial mining enterprise of speculators Bennett and Ward had failed to convert the sulfur into English gold (60). Unlike the Plunketts, these exploiters failed back in 1836 and returned to their mother country. Observing these sights along the road leads the Major's train of thought to his own reasons for choosing St. Lucia over his birthplace.

> England seemed to him merely the place of his birth.
> How odd to prefer, over its pastoral sites—
> reasonable leaves shading reasonable earth—
>
> The loud-mouthed forests on their illiterate heights,
> these springs speaking a dialect that cooled his mind
> more than pastures with castles! To prefer the hush
>
> of a hazed Atlantic worried by the salt wind!
> Others could read it as "going back to the bush," but
>   harbour
> after crescent harbour closed his wound.
>
>                                                   (61)

Here in brief are the stereotypical denominators of temperate and tropical climates that are supposed to divide light and dark races. In this subtle way, the Major justifies his chosen exile. Maud herself—who despises the humidity, pestilent insects, barefooted poor, religious converts with their "joy of sects," careering transports, and the merciless sun—much as she would like to see Ireland again, revels in the burgeoning flowers of her garden. As she recalls wryly the misspelling on Achille's *In God We Troust,* she reflects, "But then we all trust in Him, and that's why we know / the peace of a wandering heart when it is housed" (67).

Even as they pause to contemplate the Edenic quality of their life, the Major's thoughts are haunted by the butterfly-yellow of Helen's frock. Killing the engine of the Land Rover, he wonders whether her questionable acquisition of the dress could be exorcised by History, or whether she desires anyone's pardon. Without resolving that ethical issue, he concludes that since "All roots have their histories," (63) he would speak for Helen.

> So Plunkett decided that what the place needed
> was its true place in history, that he'd spend hours
> for Helen's sake on research, so he proceeded
>
> to the whirr of enormous moths in the still house.
> Memory's engines. The butterfly dress was hers,
> at least her namesake's, in the Battle of the Saints.
>
>                                                   (64)

Having thus isolated two functions of history, those of legitimizing and generating narrative, Walcott has prepared the foundation for the three subplots that make up the remainder of books one and two. They involve, first, Walcott's exposition of his own attachment to the island; second, Major Plunkett's quest for historical fragments that may be assimilated into his and Helen's organic, written history; and third, the struggle of Philoctete, Achille, Hector, and other islanders to bear the political and social consequences of colonial independence.

Continuing the kaleidoscopic segmentation of his story, Walcott shifts easily from the Plunketts' intimate self-examination to his highly personal reveries in the twelfth chapter. The setting is his childhood home at 17 Chaussee Road in Castries, the house mentioned in his 1965 article "Leaving School" and lovingly described with its "carpenter's Gothic" trim surrounded with flowering bougainvillea and allamanda in the second chapter of *Another Life.*[12] When he returns in *Omeros,* the front porch is gone and his former residence has been converted to a printery. This visit may have begun with a touch of nostalgia, but while the presses roll out handbills on machines where cherished furniture once stood, the ghost of Warwick Walcott, his father, materializes.

This evocation of his father gives Walcott a useful vehicle for establishing literary roots uncannily deep in English tradition. Warwick not only is conveniently named after Shakespeare's home shire but also succumbed to an ear ailment (as Hamlet's father had) on the Bard's accepted April 23 date of birth. The father puns that his own "Will" to produce verse in Caribbean obscurity is his son's legacy, and that the explicit Shakespearean parallels have already afforded Walcott some peace: "Death imitating Art, eh?" (69). Warwick is the first to raise the issue of influence and the anomaly of their respective ages, an ironic point that Walcott will develop later himself.

> "In this pale notebook where you found my verses"—
> my father smiled—"I appeared to make your life's
>   choice,
> and the calling that you practise both reverses
>
> and honours mine from the moment it blent with
>   yours.
> Now that you are twice my age, which is the boy's,
> which the father's?"
>                "Sir"—I swallowed—"they are one voice."
>
>                                              (68)

His answer to Warwick's query effectively seals the continuity of their shared calling. In a scene reminiscent of Anchises guiding Aeneas through the underworld until he charges him with his mission in life, Warwick leads his son out of the house, down Grass Street toward the port of Castries. Unlike Virgil, however, who maintains the integrity of his closed narrative, Walcott reminds us of the fictive nature of his tour. He explains to the curious reader that he does not venture to inquire of the ghost about the life beyond death,

> because the white shadow I had made from my mind
>
> was vague in its origin and thin as belief,
> unsinged as an Easter lily, fresh as the wind,
> its whisper as soft as a pavement-scratching leaf.
>
>                                           (70-71)

As this pair make their way toward the harbor, none of the individuals they pass is able to see the invisible father until they encounter the shade of Warwick's late barber. Referring to him as his chamberlain, Warwick fondly recalls quoting from his collection of *The World's Great Classics*,[13] prominently displayed on a varnished rack across from his elevated barber's chair.

Although the barber is one of the minor characters in the story, Walcott makes significant use of his appearance and repeatedly cites his collection of *The World's Great Classics*. As a Seventh Day Adventist and a follower of Marcus Garvey, the barber, a frustrated anarchist, had served two messiahs in life. Describing him to his son, Warwick says "The rock he lived on was nothing. Not a nation / or a people," and as a result of the curse of his birth, the "paradise" he proclaimed from his barber's throne was "a phantom Africa" (72). Because Warwick is determined that his son should not likewise set his eyes on some distant, mythical home, he shifts his attention away from the barber to the magnificent ocean liner anchored in the harbor. It is at this moment, poised literally on the corner of Bridge Street between an illusory past (whether of Christian or African origins) and a future geared to tourism, that Warwick most clearly emulates the role of An-

chises, instructing his son about his destiny. Warwick prepares for an essential transition with a warning against the corruptive power of foreign values.

> Measure the days you have left. Do just that labour
> which marries your heart to your right hand: simplify
> your life to one emblem, a sail leaving harbour
>
> and a sail coming in. All corruption will cry
> to be taken aboard. Fame is that white liner
> at the end of your street, a city to itself,
>
> taller than the Fire Station, and much finer,
> with its brass-ringed portholes, mounting shelf after
>   shelf,
> than anything Castries could ever hope to build."
>
>                                              (72-73)

After these cautionary remarks, Warwick recalls the female colliers from his childhood who had trekked like ants down to this same harbor to fuel visiting ships.

Part of their curse is that these women drifted out of existence without leaving a record of their names. Warwick himself died too young to remedy that omission; however, he is convinced that their anonymity is not the equivalent of nothingness. Addressing his son as "O Thou, my Zero," he works one more variation on the "O" image. As he does so in this instance, he echoes the fool in *King Lear* who criticizes his powerless old master for having relinquished his identity in the process of abdicating his crown.[14] The major difference is that Lear is responsible for his own predicament, and it is history that has failed to do justice to the forgotten women of St. Lucia. Calling them "Helens from an earlier time," he extols their unrecorded labor.

> The carriers were women, not the fair, gentler sex.
> Instead, they were darker and stronger, and their gait
> was made beautiful by balance, in their ascending
>
> the narrow wooden ramp built steeply to the hull
> of a liner tall as a cloud . . ."
>
>                                              (74)

Then, as a powerful climax to the first book of *Omeros*, Warwick charges his son with his sacred duty. Walcott's business is to follow in the footsteps of these women, using his pen as they had used their strong backs and feet.

> "Kneel to your load, then balance your staggering feet
> and walk up that coal ladder as they do in time,
> one bare foot after the next in ancestral rhyme. . . .
>              · · · · ·
>
> keep to that narrow causeway without looking down,
> climbing in their footsteps, that slow, ancestral beat
> of those used to climbing roads; your own work owes
>   them
>
> because the couplet of those multiplying feet
> made your first rhymes. Look, they climb, and no one
>   knows them;

they take their copper pittances, and your duty

from the time you watched them from your grandmoth-
    er's house
as a child wounded by their power and beauty
is the chance you now have, to give those feet a
    voice."

                                                            (75-76)

Situated as it is, emphatically at the end of book one, Warwick's challenge forms the central theme of *Omeros*. The
meeting with the ghost of his father also sets the scene for
Walcott to begin the crucial subplots that constitute most
of book two, separate ancestral quests for Major Plunkett
and Achille that eventually lead to their common St. Lucian identities.

### Notes

1. Walcott, "What the Twilight Says," 19; White, "An
   Interview with Derek Walcott," 35-36; Bruckner,
   "Poem in Homage," 13; Presson, "Man," 9.

2. Bruckner, "Poem in Homage," 13.

3. Froude, *The English in the West Indies,* 9-13.

4. Bruckner, "Poem in Homage," 17; Arun Mukherjee,
   *Towards an Aesthetic of Opposition: Essays on
   Literature, Criticism and Cultural Imperialism,* 17.

5. In a telephone conversation, September 6, 1996,
   Derek Walcott told me that he observed *In God We
   Trust* at Choc Bay, St. Lucia; Presson, "Man," 10;
   Walcott, "Caligula's Horse," 138.

6. Derek Walcott, in a telephone conversation with the
   author on October 11, 1993, asserted the authenticity
   of the encounter depicted here, claiming poetic
   license for the name "Antigone" to enhance the
   mythical dimensions of the poem.

7. November 11 coincides with Armistice Day in Great
   Britain, Veteran's Day in the United States, and
   Remembrance Day in Canada—to commemorate the
   end of World War I, November 11, 1918.

8. Virgil, *The Aeneid of Virgil,* translated by C. Day
   Lewis, 64, 167.

9. Hamner, "Conversation with Derek Walcott," 411.

10. Walcott, "Leaving School," 4; *Another Life,* 19; *The
    Arkansas Testament,* 26, 27; White, "An Interview
    with Derek Walcott," 35; Walcott, *The Arkansas
    Testament,* 48, 50, 51, 101.

11. Although Walcott cites *Airs from Erin* on two occa-
    sions (56, 262), I have been unable to obtain a copy
    of such a work. Thomas Moore, the composer of
    "Bendemeer's Stream," also mentioned among Maud
    Plunkett's musical references (201), is credited with
    a collection entitled *Airs of Old Erin* (New York:
    Edward B. Marks, 1936).

12. Walcott, "Leaving School," 6, 8; Walcott, *Another
    Life,* 10-14.

13. *The World's Great Classics* (New York: Colonial
    Press, 1899-1901; Grolier, 1969 [in 50 vols.]).

14. William Shakespeare, *King Lear,* Riverside edition,
    1.6.192.

### James Wieland (essay date 1998)

SOURCE: Wieland, James. "Adam's Task . . . : Myths
and Fictions in the Poetry of Derek Walcott." In *The Ensphering Mind: History, Myth, and Fictions in the Poetry
of Allen Curnow, Nissim Ezekiel, A. D. Hope, A. M. Klein,
Christopher Okigbo, and Derek Walcott,* pp. 165-88.
Washington, D.C.: Three Continents, 1998.

[*In the following essay, Wieland explores recurring allusions to mythological and fictional themes and characters
in Walcott's body of work.*]

On the dust jacket of *Another Life,* George Lamming is
quoted as having said:

> This is not the first time that Walcott has given a hint
> that his first passion is art as the indispensable language
> for interpreting reality. He is a colonial who has spent
> a life trying to dismantle and re-define the cultural ap-
> paratus of his imperialist tutelage.

This redefining of which Lamming speaks draws attention
to Walcott's relationship with his world and to his concern
to make a comprehensive and creative word-picture of the
Caribbean. The history he seeks is not that which may be
celebrated in monuments or honored through ruins; indeed,
he faces a history of loss in which monuments are reminders of subjugation and ruins evoke memories of decay. If
history is to be celebrated, Walcott says, it is to be viewed
"as fiction or as religion, then our use of it will be
idiosyncratic, personal, and therefore, creative" ("Culture
or Mimicry?" 13). As he builds fictions around his people
and his place, naming and repeating actions, images,
metaphors, and symbols, there evolves a coherence and a
pattern to his society which moves toward the sense of
myth. And while this mythic quality stands in opposition
to the vacuum of history, his fictions attempt to give the
annihilation significance in the contemporary world.
Curnow wrote an "anti-myth" in an endeavor to provide a
more inclusive view of New Zealand history and to resist
any simplistic stereotypes, and Walcott's mythopoeia functions to negate the exclusive "myth of the uncreative
parasitic, malarial nigger, the marsh-numbed imagination
that is happiest in mud" (*Dream on Monkey Mountain,* p.
33). While his experience is expressed through allusions to
Adam, Odysseus, Crusoe, and Friday, the true "stars of
[his] mythology" (*AL,* [*Another Life*] p. 22) are the islanders—artists, lovers, fishermen, foresters, *charbonnières*—
"These dead, these derelicts / that alphabet of the emaciated" (*AL,* p. 22, and see pp. 16-22). Into the lives of
these people Walcott builds the eternal struggle of being,
until they are, if not epic, at least "pseudo-epic" (*AL,* p.

41). Out of their struggle emerges the essense of what it is to be West Indian and Man. His mythology is rooted in the reality of his islands; in their history, their landscape, their folk. And the various *figurae* he uses reflect aspects of the Caribbean experience, but they reach beyond the narrow confines of time and place: his Adam's Eden is a New World Paradise, rich in ambiguity and contradiction; his Odysseus hops Caribbean islands seeking an order and pattern, and Crusoe and Friday ultimately become metamorphosed into one figure as Crusoe's experience becomes emblematic of the West Indian, cast away into a world he did not choose but with which he must come to terms.

We have suggested that the ultimate fiction leads the reader back to the essential insights of myth. This is appropriate to Walcott who sees his search as "elemental." It leads, he says, toward a

> darkness [which] must be total, and the cave should not contain a single man-made, mnemonic object. Its noises should be elemental, the roar of rain, ocean, wind, and fire. Their first sound should be like their last, the cry. The voice must grovel in search of itself until gestures and sound fuse and the blaze of their flesh astonishes them. The children of slaves must sear their memory with a torch. The actor must break up his body and feed it as ruminatively as ancestral story-tellers fed twigs to the fire. Those who look from their darkness into the tribal fire must be bold enough to cross it.
>
> (*Dream on Monkey Mountain*, pp. 5-6)

And of the energy of a poem he is reported to have said that "it moves off the page and goes into the memory. It goes into the collective memory of the entire race."[1] He sees poetry as an embodiment of the collective memory, and his ideal movement, then, is from the private and fictive, toward the communal and mythic. As he says in *Dream on Monkey Mountain*:

> For imagination and body to move with original instinct, we must begin again from the bush. That return journey, with all its horror of rediscovery, means the annihilation of what is known. Some of our poets have pretended that journey, but with an itinerary whose resting points are predetermined. On such journeys the mind will discover what it chooses, and what these writers seek, like refugees raking debris, are heirlooms to dignify an old destitution. Even this destitution, carefully invoked, is pastoral. But if the body could be reduced once more to learning, to a rendering of things through groping mnemonic fingers, a new theatre [and a new poetry] could be made, with a delight that comes in roundly naming its object.
>
> (p. 26)

In an interview he suggests that he is seeking that metaphor called Caribbean or West Indian, for "one had a metaphor called Ireland and a metaphor called America. . . . They were on solid ground with no broken islands," but in the West Indies, the

> . . . only historical legends that one individual writer would have are ethnic legends of sorts. Each of them is separate because the Indian would have India, the

African would have Africa. But the point of this is that all of these have been erased from the memory or experience of the writer. So, what has not yet been created or is actually being created by its absence, by the chaos, by the necessity for it to be created—is a West Indies, a West Indian literature. Now that is being made out of the very knowledge that there is not one.[2]

Just as we have seen Walcott's protagonists experience the necessary progression through exile and alienation to indifference and, then, to a sense of belonging, so the naming of the "nothing" of history is a necessary preamble to celebrating what is there: this entails going beyond the fact of history to emotion, and writing a comprehensive fiction of his people.[3] At this early stage of naming their existence, he suggests that they

> may not even need literature, not that [they] are beyond it, but in the archipelago particularly, nature, the elements if you want, are so new, so overpowering in their presence that awe is deeper than articulation of awe. To name is to contradict. The awe of God or of the universe is the unnameable, and this has nothing to do with literacy. It is better for us to be a race of illiterates who retain this awe than to be godless, without mystery.
>
> ("Culture or Mimicry?" 12)

\* \* \*

To consider the possibility that his people "may not even need literature" is to look for the communal and essential which may be intuited rather than learned or logically acquired. Nowhere in Walcott's work is there a denial of reason, but we sense him always reaching toward the mystery at the center of being which ultimately is beyond reason. In *Dream on Monkey Mountain* he says, "we begin again, with the vigour of a curiosity that gave the old names life, that charged an old language, from the depth of suffering, with awe" (p. 11). The negation of history has been a rape of body and mind:

> When they conquer you, you have to read their books.
> Then violently, false folklorique follows;
> Maidenheads or otherwise, arrowheads,
> Their two archaeological pursuits.
>
> ("Roots," *IAGN*, [*In A Green Night*] p. 60)[4]

And before "our Homer with truer perception erect it," every memory must be stripped bare, and the poet "make without pomp, with stone acanthus, / In our time, in the time of this phrase, a 'flowering of islands.'" To so remake the islands, which is the function of his fictions, "All else will go down," all old "ambitions," "divisions," other mythologies—Helen is shorn of her eternal beauty to become "old Helen, lying alone in bed"—and all ruins save one, "Our Sirmio" at Vigie, which is transformed by the elements from a thing of sorrow to an object of beauty.

The need to name the losses before he can remake his world is a continual energizing force behind the poetry. In doing so Walcott crosses personal and national boundaries, for his own integrity and faith are under focus in addition to the identity of his people and their relationship to other countries. As we read *In A Green Night* we sense Walcott working deeper into his own being and into his heritage, groping for what he seems to glimpse at times, a kind of elemental memory or consciousness. As he studies his "historylessness"—that "stigmata of the void," as Harris calls it[5]—he brings back reminders of the "fruitful" interaction "between man and man, man and nature—a salvage which seeks never to block its own agencies of vision by idolatrous fixations."[6] He translates the reality of absences into the reality of presences, salvaging a history of emotion from the amnesia.

Walcott's probing of reality gravitates to opposite poles; to man's finiteness and his potential for infinity. The finite being is defined by such things as color, language, religion, vocation; but a concept of infinity is grasped by locating what is elemental in being. The epitome of this groping toward infinity in Walcott's poetry is the sense we have of a mind trying to grasp, through image and metaphor, what is both external and instinctive to its consciousness. It is through the release of faith, of myth, of literature, through searching for the basic rhythm of life, that one makes contact with the unknown. And while we become progressively aware that Walcott's quest is an ongoing thing, his approach to the search is fundamentally mythopoeic. Like Curnow he bathes man, landscape, and event in his imagination, giving all that constitutes his people a continuing life in time.[7] Out of the anguish of naming the losses, out of the powerful credibility of the natural world, out of the ambivalences and contradictions of the past and present, an inchoate myth of the Caribbean begins to form. Any such myth must be inclusive, and, like the painter in **"To A Painter in England,"** Walcott wishes to define "the several postures of this virginal island" (*IAGN,* p. 16). He wants to "put down . . . in words"

> all of its sunken, leaf-choked ravines,
> every neglected, self-pitying inlet
> muttering in brackish dialect . . .

> (*AL*, p. 52)

As the epigraph to Section Two of *Another Life* suggests, the poet had assumed "Adam's task of giving things their names,"[8] and this entails naming the ruins of history, the broken men, and the natural world.

And yet this naming will be tinged with silence and humility, for the poet is concerned that "to name is to contradict"; so that, while naming may give a meaning to the presences and breathe life into the losses, it must also submit to the "awe of God or of the universe [which] is unnameable." The need to name will continue, and the names will change as the sense of the world changes and as the namers succeed to more wisdom, beginning again in the world.

In **"The Royal Palms"** he says, "Here there are no heroic palaces," and if "art is where the greatest ruins are, / Our art is in those ruins we became":[9] which is the initial posi-

tion of **"Ruins of a Great House,"** for the sense of history is conveyed through the *disjecta membra,* the decadence of the "moth-like girls," through the neglect, decay, and stench of death. But the ruins are more than a reminder of the subjugation of slaves and of a people; they become a reminder of the decline of Empire, and thus seem to take their place in a larger scheme of rise and fall. For, in compassion, the poet emerges from his "rage" into the awareness "That Albion too, was once, / A colony like ours." **"Ruins of a Great House"** brings out the ambiguities of Walcott's world and points to many of the tensions which lie behind the poetry of *In A Green Night*. It has an open-ended quality by virtue of its allusions and the multi-leveled meanings of much of the language, and it draws the reader into active contemplation with the poem, with its place in the canon, and with the various allusions. Written below an epigraph taken from Browne's *Urne Burial,* and with further allusions to it in the body of the poem, there is a complex emotional tone created out of the connotations of the "Great House" as an emblem of Britain's imperial power, its contrast with the present day, and the humility called for in the passage from *Urne Burial.* There is the additional irony that the age which produced Browne and Donne gave rise also to such exploitations as the slave trade to feed the energy of the age. In the very mention of "men like Hawkins, Walter Raleigh, Drake / Ancestral murderers and poets," Walcott catches the ambiguity of history, for, depending upon the perspective, the allusions open the way to a simultaneous naming of losses and gains, of heroism and cruelty. The essence of such contradictions is summed up in the implied contrast between Marvell's use of "green" and Walcott's, in the line: "The world's green age then was a rotting lime." The poem is suffused with the ambience of the seventeenth century; but the glory is tainted with horror, the richness with decay. And the allusions to Blake's "Night" and to "Faulkner's south" invoke worlds of exploitation and loss of innocence. Furthermore, behind the second verse paragraph, which draws on the thought of the epigraph, stands an allusion to the Book of Job and to Satan's words to God: "And touch his flesh, / And he will renounce thee to thy voice," which points to the despair of the downtrodden and the conviction to endure. And Walcott picks up the ambivalence of some of Kipling's observations of Empire, for, despite his songs of Empire, Kipling also understood something of its excesses.

We attend to puns on "spade" and "rakes"—the antagonists—to the ambiguity of the fall from "evil times," and to the faith which can conceive of death as the precursor to life. The allusions and the puns expose levels of reality that must be located and discerned, and Walcott develops a richly ambiguous world which, while it focuses on the central symbol, radiates out through the allusions to a comprehensive picture of an age and its effect on the present. Whether we pick up a direct allusion, or sense the ambience, we must bring these externals to the poem. The effect is not to diffuse the energy of the poem but to deepen its implications. The poem as a consequence is never static, it has no one meaning—we attend to the open-endedness of the final allusion to John Donne[10]—and even as the poem reaches toward certain essential truths, by its very movement and vitality and its interaction with much else that he has written, these "truths" are continually to be re-opened and studied. Further, out of the ashes rises a rich and complex fiction that captures the compassion lying at the root of Walcott's poetry, while exposing the complexities of his world.[11]

Walcott names numerous other losses and ruins: the lonely, lost and exiled, who stand in contrast to his essential men; the failure of the West Indian Federation and the American Dream; and the need to find a faith which can give reason and order to living.

In **"Roots," "Pays Natal,"** and **"The Harbour,"** the fishermen have an innate reciprocity with their home and the poet can wish that he "might have gathered those senses in [his] arms, / As weary fishermen their honest seines." In **"The Harbour"** they stand contrasted to the "secure from thinking [who] . . . climb safe to liners," escaping the adventures and risks of being. For the fishermen the harbor is a point of departure, not a haven, and they move through a world of mystery, terror, and beauty. But there is no attempt to make of these fundamental men, gods; they need "the Virgin" and "cast their hopes with care" (**"Choc Bay," IAGN,** p. 23). They are

> The Blackhanded
> Hate-bridled
> Fishermen with their haul of sprats,

but they endure and, like Hemingway's "old man," the sea is their element, they respect it, and they know it. They stand for a world, primal, vital, and enduring, transforming the outward signs of isolation, exile, negation, and the veneer "Found only / In tourist booklets" (**"Prelude," IAGN,** p. 11) into a world of meaning which the poet celebrates for its reality; its ambiguities; its ugliness and beauty; and its absences and presences.

Walcott's West Indies is defined in terms of a struggle between the dualities of heaven and hell: "The uncouth features of this my prone island" (**"Prelude," IAGN,** p. 11) are transformed into a "heaven" in the next poem (**"As John to Patmos,"** p. 12), and in the beautiful lyric **"Choc Bay"** (p. 23), the poet flees "from [the] paradise" he has painted in the opening stanzas into a portrayal of the "dead and the derelict" of the sonnet sequence, **"Tales of the Islands"** (p. 26). Personally and collectively the West Indian seems confounded by dualities and there is no certainty that they can be synthesized:

> . . . to find the true self is still arduous
> And for us, especially, the elation can be useless and
>    empty
> As this pale blue, ewer of the sky,
> Loveliest in drought.

> (**"Allegre," IAGN,** p. 58)

And in **"Sea Grapes,"** the title poem of a volume to which the sense of balance is central, Walcott isolates the dualities into what he contends is an immemorial struggle "between obsession and responsibility / [which] will never finish" (p. 3). And yet this position is a considerable advance over that of **"Allegre,"** for it accepts man's capacity to endure while realizing that there may be no one "true self" to be defined.

The classical world enters the poetry in **"Choc Bay"**: "Mary, the sea-lost, Venus, the sea-born." Both are the heritage of islanders:

> . . . the waves
> Bearing Time's bitter legends gave [them]
> To those whose lives are circled by the sea.

The **"Hate-bridled Fishermen,"** with a prayer, give their allegiance to Mary, for "Venus lives with aristocrats," but the speaker can give allegiance to neither. He feels caught between the white goddesses and what they stand for: Christian and pagan, spirit and beauty, moral and aesthetic values, containment and release, a love which leads toward charity and selflessness and that which projects an aristocratic power and self-confidence. His "mind rides anchor" in "the rare / Width of blue air"; he feels with the hawk, prays "for the wheeling spokes / Of gulls," kneels "to the shell's mass," and pays respect to "the crab in hiding in salt grass." He flies "above time's reach," basking in the heady realm of the imagination, but "dead Venus" and the Virgin "showed / It was all a wise / Hoax" to his Daedalian dream. For all he wants "are words" to name the nothingness, and, as he says in **"Lampfall"** (**The Castaway,** p. 58), invoking Penelope—the faithful wife of Ulysses, waiting and weaving—he will sing of his island. But he will catch not only the "windy leaves" and the wave's wash, for he would troll deep to the essences of his island existence to capture a sense of its enduring presence.[12]

In a number of poems the poet gives himself to his environment, naming its presences: the amethyst sea, "the pale, blue ewer of the sky," the "wing'd sound of trees," the beaches, fish flashing, and birds diving. But in naming his environment, Walcott aims at an inclusive picture also, and a poem such as **"Return to D'Ennery, Rain"** should be read in the context of the exquisite celebration of the incantatory **"A Sea Chantey."**

> Anguilla, Adina,
> Antigua, Cannelles,
> Andreuille, all the l's,
> Voyelles, of the liquid Antilles,
> The names tremble like needles
> Of anchored frigates . . .

> (**IAGN,** p. 64)

The poem is suffused with a profound sense of beauty and love and it evokes the emotional quotient which Walcott suggests was missing from the plans for federation in **"Map of the Antilles."** By way of contrast, through the extended metaphor of a cripple, **"Return to D'Ennery, Rain"** projects a vision of the Caribbean as a physical and spiritual dependent.

Imprisoned in these wires of rain, I watch
This village stricken with a single street,
Each weathered shack leans on a wooden crutch,
Contented as a cripple in defeat.

(IAGN, p. 33)

Both visions must be held; it is crucial that the West Indian make a virtue of his losses, for love is born of pain:

> . . . greater than death is death's gift, that can,
> Behind the bright dust that was the skeleton,
> (Who drank the wine and believed the blessed bread)
> Can make us see the forgotten price of man
> Shine from the perverse beauty of the dead.

("Elegy," IAGN, p. 13)[13]

But such a compassion cannot be won through until we "leave the mind's dark cave," stop "praising death in life" (**"Pocomania,"** p. 35), and reach that mystery which is at the center of being, and to which, echoing Baudelaire, he alludes in **"A Sea Chantey"**: "Repos donnez a cils . . ."[14] It is a peace beyond understanding, an immaculate balance: "The omen of calm waters" (**"A Sea Chantey"**).

By the last poem of *In A Green Night,* having expressed his admiration of "those mottled marbles" of Europe, the "Aphrodite," "Venus," "Dianas," and "Ledas," he can celebrate his race:

> Not one of those in such fierce sex was fired
> Or holds its cunning secret as this one
> Of lasting bronze, art of a savage race,
> Marble, bronze, ebonwood, white, creole, black.

(**"Bronze"**)

The bronze mask stands as a synthesis, both qualitative and quantitative, for the West Indian people. Similarly La Guaira, gateway to El Dorado (with its dual connotations of physical and mental quest) and entrance to the West Indies, is "nothing": "it means nothing" (**"Nearing La Guaira"**), grinned the sailor. But as the next stanza establishes, this nothing is everything: it is the "green water," the "sun . . . like a starfish," "the moon," "a cornet in the plaza," "the Morro, / Where the garbage drifts," the roaring fans at a bullfight, and the empty cathedral; it is the "soldiers drilling in the square, / And the green fountain with its sacrament." In this nadir of despair, as the vein of sexual imagery suggests, it stands also for the personal gulf felt between lovers. In the ambiguity of the last line, it is essential that two readings be held: "Nothing *is* bitter and *is* very deep" (my italics), but also, in the colloquial sense of "it doesn't matter," nothing is so deep or so bitter that it cannot be weathered. We are not, however, left with the same feeling of utter resignation and isolation that A. D. Hope offers at the end of **"The Wandering Islands"**:

> Around him he hears the monotonous voices
> Of wave and wind:
> "The rescue will not take place."

Introduced in the opening poem of *In A Green Night,* the journey motif is central to the poetry. In the allusion to Dante in **"Prelude"** the dimensions of the journey are suggested: it is at once a spiritual and physical quest in which he experiences, names, and places the hell, purgatory, and paradise of his own existence and of that of his people. The Odysseus archetype is directed toward uncovering the mystery which lies at the center of Caribbean existence. In **"Map of the Antilles,"** Walcott's odyssey is explicitly compared to that of Odysseus, in which the objective is "that sense of cultural unity and purpose which could replace petty insularity."[14] And in **"A Sea Chantey,"** although the passage through the islands may evoke Odysseus, the Caribbean archipelago has its own "Refracted embroidery," its "own histories / [and] . . . peace of green harbourage." In their association with new beginnings the Odysseus, Adam, and Crusoe-Friday figures are drawn together, throwing a complex of perspectives on the Caribbean situation.

Adam as lover and *poiet,* Odysseus as sea-farer and fisherman-hero, Crusoe as castaway and namer, and Friday as adaptor, exemplify the primary nature of Walcott's mythic figures who face the isolations of love and culture but who, like the old sailor, can grin at "nothing." And in doing so this consciousness appears to fuse with the poet's as this nothing is transformed into a beautiful and vibrant world (**"Nearing La Guaira"**). But the world through which his Adam-Odysseus-Crusoe figure moves is stricken with "the old original curse" (**"A Careful Passion,"** *IAGN,* p. 43), and they are continually reminded that it is their destiny to wander isolated and alone.

Walcott's local figures are important, but what they stand for must not be seen as exclusive.[15] To the poet, the simple "washing faiths" (**"Elegy,"** p. 13) of his father could not be held, nor could he share the divine Mary with the fishermen. But while he does not deny faith, it is a part of his concept of life and art; his access to the infinite must be through his art and, in *Another Life,* his faith is at once more intellectual and elemental than any he gives us in the earlier poetry. In the long poem there is a profound sense of relationship between the poet and his universe; it is explored through his psychic and physical interactions with his place. His growth is seen both in terms of his search for love and beauty, and his understanding of the light that illuminates Gregorias "within that moment where he died" (*AL,* p. 131), or that expansiveness of mind which can image Harry Simmons in terms of what is elemental in life (*AL,* pp. 132-134). His delight is to "have shared":

> I was struck like rock, and I opened
> to His gift!
> I laughed at my death-grasp in the rattle
> of the sea-shoal.
> You want to see my medals? Ask the stars.
> You want to hear my history? Ask the sea.
> And you, master and friend,
> forgive me!

(*AL,* p. 140)

Hence, while isolation may lead to the abject futility of Hope's castaway masturbating on the beach, it may lead also to the rich

Pleasures of an old man:
Morning: contemplative evacuation, considering
The dried leaf, nature's plan.

("**The Castaway,**" *The Castaway,* p. 9)

In his solitude he reaches to the mystery of "nature's plan," confronts his own humanity—"We end in earth, from earth began. / In our own entrails genesis"—and comprehends, in humility and joy, his place in the order of things.

> If I listen I can hear the polyp build,
> The silence thwanged by two waves of the sea.
> Cracking a sea-louse, I make thunder split.
> Godlike, annihilating godhead, art
> And self, I abandon
> Dead metaphors

to celebrate, as Curnow has it, "birth smell, death smell."

In moving from the Old to the New World, Walcott's Crusoe undergoes a sea-change; he becomes West Indian man, and a type for all castaways. And into this figure are to be read the poets, artists, lovers, fishermen, and all those isolated souls who populate Walcott's world but who share one common characteristic: their isolation offers the possibility, if never the certainty, of access into vision. As we suggested in speaking of Hope's sense of isolation, built into it is the possibility of union for those who can extend themselves in love and joy. Such a union may be with the external world, the self, or other individuals. But, conversely, as Klein suggests by means of his "poet," the insight which develops out of being isolated may further isolate the artist from society. At the conclusion of "**Crusoe Island**" (*The Castaway,* p. 54), the poet cannot share in "the bell's / Transfiguring tongue" like "Friday's progeny"; rooted to man and his environment, he says, "I have lost sight of hell, / of heaven," and, as "second Adam" having built "His Eden" upon his island, he must make his poetry of his time and place. Like Curnow he wants his fictions to extend his vision of reality, hoping that any access to the truths of myth will reclaim vestiges of memory that will restore life to his islands and make sense of his time. His prayer is that this world, which is nothing and everything, will make

> . . . the mind
> Catch fire till it cleaves
> Its mould of clay at last.

The thought here looks back to "**The Harbour,**" where the fishermen resist the easy rescue from thought, and forward, through sense and verbal echo, to "**At Last**" (*SG,* [*Sea Grapes*] p. 77), where Walcott's world "flashes with living / silver." The source of the imagery derives, however, from the Bible.

As is the case with the other poets in this study Walcott's New World is rich in ambiguity: its "green" may be "a rotting lime" or it may be "a green breath / Rebuilding . . . love" ("**A City's Death by Fire,**" *IAGN,* p. 14), just as for the West Indian the promise which the Old World saw in the new is negated by the horrors of the Middle Passage. And yet, out of being cast away, the New World Crusoe-Adam

> . . . appraises
> objects surely, even the bare necessities
>     of style are turned to use,
> like those plain iron tools he salvages
>     from shipwreck, hewing a prose
> as odorous as raw wood to the adze,
>     out of such timbers
> came our first book, our profane Genesis
>     whose Adam speaks that prose
> which, blessing some sea-rock, startles itself
>     with poetry's surprise,
> in a green world, one without metaphors.

("**Crusoe's Journal,**" *The Castaway,* p. 51)

The "good Fridays," picking up Crusoe's tools, at first "parrot" his "style and voice," but then they "make his language [theirs]," and out of isolation, having gone through that "longing" for companionship, they can cry

> at last, "O happy desert!"
> and learn[-] again the self-creating peace
>     of islands.

The affirmation of these lines stands in explicit juxtaposition to the poem's epigraph[16] and suggests a further stage in fitting the self to the landscape. The compassion of this sentiment is in contrast to that blinkered vision of the island mentality which can conceive of no world outside.

The islanders transform Crusoe's language and his traditions to their own ends. It is a new and confident Friday, facing the sea and making a virtue of necessity, who now says:

> . . . so from this house
> that faces nothing but the sea, his journals
>     assume a household use,
> We learn to shape from them, where nothing was,
>     the language of a race . . .

("**Crusoe's Journal**")

With this new language they will name and place their world; and the gift of language, like the rare whale or the now invisible God of "**The Whale, His Bulwark**" (*The Castaway,* p. 21), may offer access to the great design, to the mysterious and unfathomable. Of a rumor that a whale once foundered "up the Grenadines," the poet says

> . . . when I was small
> God and a foundered whale were possible.
> Whales are rarer, God is invisible.
> Yet through His gift, I praise the unfathomable,
> Though the boy may be dead, the praise unfashion-
>     able,
> The tale apocryphal.

These fictions are to be contrasted with the "lies" of the politicians in "**The Lost Federation,**" and their unimaginative mimicry of "Whitehall" in "**Parades, Parades**" (*SG,* pp. 19, 21). For, whereas the former attempt to make sense of reality and lead toward an expansion of consciousness, the latter, he suggests, falsify the reality, and extinguish vision. In *Dream on Monkey Mountain,* Walcott contends that what would deliver the New World Negro from servitude was the forging of a language that went beyond mimicry, a dialect which had the force of revelation as it invented names for things, one which finally settled on its own mode of inflection, and which began to create an oral culture of chants, jokes, folk songs and fables; this, not merely the debt of history was his proper claim to the New World.

(p. 17)

And in **"Names"** (*SG,* p. 32), Walcott celebrates the adaptation; for gradually "the names held" and began to acquire their "natural inflections."

> These palms are greater than Versailles,
> for no man made them,
> their fallen columns greater than Castille,
> no man unmade them
> except the worm, who has no helmet,
> but was always the emperor,
> and children, look at those stars
> over Valencia's forest!

It is in *The Castaway* and *The Gulf* that Walcott most consciously picks up the New World myth and turns it over in his mind. As we have suggested he looks at it *per medium* of the American Dream, and, like Allen Curnow, he executes a defoliation of the myth. What he is seeking is a more comprehensive reading of the myth than that contained in the "Dream" and, by drawing on past and contemporary history of the United States, he outlines some of the ambiguities and contradictions which should be included in any analysis of the New World. The ideals of freedom, innocence, and equality are linked with the alienation betrayal, and guilt of his "American" poems: the cry at the opening of **"Elegy"** (*The Gulf,* p. 63) is: "we miss you, Liberty." No less than the Caribbean, Walcott suggests in **"Elegy,"** the American Dream has been fraught with ambiguity and contradiction from the outset, and the consequences of these ambiguities carry forward into the present.

> . . . Che's
> bullet-riddled body falls,
> and those who cried the Republic must first die
> to be reborn are dead,
> the freeborn citizen's ballot in the head. . . .
> Some splintered arrowhead lodged in her brain
> sets the black singer howling in his bear trap . . .
> and the cherry orchard's surf
> blinds Washington and whispers
> to the assassin in his furnished room
> of an ideal America, whose flickering screens
> show, in slow herds, the ghost of the Cheyennes
> scuffling across the staked and wired plains
> with whispering, rag-bound feet,
> while the farm couple framed in their Gothic door
> like Calvin's saints, waspish, pragmatic, poor,
> gripping the devil's pitchfork
> stare rigidly toward the immortal wheat.

As the allusions to Eliot, Chekhov, and Traherne in the long third verse paragraph suggest, out of death or corruption may come rebirth or a new innocence, and this elegy

to the United States is thematically linked to **"Veranda"** and **"Ruins of a Great House"** by this recognition.[17] Walcott will not deny the past but, as he says in "Culture or Mimicry?" as a poet he is "afflicted with the superior stupidity which believes that societies can be renewed," and out of the corruption of the New World ideal may flower new promise. Any vision of a renewed world, for Walcott, must come out of the ruins of the old. This is a densely packed poem, words carrying multiple meanings and pointing to the paradox and irony which underlies it, as, in the ambience of the poem, it gains in resonance by virtue of its richness of language, its allusions, and its thematic relationship to the entire *oeuvre*. **"Elegy"** is, then, one further view of a broad cultural and spiritual decay of which Walcott, because of the accidents of history, is inextricably a part, and yet which acts as a catalyst to his quest for the meaning of the New World experience. In his moral indignation, like Eliot and Chekhov in theirs, he senses the loneliness of his search for value.

Balancing this malaise are Walcott's folk of integrity, his "lovely inheritors" of a "fallen" world (**"Veranda,"** *The Castaway,* p. 38), who endure and

> . . . stretch a darkening hand to greet those friends
> who share . . . the last inheritance
> of earth . . .

Around them Walcott weaves his fictions, and the insights which flow through them are rooted in the realities of the physical world. Walcott's vision is built on differences, evil, and negation, but as his celebrations of integrity, of the complexity of being, and of the richness of his environment suggest, out of the contradictions of existence vision is born.

Walcott draws on Greek and Christian myths and the Western literary tradition, while the rhythms of his language—its music and its beat—reach back into his folk heritage that derives ultimately from Africa.[18] As he says of his "schizophrenia": "I have one tradition inside me going in one way, and another going another. The mimetic, the narrative, and dance element is strong on one side, and the literary, the classic tradition is strong on the other" ("Meanings," p. 48). In another essay, speaking of his duality and a general West Indian psyche, he says "our bodies think in one language and move in another" (*Dream on Monkey Mountain,* p. 31), while, earlier in the same essay, he explains that in his "simple schizophrenic boyhood one could lead two lives. The interior life of poetry, the outward life of action and dialect" (p. 4). Both heritages put him into contact with what Harris calls "dark energies,"[19] beyond consciousness; it is "a fusion of formalism with exuberance, a delight in both the precision and power of language, . . . [and] a panache about life that is particularly ours" ("Meanings," p. 51). Out of this synthesis evolve fictions which often aspire toward the surface clarity of prose while retaining the compactness and fused energy of poetry that seems more readily to lead toward the incandescence of myth.

In this poetry we rarely lose sight of the physical being, since it is through his experience of the external world that we see the mind in action: now studying the minute, now dilating to infinity, seeking always to hold, as the metaphysical did, a simultaneity of vision in one image, in one idea. That he can do this, is due perhaps to his breadth of soul, to "the comprehending heart" (**"In A Green Night,"** *IAGN,* p. 73), which knows the need to "make us see the forgotten price of man" (**"Elegy,"** *IAGN,* p. 13). Walcott's poetry, then, as Owen Barfield says of all poetry, "exists . . . not by affirming but by actually experiencing, however slightly, the ultimate homogeneity of world and mind."[20] We sense that the poet, like the actor, must go through "the anguish of self-creation." To do so, the imagination must glimpse once again what is most essential to being, naming its universe by inclusion and not by exclusion; by embracing the dualities and attempting to ensphere all (see *Dream on Monkey Mountain,* pp. 25-26). And it is through imagery and metaphor that this interaction is recorded.

Metaphor provides Walcott with a means of incorporating both inner and outer reality in vision; as we have noted it functions as a means of embodying relationship. Near the end of *Another Life,* he writes:

> I lolled in the shallows like an ageing hammerhead
> afraid of my own shadow, hungering there.
> When my foot struck sand, the sky rang,
> as I inhaled, a million leaves drew inward.
> I bent towards what I remembered,
> all was inevitable shrunken,
> it was I who first extended my hand
> to nameless arthritic twigs,
> and a bush would turn in the wind
> with a toothless giggle, and
> certain roots refused English.
> But I was the one in awe.

(*AL,* p. 149.)

As they do for Curnow, imagery and metaphor contribute to the immediacy of Walcott's poetry, and, as Baugh says, to its "concentratedness,"[21] giving cohesion to individual works and a unity to the canon. Metaphor leads always toward myth and in this poetry we sense it organically coalescing and fusing, and shaping our vision. The repetitive pattern of image and metaphor in *Another Life* works toward the unity of mind and matter; it suggests that life is rooted in primordial nature, having memory-links with the mythic and the essential.[22] This primal world becomes Walcott's *locus,* that "buried original form of society, now concealed under the historical layers of civilisation,"[23] out of which he draws, through his creative imagination, what is eternal and essential to mankind. It is this "vision of consciousness," expanding through time and space, which in the end informs *Another Life,* and that underlies the explorations of the previous volumes.

The resonances of this search into a collective unconscious stand as a bulwark to the ever-present fear of fragmentation and alienation that is a central concern of the poetry.

The search hinges on two factors elemental to man: faith and art. Both of these are dependent upon the creative imagination and both are rooted in the world of actualities while offering access to a world of the pure essences of love, truth and beauty. To deny, however, the place of hatred, evil, and ugliness, is to exclude a vital aspect of any such inward search, and the tension between these essences is the stuff of Walcott's poetry. It is, further, a journey of exploration which is ever a beginning; as another West Indian poet says of their search for identity: "To conclude with / There is no conclusion."[24] This is an eternal quest by the mind, for we feel that in the paradoxes and ambiguities which are central to Walcott's whole mode of procedure, to arrive at a solution is to face dissolution.

Although we are drawn to details of time and place from the opening lines of *Another Life,* there is an almost simultaneous contraction and dilation of the temporal and the spatial spheres of the poem. The achieved effect of this is to make of one time, all time, and of one place an archetype for all places. It is as if the seeming temporal and spatial life of the poem is unlimited; that the life being dealt with is a mask for all life; that any place is one with infinite space; and that Walcott's recognized concern for history is being transformed into an ongoing and inclusive fiction, and that through the repeated naming of his place and people his fictions are reaching toward the mythic, making them, as Browning has it, "eternity's concern." The medium for this expansion in time and space is language, and the source of this language is, of course, the creative imagination.

*Another Life* opens at a specific moment in the life of the poet, that moment of the poem's inception—"I begin here." It is twilight.[25] And the twilight becomes a metaphor not only for the end of the day, but for the decline of the British Empire. This moment in personal and social history is further seen in terms of the timeless dimension of the eternal setting of suns and the motion of the ocean: it becomes a timeless moment. Attention is drawn to the eternal context by the rhetorical pattern: "I begin . . . begin . . . Begin" (in lines 4, 5, and 8), and by the placement and rhyming of "again." He will begin until "the moon's filaments wane" (*AL,* p. 3). The figure in the landscape, gazing out at the sea from his prospect, becomes subsumed into the cosmic dimensions of the scene, as sky joins sea, and the moon and sea become the measures of time.[26] Spatially we follow the poet's eye from the vantage point to the sea, to the horizon, to the vast sky filling with an amber light.[27] The sea has both a material presence, and is "a book left open by an absent master." By a fusion of connotations—sea/book/imagination/poet—the poet becomes as one with the sea just as he becomes absorbed into the light: he is simultaneously both a speck in, and center of, the universe. Despite the vast space by which he is enveloped there is no loss of his own sense of being which he endeavors to integrate with the external world into, what Harris calls, "a vision of Consciousness."[28] The heaven seemed the "glaze of another life" (*AL,* p. 3), and the twilight, almost physically, "drew a girl's figure to the open door . . . with a single stroke" (*AL,* p. 4).[29]

We move repeatedly from the figure, or from the village, out into boundless time and space and back again; now embracing a part, now spanning a whole. In the silhouette of twilight (*AL,* pp. 3-4), the poet sketches the girl's figure at the open door and as he lifts his head he glimpses details of the Hotel, Government House, the shacks on the mountain side, and, gazing until the "vision died," the "black hills simplified / to humps of coal." This spatial extension then brings the focus back to the girl whose hair becomes a vehicle for a reference to time. It is as though she too has become subsumed into the whole meaning of twilight. In the next verse-paragraph there is a similar opening out of scene—hill/sea/moon—but by the use of "burned," "foil," and "ballooned," the vastness of the scene is contained, until the moon whitewashes all below her and the entire landscape is shrunken to a miniature. At the same time, however, through a careful attention to detail, the integrity of each object is retained (even to the "earringed portrait: Albertina," *AL,* p. 5), giving a sense of order and relation between place and the vast cosmos.

Walcott's natural impulse is similar to that which Coleridge pleaded for the transcendental philosopher:

> Grant me a nature having two contrary forces, the one which tends to expand infinitely, while the other strives to apprehend or find itself in this infinity, and I will cause the world of intelligences with the whole system of their representatives to rise up before you.[30]

Out of sheer necessity to hold the many dualities of his own personal and communal, aesthetic, religious, and historic genesis in balance, Walcott struggles to retain the essence of the components which constitute these dualities. At the same time, in the Coleridgean sense, he seeks to "dissolve, diffuse, dissipate" the boundaries in order to recreate, or to "idealize and to unify" (*BL,* p. 167). The necessity to discover imaginatively himself and his people becomes the virtue which can liberate them all "to walk calm, renewed, [if] exhausted" (*AL,* p. 142). Out of this comes Walcott's balance, his poise and compassion. The renewal which the poet envisages is, like that expressed by Wallace Stevens, "a renewal of earth," not a "surrender to heaven."

Edward Baugh suggests that *Another Life* is similar "in kind" to Wordsworth's *The Prelude* and Joyce's *Portrait:*[31] it traces the growth of an artist's mind and it conveys a picture of man "'pledged to life,'" encountering reality and bent on forging in his soul "'the uncreated conscience of [a] race.'" It deals with various "spots of time" in the growth of the poet's mind from early childhood to the virtual "now" of the poem's completion in April 1972. And while there is a high degree of verifiable fact and detail in the poem (more so than *The Prelude,* as Baugh points out), through reverberations and repetitions of image, metaphor, event, and character it overleaps fixed time and place to touch what is elemental. Comparing *Another Life* with his earlier poems, **"Epitaph for the Young"**—a "sort of Urtext"—Walcott says he has "re-essentialised it, given it more of an essence in fact, made it more focal":[32]

a statement which points to the realistic and the mythic quality of the later work. Both concerns are united in Walcott's integrity for "the rightness of placed things" (*AL,* p. 15), which links a concern with the placing and naming of things to the senses and to language, and thus to the larger reality which they hold in potential. His attention to detail blended with rich metaphorical invention enables him to strike to deep layers of reality while retaining both the kind of immediacy Curnow sought and the intensity of the poetry.[33]

Through the imagination Walcott senses his unity with people and places. Of the ancient Carib Indians leaping to folly/heroism, he says:

> I leapt for the pride of that race
> at Sauteurs! An urge more than mine,
> so, see them as heroes or as the Gadarene swine.

>> (*AL,* pp. 139-140)

He projects the kind of holistic and religious mind which can find "a hermitage" in what is essential to life. The quality, he tells us, which pervades his mother, is silence: she sits "folded in silence," and in this silence "the revered, silent objects ring like glass" (*AL,* p. 11). She exudes a serenity, a rightness, a solitude; her presence has the same quality of endurance which he attributes to his Caribbean heroes. The silence of solitude is the ultimate union between the self and some other; it is an absence which holds all presences. Something of this same sense of order suffuses Anna, Harry, Gregorias, and Margaret ("For I have married one whose / darkness is a tree," *AL,* p. 140), and it rubs off on the poet, who "emerges" out of a world of explosive rhetoric, corruption, and self-aggrandizement as "out of [a] . . . mist . . . and staggers towards his lineaments" (*AL,* p. 128).[34] And in his inclusive vision of his world—one which is growing with each volume we sense—he reiterates, what earlier was implicit, the need to name his losses and despair as well as his presences and affirmations: "Pour la derniere fois, nommez! Nommez!" (p. 146). He names the evil, "Manoir . . . that dog" (p. 28); the great; and the holy:

> holy is Rampanalgas and its high-circling hawks,
> holy are the rusted, tortured, rust-caked, blind almond
>   trees,
> your great-grandfather's, and your father's torturing
>   limbs,
> holy the small, the almond-leaf-shadowed bridge
> by the small red shop, where everything smells of
>   salt,
> and holiest the break of the blue sea below the trees,
> and the rock that takes blows on its back
> and is more rock,
> and the tireless hoarse anger of the waters
> by which I can walk calm, a renewed, exhausted man,
> balanced at its edge by the weight of two dear
>   daughters.
> Holy were you, Margaret,
> and holy our calm.

>> (*AL,* pp. 147-148)

Out of the absences and presences, like a creative wind blowing off the sea—element of islanders, emblem of the creative mind and local reminder of the Middle Passage—grows a wisdom and a visionary hope of renewal which wants to "begin again": begin

> from what we have always known, nothing,
> from that carnal slime of the garden,
> from the incarnate subtlety of the snake,
> from the Egyptian moment of the heron's foot
> on the mud's entablature,
> by this augury of ibises
> flying at evening from the melting trees,
> while the silver-hammered charger of the marsh light
> brings towards us, again and again, in beaten scrolls,
> nothing, then nothing,
> and then nothing.

> (*AL,* pp. 144-145)

Out of the "amnesia" of history, out of

> . . . the untroubled ocean, the moon
> . . . swing[ing] its lantern
> and evening fold[ing] the pages of the sea

float "the lost names / of Caribs, slaves and fishermen." An essential life evolves, which reaches toward a mythic core, while trying, also, to make sense of the present.

As we read *Another Life* and turn to *Sea Grapes,* there is a deepening concern with change and with fictions that can make sense of it; but this is no new presence in the poetry. As we have suggested, central to the Adam/Odysseus/Crusoe motif is the notion of new beginnings, of transforming Old World systems into the New, and behind Walcott's preoccupation with history is the recognition that it is in continual process. It is this sense of process which characterizes Walcott's understanding of the relationship of the Caribbean to the outside world: to England, Asia, Africa, the United States. Similarly, those poems which focus on, say, England, Africa, or the United States highlight aspects of their evolution; his history is one of change, of process. To give oneself to change and transition is, however, to risk fragmentation—and we sense Curnow's precarious grasp of a language which can describe his world—and Walcott's fictions, like Hope's, are directed toward a rightness, toward the "toil that is balance" (**"To Return to the Trees,"** *SG,* p. 82). This is toward a serenity in solitude which recognizes the permanence of change and can celebrate man's achievement in merely surviving; for Walcott speaks of this survival with a profound "awe"—to use his word. In **"At Last"** (*SG,* p. 77), he sings of those of his people who have no need of fictions; who, like

> . . . the pelican beat[-]
> to the rock of the Soledad
> to a beat which is neither
> poetry nor prose.

And employing an image cluster, used also by Hope, Curnow, and Ezekiel, drawn from the visionary books of

the Old Testament, he looks forward to the flowering of his generations "from the bitterest root / and the earth that soured."[35]

As visions blossomed out of the harsh ground of an Old Testament world, so vision may find its source in this "heartbreaking past." As Walcott says, "it is not a question for us, of returning to an Eden or of creating Utopia" ("Culture or Mimicry?" 13); however, Edens are available to those who can "enter the silence" (**"Volcano,"** *SG,* p. 56), for they retain that primal "awe" which gives them contact with the fundamental rhythms of existence; this

> . . . has been lost to our time;
> so many people have seen everything,
> so many people can predict,
> so many refuse to enter the silence
> of victory, the indolence
> that burns at the core,
> so many are no more than
> erect ash, like the cigar,
> so many take thunder for granted.
> How common is the lightning,
> how lost the leviathans
> we no longer look for!

These folk stand in contrast to the unthinking and the scheming, and Walcott makes no effort to simplify his New World. He returns to the Eden archetype, but, as he says in **"For the Altarpiece of the Roseau Valley Church, Saint Lucia,"** having worked toward a vision of Eden,

> . . . okay,
> okay, not absolute Adamic silence,
> the valley of Roseau is not the Garden of Eden,
> and those who inhabit it are not in heaven.

> (*SG,* p. 46)

And his description of Dunstan St. Omar's altarpiece (which admits ambiguity into a vision of Eden) transmutes the contradictory joy and pain, beauty and ugliness, into a vibrant fiction of "the folk" of St. Lucia. The "massive altarpiece, / like a dull mirror" catches the "rich valley," the "cursed valley," the natural beauty and the broken animals and people. But it is also in Eden, he suggests in **"The Brother"** (*SG,* p. 15), where the "serpent . . . sleeps happiest," and Adam and "the snake"—colonizer and entrepreneur—

> . . . share

> the loss of Eden for a profit.
> So both made the New World. And it looked good.

> (**"New World,"** *SG,* p. 12)

The opening poems of *Sea Grapes*—**"The Virgins," "Fredericksted Nights," "Fredericksted, Dusk," "Sunday Lemons,"** and the **"Eden"** poems—constitute a powerful lament for those of his people who are "lost to the American Dream" (**"The Virgins,"** *SG,* p. 4). Instead of finding the essential truth at the bottom of the myth, the fictions they follow are false, and the poet, like Joshua, cries for his tribe following a formula of **"Economics and Exodus"** that will lead to a spiritual imprisonment bearing the burden of "no vision, no flame, / no deepness, no danger . . ."

But in spite of his harangue, or perhaps because of it, he believes that the American archipelago can be renewed ("Culture or Mimicry?" 13). And throughout *Sea Grapes* there is a deep sense of awe and a humble affirmation of his people who have survived. So that in **"Natural History II,"** he writes, picking up the moon as image of change,

> . . . History
> is natural—famine, genocide,
> as natural as moonlight—
> and man is great who rises at this cost.
>
> (p. 30)

We witness an understanding and acceptance of placed things, of the larger design, of "balance," but this is not easily won, and when it is attained it is a matter of "Hold hard then heart. This way at least you live" (**"The Fist,"** p. 65). But the pain of loving self, some other, or country, leads to a sense of living (see also **"Love after Love"**). What emerges is a kind of primitive affinity between the mind of the poet and the essential rhythms of the universe: it amounts to an acceptance but not a submission to life's process, and "out of what is lost grows something stronger / that has the rational radiance of stone" (**"Sea Canes,"** p. 70).[36]

It is as though, as he probes the mystery of being, he would move to the other side of language, to where "the silence is all." Such a silence "is deeper than the readiness"; the readiness may be articulated and suggests a choice, a logical awareness of preparedness, while the other is a felt awareness unconsciously learned, but ultimately beyond reason. It stems from a felt communion between the self and his world. With this knowledge, in which man becomes one with the world, where his sense of "home" is a mental and emotional awareness, man "can never be dispossessed."

Out of the stasis and negation which he sees around him grows a sense of movement and creative change, and he traces his odyssey through hatred, indifference, to affirmation, making of the fiction that he weaves around this journey and around his society a vision which occasionally rises to the clarity of the mythic. The temporal and particular are transformed into a seemingly eternal world:

> That child who puts the shell's bowl to his ear,
> hears nothing, hears everything
> that the historian cannot hear, the howls
> of all the races that crossed the water,
> the howls of grandfathers drowned
> in the intricately swivelled Babel,
> hears the fellaheen, the Madrasi, the Mandingo, the
>    Ashanti.
>
> (*AL*, p. 143)

If the sea is "a book left open," it is to be read, and the story which evolves from Walcott's vast ocean is a comprehensive and continuing fiction of the place of his people in some larger order. Personal and national history, then, becomes an emotive fiction of process, and Walcott draws a line from Homer's Odysseus to Joyce's Ulysses and Hemingway's "old man," through Virgil, Dante, Marvell, Cowper, Chekhov, Conrad, and Eliot, who seek to make sense of the larger reality through a dedication to language.

**"Sea Grapes"** opens with the Odysseus-figure "beating up the Caribbean," thus linking this volume with all that has gone before, but the fictional use of Odysseus is made explicit. This "could be Odysseus," but equally it could be any other wanderer caught in the "ancient war / between obsession and responsibility," the solution to which is irresolvable—"will never finish and has been the same . . . since Troy sighed its last flame"—but it must continually be faced. And the poet says: "The classics can console. But not enough." As the allusions to both **"Prelude"** and **"The Banyan Tree, Old Year's Night"** (both from his first major volume) suggest, it is up to the individual to find a way in this eternal quest, making and discarding fictions, seeking what will suffice. Man must make his own fictions of consolation, or find new relevance in the old. This is not a repudiation of the "classics," for, as he insists in **"Volcano"** (*SG*, p. 56), man must be open to the "masterpieces," not expecting to find solutions in them but a continuing relevance and wonder: as Klein has it, they are to point directions; they do not pose destinations.

The theme of change unifies the three poems which make up the short sequence **"Natural History"** (pp. 28-31). The walking fish adapts from one medium to another as, in an impressionistic synthesis of history, fish turn to vertebrate, mastodon's atrophy, and the pterodactyl shrinks to a bat, and, suggesting an erosion of imagination, "Dragons no longer fly." But as the fish endures through time, waiting his "geological epoch" and changing and adapting to his continually new world, it becomes associated with the poet who, likewise, can at last

> . . . name
> this foothold, with a grateful croak
> earth. I can arch my back.

He "can squat . . . Lurch up. . . . Up . . . walk," aware that

> everything has changed
> or has changed us.
> Or, as I
> paddle this air, breathe this new sun, am I
> still swimming through one gigantic eye?

As is the case with **"Force"** (p. 73), even as the poet tries to understand what he intuits or reasons, the fiction leads ultimately toward the poet's awe at the mystery of evolution.

In **"Names"** (p. 32), Walcott suggests that change is a component of his people; it is part of being a transplanted people who began "with a different fix on the stars." All they had to shape their lives, as the sky, sea, and history "foreclosed / with nothing in [their] hands," was

> . . . this stick
> to trace [their] names on the sand
> which the sea erased again, to [their] indifference.

And, as he suggests in the **"Crusoe"** poems, they named their worlds. Was it out of "nostalgia or irony?" he asks in **"Names."** However, in time, "the names held" and the developing consciousness transformed language to their own needs.

The more Walcott struggles to make sense of his world, the more he ponders it; and the better his tools, the more, it seems, he is conscious of "something always being missed / between the floating shadow and the pelican" (**"The Village,"** p. 35). Reality seems continually to be shifting, but by exerting his imagination on his village, objects, and people, he strives to find more precise ways of expressing it and of drawing out its essential quality. He arrives at a position where belief is possible, but never certain:

> so that, from time to time, on Sundays
> between adorations, one might see,
> if one were there, and not there,
> looking in at the windows
> the real faces of angels.

> (**"For the Altarpiece of the Roseau Valley Church, St. Lucia,"** p. 46)

Nevertheless, the poet's relationship to his world is always in process: "we shed freight," he says, "but not our need / for encumbrances," and feeling and poetry must be unlearned so that "true feeling" and truer poetry can endure. Such a survival may be beyond language,

> beyond joy,
> beyond lyrical utterance
> this obdurate almond
> going under the sand
> with this language, slowly,
> by sand grains, by centuries.

Walcott's fictions lead ultimately toward this kind of elemental understanding of reality; it is an annihilation—the journey back to the ape—in which "the voice must grovel in search of itself until gestures and sound fuse and the blaze of their flesh astonishes them" (*Dream on Monkey Mountain*, p. 5). But the journey he enacts, the journey into silence, into solitude, is in the end into the reality of myth, and out of it grows the wisdom and compassion which is humanity's right.

* * *

When we look at the major volumes we sense that history, or its absence, has been transformed into a body of knowledge open to the emotional intuition of value, as well as to reason. We apprehend the present and the past

as simultaneous realities and absorb the public and private worlds which have expanded to epic proportions without losing sight of the immediate realities of poverty, hardship, and pain. He has peopled the future with heroes; made of his "folk," "heraldic men" (*AL,* p. 75); and in remaking a place and a people, drawing on their ambiguities and contradictions, he has created the image of a civilization. His art grows toward myth, transcending the limits of its creator and reaching toward the limits of being.

Caribbean man is New World man, but with affinities to Adam, to Odysseus, to the vanished Caribs, to Africa, to Crusoe, to the whole imperial ethos of Britain from the seventeenth to twentieth centuries, and to the New World ethos of the Americas generally. Like Curnow, Walcott is conscious of being "not in *narrow* seas." The gulf between people has a tangible reality for islanders, for the sea defines human loneliness, and yet, while the sea may sunder, it also links, and in his loneliness man may come to terms with his humanity. For, like Hope, Walcott makes the journey into his own being and into the collective mind of his people, and the catalysts for such explorations are the accidents of history. And, as is the case with the other poets so far treated, Walcott's world finds parallels with the harsh environment of the Old Testament, the facing of which may lead to vision. His God is a harsh God who is largely absent, looking on with the indifference which Klein, in his despair, felt characterized his God. But, for both men, he was an "absent master" (*AL,* p. 3), and like the ruins left behind by that other "absent master," the Imperium, mementos remain. Both leave some positive legacies, a sense of love, a language, and vestiges of ritual which may give order and coherence to life. And Walcott draws on them.

Walcott's world, like Hope's Australia and Curnow's New Zealand, is both a paradise and a hell, and the contradictions which have accrued to Australia, to a lesser extent New Zealand and Canada, accrue to the West Indies and have transacted a powerful shaping force upon the people. With a direct affinity to Klein's Adam, naming and praising his New World, and to Ezekiel's search for a sense of "season," Walcott traces the steps which lie behind the shifts in consciousness which are prior to the attainment of that "balance" which can name the complexity and praise the hardship without a longing for a pastoral simplicity or without giving oneself to hatred. Walcott's celebrations, both of the elemental sublimity of land, sky, and water, and of the stifling sense of decay and nothingness which may lead toward a capitulation to the spiritual atrophy of *nada,* assume to the proportions of myth, and his castaway is like original man cast out of Eden and facing a hostile world with imperfect tools.

But Walcott's Adam-Crusoe, who brought a language and a style to the Caribbean and to the good Fridays, like some Promethean fire, now serves as a paradigm for universal man facing his destiny. The fragmentation of the Caribbean islands, its sense of history-in-transition, its continual process of growth and decay through time, stands as a type for an ever fragmenting world, as the great monolithic societies of the past, from whom Australia, Canada, New Zealand, and the Caribbean were spawned, break up; and individual man faces the isolation and cosmic loneliness of Walcott's figures on the beach. But out of this loneliness, the poets of this study suggest, may come wisdom and faith, and a stay against a submission to a seemingly hostile and chaotic world. For, by making fictions which strive to make sense of reality out of their very act of naming the presences and absences of society, and out of their variations on particular themes, the poet rises toward the mythic and he gives to the mundane and the ordinary an illumination: and "where that moment is made radiant, epiphany happens."[37]

In a world which is confronted with the permanence of change, in which social, cultural, and religious values have withered, Walcott asserts that history must be taught as either morality, in which case it "is religion," or as action, in which case it "is art" ("Culture or Mimicry?" 13). And to treat their respective histories, the poets in this study have sought a style and a language which can make sense of this reality; to each of them it is idiosyncratic, personal, and creative, like their reading of their people and place in time, but in each case, as Walcott says, it is "beyond mimicry."

> The stripped and naked man, however abused, however disabused of old beliefs, instinctively, even desperately begins again as craftsman. In the indication of the slightest necessary gesture of ordering the world around him, of losing his old name and rechristening himself, in the arduous enunciation of a dimmed alphabet, in the shaping of tools, pen or spade, is the whole, profound sigh of human optimism, of what we in the archipelago still believe in: work and hope. It is out of this that the New World, or the Third World, should begin.
>
> ("Culture or Mimicry?" 13)

### Notes

1. Robert D. Hamner, "Conversation with Derek Walcott," *WLWE,* [*World Literature Written in English*] 16, ii (1977), 417. Recorded in 1975.

2. *Ibid.,* 415-416. See also, "Culture or Mimicry?" 4: "Many of us in the Caribbean still hold the ideal of the archipelago, just as you here [his audience in Miami] hold to the metaphor named America. If I speak in the tone of metaphor among men who are more practical in their approach to problems, it is because I do not think that as men of the Americas, we are different. Our society may be less complex. It is obviously powerless. What I hope to explore is that society's validity, its reality."

3. This returns to the question of the relationship between poetry and history, and draws on the distinction which governs Aristotle's *Poetics,* Chapter Nine: "poetry refers to a possible and history to an actual order of things." But Walcott's position seems to

have some affinity to Wordsworth's statement in a note to "The Thorn": "Poetry is passion: it is the history or science of feelings." We think of Walcott's "history of emotion" and his *AL* which, he has said, was an attempt to write a "spiritual history of his region," or to capture the "intelligence" of the West Indian (see *Dream on Monkey Mountain,* p. 6; Baugh, "The Poem as Autobiographical Novel," quoting from MS.1 of *AL;* and Hamner, "Conversation with Derek Walcott," 411). See G. G[iovanninni], "History and Poetry," *Princeton Encyclopedia of Poetry and Poetics,* pp. 348-352. It is also probable that Walcott draws on the ancient conception, given new currency by Pound, that "poetry is a record of useful and memorable things" ("History and Poetry," p. 349), but he uses it for ironic effect while not denying the association which poetry has with history.

4. See also, *AL,* pp. 144-146.

5. "Interior of the Novel," p. 140: "The survivors [of a history of implosion]—a long and precarious line extending into the twentieth century—possess all the symptoms of 'historylessness,' rootlessness— stigmata of the void."

6. *loc. cit.*

7. See also, Gerald Moore, *The Chosen Tongue,* p. 21.

8. *AL,* p. 47. Walcott quotes from Alejo Carpentier's *The Lost Steps.*

9. *London Magazine,* February 1962, 12.

10. The allusion to Donne (referred to in Chapter Two) enacts what we see as the dual motion of the poem: it opens out by means of the allusions and they become a crucial element in the experience of the poem, and it rounds back to the manor house of the poem's title.

11. The poem anticipates "Veranda" and *AL,* and there is a strong verbal echo of "To A Painter in England" (see C. King, "The Poems of Derek Walcott," *Caribbean Quarterly,* X, iii [1964], 22), while it has thematic concerns with much in the canon. See also, Wilson Harris, "Interior of the Novel," p. 145: "[The] ambivalence of gains and losses is a painful one, I agree, but to deny it expression may well be to block our immersion in a ruined fabric which may constitute a new breakthrough of a power of endurance; endurance of mystique, mystique of idols, *hubris,* self-enchantment, trickster, priest: an endurance, however, which in this context subsists upon erosions rather than concretisation of violence, which accepts the hollow ground of conquest as a new dimension, an 'immaterial' function for the antagonistic fixations of monolithic convection or tribal superstition."

12. See *Dream on Monkey Mountain,* p. 4: "If there was nothing, there was everything to be made"; "A Map of the Continent" (*The Gulf,* p. 75): "Trunks that wait for names"; and *AL,* p. 89: "And now we were

the first guests of the earth / and everything stood still for us to name"; and p. 152: "We were blest with a virginal, unpainted world / with Adam's task of giving things their names . . . with nothing so old / that it could not be invented." And see also, Edward Braithwaite's "Negus": "fill me with words / and I will blind your God." Walcott is filling the void with words, making a virtue of necessity.

13. See also, the sequence "Guyana" in *The Gulf*, pp. 71-80, in particular, "Georgetown Journal" (p. 76); and *Another Life*, pp. 75, 89-90.

14. Brown, "Caribbean Castaway," 157.

15. See Gerald Moore, *The Chosen Tongue*, p. 45, who says of the fisherman: his "love is ancient, savage and strong, [he] is master of the ocean which limits the action and imagination of his fellows. . . . He alone, it seems, escapes a mentality still deeply marked by slavery and colonialism. He alone is freed from what Walcott has called 'the search of our own sadness'. He alone does not appear marooned by time on a shore that does not yet belong to him. And he is master of the element which defines, if nothing else does, the status of the Caribbean islander."

16. Walcott quotes from *Robinson Crusoe*: "I looked now upon the world as a thing remote, which I had nothing to do with, no expectation from, and, indeed, no desires about. In a word, I had nothing indeed to do with it, nor was ever like to have; so I thought it looked as we may perhaps look upon it hereafter, viz., as a place I had lived in but was come out of it; and well might I say, as Father Abraham to Dives, 'Between me and thee is a great gulf fixed.'"

17. See Eliot's *The Waste Land*, pp. 1-3; Chekhov's *The Cherry Orchard;* and Thomas Traherne's *Centuries of Meditation*. See also, "Orient and Immortal Wheat" (*IAGN*, p. 48). See also, Brown, "Caribbean Castaway," 150-152, who draws attention to the allusions to Chekhov and Eliot.

18. See Derek Walcott's "Leaving School," *London Magazine* (September 1965), 4-15; and his "Meanings," *Savacou*, 2 (1971), 46, 48, and 51, in which he writes: ". . . our early education must have ranked with the best in the world. The grounding was rigid—Latin, Greek, and the essential masterpieces, but there was this elation of discovery. Shakespeare, Marlowe, Horace, Vergil—these writers weren't jaded by immediate experiences" (51). References to both essays will hereafter be included in the text.

19. *Tradition the Writer and Society*, p. 34.

20. *Poetic Diction*, 3rd edn. (1932; rpt. Connecticut: Wesleyan University Press, 1973), p. 225.

21. "The Poem as Autobiographical Novel," p. 13. See also, p. 14.

22. See Wilson Harris, "The Native Phenomenon," pp. 144-150, *passim*.

23. Frye, *Fables of Identity* (New York: Harcourt, Brace and World, 1963), p. 64. See also, Harris, *op. cit.*

24. Samuel Selvon, "Discovering Tropic," *CV,* [*Caribbean Voices*] II, p. 165.

25. On twilight, the hour and the mood, see Walcott's essay in *Dream on Monkey Mountain:* "[And] twilight, with the patience of alchemy, almost transmutes despair into virtue" (p. 3). See also, Wilson Harris, "The Writer and Society," *Tradition the Writer and Society,* where he says of the West Indian situation, "[W]e live in a twilight situation which half-remembers, half-forgets." (p. 64)

26. In using "gazing," which is explicitly echoed in treating similar aspects of Allen Curnow's work, we have in mind both the Coleridgean sense and Wordsworth's usage, where it is analogous in intensity to the mind "working like a sea."

27. See "Leaving School," *passim,* for the details behind the poetic rendering, or the thematic and metaphoric link with the lines from "The Castaway":

   The starved eye devours the seascape for the morsel
   Of a sail.
   The horizon threads it infinitely.
   Anchored to the beach the mind behind the isolated "eye" ("I"?)
   comprehends the infinity of the landscape.

28. *Tradition the Writer and Society,* p. 32.

29. We attend to the personification of twilight; the use of this literary device endorses the point being made here of the simultaneous presence of a visible twilight and the fusion of the human into that landscape.

30. Cited by Barfield, p. 39. We quote from the single volume, Everyman edition of the *Biographia,* p. 162.

31. "The Poem as Autobiographical Novel," p. 1.

32. Hamner, "Conversation with Derek Walcott," 411. Of the concern with detail he says: "I had a professor friend come in here and point out to me many errors of chronology, of place, of names that he had researched." Of *AL,* Walcott says, that "in a sense it is a biography of an 'intelligence,' a West Indian intelligence, using it in the Latin sense of spirit. So, the biographical chronicle is not a physical one so much. Other intelligences are in the poem."

33. Edward Baugh, in his essay "The Poem as Autobiographical Novel," explores in some depth, and to great point, the poetic and prose elements of *AL*. He links *AL* to the much earlier "Tales of the Islands" and outlines the manner in which he sees Walcott "taking poetry towards prose fiction" (pp. 9-11).

34. The rightness and order of these figures stands in contrast to the "circle of hell" he depicts as part of his "Frescoes of the New World II" (*AL*, p. 127).

35. See Isaiah, 13: 11-20.

36. Wilson Harris, "Interior of the Novel," p. 141, conceives of "an art of fiction where the agents of time begin to subsist upon the real reverses the human spirit has endured, the real chasm of pain it has entered, rather than the apparent consolation, victories and battles it has won."

37. Hamner, "Conversation with Derek Walcott," 419.

SELECTED BIBLIOGRAPHY

PRIMARY SOURCES

Walcott, Derek. "Leaving School." *London Magazine* (September 1965), 4-15.

———. "Meanings." *Savacou,* 2 (1971), 45-51.

SECONDARY SOURCES

Barfield, Owen. *Poetic Diction, a study in meaning.* 3rd edn. 1932; rpt. Middletown, Connecticut: Wesleyan University Press, 1973.

Baugh, Edward. "The Poem as Autobiographical Novel: Derek Walcott's Another Life in Relation to Wordsworth's Prelude and Joyce's Portrait." *Awakened Conscience. Studies in Commonwealth Literature.* Ed. C. D. Narasimhaiah. New Delhi: Sterling Publishers, 1978.

Brown, Lloyd. "Caribbean Castaway New World Odyssey." *The Journal of Commonwealth Literature,* XI, ii (1976), 149-159.

Figueroa, John, ed. *Caribbean Voices.* 2 vols. London: Evans Brothers, 1970.

Hamner, Robert. "Conversations with Derek Walcott." *World Literature Written in English,* 16, ii (1977), 409-421.

Harris, Wilson. "Interior of the Novel: Amerindian/European/African Relations." *National Identity.* Ed. K. L. Goodwin. London and Melbourne: Heinemann, 1970.

———. *Tradition the Writer and Society. Critical Essays.* London and Port of Spain, Trinidad: New Beacon Publishers, 1967.

**John Thieme (essay date 1999)**

SOURCE: Thieme, John. "The Poet as Castaway." In *Derek Walcott,* pp. 77-100. Manchester: Manchester University Press, 1999.

[*In the following essay, Thieme analyzes the recurring motif of the Robinson Crusoe archetype in Walcott's poetry.*]

While Walcott's plays from *Ti-Jean and His Brothers* onwards demonstrate an increasing engagement with folk forms and community values, his poetry of the 1960s and early 1970s remains very much that of an individual, isolated observer. Such a figure is the central protagonist in his next collection, *The Castaway* (1965), where three poems, **'The Castaway'**, **'Crusoe's Journal'** and **'Crusoe's Island',** are focused on the character that gives the volume its title, while others are filtered through a persona who is also cast away in the sense that he seems to see life as an onlooker. Whether in the Caribbean:

> In our treacherous
> seasonless climate's
> dry heat or muggy heat or rain
> I'm measuring winter by this November sun's
> diagonals shafting the window pane . . .
>
> (**'November Sun'**)[1]

or in North America:

> Through the wide, grey loft window,
> I watched that winter morning, my first snow
> crusting the sill, puzzle the black,
> nuzzling tom.
>
> (**'A Village Life'**, *Castaway,* 16)

this figure repeatedly appears as a man alone in a room, looking at the world through a window. The emphasis on perception frequently leads to reflections on themes that had dominated Walcott's earlier work. Shafts of Caribbean sunlight and American snowfalls both bring intimations of mortality; a meditation on *Othello* (in **'Goats and Monkeys'**) rekindles the mood of racial angst and the tussle with Manichean binaries that had been so prominent in the early plays; and, while the verse now sometimes incorporates intertexts from the growing body of Caribbean literature,[2] there is the continued wrestling-match with European discourses, confirming the writer's own assessment of himself as someone who is '[s]chizophrenic, wrenched by two styles' (**'Codicil'**, *Castaway,* 61).

The use of the Crusoe figure foregrounds the struggle to construct a tradition. Along with texts such as *The Tempest* and *Heart of Darkness, Robinson Crusoe* is one of a group of canonical English texts which deal with colonialism explicitly and in a Caribbean context the decision to take such texts as departure-points inevitably raises expectations that the resultant 'counter-discourse' will contest the hegemonic authority of the English master-narratives that provide its supposed sources. One might therefore expect a Caribbean reworking of Defoe's archetypal imperialist to adopt an adversarial response, but predictably perhaps Walcott's Crusoe proves to be far more complex. In a talk he gave on 'The Figure of Crusoe' in 1965, Walcott offered a reading of the character in which he is simultaneously Adam, Columbus, God, Ben Gunn, Prospero, a missionary who instructs Friday and a beachcomber from Conrad, Stevenson or Marryat;[3] and ultimately his Crusoe is Proteus, constantly changing his shape to a point where he is as much Caliban as Prospero, as much Friday as Defoe's prototypical colonizer, as much 'the distorted, surrealist Crusoe of Bunuel'[4] as that of Defoe. In the talk, the figure of Crusoe emerges as both a Caribbean Everyman and more specifically as a type of the Caribbean writer, constructing a discursive universe from an apparent vacuum, and the shipwrecked protagonists of *The Castaway,* particularly '**Crusoe's Journal**', are very similar in conception. '**Crusoe's Journal**' also takes the view that 'All shapes, all objects multiplied from his, / our ocean's Proteus (*Castaway,* 51). So, instead of contrasting or inverting the assumed hierarchies of the colonial text, Walcott creates a multiplicity of Crusoes who collectively dismantle the very idea of hierarchical positioning.

In '**Crusoe's Journal**' Walcott begins by stressing the pragmatism of Defoe's text:

> even the bare necessities
> of style are turned to use,
> like those plain tools he salvages
> from shipwreck, hewing a prose
> as odorous as raw wood to the adze.

> (*Castaway,* 51)

Defoe and Crusoe are, then, seen as giving practical expression to 'Adam's task of giving things their names',[5] the role which Walcott had taken upon himself as an artist committed to making the St. Lucian landscape possible. Walcott also identified with the plain carpentry of Defoe's prose style for another reason. Talking about the influence of his Methodist upbringing in a 1986 interview, he says:

> Decency and understanding are what I've learned from being a Methodist. Always, one was responsible to God for one's inner conduct and not to any immense hierarchy of angels and saints. In a way I think I tried to say that in some earlier poems. There's also a very strong sense of carpentry in Protestantism, in making things simply and in a utilitarian way.[6]

Elsewhere in the same interview, he talks of 'the metaphor of the shipwreck' as '[o]ne of the more positive aspects of the Crusoe idea', saying that because all the races that have come to the region have 'been brought here under situations of servitude or rejection . . . you look around you and you have to make your own tools',[7] a view which suggests the relevance of Defoe's Protestant ethic in Caribbean contexts.

As '**Crusoe's Journal**' continues, irony is directed at the castaway figure when he is seen as a Columbus turning 'savages' into 'good Fridays', 'converted cannibals [who] learn with him to eat the flesh of Christ' (*Castaway,* 51), but this is only temporary and the poem subsequently returns to the trope of the artist as castaway, using the model of Crusoe's journals to create from a vacuum: 'We learn to shape from them, where nothing was / The language of a race' (*Castaway,* 52). So what might seem to be a private solipsistic vision comes to assume a communal significance.

In the other poems in the collection that focus explicitly on the figure of the castaway, the emphasis is more on the marooned predicament of the Caribbean artist. In '**The Castaway**' his 'starved eye devours the seascape for the morsel / Of a sail' (*Castaway,* 9). In '**Crusoe's Island**' he is a fallen Adam, '[c]razed' by the 'paradisal calm' (*Castaway,* 55) of his solitary situation, who seems to despair as he reflects on his inability to return to the purity of his youth or to produce a transfigurative art which will bless the local world, here personified by black girls on a Tobago beach.

'**The Almond Trees**' uses the image of women on a Caribbean beach in a more sustained way to provide commentary on the evolution of the region's culture and society. The poem opens with an allusion to Naipaul's *Middle Passage* comment on Caribbean history, 'History is built around achievement and creation and nothing was created in the West Indies',[8] which makes it clear that history is the subject of the poem:

> There's nothing here
> this early;
> cold sand
> cold churning ocean, the Atlantic,
> no visible history,
>
> except this stand
> of twisted, coppery sea-almond trees.

> (*Castaway,* 36)

The trees, then, are the Caribbean alternative to history. As the poem proceeds, they are likened to 'brown daphnes' sunbathing on 'this further shore of Africa' (*Castaway,* 36), personification which draws on Greek myths of woodnymphs and more specifically the legend that Daphne, pursued by Apollo, was turned into a tree. If the women initially seem to be tourists 'toasting their flesh' in 'fierce, acetylene air' which will 'sear a pale skin copper' (*Castaway,* 36-7), as the poem progresses it becomes clear that something else is intended. The 'Almond Trees' charts the movement of Caribbean society since colonization, suggesting that a gradual darkening process has taken place. Trees and women endure a furnace which seems to be the crucible of Caribbean history. Divested of identity by the experience of the Middle Passage and slavery, the women have had 'Greek or Roman tags', slave names analogous to the Latin botanical names used for trees conferred on them, but have nevertheless become '[w]elded in one flame' (*Castaway,* 37). The suggestion is that through suffering, and *pace* Naipaul, the traumas of the Middle Passage and slavery have been transformed into a history of endurance and cultural pride. Walcott does not here, as in 'The Muse of History', wipe the cultural slate clean. Instead he suggests a coming to terms with Caribbean history, which once again will obliterate hurt:

> One sunburnt body now acknowledges
> that past and its own metamorphosis
> as, moving from the sun, she kneels to spread
> her wrap within the bent arms of this grove
> that grieves in silence, like parental love.

> (*Castaway,* 37)

Other poems in *The Castaway* also survey the Caribbean past from a present vantage point. In '**Laventville**', the view is from the hill on the east side of Port of Spain,[9] where the city's poorer districts are located. The poet looks down 'on the hot, corrugated iron sea / whose horrors we all / shared' (*Castaway,* 33) and reflects that little has changed in the situation of 'the inheritors of the middle passage', who now find themselves 'stewed / five to a room, still clamped below their hatch, / breeding like felonies' (*Castaway,* 32). Despite having been 'rescued from original sin' (*Castaway,* 34) by Christianity, they remain typical Walcott protagonists in that they are caught between worlds: 'We left / somewhere a life we never found' (*Castaway,* 35). In **'Veranda'** Walcott turns to the opposite end of the Caribbean social spectrum for the vantage point, for a poem about the end of Empire[10] which provides an interesting companion-piece to **'Ruins of a Great House'.** As in the earlier poem and as in **'A Far Cry from Africa'**, **'Veranda'** initially adopts a critical attitude towards Empire, in this case treating its various 'grey apparitions' with punning irony rather than overt hostility:

> Colonels, hard as the commonwealth's greenheart,
> middlemen, usurers whose art
> kept an empire in the red,
>
> Upholders of Victoria's china seas . . .
>
> To the tarantara of the bugler, the sunset furled
> round the last post.
>
> (Castaway, 38)

Again, however, as in **'Ruins of a Great House'** and **'A Far Cry from Africa',** this mood is replaced by a gentler, more elegiac tone and an overriding compassion. As in **'Laventville',** the poet contemplates a sea crossing which seems to be both the Middle Passage and the process of living itself and this collapsing together of historical and existential conditions has the effect of breaking down the distance between colonizer and colonized. Midway through the poem Walcott again introduces an 'I' persona who invokes the ghost of a white grandfather in a spirit of tenderness which has a healing effect. Although, as in **'The Almond Trees',** burning is the central metaphor for the passage of Caribbean history, the 'I' protagonist finds beauty in the house which represents the survival of this strain of his—and the Caribbean's—ancestry:

> Your house has voices, your burnt house,
> shrills with unguessed, lovely inheritors,
> your genealogical roof tree, fallen, survives,
> like seasoned timber through green, little lives.
>
> (Castaway, 39)

While *The Castaway* continues to explore many of the same concerns as Walcott's earlier verse, its poems, although still highly personal at times, generally have external correlatives, such as shared social concerns. The result is a movement away from the often cryptic subjectivity of his 'apprenticeship' period, which had continued to characterize several of the poems in *In a Green Night,* towards verse which is generally both more accessible and more powerful.

After the publication of ***The Castaway,*** Walcott seems to have, at least temporarily, lost interest in the Crusoe figure. In 1968 he told the Jamaican writer Dennis Scott, 'two, three years ago I was attracted to the Robinson Crusoe idea . . . but I am not interested in that idea anymore'.[11] The controlling image of his next collection was, however, again indicated by its title, ***The Gulf,*** a signifier which also has multiple resonances. In the title-poem the gulf is most obviously the Gulf of Mexico—the poet is on a flight above Texas—and Gulf gas-stations are also mentioned, but more generally the poem discusses the social divides that are threatening an impending apocalypse in the United States of the 1960s:

> The Gulf, your gulf, is daily widening.
>
> each blood-red rose warns of that coming night
> when there's no rock cleft to go hidin' in
> and all the rocks catch fire . . .[12]

and then moves beyond this to suggest the more general sense of psychological displacement felt by a poet who feels he has 'no home' (*Gulf,* 29) as long as religious and racial divisions promote a clamour for revenge.

American experience is equally important in a number of other poems in the volume. **'Blues',** an untypically direct piece, describes an inter-racial encounter in which the poet sees himself as being beaten 'black and blue' because of his in-between situation, here specifically his skin-colour; 'not too bright / for a nigger, and not too dark' (*Gulf,* 34). The ostensible occasion for **'Elegy'** is the assassination of Robert Kennedy, but more generally it is a lament for America and Walcott reflects on the contemporary social inequalities in the country:

> Still, everybody wants to go to bed
> with Miss America. And if there's no bread,
> let them eat cherry pie.
>
> (Gulf, 31)

and the impossibility of a Natty-Bumppo-like retreat from the collective cover-up of the dark side of the American Dream:

> the old choice of running, howling, wounded
> wolf-deep in her woods,
> while the white papers snow on
> genocide is gone.
>
> (Gulf, 31)

The poem echoes another classic elegy, Whitman's lament for Abraham Lincoln, 'When Lilacs Last in the Dooryard Bloomed', before suggesting how contemporary media images of dead Native Americans and Puritan settlers construct binaries that perpetuate violence:

> the cherry orchard's surf
> blinds Washington and whispers
> to the assassin in his furnished room
> of an ideal America, whose flickering screens

show, in slow herds, the ghosts of the Cheyennes
scuffling across the staked and wired plains
with whispering, rag-bound feet,

while the farm couple framed in their Gothic door
like Calvin's saints, waspish, pragmatic, poor,
gripping the devil's pitchfork
stare rigidly towards the immortal wheat.

(*Gulf,* 31)[13]

The implications would seem to be that the contemporary assassin is a product of the gulf dividing contemporary American society, a situation which belies the ideals on which the nation was founded, but the poem also questions whether these ideals *ever* really obtained.

In a sense this may seem to replicate the Manichean situation in which Walcott had felt he was growing up in colonial St. Lucia and which he had related to revolutionary Haiti; and **'Elegy'** begins with a passage in which it is the Caribbean that is seen as existing in a gulf, as a 'hammock swung between Americas' (*Gulf,* 31). The range of references to the Americas as a whole is also extended by a parallel with the death of Che Guevara and the poem, like several others in the volume, charts a restless movement between 'north' and 'south',[14] an axis that becomes central in Walcott's later verse, particularly after he took up appointments in the United States. Throughout, *The Gulf* is notable for its emphasis on journeying which leaves the persona perennially between worlds. Its poems move between the Caribbean, America and England and it is the first Walcott collection in which the figure of the Odyssean traveller that dominates his later verse becomes a leading protagonist.[15] So the stasis engrained in the trope of the Caribbean artist as a contemplative Crusoe is replaced by an emphasis on the constant movement and migrations of this travelling protagonist, and while this is most vividly expressed in the mid-air predicament of the title-poem, it is a situation which informs the whole of *The Gulf.*

In his 1968 interview with Dennis Scott, Walcott also spoke of his sense that his writing was becoming 'terrifyingly plain', saying that he now found himself 'writing so directly that I wish I were . . . more "important" or complicated'.[16] However, although the language of *The Gulf* may be superficially simpler than his earlier poetry, it has lost nothing in metaphorical density. In fact, to an even greater extent than hitherto, metaphor becomes the subject of much of the poetry, since it is about transformations of one kind or another, a subject which is linguistically enacted through metaphor, the language of transformation. While some of the poems are again intensely personal, generalized metapoetic concerns are also very much to the fore. In **'Moon'**, a poem in an early sequence entitled **'Metamorphoses'**, the poet dons the role of Orpheus and envisages his body transformed first into a vowel and then a whole poem—and more generally the poem is about revitalizing a range of experience through a practice rooted in metaphorical transformation. Thus in

**'Hawk'** there is the same kind of analogy between the eponymous bird and human counterparts as one finds in Ted Hughes's *Hawk in the Rain* (1957), but the human counterparts occupying the role here are *both* Carib Indians and white planters and a further metamorphosis is anticipated at the end, where:

Slaves yearn for their master's talons
the spur and the cold, gold eyes,
for the whips, whistling like wires,

(*Gulf,* 16)

while an actual hawk circling in the sky over a Trinidadian beach is said to 'have no music' (*Gulf,* 17), as it were to exist (paradoxically, since the poem has transformed it through metaphor) in a world beyond poetry.

In **'Mass Man'** the link between metaphor and transformation, this time in the context of carnival masquerading is explicit:

Through a great lion's head clouded by mange
a black clerk growls.
Next, a gold-wired peacock withholds a man,
a fan, flaunting its oval, jewelled eyes,
What metaphors!
What coruscating, mincing fancies!

(*Gulf,* 19)

although no opinion is given on whether such role-playing contains real potential for change or whether it is mere escapism, offering only temporary release. In **'Junta'** the theme of Carnival transformation is given another wry, metaphorical twist as a masquerader who has won the title of Individual of the Year, playing the role of the barbarian king Vercingetorix, turns his talents to politics.

Ultimately, however, the transformations of *The Gulf* are more concerned with the poet himself than with social issues. **'Mass Man'** depicts a split persona, who can stand outside himself even as he appears to be caught up in the frenzy of Carnival:

But I am dancing, look, from an old gibbet
my bull-whipped body swings, a metronome!
Like a fruit-bat dropped in the silk cotton's shade
my mania, my mania is a terrible calm.

(*Gulf,* 19)

and several other poems stage a similar conflict between active involvement and the detachment of the onlooker. This two-way movement relates to the theme of Odyssean wandering, as the poet finds himself, for example in **'Homecoming: Anse La Raye',** torn between north and south, between exile and ambivalent 'homecomings without home' (*Gulf,* 51). The theme comes to a head in the final poem **'Hic Jacet',** which responds to the question, asked in its opening line, 'why did you remain?' (*Gulf,* 70). In a reference which is suggestive of a comparison with V. S. Naipaul's attitude to the Caribbean, the poet says he has stayed:

Not to spite some winter-bitten novelist
praised for his accuracy of phlegm,
but for something rooted, unwritten
that gave us its benediction,
its particular pain.

*(Gulf, 70)*

He commits himself to 'the power of provincialism' (*Gulf,* 70) and the poem concludes with his portraying himself seeking 'more power' (*Gulf,* 71) than the Caribbean's expatriate writers through this commitment—a goal which would be achieved by his creator, at least in one sense, when Walcott became a Nobel Laureate. In the closing lines of **'Hic Jacet'** he achieves the volume's ultimate act of transformation, a quasi-spiritual 'second birth' (*Gulf,* 71) made possible by remaining within the region rather than becoming an exile. Although the poems of *The Gulf* wander more widely than Walcott's earlier verse and dramatize the sense of in-betweenness that characterizes all his responses to experience in a wider range of contexts, they remain rooted within a Caribbean world-view and, although they are major work in their own right, provide a fitting prolegomenon to *Another Life,* the work in which he has most fully fulfilled his vow to realize St. Lucia on the printed page.

As will be clear from the discussion above, there had been a strong autobiographical thrust in all Walcott's poetry thus far and this impulse came to a head in *Another Life* (1973), ostensibly a poetic autobiography of the same kind as Wordsworth's *Prelude* in that its central subject is the 'growth of a poet's mind'. However, while the poem is very personal in some respects, particularly in its treatment of an early love affair, and it is certainly about the development of the poet's artistic sensibility, it is again a work about the problem of tradition and its canvas expands to incorporate a consideration of Caribbean history and aesthetics more generally. Later, Walcott would subsume autobiographical elements into his epic poem *Omeros,* sometimes revisiting personal territory he had already mapped out in *Another Life;* here the movement is in the opposite direction, with autobiography incorporating history and epic, as Walcott relates the situation of the artist to the cultural life of the society at large. The main emphasis in the discussion which follows will, however, be on the way he uses the autobiographical form for a continuing exploration of the problem of constructing a Caribbean tradition.

Initially the main focus of *Another Life* is on the poet himself, represented as a 'divided child'[17] torn between the undocumented experiences of the St. Lucian landscape and the *other* life offered by European literature and art, but as the poem proceeds the growth of the individual artist's mind is located within the supposedly 'history-less' (*AL,* [*Another Life*] 6) predicament of the Caribbean and a more general response to the situation of the artist who is, at least potentially, 'growing up stupid under the Union Jack'.[18]

*Another Life* adopts an intertextual approach to autobiography, devoting more space to examining Walcott's forma-

tive artistic influences than to attempting to provide a transcription of 'lived' experiences. Such an approach has much in common with the view of autobiography taken by post-Barthean 'death of the author' theorists. In Julia Kristeva's words: 'any text is constructed as a mosaic of quotations; any text is the absorption and transformation of another. The notion of intertextuality replaces that of intersubjectivity.'[19] While, in one sense, all Walcott's work could be seen to be moving towards such a view of textual production, *Another Life* involves a more comprehensive and searching account of his discursive formation than his other poetry and so particularly lends itself to such an intertextual reading.

From the outset the stress on the 'divided child' marks a departure from the practice of conventional autobiographies which attempt to recapture the essence of a unitary self. Instead the poem presents its subject as an intertextual construct: less a 'divided child' because of his mixed racial ancestry than because of his split responses to the two kinds of discourse which influence his character from an early age: the vernacular, hitherto extra-literary discourse of the St. Lucian people and landscape and the much more traditional 'literary' idioms of European culture. While the poem dramatizes a split between these two discursive spheres, it gradually erodes this, creating its own syncretic continuum from a fusion of elements. The title of the whole poem encompasses several meanings and prominent among them is the notion that the world of art is 'another life' away from the island location in which the child is growing up. However, even as the poem portrays the child as a construct of different discourses, it is itself creating an image of him and this image is 'another life', another textual construct, which exists at the interface of the various discourses that are being combined together in the text.

The poem's concern with investigating the processes by which autobiography comes into existence is immediately apparent in the metaliterary opening lines:

Verandahs, where the pages of the sea
are a book left open by an absent master
in the middle of another life—
I begin here again,
begin until the ocean's
a shut book, and, like a bulb
the white moon's filaments wane.

Begin with twilight, when a glare
which held the cry of bugles lowered
the coconut lances of the inlet,
as a sun, tired of empire, declined.

*(AL,* 3)

As in **'Veranda',** the moment is the twilight of Empire, but the particular force of the passage relies on the reader's making out certain associations, recognizing how other texts, phrases and images are being redeployed to produce the distinctive effect of this 'mosaic of quotations'. The line 'in the middle of another life—', alludes to the opening of the *Divine Comedy,*[20] and in so doing immediately suggests a debt to one of the greatest of European allegories, while changing a word to make it clear that it describes *another* life, one which has an ambivalent relationship to European cultural codes. As in *Dream on Monkey Mountain,* the white moon image suggests a European muse—a meaning which becomes clearer as the poem develops—and the reference to its waning filaments anticipates the gradual movement away from this Muse that will occur in the poem as a whole. The 'verandahs', 'bugles' and 'lances' all confirm the moment of the opening as the twilight of Empire; and the 'absent master' seems to suggest the 'cultural absenteeism'[21] which was a legacy of the Caribbean plantocracy that persisted into the late colonial period and beyond. So the problem of tradition is introduced in the opening sentence and the reference to 'pages' and 'book' provide a clear index of the poet's awareness of the extent to which his perception of his natural surroundings is mediated by his colonial, 'literary' upbringing. At the same time the self-referential dimension is accentuated by the analogy that is being drawn between the act of perceiving the natural world and that of reading a text. It soon becomes clear that the poet is creating a pictorial tableau, 'a landscape locked in amber', but there is irony since this 'clear / glaze of another life' has been produced by a 'monster / a prodigy of the wrong age and colour' (*AL,* 3).

Subsequent details repeatedly stress how the child's vision has been shaped by European texts, phrases and imagery: his mother's brooms remind him of 'drooping ostrich crests' and the Prince of Wales's motto, 'ICH DIEN, I SERVE' (*AL,* 10); washday bubbles bring on envious thoughts of the Bubbles frontispiece of *Pears Cyclopedia* (*AL,* 12); he sees 'autumn in a rusted leaf' (*AL,* 41). In short, a concern with tradition informs the description of even the most routine everyday occurrences. Sometimes the poet's response to the world of his youth seems to be entirely shaped by imported language and imagery:

> I saw, as through the glass of some provincial gallery
> the hieratic objects which my father loved:
> the stuffed dark nightingale of Keats,
> bead-eyed, snow-headed eagles,
> all that romantic taxidermy.
>
> (*AL,* 41)

At the same time the landscape is depicted as 'virginal, unpainted' (*AL,* 152), awaiting Adamic naming by its artists and *Another Life* embarks on this project. So, although the colonial filter threatens to colour the poet's vision to the point of distortion, another lens offers an entirely different perspective:

> no one had yet written of this landscape
> that it was possible, though there were sounds
> given to its varieties of wood;
>
> the *bois-canot* responded to its echo,
> when the axe spoke, weeds ran up to the knee
> like bastard children, hiding in their names,
>
> . . . . .

> trees and men
> laboured assiduously, silently to become
>
> whatever their given sounds resembled,
> ironwood, logwood-heart, golden apples, cedars,
> and were nearly
>
> Ironwood, logwood-heart, golden apples, cedars,
> men.
>
> (*AL,* 53-4)

In passages like this which establish the validity of particular signifiers, the poem is very obviously performing the Adamic task, but in making an 'unwritten' landscape 'possible'[22] it is also doing so in its entirety. Throughout, *Another Life* documents a tension between metropolitan and local St. Lucian influences, but although Walcott seldom forsakes European verse forms—pentameters predominate even towards the end—there is a gradual movement away from 'romantic taxidermy'.

The Russian formalist critic Boris Tomashevsky has spoken of tradition as the problem which confronts all writers: 'The writer constantly tries to solve the problem of artistic tradition which in literary experience is like the encumbrance of an ancestral heirloom'.[23] *Another Life* uses the image of the heirloom very similarly in a passage which once again foregrounds Walcott's ambivalent colonial situation:

> I had entered the house of literature as a houseboy,
> filched as the slum child stole,
> as the young slave appropriated
> those heirlooms temptingly left
> with the Victorian homilies of *Noli tangere.*
>
> (*AL,* 77)

While, like Tomashevsky, Walcott envisages tradition as an ancestral heirloom, it is not one which has been bequeathed to the colonial 'houseboy' and so he has to steal and appropriate for his own uses. In so doing he is not assimilated, but rather assimilates for his own ends. And this is exactly how *Another Life* works, with potent images of the local landscape gradually supplanting those of European literature. Formerly he has seen autumn in a rusted leaf, but this process is reversed when he finds the smell of local hogplums, 'exuding / a memory stronger than [Proustian] madeleines' (*AL,* 76).

*Another Life* is unequivocally a Caribbean poem, but the intertexts that contribute to its making are primarily European in origin. A consideration of the poet's account of his early love for a woman called 'Anna' illustrates this further. This narrative is once again less an attempt to give the illusion of transferring a past reality to the page than an exploration of the ways images of self are constituted—in this case an investigation of the discourse of love. This functions in two ways: the poet foregrounds the extent to which 'Anna' is a construct of the text, formed by his own memory and perceptions and by the act of writing, but in addition the love which is now being transformed through writing is seen as having originally been a product of the two young St. Lucians' image-making. Where the poet himself is concerned, love appears to be an intertextual creation long before he turns to rendering it in his writing. His love for 'Anna' clearly owes something to literary texts when he imagines her as Anna Christie and Anna Karenina (*AL,* 96) and earlier in the poem he has approached her through the mediation of the Book of Hours and the Biblical figures of Ruth and Judith (*AL,* 60-1).[24] There is an interesting moment when 'Anna' resists such analogical categorization, turning on the poet and complaining: 'I became a metaphor, but / believe me I was unsubtle as salt' (*AL,* 101). However, since the method of the whole poem is once again founded on metaphorical transformation,[25] this seems to be an alternative viewpoint in a dialectical debate which is not finally endorsed. The main thrust of *Another Life* suggests that all discourse is metaphorical and this particularly comes in a passage where the young lovers are seen walking beside the sea:

> Where they now stood, others before had stood,
> the same lens held them, the repeated wood,
> then there grew on each one
> the self-delighting, self-transfiguring stone
> stare of the demi-god.
> Stunned by their images they strolled on, content
> that the black film of water kept the print
> of their locked images when they passed on.
>
> (*AL,* 94)

Here the photographic metaphors seem to be less a formulation of the text than a product of the imaginations of the lovers (as characters *within* the text). As they realize that they are reenacting their own version of the behaviour of other lovers, they in effect become engaged in a form of role-playing which is analogous to the transformations of the intertextual process, even if no earlier *written* texts are explicitly mentioned at this point. Clearly they can conceive of their love as achieving the stasis of art, as the camera-like water appears to perform the function of a modern-day grecian urn. At the same time, of course, the fluidity and transience of the water cannot preserve their image for posterity; on the other hand, the poem *Another Life* can, and does, do exactly this.

So, even when the subject of tradition is not overtly to the fore, *Another Life* still suggests that fictions of self are original, but derivative reworkings of received fictions. The particular creative tension of the poem emerges from its auto-referential dimension, its investigation of the processes of autobiography and specifically of the ways in which images of self are generated. Walcott's conception of himself as a 'split writer' results in the production of an autobiography that has more in common with such works as *The Life of Giambattista Vico Written by Himself* and Roland Barthes's *Roland Barthes,* texts which question the notion of the unitary Cartesian self, than with Wordsworth's *Prelude,* which may initially seem a more obvious departure-point for *Another Life.* While he has never

shown any inclination to make common cause with post-structuralist theorists, Walcott's practice in the poem effectively promotes a view of subjectivity as a discursive formation which has much in common with theirs. His problematization of issues of self-representation and his implicit distrust of transparent accounts of unitary selves seem to arise primarily from his awareness of writing from a hybrid heritage, but this makes his autobiography every bit as much a writerly text as those mentioned above—and as such it offers a radical challenge to versions of identity predicated upon linear, essentialist conceptions of the self.

Walcott's next collection, *Sea Grapes* (1976), is notable for its unity of tone and theme. Again the title-image is central to the whole volume, which offers Walcott's most sustained set of variations on his view, powerfully expressed in 'The Muse of History' published two years previously, that the American Adamic situation is a bitter-sweet predicament. A certain astringency of tone had been prominent in much of Walcott's previous verse. *Sea Grapes* develops this with bouts of acrimony, as when he writes about exiled novelists:

> You spit on your people,
> your people applaud,
> your former oppressors
> laurel you.
> The thorns biting your forehead
> are contempt
> disguised as concern . . .
>
> ('At Last',[26] *SG,* [*Sea Grapes*] 88)

and mordant imagery such as:

> Desolate lemons, hold
> tight, in your bowl of earth,
> the light of your bitter flesh.
>
> ('Lemons', *SG,* 14)

From the outset, however, the title-poem makes it clear that this acerbity is a response to the island predicament of 'gnarled sour grapes' (*SG,* 9) and that the grapes image is being used as a metaphor for the New World experience.

In 'The Muse of History' Walcott says of the 'great poetry of the New World':

> [I]ts savour is a mixture of the acid and the sweet, the apples of its second Eden have the tartness of experience. . . . It is the acidulous that supplies its energy. The golden apples of this sun are shot with acid. The taste of Neruda is citric, the *Pomme de Cythère* of Césaire sets the teeth on edge, the savor of Perse is of salt fruit at the sea's edge, the sea grape, the 'fat-poke', the sea almond.[27]

Like St.-John Perse's salt fruit, Walcott's sea grapes also 'set the teeth on edge'. Through the volume the sourness outweighs the sweetness, but the two are seldom extricable from one another. In **'The Wind in the Dooryard'**, which is dedicated to the Tobagonian poet E. M. Roach, who drowned himself in 1974, the admixture of sour and sweet is particularly complex. Walcott begins by speaking of the poem as an involuntary creation, which he has not wanted to come either from his own 'torn mouth' or Roach's 'salt body' (*SG,* 64). Initially, this reluctance seems to stem from his grief at the drowning of a fellow island-poet whose death, like Harold Simmons's, has provided a literal instance of his early belief that the pursuit of an artistic career in the Caribbean was tantamount to suicide.[28] However, as the poem proceeds, the sense of possible identification with Roach is problematized as he implicitly criticizes what Roach's poetry 'celebrated'—'the wall with spilling coralita . . . and the clean dirt yard' (*SG,* 64)—which seem to represent a sanitized version of Caribbean social realities. And at this point, it begins to appear as if Walcott's reluctance may result from a feeling that his criticism is improper in what is, at least in one sense, another Walcott elegy. However, the last stanza of the poem involves another shift in direction, as it almost grudgingly admits:

> sometimes, under the armpit
> of the hot sky over the country
> the wind smells of salt
> and a certain breeze lifts the sprigs of coralita
> as if, like us,
> lifting our heads, at our happiest,
> it too smells the freshness of life.
>
> (*SG,* 65-6)

So, although at the outset the poem seems to engage in a repudiation of Roach's late Romanticism, still a significant strain in Caribbean verse when Walcott began his writing career in the 1940s,[29] by the conclusion it is conceding that such verse does express a particular, if limited, dimension of island experience; and in acknowledging the validity of Roach's 'freshness of life' amid the armpit smells, Walcott suggests a compound of tones that can be related to the mood of bitter-sweetness prevalent throughout *Sea Grapes.*

In much the same way as Crusoe had been the main protagonist in *The Castaway,* the related figure of Adam[30] is the central character in *Sea Grapes.* The first of several poems in which he appears, **'The Cloud'**, portrays him at the moment of the Fall possessed of a curious kind of innocence in that his initiation into the postlapsarian state *liberates* him from the Manichean binary of bondage to either God or the Devil, instead of sentencing him, as in orthodox Christian theology, to a world of sin and death. Demythologized, such an Adam is humanity able to discover the New World emancipated from the dualistic moral imperatives of Western thought and free to write its signature as it chooses on the *tabula rasa* continent. However, lest this vision of being able to name the world anew seem unduly optimistic, the next poem **'New World'** immediately provides a counter-balance. It concludes by showing Adam and the serpent working together as capitalist entrepreneurs to invent the New World:

> Adam had an idea.
> He and the snake would share

the loss of Eden for a profit.
So both made the New World. And it looked good.

> (*SG,* 19)

Taken together, **'The Cloud'** and **'New World'** express Walcott's complex and ambivalent view of the American Adamic experience. As he constructs it, it is both a postlapsarian 'sour grapes' condition and a predicament which offers the possibility of liberation from the crippling moral dualism he here particularly associates with Europe.

In 'The Muse of History', where he argues the case for a cyclic view of history which will offer release from the determinism implicit in linear historiography with its emphasis on causality, Walcott relates such a view to the Adamic vision of the 'great poets of the New World, from Whitman to Neruda',[31] saying that it is their 'awe of the numinous, this elemental privilege of naming the new world [*sic*] which annihilates history in our great poets, an elation common to all of them, whether they are aligned by heritage to Crusoe and Prospero or to Friday and Caliban'.[32] In *Sea Grapes,* particular poems pay homage to Whitman and Neruda, but the Adamic vision is integral to the whole volume—and most of Walcott's other poetry—since, as discussed above, Walcott's poetic practice again performs the Adamic task of bestowing names. In a poem actually entitled **'Names'**, which is dedicated to Brathwaite (presumably as a response to his project of *Afro*-Caribbean renaming), Walcott argues the complex case that the 'belittling diminutives' (*SG,* 41) of the names bestowed upon slaves by exiled European courtiers were gradually dignified by later creolization, in which 'The African acquiesced, / repeated, and changed them' (*SG,* 42). And **'Sainte Lucie'**, in which the poet attempts to reclaim the folk speech of his youth, offers an inventory of Caribbean signifiers, which, if it does not exactly name the world *anew,* nonetheless contributes to the Adamic project by putting a distillation of aspects of the island's speech (and its natural phenomena) on the printed page for the first time:

> Pomme arac,
> otaheite apple,
> pomme cythere,
> pomme granate,
> moubain,
> z'ananas
> the pine apple's
> Aztec helmet,
> pomme,
> I have forgotten
> what pomme for
> the Irish potato,
> cerise,
> the cherry,
> z'aman
> sea-almonds
> by the crisp
> sea-bursts,
> au bord de la 'ouviere.
> Come back to me my language.
>
> (*SG,* 43-4)

Where earlier Walcott collections had referred to the onset of middle age,[33] in *Sea Grapes,* though still only in his mid-forties, Walcott looks forward to the approach of *old age* and asks himself, in **'To Return to the Trees',** whether he will soon, like the venerable Jamaican poet John Figueroa,[34] who had been one of his tutors during his undergraduate days,[35] be 'a gnarled poet / bearded with the whirlwind, / his metres like thunder?' (*SG,* 93).

Ageing is important in the collection in another sense, as Walcott finds himself in the ironic situation of a former angry young man who is now beginning to be regarded as insufficiently radical by a new generation of highly politicized poets. His reaction to their rhetoric comes out most clearly in the poems **'The Brother'** and **'Dread Song'.** The savage imagery of the former is not untypical of *Sea Grapes,* though its language is more uncompromisingly direct than that of most of the volume:

> That smiler next to you who whispers
> brother
>
> knife him
>
> That man who borrowed your coat
> the one of many colours
>
> reclaim it as yours.
>
> (*SG,* 23)

While the poem's biblical references, such as the allusion to Joseph's coat here, suggest that false brotherhood is far from being a peculiarly Caribbean phenomenon, the primary object of attack is the political exclusiveness of contemporary black 'brothers'. Questioned on this in a 1973 interview, Walcott spoke of having become disenchanted with the black revolutionary movement in Trinidad, because of the 'blacker than thou' character it had assumed:

> The rhetoric began to take over. And so the thing was deflected. But the validity of the young uprising and the unemployed people, it was a genuine and worthwhile thing. . . . And a lot of people use the slogans, naturally, to cover up their own inadequacies and so on. So a guy who calls you brother, after a while if he's just saying the thing, you should watch out for him.[36]

**'Dread Song'** is a subtler poem which expresses a similar disillusion. Ostensibly it is a Rastafarian song of praise and it is not difficult to take the opening at face value:

> Forged from the fire of Exodus
> the iron of the tribe,
>
> Bright as the lion light, Isaiah,
> the anger of the tribe.
>
> (*SG,* 32)

After a few lines, however, the tone changes as Walcott tells how the 'tribe' now buys the lies of 'lizard-smart poets' (*SG,* 32), who have usurped the religious leader's

role. As in **'The Brother',** it is the subversion of a powerful ideal by cheap rhetoric which is the central object of attack and the point is neatly clinched in the final lines of the poem where the loss of true revolutionary fire is mirrored by a descent into incantatory banality.

Walcott is not completely unsympathetic towards either of the extremes represented by E. M. Roach and the Rasta rhetoric, but he eschews both for a middle style which ranges across the Caribbean linguistic continuum. This is not, however, simply the style of an 'ironic mulatto', who chooses to keep his distance from opposing poles of the Caribbean racial and cultural spectrum. It is once again a commitment to the plurality of Caribbean life and to a stance which rejects binary oppositions and the kind of thinking that precludes movement and dialogue between positions:

In the final poem, **'Return to the Trees',** he reflects:

> grey has grown strong to me,
>
> it's no longer neutral,
> no longer the dirty flag
> of courage going under,
>
> it is specked with hues
> like quartz; it's as
> various as boredom, . . .
>
> grey is the heart at peace,
> tougher than the warrior
> as it bestrides factions.
>
> (*SG,* 93-4)

This 'grey' is said to involve 'the toil that is balance' (*SG,* 94) and *Sea Grapes* works towards such balance through its combination of an acerbic manner and its expression of a reverential attitude towards Caribbean life. Again there is a sense of 'obliterating hurt', but the bitter-sweet tensions are less often and less comfortably resolved than hitherto and it is the image of the acidulous sea grapes that lingers longest in the mind.

### Notes

1. *The Castaway and Other Poems,* London: Jonathan Cape, 1965, 45. Subsequent references are to this edition and cite *Castaway.*

2. The poems 'Laventville' and 'The Voyage Up River' (*Castaway,* 32-5 and 50) are dedicated to V. S. Naipaul and Wilson Harris respectively. The whole collection is dedicated to John Hearne ([7]).

3. 'The Figure of Crusoe', an edited version of Walcott's 1965 paper edited by Robert D. Hamner, *Critical Perspectives on Derek Walcott,* Washington: Three Continents Press, 1993, 35-6.

4. Ibid., 38

5. *AL,* [*Another Life,* London: Jonathan Cape, 1973; New York: Farrar Straus and Giroux, 1976] 152.

6. 'The Art of Poetry', Walcott interviewed by Edward Hirsch, in Hamner (ed.), *Critical Perspectives,* 70.

7. *Ibid.,* 74.

8. V. S. Naipaul, *The Middle Passage,* London: André Deutsch, 1962, 29.

9. The area is actually called Laventille.

10. Cf. the use of the same vantage point in the opening words *of Another Life,* 'Verandahs, where the pages of the sea / are a book left open by an absent master . . .', *AL,* 3.

11. 'Walcott on Walcott', Walcott interviewed by Dennis Scott, *Caribbean Quarterly,* 14:1 and 2, 1968, 141.

12. *The Gulf and Other Poems,* London: Jonathan Cape, 1969, 29. Subsequent references are to this edition and cite *Gulf.* The poem draws on rhetoric popular among Afro-American liberation writers of the period, for example, Cf. Eldridge Cleaver, *Soul on Ice,* London: Panther, 1970.

13. Cf. 'Orient and Immortal Wheat', *IGN,* [*In a Green Light,* London: Jonathon Cape, 1962] 48. The phrase 'orient and immortal wheat' is taken from Traherne's *Centuries of Meditation.*

14. Cf. *The Fortunate Traveller* [New York: Farrar Straus and Giroux, 1981; London: Jonathan Cape] (1982), where Walcott uses 'North' and 'South' as titles for the sections of the volume.

15. See Chapter 6.

16. 'Walcott on Walcott', Walcott interviewed by Dennis Scott, *Caribbean Quarterly,* 14:1 and 2, 1968, 137.

17. The title of the first section of the poem.

18. The title of Barbadian-born novelist Austin Clarke's autobiographical memoir of his early years, Toronto: McClelland and Stewart, 1980.

19. *Desire in Language: A Semiotic Approach to Literature and Art,* ed. Leon S. Roudiez, trans. Thomas Gora, Alice Jardine and Leon S. Roudiez, New York: Columbia University Press, 1980, 66.

20. Dante's *Inferno* begins '*Nel mezzo del cammin di nostra vita . . .*'.

21. Kenneth Ramchand's phrase, *The West Indian Novel and Its Background,* London: Faber, 1970. See particularly, 32-8.

22. See Chapter 2 [in Thieme, John. *Derek Walcott.* Manchester: Manchester University Press, 1999] for a discussion of poems in *IGN* which pursue this project.

23. 'Thematics' in *Russian Formalist Criticism: Four Essays,* trans. Lee T. Lemon and Marion J. Reis, Lincoln, Nebraska: University of Nebraska Press, 1965, 64; quoted in Shirely Neuman and Robert Wilson, *Labyrinths of Voice: Conversations with Robert Kroetsch,* Edmonton: NeWest Press, 1982, 3.

24. Cf. *AL,* 89 and 133.

25. NB the poet's abandonment of his attempts to become a painter when he realizes, 'I lived in a different gift, / its element metaphor' (*AL,* 59). Cf. also the emphasis on metaphorical transformation in *The Gulf,* discussed above.

26. Probably an allusion to the title of Charles Kingsley's *At Last: A Christmas in the West Indies* (1871).

27. 'Muse', ['The Muse of History', *Is Massa Day Dead?,* Derek Walcott ed. Orde Coombs, Garden City, New York: Anchor/Doubleday, 1976] 4-5.

28. See Chapter 1, [in Thieme, John. *Derek Walcott.* Manchester: Manchester University Press, 1999] notes 25 and 39.

29. See Edward Baugh, *West Indian Poetry, 1900-1970: A Study in Cultural Decolonisation,* Kingston: Savacou Publications, n.d. (1971?).

30. Walcott links the two in his 'Figure of Crusoe' essay, Hamner (ed.), *Critical Perspectives,* 35.

31. 'Muse', 2.

32. *Ibid.,* 5.

33. For example, 'Nearing Forty', *Gulf,* 67-8 and the opening line of *AL.*

34. Both 'Nearing Forty' and 'To Return to the Trees' are dedicated to John Figueroa.

35. I am grateful to John Figueroa for confirming this.

36. 'Any Revolution Based on Race is Suicidal', *Caribbean Contact,* 1:8, August 1973, 14. Cf. the treatment of Trinidad's 1970 Black Power rebellion in *The Last Carnival.*

## Charles Lock (essay date spring 2000)

SOURCE: Lock, Charles. "Derek Walcott's *Omeros:* Echoes from a White-throated Vase." *Massachusetts Review* 41, no. 1 (spring 2000): 9-31.

[*In the following essay, Lock presents an analysis of the depiction of women in the language and structure of Walcott's* Omeros.]

In reading *Omeros* we are struck, as we are in the *Iliad,* by the silence of Helen. What is this silence, and how in a poem is silence to be figured? To depict the woman, without representing her voice, is for the poet to exercise his (specifically *his*) descriptive powers, and to render the woman an object, whose silence is matched by its/her passivity. What remains is of course beautiful, but it is a beauty achieved at the expense of the person. The familiar narrative is announced in terms of her (or its) shadow, appearance rather than substance, object rather than subject:

> The duel of these fishermen
> was over a shadow and its name was Helen.[1]

The entire poem is written in hexameters, and Helen's (or "its") second utterance is made of a hexameter famously not her own:

> "Yesterday, all my troubles seemed so far away,"
> she croons, her clear plastic sandals swung by one hand.[2]

The woman's voice is traditionally and, to us, offensively subordinated to her beauty, and it is a mere truism to say that, in Western art and literature, men act and speak, women are, and are looked at. The one who represents has been normatively male; the one represented, whether as nude or Virgin, heroine or slut, has been female, not so much, we might argue, for thematic reasons than as a function of the division between the one who represents and the one who is represented.

That division would lead us to understand that the Madonna became the dominant theme of medieval painting not as a result of an otherwise inexplicable cult of the Virgin, but as the cause of that cult: male artisans and craftsmen, charged with the task of representation, define themselves and their craft by opposition. What is represented is not craft but grace.

This constitutive division of gender between the male who represents and the female who is represented takes on a thematic rendering from the very beginning. Just as the Madonna is surrounded by male saints whose adoring gaze replicates within the pictorial space the gaze and the veneration of the (male) viewer, so Homer presents Helen not directly to the reader but as she is presented to the old men of Troy, and indirectly through their reactions:

> And catching sight of Helen moving among the
>   ramparts,
> they murmured one to another, gentle, winged words:
> "Who on earth could blame them? Ah, no wonder
> the men of Troy and Argives under arms have suffered
> years of agony all for her, for such a woman.
> Beauty, terrible beauty!
> A deathless goddess—so she strikes our eyes!"[3]

Thus, within a work of art or literature, the figure of a woman becomes a second-order work of art, admired within the work we are reading or viewing, by a male figure himself represented therein. Rather than lamenting this fact, which we may do, from a historical and political perspective, we should acknowledge that, aesthetically, the internal, represented spectator, and the internal, doubly-represented aesthetic object (the woman), make for the most intricate aesthetic and cognitive challenges. Henry James's *The Portrait of a Lady* (1881) is exemplary of the playful, self-reflexive and, at the same time, intensely ethical exercise in the aesthetic sacrifice of the person to the object, of the (representing) voice to the (represented) silence.

"Sacrifice" is of course a charged term, for it implies that necessity or beneficial consequence is involved. In political terms we had better say subordination, or repression, or worse. But in aesthetic terms we are right to speak of sacrifice, for it is the work of art which we honour and value even as we deplore the object-hood to which the person has been reduced or "sacrificed." (To the extent, of course, that "the person" has any "ethical being": here the hold of mimesis continues to cloud our thinking.)

The voice of the one who represents is strongly contrasted with the silence of the one represented: the mysterious and enigmatic silence of the Mona Lisa is emblematic of the very deed of representation. Yet there is, we should note, a difference between the figuring of silence in fiction and in poetry, especially in epic. Novelistic prose is possessed of the remarkable linguistic feature known as *erlebte Rede* or *style indirect libre,* or free indirect discourse, whereby the voice of another may be incorporated into the narrator's speech, two voices fused indistinguishably. Not only other persons, but even inanimate objects may be said to have thoughts. That is after all the point and theme of Chapter 42 of *The Portrait of a Lady,* Isabel in front of the fire, meditating, and apprehending all, without voicing a single word.

Free indirect discourse is not an effect to be striven for, but rather something that occurs almost inevitably with fiction. It may explain why *ekphrasis,* such a prestigious topos of poetry, is so seldom found in fiction. An object of description refuses in fiction to remain an object, to stay passive, but somehow answers back, becomes animated, acquires, as we say, a life and a voice of its own, interfering verbally with the narrator's voice. We see this occurring with the buildings in Dickens's London, the wind and the moorland in *Wuthering Heights,* Hardy's Egdon Heath, or any number of fictional landscapes. This is, one could argue, not a calculated thematic effect on the part of the novelist, so much as the result of the conjunction of "descriptive prose" and "novelistic discourse." What is described takes on a voice—which might explain why people in "real life" are no less interesting than their fictional equivalents, while actual landscapes, cityscapes, furniture, things, are always, after and outside a novel, somewhat disappointing.

Poetry, we might say, has as its task to keep subject and object distinct because it is the literary form of Greek philosophy: Aristotle's *Poetics* are in some sense the guarantor of Aristotle's *Metaphysics.* The novel, by contrast, confuses them and us, and is the literary form of modernity, of both imperialism and democracy.

Bakhtin argues that the novel arises from the breakdown of the "classical public wholeness of the individual . . . A differentiation between biographical and autobiographical forms had begun."[4] In Homer, Bakhtin continues, "There was as yet no internal man, no 'man for himself' (I for myself), nor any individualized approach to one's own self. An individual's unity and his self-consciousness were exclusively public. . . . The individual was completely on the surface, in the most literal sense of the word." In short, there is in Homer no thinking without speaking, and no speaking without addressing. There is therefore no possibility for representing silence.[5] Isabel by the fire is an impossible scene in epic; it (or she) is the very consummation of the possibilities of the novel.

And what is forever refreshing in Homer is the sense of narrative without internal motivation, a narrative determined purely by external factors, the visible and the vocal. As Schiller discerned, in the discontent of his awed fascination with Homer:

> even in reading, our hearts pause, and gladly detach themselves from the object in order to look within. But of all this, not a trace in Homer. . . . As though he possessed no heart in his bosom, he continues in his dry truthfulness.[6]

Our pleasure in reading novels is in part to be derived from the illusion, or the assurance, that we might have access to another person's mind and heart. The fictional representation becomes itself the best evidence (as in Schiller) for the presumption of a heart in the characters, as in the writer: a "look within."

Such access to another's mind in fiction, rather than in epic, tends to open up also an access to the mind of things, or of the landscape: that such things or views should have a heart is no more absurd than that people should—and in fiction no more infrequent.

The novel, it is often remarked, is the most successful form of cultural export: post-colonial politics is seldom embarrassed by the novel as genre, not even by the novel as vehicle of grievance. Newly-independent nations have founded their traditions on works of fiction as Greece and Rome grounded themselves on epic. Poetry, by contrast, seems always archaic (its perpetual, designated weakness vis-a-vis the novel). Modern poetry (Eliot, Pound, David Jones) insists on its modernity by keeping up with the novel, in a process which Bakhtin labelled "novelization," while at the same time unbaring its archaic traces. Yet, even in modernist verse, the dialogism so distinctive of the novel, and so central to the loose unstructured texture that typifies the genre, is not often to be noticed.

In *Omeros* we find harmony, closure, structure, thematic unity, everything that we hope to find in poetry and in epic, with none of the ironic disclaimers and compositional disruptions to which modern poetry has accustomed us. Its play with voices appears to be conventional, its distinction between diegesis and dialogue would seem recognizable to Aristotle.

> "This is how, one sunrise, we cut down them canoes."
> Philocete smiles for the tourists, who try taking
> his soul with their cameras. "Once wind bring the news

to the *laurier-canelles,* their leaves start shaking
the minute the axe of sunlight hit the cedars,
because they could see the axes in our own eyes.

Wind lift the ferns. They sound like the sea that feed us
fishermen all our life, and the ferns nodded 'Yes,
the trees have to die.' So, fists jam in our jacket,

cause the heights was cold and our breath making feathers
like the mist, we pass the rum. When it came back, it
give us the spirit to turn into murderers. . . ."[7]

Already we find in this introductory passage a sort of phonetic or accentual disruption. The effect is dramatic, in the sense that one cannot read aloud Philoctete's speech without assuming an accent: "Wind lift the fern" is not speakable in Received Pronunciation.[8] This passage is ascribed to Philoctete: by contrast, the narrator's own language, the diegesis, is always "correct." Yet it is through the narrator's voice that we learn of "the tourists, who try taking his soul with their cameras." The syntax is correct, but the sentiment, whether ascribed or shared, is "primitive," as is the idea that the ferns might nod their assent. (It would be a mistake to treat this as an instance of Ruskin's "pathetic fallacy.") On first reading, one might decode the phrase to separate our narrator from Philoctete, and to restrict to Philoctete the savage belief, of "the primitive mind," that a photograph can steal the soul. Yet in the very next section we have the narrator's description of the chopping down of trees—playing with Horace, *Satires,* Book I, 8: "Olim truncus eram"—and the building of canoes, a narration uninterrupted by dialogue:

>                                       The logs gathered that thirst
>
> for the sea which their own vined bodies were born with.
> Now the trunks in eagerness to become canoes
> ploughed into breakers of bushes, making raw holes
>
> of boulders, feeling not death inside them, but use—[9]

Here the trees are animated even in their death, animated by a desire to be of use, and through that desire, presumably, they become canoes. We must now reconsider the poem's opening verse, because if our narrator believes this about trees, he may as well believe that the camera steals the soul.

We have already said, after Bakhtin, that the Homeric world knows no interior life or inner world, that the unity of the individual is complete on the surface. Here in *Omeros* we have a world full of Homeric echoes, yet one with a rich and mystifying inwardness: epic and novel combined without the obvious signs of "novelization." And we must make explicit our view that the novel is, at the linguistic level, considerably more animistic and primitive than the Homeric epic: access to another's mind—the staple of fiction—is the very condition of animism.

Where there is inwardness, there will be echo. Where there is echo there must be an inner space, the recess of its latency.

The figure of echo is complicated. It is both outward: there is no real voice there, no presence of a person; and it is inward, in that what produces an echo must contain it.[10] The figure of synecdoche is in this way a type of echo, and we see how echo poems (George Herbert's "Heaven" is a well-known example) are constructed by removing one word from within an outer enclosing word: delight/ light, enjoy/joy, pleasure/leisure, persever/ever.[11] Echo is thus a literal or phonetic synecdoche, a word contained within a word, part of one word that can be taken for the whole of another.

Helen's very first words in **Omeros** are subject to this sort of echoic repetition:

> Helen said: "Girl, I pregnant,
> but I don't know for who." "For who," she heard an
>   echoing call, as
> with *oo*'s for rings a dove moaned in the manchineel.[12]

And the poem's title is unfolded in the same fashion:

> A wind turns the harbour's pages back to the voice
> that hummed in the vase of a girl's throat: "Omeros."
>
> "O-meros," she laughed. "That's what we call him in
>   Greek,"
> stroking the small bust with its boxer's broken
>   nose. . . .
>
>                              . . . I said, "Omeros,"
>
> and *O* was the conch-shell's invocation, *mer* was
> both mother and sea in our Antillean patois,
> *os,* a grey bone, and the white surf as it crashes
>
> and spreads its sibilant collar on a lace shore.
> Omeros was the crunch of dry leaves, and the washes
> that echoed from a cave-mouth when the tide has
>   ebbed.
>
> The name stayed in my mouth.[13]

We find in this remarkable passage the word "Omeros" being emptied of its component sounds, and the word that contains—as envelope/synecdoche—is figured in "the vase of a girl's throat," a conch-shell, a cave-mouth, and "my mouth." Catachresis (known misleadingly as incorrect usage, or as dead metaphor) is never deliberate, and needs no motive: it is always the child of necessity.[14] Yet its use here is insistent: what else can we call the entrance to a cave but its "mouth"? And what else to call "my mouth"? Other things in this poem have mouths, though they speak not: the cannon, itself an "iron log," "mounting, mounting, until its mouth touched the very first branch" (83), and the conventional catachresis of the "cannon's mouth" (102). At first the canoes do not speak, though "their nodding prows / agreed with the waves to forget their lives as

trees" (8); but when Achille is in his entranced Africa, or Lethe, "For hours the river gave the same show / for nothing, the canoe's mouth muttered its lie" (134). We attend to "the mouth of the cauldron" (246) and the mouth of sundry other vessels, one of which vessels is this craft, of poetry. The poem's dedication alerts us to this recurrent pun: "For my shipmates in this craft. . . ."[15]

The mouth is not only that through which we speak; it is the opening in any vessel, necessary if an echo is to be produced. The mouth is for both speech and echo, the sign of either a presence or an absence within the vessel. It is only by convention that words denoting parts of the human body are considered not to be catachresis, to be as it were the literal terms from which metaphor spreads, or takes off. Only by convention, by our blindness to catachresis, does a human mouth signify a presence within. Yet the mouth of a beautiful woman, aesthetically objectified, begins to resume its status as catachresis for, say, the opening of a vase.[16]

The same Greek girl from whom the narrator first heard the name of Homer is recalled at the end of Book 5 (out of 7), in Boston:

> I climbed steps, I read buzzers,
> searched from the pavement again for that attic where
>
> a curved statue had rolled black stocking down its
>   knees,
> unclipped and then shaken the black rain of its hair,
> and "Omeros" echoed from a white-throated vase.[17]

Just a few pages later, the poet/narrator is proposing a cinematic version of this poem's story:

>                              Cut to a woman's hands
> Clenched towards her mouth with no sound. Cut to
>   the wheel
> of a chariot's spiked hubcap. Cut to the face
>
> of his muscling jaw, then flashback to Achille
> hurling a red tin and a cutlass. Next, a vase
> with a girl's hoarse whisper echoing "Omeros,"
>
> as in a conch-shell.[18]

We began with "the vase of a girl's throat" and we have arrived at "a vase with a girl's hoarse whisper"; the only mouth in this section of cuts is that to which the woman clenches her hands "with no sound."

These transformations, in what the poet calls "my reversible world,"[19] have been achieved by catachresis and synecdoche. It is worth noting that synecdoche is the very trope of reversibility, by which container may stand for contained, and vice versa. We should insist that catechresis is not "dead metaphor"—as a kind of lazy deviation from the "literal"—but rather involuntary or unmotivated metaphor; it is equally important to insist that synecdoche is a type of metonymy. We thus find, in the play of catachresis and synecdoche on the figure of the vase, an elaborated model of Roman Jakobson's theory of poetic language as the transposition of—or the interference between—the metaphoric and metonymic poles.[20]

Presented with the figure of a vase, we are no longer surprised at the silence of Helen—a silence which does not exclude a capacity for echo. Yet the girl-vase-vessel who speaks the name "Omeros" is an unnamed Greek girl, with Asiatic features, not the Helen of St. Lucia (that island's name, Walcott's own birth-place, is a gift to one who would claim kinship with Homer and Milton). The named, dark Helen is introduced thus, at a café:

> I felt like standing in homage to a beauty
>
> that left, like a ship [vessel], widening eyes in its
>   wake.
> "Who the hell is that?" a tourist near my table
> asked a waitress. The waitress said, "She? She too
>   proud!"
>
> As the carved lids of the unimaginable
> ebony mask unwrapped from its cotton-wool cloud,
> the waitress sneered, "Helen." And all the rest fol-
>   lowed.
>
> (24)

Among its many senses, that last sentence almost caps, by its own subtle echo, Yeats's astonishing half-line:

> The broken wall, the burning roof and tower,
> And Agamemnon dead.

The indirect presentation of Helen by way of the tourists and the waitress accords with Lessing's observation that Helen's beauty is not described directly but must be inferred from the responses of those around her.[21]

Walcott's presentation of his Helen is not only indirect, but it makes explicit its means of indirection, its masks, shadows, and echoes:

> I saw her once after that moment on the beach
> when her face shook my heart, and that incredible
> stare paralysed me past any figure of speech,
>
> when, because they thought her moods uncontrollable,
> her tongue too tart for a waitress to take orders,
> she set up shop: beads, hair-pick, and trestle-table
>   . . .
>
> Her carved face flickering with light-wave patterns
>   cast
>
> among the coconut masks, the coral earrings
> reflected the sea's patience. Once, when I passed
> her shadow mixed with those shadows, I saw the rage
>
> of her measuring eyes, and felt again the chill
> of a panther hidden in the dark of its cage

> that drew me towards its shape as it did Achille.
> I stopped, but it took me all the strength in the world
> to approach her stall, as it takes for a hunter
> to approach a branch were a pantheress lies curled
> with leaf-light on its black silk. To stand in front of
>   her
> and pretend I was interested in the sale
> of a mask or a T-shirt? Her gaze looked too bored,
>
> and just as a pantheress stops swinging its tail
> to lightly leap into grass, she yawned and entered
> a thicket of palm-printed cloth, while I stood there
>
> stunned by that feline swiftness, by the speed
> of her vanishing, and behind her, trembling air
> divided by her echo that shook like a reed.[22]

The insistence on echo and shadow is, however, not just a tribute to Homeric indirection. It also gives us a clue to a further complexity, for *Omeros* seems to rank itself among those recensions of the Homeric story that suppose Helen to have been a figment: "Helen the *Eidolon* or 'Phantom,' whose story is that there was no such story."[23] There are two Helens in *Omeros,* the named black girl, and the unnamed Greek one. The poem thus exploits the non-Homeric story, first told by Stesichorus, mentioned by Herodotus and Euripides, treated by Sophocles in *Philoctetes,*[24] and twice cited by Plato in the *Phaedrus,* that is was only a phantom, a mask, a shadow that caused the trouble between Menelaus and Paris, and that the real, substantial Helen stayed all the while in Egypt. This tradition was given renewed life by Flaubert in *The Temptation of St. Antony,* where her presence is conjured into being by Simon Magus. That, incidentally, should give a clue to Helen's presence in Marlowe's *Doctor Faustus:* as a vision, a shadow, a phantom, she is there less for her beauty than for her "conjurability." Ernst Bloch suggests that the motivation of the myth may be ascribed to the absolute or utopian hope which can be vested only outside of objective reality.[25] The one serious attempt in modern English literature to address this theme is H.D.'s much-neglected *Helen in Egypt* published in 1961, whose prefatory note is worth citing at length:

> We all know the story of Helen of Troy but few of us have followed her to Egypt. How did she get there? Stesichorus of Sicily in his *Pallinode,* was the first to tell us. Some centuries later, Euripides repeats the story. Stesichorus was said to have been struck blind because of his invective against Helen, but later was restored to sight, when he reinstated her in his *Pallinode.* . . . According to the *Pallinode,* Helen was never in Troy. She had been transposed or translated from Greece into Egypt. Helen of Troy was a phantom, substituted for the real Helen, by jealous deities. The Greeks and the Trojans alike fought for an illusion.[26]

And H.D.'s poem takes up the theme of the phantom, shadow, reflection:

> Alas, my brothers,
> Helen did not walk
> upon the ramparts,

she whom you cursed
was but the phantom and the shadow thrown
of a reflection[27]

The two Helens in *Omeros,* Asiatic and African, Greek and Egyptian, seem to be shades, if one can put it so, of the dark and fair Iseults of the Tristan legend:

You were never in Troy, and, between two Helens,
yours is here and alive; their classic features
were turned into silhouettes from the lightning bolt
of a glance. These Helens are different creatures,

one marble, one ebony. . . .

but each draws an elbow slowly over her face
and offers the gift of her sculptured nakedness,
parting her mouth.[28]

And where there are two, there is not one original and one copy; or if there are, we cannot tell the copy from the original, the shadow from the form that casts it. It is the predicament of Narcissus:

He [Achille] brooded on the river. The canoe at its
  pole,
doubled by its stillness, looked no different
from its reflection, nor the pier stakes, nor the thick
trees inverted at the riverline, but the shadow-face

swayed by the ochre ripples seemed homesick
for the history ahead, as if its proper place
lay in unsettlement. So, to Achille, it appeared

they were not one reflection but separate men—[29]

Nor can we tell from the shadow whether it is cast by flesh or marble:

      any statue is a greater actor
than its original by its longer shadow[30]

and "Only silhouettes last."[31] We might speculate that the confusion occasioned by reflection is not unlike, and may itself reflect, the impossibility of ascribing identity to voices in the free indirect discourse of dialogism.[32]

Helen is employed as a maid by the Plunketts, an expatriate couple, he a retired Major who fought with Montgomery in North Africa, she (Maud) of Irish origin: Plunkett serves the function of the internalized male gaze, the represented gaze of admiration and desire which makes of Helen a representation within a representation. Helen, as seen by the Major, is described in terms of her shadow, and in terms of the confusion, or identity, between her shadow and herself:

he could see her shadow through the sheets of laundry
and since she and her shadow were the same, the sun
behind her often made her blent silhouette seem

naked. . . .[33]

The next time we see Helen, through the eyes of the fisherman, Achille, the presentation is slightly different, for it is the shadow rather than the body that is possessed of agency:

It was still moonlight, and the moonlight filled the
  sheen

of the nightgown she entered like water as her pride
shook free of the neck. He saw the lifted wick shine
on the ebony face, and the shadow she made

on the wall. Now the shadow unpinned one earring,
its head tilted, and smiled. It was in a good mood.
It checked its teeth in a mirror, he watched it bring

the mirror close to its eyes.

                            (114)

What is a shadow but an entirely exteriorized body, a body without inwardness, without a mind? "A shadow of himself," we say of someone numbed to silence. Yet this shadow is substantial, a body. As we have watched the transformation of an echo into the vase from which it issued, so we witness here a shadow becoming its own substance. Insubstantiality has been transformed into statuesque solidity, by the reversibility of synecdoche, and by the doubling of metonymy.

Shadows, like reflections, should be given privileged linguistic status, for they involve both likeness and proximity, both metaphor and metonymy. That is to say, there are two necessary conditions for shadows and reflections: that the shadow or reflection *resemble* what causes it, and that the shadow or reflection exist only in *proximity* to or in *contiguity* with that which is its cause. Nothing else visually, apart from shadows and reflections, so insists on the holding together of the metaphoric and the metonymic.[34]

Yet if we leave the spatial, visual field, and enter into the acoustic and temporal realm (the world of those under the patronage of St. Lucia), we must admit, to a most exclusive linguistic club, the echo. The condition of membership is that the phonetic effect depends on both resemblance and contiguity. The echo must acoustically *resemble* the word which is its cause, and it must fade, pine away into nonbeing, when not in *proximity* to its cause. As the twoness of the original and the copy (in the visual-spatial world) leads, duplicitously, to a confusion between them, or (same thing) to an identity of one with the other, so (in the aural-temporal world) an echo after a voice makes it hard to tell voice and echo apart.

Again we listen in to the acoustic chain of echoes, and understand why the echo issues from a container, and why that container has a throat. And we can attempt an answer to the sharp question posed by Maud Plunkett:

What was it in men that made such beauty evil?

                            (124)

Beauty (the feminine, the represented) is objectified, silenced, permitted only to echo the male voice. Yet this is no simple tale of the oppressors and the oppressed. As we are also told: no colony can be free of the Empire's guilt. If every poem is an echo, then all our cultural and aesthetic training teaches us to look for echoes, whether we are post-colonial poets or expatriate retired officers:

> He [Plunkett] found his Homeric coincidence.
>                         "Look, love, for instance,
> near sunset, on April 12, hear this, the *Ville de Paris*
>
> struck her colours to Rodney. Surrendered. Is this
>      chance
> or an echo? Paris gives the golden apple, a war is
> fought for an island called Helen?"[35]

Plunkett, the British expatriate, decides that their maid, Helen, is part of the pattern of echoes:

>                                    If she
> hid in their net of myths, knotted entanglements
>
> of figures and dates, she was not a fantasy
> but a webbed connection. . . .[36]

He undertakes his historical research on the War of the Antilles precisely out of his fascination not with Helen "herself" (he would not admit to that sort of improper personal interest) but with Helen as figure and echo:

> So Plunkett decided that what the place needed
> was its true place in history, that he'd spend hours
> for Helen's sake on research.[37]

Our narrator, a native of the islands, in contrast to Plunkett, is complicit with Plunkett in the silencing of Helen, even in "Not his, but her story. Not theirs, but Helen's war."[38] For even the concession of "Not his, but her story" will only place her in the focus of his gaze, so that Plunkett will enact yet again the representation of Helen as the type of beauty. It is men who make the beauty evil by representing it, though they have little choice when representation is figured as a masculine craft, and when our entire civilisation endorses the echoing of aesthetic values.

Meditating on the vase as the figure for Helen in *Omeros* one is tempted to outline a topos with a tradition: the vase as the figure of the silenced woman. Keats's urn is the epitome of the silent: "Thou still unravished bride of quietness, / Thou foster-child of silence and slow time." Its compound synecdoche (unseen emptiness of town, unseen emptiness of unseen urn) makes silence both reflective and contained, as if we might one morning hear an echo of silence:

> What little town, by river or sea shore,
>    or mountain-built with peaceful citadel,
>       Is emptied of this folk, this pious morn?

And its punning catachresis: "O Attic shape! Fair attitude!" guides us echoically to hear an apostrophe to Helen in:

> Thou, silent form, dost tease us . . . out of thought
>    As doth Eternity . . .

Browning's "The Statue and the Bust" (one of the few English poems in consistent terza rima, to which Walcott's poem alludes and from which it strikes echoes) knows almost too well what is involved in the animation of art:

> The true has no value beyond the sham:
> As well the counter as coin. . . .
>
>                                    (II, 235-36)

Browning's example would be indispensable for Henry James's portraits and representations. We should also invoke Stevens's "Anecdote of the Jar" in this line of figuration whose argument is that the vase, shapely, beautiful woman, is the woman portrayed, and thereby silenced. A singularly clear instance, transparent in its own almost embarrassing directness, is William Cowper's ode "On the Receipt of my Mother's Picture Out of Norfolk" which opens precisely with a lament at the silence of the woman portrayed:

> Oh that those lips had language! Life has passed
> With me but roughly since I heard thee last.
> Those lips are thine—thy own sweet smiles I see,
> The same that oft in childhood solaced me;
> Voice only fails, else how distinct they say,
> "Grieve not, my child. . . ."

The unspeaking lips of a portrait are not far from the unspeaking lips, and the throat, of a vase. Most dramatically, there is in *The Winter's Tale* the transubstantiation of Hermione—not a transformation, for her shape, her outline, her silhouette, that which would cast a shadow, remains unchanged. The negation of the difference between that which lives and that which is its copy, between object and subject, between voice and echo, is most poignantly posed in Leontes's question:

>                         What fine chisel
> Could ever yet cut breath?[39]

(A question which we may have heard echoed in "the trembling air / divided by her echo.") The cutting of breath—the manifestation and utterance of animation—is forever beyond the artist's power, an enduring taunt of artistic futility.

But it is equally impossible to pursue the opposite line, to see the world artlessly, without figures, beyond figuration. Just as the narrator of *Omeros* is unable to forget Homer:

>                         When would it stop,
> the echo in the throat, insisting, "Omeros";
> when would I enter that light beyond metaphor?[40]
>
>                         For three years,
> phantom hearer, I kept wandering to a voice
> hoarse as winter's echo in the throat of a vase![41]

so the narrator is unable to see the Plunketts' black maid as merely a woman, whose name is merely her name, without echo or resonance.

The narrator again acknowledges the similarities between Plunkett and himself—what all men share—similarities that extend to the research of the one and the epic of the other:

> Plunkett, in his innocence,
>
> had tried to change History to a metaphor,
> in the name of a housemaid; I, in self-defence,
> altered her opposite. Yet it was all for her.
>
> Except we had used two opposing stratagems
> in praise of her and the island; cannonballs rolled
> in the fort grass were not from Olympian games,
>
> nor the wine-bottle, crusted with its fool's gold,
> from the sunken *Ville de Paris,* legendary
> emblems; nor all their names the forced coincidence
>
> we had made them. There, in her head of ebony,
> there was no real need for the historian's
> remorse, nor for literature's. Why not see Helen
>
> as the sun saw her, with no Homeric shadow,
> swinging her plastic sandals on that beach alone,
> as fresh as the sea-wind?[42]

The sun, light, St. Lucia, is matched by the sea, *mer,* for these are the inhuman elements of light and life, innocent of human tradition, culture, memory, aesthetics, poetics:

> The ocean had
> no memory of the wanderings of Gilgamesh,
> or whose sword severed whose head in the *Iliad.*
> It was an epic where every line was erased
>
> yet freshly written in sheets of exploding surf. . . .
> It never altered its metre
> to suit the age, a wide page without metaphors.[43]

A world without metaphors, humanity as free of figures as the sea and the sun would be, were they "truly" represented: the desire for this is the theme rehearsed with elegant obsessiveness by Wallace Stevens. The peculiar fun of Stevens's poetry lies in its cheerful confidence in its own failure to reach "that light beyond metaphor," that one can practise for ever and without risk a poetic quest whose goal is securely unattainable:

> The poem of pure reality, untouched
> By trope or deviation.[44]

Yet, in Stevens, one cannot desist, and one must look down on those who abandon the quest. Likewise in Walcott, the recognition that one's subject has been objectified is of no help at all in restoring the subject, in seeing the person (in Arnoldian phrase) as in herself she really is. Tropes objectify, but they alone make representation and knowledge possible; at their most subtle, intricate, devious, the trope of echo transforms a woman into a vase, herself/itself both sculpture and echo. The poet's question:

> Why not see Helen
> as the sun saw her, with no Homeric shadow,
> swinging her plastic sandals on that beach alone . . .
> ?

may then serve as a most luminous gloss on Stevens's disdain for Mrs. Pappadopoulos, "So-and-So Reclining on her Couch," who is heard to say:

> One walks easily
> The unpainted shore, accepts the world
> As anything but sculpture. Good-bye,
> Mrs. Pappadopoulos, and thanks.

One cannot walk the unpainted shore, any more than one can see what the sun sees, or follow the rhythm of the ocean. Nor can one figure a beautiful woman as anything but a reflection of Helen and an echo of Homer—a vase, with a throat, an echo-chamber, or an echo-chamber-maid. More disturbing is the converse: one can hardly figure anything except as a woman. We might say, recalling Bakhtin, that the condition of primal epic is precisely to be free from echo, and that "novelization" takes over as soon as echo is heard. With echo all language becomes potentially parodic. Echo is the first parody, and the novel begins in parody. Epic is the vase, whose echo is the novel. That is the irreversible synecdoche, that Walcott must follow Homer, must be contained within Homer, to be detached and individualized only as an echo. They meet, climactically, and Omeros, or rather *his* marble bust, speaks:

> "Love is good, but the love of your own people is
>
> greater."
>
> "Yes," I said. "That's why I walk behind you.
> Your name in her throat's white vase sent me to find
> you."[45]

And as Walcott comes after Homer, he becomes himself as the woman or the child to the originary voice of the man:

> And my cheeks were salt with tears, but those of a
> boy,
> and he saw how deeply I had loved the island.
>    . . . . .
>
> And Omeros nodded: "We will both praise it now."
> But I could not before him. My tongue was a stone
> at the bottom of the sea, my mouth a parted conch
>
> from which nothing sounded. . . .[46]

As for those plastic sandals, even such a banal detail holds echoes that reverberate through the poem. The plasticity belongs of course with the metamorphic, Ovidian theme. And one may venture that Helen carries or wears sandals for the same reason that monastics wear them. The silence that Helen shares with monastics may be, in an unfigured sense, mere coincidence, but there is a deep logic in catachresis: a sandal, unlike a shoe, has no tongue.

By contrast, the women carrying coal are not objects of aesthetic representation, though, in an echo of Helen on the ramparts, it is an old man, the poet's father, who "spoke for those Helens of an earlier time":

> The carriers were women, not the fair, gentler sex.
> Instead, they were darker and stronger, and their gait
> was made beautiful by balance. . . .[47]

In a remarkable elaboration of the metaphorics of poetic metre, the poet's father assigns the task:

> "Kneel to your load, then balance your staggering feet
> and walk up that coal ladder as they do in time,
> one bare foot after the next in ancestral rhyme. . . .
>
> 　　　　Look, they climb, and no one knows them;
> they take their copper pittances, and your duty
>
> from the time you watched them from your grandmoth-
> 　er's house
> as a child wounded by their power and beauty
> is the chance you now have, to give those feet a
> 　voice."

Even to those women, slaves, victims, the exploited and, for all their treading, the down-trodden, can a voice be given. But to Helen, to fair Helen, the beautiful, the aesthetic, the very type and first occasion of representation, no voice can be given: throughout western history, from Homer to **Omeros,** the representation of beauty depends on a central cavernous silence. In tongueless plastic sandals lurks an echo of many scandals.

### Notes

I am grateful to Line Henriksen for bibliographical assistance in the preparation of this essay.

1. Derek Walcott, *Omeros* (London: Faber, 1990), Book One, Chapter III, Part I, p. 17.

2. *Omeros,* Book One, Chapter VI, Part II, p. 34.

3. Homer, *The Iliad,* translated by Robert Fagles (Harmondsworth: Penguin, 1990), pp. 133-34 (Book III, lines 185-190).

4. M. M. Bakhtin, *The Dialogic Imagination,* translated by Caryl Emerson and Michael Holquist, edited by Michael Holquist (Austin, TX and London: University of Texas Press, 1981), p. 133.

5. See G. E. Lessing's discussion of inarticulate noise (rather than of silence) in the "piteous outcries" and "whimperings" in the *Philoctetes* of Sophocles: "whole long lines full of *papa, papa* . . . which must have been declaimed with quite other hesitations and drawings-out of utterance than are needful in a connected speech." *Laocoön,* translated by W.A. Steel in *Laocoön, Nathan the Wise, Minne von Barnhelm* (London: Dent, 1930), ch. 1, p. 7. Sophocles's *Philoctetes* treats of the "shadow-Helen"; see nn. 23-6. For a useful account of the role of Philoctete in *Omeros,* see Carol Dougherty, "Homer after *Omeros:* Reading a H/Omeric Text," in Gregson Davis, ed., *The Poet-*

ics of Derek Walcott: Intertextual Perspectives, special issue of *South Atlantic Quarterly,* Vol. 96, no. 2 (Spring 1997), pp. 339-47.

6. Friedrich Schiller, "Naive and Sentimental Poetry," in *Naive and Sentimental Poetry and On the Sublime: Two Essays,* translated by Julias A. Elias (New York: Ungar, 1966), p. 109.

7. *Omeros,* Book One, Chapter I, Part I, p. 3.

8. As Walcott himself has noted of the poem's opening line: "There are people at Oxford, or Harvard maybe, who are going to have to read this thing [*line repeated in broad Creole accent*]. And then I said, yes, that's how it has to be—but the Empire doesn't give in that easily." "Reflections on *Omeros*" (edited transcript of lecture given at Duke University on 19 April 1995), in Gregson Davis, ed., *The Poetics of Derek Walcott,* p. 246.

9. *Omeros,* Book One, Chapter I, Part II, p. 7.

10. See, more than once, John Hollander, *The Figure of Echo: A Mode of Allusion in Milton and After* (Berkeley, CA: University of California Press, 1981).

11. One of the most memorable, if not the most delicate of these envelope-words, a visual rather than acoustic echo-pair, is Humbert Humbert's: "The rapist was Charlie Holmes; I am the therapist." Vladimir Nabokov, *Lolita* (London: Weidenfeld & Nicolson, 1955), Part 2, chapter 1, p. 147; see also Part 1, chapter 27, p. 112.

12. *Omeros,* Book One, Chapter VI, Part I, p. 34.

13. *Omeros,* Book One, Chapter II, Part III, p. 14.

14. For an excellent discussion of catachresis, see Jean-Jacques Lecercle, *The Violence of Language* (London: Routledge, 1990), pp. 55-60.

15. See also *Omeros,* Book Six, Chapter XLV, Part II, p. 227: "My craft required the same / crouching care . . ." and Book Seven, Chapter LVIII, Part II, p. 291: "a desk is a raft / for one, foaming with paper, and dipping the beak / / of a pen in its foam, while an actual craft / carries the other. . . ." Note how "craft" generates from within, by an echo-rhyme, its own metaphorical "vehicle," "raft"; and see, on "c/raft," Carol Dougherty, "Homer after *Omeros,*" p. 353.

16. See the outstanding essay by Owen Barfield, "The Meaning of Literal" in *The Rediscovery of Meaning and Other Essays* (Middletown, CT: Wesleyan University Press, 1977), pp. 32-43. What Barfield calls the achieved literal—"literalness is a quality which some words have achieved . . . it is not a quality with which the first words were born" (p. 41)—we will call catachresis.

17. *Omeros,* Book Five, Chapter XLIII, Part III, p. 219.

18. *Omeros,* Book Six, Chapter XLV, Part III, p. 230.

19. The "reversible world" translates "le monde renversé," a term often associated with the Baroque, ultimately to be derived from Baltasar Gracian. See Barbara Babcock, ed., *The Reversible World: Symbolic Inversion in Art and Society* (Ithaca, NY: Cornell University Press, 1978).

20. On Jakobson, metaphor and metonymy, see Charles Lock, "Debts and Displacements: on Metaphor and Metonymy," *Acta Linguistica Hafniensia* (C. A. Reitzel, Copenhagen: special issue on Roman Jakobson), Vol. 29 (1997), pp. 321-37.

21. G. E. Lessing, *Laocoön,* ch. 21, p. 79, and n. 5 above. See also Bakhtin, *Dialogic Imagination,* p. 351.

22. *Omeros,* Book One, Chapter VI, Part III, pp. 36-7. This passage exemplifies Lessing's account of Homer's technique: "Homer, I find, paints nothing but continuous actions, and all bodies, all single things, he paints only by their share in those actions, and in general only by one feature," *Laocoön,* ch. 16, p. 56.

23. In the phrase of Gregory Nagy, "Foreword" to Norman Austin, *Helen of Troy and Her Shameless Phantom* (Ithaca, NY: Cornell University Press, 1995), p. xi. Austin's work provides the most thorough scholarly treatment of the topic.

24. Walcott discloses: ". . . to have Philoctete as a character, although Philoctetes is not, as far as I remember, a major character in the *Odyssey,* is to have a play by Sophocles jamming with a poem by Homer." "Reflections on *Omeros*," p. 242.

25. Ernst Bloch, *The Principle of Hope,* translated by Neville Plaice, Stephen Plaice and Paul Knight (Cambridge, MA: MIT Press, 1986), Volume One, pp. 184-86.

26. H.D., *Helen in Egypt* (New York: Grove Press, 1961; New York: New Directions, 1974), p. 1. H.D. died on 27 September 1961, just after the poem's publication: see *The Letters of John Cowper Powys to Frances Gregg,* edited by Oliver M. Wilkinson (London: Cecil Woolf, 1994), Volume One, p. 237. A popular treatment of this theme was a romantic novel, *The World's Desire* (1890), written by Andrew Lang and H. Rider Haggard. The collaboration was initiated when Lang had written to Haggard: "I can't feel *quite* certain that Helen ever went to Troy. In Herodotus and Euripides only her shadow goes." See Roger Lancelyn Green, *Andrew Lang: A Critical Biography* (Leicester, UK: Edmund Ward, 1946), pp. 124-37. It is reported by the Egyptian poet M. M. Badawi that the English poet and scholar John Heath-Stubbs, while working in Alexandria from 1955 to 1958, wrote a verse-drama, "Helen in Egypt," "of which a dramatic reading was given before its publication in the house of a friend"; I have not been able to locate a copy of this work. See *Aquarius,* no. 10 ("in honour of John Heath-Stubbs," 1978), pp. 25-7.

27. H.D., *Helen in Egypt,* p. 5. The link between *Omeros* and H.D.'s *Helen in Egypt* has been made by Charlotte S. McClure in "Helen of the 'West Indies': History or Poetry of a Caribbean Realm," *Studies in the Literary Imagination,* Vol. XXVI, no. 2 (Fall 1993), pp. 15-6.

28. *Omeros,* Book Seven, Chapter LXII, Part II, p. 313.

29. *Omeros,* Book Three, Chapter XXVI, Part II, p. 141.

30. *Omeros,* Book Five, Chapter XLI, Part III, p. 210.

31. *Omeros,* Book One, Chapter VI, Part I, p. 33.

32. That Bakhtin's "dialogism" corresponds in large part to free indirect discourse may be deduced from V. N. Volosinov, *Marxism and the Philosophy of Language,* translated by L. Matejka and I. R. Titunik (Cambridge, MA: Harvard University Press, 1986); see Charles Lock, "Double Voicing, Sharing Words: Bakhtin's Dialogism and the History of the Theory of Free Indirect Discourse" in the journal *Dialogics* (Sheffield, UK), forthcoming.

33. *Omeros,* Book Two, Chapter XVIII, Part II, p. 97.

34. Further on shadows, see Charles Lock, "A Returning of Shadows," *Literary Research/Recherche Littéraire* (No. 29: Spring-Summer 1998), pp. 15-26.

35. *Omeros,* Book Two, Chapter XIX, Part I, p. 100; see also Book One, Chapter V, Part III, p. 31: "the island was once / named Helen; its Homeric association / / rose like smoke from a siege."

36. *Omeros,* Book Two, Chapter XVIII, Part I, p. 95; "webbed" plays and plies between text as texture and Zeus as swan, whose copulation with Leda engendered Helen of Troy.

37. *Omeros,* Book One, Chapter XI, Part I, p. 64.

38. *Omeros,* Book One, Chapter V, Part III, p. 30.

39. Shakespeare, *The Winter's Tale,* Act V, scene iii, line 78.

40. *Omeros,* Book Six, Chapter LIV, Part III, p. 271.

41. *Omeros,* Book Seven, Chapter LXIV, Part II, p. 323.

42. *Omeros,* Book Six, Chapter LIV, Part II, p. 271.

43. *Omeros,* Book Seven, Chapter LIX, Part I, pp. 295-96.

44. Wallace Stevens, "An Ordinary Evening in New Haven," ix.

45. *Omeros,* Book Seven, Chapter LVI, Part III, p. 284.

46. *Omeros,* Book Seven, Chapter LVII, Part I, p. 286.

47. *Omeros,* Book One, Chapter XIII, Part II, p. 74.

**Derek Walcott and William R. Ferris (interview date November-December 2001)**

SOURCE: Walcott, Derek, and William R. Ferris. "A Multiplicity of Voices: A Conversation with Derek Walcott." *Humanities* 22, no. 6 (November-December 2001): 4-7, 50-53.

*[The following interview focuses on influences on Walcott's literary career including Caribbean history, Daniel Defoe's* Robinson Crusoe, *and the language of Shakespeare.]*

*[Ferris]: I want to begin by quoting Joseph Brodsky's remark that "The West Indies were discovered by Columbus, colonized by the British, and immortalized by Walcott."*

*You were born and raised in the West Indies and spend a good bit of each year in St. Lucia. What do you feel are the basic elements that make up the Caribbean culture?*

[Walcott]: I think its multiracial character is a basic component, particularly in cases like Trinidad and the larger islands. All the races are represented here, not only the African, but the East Indian and the Chinese and the Mediterranean and the European. You can trace their influence in the music, as well as in the language.

*Is there such a thing as a Caribbean voice? If so, what does it say?*

I think the identity of the Caribbean voice is the multiplicity of voices here in the Caribbean. These languages are derived from dialects of the original languages—Spanish, French, English, Portuguese. They are all represented in this space.

*How have you seen Caribbean culture change over the last fifty years?*

Like any part of the world, it can't escape the technological advances that have happened, and not necessarily all to the good. You know, the whole idea of the global village is true. The strongest influence culturally, of course, is America. It's very hard to retain individuality since there is a kind of third empire now, which is the commercial empire that America represents in the export of its culture through television and film.

*What elements of Caribbean culture has the United States embraced and which elements of our culture has the Caribbean embraced?*

Popular culture through television, particularly with the young, is a very strong presence. A lot of the young people in the Caribbean are self-deluded into pretending that they are American. That's part of the attraction of the American technical culture, particularly in music.

As to what America itself has received and used from the Caribbean, I don't think there's much visible evidence of that because America still exercises prejudicial judgment on what influence the third world or its people of color can have. They are blocked by all sorts of forces of habit that prevent the expansion of our culture, as well as black culture, in America.

Our influence is relegated particularly to music, jazz or park music or rap, so that if the culture in America were broader, then one could say that it might include Caribbean culture. There is a struggle for the black artist in America anyway to try and have influence, or just simply to be present. So it's not easy to say that there is an influence from the Caribbean on American culture.

*The National Endowment for the Humanities supported the biography that Bruce King wrote about you and your life. I understand you were initially reluctant to allow a biography.*

Frankly, I haven't read it. But I guess it's of importance. You know, one can't avoid the idea that eventually someone is going to write about your life.

*At the time that King was writing your biography, you were working on* **Tiepolo's Hound.** *Some see that as something of an autobiography. You wrote about the life of the artist, about exile, about the relationship of new world art to Europe and other cultures. I was fascinated to see your own artwork illustrating the poem. How do the paintings and the words relate? Is a syllable like a brush stroke, as has been suggested?*

In a way. It depends on the painting itself and what medium you're using. I don't paint in a manner that, say, Cézanne painted in, his brush strokes and so on. My gouaches are more fluid.

But, yes, I have always found a great relationship between painting and writing words. I don't think that writing words can help your painting, but I think that knowing what color you're going to use and having an idea of symmetry and structure and light from the practice of painting certainly helps craft verse. So that relationship continues.

*Do you see yourself as a painter as much as you see yourself as a writer?*

No. I'm very tough on my own self as a painter. I'm much more dissatisfied and more restless and more angry and more conscious of failure in painting than I am in either theater or in verse.

The good thing about painting is that you can see that you're a flop immediately. You don't always know that you're not doing well in either a theater piece or poem.

*When John Millington Synge wrote* The Aran Islands, *Jack Yeats joined him to do an accompanying set of paintings. Synge later complained that it was much quicker and easier for Yeats to do the paintings than for him to do the writing. But you have embraced both of these worlds.*

Right. I consider Synge a more permanent artist than Yeats, though.

*By the time you were fourteen you were a published poet, and by the age of sixteen, a dramatist. Where did your urge to write come from?*

The example was from my father who was a painter, a very good watercolorist, who died very young, and my mother, who was a schoolteacher and recited Shakespeare. She was an amateur actress and my father did theatrical shows. I think it's a sort of direct inheritance.

*There is a central theme in your work of the search for identity. How would you describe your own identity?*

I could describe myself in detail down to my heel and the color of my eyes and my skin, but that's not what one means by identity in the Caribbean. It took me a long and searching time to resolve what it is to be a St. Lucian and a West Indian. The experience, of course, comes from the political pattern of the Caribbean—colonialism to independence. If you can equate adolescence to colonialism, and so forth, until you get to maturity and independence, then there's a parallel.

I knew from the time I was very, very young that I wanted to try to describe things that were Caribbean because they were new and they were exciting and they were virginal in that sense.

*Why do you find such a compelling issue in the search for identity?*

The whole mission for a writer or painter or any artist—it's true of any culture—is to find out what you mean. And you can only know what you mean by knowing who you are. That's true of a Jewish writer or an Indian writer or anyone.

We have a very complicated situation in the Caribbean because there is a lot of quarreling going on now. We have proven through our experience that people can survive next to each other, that the Muslim and the Hindu can live in Trinidad in proximity without any violence. So, even if it is a microcosm, we have these examples of harmony that can happen between the races. I'm not painting an ideal picture, but the practicality and the reality of it has been that we have lived together very amicably, and that's not the same for the rest of the world.

Now, it is small and people may say, "Well, that's not entirely true," but I think one of the political validities of the Caribbean culture is that its variety is its identity.

*The theme of discovery and exploration comes through again and again in your work. Many of your works make allusion to Daniel Defoe's* Robinson Crusoe. *When did you first encounter* Crusoe?

The Crusoe fable, as presented by Defoe, is a thing every Caribbean child knew, and maybe still knows—the idea of Friday's footprint in the sand and then the relationship with Friday, Crusoe's servant and companion. We all learned that very early, from childhood.

*Why is Crusoe such a fascinating character for you?*

Because the legend of Crusoe is set in the Caribbean. It is supposed to have taken place in Tobago. I guess the attraction is that it's an island fable. But also it's the idea of the isolated person, shipwrecked. That's a very old fable.

*You're an accomplished poet and a playwright and a painter. I want to talk with you for a moment about your poetry for which you won the Nobel Prize for Literature in 1992. Why does poetry appeal to you as a form of expression?*

I knew I wanted to write verse from very early. I can't say how far back I found myself writing verse. I think I got it from my father and from my mother's presence as a teacher. It wasn't a question of a calling; it was endemic, it was there, and I found myself working and trying to write good verse from a very early age.

Painting came a little later, but not much later. And the theater, of course, requires other people, actors and so on, and that came in school. But the poetry is something I always knew that I was going to do.

*That's beautiful. Which poets influenced your work?*

Well, the thing about a Caribbean education is that it was very classic in terms of its sources. We did Shakespeare. We did Dickens and Scott and all the given names. The same system of teaching, which is a sort of British public school curriculum, is the one that we had in the Caribbean.

We did Latin, as well, and in some islands they did Latin and the Greek. I never did Greek, but Barbados taught Latin and Greek. I'm very happy that I did Latin and I'm very sorry that Latin has been lost to all these schools now, because it is a fundamental language and it's beautiful.

*Was Dylan Thomas a poet you encountered?*

Yes, yes. I didn't consider myself to be influenced so as much as an apprentice trying to learn from everyone. I modeled my work at a very early age on all the writers that I admired, from Auden and Dylan Thomas and so on. I had the freedom, as far as I was concerned, not to have the sense of time that, say, an English schoolboy or an American might have in terms of the chronology of time and dates.

That chronology of history did not apply for me. I was free to roam any period that I liked and free to imitate and model myself on any period, whether it was Shakespeare or whether it was translations of Ovid or Dante. I don't want to sound too pretentious. I'm just saying I just felt free and entitled to all those things.

*Which poets are you still reading?*

I recently read Philip Larkin and Seamus Heaney, a contemporary. I like Paul Muldoon a lot. There are a lot of different names. It's hard to list all of them.

*You've written more than twenty-five plays since you began as a teenager. Where did your interest in the theater come from?*

My mother used to recite a lot of Shakespeare. She had acted in Shakespeare. So she recited great poetry around the house. I would hear that and feel like, yes, maybe I'll be able to get her to recite something by me sometime. And my father did amateur theatricals.

I'm a great believer in genetics. Because of environment, because of habit or direction, I inherited this theatrical sense mainly from my mother's acting, but also because I felt very strongly about poetic theater, about theater that was not prosaic and ordinary.

I was also in a very free-form environment. The privilege of being able to say, "All right, I'm going to do a play that has this or that in it"—and you perform it in an obscure little island like St. Lucia—is a kind of freedom, more than if I were in a regimented idea of an inherited style.

*What does a play allow you to express that poetry cannot?*

I think poetry can do anything. Some of the greatest theater in the world is poetry.

*Which playwrights influenced you?*

Again, answers sound pompous, but for a young man, they're not pompous. Shakespeare is an obvious influence because of the poetry, and the Jacobeans to some degree. Later on, Bertolt Brecht. Who else? Synge, the Irish revival, the Irish writers.

*You wrote the epic poem,* **Omeros,** *a twentieth-century retelling of Homer's* Iliad *and* Odyssey *set in the Caribbean, and you also did a play based on the* Odyssey.

I'd like to correct that, which I've been doing relentlessly lately. The book is not based on Homer's *Iliad* and *Odyssey.* They are associations, inferences and associations, and that's what the book says. A fisherman named Achille—and there is such a person and there is a man called Hector—they have no idea who they are.

And the plot does not imitate. The evocation is what it is, the echo and the evocation of Homer's legend is what's here—in the same way that an island may, in a sense, convey an echo of another island on the horizon. That's what it's based on mainly, not on an attempt to rewrite Homer in the Caribbean. That would be absurd. It's not designed like, say, Joyce's *Ulysses,* line by line to represent something that happened in the *Odyssey,* particularly.

*Right.*

But it is evocation and meaning. That's what it is mainly about. At the end of the book, the book turns on the author to say, stop doing this classical stuff and try and face reality where you are.

*In* Portrait of the Artist as a Young Man, *Joyce says that he fled the nets of family, religion, and politics. Joyce himself left his island and was forever an expatriate. You've come home again and you've made a reconciliation with your own culture.*

I never really separated myself from it. I never had any desire to leave it, really. The restlessness and the impatience and the anger—don't have any point, I think, in my work. I couldn't leave because I was committed to the theater primarily, and I couldn't take West Indian theater into the places that I had gone to.

*Why were you drawn to the* Odyssey *and the* Iliad *as stories?*

You live in an archipelago and so does Ulysses, so does Homer. These islands have their parallel. All literature is indebted to the *Odyssey,* so this literature is no less indebted.

Of course, this literature comes out of an even more physical resemblance to, say, the Aegean or to the fables of wandering and return that are physically present every day if we look out in the Caribbean and see a sail going out or coming back in. This would be true anywhere. It's such a powerful iconic thing that no matter where you are, you think of a single sailor as Ulysses. That has become a global metaphor.

I think maybe what I wanted to do is to write about the fishermen in St. Lucia and their way of life. That's principally it. It's a book about the sea. It's a book about memory. But it's not based on the adventures of Ulysses.

*What attracted you to writing an epic poem? What did it allow you to do?*

I didn't set out to write an epic. It just got very long and very big, and I guess that's why it's called an epic. The destination of an epic used to be a sort of political destination. It used to be to elevate the race out of which the hero came or to do X or Y, you know? We are too powerless to have that kind of hero. So the width of the book, the length of the book, really is a matter of accretion. It just got longer and wider.

But it was a great joy to write it, because the design of it meant that I could get up every morning and go towards it as if one might go to a large fiction, and the design of it was already there on a grid. It was very exciting to come to it every day, and it got to expand itself more.

*The poem and the play both are filled with historical references and allusions. What role does history play in your work?*

The history of the Caribbean is a very unhappy history. It's a history of genocide, of slavery, of indenture. As beautiful as the Caribbean is, the contrast of the history is that it has a very sad and ravaged past.

History in that sense has a malevolent kind of aura in the Caribbean, because the things that were done in the Caribbean were done in the name of history, in the name of progress and expansion, from the conquistadors or from the conquerors, you know, through the different empires that owned the islands. The battles that happened, for the sake of each individual empire, resulted in the exploitation of the obvious people, the Indians and then the Africans and so on.

*Do you think that our current culture today is historically conscious, in the Caribbean, and more broadly, globally? Are we aware of history in the way that people in earlier generations were?*

I don't think we see it as a threat or a force that dominates our lives. Whether it was British, French, or Spanish or Portuguese, when you were colonial, the history didn't belong to you. It belonged to the person who was ruling you or supervising you.

That doesn't exist anymore except in an oblique way. It exists very forcefully and it may be the most powerful influence we have, in the American influence on what we should do or what we should buy or what we should become. That's an imperial threat, too, and we have to be careful that we don't succumb to that.

*You've acknowledged your debt to Shakespeare and to other writers. I think of my old friend, Jacob Elder, in Tobago, who's done a lot of work on folklore there. How did folklore and the stories you were told shape your work?*

I incorporated them into theater, into the plays. I think it's a matter of rhythm. It is a matter of technique of folk stories, the concept of repetition and variety and the symmetry that comes in folk-telling. I think I tried to incorporate those in some of the plays, and the music.

*As you look back on a career of more than fifty years, is there a project that you wish that you had taken on?*

I would like to make films about the Caribbean, feature films. I think there is an immense amount of material from Caribbean novelists and theater people that would make excellent film material.

*That would be a wonderful step, from writing the novel to filming it.*

Yes.

*I am forever grateful to you for taking the time to speak with me and to share your thoughts in this way.*

Thank you very much.

## William A. Shullenberger (essay date November-December 2001)

SOURCE: Shullenberger, William A. "An *Iliad* for Our Time: Walcott's Caribbean Epic." *Humanities* 22, no. 6 (November-December 2001): 47-49.

[*In the following essay, Shullenberger compares Walcott's epic poem* Omeros *to Homer's* Iliad.]

Although we tend to assign the epic to the literary past as a bygone genre, Derek Walcott's **Omeros,** published in 1990, asserts the ongoing power of the epic to claim our attention and shape our understanding. The epic is a monumental literary form—an index to the depth and richness of a culture and the ultimate test of a writer's creative power. Homer's *Iliad* stands at the beginning of the epic tradition in western culture, and Walcott's **Omeros** is that tradition's most recent expression.

The epic is the collective memory of a people, offering poetic memory as a way to transcend the afflictions and losses of history. Homer, for instance, marks the differences and continuities between Greeks and Trojans, and Walcott represents the lives of Caribbean people in the waning of the colonial period.

The grace, beauty, and imaginative strength of **Omeros** depends in good part on Walcott's insightful reading and rewriting of Homer. Walcott is an example of how a contemporary writer can make a place for himself in the literary tradition and harvest its power for his own creative authority. But literary influence is not a one-way street. T. S. Eliot describes the relationship this way: "What happens when a new work of art is created is something that happens simultaneously to all the works of art which preceded it. The existing monuments form an ideal order among themselves, which is modified by the introduction of the new (the really new) work of art among them."

So Walcott, in his "really new work," revises our relation to Homer. Walcott's rewriting of Homer's epics leads contemporary readers back to the ancient texts to discover persisting human themes and complex literary strategies. It sharpens our attention to structures of imaginative, moral, and social power articulated in the *Iliad*. Reading the two poems together renews our awareness of the *Iliad*'s pertinence to our times, and renews our sympathy for those remote and god like, yet deeply vulnerable, characters who enact and suffer our ultimate concerns.

Whoever he may have been, whether a single integrative genius or a convenient fiction to pin together the accumulated work of generations of anonymous bards, "Homer" sets the standard of the epic in western culture. Walcott absorbs both the *Iliad* and the *Odyssey* in his story, but the *Iliad* establishes the high tragic tone that resonates through **Omeros** and provides the central characters and conflicts that Walcott refigures in his story.

In the *Iliad*, ten years of war at Troy are condensed into several weeks. The savagery escalates at the time of Achilles's sullen withdrawal from the fighting, and climaxes in his explosive, terrible return. In Achilles's absence, the battle shifts back and forth, affected in unpredictable ways by divine interventions and sudden outbursts of courage and skill by heroes on both sides. Achilles reluctantly permits his beloved comrade Patroclus to enter the fighting as a surrogate. His death at the hands of Hector outrages Achilles, who blazes back into the action with a bloodthirsty fury great enough to terrify even the gods.

The poem abounds in ironies. The culture is founded and defended by the very virtues which threaten to destroy it. Homer displays heroic self-assertion as a double-edged virtue, a courageous gesture of individual defiance against mortality and all human contingency. But because one person's aristeia is another's undoing, heroism ultimately serves the impersonal and destructive force it defies. Gift-giving and hospitality are binding counterforces against individual heroism; for the friendships forged by gifts and guests have a stronger claim [on] the hero than even kinship or tribal loyalties. This is what made Paris's abduction of Helen from Menelaus's household a blasphemy great enough in the Greek estimation to warrant ten years of slaughter.

Walcott has frequently developed analogies between the cultures of Homer's Mediterranean and his own Caribbean; *Omeros* relocates Homer's epic scene from ancient Troy to the backwater Antillean island of St. Lucia, and discovers the tragic grandeur and mythic power of Homer's heroes in the fishermen and villagers who harvest the all-nurturing sea and the fertile but fickle earth for their lives' subsistence. The central Homeric characters of *Omeros* are Helen, and Achille and Hector, brothers of the fishing trade whose rivalry for Helen's extraordinary beauty turns their friendship to murderous anger.

Women occupy particularly perilous and vulnerable positions in the *Iliad*. From the fight over Helen, which is the manifest cause of the war, to the sparring between Agamemnon and Achilles over the possession of the mute captive Briseis, Homer shows women as trophies, objects of exchange and contention—an extreme form of the dehumanization to which all are subject.

In *Omeros,* Helen, like her Greek prototype, is the great enigma and driving force behind men's acts of courage and desperation. Walcott heightens her mystery by providing the reader little access to her thoughts. This paradoxically, humanizes her by allowing Helen a kind of privacy of conscience unusual for a literary character. The poet refuses to intrude upon or speak for her experience, as he does for his male heroes.

Achille's desolation upon Helen's abandonment of him takes him further and further out to sea—the "mer" in O-mer-os—until the search compels him on an odyssey through time and space to an inland village of upriver Benin. Here he relives the slave raid that dispossessed his ancestors of home, name, and past. He returns to St. Lucia a changed, self-possessed man, ready to live with his losses. Meanwhile, Hector's anxiety about Helen's love and his compulsion to keep her in modern style drive him to give up the sea, to sell his canoe and to buy a souped-up transport van, with space-age customized painting and leopard skin seats, to taxi people about the island. The pressure for money, the longing for the sea, and remorse over his fight with Achille ultimately propel Hector over a sea cliff to his death. Helen and Achille are reconciled, and the poem ends with Helen preparing to give birth and Achille returning to harvest the thrashing silver of the inexhaustible sea.

Walcott crosscuts several other stories into the primary tale, among them that of the lame Philoctete waiting for a cure for the festering sore on his foot, emblematic of the psychological wound of slavery. Other stories show the deep love for the island cultivated by the expatriates Dennis and Maud Plunkett, and the displaced poet's own odyssey in search of a place to call home. The poet's journey, like Achille's, is temporal as well as geographical: he goes back in time to encounter his mother and father, and out into the world to confront the imposing cultural mystique and trace the waning boundaries of a European empire.

Homer appears as a character in various guises in *Omeros:* as the blind grizzled fisherman Seven Seas, as a crazy vagrant kicked about Trafalgar Square, as the great American painter Winslow Homer, as the Liffey-haunting, dandified ghost of James Joyce, as the griot of a West African village, and as a Sioux prophet at the time of the Ghost Dance. But Homer surfaces most powerfully in the sublime hexameters of Walcott's verse, making the poet himself the most inclusive and self-conscious of the Homeric figures he stitches into the poem.

Walcott employs what T. S. Eliot called the "mythic method," using the narrative spell of myth to organize and dignify the potential chaos and insignificance of modern secular life. But he does so in the self-questioning way of a modernist aware of the potential falsehoods and nostalgias of mythmaking. He creates a poem on a heroic scale, with the scope of the Homeric epics, but also with the self-conscious interventions and the narrative fragmentation characteristic of modernism. He sustains the tone of grandeur, weaving together a fabric of seemingly incompatible styles: the high sublime of Homeric declamation and of English visionary poetry with the nimble, syncopated Creole patois, chants, and challenges of St. Lucia's streets, bars, and seafronts.

Walcott achieves that blend of objectivity and implicit compassion that gives Homer's poems such tragic dignity, and, like Homer, he imagines the poem itself as a heroic act, a sustained meditation on history, capacious enough to register its deepest losses and powerful enough to claim that art can transcend them. In *Omeros,* . . . we see history transfigured into myth, even at the moment of its fading, and Helen's bitter lament in the *Iliad* for herself and Paris could stand as an epigraph for the central figures of both poems: "Zeus planted a killing doom within us both, / so even for generations still unborn / we will live in song."

**Jahan Ramazani (essay date 2001)**

SOURCE: Ramazani, Jahan. "The Wound of Postcolonial History: Derek Walcott's *Omeros*." In *The Hybrid Muse: Postcolonial Poetry in English,* pp. 49-71. Chicago: University of Chicago Press, 2001.

[*In the following essay, Ramazani traces the theme of postcolonial Afro-Caribbean cultural identity in Walcott's* Omeros.]

From an early age Derek Walcott felt a special "intimacy with the Irish poets" as "colonials with the same kind of problems that existed in the Caribbean. They were the niggers of Britain."[1] Passionately identifying with Yeats, Joyce, Synge, and other Irish writers, Walcott shared especially in their conflicted response to the cultural inheritances of the British empire—its literature, religion, and language. At school, Walcott recalls, Joyce's Stephen Dedalus was his "hero": "Like him, I was a knot of paradoxes," among other things "learning to hate England as I worshipped her language."[2] His best known lyric, **"A Far Cry from Africa"** (1956), elaborates the poem of ambivalence toward imperial and anti-imperial bloodshed, building on Yeats's simultaneously anticolonial and anti-anti-colonial stance in works such as **"Easter, 1916"** and **"Nineteen Hundred and Nineteen."**[3] As Yeats used a series of counterbalanced questions to dramatize his inner divisions after the Easter Rising, Walcott forty years later responds to the Mau Mau rebellion with a spiral of questions that "turn" on each other with ever stronger torque:

> I who am poisoned with the blood of both,
> Where shall I turn, divided to the vein?
> I who have cursed
> The drunken officer of British rule, how choose
> Between this Africa and the English tongue I love?
> Betray them both, or give back what they give?
> How can I face such slaughter and be cool?
> How can I turn from Africa and live?

Another thirty-four years later, in his Caribbean epic, *Omeros* (1990), Walcott is still puzzling out what it means to love the English language yet hate English imperialism. As a character within his own narrative, Walcott travels to Ireland, literalizing his revisitation of Joyce and Yeats as precursors, and there—struck anew by the shared postcolonial problem of linguistic and literary inheritance—he memorably declares Ireland "a nation / split by a glottal scream."[4]

An epic divided to the vein, a poem split by a glottal scream, *Omeros* asks how the postcolonial poet can both grieve the agonizing harm of British colonialism and celebrate the empire's literary bequest. Walcott's pervasive figure of the wound can help us to understand his answer to this question, as the figurative site where concerns with imperial injury, literary archetype, and linguistic heritage most graphically intersect. "This wound I have stitched into Plunkett's character," ventures the poet early in *Omeros.* Conflating wound and suture, Walcott suggests

that the odd surgery of poetry may have to disfigure a character with wounds to repair historical injuries. "He has to be wounded," continues the poet defensively. Why must the poet stitch some kind of wound into all of his major characters, from Philoctete, the emblematic black descendant of slaves, to Plunkett, the representative white colonial; from the lovelorn Achille to Hector, Helen, even himself? Because, the poet explains, "affliction is one theme / of this work, this fiction," as indeed of Afro-Caribbean literature and much Third World literature in general (28). That the wound trope is central to *Omeros* suits preconceptions of postcolonial writing as either "victim's literature" or "resistance literature." But Walcott's use of the figure—for example, attaching it here to the white colonial Plunkett—frustrates the assumptions it elicits. Indeed, this seemingly unsurprising motif continually turns strange and unpredictable in Walcott's hands; this strangeness starts with his willingness to embrace the motif after having denounced the literature of Third World suffering for decades.

In examining Walcott's elaboration of the wound in *Omeros,* I trace the complex genealogy of its primary bearer, the black fisherman Philoctete. Appropriating the classical type of the wound-tormented Philoctetes paradoxically enables Walcott to give new voice to the suffering of Afro-Caribbean peoples under European colonialism and slavery.[5] In this character, Walcott fuses still other literary prototypes of North and South, Old World and New. The astonishing hybridity of Walcott's black victim exemplifies the cross-cultural fabric of postcolonial poetry and contravenes the widespread assumption that postcolonial literature develops by sloughing off Eurocentrism for indigeneity. Repudiating a separatist aesthetic of affliction, Walcott turns the wound into a resonant site of interethnic connection within *Omeros,* vivifying the black Caribbean inheritance of colonial injury and at the same time deconstructing the uniqueness of suffering. Hybrid, polyvalent, and unpredictable in its knitting together of different histories of affliction, Walcott's radiant metaphor of the wound helps to dramatize poetry's promise as one of the richest and most vibrant genres of postcolonial writing.

Perhaps the most ambitious English-language poem of the decolonized Third World, Walcott's massive *Omeros* is written in long rolling lines—typically of twelve syllables—grouped in loose terza rima stanzas; alludes abundantly to Homer, Joyce, and Aimé Césaire; and ranges from precolonial Africa to eighteenth-century Saint Lucia, from the nineteenth-century United States to contemporary Ireland. Interwoven with its story of Philoctete's wound are plots of a Saint Lucian Achille and Hector struggling over a beautiful Helen, of an English Plunkett and Irish Maud seeking peace in the Caribbean, and of a composite poet—part Walcott, part blind pensioner—striving to tell the history of his island. Of Afro-Caribbean poems in English, only Kamau Brathwaite's *The Arrivants* (1967-69) is a work of comparable scope, size, and aspiration. Brathwaite's fragmentary trilogy also revisits the trauma of the Middle Passage and looks back to Africa, bases characters on inherited literary types and intermingles West Indian creole with literary English. But whereas an epic poem of Caribbean "wounds" or "hurts of history" might be expected of Brathwaite, professional historian and poet of New World African dispossession and survival, Walcott in the 1960s and 1970s declared his hostility to Afro-Caribbean literature about "the suffering of the victim."[6] While many Caribbean writers of this period chronicled the inherited devastation of European slavery and colonialism, Walcott, accusing Brathwaite among others of being absorbed in "self-pity," "rage," and "masochistic recollection," called instead for an artistic celebration of the Adamic potential of the New World African: perpetual exile was, in his view, the condition for a new creativity.[7]

In Walcott's poetry of this period, the wound or scar is often the figurative locus of such criticisms. Toward the end of his grand autobiographical poem *Another Life* (1973), Walcott blasts Caribbean artists for their "masochistic veneration of / chains," for revering "the festering roses made from their fathers' manacles."[8] He casts into the volcanic pit of his Antillean hell "the syntactical apologists of the Third World":

> Those who peel, from their own leprous flesh, their names,
> who chafe and nurture the scars of rusted chains,
> like primates favouring scabs, those who charge tickets
> for another free ride on the middle passage. . . .
>
> . . . . .
> they measure each other's sores
> to boast who has suffered most,
> and their artists keep dying,
> they are the saints of self-torture,
> their stars are pimples of pus
> on the night of our grandfathers,
> they are hired like dogs to lick the sores of their
>   people. . . .[9]

Pitching his voice in a willfully intemperate tone, Walcott attributes the scars, scabs, and sores of his damned not only to slavery but to recent masochistic indulgences. Grimly yet gleefully analogizing, Walcott maps onto Africanist returns to the trauma of slavery the Dantean figuration of hell as compulsive repetition of the past.

But in writing an epic poem of his native Saint Lucia, Walcott takes up the postcolonial poetics of affliction he once condemned, anatomizing the wounded body of Caribbean history through Philoctete,[10] injured by a rusted anchor:

> He believed the swelling came from the chained ankles
> of his grandfathers. Or else why was there no cure?
> That the cross he carried was not only the anchor's
>
> but that of his race, for a village black and poor
> as the pigs that rooted in its burning garbage,
> then were hooked on the anchors of the abattoir.
>
> (19)

Walcott makes an oblique reference to colonialism, comparing the wound to the "puffed blister of Portuguese man-o'-war" (19); and he also evokes "a wounded race" (299) and "the tribal / sorrow that Philoctete could not drown in alcohol" (129). Even after he is supposedly healed, Philoctete joins Achille in a Boxing Day rite that, like the Caribbean limbo dance, recapitulates the trauma of the Middle Passage, including the primordial deracination that Philoctete reenacts when he slaughters the yams:

> All the pain
>
> re-entered Philoctete, of the hacked yams, the hold
> closing over their heads, the bolt-closing iron. . . .
>
> (277)

In using the wound motif to signify slavery and colonialism, *Omeros* resembles countless other texts of African diaspora literature, and the reason for this prominence and pervasiveness is far from obscure. As C. L. R. James recalls in his discussion of the vicious treatment of Caribbean slaves, wounds were inflicted in many gruesome ways, and even "salt, pepper, citron, cinders, aloes, and hot ashes were poured on the bleeding wounds."[11] Early on in *Omeros,* Walcott uses one of Philoctete's seizures to suggest that the inexpressible physical suffering of enslaved Africans is retained in the bodies of their descendants and that the pain still presses urgently for an impossible verbal release:

> His knee was radiant iron,
> his chest was a sack of ice, and behind the bars
>
> of his rusted teeth, like a mongoose in a cage,
> a scream was mad to come out; his tongue tickled its claws
> on the roof of his mouth, rattling its bars in rage.
>
> (21)

Naming conditions of black enslavement with the words "iron," "bars," "rusted," and "cage," Walcott portrays the pain of the wound as colonizing Philoctete's entire body. More than any of Walcott's previous works, *Omeros* memorializes the institutionalized atrocity of New World African slavery. Though as late as the 1980s Walcott continued to castigate West Indian literature for sulking— "Look what the slave-owner did"[12]—at the beginning of *Omeros,* Philoctete rolls up his trouser leg and "shows" his punctured shin to paying tourists, figuring, by extension, the poem's large-scale exhibition of Afro-Caribbean pain to the touristic reader (4). And whereas Walcott once locked in hell "those who peel, from their own leprous flesh, their names," Philoctete refers to the colonially imposed name as one source of the ancestral wound:

> What did it mean,
>
> this name that felt like a fever? Well, one good heft
> of his garden-cutlass would slice the damned name clean
> from its rotting yam.
>
> (20)

Nursed and inspected, magnified and proliferated, the metaphor of the wound forms the vivid nucleus of Walcott's magnum opus. In an interview, Walcott indicates that the figure was the germ of *Omeros:* "A very good friend of mine had died," he recounts, "an actor, and I was thinking about that. And where this poem started was with the figure of Philoctetes, the man with the wound, alone on the beach: Philoctetes from the Greek legend and Timon of Athens as well."[13] How can we reconcile Walcott's earlier and later positions? Part of the answer is that they are less antithetical than my juxtapositions make them appear to be. In spite of his pronouncements, Walcott was already mourning early on what he memorably called the "wound," the "deep, amnesiac blow" of slavery and colonialism.[14] He was deeply aware of the central trauma of Afro-Caribbean history and drawn to bodily figurations of it. Even so, he remained hesitant about fully sounding this theme before *Omeros,* so what made it possible for him to shift from one self-defined stance on the literature of Third World suffering to its apparent opposite? The classical figure of Philoctetes is an important part of the answer, the bridge by which Walcott crosses his own divide. His Afro-Greek Philoctete is a compromise formation, the venerable vehicle legitimizing the tenor of black rage and suffering. While still granting cultural authority to Europe, Walcott also reclaims it for Caribbean blacks more vigorously than before, tropicalizing and twisting an ancient Greek hero into a vibrant new figure for Afro-Caribbean pain. One of the oldest dead white European males is reborn in a wounded black body; a member of the colonizing tribe resigns his part to limp among the colonized.

Walcott's appropriation of the wounded Philoctete broadly resembles other well-known indigenizations of canonical Western characters. To dramatize Caribbean suffering and anticolonialism, Aimé Césaire remakes the doltish Caliban in his play *Une tempête,* Kamau Brathwaite the submissive Uncle Tom in *The Arrivants,* and Jean Rhys the raving Bertha Rochester in *Wide Sargasso Sea.* Racked by an unhealing wound, Philoctete's body literalizes the anguish and anger of his celebrated West Indian counterparts. Like these writers, Walcott poetically inverts the material transfers of colonization, abducting a major character from the Western canon to dramatize the legacy of the West's atrocities. Just as "empires are smart enough to steal from the people they conquer," Walcott has remarked, "the people who have been conquered should have enough sense to steal back."[15]

But whereas Césaire, Brathwaite, and Rhys appropriate characters already oppressed by virtue of their gender, class, or race, Walcott strangely blacks up the classical white male war hero responsible for victory in the Trojan War. Like Walcott's seemingly perverse use of Crusoe instead of Friday to personify the Caribbean condition, the metamorphosis of this wounded Greek castaway is more violent and tangled than that of Caliban, Tom, or Bertha—white to black, colonizer to colonized, classic to contemporary.[16] These dislocations are not merely subversive or "exotic" but emphatically defamiliarizing.[17] Keeping the ironies acute, Walcott presents his Philoctete as even less a self-standing character, even more a signifier of the work of postcolonial reinscription—a Mona Lisa with a distinctively Caribbean mustache.[18] With only minimal credibility as a naturalistic Caribbean fisherman, Walcott's Philoctete seems to have wandered out of Greek literature and stumbled into a textual universe where he suddenly embodies the colonial horrors perpetrated by the West. To highlight his reliance on a culture of slavery to indict the practice of slavery, Walcott pointedly refers to the institution as "Greek" (177) and ironically adduces "the Attic ideal of the first slave-settlement" (63), even as he turns a Greek hero into his synecdoche for all the damage wrought by slavery and colonialism. He repeatedly signals the seeming oddity of Philoctete's name in the Saint Lucian context (greater than that of the simpler Achille or Hector or Helen), as if to make of the name a foreign-language sign hung around his neck. "Pheeloh! Pheelosophee!" scream boys on their way to school (19), and sheep bleat "Beeeeeh, Philoctete!" (20); only at the moment of his apparent cure, "The yoke of the wrong name lifted from his shoulders" (247). Instead of naturalizing the name, Walcott turns it into a trope for violent colonial imposition, a partial cause of the wound to which it is metonymically linked.

Most familiar from Sophocles' eponymous play but also portrayed in countless other retellings from Homer to Seamus Heaney and in the visual arts from Attic vase painting to neoclassical sculpture, Philoctetes, with his exquisitely elaborated pain, has long served as the classical alternative to Christ in the Western iconography of pathos and innocent victimhood. Bitten by a venomous snake and abandoned on the isle of Lemnos by his Greek compatriots, the groaning, shrieking Philoctetes languishes for nine years, his wound stinking, his body convulsed with pain, his flesh covered only with rags.[19] If Philoctetes enabled Lessing to affirm his neoclassical faith in the "moral greatness" of heroic endurance and helped Edmund Wilson to advance a psychological conception of artistic genius as "inextricably bound up" with "disability" and "disease," he becomes for Walcott, as for Heaney in *The Cure at Troy* (1991), an allegorical figure for the postcolonial condition.[20] As agent of Troy's defeat, Philoctetes might seem a dubious choice to represent the colonial victim, yet it is also true that the Greeks exploit him to conquer Troy, that he is transported to an island and abandoned there, and that he lives in poverty, hunger, and pain. Unintelligible stammerings—literally the discourse of the *barbaric*—interrupt his Greek when he suffers spasms of pain. And his wound suggests not only affliction but also colonial penetration, evacuation, and forgetting. Faithful to the classical Philoctetes in remembering his stinking wound, island fate, physical misery, and eventual cure, Walcott nevertheless transports him to a different archipelago, darkens his skin, trades his bow for a fisherman's net, transcribes his pained ejaculations in creole, and effects his cure through an obeah woman. While it might be a tempting, if pedantic, exercise to dissect each of these modifications, the risk would lie in trapping Walcott's Philoctete in an exclusive relation to his Greek namesake;

but his affinities are more culturally polyphonous than such a narrowly typological analysis could allow.

Despite the apparently obvious line of descent signaled by his name, from Philoctetes to Philoctete, Walcott has spliced a variety of literary genes and even antithetical cultures to create a surprisingly motley character. Like a composite character in one of Freud's dreams, the wound-bearing Philoctete encompasses a strange array of penumbral literary figures. Rei Terada discerns the "variegated" and even "confusingly overdetermined" models behind characters in *Omeros,* but critics have tended to see Philoctete as a character with a simple pedigree.[21] If even the character in *Omeros* who appears to be simplest in his cultural inheritance turns out to have a multiple and contradictory parentage, then perhaps the postcolonial poet's seeming capitulation to or seeming subversion of Western influences needs to be rethought as a more ambiguous and ambivalent synthesis than is usually acknowledged.

Philoctete represents Walcott's absorption and refiguration not only of Philoctetes but also, strangely enough, of Caliban. Caliban? Doesn't Walcott scorn the postcolonial transvaluation of Caliban as West Indian hero? Doesn't this poet, who saw himself in youth as "legitimately prolonging the mighty line of Marlowe, of Milton," belong, unlike George Lamming, Aimé Césaire, and Kamau Brathwaite, among the adherents of Prospero, whose Caribbean makeover as "white imperialist" he debunks as "fashionable, Marxist-evolved" revisionism?[22] Walcott's seemingly shameless mimicry of a character out of the classical tradition distracts us, I believe, from his covert refashioning of the Caribbean paradigm of anticolonial defiance. Philoctete, when we first meet him, describes the cutting down of trees, though for making canoes rather than firewood. Closely associated with the land, he mirrors, as if by magical sympathy, his natural island environment in the Caribbean. He personifies his entire race's grievance against the colonizers. He launches an abortive revolution by demolishing the garden that sustains him. He "curse[s]" because never *black people go get rest / from God,*" much as Caliban curses and rues his compulsory hard labor (21). At the moment of Philoctete's cursing, "a fierce cluster of arrows / targeted the sore, and he screamed"; similarly, Caliban's curses prompt his master to promise, "I'll rack thee with old cramps, / Fill all thy bones with aches, make thee roar."[23] Seized by the unpredictable onset of physical torment, Walcott's Philoctete fuses a classical paradigm with the Third World's transvaluation of Shakespeare's wretch. But whereas the new Caliban was already becoming a West Indian cliché a couple of decades earlier, Walcott paradoxically refreshes the symbol of postcolonial agony and anger by reaching for a still more wizened prototype. His career-long resistance to Caliban, as to the wound trope, helps him to flush these literary inheritances with new power and complexity.

As figures of Caribbean oppression, Philoctetes and Caliban complement each other: one of them, tormented on an island that is rightly his, is especially well-suited to al-legorizing colonization, while the other, transported to an alien island, easily figures the displacement and deracination of West Indian slavery. But whereas Philoctetes has remained the cultural property of the West, Caliban's postcolonial indigenization has been so vigorous that, at least regionally, he is as much a Caribbean as a Shakespearean figure. Walcott's closet Caliban bears the impress of postcolonial revisionism or what he concedes are the often "brilliant re-creations" by fellow Caribbean authors.[24] Unlike Shakespeare's but like Césaire's Caliban, for example, Walcott's Philoctete is suspicious of his cumbersome name and even wants, as we have seen, to slice it from his body. In Césaire's *Une tempête,* Caliban decides he doesn't "want to be called Caliban any longer" because Caliban "isn't [his] name" and his real "name has been *stolen.*"[25] To perpetuate Caliban, Walcott paradoxically de-indigenizes him, reroutes the figure back through colonial culture, and thus makes him new. Exemplifying the twists and turns of intercultural inheritance, this literary maneuver belies the narrative of postcolonial literary development as progression from alien metropolitan influence to complete incorporation within the native cultural body. The culturally alien and native, outside and inside can, it seems, stage a polyrhythmic dance.

Nevertheless, to see Walcott's wounded character as a combination of the classical Philoctetes and the Caribbean Caliban still oversimplifies his genesis. When Walcott yanked Philoctetes out of antiquity to recast him, still other figures from other cultures stuck to the prototype. Philoctete, as Walcott remarks of Crusoe, "changes shape . . . with Protean cunning."[26] Drawing on Western classicism for his character's base, veering homeward for a Caribbean admixture, Walcott spins the globe again and picks up other traces from Western modernism. Caliban may seem fishlike, but a Euromodernist text that also interpolates *The Tempest* provides a closer antecedent for Walcott's wounded fisherman, who, with his "unhealed" wound, "limp[s]" and languishes at the waterside, feeling his "sore twitch / its wires up to his groin"—a mysteriously unhealed wound that reflects the wounded condition of the land and indeed the entire region (9, 10). Like the Fisher King in Eliot's *Waste Land,* Philoctete is a synecdochic figure for a general loss, injury, and impotence that must be healed for the (is)lands to be set in order. If Philoctete is a kind of Caribbean Fisher King, Achille plays the role of questing knight who must journey to the Chapel Perilous—in *Omeros,* Africa, site of ancestral enslavement—to rejuvenate the wounded fisherman, the land, and its people.

Remembering the modernist metamyth of the wounded vegetation god, Walcott places *Omeros* in a line that stems not only from Eliot but from a throng of Western artists and anthropologists as well. The animistic opening scene of *Omeros* recalls, for example, Sir James Frazer and Robert Graves in its description of the sacrificial felling of godlike trees for the making of canoes. Philoctete narrates how he and his companions steeled themselves "to turn into murderers," "to wound" the trees they depend on for their livelihood (3). As a tree fell, the sun rose, "blood splashed on the cedars, / / and the grove flooded with the light of sacrifice" (5). Achille "hacked the limbs from the dead god, knot after knot, / wrenching the severed veins from the trunk" (6), but once the tree is reborn on the water as a canoe, it and Hector's canoe "agreed with the waves to forget their lives as trees" (8). Alluding to the annihilation of the Arawaks, Walcott adapts the vegetation myths of the aboriginal inhabitants of the island, as mediated through archetypalist modernism: "The first god was a gommier." He metaphorically reenacts a sacrificial rite to open the way for his own tale: much as the fishermen must kill trees to remake them as canoes, so the poet must hew the linguistic timber of his forebears to remake it as his own vehicle. Introducing the character Philoctete before anyone else, the poem insists on the analogy between his representative wound and what it repeatedly calls the "wound" suffered by the trees. Thus it makes of him the poem's spirit of life, of nature, and of the island, and his wounded body the synecdoche for all the wounds suffered by the island's natives, slaves, and natural beings, possibly even its epic poet.

Like Osiris and other vegetation deities in the modernist metamyth, Philoctete requires the ministrations of a female counterpart to be healed, in his case the obeah woman or sibyl Ma Kilman. Paralleling Achille's magical return to Africa, Ma Kilman discovers an herbal antidote of African origins, transplanted by a sea swift, and she brews the remedy in an old sugar cauldron, allegorized as "the basin / of the rusted Caribbean" (247). His "knuckled spine like islands," Philoctete emerges from his healing bath "like a boy . . . with the first clay's / innocent prick"—the new Caribbean "Adam" (248). But whereas the concept of the New World Adam resonates throughout Walcott's earlier work, he is now an aspiration, a potential achievement in the New World; the wounded, impotent Adonis, Parsifal, Fisher King, or Philoctetes more nearly represents the New World condition, overcome provisionally and strenuously. Philoctete becomes Adamic because an African flower rejoins him to the African past, not, as in the earlier Walcott, because of his "amnesia." Indeed, at the risk of crowding the field of prototypes still further, we can gauge Walcott's change in the difference between his earlier tendency to imagine the West Indian as healthy castaway and Crusoe's replacement in *Omeros* by another sort of castaway—this one harboring a stinking, ulcerous wound, his body tormented by the persistence of the past, ameliorated only by the retrieval of a precolonial inheritance.[27]

For all Philoctete's links with the Euromodernist figure of the vegetation god, we must spin the globe again to appreciate why the wound-healing quest in *Omeros* turns to Africa. Responsible not only for the postcolonial reappraisal of Caliban but also, of course, for the Caribbean recuperation of African aesthetics and values, negritude might seem an unlikely influence on Walcott, given his testy assessment of it in essay like the grudgingly titled "Necessity of Negritude" (1964).[28] While granting that

negritude helped to restore "a purpose and dignity to the descendants of slaves," Walcott suggests that "nostalgia" and uniquely French pressures of "assimilation" produced the movement's "artificial" reconstruction of a black identity rooted in Africa. "Return," Walcott later writes, is "impossible, for we cannot return to what we have never been."[29] Yet in *Omeros* the return to Africa is key to healing the torn black body and racial memory of the Caribbean, as personified by Philoctete. Walcott describes in loving detail how "centuries ago" an African swift managed, in bringing a special seed across the ocean, "to carry the cure / that precedes every wound" (238, 239). This curative plot of return to a precolonial Africa would have been unimaginable without negritude, however long past its heyday and however often resisted by Walcott. Moreover, Ma Kilman commits what would seem to be another cardinal Walcottian sin in reviving the African gods "Erzulie, / / Shango, and Ogun" to find the African flower that will cure Philoctete (242). For "the new magnifiers of Africa," Walcott had tartly stated, the "deepest loss is of the old gods," and poets who look "to a catalogue of forgotten gods . . . engage in masochistic recollection."[30] True, the narrator of *Omeros* emphasizes that the gods, "their features obscured" and "thinned," "had lost their names / / and, therefore, considerable presence" (242). Nevertheless, he assures us, "They were there" (243). In one of the most memorable scenes of *Omeros,* the gods, having earlier "rushed / across an ocean" in "loud migration," swarm like bats in Ma Kilman's grove, their wings forming "crisscrossing stitches" that presage the closing of Philoctete's wound (242). Walcott even flirts momentarily with the concept of race-based blood inheritance of African belief: the old gods sprout through Ma Kilman's body, "as if her veins were their roots" and her arms their branches (242).[31]

While negritude overcomes Walcott's resistances in his mythologizing of Africa as site of wholeness and cure, it also plays a part in engendering the wound figure itself. Since Walcott is seldom thought to owe much to negritude poetry, it might be worth pausing on this seemingly improbable point of connection, for all the obvious differences. In *Cahier d'un retour au pays natal* (1947), called by Walcott "the most powerful expression of Negritude," Césaire repeatedly personifies his West Indian homeland as a wounded body.[32] The speaker reconciles himself to returning to and even embracing a land disfigured by its forgotten wounds ("je reviens vers la hideur désertée de vos plaies"; "je dénombre les plaies avec une sorte d'allégresse").[33] Even as he celebrates and idealizes the black body, he also remembers its wounds cut by the slavemaster's whip and brand, wounds that still sound like tomtoms ("tam-tams inanes de plaies sonores").[34] One year after the first French edition of the *Cahier* was published, another crucial text of negritude followed hard on its heels in 1948, an anthology of francophone African and West Indian poets, prefaced by Jean-Paul Sartre's influential essay "Orphée Noir." The black poet, according to Sartre, writes great collective poetry when, in part, "exhibiting his wounds."[35] The black poet's capacity for articulation is so fused with a historical condition of pain and injury that, in one of the poems Sartre cites, the Haitian writer Jacques Roumain pleads in an apostrophe to Africa, "make . . . / of my mouth the lips of your wound [*plaie*]."[36] The collective memory that unites black poets of different languages and regions, according to Sartre, is one of untold, massive suffering. Slavery, despite its abolition half a century before the negritude poets were born, "lingers on as a very real memory," a point that he supports by quoting first Léon Damas of French Guyana:

> Still real is my stunned condition of the past
> of
> blows from knotted cords of bodies calcinated
> from toe to calcinated back
> of dead flesh of red iron firebrands of arms
> broken under the whip which is breaking loose . . .

and, second, the Haitian poet Jean-François Brierre:

> . . . Often like me you feel stiffnesses
> Awaken after murderous centuries
> And old wounds bleed in your flesh . . .
> [Et saigner dans ta chair les anciennes blessures . . .][37]

The vividness of the trope of the wounded black body in these influential negritude texts should prompt us to reconsider the assumption that in *Omeros* Walcott has simply transported the classical Philoctetes among other Homeric types to the Caribbean, reincarnating him in a black body, encasing him in African skin. It may be equally plausible to argue that Walcott places a Greek mask on the wounded black body of negritude.

Yet neither of these paradigms offers the definitive solution to the implicit question I have sought to complicate by oscillating between North and South, West and East, Europe, Africa, and the Caribbean: simply put, where does Philoctete's wound come from? Literally, from a rusty anchor, and allegorically, from slavery; but once the question is shifted from the mimetic to the literary historical register, the puzzle of origins multiplies. Does it come from the wounded black body of Afro-Caribbean negritude or the Euromodernist fertility god? From the Caribbean Caliban or the Greek Philoctetes? Yet even these regional designations are reductive: the Caribbean Caliban evolved from a Western canonical figure; many vegetation gods appropriated by Western modernists were originally Eastern; and negritude developed in part as a dialectical reversal of Western colonialist stereotypes. In intermingling Caribbean and European literary paradigms, Walcott thickens the cultural hybridity of each. Rather than purify what might be called the "dialectic" of the tribe, Walcott accelerates, complicates, and widens it.

One of Walcott's recurrent metaphors for cultural hybridity may seem, at this point, unsurprising: the scar. Comparing the cultural heterogeneity of the Antilles to a shattered but reassembled vase, Walcott said in his Nobel address that the "restoration shows its white scars" and that "if the pieces are disparate, ill-fitting, they contain more pain than

their original sculpture."[38] More somber than Walcott's tropes of webbing and weaving, let alone popular metaphors like melting pot, salad bowl, or callaloo, the scar signifies cultural convergence in the Americas without effacing its violent genesis. At the end of "The Muse of History," Walcott movingly recalls the violent past deposited in his body, apostrophizing a white forefather, "slave seller and slave buyer," and a black forefather "in the filth-ridden gut of the slave ship." But the scars left by the slavemaster's "whip" are metamorphosed in Walcott's magnificent image for his and the Caribbean's fusion of black and white skins, of Northern and Southern Hemispheres: "the monumental groaning and soldering of two great worlds, like the halves of a fruit seamed by its own bitter juice."[39] Even though the wound has scarified in these descriptions, Walcott never reduces the bitterness or pain to a condition that can be repaired completely; rather, it is constitutive of the new synthesis. Walcott returns to this figure near the end of *Omeros,* when he represents the intercultural labor of his poem as having

> followed a sea-swift to both sides of this text;
> her hyphen stitched its seam, like the interlocking
> basins of a globe in which one half fits the next. . . .

(319)

In Yeats's words, Walcott suggests that "nothing can be sole or whole / That has not been rent."[40]

Seaming black skin and white masks, white skin and black masks, Walcott's Philoctete stands in a long line of Walcottian personifications of cultural and racial hybridity. His name taken from the culture of colonizer and slaver, yet his wounded black body allegorizing their cruelty, Philoctete recalls the "divided" speaker of **"A Far Cry from Africa,"** cursing the brutality of the colonizers yet cursing them in the language they have given him. Greco-Caribbean, Euro-African, Anglo-Hebraic, Philoctete is a boldly intercultural amalgamation, like the self-defined Shabine of **"The Schooner *Flight*":**

> I have Dutch, nigger, and English in me,
> and either I'm nobody, or I'm a nation.[41]

Although Philoctete seems at first to represent but one cultural and racial pole of the Caribbean and thus to differ from Shabine and from Walcott's other early hybrids, Walcott suggests that even in constructing a seemingly monocultural character, in this case to allegorize black pain, the Caribbean poet builds into his aesthetic construct inevitably mixed cultural inheritances. Even Philoctete's cure, like his wound, turns out to be transcultural. Ma Kilman relies, as we have seen, on a specifically African plant and on African gods to heal Philoctete's wound. But she attends five o'clock Mass on the day she delivers Philoctete of gangrene. When she finds the curative African flower, she still wears her Sunday clothes. Vacillating between Greece and the Caribbean, the poem calls Ma Kilman "the sibyl, the obeah-woman." This apposition reverses the presumably literal and metaphoric, and succeeding lines perpetuate the whirligig in naming her "the spidery sibyl / / hanging in a sack from the cave at Cumae, the obeah / . . . possessed" woman (245).

Decades before the academic dissemination of such concepts as hybridity, creolization, cross-culturality, post-ethnicity, postnationalism, *métissage,* and *mestizaje,* Walcott argued vehemently for an intercultural model of post-colonial literature.[42] Against a "separatist" black literature that "belligerently asserts its isolation, its difference," he counterposes a vision of the Caribbean writer as inevitably "mixed": New World blacks must use what Walcott ironically calls "the white man's words" as well as "his God, his dress, his machinery, his food. And, of course, his literature."[43] But Walcott also attacks pervasive assumptions about so-called white American literature—a more powerful if less visible identitarian counterpart to negritude and nativism: "To talk about the contribution of the black man to American culture or civilization is absurd, because it is the black who energized that culture, who styles it, just as it is the black who preserved and energized its faith."[44] For Walcott, as for other Caribbean writers such as Wilson Harris and Edouard Glissant, tribalist views from either extreme disfigure the mixed reality of New World culture, repressing it in favor of simplistic narratives of cultural origin.

The twisted skein of intercultural influences in Philocte reveals the distortion involved in conceiving of postcolonial literature as a progression from colonial dominance to indigeneity, European subordination to nativist freedom.[45] According to this standard narrative, Walcott's use of the Philoctetes type would seem to be a regression to an earlier phase of Eurocentric indebtedness; yet the same linear narrative would also have to note in the figure a progressive step toward indigenous articulation of West Indian suffering. Is Walcott recolonizing Caribbean literature for Europeans by using this and other Greek types? Or is he decolonizing it by representing Caribbean agony? Does the poet reenslave the descendant of slaves by shackling him with a European name and prototype? Or does he liberate the Afro-Caribbean by stealing a literary type from former slavers and making it signify their brutality? Too simplistic for the cultural entanglements of a poem like *Omeros,* the evolutionary model of postcolonial literature is rooted in a discredited model of national development. We need a more flexible language to describe how a poet like Walcott can put into dialectical interrelation literary and cultural influences that may seem incompatible. Critics have seen an evolution in Walcott's work from literary Eurocentrism to Afrocentrism, from denying to embracing African influences on his and others' Caribbean art. Yet Philocte's wound and cure show Walcott not shedding but deepening his European interests as he explores his African commitments, becoming neither a Eurocentric nor an Afrocentric poet but an ever more multicentric poet of the contemporary world.

Having traced the cross-cultural literary genealogies of the wound and its bearer in *Omeros,* I would like to turn from the vertical axis and questions of literary sedimentation to the horizontal and the wound's intratextual resonances, and here too the profoundly intercultural character of Walcott's trope emerges. Once again this hybridity may be surprising, since the wound in *Omeros* at first seems to encode unambiguously the painful Afro-Caribbean legacy of slavery and colonialism. While using the wound motif to honor the uniqueness of this black experience, Walcott nevertheless cross-fertilizes the trope, extending it to other peoples as well. Hybrid in its intertextual ancestry, the wound is also a trope of polymorphous diversity within the text. No sooner has Walcott identified the wound motif with the black experience than he introduces his principal white character, who also happens to be wounded. "He has to be wounded," because of the poem's cross-racial thematics: "affliction is one theme / of this work" (28). What caused Plunkett's wound, other than Walcott's desire to create a cross-cultural echo? Like Philocte's wound, Plunkett's has only the bare outlines of a literal pathogenesis. Major Plunkett, wounded in the head by an explosion during the North African campaign of World War II (27), also seems to bear the inherited wound of European colonialism. He even discovers that a midshipman with his name suffered a "fatal wound" in the Battle of the Saints, the famed eighteenth-century battle for Saint Lucia (86). Certainly, Plunkett's wound differs suggestively from Philocte's: it is to his head, not his body, and it never induces spasms of uncontrollable physical pain. These and other differences point up the more cerebral nature of white suffering in the aftermath of colonialism. Even so, Walcott insists by emblem and analogy that both colonizer and colonized inherit a legacy of affliction in the Caribbean.

As if repeated application of the word "wound" to a Euro-Caribbean and an Afro-Caribbean were not enough to reveal their commonality, Walcott rhymes Plunkett and Philocte in a variety of ways. Their names may not literally rhyme, except perhaps for the final syllable, but they share an initial *p,* an *l,* and the nearly anagrammatic final letters *-kett* and *-ctete.* Though the men differ predictably in appearance, Plunkett, with "a cloud wrapped around his head" during convalescence, recalls the "foam-haired Philocte" (28, 9). The stoic Philocte resolves to "endure" his affliction with the patience of an "old horse" (22), even as Plunkett, true to his own stiff-lipped heritage, rejects the "easy excuse" of blaming his temper on his injury (22, 56). Philocte's wound apparently renders him impotent, and the great sorrow of Plunkett's life is his inability to father a son (29). Like Ma Kilman, the female anointer of Philocte's wound, Plunkett's wife, Maud, his nurse in the war, looks after his head injury.[46] After Maud dies, Ma Kilman acts as a medium in Plunkett's effort to contact her. Whether these links are instances of "Homeric repetition," "coincidence," or Joycean counterpoint (96), they make inescapable the connections between one affliction and the other. As early as **"Ruins of a Great House"** (1962), Walcott tries to hold in a single work the bitter knowledge that "some slave is rotting in this manorial lake" and "that Albion too was once / A colony like ours," that both slave and master inherit histories of excruciating pain, cruelty, and abuse.[47] As Walcott says of "doubt," the wound "isn't the privilege of one complexion" (182).

Walcott's use of the wound at first seems to satisfy Fredric Jameson's well-known generalization: "All third-world texts are necessarily . . . allegorical, and in a very specific way: they are to be read as what I will call *national allegories*."[48] Read thus, the Walcottian wound would be a trope of unproblematic referentiality and stand for the particular historical experience of a particular race in a particular part of the world. Long codified as a dominant trope for black enslavement and mimetic of real wounds perpetrated on real black bodies for hundreds of years, the wound would seem to be the perfect, unambiguous allegory of Afro-Caribbean history. But Walcott plays energetically on the instabilities of the trope. For the wound also has, as Elaine Scarry observes, "a nonreferentiality that rather than eliminating all referential activity instead gives it a frightening freedom of referential activity."[49] Discourses of realist fiction and of nationalist politics might seek to control and even defeat the "referential instability" of the wound, affixing it to a particular people, motive, or cause. But by attaching the wound trope to the name Philoctete and to a black body, Walcott already contaminates and disrupts the specificities demanded by "national allegory." Moreover, the lancet wound that Philoctete suffers from confounds inside and outside; it is the point at which racially unmarked interiority erupts as exteriority and the world within breaks through the epidermal surface. While much contemporary criticism views postcolonial texts, more than their metropolitan counterparts, as preeminent examples of the literature of national and ethnographic specificity, Walcott devises a transnational allegory about both the wound of black Saint Lucian history and a larger subject—what he calls "the incurable / / wound of time" (319).

To write about pain and mortality as transcultural experiences may seem to risk an easy humanism or discredited universalism. Walcott keeps this tendency in check by reserving for the wound an interpretive opacity. Philoctete's wound is a piece of body language that, like many literary wounds, signifies its status as polyvalent sign by resembling a "mouth" (18). But it is a dumb mouth, a sign that also signifies its inarticulateness. Although it is an external mark that tourists, associated elsewhere in the poem with neocolonialism, pay "extra silver" to see, it remains mysterious, turned inward, folded and guarded. Walcott describes it as "puckered like the corolla / of a sea-urchin," in contrast to "a garrulous waterfall" that tourists hear "pour out its secret." Philoctete "does not explain [the wound's] cure. / 'It have some things'—he smiles—'worth more than a dollar'" (4). Hovering between dumbness and communication, the wound offers touristic readers an entryway into Afro-Caribbean experience even as it reminds them that they can never fully comprehend the local burden of historical pain, that they must remain voyeurs peering from without. Philoctete's wound elicits from him a scream that is "mad to come out" but that is held back "behind the bars / / of his rusted teeth" (21).

Inducing yet disabling speech, the wound figures both the promise and the limits of language as vehicle of interpersonal and intercultural understanding.

Walcott can thematize Philoctete's wound as language without betraying the Afro-Caribbean experience because Caribbean blacks also suffered the wound of colonially imposed languages, such as French and English, which are interwoven (sometimes in creole) throughout the poem. Just as Philoctete experiences his alien and inscrutable name as a festering wound he wishes he could cut from his body, Achille realizes that he does not share his forebears' belief in an essential connection between names and things, that he does "not know" what his name means: "Trees, men, we yearn for a sound that is missing" (137). If Philoctete's wound is a language—partly readable, partly opaque—his language is also a kind of painful wound haunted by the memory of an Adamic language it has displaced. But this woundlike language is also potentially its own cure: as the narrator remarks near the end of **Omeros**, "Like Philoctete's wound, this language carries its cure, / Its radiant affliction" (323). The line break, in a pregnant syntactic ambiguity, hovers between an elided conjunction (which would make the cure and affliction opposites) and a relation of apposition (in which the cure would be the affliction). The metaphor of light, repeated from earlier descriptions of the wound as "radiant" (9, 21), tips the seeming antithesis toward identity, much as the poet has done earlier in punningly mistranslating Philoctete's complaint in French creole that he is wounded, "*Moin blessé*," as "I am blest" (18). The poet's discovery of likeness between the words *blessé* and "blest," like his monolingual play on "affliction" and "fiction" (28), demonstrates how the European languages inflicted on West Indians can be turned from curses into blessings. Like Yeats, who could never give up his "love," in spite of his "hatred," for the English language, the poet of **Omeros** refers to "the wound of a language I'd no wish to remove," even after the poet character and Plunkett mimic upper-class accents in a linguistic charade (270).

Philoctete's wound, no less than the colonial language it partly figures, carries its cure dialectically within itself. Indeed, wound, weapon, and cure belong to a metonymic family that Walcott strengthens by metaphoric substitutions throughout the poem. When Walcott compares a "running wound" to "the rusty anchor / that scabbed Philoctete's shin," for example, he identifies the shape and color of the wound with the weapon, and the word "scabbed" suggests both the injury and its cure (178). As if to close the gap between a punctured leg and the healing agent, Walcott chants their prepositional coalescence: "the flower on his shin," "the flower on his shin-blade," "the foul flower / on his shin" (235, 244, 247). The tropological binding up of seeming antitheses also works in the opposite direction. In writing that the "pronged flower / / sprang like a buried anchor," Walcott identifies the curative African plant with the weapon whose injury it reverses, as later with the wound it heals: "The wound of the flower, its gangrene, its rage / festering for centuries, reeked with corrupted blood, / / seeped the pustular drops instead of sunlit dew" (237, 244). Using metaphor to leap the gap between destruction and healing, Walcott's language performatively converts injury into remedy. The only flower that can heal Philoctete's wound must match, perhaps even exceed, the wound's "bitterness," "reek," and "stench" (237); thus Walcott suggests that the poem cannot contribute to healing the wounds of Afro-Caribbean history without reproducing their pain. Like the Boxing Day rite in which "all the pain / / reentered Philoctete," the poet's language carries a cure that must continually reopen and expose the wound (277). In fashioning a mirror relation between injury and remedy, Walcott represents within *Omeros* the poem's homeopathic relation to the traumatic history of the West Indies. Joining black and white, Old World and New, the wound's cross-cultural metaphoricity exhibits the structural doubleness that is fundamental to the poem's logic.

The wound motif exemplifies the slipperiness and polyvalence of poetic discourse that circulates between races, crossing lines of class and community, bridging differences between West Indian fisherman and Greek warrior. With its resonance and punning, imagistic doubling and metaphoric webbing, Walcott's poetry demonstrates the kinds of imaginative connections and transgressions that have ironically made poetry a minor field in postcolonial literary studies. For poetry, at least in Walcott's hands, is less respectful than prose fiction of racial, regional, national, and gender loyalties.[50]

The lancet wound migrates from Philoctete to a white American woman, when Walcott attributes to Catherine Weldon "the wound of her son's / / death from a rusty nail" (176). By means of the wound trope and others, Walcott crosses and recrosses lines of race, nation, and gender. Moreover, Walcott rides the trope across the line between narrative and lyric poetry as he compares his personal loss in a failed marriage to Philoctete's historical and communal injury: "There was no difference / between me and Philoctete" (245), he says, later coupling himself and Philoctete in a mirror image when they wave in greeting: "We shared the one wound, the same cure" (295). Although postuniversalist sensibilities might bridle at such assertions of identity, Walcott signals the distances he traverses by trope. The poet stays at a hotel; the fisherman lives in a poor village. The estranged poet looks "down" from a "height" at his island, "not like Philoctete / / limping among his yams and the yam flowers" (250). Philoctete is a contemporary black man; Catherine Weldon is a nineteenth-century white woman. But Walcott refuses to accept the identitarian fear that shuttling across these enormous differences erases them; he shoots the gulf (in Emerson's phrase), suggesting that the greater danger lies in becoming captivated by the narcissism of differences. As the poem's primary wound-bearer, Philoctete embodies the principle of metaphorical coupling, mediating not only between Greece and Africa, white and black, wound and cure but also between Achille and Hector ("Philoctete tried to make peace between them" [47]), between capitalist and Marxist parties (he campaigns for "United Love" [107]), and between the living and the dead (he names drowned fishermen [128]), as well as between male and female (he and Achille become "androgynous / warriors" during their Boxing Day dance [276]).

The wound joins the major characters of *Omeros* in a large metaphorical company. The pervasive love wound is one example of this effect: Hector's transport or minivan is like a "flaming wound" because he fears Helen still loves Achille (118); Achille "believed he smelt as badly as Philoctete / from the rotting loneliness" (116); Helen so misses Achille that it seems the nightingale's "monodic moan / / came from the hole in her heart" (152); Plunkett is afflicted with another wound on the death of his wife (309); and Saint Lucia's fishermen suffer "that obvious wound / made from loving the sea over their own country" (302). Promiscuously linking various characters in amorous anguish, the wound trope also comes to signify the love that poets like Shelley have long associated with metaphor. A metaphor for metaphor, the wound even circulates through various parts of the nonhuman world, from the volcano whose "wound closed in smoke" (59) to the French colonial ship *Ville de Paris* "wallowing in her wounded pride" (85), and from a field (170), a bay (238), a cauldron (246), and a hut (272), to shacks (178), coves (249), the entire island (249), the sky (313), even the whole Caribbean basin (247). Unleashing the pathetic fallacy, Walcott sees the region's brutal history reflected throughout its natural and human landscape. While a prodigious passion for likeness is characteristic of Walcott's poetry, this passion also typifies a much older and larger propensity of poetry, harnessing the metaphorical play of resemblance within language to amplify and free it. Acknowledging this legacy, he presents the phantasmagoria of the poet, Omeros, as the ideal embodiment of metaphorical conjuncture. Omeros's language is a "Greek calypso," and his images flicker between black and white, the living and the dead, the real and the fantastic (286).

From the perspective of the identity politics that sometimes underwrites the study of Third World literatures, metaphor and postcoloniality might seem to be strange bedfellows, but they should be regarded as reciprocal, interwoven, and mutually enlarging. The movement of metaphor across ethnic, regional, and gender boundaries is well suited to the openly hybrid and intercultural character of postcolonial literature and finds perhaps its fullest articulation in poetry, from Walcott to Ramanujan, Soyinka, and Agha Shahid Ali. Forced and voluntary migration, crossings of one people with another, linguistic creolization, and racial miscegenation—these are the sorts of displacements, wanderings, and interminglings that poetic metaphor can powerfully encode in the fabric of a postcolonial text. To trace the spiralings of the wound motif in *Omeros* is to begin to understand how a poetic imagination as fecund as Walcott's can, in its restless work of discovering and creating resemblance, confound tribal, ethnic, or national limits.

"Trauma" is, of course, Greek for wound, and Walcott's *Omeros* could be said—extending a psychological analogy of Glissant's—to remember, repeat, and work through the trauma of Afro-Caribbean history.⁵¹ But this ameliorative work should not be confused with a definitive healing. Although both the character Philocte and the "phantom narrator" are represented as being cured, Walcott so proliferates and disperses the trope that, even after the climactic scene of healing, the wounds of history and language are shown to persist. As early as the opening of *Omeros,* to which I return by way of conclusion, we can already see that Walcott turns the trope with such vigor that no fictive cure will ever put a stop to its motion. Even in this first canto, the wound bounces from trees to earth to blacks to native people. In the poem's scene of origination, Walcott wants to show victimizer and victimized to be ambiguous, shifting positions.⁵² Philocte starts out as neocolonial victim: he "smiles for the tourists, who try taking / his soul with their cameras." Walcott suggests that the neocolonial tourist and, by implication, the touristic reader perpetuate the colonial trauma in trying to penetrate the interior of the Caribbean descendant of slaves ("trauma" derives from a word for "to pierce" [*tetrainein*]). But soon enough Philocte is telling how he and the other fishermen had "axes" in their "eyes," as the tourists have piercing gazes. Indeed, he and his comrades, like latter-day colonizers, become "murderers": "'I lift up the axe and pray for strength in my hands / to wound the first cedar'" (3). Suddenly reader, tourist, and colonizer become vulnerable to the wounding they at first seemed accused of committing. If metaphor turns Philocte's wounds into weapons, it also inverts his black victimization as soon as that status is established. But neither is the alternative role stable, for Philocte now reveals his own painful scar, which identifies him with the wounds that he will perpetrate on the trees. And as Walcott alludes to the annihilation of the Arawaks and their language, he recalls a still-earlier trauma from which there can be no question of recovery. Sharing a fate of island suffering yet surviving it to replace the native population, Philocte and the other black fishermen soon resume the role of inflicting, not receiving, wounds: they turn off the chain saw and then, ripping "the wound clear" of vines, "examine the wound it / had made," as the blood of a Saint Lucian sunrise "trickled" and "splashed" on the trees (5).

Is Walcott, as poet of cross-cultural affliction, a "fortunate traveller" of transnational trope? Because he sets this most politically loaded of metaphors spinning, does he irresponsibly confound distinctions between colonizer and colonized, oppressor and oppressed? How can this cross-racializing of the wound be reconciled with the asymmetrical suffering that marks colonialism and postcoloniality, let alone slavery? These are the undeniable risks of Walcott's free riding of the wound trope across moral and historical divisions, but his wager is that they are risks worth taking.

If exclusive fidelity to a single history of affliction is required of the Third World poet, then Walcott certainly fails this test. But Walcott conceives the Antilles as a site of multiple and inextricable histories of victimization and cruelty, histories deposited not only in its landscape and its languages but even in his body. From an identitarian perspective, poets like Walcott who metaphorically enact interethnic connections falsify the historical specificity of their people's experience. But for Walcott, the greater falsification would lie in an aesthetic separatism blind to the culturally webbed history of the Caribbean, of his ancestors, and of his imagination, in a viewpoint hostile to the cross-racial and cross-historical identifications the New World offers.

As graphic emblem of convulsive, bodily pain, the wound in *Omeros* memorializes the untold suffering of Afro-Caribbeans, yet as trope, it inevitably poeticizes pain, compares this particular experience with others, and thus must either mar or deconstruct experiential uniqueness by plunging it into the whirlpool of metaphorical resemblance and difference. Anchor-like in shape and origins, the wound trope in *Omeros* drifts from the ground of a particular people's experience to the afflictions of native peoples, Greeks, Jews, colonial Americans, even the English. Because Walcott's intermappings of suffering never occlude Philocte's primacy and never sugarcoat the trauma of slavery, they keep in view differences between oppressor and oppressed, even as they open up and reveal the connections between the experiences of Afro-Caribbeans and others. Appropriating a Western icon of suffering and refashioning a polysemous and multi-parented trope, Walcott's *Omeros* champions a postcolonial poetics of affliction that unravels the distinction between "victim's literature" and its supposed opposite.

*Notes*

1. Derek Walcott, *Conversations with Derek Walcott,* ed. William Baer (Jackson: University Press of Mississippi, 1996), 59.

2. Derek Walcott, "Leaving School" (1965), in *Critical Perspectives on Derek Walcott,* ed. Robert D. Hamner (Washington, D.C.: Three Continents Press, 1993), 32.

3. Recalling Yeats's description of the Black and Tans as "drunken soldiery" ("drunken officer of British rule"), Walcott also transmutes Yeats's lines, "All men are dancers and their tread / Goes to the barbarous clangour of a gong," into a similarly bleak description of the compulsive brutality of "man": "Delirious as these worried beasts, his wars / Dance to the tightened carcass of a drum." See W. B. Yeats, *The Poems,* rev. ed., ed. Richard J. Finneran (New York: Macmillan, 1989), 207, 208; Derek Walcott, *Collected Poems, 1948-1984* (New York: Noonday-Farrar, Straus & Giroux, 1986), 17-18. Laurence A. Breiner dates the first publication of "A Far Cry from Africa" in *An Introduction to West Indian Poetry* (Cambridge: Cambridge University Press, 1998), 159; 247, n. 20.

4. Derek Walcott, *Omeros* (New York: Farrar, Straus & Giroux, 1990), 199. All further references to *Omeros* appear parenthetically in the text. Although Joyce is

the more direct influence on *Omeros,* Yeats's presence is evident from the introduction of the two major female characters in the story: an Irishwoman notably named Maud and a local woman named Helen, who caribbeanizes a Greek paradigm as Yeats had earlier "irished" her.

Walcott has often been fruitfully discussed as a poet of "mixed" culture, "divided" inheritance, and "schizophrenic" allegiance; see Paul Breslin, "'I Met History Once, But He Ain't Recognize Me': The Poetry of Derek Walcott," *Triquarterly* 68 (1987): 168-83; Joseph Brodsky, "On Derek Walcott," *New York Review of Books,* 10 November 1983, 39-41; James Dickey, review of *Collected Poems, 1948-1984,* by Derek Walcott, *New York Times Book Review,* 2 February 1986, 8; Rita Dove, "'Either I'm Nobody, or I'm a Nation,'" review of *Collected Poems, 1948-1984,* by Derek Walcott, *Parnassus* 14, no. 1 (1987): 49-76; J. D. McClatchy, review of *Collected Poems, 1948-1984,* by Derek Walcott, *New Republic,* 24 March 1986, 36-38; James McCorkle, "'The Sigh of History': The Poetry of Derek Walcott," *Verse* ("Derek Walcott Feature Issue," ed. Susan M. Schultz) 11, no. 2 (1994): 104-12; J. A. Ramsaran, "Derek Walcott: New World Mediterranean Poet," *World Literature Written in English* 21, no. 1 (1982): 133-47; Rei Terada, *Walcott's Poetry: American Mimicry* (Boston: Northeastern University Press, 1992); Helen Vendler, "Poet of Two Worlds," review of *The Fortunate Traveller,* by Derek Walcott, *New York Review of Books,* 4 March 1982, 23+; Clement H. Wyke, "'Divided to the Vein': Patterns of Tormented Ambivalence in Walcott's *The Fortunate Traveller,*" *Ariel* 20, no. 3 (1989): 55-71; and John Thieme, *Derek Walcott* (New York: Manchester University Press, 1999).

A biographical synopsis may be helpful for readers new to Walcott. He was born in Castries, Saint Lucia, on January 23, 1930. His father, a civil servant and amateur painter, died before he was a year old. His mother was the head teacher at a Methodist infant school on the predominantly Catholic island. His background was racially and culturally mixed. His grandmothers were of African descent, his white grandfathers a Dutchman and an Englishman. Speaking the Standard English that is the official language of the island, Walcott also grew up speaking the predominant French creole (or patois) that is the primary language of the street. At the age of fifteen, Walcott published a poem in the local newspaper, drawing a sharp rebuke in rhyme from a Catholic priest for his heretical pantheism and animism. A few years later, he borrowed money from his mother to print a booklet of twenty-five poems, hawking it on the streets to earn the money back. This book and his first major play, *Henri Christophe,* also met with disapprobation from the Catholic church.

In 1950 he left Saint Lucia to enter the University of the West Indies in Mona, Jamaica, where he was a

vibrant literary entrepreneur among the university's first graduating class in liberal arts. Staying on in Jamaica, he made his living through teaching and journalism. He moved to Trinidad in 1958, still working as a reviewer and art critic but also pouring energy into directing and writing plays for the Trinidad Theater Workshop until 1976. His poetry began to receive international attention with *In a Green Night* (1962).

Since 1981, he has been teaching regularly at Boston University. He recently built a home on the northwest coast of Saint Lucia where he paints and writes. Among his major plays are *Ti-Jean and His Brothers* (1958), *Dream on Monkey Mountain* (1967), and *The Odyssey* (1993). He received the Nobel Prize for literature in 1992. See Bruce King, *Derek Walcott: A Caribbean Life* (New York: Oxford University Press, 2000); and Paul Breslin, *Nobody's Nation: Reading Derek Walcott* (Chicago: University of Chicago Press, in press).

5. In *Omeros* the name is spelled "Philoctete" and pronounced "Fee-lock-TET," in accordance with the French creole of Saint Lucia.

6. Edward [Kamau] Brathwaite, *The Arrivants: A New World Trilogy* (Oxford: Oxford University Press, 1973), 210, 249, 265; Walcott, "The Muse of History: An Essay," in *Is Massa Day Dead? Black Moods in the Caribbean,* ed. Orde Coombs (Garden City, N.Y.: Anchor-Doubleday, 1974), 3.

7. Walcott, "Tribal Flutes" (1967), in *Critical Perspectives,* ed. Hamner, 43, and "The Muse of History," 8, 2-3. Brathwaite and Walcott have often been compared; see, e.g., Patricia Ismond, "Walcott versus Brathwaite," in *Critical Perspectives,* ed. Hamner, 220-36; and J. Edward Chamberlin, *Come Back to Me My Language: Poetry and the West Indies* (Urbana: University of Illinois Press, 1993), 154-55.

8. Walcott, *Collected Poems,* 269, 286.

9. Ibid., 269, 270.

10. Walcott uses the Philoctetes type in his unpublished play *The Isle Is Full of Noises* (1982), but there the wound signifies indigenous political corruption, not inherited colonial injury. I am grateful to Paul Breslin for sharing with me the play's typescript.

11. C. L. R. James, *The Black Jacobins: Toussaint L'Ouverture and the San Domingo Revolution,* 2d ed. (New York: Vintage-Random House, 1989), 12.

12. Walcott complains bitterly that such "historical sullenness" results in "morose poems and novels" of "one mood, which is in too much of Caribbean writing: that sort of chafing and rubbing of an old sore." See Edward Hirsch, "The Art of Poetry" (1986 interview), in *Critical Perspectives,* ed. Hamner, 79.

13. D. J. Bruckner, "A Poem in Homage to an Unwanted Man" (1990 interview), in *Critical Perspectives,* ed. Hamner, 397.

14. Walcott, "Laventille," in *Collected Poems,* 88.

15. Anthony Milne, "Derek Walcott" (1982 interview), in *Critical Perspectives,* ed. Hamner, 62.

16. On Walcott's use of Crusoe instead of Friday, see his "The Figure of Crusoe" (1965 lecture), in *Critical Perspectives,* ed. Hamner, 33-40.

17. Walcott earlier belittles "exotic," cross-racial recasting of characters like Hamlet; see "Meanings" (1970), in *Critical Perspectives,* ed. Hamner, 47.

18. Other Greek-named characters in *Omeros* share a similar genealogy, but their looser affinities with their namesakes make them more independent characters than the allegorical Philoctete. On the relationships between Walcott's characters and their Homeric counterparts, see Robert Hamner, *Epic of the Dispossessed: Derek Walcott's "Omeros"* (Columbia: University of Missouri Press, 1997); Terada, *Walcott's Poetry,* 183-212; Geert Lernout, "Derek Walcott's *Omeros:* The Isle Is Full of Voices," *Kunapipi* 14, no 2 (1992): 95-97; and Oliver Taplin, "Derek Walcott's *Omeros* and Derek Walcott's Homer," *Arion,* 3d ser., 1, no. 2 (1991): 213-26.

19. On the traditional fascination with Philoctetes' pain, see Oscar Mandel, *Philoctetes and the Fall of Troy* (Lincoln: University of Nebraska Press, 1981), 35-36. Mandel surveys Philoctetes' iconography (123-49).

20. Gotthold Ephraim Lessing, *Laocoön,* trans. Edward Allen McCormick (Baltimore: Johns Hopkins University Press, 1984), 29; Edmund Wilson, *The Wound and the Bow* (London: W. H. Allen, 1952), 257, 259; Seamus Heaney, *The Cure at Troy: A Version of Sophocles' "Philoctetes"* (New York: Noonday-Farrar, Straus & Giroux, 1991).

21. Terada, *Walcott's Poetry,* 188, 187.

22. Derek Walcott, "What the Twilight Says: An Overture," in *"Dream on Monkey Mountain" and Other Plays* (New York: Farrar, Straus & Giroux, 1970), 31, "The Figure of Crusoe," 36, and see also "The Muse of History," 4; Rob Nixon, "Caribbean and African Appropriations of *The Tempest,*" *Critical Inquiry* 13 (1987): 557-78; and A. James Arnold, "Caliban, Culture, and Nation-Building in the Caribbean," in *Constellation Caliban: Figurations of a Character,* ed. Nadia Lie and Theo D'haen (Amsterdam and Atlanta, Ga.: Rodopi, 1997), 231-44, and other essays in the latter collection.

23. Shakespeare, *The Tempest,* 1.2.369-70. Walcott's remark about Timon of Athens and his script for *The Isle Is Full of Noises* indicate an additional Shakespearean prototype for the cursing Philoctete.

24. Walcott, "The Figure of Crusoe," 36.

25. Aimé Césaire, *A Tempest,* trans. Richard Miller (Paris: Editions du Seuil, 1986), 17, 18.

26. Walcott, "The Figure of Crusoe," 37, 35.

27. As an indication that Walcott closely associates Philoctetes and Crusoe, he gives the nickname "Crusoe" to the Philoctetes character in *The Isle Is Full of Noises.* Carol Dougherty argues for yet another Western prototype: Walcott introduces the scar-bearing Philoctete "as an Odysseus of sorts" ("Homer after *Omeros:* Reading a H/Omeric Text," *South Atlantic Quarterly* 96 [1997]: 339-47).

28. Walcott, "Necessity of Negritude," in *Critical Perspectives,* ed. Hamner, 20-23. On negritude and various conceptions of Africa in West Indian poetry, see Breiner, *An Introduction to West Indian Poetry,* 156-64.

29. Walcott, "The Caribbean: Culture or Mimicry?" (1974), in *Critical Perspectives,* ed. Hamner, 53.

30. Walcott, "The Muse of History, 7, 8.

31. At a more general level, Walcott follows the lead of negritude writers insofar as he, like them, dialectically inverts colonial stereotypes. Fanon, who worried about negritude's tendency to duplicate colonial views through such inversion, mentions as one of colonialism's dehumanizing terms the "stink" of the native. When Walcott stresses the foul "smell" of Philoctete's wound, he not only remembers the Greek prototype but also flouts a repressive stereotype (10). See Frantz Fanon, *The Wretched of the Earth,* trans. Constance Farrington (New York: Grove Press-Présence Africaine, 1963), 212-13, 42.

32. Walcott, "Necessity of Negritude," 21.

33. Aimé Césaire, *Cahier d'un retour au pays natal,* 2d ed. (bilingual), English trans. Emile Snyders (Paris: Présence Africaine, 1968), 40, 126.

34. Ibid.: "whip" (130), "brand" (114), "tom-toms" (94).

35. Jean-Paul Sartre, "Black Orpheus" (1948), trans. John MacCombie, reprinted in *The Black American Writer,* ed. C. W. E. Bigsby (Deland, Fla.: Everett/Edward, 1969), 2:13. The anthology in which Sartre's "Orphée Noir" was originally published is *Anthologie de la nouvelle poésie nègre et malgache de langue française,* ed. Léopold Sédar Senghor (Paris: Presses Universitaires de France, 1948).

36. Sartre, "Black Orpheus," 36; "Orphée Noir," 41.

37. Sartre, "Black Orpheus," 31-32; "Orphée Noir," 36.

38. Walcott, "The Antilles: Fragments of Epic Memory," reprinted in *Dictionary of Literary Biography Yearbook* (Detroit: Gale Research Co., 1992), 14.

39. Walcott, "The Muse of History," 27.

40. Yeats, "Crazy Jane Talks with the Bishop," in *Poems,* 260.

41. Walcott, *Collected Poems,* 346.

42. See Edward Kamau Brathwaite, *The Development of Creole Society in Jamaica, 1770-1820* (Oxford: Oxford University Press, 1971), and *Roots* (Ann Arbor: University of Michigan Press, 1993); Homi K. Bhabha, *The Location of Culture* (New York: Routledge, 1994); Edouard Glissant, *Caribbean Discourse: Selected Essays,* trans. J. Michael Dash (Charlottesville: University Press of Virginia, 1989); Roberto Fernández Retamar, *Caliban and Other Essays* (Minneapolis: University of Minnesota Press, 1989); and David A. Hollinger, *Postethnic America: Beyond Multiculturalism* (New York: Basic, 1995). The mixture in some models is primarily cultural, in others racial, and Walcott often conflates the two. Regarding the West Indies, "almost all contemporary approaches to Afro-Caribbean culture(s)," according to Richard D. E. Burton, "stress its (their) syncretistic or mosaic character," with significant differences in emphasis (*Afro-Creole: Power, Opposition, and Play in the Caribbean* [Ithaca, N.Y.: Cornell University Press, 1997], 3). On the hybridity of Caribbean literature, see Antonio Benítez-Rojo, *The Repeating Island: The Caribbean and the Postmodern Perspective,* trans. James Maraniss (Durham, N.C.: Duke University Press, 1992); Silvio Torres-Saillant, *Caribbean Poetics: Toward an Aesthetics of West Indian Literature* (Cambridge: Cambridge University Press, 1997); and J. Michael Dash, *The Other America: Caribbean Literature in a New World Context,* New World Studies (Charlottesville: University Press of Virginia, 1998).

43. Walcott, "Necessity of Negritude," 20.

44. Walcott, "The Caribbean," 52.

45. See Frantz Fanon's classic formulation of the three-stage "evolution" of native writing, from "unqualified assimilation" to nativist "exoticism" to "revolutionary," truly "national literature" (*The Wretched of the Earth,* trans. Constance Farrington [New York: Grove, 1963], 222-23). For a more recent example, see Bill Ashcroft, Gareth Griffiths, and Helen Tiffin, *The Empire Writes Back: Theory and Practice in Post-colonial Literatures* (New York: Routledge, 1989), 4-5: "Post-colonial literatures developed through several stages which can be seen to correspond to stages both of national or regional consciousness and of the project of asserting difference from the imperial centre." For Ashcroft, Griffiths, and Tiffin, as for many other critics, this literary historical narrative remains fundamental, despite a growing interest in "models of hybridity and syncreticity" (33-37).

46. According to John Barrell, the traditional image of Philoctetes, "with his wounded and unsupported foot, . . . express[es] the fear of castration," which "derives from the belief that the woman is castrated" and thus "produces the need for the companion representation" of a female figure (*The Birth of Pandora and the Division of Knowledge* [Philadelphia: University of Pennsylvania Press, 1992], 213).

47. Walcott, *Collected Poems,* 20. Joseph Farrell comments on the "unending succession whereby formerly enslaved and colonized peoples become oppressors in their own right" ("Walcott's *Omeros:* The Classical Epic in a Postmodern World," *South Atlantic Quarterly* 96 [1997]: 265).

48. Frederic Jameson, "Third-World Literature in the Era of Multinational Capitalism," *Social Text* 15 (1986): 69.

49. Elaine Scarry, *The Body in Pain: The Making and Unmaking of the World* (New York: Oxford University Press, 1985), 119; and see 121 for the ensuing quotation.

50. Arguably, even postcolonial novels such as Michelle Cliff's *No Telephone to Heaven* and J. M. Coetzee's *Waiting for the Barbarians,* which like *Omeros* allegorize the wound and scar, more readily satisfy the imperatives of much postcolonial criticism than poetry does.

51. Glissant, *Caribbean Discourse,* 65-66.

52. On the ambiguous historicity and positionality of trauma, see Cathy Caruth, introduction to *Trauma: Explorations in Memory,* ed. Cathy Caruth (Baltimore: Johns Hopkins University Press, 1995), 3-11; and Dori Laub, "Bearing Witness; or, The Vicissitudes of Listening," in *Testimony: Crises of Witnessing in Literature, Psychoanalysis, and History,* ed. Shoshana Felman and Dori Laub (Routledge: New York, 1992), 57-74.

## Isidore Okpewho (essay date 2002)

SOURCE: Okpewho, Isidore. "Walcott, Homer, and the 'Black Atlantic.'" *Research in African Literatures* 33, no. 1 (2002): 27-44.

[*In the following essay, Okpewho examines Walcott's themes of journey, voyage, and cultural identity within the context of African Caribbean literary discourse.*]

I

In exploring Derek Walcott's abiding recourse to Homer in his creative writing, I have chosen to invoke the discursive paradigm recently advertised by Paul Gilroy in his book because whatever problems we may agree it creates in its analysis of the condition of blacks in Western society, the book has at any rate invited us to rethink familiar assumptions about questions of self-apprehension created by centuries of stressful relations between peoples of African and European descent. In formulating his concept of a "black Atlantic," Gilroy abjures all obsessive attachment to an African racial antecedence, embracing in the process a *modernist* consciousness that entails, as he puts it (following Habermas), "a rift between secular and sacred spheres of action" whereby contemporary artists feel "a sense of artistic practice as an autonomous domain either reluctantly or happily divorced from the everyday life-world" (50, 73). Gilroy especially celebrates the "rhizomorphic, fractal structure" (4) of this unique formation because in "[transcending] both the structures of the nation state and the constraints of ethnicity and national particularity" (19), it enables us "to construct an intercultural and anti-ethnocentric account of modern black history and political culture" (4). In this project, he adopts the image of "ships" as a guiding metaphor in their signification far less of "the triangular trade" (16-17) than of "the unfinished history of blacks in the modern world" (80).

Gilroy's book provides us a point of departure here because it foregrounds the interplay of issues of history and identity that characterize Caribbean discourse generally. This discourse may be reduced to two main strands. The first of these is represented by European travel accounts and histories (Columbus, Trollope, Froude, etc.) that present a uniformly negative portrait of minority American peoples. This imperialist outlook, designed to support planter/mercantile adventurism and the exploitation of Caribbean society and economy, poses a denial of Caribbean history and culture and makes no concessions whatever to the innate humanity of the people. "There has been splendour and luxurious living," says Froude, "and there have been crimes and horrors, and revolts and massacres. There has been romance, but it has been the romance of pirates and outlaws. The natural graces of life do not show themselves under these conditions [. . .]. There are no people in the true sense of the word, with a character and purpose of their own" (305-06). Have they made any contributions to science and technology? "Rocks and trees and flowers remain as they always were, and Nature is constant to herself; but the traveller whose heart is with his land, and cares only to see his brother mortals making their corner of the planet an orderly and rational home, had better choose some other object for his pilgrimage" (306). Needless to say, the more humane interventions of contemporary writers (de las Casas, Sewell) did little to dent the image enshrined by this dominant imperialist discourse.

The second strand of Caribbean discourse involves responses by native Caribbean artists and intellectuals to the above position. Between the two strands, however, lies an intermediate position represented by a writer like V. S. Naipaul who, in castigating (from his British exile) the failures of Caribbean society, has not hesitated to preface his portraits of it with passages such as those quoted above from the likes of Froude and Trollope. We may call this the tough love of someone saddened by the wasted promise of his native land; but nothing excuses the readiness with which he echoes the imperialist sneer. "How can the history of this West Indian futility be written?" he asks in *The Middle Passage,* then answers: "The history of the islands can never be satisfactorily told. Brutality is not the only difficulty. History is built around achievement and creation; and nothing was created in the West Indies" (28-29).

Most of the prominent Caribbean writers are, unlike Naipaul, of part-African descent and, though they have often condemned some of the shortcomings of Caribbean society that Naipaul addresses, have nonetheless shown considerable sympathy for and commitment to the fortunes of the region. In his *Cahiers d'un retour au pays natal,* Aimé Césaire debunks European claims to rationality and civilization, and extols the indigenous cultural propensities of African descended peoples (animism, idolatry, etc.), even the absence of Western technology. Black people may never have invented things or brought the world under exploitative control, posits Césaire; but they remain the final guarantee of the humane sensibility. Hence, while proclaiming the richness both of nature and of Africa's cultural traditions, he pursues a broad humanist agenda that entails a "celebration of universal love and a plea for recognition of man's universal ties in a world beset by hatred and divisiveness" (Cudjoe 136).

In his Afrocentrist trilogy titled *Arrivants,* Kamau Brathwaite proudly acknowledges that

> we
> who have cre-
> ated nothing,
> must exist
> On nothing.

("Postlude/Home," *Arrivants* 79)

Here he makes a determined connection with his African roots, subjecting himself to ritual seances that renew his ties to ancestral spirits and customs and prepare him, upon his return, to revitalize his Caribbean society with creative essences derived from Africa. In an earlier effort, *History of the Voice,* he asserts the persistence of Africa in Caribbean expressive arts and recognizes in the entire culture a substratum of religious sensibility. And he is so forceful in arguing a fundamental African quality to Caribbean oral arts that he finds ethnic peculiarities in the folk speech of the region, using the phrase "nation language" to acknowledge the ethnic identities that cohere in the Caribbean. Hence he tries to document the ways in which "the native language as spoken by Africans" (5) have left their impress on English as spoken in various Caribbean communities.

Wilson Harris offers a slightly different though cognate perspective on Caribbean reality. Like many of his contemporaries, he is a scion of mixed racial backgrounds (vividly reflected in the hybrid worlds of his novels)—so mixed, in fact, that he deserves to be taken seriously when in "History, Fable, and Myth" he claims he has "no racial biases" (*Selected Essays* 156). Also like them, he is a product of a British colonial education that put tremendous emphasis on the classics and encouraged a propensity for crosscultural, universalist insights. But two other aspects of his life are especially pivotal to the contributions he has made to Caribbean discourse. One, working as a land and river surveyor in the interior of Guyana brought him to encounter the sheer *organum* of its centuries-old ecology and native peoples, filling him with a sense not only of history in continuity but of the numinous interfusion of various forces—organic, inorganic, and especially nonsubstantial—with human life in a way that transcends temporal reality.[1] Two, his readings in German philosophy and metaphysics disposed his mind to an "inner time" undergirding temporal reality in much the same sphere as dreams and other forms of supraconscious experience. No wonder, then, that Harris—as he again states in "History, Fable, and Myth"—is intellectually attracted to the symbolic kinship of limbo and Haitian *vodun* as "variables of an underworld imagination," or that for him Jean Rhys's *Wide Sargasso Sea* and Charlotte Bronte's *Jane Eyre* are linked by "a universal heritage" of the "nightmare" consciousness (159-60). History as a linear continuum, as well as political ideologies guided by it, has little place in his search for "the life of the imagination" ("Continuity and Discontinuity," *Selected Essays* 177). Rather, he has a cyclic sense of time that sets no barriers between peoples and epochs in the fluid and ongoing history of the Caribbean world ("Tradition and the West Indian Novel," *Selected Essays* 141).

This reaction to "history" finally brings us to a recognition, in some segments of Caribbean thought, of a separate reality characterizing the region, as amply articulated by the writer/scholar Edouard Glissant. This consciousness is represented, in large degree, by the rejection of History (with a capital H) as a totalizing project in Western (colonial, imperial) discourse which, utilizing the privilege of its literate resources, constructs a universal narrative that sets Europe at the center of humanity and thrusts the peoples without writing to the margins. Glissant advocates a strategy that puts emphasis on the "lived reality" of the Caribbean world, rather than on an hegemonist epistemology that relies on the myth of Europe's manifest destiny. This theory of the uniqueness of Caribbean fortunes, generally referred to as *antillanité,* does not exactly disown an African antecedence, but it sets its real historical sights on the experiences that constitute the sources of a peculiar Caribbean world, beginning with the slave trade:

> The journey that has fixed in us the unceasing tug of Africa against which we must paradoxically struggle today in order to take root in our rightful land. The motherland is also for us the inaccessible land.
>
> Slavery, a struggle with no witnesses from which we perhaps have acquired the taste for repeating words that recall those rasping whispers deep in our throats, in the huts of the implacably hostile world of slavery.
>
> The loss of collective memory, the careful erasing of the past, which often makes our calendar nothing more than a series of natural calamities, not a linear progression, and so time keeps turning around in us.
>
> (160-61)

In the circumstances the Caribbean, no longer able to see the world through the same experiential lens as African countries (62-63), has been forced to realize "the creative energy of a dialectic reestablished between nature and culture" (65) in the New World. "The creative link between nature and culture," says Glissant, "is vital to the formation of a community" (63); despite their diverse histories, Caribbean peoples have survived the traumas of the Middle Passage and kindred historical struggles in the New World, and are today "the roots of a cross-cultural relationship" (67). "[This] past, to which we were subjected, which has not yet emerged as history for us, is, however, obsessively present. The duty of the writer is to explore this obsession, to show its relevance in a continuous fashion to the immediate present" (63-64).

We might say, then, that Caribbean discourse hinges on two principal axes, each of which is committed to seeking a viable aesthetic as well as political identity: one that affirms Africa as its ultimate point of reference, and another whereby Africa is recognized as an inevitable but hardly dominant source of the larger Caribbean or Antillean universe. A writer like V. S. Naipaul stands somewhat outside of this discourse, especially because he has shown very little sympathy for the region's fortunes and aspirations.

II

Where does Walcott belong in this configuration? His backgrounds and his earlier career definitely evince a personality more akin to Harris than to Césaire or Brathwaite. Like Harris, he comes of a hybrid racial stock (less so, perhaps) and a classically grounded colonial education. Walcott's writing reveals an appreciation for the Caribbean's natural environment as deeply felt as Harris's, though the visual artist in him seemed at first attracted more to the open topography of an all too accessible island universe than to the recessed inner life of Harris's tropical forests. Finally, although like Harris he observed a guarded distance from radical political ideologies, and was especially disdainful of strident demagoguery (*Gulf* 110) and rabid, opportunistic Afrocentrism (*O Babylon!;* "Muse of History," What the Twilight Says), there is nonetheless greater evidence in his work than in Harris's of a sympathy with proletarian interests.

Whatever his ideological leanings, Walcott in his early work was no less determined than his contemporaries in responding to issues of history and identity foregrounded by the antecedent colonialist discourse. In the poem **"Air"** (*Gulf* 69-70), he mocks the colonialists' denial of history and achievement in the Caribbean, working through a parody of Euro-Christian presumptions to assert the challenges posed by the native environment and ending with a clinching laugh, "there is too much nothing here"! And in ***Another Life,*** he ridicules those who, while waving as trophies of achievement the elimination of indigenous races, charge "nothing" was ever created in the region (144-45). He disdains the sorts of "history" by which the Caribbean has been conventionally defined—the bloody, exploitative careers of adventurers and colonists—and sees his generation as exiles positioned, like Adam in a virgin Eden, and certainly more like Crusoe than Prospero, to give a fresh cultural identity and dignity to their inherited world ("The Figure of Crusoe," *Critical Perspectives on Derek Walcott* 36).[2]

The search for a proper identity for the Caribbean is itself beset with obstacles that must needs be overcome. For Walcott, the answer lies neither in the all too easy but false image of the Caribbean as a tourist paradise (**"Prelude,"** *Green Night* 11), nor in an appeal to the discredited survivors of European vandalism—the Indians and their violated sanctuaries (**"The Voyage Up River,"** *Castaway* 50). Nor does Walcott find Africa any more attractive as a point of reference. Although his roots lie partly there, he feels considerable distrust of it especially in light of the contemporary postindependence record of horrors (**"A Far Cry from Africa,"** *Green Night 18*). In *Dream on Monkey Mountain,* Makak recovers from his hallucinations of a royal African past to confront once again his oppressed proletarian lot and real-life (servile) identity, Felix Hobain. Clearly Shabine, in **"The Schooner Flight,"** articulates Walcott's sentiment when, confronting the phantoms of his ancestors, he dismisses the epiphany with the question, "Who knows / who his grandfather is, much less his name?" (*Star-Apple Kingdom* 11).

Having rejected the panoply of ancestors usually employed in defining Caribbean identity, Walcott opts for an inclusive geopolitical framework that recognizes contemporary realities. For instance, in **"A Map of the Antilles,"** he acknowledges the unity of an Antillean universe despite the divisions forced upon it by history and politics (*Green Night* 55). In **"Bronze,"** he affirms the essential hybridity of a Caribbean society blended from old-world and new-world sources, best captured perhaps in the icon of a Caribbean beauty as a multiracial monument greater than the masterpieces of Grecian art or myth—unbroken by imperial rape, and proudly projecting the stubborn hopes of a people struggling to be unified (*Green Night* 78-79). He then recognizes the reality of a larger *American* world, wherein the Caribbean is seen as united with the mainland by common experiences of a historic colonialism ("Muse of History," Twilight Says 36) and present-day racial prejudice (**"Lines in New England,"** *Castaway* 48-49; **"The Gulf,"** *Gulf* 58-62). This ever-widening landscape finally leads Walcott, especially in the later travel poems, to a certain universalist sensibility. Hence, in **"The Schooner *Flight*,"** a social critic like Shabine would conclude that "this earth is one / island in archipelagoes of stars" (*Star-Apple Kingdom* 20), while in **"Spoiler's Return"** the calypso king (Spoiler) summons the aid of a (European) "Old Brigade" in castigating the dog-eat-dog, doom-bound excesses of Caribbean society (*Fortunate Traveller* 53-60). Sadly, at this point Walcott's Caribbean critics are moved to lament, with Fred D'Aguiar in a review of *Midsummer,* that the poet's universalist forays have cost him his "sense of purpose and resolve."

Walcott's progression from a local to an ecumenical vision should perhaps be read as a "need to escape static, essentialist constructions of personality" (Thieme 152). A less sympathetic view might, however, see in this the influence of colonial education, with its notorious record in orienting the native youth away from their roots in pursuit of models offered by the imperial system. Some of this, at any rate, is evident in Walcott's early immersion, with his friend Dunstan St. Omer (**"Gregorias"** of *Another Life*), in the fine arts under their apprenticeship of Harry Simmons, who guided his wards in internalizing the traditions of European Renaissance art to a level amply revealed in Walcott's *oeuvre* especially from *Another Life* and *Midsummer* to the more recent *Tiepolo's Hound.* Equally significant is his attitude to language, where he reveals an interesting ambivalence. In "What the Twilight Says," he is so "madly in love with English" he sees himself as "prolonging the mighty line of Marlowe, of Milton" (*Twilight Says* 10); yet he can hardly escape the aesthetic tug of the local environment, where "in the dialect-loud dusk of water-buckets and fish-sellers, conscious of the naked, voluble poetry around me, I felt a fear of that darkness which had swallowed up all fathers" (28). The result of this ambivalence is a studied lexical management of English and Creole on a separate but hardly equal basis in much of Walcott's earlier poetry. There is little of the bold experimentation we find in the poetries of Kamau Brathwaite and Louisse Bennett. Indeed, Walcott sees these revolutionary ventures in language as pointless because they can never capture the essence of the old tribal traditions, and concedes the superiority of standard European grammar by suggesting that "the great poem of Césaire's could not be written in a French Creole because there are no words for some of its concepts" ("Muse of History," *Twilight Says* 51).

A similar crisis is evident in Walcott's embrace of the European classics. Of his education he admits the "grounding was rigid—Latin, Greek, and the essential masterpieces" ("Meanings," *Critical Perspectives* 50). So binding, indeed, was the hold of the classics that in St. Lucia, as he tells us, while folk and Christian songs and pageants were performed in open-air festivals, "On the verandah, with his back to the street, he began marathon poems on Greek heroes which ran out of breath, lute songs, heroic tragedies, but . . . the rhythms of the street were entering the pulse beat of the wrist" ("What the Twilight Says" 20). So we are not surprised to find troubling images of classical civilization here and there, as in the poem **"Statues,"** which castigates Roman imperialism enshrined in stone (*Castaway* 40-41). In "C. L. R. James," he compares the British empire of James's day with Greece as slavocracies (*Twilight Says* 116); and in **"Ruins of a Great House"** he presents a tragic image of imperial demise: "Marble as Greece, like Faulkner's South in stone, / Deciduous beauty prospered and is gone" (*Green Night* 19).

The commanding guide in Walcott's explorations of classical European literature is, of course, Homer. So deeply did Walcott internalize his model that he saw himself as the Homer of the Antilles, appointed—by genius or by fate, it's not quite clear—to record the region's virtues, its woes, and its destiny. Hence he is convinced St. Lucia would remain "a naturalist's scrapbook"

till our Homer with truer perception erect it,
Stripped of all memory or rhetoric,
As the peeled bark shows white.

             ("Roots," *Green Night* 60)

And we may well hear Walcott in the voice of the Odyssean voyager Shabine, declaring, "I am satisfied / if my hand gave voice to one people's grief" (**"The Schooner Flight"** 19). There is a wide range of images in Walcott's *oeuvre* taken from the *Iliad* and *Odyssey,* not the least of which is the figure of St. Lucia as the "Helen of the West" ("Leaving School," *Critical Perspectives* 24). But far the most prominent theme in Walcott is the Ulyssean—influenced either by direct classical reading or by the modernist tradition of Joyce, who may be judged Walcott's immediate model in seeking to articulate "the uncreated conscience of his race." In fact, the Odyssean journey may be seen as the commanding paradigm in most of Walcott's middle period—*Gulf, Sea Grapes, Star-Apple Kingdom, Fortunate Traveller, Midsummer,* and *Arkansas Testament*—in which we see either the poet himself or some alter ego traveling through the Caribbean/American region and lamenting the fallen world of its sociopolitical life, though not without a touch of chastened optimism. *Sea Grapes,* for instance, sees the voyager home to a cherished native earth, to reconciliation, and to the peace of old age very much as in Homer's *Odyssey.*

### III

Who was this Homer, by whom Walcott sets so much store? There already exists today an enormous body of well-informed conjecture and comment on Homer's backgrounds and identity. Despite the volume of more recent opinion on the issue, it remains safe to invoke T. W. Allen's detailed review of a broad range of *loci classici* relating to Homer and the post-Homeric guild of minstrels called *Homeridae* (descendants of Homer), which led him to various conclusions, such as (I) that Homer was a traditional bard from the Aegean island of Chios, and (ii) that the so-called progeny of minstrels may have originally been family though other guild members became attached to the family through stages of professional affiliation (11-50).[3] The classic image of Homer as a *blind* singer—not the least aided by evidence from the first *Hymn to Apollo*—may have come either by eponymization of the word *homeros* or by deduction from contrast with the deep inner vision *homeros* by the bard's tales. This biographical point is significant because of Walcott's focalization of the blind minstrel in his two adaptations of Homer. I will be concerned here, therefore, mainly with the ramifications of the Homeric identity for the use to which it has been put by Walcott.

For instance, one implication of Chios is to make Homer either a colonial pandering, with his songs, to the glory of the imperial rulers of his region, or else a Greek colonist celebrating the traditions and triumphs of his mainland home with a touch of patriotic pride. At any rate, the epics reveal a tremendous familiarity with a universe defined as much by the mainland regions of Greece and the Troad as by the archipelago of islands especially in the Aegean. There is a comprehensive feel for the variety of peoples in that universe even when they are marshaled against one another: thus the recognition scene between Diomedes and Glaukos (*Iliad* 6.119-236) reveals a network of kinship and hospitality ties unifying cross-regional class and other interests. Homer also shows a deep empathy with the marine world by his graphic representations of color and activity around it, so that "the archipelago comes alive," despite the toll of dying nearby, "in a sort of animate relief" and "a certain order, a certain rhythm" (Vivante 103).

Another implication of a Homer from the outposts has some bearing with the language of his epics, with their intricate layering of dialects. Whether this palimpsest arose from an itinerant Homer adjusting his performances to the dialects of many host peoples, or from a harmonization of episodes performed by rhapsodes across regions (as the Pisistratean recensionists would have it) and especially their standardization for performance at regional or national festivals (as Wade-Gery and, more recently, Nagy would have it[4]), the implications of such a dialectical relationship between the center and the margins in the use of language is certainly of interest to a postcolonial poet like Walcott.

But what kinds of audience did Homer perform for? The evidence of bards in the *Odyssey* (Phemios, Demodokos) would suggest he sang for royal or aristocratic hosts. The blind Chian of the *Hymn to Apollo* would signify, rather, an itinerant bard who sang to all and sundry. What we have here is a possible polarity between class interests. On the one hand the blind Chian, whose sympathy seems to lie with the unaccountable folk "whose suffering never ends" (167-68)—a sympathy augmented by Homer's frequent punctuation of the lofty aristocratic world with similes of humble life and occupations especially in the *Iliad*—evidently identifies the epics no more as a celebration of the *klea andron* (*Iliad* 9.189) than as a general reflection on the human condition, so that the plight of proletarian characters like the hapless Thersites in *Iliad* 2 and the servants on Odysseus's Ithakan estate loom larger in the poet's ideological consciousness than we are inclined to think. On the other hand, recent radical scholarship has argued the basic hegemonist ideology of Homer's epics by suggesting that, whatever solace the images of the lowly and underprivileged may offer either to the bard or to his non-elite audiences, the underlying outlook of those tales is elitist (Rose, Thalmann) and sexist (Murnaghan); the marginalized characters, male or female, are too easily led to accept their submission or are in any case in no position to stand up to, or enjoy meaningful support from any quarters against, the inequities imposed on them by a largely slave-owning, feudal, and patriarchal system. Again, such arguments have implications for ideological stresses evident in the use of which Walcott has put Homer in his work.

## IV

By the time Walcott came to adapt Homer's epics, he had been compelled by various factors to adjust his outlook somewhat. Persisting racial conflict across the world involving black peoples—as much in the U.S. as elsewhere—must have urged a firmer commitment.[5] Walcott also came under considerable attack for his elitist portraits of popular culture and his increasing Euro-modernist leanings. As revolutionary movements in the Caribbean gained in popularity and commanded the respect even of the political class,[6] it became increasingly risky to be seen as opposing such forces, especially for a writer who aspired to be the conscience of his people. Even the scholars were gaining greater prominence in their pursuit of research into African connections, thus tilting the scales of critical opinion—in the debate highlighted by the likes of Edward Lucie-Smith, Gordon Collier, Arthur Drayton, Patricia Ismond, and more recently June Bobb—on the side of Brathwaite against Walcott. Finally, despite continuing social and political woes, it would seem that Africa was at last getting the attention of Walcott, not least with achievements recorded by artists like Wole Soyinka, the first black writer to win the Nobel Prize for Literature (1986).

Walcott must thus have come to a point where he needed to resolve the tensions between his ecumenical instincts and his growing black consciousness. As early as the title poem of *Sea Grapes,* he admits, "The classics can console. But not enough" (3). In reviewing Walcott's adaptations of Homer's epics, however, we must begin by acknowledging his deep indebtedness to the Greek poet. For a start, he was aware that, in being positioned at the cross-currents of the world's political, cultural, and other forces, the two archipelagos of the Aegean and the Caribbean have been subject to comparable tides of history as well as heirs to analogous fortunes: in *Omeros* he tells Homer that these "tides," of both sea and history, are "Our last resort as much as yours" (296). From Homer, also, Walcott absorbed a touching regard for the marine environment in both its positive and negative aspects: its prepossessing natural beauty (as in "conch-coloured dusk," *Omeros* 11) as well as its menace to life ("variegated fists of clouds," *Green Night* 11). Like their "blind" Chian counterpart, the itinerant bards of Walcott's versions (Seven Seas in *Omeros* and Billy Blue in the stage *Odyssey*) distill life's deeper truths—the limitations of human aspiration, and especially the subordination (despite the modernist creed) of human life to a supernatural network of forces—from communities across time and space, for the benefit of contemporary audiences.

In *Omeros,* Walcott uses the interesting figure of "the fallen schism / of a starfish" (294) to characterize his "homage to Homer" as an act of "exorcism." Whatever else this figure implies, it appears that in his adaptations of Homer he is finally able to resolve what in *Sea Grapes* he calls "the ancient war / between obsession and responsibility" (3). I drew attention above to the stresses in Homer's epics between, on the one hand, an obvious deference to

the aristocracy and, on the other, an arguable sympathy with the proletarian class. In his case, the tensions Walcott addresses are evidently between, on the one hand, a sustained cultivation of an elitist Eurocentric sensibility and, on the other, an increasing sympathy for elements in his society fundamentally excluded, by structures of control enshrined by European colonialism, from attainment of the basic privileges of human existence.

But Walcott's departures from his model are just as striking. In the first place, despite the colossal scope of a work like *Omeros,* he feels a certain ambivalence about the convention of the "epic" as a medium for articulating the antihegemonist sentiments that would form the bedrock of his vision of Caribbean history and culture. Admittedly, there is a certain stoic regularity, even "high seriousness," in the stanzaic design—*terza rima,* with varying rhyme schemes—that propels the narrative, analogous perhaps to the steady hexametric movement of the Homeric epic. But in terms of poetic form, it would be fair to say that Walcott is somewhat less beholden to Homer than to latter-day transformations of the genre, if not exactly in Callimachus, Vergil, and Dante, at least in the modernist poetic of the generation of Ezra Pound, in whose hands the epic edge tends to have suffered some blunting. Rei Terada thinks that "Walcott does [. . .] pastoralize the Homeric poems in *Omeros*" (186). Gregson Davis also draws attention to "the centrality of pastoral motifs and obsessions in the economy of [*Omeros*]" ("Pastoral Sites" 43), and judges the poem "a multilayered palimpsest" that, in mixing the creole of characters like Philoctete with the "elegant musings of the phantom narrator" (49), altogether abdicates the high seriousness of the Homeric model. Although Davis earlier saw something of a generic sleight of hand in Walcott's disavowing the Homeric form even when he is most indebted to it ("'With No Homeric Shadow'"), it is fair to conclude that in *Omeros* Walcott succeeds considerably in distancing himself ideologically from his model and creating "a polysemous, demotic narrative" (Hamner, *Epic* 32).

In placing Creole speech and culture on equal footing with the dominant colonialist style, *Omeros* indeed gives Walcott an opportunity to descend from his elitist high horse more decidedly than he ever did in his earlier work. Here, distortions of standard English forms are indulged both by characters (Achille christens his boat "In God We Troust") and the narrator himself (of Helen: "Were both hemispheres part of the split breadfruit of her African ass . . . ?" 312), from a clearly anti-imperialist impulse (compare Hofmeister 52); and now and then Walcott uses the unglossed names of local Caribbean cultural items (e.g., "acajou," 18). In *Omeros,* he is finally able to demonstrate his belief that "the speeches of Caliban are equal in their elemental power to those of his tutor" ("Muse of History" 39).

It is in dignifying the dispossessed of the Caribbean that Walcott makes his clinching departure from the superior claims of Homer's aristocratic culture. The "epic" battle of *Omeros* pits not highborn warlords leading national armies in a contest over a woman, but two fishermen, descendants of slaves, in a fight over the mere means of survival. Although the animosity between Achille and Hector has its roots in their rivalry over Helen—so much for Walcott's adoption of the Homeric motif—the point at issue is really a bailing tin. The two rivals never quite get the chance to make up, because Hector dies in a car accident; but Achille mourns the man in a way Homer's Achilles is incapable of—a token no doubt of Walcott's recognition of the pacifist instincts of these humble folk (compare Terada 186). In dealing with their fellow men they also reveal a basic nobility and humaneness that their more elitist counterparts like the Plunketts are less capable of; we see these qualities clearly in their rallying around Plunkett upon the death of his wife, Maude. If there is anything "epic" in these humble folk, it is the way they tower above the haughty colonial elite by the largeness of heart and consideration they show for the plight of their fellow men, whatever the social or other distinctions between them.

Equally significant in *Omeros*'s revisionism is the identity of the marginalized. In Homer's epics, there is an obvious fetish in the detailed recognition of the principal figures by patronymics and other tokens of distinguished affiliation. But very few of the rank and file are given detailed identification; thus, in the fight sequences many are acknowledged only by name as they fall to the onslaught of the likes of Patroklos and Hector. In Achille's "journey" to Africa, however, Walcott takes the symbolic step of restoring the erased identity of the dispossessed elements of Caribbean society. The colonial elite are also given an opportunity, with the Plunketts, to revisit their native homes, but the reconnection is uneasy and ultimately aborted; Achille, on the contrary, is able to rediscover his ancestral name (Afolabe) as well as his native African land, albeit filtered through a kaleidoscope of scenes recalling the tragic history of enslavement and expatriation. In this event, Walcott also manages to correct a flaw in Makak's earlier "journey" to the same source in *Dream on Monkey Mountain*. After Achille's journey, it will no longer do to lament, as Philoctete early in *Omeros,* "what it's like without roots in this world" (21).

The vindication of these marginalized elements is ultimately a comment on the structures of domination that constrain their existence. Walcott has, of course, been consistent in exposing the ugliness, sham, and futility of the imperial enterprise that put these hegemonic structures in place, as witness poems like **"Ruins of a Great House"** and **"Roots"** in *Green Night,* as well as **"Air"** and the **"Guyana"** sequence in *Gulf.* In *Omeros* and the stage *Odyssey* he is able to weave this theme into a broad historical and mythic tapestry. In *Omeros,* the ravages of the U.S. army against native Americans and the slave raids in Africa expose the horrors of imperial domination; in the stage *Odyssey,* Odysseus' acquisitive greed and the paranoia that assails him upon his return to his Ithakan home reveal the sheer emptiness of these foreign exertions. Between them, these adaptations give Walcott an opportunity to rethink his relations with his model by tak-

ing an anti-hegemonist stand against whatever role the tale of Troy, as the prime text of the European literary canon, has played in enshrining the claims of the West over the rest of us.

Of the dispossessed, it is clearly Helen who—despite Walcott's well-advertised problems with real-life women—has triumphed the most against the sexist fate imposed upon her by Greek myth and history through the Homeric epos. In both the *Iliad* and the *Odyssey,* she groans with self-reproach for the tragedy she has caused the embattled peoples by breaking her marital faith. On the contrary, in both *Omeros* and his stage *Odyssey,* Walcott gives us a Helen who is poor but proud, a saucy and irrepressible will-o'-the-wisp who chooses her affiliations between Achille and Hector with a random sense of independence, though she is humane enough to spare a tear when one of them (Hector) dies in an accident. She flaunts her charms and enthralls men in them, not least her former employer Plunkett who, seeing her as symbolizing the much-contested island of St Lucia, tries but fails to construct a coherent narrative of her historical fortunes. For Walcott, Helen thus represents "the evasiveness of the signified," a clear proof not only of the inadequacy of history but even of "the infirmity of his [Walcott's] own medium" of art (Terada 196-97) in attempting to arrest the shifting signs of temporal reality.

## V

What, then, is Walcott's place in black New World discourse? It is, perhaps, fair to start by saying that he is one with the likes of Harris and Gilroy in seeing New World history as an ongoing process, its identity as continually evolving, rather than as something to be arrested at a point in time decreed by a dominant imperial culture. In *Omeros,* as Achille hangs up his fishing net and walks home with "the odours of the sea in him," we are told in the very last line, "When he left the beach, the sea was still going on" (325). This metaphor of the sea as history, which Walcott uses in *The Star-Apple Kingdom* to mock the touted trophies of imperial adventurism, serves also to inscribe the fluidity of time and the unfinished nature of all efforts in personal or national self-fashioning. But the fact that Achille bears this element *in* him suggests that he and his kind, once erased from the privileged accounts of the imperial establishment, will in the end have taken their proud proprietary place when the intruders' grand edifices have been flushed down the flood of time.

In *Omeros,* Walcott mocks the concept of "history" in the sense it has statutorily assumed in master chronicles. Imperial history is, in the final analysis, official record documenting the systematic appropriations of other peoples' territory and selfhood by adventurers with superior tools of control, technological and otherwise, which is why Hegel and Trevor-Roper have variously pronounced that African history begins only with the coming of white people to the continent (Fage 7). Walcott delivers a double blow at such presumptions. To begin with, he demonstrates that if we look hard enough among various sites of the natural environment, we will find evidence of the pristine cultural history that the imperial machinery tried to erase in the process of its appropriation. People have *always* lived here since the dawn of time, and have *always* carried on a viable existence; they will never forget who they are or the things that have always sustained them. More than that, in his survey of the record of imperial dispossession of peoples in the Americas, Walcott revises the conventions of geographic partitioning of the world that suits the exploitative designs of empire. Although they are different peoples culturally, blacks and Amerindians are united in one fate as the wretched of the American earth under the European machinery of exploitation.

In endorsing the concept of unfinished history, Walcott has nonetheless come to recognize the primacy of the African factor in Caribbean identity. In sending Achille on an African "journey" to recover his identity, Walcott ultimately embraces the archeology of knowledge that has been central to the thought of Césaire and Brathwaite. Even more, in integrating elements of African metaphysics and theology in the enterprise of "recovery" by Achille and Ma Kilman (*Omeros*) and in the foreign worlds of Odysseus's appropriative ventures (stage *Odyssey*), Walcott would seem to contest the separation of the secular from the supernatural that is central to Gilroy's conception of the "modern." Above all, although Walcott reconciles the races in his vision of a harmonious Antillean universe, his centralization of dispossessed elements like Achille, son of Afolabe, who plies the waves in an African-style canoe (*Omeros* 287)—not in a ship (*pace* Gilroy) that cargoed his ancestors to the Americas—is Walcott's deft Afrocentric move in foregrounding the black identity and coming to terms with the dominant structures of feeling in the Caribbean.[7]

Finally, I think it would be fair to say that, although Walcott recognizes the disparate identities from which the Caribbean is constituted, his work seems to have moved steadily beyond the paranoia of fragmentation, the sense of what Gilroy calls a "rhizomorphic, fractal structure" which does not recognize such an entity as the nation. *Omeros* shows the poet returning to his home region, prodigal-like (to borrow a thought from Dan Izevbaye), and here using St Lucia as a microcosm for the larger Caribbean world. It represents his hopes for a universe self-sufficient and at peace with itself; a unified society in which the varied cultural identities, the Plunketts as well as the Philoctetes, find a welcome home however they may have been brought there by the vagaries of history; most of all, a society in which the dispossessed elements are finally restored to their due place as the true energies driving Caribbean society. That pride of place basically privileges the Black factor in the Caribbean. In *Omeros* Walcott, unlike Gilroy, finally comes to recognize the "image" of Africa that continually "insists"—to borrow a phrase from the late Nigerian poet Christopher Okigbo, whose work Walcott grew to respect (King, *Caribbean*

*Life* 356)—on being credited as the basic substratum of Caribbean identity.

*Notes*

1. The stories in *The Guyana Quartet* are, without question, Harris's deep-felt acknowledgment of the interpenetration of the temporal and the timeless in the native cultures of the Caribbean. The stories were designed, he tells us in his somewhat nuanced introduction to the *Quartet,* to uncover the inherent truth of works outside the canons of (Western) realism, "by bringing the fictions I had in mind into parallel with profound myth that lies apparently eclipsed in largely forgotten so-called savage cultures" (7). With a writer like Harris, we are introduced to a tradition of writing that has become very much a staple of 'Third World' fiction—magical realism—in which "the entire apparatus of verisimilitude, which was the focal point of nineteenth-century European realism, proves inadequate as a medium for registering the difference of the colonial subject" (Wilson-Tagoe 5).

2. The figure of Robinson Crusoe evidently served Walcott's programmatic conception of the Caribbean artist struggling to fashion something out of the apparent cultural vacuum in which he has been marooned. But the figure itself—derived as it is from a classic work of colonial fiction—comes saddled with a curious political baggage of which Walcott seems to have been aware early enough in his work. For a "black" artist to use a "white" colonial figure as a prototype of the Caribbean creative imagination does raise questions as to what side the artist is really on. Indeed, so much is invested in Crusoe as the focal figure of *The Castaway*—a focalization hardly redeemed by his equation with Columbus, Adam, even God in the essay "The Figure of Crusoe" (*Critical Perspectives* 35-36)—that the radical reader soon flinches at the writer's "continued wrestling-match with European discourses" (Thieme 78). In time, however, the excesses of the figuration soon dawn on Walcott, as the Crusoe persona is thrown into increasing self-contestation of his hegemonist relations with the dispossessed of his new world. Bruce King gives some background to Walcott's composition of the play *Pantomime* (*Walcott and West Indian Drama* 295), which sheds light on the interesting dissolution of the hegemonist gulf in the running argument between the English (white) hotel manager Harry (Crusoe) and his black employee Jackson (Friday).

3. There is, of course, an enormous amount of critical opinion, both attesting to and questioning the historicity of the poet "Homer," but the balance of judgment seems to uphold popular (which does not exclude scholarly) habit—as well as classical iconography—in seeing the "blind Chian" as the creator of both the *Iliad* and *Odyssey*. No less contested has been the issue whether Homer was an

oral or a literate poet; in this regard, I find Nagy's arguments about Homer as a "stitcher," "weaver," or "joiner" of songs—in the same artisanal convention as a traditional carpenter (*Best of the Achaeans* 296-333, *Homeric Questions* 89-93, and *Poetry as Performance* 74-75)—rather convincing in demonstrating the poet's status as a member of a traditional, oral culture, whatever shape may have been given to his compositions in later times for arguable festival performances. I think West has, in his recent article, made a forceful attempt to prove that the name "Homer" was only an eponymous coinage, especially by the so-called "Homeridae," designed to dignify their guild with an ancestry of sorts; there was no such ancestor from whom they traced their descent; and the idea that Homer was a blind poet was only a claim made on the basis of minstrelsy being "a favored occupation for the blind in many societies" (374). Unfortunately, even were we to overlook some notable flaws in his argument, the idea of Homer as an oral poet has become too well established by the Parry-Lord tradition of scholarship for West's erudite thesis to elicit more a deferential nod. And some of the authorities that he cites in support of his case, such as Janko and Nagy, are really more inclined toward the oral hypothesis than West seems to acknowledge; a close reading of Janko's chapter 2 is especially rewarding.

4. See Wade-Gery, *The Poet of the Iliad* 14-18; Nagy, *Best of* 6-7, *Questions* 42-43 and 80-81, *Pindar's Homer* 21-24, 60-73. The idea that Homer's narrative songs, originally performed by him or by later singers in independent episodes, were ultimately cobbled together into continuous wholes at some point in time—possibly under commission from the sixth-century BC Athenian tyrant Pisistratos—has some respectable ancient authority behind it: e.g., Plato, *Hipparchus* 228b; Cicero, *De Oratore* 3.137; Josephus, *Contra Apionem* 1.12. In 1795 a German scholar by the name of Friedrich August Wolf published a essay titled *Prolegomena ad Homerum* (the actual Latin title is much longer!), which put a whole new spin on the theory of Homer's songs being in scattered and later unified forms. It caused a rift, for over a century, between "Analysts," who treated Homer's texts as curious pieces of patchwork, and "Unitarians," who saw a coherent pattern and genius in the poems. For a useful discussion of this issue, see at least Davison, "The Homeric Question"; Adam Parry's introduction (x-xxi) to his father Milman Parry's collected essays; and Foley 2-6.

5. The title poem of *The Arkansas Testament,* a meditation on racial prejudice in the US inspired by a visit to Fayetteville, Arkansas, contains some of the strongest language ever used by a writer who has, to this point (1987), embraced an identity pretty evenly shared between black and white ancestries. Images of cross burning and other emblems of segregation shake Walcott gruffly from his color-blind liberalism,

forcing him to seek comfort in his kind—"my race" (110), "my people's predicament" (116)—and wonder what has become of the foundations of "this aging Democracy" (114). The effect of his encounters is altogether devastating: "My metre dropped its limp . . . ," he confesses,

> hairs
> fall on my collar as I write this
> in shorter days, darker years,
> more hatred, more racial rage.

> (112-13)

6. Walcott's play *O Babylon!* was seen by some Caribbean critics as being either out of touch with the real aspirations and culture of the Rastafarian elements of Jamaica, the subjects of the play, or else unconscionably elitist: see, for instance, reviews of it by Earl Lovelace and "Sule Mombara" (Horace Campbell). Indeed, after the Rastafarian reggae superstars Bob Marley and Peter Tosh showed such a strong presence at Marley's "One Love Peace Concert" in Kingston (1978), which brought together Jamaica's warring political leaders Michael Manley and Edward Seaga in a momentary show of accord (Barrett 223), no one could ignore the influence of these revolutionary elements in Jamaican society, despite their periodic clashes with law enforcement authorities. In prefacing one of his poems, "The Light of the World," with lines from Marley's song "Kaya" (*Arkansas Testament* 48), Walcott is clearly acknowledging the pervasive influence of Rasta music and culture not only in Jamaica but across the Caribbean.

7. Compare Thieme: "*Omeros* concludes with a message which revitalizes Walcott's life-long preoccupation with classical epic and nervous engagement with the anxiety of influence. It [. . .] admits the importance of African retentions in the Caribbean in a way that has hitherto been rare in Walcott's verse" (187); and Hamner: "Achille's odyssey reestablishes African roots and affirms their influence in island customs" (*Derek Walcott* 147).

*Works Cited*

Allen, T. W. *Homer: The Origins and the Transmission.* Oxford: Clarendon, 1924.

Barrett Leonard E., Sr. *The Rastafarians: Sounds of Cultural Dissonance.* Revised and updated edition. Boston: Beacon, 1988.

Bobb, June D. *Beating a Restless Drum: The Poetics of Kamau Brathwaite and Derek Walcott.* Trenton: Africa World P, 1998.

Brathwaite, Edward [Kamau]. *The Arrivants: A New World Trilogy.* London: Oxford UP, 1973.

Brathwaite, Edward Kamau. *History of the Voice: The Development of Nation Language in Anglophone Caribbean Poetry.* London: New Beacon, 1984.

Casas, Bartolome de las. *The Devastation of the Indies.* Trans. Herman Briffault. Baltimore: Johns Hopkins UP, 1974.

Césaire, Aimé. *Cahiers d'un retour au pays natal.* Trans. as *Return to My Native Land.* Harmondsworth: Penguin, 1970.

Collier, Gordon. "Artistic Autonomy and Cultural Allegiance: Aspects of the Walcott-Brathwaite Debate Reexamined." *The Literary Half-Yearly* 20 (1979): 93-105.

Columbus, Christopher. *The Voyage of Christopher Columbus.* Trans. John Cummins. New York: St. Martin's, 1992.

*Critical Perspectives on Derek Walcott.* Ed. Robert D. Hamner. Washington, DC: Three Continents, 1993.

Cudjoe, Selwyn R. *Resistance and Caribbean Literature.* Athens: Ohio UP, 1980.

D'Aguiar, Fred. "'Lines with Their Knots Left in': *Third World Poems* by Edward Kamau Brathwaite and *Midsummer* by Derek Walcott." *Wasafiri* 1 (1985): 37-38.

Davis, Gregson. "'Pastoral Sites': Aspects of Bucolic Transformation in Derek Walcott's *Omeros.*" *Classical World* 93 (1999): 43-49.

———. "'With No Homeric Shadow': The Disavowal of Epic in Derek Walcott's *Omeros.*" *South Atlantic Quarterly* 96 (1997): 321-33.

Davison J. A. "The Homeric Question." *A Companion to Homer.* Ed. A. J. B. Wace and F. H. Stubbings. London: Macmillan, 1962. 234-65.

Drayton, Arthur D. "The European Factor in West Indian Literature." *The Literary Half-Yearly* 11 (1970): 71-95.

Fage, J. D. *Africa Discovers Her Past.* London: Oxford UP, 1970.

Foley, John Miles. *The Theory of Oral Composition: History and Methodology.* Bloomington: Indiana UP, 1988.

Froude, James Anthony. *The English in the West Indies, or The Bow of Ulysses.* London: Longmans, Green, 1888.

Gilroy, Paul. *The Black Atlantic: Modernity and Double Consciousness.* Cambridge: Harvard UP, 1993.

Glissant, Edouard. *Caribbean Discourse: Selected Essays.* Trans. J. Michael Dash. Charlottesville: UP of Virginia, 1989.

Hamner, Robert D. *Derek Walcott.* Updated edition. New York: Twayne, 1993.

———. *Epic of the Dispossessed: Derek Walcott's Omeros.* Columbia: U of Missouri P, 1997.

Harris, Wilson. *Palace of the Peacock.* In *The Guyana Quartet.* London: Faber and Faber, 1985.

———. *Selected Essays of Wilson Harris: The Unfinished Genesis of the Imagination.* Ed. Andrew J. M. Bundy. London: Routledge, 1999.

Hofmeister, Timothy. "'This Is We Calypso': An Ithacan and Antillean *Topos* in Derek Walcott's *Omeros.*" *Classical World,* 93 (1999): 51-70.

Ismond, Patricia. "Walcott versus Brathwaite." *Critical Perspectives on Derek Walcott.* 220-236.

Izevbaye, D. S. "The Exile and the Prodigal: Derek Walcott as West Indian Poet." *Caribbean Quarterly* 26 (1980): 70-82.

Janko, Richard. *Homer, Hesiod, and the Hymns: Diachronic Development in Epic Diction.* Cambridge: Cambridge UP, 1982.

King, Bruce. *Derek Walcott: A Caribbean Life.* Oxford: Oxford UP, 2000.———. *Derek Walcott and West Indian Drama.* Oxford: Clarendon, 1995.

Lovelace, Earl. "Rude Bwoy Walcott." (Review of *O Babylon!*). *People* 1.2 (1976): 37-39.

Lucie-Smith, Edward. "West Indian Writing." *The London Magazine* 8 (1968): 96-102.

Mombara, Sule. "'*O Babylon!*': Where It Went Wrong." (Review of *O Babylon!*). *Critical Perspectives on Derek Walcott.* 268-71.

Murnaghan, Sheila. *Disguise and Recognition in the Odyssey.* Princeton: Princeton UP, 1987.

———. "The Plan of Athena." *The Distaff Side: Representing the Female in Homer's Odyssey.* Ed. Beth Cohen. New York: Oxford UP, 1995, 61-80.

Nagy, Gregory. *Homeric Questions.* Austin: U of Texas P, 1996.

———. *Pindar's Homer: The Lyric Possession of an Epic Past.* Baltimore: Johns Hopkins UP, 1990.

———. *Poetry as Performance: Homer and Beyond.* Cambridge: Cambridge UP, 1996.

———. *The Best of the Achaeans: Concepts of the Hero in Archaic Greek Poetry.* Baltimore: Johns Hopkins UP, 1979.

Naipaul, V. S. *The Middle Passage.* London: Andre Deutsch, 1962.

Parry, Adam, ed. *The Making of Homeric Verse: The Collected Papers of Milman Parry.* 1971. New York: Oxford UP, 1987.

Rose, Peter W. *Sons of the Gods, Children of Earth: Ideology and Literary Form in Ancient Greece.* Ithaca: Cornell UP, 1992.

Sewell, W. G. *The Ordeal of Free Labour in the West Indies.* London: Sampson Low, 1862.

Terada, Rei. *Derek Walcott's Poetry: American Mimicry.* Boston: Northeastern UP, 1992.

Thalmann, William G. *The Swineherd and the Bow: Representations of Class in the "Odyssey."* Ithaca: Cornell UP, 1998.

Thieme, John. *Derek Walcott.* Contemporary World Writers. Manchester: Manchester UP, 1999.

Trollope, Anthony. *The West Indies and the Spanish Main.* 1860. London: Frank Cass, 1968.

Vivante, Paolo. *The Homeric Imagination: A Study of Homer's Poetic Perception of Reality.* Bloomington: Indiana UP, 1970.

Wade-Gery, H.T. *The Poet of the Iliad.* Cambridge: Cambridge UP, 1952.

Walcott, Derek. *Another Life.* New York: Farrar, 1973.

———. *Dream on Monkey Mountain and Other Plays.* New York: Farrar, 1972.

———. *In a Green Night.* London: Jonathan Cape, 1962.

———. *Midsummer.* New York: Farrar, 1984.

———. *O Babylon!* In *The Joker of Seville and O Babylon!* New York: Farrar, 1978.

———. *Omeros.* New York: Farrar, 1990.

———. *Sea Grapes.* New York: Farrar, 1976.

———. *The Arkansas Testament.* New York: Farrar, 1987.

———. *The Castaway.* London: Jonathan Cape, 1965.

———. *The Fortunate Traveller.* New York: Farrar, 1981.

———. *The Gulf.* New York: Farrar, 1970.

———. *The Odyssey: A Stage Version.* New York: Farrar, 1993.

———. *The Star-Apple Kingdom.* New York: Farrar, 1979.

———. *Tiepolo's Hound.* New York: Farrar, 2000.

———. *What the Twilight Says: Essays.* New York: Farrar, 1998.

West, M. L. "The Invention of Homer." *Classical Quarterly.* New Series 49 (1999): 364-82.

Wilson-Tagoe, Nana. *Historical Thought and Literary Representation in West Indian Literature.* Gainsville: UP of Florida, 1998.

# FURTHER READING

## Criticism

Breslin, Paul. "Tracking *Tiepolo's Hound.*" *Poetry* 178, no. 1 (April 2001): 38-40.

In a positive review of *Tiepolo's Hound,* Breslin calls the work "strikingly beautiful."

Cribb, T. J. "Walcott, Poet and Painter." *Kenyon Review* 23, no. 2 (spring 2001): 176-84.

Examines the interrelationship between Walcott's poetry and painting, as evident in *Another Life, Omeros,* and *Tiepolo's Hound.*

Davis, Gregson. *The Poetics of Derek Walcott: Intertextual Perspectives. The South Atlantic Quarterly* 96, no. 2 (spring 1997).

This collection of essays by North American and Caribbean literary scholars includes a previously unpublished essay by Derek Walcott, "Reflections on *Omeros.*"

Dentith, Simon. "Heaney and Walcott: Two Poems." *Critical Survey* 11, no. 3 (1999): 92-9.

Offers a critical comparison of Seamus Heaney's "The Ministry of Fear," and Derek Walcott's "Homecoming: Anse La Raye," which first appeared in *The Gulf and Other Poems* in 1969.

Donoghue, Denis. "Themes from Derek Walcott." *Parnassus: Poetry in Review* 6, no. 1 (1977): 88-100.

Traces themes of exile and identity in a discussion of Walcott's works that includes particular focus on *Sea Grapes.*

King, Bruce. *Derek Walcott: A Caribbean Life.* Oxford: Oxford University Press, 2000, 714 p.

Presents a book-length critical biography of Walcott.

---

# How to Use This Index

*CMW* = *St. James Guide to Crime & Mystery Writers*
*CN* = *Contemporary Novelists*
*CP* = *Contemporary Poets*
*CPW* = *Contemporary Popular Writers*
*CSW* = *Contemporary Southern Writers*
*CWD* = *Contemporary Women Dramatists*
*CWP* = *Contemporary Women Poets*
*CWRI* = *St. James Guide to Children's Writers*
*CWW* = *Contemporary World Writers*
*DA* = *DISCovering Authors*
*DA3* = *DISCovering Authors 3.0*
*DAB* = *DISCovering Authors: British Edition*
*DAC* = *DISCovering Authors: Canadian Edition*
*DAM* = *DISCovering Authors: Modules*
   *DRAM: Dramatists Module; MST: Most-studied Authors Module;*
   *MULT: Multicultural Authors Module; NOV: Novelists Module;*
   *POET: Poets Module; POP: Popular Fiction and Genre Authors Module*
*DFS* = *Drama for Students*
*DLB* = *Dictionary of Literary Biography*
*DLBD* = *Dictionary of Literary Biography Documentary Series*
*DLBY* = *Dictionary of Literary Biography Yearbook*
*DNFS* = *Literature of Developing Nations for Students*
*EFS* = *Epics for Students*
*EXPN* = *Exploring Novels*
*EXPP* = *Exploring Poetry*
*EXPS* = *Exploring Short Stories*
*EW* = *European Writers*
*FANT* = *St. James Guide to Fantasy Writers*
*FW* = *Feminist Writers*
*GFL* = *Guide to French Literature,* Beginnings to 1789, 1798 to the Present
*GLL* = *Gay and Lesbian Literature*
*HGG* = *St. James Guide to Horror, Ghost & Gothic Writers*
*HW* = *Hispanic Writers*
*IDFW* = *International Dictionary of Films and Filmmakers: Writers and Production Artists*
*IDTP* = *International Dictionary of Theatre: Playwrights*
*LAIT* = *Literature and Its Times*
*LAW* = *Latin American Writers*
*JRDA* = *Junior DISCovering Authors*
*MAICYA* = *Major Authors and Illustrators for Children and Young Adults*
*MAICYAS* = *Major Authors and Illustrators for Children and Young Adults Supplement*
*MAWW* = *Modern American Women Writers*
*MJW* = *Modern Japanese Writers*
*MTCW* = *Major 20th-Century Writers*
*NCFS* = *Nonfiction Classics for Students*
*NFS* = *Novels for Students*
*PAB* = *Poets: American and British*
*PFS* = *Poetry for Students*
*RGAL* = *Reference Guide to American Literature*
*RGEL* = *Reference Guide to English Literature*
*RGSF* = *Reference Guide to Short Fiction*
*RGWL* = *Reference Guide to World Literature*
*RHW* = *Twentieth-Century Romance and Historical Writers*
*SAAS* = *Something about the Author Autobiography Series*
*SATA* = *Something about the Author*
*SFW* = *St. James Guide to Science Fiction Writers*
*SSFS* = *Short Stories for Students*
*TCWW* = *Twentieth-Century Western Writers*
*WLIT* = *World Literature and Its Times*
*WP* = *World Poets*
*YABC* = *Yesterday's Authors of Books for Children*
*YAW* = *St. James Guide to Young Adult Writers*

# Literary Criticism Series
# Cumulative Author Index

**Aguilera Malta, Demetrio** 1909-1981 **HLCS 1**
See also CA 124; 111; CANR 87; DAM MULT, NOV; DLB 145; EWL 3; HW 1; RGWL 3

**Agustini, Delmira** 1886-1914 **HLCS 1**
See also CA 166; HW 1, 2; LAW

**Aherne, Owen**
See Cassill, R(onald) V(erlin)

**Ai** 1947- **CLC 4, 14, 69**
See also CA 85-88; CAAS 13; CANR 70; DLB 120; PFS 16

**Aickman, Robert (Fordyce)** 1914-1981 **CLC 57**
See also CA 5-8R; CANR 3, 72, 100; DLB 261; HGG; SUFW 1, 2

**Aidoo, (Christina) Ama Ata** 1942- **BLCS**
See also AFW; BW 1; CA 101; CANR 62; CD 5; CDWLB 3; CN 7; CWD; CWP; DLB 117; DNFS 1, 2; EWL 3; FW; WLIT 2

**Aiken, Conrad (Potter)** 1889-1973 **CLC 1, 3, 5, 10, 52; PC 26; SSC 9**
See also AMW; CA 45-48; 5-8R; CANR 4, 60; CDALB 1929-1941; DAM NOV, POET; DLB 9, 45, 102; EWL 3; EXPS; HGG; MTCW 1, 2; RGAL 4; RGSF 2; SATA 3, 30; SSFS 8; TUS

**Aiken, Joan (Delano)** 1924- **CLC 35**
See also AAYA 1, 25; CA 9-12R, 182; CAAE 182; CANR 4, 23, 34, 64; CLR 1, 19; DLB 161; FANT; HGG; JRDA; MAICYA 1, 2; MTCW 1; RHW; SAAS 1; SATA 2, 30, 73; SATA-Essay 109; SUFW 2; WYA; YAW

**Ainsworth, William Harrison** 1805-1882 **NCLC 13**
See also DLB 21; HGG; RGEL 2; SATA 24; SUFW 1

**Aitmatov, Chingiz (Torekulovich)** 1928- **CLC 71**
See Aytmatov, Chingiz
See also CA 103; CANR 38; MTCW 1; RGSF 2; SATA 56

**Akers, Floyd**
See Baum, L(yman) Frank

**Akhmadulina, Bella Akhatovna** 1937- **CLC 53; PC 43**
See also CA 65-68; CWP; CWW 2; DAM POET; EWL 3

**Akhmatova, Anna** 1888-1966 **CLC 11, 25, 64, 126; PC 2**
See also CA 25-28R; 19-20; CANR 35; CAP 1; DA3; DAM POET; EW 10; EWL 3; MTCW 1, 2; RGWL 2, 3

**Aksakov, Sergei Timofeyvich** 1791-1859 **NCLC 2**
See also DLB 198

**Aksenov, Vassily**
See Aksyonov, Vassily (Pavlovich)

**Akst, Daniel** 1956- **CLC 109**
See also CA 161; CANR 110

**Aksyonov, Vassily (Pavlovich)** 1932- **CLC 22, 37, 101**
See also CA 53-56; CANR 12, 48, 77; CWW 2; EWL 3

**Akutagawa Ryunosuke** 1892-1927 **SSC 44; TCLC 16**
See also CA 154; 117; DLB 180; EWL 3; MJW; RGSF 2; RGWL 2, 3

**Alain** 1868-1951 **TCLC 41**
See also CA 163; EWL 3; GFL 1789 to the Present

**Alain de Lille** c. 1116-c. 1203 **CMLC 53**
See also DLB 208

**Alain-Fournier TCLC 6**
See Fournier, Henri-Alban
See also DLB 65; EWL 3; GFL 1789 to the Present; RGWL 2, 3

**Al-Amin, Jamil Abdullah** 1943- **BLC 1**
See also BW 1, 3; CA 125; 112; CANR 82; DAM MULT

**Alanus de Insluis**
See Alain de Lille

**Alarcon, Pedro Antonio de** 1833-1891 **NCLC 1**

**Alas (y Urena), Leopoldo (Enrique Garcia)** 1852-1901 **TCLC 29**
See also CA 131; 113; HW 1; RGSF 2

**Albee, Edward (Franklin III)** 1928- **CLC 1, 2, 3, 5, 9, 11, 13, 25, 53, 86, 113; DC 11; WLC**
See also AITN 1; AMW; CA 5-8R; CABS 3; CAD; CANR 8, 54, 74; CD 5; CDALB 1941-1968; DA; DA3; DAB; DAC; DAM DRAM, MST; DFS 2, 3, 8, 10, 13, 14; DLB 7, 266; EWL 3; INT CANR-8; LAIT 4; LMFS 2; MTCW 1, 2; RGAL 4; TUS

**Alberti, Rafael** 1902-1999 **CLC 7**
See also CA 185; 85-88; CANR 81; DLB 108; EWL 3; HW 2; RGWL 2, 3

**Albert the Great** 1193(?)-1280 **CMLC 16**
See also DLB 115

**Alcala-Galiano, Juan Valera y**
See Valera y Alcala-Galiano, Juan

**Alcayaga, Lucila Godoy**
See Godoy Alcayaga, Lucila

**Alcott, Amos Bronson** 1799-1888 **NCLC 1**
See also DLB 1, 223

**Alcott, Louisa May** 1832-1888 **NCLC 6, 58, 83; SSC 27; WLC**
See also AAYA 20; AMWS 1; BPFB 1; BYA 2; CDALB 1865-1917; CLR 1, 38; DA; DA3; DAB; DAC; DAM MST, NOV; DLB 1, 42, 79, 223, 239, 242; DLBD 14; FW; JRDA; LAIT 2; MAICYA 1, 2; NFS 12; RGAL 4; SATA 100; TUS; WCH; WYA; YABC 1; YAW

**Aldanov, M. A.**
See Aldanov, Mark (Alexandrovich)

**Aldanov, Mark (Alexandrovich)** 1886(?)-1957 **TCLC 23**
See also CA 181; 118

**Aldington, Richard** 1892-1962 **CLC 49**
See also CA 85-88; CANR 45; DLB 20, 36, 100, 149; LMFS 2; RGEL 2

**Aldiss, Brian W(ilson)** 1925- **CLC 5, 14, 40; SSC 36**
See also AAYA 42; CA 5-8R; CAAE 190; CAAS 2; CANR 5, 28, 64; CN 7; DAM NOV; DLB 14, 261, 271; MTCW 1, 2; SATA 34; SFW 4

**Aldrich, Bess Streeter** 1881-1954 **TCLC 125**
See also CLR 70

**Alegria, Claribel** 1924- **CLC 75; HLCS 1; PC 26**
See also CA 131; CAAS 15; CANR 66, 94; CWW 2; DAM MULT; DLB 145; EWL 3; HW 1; MTCW 1

**Alegria, Fernando** 1918- **CLC 57**
See also CA 9-12R; CANR 5, 32, 72; EWL 3; HW 1, 2

**Aleichem, Sholom SSC 33; TCLC 1, 35**
See Rabinovitch, Sholem
See also TWA

**Aleixandre, Vicente** 1898-1984 **HLCS 1; TCLC 113**
See also CANR 81; DLB 108; EWL 3; HW 2; RGWL 2, 3

**Aleman, Mateo** 1547-1615(?) **LC 81**

**Alencon, Marguerite d'**
See de Navarre, Marguerite

**Alepoudelis, Odysseus**
See Elytis, Odysseus
See also CWW 2

**Aleshkovsky, Joseph** 1929-
See Aleshkovsky, Yuz
See also CA 128; 121

**Aleshkovsky, Yuz CLC 44**
See Aleshkovsky, Joseph

**Alexander, Lloyd (Chudley)** 1924- **CLC 35**
See also AAYA 1, 27; BPFB 1; BYA 5, 6, 7, 9, 10, 11; CA 1-4R; CANR 1, 24, 38, 55, 113; CLR 1, 5, 48; CWRI 5; DLB 52; FANT; JRDA; MAICYA 1, 2; MAICYAS 1; MTCW 1; SAAS 19; SATA 3, 49, 81, 129, 135; SUFW; TUS; WYA; YAW

**Alexander, Meena** 1951- **CLC 121**
See also CA 115; CANR 38, 70; CP 7; CWP; FW

**Alexander, Samuel** 1859-1938 **TCLC 77**

**Alexie, Sherman (Joseph, Jr.)** 1966- **CLC 96, 154; NNAL**
See also AAYA 28; CA 138; CANR 95; DA3; DAM MULT; DLB 175, 206, 278; MTCW 1; NFS 17

**al-Farabi** 870(?)-950 **CMLC 58**
See also DLB 115

**Alfau, Felipe** 1902-1999 **CLC 66**
See also CA 137

**Alfieri, Vittorio** 1749-1803 **NCLC 101**
See also EW 4; RGWL 2, 3

**Alfred, Jean Gaston**
See Ponge, Francis

**Alger, Horatio, Jr.** 1832-1899 **NCLC 8, 83**
See also DLB 42; LAIT 2; RGAL 4; SATA 16; TUS

**Al-Ghazali, Muhammad ibn Muhammad** 1058-1111 **CMLC 50**
See also DLB 115

**Algren, Nelson** 1909-1981 **CLC 4, 10, 33; SSC 33**
See also AMWS 9; BPFB 1; CA 103; 13-16R; CANR 20, 61; CDALB 1941-1968; DLB 9; DLBY 1981, 1982, 2000; EWL 3; MTCW 1, 2; RGAL 4; RGSF 2

**Ali, Ahmed** 1908-1998 **CLC 69**
See also CA 25-28R; CANR 15, 34; EWL 3

**Alighieri, Dante**
See Dante

**Allan, John B.**
See Westlake, Donald E(dwin)

**Allan, Sidney**
See Hartmann, Sadakichi

**Allan, Sydney**
See Hartmann, Sadakichi

**Allard, Janet CLC 59**

**Allen, Edward** 1948- **CLC 59**

**Allen, Fred** 1894-1956 **TCLC 87**

**Allen, Paula Gunn** 1939- **CLC 84; NNAL**
See also AMWS 4; CA 143; 112; CANR 63; CWP; DA3; DAM MULT; DLB 175; FW; MTCW 1; RGAL 4

**Allen, Roland**
See Ayckbourn, Alan

**Allen, Sarah A.**
See Hopkins, Pauline Elizabeth

**Allen, Sidney H.**
See Hartmann, Sadakichi

**Allen, Woody** 1935- **CLC 16, 52**
See also AAYA 10; CA 33-36R; CANR 27, 38, 63; DAM POP; DLB 44; MTCW 1

**Allende, Isabel** 1942- **CLC 39, 57, 97, 170; HLC 1; WLCS**
See also AAYA 18; CA 130; 125; CANR 51, 74; CDWLB 3; CWW 2; DA3; DAM MULT, NOV; DLB 145; DNFS 1; EWL 3; FW; HW 1, 2; INT CA-130; LAIT 5; LAWS 1; LMFS 2; MTCW 1, 2; NCFS 1; NFS 6; RGSF 2; RGWL 3; SSFS 11, 16; WLIT 1

**Alleyn, Ellen**
See Rossetti, Christina (Georgina)

**Alleyne, Carla D. CLC 65**

**Anthony, Florence**
See Ai
**Anthony, John**
See Ciardi, John (Anthony)
**Anthony, Peter**
See Shaffer, Anthony (Joshua); Shaffer, Peter (Levin)
**Anthony, Piers** 1934- **CLC 35**
See also AAYA 11; BYA 7; CA 21-24R; CAAE 200; CANR 28, 56, 73, 102; CPW; DAM POP; DLB 8; FANT; MAICYA 2; MAICYAS 1; MTCW 1, 2; SAAS 22; SATA 84; SATA-Essay 129; SFW 4; SUFW 1, 2; YAW
**Anthony, Susan B(rownell)** 1820-1906 **TCLC 84**
See also FW
**Antiphon** c. 480B.C.-c. 411B.C. **CMLC 55**
**Antoine, Marc**
See Proust, (Valentin-Louis-George-Eugene-)Marcel
**Antoninus, Brother**
See Everson, William (Oliver)
**Antonioni, Michelangelo** 1912- **CLC 20, 144**
See also CA 73-76; CANR 45, 77
**Antschel, Paul** 1920-1970
See Celan, Paul
See also CA 85-88; CANR 33, 61; MTCW 1
**Anwar, Chairil** 1922-1949 **TCLC 22**
See Chairil Anwar
See also CA 121; RGWL 3
**Anzaldua, Gloria (Evanjelina)** 1942- **HLCS 1**
See also CA 175; CSW; CWP; DLB 122; FW; RGAL 4
**Apess, William** 1798-1839(?) **NCLC 73; NNAL**
See also DAM MULT; DLB 175, 243
**Apollinaire, Guillaume** 1880-1918 **PC 7; TCLC 3, 8, 51**
See Kostrowitzki, Wilhelm Apollinaris de
See also CA 152; DAM POET; DLB 258; EW 9; EWL 3; GFL 1789 to the Present; MTCW 1; RGWL 2, 3; TWA; WP
**Apollonius of Rhodes**
See Apollonius Rhodius
See also AW 1; RGWL 2, 3
**Apollonius Rhodius** c. 300B.C.-c. 220B.C. **CMLC 28**
See Apollonius of Rhodes
See also DLB 176
**Appelfeld, Aharon** 1932- **CLC 23, 47; SSC 42**
See also CA 133; 112; CANR 86; CWW 2; EWL 3; RGSF 2
**Apple, Max (Isaac)** 1941- **CLC 9, 33; SSC 50**
See also CA 81-84; CANR 19, 54; DLB 130
**Appleman, Philip (Dean)** 1926- **CLC 51**
See also CA 13-16R; CAAS 18; CANR 6, 29, 56
**Appleton, Lawrence**
See Lovecraft, H(oward) P(hillips)
**Apteryx**
See Eliot, T(homas) S(tearns)
**Apuleius, (Lucius Madaurensis)** 125(?)-175(?) **CMLC 1**
See also AW 2; CDWLB 1; DLB 211; RGWL 2, 3; SUFW
**Aquin, Hubert** 1929-1977 **CLC 15**
See also CA 105; DLB 53; EWL 3
**Aquinas, Thomas** 1224(?)-1274 **CMLC 33**
See also DLB 115; EW 1; TWA
**Aragon, Louis** 1897-1982 **CLC 3, 22; TCLC 123**
See also CA 108; 69-72; CANR 28, 71; DAM NOV, POET; DLB 72, 258; EW 11; EWL 3; GFL 1789 to the Present; GLL 2; MTCW 1, 2; RGWL 2, 3

**Arany, Janos** 1817-1882 **NCLC 34**
**Aranyos, Kakay** 1847-1910
See Mikszath, Kalman
**Arbuthnot, John** 1667-1735 **LC 1**
See also DLB 101
**Archer, Herbert Winslow**
See Mencken, H(enry) L(ouis)
**Archer, Jeffrey (Howard)** 1940- **CLC 28**
See also AAYA 16; BEST 89:3; BPFB 1; CA 77-80; CANR 22, 52, 95; CPW; DA3; DAM POP; INT CANR-22
**Archer, Jules** 1915- **CLC 12**
See also CA 9-12R; CANR 6, 69; SAAS 5; SATA 4, 85
**Archer, Lee**
See Ellison, Harlan (Jay)
**Archilochus** c. 7th cent. B.C.- **CMLC 44**
See also DLB 176
**Arden, John** 1930- **CLC 6, 13, 15**
See also BRWS 2; CA 13-16R; CAAS 4; CANR 31, 65, 67; CBD; CD 5; DAM DRAM; DFS 9; DLB 13, 245; EWL 3; MTCW 1
**Arenas, Reinaldo** 1943-1990 **CLC 41; HLC 1**
See also CA 133; 128; 124; CANR 73, 106; DAM MULT; DLB 145; EWL 3; GLL 2; HW 1; LAW; LAWS 1; MTCW 1; RGSF 2; RGWL 3; WLIT 1
**Arendt, Hannah** 1906-1975 **CLC 66, 98**
See also CA 61-64; 17-20R; CANR 26, 60; DLB 242; MTCW 1, 2
**Aretino, Pietro** 1492-1556 **LC 12**
See also RGWL 2, 3
**Arghezi, Tudor CLC 80**
See Theodorescu, Ion N.
See also CA 167; CDWLB 4; DLB 220; EWL 3
**Arguedas, Jose Maria** 1911-1969 **CLC 10, 18; HLCS 1**
See also CA 89-92; CANR 73; DLB 113; EWL 3; HW 1; LAW; RGWL 2, 3; WLIT 1
**Argueta, Manlio** 1936- **CLC 31**
See also CA 131; CANR 73; CWW 2; DLB 145; EWL 3; HW 1; RGWL 3
**Arias, Ron(ald Francis)** 1941- **HLC 1**
See also CA 131; CANR 81; DAM MULT; DLB 82; HW 1, 2; MTCW 2
**Ariosto, Ludovico** 1474-1533 **LC 6, 87; PC 42**
See also EW 2; RGWL 2, 3
**Aristides**
See Epstein, Joseph
**Aristophanes** 450B.C.-385B.C. **CMLC 4, 51; DC 2; WLCS**
See also AW 1; CDWLB 1; DA; DA3; DAB; DAC; DAM DRAM, MST; DFS 10; DLB 176; RGWL 2, 3; TWA
**Aristotle** 384B.C.-322B.C. **CMLC 31; WLCS**
See also AW 1; CDWLB 1; DA; DA3; DAB; DAC; DAM MST; DLB 176; RGWL 2, 3; TWA
**Arlt, Roberto (Godofredo Christophersen)** 1900-1942 **HLC 1; TCLC 29**
See also CA 131; 123; CANR 67; DAM MULT; EWL 3; HW 1, 2; LAW
**Armah, Ayi Kwei** 1939- **BLC 1; CLC 5, 33, 136**
See also AFW; BW 1; CA 61-64; CANR 21, 64; CDWLB 3; CN 7; DAM MULT, POET; DLB 117; EWL 3; MTCW 1; WLIT 2
**Armatrading, Joan** 1950- **CLC 17**
See also CA 186; 114
**Armitage, Frank**
See Carpenter, John (Howard)
**Armstrong, Jeannette (C.)** 1948- **NNAL**
See also CA 149; CCA 1; CN 7; DAC; SATA 102

**Arnette, Robert**
See Silverberg, Robert
**Arnim, Achim von (Ludwig Joachim von Arnim)** 1781-1831 **NCLC 5; SSC 29**
See also DLB 90
**Arnim, Bettina von** 1785-1859 **NCLC 38, 123**
See also DLB 90; RGWL 2, 3
**Arnold, Matthew** 1822-1888 **NCLC 6, 29, 89; PC 5; WLC**
See also BRW 5; CDBLB 1832-1890; DA; DAB; DAC; DAM MST, POET; DLB 32, 57; EXPP; PAB; PFS 2; TEA; WP
**Arnold, Thomas** 1795-1842 **NCLC 18**
See also DLB 55
**Arnow, Harriette (Louisa) Simpson** 1908-1986 **CLC 2, 7, 18**
See also BPFB 1; CA 118; 9-12R; CANR 14; DLB 6; FW; MTCW 1, 2; RHW; SATA 42; SATA-Obit 47
**Arouet, Francois-Marie**
See Voltaire
**Arp, Hans**
See Arp, Jean
**Arp, Jean** 1887-1966 **CLC 5; TCLC 115**
See also CA 25-28R; 81-84; CANR 42, 77; EW 10
**Arrabal**
See Arrabal, Fernando
**Arrabal, Fernando** 1932- **CLC 2, 9, 18, 58**
See also CA 9-12R; CANR 15; EWL 3; LMFS 2
**Arreola, Juan Jose** 1918-2001 **CLC 147; HLC 1; SSC 38**
See also CA 200; 131; 113; CANR 81; DAM MULT; DLB 113; DNFS 2; EWL 3; HW 1, 2; LAW; RGSF 2
**Arrian** c. 89(?)-c. 155(?) **CMLC 43**
See also DLB 176
**Arrick, Fran CLC 30**
See Gaberman, Judie Angell
See also BYA 6
**Arriey, Richmond**
See Delany, Samuel R(ay), Jr.
**Artaud, Antonin (Marie Joseph)** 1896-1948 **DC 14; TCLC 3, 36**
See also CA 149; 104; DA3; DAM DRAM; DLB 258; EW 11; EWL 3; GFL 1789 to the Present; MTCW 1; RGWL 2, 3
**Arthur, Ruth M(abel)** 1905-1979 **CLC 12**
See also CA 85-88; 9-12R; CANR 4; CWRI 5; SATA 7, 26
**Artsybashev, Mikhail (Petrovich)** 1878-1927 **TCLC 31**
See also CA 170
**Arundel, Honor (Morfydd)** 1919-1973 **CLC 17**
See also CA 41-44R; 21-22; CAP 2; CLR 35; CWRI 5; SATA 4; SATA-Obit 24
**Arzner, Dorothy** 1900-1979 **CLC 98**
**Asch, Sholem** 1880-1957 **TCLC 3**
See also CA 105; EWL 3; GLL 2
**Ash, Shalom**
See Asch, Sholem
**Ashbery, John (Lawrence)** 1927- **CLC 2, 3, 4, 6, 9, 13, 15, 25, 41, 77, 125; PC 26**
See Berry, Jonas
See also AMWS 3; CA 5-8R; CANR 9, 37, 66, 102; CP 7; DA3; DAM POET; DLB 5, 165; DLBY 1981; EWL 3; INT CANR-9; MTCW 1, 2; PAB; PFS 11; RGAL 4; WP
**Ashdown, Clifford**
See Freeman, R(ichard) Austin
**Ashe, Gordon**
See Creasey, John
**Ashton-Warner, Sylvia (Constance)** 1908-1984 **CLC 19**
See also CA 112; 69-72; CANR 29; MTCW 1, 2

**Asimov, Isaac** 1920-1992 **CLC 1, 3, 9, 19, 26, 76, 92**
See also AAYA 13; BEST 90:2; BPFB 1; BYA 4, 6, 7, 9; CA 137; 1-4R; CANR 2, 19, 36, 60; CLR 12, 79; CMW 4; CPW; DA3; DAM POP; DLB 8; DLBY 1992; INT CANR-19; JRDA; LAIT 5; MAICYA 1, 2; MTCW 1, 2; RGAL 4; SATA 1, 26, 74; SCFW 2; SFW 4; SSFS 17; TUS; YAW

**Askew, Anne** 1521(?)-1546 **LC 81**
See also DLB 136

**Assis, Joaquim Maria Machado de**
See Machado de Assis, Joaquim Maria

**Astell, Mary** 1666-1731 **LC 68**
See also DLB 252; FW

**Astley, Thea (Beatrice May)** 1925- **CLC 41**
See also CA 65-68; CANR 11, 43, 78; CN 7; EWL 3

**Astley, William** 1855-1911
See Warung, Price

**Aston, James**
See White, T(erence) H(anbury)

**Asturias, Miguel Angel** 1899-1974 **CLC 3, 8, 13; HLC 1**
See also CA 49-52; 25-28; CANR 32; CAP 2; CDWLB 3; DA3; DAM MULT, NOV; DLB 113; EWL 3; HW 1; LAW; LMFS 2; MTCW 1, 2; RGWL 2, 3; WLIT 1

**Atares, Carlos Saura**
See Saura (Atares), Carlos

**Athanasius** c. 295-c. 373 **CMLC 48**

**Atheling, William**
See Pound, Ezra (Weston Loomis)

**Atheling, William, Jr.**
See Blish, James (Benjamin)

**Atherton, Gertrude (Franklin Horn)** 1857-1948 **TCLC 2**
See also CA 155; 104; DLB 9, 78, 186; HGG; RGAL 4; SUFW 1; TCWW 2

**Atherton, Lucius**
See Masters, Edgar Lee

**Atkins, Jack**
See Harris, Mark

**Atkinson, Kate** 1951- **CLC 99**
See also CA 166; CANR 101; DLB 267

**Attaway, William (Alexander)** 1911-1986 **BLC 1; CLC 92**
See also BW 2, 3; CA 143; CANR 82; DAM MULT; DLB 76

**Atticus**
See Fleming, Ian (Lancaster); Wilson, (Thomas) Woodrow

**Atwood, Margaret (Eleanor)** 1939- **CLC 2, 3, 4, 8, 13, 15, 25, 44, 84, 135; PC 8; SSC 2, 46; WLC**
See also AAYA 12, 47; BEST 89:2; BPFB 1; CA 49-52; CANR 3, 24, 33, 59, 95; CN 7; CP 7; CPW; CWP; DA; DA3; DAB; DAC; DAM MST, NOV, POET; DLB 53, 251; EWL 3; EXPN; FW; INT CANR-24; LAIT 5; MTCW 1, 2; NFS 4, 12, 13, 14; PFS 7; RGSF 2; SATA 50; SSFS 3, 13; TWA; YAW

**Aubigny, Pierre d'**
See Mencken, H(enry) L(ouis)

**Aubin, Penelope** 1685-1731(?) **LC 9**
See also DLB 39

**Auchincloss, Louis (Stanton)** 1917- **CLC 4, 6, 9, 18, 45; SSC 22**
See also AMWS 4; CA 1-4R; CANR 6, 29, 55, 87; CN 7; DAM NOV; DLB 2, 244; DLBY 1980; EWL 3; INT CANR-29; MTCW 1; RGAL 4

**Auden, W(ystan) H(ugh)** 1907-1973 **CLC 1, 2, 3, 4, 6, 9, 11, 14, 43, 123; PC 1; WLC**
See also AAYA 18; AMWS 2; BRW 7; BRWR 1; CA 45-48; 9-12R; CANR 5, 61, 105; CDBLB 1914-1945; DA; DA3;

DAB; DAC; DAM DRAM, MST, POET; DLB 10, 20; EWL 3; EXPP; MTCW 1, 2; PAB; PFS 1, 3, 4, 10; TUS; WP

**Audiberti, Jacques** 1900-1965 **CLC 38**
See also CA 25-28R; DAM DRAM; EWL 3

**Audubon, John James** 1785-1851 **NCLC 47**
See also ANW; DLB 248

**Auel, Jean M(arie)** 1936- **CLC 31, 107**
See also AAYA 7; BEST 90:4; BPFB 1; CA 103; CANR 21, 64, 115; CPW; DA3; DAM POP; INT CANR-21; NFS 11; RHW; SATA 91

**Auerbach, Erich** 1892-1957 **TCLC 43**
See also CA 155; 118; EWL 3

**Augier, Emile** 1820-1889 **NCLC 31**
See also DLB 192; GFL 1789 to the Present

**August, John**
See De Voto, Bernard (Augustine)

**Augustine, St.** 354-430 **CMLC 6; WLCS**
See also DA; DA3; DAB; DAC; DAM MST; DLB 115; EW 1; RGWL 2, 3

**Aunt Belinda**
See Braddon, Mary Elizabeth

**Aunt Weedy**
See Alcott, Louisa May

**Aurelius**
See Bourne, Randolph S(illiman)

**Aurelius, Marcus** 121-180 **CMLC 45**
See Marcus Aurelius
See also RGWL 2, 3

**Aurobindo, Sri**
See Ghose, Aurabinda

**Aurobindo Ghose**
See Ghose, Aurabinda

**Austen, Jane** 1775-1817 **NCLC 1, 13, 19, 33, 51, 81, 95, 119; WLC**
See also AAYA 19; BRW 4; BRWC 1; BRWR 2; BYA 3; CDBLB 1789-1832; DA; DA3; DAB; DAC; DAM MST, NOV; DLB 116; EXPN; LAIT 2; NFS 1, 14; TEA; WLIT 3; WYAS 1

**Auster, Paul** 1947- **CLC 47, 131**
See also AMWS 12; CA 69-72; CANR 23, 52, 75; CMW 4; CN 7; DA3; DLB 227; MTCW 1; SUFW 2

**Austin, Frank**
See Faust, Frederick (Schiller)
See also TCWW 2

**Austin, Mary (Hunter)** 1868-1934 **TCLC 25**
See Stairs, Gordon
See also ANW; CA 178; 109; DLB 9, 78, 206, 221, 275; FW; TCWW 2

**Averroes** 1126-1198 **CMLC 7**
See also DLB 115

**Avicenna** 980-1037 **CMLC 16**
See also DLB 115

**Avison, Margaret** 1918- **CLC 2, 4, 97**
See also CA 17-20R; CP 7; DAC; DAM POET; DLB 53; MTCW 1

**Axton, David**
See Koontz, Dean R(ay)

**Ayckbourn, Alan** 1939- **CLC 5, 8, 18, 33, 74; DC 13**
See also BRWS 5; CA 21-24R; CANR 31, 59; CBD; CD 5; DAB; DAM DRAM; DFS 7; DLB 13, 245; EWL 3; MTCW 1, 2

**Aydy, Catherine**
See Tennant, Emma (Christina)

**Ayme, Marcel (Andre)** 1902-1967 **CLC 11; SSC 41**
See also CA 89-92; CANR 67; CLR 25; DLB 72; EW 12; EWL 3; GFL 1789 to the Present; RGSF 2; RGWL 2, 3; SATA 91

**Ayrton, Michael** 1921-1975 **CLC 7**
See also CA 61-64; 5-8R; CANR 9, 21

**Aytmatov, Chingiz**
See Aitmatov, Chingiz (Torekulovich)
See also EWL 3

**Azorin CLC 11**
See Martinez Ruiz, Jose
See also EW 9; EWL 3

**Azuela, Mariano** 1873-1952 **HLC 1; TCLC 3**
See also CA 131; 104; CANR 81; DAM MULT; EWL 3; HW 1, 2; LAW; MTCW 1, 2

**Ba, Mariama** 1929-1981 **BLCS**
See also AFW; BW 2; CA 141; CANR 87; DNFS 2; WLIT 2

**Baastad, Babbis Friis**
See Friis-Baastad, Babbis Ellinor

**Bab**
See Gilbert, W(illiam) S(chwenck)

**Babbis, Eleanor**
See Friis-Baastad, Babbis Ellinor

**Babel, Isaac**
See Babel, Isaak (Emmanuilovich)
See also EW 11; SSFS 10

**Babel, Isaak (Emmanuilovich)** 1894-1941(?) **SSC 16; TCLC 2, 13**
See Babel, Isaac
See also CA 155; 104; CANR 113; DLB 272; EWL 3; MTCW 1; RGSF 2; RGWL 2, 3; TWA

**Babits, Mihaly** 1883-1941 **TCLC 14**
See also CA 114; CDWLB 4; DLB 215; EWL 3

**Babur** 1483-1530 **LC 18**

**Babylas** 1898-1962
See Ghelderode, Michel de

**Baca, Jimmy Santiago** 1952- **HLC 1; PC 41**
See also CA 131; CANR 81, 90; CP 7; DAM MULT; DLB 122; HW 1, 2

**Baca, Jose Santiago**
See Baca, Jimmy Santiago

**Bacchelli, Riccardo** 1891-1985 **CLC 19**
See also CA 117; 29-32R; DLB 264; EWL 3

**Bach, Richard (David)** 1936- **CLC 14**
See also AITN 1; BEST 89:2; BPFB 1; BYA 5; CA 9-12R; CANR 18, 93; CPW; DAM NOV, POP; FANT; MTCW 1; SATA 13

**Bache, Benjamin Franklin** 1769-1798 **LC 74**
See also DLB 43

**Bachelard, Gaston** 1884-1962 **TCLC 128**
See also CA 89-92; 97-100; GFL 1789 to the Present

**Bachman, Richard**
See King, Stephen (Edwin)

**Bachmann, Ingeborg** 1926-1973 **CLC 69**
See also CA 45-48; 93-96; CANR 69; DLB 85; EWL 3; RGWL 2, 3

**Bacon, Francis** 1561-1626 **LC 18, 32**
See also BRW 1; CDBLB Before 1660; DLB 151, 236, 252; RGEL 2; TEA

**Bacon, Roger** 1214(?)-1294 **CMLC 14**
See also DLB 115

**Bacovia, George** 1881-1957 **TCLC 24**
See Vasiliu, Gheorghe
See also CDWLB 4; DLB 220; EWL 3

**Badanes, Jerome** 1937- **CLC 59**

**Bagehot, Walter** 1826-1877 **NCLC 10**
See also DLB 55

**Bagnold, Enid** 1889-1981 **CLC 25**
See also BYA 2; CA 103; 5-8R; CANR 5, 40; CBD; CWD; CWRI 5; DAM DRAM; DLB 13, 160, 191, 245; FW; MAICYA 1, 2; RGEL 2; SATA 1, 25

**Bagritsky, Eduard TCLC 60**
See Dzyubin, Eduard Georgievich

**Bagrjana, Elisaveta**
See Belcheva, Elisaveta Lyubomirova

**Bagryana, Elisaveta CLC 10**
See Belcheva, Elisaveta Lyubomirova
See also CA 178; CDWLB 4; DLB 147;
EWL 3

**Bailey, Paul** 1937- **CLC 45**
See also CA 21-24R; CANR 16, 62; CN 7;
DLB 14, 271; GLL 2

**Baillie, Joanna** 1762-1851 **NCLC 71**
See also DLB 93; RGEL 2

**Bainbridge, Beryl (Margaret)** 1934- **CLC 4,
5, 8, 10, 14, 18, 22, 62, 130**
See also BRWS 6; CA 21-24R; CANR 24,
55, 75, 88; CN 7; DAM NOV; DLB 14,
231; EWL 3; MTCW 1, 2

**Baker, Carlos (Heard)** 1909-1987 **TCLC 119**
See also CA 122; 5-8R; CANR 3, 63; DLB
103

**Baker, Elliott** 1922- **CLC 8**
See also CA 45-48; CANR 2, 63; CN 7

**Baker, Jean H. TCLC 3, 10**
See Russell, George William

**Baker, Nicholson** 1957- **CLC 61, 165**
See also CA 135; CANR 63; CN 7; CPW;
DA3; DAM POP; DLB 227

**Baker, Ray Stannard** 1870-1946 **TCLC 47**
See also CA 118

**Baker, Russell (Wayne)** 1925- **CLC 31**
See also BEST 89:4; CA 57-60; CANR 11,
41, 59; MTCW 1, 2

**Bakhtin, M.**
See Bakhtin, Mikhail Mikhailovich

**Bakhtin, M. M.**
See Bakhtin, Mikhail Mikhailovich

**Bakhtin, Mikhail**
See Bakhtin, Mikhail Mikhailovich

**Bakhtin, Mikhail Mikhailovich** 1895-1975
**CLC 83**
See also CA 113; 128; DLB 242; EWL 3

**Bakshi, Ralph** 1938(?)- **CLC 26**
See also CA 138; 112; IDFW 3

**Bakunin, Mikhail (Alexandrovich)**
1814-1876 **NCLC 25, 58**
See also DLB 277

**Baldwin, James (Arthur)** 1924-1987 **BLC 1;
CLC 1, 2, 3, 4, 5, 8, 13, 15, 17, 42, 50,
67, 90, 127; DC 1; SSC 10, 33; WLC**
See also AAYA 4, 34; AFAW 1, 2; AMWR
2; AMWS 1; BPFB 1; BW 1; CA 124;
1-4R; CABS 1; CAD; CANR 3, 24;
CDALB 1941-1968; CPW; DA; DA3;
DAB; DAC; DAM MST, MULT, NOV,
POP; DFS 15; DLB 2, 7, 33, 249, 278;
DLBY 1987; EWL 3; EXPS; LAIT 5;
MTCW 1, 2; NCFS 4; NFS 4; RGAL 4;
RGSF 2; SATA 9; SATA-Obit 54; SSFS
2; TUS

**Bale, John** 1495-1563 **LC 62**
See also DLB 132; RGEL 2; TEA

**Ball, Hugo** 1886-1927 **TCLC 104**

**Ballard, J(ames) G(raham)** 1930- **CLC 3, 6,
14, 36, 137; SSC 1, 53**
See also AAYA 3; BRWS 5; CA 5-8R;
CANR 15, 39, 65, 107; CN 7; DA3; DAM
NOV, POP; DLB 14, 207, 261; EWL 3;
HGG; MTCW 1, 2; NFS 8; RGEL 2;
RGSF 2; SATA 93; SFW 4

**Balmont, Konstantin (Dmitriyevich)**
1867-1943 **TCLC 11**
See also CA 155; 109; EWL 3

**Baltausis, Vincas** 1847-1910
See Mikszath, Kalman

**Balzac, Honore de** 1799-1850 **NCLC 5, 35,
53; SSC 5, 59; WLC**
See also DA; DA3; DAB; DAC; DAM
MST, NOV; DLB 119; EW 5; GFL 1789
to the Present; RGSF 2; RGWL 2, 3;
SSFS 10; SUFW; TWA

**Bambara, Toni Cade** 1939-1995 **BLC 1; CLC
19, 88; SSC 35; TCLC 116; WLCS**
See also AAYA 5; AFAW 2; AMWS 11; BW
2, 3; BYA 12, 14; CA 150; 29-32R;
CANR 24, 49, 81; CDALBS; DA; DA3;
DAC; DAM MST, MULT; DLB 38, 218;
EXPS; MTCW 1, 2; RGAL 4; RGSF 2;
SATA 112; SSFS 4, 7, 12

**Bamdad, A.**
See Shamlu, Ahmad

**Banat, D. R.**
See Bradbury, Ray (Douglas)

**Bancroft, Laura**
See Baum, L(yman) Frank

**Banim, John** 1798-1842 **NCLC 13**
See also DLB 116, 158, 159; RGEL 2

**Banim, Michael** 1796-1874 **NCLC 13**
See also DLB 158, 159

**Banjo, The**
See Paterson, A(ndrew) B(arton)

**Banks, Iain**
See Banks, Iain M(enzies)

**Banks, Iain M(enzies)** 1954- **CLC 34**
See also CA 128; 123; CANR 61, 106; DLB
194, 261; EWL 3; HGG; INT 128; SFW 4

**Banks, Lynne Reid CLC 23**
See Reid Banks, Lynne
See also AAYA 6; BYA 7; CLR 86

**Banks, Russell** 1940- **CLC 37, 72; SSC 42**
See also AAYA 45; AMWS 5; CA 65-68;
CAAS 15; CANR 19, 52, 73; CN 7; DLB
130, 278; EWL 3; NFS 13

**Banville, John** 1945- **CLC 46, 118**
See also CA 128; 117; CANR 104; CN 7;
DLB 14, 271; INT 128

**Banville, Theodore (Faullain) de** 1832-1891
**NCLC 9**
See also DLB 217; GFL 1789 to the Present

**Baraka, Amiri** 1934- **BLC 1; CLC 1, 2, 3, 5,
10, 14, 33, 115; DC 6; PC 4; WLCS**
See Jones, LeRoi
See also AFAW 1, 2; AMWS 2; BW 2, 3;
CA 21-24R; CABS 3; CAD; CANR 27,
38, 61; CD 5; CDALB 1941-1968; CP 7;
CPW; DA; DA3; DAC; DAM MST,
MULT, POET, POP; DFS 3, 11, 16; DLB
5, 7, 16, 38; DLBD 8; EWL 3; MTCW 1,
2; PFS 9; RGAL 4; TUS; WP

**Baratynsky, Evgenii Abramovich** 1800-1844
**NCLC 103**
See also DLB 205

**Barbauld, Anna Laetitia** 1743-1825 **NCLC
50**
See also DLB 107, 109, 142, 158; RGEL 2

**Barbellion, W. N. P. TCLC 24**
See Cummings, Bruce F(rederick)

**Barber, Benjamin R.** 1939- **CLC 141**
See also CA 29-32R; CANR 12, 32, 64

**Barbera, Jack (Vincent)** 1945- **CLC 44**
See also CA 110; CANR 45

**Barbey d'Aurevilly, Jules-Amedee** 1808-1889
**NCLC 1; SSC 17**
See also DLB 119; GFL 1789 to the Present

**Barbour, John** c. 1316-1395 **CMLC 33**
See also DLB 146

**Barbusse, Henri** 1873-1935 **TCLC 5**
See also CA 154; 105; DLB 65; EWL 3;
RGWL 2, 3

**Barclay, Bill**
See Moorcock, Michael (John)

**Barclay, William Ewert**
See Moorcock, Michael (John)

**Barea, Arturo** 1897-1957 **TCLC 14**
See also CA 201; 111

**Barfoot, Joan** 1946- **CLC 18**
See also CA 105

**Barham, Richard Harris** 1788-1845 **NCLC
77**
See also DLB 159

**Baring, Maurice** 1874-1945 **TCLC 8**
See also CA 168; 105; DLB 34; HGG

**Baring-Gould, Sabine** 1834-1924 **TCLC 88**
See also DLB 156, 190

**Barker, Clive** 1952- **CLC 52; SSC 53**
See also AAYA 10; BEST 90:3; BPFB 1;
CA 129; 121; CANR 71, 111; CPW; DA3;
DAM POP; DLB 261; HGG; INT 129;
MTCW 1, 2; SUFW 2

**Barker, George Granville** 1913-1991 **CLC 8,
48**
See also CA 135; 9-12R; CANR 7, 38;
DAM POET; DLB 20; EWL 3; MTCW 1

**Barker, Harley Granville**
See Granville-Barker, Harley
See also DLB 10

**Barker, Howard** 1946- **CLC 37**
See also CA 102; CBD; CD 5; DLB 13,
233

**Barker, Jane** 1652-1732 **LC 42, 82**
See also DLB 39, 131

**Barker, Pat(ricia)** 1943- **CLC 32, 94, 146**
See also BRWS 4; CA 122; 117; CANR 50,
101; CN 7; DLB 271; INT 122

**Barlach, Ernst (Heinrich)** 1870-1938 **TCLC
84**
See also CA 178; DLB 56, 118; EWL 3

**Barlow, Joel** 1754-1812 **NCLC 23**
See also AMWS 2; DLB 37; RGAL 4

**Barnard, Mary (Ethel)** 1909- **CLC 48**
See also CA 21-22; CAP 2

**Barnes, Djuna** 1892-1982 **CLC 3, 4, 8, 11, 29,
127; SSC 3**
See Steptoe, Lydia
See also AMWS 3; CA 107; 9-12R; CAD;
CANR 16, 55; CWD; DLB 4, 9, 45; EWL
3; GLL 1; MTCW 1, 2; RGAL 4; TUS

**Barnes, Jim** 1933- **NNAL**
See also CA 108; 175; CAAE 175; CAAS
28; DLB 175

**Barnes, Julian (Patrick)** 1946- **CLC 42, 141**
See also BRWS 4; CA 102; CANR 19, 54,
115; CN 7; DAB; DLB 194; DLBY 1993;
EWL 3; MTCW 1

**Barnes, Peter** 1931- **CLC 5, 56**
See also CA 65-68; CAAS 12; CANR 33,
34, 64, 113; CBD; CD 5; DFS 6; DLB
13, 233; MTCW 1

**Barnes, William** 1801-1886 **NCLC 75**
See also DLB 32

**Baroja (y Nessi), Pio** 1872-1956 **HLC 1;
TCLC 8**
See also CA 104; EW 9

**Baron, David**
See Pinter, Harold

**Baron Corvo**
See Rolfe, Frederick (William Serafino
Austin Lewis Mary)

**Barondess, Sue K(aufman)** 1926-1977 **CLC 8**
See Kaufman, Sue
See also CA 69-72; 1-4R; CANR 1

**Baron de Teive**
See Pessoa, Fernando (Antonio Nogueira)

**Baroness Von S.**
See Zangwill, Israel

**Barres, (Auguste-)Maurice** 1862-1923 **TCLC
47**
See also CA 164; DLB 123; GFL 1789 to
the Present

**Barreto, Afonso Henrique de Lima**
See Lima Barreto, Afonso Henrique de

**Barrett, Andrea** 1954- **CLC 150**
See also CA 156; CANR 92

**Barrett, Michele CLC 65**

**Barrett, (Roger) Syd** 1946- **CLC 35**

**Barrett, William (Christopher)** 1913-1992
**CLC 27**
See also CA 139; 13-16R; CANR 11, 67;
INT CANR-11

**Barrie, J(ames) M(atthew)** 1860-1937 **TCLC 2**
See also BRWS 3; BYA 4, 5; CA 136; 104; CANR 77; CDBLB 1890-1914; CLR 16; CWRI 5; DA3; DAB; DAM DRAM; DFS 7; DLB 10, 141, 156; EWL 3; FANT; MAICYA 1, 2; MTCW 1; SATA 100; SUFW; WCH; WLIT 4; YABC 1

**Barrington, Michael**
See Moorcock, Michael (John)

**Barrol, Grady**
See Bograd, Larry

**Barry, Mike**
See Malzberg, Barry N(athaniel)

**Barry, Philip** 1896-1949 **TCLC 11**
See also CA 199; 109; DFS 9; DLB 7, 228; RGAL 4

**Bart, Andre Schwarz**
See Schwarz-Bart, Andre

**Barth, John (Simmons)** 1930- **CLC 1, 2, 3, 5, 7, 9, 10, 14, 27, 51, 89; SSC 10**
See also AITN 1, 2; AMW; BPFB 1; CA 1-4R; CABS 1; CANR 5, 23, 49, 64, 113; CN 7; DAM NOV; DLB 2, 227; EWL 3; FANT; MTCW 1; RGAL 4; RGSF 2; RHW; SSFS 6; TUS

**Barthelme, Donald** 1931-1989 **CLC 1, 2, 3, 5, 6, 8, 13, 23, 46, 59, 115; SSC 2, 55**
See also AMWS 4; BPFB 1; CA 129; 21-24R; CANR 20, 58; DA3; DAM NOV; DLB 2, 234; DLBY 1980, 1989; EWL 3; FANT; MTCW 1, 2; RGAL 4; RGSF 2; SATA 7; SATA-Obit 62; SSFS 17

**Barthelme, Frederick** 1943- **CLC 36, 117**
See also AMWS 11; CA 122; 114; CANR 77; CN 7; CSW; DLB 244; DLBY 1985; EWL 3; INT CA-122

**Barthes, Roland (Gerard)** 1915-1980 **CLC 24, 83**
See also CA 97-100; 130; CANR 66; EW 13; EWL 3; GFL 1789 to the Present; MTCW 1, 2; TWA

**Barzun, Jacques (Martin)** 1907- **CLC 51, 145**
See also CA 61-64; CANR 22, 95

**Bashevis, Isaac**
See Singer, Isaac Bashevis

**Bashkirtseff, Marie** 1859-1884 **NCLC 27**

**Basho, Matsuo**
See Matsuo Basho
See also RGWL 2, 3; WP

**Basil of Caesaria** c. 330-379 **CMLC 35**

**Bass, Kingsley B., Jr.**
See Bullins, Ed

**Bass, Rick** 1958- **CLC 79, 143**
See also ANW; CA 126; CANR 53, 93; CSW; DLB 212, 275

**Bassani, Giorgio** 1916-2000 **CLC 9**
See also CA 190; 65-68; CANR 33; CWW 2; DLB 128, 177; EWL 3; MTCW 1; RGWL 2, 3

**Bastian, Ann CLC 70**

**Bastos, Augusto (Antonio) Roa**
See Roa Bastos, Augusto (Antonio)

**Bataille, Georges** 1897-1962 **CLC 29**
See also CA 89-92; 101; EWL 3

**Bates, H(erbert) E(rnest)** 1905-1974 **CLC 46; SSC 10**
See also CA 45-48; 93-96; CANR 34; DA3; DAB; DAM POP; DLB 162, 191; EWL 3; EXPS; MTCW 1, 2; RGSF 2; SSFS 7

**Bauchart**
See Camus, Albert

**Baudelaire, Charles** 1821-1867 **NCLC 6, 29, 55; PC 1; SSC 18; WLC**
See also DA; DA3; DAB; DAC; DAM MST, POET; DLB 217; EW 7; GFL 1789 to the Present; RGWL 2, 3; TWA

**Baudouin, Marcel**
See Peguy, Charles (Pierre)

**Baudouin, Pierre**
See Peguy, Charles (Pierre)

**Baudrillard, Jean** 1929- **CLC 60**

**Baum, L(yman) Frank** 1856-1919 **TCLC 7, 132**
See also AAYA 46; CA 133; 108; CLR 15; CWRI 5; DLB 22; FANT; JRDA; MAICYA 1, 2; MTCW 1, 2; NFS 13; RGAL 4; SATA 18, 100; WCH

**Baum, Louis F.**
See Baum, L(yman) Frank

**Baumbach, Jonathan** 1933- **CLC 6, 23**
See also CA 13-16R; CAAS 5; CANR 12, 66; CN 7; DLBY 1980; INT CANR-12; MTCW 1

**Bausch, Richard (Carl)** 1945- **CLC 51**
See also AMWS 7; CA 101; CAAS 14; CANR 43, 61, 87; CSW; DLB 130

**Baxter, Charles (Morley)** 1947- **CLC 45, 78**
See also CA 57-60; CANR 40, 64, 104; CPW; DAM POP; DLB 130; MTCW 2

**Baxter, George Owen**
See Faust, Frederick (Schiller)

**Baxter, James K(eir)** 1926-1972 **CLC 14**
See also CA 77-80; EWL 3

**Baxter, John**
See Hunt, E(verette) Howard, (Jr.)

**Bayer, Sylvia**
See Glassco, John

**Baynton, Barbara** 1857-1929 **TCLC 57**
See also DLB 230; RGSF 2

**Beagle, Peter S(oyer)** 1939- **CLC 7, 104**
See also AAYA 47; BPFB 1; BYA 9, 10; CA 9-12R; CANR 4, 51, 73, 110; DA3; DLBY 1980; FANT; INT CANR-4; MTCW 1; SATA 60, 130; SUFW 1, 2; YAW

**Bean, Normal**
See Burroughs, Edgar Rice

**Beard, Charles A(ustin)** 1874-1948 **TCLC 15**
See also CA 189; 115; DLB 17; SATA 18

**Beardsley, Aubrey** 1872-1898 **NCLC 6**

**Beattie, Ann** 1947- **CLC 8, 13, 18, 40, 63, 146; SSC 11**
See also AMWS 5; BEST 90:2; BPFB 1; CA 81-84; CANR 53, 73; CN 7; CPW; DA3; DAM NOV, POP; DLB 218, 278; DLBY 1982; EWL 3; MTCW 1, 2; RGAL 4; RGSF 2; SSFS 9; TUS

**Beattie, James** 1735-1803 **NCLC 25**
See also DLB 109

**Beauchamp, Kathleen Mansfield** 1888-1923
See Mansfield, Katherine
See also CA 134; 104; DA; DA3; DAC; DAM MST; MTCW 2; TEA

**Beaumarchais, Pierre-Augustin Caron de** 1732-1799 **DC 4; LC 61**
See also DAM DRAM; DFS 14, 16; EW 4; GFL Beginnings to 1789; RGWL 2, 3

**Beaumont, Francis** 1584(?)-1616 **DC 6; LC 33**
See also BRW 2; CDBLB Before 1660; DLB 58; TEA

**Beauvoir, Simone (Lucie Ernestine Marie Bertrand) de** 1908-1986 **CLC 1, 2, 4, 8, 14, 31, 44, 50, 71, 124; SSC 35; WLC**
See also BPFB 1; CA 118; 9-12R; CANR 28, 61; DA; DA3; DAB; DAC; DAM MST, NOV; DLB 72; DLBY 1986; EW 12; EWL 3; FW; GFL 1789 to the Present; LMFS 2; MTCW 1, 2; RGSF 2; RGWL 2, 3; TWA

**Becker, Carl (Lotus)** 1873-1945 **TCLC 63**
See also CA 157; DLB 17

**Becker, Jurek** 1937-1997 **CLC 7, 19**
See also CA 157; 85-88; CANR 60, 117; CWW 2; DLB 75; EWL 3

**Becker, Walter** 1950- **CLC 26**

**Beckett, Samuel (Barclay)** 1906-1989 **CLC 1, 2, 3, 4, 6, 9, 10, 11, 14, 18, 29, 57, 59, 83; SSC 16; WLC**
See also BRWR 1; BRWS 1; CA 130; 5-8R; CANR 33, 61; CBD; CDBLB 1945-1960; DA; DA3; DAB; DAC; DAM DRAM, MST, NOV; DFS 2, 7; DLB 13, 15, 233; DLBY 1990; EWL 3; GFL 1789 to the Present; LMFS 2; MTCW 1, 2; RGSF 2; RGWL 2, 3; SSFS 15; TEA; WLIT 4

**Beckford, William** 1760-1844 **NCLC 16**
See also BRW 3; DLB 39, 213; HGG; SUFW

**Beckham, Barry (Earl)** 1944- **BLC 1**
See also BW 1; CA 29-32R; CANR 26, 62; CN 7; DAM MULT; DLB 33

**Beckman, Gunnel** 1910- **CLC 26**
See also CA 33-36R; CANR 15, 114; CLR 25; MAICYA 1, 2; SAAS 9; SATA 6

**Becque, Henri** 1837-1899 **NCLC 3**
See also DLB 192; GFL 1789 to the Present

**Becquer, Gustavo Adolfo** 1836-1870 **HLCS 1; NCLC 106**
See also DAM MULT

**Beddoes, Thomas Lovell** 1803-1849 **DC 15; NCLC 3**
See also DLB 96

**Bede** c. 673-735 **CMLC 20**
See also DLB 146; TEA

**Bedford, Denton R.** 1907-(?) **NNAL**

**Bedford, Donald F.**
See Fearing, Kenneth (Flexner)

**Beecher, Catharine Esther** 1800-1878 **NCLC 30**
See also DLB 1, 243

**Beecher, John** 1904-1980 **CLC 6**
See also AITN 1; CA 105; 5-8R; CANR 8

**Beer, Johann** 1655-1700 **LC 5**
See also DLB 168

**Beer, Patricia** 1924- **CLC 58**
See also CA 183; 61-64; CANR 13, 46; CP 7; CWP; DLB 40; FW

**Beerbohm, Max**
See Beerbohm, (Henry) Max(imilian)

**Beerbohm, (Henry) Max(imilian)** 1872-1956 **TCLC 1, 24**
See also BRWS 2; CA 154; 104; CANR 79; DLB 34, 100; FANT

**Beer-Hofmann, Richard** 1866-1945 **TCLC 60**
See also CA 160; DLB 81

**Beg, Shemus**
See Stephens, James

**Begiebing, Robert J(ohn)** 1946- **CLC 70**
See also CA 122; CANR 40, 88

**Behan, Brendan** 1923-1964 **CLC 1, 8, 11, 15, 79**
See also BRWS 2; CA 73-76; CANR 33; CBD; CDBLB 1945-1960; DAM DRAM; DFS 7; DLB 13, 233; EWL 3; MTCW 1, 2

**Behn, Aphra** 1640(?)-1689 **DC 4; LC 1, 30, 42; PC 13; WLC**
See also BRWS 3; DA; DA3; DAB; DAC; DAM DRAM, MST, NOV, POET; DFS 16; DLB 39, 80, 131; FW; TEA; WLIT 3

**Behrman, S(amuel) N(athaniel)** 1893-1973 **CLC 40**
See also CA 45-48; 13-16; CAD; CAP 1; DLB 7, 44; IDFW 3; RGAL 4

**Belasco, David** 1853-1931 **TCLC 3**
See also CA 168; 104; DLB 7; RGAL 4

**Belcheva, Elisaveta Lyubomirova** 1893-1991 **CLC 10**
See Bagryana, Elisaveta

**Beldone, Phil "Cheech"**
See Ellison, Harlan (Jay)

**Beleno**
See Azuela, Mariano

**Belinski, Vissarion Grigoryevich** 1811-1848
**NCLC 5**
See also DLB 198

**Belitt, Ben** 1911- **CLC 22**
See also CA 13-16R; CAAS 4; CANR 7,
77; CP 7; DLB 5

**Bell, Gertrude (Margaret Lowthian)**
1868-1926 **TCLC 67**
See also CA 167; CANR 110; DLB 174

**Bell, J. Freeman**
See Zangwill, Israel

**Bell, James Madison** 1826-1902 **BLC 1;
TCLC 43**
See also BW 1; CA 124; 122; DAM MULT;
DLB 50

**Bell, Madison Smartt** 1957- **CLC 41, 102**
See also AMWS 10; BPFB 1; CA 111, 183;
CAAE 183; CANR 28, 54, 73; CN 7;
CSW; DLB 218, 278; MTCW 1

**Bell, Marvin (Hartley)** 1937- **CLC 8, 31**
See also CA 21-24R; CAAS 14; CANR 59,
102; CP 7; DAM POET; DLB 5; MTCW
1

**Bell, W. L. D.**
See Mencken, H(enry) L(ouis)

**Bellamy, Atwood C.**
See Mencken, H(enry) L(ouis)

**Bellamy, Edward** 1850-1898 **NCLC 4, 86**
See also DLB 12; NFS 15; RGAL 4; SFW
4

**Belli, Gioconda** 1949- **HLCS 1**
See also CA 152; CWW 2; EWL 3; RGWL
3

**Bellin, Edward J.**
See Kuttner, Henry

**Belloc, (Joseph) Hilaire (Pierre Sebastien
Rene Swanton)** 1870-1953 **PC 24; TCLC
7, 18**
See also CA 152; 106; CWRI 5; DAM
POET; DLB 19, 100, 141, 174; EWL 3;
MTCW 1; SATA 112; WCH; YABC 1

**Belloc, Joseph Peter Rene Hilaire**
See Belloc, (Joseph) Hilaire (Pierre Sebastien Rene Swanton)

**Belloc, Joseph Pierre Hilaire**
See Belloc, (Joseph) Hilaire (Pierre Sebastien Rene Swanton)

**Belloc, M. A.**
See Lowndes, Marie Adelaide (Belloc)

**Belloc-Lowndes, Mrs.**
See Lowndes, Marie Adelaide (Belloc)

**Bellow, Saul** 1915- **CLC 1, 2, 3, 6, 8, 10, 13,
15, 25, 33, 34, 63, 79; SSC 14; WLC**
See also AITN 2; AMW; AMWR 2; BEST
89:3; BPFB 1; CA 5-8R; CABS 1; CANR
29, 53, 95; CDALB 1941-1968; CN 7;
DA; DA3; DAB; DAC; DAM MST, NOV,
POP; DLB 2, 28; DLBD 3; DLBY 1982;
EWL 3; MTCW 1, 2; NFS 4, 14; RGAL
4; RGSF 2; SSFS 12; TUS

**Belser, Reimond Karel Maria de** 1929-
See Ruyslinck, Ward
See also CA 152

**Bely, Andrey PC 11; TCLC 7**
See Bugayev, Boris Nikolayevich
See also EW 9; EWL 3; MTCW 1

**Belyi, Andrei**
See Bugayev, Boris Nikolayevich
See also RGWL 2, 3

**Bembo, Pietro** 1470-1547 **LC 79**
See also RGWL 2, 3

**Benary, Margot**
See Benary-Isbert, Margot

**Benary-Isbert, Margot** 1889-1979 **CLC 12**
See also CA 89-92; 5-8R; CANR 4, 72;
CLR 12; MAICYA 1, 2; SATA 2; SATA-
Obit 21

**Benavente (y Martinez), Jacinto** 1866-1954
**HLCS 1; TCLC 3**
See also CA 131; 106; CANR 81; DAM
DRAM, MULT; EWL 3; GLL 2; HW 1,
2; MTCW 1, 2

**Benchley, Peter (Bradford)** 1940- **CLC 4, 8**
See also AAYA 14; AITN 2; BPFB 1; CA
17-20R; CANR 12, 35, 66, 115; CPW;
DAM NOV, POP; HGG; MTCW 1, 2;
SATA 3, 89

**Benchley, Robert (Charles)** 1889-1945 **TCLC
1, 55**
See also CA 153; 105; DLB 11; RGAL 4

**Benda, Julien** 1867-1956 **TCLC 60**
See also CA 154; 120; GFL 1789 to the
Present

**Benedict, Ruth (Fulton)** 1887-1948 **TCLC 60**
See also CA 158; DLB 246

**Benedikt, Michael** 1935- **CLC 4, 14**
See also CA 13-16R; CANR 7; CP 7; DLB
5

**Benet, Juan** 1927-1993 **CLC 28**
See also CA 143; EWL 3

**Benet, Stephen Vincent** 1898-1943 **SSC 10;
TCLC 7**
See also AMWS 11; CA 152; 104; DA3;
DAM POET; DLB 4, 48, 102, 249; DLBY
1997; EWL 3; HGG; MTCW 1; RGAL 4;
RGSF 2; SUFW; WP; YABC 1

**Benet, William Rose** 1886-1950 **TCLC 28**
See also CA 152; 118; DAM POET; DLB
45; RGAL 4

**Benford, Gregory (Albert)** 1941- **CLC 52**
See also BPFB 1; CA 69-72, 175; CAAE
175; CAAS 27; CANR 12, 24, 49, 95;
CSW; DLBY 1982; SCFW 2; SFW 4

**Bengtsson, Frans (Gunnar)** 1894-1954 **TCLC
48**
See also CA 170; EWL 3

**Benjamin, David**
See Slavitt, David R(ytman)

**Benjamin, Lois**
See Gould, Lois

**Benjamin, Walter** 1892-1940 **TCLC 39**
See also CA 164; DLB 242; EW 11; EWL
3

**Benn, Gottfried** 1886-1956 **PC 35; TCLC 3**
See also CA 153; 106; DLB 56; EWL 3;
RGWL 2, 3

**Bennett, Alan** 1934- **CLC 45, 77**
See also BRWS 8; CA 103; CANR 35, 55,
106; CBD; CD 5; DAB; DAM MST;
MTCW 1, 2

**Bennett, (Enoch) Arnold** 1867-1931 **TCLC 5,
20**
See also BRW 6; CA 155; 106; CDBLB
1890-1914; DLB 10, 34, 98, 135; EWL 3;
MTCW 2

**Bennett, Elizabeth**
See Mitchell, Margaret (Munnerlyn)

**Bennett, George Harold** 1930-
See Bennett, Hal
See also BW 1; CA 97-100; CANR 87

**Bennett, Gwendolyn B.** 1902-1981 **HR 2**
See also BW 1; CA 125; DLB 51; WP

**Bennett, Hal CLC 5**
See Bennett, George Harold
See also DLB 33

**Bennett, Jay** 1912- **CLC 35**
See also AAYA 10; CA 69-72; CANR 11,
42, 79; JRDA; SAAS 4; SATA 41, 87;
SATA-Brief 27; WYA; YAW

**Bennett, Louise (Simone)** 1919- **BLC 1; CLC
28**
See also BW 2, 3; CA 151; CDWLB 3; CP
7; DAM MULT; DLB 117; EWL 3

**Benson, A. C.** 1862-1925 **TCLC 123**
See also DLB 98

**Benson, E(dward) F(rederic)** 1867-1940
**TCLC 27**
See also CA 157; 114; DLB 135, 153;
HGG; SUFW 1

**Benson, Jackson J.** 1930- **CLC 34**
See also CA 25-28R; DLB 111

**Benson, Sally** 1900-1972 **CLC 17**
See also CA 37-40R; 19-20; CAP 1; SATA
1, 35; SATA-Obit 27

**Benson, Stella** 1892-1933 **TCLC 17**
See also CA 154, 155; 117; DLB 36, 162;
FANT; TEA

**Bentham, Jeremy** 1748-1832 **NCLC 38**
See also DLB 107, 158, 252

**Bentley, E(dmund) C(lerihew)** 1875-1956
**TCLC 12**
See also CA 108; DLB 70; MSW

**Bentley, Eric (Russell)** 1916- **CLC 24**
See also CA 5-8R; CAD; CANR 6, 67;
CBD; CD 5; INT CANR-6

**Beranger, Pierre Jean de** 1780-1857 **NCLC
34**

**Berdyaev, Nicolas**
See Berdyaev, Nikolai (Aleksandrovich)

**Berdyaev, Nikolai (Aleksandrovich)**
1874-1948 **TCLC 67**
See also CA 157; 120

**Berdyayev, Nikolai (Aleksandrovich)**
See Berdyaev, Nikolai (Aleksandrovich)

**Berendt, John (Lawrence)** 1939- **CLC 86**
See also CA 146; CANR 75, 93; DA3;
MTCW 1

**Beresford, J(ohn) D(avys)** 1873-1947 **TCLC
81**
See also CA 155; 112; DLB 162, 178, 197;
SFW 4; SUFW 1

**Bergelson, David** 1884-1952 **TCLC 81**
See Bergelson, Dovid

**Bergelson, Dovid**
See Bergelson, David
See also EWL 3

**Berger, Colonel**
See Malraux, (Georges-)Andre

**Berger, John (Peter)** 1926- **CLC 2, 19**
See also BRWS 4; CA 81-84; CANR 51,
78, 117; CN 7; DLB 14, 207

**Berger, Melvin H.** 1927- **CLC 12**
See also CA 5-8R; CANR 4; CLR 32;
SAAS 2; SATA 5, 88; SATA-Essay 124

**Berger, Thomas (Louis)** 1924- **CLC 3, 5, 8,
11, 18, 38**
See also BPFB 1; CA 1-4R; CANR 5, 28,
51; CN 7; DAM NOV; DLB 2; DLBY
1980; EWL 3; FANT; INT CANR-28;
MTCW 1, 2; RHW; TCWW 2

**Bergman, (Ernst) Ingmar** 1918- **CLC 16, 72**
See also CA 81-84; CANR 33, 70; DLB
257; MTCW 2

**Bergson, Henri(-Louis)** 1859-1941 **TCLC 32**
See also CA 164; EW 8; EWL 3; GFL 1789
to the Present

**Bergstein, Eleanor** 1938- **CLC 4**
See also CA 53-56; CANR 5

**Berkeley, George** 1685-1753 **LC 65**
See also DLB 31, 101, 252

**Berkoff, Steven** 1937- **CLC 56**
See also CA 104; CANR 72; CBD; CD 5

**Berlin, Isaiah** 1909-1997 **TCLC 105**
See also CA 162; 85-88

**Bermant, Chaim (Icyk)** 1929-1998 **CLC 40**
See also CA 57-60; CANR 6, 31, 57, 105;
CN 7

**Bern, Victoria**
See Fisher, M(ary) F(rances) K(ennedy)

**Bernanos, (Paul Louis) Georges** 1888-1948
**TCLC 3**
See also CA 130; 104; CANR 94; DLB 72;
EWL 3; GFL 1789 to the Present; RGWL
2, 3

**Bernard, April** 1956- **CLC 59**
See also CA 131
**Berne, Victoria**
See Fisher, M(ary) F(rances) K(ennedy)
**Bernhard, Thomas** 1931-1989 **CLC 3, 32, 61; DC 14**
See also CA 127; 85-88; CANR 32, 57; CD-WLB 2; DLB 85, 124; EWL 3; MTCW 1; RGWL 2, 3
**Bernhardt, Sarah (Henriette Rosine)** 1844-1923 **TCLC 75**
See also CA 157
**Bernstein, Charles** 1950- **CLC 142,**
See also CA 129; CAAS 24; CANR 90; CP 7; DLB 169
**Berriault, Gina** 1926-1999 **CLC 54, 109; SSC 30**
See also CA 185; 129; 116; CANR 66; DLB 130; SSFS 7,11
**Berrigan, Daniel** 1921- **CLC 4**
See also CA 33-36R; CAAE 187; CAAS 1; CANR 11, 43, 78; CP 7; DLB 5
**Berrigan, Edmund Joseph Michael, Jr.** 1934-1983
See Berrigan, Ted
See also CA 110; 61-64; CANR 14, 102
**Berrigan, Ted CLC 37**
See Berrigan, Edmund Joseph Michael, Jr.
See also DLB 5, 169; WP
**Berry, Charles Edward Anderson** 1931-
See Berry, Chuck
See also CA 115
**Berry, Chuck CLC 17**
See Berry, Charles Edward Anderson
**Berry, Jonas**
See Ashbery, John (Lawrence)
See also GLL 1
**Berry, Wendell (Erdman)** 1934- **CLC 4, 6, 8, 27, 46; PC 28**
See also AITN 1; AMWS 10; ANW; CA 73-76; CANR 50, 73, 101; CP 7; CSW; DAM POET; DLB 5, 6, 234, 275; MTCW 1
**Berryman, John** 1914-1972 **CLC 1, 2, 3, 4, 6, 8, 10, 13, 25, 62**
See also AMW; CA 33-36R; 13-16; CABS 2; CANR 35; CAP 1; CDALB 1941-1968; DAM POET; DLB 48; EWL 3; MTCW 1, 2; PAB; RGAL 4; WP
**Bertolucci, Bernardo** 1940- **CLC 16, 157**
See also CA 106
**Berton, Pierre (Francis Demarigny)** 1920-**CLC 104**
See also CA 1-4R; CANR 2, 56; CPW; DLB 68; SATA 99
**Bertrand, Aloysius** 1807-1841 **NCLC 31**
See Bertrand, Louis oAloysiusc
**Bertrand, Louis oAloysiusc**
See Bertrand, Aloysius
See also DLB 217
**Bertran de Born** c. 1140-1215 **CMLC 5**
**Besant, Annie (Wood)** 1847-1933 **TCLC 9**
See also CA 185; 105
**Bessie, Alvah** 1904-1985 **CLC 23**
See also CA 116; 5-8R; CANR 2, 80; DLB 26
**Bethlen, T. D.**
See Silverberg, Robert
**Beti, Mongo BLC 1; CLC 27**
See Biyidi, Alexandre
See also AFW; CANR 79; DAM MULT; EWL 3; WLIT 2
**Betjeman, John** 1906-1984 **CLC 2, 6, 10, 34, 43**
See also BRW 7; CA 112; 9-12R; CANR 33, 56; CDBLB 1945-1960; DA3; DAB; DAM MST, POET; DLB 20; DLBY 1984; EWL 3; MTCW 1, 2

**Bettelheim, Bruno** 1903-1990 **CLC 79**
See also CA 131; 81-84; CANR 23, 61; DA3; MTCW 1, 2
**Betti, Ugo** 1892-1953 **TCLC 5**
See also CA 155; 104; EWL 3; RGWL 2, 3
**Betts, Doris (Waugh)** 1932- **CLC 3, 6, 28; SSC 45**
See also CA 13-16R; CANR 9, 66, 77; CN 7; CSW; DLB 218; DLBY 1982; INT CANR-9; RGAL 4
**Bevan, Alistair**
See Roberts, Keith (John Kingston)
**Bey, Pilaff**
See Douglas, (George) Norman
**Bialik, Chaim Nachman** 1873-1934 **TCLC 25**
See also CA 170; EWL 3
**Bickerstaff, Isaac**
See Swift, Jonathan
**Bidart, Frank** 1939- **CLC 33**
See also CA 140; CANR 106; CP 7
**Bienek, Horst** 1930- **CLC 7, 11**
See also CA 73-76; DLB 75
**Bierce, Ambrose (Gwinett)** 1842-1914(?) **SSC 9; TCLC 1, 7, 44; WLC**
See also AMW; BYA 11; CA 139; 104; CANR 78; CDALB 1865-1917; DA; DA3; DAC; DAM MST; DLB 11, 12, 23, 71, 74, 186; EWL 3; EXPS; HGG; LAIT 2; RGAL 4; RGSF 2; SSFS 9; SUFW 1
**Biggers, Earl Derr** 1884-1933 **TCLC 65**
See also CA 153; 108
**Billiken, Bud**
See Motley, Willard (Francis)
**Billings, Josh**
See Shaw, Henry Wheeler
**Billington, (Lady) Rachel (Mary)** 1942- **CLC 43**
See also AITN 2; CA 33-36R; CANR 44; CN 7
**Binchy, Maeve** 1940- **CLC 153**
See also BEST 90:1; BPFB 1; CA 134; 127; CANR 50, 96; CN 7; CPW; DA3; DAM POP; INT CA-134; MTCW 1; RHW
**Binyon, T(imothy) J(ohn)** 1936- **CLC 34**
See also CA 111; CANR 28
**Bion** 335B.C.-245B.C. **CMLC 39**
**Bioy Casares, Adolfo** 1914-1999 **CLC 4, 8, 13, 88; HLC 1; SSC 17**
See Casares, Adolfo Bioy; Miranda, Javier; Sacastru, Martin
See also CA 177; 29-32R; CANR 19, 43, 66; DAM MULT; DLB 113; EWL 3; HW 1, 2; LAW; MTCW 1, 2
**Birch, Allison CLC 65**
**Bird, Cordwainer**
See Ellison, Harlan (Jay)
**Bird, Robert Montgomery** 1806-1854 **NCLC 1**
See also DLB 202; RGAL 4
**Birkerts, Sven** 1951- **CLC 116**
See also CA 133, 176; 128; CAAE 176; CAAS 29; INT 133
**Birney, (Alfred) Earle** 1904-1995 **CLC 1, 4, 6, 11**
See also CA 1-4R; CANR 5, 20; CP 7; DAC; DAM MST, POET; DLB 88; MTCW 1; PFS 8; RGEL 2
**Biruni, al** 973-1048(?) **CMLC 28**
**Bishop, Elizabeth** 1911-1979 **CLC 1, 4, 9, 13, 15, 32; PC 3, 34; TCLC 121**
See also AMWR 1; AMWS 1; CA 89-92; 5-8R; CABS 2; CANR 26, 61, 108; CDALB 1968-1988; DA; DA3; DAC; DAM MST, POET; DLB 5, 169; EWL 3; GLL 2; MAWW; MTCW 1, 2; PAB; PFS 6, 12; RGAL 4; SATA-Obit 24; TUS; WP
**Bishop, John** 1935- **CLC 10**
See also CA 105

**Bishop, John Peale** 1892-1944 **TCLC 103**
See also CA 155; 107; DLB 4, 9, 45; RGAL 4
**Bissett, Bill** 1939- **CLC 18; PC 14**
See also CA 69-72; CAAS 19; CANR 15; CCA 1; CP 7; DLB 53; MTCW 1
**Bissoondath, Neil (Devindra)** 1955- **CLC 120**
See also CA 136; CN 7; DAC
**Bitov, Andrei (Georgievich)** 1937- **CLC 57**
See also CA 142
**Biyidi, Alexandre** 1932-
See Beti, Mongo
See also BW 1, 3; CA 124; 114; CANR 81; DA3; MTCW 1, 2
**Bjarme, Brynjolf**
See Ibsen, Henrik (Johan)
**Bjoernson, Bjoernstjerne (Martinius)** 1832-1910 **TCLC 7, 37**
See also CA 104
**Black, Robert**
See Holdstock, Robert P.
**Blackburn, Paul** 1926-1971 **CLC 9, 43**
See also BG 2; CA 33-36R; 81-84; CANR 34; DLB 16; DLBY 1981
**Black Elk** 1863-1950 **NNAL; TCLC 33**
See also CA 144; DAM MULT; MTCW 1; WP
**Black Hawk** 1767-1838 **NNAL**
**Black Hobart**
See Sanders, (James) Ed(ward)
**Blacklin, Malcolm**
See Chambers, Aidan
**Blackmore, R(ichard) D(oddridge)** 1825-1900 **TCLC 27**
See also CA 120; DLB 18; RGEL 2
**Blackmur, R(ichard) P(almer)** 1904-1965 **CLC 2, 24**
See also AMWS 2; CA 25-28R; 11-12; CANR 71; CAP 1; DLB 63; EWL 3
**Black Tarantula**
See Acker, Kathy
**Blackwood, Algernon (Henry)** 1869-1951 **TCLC 5**
See also CA 150; 105; DLB 153, 156, 178; HGG; SUFW 1
**Blackwood, Caroline** 1931-1996 **CLC 6, 9, 100**
See also CA 151; 85-88; CANR 32, 61, 65; CN 7; DLB 14, 207; HGG; MTCW 1
**Blade, Alexander**
See Hamilton, Edmond; Silverberg, Robert
**Blaga, Lucian** 1895-1961 **CLC 75**
See also CA 157; DLB 220; EWL 3
**Blair, Eric (Arthur)** 1903-1950 **TCLC 123**
See Orwell, George
See also CA 132; 104; DA; DA3; DAB; DAC; DAM MST, NOV; MTCW 1, 2; SATA 29
**Blair, Hugh** 1718-1800 **NCLC 75**
**Blais, Marie-Claire** 1939- **CLC 2, 4, 6, 13, 22**
See also CA 21-24R; CAAS 4; CANR 38, 75, 93; DAC; DAM MST; DLB 53; EWL 3; FW; MTCW 1, 2; TWA
**Blaise, Clark** 1940- **CLC 29**
See also AITN 2; CA 53-56; CAAS 3; CANR 5, 66, 106; CN 7; DLB 53; RGSF 2
**Blake, Fairley**
See De Voto, Bernard (Augustine)
**Blake, Nicholas**
See Day Lewis, C(ecil)
See also DLB 77; MSW
**Blake, Sterling**
See Benford, Gregory (Albert)
**Blake, William** 1757-1827 **NCLC 13, 37, 57; PC 12; WLC**
See also AAYA 47; BRW 3; BRWR 1; CD-BLB 1789-1832; CLR 52; DA; DA3; DAB; DAC; DAM MST, POET; DLB 93,

163; EXPP; MAICYA 1, 2; PAB; PFS 2, 12; SATA 30; TEA; WCH; WLIT 3; WP

**Blanchot, Maurice** 1907- **CLC 135**
See also CA 144; 117; DLB 72; EWL 3

**Blasco Ibanez, Vicente** 1867-1928 **TCLC 12**
See also BPFB 1; CA 131; 110; CANR 81; DA3; DAM NOV; EW 8; EWL 3; HW 1, 2; MTCW 1

**Blatty, William Peter** 1928- **CLC 2**
See also CA 5-8R; CANR 9; DAM POP; HGG

**Bleeck, Oliver**
See Thomas, Ross (Elmore)

**Blessing, Lee** 1949- **CLC 54**
See also CAD; CD 5

**Blight, Rose**
See Greer, Germaine

**Blish, James (Benjamin)** 1921-1975 **CLC 14**
See also BPFB 1; CA 57-60; 1-4R; CANR 3; DLB 8; MTCW 1; SATA 66; SCFW 2; SFW 4

**Bliss, Reginald**
See Wells, H(erbert) G(eorge)

**Blixen, Karen (Christentze Dinesen)** 1885-1962
See Dinesen, Isak
See also CA 25-28; CANR 22, 50; CAP 2; DA3; DLB 214; MTCW 1, 2; SATA 44

**Bloch, Robert (Albert)** 1917-1994 **CLC 33**
See also AAYA 29; CA 146; 5-8R, 179; CAAS 20; CAAS 20; CANR 5, 78; DA3; DLB 44; HGG; INT CANR-5; MTCW 1; SATA 12; SATA-Obit 82; SFW 4; SUFW 1, 2

**Blok, Alexander (Alexandrovich)** 1880-1921 **PC 21; TCLC 5**
See also CA 183; 104; EW 9; EWL 3; RGWL 2, 3

**Blom, Jan**
See Breytenbach, Breyten

**Bloom, Harold** 1930- **CLC 24, 103**
See also CA 13-16R; CANR 39, 75, 92; DLB 67; EWL 3; MTCW 1; RGAL 4

**Bloomfield, Aurelius**
See Bourne, Randolph S(illiman)

**Blount, Roy (Alton), Jr.** 1941- **CLC 38**
See also CA 53-56; CANR 10, 28, 61; CSW; INT CANR-28; MTCW 1, 2

**Blowsnake, Sam** 1875-(?) **NNAL**

**Bloy, Leon** 1846-1917 **TCLC 22**
See also CA 183; 121; DLB 123; GFL 1789 to the Present

**Blue Cloud, Peter (Aroniawenrate)** 1933- **NNAL**
See also CA 117; CANR 40; DAM MULT

**Bluggage, Oranthy**
See Alcott, Louisa May

**Blume, Judy (Sussman)** 1938- **CLC 12, 30**
See also AAYA 3, 26; BYA 1, 8, 12; CA 29-32R; CANR 13, 37, 66; CLR 2, 15, 69; CPW; DA3; DAM NOV, POP; DLB 52; JRDA; MAICYA 1, 2; MAICYAS 1; MTCW 1, 2; SATA 2, 31, 79; WYA; YAW

**Blunden, Edmund (Charles)** 1896-1974 **CLC 2, 56**
See also BRW 6; CA 45-48; 17-18; CANR 54; CAP 2; DLB 20, 100, 155; MTCW 1; PAB

**Bly, Robert (Elwood)** 1926- **CLC 1, 2, 5, 10, 15, 38, 128; PC 39**
See also AMWS 4; CA 5-8R; CANR 41, 73; CP 7; DA3; DAM POET; DLB 5; EWL 3; MTCW 1, 2; PFS 17; RGAL 4

**Boas, Franz** 1858-1942 **TCLC 56**
See also CA 181; 115

**Bobette**
See Simenon, Georges (Jacques Christian)

**Boccaccio, Giovanni** 1313-1375 **CMLC 13, 57; SSC 10**
See also EW 2; RGSF 2; RGWL 2, 3; TWA

**Bochco, Steven** 1943- **CLC 35**
See also AAYA 11; CA 138; 124

**Bode, Sigmund**
See O'Doherty, Brian

**Bodel, Jean** 1167(?)-1210 **CMLC 28**

**Bodenheim, Maxwell** 1892-1954 **TCLC 44**
See also CA 187; 110; DLB 9, 45; RGAL 4

**Bodenheimer, Maxwell**
See Bodenheim, Maxwell

**Bodker, Cecil** 1927-
See Bodker, Cecil

**Bodker, Cecil** 1927- **CLC 21**
See also CA 73-76; CANR 13, 44, 111; CLR 23; MAICYA 1, 2; SATA 14, 133

**Boell, Heinrich (Theodor)** 1917-1985 **CLC 2, 3, 6, 9, 11, 15, 27, 32, 72; SSC 23; WLC**
See Boll, Heinrich
See also CA 116; 21-24R; CANR 24; DA; DA3; DAB; DAC; DAM MST, NOV; DLB 69; DLBY 1985; MTCW 1, 2; TWA

**Boerne, Alfred**
See Doeblin, Alfred

**Boethius** c. 480-c. 524 **CMLC 15**
See also DLB 115; RGWL 2, 3

**Boff, Leonardo (Genezio Darci)** 1938- **CLC 70; HLC 1**
See also CA 150; DAM MULT; HW 2

**Bogan, Louise** 1897-1970 **CLC 4, 39, 46, 93; PC 12**
See also AMWS 3; CA 25-28R; 73-76; CANR 33, 82; DAM POET; DLB 45, 169; EWL 3; MAWW; MTCW 1, 2; RGAL 4

**Bogarde, Dirk**
See Van Den Bogarde, Derek Jules Gaspard Ulric Niven
See also DLB 14

**Bogosian, Eric** 1953- **CLC 45, 141**
See also CA 138; CAD; CANR 102; CD 5

**Bograd, Larry** 1953- **CLC 35**
See also CA 93-96; CANR 57; SAAS 21; SATA 33, 89; WYA

**Boiardo, Matteo Maria** 1441-1494 **LC 6**

**Boileau-Despreaux, Nicolas** 1636-1711 **LC 3**
See also DLB 268; EW 3; GFL Beginnings to 1789; RGWL 2, 3

**Boissard, Maurice**
See Leautaud, Paul

**Bojer, Johan** 1872-1959 **TCLC 64**
See also CA 189; EWL 3

**Bok, Edward W.** 1863-1930 **TCLC 101**
See also DLB 91; DLBD 16

**Boland, Eavan (Aisling)** 1944- **CLC 40, 67, 113**
See also BRWS 5; CA 143; CAAE 207; CANR 61; CP 7; CWP; DAM POET; DLB 40; FW; MTCW 2; PFS 12

**Boll, Heinrich**
See Boell, Heinrich (Theodor)
See also BPFB 1; CDWLB 2; EW 13; EWL 3; RGSF 2; RGWL 2, 3

**Bolt, Lee**
See Faust, Frederick (Schiller)

**Bolt, Robert (Oxton)** 1924-1995 **CLC 14**
See also CA 147; 17-20R; CANR 35, 67; CBD; DAM DRAM; DFS 2; DLB 13, 233; EWL 3; LAIT 1; MTCW 1

**Bombal, Maria Luisa** 1910-1980 **HLCS 1; SSC 37**
See also CA 127; CANR 72; EWL 3; HW 1; LAW; RGSF 2

**Bombet, Louis-Alexandre-Cesar**
See Stendhal

**Bomkauf**
See Kaufman, Bob (Garnell)

**Bonaventura NCLC 35**
See also DLB 90

**Bond, Edward** 1934- **CLC 4, 6, 13, 23**
See also BRWS 1; CA 25-28R; CANR 38, 67, 106; CBD; CD 5; DAM DRAM; DFS 3,8; DLB 13; EWL 3; MTCW 1

**Bonham, Frank** 1914-1989 **CLC 12**
See also AAYA 1; BYA 1, 3; CA 9-12R; CANR 4, 36; JRDA; MAICYA 1, 2; SAAS 3; SATA 1, 49; SATA-Obit 62; TCWW 2; YAW

**Bonnefoy, Yves** 1923- **CLC 9, 15, 58**
See also CA 85-88; CANR 33, 75, 97; CWW 2; DAM MST, POET; DLB 258; EWL 3; GFL 1789 to the Present; MTCW 1, 2

**Bonner, Marita HR 2**
See Occomy, Marita (Odette) Bonner

**Bonnin, Gertrude** 1876-1938 **NNAL**
See Zitkala-Sa
See also CA 150; DAM MULT

**Bontemps, Arna(ud Wendell)** 1902-1973 **BLC 1; CLC 1, 18; HR 2**
See also BW 1; CA 41-44R; 1-4R; CANR 4, 35; CLR 6; CWRI 5; DA3; DAM MULT, NOV, POET; DLB 48, 51; JRDA; MAICYA 1, 2; MTCW 1, 2; SATA 2, 44; SATA-Obit 24; WCH; WP

**Booth, Martin** 1944- **CLC 13**
See also CA 93-96; CAAE 188; CAAS 2; CANR 92

**Booth, Philip** 1925- **CLC 23**
See also CA 5-8R; CANR 5, 88; CP 7; DLBY 1982

**Booth, Wayne C(layson)** 1921- **CLC 24**
See also CA 1-4R; CAAS 5; CANR 3, 43, 117; DLB 67

**Borchert, Wolfgang** 1921-1947 **TCLC 5**
See also CA 188; 104; DLB 69, 124; EWL 3

**Borel, Petrus** 1809-1859 **NCLC 41**
See also DLB 119; GFL 1789 to the Present

**Borges, Jorge Luis** 1899-1986 **CLC 1, 2, 3, 4, 6, 8, 9, 10, 13, 19, 44, 48, 83; HLC 1; PC 22, 32; SSC 4, 41; TCLC 109; WLC**
See also AAYA 26; BPFB 1; CA 21-24R; CANR 19, 33, 75, 105; CDWLB 3; DA; DA3; DAB; DAC; DAM MST, MULT; DLB 113; DLBY 1986; DNFS 1, 2; EWL 3; HW 1, 2; LAW; LMFS 2; MSW; MTCW 1, 2; RGSF 2; RGWL 2, 3; SFW 4; SSFS 17; TWA; WLIT 1

**Borowski, Tadeusz** 1922-1951 **SSC 48; TCLC 9**
See also CA 154; 106; CDWLB 4; DLB 215; EWL 3; RGSF 2; RGWL 3; SSFS 13

**Borrow, George (Henry)** 1803-1881 **NCLC 9**
See also DLB 21, 55, 166

**Bosch (Gavino), Juan** 1909-2001 **HLCS 1**
See also CA 204; 151; DAM MST, MULT; DLB 145; HW 1, 2

**Bosman, Herman Charles** 1905-1951 **TCLC 49**
See Malan, Herman
See also CA 160; DLB 225; RGSF 2

**Bosschere, Jean de** 1878(?)-1953 **TCLC 19**
See also CA 186; 115

**Boswell, James** 1740-1795 **LC 4, 50; WLC**
See also BRW 3; CDBLB 1660-1789; DA; DAB; DAC; DAM MST; DLB 104, 142; TEA; WLIT 3

**Bottomley, Gordon** 1874-1948 **TCLC 107**
See also CA 192; 120; DLB 10

**Bottoms, David** 1949- **CLC 53**
See also CA 105; CANR 22; CSW; DLB 120; DLBY 1983

**Boucicault, Dion** 1820-1890 **NCLC 41**

**Boucolon, Maryse**
See Conde, Maryse

**Bourget, Paul (Charles Joseph)** 1852-1935 **TCLC 12**
See also CA 196; 107; DLB 123; GFL 1789 to the Present

**Bourjaily, Vance (Nye)** 1922- **CLC 8, 62**
See also CA 1-4R; CAAS 1; CANR 2, 72; CN 7; DLB 2, 143

**Bourne, Randolph S(illiman)** 1886-1918 **TCLC 16**
See also AMW; CA 155; 117; DLB 63

**Bova, Ben(jamin William)** 1932- **CLC 45**
See also AAYA 16; CA 5-8R; CAAS 18; CANR 11, 56, 94, 111; CLR 3; DLBY 1981; INT CANR-11; MAICYA 1, 2; MTCW 1; SATA 6, 68, 133; SFW 4

**Bowen, Elizabeth (Dorothea Cole)** 1899-1973 **CLC 1, 3, 6, 11, 15, 22, 118; SSC 3, 28**
See also BRWS 2; CA 41-44R; 17-18; CANR 35, 105; CAP 2; CDBLB 1945-1960; DA3; DAM NOV; DLB 15, 162; EWL 3; EXPS; FW; HGG; MTCW 1, 2; NFS 13; RGSF 2; SSFS 5; SUFW 1; TEA; WLIT 4

**Bowering, George** 1935- **CLC 15, 47**
See also CA 21-24R; CAAS 16; CANR 10; CP 7; DLB 53

**Bowering, Marilyn R(uthe)** 1949- **CLC 32**
See also CA 101; CANR 49; CP 7; CWP

**Bowers, Edgar** 1924-2000 **CLC 9**
See also CA 188; 5-8R; CANR 24; CP 7; CSW; DLB 5

**Bowers, Mrs. J. Milton** 1842-1914
See Bierce, Ambrose (Gwinett)

**Bowie, David CLC 17**
See Jones, David Robert

**Bowles, Jane (Sydney)** 1917-1973 **CLC 3, 68**
See Bowles, Jane Auer
See also CA 41-44R; 19-20; CAP 2

**Bowles, Jane Auer**
See Bowles, Jane (Sydney)
See also EWL 3

**Bowles, Paul (Frederick)** 1910-1999 **CLC 1, 2, 19, 53; SSC 3**
See also AMWS 4; CA 186; 1-4R; CAAS 1; CANR 1, 19, 50, 75; CN 7; DA3; DLB 5, 6, 218; EWL 3; MTCW 1, 2; RGAL 4; SSFS 17

**Bowles, William Lisle** 1762-1850 **NCLC 103**
See also DLB 93

**Box, Edgar**
See Vidal, Gore
See also GLL 1

**Boyd, James** 1888-1944 **TCLC 115**
See also CA 186; DLB 9; DLBD 16; RGAL 4; RHW

**Boyd, Nancy**
See Millay, Edna St. Vincent
See also GLL 1

**Boyd, Thomas (Alexander)** 1898-1935 **TCLC 111**
See also CA 183; 111; DLB 9; DLBD 16

**Boyd, William** 1952- **CLC 28, 53, 70**
See also CA 120; 114; CANR 51, 71; CN 7; DLB 231

**Boyle, Kay** 1902-1992 **CLC 1, 5, 19, 58, 121; SSC 5**
See also CA 140; 13-16R; CAAS 1; CANR 29, 61, 110; DLB 4, 9, 48, 86; DLBY 1993; EWL 3; MTCW 1, 2; RGAL 4; RGSF 2; SSFS 10, 13, 14

**Boyle, Mark**
See Kienzle, William X(avier)

**Boyle, Patrick** 1905-1982 **CLC 19**
See also CA 127

**Boyle, T. C.**
See Boyle, T(homas) Coraghessan
See also AMWS 8

**Boyle, T(homas) Coraghessan** 1948- **CLC 36, 55, 90; SSC 16**
See Boyle, T. C.
See also AAYA 47; BEST 90:4; BPFB 1; CA 120; CANR 44, 76, 89; CN 7; CPW; DA3; DAM POP; DLB 218, 278; DLBY 1986; EWL 3; MTCW 2; SSFS 13

**Boz**
See Dickens, Charles (John Huffam)

**Brackenridge, Hugh Henry** 1748-1816 **NCLC 7**
See also DLB 11, 37; RGAL 4

**Bradbury, Edward P.**
See Moorcock, Michael (John)
See also MTCW 2

**Bradbury, Malcolm (Stanley)** 1932-2000 **CLC 32, 61**
See also CA 1-4R; CANR 1, 33, 91, 98; CN 7; DA3; DAM NOV; DLB 14, 207; EWL 3; MTCW 1, 2

**Bradbury, Ray (Douglas)** 1920- **CLC 1, 3, 10, 15, 42, 98; SSC 29, 53; WLC**
See also AAYA 15; AITN 1, 2; AMWS 4; BPFB 1; BYA 4, 5, 11; CA 1-4R; CANR 2, 30, 75; CDALB 1968-1988; CN 7; CPW; DA; DA3; DAB; DAC; DAM MST, NOV, POP; DLB 2, 8; EXPN; EXPS; HGG; LAIT 3, 5; MTCW 1, 2; NFS 1; RGAL 4; RGSF 2; SATA 11, 64, 123; SCFW 2; SFW 4; SSFS 1; SUFW 1, 2; TUS; YAW

**Braddon, Mary Elizabeth** 1837-1915 **TCLC 111**
See also BRWS 8; CA 179; 108; CMW 4; DLB 18, 70, 156; HGG

**Bradford, Gamaliel** 1863-1932 **TCLC 36**
See also CA 160; DLB 17

**Bradford, William** 1590-1657 **LC 64**
See also DLB 24, 30; RGAL 4

**Bradley, David (Henry), Jr.** 1950- **BLC 1; CLC 23, 118**
See also BW 1, 3; CA 104; CANR 26, 81; CN 7; DAM MULT; DLB 33

**Bradley, John Ed(mund, Jr.)** 1958- **CLC 55**
See also CA 139; CANR 99; CN 7; CSW

**Bradley, Marion Zimmer** 1930-1999 **CLC 30**
See Chapman, Lee; Dexter, John; Gardner, Miriam; Ives, Morgan; Rivers, Elfrida
See also AAYA 40; BPFB 1; CA 185; 57-60; CAAS 10; CANR 7, 31, 51, 75, 107; CPW; DA3; DAM POP; DLB 8; FANT; FW; MTCW 1, 2; SATA 90; SATA-Obit 116; SFW 4; SUFW 2; YAW

**Bradshaw, John** 1933- **CLC 70**
See also CA 138; CANR 61

**Bradstreet, Anne** 1612(?)-1672 **LC 4, 30; PC 10**
See also AMWS 1; CDALB 1640-1865; DA; DA3; DAC; DAM MST, POET; DLB 24; EXPP; FW; PFS 6; RGAL 4; TUS; WP

**Brady, Joan** 1939- **CLC 86**
See also CA 141

**Bragg, Melvyn** 1939- **CLC 10**
See also BEST 89:3; CA 57-60; CANR 10, 48, 89; CN 7; DLB 14, 271; RHW

**Brahe, Tycho** 1546-1601 **LC 45**

**Braine, John (Gerard)** 1922-1986 **CLC 1, 3, 41**
See also CA 120; 1-4R; CANR 1, 33; CDBLB 1945-1960; DLB 15; DLBY 1986; EWL 3; MTCW 1

**Braithwaite, William Stanley (Beaumont)** 1878-1962 **BLC 1; HR 2**
See also BW 1; CA 125; DAM MULT; DLB 50, 54

**Bramah, Ernest** 1868-1942 **TCLC 72**
See also CA 156; CMW 4; DLB 70; FANT

**Brammer, William** 1930(?)-1978 **CLC 31**
See also CA 77-80

**Brancati, Vitaliano** 1907-1954 **TCLC 12**
See also CA 109; DLB 264; EWL 3

**Brancato, Robin F(idler)** 1936- **CLC 35**
See also AAYA 9; BYA 6; CA 69-72; CANR 11, 45; CLR 32; JRDA; MAICYA 2; MAICYAS 1; SAAS 9; SATA 97; WYA; YAW

**Brand, Max**
See Faust, Frederick (Schiller)
See also BPFB 1; TCWW 2

**Brand, Millen** 1906-1980 **CLC 7**
See also CA 97-100; 21-24R; CANR 72

**Branden, Barbara CLC 44**
See also CA 148

**Brandes, Georg (Morris Cohen)** 1842-1927 **TCLC 10**
See also CA 189; 105

**Brandys, Kazimierz** 1916-2000 **CLC 62**
See also EWL 3

**Branley, Franklyn M(ansfield)** 1915-2002 **CLC 21**
See also CA 207; 33-36R; CANR 14, 39; CLR 13; MAICYA 1, 2; SAAS 16; SATA 4, 68, 136

**Brant, Beth (E.)** 1941- **NNAL**
See also CA 144; FW

**Brathwaite, Edward Kamau** 1930- **BLCS; CLC 11**
See also BW 2, 3; CA 25-28R; CANR 11, 26, 47, 107; CDWLB 3; CP 7; DAM POET; DLB 125; EWL 3

**Brathwaite, Kamau**
See Brathwaite, Edward Kamau

**Brautigan, Richard (Gary)** 1935-1984 **CLC 1, 3, 5, 9, 12, 34, 42; TCLC 133**
See also BPFB 1; CA 113; 53-56; CANR 34; DA3; DAM NOV; DLB 2, 5, 206; DLBY 1980, 1984; FANT; MTCW 1; RGAL 4; SATA 56

**Brave Bird, Mary NNAL**
See Crow Dog, Mary (Ellen)

**Braverman, Kate** 1950- **CLC 67**
See also CA 89-92

**Brecht, (Eugen) Bertolt (Friedrich)** 1898-1956 **DC 3; TCLC 1, 6, 13, 35; WLC**
See also CA 133; 104; CANR 62; CDWLB 2; DA; DA3; DAB; DAC; DAM DRAM, MST; DFS 4, 5, 9; DLB 56, 124; EW 11; EWL 3; IDTP; MTCW 1, 2; RGWL 2, 3; TWA

**Brecht, Eugen Berthold Friedrich**
See Brecht, (Eugen) Bertolt (Friedrich)

**Bremer, Fredrika** 1801-1865 **NCLC 11**
See also DLB 254

**Brennan, Christopher John** 1870-1932 **TCLC 17**
See also CA 188; 117; DLB 230; EWL 3

**Brennan, Maeve** 1917-1993 **CLC 5; TCLC 124**
See also CA 81-84; CANR 72, 100

**Brent, Linda**
See Jacobs, Harriet A(nn)

**Brentano, Clemens (Maria)** 1778-1842 **NCLC 1**
See also DLB 90; RGWL 2, 3

**Brent of Bin Bin**
See Franklin, (Stella Maria Sarah) Miles (Lampe)

**Brenton, Howard** 1942- **CLC 31**
See also CA 69-72; CANR 33, 67; CBD; CD 5; DLB 13; MTCW 1

**Breslin, James** 1930-
See Breslin, Jimmy
See also CA 73-76; CANR 31, 75; DAM NOV; MTCW 1, 2

**Breslin, Jimmy CLC 4, 43**
See Breslin, James
See also AITN 1; DLB 185; MTCW 2

**Bresson, Robert** 1901(?)-1999 **CLC 16**
See also CA 187; 110; CANR 49
**Breton, Andre** 1896-1966 **CLC 2, 9, 15, 54; PC 15**
See also CA 25-28R; 19-20; CANR 40, 60; CAP 2; DLB 65, 258; EW 11; EWL 3; GFL 1789 to the Present; MTCW 1, 2; RGWL 2, 3; TWA; WP
**Breytenbach, Breyten** 1939(?)- **CLC 23, 37, 126**
See also CA 129; 113; CANR 61; CWW 2; DAM POET; DLB 225; EWL 3
**Bridgers, Sue Ellen** 1942- **CLC 26**
See also AAYA 8; BYA 7, 8; CA 65-68; CANR 11, 36; CLR 18; DLB 52; JRDA; MAICYA 1, 2; SAAS 1; SATA 22, 90; SATA-Essay 109; WYA; YAW
**Bridges, Robert (Seymour)** 1844-1930 **PC 28; TCLC 1**
See also BRW 6; CA 152; 104; CDBLB 1890-1914; DAM POET; DLB 19, 98
**Bridie, James TCLC 3**
See Mavor, Osborne Henry
See also DLB 10; EWL 3
**Brin, David** 1950- **CLC 34**
See also AAYA 21; CA 102; CANR 24, 70; INT CANR-24; SATA 65; SCFW 2; SFW 4
**Brink, Andre (Philippus)** 1935- **CLC 18, 36, 106**
See also AFW; BRWS 6; CA 104; CANR 39, 62, 109; CN 7; DLB 225; EWL 3; INT CA-103; MTCW 1, 2; WLIT 2
**Brinsmead, H. F(ay)**
See Brinsmead, H(esba) F(ay)
**Brinsmead, H. F.**
See Brinsmead, H(esba) F(ay)
**Brinsmead, H(esba) F(ay)** 1922- **CLC 21**
See also CA 21-24R; CANR 10; CLR 47; CWRI 5; MAICYA 1, 2; SAAS 5; SATA 18, 78
**Brittain, Vera (Mary)** 1893(?)-1970 **CLC 23**
See also CA 25-28R; 13-16; CANR 58; CAP 1; DLB 191; FW; MTCW 1, 2
**Broch, Hermann** 1886-1951 **TCLC 20**
See also CA 117; CDWLB 2; DLB 85, 124; EW 10; EWL 3; RGWL 2, 3
**Brock, Rose**
See Hansen, Joseph
See also GLL 1
**Brod, Max** 1884-1968 **TCLC 115**
See also CA 25-28R; 5-8R; CANR 7; DLB 81; EWL 3
**Brodkey, Harold (Roy)** 1930-1996 **CLC 56; TCLC 123**
See also CA 151; 111; CANR 71; CN 7; DLB 130
**Brodskii, Iosif**
See Brodsky, Joseph
**Brodsky, Iosif Alexandrovich** 1940-1996
See Brodsky, Joseph
See also AITN 1; CA 151; 41-44R; CANR 37, 106; DA3; DAM POET; MTCW 1, 2; RGWL 2, 3
**Brodsky, Joseph CLC 4, 6, 13, 36, 100; PC 9**
See Brodsky, Iosif Alexandrovich
See also AMWS 8; CWW 2; EWL 3; MTCW 1
**Brodsky, Michael (Mark)** 1948- **CLC 19**
See also CA 102; CANR 18, 41, 58; DLB 244
**Brodzki, Bella ed. CLC 65**
**Brome, Richard** 1590(?)-1652 **LC 61**
See also DLB 58
**Bromell, Henry** 1947- **CLC 5**
See also CA 53-56; CANR 9, 115, 116

**Bromfield, Louis (Brucker)** 1896-1956 **TCLC 11**
See also CA 155; 107; DLB 4, 9, 86; RGAL 4; RHW
**Broner, E(sther) M(asserman)** 1930- **CLC 19**
See also CA 17-20R; CANR 8, 25, 72; CN 7; DLB 28
**Bronk, William (M.)** 1918-1999 **CLC 10**
See also CA 177; 89-92; CANR 23; CP 7; DLB 165
**Bronstein, Lev Davidovich**
See Trotsky, Leon
**Bronte, Anne** 1820-1849 **NCLC 4, 71, 102**
See also BRW 5; BRWR 1; DA3; DLB 21, 199; TEA
**Bronte, (Patrick) Branwell** 1817-1848 **NCLC 109**
**Bronte, Charlotte** 1816-1855 **NCLC 3, 8, 33, 58, 105; WLC**
See also AAYA 17; BRW 5; BRWR 1; BYA 2; CDBLB 1832-1890; DA; DA3; DAB; DAC; DAM MST, NOV; DLB 21, 159, 199; EXPN; LAIT 2; NFS 4; TEA; WLIT 4
**Bronte, Emily (Jane)** 1818-1848 **NCLC 16, 35; PC 8; WLC**
See also AAYA 17; BPFB 1; BRW 5; BRWC 1; BRWR 1; BYA 3; CDBLB 1832-1890; DA; DA3; DAB; DAC; DAM MST, NOV, POET; DLB 21, 32, 199; EXPN; LAIT 1; TEA; WLIT 3
**Brontes**
See Bronte, Anne; Bronte, Charlotte; Bronte, Emily (Jane)
**Brooke, Frances** 1724-1789 **LC 6, 48**
See also DLB 39, 99
**Brooke, Henry** 1703(?)-1783 **LC 1**
See also DLB 39
**Brooke, Rupert (Chawner)** 1887-1915 **PC 24; TCLC 2, 7; WLC**
See also BRWS 3; CA 132; 104; CANR 61; CDBLB 1914-1945; DA; DAB; DAC; DAM MST, POET; DLB 19, 216; EXPP; GLL 2; MTCW 1, 2; PFS 7; TEA
**Brooke-Haven, P.**
See Wodehouse, P(elham) G(renville)
**Brooke-Rose, Christine** 1926(?)- **CLC 40**
See also BRWS 4; CA 13-16R; CANR 58; CN 7; DLB 14, 231; EWL 3; SFW 4
**Brookner, Anita** 1928- **CLC 32, 34, 51, 136**
See also BRWS 4; CA 120; 114; CANR 37, 56, 87; CN 7; CPW; DA3; DAB; DAM POP; DLB 194; DLBY 1987; EWL 3; MTCW 1, 2; TEA
**Brooks, Cleanth** 1906-1994 **CLC 24, 86, 110**
See also CA 145; 17-20R; CANR 33, 35; CSW; DLB 63; DLBY 1994; EWL 3; INT CANR-35; MTCW 1, 2
**Brooks, George**
See Baum, L(yman) Frank
**Brooks, Gwendolyn (Elizabeth)** 1917-2000 **BLC 1; CLC 1, 2, 4, 5, 15, 49, 125; PC 7; WLC**
See also AAYA 20; AFAW 1, 2; AITN 1; AMWS 3; BW 2, 3; CA 190; 1-4R; CANR 1, 27, 52, 75; CDALB 1941-1968; CLR 27; CP 7; CWP; DA; DA3; DAC; DAM MST, MULT, POET; DLB 5, 76, 165; EWL 3; EXPP; MAWW; MTCW 1, 2; PFS 1, 2, 4, 6; RGAL 4; SATA 6; SATA-Obit 123; TUS; WP
**Brooks, Mel CLC 12**
See Kaminsky, Melvin
See also AAYA 13; DLB 26
**Brooks, Peter (Preston)** 1938- **CLC 34**
See also CA 45-48; CANR 1, 107
**Brooks, Van Wyck** 1886-1963 **CLC 29**
See also AMW; CA 1-4R; CANR 6; DLB 45, 63, 103; TUS

**Brophy, Brigid (Antonia)** 1929-1995 **CLC 6, 11, 29, 105**
See also CA 149; 5-8R; CAAS 4; CANR 25, 53; CBD; CN 7; CWD; DA3; DLB 14, 271; EWL 3; MTCW 1, 2
**Brosman, Catharine Savage** 1934- **CLC 9**
See also CA 61-64; CANR 21, 46
**Brossard, Nicole** 1943- **CLC 115, 169**
See also CA 122; CAAS 16; CCA 1; CWP; CWW 2; DLB 53; EWL 3; FW; GLL 2; RGWL 3
**Brother Antoninus**
See Everson, William (Oliver)
**The Brothers Quay**
See Quay, Stephen; Quay, Timothy
**Broughton, T(homas) Alan** 1936- **CLC 19**
See also CA 45-48; CANR 2, 23, 48, 111
**Broumas, Olga** 1949- **CLC 10, 73**
See also CA 85-88; CANR 20, 69, 110; CP 7; CWP; GLL 2
**Broun, Heywood** 1888-1939 **TCLC 104**
See also DLB 29, 171
**Brown, Alan** 1950- **CLC 99**
See also CA 156
**Brown, Charles Brockden** 1771-1810 **NCLC 22, 74, 122**
See also AMWS 1; CDALB 1640-1865; DLB 37, 59, 73; FW; HGG; RGAL 4; TUS
**Brown, Christy** 1932-1981 **CLC 63**
See also BYA 13; CA 104; 105; CANR 72; DLB 14
**Brown, Claude** 1937-2002 **BLC 1; CLC 30**
See also AAYA 7; BW 1, 3; CA 205; 73-76; CANR 81; DAM MULT
**Brown, Dee (Alexander)** 1908- **CLC 18, 47**
See also AAYA 30; CA 13-16R; CAAS 6; CANR 11, 45, 60; CPW; CSW; DA3; DAM POP; DLBY 1980; LAIT 2; MTCW 1, 2; SATA 5, 110; TCWW 2
**Brown, George**
See Wertmueller, Lina
**Brown, George Douglas** 1869-1902 **TCLC 28**
See Douglas, George
See also CA 162
**Brown, George Mackay** 1921-1996 **CLC 5, 48, 100**
See also BRWS 6; CA 151; 21-24R; CAAS 6; CANR 12, 37, 67; CN 7; CP 7; DLB 14, 27, 139, 271; MTCW 1; RGSF 2; SATA 35
**Brown, (William) Larry** 1951- **CLC 73**
See also CA 134; 130; CANR 117; CSW; DLB 234; INT 133
**Brown, Moses**
See Barrett, William (Christopher)
**Brown, Rita Mae** 1944- **CLC 18, 43, 79**
See also BPFB 1; CA 45-48; CANR 2, 11, 35, 62, 95; CN 7; CPW; CSW; DA3; DAM NOV, POP; FW; INT CANR-11; MTCW 1, 2; NFS 9; RGAL 4; TUS
**Brown, Roderick (Langmere) Haig-**
See Haig-Brown, Roderick (Langmere)
**Brown, Rosellen** 1939- **CLC 32, 170**
See also CA 77-80; CAAS 10; CANR 14, 44, 98; CN 7
**Brown, Sterling Allen** 1901-1989 **BLC 1; CLC 1, 23, 59; HR 2**
See also AFAW 1, 2; BW 1, 3; CA 127; 85-88; CANR 26; DA3; DAM MULT, POET; DLB 48, 51, 63; MTCW 1, 2; RGAL 4; WP
**Brown, Will**
See Ainsworth, William Harrison
**Brown, William Wells** 1815-1884 **BLC 1; DC 1; NCLC 2, 89**
See also DAM MULT; DLB 3, 50, 183, 248; RGAL 4

**Browne, (Clyde) Jackson** 1948(?)- **CLC 21**
See also CA 120

**Browning, Elizabeth Barrett** 1806-1861
**NCLC 1, 16, 61, 66; PC 6; WLC**
See also BRW 4; CDBLB 1832-1890; DA;
DA3; DAB; DAC; DAM MST, POET;
DLB 32, 199; EXPP; PAB; PFS 2, 16;
TEA; WLIT 4; WP

**Browning, Robert** 1812-1889 **NCLC 19, 79;
PC 2; WLCS**
See also BRW 4; BRWR 2; CDBLB 1832-
1890; DA; DA3; DAB; DAC; DAM MST,
POET; DLB 32, 163; EXPP; PAB; PFS 1,
15; RGEL 2; TEA; WLIT 4; WP; YABC
1

**Browning, Tod** 1882-1962 **CLC 16**
See also CA 117; 141

**Brownmiller, Susan** 1935- **CLC 159**
See also CA 103; CANR 35, 75; DAM
NOV; FW; MTCW 1, 2

**Brownson, Orestes Augustus** 1803-1876
**NCLC 50**
See also DLB 1, 59, 73, 243

**Bruccoli, Matthew J(oseph)** 1931- **CLC 34**
See also CA 9-12R; CANR 7, 87; DLB 103

**Bruce, Lenny CLC 21**
See Schneider, Leonard Alfred

**Bruchac, Joseph III** 1942- **NNAL**
See also AAYA 19; CA 33-36R; CANR 13,
47, 75, 94; CLR 46; CWRI 5; DAM
MULT; JRDA; MAICYA 2; MAICYAS 1;
MTCW 1; SATA 42, 89, 131

**Bruin, John**
See Brutus, Dennis

**Brulard, Henri**
See Stendhal

**Brulls, Christian**
See Simenon, Georges (Jacques Christian)

**Brunner, John (Kilian Houston)** 1934-1995
**CLC 8, 10**
See also CA 149; 1-4R; CAAS 8; CANR 2,
37; CPW; DAM POP; DLB 261; MTCW
1, 2; SCFW 2; SFW 4

**Bruno, Giordano** 1548-1600 **LC 27**
See also RGWL 2, 3

**Brutus, Dennis** 1924- **BLC 1; CLC 43; PC
24**
See also AFW; BW 2, 3; CA 49-52; CAAS
14; CANR 2, 27, 42, 81; CDWLB 3; CP
7; DAM MULT, POET; DLB 117, 225;
EWL 3

**Bryan, C(ourtlandt) D(ixon) B(arnes)** 1936-
**CLC 29**
See also CA 73-76; CANR 13, 68; DLB
185; INT CANR-13

**Bryan, Michael**
See Moore, Brian
See also CCA 1

**Bryan, William Jennings** 1860-1925 **TCLC
99**

**Bryant, William Cullen** 1794-1878 **NCLC 6,
46; PC 20**
See also AMWS 1; CDALB 1640-1865;
DA; DAB; DAC; DAM MST, POET;
DLB 3, 43, 59, 189, 250; EXPP; PAB;
RGAL 4; TUS

**Bryusov, Valery Yakovlevich** 1873-1924
**TCLC 10**
See also CA 155; 107; EWL 3; SFW 4

**Buchan, John** 1875-1940 **TCLC 41**
See also CA 145; 108; CMW 4; DAB;
DAM POP; DLB 34, 70, 156; HGG;
MSW; MTCW 1; RGEL 2; RHW; YABC
2

**Buchanan, George** 1506-1582 **LC 4**
See also DLB 132

**Buchanan, Robert** 1841-1901 **TCLC 107**
See also CA 179; DLB 18, 35

**Buchheim, Lothar-Guenther** 1918- **CLC 6**
See also CA 85-88

**Buchner, (Karl) Georg** 1813-1837 **NCLC 26**
See also CDWLB 2; DLB 133; EW 6;
RGSF 2; RGWL 2, 3; TWA

**Buchwald, Art(hur)** 1925- **CLC 33**
See also AITN 1; CA 5-8R; CANR 21, 67,
107; MTCW 1, 2; SATA 10

**Buck, Pearl S(ydenstricker)** 1892-1973 **CLC
7, 11, 18, 127**
See also AAYA 42; AITN 1; AMWS 2;
BPFB 1; CA 41-44R; 1-4R; CANR 1, 34;
CDALBS; DA; DA3; DAB; DAC; DAM
MST, NOV; DLB 9, 102; EWL 3; LAIT
3; MTCW 1, 2; RGAL 4; RHW; SATA 1,
25; TUS

**Buckler, Ernest** 1908-1984 **CLC 13**
See also CA 114; 11-12; CAP 1; CCA 1;
DAC; DAM MST; DLB 68; SATA 47

**Buckley, Christopher (Taylor)** 1952- **CLC
165**
See also CA 139

**Buckley, Vincent (Thomas)** 1925-1988 **CLC
57**
See also CA 101

**Buckley, William F(rank), Jr.** 1925- **CLC 7,
18, 37**
See also AITN 1; BPFB 1; CA 1-4R; CANR
1, 24, 53, 93; CMW 4; CPW; DA3; DAM
POP; DLB 137; DLBY 1980; INT CANR-
24; MTCW 1, 2; TUS

**Buechner, (Carl) Frederick** 1926- **CLC 2, 4,
6, 9**
See also AMWS 12; BPFB 1; CA 13-16R;
CANR 11, 39, 64, 114; CN 7; DAM NOV;
DLBY 1980; INT CANR-11; MTCW 1, 2

**Buell, John (Edward)** 1927- **CLC 10**
See also CA 1-4R; CANR 71; DLB 53

**Buero Vallejo, Antonio** 1916-2000 **CLC 15,
46, 139; DC 18**
See also CA 189; 106; CANR 24, 49, 75;
DFS 11; EWL 3; HW 1; MTCW 1, 2

**Bufalino, Gesualdo** 1920(?)-1990 **CLC 74**
See also CWW 2; DLB 196

**Bugayev, Boris Nikolayevich** 1880-1934 **PC
11; TCLC 7**
See Bely, Andrey; Belyi, Andrei
See also CA 165; 104; MTCW 1

**Bukowski, Charles** 1920-1994 **CLC 2, 5, 9,
41, 82, 108; PC 18; SSC 45**
See also CA 144; 17-20R; CANR 40, 62,
105; CPW; DA3; DAM NOV, POET;
DLB 5, 130, 169; EWL 3; MTCW 1, 2

**Bulgakov, Mikhail (Afanas'evich)** 1891-1940
**SSC 18; TCLC 2, 16**
See also BPFB 1; CA 152; 105; DAM
DRAM, NOV; DLB 272; EWL 3; NFS 8;
RGSF 2; RGWL 2, 3; SFW 4; TWA

**Bulgya, Alexander Alexandrovich** 1901-1956
**TCLC 53**
See Fadeev, Aleksandr Aleksandrovich;
Fadeev, Alexandr Alexandrovich; Fadeyev,
Alexander
See also CA 181; 117

**Bullins, Ed** 1935- **BLC 1; CLC 1, 5, 7; DC 6**
See also BW 2, 3; CA 49-52; CAAS 16;
CAD; CANR 24, 46, 73; CD 5; DAM
DRAM, MULT; DLB 7, 38, 249; EWL 3;
MTCW 1, 2; RGAL 4

**Bulosan, Carlos** 1911-1956 **AAL**
See also RGAL 4

**Bulwer-Lytton, Edward (George Earle
Lytton)** 1803-1873 **NCLC 1, 45**
See also DLB 21; RGEL 2; SFW 4; SUFW
1; TEA

**Bunin, Ivan Alexeyevich** 1870-1953 **SSC 5;
TCLC 6**
See also CA 104; EWL 3; RGSF 2; RGWL
2, 3; TWA

**Bunting, Basil** 1900-1985 **CLC 10, 39, 47**
See also BRWS 7; CA 115; 53-56; CANR
7; DAM POET; DLB 20; EWL 3; RGEL
2

**Bunuel, Luis** 1900-1983 **CLC 16, 80; HLC 1**
See also CA 110; 101; CANR 32, 77; DAM
MULT; HW 1

**Bunyan, John** 1628-1688 **LC 4, 69; WLC**
See also BRW 2; BYA 5; CDBLB 1660-
1789; DA; DAB; DAC; DAM MST; DLB
39; RGEL 2; TEA; WCH; WLIT 3

**Buravsky, Alexandr CLC 59**

**Burckhardt, Jacob (Christoph)** 1818-1897
**NCLC 49**
See also EW 6

**Burford, Eleanor**
See Hibbert, Eleanor Alice Burford

**Burgess, Anthony CLC 1, 2, 4, 5, 8, 10, 13,
15, 22, 40, 62, 81, 94**
See Wilson, John (Anthony) Burgess
See also AAYA 25; AITN 1; BRWS 1; CD-
BLB 1960 to Present; DAB; DLB 14, 194,
261; DLBY 1998; EWL 3; MTCW 1;
RGEL 2; RHW; SFW 4; YAW

**Burke, Edmund** 1729(?)-1797 **LC 7, 36;
WLC**
See also BRW 3; DA; DA3; DAB; DAC;
DAM MST; DLB 104, 252; RGEL 2;
TEA

**Burke, Kenneth (Duva)** 1897-1993 **CLC 2,
24**
See also AMW; CA 143; 5-8R; CANR 39,
74; DLB 45, 63; EWL 3; MTCW 1, 2;
RGAL 4

**Burke, Leda**
See Garnett, David

**Burke, Ralph**
See Silverberg, Robert

**Burke, Thomas** 1886-1945 **TCLC 63**
See also CA 155; 113; CMW 4; DLB 197

**Burney, Fanny** 1752-1840 **NCLC 12, 54, 107**
See also BRWS 3; DLB 39; NFS 16; RGEL
2; TEA

**Burney, Frances**
See Burney, Fanny

**Burns, Robert** 1759-1796 **LC 3, 29, 40; PC 6;
WLC**
See also BRW 3; CDBLB 1789-1832; DA;
DA3; DAB; DAC; DAM MST, POET;
DLB 109; EXPP; PAB; RGEL 2; TEA;
WP

**Burns, Tex**
See L'Amour, Louis (Dearborn)
See also TCWW 2

**Burnshaw, Stanley** 1906- **CLC 3, 13, 44**
See also CA 9-12R; CP 7; DLB 48; DLBY
1997

**Burr, Anne** 1937- **CLC 6**
See also CA 25-28R

**Burroughs, Edgar Rice** 1875-1950 **TCLC 2,
32**
See also AAYA 11; BPFB 1; BYA 4, 9; CA
132; 104; DA3; DAM NOV; DLB 8;
FANT; MTCW 1, 2; RGAL 4; SATA 41;
SCFW 2; SFW 4; TUS; YAW

**Burroughs, William S(eward)** 1914-1997
**CLC 1, 2, 5, 15, 22, 42, 75, 109; TCLC
121; WLC**
See Lee, William; Lee, Willy
See also AITN 2; AMWS 3; BG 2; BPFB
1; CA 160; 9-12R; CANR 20, 52, 104;
CN 7; CPW; DA; DA3; DAB; DAC;
DAM MST, NOV, POP; DLB 2, 8, 16,
152, 237; DLBY 1981, 1997; EWL 3;
HGG; LMFS 2; MTCW 1, 2; RGAL 4;
SFW 4

**Burton, Sir Richard F(rancis)** 1821-1890
**NCLC 42**
See also DLB 55, 166, 184

WLB 3; DAM MULT; DLB 113; EWL 3; FW; HW 1; LAW; MTCW 1; RGSF 2; RGWL 2, 3

**Castelvetro, Lodovico** 1505-1571 **LC 12**

**Castiglione, Baldassare** 1478-1529 **LC 12**
See Castiglione, Baldesar
See also RGWL 2, 3

**Castiglione, Baldesar**
See Castiglione, Baldassare
See also EW 2

**Castillo, Ana (Hernandez Del)** 1953- **CLC 151**
See also AAYA 42; CA 131; CANR 51, 86; CWP; DLB 122, 227; DNFS 2; FW; HW 1

**Castle, Robert**
See Hamilton, Edmond

**Castro (Ruz), Fidel** 1926(?)- **HLC 1**
See also CA 129; 110; CANR 81; DAM MULT; HW 2

**Castro, Guillen de** 1569-1631 **LC 19**

**Castro, Rosalia de** 1837-1885 **NCLC 3, 78; PC 41**
See also DAM MULT

**Cather, Willa (Sibert)** 1873-1947 **SSC 2, 50; TCLC 1, 11, 31, 99, 132; WLC**
See also AAYA 24; AMW; AMWC 1; AMWR 1; BPFB 1; CA 128; 104; CDALB 1865-1917; DA; DA3; DAB; DAC; DAM MST, NOV; DLB 9, 54, 78, 256; DLBD 1; EWL 3; EXPN; EXPS; LAIT 3; MAWW; MTCW 1, 2; NFS 2; RGAL 4; RGSF 2; RHW; SATA 30; SSFS 2, 7, 16; TCWW 2; TUS

**Catherine II**
See Catherine the Great
See also DLB 150

**Catherine the Great** 1729-1796 **LC 69**
See Catherine II

**Cato, Marcus Porcius** 234B.C.-149B.C. **CMLC 21**
See Cato the Elder

**Cato, Marcus Porcius, the Elder**
See Cato, Marcus Porcius

**Cato the Elder**
See Cato, Marcus Porcius
See also DLB 211

**Catton, (Charles) Bruce** 1899-1978 **CLC 35**
See also AITN 1; CA 81-84; 5-8R; CANR 7, 74; DLB 17; SATA 2; SATA-Obit 24

**Catullus** c. 84B.C.-54B.C. **CMLC 18**
See also AW 2; CDWLB 1; DLB 211; RGWL 2, 3

**Cauldwell, Frank**
See King, Francis (Henry)

**Caunitz, William J.** 1933-1996 **CLC 34**
See also BEST 89:3; CA 152; 130; 125; CANR 73; INT 130

**Causley, Charles (Stanley)** 1917- **CLC 7**
See also CA 9-12R; CANR 5, 35, 94; CLR 30; CWRI 5; DLB 27; MTCW 1; SATA 3, 66

**Caute, (John) David** 1936- **CLC 29**
See also CA 1-4R; CAAS 4; CANR 1, 33, 64; CBD; CD 5; CN 7; DAM NOV; DLB 14, 231

**Cavafy, C(onstantine) P(eter)** **PC 36; TCLC 2, 7**
See Kavafis, Konstantinos Petrou
See also CA 148; DA3; DAM POET; EW 8; EWL 3; MTCW 1; RGWL 2, 3; WP

**Cavalcanti, Guido** c. 1250-c. 1300 **CMLC 54**

**Cavallo, Evelyn**
See Spark, Muriel (Sarah)

**Cavanna, Betty** **CLC 12**
See Harrison, Elizabeth (Allen) Cavanna
See also JRDA; MAICYA 1; SAAS 4; SATA 1, 30

**Cavendish, Margaret Lucas** 1623-1673 **LC 30**
See also DLB 131, 252; RGEL 2

**Caxton, William** 1421(?)-1491(?) **LC 17**
See also DLB 170

**Cayer, D. M.**
See Duffy, Maureen

**Cayrol, Jean** 1911- **CLC 11**
See also CA 89-92; DLB 83; EWL 3

**Cela, Camilo Jose** 1916-2002 **CLC 4, 13, 59, 122; HLC 1**
See also BEST 90:2; CA 206; 21-24R; CAAS 10; CANR 21, 32, 76; DAM MULT; DLBY 1989; EW 13; EWL 3; HW 1; MTCW 1, 2; RGSF 2; RGWL 2, 3

**Celan, Paul** **CLC 10, 19, 53, 82; PC 10**
See Antschel, Paul
See also CDWLB 2; DLB 69; EWL 3; RGWL 2, 3

**Celine, Louis-Ferdinand** **CLC 1, 3, 4, 7, 9, 15, 47, 124**
See Destouches, Louis-Ferdinand
See also DLB 72; EW 11; EWL 3; GFL 1789 to the Present; RGWL 2, 3

**Cellini, Benvenuto** 1500-1571 **LC 7**

**Cendrars, Blaise** **CLC 18, 106**
See Sauser-Hall, Frederic
See also DLB 258; EWL 3; GFL 1789 to the Present; RGWL 2, 3; WP

**Centlivre, Susanna** 1669(?)-1723 **LC 65**
See also DLB 84; RGEL 2

**Cernuda (y Bidon), Luis** 1902-1963 **CLC 54**
See also CA 89-92; 131; DAM POET; DLB 134; EWL 3; GLL 1; HW 1; RGWL 2, 3

**Cervantes, Lorna Dee** 1954- **HLCS 1; PC 35**
See also CA 131; CANR 80; CWP; DLB 82; EXPP; HW 1

**Cervantes (Saavedra), Miguel de** 1547-1616 **HLCS; LC 6, 23; SSC 12; WLC**
See also BYA 1, 14; DA; DAB; DAC; DAM MST, NOV; EW 2; LAIT 1; NFS 8; RGSF 2; RGWL 2, 3; TWA

**Chabon, Michael** 1963- **CLC 55, 149; SSC 59**
See also AAYA 45; AMWS 11; CA 139; CANR 57, 96; DLB 278

**Chabrol, Claude** 1930- **CLC 16**
See also CA 110

**Chairil Anwar**
See Anwar, Chairil
See also EWL 3

**Challans, Mary** 1905-1983
See Renault, Mary
See also CA 111; 81-84; CANR 74; DA3; MTCW 2; SATA 23; SATA-Obit 36; TEA

**Challis, George**
See Faust, Frederick (Schiller)
See also TCWW 2

**Chambers, Aidan** 1934- **CLC 35**
See also AAYA 27; CA 25-28R; CANR 12, 31, 58, 116; JRDA; MAICYA 1, 2; SAAS 12; SATA 1, 69, 108; WYA; YAW

**Chambers, James** 1948-
See Cliff, Jimmy
See also CA 124

**Chambers, Jessie**
See Lawrence, D(avid) H(erbert Richards)
See also GLL 1

**Chambers, Robert W(illiam)** 1865-1933 **TCLC 41**
See also CA 165; DLB 202; HGG; SATA 107; SUFW 1

**Chambers, (David) Whittaker** 1901-1961 **TCLC 129**
See also CA 89-92

**Chamisso, Adelbert von** 1781-1838 **NCLC 82**
See also DLB 90; RGWL 2, 3; SUFW 1

**Chance, James T.**
See Carpenter, John (Howard)

**Chance, John T.**
See Carpenter, John (Howard)

**Chandler, Raymond (Thornton)** 1888-1959 **SSC 23; TCLC 1, 7**
See also AAYA 25; AMWS 4; BPFB 1; CA 129; 104; CANR 60, 107; CDALB 1929-1941; CMW 4; DA3; DLB 226, 253; DLBD 6; EWL 3; MSW; MTCW 1, 2; NFS 17; RGAL 4; TUS

**Chang, Diana** 1934- **AAL**
See also CWP; EXPP

**Chang, Eileen** 1921-1995 **AAL; SSC 28**
See Chang Ai-Ling
See also CA 166; CWW 2

**Chang, Jung** 1952- **CLC 71**
See also CA 142

**Chang Ai-Ling**
See Chang, Eileen
See also EWL 3

**Channing, William Ellery** 1780-1842 **NCLC 17**
See also DLB 1, 59, 235; RGAL 4

**Chao, Patricia** 1955- **CLC 119**
See also CA 163

**Chaplin, Charles Spencer** 1889-1977 **CLC 16**
See Chaplin, Charlie
See also CA 73-76; 81-84

**Chaplin, Charlie**
See Chaplin, Charles Spencer
See also DLB 44

**Chapman, George** 1559(?)-1634 **DC 19; LC 22**
See also BRW 1; DAM DRAM; DLB 62, 121; RGEL 2

**Chapman, Graham** 1941-1989 **CLC 21**
See Monty Python
See also CA 129; 116; CANR 35, 95

**Chapman, John Jay** 1862-1933 **TCLC 7**
See also CA 191; 104

**Chapman, Lee**
See Bradley, Marion Zimmer
See also GLL 1

**Chapman, Walker**
See Silverberg, Robert

**Chappell, Fred (Davis)** 1936- **CLC 40, 78, 162**
See also CA 5-8R; CAAE 198; CAAS 4; CANR 8, 33, 67, 110; CN 7; CP 7; CSW; DLB 6, 105; HGG

**Char, Rene(-Emile)** 1907-1988 **CLC 9, 11, 14, 55**
See also CA 124; 13-16R; CANR 32; DAM POET; DLB 258; EWL 3; GFL 1789 to the Present; MTCW 1, 2; RGWL 2, 3

**Charby, Jay**
See Ellison, Harlan (Jay)

**Chardin, Pierre Teilhard de**
See Teilhard de Chardin, (Marie Joseph) Pierre

**Chariton** fl. 1st cent. (?)- **CMLC 49**

**Charlemagne** 742-814 **CMLC 37**

**Charles I** 1600-1649 **LC 13**

**Charriere, Isabelle de** 1740-1805 **NCLC 66**

**Chartier, Emile-Auguste**
See Alain

**Charyn, Jerome** 1937- **CLC 5, 8, 18**
See also CA 5-8R; CAAS 1; CANR 7, 61, 101; CMW 4; CN 7; DLBY 1983; MTCW 1

**Chase, Adam**
See Marlowe, Stephen
**Chase, Mary (Coyle)** 1907-1981 **DC 1**
See also CA 105; 77-80; CAD; CWD; DFS
11; DLB 228; SATA 17; SATA-Obit 29
**Chase, Mary Ellen** 1887-1973 **CLC 2; TCLC 124**
See also CA 41-44R; 13-16; CAP 1; SATA 10
**Chase, Nicholas**
See Hyde, Anthony
See also CCA 1
**Chateaubriand, Francois Rene de** 1768-1848 **NCLC 3**
See also DLB 119; EW 5; GFL 1789 to the Present; RGWL 2, 3; TWA
**Chatterje, Sarat Chandra** 1876-1936(?)
See Chatterji, Saratchandra
See also CA 109
**Chatterji, Bankim Chandra** 1838-1894 **NCLC 19**
**Chatterji, Saratchandra TCLC 13**
See Chatterje, Sarat Chandra
See also CA 186; EWL 3
**Chatterton, Thomas** 1752-1770 **LC 3, 54**
See also DAM POET; DLB 109; RGEL 2
**Chatwin, (Charles) Bruce** 1940-1989 **CLC 28, 57, 59**
See also AAYA 4; BEST 90:1; BRWS 4;
CA 127; 85-88; CPW; DAM POP; DLB 194, 204; EWL 3
**Chaucer, Daniel**
See Ford, Ford Madox
See also RHW
**Chaucer, Geoffrey** 1340(?)-1400 **LC 17, 56; PC 19; WLCS**
See also BRW 1; BRWC 1; BRWR 2; CD-
BLB Before 1660; DA; DA3; DAB;
DAC; DAM MST, POET; DLB 146;
LAIT 1; PAB; PFS 14; RGEL 2; TEA;
WLIT 3; WP
**Chavez, Denise (Elia)** 1948- **HLC 1**
See also CA 131; CANR 56, 81; DAM
MULT; DLB 122; FW; HW 1, 2; MTCW 2
**Chaviaras, Strates** 1935-
See Haviaras, Stratis
See also CA 105
**Chayefsky, Paddy CLC 23**
See Chayefsky, Sidney
See also CAD; DLB 7, 44; DLBY 1981;
RGAL 4
**Chayefsky, Sidney** 1923-1981
See Chayefsky, Paddy
See also CA 104; 9-12R; CANR 18; DAM
DRAM
**Chedid, Andree** 1920- **CLC 47**
See also CA 145; CANR 95; EWL 3
**Cheever, John** 1912-1982 **CLC 3, 7, 8, 11, 15, 25, 64; SSC 1, 38, 57; WLC**
See also AMWS 1; BPFB 1; CA 106; 5-8R;
CABS 1; CANR 5, 27, 76; CDALB 1941-
1968; CPW; DA; DA3; DAB; DAC;
DAM MST, NOV, POP; DLB 2, 102, 227;
DLBY 1980, 1982; EWL 3; EXPS; INT
CANR-5; MTCW 1, 2; RGAL 4; RGSF
2; SSFS 2, 14; TUS
**Cheever, Susan** 1943- **CLC 18, 48**
See also CA 103; CANR 27, 51, 92; DLBY
1982; INT CANR-27
**Chekhonte, Antosha**
See Chekhov, Anton (Pavlovich)
**Chekhov, Anton (Pavlovich)** 1860-1904 **DC 9; SSC 2, 28, 41, 51; TCLC 3, 10, 31, 55, 96; WLC**
See also BYA 14; CA 124; 104; DA; DA3;
DAB; DAC; DAM DRAM, MST; DFS 1,
5, 10, 12; DLB 277; EW 7; EWL 3;
EXPS; LAIT 3; RGSF 2; RGWL 2, 3;
SATA 90; SSFS 5, 13, 14; TWA

**Cheney, Lynne V.** 1941- **CLC 70**
See also CA 89-92; CANR 58, 117
**Chernyshevsky, Nikolai Gavrilovich**
See Chernyshevsky, Nikolay Gavrilovich
See also DLB 238
**Chernyshevsky, Nikolay Gavrilovich** 1828-1889 **NCLC 1**
See Chernyshevsky, Nikolai Gavrilovich
**Cherry, Carolyn Janice** 1942-
See Cherryh, C. J.
See also CA 65-68; CANR 10
**Cherryh, C. J. CLC 35**
See Cherry, Carolyn Janice
See also AAYA 24; BPFB 1; DLBY 1980;
FANT; SATA 93; SCFW 2; SFW 4; YAW
**Chesnutt, Charles W(addell)** 1858-1932 **BLC 1; SSC 7, 54; TCLC 5, 39**
See also AFAW 1, 2; BW 1, 3; CA 125;
106; CANR 76; DAM MULT; DLB 12,
50, 78; EWL 3; MTCW 1, 2; RGAL 4;
RGSF 2; SSFS 11
**Chester, Alfred** 1929(?)-1971 **CLC 49**
See also CA 33-36R; 196; DLB 130
**Chesterton, G(ilbert) K(eith)** 1874-1936 **PC 28; SSC 1, 46; TCLC 1, 6, 64**
See also BRW 6; CA 132; 104; CANR 73;
CDBLB 1914-1945; CMW 4; DAM NOV,
POET; DLB 10, 19, 34, 70, 98, 149, 178;
EWL 3; FANT; MSW; MTCW 1, 2;
RGEL 2; RGSF 2; SATA 27; SUFW 1
**Chiang, Pin-chin** 1904-1986
See Ding Ling
See also CA 118
**Chief Joseph** 1840-1904 **NNAL**
See also CA 152; DA3; DAM MULT
**Chief Seattle** 1786(?)-1866 **NNAL**
See also DA3; DAM MULT
**Ch'ien, Chung-shu** 1910-1998 **CLC 22**
See also CA 130; CANR 73; MTCW 1, 2
**Chikamatsu Monzaemon** 1653-1724 **LC 66**
See also RGWL 2, 3
**Child, L. Maria**
See Child, Lydia Maria
**Child, Lydia Maria** 1802-1880 **NCLC 6, 73**
See also DLB 1, 74, 243; RGAL 4; SATA 67
**Child, Mrs.**
See Child, Lydia Maria
**Child, Philip** 1898-1978 **CLC 19, 68**
See also CA 13-14; CAP 1; DLB 68; RHW;
SATA 47
**Childers, (Robert) Erskine** 1870-1922 **TCLC 65**
See also CA 153; 113; DLB 70
**Childress, Alice** 1920-1994 **BLC 1; CLC 12, 15, 86, 96; DC 4; TCLC 116**
See also AAYA 8; BW 2, 3; BYA 2; CA
146; 45-48; CAD; CANR 3, 27, 50, 74;
CLR 14; CWD; DA3; DAM DRAM,
MULT, NOV; DFS 2, 8, 14; DLB 7, 38,
249; JRDA; LAIT 5; MAICYA 1, 2; MAI-
CYAS 1; MTCW 1, 2; RGAL 4; SATA 7,
48, 81; TUS; WYA; YAW
**Chin, Frank (Chew, Jr.)** 1940- **CLC 135; DC 7**
See also CA 33-36R; CANR 71; CD 5;
DAM MULT; DLB 206; LAIT 5; RGAL 4
**Chin, Marilyn (Mei Ling)** 1955- **PC 40**
See also CA 129; CANR 70, 113; CWP
**Chislett, (Margaret) Anne** 1943- **CLC 34**
See also CA 151
**Chitty, Thomas Willes** 1926- **CLC 11**
See Hinde, Thomas
See also CA 5-8R; CN 7
**Chivers, Thomas Holley** 1809-1858 **NCLC 49**
See also DLB 3, 248; RGAL 4
**Choi, Susan CLC 119**

**Chomette, Rene Lucien** 1898-1981
See Clair, Rene
See also CA 103
**Chomsky, (Avram) Noam** 1928- **CLC 132**
See also CA 17-20R; CANR 28, 62, 110;
DA3; DLB 246; MTCW 1, 2
**Chona, Maria** 1845(?)-1936 **NNAL**
See also CA 144
**Chopin, Kate SSC 8; TCLC 127; WLCS**
See Chopin, Katherine
See also AAYA 33; AMWR 2; AMWS 1;
CDALB 1865-1917; DA; DAB; DLB 12,
78; EXPN; EXPS; FW; LAIT 3; MAWW;
NFS 3; RGAL 4; RGSF 2; SSFS 17; TUS
**Chopin, Katherine** 1851-1904
See Chopin, Kate
See also CA 122; 104; DA3; DAC; DAM
MST, NOV
**Chretien de Troyes** c. 12th cent. - **CMLC 10**
See also DLB 208; EW 1; RGWL 2, 3;
TWA
**Christie**
See Ichikawa, Kon
**Christie, Agatha (Mary Clarissa)** 1890-1976 **CLC 1, 6, 8, 12, 39, 48, 110**
See also AAYA 9; AITN 1, 2; BPFB 1;
BRWS 2; CA 61-64; 17-20R; CANR 10,
37, 108; CBD; CDBLB 1914-1945; CMW
4; CPW; CWD; DA3; DAB; DAC; DAM
NOV; DFS 2; DLB 13, 77, 245; MSW;
MTCW 1, 2; NFS 8; RGEL 2; RHW;
SATA 36; TEA; YAW
**Christie, Philippa CLC 21**
See Pearce, Philippa
See also BYA 5; CANR 109; CLR 9; DLB
161; MAICYA 1; SATA 1, 67, 129
**Christine de Pizan** 1365(?)-1431(?) **LC 9**
See also DLB 208; RGWL 2, 3
**Chuang Tzu** c. 369B.C.-c. 286B.C. **CMLC 57**
**Chubb, Elmer**
See Masters, Edgar Lee
**Chulkov, Mikhail Dmitrievich** 1743-1792 **LC 2**
See also DLB 150
**Churchill, Caryl** 1938- **CLC 31, 55, 157; DC 5**
See also BRWS 4; CA 102; CANR 22, 46,
108; CBD; CWD; DFS 12, 16; DLB 13;
EWL 3; FW; MTCW 1; RGEL 2
**Churchill, Charles** 1731-1764 **LC 3**
See also DLB 109; RGEL 2
**Churchill, Sir Winston (Leonard Spencer)** 1874-1965 **TCLC 113**
See also BRW 6; CA 97-100; CDBLB
1890-1914; DA3; DLB 100; DLBD 16;
LAIT 4; MTCW 1, 2
**Chute, Carolyn** 1947- **CLC 39**
See also CA 123
**Ciardi, John (Anthony)** 1916-1986 **CLC 10, 40, 44, 129**
See also CA 118; 5-8R; CAAS 2; CANR 5,
33; CLR 19; CWRI 5; DAM POET; DLB
5; DLBY 1986; INT CANR-5; MAICYA
1, 2; MTCW 1, 2; RGAL 4; SAAS 26;
SATA 1, 65; SATA-Obit 46
**Cibber, Colley** 1671-1757 **LC 66**
See also DLB 84; RGEL 2
**Cicero, Marcus Tullius** 106B.C.-43B.C. **CMLC 3**
See also AW 1; CDWLB 1; DLB 211;
RGWL 2, 3
**Cimino, Michael** 1943- **CLC 16**
See also CA 105
**Cioran, E(mil) M.** 1911-1995 **CLC 64**
See also CA 149; 25-28R; CANR 91; DLB
220; EWL 3
**Cisneros, Sandra** 1954- **CLC 69, 118; HLC 1; SSC 32**
See also AAYA 9; AMWS 7; CA 131;
CANR 64; CWP; DA3; DAM MULT;

DLB 122, 152; EWL 3; EXPN; FW; HW
1, 2; LAIT 5; MAICYA 2; MTCW 2; NFS
2; RGAL 4; RGSF 2; SSFS 3, 13; WLIT
1; YAW

**Cixous, Helene** 1937- **CLC 92**
See also CA 126; CANR 55; CWW 2; DLB
83, 242; EWL 3; FW; GLL 2; MTCW 1,
2; TWA

**Clair, Rene CLC 20**
See Chomette, Rene Lucien

**Clampitt, Amy** 1920-1994 **CLC 32; PC 19**
See also AMWS 9; CA 146; 110; CANR
29, 79; DLB 105

**Clancy, Thomas L., Jr.** 1947-
See Clancy, Tom
See also CA 131; 125; CANR 62, 105;
DA3; INT CA-131; MTCW 1, 2

**Clancy, Tom CLC 45, 112**
See Clancy, Thomas L., Jr.
See also AAYA 9; BEST 89:1, 90:1; BPFB
1; BYA 10, 11; CMW 4; CPW; DAM
NOV, POP; DLB 227

**Clare, John** 1793-1864 **NCLC 9, 86; PC 23**
See also DAB; DAM POET; DLB 55, 96;
RGEL 2

**Clarin**
See Alas (y Urena), Leopoldo (Enrique
Garcia)

**Clark, Al C.**
See Goines, Donald

**Clark, (Robert) Brian** 1932- **CLC 29**
See also CA 41-44R; CANR 67; CBD; CD
5

**Clark, Curt**
See Westlake, Donald E(dwin)

**Clark, Eleanor** 1913-1996 **CLC 5, 19**
See also CA 151; 9-12R; CANR 41; CN 7;
DLB 6

**Clark, J. P.**
See Clark Bekederemo, J(ohnson) P(epper)
See also CDWLB 3; DLB 117

**Clark, John Pepper**
See Clark Bekederemo, J(ohnson) P(epper)
See also AFW; CD 5; CP 7; RGEL 2

**Clark, M. R.**
See Clark, Mavis Thorpe

**Clark, Mavis Thorpe** 1909-1999 **CLC 12**
See also CA 57-60; CANR 8, 37, 107; CLR
30; CWRI 5; MAICYA 1, 2; SAAS 5;
SATA 8, 74

**Clark, Walter Van Tilburg** 1909-1971 **CLC
28**
See also CA 33-36R; 9-12R; CANR 63,
113; DLB 9, 206; LAIT 2; RGAL 4;
SATA 8

**Clark Bekederemo, J(ohnson) P(epper)**
1935- **BLC 1; CLC 38; DC 5**
See Clark, J. P.; Clark, John Pepper
See also BW 1; CA 65-68; CANR 16, 72;
DAM DRAM, MULT; DFS 13; EWL 3;
MTCW 1

**Clarke, Arthur C(harles)** 1917- **CLC 1, 4, 13,
18, 35, 136; SSC 3**
See also AAYA 4, 33; BPFB 1; BYA 13;
CA 1-4R; CANR 2, 28, 55, 74; CN 7;
CPW; DA3; DAM POP; DLB 261; JRDA;
LAIT 5; MAICYA 1, 2; MTCW 1, 2;
SATA 13, 70, 115; SCFW; SFW 4; SSFS
4; YAW

**Clarke, Austin** 1896-1974 **CLC 6, 9**
See also CA 49-52; 29-32; CAP 2; DAM
POET; DLB 10, 20; EWL 3; RGEL 2

**Clarke, Austin C(hesterfield)** 1934- **BLC 1;
CLC 8, 53; SSC 45**
See also BW 1; CA 25-28R; CAAS 16;
CANR 14, 32, 68; CN 7; DAC; DAM
MULT; DLB 53, 125; DNFS 2; RGSF 2

**Clarke, Gillian** 1937- **CLC 61**
See also CA 106; CP 7; CWP; DLB 40

**Clarke, Marcus (Andrew Hislop)** 1846-1881
**NCLC 19**
See also DLB 230; RGEL 2; RGSF 2

**Clarke, Shirley** 1925-1997 **CLC 16**
See also CA 189

**Clash, The**
See Headon, (Nicky) Topper; Jones, Mick;
Simonon, Paul; Strummer, Joe

**Claudel, Paul (Louis Charles Marie)**
1868-1955 **TCLC 2, 10**
See also CA 165; 104; DLB 192, 258; EW
8; EWL 3; GFL 1789 to the Present;
RGWL 2, 3; TWA

**Claudian** 370(?)-404(?) **CMLC 46**
See also RGWL 2, 3

**Claudius, Matthias** 1740-1815 **NCLC 75**
See also DLB 97

**Clavell, James (duMaresq)** 1925-1994 **CLC
6, 25, 87**
See also BPFB 1; CA 146; 25-28R; CANR
26, 48; CPW; DA3; DAM NOV, POP;
MTCW 1, 2; NFS 10; RHW

**Clayman, Gregory CLC 65**

**Cleaver, (Leroy) Eldridge** 1935-1998 **BLC 1;
CLC 30, 119**
See also BW 1, 3; CA 167; 21-24R; CANR
16, 75; DA3; DAM MULT; MTCW 2;
YAW

**Cleese, John (Marwood)** 1939- **CLC 21**
See Monty Python
See also CA 116; 112; CANR 35; MTCW 1

**Cleishbotham, Jebediah**
See Scott, Sir Walter

**Cleland, John** 1710-1789 **LC 2, 48**
See also DLB 39; RGEL 2

**Clemens, Samuel Langhorne** 1835-1910
See Twain, Mark
See also CA 135; 104; CDALB 1865-1917;
DA; DA3; DAB; DAC; DAM MST, NOV;
DLB 12, 23, 64, 74, 186, 189; JRDA;
MAICYA 1, 2; NCFS 4; SATA 100; SSFS
16; YABC 2

**Clement of Alexandria** 150(?)-215(?) **CMLC
41**

**Cleophil**
See Congreve, William

**Clerihew, E.**
See Bentley, E(dmund) C(lerihew)

**Clerk, N. W.**
See Lewis, C(live) S(taples)

**Cliff, Jimmy CLC 21**
See Chambers, James
See also CA 193

**Cliff, Michelle** 1946- **BLCS; CLC 120**
See also BW 2; CA 116; CANR 39, 72; CD-
WLB 3; DLB 157; FW; GLL 2

**Clifford, Lady Anne** 1590-1676 **LC 76**
See also DLB 151

**Clifton, (Thelma) Lucille** 1936- **BLC 1; CLC
19, 66, 162; PC 17**
See also AFAW 2; BW 2, 3; CA 49-52;
CANR 2, 24, 42, 76, 97; CLR 5; CP 7;
CSW; CWP; CWRI 5; DA3; DAM MULT,
POET; DLB 5, 41; EXPP; MAICYA 1, 2;
MTCW 1, 2; PFS 1, 14; SATA 20, 69,
128; WP

**Clinton, Dirk**
See Silverberg, Robert

**Clough, Arthur Hugh** 1819-1861 **NCLC 27**
See also BRW 5; DLB 32; RGEL 2

**Clutha, Janet Paterson Frame** 1924-
See Frame, Janet
See also CA 1-4R; CANR 2, 36, 76; MTCW
1, 2; SATA 119

**Clyne, Terence**
See Blatty, William Peter

**Cobalt, Martin**
See Mayne, William (James Carter)

**Cobb, Irvin S(hrewsbury)** 1876-1944 **TCLC
77**
See also CA 175; DLB 11, 25, 86

**Cobbett, William** 1763-1835 **NCLC 49**
See also DLB 43, 107, 158; RGEL 2

**Coburn, D(onald) L(ee)** 1938- **CLC 10**
See also CA 89-92

**Cocteau, Jean (Maurice Eugene Clement)**
1889-1963 **CLC 1, 8, 15, 16, 43; DC 17;
TCLC 119; WLC**
See also CA 25-28; CANR 40; CAP 2; DA;
DA3; DAB; DAC; DAM DRAM, MST,
NOV; DLB 65, 258; EW 10; EWL 3; GFL
1789 to the Present; MTCW 1, 2; RGWL
2, 3; TWA

**Codrescu, Andrei** 1946- **CLC 46, 121**
See also CA 33-36R; CAAS 19; CANR 13,
34, 53, 76; DA3; DAM POET; MTCW 2

**Coe, Max**
See Bourne, Randolph S(illiman)

**Coe, Tucker**
See Westlake, Donald E(dwin)

**Coen, Ethan** 1958- **CLC 108**
See also CA 126; CANR 85

**Coen, Joel** 1955- **CLC 108**
See also CA 126

**The Coen Brothers**
See Coen, Ethan; Coen, Joel

**Coetzee, J(ohn) M(ichael)** 1940- **CLC 23, 33,
66, 117, 161, 162**
See also AAYA 37; AFW; BRWS 6; CA 77-
80; CANR 41, 54, 74, 114; CN 7; DA3;
DAM NOV; DLB 225; EWL 3; LMFS 2;
MTCW 1, 2; WLIT 2

**Coffey, Brian**
See Koontz, Dean R(ay)

**Coffin, Robert P(eter) Tristram** 1892-1955
**TCLC 95**
See also CA 169; 123; DLB 45

**Cohan, George M(ichael)** 1878-1942 **TCLC
60**
See also CA 157; DLB 249; RGAL 4

**Cohen, Arthur A(llen)** 1928-1986 **CLC 7, 31**
See also CA 120; 1-4R; CANR 1, 17, 42;
DLB 28

**Cohen, Leonard (Norman)** 1934- **CLC 3, 38**
See also CA 21-24R; CANR 14, 69; CN 7;
CP 7; DAC; DAM MST; DLB 53; EWL
3; MTCW 1

**Cohen, Matt(hew)** 1942-1999 **CLC 19**
See also CA 187; 61-64; CAAS 18; CANR
40; CN 7; DAC; DLB 53

**Cohen-Solal, Annie** 19(?)- **CLC 50**

**Colegate, Isabel** 1931- **CLC 36**
See also CA 17-20R; CANR 8, 22, 74; CN
7; DLB 14, 231; INT CANR-22; MTCW
1

**Coleman, Emmett**
See Reed, Ishmael

**Coleridge, Hartley** 1796-1849 **NCLC 90**
See also DLB 96

**Coleridge, M. E.**
See Coleridge, Mary E(lizabeth)

**Coleridge, Mary E(lizabeth)** 1861-1907
**TCLC 73**
See also CA 166; 116; DLB 19, 98

**Coleridge, Samuel Taylor** 1772-1834 **NCLC
9, 54, 99, 111; PC 11, 39; WLC**
See also BRW 4; BRWR 2; BYA 4; CD-
BLB 1789-1832; DA; DA3; DAB; DAC;
DAM MST, POET; DLB 93, 107; EXPP;
PAB; PFS 4, 5; RGEL 2; TEA; WLIT 3;
WP

**Coleridge, Sara** 1802-1852 **NCLC 31**
See also DLB 199

**Coles, Don** 1928- **CLC 46**
See also CA 115; CANR 38; CP 7

**Coles, Robert (Martin)** 1929- **CLC 108**
  See also CA 45-48; CANR 3, 32, 66, 70;
  INT CANR-32; SATA 23
**Colette, (Sidonie-Gabrielle)** 1873-1954 **SSC
  10; TCLC 1, 5, 16**
  See Willy, Colette
  See also CA 131; 104; DA3; DAM NOV;
  DLB 65; EW 9; EWL 3; GFL 1789 to the
  Present; MTCW 1, 2; RGWL 2, 3; TWA
**Collett, (Jacobine) Camilla (Wergeland)**
  1813-1895 **NCLC 22**
**Collier, Christopher** 1930- **CLC 30**
  See also AAYA 13; BYA 2; CA 33-36R;
  CANR 13, 33, 102; JRDA; MAICYA 1,
  2; SATA 16, 70; WYA; YAW 1
**Collier, James Lincoln** 1928- **CLC 30**
  See also AAYA 13; BYA 2; CA 9-12R;
  CANR 4, 33, 60, 102; CLR 3; DAM POP;
  JRDA; MAICYA 1, 2; SAAS 21; SATA 8,
  70; WYA; YAW 1
**Collier, Jeremy** 1650-1726 **LC 6**
**Collier, John** 1901-1980 **SSC 19; TCLC 127**
  See also CA 97-100; 65-68; CANR 10;
  DLB 77, 255; FANT; SUFW 1
**Collier, Mary** 1690-1762 **LC 86**
  See also DLB 95
**Collingwood, R(obin) G(eorge)** 1889(?)-1943
  **TCLC 67**
  See also CA 155; 117; DLB 262
**Collins, Hunt**
  See Hunter, Evan
**Collins, Linda** 1931- **CLC 44**
  See also CA 125
**Collins, Tom**
  See Furphy, Joseph
  See also RGEL 2
**Collins, (William) Wilkie** 1824-1889 **NCLC
  1, 18, 93**
  See also BRWS 6; CDBLB 1832-1890;
  CMW 4; DLB 18, 70, 159; MSW; RGEL
  2; RGSF 2; SUFW 1; WLIT 4
**Collins, William** 1721-1759 **LC 4, 40**
  See also BRW 3; DAM POET; DLB 109;
  RGEL 2
**Collodi, Carlo NCLC 54**
  See Lorenzini, Carlo
  See also CLR 5; WCH
**Colman, George**
  See Glassco, John
**Colonna, Vittoria** 1492-1547 **LC 71**
  See also RGWL 2, 3
**Colt, Winchester Remington**
  See Hubbard, L(afayette) Ron(ald)
**Colter, Cyrus J.** 1910-2002 **CLC 58**
  See also BW 1; CA 205; 65-68; CANR 10,
  66; CN 7; DLB 33
**Colton, James**
  See Hansen, Joseph
  See also GLL 1
**Colum, Padraic** 1881-1972 **CLC 28**
  See also BYA 4; CA 33-36R; 73-76; CANR
  35; CLR 36; CWRI 5; DLB 19; MAICYA
  1, 2; MTCW 1; RGEL 2; SATA 15; WCH
**Colvin, James**
  See Moorcock, Michael (John)
**Colwin, Laurie (E.)** 1944-1992 **CLC 5, 13,
  23, 84**
  See also CA 139; 89-92; CANR 20, 46;
  DLB 218; DLBY 1980; MTCW 1
**Comfort, Alex(ander)** 1920-2000 **CLC 7**
  See also CA 190; 1-4R; CANR 1, 45; CP 7;
  DAM POP; MTCW 1
**Comfort, Montgomery**
  See Campbell, (John) Ramsey
**Compton-Burnett, I(vy)** 1892(?)-1969 **CLC 1,
  3, 10, 15, 34**
  See also BRW 7; CA 25-28R; 1-4R; CANR
  4; DAM NOV; DLB 36; EWL 3; MTCW
  1; RGEL 2

**Comstock, Anthony** 1844-1915 **TCLC 13**
  See also CA 169; 110
**Comte, Auguste** 1798-1857 **NCLC 54**
**Conan Doyle, Arthur**
  See Doyle, Sir Arthur Conan
  See also BPFB 1; BYA 4, 5, 11
**Conde (Abellan), Carmen** 1901-1996 **HLCS
  1**
  See also CA 177; DLB 108; EWL 3; HW 2
**Conde, Maryse** 1937- **BLCS; CLC 52, 92**
  See also BW 2, 3; CA 110; CAAE 190;
  CANR 30, 53, 76; CWW 2; DAM MULT;
  EWL 3; MTCW 1
**Condillac, Etienne Bonnot de** 1714-1780 **LC
  26**
**Condon, Richard (Thomas)** 1915-1996 **CLC
  4, 6, 8, 10, 45, 100**
  See also BEST 90:3; BPFB 1; CA 151;
  1-4R; CAAS 1; CANR 2, 23; CMW 4;
  CN 7; DAM NOV; INT CANR-23;
  MTCW 1, 2
**Confucius** 551B.C.-479B.C. **CMLC 19;
  WLCS**
  See also DA; DA3; DAB; DAC; DAM
  MST
**Congreve, William** 1670-1729 **DC 2; LC 5,
  21; WLC**
  See also BRW 2; CDBLB 1660-1789; DA;
  DAB; DAC; DAM DRAM, MST, POET;
  DFS 15; DLB 39, 84; RGEL 2; WLIT 3
**Conley, Robert J(ackson)** 1940- **NNAL**
  See also CA 41-44R; CANR 15, 34, 45, 96;
  DAM MULT
**Connell, Evan S(helby), Jr.** 1924- **CLC 4, 6,
  45**
  See also AAYA 7; CA 1-4R; CAAS 2;
  CANR 2, 39, 76, 97; CN 7; DAM NOV;
  DLB 2; DLBY 1981; MTCW 1, 2
**Connelly, Marc(us Cook)** 1890-1980 **CLC 7**
  See also CA 102; 85-88; CANR 30; DFS
  12; DLB 7; DLBY 1980; RGAL 4; SATA-
  Obit 25
**Connor, Ralph TCLC 31**
  See Gordon, Charles William
  See also DLB 92; TCWW 2
**Conrad, Joseph** 1857-1924 **SSC 9; TCLC 1,
  6, 13, 25, 43, 57; WLC**
  See also AAYA 26; BPFB 1; BRW 6;
  BRWC 1; BRWR 2; BYA 2; CA 131; 104;
  CANR 60; CDBLB 1890-1914; DA; DA3;
  DAB; DAC; DAM MST, NOV; DLB 10,
  34, 98, 156; EWL 3; EXPN; EXPS; LAIT
  2; MTCW 1, 2; NFS 2, 16; RGEL 2;
  RGSF 2; SATA 27; SSFS 1, 12; TEA;
  WLIT 4
**Conrad, Robert Arnold**
  See Hart, Moss
**Conroy, (Donald) Pat(rick)** 1945- **CLC 30, 74**
  See also AAYA 8; AITN 1; BPFB 1; CA
  85-88; CANR 24, 53; CPW; CSW; DA3;
  DAM NOV, POP; DLB 6; LAIT 5;
  MTCW 1, 2
**Constant (de Rebecque), (Henri) Benjamin**
  1767-1830 **NCLC 6**
  See also DLB 119; EW 4; GFL 1789 to the
  Present
**Conway, Jill K(er)** 1934- **CLC 152**
  See also CA 130; CANR 94
**Conybeare, Charles Augustus**
  See Eliot, T(homas) S(tearns)
**Cook, Michael** 1933-1994 **CLC 58**
  See also CA 93-96; CANR 68; DLB 53
**Cook, Robin** 1940- **CLC 14**
  See also AAYA 32; BEST 90:2; BPFB 1;
  CA 111; 108; CANR 41, 90, 109; CPW;
  DA3; DAM POP; HGG; INT CA-111
**Cook, Roy**
  See Silverberg, Robert
**Cooke, Elizabeth** 1948- **CLC 55**
  See also CA 129

**Cooke, John Esten** 1830-1886 **NCLC 5**
  See also DLB 3, 248; RGAL 4
**Cooke, John Estes**
  See Baum, L(yman) Frank
**Cooke, M. E.**
  See Creasey, John
**Cooke, Margaret**
  See Creasey, John
**Cooke, Rose Terry** 1827-1892 **NCLC 110**
  See also DLB 12, 74
**Cook-Lynn, Elizabeth** 1930- **CLC 93; NNAL**
  See also CA 133; DAM MULT; DLB 175
**Cooney, Ray CLC 62**
  See also CBD
**Cooper, Douglas** 1960- **CLC 86**
**Cooper, Henry St. John**
  See Creasey, John
**Cooper, J(oan) California** (?)- **CLC 56**
  See also AAYA 12; BW 1; CA 125; CANR
  55; DAM MULT; DLB 212
**Cooper, James Fenimore** 1789-1851 **NCLC 1,
  27, 54**
  See also AAYA 22; AMW; BPFB 1;
  CDALB 1640-1865; DA3; DLB 3, 183,
  250, 254; LAIT 1; NFS 9; RGAL 4; SATA
  19; TUS; WCH
**Coover, Robert (Lowell)** 1932- **CLC 3, 7, 15,
  32, 46, 87, 161; SSC 15**
  See also AMWS 5; BPFB 1; CA 45-48;
  CANR 3, 37, 58, 115; CN 7; DAM NOV;
  DLB 2, 227; DLBY 1981; EWL 3;
  MTCW 1, 2; RGAL 4; RGSF 2
**Copeland, Stewart (Armstrong)** 1952- **CLC
  26**
**Copernicus, Nicolaus** 1473-1543 **LC 45**
**Coppard, A(lfred) E(dgar)** 1878-1957 **SSC
  21; TCLC 5**
  See also BRWS 8; CA 167; 114; DLB 162;
  EWL 3; HGG; RGEL 2; RGSF 2; SUFW
  1; YABC 1
**Coppee, Francois** 1842-1908 **TCLC 25**
  See also CA 170; DLB 217
**Coppola, Francis Ford** 1939- **CLC 16, 126**
  See also AAYA 39; CA 77-80; CANR 40,
  78; DLB 44
**Copway, George** 1818-1869 **NNAL**
  See also DAM MULT; DLB 175, 183
**Corbiere, Tristan** 1845-1875 **NCLC 43**
  See also DLB 217; GFL 1789 to the Present
**Corcoran, Barbara (Asenath)** 1911- **CLC 17**
  See also AAYA 14; CA 21-24R; CAAE 191;
  CAAS 20; CANR 11, 28, 48; CLR 50;
  DLB 52; JRDA; MAICYA 2; MAICYAS
  1; RHW; SAAS 20; SATA 3, 77, 125
**Cordelier, Maurice**
  See Giraudoux, Jean(-Hippolyte)
**Corelli, Marie TCLC 51**
  See Mackay, Mary
  See also DLB 34, 156; RGEL 2; SUFW 1
**Corman, Cid CLC 9**
  See Corman, Sidney
  See also CAAS 2; DLB 5, 193
**Corman, Sidney** 1924-
  See Corman, Cid
  See also CA 85-88; CANR 44; CP 7; DAM
  POET
**Cormier, Robert (Edmund)** 1925-2000 **CLC
  12, 30**
  See also AAYA 3, 19; BYA 1, 2, 6, 8, 9;
  CA 1-4R; CANR 5, 23, 76, 93; CDALB
  1968-1988; CLR 12, 55; DA; DAB; DAC;
  DAM MST, NOV; DLB 52; EXPN; INT
  CANR-23; JRDA; LAIT 5; MAICYA 1,
  2; MTCW 1, 2; NFS 2; SATA 10, 45, 83;
  SATA-Obit 122; WYA; YAW
**Corn, Alfred (DeWitt III)** 1943- **CLC 33**
  See also CA 179; CAAE 179; CAAS 25;
  CANR 44; CP 7; CSW; DLB 120; DLBY
  1980

**Cross, Amanda**
See Heilbrun, Carolyn G(old)
See also BPFB 1; CMW; CPW; MSW

**Crothers, Rachel** 1878-1958 **TCLC 19**
See also CA 194; 113; CAD; CWD; DLB 7, 266; RGAL 4

**Croves, Hal**
See Traven, B.

**Crow Dog, Mary (Ellen)** (?)- **CLC 93**
See Brave Bird, Mary
See also CA 154

**Crowfield, Christopher**
See Stowe, Harriet (Elizabeth) Beecher

**Crowley, Aleister TCLC 7**
See Crowley, Edward Alexander
See also GLL 1

**Crowley, Edward Alexander** 1875-1947
See Crowley, Aleister
See also CA 104; HGG

**Crowley, John** 1942- **CLC 57**
See also BPFB 1; CA 61-64; CANR 43, 98; DLBY 1982; SATA 65; SFW 4; SUFW 2

**Crud**
See Crumb, R(obert)

**Crumarums**
See Crumb, R(obert)

**Crumb, R(obert)** 1943- **CLC 17**
See also CA 106; CANR 107

**Crumbum**
See Crumb, R(obert)

**Crumski**
See Crumb, R(obert)

**Crum the Bum**
See Crumb, R(obert)

**Crunk**
See Crumb, R(obert)

**Crustt**
See Crumb, R(obert)

**Crutchfield, Les**
See Trumbo, Dalton

**Cruz, Victor Hernandez** 1949- **HLC 1; PC 37**
See also BW 2; CA 65-68; CAAS 17; CANR 14, 32, 74; CP 7; DAM MULT, POET; DLB 41; DNFS 1; EXPP; HW 1, 2; MTCW 1; PFS 16; WP

**Cryer, Gretchen (Kiger)** 1935- **CLC 21**
See also CA 123; 114

**Csath, Geza** 1887-1919 **TCLC 13**
See also CA 111

**Cudlip, David R(ockwell)** 1933- **CLC 34**
See also CA 177

**Cullen, Countee** 1903-1946 **BLC 1; HR 2; PC 20; TCLC 4, 37; WLCS**
See also AFAW 2; AMWS 4; BW 1; CA 124; 108; CDALB 1917-1929; DA; DA3; DAC; DAM MST, MULT, POET; DLB 4, 48, 51; EWL 3; EXPP; LMFS 2; MTCW 1, 2; PFS 3; RGAL 4; SATA 18; WP

**Culleton, Beatrice** 1949- **NNAL**
See also CA 120; CANR 83; DAC

**Cum, R.**
See Crumb, R(obert)

**Cummings, Bruce F(rederick)** 1889-1919
See Barbellion, W. N. P.
See also CA 123

**Cummings, E(dward) E(stlin)** 1894-1962
**CLC 1, 3, 8, 12, 15, 68; PC 5; WLC**
See also AAYA 41; AMW; CA 73-76; CANR 31; CDALB 1929-1941; DA; DA3; DAB; DAC; DAM MST, POET; DLB 4, 48; EWL 3; EXPP; MTCW 1, 2; PAB; PFS 1, 3, 12, 13; RGAL 4; TUS; WP

**Cunha, Euclides (Rodrigues Pimenta) da** 1866-1909 **TCLC 24**
See also CA 123; LAW; WLIT 1

**Cunningham, E. V.**
See Fast, Howard (Melvin)

**Cunningham, J(ames) V(incent)** 1911-1985 **CLC 3, 31**
See also CA 115; 1-4R; CANR 1, 72; DLB 5

**Cunningham, Julia (Woolfolk)** 1916- **CLC 12**
See also CA 9-12R; CANR 4, 19, 36; CWRI 5; JRDA; MAICYA 1, 2; SAAS 2; SATA 1, 26, 132

**Cunningham, Michael** 1952- **CLC 34**
See also CA 136; CANR 96; GLL 2

**Cunninghame Graham, R. B.**
See Cunninghame Graham, Robert (Gallnigad) Bontine

**Cunninghame Graham, Robert (Gallnigad) Bontine** 1852-1936 **TCLC 19**
See Graham, R(obert) B(ontine) Cunninghame
See also CA 184; 119

**Currie, Ellen** 19(?)- **CLC 44**

**Curtin, Philip**
See Lowndes, Marie Adelaide (Belloc)

**Curtin, Phillip**
See Lowndes, Marie Adelaide (Belloc)

**Curtis, Price**
See Ellison, Harlan (Jay)

**Cusanus, Nicolaus** 1401-1464 **LC 80**
See Nicholas of Cusa

**Cutrate, Joe**
See Spiegelman, Art

**Cynewulf** c. 770- **CMLC 23**
See also DLB 146; RGEL 2

**Cyrano de Bergerac, Savinien de** 1619-1655 **LC 65**
See also DLB 268; GFL Beginnings to 1789; RGWL 2, 3

**Czaczkes, Shmuel Yosef Halevi**
See Agnon, S(hmuel) Y(osef Halevi)

**Dabrowska, Maria (Szumska)** 1889-1965 **CLC 15**
See also CA 106; CDWLB 4; DLB 215; EWL 3

**Dabydeen, David** 1955- **CLC 34**
See also BW 1; CA 125; CANR 56, 92; CN 7; CP 7

**Dacey, Philip** 1939- **CLC 51**
See also CA 37-40R; CAAS 17; CANR 14, 32, 64; CP 7; DLB 105

**Dagerman, Stig (Halvard)** 1923-1954 **TCLC 17**
See also CA 155; 117; DLB 259; EWL 3

**D'Aguiar, Fred** 1960- **CLC 145**
See also CA 148; CANR 83, 101; CP 7; DLB 157; EWL 3

**Dahl, Roald** 1916-1990 **CLC 1, 6, 18, 79**
See also AAYA 15; BPFB 1; BRWS 4; BYA 5; CA 133; 1-4R; CANR 6, 32, 37, 62; CLR 1, 7, 41; CPW; DA3; DAB; DAC; DAM MST, NOV, POP; DLB 139, 255; HGG; JRDA; MAICYA 1, 2; MTCW 1, 2; RGSF 2; SATA 1, 26, 73; SATA-Obit 65; SSFS 4; TEA; YAW

**Dahlberg, Edward** 1900-1977 **CLC 1, 7, 14**
See also CA 69-72; 9-12R; CANR 31, 62; DLB 48; MTCW 1; RGAL 4

**Daitch, Susan** 1954- **CLC 103**
See also CA 161

**Dale, Colin TCLC 18**
See Lawrence, T(homas) E(dward)

**Dale, George E.**
See Asimov, Isaac

**Dalton, Roque** 1935-1975(?) **HLCS 1; PC 36**
See also CA 176; HW 2

**Daly, Elizabeth** 1878-1967 **CLC 52**
See also CA 25-28R; 23-24; CANR 60; CAP 2; CMW 4

**Daly, Maureen** 1921- **CLC 17**
See also AAYA 5; BYA 6; CANR 37, 83, 108; JRDA; MAICYA 1, 2; SAAS 1; SATA 2, 129; WYA; YAW

**Damas, Leon-Gontran** 1912-1978 **CLC 84**
See also BW 1; CA 73-76; 125; EWL 3

**Dana, Richard Henry Sr.** 1787-1879 **NCLC 53**

**Daniel, Samuel** 1562(?)-1619 **LC 24**
See also DLB 62; RGEL 2

**Daniels, Brett**
See Adler, Renata

**Dannay, Frederic** 1905-1982 **CLC 11**
See Queen, Ellery
See also CA 107; 1-4R; CANR 1, 39; CMW 4; DAM POP; DLB 137; MTCW 1

**D'Annunzio, Gabriele** 1863-1938 **TCLC 6, 40**
See also CA 155; 104; EW 8; EWL 3; RGWL 2, 3; TWA

**Danois, N. le**
See Gourmont, Remy(-Marie-Charles) de

**Dante** 1265-1321 **CMLC 3, 18, 39; PC 21; WLCS**
See also DA; DA3; DAB; DAC; DAM MST, POET; EFS 1; EW 1; LAIT 1; RGWL 2, 3; TWA; WP

**d'Antibes, Germain**
See Simenon, Georges (Jacques Christian)

**Danticat, Edwidge** 1969- **CLC 94, 139**
See also AAYA 29; CA 152; CAAE 192; CANR 73; DNFS 1; EXPS; MTCW 1; SSFS 1; YAW

**Danvers, Dennis** 1947- **CLC 70**

**Danziger, Paula** 1944- **CLC 21**
See also AAYA 4, 36; BYA 6, 7, 14; CA 115; 112; CANR 37; CLR 20; JRDA; MAICYA 1, 2; SATA 36, 63, 102; SATA-Brief 30; WYA; YAW

**Da Ponte, Lorenzo** 1749-1838 **NCLC 50**

**Dario, Ruben** 1867-1916 **HLC 1; PC 15; TCLC 4**
See also CA 131; CANR 81; DAM MULT; EWL 3; HW 1, 2; LAW; MTCW 1, 2; RGWL 2, 3

**Darley, George** 1795-1846 **NCLC 2**
See also DLB 96; RGEL 2

**Darrow, Clarence (Seward)** 1857-1938 **TCLC 81**
See also CA 164

**Darwin, Charles** 1809-1882 **NCLC 57**
See also BRWS 7; DLB 57, 166; RGEL 2; TEA; WLIT 4

**Darwin, Erasmus** 1731-1802 **NCLC 106**
See also DLB 93; RGEL 2

**Daryush, Elizabeth** 1887-1977 **CLC 6, 19**
See also CA 49-52; CANR 3, 81; DLB 20

**Das, Kamala** 1934- **PC 43**
See also CA 101; CANR 27, 59; CP 7; CWP; FW

**Dasgupta, Surendranath** 1887-1952 **TCLC 81**
See also CA 157

**Dashwood, Edmee Elizabeth Monica de la Pasture** 1890-1943
See Delafield, E. M.
See also CA 154; 119

**da Silva, Antonio Jose** 1705-1739 **NCLC 114**
See Silva, Jose Asuncion

**Daudet, (Louis Marie) Alphonse** 1840-1897 **NCLC 1**
See also DLB 123; GFL 1789 to the Present; RGSF 2

**Daumal, Rene** 1908-1944 **TCLC 14**
See also CA 114; EWL 3

**Davenant, William** 1606-1668 **LC 13**
See also DLB 58, 126; RGEL 2

**Davenport, Guy (Mattison, Jr.)** 1927- **CLC 6, 14, 38; SSC 16**
See also CA 33-36R; CANR 23, 73; CN 7; CSW; DLB 130

**David, Robert**
See Nezval, Vitezslav

**De Lisser, H(erbert) G(eorge)** 1878-1944
  **TCLC 12**
    See de Lisser, H. G.
    See also BW 2; CA 152; 109
**Deloire, Pierre**
    See Peguy, Charles (Pierre)
**Deloney, Thomas** 1543(?)-1600 **LC 41**
    See also DLB 167; RGEL 2
**Deloria, Ella (Cara)** 1889-1971(?) **NNAL**
    See also CA 152; DAM MULT; DLB 175
**Deloria, Vine (Victor), Jr.** 1933- **CLC 21, 122;**
  **NNAL**
    See also CA 53-56; CANR 5, 20, 48, 98;
    DAM MULT; DLB 175; MTCW 1; SATA
    21
**del Valle-Inclan, Ramon (Maria)**
    See Valle-Inclan, Ramon (Maria) del
**Del Vecchio, John M(ichael)** 1947- **CLC 29**
    See also CA 110; DLBD 9
**de Man, Paul (Adolph Michel)** 1919-1983
  **CLC 55**
    See also CA 111; 128; CANR 61; DLB 67;
    MTCW 1, 2
**DeMarinis, Rick** 1934- **CLC 54**
    See also CA 57-60, 184; CAAE 184; CAAS
    24; CANR 9, 25, 50; DLB 218
**de Maupassant, (Henri Rene Albert) Guy**
    See Maupassant, (Henri Rene Albert) Guy
    de
**Dembry, R. Emmet**
    See Murfree, Mary Noailles
**Demby, William** 1922- **BLC 1; CLC 53**
    See also BW 1, 3; CA 81-84; CANR 81;
    DAM MULT; DLB 33
**de Menton, Francisco**
    See Chin, Frank (Chew, Jr.)
**Demetrius of Phalerum** c. 307B.C.- **CMLC**
  **34**
**Demijohn, Thom**
    See Disch, Thomas M(ichael)
**De Mille, James** 1833-1880 **NCLC 123**
    See also DLB 99, 251
**Deming, Richard** 1915-1983
    See Queen, Ellery
    See also CA 9-12R; CANR 3, 94; SATA 24
**Democritus** c. 460B.C.-c. 370B.C. **CMLC 47**
**de Montaigne, Michel (Eyquem)**
    See Montaigne, Michel (Eyquem) de
**de Montherlant, Henry (Milon)**
    See Montherlant, Henry (Milon) de
**Demosthenes** 384B.C.-322B.C. **CMLC 13**
    See also AW 1; DLB 176; RGWL 2, 3
**de Musset, (Louis Charles) Alfred**
    See Musset, (Louis Charles) Alfred de
**de Natale, Francine**
    See Malzberg, Barry N(athaniel)
**de Navarre, Marguerite** 1492-1549 **LC 61**
    See Marguerite d'Angouleme; Marguerite
    de Navarre
**Denby, Edwin (Orr)** 1903-1983 **CLC 48**
    See also CA 110; 138
**de Nerval, Gerard**
    See Nerval, Gerard de
**Denham, John** 1615-1669 **LC 73**
    See also DLB 58, 126; RGEL 2
**Denis, Julio**
    See Cortazar, Julio
**Denmark, Harrison**
    See Zelazny, Roger (Joseph)
**Dennis, John** 1658-1734 **LC 11**
    See also DLB 101; RGEL 2
**Dennis, Nigel (Forbes)** 1912-1989 **CLC 8**
    See also CA 129; 25-28R; DLB 13, 15, 233;
    EWL 3; MTCW 1
**Dent, Lester** 1904(?)-1959 **TCLC 72**
    See also CA 161; 112; CMW 4; SFW 4
**De Palma, Brian (Russell)** 1940- **CLC 20**
    See also CA 109

**De Quincey, Thomas** 1785-1859 **NCLC 4, 87**
    See also BRW 4; CDBLB 1789-1832; DLB
    110, 144; RGEL 2
**Deren, Eleanora** 1908(?)-1961
    See Deren, Maya
    See also CA 111; 192
**Deren, Maya CLC 16, 102**
    See Deren, Eleanora
**Derleth, August (William)** 1909-1971 **CLC**
  **31**
    See also BPFB 1; BYA 9, 10; CA 29-32R;
    1-4R; CANR 4; CMW 4; DLB 9; DLBD
    17; HGG; SATA 5; SUFW 1
**Der Nister** 1884-1950 **TCLC 56**
    See Nister, Der
**de Routisie, Albert**
    See Aragon, Louis
**Derrida, Jacques** 1930- **CLC 24, 87**
    See also CA 127; 124; CANR 76, 98; DLB
    242; EWL 3; MTCW 1; TWA
**Derry Down Derry**
    See Lear, Edward
**Dersonnes, Jacques**
    See Simenon, Georges (Jacques Christian)
**Desai, Anita** 1937- **CLC 19, 37, 97**
    See also BRWS 5; CA 81-84; CANR 33,
    53, 95; CN 7; CWRI 5; DA3; DAB; DAM
    NOV; DLB 271; DNFS 2; EWL 3; FW;
    MTCW 1, 2; SATA 63, 126
**Desai, Kiran** 1971- **CLC 119**
    See also CA 171
**de Saint-Luc, Jean**
    See Glassco, John
**de Saint Roman, Arnaud**
    See Aragon, Louis
**Desbordes-Valmore, Marceline** 1786-1859
  **NCLC 97**
    See also DLB 217
**Descartes, Rene** 1596-1650 **LC 20, 35**
    See also DLB 268; EW 3; GFL Beginnings
    to 1789
**De Sica, Vittorio** 1901(?)-1974 **CLC 20**
    See also CA 117
**Desnos, Robert** 1900-1945 **TCLC 22**
    See also CA 151; 121; CANR 107; DLB
    258; EWL 3
**Destouches, Louis-Ferdinand** 1894-1961 **CLC**
  **9, 15**
    See Celine, Louis-Ferdinand
    See also CA 85-88; CANR 28; MTCW 1
**de Tolignac, Gaston**
    See Griffith, D(avid Lewelyn) W(ark)
**Deutsch, Babette** 1895-1982 **CLC 18**
    See also BYA 3; CA 108; 1-4R; CANR 4,
    79; DLB 45; SATA 1; SATA-Obit 33
**Devenant, William** 1606-1649 **LC 13**
**Devkota, Laxmiprasad** 1909-1959 **TCLC 23**
    See also CA 123
**De Voto, Bernard (Augustine)** 1897-1955
  **TCLC 29**
    See also CA 160; 113; DLB 9, 256
**De Vries, Peter** 1910-1993 **CLC 1, 2, 3, 7, 10,**
  **28, 46**
    See also CA 142; 17-20R; CANR 41; DAM
    NOV; DLB 6; DLBY 1982; MTCW 1, 2
**Dewey, John** 1859-1952 **TCLC 95**
    See also CA 170; 114; DLB 246, 270;
    RGAL 4
**Dexter, John**
    See Bradley, Marion Zimmer
    See also GLL 1
**Dexter, Martin**
    See Faust, Frederick (Schiller)
    See also TCWW 2
**Dexter, Pete** 1943- **CLC 34, 55**
    See also BEST 89:2; CA 131; 127; CPW;
    DAM POP; INT 131; MTCW 1

**Diamano, Silmang**
    See Senghor, Leopold Sedar
**Diamond, Neil** 1941- **CLC 30**
    See also CA 108
**Diaz del Castillo, Bernal** 1496-1584 **HLCS 1;**
  **LC 31**
    See also LAW
**di Bassetto, Corno**
    See Shaw, George Bernard
**Dick, Philip K(indred)** 1928-1982 **CLC 10,**
  **30, 72; SSC 57**
    See also AAYA 24; BPFB 1; BYA 11; CA
    106; 49-52; CANR 2, 16; CPW; DA3;
    DAM NOV, POP; DLB 8; MTCW 1, 2;
    NFS 5; SCFW 4; SFW 4
**Dickens, Charles (John Huffam)** 1812-1870
  **NCLC 3, 8, 18, 26, 37, 50, 86, 105, 113;**
  **SSC 17, 49; WLC**
    See also AAYA 23; BRW 5; BRWC 1; BYA
    1, 2, 3, 13, 14; CDBLB 1832-1890; CMW
    4; DA; DA3; DAB; DAC; DAM MST,
    NOV; DLB 21, 55, 70, 159, 166; EXPN;
    HGG; JRDA; LAIT 1, 2; MAICYA 1, 2;
    NFS 4, 5, 10, 14; RGEL 2; RGSF 2;
    SATA 15; SUFW 1; TEA; WCH; WLIT
    4; WYA
**Dickey, James (Lafayette)** 1923-1997 **CLC 1,**
  **2, 4, 7, 10, 15, 47, 109; PC 40**
    See also AITN 1, 2; AMWS 4; BPFB 1;
    CA 156; 9-12R; CABS 2; CANR 10, 48,
    61, 105; CDALB 1968-1988; CP 7; CPW;
    CSW; DA3; DAM NOV, POET, POP;
    DLB 5, 193; DLBD 7; DLBY 1982, 1993,
    1996, 1997, 1998; EWL 3; INT CANR-
    10; MTCW 1, 2; NFS 9; PFS 6, 11;
    RGAL 4; TUS
**Dickey, William** 1928-1994 **CLC 3, 28**
    See also CA 145; 9-12R; CANR 24, 79;
    DLB 5
**Dickinson, Charles** 1951- **CLC 49**
    See also CA 128
**Dickinson, Emily (Elizabeth)** 1830-1886
  **NCLC 21, 77; PC 1; WLC**
    See also AAYA 22; AMW; AMWR 1;
    CDALB 1865-1917; DA; DA3; DAB;
    DAC; DAM MST, POET; DLB 1, 243;
    EXPP; MAWW; PFS 1, 2, 3, 4, 5,
    6, 8, 10, 11, 13, 16; RGAL 4; SATA 29;
    TUS; WP; WYA
**Dickinson, Mrs. Herbert Ward**
    See Phelps, Elizabeth Stuart
**Dickinson, Peter (Malcolm)** 1927- **CLC 12,**
  **35**
    See also AAYA 9; BYA 5; CA 41-44R;
    CANR 31, 58, 88; CLR 29; CMW 4; DLB
    87, 161, 276; JRDA; MAICYA 1, 2;
    SATA 5, 62, 95; SFW 4; WYA; YAW
**Dickson, Carr**
    See Carr, John Dickson
**Dickson, Carter**
    See Carr, John Dickson
**Diderot, Denis** 1713-1784 **LC 26**
    See also EW 4; GFL Beginnings to 1789;
    RGWL 2, 3
**Didion, Joan** 1934- **CLC 1, 3, 8, 14, 32, 129**
    See also AITN 1; AMWS 4; CA 5-8R;
    CANR 14, 52, 76; CDALB 1968-1988;
    CN 7; DA3; DAM NOV; DLB 2, 173,
    185; DLBY 1981, 1986; EWL 3; MAWW;
    MTCW 1, 2; NFS 3; RGAL 4; TCWW 2;
    TUS
**Dietrich, Robert**
    See Hunt, E(verette) Howard, (Jr.)
**Difusa, Pati**
    See Almodovar, Pedro
**Dillard, Annie** 1945- **CLC 9, 60, 115**
    See also AAYA 6, 43; AMWS 6; ANW; CA
    49-52; CANR 3, 43, 62, 90; DA3; DAM

NOV; DLB 275, 278; DLBY 1980; LAIT
4, 5; MTCW 1, 2; NCFS 1; RGAL 4;
SATA 10; TUS

**Dillard, R(ichard) H(enry) W(ilde)** 1937-
**CLC 5**
See also CA 21-24R; CAAS 7; CANR 10;
CP 7; CSW; DLB 5, 244

**Dillon, Eilis** 1920-1994 **CLC 17**
See also CA 147; 9-12R, 182; CAAE 182;
CAAS 3; CANR 4, 38, 78; CLR 26; MAI-
CYA 1, 2; MAICYAS 1; SATA 2, 74;
SATA-Essay 105; SATA-Obit 83; YAW

**Dimont, Penelope**
See Mortimer, Penelope (Ruth)

**Dinesen, Isak CLC 10, 29, 95; SSC 7**
See Blixen, Karen (Christentze Dinesen)
See also EW 10; EWL 3; EXPS; FW; HGG;
LAIT 3; MTCW 1; NCFS 2; NFS 9;
RGSF 2; RGWL 2, 3; SSFS 3, 6, 13;
WLIT 2

**Ding Ling CLC 68**
See Chiang, Pin-chin
See also RGWL 3

**Diphusa, Patty**
See Almodovar, Pedro

**Disch, Thomas M(ichael)** 1940- **CLC 7, 36**
See also AAYA 17; BPFB 1; CA 21-24R;
CAAS 4; CANR 17, 36, 54, 89; CLR 18;
CP 7; DA3; DLB 8; HGG; MAICYA 1, 2;
MTCW 1, 2; SAAS 15; SATA 92; SCFW;
SFW 4; SUFW 2

**Disch, Tom**
See Disch, Thomas M(ichael)

**d'Isly, Georges**
See Simenon, Georges (Jacques Christian)

**Disraeli, Benjamin** 1804-1881 **NCLC 2, 39,
79**
See also BRW 4; DLB 21, 55; RGEL 2

**Ditcum, Steve**
See Crumb, R(obert)

**Dixon, Paige**
See Corcoran, Barbara (Asenath)

**Dixon, Stephen** 1936- **CLC 52; SSC 16**
See also AMWS 12; CA 89-92; CANR 17,
40, 54, 91; CN 7; DLB 130

**Doak, Annie**
See Dillard, Annie

**Dobell, Sydney Thompson** 1824-1874 **NCLC
43**
See also DLB 32; RGEL 2

**Doblin, Alfred TCLC 13**
See Doeblin, Alfred
See also CDWLB 2; EWL 3; RGWL 2, 3

**Dobroliubov, Nikolai Aleksandrovich**
See Dobrolyubov, Nikolai Alexandrovich
See also DLB 277

**Dobrolyubov, Nikolai Alexandrovich**
1836-1861 **NCLC 5**
See Dobroliubov, Nikolai Aleksandrovich

**Dobson, Austin** 1840-1921 **TCLC 79**
See also DLB 35, 144

**Dobyns, Stephen** 1941- **CLC 37**
See also CA 45-48; CANR 2, 18, 99; CMW
4; CP 7

**Doctorow, E(dgar) L(aurence)** 1931- **CLC 6,
11, 15, 18, 37, 44, 65, 113**
See also AAYA 22; AITN 2; AMWS 4;
BEST 89:3; BPFB 1; CA 45-48; CANR
2, 33, 51, 76, 97; CDALB 1968-1988; CN
7; CPW; DA3; DAM NOV, POP; DLB 2,
28, 173; DLBY 1980; EWL 3; LAIT 3;
MTCW 1, 2; NFS 6; RGAL 4; RHW;
TUS

**Dodgson, Charles L(utwidge)** 1832-1898
See Carroll, Lewis
See also CLR 2; DA; DA3; DAB; DAC;
DAM MST, NOV, POET; MAICYA 1, 2;
SATA 100; YABC 2

**Dodson, Owen (Vincent)** 1914-1983 **BLC 1;
CLC 79**
See also BW 1; CA 110; 65-68; CANR 24;
DAM MULT; DLB 76

**Doeblin, Alfred** 1878-1957 **TCLC 13**
See Doblin, Alfred
See also CA 141; 110; DLB 66

**Doerr, Harriet** 1910- **CLC 34**
See also CA 122; 117; CANR 47; INT 122

**Domecq, H(onorio Bustos)**
See Bioy Casares, Adolfo

**Domecq, H(onorio) Bustos**
See Bioy Casares, Adolfo; Borges, Jorge
Luis

**Domini, Rey**
See Lorde, Audre (Geraldine)
See also GLL 1

**Dominique**
See Proust, (Valentin-Louis-George-Eugene-
)Marcel

**Don, A**
See Stephen, Sir Leslie

**Donaldson, Stephen R(eeder)** 1947- **CLC 46,
138**
See also AAYA 36; BPFB 1; CA 89-92;
CANR 13, 55, 99; CPW; DAM POP;
FANT; INT CANR-13; SATA 121; SFW
4; SUFW 1, 2

**Donleavy, J(ames) P(atrick)** 1926- **CLC 1, 4,
6, 10, 45**
See also AITN 2; BPFB 1; CA 9-12R;
CANR 24, 49, 62, 80; CBD; CD 5; CN 7;
DLB 6, 173; INT CANR-24; MTCW 1,
2; RGAL 4

**Donnadieu, Marguerite**
See Duras, Marguerite
See also CWW 2

**Donne, John** 1572-1631 **LC 10, 24; PC 1, 43;
WLC**
See also BRW 1; BRWC 1; BRWR 2; CD-
BLB Before 1660; DA; DAB; DAC;
DAM MST, POET; DLB 121, 151; EXPP;
PAB; PFS 2, 11; RGEL 2; TEA; WLIT 3;
WP

**Donnell, David** 1939(?)- **CLC 34**
See also CA 197

**Donoghue, P. S.**
See Hunt, E(verette) Howard, (Jr.)

**Donoso (Yanez), Jose** 1924-1996 **CLC 4, 8,
11, 32, 99; HLC 1; SSC 34; TCLC 133**
See also CA 155; 81-84; CANR 32, 73; CD-
WLB 3; DAM MULT; DLB 113; EWL 3;
HW 1, 2; LAW; LAWS 1; MTCW 1, 2;
RGSF 2; WLIT 1

**Donovan, John** 1928-1992 **CLC 35**
See also AAYA 20; CA 137; 97-100; CLR
3; MAICYA 1, 2; SATA 72; SATA-Brief
29; YAW

**Don Roberto**
See Cunninghame Graham, Robert
(Gallnigad) Bontine

**Doolittle, Hilda** 1886-1961 **CLC 3, 8, 14, 31,
34, 73; PC 5; WLC**
See H. D.
See also AMWS 1; CA 97-100; CANR 35;
DA; DAC; DAM MST, POET; DLB 4,
45; EWL 3; FW; GLL 1; LMFS 2;
MAWW; MTCW 1, 2; PFS 6; RGAL 4

**Doppo, Kunikida TCLC 99**
See Kunikida Doppo

**Dorfman, Ariel** 1942- **CLC 48, 77; HLC 1**
See also CA 130; 124; CANR 67, 70; CWW
2; DAM MULT; DFS 4; EWL 3; HW 1,
2; INT CA-130; WLIT 1

**Dorn, Edward (Merton)** 1929-1999 **CLC 10,
18**
See also CA 187; 93-96; CANR 42, 79; CP
7; DLB 5; INT 93-96; WP

**Dor-Ner, Zvi CLC 70**

**Dorris, Michael (Anthony)** 1945-1997 **CLC
109; NNAL**
See also AAYA 20; BEST 90:1; BYA 12;
CA 157; 102; CANR 19, 46, 75; CLR 58;
DA3; DAM MULT, NOV; DLB 175;
LAIT 5; MTCW 2; NFS 3; RGAL 4;
SATA 75; SATA-Obit 94; TCWW 2; YAW

**Dorris, Michael A.**
See Dorris, Michael (Anthony)

**Dorsan, Luc**
See Simenon, Georges (Jacques Christian)

**Dorsange, Jean**
See Simenon, Georges (Jacques Christian)

**Dos Passos, John (Roderigo)** 1896-1970 **CLC
1, 4, 8, 11, 15, 25, 34, 82; WLC**
See also AMW; BPFB 1; CA 29-32R; 1-4R;
CANR 3; CDALB 1929-1941; DA; DA3;
DAB; DAC; DAM MST, NOV; DLB 4,
9, 274; DLBD 1, 15; DLBY 1996; EWL
3; MTCW 1, 2; NFS 14; RGAL 4; TUS

**Dossage, Jean**
See Simenon, Georges (Jacques Christian)

**Dostoevsky, Fedor Mikhailovich** 1821-1881
**NCLC 2, 7, 21, 33, 43, 119; SSC 2, 33,
44; WLC**
See Dostoevsky, Fyodor
See also AAYA 40; DA; DA3; DAB; DAC;
DAM MST, NOV; EW 7; EXPN; NFS 3,
8; RGSF 2; RGWL 2, 3; SSFS 8; TWA

**Dostoevsky, Fyodor**
See Dostoevsky, Fedor Mikhailovich
See also DLB 238; LMFS 2

**Doughty, Charles M(ontagu)** 1843-1926
**TCLC 27**
See also CA 178; 115; DLB 19, 57, 174

**Douglas, Ellen CLC 73**
See Haxton, Josephine Ayres; Williamson,
Ellen Douglas
See also CN 7; CSW

**Douglas, Gavin** 1475(?)-1522 **LC 20**
See also DLB 132; RGEL 2

**Douglas, George**
See Brown, George Douglas
See also RGEL 2

**Douglas, Keith (Castellain)** 1920-1944 **TCLC
40**
See also BRW 7; CA 160; DLB 27; EWL
3; PAB; RGEL 2

**Douglas, Leonard**
See Bradbury, Ray (Douglas)

**Douglas, Michael**
See Crichton, (John) Michael

**Douglas, (George) Norman** 1868-1952 **TCLC
68**
See also BRW 6; CA 157; 119; DLB 34,
195; RGEL 2

**Douglas, William**
See Brown, George Douglas

**Douglass, Frederick** 1817(?)-1895 **BLC 1;
NCLC 7, 55; WLC**
See also AFAW 1, 2; AMWC 1; AMWS 3;
CDALB 1640-1865; DA; DA3; DAC;
DAM MST, MULT; DLB 1, 43, 50, 79,
243; FW; LAIT 2; NCFS 2; RGAL 4;
SATA 29

**Dourado, (Waldomiro Freitas) Autran** 1926-
**CLC 23, 60**
See also CA 25-28R, 179; CANR 34, 81;
DLB 145; HW 2

**Dourado, Waldomiro Autran**
See Dourado, (Waldomiro Freitas) Autran
See also CA 179

**Dove, Rita (Frances)** 1952- **BLCS; CLC 50,
81; PC 6**
See also AAYA 46; AMWS 4; BW 2; CA
109; CAAS 19; CANR 27, 42, 68, 76, 97;
CDALBS; CP 7; CSW; CWP; DA3; DAM
MULT, POET; DLB 120; EWL 3; EXPP;
MTCW 1; PFS 1, 15; RGAL 4

**Doveglion**
See Villa, Jose Garcia
**Dowell, Coleman** 1925-1985 **CLC 60**
See also CA 117; 25-28R; CANR 10; DLB 130; GLL 2
**Dowson, Ernest (Christopher)** 1867-1900 **TCLC 4**
See also CA 150; 105; DLB 19, 135; RGEL 2
**Doyle, A. Conan**
See Doyle, Sir Arthur Conan
**Doyle, Sir Arthur Conan** 1859-1930 **SSC 12; TCLC 7; WLC**
See Conan Doyle, Arthur
See also AAYA 14; BRWS 2; CA 122; 104; CDBLB 1890-1914; CMW 4; DA; DA3; DAB; DAC; DAM MST, NOV; DLB 18, 70, 156, 178; EXPS; HGG; LAIT 2; MSW; MTCW 1, 2; RGEL 2; RGSF 2; RHW; SATA 24; SCFW 2; SFW 4; SSFS 2; TEA; WCH; WLIT 4; WYA; YAW
**Doyle, Conan**
See Doyle, Sir Arthur Conan
**Doyle, John**
See Graves, Robert (von Ranke)
**Doyle, Roddy** 1958(?)- **CLC 81**
See also AAYA 14; BRWS 5; CA 143; CANR 73; CN 7; DA3; DLB 194
**Doyle, Sir A. Conan**
See Doyle, Sir Arthur Conan
**Dr. A**
See Asimov, Isaac; Silverstein, Alvin; Silverstein, Virginia B(arbara Opshelor)
**Drabble, Margaret** 1939- **CLC 2, 3, 5, 8, 10, 22, 53, 129**
See also BRWS 4; CA 13-16R; CANR 18, 35, 63, 112; CDBLB 1960 to Present; CN 7; CPW; DA3; DAB; DAC; DAM MST, NOV, POP; DLB 14, 155, 231; EWL 3; FW; MTCW 1, 2; RGEL 2; SATA 48; TEA
**Drapier, M. B.**
See Swift, Jonathan
**Drayham, James**
See Mencken, H(enry) L(ouis)
**Drayton, Michael** 1563-1631 **LC 8**
See also DAM POET; DLB 121; RGEL 2
**Dreadstone, Carl**
See Campbell, (John) Ramsey
**Dreiser, Theodore (Herman Albert)** 1871-1945 **SSC 30; TCLC 10, 18, 35, 83; WLC**
See also AMW; AMWR 2; CA 132; 106; CDALB 1865-1917; DA; DA3; DAC; DAM MST, NOV; DLB 9, 12, 102, 137; DLBD 1; EWL 3; LAIT 2; LMFS 2; MTCW 1, 2; NFS 17; RGAL 4; TUS
**Drexler, Rosalyn** 1926- **CLC 2, 6**
See also CA 81-84; CAD; CANR 68; CD 5; CWD
**Dreyer, Carl Theodor** 1889-1968 **CLC 16**
See also CA 116
**Drieu la Rochelle, Pierre(-Eugene)** 1893-1945 **TCLC 21**
See also CA 117; DLB 72; EWL 3; GFL 1789 to the Present
**Drinkwater, John** 1882-1937 **TCLC 57**
See also CA 149; 109; DLB 10, 19, 149; RGEL 2
**Drop Shot**
See Cable, George Washington
**Droste-Hulshoff, Annette Freiin von** 1797-1848 **NCLC 3**
See also CDWLB 2; DLB 133; RGSF 2; RGWL 2, 3
**Drummond, Walter**
See Silverberg, Robert
**Drummond, William Henry** 1854-1907 **TCLC 25**
See also CA 160; DLB 92

**Drummond de Andrade, Carlos** 1902-1987 **CLC 18**
See Andrade, Carlos Drummond de
See also CA 123; 132; LAW
**Drummond of Hawthornden, William** 1585-1649 **LC 83**
See also DLB 121, 213; RGEL 2
**Drury, Allen (Stuart)** 1918-1998 **CLC 37**
See also CA 170; 57-60; CANR 18, 52; CN 7; INT CANR-18
**Dryden, John** 1631-1700 **DC 3; LC 3, 21; PC 25; WLC**
See also BRW 2; CDBLB 1660-1789; DA; DAB; DAC; DAM DRAM, MST, POET; DLB 80, 101, 131; EXPP; IDTP; RGEL 2; TEA; WLIT 3
**Duberman, Martin (Bauml)** 1930- **CLC 8**
See also CA 1-4R; CAD; CANR 2, 63; CD 5
**Dubie, Norman (Evans)** 1945- **CLC 36**
See also CA 69-72; CANR 12, 115; CP 7; DLB 120; PFS 12
**Du Bois, W(illiam) E(dward) B(urghardt)** 1868-1963 **BLC 1; CLC 1, 2, 13, 64, 96; HR 2; WLC**
See also AAYA 40; AFAW 1, 2; AMWC 1; AMWS 2; BW 1, 3; CA 85-88; CANR 34, 82; CDALB 1865-1917; DA; DA3; DAC; DAM MST, MULT, NOV; DLB 47, 50, 91, 246; EWL 3; EXPP; LAIT 2; LMFS 2; MTCW 1, 2; NCFS 1; PFS 13; RGAL 4; SATA 42
**Dubus, Andre** 1936-1999 **CLC 13, 36, 97; SSC 15**
See also AMWS 7; CA 177; 21-24R; CANR 17; CN 7; CSW; DLB 130; INT CANR-17; RGAL 4; SSFS 10
**Duca Minimo**
See D'Annunzio, Gabriele
**Ducharme, Rejean** 1941- **CLC 74**
See also CA 165; DLB 60
**Duchen, Claire CLC 65**
**Duclos, Charles Pinot-** 1704-1772 **LC 1**
See also GFL Beginnings to 1789
**Dudek, Louis** 1918- **CLC 11, 19**
See also CA 45-48; CAAS 14; CANR 1; CP 7; DLB 88
**Duerrenmatt, Friedrich** 1921-1990 **CLC 1, 4, 8, 11, 15, 43, 102**
See Durrenmatt, Friedrich
See also CA 17-20R; CANR 33; CMW 4; DAM DRAM; DLB 69, 124; MTCW 1, 2
**Duffy, Bruce** 1953(?)- **CLC 50**
See also CA 172
**Duffy, Maureen** 1933- **CLC 37**
See also CA 25-28R; CANR 33, 68; CBD; CN 7; CP 7; CWD; CWP; DFS 15; DLB 14; FW; MTCW 1
**Du Fu**
See Tu Fu
See also RGWL 2, 3
**Dugan, Alan** 1923- **CLC 2, 6**
See also CA 81-84; CP 7; DLB 5; PFS 10
**du Gard, Roger Martin**
See Martin du Gard, Roger
**Duhamel, Georges** 1884-1966 **CLC 8**
See also CA 25-28R; 81-84; CANR 35; DLB 65; EWL 3; GFL 1789 to the Present; MTCW 1
**Dujardin, Edouard (Emile Louis)** 1861-1949 **TCLC 13**
See also CA 109; DLB 123
**Duke, Raoul**
See Thompson, Hunter S(tockton)
**Dulles, John Foster** 1888-1959 **TCLC 72**
See also CA 149; 115

**Dumas, Alexandre (pere)** 1802-1870 **NCLC 11, 71; WLC**
See also AAYA 22; BYA 3; DA; DA3; DAB; DAC; DAM MST, NOV; DLB 119, 192; EW 6; GFL 1789 to the Present; LAIT 1, 2; NFS 14; RGWL 2, 3; SATA 18; TWA; WCH
**Dumas, Alexandre (fils)** 1824-1895 **DC 1; NCLC 9**
See also DLB 192; GFL 1789 to the Present; RGWL 2, 3
**Dumas, Claudine**
See Malzberg, Barry N(athaniel)
**Dumas, Henry L.** 1934-1968 **CLC 6, 62**
See also BW 1; CA 85-88; DLB 41; RGAL 4
**du Maurier, Daphne** 1907-1989 **CLC 6, 11, 59; SSC 18**
See also AAYA 37; BPFB 1; BRWS 3; CA 128; 5-8R; CANR 6, 55; CMW 4; CPW; DA3; DAB; DAC; DAM MST, POP; DLB 191; HGG; LAIT 1; MSW; MTCW 1, 2; NFS 12; RGEL 2; RGSF 2; RHW; SATA 27; SATA-Obit 60; SSFS 14, 16; TEA
**Du Maurier, George** 1834-1896 **NCLC 86**
See also DLB 153, 178; RGEL 2
**Dunbar, Paul Laurence** 1872-1906 **BLC 1; PC 5; SSC 8; TCLC 2, 12; WLC**
See also AFAW 1, 2; AMWS 2; BW 1, 3; CA 124; 104; CANR 79; CDALB 1865-1917; DA; DA3; DAC; DAM MST, MULT, POET; DLB 50, 54, 78; EXPP; RGAL 4; SATA 34
**Dunbar, William** 1460(?)-1520(?) **LC 20**
See also BRWS 8; DLB 132, 146; RGEL 2
**Dunbar-Nelson, Alice HR 2**
See Nelson, Alice Ruth Moore Dunbar
**Duncan, Dora Angela**
See Duncan, Isadora
**Duncan, Isadora** 1877(?)-1927 **TCLC 68**
See also CA 149; 118
**Duncan, Lois** 1934- **CLC 26**
See also AAYA 4, 34; BYA 6, 8; CA 1-4R; CANR 2, 23, 36, 111; CLR 29; JRDA; MAICYA 1, 2; MAICYAS 1; SAAS 2; SATA 1, 36, 75, 133; WYA; YAW
**Duncan, Robert (Edward)** 1919-1988 **CLC 1, 2, 4, 7, 15, 41, 55; PC 2**
See also BG 2; CA 124; 9-12R; CANR 28, 62; DAM POET; DLB 5, 16, 193; EWL 3; MTCW 1, 2; PFS 13; RGAL 4; WP
**Duncan, Sara Jeannette** 1861-1922 **TCLC 60**
See also CA 157; DLB 92
**Dunlap, William** 1766-1839 **NCLC 2**
See also DLB 30, 37, 59; RGAL 4
**Dunn, Douglas (Eaglesham)** 1942- **CLC 6, 40**
See also CA 45-48; CANR 2, 33; CP 7; DLB 40; MTCW 1
**Dunn, Katherine (Karen)** 1945- **CLC 71**
See also CA 33-36R; CANR 72; HGG; MTCW 1
**Dunn, Stephen (Elliott)** 1939- **CLC 36**
See also AMWS 11; CA 33-36R; CANR 12, 48, 53, 105; CP 7; DLB 105
**Dunne, Finley Peter** 1867-1936 **TCLC 28**
See also CA 178; 108; DLB 11, 23; RGAL 4
**Dunne, John Gregory** 1932- **CLC 28**
See also CA 25-28R; CANR 14, 50; CN 7; DLBY 1980
**Dunsany, Lord TCLC 2, 59**
See Dunsany, Edward John Moreton Drax Plunkett
See also DLB 77, 153, 156, 255; FANT; IDTP; RGEL 2; SFW 4; SUFW 1
**Dunsany, Edward John Moreton Drax Plunkett** 1878-1957
See Dunsany, Lord
See also CA 148; 104; DLB 10; MTCW 1

**El Crummo**
See Crumb, R(obert)

**Elder, Lonne III** 1931-1996 **BLC 1; DC 8**
See also BW 1, 3; CA 152; 81-84; CAD; CANR 25; DAM MULT; DLB 7, 38, 44

**Eleanor of Aquitaine** 1122-1204 **CMLC 39**

**Elia**
See Lamb, Charles

**Eliade, Mircea** 1907-1986 **CLC 19**
See also CA 119; 65-68; CANR 30, 62; CD-WLB 4; DLB 220; EWL 3; MTCW 1; RGWL 3; SFW 4

**Eliot, A. D.**
See Jewett, (Theodora) Sarah Orne

**Eliot, Alice**
See Jewett, (Theodora) Sarah Orne

**Eliot, Dan**
See Silverberg, Robert

**Eliot, George** 1819-1880 **NCLC 4, 13, 23, 41, 49, 89, 118; PC 20; WLC**
See also BRW 5; BRWC 1; BRWR 2; CD-BLB 1832-1890; CN 7; CPW; DA; DA3; DAB; DAC; DAM MST, NOV; DLB 21, 35, 55; NFS 17; RGEL 2; RGSF 2; SSFS 8; TEA; WLIT 3

**Eliot, John** 1604-1690 **LC 5**
See also DLB 24

**Eliot, T(homas) S(tearns)** 1888-1965 **CLC 1, 2, 3, 6, 9, 10, 13, 15, 24, 34, 41, 55, 57, 113; PC 5, 31; WLC**
See also AAYA 28; AMW; AMWC 1; AMWR 1; BRW 7; BRWR 2; CA 25-28R; 5-8R; CANR 41; CDALB 1929-1941; DA; DA3; DAB; DAC; DAM DRAM, MST, POET; DFS 4, 13; DLB 7, 10, 45, 63, 245; DLBY 1988; EWL 3; EXPP; LAIT 3; LMFS 2; MTCW 1, 2; PAB; PFS 1, 7; RGAL 4; RGEL 2; TUS; WLIT 4; WP

**Elizabeth** 1866-1941 **TCLC 41**

**Elkin, Stanley L(awrence)** 1930-1995 **CLC 4, 6, 9, 14, 27, 51, 91; SSC 12**
See also AMWS 6; BPFB 1; CA 148; 9-12R; CANR 8, 46; CN 7; CPW; DAM NOV, POP; DLB 2, 28, 218, 278; DLBY 1980; EWL 3; INT CANR-8; MTCW 1, 2; RGAL 4

**Elledge, Scott CLC 34**

**Elliot, Don**
See Silverberg, Robert

**Elliott, Don**
See Silverberg, Robert

**Elliott, George P(aul)** 1918-1980 **CLC 2**
See also CA 97-100; 1-4R; CANR 2; DLB 244

**Elliott, Janice** 1931-1995 **CLC 47**
See also CA 13-16R; CANR 8, 29, 84; CN 7; DLB 14; SATA 119

**Elliott, Sumner Locke** 1917-1991 **CLC 38**
See also CA 134; 5-8R; CANR 2, 21

**Elliott, William**
See Bradbury, Ray (Douglas)

**Ellis, A. E. CLC 7**

**Ellis, Alice Thomas CLC 40**
See Haycraft, Anna (Margaret)
See also DLB 194; MTCW 1

**Ellis, Bret Easton** 1964- **CLC 39, 71, 117**
See also AAYA 2, 43; CA 123; 118; CANR 51, 74; CN 7; CPW; DA3; DAM POP; HGG; INT CA-123; MTCW 1; NFS 11

**Ellis, (Henry) Havelock** 1859-1939 **TCLC 14**
See also CA 169; 109; DLB 190

**Ellis, Landon**
See Ellison, Harlan (Jay)

**Ellis, Trey** 1962- **CLC 55**
See also CA 146; CANR 92

**Ellison, Harlan (Jay)** 1934- **CLC 1, 13, 42, 139; SSC 14**
See also AAYA 29; BPFB 1; BYA 14; CA 5-8R; CANR 5, 46, 115; CPW; DAM POP; DLB 8; HGG; INT CANR-5; MTCW 1, 2; SCFW 2; SFW 4; SSFS 13, 14, 15; SUFW 1, 2

**Ellison, Ralph (Waldo)** 1914-1994 **BLC 1; CLC 1, 3, 11, 54, 86, 114; SSC 26; WLC**
See also AAYA 19; AFAW 1, 2; AMWR 2; AMWS 2; BPFB 1; BW 1, 3; BYA 2; CA 145; 9-12R; CANR 24, 53; CDALB 1941-1968; CSW; DA; DA3; DAB; DAC; DAM MST, MULT, NOV; DLB 2, 76, 227; DLBY 1994; EWL 3; EXPN; EXPS; LAIT 4; MTCW 1, 2; NCFS 3; NFS 2; RGAL 4; RGSF 2; SSFS 1, 11; YAW

**Ellmann, Lucy (Elizabeth)** 1956- **CLC 61**
See also CA 128

**Ellmann, Richard (David)** 1918-1987 **CLC 50**
See also BEST 89:2; CA 122; 1-4R; CANR 2, 28, 61; DLB 103; DLBY 1987; MTCW 1, 2

**Elman, Richard (Martin)** 1934-1997 **CLC 19**
See also CA 163; 17-20R; CAAS 3; CANR 47

**Elron**
See Hubbard, L(afayette) Ron(ald)

**Eluard, Paul PC 38; TCLC 7, 41**
See Grindel, Eugene
See also EWL 3; GFL 1789 to the Present; RGWL 2, 3

**Elyot, Thomas** 1490(?)-1546 **LC 11**
See also DLB 136; RGEL 2

**Elytis, Odysseus** 1911-1996 **CLC 15, 49, 100; PC 21**
See Alepoudelis, Odysseus
See also CA 151; 102; CANR 94; CWW 2; DAM POET; EW 13; EWL 3; MTCW 1, 2; RGWL 2, 3

**Emecheta, (Florence Onye) Buchi** 1944- **BLC 2; CLC 14, 48, 128**
See also AFW; BW 2, 3; CA 81-84; CANR 27, 81; CDWLB 3; CN 7; CWRI 5; DA3; DAM MULT; DLB 117; EWL 3; FW; MTCW 1, 2; NFS 12, 14; SATA 66; WLIT 2

**Emerson, Mary Moody** 1774-1863 **NCLC 66**

**Emerson, Ralph Waldo** 1803-1882 **NCLC 1, 38, 98; PC 18; WLC**
See also AMW; ANW; CDALB 1640-1865; DA; DA3; DAB; DAC; DAM MST, POET; DLB 1, 59, 73, 183, 223, 270; EXPP; LAIT 2; NCFS 3; PFS 4, 17; RGAL 4; TUS; WP

**Eminescu, Mihail** 1850-1889 **NCLC 33**

**Empedocles** 5th cent. B.C.- **CMLC 50**
See also DLB 176

**Empson, William** 1906-1984 **CLC 3, 8, 19, 33, 34**
See also BRWS 2; CA 112; 17-20R; CANR 31, 61; DLB 20; EWL 3; MTCW 1, 2; RGEL 2

**Enchi, Fumiko (Ueda)** 1905-1986 **CLC 31**
See Enchi Fumiko
See also CA 121; 129; FW; MJW

**Enchi Fumiko**
See Enchi, Fumiko (Ueda)
See also DLB 182; EWL 3

**Ende, Michael (Andreas Helmuth)** 1929-1995 **CLC 31**
See also BYA 5; CA 149; 124; 118; CANR 36, 110; CLR 14; DLB 75; MAICYA 1, 2; MAICYAS 1; SATA 61, 130; SATA-Brief 42; SATA-Obit 86

**Endo, Shusaku** 1923-1996 **CLC 7, 14, 19, 54, 99; SSC 48**
See Endo Shusaku
See also CA 153; 29-32R; CANR 21, 54; DA3; DAM NOV; MTCW 1, 2; RGSF 2; RGWL 2, 3

**Endo Shusaku**
See Endo, Shusaku
See also DLB 182; EWL 3

**Engel, Marian** 1933-1985 **CLC 36**
See also CA 25-28R; CANR 12; DLB 53; FW; INT CANR-12

**Engelhardt, Frederick**
See Hubbard, L(afayette) Ron(ald)

**Engels, Friedrich** 1820-1895 **NCLC 85, 114**
See also DLB 129

**Enright, D(ennis) J(oseph)** 1920- **CLC 4, 8, 31**
See also CA 1-4R; CANR 1, 42, 83; CP 7; DLB 27; EWL 3; SATA 25

**Enzensberger, Hans Magnus** 1929- **CLC 43; PC 28**
See also CA 119; 116; CANR 103; EWL 3

**Ephron, Nora** 1941- **CLC 17, 31**
See also AAYA 35; AITN 2; CA 65-68; CANR 12, 39, 83

**Epicurus** 341B.C.-270B.C. **CMLC 21**
See also DLB 176

**Epsilon**
See Betjeman, John

**Epstein, Daniel Mark** 1948- **CLC 7**
See also CA 49-52; CANR 2, 53, 90

**Epstein, Jacob** 1956- **CLC 19**
See also CA 114

**Epstein, Jean** 1897-1953 **TCLC 92**

**Epstein, Joseph** 1937- **CLC 39**
See also CA 119; 112; CANR 50, 65, 117

**Epstein, Leslie** 1938- **CLC 27**
See also AMWS 12; CA 73-76; CAAS 12; CANR 23, 69

**Equiano, Olaudah** 1745(?)-1797 **BLC 2; LC 16**
See also AFAW 1, 2; CDWLB 3; DAM MULT; DLB 37, 50; WLIT 2

**Erasmus, Desiderius** 1469(?)-1536 **LC 16**
See also DLB 136; EW 2; RGWL 2, 3; TWA

**Erdman, Paul E(mil)** 1932- **CLC 25**
See also AITN 1; CA 61-64; CANR 13, 43, 84

**Erdrich, Louise** 1954- **CLC 39, 54, 120; NNAL**
See also AAYA 10, 47; AMWS 4; BEST 89:1; BPFB 1; CA 114; CANR 41, 62; CDALBS; CN 7; CP 7; CPW; CWP; DA3; DAM MULT, NOV, POP; DLB 152, 175, 206; EWL 3; EXPP; LAIT 5; MTCW 1; NFS 5; PFS 14; RGAL 4; SATA 94; SSFS 14; TCWW 2

**Erenburg, Ilya (Grigoryevich)**
See Ehrenburg, Ilya (Grigoryevich)

**Erickson, Stephen Michael** 1950-
See Erickson, Steve
See also CA 129; SFW 4

**Erickson, Steve CLC 64**
See Erickson, Stephen Michael
See also CANR 60, 68; SUFW 2

**Ericson, Walter**
See Fast, Howard (Melvin)

**Eriksson, Buntel**
See Bergman, (Ernst) Ingmar

**Ernaux, Annie** 1940- **CLC 88**
See also CA 147; CANR 93; NCFS 3

**Erskine, John** 1879-1951 **TCLC 84**
See also CA 159; 112; DLB 9, 102; FANT

**Eschenbach, Wolfram von**
See Wolfram von Eschenbach
See also RGWL 3

**Eseki, Bruno**
See Mphahlele, Ezekiel

**Esenin, Sergei (Alexandrovich)** 1895-1925 **TCLC 4**
See also CA 104; RGWL 2, 3

**Eshleman, Clayton** 1935- **CLC 7**
See also CA 33-36R; CAAS 6; CANR 93; CP 7; DLB 5

**Espriella, Don Manuel Alvarez**
See Southey, Robert

**Espriu, Salvador** 1913-1985 **CLC 9**
See also CA 115; 154; DLB 134; EWL 3

**Espronceda, Jose de** 1808-1842 **NCLC 39**

**Esquivel, Laura** 1951(?)- **CLC 141; HLCS 1**
See also AAYA 29; CA 143; CANR 68, 113; DA3; DNFS 2; LAIT 3; LMFS 2; MTCW 1; NFS 5; WLIT 1

**Esse, James**
See Stephens, James

**Esterbrook, Tom**
See Hubbard, L(afayette) Ron(ald)

**Estleman, Loren D.** 1952- **CLC 48**
See also AAYA 27; CA 85-88; CANR 27, 74; CMW 4; CPW; DA3; DAM NOV, POP; DLB 226; INT CANR-27; MTCW 1, 2

**Etherege, Sir George** 1636-1692 **LC 78**
See also BRW 2; DAM DRAM; DLB 80; PAB; RGEL 2

**Euclid** 306B.C.-283B.C. **CMLC 25**

**Eugenides, Jeffrey** 1960(?)- **CLC 81**
See also CA 144

**Euripides** c. 484B.C.-406B.C. **CMLC 23, 51; DC 4; WLCS**
See also AW 1; CDWLB 1; DA; DA3; DAB; DAC; DAM DRAM, MST; DFS 1, 4, 6; DLB 176; LAIT 1; RGWL 2, 3

**Evan, Evin**
See Faust, Frederick (Schiller)

**Evans, Caradoc** 1878-1945 **SSC 43; TCLC 85**
See also DLB 162

**Evans, Evan**
See Faust, Frederick (Schiller)
See also TCWW 2

**Evans, Marian**
See Eliot, George

**Evans, Mary Ann**
See Eliot, George

**Evarts, Esther**
See Benson, Sally

**Everett, Percival**
See Everett, Percival L.
See also CSW

**Everett, Percival L.** 1956- **CLC 57**
See Everett, Percival
See also BW 2; CA 129; CANR 94

**Everson, R(onald) G(ilmour)** 1903-1992 **CLC 27**
See also CA 17-20R; DLB 88

**Everson, William (Oliver)** 1912-1994 **CLC 1, 5, 14**
See also BG 2; CA 145; 9-12R; CANR 20; DLB 5, 16, 212; MTCW 1

**Evtushenko, Evgenii Aleksandrovich**
See Yevtushenko, Yevgeny (Alexandrovich)
See also RGWL 2, 3

**Ewart, Gavin (Buchanan)** 1916-1995 **CLC 13, 46**
See also BRWS 7; CA 150; 89-92; CANR 17, 46; CP 7; DLB 40; MTCW 1

**Ewers, Hanns Heinz** 1871-1943 **TCLC 12**
See also CA 149; 109

**Ewing, Frederick R.**
See Sturgeon, Theodore (Hamilton)

**Exley, Frederick (Earl)** 1929-1992 **CLC 6, 11**
See also AITN 2; BPFB 1; CA 138; 81-84; CANR 117; DLB 143; DLBY 1981

**Eynhardt, Guillermo**
See Quiroga, Horacio (Sylvestre)

**Ezekiel, Nissim** 1924- **CLC 61**
See also CA 61-64; CP 7; EWL 3

**Ezekiel, Tish O'Dowd** 1943- **CLC 34**
See also CA 129

**Fadeev, Aleksandr Aleksandrovich**
See Bulgya, Alexander Alexandrovich
See also DLB 272

**Fadeev, Alexandr Alexandrovich**
See Bulgya, Alexander Alexandrovich
See also EWL 3

**Fadeyev, A.**
See Bulgya, Alexander Alexandrovich

**Fadeyev, Alexander TCLC 53**
See Bulgya, Alexander Alexandrovich

**Fagen, Donald** 1948- **CLC 26**

**Fainzilberg, Ilya Arnoldovich** 1897-1937
See Ilf, Ilya
See also CA 165; 120

**Fair, Ronald L.** 1932- **CLC 18**
See also BW 1; CA 69-72; CANR 25; DLB 33

**Fairbairn, Roger**
See Carr, John Dickson

**Fairbairns, Zoe (Ann)** 1948- **CLC 32**
See also CA 103; CANR 21, 85; CN 7

**Fairfield, Flora**
See Alcott, Louisa May

**Fairman, Paul W.** 1916-1977
See Queen, Ellery
See also CA 114; SFW 4

**Falco, Gian**
See Papini, Giovanni

**Falconer, James**
See Kirkup, James

**Falconer, Kenneth**
See Kornbluth, C(yril) M.

**Falkland, Samuel**
See Heijermans, Herman

**Fallaci, Oriana** 1930- **CLC 11, 110**
See also CA 77-80; CANR 15, 58; FW; MTCW 1

**Faludi, Susan** 1959- **CLC 140**
See also CA 138; FW; MTCW 1; NCFS 3

**Faludy, George** 1913- **CLC 42**
See also CA 21-24R

**Faludy, Gyoergy**
See Faludy, George

**Fanon, Frantz** 1925-1961 **BLC 2; CLC 74**
See also BW 1; CA 89-92; 116; DAM MULT; LMFS 2; WLIT 2

**Fanshawe, Ann** 1625-1680 **LC 11**

**Fante, John (Thomas)** 1911-1983 **CLC 60**
See also AMWS 11; CA 109; 69-72; CANR 23, 104; DLB 130; DLBY 1983

**Farah, Nuruddin** 1945- **BLC 2; CLC 53, 137**
See also AFW; BW 2, 3; CA 106; CANR 81; CDWLB 3; CN 7; DAM MULT; DLB 125; EWL 3; WLIT 2

**Fargue, Leon-Paul** 1876(?)-1947 **TCLC 11**
See also CA 109; CANR 107; DLB 258; EWL 3

**Farigoule, Louis**
See Romains, Jules

**Farina, Richard** 1936(?)-1966 **CLC 9**
See also CA 25-28R; 81-84

**Farley, Walter (Lorimer)** 1915-1989 **CLC 17**
See also BYA 14; CA 17-20R; CANR 8, 29, 84; DLB 22; JRDA; MAICYA 1, 2; SATA 2, 43, 132; YAW

**Farmer, Philip Jose** 1918- **CLC 1, 19**
See also AAYA 28; BPFB 1; CA 1-4R; CANR 4, 35, 111; DLB 8; MTCW 1; SATA 93; SCFW 2; SFW 4

**Farquhar, George** 1677-1707 **LC 21**
See also BRW 2; DAM DRAM; DLB 84; RGEL 2

**Farrell, J(ames) G(ordon)** 1935-1979 **CLC 6**
See also CA 89-92; 73-76; CANR 36; DLB 14, 271; MTCW 1; RGEL 2; RHW; WLIT 4

**Farrell, James T(homas)** 1904-1979 **CLC 1, 4, 8, 11, 66; SSC 28**
See also AMW; BPFB 1; CA 89-92; 5-8R; CANR 9, 61; DLB 4, 9, 86; DLBD 2; EWL 3; MTCW 1, 2; RGAL 4

**Farrell, Warren (Thomas)** 1943- **CLC 70**
See also CA 146

**Farren, Richard J.**
See Betjeman, John

**Farren, Richard M.**
See Betjeman, John

**Fassbinder, Rainer Werner** 1946-1982 **CLC 20**
See also CA 106; 93-96; CANR 31

**Fast, Howard (Melvin)** 1914-2003 **CLC 23, 131**
See also AAYA 16; BPFB 1; CA 1-4R, 181; CAAE 181; CAAS 18; CANR 1, 33, 54, 75, 98; CMW 4; CN 7; CPW; DAM NOV; DLB 9; INT CANR-33; MTCW 1; RHW; SATA 7; SATA-Essay 107; TCWW 2; YAW

**Faulcon, Robert**
See Holdstock, Robert P.

**Faulkner, William (Cuthbert)** 1897-1962
**CLC 1, 3, 6, 8, 9, 11, 14, 18, 28, 52, 68; SSC 1, 35, 42; WLC**
See also AAYA 7; AMW; AMWR 1; BPFB 1; BYA 5; CA 81-84; CANR 33; CDALB 1929-1941; DA; DA3; DAB; DAC; DAM MST, NOV; DLB 9, 11, 44, 102; DLBD 2; DLBY 1986, 1997; EWL 3; EXPN; EXPS; LAIT 2; LMFS 2; MTCW 1, 2; NFS 4, 8, 13; RGAL 4; RGSF 2; SSFS 2, 5, 6, 12; TUS

**Fauset, Jessie Redmon** 1882(?)-1961 **BLC 2; CLC 19, 54; HR 2**
See also AFAW 2; BW 1; CA 109; CANR 83; DAM MULT; DLB 51; FW; LMFS 2; MAWW

**Faust, Frederick (Schiller)** 1892-1944(?) **TCLC 49**
See Austin, Frank; Brand, Max; Challis, George; Dawson, Peter; Dexter, Martin; Evans, Evan; Frederick, John; Frost, Frederick; Manning, David; Silver, Nicholas
See also CA 152; 108; DAM POP; DLB 256; TUS

**Faust, Irvin** 1924- **CLC 8**
See also CA 33-36R; CANR 28, 67; CN 7; DLB 2, 28, 218, 278; DLBY 1980

**Faustino, Domingo** 1811-1888 **NCLC 123**

**Fawkes, Guy**
See Benchley, Robert (Charles)

**Fearing, Kenneth (Flexner)** 1902-1961 **CLC 51**
See also CA 93-96; CANR 59; CMW 4; DLB 9; RGAL 4

**Fecamps, Elise**
See Creasey, John

**Federman, Raymond** 1928- **CLC 6, 47**
See also CA 17-20R; CAAE 208; CAAS 8; CANR 10, 43, 83, 108; CN 7; DLBY 1980

**Federspiel, J(uerg) F.** 1931- **CLC 42**
See also CA 146

**Feiffer, Jules (Ralph)** 1929- **CLC 2, 8, 64**
See also AAYA 3; CA 17-20R; CAD; CANR 30, 59; CD 5; DAM DRAM; DLB 7, 44; INT CANR-30; MTCW 1; SATA 8, 61, 111

**Feige, Hermann Albert Otto Maximilian**
See Traven, B.

**Feinberg, David B.** 1956-1994 **CLC 59**
See also CA 147; 135

**Feinstein, Elaine** 1930- **CLC 36**
See also CA 69-72; CAAS 1; CANR 31, 68; CN 7; CP 7; CWP; DLB 14, 40; MTCW 1

**Feke, Gilbert David CLC 65**

**Feldman, Irving (Mordecai)** 1928- **CLC 7**
See also CA 1-4R; CANR 1; CP 7; DLB 169

**Felix-Tchicaya, Gerald**
See Tchicaya, Gerald Felix

**Fellini, Federico** 1920-1993 **CLC 16, 85**
See also CA 143; 65-68; CANR 33

**Felsen, Henry Gregor** 1916-1995 **CLC 17**
See also CA 180; 1-4R; CANR 1; SAAS 2; SATA 1

**Felski, Rita CLC 65**

**Fenno, Jack**
See Calisher, Hortense

**Fenollosa, Ernest (Francisco)** 1853-1908 **TCLC 91**

**Fenton, James Martin** 1949- **CLC 32**
See also CA 102; CANR 108; CP 7; DLB 40; PFS 11

**Ferber, Edna** 1887-1968 **CLC 18, 93**
See also AITN 1; CA 25-28R; 5-8R; CANR 68, 105; DLB 9, 28, 86, 266; MTCW 1, 2; RGAL 4; RHW; SATA 7; TCWW 2

**Ferdowsi, Abu'l Qasem** 940-1020 **CMLC 43**
See also RGWL 2, 3

**Ferguson, Helen**
See Kavan, Anna

**Ferguson, Niall** 1964- **CLC 134**
See also CA 190

**Ferguson, Samuel** 1810-1886 **NCLC 33**
See also DLB 32; RGEL 2

**Fergusson, Robert** 1750-1774 **LC 29**
See also DLB 109; RGEL 2

**Ferling, Lawrence**
See Ferlinghetti, Lawrence (Monsanto)

**Ferlinghetti, Lawrence (Monsanto)** 1919(?)- **CLC 2, 6, 10, 27, 111; PC 1**
See also CA 5-8R; CANR 3, 41, 73; CDALB 1941-1968; CP 7; DA3; DAM POET; DLB 5, 16; MTCW 1, 2; RGAL 4; WP

**Fern, Fanny**
See Parton, Sara Payson Willis

**Fernandez, Vicente Garcia Huidobro**
See Huidobro Fernandez, Vicente Garcia

**Fernandez-Armesto, Felipe CLC 70**

**Fernandez de Lizardi, Jose Joaquin**
See Lizardi, Jose Joaquin Fernandez de

**Ferre, Rosario** 1938- **CLC 139; HLCS 1; SSC 36**
See also CA 131; CANR 55, 81; CWW 2; DLB 145; EWL 3; HW 1, 2; LAWS 1; MTCW 1; WLIT 1

**Ferrer, Gabriel (Francisco Victor) Miro**
See Miro (Ferrer), Gabriel (Francisco Victor)

**Ferrier, Susan (Edmonstone)** 1782-1854 **NCLC 8**
See also DLB 116; RGEL 2

**Ferrigno, Robert** 1948(?)- **CLC 65**
See also CA 140

**Ferron, Jacques** 1921-1985 **CLC 94**
See also CA 129; 117; CCA 1; DAC; DLB 60; EWL 3

**Feuchtwanger, Lion** 1884-1958 **TCLC 3**
See also CA 187; 104; DLB 66; EWL 3

**Feuillet, Octave** 1821-1890 **NCLC 45**
See also DLB 192

**Feydeau, Georges (Leon Jules Marie)** 1862-1921 **TCLC 22**
See also CA 152; 113; CANR 84; DAM DRAM; DLB 192; EWL 3; GFL 1789 to the Present; RGWL 2, 3

**Fichte, Johann Gottlieb** 1762-1814 **NCLC 62**
See also DLB 90

**Ficino, Marsilio** 1433-1499 **LC 12**

**Fiedeler, Hans**
See Doeblin, Alfred

**Fiedler, Leslie A(aron)** 1917-2003 **CLC 4, 13, 24**
See also CA 9-12R; CANR 7, 63; CN 7; DLB 28, 67; EWL 3; MTCW 1, 2; RGAL 4; TUS

**Field, Andrew** 1938- **CLC 44**
See also CA 97-100; CANR 25

**Field, Eugene** 1850-1895 **NCLC 3**
See also DLB 23, 42, 140; DLBD 13; MAICYA 1, 2; RGAL 4; SATA 16

**Field, Gans T.**
See Wellman, Manly Wade

**Field, Michael** 1915-1971 **TCLC 43**
See also CA 29-32R

**Field, Peter**
See Hobson, Laura Z(ametkin)
See also TCWW 2

**Fielding, Helen** 1959(?)- **CLC 146**
See also CA 172; DLB 231

**Fielding, Henry** 1707-1754 **LC 1, 46, 85; WLC**
See also BRW 3; BRWR 1; CDBLB 1660-1789; DA; DA3; DAB; DAC; DAM DRAM, MST, NOV; DLB 39, 84, 101; RGEL 2; TEA; WLIT 3

**Fielding, Sarah** 1710-1768 **LC 1, 44**
See also DLB 39; RGEL 2; TEA

**Fields, W. C.** 1880-1946 **TCLC 80**
See also DLB 44

**Fierstein, Harvey (Forbes)** 1954- **CLC 33**
See also CA 129; 123; CAD; CD 5; CPW; DA3; DAM DRAM, POP; DFS 6; DLB 266; GLL

**Figes, Eva** 1932- **CLC 31**
See also CA 53-56; CANR 4, 44, 83; CN 7; DLB 14, 271; FW

**Filippo, Eduardo de**
See de Filippo, Eduardo

**Finch, Anne** 1661-1720 **LC 3; PC 21**
See also DLB 95

**Finch, Robert (Duer Claydon)** 1900-1995 **CLC 18**
See also CA 57-60; CANR 9, 24, 49; CP 7; DLB 88

**Findley, Timothy (Irving Frederick)** 1930-2002 **CLC 27, 102**
See also CA 206; 25-28R; CANR 12, 42, 69, 109; CCA 1; CN 7; DAC; DAM MST; DLB 53; FANT; RHW

**Fink, William**
See Mencken, H(enry) L(ouis)

**Firbank, Louis** 1942-
See Reed, Lou
See also CA 117

**Firbank, (Arthur Annesley) Ronald** 1886-1926 **TCLC 1**
See also BRWS 2; CA 177; 104; DLB 36; EWL 3; RGEL 2

**Fish, Stanley**
See Fish, Stanley Eugene

**Fish, Stanley E.**
See Fish, Stanley Eugene

**Fish, Stanley Eugene** 1938- **CLC 142**
See also CA 132; 112; CANR 90; DLB 67

**Fisher, Dorothy (Frances) Canfield** 1879-1958 **TCLC 87**
See also CA 136; 114; CANR 80; CLR 71,; CWRI 5; DLB 9, 102; MAICYA 1, 2; YABC 1

**Fisher, M(ary) F(rances) K(ennedy)** 1908-1992 **CLC 76, 87**
See also CA 138; 77-80; CANR 44; MTCW 1

**Fisher, Roy** 1930- **CLC 25**
See also CA 81-84; CAAS 10; CANR 16; CP 7; DLB 40

**Fisher, Rudolph** 1897-1934 **BLC 2; HR 2; SSC 25; TCLC 11**
See also BW 1, 3; CA 124; 107; CANR 80; DAM MULT; DLB 51, 102

**Fisher, Vardis (Alvero)** 1895-1968 **CLC 7**
See also CA 25-28R; 5-8R; CANR 68; DLB 9, 206; RGAL 4; TCWW 2

**Fiske, Tarleton**
See Bloch, Robert (Albert)

**Fitch, Clarke**
See Sinclair, Upton (Beall)

**Fitch, John IV**
See Cormier, Robert (Edmund)

**Fitzgerald, Captain Hugh**
See Baum, L(yman) Frank

**FitzGerald, Edward** 1809-1883 **NCLC 9**
See also BRW 4; DLB 32; RGEL 2

**Fitzgerald, F(rancis) Scott (Key)** 1896-1940 **SSC 6, 31; TCLC 1, 6, 14, 28, 55; WLC**
See also AAYA 24; AITN 1; AMW; AMWR 1; BPFB 1; CA 123; 110; CDALB 1917-1929; DA; DA3; DAB; DAC; DAM MST, NOV; DLB 4, 9, 86, 219, 273; DLBD 1, 15, 16; DLBY 1981, 1996; EWL 3; EXPN; EXPS; LAIT 3; MTCW 1, 2; NFS 2; RGAL 4; RGSF 2; SSFS 4, 15; TUS

**Fitzgerald, Penelope** 1916-2000 **CLC 19, 51, 61, 143**
See also BRWS 5; CA 190; 85-88; CAAS 10; CANR 56, 86; CN 7; DLB 14, 194; EWL 3; MTCW 2

**Fitzgerald, Robert (Stuart)** 1910-1985 **CLC 39**
See also CA 114; 1-4R; CANR 1; DLBY 1980

**FitzGerald, Robert D(avid)** 1902-1987 **CLC 19**
See also CA 17-20R; DLB 260; RGEL 2

**Fitzgerald, Zelda (Sayre)** 1900-1948 **TCLC 52**
See also AMWS 9; CA 126; 117; DLBY 1984

**Flanagan, Thomas (James Bonner)** 1923-2002 **CLC 25, 52**
See also CA 206; 108; CANR 55; CN 7; DLBY 1980; INT 108; MTCW 1; RHW

**Flaubert, Gustave** 1821-1880 **NCLC 2, 10, 19, 62, 66; SSC 11; WLC**
See also DA; DA3; DAB; DAC; DAM MST, NOV; DLB 119; EW 7; EXPS; GFL 1789 to the Present; LAIT 2; NFS 14; RGSF 2; RGWL 2, 3; SSFS 6; TWA

**Flavius Josephus**
See Josephus, Flavius

**Flecker, Herman Elroy**
See Flecker, (Herman) James Elroy

**Flecker, (Herman) James Elroy** 1884-1915 **TCLC 43**
See also CA 150; 109; DLB 10, 19; RGEL 2

**Fleming, Ian (Lancaster)** 1908-1964 **CLC 3, 30**
See also AAYA 26; BPFB 1; CA 5-8R; CANR 59; CDBLB 1945-1960; CMW 4; CPW; DA3; DAM POP; DLB 87, 201; MSW; MTCW 1, 2; RGEL 2; SATA 9; TEA; YAW

**Fleming, Thomas (James)** 1927- **CLC 37**
See also CA 5-8R; CANR 10, 102; INT CANR-10; SATA 8

**Fletcher, John** 1579-1625 **DC 6; LC 33**
See also BRW 2; CDBLB Before 1660; DLB 58; RGEL 2; TEA

**Fletcher, John Gould** 1886-1950 **TCLC 35**
See also CA 167; 107; DLB 4, 45; LMFS 2; RGAL 4

**Fleur, Paul**
　See Pohl, Frederik
**Flooglebuckle, Al**
　See Spiegelman, Art
**Flora, Fletcher** 1914-1969
　See Queen, Ellery
　See also CA 1-4R; CANR 3, 85
**Flying Officer X**
　See Bates, H(erbert) E(rnest)
**Fo, Dario** 1926- **CLC 32, 109; DC 10**
　See also CA 128; 116; CANR 68, 114;
　　CWW 2; DA3; DAM DRAM; DLBY
　　1997; EWL 3; MTCW 1, 2
**Fogarty, Jonathan Titulescu Esq.**
　See Farrell, James T(homas)
**Follett, Ken(neth Martin)** 1949- **CLC 18**
　See also AAYA 6; BEST 89:4; BPFB 1; CA
　　81-84; CANR 13, 33, 54, 102; CMW 4;
　　CPW; DA3; DAM NOV, POP; DLB 87;
　　DLBY 1981; INT CANR-33; MTCW 1
**Fontane, Theodor** 1819-1898 **NCLC 26**
　See also CDWLB 2; DLB 129; EW 6;
　　RGWL 2, 3; TWA
**Fontenot, Chester CLC 65**
**Fonvizin, Denis Ivanovich** 1744(?)-1792 **LC
81**
　See also DLB 150; RGWL 2, 3
**Foote, Horton** 1916- **CLC 51, 91**
　See also CA 73-76; CAD; CANR 34, 51,
　　110; CD 5; CSW; DA3; DAM DRAM;
　　DLB 26, 266; EWL 3; INT CANR-34
**Foote, Mary Hallock** 1847-1938 **TCLC 108**
　See also DLB 186, 188, 202, 221
**Foote, Shelby** 1916- **CLC 75**
　See also AAYA 40; CA 5-8R; CANR 3, 45,
　　74; CN 7; CPW; CSW; DA3; DAM NOV,
　　POP; DLB 2, 17; MTCW 2; RHW
**Forbes, Cosmo**
　See Lewton, Val
**Forbes, Esther** 1891-1967 **CLC 12**
　See also AAYA 17; BYA 2; CA 25-28R; 13-
　　14; CAP 1; CLR 27; DLB 22; JRDA;
　　MAICYA 1, 2; RHW; SATA 2, 100; YAW
**Forche, Carolyn (Louise)** 1950- **CLC 25, 83,
86; PC 10**
　See also CA 117; 109; CANR 50, 74; CP 7;
　　CWP; DA3; DAM POET; DLB 5, 193;
　　INT CA-117; MTCW 1; RGAL 4
**Ford, Elbur**
　See Hibbert, Eleanor Alice Burford
**Ford, Ford Madox** 1873-1939 **TCLC 1, 15,
39, 57**
　See Chaucer, Daniel
　See also BRW 6; CA 132; 104; CANR 74;
　　CDBLB 1914-1945; DA3; DAM NOV;
　　DLB 34, 98, 162; EWL 3; MTCW 1, 2;
　　RGEL 2; TEA
**Ford, Henry** 1863-1947 **TCLC 73**
　See also CA 148; 115
**Ford, Jack**
　See Ford, John
**Ford, John** 1586-1639 **DC 8; LC 68**
　See also BRW 2; CDBLB Before 1660;
　　DA3; DAM DRAM; DFS 7; DLB 58;
　　IDTP; RGEL 2
**Ford, John** 1895-1973 **CLC 16**
　See also CA 45-48; 187
**Ford, Richard** 1944- **CLC 46, 99**
　See also AMWS 5; CA 69-72; CANR 11,
　　47, 86; CN 7; CSW; DLB 227; EWL 3;
　　MTCW 1; RGAL 4; RGSF 2
**Ford, Webster**
　See Masters, Edgar Lee
**Foreman, Richard** 1937- **CLC 50**
　See also CA 65-68; CAD; CANR 32, 63;
　　CD 5
**Forester, C(ecil) S(cott)** 1899-1966 **CLC 35**
　See also CA 25-28R; 73-76; CANR 83;
　　DLB 191; RGEL 2; RHW; SATA 13

**Forez**
　See Mauriac, Francois (Charles)
**Forman, James**
　See Forman, James D(ouglas)
**Forman, James D(ouglas)** 1932- **CLC 21**
　See also AAYA 17; CA 9-12R; CANR 4,
　　19, 42; JRDA; MAICYA 1, 2; SATA 8,
　　70; YAW
**Forman, Milos** 1932- **CLC 164**
　See also CA 109
**Fornes, Maria Irene** 1930- **CLC 39, 61; DC
10; HLCS 1**
　See also CA 25-28R; CAD; CANR 28, 81;
　　CD 5; CWD; DLB 7; HW 1, 2; INT
　　CANR-28; MTCW 1; RGAL 4
**Forrest, Leon (Richard)** 1937-1997 **BLCS;
CLC 4**
　See also AFAW 2; BW 2; CA 162; 89-92;
　　CAAS 7; CANR 25, 52, 87; CN 7; DLB
　　33
**Forster, E(dward) M(organ)** 1879-1970 **CLC
1, 2, 3, 4, 9, 10, 13, 15, 22, 45, 77; SSC
27; TCLC 125; WLC**
　See also AAYA 2, 37; BRW 6; BRWR 2;
　　CA 25-28R; 13-14; CANR 45; CAP 1;
　　CDBLB 1914-1945; DA; DA3; DAB;
　　DAC; DAM MST, NOV; DLB 34, 98,
　　162, 178, 195; DLBD 10; EWL 3; EXPN;
　　LAIT 3; MTCW 1, 2; NCFS 1; NFS 3,
　　10, 11; RGEL 2; RGSF 2; SATA 57;
　　SUFW 1; TEA; WLIT 4
**Forster, John** 1812-1876 **NCLC 11**
　See also DLB 144, 184
**Forster, Margaret** 1938- **CLC 149**
　See also CA 133; CANR 62, 115; CN 7;
　　DLB 155, 271
**Forsyth, Frederick** 1938- **CLC 2, 5, 36**
　See also BEST 89:4; CA 85-88; CANR 38,
　　62, 115; CMW 4; CN 7; CPW; DAM
　　NOV, POP; DLB 87; MTCW 1, 2
**Forten, Charlotte L.** 1837-1914 **BLC 2;
TCLC 16**
　See Grimke, Charlotte L(ottie) Forten
　See also DLB 50, 239
**Fortinbras**
　See Grieg, (Johan) Nordahl (Brun)
**Foscolo, Ugo** 1778-1827 **NCLC 8, 97**
　See also EW 5
**Fosse, Bob CLC 20**
　See Fosse, Robert Louis
**Fosse, Robert Louis** 1927-1987
　See Fosse, Bob
　See also CA 123; 110
**Foster, Hannah Webster** 1758-1840 **NCLC
99**
　See also DLB 37, 200; RGAL 4
**Foster, Stephen Collins** 1826-1864 **NCLC 26**
　See also RGAL 4
**Foucault, Michel** 1926-1984 **CLC 31, 34, 69**
　See also CA 113; 105; CANR 34; DLB 242;
　　EW 13; EWL 3; GFL 1789 to the Present;
　　GLL 1; MTCW 1, 2; TWA
**Fouque, Friedrich (Heinrich Karl) de la
Motte** 1777-1843 **NCLC 2**
　See also DLB 90; RGWL 2, 3; SUFW 1
**Fourier, Charles** 1772-1837 **NCLC 51**
**Fournier, Henri-Alban** 1886-1914
　See Alain-Fournier
　See also CA 179; 104
**Fournier, Pierre** 1916- **CLC 11**
　See Gascar, Pierre
　See also CA 89-92; CANR 16, 40
**Fowles, John (Robert)** 1926- **CLC 1, 2, 3, 4,
6, 9, 10, 15, 33, 87; SSC 33**
　See also BPFB 1; BRWS 1; CA 5-8R;
　　CANR 25, 71, 103; CDBLB 1960 to
　　Present; CN 7; DA3; DAB; DAC; DAM

MST; DLB 14, 139, 207; EWL 3; HGG;
　　MTCW 1, 2; RGEL 2; RHW; SATA 22;
　　TEA; WLIT 4
**Fox, Paula** 1923- **CLC 2, 8, 121**
　See also AAYA 3, 37; BYA 3, 8; CA 73-76;
　　CANR 20, 36, 62, 105; CLR 1, 44; DLB
　　52; JRDA; MAICYA 1, 2; MTCW 1; NFS
　　12; SATA 17, 60, 120; WYA; YAW
**Fox, William Price (Jr.)** 1926- **CLC 22**
　See also CA 17-20R; CAAS 19; CANR 11;
　　CSW; DLB 2; DLBY 1981
**Foxe, John** 1517(?)-1587 **LC 14**
　See also DLB 132
**Frame, Janet CLC 2, 3, 6, 22, 66, 96; SSC 29**
　See Clutha, Janet Paterson Frame
　See also CN 7; CWP; EWL 3; RGEL 2;
　　RGSF 2; TWA
**France, Anatole TCLC 9**
　See Thibault, Jacques Anatole Francois
　See also DLB 123; EWL 3; GFL 1789 to
　　the Present; MTCW 1; RGWL 2, 3;
　　SUFW 1
**Francis, Claude CLC 50**
　See also CA 192
**Francis, Dick** 1920- **CLC 2, 22, 42, 102**
　See also AAYA 5, 21; BEST 89:3; BPFB 1;
　　CA 5-8R; CANR 9, 42, 68, 100; CDBLB
　　1960 to Present; CMW 4; CN 7; DA3;
　　DAM POP; DLB 87; INT CANR-9;
　　MSW; MTCW 1, 2
**Francis, Robert (Churchill)** 1901-1987 **CLC
15; PC 34**
　See also AMWS 9; CA 123; 1-4R; CANR
　　1; EXPP; PFS 12
**Francis, Lord Jeffrey**
　See Jeffrey, Francis
　See also DLB 107
**Frank, Anne(lies Marie)** 1929-1945 **TCLC
17; WLC**
　See also AAYA 12; BYA 1; CA 133; 113;
　　CANR 68; DA; DA3; DAB; DAC; DAM
　　MST; LAIT 4; MAICYA 2; MAICYAS 1;
　　MTCW 1, 2; NCFS 2; SATA 87; SATA-
　　Brief 42; WYA; YAW
**Frank, Bruno** 1887-1945 **TCLC 81**
　See also CA 189; DLB 118; EWL 3
**Frank, Elizabeth** 1945- **CLC 39**
　See also CA 126; 121; CANR 78; INT 126
**Frankl, Viktor E(mil)** 1905-1997 **CLC 93**
　See also CA 161; 65-68
**Franklin, Benjamin**
　See Hasek, Jaroslav (Matej Frantisek)
**Franklin, Benjamin** 1706-1790 **LC 25; WLCS**
　See also AMW; CDALB 1640-1865; DA;
　　DA3; DAB; DAC; DAM MST; DLB 24,
　　43, 73, 183; LAIT 1; RGAL 4; TUS
**Franklin, (Stella Maria Sarah) Miles
(Lampe)** 1879-1954 **TCLC 7**
　See also CA 164; 104; DLB 230; FW;
　　MTCW 2; RGEL 2; TWA
**Fraser, (Lady) Antonia (Pakenham)** 1932-
**CLC 32, 107**
　See also CA 85-88; CANR 44, 65; CMW;
　　DLB 276; MTCW 1, 2; SATA-Brief 32
**Fraser, George MacDonald** 1925- **CLC 7**
　See also CA 45-48; 180; CAAE 180; CANR
　　2, 48, 74; MTCW 1; RHW
**Fraser, Sylvia** 1935- **CLC 64**
　See also CA 45-48; CANR 1, 16, 60; CCA
　　1
**Frayn, Michael** 1933- **CLC 3, 7, 31, 47**
　See also BRWS 7; CA 5-8R; CANR 30, 69,
　　114; CBD; CD 5; CN 7; DAM DRAM,
　　NOV; DLB 13, 14, 194, 245; FANT;
　　MTCW 1, 2; SFW 4
**Fraze, Candida (Merrill)** 1945- **CLC 50**
　See also CA 126

**Frazer, Andrew**
See Marlowe, Stephen

**Frazer, J(ames) G(eorge)** 1854-1941 **TCLC 32**
See also BRWS 3; CA 118

**Frazer, Robert Caine**
See Creasey, John

**Frazer, Sir James George**
See Frazer, J(ames) G(eorge)

**Frazier, Charles** 1950- **CLC 109**
See also AAYA 34; CA 161; CSW

**Frazier, Ian** 1951- **CLC 46**
See also CA 130; CANR 54, 93

**Frederic, Harold** 1856-1898 **NCLC 10**
See also AMW; DLB 12, 23; DLBD 13; RGAL 4

**Frederick, John**
See Faust, Frederick (Schiller)
See also TCWW 2

**Frederick the Great** 1712-1786 **LC 14**

**Fredro, Aleksander** 1793-1876 **NCLC 8**

**Freeling, Nicolas** 1927- **CLC 38**
See also CA 49-52; CAAS 12; CANR 1, 17, 50, 84; CMW 4; CN 7; DLB 87

**Freeman, Douglas Southall** 1886-1953 **TCLC 11**
See also CA 195; 109; DLB 17; DLBD 17

**Freeman, Judith** 1946- **CLC 55**
See also CA 148; DLB 256

**Freeman, Mary E(leanor) Wilkins** 1852-1930 **SSC 1, 47; TCLC 9**
See also CA 177; 106; DLB 12, 78, 221; EXPS; FW; HGG; MAWW; RGAL 4; RGSF 2; SSFS 4, 8; SUFW 1; TUS

**Freeman, R(ichard) Austin** 1862-1943 **TCLC 21**
See also CA 113; CANR 84; CMW 4; DLB 70

**French, Albert** 1943- **CLC 86**
See also BW 3; CA 167

**French, Antonia**
See Kureishi, Hanif

**French, Marilyn** 1929- **CLC 10, 18, 60**
See also BPFB 1; CA 69-72; CANR 3, 31; CN 7; CPW; DAM DRAM, NOV, POP; FW; INT CANR-31; MTCW 1, 2

**French, Paul**
See Asimov, Isaac

**Freneau, Philip Morin** 1752-1832 **NCLC 1, 111**
See also AMWS 2; DLB 37, 43; RGAL 4

**Freud, Sigmund** 1856-1939 **TCLC 52**
See also CA 133; 115; CANR 69; EW 8; EWL 3; MTCW 1, 2; NCFS 3; TWA

**Freytag, Gustav** 1816-1895 **NCLC 109**
See also DLB 129

**Friedan, Betty (Naomi)** 1921- **CLC 74**
See also CA 65-68; CANR 18, 45, 74; DLB 246; FW; MTCW 1, 2

**Friedlander, Saul** 1932- **CLC 90**
See also CA 130; 117; CANR 72

**Friedman, B(ernard) H(arper)** 1926- **CLC 7**
See also CA 1-4R; CANR 3, 48

**Friedman, Bruce Jay** 1930- **CLC 3, 5, 56**
See also CA 9-12R; CAD; CANR 25, 52, 101; CD 5; CN 7; DLB 2, 28, 244; INT CANR-25

**Friel, Brian** 1929- **CLC 5, 42, 59, 115; DC 8**
See also BRWS 5; CA 21-24R; CANR 33, 69; CBD; CD 5; DFS 11; DLB 13; EWL 3; MTCW 1, 2; RGEL 2; TEA

**Friis-Baastad, Babbis Ellinor** 1921-1970 **CLC 12**
See also CA 134; 17-20R; SATA 7

**Frisch, Max (Rudolf)** 1911-1991 **CLC 3, 9, 14, 18, 32, 44; TCLC 121**
See also CA 134; 85-88; CANR 32, 74; CD-WLB 2; DAM DRAM, NOV; DLB 69, 124; EW 13; EWL 3; MTCW 1, 2; RGWL 2, 3

**Fromentin, Eugene (Samuel Auguste)** 1820-1876 **NCLC 10**
See also DLB 123; GFL 1789 to the Present

**Frost, Frederick**
See Faust, Frederick (Schiller)
See also TCWW 2

**Frost, Robert (Lee)** 1874-1963 **CLC 1, 3, 4, 9, 10, 13, 15, 26, 34, 44; PC 1, 39; WLC**
See also AAYA 21; AMW; AMWR 1; CA 89-92; CANR 33; CDALB 1917-1929; CLR 67; DA; DA3; DAB; DAC; DAM MST, POET; DLB 54; DLBD 7; EWL 3; EXPP; MTCW 1, 2; PAB; PFS 1, 2, 3, 4, 5, 6, 7, 10, 13; RGAL 4; SATA 14; TUS; WP; WYA

**Froude, James Anthony** 1818-1894 **NCLC 43**
See also DLB 18, 57, 144

**Froy, Herald**
See Waterhouse, Keith (Spencer)

**Fry, Christopher** 1907- **CLC 2, 10, 14**
See also BRWS 3; CA 17-20R; CAAS 23; CANR 9, 30, 74; CBD; CD 5; CP 7; DAM DRAM; DLB 13; EWL 3; MTCW 1, 2; RGEL 2; SATA 66; TEA

**Frye, (Herman) Northrop** 1912-1991 **CLC 24, 70**
See also CA 133; 5-8R; CANR 8, 37; DLB 67, 68, 246; EWL 3; MTCW 1, 2; RGAL 4; TWA

**Fuchs, Daniel** 1909-1993 **CLC 8, 22**
See also CA 142; 81-84; CAAS 5; CANR 40; DLB 9, 26, 28; DLBY 1993

**Fuchs, Daniel** 1934- **CLC 34**
See also CA 37-40R; CANR 14, 48

**Fuentes, Carlos** 1928- **CLC 3, 8, 10, 13, 22, 41, 60, 113; HLC 1; SSC 24; WLC**
See also AAYA 4, 45; AITN 2; BPFB 1; CA 69-72; CANR 10, 32, 68, 104; CD-WLB 3; CWW 2; DA; DA3; DAB; DAC; DAM MST, MULT, NOV; DLB 113; DNFS 2; EWL 3; HW 1, 2; LAIT 3; LAW; LAWS 1; LMFS 2; MTCW 1, 2; NFS 8; RGSF 2; RGWL 2, 3; TWA; WLIT 1

**Fuentes, Gregorio Lopez y**
See Lopez y Fuentes, Gregorio

**Fuertes, Gloria** 1918-1998 **PC 27**
See also CA 178, 180; DLB 108; HW 2; SATA 115

**Fugard, (Harold) Athol** 1932- **CLC 5, 9, 14, 25, 40, 80; DC 3**
See also AAYA 17; AFW; CA 85-88; CANR 32, 54; CD 5; DAM DRAM; DFS 3, 6, 10; DLB 225; DNFS 1, 2; EWL 3; MTCW 1; RGEL 2; WLIT 2

**Fugard, Sheila** 1932- **CLC 48**
See also CA 125

**Fukuyama, Francis** 1952- **CLC 131**
See also CA 140; CANR 72

**Fuller, Charles (H., Jr.)** 1939- **BLC 2; CLC 25; DC 1**
See also BW 2; CA 112; 108; CAD; CANR 87; CD 5; DAM DRAM, MULT; DFS 8; DLB 38, 266; EWL 3; INT CA-112; MTCW 1

**Fuller, Henry Blake** 1857-1929 **TCLC 103**
See also CA 177; 108; DLB 12; RGAL 4

**Fuller, John (Leopold)** 1937- **CLC 62**
See also CA 21-24R; CANR 9, 44; CP 7; DLB 40

**Fuller, Margaret**
See Ossoli, Sarah Margaret (Fuller)
See also AMWS 2; DLB 183, 223, 239

**Fuller, Roy (Broadbent)** 1912-1991 **CLC 4, 28**
See also BRWS 7; CA 135; 5-8R; CAAS 10; CANR 53, 83; CWRI 5; DLB 15, 20; EWL 3; RGEL 2; SATA 87

**Fuller, Sarah Margaret**
See Ossoli, Sarah Margaret (Fuller)

**Fuller, Sarah Margaret**
See Ossoli, Sarah Margaret (Fuller)
See also DLB 1, 59, 73

**Fulton, Alice** 1952- **CLC 52**
See also CA 116; CANR 57, 88; CP 7; CWP; DLB 193

**Furphy, Joseph** 1843-1912 **TCLC 25**
See Collins, Tom
See also CA 163; DLB 230; EWL 3; RGEL 2

**Fuson, Robert H(enderson)** 1927- **CLC 70**
See also CA 89-92; CANR 103

**Fussell, Paul** 1924- **CLC 74**
See also BEST 90:1; CA 17-20R; CANR 8, 21, 35, 69; INT CANR-21; MTCW 1, 2

**Futabatei, Shimei** 1864-1909 **TCLC 44**
See Futabatei Shimei
See also CA 162; MJW

**Futabatei Shimei**
See Futabatei, Shimei
See also DLB 180; EWL 3

**Futrelle, Jacques** 1875-1912 **TCLC 19**
See also CA 155; 113; CMW 4

**Gaboriau, Emile** 1835-1873 **NCLC 14**
See also CMW 4; MSW

**Gadda, Carlo Emilio** 1893-1973 **CLC 11**
See also CA 89-92; DLB 177; EWL 3

**Gaddis, William** 1922-1998 **CLC 1, 3, 6, 8, 10, 19, 43, 86**
See also AMWS 4; BPFB 1; CA 172; 17-20R; CANR 21, 48; CN 7; DLB 2, 278; EWL 3; MTCW 1, 2; RGAL 4

**Gaelique, Moruen le**
See Jacob, (Cyprien-)Max

**Gage, Walter**
See Inge, William (Motter)

**Gaines, Ernest J(ames)** 1933- **BLC 2; CLC 3, 11, 18, 86**
See also AAYA 18; AFAW 1, 2; AITN 1; BPFB 2; BW 2, 3; BYA 6; CA 9-12R; CANR 6, 24, 42, 75; CDALB 1968-1988; CLR 62; CN 7; CSW; DA3; DAM MULT; DLB 2, 33, 152; DLBY 1980; EWL 3; EXPN; LAIT 5; MTCW 1, 2; NFS 5, 7, 16; RGAL 4; RGSF 2; RHW; SATA 86; SSFS 5; YAW

**Gaitskill, Mary** 1954- **CLC 69**
See also CA 128; CANR 61; DLB 244

**Galdos, Benito Perez**
See Perez Galdos, Benito
See also EW 7

**Gale, Zona** 1874-1938 **TCLC 7**
See also CA 153; 105; CANR 84; DAM DRAM; DFS 17; DLB 9, 78, 228; RGAL 4

**Galeano, Eduardo (Hughes)** 1940- **CLC 72; HLCS 1**
See also CA 29-32R; CANR 13, 32, 100; HW 1

**Galiano, Juan Valera y Alcala**
See Valera y Alcala-Galiano, Juan

**Galilei, Galileo** 1564-1642 **LC 45**

**Gallagher, Tess** 1943- **CLC 18, 63; PC 9**
See also CA 106; CP 7; CWP; DAM POET; DLB 120, 212, 244; PFS 16

**Gallant, Mavis** 1922- **CLC 7, 18, 38, 172; SSC 5**
See also CA 69-72; CANR 29, 69, 117; CCA 1; CN 7; DAC; DAM MST; DLB 53; EWL 3; MTCW 1, 2; RGEL 2; RGSF 2

**Grade, Chaim** 1910-1982 **CLC 10**
  See also CA 107; 93-96; EWL 3
**Graduate of Oxford, A**
  See Ruskin, John
**Grafton, Garth**
  See Duncan, Sara Jeannette
**Grafton, Sue** 1940- **CLC 163**
  See also AAYA 11; BEST 90:3; CA 108;
  CANR 31, 55, 111; CMW 4; CPW; CSW;
  DA3; DAM POP; DLB 226; FW; MSW
**Graham, John**
  See Phillips, David Graham
**Graham, Jorie** 1951- **CLC 48, 118**
  See also CA 111; CANR 63; CP 7; CWP;
  DLB 120; EWL 3; PFS 10, 17
**Graham, R(obert) B(ontine) Cunninghame**
  See Cunninghame Graham, Robert
  (Gallnigad) Bontine
  See also DLB 98, 135, 174; RGEL 2; RGSF
  2
**Graham, Robert**
  See Haldeman, Joe (William)
**Graham, Tom**
  See Lewis, (Harry) Sinclair
**Graham, W(illiam) S(idney)** 1918-1986 **CLC
29**
  See also BRWS 7; CA 118; 73-76; DLB 20;
  RGEL 2
**Graham, Winston (Mawdsley)** 1910- **CLC 23**
  See also CA 49-52; CANR 2, 22, 45, 66;
  CMW 4; CN 7; DLB 77; RHW
**Grahame, Kenneth** 1859-1932 **TCLC 64**
  See also BYA 5; CA 136; DLB 34; CANR 80;
  CLR 5; CWRI 5; DA3; DAB; DLB 34,
  141, 178; FANT; MAICYA 1, 2; MTCW
  2; RGEL 2; SATA 100; TEA; WCH;
  YABC 1
**Granger, Darius John**
  See Marlowe, Stephen
**Granin, Daniil CLC 59**
**Granovsky, Timofei Nikolaevich** 1813-1855
**NCLC 75**
  See also DLB 198
**Grant, Skeeter**
  See Spiegelman, Art
**Granville-Barker, Harley** 1877-1946 **TCLC 2**
  See Barker, Harley Granville
  See also CA 204; 104; DAM DRAM;
  RGEL 2
**Granzotto, Gianni**
  See Granzotto, Giovanni Battista
**Granzotto, Giovanni Battista** 1914-1985 **CLC
70**
  See also CA 166
**Grass, Guenter (Wilhelm)** 1927- **CLC 1, 2, 4,
6, 11, 15, 22, 32, 49, 88; WLC**
  See also BPFB 2; CA 13-16R; CANR 20,
  75, 93; CDWLB 2; DA; DA3; DAB;
  DAC; DAM MST, NOV; DLB 75, 124;
  EW 13; EWL 3; MTCW 1, 2; RGWL 2,
  3; TWA
**Gratton, Thomas**
  See Hulme, T(homas) E(rnest)
**Grau, Shirley Ann** 1929- **CLC 4, 9, 146; SSC
15**
  See also CA 89-92; CANR 22, 69; CN 7;
  CSW; DLB 2, 218; INT CA-89-92,
  CANR-22; MTCW 1
**Gravel, Fern**
  See Hall, James Norman
**Graver, Elizabeth** 1964- **CLC 70**
  See also CA 135; CANR 71
**Graves, Richard Perceval** 1895-1985 **CLC 44**
  See also CA 65-68; CANR 9, 26, 51
**Graves, Robert (von Ranke)** 1895-1985 **CLC
1, 2, 6, 11, 39, 44, 45; PC 6**
  See also BPFB 2; BRW 7; BYA 4; CA 117;
  5-8R; CANR 5, 36; CDBLB 1914-1945;
  DA3; DAB; DAC; DAM MST, POET;

DLB 20, 100, 191; DLBD 18; DLBY
1985; EWL 3; MTCW 1, 2; NCFS 2;
RGEL 2; RHW; SATA 45; TEA
**Graves, Valerie**
  See Bradley, Marion Zimmer
**Gray, Alasdair (James)** 1934- **CLC 41**
  See also CA 126; CANR 47, 69, 106; CN
  7; DLB 194, 261; HGG; INT CA-126;
  MTCW 1, 2; RGSF 2; SUFW 2
**Gray, Amlin** 1946- **CLC 29**
  See also CA 138
**Gray, Francine du Plessix** 1930- **CLC 22, 153**
  See also BEST 90:3; CA 61-64; CAAS 2;
  CANR 11, 33, 75, 81; DAM NOV; INT
  CANR-11; MTCW 1, 2
**Gray, John (Henry)** 1866-1934 **TCLC 19**
  See also CA 162; 119; RGEL 2
**Gray, Simon (James Holliday)** 1936- **CLC 9,
14, 36**
  See also AITN 1; CA 21-24R; CAAS 3;
  CANR 32, 69; CD 5; DLB 13; EWL 3;
  MTCW 1; RGEL 2
**Gray, Spalding** 1941- **CLC 49, 112; DC 7**
  See also CA 128; CAD; CANR 74; CD 5;
  CPW; DAM POP; MTCW 2
**Gray, Thomas** 1716-1771 **LC 4, 40; PC 2;
WLC**
  See also BRW 3; CDBLB 1660-1789; DA;
  DA3; DAB; DAC; DAM MST; DLB 109;
  EXPP; PAB; PFS 9; RGEL 2; TEA; WP
**Grayson, David**
  See Baker, Ray Stannard
**Grayson, Richard (A.)** 1951- **CLC 38**
  See also CA 85-88; CANR 14, 31, 57; DLB
  234
**Greeley, Andrew M(oran)** 1928- **CLC 28**
  See also BPFB 2; CA 5-8R; CAAS 7;
  CANR 7, 43, 69, 104; CMW 4; CPW;
  DA3; DAM POP; MTCW 1, 2
**Green, Anna Katharine** 1846-1935 **TCLC 63**
  See also CA 159; 112; CMW 4; DLB 202,
  221; MSW
**Green, Brian**
  See Card, Orson Scott
**Green, Hannah**
  See Greenberg, Joanne (Goldenberg)
**Green, Hannah** 1927(?)-1996 **CLC 3**
  See also CA 73-76; CANR 59, 93; NFS 10
**Green, Henry CLC 2, 13, 97**
  See Yorke, Henry Vincent
  See also BRWS 2; CA 175; DLB 15; EWL
  3; RGEL 2
**Green, Julian (Hartridge)** 1900-1998
  See Green, Julien
  See also CA 169; 21-24R; CANR 33, 87;
  DLB 4, 72; MTCW 1
**Green, Julien CLC 3, 11, 77**
  See Green, Julian (Hartridge)
  See also EWL 3; GFL 1789 to the Present;
  MTCW 2
**Green, Paul (Eliot)** 1894-1981 **CLC 25**
  See also AITN 1; CA 103; 5-8R; CANR 3;
  DAM DRAM; DLB 7, 9, 249; DLBY
  1981; RGAL 4
**Greenaway, Peter** 1942- **CLC 159**
  See also CA 127
**Greenberg, Ivan** 1908-1973
  See Rahv, Philip
  See also CA 85-88
**Greenberg, Joanne (Goldenberg)** 1932- **CLC
7, 30**
  See also AAYA 12; CA 5-8R; CANR 14,
  32, 69; CN 7; SATA 25; YAW
**Greenberg, Richard** 1959(?)- **CLC 57**
  See also CA 138; CAD; CD 5
**Greenblatt, Stephen J(ay)** 1943- **CLC 70**
  See also CA 49-52; CANR 115

**Greene, Bette** 1934- **CLC 30**
  See also AAYA 7; BYA 3; CA 53-56; CANR
  4; CLR 2; CWRI 5; JRDA; LAIT 4; MAI-
  CYA 1, 2; NFS 10; SAAS 16; SATA 8,
  102; WYA; YAW
**Greene, Gael CLC 8**
  See also CA 13-16R; CANR 10
**Greene, Graham (Henry)** 1904-1991 **CLC 1,
3, 6, 9, 14, 18, 27, 37, 70, 72, 125; SSC
29; WLC**
  See also AITN 2; BPFB 2; BRWR 2; BRWS
  1; BYA 3; CA 133; 13-16R; CANR 35,
  61; CBD; CDBLB 1945-1960; CMW 4;
  DA; DA3; DAB; DAC; DAM MST, NOV;
  DLB 13, 15, 77, 100, 162, 201, 204;
  DLBY 1991; EWL 3; MSW; MTCW 1, 2;
  NFS 16; RGEL 2; SATA 20; SSFS 14;
  TEA; WLIT 4
**Greene, Robert** 1558-1592 **LC 41**
  See also BRWS 8; DLB 62, 167; IDTP;
  RGEL 2; TEA
**Greer, Germaine** 1939- **CLC 131**
  See also AITN 1; CA 81-84; CANR 33, 70,
  115; FW; MTCW 1, 2
**Greer, Richard**
  See Silverberg, Robert
**Gregor, Arthur** 1923- **CLC 9**
  See also CA 25-28R; CAAS 10; CANR 11;
  CP 7; SATA 36
**Gregor, Lee**
  See Pohl, Frederik
**Gregory, Lady Isabella Augusta (Persse)**
  1852-1932 **TCLC 1**
  See also BRW 6; CA 184; 104; DLB 10;
  IDTP; RGEL 2
**Gregory, J. Dennis**
  See Williams, John A(lfred)
**Grekova, I. CLC 59**
**Grendon, Stephen**
  See Derleth, August (William)
**Grenville, Kate** 1950- **CLC 61**
  See also CA 118; CANR 53, 93
**Grenville, Pelham**
  See Wodehouse, P(elham) G(renville)
**Greve, Felix Paul (Berthold Friedrich)**
  1879-1948
  See Grove, Frederick Philip
  See also CA 141, 175; 104; CANR 79;
  DAC; DAM MST
**Greville, Fulke** 1554-1628 **LC 79**
  See also DLB 62, 172; RGEL 2
**Grey, Zane** 1872-1939 **TCLC 6**
  See also BPFB 2; CA 132; 104; DA3; DAM
  POP; DLB 9, 212; MTCW 1, 2; RGAL 4;
  TCWW 2; TUS
**Grieg, (Johan) Nordahl (Brun)** 1902-1943
**TCLC 10**
  See also CA 189; 107; EWL 3
**Grieve, C(hristopher) M(urray)** 1892-1978
**CLC 11, 19**
  See MacDiarmid, Hugh; Pteleon
  See also CA 85-88; 5-8R; CANR 33, 107;
  DAM POET; MTCW 1; RGEL 2
**Griffin, Gerald** 1803-1840 **NCLC 7**
  See also DLB 159; RGEL 2
**Griffin, John Howard** 1920-1980 **CLC 68**
  See also AITN 1; CA 101; 1-4R; CANR 2
**Griffin, Peter** 1942- **CLC 39**
  See also CA 136
**Griffith, D(avid Lewelyn) W(ark)**
  1875(?)-1948 **TCLC 68**
  See also CA 150; 119; CANR 80
**Griffith, Lawrence**
  See Griffith, D(avid Lewelyn) W(ark)
**Griffiths, Trevor** 1935- **CLC 13, 52**
  See also CA 97-100; CANR 45; CBD; CD
  5; DLB 13, 245
**Griggs, Sutton (Elbert)** 1872-1930 **TCLC 77**
  See also CA 186; 123; DLB 50

**Harris, Christie** 1907-
See Harris, Christie (Lucy) Irwin
**Harris, Christie (Lucy) Irwin** 1907-2002 **CLC 12**
See also CA 5-8R; CANR 6, 83; CLR 47; DLB 88; JRDA; MAICYA 1, 2; SAAS 10; SATA 6, 74; SATA-Essay 116
**Harris, Frank** 1856-1931 **TCLC 24**
See also CA 150; 109; CANR 80; DLB 156, 197; RGEL 2
**Harris, George Washington** 1814-1869 **NCLC 23**
See also DLB 3, 11, 248; RGAL 4
**Harris, Joel Chandler** 1848-1908 **SSC 19; TCLC 2**
See also CA 137; 104; CANR 80; CLR 49; DLB 11, 23, 42, 78, 91; LAIT 2; MAICYA 1, 2; RGSF 2; SATA 100; WCH; YABC 1
**Harris, John (Wyndham Parkes Lucas) Beynon** 1903-1969
See Wyndham, John
See also CA 89-92; 102; CANR 84; SATA 118; SFW 4
**Harris, MacDonald CLC 9**
See Heiney, Donald (William)
**Harris, Mark** 1922- **CLC 19**
See also CA 5-8R; CAAS 3; CANR 2, 55, 83; CN 7; DLB 2; DLBY 1980
**Harris, Norman CLC 65**
**Harris, (Theodore) Wilson** 1921- **CLC 25, 159**
See also BRWS 5; BW 2, 3; CA 65-68; CAAS 16; CANR 11, 27, 69, 114; CD-WLB 3; CN 7; CP 7; DLB 117; EWL 3; MTCW 1; RGEL 2
**Harrison, Barbara Grizzuti** 1934-2002 **CLC 144**
See also CA 205; 77-80; CANR 15, 48; INT CANR-15
**Harrison, Elizabeth (Allen) Cavanna** 1909-2001
See Cavanna, Betty
See also CA 200; 9-12R; CANR 6, 27, 85, 104; MAICYA 2; YAW
**Harrison, Harry (Max)** 1925- **CLC 42**
See also CA 1-4R; CANR 5, 21, 84; DLB 8; SATA 4; SCFW 2; SFW 4
**Harrison, James (Thomas)** 1937- **CLC 6, 14, 33, 66, 143; SSC 19**
See Harrison, Jim
See also CA 13-16R; CANR 8, 51, 79; CN 7; CP 7; DLBY 1982; INT CANR-8
**Harrison, Jim**
See Harrison, James (Thomas)
See also AMWS 8; RGAL 4; TCWW 2; TUS
**Harrison, Kathryn** 1961- **CLC 70, 151**
See also CA 144; CANR 68
**Harrison, Tony** 1937- **CLC 43, 129**
See also BRWS 5; CA 65-68; CANR 44, 98; CBD; CD 5; CP 7; DLB 40, 245; MTCW 1; RGEL 2
**Harriss, Will(ard Irvin)** 1922- **CLC 34**
See also CA 111
**Hart, Ellis**
See Ellison, Harlan (Jay)
**Hart, Josephine** 1942(?)- **CLC 70**
See also CA 138; CANR 70; CPW; DAM POP
**Hart, Moss** 1904-1961 **CLC 66**
See also CA 89-92; 109; CANR 84; DAM DRAM; DFS 1; DLB 7, 266; RGAL 4
**Harte, (Francis) Bret(t)** 1836(?)-1902 **SSC 8, 59; TCLC 1, 25; WLC**
See also AMWS 2; CA 140; 104; CANR 80; CDALB 1865-1917; DA; DA3; DAC;

DAM MST; DLB 12, 64, 74, 79, 186; EXPS; LAIT 2; RGAL 4; RGSF 2; SATA 26; SSFS 3; TUS
**Hartley, L(eslie) P(oles)** 1895-1972 **CLC 2, 22**
See also BRWS 7; CA 37-40R; 45-48; CANR 33; DLB 15, 139; EWL 3; HGG; MTCW 1, 2; RGEL 2; RGSF 2; SUFW 1
**Hartman, Geoffrey H.** 1929- **CLC 27**
See also CA 125; 117; CANR 79; DLB 67
**Hartmann, Sadakichi** 1869-1944 **TCLC 73**
See also CA 157; DLB 54
**Hartmann von Aue** c. 1170-c. 1210 **CMLC 15**
See also CDWLB 2; DLB 138; RGWL 2, 3
**Hartog, Jan de**
See de Hartog, Jan
**Haruf, Kent** 1943- **CLC 34**
See also AAYA 44; CA 149; CANR 91
**Harvey, Gabriel** 1550(?)-1631 **LC 88**
See also DLB 167, 213
**Harwood, Ronald** 1934- **CLC 32**
See also CA 1-4R; CANR 4, 55; CBD; CD 5; DAM DRAM, MST; DLB 13
**Hasegawa Tatsunosuke**
See Futabatei, Shimei
**Hasek, Jaroslav (Matej Frantisek)** 1883-1923 **TCLC 4**
See also CA 129; 104; CDWLB 4; DLB 215; EW 9; EWL 3; MTCW 1, 2; RGSF 2; RGWL 2, 3
**Hass, Robert** 1941- **CLC 18, 39, 99; PC 16**
See also AMWS 6; CA 111; CANR 30, 50, 71; CP 7; DLB 105, 206; EWL 3; RGAL 4; SATA 94
**Hastings, Hudson**
See Kuttner, Henry
**Hastings, Selina CLC 44**
**Hathorne, John** 1641-1717 **LC 38**
**Hatteras, Amelia**
See Mencken, H(enry) L(ouis)
**Hatteras, Owen TCLC 18**
See Mencken, H(enry) L(ouis); Nathan, George Jean
**Hauptmann, Gerhart (Johann Robert)** 1862-1946 **SSC 37; TCLC 4**
See also CA 153; 104; CDWLB 2; DAM DRAM; DLB 66, 118; EW 8; EWL 3; RGSF 2; RGWL 2, 3; TWA
**Havel, Vaclav** 1936- **CLC 25, 58, 65, 123; DC 6**
See also CA 104; CANR 36, 63; CDWLB 4; CWW 2; DA3; DAM DRAM; DFS 10; DLB 232; EWL 3; LMFS 2; MTCW 1, 2; RGWL 3
**Haviaras, Stratis CLC 33**
See Chaviaras, Strates
**Hawes, Stephen** 1475(?)-1529(?) **LC 17**
See also DLB 132; RGEL 2
**Hawkes, John (Clendennin Burne, Jr.)** 1925-1998 **CLC 1, 2, 3, 4, 7, 9, 14, 15, 27, 49**
See also BPFB 2; CA 167; 1-4R; CANR 2, 47, 64; CN 7; DLB 2, 7, 227; DLBY 1980, 1998; EWL 3; MTCW 1, 2; RGAL 4
**Hawking, S. W.**
See Hawking, Stephen W(illiam)
**Hawking, Stephen W(illiam)** 1942- **CLC 63, 105**
See also AAYA 13; BEST 89:1; CA 129; 126; CANR 48, 115; CPW; DA3; MTCW 2
**Hawkins, Anthony Hope**
See Hope, Anthony
**Hawthorne, Julian** 1846-1934 **TCLC 25**
See also CA 165; HGG

**Hawthorne, Nathaniel** 1804-1864 **NCLC 2, 10, 17, 23, 39, 79, 95; SSC 3, 29, 39; WLC**
See also AAYA 18; AMW; AMWC 1; AMWR 1; BPFB 2; BYA 3; CDALB 1640-1865; DA; DA3; DAB; DAC; DAM MST, NOV; DLB 1, 74, 183, 223, 269; EXPN; EXPS; HGG; LAIT 1; NFS 1; RGAL 4; RGSF 2; SSFS 1, 7, 11, 15; SUFW 1; TUS; WCH; YABC 2
**Haxton, Josephine Ayres** 1921-
See Douglas, Ellen
See also CA 115; CANR 41, 83
**Hayaseca y Eizaguirre, Jorge**
See Echegaray (y Eizaguirre), Jose (Maria Waldo)
**Hayashi, Fumiko** 1904-1951 **TCLC 27**
See Hayashi Fumiko
See also CA 161
**Hayashi Fumiko**
See Hayashi, Fumiko
See also DLB 180; EWL 3
**Haycraft, Anna (Margaret)** 1932-
See Ellis, Alice Thomas
See also CA 122; CANR 85, 90; MTCW 2
**Hayden, Robert E(arl)** 1913-1980 **BLC 2; CLC 5, 9, 14, 37; PC 6**
See also AFAW 1, 2; AMWS 2; BW 1, 3; CA 97-100; 69-72; CABS 2; CANR 24, 75, 82; CDALB 1941-1968; DA; DAC; DAM MST, MULT, POET; DLB 5, 76; EWL 3; EXPP; MTCW 1, 2; PFS 1; RGAL 4; SATA 19; SATA-Obit 26; WP
**Hayek, F(riedrich) A(ugust von)** 1899-1992 **TCLC 109**
See also CA 137; 93-96; CANR 20; MTCW 1, 2
**Hayford, J(oseph) E(phraim) Casely**
See Casely-Hayford, J(oseph) E(phraim)
**Hayman, Ronald** 1932- **CLC 44**
See also CA 25-28R; CANR 18, 50, 88; CD 5; DLB 155
**Hayne, Paul Hamilton** 1830-1886 **NCLC 94**
See also DLB 3, 64, 79, 248; RGAL 4
**Hays, Mary** 1760-1843 **NCLC 114**
See also DLB 142, 158; RGEL 2
**Haywood, Eliza (Fowler)** 1693(?)-1756 **LC 1, 44**
See also DLB 39; RGEL 2
**Hazlitt, William** 1778-1830 **NCLC 29, 82**
See also BRW 4; DLB 110, 158; RGEL 2; TEA
**Hazzard, Shirley** 1931- **CLC 18**
See also CA 9-12R; CANR 4, 70; CN 7; DLBY 1982; MTCW 1
**Head, Bessie** 1937-1986 **BLC 2; CLC 25, 67; SSC 52**
See also AFW; BW 2, 3; CA 119; 29-32R; CANR 25, 82; CDWLB 3; DA3; DAM MULT; DLB 117, 225; EWL 3; EXPS; FW; MTCW 1, 2; RGSF 2; SSFS 5, 13; WLIT 2
**Headon, (Nicky) Topper** 1956(?)- **CLC 30**
**Heaney, Seamus (Justin)** 1939- **CLC 5, 7, 14, 25, 37, 74, 91, 171; PC 18; WLCS**
See also BRWR 1; BRWS 2; CA 85-88; CANR 25, 48, 75, 91; CDBLB 1960 to Present; CP 7; DA3; DAB; DAM POET; DLB 40; DLBY 1995; EWL 3; EXPP; MTCW 1, 2; PAB; PFS 2, 5, 8, 17; RGEL 2; TEA; WLIT 4
**Hearn, (Patricio) Lafcadio (Tessima Carlos)** 1850-1904 **TCLC 9**
See also CA 166; 105; DLB 12, 78, 189; HGG; RGAL 4
**Hearne, Vicki** 1946-2001 **CLC 56**
See also CA 201; 139
**Hearon, Shelby** 1931- **CLC 63**
See also AITN 2; AMWS 8; CA 25-28R; CANR 18, 48, 103; CSW

**Heat-Moon, William Least CLC 29**
See Trogdon, William (Lewis)
See also AAYA 9
**Hebbel, Friedrich** 1813-1863 **NCLC 43**
See also CDWLB 2; DAM DRAM; DLB
129; EW 6; RGWL 2, 3
**Hebert, Anne** 1916-2000 **CLC 4, 13, 29**
See also CA 187; 85-88; CANR 69; CCA
1; CWP; CWW 2; DA3; DAC; DAM
MST, POET; DLB 68; EWL 3; GFL 1789
to the Present; MTCW 1, 2
**Hecht, Anthony (Evan)** 1923- **CLC 8, 13, 19**
See also AMWS 10; CA 9-12R; CANR 6,
108; CP 7; DAM POET; DLB 5, 169;
EWL 3; PFS 6; WP
**Hecht, Ben** 1894-1964 **CLC 8; TCLC 101**
See also CA 85-88; DFS 9; DLB 7, 9, 25,
26, 28, 86; FANT; IDFW 3, 4; RGAL 4
**Hedayat, Sadeq** 1903-1951 **TCLC 21**
See also CA 120; EWL 3; RGSF 2
**Hegel, Georg Wilhelm Friedrich** 1770-1831
**NCLC 46**
See also DLB 90; TWA
**Heidegger, Martin** 1889-1976 **CLC 24**
See also CA 65-68; 81-84; CANR 34;
MTCW 1, 2
**Heidenstam, (Carl Gustaf) Verner von**
1859-1940 **TCLC 5**
See also CA 104
**Heifner, Jack** 1946- **CLC 11**
See also CA 105; CANR 47
**Heijermans, Herman** 1864-1924 **TCLC 24**
See also CA 123; EWL 3
**Heilbrun, Carolyn G(old)** 1926- **CLC 25**
See Cross, Amanda
See also CA 45-48; CANR 1, 28, 58, 94;
FW
**Hein, Christoph** 1944- **CLC 154**
See also CA 158; CANR 108; CDWLB 2;
CWW 2; DLB 124
**Heine, Heinrich** 1797-1856 **NCLC 4, 54; PC 25**
See also CDWLB 2; DLB 90; EW 5; RGWL
2, 3; TWA
**Heinemann, Larry (Curtiss)** 1944- **CLC 50**
See also CA 110; CAAS 21; CANR 31, 81;
DLBD 9; INT CANR-31
**Heiney, Donald (William)** 1921-1993
See Harris, MacDonald
See also CA 142; 1-4R; CANR 3, 58; FANT
**Heinlein, Robert A(nson)** 1907-1988 **CLC 1, 3, 8, 14, 26, 55; SSC 55**
See also AAYA 17; BPFB 2; BYA 4, 13;
CA 125; 1-4R; CANR 1, 20, 53; CLR 75;
CPW; DA3; DAM POP; DLB 8; EXPS;
JRDA; LAIT 5; MAICYA 1, 2; MTCW 1,
2; RGAL 4; SATA 9, 69; SATA-Obit 56;
SCFW; SFW 4; SSFS 7; YAW
**Helforth, John**
See Doolittle, Hilda
**Heliodorus** fl. 3rd cent. - **CMLC 52**
**Hellenhofferu, Vojtech Kapristian z**
See Hasek, Jaroslav (Matej Frantisek)
**Heller, Joseph** 1923-1999 **CLC 1, 3, 5, 8, 11, 36, 63; TCLC 131; WLC**
See also AAYA 24; AITN 1; AMWS 4;
BPFB 2; BYA 1; CA 187; 5-8R; CABS 1;
CANR 8, 42, 66; CN 7; CPW; DA; DA3;
DAB; DAC; DAM MST, NOV, POP;
DLB 2, 28, 227; DLBY 1980; EWL 3;
EXPN; INT CANR-8; LAIT 4; MTCW 1,
2; NFS 1; RGAL 4; TUS; YAW
**Hellman, Lillian (Florence)** 1906-1984 **CLC 2, 4, 8, 14, 18, 34, 44, 52; DC 1; TCLC 119**
See also AAYA 47; AITN 1, 2; AMWS 1;
CA 112; 13-16R; CAD; CANR 33; CWD;
DA3; DAM DRAM; DFS 1, 3, 14; DLB

7, 228; DLBY 1984; EWL 3; FW; LAIT
3; MAWW; MTCW 1, 2; RGAL 4; TUS
**Helprin, Mark** 1947- **CLC 7, 10, 22, 32**
See also CA 81-84; CANR 47, 64;
CDALBS; CPW; DA3; DAM NOV, POP;
DLBY 1985; FANT; MTCW 1, 2; SUFW
2
**Helvetius, Claude-Adrien** 1715-1771 **LC 26**
**Helyar, Jane Penelope Josephine** 1933-
See Poole, Josephine
See also CA 21-24R; CANR 10, 26; CWRI
5; SATA 82
**Hemans, Felicia** 1793-1835 **NCLC 29, 71**
See also DLB 96; RGEL 2
**Hemingway, Ernest (Miller)** 1899-1961 **CLC 1, 3, 6, 8, 10, 13, 19, 30, 34, 39, 41, 44, 50, 61, 80; SSC 1, 25, 36, 40; TCLC 115; WLC**
See also AAYA 19; AMW; AMWC 1;
AMWR 1; BPFB 2; BYA 2, 3, 13; CA
77-80; CANR 34; CDALB 1917-1929;
DA; DA3; DAB; DAC; DAM MST, NOV,
DLB 4, 9, 102, 210; DLBD 1, 15, 16;
DLBY 1981, 1987, 1996, 1998; EWL 3;
EXPN; EXPS; LAIT 3, 4; MTCW 1, 2;
NFS 1, 5, 6, 14; RGAL 4; RGSF 2; SSFS
17; TUS; WYA
**Hempel, Amy** 1951- **CLC 39**
See also CA 137; 118; CANR 70; DA3;
DLB 218; EXPS; MTCW 2; SSFS 2
**Henderson, F. C.**
See Mencken, H(enry) L(ouis)
**Henderson, Sylvia**
See Ashton-Warner, Sylvia (Constance)
**Henderson, Zenna (Chlarson)** 1917-1983 **SSC 29**
See also CA 133; 1-4R; CANR 1, 84; DLB
8; SATA 5; SFW 4
**Henkin, Joshua CLC 119**
See also CA 161
**Henley, Beth CLC 23; DC 6, 14**
See Henley, Elizabeth Becker
See also CABS 3; CAD; CD 5; CSW;
CWD; DFS 2; DLBY 1986; FW
**Henley, Elizabeth Becker** 1952-
See Henley, Beth
See also CA 107; CANR 32, 73; DA3;
DAM DRAM, MST; MTCW 1, 2
**Henley, William Ernest** 1849-1903 **TCLC 8**
See also CA 105; DLB 19; RGEL 2
**Hennissart, Martha**
See Lathen, Emma
See also CA 85-88; CANR 64
**Henry VIII** 1491-1547 **LC 10**
See also DLB 132
**Henry, O. SSC 5, 49; TCLC 1, 19; WLC**
See Porter, William Sydney
See also AAYA 41; AMWS 2; EXPS; RGAL
4; RGSF 2; SSFS 2
**Henry, Patrick** 1736-1799 **LC 25**
See also LAIT 1
**Henryson, Robert** 1430(?)-1506(?) **LC 20**
See also BRWS 7; DLB 146; RGEL 2
**Henschke, Alfred**
See Klabund
**Henson, Lance** 1944- **NNAL**
See also CA 146; DLB 175
**Hentoff, Nat(han Irving)** 1925- **CLC 26**
See also AAYA 4, 42; BYA 6; CA 1-4R;
CAAS 6; CANR 5, 25, 77, 114; CLR 1,
52; INT CANR-25; JRDA; MAICYA 1,
2; SATA 42, 69, 133; SATA-Brief 27;
WYA; YAW
**Heppenstall, (John) Rayner** 1911-1981 **CLC 10**
See also CA 103; 1-4R; CANR 29; EWL 3
**Heraclitus** c. 540B.C.-c. 450B.C. **CMLC 22**
See also DLB 176

**Herbert, Frank (Patrick)** 1920-1986 **CLC 12, 23, 35, 44, 85**
See also AAYA 21; BPFB 2; BYA 4, 14;
CA 118; 53-56; CANR 5, 43; CDALBS;
CPW; DAM POP; DLB 8; INT CANR-5;
LAIT 5; MTCW 1, 2; NFS 17; SATA 9,
37; SATA-Obit 47; SCFW 2; SFW 4;
YAW
**Herbert, George** 1593-1633 **LC 24; PC 4**
See also BRW 2; BRWR 2; CDBLB Before
1660; DAB; DAM POET; DLB 126;
EXPP; RGEL 2; TEA; WP
**Herbert, Zbigniew** 1924-1998 **CLC 9, 43**
See also CA 169; 89-92; CANR 36, 74; CD-
WLB 4; CWW 2; DAM POET; DLB 232;
EWL 3; MTCW 1
**Herbst, Josephine (Frey)** 1897-1969 **CLC 34**
See also CA 25-28R; 5-8R; DLB 9
**Herder, Johann Gottfried von** 1744-1803
**NCLC 8**
See also DLB 97; EW 4; TWA
**Heredia, Jose Maria** 1803-1839 **HLCS 2**
See also LAW
**Hergesheimer, Joseph** 1880-1954 **TCLC 11**
See also CA 194; 109; DLB 102, 9; RGAL
4
**Herlihy, James Leo** 1927-1993 **CLC 6**
See also CA 143; 1-4R; CAD; CANR 2
**Herman, William**
See Bierce, Ambrose (Gwinett)
**Hermogenes** fl. c. 175- **CMLC 6**
**Hernandez, Jose** 1834-1886 **NCLC 17**
See also LAW; RGWL 2, 3; WLIT 1
**Herodotus** c. 484B.C.-c. 420B.C. **CMLC 17**
See also AW 1; CDWLB 1; DLB 176;
RGWL 2, 3; TWA
**Herrick, Robert** 1591-1674 **LC 13; PC 9**
See also BRW 2; DA; DAB; DAC; DAM
MST, POP; DLB 126; EXPP; PFS 13;
RGAL 4; RGEL 2; TEA; WP
**Herring, Guilles**
See Somerville, Edith Oenone
**Herriot, James** 1916-1995 **CLC 12**
See Wight, James Alfred
See also AAYA 1; BPFB 2; CA 148; CANR
40; CLR 80; CPW; DAM POP; LAIT 3;
MAICYA 2; MAICYAS 1; MTCW 2;
SATA 86, 135; TEA; YAW
**Herris, Violet**
See Hunt, Violet
**Herrmann, Dorothy** 1941- **CLC 44**
See also CA 107
**Herrmann, Taffy**
See Herrmann, Dorothy
**Hersey, John (Richard)** 1914-1993 **CLC 1, 2, 7, 9, 40, 81, 97**
See also AAYA 29; BPFB 2; CA 140; 17-
20R; CANR 33; CDALBS; CPW; DAM
POP; DLB 6, 185, 278; MTCW 1, 2;
SATA 25; SATA-Obit 76; TUS
**Herzen, Aleksandr Ivanovich** 1812-1870
**NCLC 10, 61**
See Herzen, Alexander
**Herzen, Alexander**
See Herzen, Aleksandr Ivanovich
See also DLB 277
**Herzl, Theodor** 1860-1904 **TCLC 36**
See also CA 168
**Herzog, Werner** 1942- **CLC 16**
See also CA 89-92
**Hesiod** c. 8th cent. B.C.- **CMLC 5**
See also AW 1; DLB 176; RGWL 2, 3
**Hesse, Hermann** 1877-1962 **CLC 1, 2, 3, 6, 11, 17, 25, 69; SSC 9, 49; WLC**
See also AAYA 43; BPFB 2; CA 17-18;
CAP 2; CDWLB 2; DA; DA3; DAB;
DAC; DAM MST, NOV; DLB 66; EW 9;
EWL 3; EXPN; LAIT 1; MTCW 1, 2;
NFS 6, 15; RGWL 2, 3; SATA 50; TWA

**Howells, William D.**
See Howells, William Dean

**Howells, William Dean** 1837-1920 **SSC 36; TCLC 7, 17, 41**
See also AMW; CA 134; 104; CDALB 1865-1917; DLB 12, 64, 74, 79, 189; MTCW 2; RGAL 4; TUS

**Howes, Barbara** 1914-1996 **CLC 15**
See also CA 151; 9-12R; CAAS 3; CANR 53; CP 7; SATA 5

**Hrabal, Bohumil** 1914-1997 **CLC 13, 67**
See also CA 156; 106; CAAS 12; CANR 57; CWW 2; DLB 232; EWL 3; RGSF 2

**Hrotsvit of Gandersheim** c. 935-c. 1000 **CMLC 29**
See also DLB 148

**Hsi, Chu** 1130-1200 **CMLC 42**

**Hsun, Lu**
See Lu Hsun

**Hubbard, L(afayette) Ron(ald)** 1911-1986 **CLC 43**
See also CA 118; 77-80; CANR 52; CPW; DA3; DAM POP; FANT; MTCW 2; SFW 4

**Huch, Ricarda (Octavia)** 1864-1947 **TCLC 13**
See also CA 189; 111; DLB 66; EWL 3

**Huddle, David** 1942- **CLC 49**
See also CA 57-60; CAAS 20; CANR 89; DLB 130

**Hudson, Jeffrey**
See Crichton, (John) Michael

**Hudson, W(illiam) H(enry)** 1841-1922 **TCLC 29**
See also CA 190; 115; DLB 98, 153, 174; RGEL 2; SATA 35

**Hueffer, Ford Madox**
See Ford, Ford Madox

**Hughart, Barry** 1934- **CLC 39**
See also CA 137; FANT; SFW 4; SUFW 2

**Hughes, Colin**
See Creasey, John

**Hughes, David (John)** 1930- **CLC 48**
See also CA 129; 116; CN 7; DLB 14

**Hughes, Edward James**
See Hughes, Ted
See also DA3; DAM MST, POET

**Hughes, (James Mercer) Langston** 1902-1967 **BLC 2; CLC 1, 5, 10, 15, 35, 44, 108; DC 3; HR 2; PC 1; SSC 6; WLC**
See also AAYA 12; AFAW 1, 2; AMWR 1; AMWS 1; BW 1, 3; CA 25-28R; 1-4R; CANR 1, 34, 82; CDALB 1929-1941; CLR 17; DA; DA3; DAB; DAC; DAM DRAM, MST, MULT, POET; DLB 4, 7, 48, 51, 86, 228; EWL 3; EXPP; EXPS; JRDA; LAIT 3; LMFS 2; MAICYA 1, 2; MTCW 1, 2; PAB; PFS 1, 3, 6, 10, 15; RGAL 4; RGSF 2; SATA 4, 33; SSFS 4, 7; TUS; WCH; WP; YAW

**Hughes, Richard (Arthur Warren)** 1900-1976 **CLC 1, 11**
See also CA 65-68; 5-8R; CANR 4; DAM NOV; DLB 15, 161; EWL 3; MTCW 1; RGEL 2; SATA 8; SATA-Obit 25

**Hughes, Ted** 1930-1998 **CLC 2, 4, 9, 14, 37, 119; PC 7**
See Hughes, Edward James
See also BRWR 2; BRWS 1; CA 171; 1-4R; CANR 1, 33, 66, 108; CLR 3; CP 7; DAB; DAC; DLB 40, 161; EWL 3; EXPP; MAICYA 1, 2; MTCW 1, 2; PAB; PFS 4; RGEL 2; SATA 49; SATA-Brief 27; SATA-Obit 107; TEA; YAW

**Hugo, Richard**
See Huch, Ricarda (Octavia)

**Hugo, Richard F(ranklin)** 1923-1982 **CLC 6, 18, 32**
See also AMWS 6; CA 108; 49-52; CANR 3; DAM POET; DLB 5, 206; EWL 3; PFS 17; RGAL 4

**Hugo, Victor (Marie)** 1802-1885 **NCLC 3, 10, 21; PC 17; WLC**
See also AAYA 28; DA; DA3; DAB; DAC; DAM DRAM, MST, NOV, POET; DLB 119, 192, 217; EFS 2; EW 6; EXPN; GFL 1789 to the Present; LAIT 1, 2; NFS 5; RGWL 2, 3; SATA 47; TWA

**Huidobro, Vicente**
See Huidobro Fernandez, Vicente Garcia
See also EWL 3; LAW

**Huidobro Fernandez, Vicente Garcia** 1893-1948 **TCLC 31**
See Huidobro, Vicente
See also CA 131; HW 1

**Hulme, Keri** 1947- **CLC 39, 130**
See also CA 125; CANR 69; CN 7; CP 7; CWP; EWL 3; FW; INT 125

**Hulme, T(homas) E(rnest)** 1883-1917 **TCLC 21**
See also BRWS 6; CA 203; 117; DLB 19

**Hume, David** 1711-1776 **LC 7, 56**
See also BRWS 3; DLB 104, 252; TEA

**Humphrey, William** 1924-1997 **CLC 45**
See also AMWS 9; CA 160; 77-80; CANR 68; CN 7; CSW; DLB 6, 212, 234, 278; TCWW 2

**Humphreys, Emyr Owen** 1919- **CLC 47**
See also CA 5-8R; CANR 3, 24; CN 7; DLB 15

**Humphreys, Josephine** 1945- **CLC 34, 57**
See also CA 127; 121; CANR 97; CSW; INT 127

**Huneker, James Gibbons** 1860-1921 **TCLC 65**
See also CA 193; DLB 71; RGAL 4

**Hungerford, Hesba Fay**
See Brinsmead, H(esba) F(ay)

**Hungerford, Pixie**
See Brinsmead, H(esba) F(ay)

**Hunt, E(verette) Howard, (Jr.)** 1918- **CLC 3**
See also AITN 1; CA 45-48; CANR 2, 47, 103; CMW 4

**Hunt, Francesca**
See Holland, Isabelle (Christian)

**Hunt, Howard**
See Hunt, E(verette) Howard, (Jr.)

**Hunt, Kyle**
See Creasey, John

**Hunt, (James Henry) Leigh** 1784-1859 **NCLC 1, 70**
See also DAM POET; DLB 96, 110, 144; RGEL 2; TEA

**Hunt, Marsha** 1946- **CLC 70**
See also BW 2, 3; CA 143; CANR 79

**Hunt, Violet** 1866(?)-1942 **TCLC 53**
See also CA 184; DLB 162, 197

**Hunter, E. Waldo**
See Sturgeon, Theodore (Hamilton)

**Hunter, Evan** 1926- **CLC 11, 31**
See McBain, Ed
See also AAYA 39; BPFB 2; CA 5-8R; CANR 5, 38, 62, 97; CMW 4; CN 7; CPW; DAM POP; DLBY 1982; INT CANR-5; MSW; MTCW 1; SATA 25; SFW 4

**Hunter, Kristin** 1931-
See Lattany, Kristin (Elaine Eggleston) Hunter

**Hunter, Mary**
See Austin, Mary (Hunter)

**Hunter, Mollie** 1922- **CLC 21**
See McIlwraith, Maureen Mollie Hunter
See also AAYA 13; BYA 6; CANR 37, 78; CLR 25; DLB 161; JRDA; MAICYA 1, 2; SAAS 7; SATA 54, 106; WYA; YAW

**Hunter, Robert** (?)-1734 **LC 7**

**Hurston, Zora Neale** 1891-1960 **BLC 2; CLC 7, 30, 61; DC 12; HR 2; SSC 4; TCLC 121, 131; WLCS**
See also AAYA 15; AFAW 1, 2; AMWS 6; BW 1, 3; BYA 12; CA 85-88; CANR 61; CDALBS; DA; DA3; DAC; DAM MST, MULT, NOV; DFS 6; DLB 51, 86; EWL 3; EXPN; EXPS; FW; LAIT 3; LMFS 2; MAWW; MTCW 1, 2; NFS 3; RGAL 4; RGSF 2; SSFS 1, 6, 11; TUS; YAW

**Husserl, E. G.**
See Husserl, Edmund (Gustav Albrecht)

**Husserl, Edmund (Gustav Albrecht)** 1859-1938 **TCLC 100**
See also CA 133; 116

**Huston, John (Marcellus)** 1906-1987 **CLC 20**
See also CA 123; 73-76; CANR 34; DLB 26

**Hustvedt, Siri** 1955- **CLC 76**
See also CA 137

**Hutten, Ulrich von** 1488-1523 **LC 16**
See also DLB 179

**Huxley, Aldous (Leonard)** 1894-1963 **CLC 1, 3, 4, 5, 8, 11, 18, 35, 79; WLC**
See also AAYA 11; BPFB 2; BRW 7; CA 85-88; CANR 44, 99; CDBLB 1914-1945; DA; DA3; DAB; DAC; DAM MST, NOV; DLB 36, 100, 162, 195, 255; EWL 3; EXPN; LAIT 5; MTCW 1, 2; NFS 6; RGEL 2; SATA 63; SCFW 2; SFW 4; TEA; YAW

**Huxley, T(homas) H(enry)** 1825-1895 **NCLC 67**
See also DLB 57; TEA

**Huysmans, Joris-Karl** 1848-1907 **TCLC 7, 69**
See also CA 165; 104; DLB 123; EW 7; GFL 1789 to the Present; RGWL 2, 3

**Hwang, David Henry** 1957- **CLC 55; DC 4**
See also CA 132; 127; CAD; CANR 76; CD 5; DA3; DAM DRAM; DFS 11; DLB 212, 228; INT CA-132; MTCW 2; RGAL 4

**Hyde, Anthony** 1946- **CLC 42**
See Chase, Nicholas
See also CA 136; CCA 1

**Hyde, Margaret O(ldroyd)** 1917- **CLC 21**
See also CA 1-4R; CANR 1, 36; CLR 23; JRDA; MAICYA 1, 2; SAAS 8; SATA 1, 42, 76

**Hynes, James** 1956(?)- **CLC 65**
See also CA 164; CANR 105

**Hypatia** c. 370-415 **CMLC 35**

**Ian, Janis** 1951- **CLC 21**
See also CA 187; 105

**Ibanez, Vicente Blasco**
See Blasco Ibanez, Vicente

**Ibarbourou, Juana de** 1895-1979 **HLCS 2**
See also HW 1; LAW

**Ibarguengoitia, Jorge** 1928-1983 **CLC 37**
See also CA 113; 124; EWL 3; HW 1

**Ibn Battuta, Abu Abdalla** 1304-1368(?) **CMLC 57**
See also WLIT 2

**Ibsen, Henrik (Johan)** 1828-1906 **DC 2; TCLC 2, 8, 16, 37, 52; WLC**
See also AAYA 46; CA 141; 104; DA; DA3; DAB; DAC; DAM DRAM, MST; DFS 1, 6, 8, 10, 11, 15, 16; EW 7; LAIT 2; RGWL 2, 3

**Ibuse, Masuji** 1898-1993 **CLC 22**
See Ibuse Masuji
See also CA 141; 127; MJW; RGWL 3

**Ibuse Masuji**
See Ibuse, Masuji
See also DLB 180; EWL 3

**Ichikawa, Kon** 1915- **CLC 20**
See also CA 121

**Author Index**

**Jones, Arthur Llewellyn** 1863-1947
See Machen, Arthur
See also CA 179; 104; HGG

**Jones, D(ouglas) G(ordon)** 1929- **CLC 10**
See also CA 29-32R; CANR 13, 90; CP 7;
DLB 53

**Jones, David (Michael)** 1895-1974 **CLC 2, 4,
7, 13, 42**
See also BRW 6; BRWS 7; CA 53-56;
9-12R; CANR 28; CDBLB 1945-1960;
DLB 20, 100; EWL 3; MTCW 1; PAB;
RGEL 2

**Jones, David Robert** 1947-
See Bowie, David
See also CA 103; CANR 104

**Jones, Diana Wynne** 1934- **CLC 26**
See also AAYA 12; BYA 6, 7, 9, 11, 13; CA
49-52; CANR 4, 26, 56; CLR 23; DLB
161; FANT; JRDA; MAICYA 1, 2; SAAS
7; SATA 9, 70, 108; SFW 4; SUFW 2;
YAW

**Jones, Edward P.** 1950- **CLC 76**
See also BW 2, 3; CA 142; CANR 79; CSW

**Jones, Gayl** 1949- **BLC 2; CLC 6, 9, 131**
See also AFAW 1, 2; BW 2, 3; CA 77-80;
CANR 27, 66; CN 7; CSW; DA3; DAM
MULT; DLB 33, 278; MTCW 1, 2; RGAL
4

**Jones, James** 1921-1977 **CLC 1, 3, 10, 39**
See also AITN 1, 2; AMWS 11; BPFB 2;
CA 69-72; 1-4R; CANR 6; DLB 2, 143;
DLBD 17; DLBY 1998; EWL 3; MTCW
1; RGAL 4

**Jones, John J.**
See Lovecraft, H(oward) P(hillips)

**Jones, LeRoi CLC 1, 2, 3, 5, 10, 14**
See Baraka, Amiri
See also MTCW 2

**Jones, Louis B.** 1953- **CLC 65**
See also CA 141; CANR 73

**Jones, Madison (Percy, Jr.)** 1925- **CLC 4**
See also CA 13-16R; CAAS 11; CANR 7,
54, 83; CN 7; CSW; DLB 152

**Jones, Mervyn** 1922- **CLC 10, 52**
See also CA 45-48; CAAS 5; CANR 1, 91;
CN 7; MTCW 1

**Jones, Mick** 1956(?)- **CLC 30**

**Jones, Nettie (Pearl)** 1941- **CLC 34**
See also BW 2; CA 137; CAAS 20; CANR
88

**Jones, Peter** 1802-1856 **NNAL**

**Jones, Preston** 1936-1979 **CLC 10**
See also CA 89-92; 73-76; DLB 7

**Jones, Robert F(rancis)** 1934- **CLC 7**
See also CA 49-52; CANR 2, 61

**Jones, Rod** 1953- **CLC 50**
See also CA 128

**Jones, Terence Graham Parry** 1942- **CLC 21**
See Jones, Terry; Monty Python
See also CA 116; 112; CANR 35, 93; INT
116; SATA 127

**Jones, Terry**
See Jones, Terence Graham Parry
See also SATA 67; SATA-Brief 51

**Jones, Thom (Douglas)** 1945(?)- **CLC 81;
SSC 56**
See also CA 157; CANR 88; DLB 244

**Jong, Erica** 1942- **CLC 4, 6, 8, 18, 83**
See also AITN 1; AMWS 5; BEST 90:2;
BPFB 2; CA 73-76; CANR 26, 52, 75;
CN 7; CP 7; CPW; DA3; DAM NOV,
POP; DLB 2, 5, 28, 152; FW; INT CANR-
26; MTCW 1, 2

**Jonson, Ben(jamin)** 1572(?)-1637 **DC 4; LC
6, 33; PC 17; WLC**
See also BRW 1; BRWC 1; BRWR 1; CD-
BLB Before 1660; DA; DAB; DAC;
DAM DRAM, MST, POET; DFS 4, 10;
DLB 62, 121; RGEL 2; TEA; WLIT 3

**Jordan, June (Meyer)** 1936-2002 **BLCS;
CLC 5, 11, 23, 114; PC 38**
See also AAYA 2; AFAW 1, 2; BW 2, 3;
CA 206; 33-36R; CANR 25, 70, 114; CLR
10; CP 7; CWP; DAM MULT, POET;
DLB 38; GLL 2; LAIT 5; MAICYA 1, 2;
MTCW 1; SATA 4, 136; YAW

**Jordan, Neil (Patrick)** 1950- **CLC 110**
See also CA 130; 124; CANR 54; CN 7;
GLL 2; INT 130

**Jordan, Pat(rick M.)** 1941- **CLC 37**
See also CA 33-36R

**Jorgensen, Ivar**
See Ellison, Harlan (Jay)

**Jorgenson, Ivar**
See Silverberg, Robert

**Joseph, George Ghevarughese CLC 70**

**Josephson, Mary**
See O'Doherty, Brian

**Josephus, Flavius** c. 37-100 **CMLC 13**
See also AW 2; DLB 176

**Josiah Allen's Wife**
See Holley, Marietta

**Josipovici, Gabriel (David)** 1940- **CLC 6, 43,
153**
See also CA 37-40R; CAAS 8; CANR 47,
84; CN 7; DLB 14

**Joubert, Joseph** 1754-1824 **NCLC 9**

**Jouve, Pierre Jean** 1887-1976 **CLC 47**
See also CA 65-68; DLB 258; EWL 3

**Jovine, Francesco** 1902-1950 **TCLC 79**
See also DLB 264; EWL 3

**Joyce, James (Augustine Aloysius)**
1882-1941 **DC 16; PC 22; SSC 3, 26,
44; TCLC 3, 8, 16, 35, 52; WLC**
See also AAYA 42; BRW 7; BRWC 1;
BRWR 1; BYA 11, 13; CA 126; 104; CD-
BLB 1914-1945; DA; DA3; DAB; DAC;
DAM MST, NOV, POET; DLB 10, 19,
36, 162, 247; EWL 3; EXPN; EXPS;
LAIT 3; LMFS 2; MTCW 1, 2; NFS 7;
RGSF 2; SSFS 1; TEA; WLIT 4

**Jozsef, Attila** 1905-1937 **TCLC 22**
See also CA 116; CDWLB 4; DLB 215;
EWL 3

**Juana Ines de la Cruz, Sor** 1651(?)-1695
**HLCS 1; LC 5; PC 24**
See also FW; LAW; RGWL 2, 3; WLIT 1

**Juana Inez de La Cruz, Sor**
See Juana Ines de la Cruz, Sor

**Judd, Cyril**
See Kornbluth, C(yril) M.; Pohl, Frederik

**Juenger, Ernst** 1895-1998 **CLC 125**
See Junger, Ernst
See also CA 167; 101; CANR 21, 47, 106;
DLB 56

**Julian of Norwich** 1342(?)-1416(?) **LC 6, 52**
See also DLB 146

**Julius Caesar** 100B.C.-44B.C.
See Caesar, Julius
See also CDWLB 1; DLB 211

**Junger, Ernst**
See Juenger, Ernst
See also CDWLB 2; EWL 3; RGWL 2, 3

**Junger, Sebastian** 1962- **CLC 109**
See also AAYA 28; CA 165

**Juniper, Alex**
See Hospital, Janette Turner

**Junius**
See Luxemburg, Rosa

**Just, Ward (Swift)** 1935- **CLC 4, 27**
See also CA 25-28R; CANR 32, 87; CN 7;
INT CANR-32

**Justice, Donald (Rodney)** 1925- **CLC 6, 19,
102**
See also AMWS 7; CA 5-8R; CANR 26,
54, 74; CP 7; CSW; DAM POET; DLBY
1983; EWL 3; INT CANR-26; MTCW 2;
PFS 14

**Juvenal** c. 60-c. 130 **CMLC 8**
See also AW 2; CDWLB 1; DLB 211;
RGWL 2, 3

**Juvenis**
See Bourne, Randolph S(illiman)

**K., Alice**
See Knapp, Caroline

**Kabakov, Sasha CLC 59**

**Kacew, Romain** 1914-1980
See Gary, Romain
See also CA 102; 108

**Kadare, Ismail** 1936- **CLC 52**
See also CA 161; EWL 3; RGWL 3

**Kadohata, Cynthia CLC 59, 122**
See also CA 140

**Kafka, Franz** 1883-1924 **SSC 5, 29, 35;
TCLC 2, 6, 13, 29, 47, 53, 112; WLC**
See also AAYA 31; BPFB 2; CA 126; 105;
CDWLB 2; DA; DA3; DAB; DAC; DAM
MST, NOV; DLB 81; EW 9; EWL 3;
EXPS; LMFS 1; MTCW 1, 2; NFS 7;
RGSF 2; RGWL 2, 3; SFW 4; SSFS 3, 7,
12; TWA

**Kahanovitsch, Pinkhes**
See Der Nister

**Kahn, Roger** 1927- **CLC 30**
See also CA 25-28R; CANR 44, 69; DLB
171; SATA 37

**Kain, Saul**
See Sassoon, Siegfried (Lorraine)

**Kaiser, Georg** 1878-1945 **TCLC 9**
See also CA 190; 106; CDWLB 2; DLB
124; EWL 3; LMFS 2; RGWL 2, 3

**Kaledin, Sergei CLC 59**

**Kaletski, Alexander** 1946- **CLC 39**
See also CA 143; 118

**Kalidasa** fl. c. 400-455 **CMLC 9; PC 22**
See also RGWL 2, 3

**Kallman, Chester (Simon)** 1921-1975 **CLC 2**
See also CA 53-56; 45-48; CANR 3

**Kaminsky, Melvin** 1926-
See Brooks, Mel
See also CA 65-68; CANR 16

**Kaminsky, Stuart M(elvin)** 1934- **CLC 59**
See also CA 73-76; CANR 29, 53, 89;
CMW 4

**Kandinsky, Wassily** 1866-1944 **TCLC 92**
See also CA 155; 118

**Kane, Francis**
See Robbins, Harold

**Kane, Henry** 1918-
See Queen, Ellery
See also CA 156; CMW 4

**Kane, Paul**
See Simon, Paul (Frederick)

**Kanin, Garson** 1912-1999 **CLC 22**
See also AITN 1; CA 177; 5-8R; CAD;
CANR 7, 78; DLB 7; IDFW 3, 4

**Kaniuk, Yoram** 1930- **CLC 19**
See also CA 134

**Kant, Immanuel** 1724-1804 **NCLC 27, 67**
See also DLB 94

**Kantor, MacKinlay** 1904-1977 **CLC 7**
See also CA 73-76; 61-64; CANR 60, 63;
DLB 9, 102; MTCW 2; RHW; TCWW 2

**Kanze Motokiyo**
See Zeami

**Kaplan, David Michael** 1946- **CLC 50**
See also CA 187

**Kaplan, James** 1951- **CLC 59**
See also CA 135

**Karadzic, Vuk Stefanovic** 1787-1864 **NCLC
115**
See also CDWLB 4; DLB 147

**Karageorge, Michael**
See Anderson, Poul (William)

**Key, Ellen (Karolina Sofia)** 1849-1926 **TCLC 65**
See also DLB 259

**Keyber, Conny**
See Fielding, Henry

**Keyes, Daniel** 1927- **CLC 80**
See also AAYA 23; BYA 11; CA 17-20R, 181; CAAE 181; CANR 10, 26, 54, 74; DA; DA3; DAC; DAM MST, NOV; EXPN; LAIT 4; MTCW 2; NFS 2; SATA 37; SFW 4

**Keynes, John Maynard** 1883-1946 **TCLC 64**
See also CA 162, 163; 114; DLBD 10; MTCW 2

**Khanshendel, Chiron**
See Rose, Wendy

**Khayyam, Omar** 1048-1131 **CMLC 11; PC 8**
See Omar Khayyam
See also DA3; DAM POET

**Kherdian, David** 1931- **CLC 6, 9**
See also AAYA 42; CA 21-24R; CAAE 192; CAAS 2; CANR 39, 78; CLR 24; JRDA; LAIT 3; MAICYA 1, 2; SATA 16, 74; SATA-Essay 125

**Khlebnikov, Velimir TCLC 20**
See Khlebnikov, Viktor Vladimirovich
See also EW 10; EWL 3; RGWL 2, 3

**Khlebnikov, Viktor Vladimirovich** 1885-1922
See Khlebnikov, Velimir
See also CA 117

**Khodasevich, Vladislav (Felitsianovich)** 1886-1939 **TCLC 15**
See also CA 115; EWL 3

**Kielland, Alexander Lange** 1849-1906 **TCLC 5**
See also CA 104

**Kiely, Benedict** 1919- **CLC 23, 43; SSC 58**
See also CA 1-4R; CANR 2, 84; CN 7; DLB 15

**Kienzle, William X(avier)** 1928-2001 **CLC 25**
See also CA 203; 93-96; CAAS 1; CANR 9, 31, 59, 111; CMW 4; DA3; DAM POP; INT CANR-31; MSW; MTCW 1, 2

**Kierkegaard, Soren** 1813-1855 **NCLC 34, 78**
See also EW 6; LMFS 2; RGWL 3; TWA

**Kieslowski, Krzysztof** 1941-1996 **CLC 120**
See also CA 151; 147

**Killens, John Oliver** 1916-1987 **CLC 10**
See also BW 2; CA 123; 77-80; CAAS 2; CANR 26; DLB 33; EWL 3

**Killigrew, Anne** 1660-1685 **LC 4, 73**
See also DLB 131

**Killigrew, Thomas** 1612-1683 **LC 57**
See also DLB 58; RGEL 2

**Kim**
See Simenon, Georges (Jacques Christian)

**Kincaid, Jamaica** 1949- **BLC 2; CLC 43, 68, 137**
See also AAYA 13; AFAW 2; AMWS 7; BRWS 7; BW 2, 3; CA 125; CANR 47, 59, 95; CDALBS; CDWLB 3; CLR 63; CN 7; DA3; DAM MULT, NOV; DLB 157, 227; DNFS 1; EWL 3; EXPS; FW; LMFS 2; MTCW 2; NCFS 1; NFS 3; SSFS 5, 7; TUS; YAW

**King, Francis (Henry)** 1923- **CLC 8, 53, 145**
See also CA 1-4R; CANR 1, 33, 86; CN 7; DAM NOV; DLB 15, 139; MTCW 1

**King, Kennedy**
See Brown, George Douglas

**King, Martin Luther, Jr.** 1929-1968 **BLC 2; CLC 83; WLCS**
See also BW 2, 3; CA 25-28; CANR 27, 44; CAP 2; DA; DA3; DAB; DAC; DAM MST, MULT; LAIT 5; MTCW 1, 2; SATA 14

**King, Stephen (Edwin)** 1947- **CLC 12, 26, 37, 61, 113; SSC 17, 55**
See also AAYA 1, 17; AMWS 5; BEST 90:1; BPFB 2; CA 61-64; CANR 1, 30, 52, 76; CPW; DA3; DAM NOV, POP; DLB 143; DLBY 1980; HGG; JRDA; LAIT 5; MTCW 1, 2; RGAL 4; SATA 9, 55; SUFW 1, 2; WYAS 1; YAW

**King, Steve**
See King, Stephen (Edwin)

**King, Thomas** 1943- **CLC 89, 171; NNAL**
See also CA 144; CANR 95; CCA 1; CN 7; DAC; DAM MULT; DLB 175; SATA 96

**Kingman, Lee CLC 17**
See Natti, (Mary) Lee
See also CWRI 5; SAAS 3; SATA 1, 67

**Kingsley, Charles** 1819-1875 **NCLC 35**
See also CLR 77; DLB 21, 32, 163, 178, 190; FANT; MAICYA 2; MAICYAS 1; RGEL 2; WCH; YABC 2

**Kingsley, Henry** 1830-1876 **NCLC 107**
See also DLB 21, 230; RGEL 2

**Kingsley, Sidney** 1906-1995 **CLC 44**
See also CA 147; 85-88; CAD; DFS 14; DLB 7; RGAL 4

**Kingsolver, Barbara** 1955- **CLC 55, 81, 130**
See also AAYA 15; AMWS 7; CA 134; 129; CANR 60, 96; CDALBS; CPW; CSW; DA3; DAM POP; DLB 206; INT CA-134; LAIT 5; MTCW 2; NFS 5, 10, 12; RGAL 4

**Kingston, Maxine (Ting Ting) Hong** 1940- **AAL; CLC 12, 19, 58, 121; WLCS**
See also AAYA 8; AMWS 5; BPFB 2; CA 69-72; CANR 13, 38, 74, 87; CDALBS; CN 7; DA3; DAM MULT, NOV; DLB 173, 212; DLBY 1980; EWL 3; FW; INT CANR-13; LAIT 5; MAWW; MTCW 1, 2; NFS 6; RGAL 4; SATA 53; SSFS 3

**Kinnell, Galway** 1927- **CLC 1, 2, 3, 5, 13, 29, 129; PC 26**
See also AMWS 3; CA 9-12R; CANR 10, 34, 66, 116; CP 7; DLB 5; DLBY 1987; EWL 3; INT CANR-34; MTCW 1, 2; PAB; PFS 9; RGAL 4; WP

**Kinsella, Thomas** 1928- **CLC 4, 19, 138**
See also BRWS 5; CA 17-20R; CANR 15; CP 7; DLB 27; EWL 3; MTCW 1, 2; RGEL 2; TEA

**Kinsella, W(illiam) P(atrick)** 1935- **CLC 27, 43, 166**
See also AAYA 7; BPFB 2; CA 97-100; CAAS 7; CANR 21, 35, 66, 75; CN 7; CPW; DAC; DAM NOV, POP; FANT; INT CANR-21; LAIT 5; MTCW 1, 2; NFS 15; RGSF 2

**Kinsey, Alfred C(harles)** 1894-1956 **TCLC 91**
See also CA 170; 115; MTCW 2

**Kipling, (Joseph) Rudyard** 1865-1936 **PC 3; SSC 5, 54; TCLC 8, 17; WLC**
See also AAYA 32; BRW 6; BRWC 1; BYA 4; CA 120; 105; CANR 33; CDBLB 1890-1914; CLR 39, 65; CWRI 5; DA; DA3; DAB; DAC; DAM MST, POET; DLB 19, 34, 141, 156; EWL 3; EXPS; FANT; LAIT 3; MAICYA 1, 2; MTCW 1, 2; RGEL 2; RGSF 2; SATA 100; SFW 4; SSFS 8; SUFW 1; TEA; WCH; WLIT 4; YABC 2

**Kirk, Russell (Amos)** 1918-1994 **TCLC 119**
See also AITN 1; CA 145; 1-4R; CAAS 9; CANR 1, 20, 60; HGG; INT CANR-20; MTCW 1, 2

**Kirkland, Caroline M.** 1801-1864 **NCLC 85**
See also DLB 3, 73, 74, 250, 254; DLBD 13

**Kirkup, James** 1918- **CLC 1**
See also CA 1-4R; CAAS 4; CANR 2; CP 7; DLB 27; SATA 12

**Kirkwood, James** 1930(?)-1989 **CLC 9**
See also AITN 2; CA 128; 1-4R; CANR 6, 40; GLL 2

**Kirshner, Sidney**
See Kingsley, Sidney

**Kis, Danilo** 1935-1989 **CLC 57**
See also CA 129; 118; 109; CANR 61; CDWLB 4; DLB 181; EWL 3; MTCW 1; RGSF 2; RGWL 2, 3

**Kissinger, Henry A(lfred)** 1923- **CLC 137**
See also CA 1-4R; CANR 2, 33, 66, 109; MTCW 1

**Kivi, Aleksis** 1834-1872 **NCLC 30**

**Kizer, Carolyn (Ashley)** 1925- **CLC 15, 39, 80**
See also CA 65-68; CAAS 5; CANR 24, 70; CP 7; CWP; DAM POET; DLB 5, 169; EWL 3; MTCW 1

**Klabund** 1890-1928 **TCLC 44**
See also CA 162; DLB 66

**Klappert, Peter** 1942- **CLC 57**
See also CA 33-36R; CSW; DLB 5

**Klein, A(braham) M(oses)** 1909-1972 **CLC 19**
See also CA 37-40R; 101; DAB; DAC; DAM MST; DLB 68; EWL 3; RGEL 2

**Klein, Joe**
See Klein, Joseph

**Klein, Joseph** 1946- **CLC 154**
See also CA 85-88; CANR 55

**Klein, Norma** 1938-1989 **CLC 30**
See also AAYA 2, 35; BPFB 2; BYA 6, 7, 8; CA 128; 41-44R; CANR 15, 37; CLR 2, 19; INT CANR-15; JRDA; MAICYA 1, 2; SAAS 1; SATA 7, 57; WYA; YAW

**Klein, T(heodore) E(ibon) D(onald)** 1947- **CLC 34**
See also CA 119; CANR 44, 75; HGG

**Kleist, Heinrich von** 1777-1811 **NCLC 2, 37; SSC 22**
See also CDWLB 2; DAM DRAM; DLB 90; EW 5; RGSF 2; RGWL 2, 3

**Klima, Ivan** 1931- **CLC 56, 172**
See also CA 25-28R; CANR 17, 50, 91; CDWLB 4; CWW 2; DAM NOV; DLB 232; EWL 3; RGWL 3

**Klimentev, Andrei Platonovich**
See Klimentov, Andrei Platonovich

**Klimentov, Andrei Platonovich** 1899-1951 **SSC 42; TCLC 14**
See Platonov, Andrei Platonovich; Platonov, Andrey Platonovich
See also CA 108

**Klinger, Friedrich Maximilian von** 1752-1831 **NCLC 1**
See also DLB 94

**Klingsor the Magician**
See Hartmann, Sadakichi

**Klopstock, Friedrich Gottlieb** 1724-1803 **NCLC 11**
See also DLB 97; EW 4; RGWL 2, 3

**Knapp, Caroline** 1959-2002 **CLC 99**
See also CA 207; 154

**Knebel, Fletcher** 1911-1993 **CLC 14**
See also AITN 1; CA 140; 1-4R; CAAS 3; CANR 1, 36; SATA 36; SATA-Obit 75

**Knickerbocker, Diedrich**
See Irving, Washington

**Knight, Etheridge** 1931-1991 **BLC 2; CLC 40; PC 14**
See also BW 1, 3; CA 133; 21-24R; CANR 23, 82; DAM POET; DLB 41; MTCW 2; RGAL 4

**Knight, Sarah Kemble** 1666-1727 **LC 7**
See also DLB 24, 200

**Knister, Raymond** 1899-1932 **TCLC 56**
See also CA 186; DLB 68; RGEL 2

**Knowles, John** 1926-2001 **CLC 1, 4, 10, 26**
See also AAYA 10; AMWS 12; BPFB 2;
BYA 3; CA 203; 17-20R; CANR 40, 74,
76; CDALB 1968-1988; CN 7; DA; DAC;
DAM MST, NOV; DLB 6; EXPN; MTCW
1, 2; NFS 2; RGAL 4; SATA 8, 89; SATA-
Obit 134; YAW

**Knox, Calvin M.**
See Silverberg, Robert

**Knox, John** c. 1505-1572 **LC 37**
See also DLB 132

**Knye, Cassandra**
See Disch, Thomas M(ichael)

**Koch, C(hristopher) J(ohn)** 1932- **CLC 42**
See also CA 127; CANR 84; CN 7

**Koch, Christopher**
See Koch, C(hristopher) J(ohn)

**Koch, Kenneth (Jay)** 1925-2002 **CLC 5, 8, 44**
See also CA 207; 1-4R; CAD; CANR 6,
36, 57, 97; CD 5; CP 7; DAM POET;
DLB 5; INT CANR-36; MTCW 2; SATA
65; WP

**Kochanowski, Jan** 1530-1584 **LC 10**
See also RGWL 2, 3

**Kock, Charles Paul de** 1794-1871 **NCLC 16**

**Koda Rohan**
See Koda Shigeyuki

**Koda Rohan**
See Koda Shigeyuki
See also DLB 180

**Koda Shigeyuki** 1867-1947 **TCLC 22**
See Koda Rohan
See also CA 183; 121

**Koestler, Arthur** 1905-1983 **CLC 1, 3, 6, 8, 15, 33**
See also BRWS 1; CA 109; 1-4R; CANR 1,
33; CDBLB 1945-1960; DLBY 1983;
EWL 3; MTCW 1, 2; RGEL 2

**Kogawa, Joy Nozomi** 1935- **CLC 78, 129**
See also AAYA 47; CA 101; CANR 19, 62;
CN 7; CWP; DAC; DAM MST, MULT;
FW; MTCW 2; NFS 3; SATA 99

**Kohout, Pavel** 1928- **CLC 13**
See also CA 45-48; CANR 3

**Koizumi, Yakumo**
See Hearn, (Patricio) Lafcadio (Tessima
Carlos)

**Kolmar, Gertrud** 1894-1943 **TCLC 40**
See also CA 167; EWL 3

**Komunyakaa, Yusef** 1947- **BLCS; CLC 86, 94**
See also AFAW 2; CA 147; CANR 83; CP
7; CSW; DLB 120; EWL 3; PFS 5; RGAL
4

**Konrad, George**
See Konrad, Gyorgy
See also CWW 2

**Konrad, Gyorgy** 1933- **CLC 4, 10, 73**
See Konrad, George
See also CA 85-88; CANR 97; CDWLB 4;
CWW 2; DLB 232; EWL 3

**Konwicki, Tadeusz** 1926- **CLC 8, 28, 54, 117**
See also CA 101; CAAS 9; CANR 39, 59;
CWW 2; DLB 232; EWL 3; IDFW 3;
MTCW 1

**Koontz, Dean R(ay)** 1945- **CLC 78**
See also AAYA 9, 31; BEST 89:3, 90:2; CA
108; CANR 19, 36, 52, 95; CMW 4;
CPW; DA3; DAM NOV, POP; HGG;
MTCW 1; SATA 92; SFW 4; SUFW 2;
YAW

**Kopernik, Mikolaj**
See Copernicus, Nicolaus

**Kopit, Arthur (Lee)** 1937- **CLC 1, 18, 33**
See also AITN 1; CA 81-84; CABS 3; CD
5; DAM DRAM; DFS 7, 14; DLB 7;
MTCW 1; RGAL 4

**Kopitar, Jernej (Bartholomaus)** 1780-1844
**NCLC 117**

**Kops, Bernard** 1926- **CLC 4**
See also CA 5-8R; CANR 84; CBD; CN 7;
CP 7; DLB 13

**Kornbluth, C(yril) M.** 1923-1958 **TCLC 8**
See also CA 160; 105; DLB 8; SFW 4

**Korolenko, V. G.**
See Korolenko, Vladimir Galaktionovich

**Korolenko, Vladimir**
See Korolenko, Vladimir Galaktionovich

**Korolenko, Vladimir G.**
See Korolenko, Vladimir Galaktionovich

**Korolenko, Vladimir Galaktionovich**
1853-1921 **TCLC 22**
See also CA 121; DLB 277

**Korzybski, Alfred (Habdank Skarbek)**
1879-1950 **TCLC 61**
See also CA 160; 123

**Kosinski, Jerzy (Nikodem)** 1933-1991 **CLC 1, 2, 3, 6, 10, 15, 53, 70**
See also AMWS 7; BPFB 2; CA 134; 17-
20R; CANR 9, 46; DA3; DAM NOV;
DLB 2; DLBY 1982; EWL 3; HGG;
MTCW 1, 2; NFS 12; RGAL 4; TUS

**Kostelanetz, Richard (Cory)** 1940- **CLC 28**
See also CA 13-16R; CAAS 8; CANR 38,
77; CN 7; CP 7

**Kostrowitzki, Wilhelm Apollinaris de**
1880-1918
See Apollinaire, Guillaume
See also CA 104

**Kotlowitz, Robert** 1924- **CLC 4**
See also CA 33-36R; CANR 36

**Kotzebue, August (Friedrich Ferdinand) von**
1761-1819 **NCLC 25**
See also DLB 94

**Kotzwinkle, William** 1938- **CLC 5, 14, 35**
See also BPFB 2; CA 45-48; CANR 3, 44,
84; CLR 6; DLB 173; FANT; MAICYA
1, 2; SATA 24, 70; SFW 4; SUFW 2;
YAW

**Kowna, Stancy**
See Szymborska, Wislawa

**Kozol, Jonathan** 1936- **CLC 17**
See also AAYA 46; CA 61-64; CANR 16,
45, 96

**Kozoll, Michael** 1940(?)- **CLC 35**

**Kramer, Kathryn** 19(?)- **CLC 34**

**Kramer, Larry** 1935- **CLC 42; DC 8**
See also CA 126; 124; CANR 60; DAM
POP; DLB 249; GLL 1

**Krasicki, Ignacy** 1735-1801 **NCLC 8**

**Krasinski, Zygmunt** 1812-1859 **NCLC 4**
See also RGWL 2, 3

**Kraus, Karl** 1874-1936 **TCLC 5**
See also CA 104; DLB 118; EWL 3

**Kreve (Mickevicius), Vincas** 1882-1954
**TCLC 27**
See also CA 170; DLB 220; EWL 3

**Kristeva, Julia** 1941- **CLC 77, 140**
See also CA 154; CANR 99; DLB 242;
EWL 3; FW

**Kristofferson, Kris** 1936- **CLC 26**
See also CA 104

**Krizanc, John** 1956- **CLC 57**
See also CA 187

**Krleza, Miroslav** 1893-1981 **CLC 8, 114**
See also CA 105; 97-100; CANR 50; CD-
WLB 4; DLB 147; EW 11; RGWL 2, 3

**Kroetsch, Robert** 1927- **CLC 5, 23, 57, 132**
See also CA 17-20R; CANR 8, 38; CCA 1;
CN 7; CP 7; DAC; DAM POET; DLB 53;
MTCW 1

**Kroetz, Franz**
See Kroetz, Franz Xaver

**Kroetz, Franz Xaver** 1946- **CLC 41**
See also CA 130; EWL 3

**Kroker, Arthur (W.)** 1945- **CLC 77**
See also CA 161

**Kropotkin, Peter (Aleksieevich)** 1842-1921
**TCLC 36**
See Kropotkin, Petr Alekseevich
See also CA 119

**Kropotkin, Petr Alekseevich**
See Kropotkin, Peter (Aleksieevich)
See also DLB 277

**Krotkov, Yuri** 1917-1981 **CLC 19**
See also CA 102

**Krumb**
See Crumb, R(obert)

**Krumgold, Joseph (Quincy)** 1908-1980 **CLC 12**
See also BYA 1, 2; CA 101; 9-12R; CANR
7; MAICYA 1, 2; SATA 1, 48; SATA-Obit
23; YAW

**Krumwitz**
See Crumb, R(obert)

**Krutch, Joseph Wood** 1893-1970 **CLC 24**
See also ANW; CA 25-28R; 1-4R; CANR
4; DLB 63, 206, 275

**Krutzch, Gus**
See Eliot, T(homas) S(tearns)

**Krylov, Ivan Andreevich** 1768(?)-1844 **NCLC 1**
See also DLB 150

**Kubin, Alfred (Leopold Isidor)** 1877-1959
**TCLC 23**
See also CA 149; 112; CANR 104; DLB 81

**Kubrick, Stanley** 1928-1999 **CLC 16; TCLC 112**
See also AAYA 30; CA 177; 81-84; CANR
33; DLB 26

**Kueng, Hans** 1928-
See Kung, Hans
See also CA 53-56; CANR 66; MTCW 1, 2

**Kumin, Maxine (Winokur)** 1925- **CLC 5, 13, 28, 164; PC 15**
See also AITN 2; AMWS 4; ANW; CA
1-4R; CAAS 8; CANR 1, 21, 69, 115; CP
7; CWP; DA3; DAM POET; DLB 5;
EWL 3; EXPP; MTCW 1, 2; PAB; SATA
12

**Kundera, Milan** 1929- **CLC 4, 9, 19, 32, 68, 115, 135; SSC 24**
See also AAYA 2; BPFB 2; CA 85-88;
CANR 19, 52, 74; CDWLB 4; CWW 2;
DA3; DAM NOV; DLB 232; EW 13;
EWL 3; MTCW 1, 2; RGSF 2; RGWL 3;
SSFS 10

**Kunene, Mazisi (Raymond)** 1930- **CLC 85**
See also BW 1, 3; CA 125; CANR 81; CP
7; DLB 117

**Kung, Hans CLC 130**
See Kueng, Hans

**Kunikida Doppo** 1869(?)-1908
See Doppo, Kunikida
See also DLB 180; EWL 3

**Kunitz, Stanley (Jasspon)** 1905- **CLC 6, 11, 14, 148; PC 19**
See also AMWS 3; CA 41-44R; CANR 26,
57, 98; CP 7; DA3; DLB 48; INT CANR-
26; MTCW 1, 2; PFS 11; RGAL 4

**Kunze, Reiner** 1933- **CLC 10**
See also CA 93-96; CWW 2; DLB 75; EWL
3

**Kuprin, Aleksander Ivanovich** 1870-1938
**TCLC 5**
See Kuprin, Alexandr Ivanovich
See also CA 182; 104

**Kuprin, Alexandr Ivanovich**
See Kuprin, Aleksander Ivanovich
See also EWL 3

**Kureishi, Hanif** 1954(?)- **CLC 64, 135**
See also CA 139; CANR 113; CBD; CD 5;
CN 7; DLB 194, 245; GLL 2; IDFW 4;
WLIT 4

**Kurosawa, Akira** 1910-1998 **CLC 16, 119**
　　See also AAYA 11; CA 170; 101; CANR 46; DAM MULT

**Kushner, Tony** 1957(?)- **CLC 81; DC 10**
　　See also AMWS 9; CA 144; CAD; CANR 74; CD 5; DA3; DAM DRAM; DFS 5; DLB 228; EWL 3; GLL 1; LAIT 5; MTCW 2; RGAL 4

**Kuttner, Henry** 1915-1958 **TCLC 10**
　　See also CA 157; 107; DLB 8; FANT; SCFW 2; SFW 4

**Kutty, Madhavi**
　　See Das, Kamala

**Kuzma, Greg** 1944- **CLC 7**
　　See also CA 33-36R; CANR 70

**Kuzmin, Mikhail** 1872(?)-1936 **TCLC 40**
　　See also CA 170; EWL 3

**Kyd, Thomas** 1558-1594 **DC 3; LC 22**
　　See also BRW 1; DAM DRAM; DLB 62; IDTP; RGEL 2; TEA; WLIT 3

**Kyprianos, Iossif**
　　See Samarakis, Antonis

**L. S.**
　　See Stephen, Sir Leslie

**Labrunie, Gerard**
　　See Nerval, Gerard de

**La Bruyere, Jean de** 1645-1696 **LC 17**
　　See also DLB 268; EW 3; GFL Beginnings to 1789

**Lacan, Jacques (Marie Emile)** 1901-1981 **CLC 75**
　　See also CA 104; 121; EWL 3; TWA

**Laclos, Pierre Ambroise Francois** 1741-1803 **NCLC 4, 87**
　　See also EW 4; GFL Beginnings to 1789; RGWL 2, 3

**La Colere, Francois**
　　See Aragon, Louis

**Lacolere, Francois**
　　See Aragon, Louis

**La Deshabilleuse**
　　See Simenon, Georges (Jacques Christian)

**Lady Gregory**
　　See Gregory, Lady Isabella Augusta (Persse)

**Lady of Quality, A**
　　See Bagnold, Enid

**La Fayette, Marie-(Madelaine Pioche de la Vergne)** 1634-1693 **LC 2**
　　See Lafayette, Marie-Madeleine
　　See also GFL Beginnings to 1789; RGWL 2, 3

**Lafayette, Marie-Madeleine**
　　See La Fayette, Marie-(Madelaine Pioche de la Vergne)
　　See also DLB 268

**Lafayette, Rene**
　　See Hubbard, L(afayette) Ron(ald)

**La Flesche, Francis** 1857(?)-1932 **NNAL**
　　See also CA 144; CANR 83; DLB 175

**La Fontaine, Jean de** 1621-1695 **LC 50**
　　See also DLB 268; EW 3; GFL Beginnings to 1789; MAICYA 1, 2; RGWL 2, 3; SATA 18

**Laforgue, Jules** 1860-1887 **NCLC 5, 53; PC 14; SSC 20**
　　See also DLB 217; EW 7; GFL 1789 to the Present; RGWL 2, 3

**Layamon**
　　See Layamon
　　See also DLB 146

**Lagerkvist, Paer (Fabian)** 1891-1974 **CLC 7, 10, 13, 54**
　　See Lagerkvist, Par
　　See also CA 49-52; 85-88; DA3; DAM DRAM, NOV; MTCW 1, 2; TWA

**Lagerkvist, Par SSC 12**
　　See Lagerkvist, Paer (Fabian)
　　See also DLB 259; EW 10; EWL 3; MTCW 2; RGSF 2; RGWL 2, 3

**Lagerloef, Selma (Ottiliana Lovisa)** 1858-1940 **TCLC 4, 36**
　　See Lagerlof, Selma (Ottiliana Lovisa)
　　See also CA 108; MTCW 2; SATA 15

**Lagerlof, Selma (Ottiliana Lovisa)**
　　See Lagerloef, Selma (Ottiliana Lovisa)
　　See also CLR 7; SATA 15

**La Guma, (Justin) Alex(ander)** 1925-1985 **BLCS; CLC 19**
　　See also AFW; BW 1, 3; CA 118; 49-52; CANR 25, 81; CDWLB 3; DAM NOV; DLB 117, 225; EWL 3; MTCW 1, 2; WLIT 2

**Laidlaw, A. K.**
　　See Grieve, C(hristopher) M(urray)

**Lainez, Manuel Mujica**
　　See Mujica Lainez, Manuel
　　See also HW 1

**Laing, R(onald) D(avid)** 1927-1989 **CLC 95**
　　See also CA 129; 107; CANR 34; MTCW 1

**Lamartine, Alphonse (Marie Louis Prat) de** 1790-1869 **NCLC 11; PC 16**
　　See also DAM POET; DLB 217; GFL 1789 to the Present; RGWL 2, 3

**Lamb, Charles** 1775-1834 **NCLC 10, 113; WLC**
　　See also BRW 4; CDBLB 1789-1832; DA; DAB; DAC; DAM MST; DLB 93, 107, 163; RGEL 2; SATA 17; TEA

**Lamb, Lady Caroline** 1785-1828 **NCLC 38**
　　See also DLB 116

**Lame Deer** 1903(?)-1976 **NNAL**
　　See also CA 69-72

**Lamming, George (William)** 1927- **BLC 2; CLC 2, 4, 66, 144**
　　See also BW 2, 3; CA 85-88; CANR 26, 76; CDWLB 3; CN 7; DAM MULT; DLB 125; EWL 3; MTCW 1, 2; NFS 15; RGEL 2

**L'Amour, Louis (Dearborn)** 1908-1988 **CLC 25, 55**
　　See Burns, Tex; Mayo, Jim
　　See also AAYA 16; AITN 2; BEST 89:2; BPFB 2; CA 125; 1-4R; CANR 3, 25, 40; CPW; DA3; DAM NOV, POP; DLB 206; DLBY 1980; MTCW 1, 2; RGAL 4

**Lampedusa, Giuseppe (Tomasi) di TCLC 13**
　　See Tomasi di Lampedusa, Giuseppe
　　See also CA 164; EW 11; MTCW 2; RGWL 2, 3

**Lampman, Archibald** 1861-1899 **NCLC 25**
　　See also DLB 92; RGEL 2; TWA

**Lancaster, Bruce** 1896-1963 **CLC 36**
　　See also CA 9-10; CANR 70; CAP 1; SATA 9

**Lanchester, John** 1962- **CLC 99**
　　See also CA 194; DLB 267

**Landau, Mark Alexandrovich**
　　See Aldanov, Mark (Alexandrovich)

**Landau-Aldanov, Mark Alexandrovich**
　　See Aldanov, Mark (Alexandrovich)

**Landis, Jerry**
　　See Simon, Paul (Frederick)

**Landis, John** 1950- **CLC 26**
　　See also CA 122; 112

**Landolfi, Tommaso** 1908-1979 **CLC 11, 49**
　　See also CA 117; 127; DLB 177; EWL 3

**Landon, Letitia Elizabeth** 1802-1838 **NCLC 15**
　　See also DLB 96

**Landor, Walter Savage** 1775-1864 **NCLC 14**
　　See also BRW 4; DLB 93, 107; RGEL 2

**Landwirth, Heinz** 1927-
　　See Lind, Jakov
　　See also CA 9-12R; CANR 7

**Lane, Patrick** 1939- **CLC 25**
　　See also CA 97-100; CANR 54; CP 7; DAM POET; DLB 53; INT 97-100

**Lang, Andrew** 1844-1912 **TCLC 16**
　　See also CA 137; 114; CANR 85; DLB 98, 141, 184; FANT; MAICYA 1, 2; RGEL 2; SATA 16; WCH

**Lang, Fritz** 1890-1976 **CLC 20, 103**
　　See also CA 69-72; 77-80; CANR 30

**Lange, John**
　　See Crichton, (John) Michael

**Langer, Elinor** 1939- **CLC 34**
　　See also CA 121

**Langland, William** 1332(?)-1400(?) **LC 19**
　　See also BRW 1; DA; DAB; DAC; DAM MST, POET; DLB 146; RGEL 2; TEA; WLIT 3

**Langstaff, Launcelot**
　　See Irving, Washington

**Lanier, Sidney** 1842-1881 **NCLC 6, 118**
　　See also AMWS 1; DAM POET; DLB 64; DLBD 13; EXPP; MAICYA 1; PFS 14; RGAL 4; SATA 18

**Lanyer, Aemilia** 1569-1645 **LC 10, 30, 83**
　　See also DLB 121

**Lao-Tzu**
　　See Lao Tzu

**Lao Tzu** c. 6th cent. B.C.-3rd cent. B.C. **CMLC 7**

**Lapine, James (Elliot)** 1949- **CLC 39**
　　See also CA 130; 123; CANR 54; INT 130

**Larbaud, Valery (Nicolas)** 1881-1957 **TCLC 9**
　　See also CA 152; 106; EWL 3; GFL 1789 to the Present

**Lardner, Ring**
　　See Lardner, Ring(gold) W(ilmer)
　　See also BPFB 2; CDALB 1917-1929; DLB 11, 25, 86, 171; DLBD 16; RGAL 4; RGSF 2

**Lardner, Ring W., Jr.**
　　See Lardner, Ring(gold) W(ilmer)

**Lardner, Ring(gold) W(ilmer)** 1885-1933 **SSC 32; TCLC 2, 14**
　　See Lardner, Ring
　　See also AMW; CA 131; 104; MTCW 1, 2; TUS

**Laredo, Betty**
　　See Codrescu, Andrei

**Larkin, Maia**
　　See Wojciechowska, Maia (Teresa)

**Larkin, Philip (Arthur)** 1922-1985 **CLC 3, 5, 8, 9, 13, 18, 33, 39, 64; PC 21**
　　See also BRWS 1; CA 117; 5-8R; CANR 24, 62; CDBLB 1960 to Present; DA3; DAB; DAM MST, POET; DLB 27; EWL 3; MTCW 1, 2; PFS 3, 4, 12; RGEL 2

**La Roche, Sophie von** 1730-1807 **NCLC 121**
　　See also DLB 94

**Larra (y Sanchez de Castro), Mariano Jose de** 1809-1837 **NCLC 17**

**Larsen, Eric** 1941- **CLC 55**
　　See also CA 132

**Larsen, Nella** 1893(?)-1963 **BLC 2; CLC 37; HR 3**
　　See also AFAW 1, 2; BW 1; CA 125; CANR 83; DAM MULT; DLB 51; FW; LMFS 2

**Larson, Charles R(aymond)** 1938- **CLC 31**
　　See also CA 53-56; CANR 4

**Larson, Jonathan** 1961-1996 **CLC 99**
　　See also AAYA 28; CA 156

**Las Casas, Bartolome de** 1474-1566 **HLCS; LC 31**
　　See Casas, Bartolome de las
　　See also LAW

**Lasch, Christopher** 1932-1994 **CLC 102**
　　See also CA 144; 73-76; CANR 25; DLB 246; MTCW 1, 2

**Lasker-Schueler, Else** 1869-1945 **TCLC 57**
　　See Lasker-Schuler, Else
　　See also CA 183; DLB 66, 124

**Le Fanu, Joseph Sheridan** 1814-1873 **NCLC 9, 58; SSC 14**
See also CMW 4; DA3; DAM POP; DLB 21, 70, 159, 178; HGG; RGEL 2; RGSF 2; SUFW 1

**Leffland, Ella** 1931- **CLC 19**
See also CA 29-32R; CANR 35, 78, 82; DLBY 1984; INT CANR-35; SATA 65

**Leger, Alexis**
See Leger, (Marie-Rene Auguste) Alexis Saint-Leger

**Leger, (Marie-Rene Auguste) Alexis Saint-Leger** 1887-1975 **CLC 4, 11, 46; PC 23**
See Perse, Saint-John; Saint-John Perse
See also CA 61-64; 13-16R; CANR 43; DAM POET; MTCW 1

**Leger, Saintleger**
See Leger, (Marie-Rene Auguste) Alexis Saint-Leger

**Le Guin, Ursula K(roeber)** 1929- **CLC 8, 13, 22, 45, 71, 136; SSC 12**
See also AAYA 9, 27; AITN 1; BPFB 2; BYA 5, 8, 11, 14; CA 21-24R; CANR 9, 32, 52, 74; CDALB 1968-1988; CLR 3, 28; CN 7; CPW; DA3; DAB; DAC; DAM MST, POP; DLB 8, 52, 256, 275; EXPS; FANT; FW; INT CANR-32; JRDA; LAIT 5; MAICYA 1, 2; MTCW 1, 2; NFS 6, 9; SATA 4, 52, 99; SCFW; SFW 4; SSFS 2; SUFW 1, 2; WYA; YAW

**Lehmann, Rosamond (Nina)** 1901-1990 **CLC 5**
See also CA 131; 77-80; CANR 8, 73; DLB 15; MTCW 2; RGEL 2; RHW

**Leiber, Fritz (Reuter, Jr.)** 1910-1992 **CLC 25**
See also BPFB 2; CA 139; 45-48; CANR 2, 40, 86; DLB 8; FANT; HGG; MTCW 1, 2; SATA 45; SATA-Obit 73; SCFW 2; SFW 4; SUFW 1, 2

**Leibniz, Gottfried Wilhelm von** 1646-1716 **LC 35**
See also DLB 168

**Leimbach, Martha** 1963-
See Leimbach, Marti
See also CA 130

**Leimbach, Marti CLC 65**
See Leimbach, Martha

**Leino, Eino TCLC 24**
See Lonnbohm, Armas Eino Leopold
See also EWL 3

**Leiris, Michel (Julien)** 1901-1990 **CLC 61**
See also CA 132; 128; 119; EWL 3; GFL 1789 to the Present

**Leithauser, Brad** 1953- **CLC 27**
See also CA 107; CANR 27, 81; CP 7; DLB 120

**Lelchuk, Alan** 1938- **CLC 5**
See also CA 45-48; CAAS 20; CANR 1, 70; CN 7

**Lem, Stanislaw** 1921- **CLC 8, 15, 40, 149**
See also CA 105; CAAS 1; CANR 32; CWW 2; MTCW 1; SCFW 2; SFW 4

**Lemann, Nancy** 1956- **CLC 39**
See also CA 136; 118

**Lemonnier, (Antoine Louis) Camille** 1844-1913 **TCLC 22**
See also CA 121

**Lenau, Nikolaus** 1802-1850 **NCLC 16**

**L'Engle, Madeleine (Camp Franklin)** 1918- **CLC 12**
See also AAYA 28; AITN 2; BPFB 2; BYA 2, 4, 5, 7; CA 1-4R; CANR 3, 21, 39, 66, 107; CLR 1, 14, 57; CPW; CWRI 5; DA3; DAM POP; DLB 52; JRDA; MAICYA 1, 2; MTCW 1, 2; SAAS 15; SATA 1, 27, 75, 128; SFW 4; WYA; YAW

**Lengyel, Jozsef** 1896-1975 **CLC 7**
See also CA 57-60; 85-88; CANR 71; RGSF 2

**Lenin** 1870-1924
See Lenin, V. I.
See also CA 168; 121

**Lenin, V. I. TCLC 67**
See Lenin

**Lennon, John (Ono)** 1940-1980 **CLC 12, 35**
See also CA 102; SATA 114

**Lennox, Charlotte Ramsay** 1729(?)-1804 **NCLC 23**
See also DLB 39; RGEL 2

**Lentricchia, Frank, (Jr.)** 1940- **CLC 34**
See also CA 25-28R; CANR 19, 106; DLB 246

**Lenz, Gunter CLC 65**

**Lenz, Siegfried** 1926- **CLC 27; SSC 33**
See also CA 89-92; CANR 80; CWW 2; DLB 75; EWL 3; RGSF 2; RGWL 2, 3

**Leon, David**
See Jacob, (Cyprien-)Max

**Leonard, Elmore (John, Jr.)** 1925- **CLC 28, 34, 71, 120**
See also AAYA 22; AITN 1; BEST 89:1, 90:4; BPFB 2; CA 81-84; CANR 12, 28, 53, 76, 96; CMW 4; CN 7; CPW; DA3; DAM POP; DLB 173, 226; INT CANR-28; MSW; MTCW 1, 2; RGAL 4; TCWW 2

**Leonard, Hugh CLC 19**
See Byrne, John Keyes
See also CBD; CD 5; DFS 13; DLB 13

**Leonov, Leonid (Maximovich)** 1899-1994 **CLC 92**
See Leonov, Leonid Maksimovich
See also CA 129; CANR 74, 76; DAM NOV; EWL 3; MTCW 1, 2

**Leonov, Leonid Maksimovich**
See Leonov, Leonid (Maximovich)
See also DLB 272

**Leopardi, (Conte) Giacomo** 1798-1837 **NCLC 22; PC 37**
See also EW 5; RGWL 2, 3; WP

**Le Reveler**
See Artaud, Antonin (Marie Joseph)

**Lerman, Eleanor** 1952- **CLC 9**
See also CA 85-88; CANR 69

**Lerman, Rhoda** 1936- **CLC 56**
See also CA 49-52; CANR 70

**Lermontov, Mikhail**
See Lermontov, Mikhail Yuryevich

**Lermontov, Mikhail Iur'evich**
See Lermontov, Mikhail Yuryevich
See also DLB 205

**Lermontov, Mikhail Yuryevich** 1814-1841 **NCLC 5, 47; PC 18**
See Lermontov, Mikhail Iur'evich
See also EW 6; RGWL 2, 3; TWA

**Leroux, Gaston** 1868-1927 **TCLC 25**
See also CA 136; 108; CANR 69; CMW 4; SATA 65

**Lesage, Alain-Rene** 1668-1747 **LC 2, 28**
See also EW 3; GFL Beginnings to 1789; RGWL 2, 3

**Leskov, N(ikolai) S(emenovich)** 1831-1895
See Leskov, Nikolai (Semyonovich)

**Leskov, Nikolai (Semyonovich)** 1831-1895 **NCLC 25; SSC 34**
See Leskov, Nikolai Semenovich

**Leskov, Nikolai Semenovich**
See Leskov, Nikolai (Semyonovich)
See also DLB 238

**Lesser, Milton**
See Marlowe, Stephen

**Lessing, Doris (May)** 1919- **CLC 1, 2, 3, 6, 10, 15, 22, 40, 94, 170; SSC 6; WLCS**
See also AFW; BRWS 1; CA 9-12R; CAAS 14; CANR 33, 54, 76; CD 5; CDBLB 1960 to Present; CN 7; DA; DA3; DAB; DAC; DAM MST, NOV; DLB 15, 139; DLBY 1985; EWL 3; EXPS; FW; LAIT

**Lessing, Gotthold Ephraim** 1729-1781 **LC 8**
See also CDWLB 2; DLB 97; EW 4; RGWL 2, 3

**Lester, Richard** 1932- **CLC 20**

**Levenson, Jay CLC 70**

**Lever, Charles (James)** 1806-1872 **NCLC 23**
See also DLB 21; RGEL 2

**Leverson, Ada Esther** 1862(?)-1933(?) **TCLC 18**
See Elaine
See also CA 202; 117; DLB 153; RGEL 2

**Levertov, Denise** 1923-1997 **CLC 1, 2, 3, 5, 8, 15, 28, 66; PC 11**
See also AMWS 3; CA 163; 1-4R; 178; CAAE 178; CAAS 19; CANR 3, 29, 50, 108; CDALBS; CP 7; DAM POET; DLB 5, 165; EWL 3; EXPP; FW; INT CANR-29; MTCW 1, 2; PAB; PFS 7, 16; RGAL 4; TUS; WP

**Levi, Carlo** 1902-1975 **TCLC 125**
See also CA 53-56; 65-68; CANR 10; EWL 3; RGWL 2, 3

**Levi, Jonathan CLC 76**
See also CA 197

**Levi, Peter (Chad Tigar)** 1931-2000 **CLC 41**
See also CA 187; 5-8R; CANR 34, 80; CP 7; DLB 40

**Levi, Primo** 1919-1987 **CLC 37, 50; SSC 12; TCLC 109**
See also CA 122; 13-16R; CANR 12, 33, 61, 70; DLB 177; EWL 3; MTCW 1, 2; RGWL 2, 3

**Levin, Ira** 1929- **CLC 3, 6**
See also CA 21-24R; CANR 17, 44, 74; CMW 4; CN 7; CPW; DA3; DAM POP; HGG; MTCW 1, 2; SATA 66; SFW 4

**Levin, Meyer** 1905-1981 **CLC 7**
See also AITN 1; CA 104; 9-12R; CANR 15; DAM POP; DLB 9, 28; DLBY 1981; SATA 21; SATA-Obit 27

**Levine, Norman** 1924- **CLC 54**
See also CA 73-76; CAAS 23; CANR 14, 70; DLB 88

**Levine, Philip** 1928- **CLC 2, 4, 5, 9, 14, 33, 118; PC 22**
See also AMWS 5; CA 9-12R; CANR 9, 37, 52, 116; CP 7; DAM POET; DLB 5; EWL 3; PFS 8

**Levinson, Deirdre** 1931- **CLC 49**
See also CA 73-76; CANR 70

**Levi-Strauss, Claude** 1908- **CLC 38**
See also CA 1-4R; CANR 6, 32, 57; DLB 242; EWL 3; GFL 1789 to the Present; MTCW 1, 2; TWA

**Levitin, Sonia (Wolff)** 1934- **CLC 17**
See also AAYA 13; CA 29-32R; CANR 14, 32, 79; CLR 53; JRDA; MAICYA 1, 2; SAAS 2; SATA 4, 68, 119; SATA-Essay 131; YAW

**Levon, O. U.**
See Kesey, Ken (Elton)

**Levy, Amy** 1861-1889 **NCLC 59**
See also DLB 156, 240

**Lewes, George Henry** 1817-1878 **NCLC 25**
See also DLB 55, 144

**Lewis, Alun** 1915-1944 **SSC 40; TCLC 3**
See also BRW 7; CA 188; 104; DLB 20, 162; PAB; RGEL 2

**Lewis, C. Day**
See Day Lewis, C(ecil)

**Lewis, C(live) S(taples)** 1898-1963 **CLC 1, 3, 6, 14, 27, 124; WLC**
See also AAYA 3, 39; BPFB 2; BRWS 3; CA 81-84; CANR 33, 71; CDBLB 1945-1960; CLR 3, 27; CWRI 5; DA; DA3; DAB; DAC; DAM MST, NOV, POP; DLB 15, 100, 160, 255; EWL 3; FANT;

JRDA; MAICYA 1, 2; MTCW 1, 2; RGEL
2; SATA 13, 100; SCFW; SFW 4; SUFW
1; TEA; WCH; WYA; YAW

**Lewis, Cecil Day**
See Day Lewis, C(ecil)

**Lewis, Janet** 1899-1998 **CLC 41**
See Winters, Janet Lewis
See also CA 172; 9-12R; CANR 29, 63;
CAP 1; CN 7; DLBY 1987; RHW;
TCWW 2

**Lewis, Matthew Gregory** 1775-1818 **NCLC
11, 62**
See also DLB 39, 158, 178; HGG; RGEL
2; SUFW

**Lewis, (Harry) Sinclair** 1885-1951 **TCLC 4,
13, 23, 39; WLC**
See also AMW; AMWC 1; BPFB 2; CA
133; 104; CDALB 1917-1929; DA; DA3;
DAB; DAC; DAM MST, NOV; DLB 9,
102; DLBD 1; EWL 3; LAIT 3; MTCW
1, 2; NFS 15; RGAL 2; TUS

**Lewis, (Percy) Wyndham** 1884(?)-1957 **SSC
34; TCLC 2, 9, 104**
See also BRW 7; CA 157; 104; DLB 15;
EWL 3; FANT; MTCW 2; RGEL 2

**Lewisohn, Ludwig** 1883-1955 **TCLC 19**
See also CA 203; 107; DLB 4, 9, 28, 102

**Lewton, Val** 1904-1951 **TCLC 76**
See also CA 199; IDFW 3, 4

**Leyner, Mark** 1956- **CLC 92**
See also CA 110; CANR 28, 53; DA3;
MTCW 2

**Lezama Lima, Jose** 1910-1976 **CLC 4, 10,
101; HLCS 2**
See also CA 77-80; CANR 71; DAM
MULT; DLB 113; EWL 3; HW 1, 2;
LAW; RGWL 2, 3

**L'Heureux, John (Clarke)** 1934- **CLC 52**
See also CA 13-16R; CANR 23, 45, 88;
DLB 244

**Liddell, C. H.**
See Kuttner, Henry

**Lie, Jonas (Lauritz Idemil)** 1833-1908(?)
**TCLC 5**
See also CA 115

**Lieber, Joel** 1937-1971 **CLC 6**
See also CA 29-32R; 73-76

**Lieber, Stanley Martin**
See Lee, Stan

**Lieberman, Laurence (James)** 1935- **CLC 4,
36**
See also CA 17-20R; CANR 8, 36, 89; CP
7

**Lieh Tzu** fl. 7th cent. B.C.-5th cent. B.C.
**CMLC 27**

**Lieksman, Anders**
See Haavikko, Paavo Juhani

**Li Fei-kan** 1904-
See Pa Chin
See also CA 105; TWA

**Lifton, Robert Jay** 1926- **CLC 67**
See also CA 17-20R; CANR 27, 78; INT
CANR-27; SATA 66

**Lightfoot, Gordon** 1938- **CLC 26**
See also CA 109

**Lightman, Alan P(aige)** 1948- **CLC 81**
See also CA 141; CANR 63, 105

**Ligotti, Thomas (Robert)** 1953- **CLC 44; SSC
16**
See also CA 123; CANR 49; HGG; SUFW
2

**Li Ho** 791-817 **PC 13**

**Liliencron, (Friedrich Adolf Axel) Detlev
von** 1844-1909 **TCLC 18**
See also CA 117

**Lille, Alain de**
See Alain de Lille

**Lilly, William** 1602-1681 **LC 27**

**Lima, Jose Lezama**
See Lezama Lima, Jose

**Lima Barreto, Afonso Henrique de**
1881-1922 **TCLC 23**
See also CA 181; 117; LAW

**Lima Barreto, Afonso Henriques de**
See Lima Barreto, Afonso Henrique de

**Limonov, Edward** 1944- **CLC 67**
See also CA 137

**Lin, Frank**
See Atherton, Gertrude (Franklin Horn)

**Lincoln, Abraham** 1809-1865 **NCLC 18**
See also LAIT 2

**Lind, Jakov CLC 1, 2, 4, 27, 82**
See Landwirth, Heinz
See also CAAS 4; EWL 3

**Lindbergh, Anne (Spencer) Morrow**
1906-2001 **CLC 82**
See also BPFB 2; CA 193; 17-20R; CANR
16, 73; DAM NOV; MTCW 1, 2; SATA
33; SATA-Obit 125; TUS

**Lindsay, David** 1878(?)-1945 **TCLC 15**
See also CA 187; 113; DLB 255; FANT;
SFW 4; SUFW 1

**Lindsay, (Nicholas) Vachel** 1879-1931 **PC 23;
TCLC 17; WLC**
See also AMWS 1; CA 135; 114; CANR
79; CDALB 1865-1917; DA; DA3; DAC;
DAM MST, POET; DLB 54; EWL 3;
EXPP; RGAL 4; SATA 40; WP

**Linke-Poot**
See Doeblin, Alfred

**Linney, Romulus** 1930- **CLC 51**
See also CA 1-4R; CAD; CANR 40, 44,
79; CD 5; CSW; RGAL 4

**Linton, Eliza Lynn** 1822-1898 **NCLC 41**
See also DLB 18

**Li Po** 701-763 **CMLC 2; PC 29**
See also WP

**Lipsius, Justus** 1547-1606 **LC 16**

**Lipsyte, Robert (Michael)** 1938- **CLC 21**
See also AAYA 7, 45; CA 17-20R; CANR
8, 57; CLR 23, 76; DA; DAC; DAM
MST, NOV; JRDA; LAIT 5; MAICYA 1,
2; SATA 5, 68, 113; WYA; YAW

**Lish, Gordon (Jay)** 1934- **CLC 45; SSC 18**
See also CA 117; 113; CANR 79; DLB 130;
INT 117

**Lispector, Clarice** 1925(?)-1977 **CLC 43;
HLCS 2; SSC 34**
See also CA 116; 139; CANR 71; CDWLB
3; DLB 113; DNFS 1; EWL 3; FW; HW
2; LAW; RGSF 2; RGWL 2, 3; WLIT 1

**Littell, Robert** 1935(?)- **CLC 42**
See also CA 112; 109; CANR 64, 115;
CMW 4

**Little, Malcolm** 1925-1965
See Malcolm X
See also BW 1, 3; CA 111; 125; CANR 82;
DA; DA3; DAB; DAC; DAM MST,
MULT; MTCW 1, 2; NCFS 3

**Littlewit, Humphrey Gent.**
See Lovecraft, H(oward) P(hillips)

**Litwos**
See Sienkiewicz, Henryk (Adam Alexander
Pius)

**Liu, E.** 1857-1909 **TCLC 15**
See also CA 190; 115

**Lively, Penelope (Margaret)** 1933- **CLC 32,
50**
See also BPFB 2; CA 41-44R; CANR 29,
67, 79; CLR 7; CN 7; CWRI 5; DAM
NOV; DLB 14, 161, 207; FANT; JRDA;
MAICYA 1, 2; MTCW 1, 2; SATA 7, 60,
101; TEA

**Livesay, Dorothy (Kathleen)** 1909-1996 **CLC
4, 15, 79**
See also AITN 2; CA 25-28R; CAAS 8;
CANR 36, 67; DAC; DAM MST, POET;
DLB 68; FW; MTCW 1; RGEL 2; TWA

**Livy** c. 59B.C.-c. 12 **CMLC 11**
See also AW 2; CDWLB 1; DLB 211;
RGWL 2, 3

**Lizardi, Jose Joaquin Fernandez de**
1776-1827 **NCLC 30**
See also LAW

**Llewellyn, Richard**
See Llewellyn Lloyd, Richard Dafydd Viv-
ian
See also DLB 15

**Llewellyn Lloyd, Richard Dafydd Vivian**
1906-1983 **CLC 7, 80**
See Llewellyn, Richard
See also CA 111; 53-56; CANR 7, 71;
SATA 11; SATA-Obit 37

**Llosa, (Jorge) Mario (Pedro) Vargas**
See Vargas Llosa, (Jorge) Mario (Pedro)
See also RGWL 3

**Lloyd, Manda**
See Mander, (Mary) Jane

**Lloyd Webber, Andrew** 1948-
See Webber, Andrew Lloyd
See also AAYA 1, 38; CA 149; 116; DAM
DRAM; SATA 56

**Llull, Ramon** c. 1235-c. 1316 **CMLC 12**

**Lobb, Ebenezer**
See Upward, Allen

**Locke, Alain (Le Roy)** 1886-1954 **BLCS; HR
3; TCLC 43**
See also BW 1, 3; CA 124; 106; CANR 79;
DLB 51; LMFS 2; RGAL 4

**Locke, John** 1632-1704 **LC 7, 35**
See also DLB 31, 101, 213, 252; RGEL 2;
WLIT 3

**Locke-Elliott, Sumner**
See Elliott, Sumner Locke

**Lockhart, John Gibson** 1794-1854 **NCLC 6**
See also DLB 110, 116, 144

**Lockridge, Ross (Franklin), Jr.** 1914-1948
**TCLC 111**
See also CA 145; 108; CANR 79; DLB 143;
DLBY 1980; RGAL 4; RHW

**Lockwood, Robert**
See Johnson, Robert

**Lodge, David (John)** 1935- **CLC 36, 141**
See also BEST 90:1; BRWS 4; CA 17-20R;
CANR 19, 53, 92; CN 7; CPW; DAM
POP; DLB 14, 194; EWL 3; INT CANR-
19; MTCW 1, 2

**Lodge, Thomas** 1558-1625 **LC 41**
See also DLB 172; RGEL 2

**Loewinsohn, Ron(ald William)** 1937- **CLC
52**
See also CA 25-28R; CANR 71

**Logan, Jake**
See Smith, Martin Cruz

**Logan, John (Burton)** 1923-1987 **CLC 5**
See also CA 124; 77-80; CANR 45; DLB 5

**Lo Kuan-chung** 1330(?)-1400(?) **LC 12**

**Lombard, Nap**
See Johnson, Pamela Hansford

**Lomotey (editor), Kofi CLC 70**

**London, Jack** 1876-1916 **SSC 4, 49; TCLC 9,
15, 39; WLC**
See London, John Griffith
See also AAYA 13; AITN 2; AMW; BPFB
2; BYA 4, 13; CDALB 1865-1917; DLB
8, 12, 78, 212; EWL 3; EXPS; LAIT 3;
NFS 8; RGAL 4; RGSF 2; SATA 18; SFW
4; SSFS 7; TCWW 2; TUS; WYA; YAW

**London, John Griffith** 1876-1916
See London, Jack
See also CA 119; 110; CANR 73; DA; DA3;
DAB; DAC; DAM MST, NOV; JRDA;
MAICYA 1, 2; MTCW 1, 2

**Long, Emmett**
See Leonard, Elmore (John, Jr.)

**Longbaugh, Harry**
See Goldman, William (W.)

**Longfellow, Henry Wadsworth** 1807-1882 **NCLC 2, 45, 101, 103; PC 30; WLCS**
See also AMW; AMWR 2; CDALB 1640-1865; DA; DA3; DAB; DAC; DAM MST, POET; DLB 1, 59, 235; EXPP; PAB; PFS 2, 7, 17; RGAL 4; SATA 19; TUS; WP

**Longinus** c. 1st cent. - **CMLC 27**
See also AW 2; DLB 176

**Longley, Michael** 1939- **CLC 29**
See also BRWS 8; CA 102; CP 7; DLB 40

**Longus** fl. c. 2nd cent. - **CMLC 7**

**Longway, A. Hugh**
See Lang, Andrew

**Lonnbohm, Armas Eino Leopold** 1878-1926
See Leino, Eino
See also CA 123

**Lonnrot, Elias** 1802-1884 **NCLC 53**
See also EFS 1

**Lonsdale, Roger** ed. **CLC 65**

**Lopate, Phillip** 1943- **CLC 29**
See also CA 97-100; CANR 88; DLBY 1980; INT 97-100

**Lopez, Barry (Holstun)** 1945- **CLC 70**
See also AAYA 9; ANW; CA 65-68; CANR 7, 23, 47, 68, 92; DLB 256, 275; INT CANR-7, -23; MTCW 1; RGAL 4; SATA 67

**Lopez Portillo (y Pacheco), Jose** 1920- **CLC 46**
See also CA 129; HW 1

**Lopez y Fuentes, Gregorio** 1897(?)-1966 **CLC 32**
See also CA 131; EWL 3; HW 1

**Lorca, Federico Garcia**
See Garcia Lorca, Federico
See also DFS 4; EW 11; RGWL 2, 3; WP

**Lord, Audre**
See Lorde, Audre (Geraldine)
See also EWL 3

**Lord, Bette Bao** 1938- **AAL; CLC 23**
See also BEST 90:3; BPFB 2; CA 107; CANR 41, 79; INT CA-107; SATA 58

**Lord Auch**
See Bataille, Georges

**Lord Brooke**
See Greville, Fulke

**Lord Byron**
See Byron, George Gordon (Noel)

**Lorde, Audre (Geraldine)** 1934-1992 **BLC 2; CLC 18, 71; PC 12**
See Domini, Rey; Lord, Audre
See also AFAW 1, 2; BW 1, 3; CA 142; 25-28R; CANR 16, 26, 46, 82; DA3; DAM MULT, POET; DLB 41; FW; MTCW 1, 2; PFS 16; RGAL 4

**Lord Houghton**
See Milnes, Richard Monckton

**Lord Jeffrey**
See Jeffrey, Francis

**Loreaux, Nichol CLC 65**

**Lorenzini, Carlo** 1826-1890
See Collodi, Carlo
See also MAICYA 1, 2; SATA 29, 100

**Lorenzo, Heberto Padilla**
See Padilla (Lorenzo), Heberto

**Loris**
See Hofmannsthal, Hugo von

**Loti, Pierre TCLC 11**
See Viaud, (Louis Marie) Julien
See also DLB 123; GFL 1789 to the Present

**Lou, Henri**
See Andreas-Salome, Lou

**Louie, David Wong** 1954- **CLC 70**
See also CA 139

**Louis, Adrian C. NNAL**

**Louis, Father M.**
See Merton, Thomas (James)

**Lovecraft, H(oward) P(hillips)** 1890-1937 **SSC 3, 52; TCLC 4, 22**
See also AAYA 14; BPFB 2; CA 133; 104; CANR 106; DA3; DAM POP; HGG; MTCW 1, 2; RGAL 4; SCFW; SFW 4; SUFW

**Lovelace, Earl** 1935- **CLC 51**
See also BW 2; CA 77-80; CANR 41, 72, 114; CD 5; CDWLB 3; CN 7; DLB 125; EWL 3; MTCW 1

**Lovelace, Richard** 1618-1657 **LC 24**
See also BRW 2; DLB 131; EXPP; PAB; RGEL 2

**Lowe, Pardee** 1904- **AAL**

**Lowell, Amy** 1874-1925 **PC 13; TCLC 1, 8**
See also AMW; CA 151; 104; DAM POET; DLB 54, 140; EWL 3; EXPP; LMFS 2; MAWW; MTCW 2; RGAL 4; TUS

**Lowell, James Russell** 1819-1891 **NCLC 2, 90**
See also AMWS 1; CDALB 1640-1865; DLB 1, 11, 64, 79, 189, 235; RGAL 4

**Lowell, Robert (Traill Spence, Jr.)** 1917-1977 **CLC 1, 2, 3, 4, 5, 8, 9, 11, 15, 37, 124; PC 3; WLC**
See also AMW; AMWR 2; CA 73-76; 9-12R; CABS 2; CANR 26, 60; CDALBS; DA; DA3; DAB; DAC; DAM MST, NOV, DLB 5, 169; EWL 3; MTCW 1, 2; PAB; PFS 6, 7; RGAL 4; WP

**Lowenthal, Michael (Francis)** 1969- **CLC 119**
See also CA 150; CANR 115

**Lowndes, Marie Adelaide (Belloc)** 1868-1947 **TCLC 12**
See also CA 107; CMW 4; DLB 70; RHW

**Lowry, (Clarence) Malcolm** 1909-1957 **SSC 31; TCLC 6, 40**
See also BPFB 2; BRWS 3; CA 131; 105; CANR 62, 105; CDBLB 1945-1960; DLB 15; EWL 3; MTCW 1, 2; RGEL 2

**Lowry, Mina Gertrude** 1882-1966
See Loy, Mina
See also CA 113

**Loxsmith, John**
See Brunner, John (Kilian Houston)

**Loy, Mina CLC 28; PC 16**
See Lowry, Mina Gertrude
See also DAM POET; DLB 4, 54

**Loyson-Bridet**
See Schwob, Marcel (Mayer Andre)

**Lucan** 39-65 **CMLC 33**
See also AW 2; DLB 211; EFS 2; RGWL 2, 3

**Lucas, Craig** 1951- **CLC 64**
See also CA 137; CAD; CANR 71, 109; CD 5; GLL 2

**Lucas, E(dward) V(errall)** 1868-1938 **TCLC 73**
See also CA 176; DLB 98, 149, 153; SATA 20

**Lucas, George** 1944- **CLC 16**
See also AAYA 1, 23; CA 77-80; CANR 30; SATA 56

**Lucas, Hans**
See Godard, Jean-Luc

**Lucas, Victoria**
See Plath, Sylvia

**Lucian** c. 125-c. 180 **CMLC 32**
See also AW 2; DLB 176; RGWL 2, 3

**Lucretius** c. 94B.C.-c. 49B.C. **CMLC 48**
See also AW 2; CDWLB 1; DLB 211; EFS 2; RGWL 2, 3

**Ludlam, Charles** 1943-1987 **CLC 46, 50**
See also CA 122; 85-88; CAD; CANR 72, 86; DLB 266

**Ludlum, Robert** 1927-2001 **CLC 22, 43**
See also AAYA 10; BEST 89:1, 90:3; BPFB 2; CA 195; 33-36R; CANR 25, 41, 68,

105; CMW 4; CPW; DA3; DAM NOV, POP; DLBY 1982; MSW; MTCW 1, 2

**Ludwig, Ken CLC 60**
See also CA 195; CAD

**Ludwig, Otto** 1813-1865 **NCLC 4**
See also DLB 129

**Lugones, Leopoldo** 1874-1938 **HLCS 2; TCLC 15**
See also CA 131; 116; CANR 104; EWL 3; HW 1; LAW

**Lu Hsun SSC 20; TCLC 3**
See Shu-Jen, Chou
See also EWL 3

**Lukacs, George CLC 24**
See Lukacs, Gyorgy (Szegeny von)

**Lukacs, Gyorgy (Szegeny von)** 1885-1971
See Lukacs, George
See also CA 29-32R; 101; CANR 62; CD-WLB 4; DLB 215, 242; EW 10; EWL 3; MTCW 2

**Luke, Peter (Ambrose Cyprian)** 1919-1995 **CLC 38**
See also CA 147; 81-84; CANR 72; CBD; CD 5; DLB 13

**Lunar, Dennis**
See Mungo, Raymond

**Lurie, Alison** 1926- **CLC 4, 5, 18, 39**
See also BPFB 2; CA 1-4R; CANR 2, 17, 50, 88; CN 7; DLB 2; MTCW 1; SATA 46, 112

**Lustig, Arnost** 1926- **CLC 56**
See also AAYA 3; CA 69-72; CANR 47, 102; CWW 2; DLB 232; EWL 3; SATA 56

**Luther, Martin** 1483-1546 **LC 9, 37**
See also CDWLB 2; DLB 179; EW 2; RGWL 2, 3

**Luxemburg, Rosa** 1870(?)-1919 **TCLC 63**
See also CA 118

**Luzi, Mario** 1914- **CLC 13**
See also CA 61-64; CANR 9, 70; CWW 2; DLB 128; EWL 3

**L'vov, Arkady CLC 59**

**Lydgate, John** c. 1370-1450(?) **LC 81**
See also BRW 1; DLB 146; RGEL 2

**Lyly, John** 1554(?)-1606 **DC 7; LC 41**
See also BRW 1; DAM DRAM; DLB 62, 167; RGEL 2

**L'Ymagier**
See Gourmont, Remy(-Marie-Charles) de

**Lynch, B. Suarez**
See Borges, Jorge Luis

**Lynch, David (Keith)** 1946- **CLC 66, 162**
See also CA 129; 124; CANR 111

**Lynch, James**
See Andreyev, Leonid (Nikolaevich)

**Lyndsay, Sir David** 1485-1555 **LC 20**
See also RGEL 2

**Lynn, Kenneth S(chuyler)** 1923-2001 **CLC 50**
See also CA 196; 1-4R; CANR 3, 27, 65

**Lynx**
See West, Rebecca

**Lyons, Marcus**
See Blish, James (Benjamin)

**Lyotard, Jean-Francois** 1924-1998 **TCLC 103**
See also DLB 242; EWL 3

**Lyre, Pinchbeck**
See Sassoon, Siegfried (Lorraine)

**Lytle, Andrew (Nelson)** 1902-1995 **CLC 22**
See also CA 150; 9-12R; CANR 70; CN 7; CSW; DLB 6; DLBY 1995; RGAL 4; RHW

**Lyttelton, George** 1709-1773 **LC 10**
See also RGEL 2

**Lytton of Knebworth, Baron**
See Bulwer-Lytton, Edward (George Earle Lytton)

**Maas, Peter** 1929-2001 **CLC 29**
    See also CA 201; 93-96; INT CA-93-96;
    MTCW 2

**Macaulay, Catherine** 1731-1791 **LC 64**
    See also DLB 104

**Macaulay, (Emilie) Rose** 1881(?)-1958 **TCLC 7, 44**
    See also CA 104; DLB 36; EWL 3; RGEL
    2; RHW

**Macaulay, Thomas Babington** 1800-1859 **NCLC 42**
    See also BRW 4; CDBLB 1832-1890; DLB
    32, 55; RGEL 2

**MacBeth, George (Mann)** 1932-1992 **CLC 2, 5, 9**
    See also CA 136; 25-28R; CANR 61, 66;
    DLB 40; MTCW 1; PFS 8; SATA 4;
    SATA-Obit 70

**MacCaig, Norman (Alexander)** 1910-1996 **CLC 36**
    See also BRWS 6; CA 9-12R; CANR 3, 34;
    CP 7; DAB; DAM POET; DLB 27; EWL
    3; RGEL 2

**MacCarthy, Sir (Charles Otto) Desmond** 1877-1952 **TCLC 36**
    See also CA 167

**MacDiarmid, Hugh** **CLC 2, 4, 11, 19, 63; PC 9**
    See Grieve, C(hristopher) M(urray)
    See also CDBLB 1945-1960; DLB 20;
    EWL 3; RGEL 2

**MacDonald, Anson**
    See Heinlein, Robert A(nson)

**Macdonald, Cynthia** 1928- **CLC 13, 19**
    See also CA 49-52; CANR 4, 44; DLB 105

**MacDonald, George** 1824-1905 **TCLC 9, 113**
    See also BYA 5; CA 137; 106; CANR 80;
    CLR 67; DLB 18, 163, 178; FANT; MAI-
    CYA 1, 2; RGEL 2; SATA 33, 100; SFW
    4; SUFW; WCH

**Macdonald, John**
    See Millar, Kenneth

**MacDonald, John D(ann)** 1916-1986 **CLC 3, 27, 44**
    See also BPFB 2; CA 121; 1-4R; CANR 1,
    19, 60; CMW 4; CPW; DAM NOV, POP;
    DLB 8; DLBY 1986; MSW; MTCW 1, 2;
    SFW 4

**Macdonald, John Ross**
    See Millar, Kenneth

**Macdonald, Ross** **CLC 1, 2, 3, 14, 34, 41**
    See Millar, Kenneth
    See also AMWS 4; BPFB 2; DLBD 6;
    MSW; RGAL 4

**MacDougal, John**
    See Blish, James (Benjamin)

**MacDougal, John**
    See Blish, James (Benjamin)

**MacDowell, John**
    See Parks, Tim(othy Harold)

**MacEwen, Gwendolyn (Margaret)** 1941-1987 **CLC 13, 55**
    See also CA 124; 9-12R; CANR 7, 22; DLB
    53, 251; SATA 50; SATA-Obit 55

**Macha, Karel Hynek** 1810-1846 **NCLC 46**

**Machado (y Ruiz), Antonio** 1875-1939 **TCLC 3**
    See also CA 174; 104; DLB 108; EW 9;
    EWL 3; HW 2; RGWL 2, 3

**Machado de Assis, Joaquim Maria** 1839-1908 **BLC 2; HLCS 2; SSC 24; TCLC 10**
    See also CA 153; 107; CANR 91; LAW;
    RGSF 2; RGWL 2, 3; TWA; WLIT 1

**Machen, Arthur** **SSC 20; TCLC 4**
    See Jones, Arthur Llewellyn
    See also CA 179; DLB 156, 178; RGEL 2;
    SUFW 1

**Machiavelli, Niccolo** 1469-1527 **DC 16; LC 8, 36; WLCS**
    See also DA; DAB; DAC; DAM MST; EW
    2; LAIT 1; NFS 9; RGWL 2, 3; TWA

**MacInnes, Colin** 1914-1976 **CLC 4, 23**
    See also CA 65-68; 69-72; CANR 21; DLB
    14; MTCW 1, 2; RGEL 2; RHW

**MacInnes, Helen (Clark)** 1907-1985 **CLC 27, 39**
    See also BPFB 2; CA 117; 1-4R; CANR 1,
    28, 58; CMW 4; CPW; DAM POP; DLB
    87; MSW; MTCW 1, 2; SATA 22; SATA-
    Obit 44

**Mackay, Mary** 1855-1924
    See Corelli, Marie
    See also CA 177; 118; FANT; RHW

**Mackenzie, Compton (Edward Montague)** 1883-1972 **CLC 18; TCLC 116**
    See also CA 37-40R; 21-22; CAP 2; DLB
    34, 100; RGEL 2

**Mackenzie, Henry** 1745-1831 **NCLC 41**
    See also DLB 39; RGEL 2

**Mackintosh, Elizabeth** 1896(?)-1952
    See Tey, Josephine
    See also CA 110; CMW 4

**MacLaren, James**
    See Grieve, C(hristopher) M(urray)

**Mac Laverty, Bernard** 1942- **CLC 31**
    See also CA 118; 116; CANR 43, 88; CN
    7; DLB 267; INT CA-118; RGSF 2

**MacLean, Alistair (Stuart)** 1922(?)-1987 **CLC 3, 13, 50, 63**
    See also CA 121; 57-60; CANR 28, 61;
    CMW 4; CPW; DAM POP; DLB 276;
    MTCW 1; SATA 23; SATA-Obit 50;
    TCWW 2

**Maclean, Norman (Fitzroy)** 1902-1990 **CLC 78; SSC 13**
    See also CA 132; 102; CANR 49; CPW;
    DAM POP; DLB 206; TCWW 2

**MacLeish, Archibald** 1892-1982 **CLC 3, 8, 14, 68**
    See also AMW; CA 106; 9-12R; CAD;
    CANR 33, 63; CDALBS; DAM POET;
    DFS 15; DLB 4, 7, 45; DLBY 1982; EWL
    3; EXPP; MTCW 1, 2; PAB; PFS 5;
    RGAL 4; TUS

**MacLennan, (John) Hugh** 1907-1990 **CLC 2, 14, 92**
    See also CA 142; 5-8R; CANR 33; DAC;
    DAM MST; DLB 68; EWL 3; MTCW 1,
    2; RGEL 2; TWA

**MacLeod, Alistair** 1936- **CLC 56, 165**
    See also CA 123; CCA 1; DAC; DAM
    MST; DLB 60; MTCW 2; RGSF 2

**Macleod, Fiona**
    See Sharp, William
    See also RGEL 2; SUFW

**MacNeice, (Frederick) Louis** 1907-1963 **CLC 1, 4, 10, 53**
    See also BRW 7; CA 85-88; CANR 61;
    DAB; DAM POET; DLB 10, 20; EWL 3;
    MTCW 1, 2; RGEL 2

**MacNeill, Dand**
    See Fraser, George MacDonald

**Macpherson, James** 1736-1796 **LC 29**
    See Ossian
    See also BRWS 8; DLB 109; RGEL 2

**Macpherson, (Jean) Jay** 1931- **CLC 14**
    See also CA 5-8R; CANR 90; CP 7; CWP;
    DLB 53

**Macrobius** fl. 430- **CMLC 48**

**MacShane, Frank** 1927-1999 **CLC 39**
    See also CA 186; 9-12R; CANR 3, 33; DLB
    111

**Macumber, Mari**
    See Sandoz, Mari(e Susette)

**Madach, Imre** 1823-1864 **NCLC 19**

**Madden, (Jerry) David** 1933- **CLC 5, 15**
    See also CA 1-4R; CAAS 3; CANR 4, 45;
    CN 7; CSW; DLB 6; MTCW 1

**Maddern, Al(an)**
    See Ellison, Harlan (Jay)

**Madhubuti, Haki R.** 1942- **BLC 2; CLC 6, 73; PC 5**
    See Lee, Don L.
    See also BW 2, 3; CA 73-76; CANR 24,
    51, 73; CP 7; CSW; DAM MULT, POET;
    DLB 5, 41; DLBD 8; EWL 3; MTCW 2;
    RGAL 4

**Maepenn, Hugh**
    See Kuttner, Henry

**Maepenn, K. H.**
    See Kuttner, Henry

**Maeterlinck, Maurice** 1862-1949 **TCLC 3**
    See also CA 136; 104; CANR 80; DAM
    DRAM; DLB 192; EW 8; EWL 3; GFL
    1789 to the Present; RGWL 2, 3; SATA
    66; TWA

**Maginn, William** 1794-1842 **NCLC 8**
    See also DLB 110, 159

**Mahapatra, Jayanta** 1928- **CLC 33**
    See also CA 73-76; CAAS 9; CANR 15,
    33, 66, 87; CP 7; DAM MULT

**Mahfouz, Naguib (Abdel Aziz Al-Sabilgi)** 1911(?)- **CLC 153**
    See Mahfuz, Najib (Abdel Aziz al-Sabilgi)
    See also BEST 89:2; CA 128; CANR 55,
    101; CWW 2; DA3; DAM NOV; MTCW
    1, 2; RGWL 2, 3; SSFS 9

**Mahfuz, Najib (Abdel Aziz al-Sabilgi)** **CLC 52, 55**
    See Mahfouz, Naguib (Abdel Aziz Al-
    Sabilgi)
    See also AFW; DLBY 1988; EWL 3; RGSF
    2; WLIT 2

**Mahon, Derek** 1941- **CLC 27**
    See also BRWS 6; CA 128; 113; CANR 88;
    CP 7; DLB 40; EWL 3

**Maiakovskii, Vladimir**
    See Mayakovski, Vladimir (Vladimirovich)
    See also IDTP; RGWL 2, 3

**Mailer, Norman** 1923- **CLC 1, 2, 3, 4, 5, 8, 11, 14, 28, 39, 74, 111**
    See also AAYA 31; AITN 2; AMW; AMWR
    2; BPFB 2; CA 9-12R; CABS 1; CANR
    28, 74, 77; CDALB 1968-1988; CN 7;
    CPW; DA; DA3; DAB; DAC; DAM MST,
    NOV, POP; DLB 2, 16, 28, 185, 278;
    DLBD 3; DLBY 1980, 1983; EWL 3;
    MTCW 1, 2; NFS 10; RGAL 4; TUS

**Maillet, Antonine** 1929- **CLC 54, 118**
    See also CA 120; 115; CANR 46, 74, 77;
    CCA 1; CWW 2; DAC; DLB 60; INT
    120; MTCW 2

**Mais, Roger** 1905-1955 **TCLC 8**
    See also BW 1, 3; CA 124; 105; CANR 82;
    CDWLB 3; DLB 125; EWL 3; MTCW 1;
    RGEL 2

**Maistre, Joseph** 1753-1821 **NCLC 37**
    See also GFL 1789 to the Present

**Maitland, Frederic William** 1850-1906 **TCLC 65**

**Maitland, Sara (Louise)** 1950- **CLC 49**
    See also CA 69-72; CANR 13, 59; DLB
    271; FW

**Major, Clarence** 1936- **BLC 2; CLC 3, 19, 48**
    See also AFAW 2; BW 2, 3; CA 21-24R;
    CAAS 6; CANR 13, 25, 53, 82; CN 7;
    CP 7; CSW; DAM MULT; DLB 33; EWL
    3; MSW

**Major, Kevin (Gerald)** 1949- **CLC 26**
    See also AAYA 16; CA 97-100; CANR 21,
    38, 112; CLR 11; DAC; DLB 60; INT
    CANR-21; JRDA; MAICYA 1, 2; MAIC-
    YAS 1; SATA 32, 82, 134; WYA; YAW

**Maki, James**
    See Ozu, Yasujiro

**Malabaila, Damiano**
See Levi, Primo

**Malamud, Bernard** 1914-1986 **CLC 1, 2, 3, 5, 8, 9, 11, 18, 27, 44, 78, 85; SSC 15; TCLC 129; WLC**
See also AAYA 16; AMWS 1; BPFB 2; CA 118; 5-8R; CABS 1; CANR 28, 62, 114; CDALB 1941-1968; CPW; DA; DA3; DAB; DAC; DAM MST, NOV, POP; DLB 2, 28, 152; DLBY 1980, 1986; EWL 3; EXPS; LAIT 4; MTCW 1, 2; NFS 4, 9; RGAL 4; RGSF 2; SSFS 8, 13, 16; TUS

**Malan, Herman**
See Bosman, Herman Charles; Bosman, Herman Charles

**Malaparte, Curzio** 1898-1957 **TCLC 52**
See also DLB 264

**Malcolm, Dan**
See Silverberg, Robert

**Malcolm X BLC 2; CLC 82, 117; WLCS**
See Little, Malcolm
See also LAIT 5

**Malherbe, Francois de** 1555-1628 **LC 5**
See also GFL Beginnings to 1789

**Mallarme, Stephane** 1842-1898 **NCLC 4, 41; PC 4**
See also DAM POET; DLB 217; EW 7; GFL 1789 to the Present; RGWL 2, 3; TWA

**Mallet-Joris, Francoise** 1930- **CLC 11**
See also CA 65-68; CANR 17; DLB 83; EWL 3; GFL 1789 to the Present

**Malley, Ern**
See McAuley, James Phillip

**Mallon, Thomas** 1951- **CLC 172**
See also CA 110; CANR 29, 57, 92

**Mallowan, Agatha Christie**
See Christie, Agatha (Mary Clarissa)

**Maloff, Saul** 1922- **CLC 5**
See also CA 33-36R

**Malone, Louis**
See MacNeice, (Frederick) Louis

**Malone, Michael (Christopher)** 1942- **CLC 43**
See also CA 77-80; CANR 14, 32, 57, 114

**Malory, Sir Thomas** 1410(?)-1471(?) **LC 11, 88; WLCS**
See also BRW 1; BRWR 2; CDBLB Before 1660; DA; DAB; DAC; DAM MST; DLB 146; EFS 2; RGEL 2; SATA 59; SATA-Brief 33; TEA; WLIT 3

**Malouf, (George Joseph) David** 1934- **CLC 28, 86**
See also CA 124; CANR 50, 76; CN 7; CP 7; EWL 3; MTCW 2

**Malraux, (Georges-)Andre** 1901-1976 **CLC 1, 4, 9, 13, 15, 57**
See also BPFB 2; CA 69-72; 21-22; CANR 34, 58; CAP 2; DA3; DAM NOV; DLB 72; EW 12; EWL 3; GFL 1789 to the Present; MTCW 1, 2; RGWL 2, 3; TWA

**Malzberg, Barry N(athaniel)** 1939- **CLC 7**
See also CA 61-64; CAAS 4; CANR 16; CMW 4; DLB 8; SFW 4

**Mamet, David (Alan)** 1947- **CLC 9, 15, 34, 46, 91, 166; DC 4**
See also AAYA 3; CA 81-84; CABS 3; CANR 15, 41, 67, 72; CD 5; DA3; DAM DRAM; DFS 15; DLB 7; EWL 3; IDFW 4; MTCW 1, 2; RGAL 4

**Mamoulian, Rouben (Zachary)** 1897-1987 **CLC 16**
See also CA 124; 25-28R; CANR 85

**Mandelshtam, Osip**
See Mandelstam, Osip (Emilievich)
See also EW 10; EWL 3; RGWL 2, 3

**Mandelstam, Osip (Emilievich)** 1891(?)-1943(?) **PC 14; TCLC 2, 6**
See Mandelshtam, Osip
See also CA 150; 104; MTCW 2; TWA

**Mander, (Mary) Jane** 1877-1949 **TCLC 31**
See also CA 162; RGEL 2

**Mandeville, Bernard** 1670-1733 **LC 82**
See also DLB 101

**Mandeville, Sir John** fl. 1350- **CMLC 19**
See also DLB 146

**Mandiargues, Andre Pieyre de CLC 41**
See Pieyre de Mandiargues, Andre
See also DLB 83

**Mandrake, Ethel Belle**
See Thurman, Wallace (Henry)

**Mangan, James Clarence** 1803-1849 **NCLC 27**
See also RGEL 2

**Maniere, J.-E.**
See Giraudoux, Jean(-Hippolyte)

**Mankiewicz, Herman (Jacob)** 1897-1953 **TCLC 85**
See also CA 169; 120; DLB 26; IDFW 3, 4

**Manley, (Mary) Delariviere** 1672(?)-1724 **LC 1, 42**
See also DLB 39, 80; RGEL 2

**Mann, Abel**
See Creasey, John

**Mann, Emily** 1952- **DC 7**
See also CA 130; CAD; CANR 55; CD 5; CWD; DLB 266

**Mann, (Luiz) Heinrich** 1871-1950 **TCLC 9**
See also CA 164, 181; 106; DLB 66, 118; EW 8; RGWL 2, 3

**Mann, (Paul) Thomas** 1875-1955 **SSC 5; TCLC 2, 8, 14, 21, 35, 44, 60; WLC**
See also BPFB 2; CA 128; 104; CDWLB 2; DA; DA3; DAB; DAC; DAM MST, NOV; DLB 66; EW 9; EWL 3; GLL 1; MTCW 1, 2; NFS 17; RGSF 2; RGWL 2, 3; SSFS 4, 9; TWA

**Mannheim, Karl** 1893-1947 **TCLC 65**
See also CA 204

**Manning, David**
See Faust, Frederick (Schiller)
See also TCWW 2

**Manning, Frederic** 1887(?)-1935 **TCLC 25**
See also CA 124; DLB 260

**Manning, Olivia** 1915-1980 **CLC 5, 19**
See also CA 101; 5-8R; CANR 29; EWL 3; FW; MTCW 1; RGEL 2

**Mano, D. Keith** 1942- **CLC 2, 10**
See also CA 25-28R; CAAS 6; CANR 26, 57; DLB 6

**Mansfield, Katherine SSC 9, 23, 38; TCLC 2, 8, 39; WLC**
See Beauchamp, Kathleen Mansfield
See also BPFB 2; BRW 7; DAB; DLB 162; EWL 3; EXPS; FW; GLL 1; RGEL 2; RGSF 2; SSFS 2, 8, 10, 11

**Manso, Peter** 1940- **CLC 39**
See also CA 29-32R; CANR 44

**Mantecon, Juan Jimenez**
See Jimenez (Mantecon), Juan Ramon

**Mantel, Hilary (Mary)** 1952- **CLC 144**
See also CA 125; CANR 54, 101; CN 7; DLB 271; RHW

**Manton, Peter**
See Creasey, John

**Man Without a Spleen, A**
See Chekhov, Anton (Pavlovich)

**Manzoni, Alessandro** 1785-1873 **NCLC 29, 98**
See also EW 5; RGWL 2, 3; TWA

**Map, Walter** 1140-1209 **CMLC 32**

**Mapu, Abraham (ben Jekutiel)** 1808-1867 **NCLC 18**

**Mara, Sally**
See Queneau, Raymond

**Maracle, Lee** 1950- **NNAL**
See also CA 149

**Marat, Jean Paul** 1743-1793 **LC 10**

**Marcel, Gabriel Honore** 1889-1973 **CLC 15**
See also CA 45-48; 102; EWL 3; MTCW 1, 2

**March, William** 1893-1954 **TCLC 96**

**Marchbanks, Samuel**
See Davies, (William) Robertson
See also CCA 1

**Marchi, Giacomo**
See Bassani, Giorgio

**Marcus Aurelius**
See Aurelius, Marcus
See also AW 2

**Marguerite**
See de Navarre, Marguerite

**Marguerite d'Angouleme**
See de Navarre, Marguerite
See also GFL Beginnings to 1789

**Marguerite de Navarre**
See de Navarre, Marguerite
See also RGWL 2, 3

**Margulies, Donald** 1954- **CLC 76**
See also CA 200; DFS 13; DLB 228

**Marie de France** c. 12th cent. - **CMLC 8; PC 22**
See also DLB 208; FW; RGWL 2, 3

**Marie de l'Incarnation** 1599-1672 **LC 10**

**Marier, Captain Victor**
See Griffith, D(avid Lewelyn) W(ark)

**Mariner, Scott**
See Pohl, Frederik

**Marinetti, Filippo Tommaso** 1876-1944 **TCLC 10**
See also CA 107; DLB 114, 264; EW 9; EWL 3

**Marivaux, Pierre Carlet de Chamblain de** 1688-1763 **DC 7; LC 4**
See also GFL Beginnings to 1789; RGWL 2, 3; TWA

**Markandaya, Kamala CLC 8, 38**
See Taylor, Kamala (Purnaiya)
See also BYA 13; CN 7; EWL 3

**Markfield, Wallace** 1926-2002 **CLC 8**
See also CA 208; 69-72; CAAS 3; CN 7; DLB 2, 28

**Markham, Edwin** 1852-1940 **TCLC 47**
See also CA 160; DLB 54, 186; RGAL 4

**Markham, Robert**
See Amis, Kingsley (William)

**Markoosie NNAL**
See Markoosie, Patsauq
See also CLR 23; DAM MULT

**Marks, J**
See Highwater, Jamake (Mamake)

**Marks, J.**
See Highwater, Jamake (Mamake)

**Marks-Highwater, J**
See Highwater, Jamake (Mamake)

**Marks-Highwater, J.**
See Highwater, Jamake (Mamake)

**Markson, David M(errill)** 1927- **CLC 67**
See also CA 49-52; CANR 1, 91; CN 7

**Marlatt, Daphne (Buckle)** 1942- **CLC 168**
See also CA 25-28R; CANR 17, 39; CN 7; CP 7; CWP; DLB 60; FW

**Marley, Bob CLC 17**
See Marley, Robert Nesta

**Marley, Robert Nesta** 1945-1981
See Marley, Bob
See also CA 103; 107

**Marlowe, Christopher** 1564-1593 **DC 1; LC 22, 47; WLC**
See also BRW 1; BRWR 1; CDBLB Before 1660; DA; DA3; DAB; DAC; DAM DRAM, MST; DFS 1, 5, 13; DLB 62; EXPP; RGEL 2; TEA; WLIT 3

**Marlowe, Stephen** 1928- **CLC 70**
See Queen, Ellery
See also CA 13-16R; CANR 6, 55; CMW 4; SFW 4

**Marmontel, Jean-Francois** 1723-1799 **LC 2**

**Maron, Monika** 1941- **CLC 165**
See also CA 201

**Marquand, John P(hillips)** 1893-1960 **CLC 2, 10**
See also AMW; BPFB 2; CA 85-88; CANR 73; CMW 4; DLB 9, 102; EWL 3; MTCW 2; RGAL 4

**Marques, Rene** 1919-1979 **CLC 96; HLC 2**
See also CA 85-88; 97-100; CANR 78; DAM MULT; DLB 113; EWL 3; HW 1, 2; LAW; RGSF 2

**Marquez, Gabriel (Jose) Garcia**
See Garcia Marquez, Gabriel (Jose)

**Marquis, Don(ald Robert Perry)** 1878-1937 **TCLC 7**
See also CA 166; 104; DLB 11, 25; RGAL 4

**Marquis de Sade**
See Sade, Donatien Alphonse Francois

**Marric, J. J.**
See Creasey, John
See also MSW

**Marryat, Frederick** 1792-1848 **NCLC 3**
See also DLB 21, 163; RGEL 2; WCH

**Marsden, James**
See Creasey, John

**Marsh, Edward** 1872-1953 **TCLC 99**

**Marsh, (Edith) Ngaio** 1899-1982 **CLC 7, 53**
See also CA 9-12R; CANR 6, 58; CMW 4; CPW; DAM POP; DLB 77; MSW; MTCW 1, 2; RGEL 2; TEA

**Marshall, Garry** 1934- **CLC 17**
See also AAYA 3; CA 111; SATA 60

**Marshall, Paule** 1929- **BLC 3; CLC 27, 72; SSC 3**
See also AFAW 1, 2; AMWS 11; BPFB 2; BW 2, 3; CA 77-80; CANR 25, 73; CN 7; DA3; DAM MULT; DLB 33, 157, 227; EWL 3; MTCW 1, 2; RGAL 4; SSFS 15

**Marshallik**
See Zangwill, Israel

**Marsten, Richard**
See Hunter, Evan

**Marston, John** 1576-1634 **LC 33**
See also BRW 2; DAM DRAM; DLB 58, 172; RGEL 2

**Martha, Henry**
See Harris, Mark

**Marti (y Perez), Jose (Julian)** 1853-1895 **HLC 2; NCLC 63**
See also DAM MULT; HW 2; LAW; RGWL 2, 3; WLIT 1

**Martial** c. 40-c. 104 **CMLC 35; PC 10**
See also AW 2; CDWLB 1; DLB 211; RGWL 2, 3

**Martin, Ken**
See Hubbard, L(afayette) Ron(ald)

**Martin, Richard**
See Creasey, John

**Martin, Steve** 1945- **CLC 30**
See also CA 97-100; CANR 30, 100; MTCW 1

**Martin, Valerie** 1948- **CLC 89**
See also BEST 90:2; CA 85-88; CANR 49, 89

**Martin, Violet Florence** 1862-1915 **SSC 56; TCLC 51**

**Martin, Webber**
See Silverberg, Robert

**Martindale, Patrick Victor**
See White, Patrick (Victor Martindale)

**Martin du Gard, Roger** 1881-1958 **TCLC 24**
See also CA 118; CANR 94; DLB 65; EWL 3; GFL 1789 to the Present; RGWL 2, 3

**Martineau, Harriet** 1802-1876 **NCLC 26**
See also DLB 21, 55, 159, 163, 166, 190; FW; RGEL 2; YABC 2

**Martines, Julia**
See O'Faolain, Julia

**Martinez, Enrique Gonzalez**
See Gonzalez Martinez, Enrique

**Martinez, Jacinto Benavente y**
See Benavente (y Martinez), Jacinto

**Martinez de la Rosa, Francisco de Paula** 1787-1862 **NCLC 102**
See also TWA

**Martinez Ruiz, Jose** 1873-1967
See Azorin; Ruiz, Jose Martinez
See also CA 93-96; HW 1

**Martinez Sierra, Gregorio** 1881-1947 **TCLC 6**
See also CA 115; EWL 3

**Martinez Sierra, Maria (de la O'LeJarraga)** 1874-1974 **TCLC 6**
See also CA 115; EWL 3

**Martinsen, Martin**
See Follett, Ken(neth Martin)

**Martinson, Harry (Edmund)** 1904-1978 **CLC 14**
See also CA 77-80; CANR 34; DLB 259; EWL 3

**Martyn, Edward** 1859-1923 **TCLC 131**
See also CA 179; DLB 10; RGEL 2

**Marut, Ret**
See Traven, B.

**Marut, Robert**
See Traven, B.

**Marvell, Andrew** 1621-1678 **LC 4, 43; PC 10; WLC**
See also BRW 2; BRWR 2; CDBLB 1660-1789; DA; DAB; DAC; DAM MST, POET; DLB 131; EXPP; PFS 5; RGEL 2; TEA; WP

**Marx, Karl (Heinrich)** 1818-1883 **NCLC 17, 114**
See also DLB 129; TWA

**Masaoka, Shiki** -1902 **TCLC 18**
See Masaoka, Tsunenori
See also RGWL 3

**Masaoka, Tsunenori** 1867-1902
See Masaoka, Shiki
See also CA 191; 117; TWA

**Masefield, John (Edward)** 1878-1967 **CLC 11, 47**
See also CA 25-28R; 19-20; CANR 33; CAP 2; CDBLB 1890-1914; DAM POET; DLB 10, 19, 153, 160; EWL 3; EXPP; FANT; MTCW 1, 2; PFS 5; RGEL 2; SATA 19

**Maso, Carole** 19(?)- **CLC 44**
See also CA 170; GLL 2; RGAL 4

**Mason, Bobbie Ann** 1940- **CLC 28, 43, 82, 154; SSC 4**
See also AAYA 5, 42; AMWS 8; BPFB 2; CA 53-56; CANR 11, 31, 58, 83; CDALBS; CN 7; CSW; DA3; DLB 173; DLBY 1987; EWL 3; EXPS; INT CANR-31; MTCW 1, 2; NFS 4; RGAL 4; RGSF 2; SSFS 3,8; YAW

**Mason, Ernst**
See Pohl, Frederik

**Mason, Hunni B.**
See Sternheim, (William Adolf) Carl

**Mason, Lee W.**
See Malzberg, Barry N(athaniel)

**Mason, Nick** 1945- **CLC 35**

**Mason, Tally**
See Derleth, August (William)

**Mass, Anna CLC 59**

**Mass, William**
See Gibson, William

**Massinger, Philip** 1583-1640 **LC 70**
See also DLB 58; RGEL 2

**Master Lao**
See Lao Tzu

**Masters, Edgar Lee** 1868-1950 **PC 1, 36; TCLC 2, 25; WLCS**
See also AMWS 1; CA 133; 104; CDALB 1865-1917; DA; DAC; DAM MST, POET; DLB 54; EWL 3; EXPP; MTCW 1, 2; RGAL 4; TUS; WP

**Masters, Hilary** 1928- **CLC 48**
See also CA 25-28R; CANR 13, 47, 97; CN 7; DLB 244

**Mastrosimone, William** 19(?)- **CLC 36**
See also CA 186; CAD; CD 5

**Mathe, Albert**
See Camus, Albert

**Mather, Cotton** 1663-1728 **LC 38**
See also AMWS 2; CDALB 1640-1865; DLB 24, 30, 140; RGAL 4; TUS

**Mather, Increase** 1639-1723 **LC 38**
See also DLB 24

**Matheson, Richard (Burton)** 1926- **CLC 37**
See also AAYA 31; CA 97-100; CANR 88, 99; DLB 8, 44; HGG; INT 97-100; SCFW 2; SFW 4; SUFW 2

**Mathews, Harry** 1930- **CLC 6, 52**
See also CA 21-24R; CAAS 6; CANR 18, 40, 98; CN 7

**Mathews, John Joseph** 1894-1979 **CLC 84; NNAL**
See also CA 142; 19-20; CANR 45; CAP 2; DAM MULT; DLB 175

**Mathias, Roland (Glyn)** 1915- **CLC 45**
See also CA 97-100; CANR 19, 41; CP 7; DLB 27

**Matsuo Basho** 1644-1694 **LC 62; PC 3**
See Basho, Matsuo
See also DAM POET; PFS 2, 7

**Mattheson, Rodney**
See Creasey, John

**Matthews, (James) Brander** 1852-1929 **TCLC 95**
See also DLB 71, 78; DLBD 13

**Matthews, Greg** 1949- **CLC 45**
See also CA 135

**Matthews, William (Procter III)** 1942-1997 **CLC 40**
See also AMWS 9; CA 162; 29-32R; CAAS 18; CANR 12, 57; CP 7; DLB 5

**Matthias, John (Edward)** 1941- **CLC 9**
See also CA 33-36R; CANR 56; CP 7

**Matthiessen, F(rancis) O(tto)** 1902-1950 **TCLC 100**
See also CA 185; DLB 63

**Matthiessen, Peter** 1927- **CLC 5, 7, 11, 32, 64**
See also AAYA 6, 40; AMWS 5; ANW; BEST 90:4; BPFB 2; CA 9-12R; CANR 21, 50, 73, 100; CN 7; DA3; DAM NOV; DLB 6, 173, 275; MTCW 1, 2; SATA 27

**Maturin, Charles Robert** 1780(?)-1824 **NCLC 6**
See also BRWS 8; DLB 178; HGG; RGEL 2; SUFW

**Matute (Ausejo), Ana Maria** 1925- **CLC 11**
See also CA 89-92; EWL 3; MTCW 1; RGSF 2

**Maugham, W. S.**
See Maugham, W(illiam) Somerset

**Maugham, W(illiam) Somerset** 1874-1965 **CLC 1, 11, 15, 67, 93; SSC 8; WLC**
See also BPFB 2; BRW 6; CA 25-28R; 5-8R; CANR 40; CDBLB 1914-1945; CMW 4; DA; DA3; DAB; DAC; DAM DRAM, MST, NOV; DLB 10, 36, 77, 100, 162, 195; EWL 3; LAIT 3; MTCW 1, 2; RGEL 2; RGSF 2; SATA 54; SSFS 17

**Maugham, William Somerset**
See Maugham, W(illiam) Somerset

Maupassant, (Henri Rene Albert) Guy de
1850-1893 **NCLC 1, 42, 83; SSC 1;**
**WLC**
See also BYA 14; DA; DA3; DAB; DAC;
DAM MST; DLB 123; EW 7; EXPS; GFL
1789 to the Present; LAIT 2; RGSF 2;
RGWL 2, 3; SSFS 4; SUFW; TWA

Maupin, Armistead (Jones, Jr.) 1944- **CLC**
**95**
See also CA 130; 125; CANR 58, 101;
CPW; DA3; DAM POP; DLB 278; GLL
1; INT 130; MTCW 2

Maurhut, Richard
See Traven, B.

Mauriac, Claude 1914-1996 **CLC 9**
See also CA 152; 89-92; CWW 2; DLB 83;
EWL 3; GFL 1789 to the Present

Mauriac, Francois (Charles) 1885-1970 **CLC**
**4, 9, 56; SSC 24**
See also CA 25-28; CAP 2; DLB 65; EW
10; EWL 3; GFL 1789 to the Present;
MTCW 1, 2; RGWL 2, 3; TWA

Mavor, Osborne Henry 1888-1951
See Bridie, James
See also CA 104

Maxwell, William (Keepers, Jr.) 1908-2000
**CLC 19**
See also AMWS 8; CA 189; 93-96; CANR
54, 95; CN 7; DLB 218, 278; DLBY
1980; INT CA-93-96; SATA-Obit 128

May, Elaine 1932- **CLC 16**
See also CA 142; 124; CAD; CWD; DLB
44

Mayakovski, Vladimir (Vladimirovich)
1893-1930 **TCLC 4, 18**
See Maiakovskii, Vladimir; Mayakovsky,
Vladimir
See also CA 158; 104; EWL 3; MTCW 2;
SFW 4; TWA

Mayakovsky, Vladimir
See Mayakovski, Vladimir (Vladimirovich)
See also EW 11; WP

Mayhew, Henry 1812-1887 **NCLC 31**
See also DLB 18, 55, 190

Mayle, Peter 1939(?)- **CLC 89**
See also CA 139; CANR 64, 109

Maynard, Joyce 1953- **CLC 23**
See also CA 129; 111; CANR 64

Mayne, William (James Carter) 1928- **CLC**
**12**
See also AAYA 20; CA 9-12R; CANR 37,
80, 100; CLR 25; FANT; JRDA; MAI-
CYA 1, 2; MAICYAS 1; SAAS 11; SATA
6, 68, 122; SUFW 2; YAW

Mayo, Jim
See L'Amour, Louis (Dearborn)
See also TCWW 2

Maysles, Albert 1926- **CLC 16**
See also CA 29-32R

Maysles, David 1932-1987 **CLC 16**
See also CA 191

Mazer, Norma Fox 1931- **CLC 26**
See also AAYA 5, 36; BYA 1, 8; CA 69-72;
CANR 12, 32, 66; CLR 23; JRDA; MAI-
CYA 1, 2; SAAS 1; SATA 24, 67, 105;
WYA; YAW

Mazzini, Guiseppe 1805-1872 **NCLC 34**

McAlmon, Robert (Menzies) 1895-1956
**TCLC 97**
See also CA 168; 107; DLB 4, 45; DLBD
15; GLL 1

McAuley, James Phillip 1917-1976 **CLC 45**
See also CA 97-100; DLB 260; RGEL 2

McBain, Ed
See Hunter, Evan
See also MSW

McBrien, William (Augustine) 1930- **CLC 44**
See also CA 107; CANR 90

McCabe, Patrick 1955- **CLC 133**
See also CA 130; CANR 50, 90; CN 7;
DLB 194

McCaffrey, Anne (Inez) 1926- **CLC 17**
See also AAYA 6, 34; AITN 2; BEST 89:2;
BPFB 2; BYA 5; CA 25-28R; CANR 15,
35, 55, 96; CLR 49; CPW; DA3; DAM
NOV, POP; DLB 8; JRDA; MAICYA 1,
2; MTCW 1, 2; SAAS 11; SATA 8, 70,
116; SFW 4; SUFW 2; WYA; YAW

McCall, Nathan 1955(?)- **CLC 86**
See also BW 3; CA 146; CANR 88

McCann, Arthur
See Campbell, John W(ood, Jr.)

McCann, Edson
See Pohl, Frederik

McCarthy, Charles, Jr. 1933-
See McCarthy, Cormac
See also CANR 42, 69, 101; CN 7; CPW;
CSW; DA3; DAM POP; MTCW 2

McCarthy, Cormac **CLC 4, 57, 59, 101**
See McCarthy, Charles, Jr.
See also AAYA 41; AMWS 8; BPFB 2; CA
13-16R; CANR 10; DLB 6, 143, 256;
EWL 3; TCWW 2

McCarthy, Mary (Therese) 1912-1989 **CLC**
**1, 3, 5, 14, 24, 39, 59; SSC 24**
See also BPFB 2; CA 129; 5-8R;
CANR 16, 50, 64; DA3; DLB 2; DLBY
1981; EWL 3; FW; INT CANR-16;
MAWW; MTCW 1, 2; RGAL 4; TUS

McCartney, (James) Paul 1942- **CLC 12, 35**
See also CA 146; CANR 111

McCauley, Stephen (D.) 1955- **CLC 50**
See also CA 141

McClaren, Peter **CLC 70**

McClure, Michael (Thomas) 1932- **CLC 6,**
**10**
See also BG 3; CA 21-24R; CAD; CANR
17, 46, 77; CD 5; CP 7; DLB 16; WP

McCorkle, Jill (Collins) 1958- **CLC 51**
See also CA 121; CANR 113; CSW; DLB
234; DLBY 1987

McCourt, Frank 1930- **CLC 109**
See also AMWS 12; CA 157; CANR 97;
NCFS 1

McCourt, James 1941- **CLC 5**
See also CA 57-60; CANR 98

McCourt, Malachy 1931- **CLC 119**
See also SATA 126

McCoy, Horace (Stanley) 1897-1955 **TCLC**
**28**
See also CA 155; 108; CMW 4; DLB 9

McCrae, John 1872-1918 **TCLC 12**
See also CA 109; DLB 92; PFS 5

McCreigh, James
See Pohl, Frederik

McCullers, (Lula) Carson (Smith) 1917-1967
**CLC 1, 4, 10, 12, 48, 100; SSC 9, 24;**
**WLC**
See also AAYA 21; AMW; BPFB 2; CA 25-
28R; 5-8R; CABS 1, 3; CANR 18;
CDALB 1941-1968; DA; DA3; DAB;
DAC; DAM MST, NOV; DFS 5; DLB 2,
7, 173, 228; EWL 3; EXPS; FW; GLL 1;
LAIT 3, 4; MAWW; MTCW 1, 2; NFS 6,
13; RGAL 4; RGSF 2; SATA 27; SSFS 5;
TUS; YAW

McCulloch, John Tyler
See Burroughs, Edgar Rice

McCullough, Colleen 1938(?)- **CLC 27, 107**
See also AAYA 36; BPFB 2; CA 81-84;
CANR 17, 46, 67, 98; CPW; DA3; DAM
NOV, POP; MTCW 1, 2; RHW

McCunn, Ruthanne Lum 1946- **AAL**
See also CA 119; CANR 43, 96; LAIT 2;
SATA 63

McDermott, Alice 1953- **CLC 90**
See also CA 109; CANR 40, 90

McElroy, Joseph 1930- **CLC 5, 47**
See also CA 17-20R; CN 7

McEwan, Ian (Russell) 1948- **CLC 13, 66,**
**169**
See also BEST 90:4; BRWS 4; CA 61-64;
CANR 14, 41, 69, 87; CN 7; DAM NOV;
DLB 14, 194; HGG; MTCW 1, 2; RGSF
2; SUFW 2; TEA

McFadden, David 1940- **CLC 48**
See also CA 104; CP 7; DLB 60; INT 104

McFarland, Dennis 1950- **CLC 65**
See also CA 165; CANR 110

McGahern, John 1934- **CLC 5, 9, 48, 156;**
**SSC 17**
See also CA 17-20R; CANR 29, 68, 113;
CN 7; DLB 14, 231; MTCW 1

McGinley, Patrick (Anthony) 1937- **CLC 41**
See also CA 127; 120; CANR 56; INT 127

McGinley, Phyllis 1905-1978 **CLC 14**
See also CA 77-80; 9-12R; CANR 19;
CWRI 5; DLB 11, 48; PFS 9, 13; SATA
2, 44; SATA-Obit 24

McGinniss, Joe 1942- **CLC 32**
See also AITN 2; BEST 89:2; CA 25-28R;
CANR 26, 70; CPW; DLB 185; INT
CANR-26

McGivern, Maureen Daly
See Daly, Maureen

McGrath, Patrick 1950- **CLC 55**
See also CA 136; CANR 65; CN 7; DLB
231; HGG; SUFW 2

McGrath, Thomas (Matthew) 1916-1990
**CLC 28, 59**
See also AMWS 10; CA 132; 9-12R; CANR
6, 33, 95; DAM POET; MTCW 1; SATA
41; SATA-Obit 66

McGuane, Thomas (Francis III) 1939- **CLC**
**3, 7, 18, 45, 127**
See also AITN 2; BPFB 2; CA 49-52;
CANR 5, 24, 49, 94; CN 7; DLB 2, 212;
DLBY 1980; EWL 3; INT CANR-24;
MTCW 1; TCWW 2

McGuckian, Medbh 1950- **CLC 48; PC 27**
See also BRWS 5; CA 143; CP 7; CWP;
DAM POET; DLB 40

McHale, Tom 1942(?)-1982 **CLC 3, 5**
See also AITN 1; CA 106; 77-80

McIlvanney, William 1936- **CLC 42**
See also CA 25-28R; CANR 61; CMW 4;
DLB 14, 207

McIlwraith, Maureen Mollie Hunter
See Hunter, Mollie
See also SATA 2

McInerney, Jay 1955- **CLC 34, 112**
See also AAYA 18; BPFB 2; CA 123; 116;
CANR 45, 68, 116; CN 7; CPW; DA3;
DAM POP; INT 123; MTCW 2

McIntyre, Vonda N(eel) 1948- **CLC 18**
See also CA 81-84; CANR 17, 34, 69;
MTCW 1; SFW 4; YAW

McKay, Claude BLC 3; HR 3; PC 2; TCLC
**7, 41; WLC**
See McKay, Festus Claudius
See also AFAW 1, 2; AMWS 10; DAB;
DLB 4, 45, 51, 117; EWL 3; EXPP; GLL
2; LAIT 3; LMFS 2; PAB; PFS 4; RGAL
4; WP

McKay, Festus Claudius 1889-1948
See McKay, Claude
See also BW 1, 3; CA 124; 104; CANR 73;
DA; DAC; DAM MST, MULT, NOV,
POET; MTCW 1, 2; TUS

McKuen, Rod 1933- **CLC 1, 3**
See also AITN 1; CA 41-44R; CANR 40

McLoughlin, R. B.
See Mencken, H(enry) L(ouis)

McLuhan, (Herbert) Marshall 1911-1980
**CLC 37, 83**
See also CA 102; 9-12R; CANR 12, 34, 61;
DLB 88; INT CANR-12; MTCW 1, 2

**McManus, Declan Patrick Aloysius**
  See Costello, Elvis
**McMillan, Terry (L.)** 1951- **BLCS; CLC 50, 61, 112**
  See also AAYA 21; BPFB 2; BW 2, 3; CA 140; CANR 60, 104; CPW; DA3; DAM MULT, NOV, POP; MTCW 2; RGAL 4; YAW
**McMurtry, Larry (Jeff)** 1936- **CLC 2, 3, 7, 11, 27, 44, 127**
  See also AAYA 15; AITN 2; AMWS 5; BEST 89:2; BPFB 2; CA 5-8R; CANR 19, 43, 64, 103; CDALB 1968-1988; CN 7; CPW; CSW; DA3; DAM NOV, POP; DLB 2, 143, 256; DLBY 1980, 1987; EWL 3; MTCW 1, 2; RGAL 4; TCWW 2
**McNally, T. M.** 1961- **CLC 82**
**McNally, Terrence** 1939- **CLC 4, 7, 41, 91**
  See also CA 45-48; CAD; CANR 2, 56, 116; CD 5; DA3; DAM DRAM; DFS 16; DLB 7, 249; EWL 3; GLL 1; MTCW 2
**McNamer, Deirdre** 1950- **CLC 70**
**McNeal, Tom CLC 119**
**McNeile, Herman Cyril** 1888-1937
  See Sapper
  See also CA 184; CMW 4; DLB 77
**McNickle, (William) D'Arcy** 1904-1977 **CLC 89; NNAL**
  See also CA 85-88; 9-12R; CANR 5, 45; DAM MULT; DLB 175, 212; RGAL 4; SATA-Obit 22
**McPhee, John (Angus)** 1931- **CLC 36**
  See also ANW; BEST 90:1; CA 65-68; CANR 20, 46, 64, 69; CPW; DLB 185, 275; MTCW 1, 2; TUS
**McPherson, James Alan** 1943- **BLCS; CLC 19, 77**
  See also BW 1, 3; CA 25-28R; CAAS 17; CANR 24, 74; CN 7; CSW; DLB 38, 244; EWL 3; MTCW 1, 2; RGAL 4; RGSF 2
**McPherson, William (Alexander)** 1933- **CLC 34**
  See also CA 69-72; CANR 28; INT CANR-28
**McTaggart, J. McT. Ellis**
  See McTaggart, John McTaggart Ellis
**McTaggart, John McTaggart Ellis** 1866-1925 **TCLC 105**
  See also CA 120; DLB 262
**Mead, George Herbert** 1863-1931 **TCLC 89**
  See also DLB 270
**Mead, Margaret** 1901-1978 **CLC 37**
  See also AITN 1; CA 81-84; 1-4R; CANR 4; DA3; FW; MTCW 1, 2; SATA-Obit 20
**Meaker, Marijane (Agnes)** 1927-
  See Kerr, M. E.
  See also CA 107; CANR 37, 63; INT 107; JRDA; MAICYA 1, 2; MAICYAS 1; MTCW 1; SATA 20, 61, 99; SATA-Essay 111; YAW
**Medoff, Mark (Howard)** 1940- **CLC 6, 23**
  See also AITN 1; CA 53-56; CAD; CANR 5; CD 5; DAM DRAM; DFS 4; DLB 7; INT CANR-5
**Medvedev, P. N.**
  See Bakhtin, Mikhail Mikhailovich
**Meged, Aharon**
  See Megged, Aharon
**Meged, Aron**
  See Megged, Aharon
**Megged, Aharon** 1920- **CLC 9**
  See also CA 49-52; CAAS 13; CANR 1; EWL 3
**Mehta, Ved (Parkash)** 1934- **CLC 37**
  See also CA 1-4R; CANR 2, 23, 69; MTCW 1
**Melanter**
  See Blackmore, R(ichard) D(oddridge)
**Meleager** c. 140B.C.-c. 70B.C. **CMLC 53**

**Melies, Georges** 1861-1938 **TCLC 81**
**Melikow, Loris**
  See Hofmannsthal, Hugo von
**Melmoth, Sebastian**
  See Wilde, Oscar (Fingal O'Flahertie Wills)
**Melo Neto, Joao Cabral de**
  See Cabral de Melo Neto, Joao
  See also EWL 3
**Meltzer, Milton** 1915- **CLC 26**
  See also AAYA 8, 45; BYA 2, 6; CA 13-16R; CANR 38, 92, 107; CLR 13; DLB 61; JRDA; MAICYA 1, 2; SAAS 1; SATA 1, 50, 80, 128; SATA-Essay 124; WYA; YAW
**Melville, Herman** 1819-1891 **NCLC 3, 12, 29, 45, 49, 91, 93, 123; SSC 1, 17, 46; WLC**
  See also AAYA 25; AMW; AMWR 1; CDALB 1640-1865; DA; DA3; DAB; DAC; DAM MST, NOV; DLB 3, 74, 250, 254; EXPN; EXPS; LAIT 1, 2; NFS 7, 9; RGAL 4; RGSF 2; SATA 59; SSFS 3; TUS
**Members, Mark**
  See Powell, Anthony (Dymoke)
**Membreno, Alejandro CLC 59**
**Menander** c. 342B.C.-c. 293B.C. **CMLC 9, 51; DC 3**
  See also AW 1; CDWLB 1; DAM DRAM; DLB 176; RGWL 2, 3
**Menchu, Rigoberta** 1959- **CLC 160; HLCS 2**
  See also CA 175; DNFS 1; WLIT 1
**Mencken, H(enry) L(ouis)** 1880-1956 **TCLC 13**
  See also AMW; CA 125; 105; CDALB 1917-1929; DLB 11, 29, 63, 137, 222; EWL 3; MTCW 1, 2; NCFS 4; RGAL 4; TUS
**Mendelsohn, Jane** 1965- **CLC 99**
  See also CA 154; CANR 94
**Menton, Francisco de**
  See Chin, Frank (Chew, Jr.)
**Mercer, David** 1928-1980 **CLC 5**
  See also CA 102; 9-12R; CANR 23; CBD; DAM DRAM; DLB 13; MTCW 1; RGEL 2
**Merchant, Paul**
  See Ellison, Harlan (Jay)
**Meredith, George** 1828-1909 **TCLC 17, 43**
  See also CA 153; 117; CANR 80; CDBLB 1832-1890; DAM POET; DLB 18, 35, 57, 159; RGEL 2; TEA
**Meredith, William (Morris)** 1919- **CLC 4, 13, 22, 55; PC 28**
  See also CA 9-12R; CAAS 14; CANR 6, 40; CP 7; DAM POET; DLB 5
**Merezhkovsky, Dmitry Sergeevich**
  See Merezhkovsky, Dmitry Sergeyevich
  See also EWL 3
**Merezhkovsky, Dmitry Sergeyevich** 1865-1941 **TCLC 29**
  See Merezhkovsky, Dmitry Sergeevich
  See also CA 169
**Merimee, Prosper** 1803-1870 **NCLC 6, 65; SSC 7**
  See also DLB 119, 192; EW 6; EXPS; GFL 1789 to the Present; RGSF 2; RGWL 2, 3; SSFS 8; SUFW
**Merkin, Daphne** 1954- **CLC 44**
  See also CA 123
**Merlin, Arthur**
  See Blish, James (Benjamin)
**Mernissi, Fatima** 1940- **CLC 171**
  See also CA 152; FW
**Merrill, James (Ingram)** 1926-1995 **CLC 2, 3, 6, 8, 13, 18, 34, 91; PC 28**
  See also AMWS 3; CA 147; 13-16R; CANR 10, 49, 63, 108; DA3; DAM POET; DLB 5, 165; DLBY 1985; EWL 3; INT CANR-10; MTCW 1, 2; PAB; RGAL 4

**Merriman, Alex**
  See Silverberg, Robert
**Merriman, Brian** 1747-1805 **NCLC 70**
**Merritt, E. B.**
  See Waddington, Miriam
**Merton, Thomas (James)** 1915-1968 **CLC 1, 3, 11, 34, 83; PC 10**
  See also AMWS 8; CA 25-28R; 5-8R; CANR 22, 53, 111; DA3; DLB 48; DLBY 1981; MTCW 1, 2
**Merwin, W(illiam) S(tanley)** 1927- **CLC 1, 2, 3, 5, 8, 13, 18, 45, 88; PC 45**
  See also AMWS 3; CA 13-16R; CANR 15, 51, 112; CP 7; DA3; DAM POET; DLB 5, 169; EWL 3; INT CANR-15; MTCW 1, 2; PAB; PFS 5, 15; RGAL 4
**Metcalf, John** 1938- **CLC 37; SSC 43**
  See also CA 113; CN 7; DLB 60; RGSF 2; TWA
**Metcalf, Suzanne**
  See Baum, L(yman) Frank
**Mew, Charlotte (Mary)** 1870-1928 **TCLC 8**
  See also CA 189; 105; DLB 19, 135; RGEL 2
**Mewshaw, Michael** 1943- **CLC 9**
  See also CA 53-56; CANR 7, 47; DLBY 1980
**Meyer, Conrad Ferdinand** 1825-1905 **NCLC 81**
  See also DLB 129; EW; RGWL 2, 3
**Meyer, Gustav** 1868-1932
  See Meyrink, Gustav
  See also CA 190; 117
**Meyer, June**
  See Jordan, June (Meyer)
**Meyer, Lynn**
  See Slavitt, David R(ytman)
**Meyers, Jeffrey** 1939- **CLC 39**
  See also CA 73-76; CAAE 186; CANR 54, 102; DLB 111
**Meynell, Alice (Christina Gertrude Thompson)** 1847-1922 **TCLC 6**
  See also CA 177; 104; DLB 19, 98; RGEL 2
**Meyrink, Gustav TCLC 21**
  See Meyer, Gustav
  See also DLB 81; EWL 3
**Michaels, Leonard** 1933- **CLC 6, 25; SSC 16**
  See also CA 61-64; CANR 21, 62; CN 7; DLB 130; MTCW 1
**Michaux, Henri** 1899-1984 **CLC 8, 19**
  See also CA 114; 85-88; DLB 258; EWL 3; GFL 1789 to the Present; RGWL 2, 3
**Micheaux, Oscar (Devereaux)** 1884-1951 **TCLC 76**
  See also BW 3; CA 174; DLB 50; TCWW 2
**Michelangelo** 1475-1564 **LC 12**
  See also AAYA 43
**Michelet, Jules** 1798-1874 **NCLC 31**
  See also EW 5; GFL 1789 to the Present
**Michels, Robert** 1876-1936 **TCLC 88**
**Michener, James A(lbert)** 1907(?)-1997 **CLC 1, 5, 11, 29, 60, 109**
  See also AAYA 27; AITN 1; BEST 90:1; BPFB 2; CA 161; 5-8R; CANR 21, 45, 68; CN 7; CPW; DA3; DAM NOV, POP; DLB 6; MTCW 1, 2; RHW
**Mickiewicz, Adam** 1798-1855 **NCLC 3, 101; PC 38**
  See also EW 5; RGWL 2, 3
**Middleton, (John) Christopher**
  See Middleton, Christopher
**Middleton, Christopher** 1926- **CLC 13**
  See also CA 13-16R; CANR 29, 54, 117; CP 7; DLB 40
**Middleton, Richard (Barham)** 1882-1911 **TCLC 56**
  See also CA 187; DLB 156; HGG

**Middleton, Stanley** 1919- **CLC 7, 38**
See also CA 25-28R; CAAS 23; CANR 21, 46, 81; CN 7; DLB 14

**Middleton, Thomas** 1580-1627 **DC 5; LC 33**
See also BRW 2; DAM DRAM, MST; DLB 58; RGEL 2

**Migueis, Jose Rodrigues** 1901- **CLC 10**

**Mikszath, Kalman** 1847-1910 **TCLC 31**
See also CA 170

**Miles, Jack CLC 100**
See also CA 200

**Miles, John Russiano**
See Miles, Jack

**Miles, Josephine (Louise)** 1911-1985 **CLC 1, 2, 14, 34, 39**
See also CA 116; 1-4R; CANR 2, 55; DAM POET; DLB 48

**Militant**
See Sandburg, Carl (August)

**Mill, Harriet (Hardy) Taylor** 1807-1858 **NCLC 102**
See also FW

**Mill, John Stuart** 1806-1873 **NCLC 11, 58**
See also CDBLB 1832-1890; DLB 55, 190, 262; FW 1; RGEL 2; TEA

**Millar, Kenneth** 1915-1983 **CLC 14**
See Macdonald, Ross
See also CA 110; 9-12R; CANR 16, 63, 107; CMW 4; CPW; DA3; DAM POP; DLB 2, 226; DLBD 6; DLBY 1983; MTCW 1, 2

**Millay, E. Vincent**
See Millay, Edna St. Vincent

**Millay, Edna St. Vincent** 1892-1950 **PC 6; TCLC 4, 49; WLCS**
See Boyd, Nancy
See also AMW; CA 130; 104; CDALB 1917-1929; DA; DA3; DAB; DAC; DAM MST, POET; DLB 45, 249; EWL 3; EXPP; MAWW; MTCW 1, 2; PAB; PFS 3, 17; RGAL 4; TUS; WP

**Miller, Arthur** 1915- **CLC 1, 2, 6, 10, 15, 26, 47, 78; DC 1; WLC**
See also AAYA 15; AITN 1; AMW; AMWC 1; CA 1-4R; CABS 3; CAD; CANR 2, 30, 54, 76; CD 5; CDALB 1941-1968; DA; DA3; DAB; DAC; DAM DRAM, MST; DFS 1, 3; DLB 7, 266; EWL 3; LAIT 1, 4; MTCW 1, 2; RGAL 4; TUS; WYAS 1

**Miller, Henry (Valentine)** 1891-1980 **CLC 1, 2, 4, 9, 14, 43, 84; WLC**
See also AMW; BPFB 2; CA 97-100; 9-12R; CANR 33, 64; CDALB 1929-1941; DA; DA3; DAB; DAC; DAM MST, NOV; DLB 4, 9; DLBY 1980; EWL 3; MTCW 1, 2; RGAL 4; TUS

**Miller, Jason** 1939(?)-2001 **CLC 2**
See also AITN 1; CA 197; 73-76; CAD; DFS 12; DLB 7

**Miller, Sue** 1943- **CLC 44**
See also AMWS 12; BEST 90:3; CA 139; CANR 59, 91; DA3; DAM POP; DLB 143

**Miller, Walter M(ichael, Jr.)** 1923-1996 **CLC 4, 30**
See also BPFB 2; CA 85-88; CANR 108; DLB 8; SCFW; SFW 4

**Millett, Kate** 1934- **CLC 67**
See also AITN 1; CA 73-76; CANR 32, 53, 76, 110; DA3; DLB 246; FW; GLL 1; MTCW 1, 2

**Millhauser, Steven (Lewis)** 1943- **CLC 21, 54, 109; SSC 57**
See also CA 111; 110; CANR 63, 114; CN 7; DA3; DLB 2; FANT; INT CA-111; MTCW 2

**Millin, Sarah Gertrude** 1889-1968 **CLC 49**
See also CA 93-96; 102; DLB 225; EWL 3

**Milne, A(lan) A(lexander)** 1882-1956 **TCLC 6, 88**
See also BRWS 5; CA 133; 104; CLR 1, 26; CMW 4; CWRI 5; DA3; DAB; DAC; DAM MST; DLB 10, 77, 100, 160; FANT; MAICYA 1, 2; MTCW 1, 2; RGEL 2; SATA 100; WCH; YABC 1

**Milner, Ron(ald)** 1938- **BLC 3; CLC 56**
See also AITN 1; BW 1; CA 73-76; CAD; CANR 24, 81; CD 5; DAM MULT; DLB 38; MTCW 1

**Milnes, Richard Monckton** 1809-1885 **NCLC 61**
See also DLB 32, 184

**Milosz, Czeslaw** 1911- **CLC 5, 11, 22, 31, 56, 82; PC 8; WLCS**
See also CA 81-84; CANR 23, 51, 91; CD-WLB 4; CWW 2; DA3; DAM MST, POET; DLB 215; EW 13; EWL 3; MTCW 1, 2; PFS 16; RGWL 2, 3

**Milton, John** 1608-1674 **LC 9, 43; PC 19, 29; WLC**
See also BRW 2; BRWR 2; CDBLB 1660-1789; DA; DA3; DAB; DAC; DAM MST, POET; DLB 131, 151; EFS 1; EXPP; LAIT 1; PAB; PFS 3, 17; RGEL 2; TEA; WLIT 3; WP

**Min, Anchee** 1957- **CLC 86**
See also CA 146; CANR 94

**Minehaha, Cornelius**
See Wedekind, (Benjamin) Frank(lin)

**Miner, Valerie** 1947- **CLC 40**
See also CA 97-100; CANR 59; FW; GLL 2

**Minimo, Duca**
See D'Annunzio, Gabriele

**Minot, Susan** 1956- **CLC 44, 159**
See also AMWS 6; CA 134; CN 7

**Minus, Ed** 1938- **CLC 39**
See also CA 185

**Miranda, Javier**
See Bioy Casares, Adolfo
See also CWW 2

**Mirbeau, Octave** 1848-1917 **TCLC 55**
See also DLB 123, 192; GFL 1789 to the Present

**Mirikitani, Janice** 1942- **AAL**
See also RGAL 4

**Miro (Ferrer), Gabriel (Francisco Victor)** 1879-1930 **TCLC 5**
See also CA 185; 104; EWL 3

**Misharin, Alexandr CLC 59**

**Mishima, Yukio CLC 2, 4, 6, 9, 27; DC 1; SSC 4**
See Hiraoka, Kimitake
See also BPFB 1; GLL 1; MJW; MTCW 2; RGSF 2; RGWL 2, 3; SSFS 5, 12

**Mistral, Frederic** 1830-1914 **TCLC 51**
See also CA 122; GFL 1789 to the Present

**Mistral, Gabriela**
See Godoy Alcayaga, Lucila
See also DNFS 1; EWL 3; LAW; RGWL 2, 3; WP

**Mistry, Rohinton** 1952- **CLC 71**
See also CA 141; CANR 86, 114; CCA 1; CN 7; DAC; SSFS 6

**Mitchell, Clyde**
See Ellison, Harlan (Jay)

**Mitchell, Emerson Blackhorse Barney** 1945- **NNAL**
See also CA 45-48

**Mitchell, James Leslie** 1901-1935
See Gibbon, Lewis Grassic
See also CA 188; 104; DLB 15

**Mitchell, Joni** 1943- **CLC 12**
See also CA 112; CCA 1

**Mitchell, Joseph (Quincy)** 1908-1996 **CLC 98**
See also CA 152; 77-80; CANR 69; CN 7; CSW; DLB 185; DLBY 1996

**Mitchell, Margaret (Munnerlyn)** 1900-1949 **TCLC 11**
See also AAYA 23; BPFB 2; BYA 1; CA 125; 109; CANR 55, 94; CDALBS; DA3; DAM NOV, POP; DLB 9; LAIT 2; MTCW 1, 2; NFS 9; RGAL 4; RHW; TUS; WYAS 1; YAW

**Mitchell, Peggy**
See Mitchell, Margaret (Munnerlyn)

**Mitchell, S(ilas) Weir** 1829-1914 **TCLC 36**
See also CA 165; DLB 202; RGAL 4

**Mitchell, W(illiam) O(rmond)** 1914-1998 **CLC 25**
See also CA 165; 77-80; CANR 15, 43; CN 7; DAC; DAM MST; DLB 88

**Mitchell, William** 1879-1936 **TCLC 81**

**Mitford, Mary Russell** 1787-1855 **NCLC 4**
See also DLB 110, 116; RGEL 2

**Mitford, Nancy** 1904-1973 **CLC 44**
See also CA 9-12R; DLB 191; RGEL 2

**Miyamoto, (Chujo) Yuriko** 1899-1951 **TCLC 37**
See Miyamoto Yuriko
See also CA 170, 174

**Miyamoto Yuriko**
See Miyamoto, (Chujo) Yuriko
See also DLB 180

**Miyazawa, Kenji** 1896-1933 **TCLC 76**
See Miyazawa Kenji
See also CA 157; RGWL 3

**Miyazawa Kenji**
See Miyazawa, Kenji
See also EWL 3

**Mizoguchi, Kenji** 1898-1956 **TCLC 72**
See also CA 167

**Mo, Timothy (Peter)** 1950(?)- **CLC 46, 134**
See also CA 117; CN 7; DLB 194; MTCW 1; WLIT 4

**Modarressi, Taghi (M.)** 1931-1997 **CLC 44**
See also CA 134; 121; INT 134

**Modiano, Patrick (Jean)** 1945- **CLC 18**
See also CA 85-88; CANR 17, 40, 115; CWW 2; DLB 83; EWL 3

**Mofolo, Thomas (Mokopu)** 1875(?)-1948 **BLC 3; TCLC 22**
See also AFW; CA 153; 121; CANR 83; DAM MULT; DLB 225; EWL 3; MTCW 2; WLIT 2

**Mohr, Nicholasa** 1938- **CLC 12; HLC 2**
See also AAYA 8, 46; CA 49-52; CANR 1, 32, 64; CLR 22; DAM MULT; DLB 145; HW 1, 2; JRDA; LAIT 5; MAICYA 1; MAICYAS 1; RGAL 4; SAAS 8; SATA 8, 97; SATA-Essay 113; WYA; YAW

**Moi, Toril** 1953- **CLC 172**
See also CA 154; CANR 102; FW

**Mojtabai, A(nn) G(race)** 1938- **CLC 5, 9, 15, 29**
See also CA 85-88; CANR 88

**Moliere** 1622-1673 **DC 13; LC 10, 28, 64; WLC**
See also DA; DA3; DAB; DAC; DAM DRAM, MST; DFS 13; DLB 268; EW 3; GFL Beginnings to 1789; RGWL 2, 3; TWA

**Molin, Charles**
See Mayne, William (James Carter)

**Molnar, Ferenc** 1878-1952 **TCLC 20**
See also CA 153; 109; CANR 83; CDWLB 4; DAM DRAM; DLB 215; EWL 3; RGWL 2, 3

**Momaday, N(avarre) Scott** 1934- **CLC 2, 19, 85, 95, 160; NNAL; PC 25; WLCS**
See also AAYA 11; AMWS 4; ANW; BPFB 2; CA 25-28R; CANR 14, 34, 68; CDALBS; CN 7; CPW; DA; DA3; DAB; DAC; DAM MST, MULT, NOV, POP; DLB 143, 175, 256; EWL 3; EXPP; INT

CANR-14; LAIT 4; MTCW 1, 2; NFS 10;
PFS 2, 11; RGAL 4; SATA 48; SATA-
Brief 30; WP; YAW
**Monette, Paul** 1945-1995 **CLC 82**
See also AMWS 10; CA 147; 139; CN 7;
GLL 1
**Monroe, Harriet** 1860-1936 **TCLC 12**
See also CA 204; 109; DLB 54, 91
**Monroe, Lyle**
See Heinlein, Robert A(nson)
**Montagu, Elizabeth** 1720-1800 **NCLC 7, 117**
See also FW
**Montagu, Mary (Pierrepont) Wortley**
1689-1762 **LC 9, 57; PC 16**
See also DLB 95, 101; RGEL 2
**Montagu, W. H.**
See Coleridge, Samuel Taylor
**Montague, John (Patrick)** 1929- **CLC 13, 46**
See also CA 9-12R; CANR 9, 69; CP 7;
DLB 40; EWL 3; MTCW 1; PFS 12;
RGEL 2
**Montaigne, Michel (Eyquem) de** 1533-1592
**LC 8; WLC**
See also DA; DAB; DAC; DAM MST; EW
2; GFL Beginnings to 1789; RGWL 2, 3;
TWA
**Montale, Eugenio** 1896-1981 **CLC 7, 9, 18; PC 13**
See also CA 104; 17-20R; CANR 30; DLB
114; EW 11; EWL 3; MTCW 1; RGWL
2, 3; TWA
**Montesquieu, Charles-Louis de Secondat**
1689-1755 **LC 7, 69**
See also EW 3; GFL Beginnings to 1789;
TWA
**Montessori, Maria** 1870-1952 **TCLC 103**
See also CA 147; 115
**Montgomery, (Robert) Bruce** 1921(?)-1978
See Crispin, Edmund
See also CA 104; 179; CMW 4
**Montgomery, L(ucy) M(aud)** 1874-1942
**TCLC 51**
See also AAYA 12; BYA 1; CA 137; 108;
CLR 8; DA3; DAC; DAM MST; DLB 92;
DLBD 14; JRDA; MAICYA 1, 2; MTCW
2; RGEL 2; SATA 100; TWA; WCH;
WYA; YABC 1
**Montgomery, Marion H., Jr.** 1925- **CLC 7**
See also AITN 1; CA 1-4R; CANR 3, 48;
CSW; DLB 6
**Montgomery, Max**
See Davenport, Guy (Mattison, Jr.)
**Montherlant, Henry (Milon) de** 1896-1972
**CLC 8, 19**
See also CA 37-40R; 85-88; DAM DRAM;
DLB 72; EW 11; EWL 3; GFL 1789 to
the Present; MTCW 1
**Monty Python**
See Chapman, Graham; Cleese, John
(Marwood); Gilliam, Terry (Vance); Idle,
Eric; Jones, Terence Graham Parry; Palin,
Michael (Edward)
See also AAYA 7
**Moodie, Susanna (Strickland)** 1803-1885
**NCLC 14, 113**
See also DLB 99
**Moody, Hiram (F. III)** 1961-
See Moody, Rick
See also CA 138; CANR 64, 112
**Moody, Minerva**
See Alcott, Louisa May
**Moody, Rick CLC 147**
See Moody, Hiram (F. III)
**Moody, William Vaughan** 1869-1910 **TCLC 105**
See also CA 178; 110; DLB 7, 54; RGAL 4
**Mooney, Edward** 1951-
See Mooney, Ted
See also CA 130

**Mooney, Ted CLC 25**
See Mooney, Edward
**Moorcock, Michael (John)** 1939- **CLC 5, 27, 58**
See Bradbury, Edward P.
See also AAYA 26; CA 45-48; CAAS 5;
CANR 2, 17, 38, 64; CN 7; DLB 14, 231,
261; FANT; MTCW 1, 2; SATA 93;
SCFW 2; SFW 4; SUFW 1, 2
**Moore, Brian** 1921-1999 **CLC 1, 3, 5, 7, 8, 19, 32, 90**
See Bryan, Michael
See also CA 174; 1-4R; CANR 1, 25, 42,
63; CCA 1; CN 7; DAB; DAC; DAM
MST; DLB 251; EWL 3; FANT; MTCW
1, 2; RGEL 2
**Moore, Edward**
See Muir, Edwin
See also RGEL 2
**Moore, G. E.** 1873-1958 **TCLC 89**
See also DLB 262
**Moore, George Augustus** 1852-1933 **SSC 19; TCLC**
See also BRW 6; CA 177; 104; DLB 10,
18, 57, 135; EWL 3; RGEL 2; RGSF 2
**Moore, Lorrie CLC 39, 45, 68**
See Moore, Marie Lorena
See also AMWS 10; DLB 234
**Moore, Marianne (Craig)** 1887-1972 **CLC 1, 2, 4, 8, 10, 13, 19, 47; PC 4; WLCS**
See also AMW; CA 33-36R; 1-4R; CANR
3, 61; CDALB 1929-1941; DA; DA3;
DAB; DAC; DAM MST, POET; DLB 45;
DLBD 7; EWL 3; EXPP; MAWW;
MTCW 1, 2; PAB; PFS 14, 17; RGAL 4;
SATA 20; TUS; WP
**Moore, Marie Lorena** 1957- **CLC 165**
See Moore, Lorrie
See also CA 116; CANR 39, 83; CN 7; DLB
234
**Moore, Thomas** 1779-1852 **NCLC 6, 110**
See also DLB 96, 144; RGEL 2
**Moorhouse, Frank** 1938- **SSC 40**
See also CA 118; CANR 92; CN 7; RGSF
2
**Mora, Pat(ricia)** 1942- **HLC 2**
See also CA 129; CANR 57, 81, 112; CLR
58; DAM MULT; DLB 209; HW 1, 2;
MAICYA 2; SATA 92, 134
**Moraga, Cherríe** 1952- **CLC 126**
See also CA 131; CANR 66; DAM MULT;
DLB 82, 249; FW; GLL 1; HW 1, 2
**Morand, Paul** 1888-1976 **CLC 41; SSC 22**
See also CA 69-72; 184; DLB 65; EWL 3
**Morante, Elsa** 1918-1985 **CLC 8, 47**
See also CA 117; 85-88; CANR 35; DLB
177; EWL 3; MTCW 1, 2; RGWL 2, 3
**Moravia, Alberto CLC 2, 7, 11, 27, 46; SSC 26**
See Pincherle, Alberto
See also DLB 177; EW 12; EWL 3; MTCW
2; RGSF 2; RGWL 2, 3
**More, Hannah** 1745-1833 **NCLC 27**
See also DLB 107, 109, 116, 158; RGEL 2
**More, Henry** 1614-1687 **LC 9**
See also DLB 126, 252
**More, Sir Thomas** 1478(?)-1535 **LC 10, 32**
See also BRWC 1; BRWS 7; DLB 136;
RGEL 2; TEA
**Moréas, Jean TCLC 18**
See Papadiamantopoulos, Johannes
See also GFL 1789 to the Present
**Moreton, Andrew Esq.**
See Defoe, Daniel
**Morgan, Berry** 1919-2002 **CLC 6**
See also CA 208; 49-52; DLB 6
**Morgan, Claire**
See Highsmith, (Mary) Patricia
See also GLL 1

**Morgan, Edwin (George)** 1920- **CLC 31**
See also CA 5-8R; CANR 3, 43, 90; CP 7;
DLB 27
**Morgan, (George) Frederick** 1922- **CLC 23**
See also CA 17-20R; CANR 21; CP 7
**Morgan, Harriet**
See Mencken, H(enry) L(ouis)
**Morgan, Jane**
See Cooper, James Fenimore
**Morgan, Janet** 1945- **CLC 39**
See also CA 65-68
**Morgan, Lady** 1776(?)-1859 **NCLC 29**
See also DLB 116, 158; RGEL 2
**Morgan, Robin (Evonne)** 1941- **CLC 2**
See also CA 69-72; CANR 29, 68; FW;
GLL 2; MTCW 1; SATA 80
**Morgan, Scott**
See Kuttner, Henry
**Morgan, Seth** 1949(?)-1990 **CLC 65**
See also CA 132; 185
**Morgenstern, Christian (Otto Josef Wolfgang)** 1871-1914 **TCLC 8**
See also CA 191; 105; EWL 3
**Morgenstern, S.**
See Goldman, William (W.)
**Mori, Rintaro**
See Mori Ogai
See also CA 110
**Moricz, Zsigmond** 1879-1942 **TCLC 33**
See also CA 165; DLB 215; EWL 3
**Morike, Eduard (Friedrich)** 1804-1875
**NCLC 10**
See also DLB 133; RGWL 2, 3
**Mori Ogai** 1862-1922 **TCLC 14**
See Ogai
See also CA 164; DLB 180; EWL 3; RGWL
3; TWA
**Moritz, Karl Philipp** 1756-1793 **LC 2**
See also DLB 94
**Morland, Peter Henry**
See Faust, Frederick (Schiller)
**Morley, Christopher (Darlington)** 1890-1957
**TCLC 87**
See also CA 112; DLB 9; RGAL 4
**Morren, Theophil**
See Hofmannsthal, Hugo von
**Morris, Bill** 1952- **CLC 76**
**Morris, Julian**
See West, Morris L(anglo)
**Morris, Steveland Judkins** 1950(?)-
See Wonder, Stevie
See also CA 111
**Morris, William** 1834-1896 **NCLC 4**
See also BRW 5; CDBLB 1832-1890; DLB
18, 35, 57, 156, 178, 184; FANT; RGEL
2; SFW 4; SUFW
**Morris, Wright** 1910-1998 **CLC 1, 3, 7, 18, 37; TCLC 107**
See also AMW; CA 167; 9-12R; CANR 21,
81; CN 7; DLB 2, 206, 218; DLBY 1981;
EWL 3; MTCW 1, 2; RGAL 4; TCWW 2
**Morrison, Arthur** 1863-1945 **SSC 40; TCLC 72**
See also CA 157; 120; CMW 4; DLB 70,
135, 197; RGEL 2
**Morrison, James Douglas** 1943-1971
See Morrison, Jim
See also CA 73-76; CANR 40
**Morrison, Jim CLC 17**
See Morrison, James Douglas
**Morrison, Toni** 1931- **BLC 3; CLC 4, 10, 22, 55, 81, 87**
See also AAYA 1, 22; AFAW 1, 2; AMWC
1; AMWS 3; BPFB 2; BW 2, 3; CA 29-
32R; CANR 27, 42, 67, 113; CDALB
1968-1988; CN 7; CPW; DA; DA3; DAB;
DAC; DAM MST, MULT, NOV, POP;
DLB 6, 33, 143; DLBY 1981; EWL 3;
EXPN; FW; LAIT 2, 4; MAWW; MTCW

DA3; DAB; DAC; DAM MST, NOV; DLB 2, 244, 278; DLBD 3; DLBY 1980, 1991; EWL 3; EXPS; MTCW 1, 2; NCFS 4; NFS 9; RGAL 4; RGSF 2; SSFS 6, 15; TUS

**Naevius c. 265B.C.-201B.C. CMLC 37**
See also DLB 211

**Nagai, Kafu TCLC 51**
See Nagai, Sokichi
See also DLB 180

**Nagai, Sokichi 1879-1959**
See Nagai, Kafu
See also CA 117

**Nagy, Laszlo 1925-1978 CLC 7**
See also CA 112; 129

**Naidu, Sarojini 1879-1949 TCLC 80**
See also EWL 3; RGEL 2

**Naipaul, Shiva(dhar Srinivasa) 1945-1985 CLC 32, 39**
See also CA 116; 112; 110; CANR 33; DA3; DAM NOV; DLB 157; DLBY 1985; EWL 3; MTCW 1, 2

**Naipaul, V(idiadhar) S(urajprasad) 1932- CLC 4, 7, 9, 13, 18, 37, 105; SSC 38**
See also BPFB 2; BRWS 1; CA 1-4R; CANR 1, 33, 51, 91; CDBLB 1960 to Present; CDWLB 3; CN 7; DA3; DAB; DAC; DAM MST, NOV; DLB 125, 204, 207; DLBY 1985, 2001; EWL 3; MTCW 1, 2; RGEL 2; RGSF 2; TWA; WLIT 4

**Nakos, Lilika 1899(?)- CLC 29**

**Narayan, R(asipuram) K(rishnaswami) 1906-2001 CLC 7, 28, 47, 121; SSC 25**
See also BPFB 2; CA 196; 81-84; CANR 33, 61, 112; CN 7; DA3; DAM NOV; DNFS 1; EWL 3; MTCW 1, 2; RGEL 2; RGSF 2; SATA 62; SSFS 5

**Nash, (Frediric) Ogden 1902-1971 CLC 23; PC 21; TCLC 109**
See also CA 29-32R; 13-14; CANR 34, 61; CAP 1; DAM POET; DLB 11; MAICYA 1, 2; MTCW 1, 2; RGAL 4; SATA 2, 46; WP

**Nashe, Thomas 1567-1601(?) LC 41**
See also DLB 167; RGEL 2

**Nathan, Daniel**
See Dannay, Frederic

**Nathan, George Jean 1882-1958 TCLC 18**
See Hatteras, Owen
See also CA 169; 114; DLB 137

**Natsume, Kinnosuke**
See Natsume, Soseki

**Natsume, Soseki 1867-1916 TCLC 2, 10**
See Natsume Soseki; Soseki
See also CA 195; 104; RGWL 2, 3; TWA

**Natsume Soseki**
See Natsume, Soseki
See also DLB 180; EWL 3

**Natti, (Mary) Lee 1919-**
See Kingman, Lee
See also CA 5-8R; CANR 2

**Navarre, Marguerite de**
See de Navarre, Marguerite

**Naylor, Gloria 1950- BLC 3; CLC 28, 52, 156; WLCS**
See also AAYA 6, 39; AFAW 1, 2; AMWS 8; BW 2, 3; CA 107; CANR 27, 51, 74; CN 7; CPW; DA; DA3; DAC; DAM MST, MULT, NOV, POP; DLB 173; EWL 3; FW; MTCW 1, 2; NFS 4, 7; RGAL 4; TUS

**Neff, Debra CLC 59**

**Neihardt, John Gneisenau 1881-1973 CLC 32**
See also CA 13-14; CANR 65; CAP 1; DLB 9, 54, 256; LAIT 2

**Nekrasov, Nikolai Alekseevich 1821-1878 NCLC 11**
See also DLB 277

**Nelligan, Emile 1879-1941 TCLC 14**
See also CA 204; 114; DLB 92; EWL 3

**Nelson, Willie 1933- CLC 17**
See also CA 107; CANR 114

**Nemerov, Howard (Stanley) 1920-1991 CLC 2, 6, 9, 36; PC 24; TCLC 124**
See also AMW; CA 134; 1-4R; CABS 2; CANR 1, 27, 53; DAM POET; DLB 5, 6; DLBY 1983; EWL 3; INT CANR-27; MTCW 1, 2; PFS 10, 14; RGAL 4

**Neruda, Pablo 1904-1973 CLC 1, 2, 5, 7, 9, 28, 62; HLC 2; PC 4; WLC**
See also CA 45-48; 19-20; CAP 2; DA; DA3; DAB; DAC; DAM MST, MULT, POET; DNFS 2; EWL 3; HW 1; LAW; MTCW 1, 2; PFS 11; RGWL 2, 3; TWA; WLIT 1; WP

**Nerval, Gerard de 1808-1855 NCLC 1, 67; PC 13; SSC 18**
See also DLB 217; EW 6; GFL 1789 to the Present; RGSF 2; RGWL 2, 3

**Nervo, (Jose) Amado (Ruiz de) 1870-1919 HLCS 2; TCLC 11**
See also CA 131; 109; EWL 3; HW 1; LAW

**Nesbit, Malcolm**
See Chester, Alfred

**Nessi, Pio Baroja y**
See Baroja (y Nessi), Pio

**Nestroy, Johann 1801-1862 NCLC 42**
See also DLB 133; RGWL 2, 3

**Netterville, Luke**
See O'Grady, Standish (James)

**Neufeld, John (Arthur) 1938- CLC 17**
See also AAYA 11; CA 25-28R; CANR 11, 37, 56; CLR 52; MAICYA 1, 2; SAAS 3; SATA 6, 81; SATA-Essay 131; YAW

**Neumann, Alfred 1895-1952 TCLC 100**
See also CA 183; DLB 56

**Neumann, Ferenc**
See Molnar, Ferenc

**Neville, Emily Cheney 1919- CLC 12**
See also BYA 2; CA 5-8R; CANR 3, 37, 85; JRDA; MAICYA 1, 2; SAAS 2; SATA 1; YAW

**Newbound, Bernard Slade 1930-**
See Slade, Bernard
See also CA 81-84; CANR 49; CD 5; DAM DRAM

**Newby, P(ercy) H(oward) 1918-1997 CLC 2, 13**
See also CA 161; 5-8R; CANR 32, 67; CN 7; DAM NOV; DLB 15; MTCW 1; RGEL 2

**Newcastle**
See Cavendish, Margaret Lucas

**Newlove, Donald 1928- CLC 6**
See also CA 29-32R; CANR 25

**Newlove, John (Herbert) 1938- CLC 14**
See also CA 21-24R; CANR 9, 25; CP 7

**Newman, Charles 1938- CLC 2, 8**
See also CA 21-24R; CANR 84; CN 7

**Newman, Edwin (Harold) 1919- CLC 14**
See also AITN 1; CA 69-72; CANR 5

**Newman, John Henry 1801-1890 NCLC 38, 99**
See also BRWS 7; DLB 18, 32, 55; RGEL 2

**Newton, (Sir) Isaac 1642-1727 LC 35, 53**
See also DLB 252

**Newton, Suzanne 1936- CLC 35**
See also BYA 7; CA 41-44R; CANR 14; JRDA; SATA 5, 77

**New York Dept. of Ed. CLC 70**

**Nexo, Martin Andersen 1869-1954 TCLC 43**
See also CA 202; DLB 214; EWL 3

**Nezval, Vitezslav 1900-1958 TCLC 44**
See also CA 123; CDWLB 4; DLB 215; EWL 3

**Ng, Fae Myenne 1957(?)- CLC 81**
See also CA 146

**Ngema, Mbongeni 1955- CLC 57**
See also BW 2; CA 143; CANR 84; CD 5

**Ngugi, James T(hiong'o) CLC 3, 7, 13**
See Ngugi wa Thiong'o

**Ngugi wa Thiong'o**
See Ngugi wa Thiong'o
See also DLB 125; EWL 3

**Ngugi wa Thiong'o 1938- BLC 3; CLC 36**
See Ngugi, James T(hiong'o); Ngugi wa Thiong'o
See also AFW; BRWS 8; BW 2; CA 81-84; CANR 27, 58; CDWLB 3; DAM MULT, NOV; DNFS 2; MTCW 1, 2; RGAL 2

**Niatum, Duane 1938- NNAL**
See also CA 41-44R; CANR 21, 45, 83; DLB 175

**Nichol, B(arrie) P(hillip) 1944-1988 CLC 18**
See also CA 53-56; DLB 53; SATA 66

**Nicholas of Cusa 1401-1464 LC 80**
See also DLB 115

**Nichols, John (Treadwell) 1940- CLC 38**
See also CA 9-12R; CAAE 190; CAAS 2; CANR 6, 70; DLBY 1982; TCWW 2

**Nichols, Leigh**
See Koontz, Dean R(ay)

**Nichols, Peter (Richard) 1927- CLC 5, 36, 65**
See also CA 104; CANR 33, 86; CBD; CD 5; DLB 13, 245; MTCW 1

**Nicholson, Linda ed. CLC 65**

**Ni Chuilleanain, Eilean 1942- PC 34**
See also CA 126; CANR 53, 83; CP 7; CWP; DLB 40

**Nicolas, F. R. E.**
See Freeling, Nicolas

**Niedecker, Lorine 1903-1970 CLC 10, 42; PC 42**
See also CA 25-28; CAP 2; DAM POET; DLB 48

**Nietzsche, Friedrich (Wilhelm) 1844-1900 TCLC 10, 18, 55**
See also CA 121; 107; CDWLB 2; DLB 129; EW 7; RGWL 2, 3; TWA

**Nievo, Ippolito 1831-1861 NCLC 22**

**Nightingale, Anne Redmon 1943-**
See Redmon, Anne
See also CA 103

**Nightingale, Florence 1820-1910 TCLC 85**
See also CA 188; DLB 166

**Nijo Yoshimoto 1320-1388 CMLC 49**
See also DLB 203

**Nik. T. O.**
See Annensky, Innokenty (Fyodorovich)

**Nin, Anais 1903-1977 CLC 1, 4, 8, 11, 14, 60, 127; SSC 10**
See also AITN 2; AMWS 10; BPFB 2; CA 69-72; 13-16R; CANR 22, 53; DAM NOV, POP; DLB 2, 4, 152; EWL 3; GLL 2; MAWW; MTCW 1, 2; RGAL 4; RGSF 2

**Nisbet, Robert A(lexander) 1913-1996 TCLC 117**
See also CA 153; 25-28R; CANR 17; INT CANR-17

**Nishida, Kitaro 1870-1945 TCLC 83**

**Nishiwaki, Junzaburo**
See Nishiwaki, Junzaburo
See also CA 194

**Nishiwaki, Junzaburo 1894-1982 PC 15**
See Nishiwaki, Junzaburo; Nishiwaki Junzaburo
See also CA 107; 194; MJW; RGWL 3

**Nishiwaki Junzaburo**
See Nishiwaki, Junzaburo
See also EWL 3

**Nissenson, Hugh 1933- CLC 4, 9**
See also CA 17-20R; CANR 27, 108; CN 7; DLB 28

**Nister, Der**
   See Der Nister
   See also EWL 3
**Niven, Larry CLC 8**
   See Niven, Laurence Van Cott
   See also AAYA 27; BPFB 2; BYA 10;
   CAAE 207; DLB 8; SCFW 2
**Niven, Laurence Van Cott 1938-**
   See Niven, Larry
   See also CA 21-24R; CAAS 12; CANR 14,
   44, 66, 113; CPW; DAM POP; MTCW 1,
   2; SATA 95; SFW 4
**Nixon, Agnes Eckhardt 1927- CLC 21**
   See also CA 110
**Nizan, Paul 1905-1940 TCLC 40**
   See also CA 161; DLB 72; EWL 3; GFL
   1789 to the Present
**Nkosi, Lewis 1936- BLC 3; CLC 45**
   See also BW 1, 3; CA 65-68; CANR 27,
   81; CBD; CD 5; DAM MULT; DLB 157,
   225
**Nodier, (Jean) Charles (Emmanuel)**
   **1780-1844 NCLC 19**
   See also DLB 119; GFL 1789 to the Present
**Noguchi, Yone 1875-1947 TCLC 80**
**Nolan, Christopher 1965- CLC 58**
   See also CA 111; CANR 88
**Noon, Jeff 1957- CLC 91**
   See also CA 148; CANR 83; DLB 267;
   SFW 4
**Norden, Charles**
   See Durrell, Lawrence (George)
**Nordhoff, Charles (Bernard) 1887-1947**
   **TCLC 23**
   See also CA 108; DLB 9; LAIT 1; RHW 1;
   SATA 23
**Norfolk, Lawrence 1963- CLC 76**
   See also CA 144; CANR 85; CN 7; DLB
   267
**Norman, Marsha 1947- CLC 28; DC 8**
   See also CA 105; CABS 3; CAD; CANR
   41; CD 5; CSW; CWD; DAM DRAM;
   DFS 2; DLB 266; DLBY 1984; FW
**Normyx**
   See Douglas, (George) Norman
**Norris, (Benjamin) Frank(lin, Jr.) 1870-1902**
   **SSC 28; TCLC 24**
   See also AMW; BPFB 2; CA 160; 110;
   CDALB 1865-1917; DLB 12, 71, 186;
   LMFS 2; NFS 12; RGAL 4; TCWW 2;
   TUS
**Norris, Leslie 1921- CLC 14**
   See also CA 11-12; CANR 14, 117; CAP 1;
   CP 7; DLB 27, 256
**North, Andrew**
   See Norton, Andre
**North, Anthony**
   See Koontz, Dean R(ay)
**North, Captain George**
   See Stevenson, Robert Louis (Balfour)
**North, Captain George**
   See Stevenson, Robert Louis (Balfour)
**North, Milou**
   See Erdrich, Louise
**Northrup, B. A.**
   See Hubbard, L(afayette) Ron(ald)
**North Staffs**
   See Hulme, T(homas) E(rnest)
**Northup, Solomon 1808-1863 NCLC 105**
**Norton, Alice Mary**
   See Norton, Andre
   See also MAICYA 1; SATA 1, 43
**Norton, Andre 1912- CLC 12**
   See Norton, Alice Mary
   See also AAYA 14; BPFB 2; BYA 4, 10,
   12; CA 1-4R; CANR 68; CLR 50; DLB
   8, 52; JRDA; MAICYA 2; MTCW 1;
   SATA 91; SUFW 1, 2; YAW

**Norton, Caroline 1808-1877 NCLC 47**
   See also DLB 21, 159, 199
**Norway, Nevil Shute 1899-1960**
   See Shute, Nevil
   See also CA 93-96; 102; CANR 85; MTCW
   2
**Norwid, Cyprian Kamil 1821-1883 NCLC 17**
   See also RGWL 3
**Nosille, Nabrah**
   See Ellison, Harlan (Jay)
**Nossack, Hans Erich 1901-1978 CLC 6**
   See also CA 85-88; 93-96; DLB 69; EWL 3
**Nostradamus 1503-1566 LC 27**
**Nosu, Chuji**
   See Ozu, Yasujiro
**Notenburg, Eleanora (Genrikhovna) von**
   See Guro, Elena
**Nova, Craig 1945- CLC 7, 31**
   See also CA 45-48; CANR 2, 53
**Novak, Joseph**
   See Kosinski, Jerzy (Nikodem)
**Novalis 1772-1801 NCLC 13**
   See also CDWLB 2; DLB 90; EW 5; RGWL
   2, 3
**Novick, Peter 1934- CLC 164**
   See also CA 188
**Novis, Emile**
   See Weil, Simone (Adolphine)
**Nowlan, Alden (Albert) 1933-1983 CLC 15**
   See also CA 9-12R; CANR 5; DAC; DAM
   MST; DLB 53; PFS 12
**Noyes, Alfred 1880-1958 PC 27; TCLC 7**
   See also CA 188; 104; DLB 20; EXPP;
   FANT; PFS 4; RGEL 2
**Nugent, Richard Bruce 1906(?)-1987 HR 3**
   See also BW 1; CA 125; DLB 51; GLL 2
**Nunn, Kem CLC 34**
   See also CA 159
**Nwapa, Flora (Nwanzuruaha) 1931-1993**
   **BLCS; CLC 133**
   See also BW 2; CA 143; CANR 83; CD-
   WLB 3; CWRI 5; DLB 125; EWL 3;
   WLIT 2
**Nye, Robert 1939- CLC 13, 42**
   See also CA 33-36R; CANR 29, 67, 107;
   CN 7; CP 7; CWRI 5; DAM NOV; DLB
   14, 271; FANT; HGG; MTCW 1; RHW;
   SATA 6
**Nyro, Laura 1947-1997 CLC 17**
   See also CA 194
**Oates, Joyce Carol 1938- CLC 1, 2, 3, 6, 9,**
   **11, 15, 19, 33, 52, 108, 134; SSC 6; WLC**
   See also AAYA 15; AITN 1; AMWS 2;
   BEST 89:2; BPFB 2; BYA 11; CA 5-8R;
   CANR 25, 45, 74, 113, 113; CDALB
   1968-1988; CN 7; CP 7; CPW; CWP; DA;
   DA3; DAB; DAC; DAM MST, NOV,
   POP; DLB 2, 5, 130; DLBY 1981; EWL
   3; EXPS; FW; HGG; INT CANR-25;
   LAIT 4; MAWW; MTCW 1, 2; NFS 8;
   RGAL 4; RGSF 2; SSFS 17; SUFW 2;
   TUS
**O'Brian, E. G.**
   See Clarke, Arthur C(harles)
**O'Brian, Patrick 1914-2000 CLC 152**
   See also CA 187; 144; CANR 74; CPW;
   MTCW 2; RHW
**O'Brien, Darcy 1939-1998 CLC 11**
   See also CA 167; 21-24R; CANR 8, 59
**O'Brien, Edna 1936- CLC 3, 5, 8, 13, 36, 65,**
   **116; SSC 10**
   See also BRWS 5; CA 1-4R; CANR 6, 41,
   65, 102; CDBLB 1960 to Present; CN 7;
   DA3; DAM NOV; DLB 14, 231; EWL 3;
   FW; MTCW 1, 2; RGSF 2; WLIT 4
**O'Brien, Fitz-James 1828-1862 NCLC 21**
   See also DLB 74; RGAL 4; SUFW

**O'Brien, Flann CLC 1, 4, 5, 7, 10, 47**
   See O Nuallain, Brian
   See also BRWS 2; DLB 231; EWL 3;
   RGEL 2
**O'Brien, Richard 1942- CLC 17**
   See also CA 124
**O'Brien, (William) Tim(othy) 1946- CLC 7,**
   **19, 40, 103**
   See also AAYA 16; AMWS 5; CA 85-88;
   CANR 40, 58; CDALBS; CN 7; CPW;
   DA3; DAM POP; DLB 152; DLBD 9;
   DLBY 1980; MTCW 2; RGAL 4; SSFS
   5, 15
**Obstfelder, Sigbjoern 1866-1900 TCLC 23**
   See also CA 123
**O'Casey, Sean 1880-1964 CLC 1, 5, 9, 11, 15,**
   **88; DC 12; WLCS**
   See also BRW 7; CA 89-92; CANR 62;
   CBD; CDBLB 1914-1945; DA3; DAB;
   DAC; DAM DRAM, MST; DLB 10;
   EWL 3; MTCW 1, 2; RGEL 2; TEA;
   WLIT 4
**O'Cathasaigh, Sean**
   See O'Casey, Sean
**Occom, Samson 1723-1792 LC 60; NNAL**
   See also DLB 175
**Ochs, Phil(ip David) 1940-1976 CLC 17**
   See also CA 65-68; 185
**O'Connor, Edwin (Greene) 1918-1968 CLC**
   **14**
   See also CA 25-28R; 93-96
**O'Connor, (Mary) Flannery 1925-1964 CLC**
   **1, 2, 3, 6, 10, 13, 15, 21, 66, 104; SSC 1,**
   **23; TCLC 132; WLC**
   See also AAYA 7; AMW; AMWR 2; BPFB
   3; CA 1-4R; CANR 3, 41; CDALB 1941-
   1968; DA; DA3; DAB; DAC; DAM MST,
   NOV; DLB 2, 152; DLBD 12; DLBY
   1980; EWL 3; EXPS; LAIT 5; MAWW;
   MTCW 1, 2; NFS 3; RGAL 4; RGSF 2;
   SSFS 2, 7, 10; TUS
**O'Connor, Frank CLC 23; SSC 5**
   See O'Donovan, Michael Francis
   See also DLB 162; EWL 3; RGSF 2; SSFS
   5
**O'Dell, Scott 1898-1989 CLC 30**
   See also AAYA 3, 44; BPFB 3; BYA 1, 2,
   3, 5; CA 129; 61-64; CANR 12, 30, 112;
   CLR 1, 16; DLB 52; JRDA; MAICYA 1,
   2; SATA 12, 60, 134; WYA; YAW
**Odets, Clifford 1906-1963 CLC 2, 28, 98; DC**
   **6**
   See also AMWS 2; CA 85-88; CAD; CANR
   62; DAM DRAM; DFS 17; DLB 7, 26;
   EWL 3; MTCW 1, 2; RGAL 4; TUS
**O'Doherty, Brian 1928- CLC 76**
   See also CA 105; CANR 108
**O'Donnell, K. M.**
   See Malzberg, Barry N(athaniel)
**O'Donnell, Lawrence**
   See Kuttner, Henry
**O'Donovan, Michael Francis 1903-1966 CLC**
   **14**
   See O'Connor, Frank
   See also CA 93-96; CANR 84
**Oe, Kenzaburo 1935- CLC 10, 36, 86; SSC**
   **20**
   See Oe Kenzaburo
   See also CA 97-100; CANR 36, 50, 74;
   CWW 2; DA3; DAM NOV; DLB 182;
   DLBY 1994; EWL 3; MJW; MTCW 1, 2;
   RGSF 2; RGWL 2, 3
**Oe Kenzaburo**
   See Oe, Kenzaburo
   See also EWL 3
**O'Faolain, Julia 1932- CLC 6, 19, 47, 108**
   See also CA 81-84; CAAS 2; CANR 12,
   61; CN 7; DLB 14, 231; FW; MTCW 1;
   RHW

**O'Faolain, Sean** 1900-1991 **CLC 1, 7, 14, 32, 70; SSC 13**
See also CA 134; 61-64; CANR 12, 66; DLB 15, 162; MTCW 1, 2; RGEL 2; RGSF 2

**O'Flaherty, Liam** 1896-1984 **CLC 5, 34; SSC 6**
See also CA 113; 101; CANR 35; DLB 36, 162; DLBY 1984; MTCW 1, 2; RGEL 2; RGSF 2; SSFS 5

**Ogai**
See Mori Ogai
See also MJW

**Ogilvy, Gavin**
See Barrie, J(ames) M(atthew)

**O'Grady, Standish (James)** 1846-1928 **TCLC 5**
See also CA 157; 104

**O'Grady, Timothy** 1951- **CLC 59**
See also CA 138

**O'Hara, Frank** 1926-1966 **CLC 2, 5, 13, 78; PC 45**
See also CA 25-28R; 9-12R; CANR 33; DA3; DAM POET; DLB 5, 16, 193; EWL 3; MTCW 1, 2; PFS 8; 12; RGAL 4; WP

**O'Hara, John (Henry)** 1905-1970 **CLC 1, 2, 3, 6, 11, 42; SSC 15**
See also AMW; BPFB 3; CA 25-28R; 5-8R; CANR 31, 60; CDALB 1929-1941; DAM NOV; DLB 9, 86; DLBD 2; EWL 3; MTCW 1, 2; NFS 11; RGAL 4; RGSF 2

**O Hehir, Diana** 1922- **CLC 41**
See also CA 93-96

**Ohiyesa**
See Eastman, Charles A(lexander)

**Okada, John** 1923-1971 **AAL**
See also BYA 14

**Okigbo, Christopher (Ifenayichukwu)** 1932-1967 **BLC 3; CLC 25, 84; PC 7**
See also AFW; BW 1, 3; CA 77-80; CANR 74; CDWLB 3; DAM MULT, POET; DLB 125; EWL 3; MTCW 1, 2; RGEL 2

**Okri, Ben** 1959- **CLC 87**
See also AFW; BRWS 5; BW 2, 3; CA 138; 130; CANR 65; CN 7; DLB 157, 231; EWL 3; INT CA-138; MTCW 2; RGSF 2; WLIT 2

**Olds, Sharon** 1942- **CLC 32, 39, 85; PC 22**
See also AMWS 10; CA 101; CANR 18, 41, 66, 98; CP 7; CPW; CWP; DAM POET; DLB 120; MTCW 2; PFS 17

**Oldstyle, Jonathan**
See Irving, Washington

**Olesha, Iurii**
See Olesha, Yuri (Karlovich)
See also RGWL 2

**Olesha, Iurii Karlovich**
See Olesha, Yuri (Karlovich)
See also DLB 272

**Olesha, Yuri (Karlovich)** 1899-1960 **CLC 8**
See Olesha, Iurii; Olesha, Iurii Karlovich; Olesha, Yury Karlovich
See also CA 85-88; EW 11; RGWL 3

**Olesha, Yury Karlovich**
See Olesha, Yuri (Karlovich)
See also EWL 3

**Oliphant, Mrs.**
See Oliphant, Margaret (Oliphant Wilson)
See also SUFW

**Oliphant, Laurence** 1829(?)-1888 **NCLC 47**
See also DLB 18, 166

**Oliphant, Margaret (Oliphant Wilson)** 1828-1897 **NCLC 11, 61; SSC 25**
See Oliphant, Mrs.
See also DLB 18, 159, 190; HGG; RGEL 2; RGSF 2

**Oliver, Mary** 1935- **CLC 19, 34, 98**
See also AMWS 7; CA 21-24R; CANR 9, 43, 84, 92; CP 7; CWP; DLB 5, 193; EWL 3; PFS 15

**Olivier, Laurence (Kerr)** 1907-1989 **CLC 20**
See also CA 129; 150; 111

**Olsen, Tillie** 1912- **CLC 4, 13, 114; SSC 11**
See also BYA 11; CA 1-4R; CANR 1, 43, 74; CDALBS; CN 7; DA; DA3; DAB; DAC; DAM MST; DLB 28, 206; DLBY 1980; EWL 3; EXPS; FW; MTCW 1, 2; RGAL 4; RGSF 2; SSFS 1; TUS

**Olson, Charles (John)** 1910-1970 **CLC 1, 2, 5, 6, 9, 11, 29; PC 19**
See also AMWS 2; CA 25-28R; 13-16; CABS 2; CANR 35, 61; CAP 1; DAM POET; DLB 5, 16, 193; EWL 3; MTCW 1, 2; RGAL 4; WP

**Olson, Toby** 1937- **CLC 28**
See also CA 65-68; CANR 9, 31, 84; CP 7

**Olyesha, Yuri**
See Olesha, Yuri (Karlovich)

**Omar Khayyam**
See Khayyam, Omar
See also RGWL 2, 3

**Ondaatje, (Philip) Michael** 1943- **CLC 14, 29, 51, 76; PC 28**
See also CA 77-80; CANR 42, 74, 109; CN 7; CP 7; DA3; DAB; DAC; DAM MST; DLB 60; EWL 3; LMFS 2; MTCW 2; PFS 8; TWA

**Oneal, Elizabeth** 1934-
See Oneal, Zibby
See also CA 106; CANR 28, 84; MAICYA 1, 2; SATA 30, 82; YAW

**Oneal, Zibby** **CLC 30**
See Oneal, Elizabeth
See also AAYA 5, 41; BYA 13; CLR 13; JRDA; WYA

**O'Neill, Eugene (Gladstone)** 1888-1953 **DC 20; TCLC 1, 6, 27, 49; WLC**
See also AITN 1; AMW; AMWC 1; CA 132; 110; CAD; CDALB 1929-1941; DA; DA3; DAB; DAC; DAM DRAM, MST; DFS 9, 11, 12, 16; DLB 7; EWL 3; LAIT 3; LMFS 2; MTCW 1, 2; RGAL 4; TUS

**Onetti, Juan Carlos** 1909-1994 **CLC 7, 10; HLCS 2; SSC 23; TCLC 131**
See also CA 145; 85-88; CANR 32, 63; CDWLB 3; DAM MULT, NOV; DLB 113; EWL 3; HW 1, 2; LAW; MTCW 1, 2; RGSF 2

**O Nuallain, Brian** 1911-1966
See O'Brien, Flann
See also CA 25-28R; 21-22; CAP 2; DLB 231; FANT; TEA

**Ophuls, Max** 1902-1957 **TCLC 79**
See also CA 113

**Opie, Amelia** 1769-1853 **NCLC 65**
See also DLB 116, 159; RGEL 2

**Oppen, George** 1908-1984 **CLC 7, 13, 34; PC 35; TCLC 107**
See also CA 113; 13-16R; CANR 8, 82; DLB 5, 165

**Oppenheim, E(dward) Phillips** 1866-1946 **TCLC 45**
See also CA 202; 111; CMW 4; DLB 70

**Opuls, Max**
See Ophuls, Max

**Origen** c. 185-c. 254 **CMLC 19**

**Orlovitz, Gil** 1918-1973 **CLC 22**
See also CA 45-48; 77-80; DLB 2, 5

**Orris**
See Ingelow, Jean

**Ortega y Gasset, Jose** 1883-1955 **HLC 2; TCLC 9**
See also CA 130; 106; DAM MULT; EW 9; EWL 3; HW 1, 2; MTCW 1, 2

**Ortese, Anna Maria** 1914-1998 **CLC 89**
See also DLB 177; EWL 3

**Ortiz, Simon J(oseph)** 1941- **CLC 45; NNAL; PC 17**
See also AMWS 4; CA 134; CANR 69; CP 7; DAM MULT, POET; DLB 120, 175, 256; EXPP; PFS 4, 16; RGAL 4

**Orton, Joe CLC 4, 13, 43; DC 3**
See Orton, John Kingsley
See also BRWS 5; CBD; CDBLB 1960 to Present; DFS 3, 6; DLB 13; GLL 1; MTCW 2; RGEL 2; TEA; WLIT 4

**Orton, John Kingsley** 1933-1967
See Orton, Joe
See also CA 85-88; CANR 35, 66; DAM DRAM; MTCW 1, 2

**Orwell, George TCLC 2, 6, 15, 31, 51, 128, 129; WLC**
See Blair, Eric (Arthur)
See also BPFB 3; BRW 7; BYA 5; CDBLB 1945-1960; CLR 68; DAB; DLB 15, 98, 195, 255; EWL 3; EXPN; LAIT 4, 5; NFS 3, 7; RGEL 2; SCFW 2; SFW 4; SSFS 4; TEA; WLIT 4; YAW

**Osborne, David**
See Silverberg, Robert

**Osborne, George**
See Silverberg, Robert

**Osborne, John (James)** 1929-1994 **CLC 1, 2, 5, 11, 45; WLC**
See also BRWS 1; CA 147; 13-16R; CANR 21, 56; CDBLB 1945-1960; DA; DAB; DAC; DAM DRAM, MST; DFS 4; DLB 13; EWL 3; MTCW 1, 2; RGEL 2

**Osborne, Lawrence** 1958- **CLC 50**
See also CA 189

**Osbourne, Lloyd** 1868-1947 **TCLC 93**

**Oshima, Nagisa** 1932- **CLC 20**
See also CA 121; 116; CANR 78

**Oskison, John Milton** 1874-1947 **NNAL; TCLC 35**
See also CA 144; CANR 84; DAM MULT; DLB 175

**Ossian** c. 3rd cent. - **CMLC 28**
See Macpherson, James

**Ossoli, Sarah Margaret (Fuller)** 1810-1850 **NCLC 5, 50**
See Fuller, Margaret; Fuller, Sarah Margaret
See also CDALB 1640-1865; FW; SATA 25

**Ostriker, Alicia (Suskin)** 1937- **CLC 132**
See also CA 25-28R; CAAS 24; CANR 10, 30, 62, 99; CWP; DLB 120; EXPP

**Ostrovsky, Aleksandr Nikolaevich**
See Ostrovsky, Alexander
See also DLB 277

**Ostrovsky, Alexander** 1823-1886 **NCLC 30, 57**
See Ostrovsky, Aleksandr Nikolaevich

**Otero, Blas de** 1916-1979 **CLC 11**
See also CA 89-92; DLB 134; EWL 3

**Otto, Rudolf** 1869-1937 **TCLC 85**

**Otto, Whitney** 1955- **CLC 70**
See also CA 140

**Ouida TCLC 43**
See De la Ramee, Marie Louise (Ouida)
See also DLB 18, 156; RGEL 2

**Ouologuem, Yambo** 1940- **CLC 146**
See also CA 176; 111

**Ousmane, Sembene** 1923- **BLC 3; CLC 66**
See Sembene, Ousmane
See also BW 1, 3; CA 125; 117; CANR 81; CWW 2; MTCW 1

**Ovid** 43B.C.-17 **CMLC 7; PC 2**
See also AW 2; CDWLB 1; DA3; DAM POET; DLB 211; RGWL 2, 3; WP

**Owen, Hugh**
See Faust, Frederick (Schiller)

**Pater, Walter (Horatio)** 1839-1894 **NCLC 7, 90**
See also BRW 5; CDBLB 1832-1890; DLB 57, 156; RGEL 2; TEA

**Paterson, A(ndrew) B(arton)** 1864-1941 **TCLC 32**
See also CA 155; DLB 230; RGEL 2; SATA 97

**Paterson, Banjo**
See Paterson, A(ndrew) B(arton)

**Paterson, Katherine (Womeldorf)** 1932- **CLC 12, 30**
See also AAYA 1, 31; BYA 1, 2, 7; CA 21-24R; CANR 28, 59, 111; CLR 7, 50; CWRI 5; DLB 52; JRDA; LAIT 4; MAICYA 1, 2; MAICYAS 1; MTCW 1; SATA 13, 53, 92, 133; WYA; YAW

**Patmore, Coventry Kersey Dighton** 1823-1896 **NCLC 9**
See also DLB 35, 98; RGEL 2; TEA

**Paton, Alan (Stewart)** 1903-1988 **CLC 4, 10, 25, 55, 106; WLC**
See also AAYA 26; AFW; BPFB 3; BRWS 2; BYA 1; CA 125; 13-16; CANR 22; CAP 1; DA; DA3; DAB; DAC; DAM MST, NOV; DLB 225; DLBD 17; EWL 3; EXPN; LAIT 4; MTCW 1, 2; NFS 3, 12; RGEL 2; SATA 11; SATA-Obit 56; TWA; WLIT 2

**Paton Walsh, Gillian** 1937- **CLC 35**
See Paton Walsh, Jill; Walsh, Jill Paton
See also AAYA 11; CANR 38, 83; CLR 2, 65; DLB 161; JRDA; MAICYA 1, 2; SAAS 3; SATA 4, 72, 109; YAW

**Paton Walsh, Jill**
See Paton Walsh, Gillian
See also AAYA 47; BYA 1, 8

**Patterson, (Horace) Orlando (Lloyd)** 1940- **BLCS**
See also BW 1; CA 65-68; CANR 27, 84; CN 7

**Patton, George S(mith), Jr.** 1885-1945 **TCLC 79**
See also CA 189

**Paulding, James Kirke** 1778-1860 **NCLC 2**
See also DLB 3, 59, 74, 250; RGAL 4

**Paulin, Thomas Neilson** 1949-
See Paulin, Tom
See also CA 128; 123; CANR 98; CP 7

**Paulin, Tom CLC 37**
See Paulin, Thomas Neilson
See also DLB 40

**Pausanias** c. 1st cent. - **CMLC 36**

**Paustovsky, Konstantin (Georgievich)** 1892-1968 **CLC 40**
See also CA 25-28R; 93-96; DLB 272; EWL 3

**Pavese, Cesare** 1908-1950 **PC 13; SSC 19; TCLC 3**
See also CA 169; 104; DLB 128, 177; EW 12; EWL 3; RGSF 2; RGWL 2, 3; TWA

**Pavic, Milorad** 1929- **CLC 60**
See also CA 136; CDWLB 4; CWW 2; DLB 181; EWL 3; RGWL 3

**Pavlov, Ivan Petrovich** 1849-1936 **TCLC 91**
See also CA 180; 118

**Payne, Alan**
See Jakes, John (William)

**Paz, Gil**
See Lugones, Leopoldo

**Paz, Octavio** 1914-1998 **CLC 3, 4, 6, 10, 19, 51, 65, 119; HLC 2; PC 1; WLC**
See also CA 165; 73-76; CANR 32, 65, 104; CWW 2; DA; DA3; DAB; DAC; DAM MST, MULT, POET; DLBY 1990, 1998; DNFS 1; EWL 3; HW 1, 2; LAW; LAWS 1; MTCW 1, 2; RGWL 2, 3; SSFS 13; TWA; WLIT 1

**p'Bitek, Okot** 1931-1982 **BLC 3; CLC 96**
See also AFW; BW 2, 3; CA 107; 124; CANR 82; DAM MULT; DLB 125; EWL 3; MTCW 1, 2; RGEL 2; WLIT 2

**Peacock, Molly** 1947- **CLC 60**
See also CA 103; CAAS 21; CANR 52, 84; CP 7; CWP; DLB 120

**Peacock, Thomas Love** 1785-1866 **NCLC 22**
See also BRW 4; DLB 96, 116; RGEL 2; RGSF 2

**Peake, Mervyn** 1911-1968 **CLC 7, 54**
See also CA 25-28R; 5-8R; CANR 3; DLB 15, 160, 255; FANT; MTCW 1; RGEL 2; SATA 23; SFW 4

**Pearce, Philippa**
See Christie, Philippa
See also CA 5-8R; CANR 4, 109; CWRI 5; FANT; MAICYA 2

**Pearl, Eric**
See Elman, Richard (Martin)

**Pearson, T(homas) R(eid)** 1956- **CLC 39**
See also CA 130; 120; CANR 97; CSW; INT 130

**Peck, Dale** 1967- **CLC 81**
See also CA 146; CANR 72; GLL 2

**Peck, John (Frederick)** 1941- **CLC 3**
See also CA 49-52; CANR 3, 100; CP 7

**Peck, Richard (Wayne)** 1934- **CLC 21**
See also AAYA 1, 24; BYA 1, 6, 8, 11; CA 85-88; CANR 19, 38; CLR 15; INT CANR-19; JRDA; MAICYA 1, 2; SAAS 2; SATA 18, 55, 97; SATA-Essay 110; WYA; YAW

**Peck, Robert Newton** 1928- **CLC 17**
See also AAYA 3, 43; BYA 1, 6; CA 81-84, 182; CAAE 182; CANR 31, 63; CLR 45; DA; DAC; DAM MST; JRDA; LAIT 3; MAICYA 1, 2; SAAS 1; SATA 21, 62, 111; SATA-Essay 108; WYA; YAW

**Peckinpah, (David) Sam(uel)** 1925-1984 **CLC 20**
See also CA 114; 109; CANR 82

**Pedersen, Knut** 1859-1952
See Hamsun, Knut
See also CA 119; 104; CANR 63; MTCW 1, 2

**Peeslake, Gaffer**
See Durrell, Lawrence (George)

**Peguy, Charles (Pierre)** 1873-1914 **TCLC 10**
See also CA 193; 107; DLB 258; EWL 3; GFL 1789 to the Present

**Peirce, Charles Sanders** 1839-1914 **TCLC 81**
See also CA 194; DLB 270

**Pellicer, Carlos** 1900(?)-1977 **HLCS 2**
See also CA 69-72; 153; EWL 3; HW 1

**Pena, Ramon del Valle y**
See Valle-Inclan, Ramon (Maria) del

**Pendennis, Arthur Esquir**
See Thackeray, William Makepeace

**Penn, William** 1644-1718 **LC 25**
See also DLB 24

**PEPECE**
See Prado (Calvo), Pedro

**Pepys, Samuel** 1633-1703 **LC 11, 58; WLC**
See also BRW 2; CDBLB 1660-1789; DA; DA3; DAB; DAC; DAM MST; DLB 101, 213; NCFS 4; RGEL 2; TEA; WLIT 3

**Percy, Thomas** 1729-1811 **NCLC 95**
See also DLB 104

**Percy, Walker** 1916-1990 **CLC 2, 3, 6, 8, 14, 18, 47, 65**
See also AMWS 3; BPFB 3; CA 131; 1-4R; CANR 1, 23, 64; CPW; CSW; DA3; DAM NOV, POP; DLB 2; DLBY 1980, 1990; EWL 3; MTCW 1, 2; RGAL 4; TUS

**Percy, William Alexander** 1885-1942 **TCLC 84**
See also CA 163; MTCW 2

**Perec, Georges** 1936-1982 **CLC 56, 116**
See also CA 141; DLB 83; EWL 3; GFL 1789 to the Present; RGWL 3

**Pereda (y Sanchez de Porrua), Jose Maria de** 1833-1906 **TCLC 16**
See also CA 117

**Pereda y Porrua, Jose Maria de**
See Pereda (y Sanchez de Porrua), Jose Maria de

**Peregoy, George Weems**
See Mencken, H(enry) L(ouis)

**Perelman, S(idney) J(oseph)** 1904-1979 **CLC 3, 5, 9, 15, 23, 44, 49; SSC 32**
See also AITN 1, 2; BPFB 3; CA 89-92; 73-76; CANR 18; DAM DRAM; DLB 11, 44; MTCW 1, 2; RGAL 4

**Peret, Benjamin** 1899-1959 **PC 33; TCLC 20**
See also CA 186; 117; GFL 1789 to the Present

**Peretz, Isaac Leib** 1851(?)-1915
See Peretz, Isaac Loeb
See also CA 201

**Peretz, Isaac Loeb** 1851(?)-1915 **SSC 26; TCLC 16**
See Peretz, Isaac Leib
See also CA 109

**Peretz, Yitzkhok Leibush**
See Peretz, Isaac Loeb

**Perez Galdos, Benito** 1843-1920 **HLCS 2; TCLC 27**
See Galdos, Benito Perez
See also CA 153; 125; EWL 3; HW 1; RGWL 2, 3

**Peri Rossi, Cristina** 1941- **CLC 156; HLCS 2**
See also CA 131; CANR 59, 81; DLB 145; EWL 3; HW 1, 2

**Perlata**
See Peret, Benjamin

**Perloff, Marjorie G(abrielle)** 1931- **CLC 137**
See also CA 57-60; CANR 7, 22, 49, 104

**Perrault, Charles** 1628-1703 **DC 12; LC 2, 56**
See also BYA 4; CLR 79; DLB 268; GFL Beginnings to 1789; MAICYA 1, 2; RGWL 2, 3; SATA 25; WCH

**Perry, Anne** 1938- **CLC 126**
See also CA 101; CANR 22, 50, 84; CMW 4; CN 7; CPW; DLB 276

**Perry, Brighton**
See Sherwood, Robert E(mmet)

**Perse, St.-John**
See Leger, (Marie-Rene Auguste) Alexis Saint-Leger

**Perse, Saint-John**
See Leger, (Marie-Rene Auguste) Alexis Saint-Leger
See also DLB 258; RGWL 3

**Perutz, Leo(pold)** 1882-1957 **TCLC 60**
See also CA 147; DLB 81

**Peseenz, Tulio F.**
See Lopez y Fuentes, Gregorio

**Pesetsky, Bette** 1932- **CLC 28**
See also CA 133; DLB 130

**Peshkov, Alexei Maximovich** 1868-1936
See Gorky, Maxim
See also CA 141; 105; CANR 83; DA; DAC; DAM DRAM, MST, NOV; MTCW 2

**Pessoa, Fernando (Antonio Nogueira)** 1898-1935 **HLC 2; PC 20; TCLC 27**
See also CA 183; 125; DAM MULT; EW 10; EWL 3; RGWL 2, 3; WP

**Peterkin, Julia Mood** 1880-1961 **CLC 31**
See also CA 102; DLB 9

**Peters, Joan K(aren)** 1945- **CLC 39**
See also CA 158; CANR 109

**Peters, Robert L(ouis)** 1924- **CLC 7**
See also CA 13-16R; CAAS 8; CP 7; DLB 105

**Petofi, Sandor** 1823-1849 **NCLC 21**
See also RGWL 2, 3

**Petrakis, Harry Mark** 1923- **CLC 3**
See also CA 9-12R; CANR 4, 30, 85; CN 7

**Petrarch** 1304-1374 **CMLC 20; PC 8**
See also DA3; DAM POET; EW 2; RGWL
2, 3

**Petronius** c. 20-66 **CMLC 34**
See also AW 2; CDWLB 1; DLB 211;
RGWL 2, 3

**Petrov, Evgeny TCLC 21**
See Kataev, Evgeny Petrovich

**Petry, Ann (Lane)** 1908-1997 **CLC 1, 7, 18;
TCLC 112**
See also AFAW 1, 2; BPFB 3; BW 1, 3;
BYA 3; CA 157; 5-8R; CAAS 6; CANR
4, 46; CLR 12; CN 7; DLB 76; EWL 3;
JRDA; LAIT 1; MAICYA 1, 2; MAIC-
YAS 1; MTCW 1; RGAL 4; SATA 5;
SATA-Obit 94; TUS

**Petursson, Halligrimur** 1614-1674 **LC 8**

**Peychinovich**
See Vazov, Ivan (Minchov)

**Phaedrus** c. 15B.C.-c. 50 **CMLC 25**
See also DLB 211

**Phelps (Ward), Elizabeth Stuart**
See Phelps, Elizabeth Stuart
See also FW

**Phelps, Elizabeth Stuart** 1844-1911 **TCLC
113**
See Phelps (Ward), Elizabeth Stuart
See also DLB 74

**Philips, Katherine** 1632-1664 **LC 30; PC 40**
See also DLB 131; RGEL 2

**Philipson, Morris H.** 1926- **CLC 53**
See also CA 1-4R; CANR 4

**Phillips, Caryl** 1958- **BLCS; CLC 96**
See also BRWS 5; BW 2; CA 141; CANR
63, 104; CBD; CD 5; CN 7; DA3; DAM
MULT; DLB 157; EWL 3; MTCW 2;
WLIT 4

**Phillips, David Graham** 1867-1911 **TCLC 44**
See also CA 176; 108; DLB 9, 12; RGAL 4

**Phillips, Jack**
See Sandburg, Carl (August)

**Phillips, Jayne Anne** 1952- **CLC 15, 33, 139;
SSC 16**
See also BPFB 3; CA 101; CANR 24, 50,
96; CN 7; CSW; DLBY 1980; INT
CANR-24; MTCW 1, 2; RGAL 4; RGSF
2; SSFS 4

**Phillips, Richard**
See Dick, Philip K(indred)

**Phillips, Robert (Schaeffer)** 1938- **CLC 28**
See also CA 17-20R; CAAS 13; CANR 8;
DLB 105

**Phillips, Ward**
See Lovecraft, H(oward) P(hillips)

**Piccolo, Lucio** 1901-1969 **CLC 13**
See also CA 97-100; DLB 114; EWL 3

**Pickthall, Marjorie L(owry) C(hristie)**
1883-1922 **TCLC 21**
See also CA 107; DLB 92

**Pico della Mirandola, Giovanni** 1463-1494
**LC 15**

**Piercy, Marge** 1936- **CLC 3, 6, 14, 18, 27, 62,
128; PC 29**
See also BPFB 3; CA 21-24R; CAAE 187;
CAAS 1; CANR 13, 43, 66, 111; CN 7;
CP 7; CWP; DLB 120, 227; EXPP; FW;
MTCW 1, 2; PFS 9; SFW 4

**Piers, Robert**
See Anthony, Piers

**Pieyre de Mandiargues, Andre** 1909-1991
See Mandiargues, Andre Pieyre de
See also CA 136; 103; CANR 22, 82; EWL
3; GFL 1789 to the Present

**Pilnyak, Boris** 1894-1938 **SSC 48; TCLC 23**
See Vogau, Boris Andreyevich
See also EWL 3

**Pinchback, Eugene**
See Toomer, Jean

**Pincherle, Alberto** 1907-1990 **CLC 11, 18**
See Moravia, Alberto
See also CA 132; 25-28R; CANR 33, 63;
DAM NOV; MTCW 1

**Pinckney, Darryl** 1953- **CLC 76**
See also BW 2, 3; CA 143; CANR 79

**Pindar** 518(?)B.C.-438(?)B.C. **CMLC 12; PC
19**
See also AW 1; CDWLB 1; DLB 176;
RGWL 2

**Pineda, Cecile** 1942- **CLC 39**
See also CA 118; DLB 209

**Pinero, Arthur Wing** 1855-1934 **TCLC 32**
See also CA 153; 110; DAM DRAM; DLB
10; RGEL 2

**Pinero, Miguel (Antonio Gomez)** 1946-1988
**CLC 4, 55**
See also CA 125; 61-64; CAD; CANR 29,
90; DLB 266; HW 1

**Pinget, Robert** 1919-1997 **CLC 7, 13, 37**
See also CA 160; 85-88; CWW 2; DLB 83;
EWL 3; GFL 1789 to the Present

**Pink Floyd**
See Barrett, (Roger) Syd; Gilmour, David;
Mason, Nick; Waters, Roger; Wright, Rick

**Pinkney, Edward** 1802-1828 **NCLC 31**
See also DLB 248

**Pinkwater, Daniel**
See Pinkwater, Daniel Manus

**Pinkwater, Daniel Manus** 1941- **CLC 35**
See also AAYA 1, 46; BYA 9; CA 29-32R;
CANR 12, 38, 89; CLR 4; CSW; FANT;
JRDA; MAICYA 1, 2; SAAS 3; SATA 8,
46, 76, 114; SFW 4; YAW

**Pinkwater, Manus**
See Pinkwater, Daniel Manus

**Pinsky, Robert** 1940- **CLC 9, 19, 38, 94, 121;
PC 27**
See also AMWS 6; CA 29-32R; CAAS 4;
CANR 58, 97; CP 7; DA3; DAM POET;
DLBY 1982, 1998; MTCW 2; RGAL 4

**Pinta, Harold**
See Pinter, Harold

**Pinter, Harold** 1930- **CLC 1, 3, 6, 9, 11, 15,
27, 58, 73; DC 15; WLC**
See also BRWR 1; BRWS 1; CA 5-8R;
CANR 33, 65, 112; CBD; CD 5; CDBLB
1960 to Present; DA; DA3; DAB; DAC;
DAM DRAM, MST; DFS 3, 5, 7, 14;
DLB 13; EWL 3; IDFW 3, 4; LMFS 2;
MTCW 1, 2; RGEL 2; TEA

**Piozzi, Hester Lynch (Thrale)** 1741-1821
**NCLC 57**
See also DLB 104, 142

**Pirandello, Luigi** 1867-1936 **DC 5; SSC 22;
TCLC 4, 29; WLC**
See also CA 153; 104; CANR 103; DA;
DA3; DAB; DAC; DAM DRAM, MST;
DFS 4, 9; DLB 264; EW 8; EWL 3;
MTCW 2; RGSF 2; RGWL 2, 3

**Pirsig, Robert M(aynard)** 1928- **CLC 4, 6, 73**
See also CA 53-56; CANR 42, 74; CPW 1;
DA3; DAM POP; MTCW 1, 2; SATA 39

**Pisarev, Dmitrii Ivanovich**
See Pisarev, Dmitry Ivanovich
See also DLB 277

**Pisarev, Dmitry Ivanovich** 1840-1868 **NCLC
25**
See Pisarev, Dmitrii Ivanovich

**Pix, Mary (Griffith)** 1666-1709 **LC 8**
See also DLB 80

**Pixerecourt, (Rene Charles) Guilbert de**
1773-1844 **NCLC 39**
See also DLB 192; GFL 1789 to the Present

**Plaatje, Sol(omon) T(shekisho)** 1878-1932
**BLCS; TCLC 73**
See also BW 2, 3; CA 141; CANR 79; DLB
125, 225

**Plaidy, Jean**
See Hibbert, Eleanor Alice Burford

**Planche, James Robinson** 1796-1880 **NCLC
42**
See also RGEL 2

**Plant, Robert** 1948- **CLC 12**

**Plante, David (Robert)** 1940- **CLC 7, 23, 38**
See also CA 37-40R; CANR 12, 36, 58, 82;
CN 7; DAM NOV; DLBY 1983; INT
CANR-12; MTCW 1

**Plath, Sylvia** 1932-1963 **CLC 1, 2, 3, 5, 9, 11,
14, 17, 50, 51, 62, 111; PC 1, 37; WLC**
See also AAYA 13; AMWR 2; AMWS 1;
BPFB 3; CA 19-20; CANR 34, 101; CAP
2; CDALB 1941-1968; DA; DA3; DAB;
DAC; DAM MST, POET; DLB 5, 6, 152;
EWL 3; EXPN; EXPP; FW; LAIT 4;
MAWW; MTCW 1, 2; NFS 1; PAB; PFS
1, 15; RGAL 4; SATA 96; TUS; WP;
YAW

**Plato** c. 428B.C.-347B.C. **CMLC 8; WLCS**
See also AW 1; CDWLB 1; DA; DA3;
DAB; DAC; DAM MST; DLB 176; LAIT
1; RGWL 2, 3

**Platonov, Andrei**
See Klimentov, Andrei Platonovich

**Platonov, Andrei Platonovich**
See Klimentov, Andrei Platonovich
See also DLB 272

**Platonov, Andrey Platonovich**
See Klimentov, Andrei Platonovich
See also EWL 3

**Platt, Kin** 1911- **CLC 26**
See also AAYA 11; CA 17-20R; CANR 11;
JRDA; SAAS 17; SATA 21, 86; WYA

**Plautus** c. 254B.C.-c. 184B.C. **CMLC 24; DC
6**
See also AW 1; CDWLB 1; DLB 211;
RGWL 2, 3

**Plick et Plock**
See Simenon, Georges (Jacques Christian)

**Plieksans, Janis**
See Rainis, Janis

**Plimpton, George (Ames)** 1927- **CLC 36**
See also AITN 1; CA 21-24R; CANR 32,
70, 103; DLB 185, 241; MTCW 1, 2;
SATA 10

**Pliny the Elder** c. 23-79 **CMLC 23**
See also DLB 211

**Plomer, William Charles Franklin** 1903-1973
**CLC 4, 8**
See also AFW; CA 21-22; CANR 34; CAP
2; DLB 20, 162, 191, 225; EWL 3;
MTCW 1; RGEL 2; RGSF 2; SATA 24

**Plotinus** 204-270 **CMLC 46**
See also CDWLB 1; DLB 176

**Plowman, Piers**
See Kavanagh, Patrick (Joseph)

**Plum, J.**
See Wodehouse, P(elham) G(renville)

**Plumly, Stanley (Ross)** 1939- **CLC 33**
See also CA 110; 108; CANR 97; CP 7;
DLB 5, 193; INT 110

**Plumpe, Friedrich Wilhelm** 1888-1931 **TCLC
53**
See also CA 112

**Po Chu-i** 772-846 **CMLC 24**

**Poe, Edgar Allan** 1809-1849 **NCLC 1, 16, 55,
78, 94, 97, 117; PC 1; SSC 1, 22, 34, 35,
54; WLC**
See also AAYA 14; AMW; AMWC 1;
AMWR 2; BPFB 3; BYA 5, 11; CDALB
1640-1865; CMW 4; DA; DA3; DAB;
DAC; DAM MST, POET; DLB 3, 59, 73,
74, 248, 254; EXPP; EXPS; HGG; LAIT

2; MSW; PAB; PFS 1, 3, 9; RGAL 4;
RGSF 2; SATA 23; SCFW 2; SFW 4;
SSFS 2, 4, 7, 8, 16; SUFW; TUS; WP;
WYA

**Poet of Titchfield Street, The**
See Pound, Ezra (Weston Loomis)

**Pohl, Frederik** 1919- **CLC 18; SSC 25**
See also AAYA 24; CA 61-64; CAAE 188;
CAAS 1; CANR 11, 37, 81; CN 7; DLB
8; INT CANR-11; MTCW 1, 2; SATA 24;
SCFW 2; SFW 4

**Poirier, Louis** 1910-
See Gracq, Julien
See also CA 126; 122; CWW 2

**Poitier, Sidney** 1927- **CLC 26**
See also BW 1; CA 117; CANR 94

**Pokagon, Simon** 1830-1899 **NNAL**
See also DAM MULT

**Polanski, Roman** 1933- **CLC 16**
See also CA 77-80

**Poliakoff, Stephen** 1952- **CLC 38**
See also CA 106; CANR 116; CBD; CD 5;
DLB 13

**Police, The**
See Copeland, Stewart (Armstrong); Summers, Andrew James; Sumner, Gordon
Matthew

**Polidori, John William** 1795-1821 **NCLC 51**
See also DLB 116; HGG

**Pollitt, Katha** 1949- **CLC 28, 122**
See also CA 122; 120; CANR 66, 108;
MTCW 1, 2

**Pollock, (Mary) Sharon** 1936- **CLC 50**
See also CA 141; CD 5; CWD; DAC; DAM
DRAM, MST; DFS 3; DLB 60; FW

**Pollock, Sharon** 1936- **DC 20**

**Polo, Marco** 1254-1324 **CMLC 15**

**Polonsky, Abraham (Lincoln)** 1910-1999
**CLC 92**
See also CA 187; 104; DLB 26; INT 104

**Polybius** c. 200B.C.-c. 118B.C. **CMLC 17**
See also AW 1; DLB 176; RGWL 2, 3

**Pomerance, Bernard** 1940- **CLC 13**
See also CA 101; CAD; CANR 49; CD 5;
DAM DRAM; DFS 9; LAIT 2

**Ponge, Francis** 1899-1988 **CLC 6, 18**
See also CA 126; 85-88; CANR 40, 86;
DAM POET; DLBY 2002; EWL 3; GFL
1789 to the Present; RGWL 2, 3

**Poniatowska, Elena** 1933- **CLC 140; HLC 2**
See also CA 101; CANR 32, 66, 107; CD-
WLB 3; DAM MULT; DLB 113; EWL 3;
HW 1, 2; LAWS 1; WLIT 1

**Pontoppidan, Henrik** 1857-1943 **TCLC 29**
See also CA 170

**Poole, Josephine** **CLC 17**
See Helyar, Jane Penelope Josephine
See also SAAS 2; SATA 5

**Popa, Vasko** 1922-1991 **CLC 19**
See also CA 148; 112; CDWLB 4; DLB
181; EWL 3; RGWL 2, 3

**Pope, Alexander** 1688-1744 **LC 3, 58, 60, 64;
PC 26; WLC**
See also BRW 3; BRWC 1; BRWR 1; CD-
BLB 1660-1789; DA; DA3; DAB; DAC;
DAM MST, POET; DLB 95, 101, 213;
EXPP; PAB; PFS 12; RGEL 2; WLIT 3;
WP

**Popov, Yevgeny** **CLC 59**

**Poquelin, Jean-Baptiste**
See Moliere

**Porter, Connie (Rose)** 1959(?)- **CLC 70**
See also BW 2, 3; CA 142; CANR 90, 109;
SATA 81, 129

**Porter, Gene(va Grace) Stratton** **TCLC 21**
See Stratton-Porter, Gene(va Grace)
See also BPFB 3; CA 112; CWRI 5; RHW

**Porter, Katherine Anne** 1890-1980 **CLC 1, 3,
7, 10, 13, 15, 27, 101; SSC 4, 31, 43**
See also AAYA 42; AITN 2; AMW; BPFB
3; CA 101; 1-4R; CANR 1, 65; CDALBS;
DA; DA3; DAB; DAC; DAM MST, NOV;
DLB 4, 9, 102; DLBD 12; DLBY 1980;
EWL 3; EXPS; LAIT 3; MAWW; MTCW
1, 2; NFS 14; RGAL 4; RGSF 2; SATA
39; SATA-Obit 23; SSFS 1, 8, 11, 16;
TUS

**Porter, Peter (Neville Frederick)** 1929- **CLC
5, 13, 33**
See also CA 85-88; CP 7; DLB 40

**Porter, William Sydney** 1862-1910
See Henry, O.
See also CA 131; 104; CDALB 1865-1917;
DA; DA3; DAB; DAC; DAM MST; DLB
12, 78, 79; MTCW 1, 2; TUS; YABC 2

**Portillo (y Pacheco), Jose Lopez**
See Lopez Portillo (y Pacheco), Jose

**Portillo Trambley, Estela** 1927-1998 **HLC 2**
See Trambley, Estela Portillo
See also CANR 32; DAM MULT; DLB
209; HW 1

**Posey, Alexander (Lawrence)** 1873-1908
**NNAL**
See also CA 144; CANR 80; DAM MULT;
DLB 175

**Posse, Abel** **CLC 70**

**Post, Melville Davisson** 1869-1930 **TCLC 39**
See also CA 202; 110; CMW 4

**Potok, Chaim** 1929-2002 **CLC 2, 7, 14, 26,
112**
See also AAYA 15; AITN 1, 2; BPFB 3;
BYA 1; CA 208; 17-20R; CANR 19, 35,
64, 98; CN 7; DA3; DAM NOV; DLB 28,
152; EXPN; INT CANR-19; LAIT 4;
MTCW 1, 2; NFS 4; SATA 33, 106;
SATA-Obit 134; TUS; YAW

**Potok, Herbert Harold** -2002
See Potok, Chaim

**Potok, Herman Harold**
See Potok, Chaim

**Potter, Dennis (Christopher George)**
1935-1994 **CLC 58, 86, 123**
See also CA 145; 107; CANR 33, 61; CBD;
DLB 233; MTCW 1

**Pound, Ezra (Weston Loomis)** 1885-1972
**CLC 1, 2, 3, 4, 5, 7, 10, 13, 18, 34, 48,
50, 112; PC 4; WLC**
See also AAYA 47; AMW; AMWR 1; CA
37-40R; 5-8R; CANR 40; CDALB 1917-
1929; DA; DA3; DAB; DAC; DAM MST,
POET; DLB 4, 45, 63; DLBD 15; EFS 2;
EWL 3; EXPP; LMFS 2; MTCW 1, 2;
PAB; PFS 2, 8, 16; RGAL 4; TUS; WP

**Povod, Reinaldo** 1959-1994 **CLC 44**
See also CA 146; 136; CANR 83

**Powell, Adam Clayton, Jr.** 1908-1972 **BLC 3;
CLC 89**
See also BW 1, 3; CA 33-36R; 102; CANR
86; DAM MULT

**Powell, Anthony (Dymoke)** 1905-2000 **CLC
1, 3, 7, 9, 10, 31**
See also BRW 7; CA 189; 1-4R; CANR 1,
32, 62, 107; CDBLB 1945-1960; CN 7;
DLB 15; EWL 3; MTCW 1, 2; RGEL 2;
TEA

**Powell, Dawn** 1896(?)-1965 **CLC 66**
See also CA 5-8R; DLBY 1997

**Powell, Padgett** 1952- **CLC 34**
See also CA 126; CANR 63, 101; CSW;
DLB 234; DLBY 01

**Powell, (Oval) Talmage** 1920-2000
See Queen, Ellery
See also CA 5-8R; CANR 2, 80

**Power, Susan** 1961- **CLC 91**
See also BYA 14; CA 160; NFS 11

**Powers, J(ames) F(arl)** 1917-1999 **CLC 1, 4,
8, 57; SSC 4**
See also CA 181; 1-4R; CANR 2, 61; CN
7; DLB 130; MTCW 1; RGAL 4; RGSF
2

**Powers, John J(ames)** 1945-
See Powers, John R.
See also CA 69-72

**Powers, John R.** **CLC 66**
See Powers, John J(ames)

**Powers, Richard (S.)** 1957- **CLC 93**
See also AMWS 9; BPFB 3; CA 148;
CANR 80; CN 7

**Pownall, David** 1938- **CLC 10**
See also CA 89-92; 180; CAAS 18; CANR
49, 101; CBD; CD 5; CN 7; DLB 14

**Powys, John Cowper** 1872-1963 **CLC 7, 9,
15, 46, 125**
See also CA 85-88; CANR 106; DLB 15,
255; EWL 3; FANT; MTCW 1, 2; RGEL
2; SUFW

**Powys, T(heodore) F(rancis)** 1875-1953
**TCLC 9**
See also BRWS 8; CA 189; 106; DLB 36,
162; EWL 3; FANT; RGEL 2; SUFW

**Prado (Calvo), Pedro** 1886-1952 **TCLC 75**
See also CA 131; HW 1; LAW

**Prager, Emily** 1952- **CLC 56**
See also CA 204

**Pratolini, Vasco** 1913-1991 **TCLC 124**
See also DLB 177; EWL 3; RGWL 2, 3

**Pratt, E(dwin) J(ohn)** 1883(?)-1964 **CLC 19**
See also CA 93-96; 141; CANR 77; DAC;
DAM POET; DLB 92; EWL 3; RGEL 2;
TWA

**Premchand** **TCLC 21**
See Srivastava, Dhanpat Rai
See also EWL 3

**Preussler, Otfried** 1923- **CLC 17**
See also CA 77-80; SATA 24

**Prevert, Jacques (Henri Marie)** 1900-1977
**CLC 15**
See also CA 69-72; 77-80; CANR 29, 61;
DLB 258; EWL 3; GFL 1789 to the
Present; IDFW 3, 4; MTCW 1; RGWL 2,
3; SATA-Obit 30

**Prevost, (Antoine Francois)** 1697-1763 **LC 1**
See also EW 4; GFL Beginnings to 1789;
RGWL 2, 3

**Price, (Edward) Reynolds** 1933- **CLC 3, 6,
13, 43, 50, 63; SSC 22**
See also AMWS 6; CA 1-4R; CANR 1, 37,
57, 87; CN 7; CSW; DAM NOV; DLB 2,
218, 278; EWL 3; INT CANR-37

**Price, Richard** 1949- **CLC 6, 12**
See also CA 49-52; CANR 3; DLBY 1981

**Prichard, Katharine Susannah** 1883-1969
**CLC 46**
See also CA 11-12; CANR 33; CAP 1; DLB
260; MTCW 1; RGEL 2; RGSF 2; SATA
66

**Priestley, J(ohn) B(oynton)** 1894-1984 **CLC
2, 5, 9, 34**
See also BRW 7; CA 113; 9-12R; CANR
33; CDBLB 1914-1945; DA3; DAM
DRAM, NOV; DLB 10, 34, 77, 100, 139;
DLBY 1984; EWL 3; MTCW 1, 2; RGEL
2; SFW 4

**Prince** 1958(?)- **CLC 35**

**Prince, F(rank) T(empleton)** 1912- **CLC 22**
See also CA 101; CANR 43, 79; CP 7; DLB
20

**Prince Kropotkin**
See Kropotkin, Peter (Aleksieevich)

**Prior, Matthew** 1664-1721 **LC 4**
See also DLB 95; RGEL 2

**Prishvin, Mikhail** 1873-1954 **TCLC 75**
See Prishvin, Mikhail Mikhailovich

**Prishvin, Mikhail Mikhailovich**
See Prishvin, Mikhail
See also DLB 272; EWL 3
**Pritchard, William H(arrison)** 1932- **CLC 34**
See also CA 65-68; CANR 23, 95; DLB 111
**Pritchett, V(ictor) S(awdon)** 1900-1997 **CLC 5, 13, 15, 41; SSC 14**
See also BPFB 3; BRWS 3; CA 157; 61-64; CANR 31, 63; CN 7; DA3; DAM NOV; DLB 15, 139; EWL 3; MTCW 1, 2; RGEL 2; RGSF 2; TEA
**Private 19022**
See Manning, Frederic
**Probst, Mark** 1925- **CLC 59**
See also CA 130
**Prokosch, Frederic** 1908-1989 **CLC 4, 48**
See also CA 128; 73-76; CANR 82; DLB 48; MTCW 2
**Propertius, Sextus** c. 50B.C.-c. 16B.C. **CMLC 32**
See also AW 2; CDWLB 1; DLB 211; RGWL 2, 3
**Prophet, The**
See Dreiser, Theodore (Herman Albert)
**Prose, Francine** 1947- **CLC 45**
See also CA 112; 109; CANR 46, 95; DLB 234; SATA 101
**Proudhon**
See Cunha, Euclides (Rodrigues Pimenta) da
**Proulx, Annie**
See Proulx, E(dna) Annie
**Proulx, E(dna) Annie** 1935- **CLC 81, 158**
See also AMWS 7; BPFB 3; CA 145; CANR 65, 110; CN 7; CPW 1; DA3; DAM POP; MTCW 2
**Proust,**
**(Valentin-Louis-George-Eugene-)Marcel** 1871-1922 **TCLC 7, 13, 33; WLC**
See also BPFB 3; CA 120; 104; CANR 110; DA; DA3; DAB; DAC; DAM MST, NOV; DLB 65; EW 8; EWL 3; GFL 1789 to the Present; MTCW 1, 2; RGWL 2, 3; TWA
**Prowler, Harley**
See Masters, Edgar Lee
**Prus, Boleslaw** 1845-1912 **TCLC 48**
See also RGWL 2, 3
**Pryor, Richard (Franklin Lenox Thomas)** 1940- **CLC 26**
See also CA 152; 122
**Przybyszewski, Stanislaw** 1868-1927 **TCLC 36**
See also CA 160; DLB 66; EWL 3
**Pteleon**
See Grieve, C(hristopher) M(urray)
See also DAM POET
**Puckett, Lute**
See Masters, Edgar Lee
**Puig, Manuel** 1932-1990 **CLC 3, 5, 10, 28, 65, 133; HLC 2**
See also BPFB 3; CA 45-48; CANR 2, 32, 63; CDWLB 3; DA3; DAM MULT; DLB 113; DNFS 1; EWL 3; GLL 1; HW 1, 2; LAW; MTCW 1, 2; RGWL 2, 3; TWA; WLIT 1
**Pulitzer, Joseph** 1847-1911 **TCLC 76**
See also CA 114; DLB 23
**Purchas, Samuel** 1577(?)-1626 **LC 70**
See also DLB 151
**Purdy, A(lfred) W(ellington)** 1918-2000 **CLC 3, 6, 14, 50**
See also CA 189; 81-84; CAAS 17; CANR 42, 66; CP 7; DAM MST, POET; DLB 88; PFS 5; RGEL 2
**Purdy, James (Amos)** 1923- **CLC 2, 4, 10, 28, 52**
See also AMWS 7; CA 33-36R; CAAS 1; CANR 19, 51; CN 7; DLB 2, 218; EWL 3; INT CANR-19; MTCW 1; RGAL 4

**Pure, Simon**
See Swinnerton, Frank Arthur
**Pushkin, Aleksandr Sergeevich**
See Pushkin, Alexander (Sergeyevich)
See also DLB 205
**Pushkin, Alexander (Sergeyevich)** 1799-1837 **NCLC 3, 27, 83; PC 10; SSC 27, 55; WLC**
See Pushkin, Aleksandr Sergeevich
See also DA; DA3; DAB; DAC; DAM DRAM, MST, POET; EW 5; EXPS; RGSF 2; RGWL 2, 3; SATA 61; SSFS 9; TWA
**P'u Sung-ling** 1640-1715 **LC 49; SSC 31**
**Putnam, Arthur Lee**
See Alger, Horatio, Jr.
**Puzo, Mario** 1920-1999 **CLC 1, 2, 6, 36, 107**
See also BPFB 3; CA 185; 65-68; CANR 4, 42, 65, 99; CN 7; CPW; DA3; DAM NOV, POP; DLB 6; MTCW 1, 2; NFS 16; RGAL 4
**Pygge, Edward**
See Barnes, Julian (Patrick)
**Pyle, Ernest Taylor** 1900-1945
See Pyle, Ernie
See also CA 160; 115
**Pyle, Ernie TCLC 75**
See Pyle, Ernest Taylor
See also DLB 29; MTCW 2
**Pyle, Howard** 1853-1911 **TCLC 81**
See also BYA 2, 4; CA 137; 109; CLR 22; DLB 42, 188; DLBD 13; LAIT 1; MAICYA 1, 2; SATA 16, 100; WCH; YAW
**Pym, Barbara (Mary Crampton)** 1913-1980 **CLC 13, 19, 37, 111**
See also BPFB 3; BRWS 2; CA 97-100; 13-14; CANR 13, 34; CAP 1; DLB 14, 207; DLBY 1987; EWL 3; MTCW 1, 2; RGEL 2; TEA
**Pynchon, Thomas (Ruggles, Jr.)** 1937- **CLC 2, 3, 6, 9, 11, 18, 33, 62, 72, 123; SSC 14; WLC**
See also AMWS 2; BEST 90:2; BPFB 3; CA 17-20R; CANR 22, 46, 73; CN 7; CPW 1; DA; DA3; DAB; DAC; DAM MST, NOV, POP; DLB 2, 173; EWL 3; MTCW 1, 2; RGAL 4; SFW 4; TUS
**Pythagoras** c. 582B.C.-c. 507B.C. **CMLC 22**
See also DLB 176
**Q**
See Quiller-Couch, Sir Arthur (Thomas)
**Qian, Chongzhu**
See Ch'ien, Chung-shu
**Qian Zhongshu**
See Ch'ien, Chung-shu
**Qroll**
See Dagerman, Stig (Halvard)
**Quarrington, Paul (Lewis)** 1953- **CLC 65**
See also CA 129; CANR 62, 95
**Quasimodo, Salvatore** 1901-1968 **CLC 10**
See also CA 25-28R; 13-16; CAP 1; DLB 114; EW 12; MTCW 1; RGWL 2, 3
**Quatermass, Martin**
See Carpenter, John (Howard)
**Quay, Stephen** 1947- **CLC 95**
See also CA 189
**Quay, Timothy** 1947- **CLC 95**
See also CA 189
**Queen, Ellery CLC 3, 11**
See Dannay, Frederic; Davidson, Avram (James); Deming, Richard; Fairman, Paul W.; Flora, Fletcher; Hoch, Edward D(entinger); Kane, Henry; Lee, Manfred B(ennington); Marlowe, Stephen; Powell, (Oval) Talmage; Sheldon, Walter J(ames); Sturgeon, Theodore (Hamilton); Tracy, Don(ald Fiske); Vance, John Holbrook
See also BPFB 3; CMW 4; MSW; RGAL 4

**Queen, Ellery, Jr.**
See Dannay, Frederic; Lee, Manfred B(ennington)
**Queneau, Raymond** 1903-1976 **CLC 2, 5, 10, 42**
See also CA 69-72; 77-80; CANR 32; DLB 72, 258; EW 12; GFL 1789 to the Present; MTCW 1, 2; RGWL 2, 3
**Quevedo, Francisco de** 1580-1645 **LC 23**
**Quiller-Couch, Sir Arthur (Thomas)** 1863-1944 **TCLC 53**
See also CA 166; 118; DLB 135, 153, 190; HGG; RGEL 2; SUFW 1
**Quin, Ann (Marie)** 1936-1973 **CLC 6**
See also CA 45-48; 9-12R; DLB 14, 231
**Quincey, Thomas de**
See De Quincey, Thomas
**Quinn, Martin**
See Smith, Martin Cruz
**Quinn, Peter** 1947- **CLC 91**
See also CA 197
**Quinn, Simon**
See Smith, Martin Cruz
**Quintana, Leroy V.** 1944- **HLC 2; PC 36**
See also CA 131; CANR 65; DAM MULT; DLB 82; HW 1, 2
**Quiroga, Horacio (Sylvestre)** 1878-1937 **HLC 2; TCLC 20**
See also CA 131; 117; DAM MULT; HW 1; LAW; MTCW 1; RGSF 2; WLIT 1
**Quoirez, Francoise** 1935- **CLC 9**
See Sagan, Francoise
See also CA 49-52; CANR 6, 39, 73; CWW 2; MTCW 1, 2; TWA
**Raabe, Wilhelm (Karl)** 1831-1910 **TCLC 45**
See also CA 167; DLB 129
**Rabe, David (William)** 1940- **CLC 4, 8, 33; DC 16**
See also CA 85-88; CABS 3; CAD; CANR 59; CD 5; DAM DRAM; DFS 3, 8, 13; DLB 7, 228
**Rabelais, Francois** 1494-1553 **LC 5, 60; WLC**
See also DA; DAB; DAC; DAM MST; EW 2; GFL Beginnings to 1789; RGWL 2, 3; TWA
**Rabinovitch, Sholem** 1859-1916
See Aleichem, Sholom
See also CA 104
**Rabinyan, Dorit** 1972- **CLC 119**
See also CA 170
**Rachilde**
See Vallette, Marguerite Eymery
**Racine, Jean** 1639-1699 **LC 28**
See also DA3; DAB; DAM MST; DLB 268; EW 3; GFL Beginnings to 1789; RGWL 2, 3; TWA
**Radcliffe, Ann (Ward)** 1764-1823 **NCLC 6, 55, 106**
See also DLB 39, 178; HGG; RGEL 2; SUFW; WLIT 3
**Radclyffe-Hall, Marguerite**
See Hall, (Marguerite) Radclyffe
**Radiguet, Raymond** 1903-1923 **TCLC 29**
See also CA 162; DLB 65; GFL 1789 to the Present; RGWL 2, 3
**Radnoti, Miklos** 1909-1944 **TCLC 16**
See also CA 118; CDWLB 4; DLB 215; RGWL 2, 3
**Rado, James** 1939- **CLC 17**
See also CA 105
**Radvanyi, Netty** 1900-1983
See Seghers, Anna
See also CA 110; 85-88; CANR 82
**Rae, Ben**
See Griffiths, Trevor
**Raeburn, John (Hay)** 1941- **CLC 34**
See also CA 57-60
**Ragni, Gerome** 1942-1991 **CLC 17**
See also CA 134; 105

**Rahv, Philip CLC 24**
See Greenberg, Ivan
See also DLB 137

**Raimund, Ferdinand Jakob** 1790-1836
**NCLC 69**
See also DLB 90

**Raine, Craig (Anthony)** 1944- **CLC 32, 103**
See also CA 108; CANR 29, 51, 103; CP 7;
DLB 40; PFS 7

**Raine, Kathleen (Jessie)** 1908- **CLC 7, 45**
See also CA 85-88; CANR 46, 109; CP 7;
DLB 20; MTCW 1; RGEL 2

**Rainis, Janis** 1865-1929 **TCLC 29**
See also CA 170; CDWLB 4; DLB 220

**Rakosi, Carl CLC 47**
See Rawley, Callman
See also CAAS 5; CP 7; DLB 193

**Ralegh, Sir Walter**
See Raleigh, Sir Walter
See also BRW 1; RGEL 2; WP

**Raleigh, Richard**
See Lovecraft, H(oward) P(hillips)

**Raleigh, Sir Walter** 1554(?)-1618 **LC 31, 39;**
**PC 31**
See Ralegh, Sir Walter
See also CDBLB Before 1660; DLB 172;
EXPP; PFS 14; TEA

**Rallentando, H. P.**
See Sayers, Dorothy L(eigh)

**Ramal, Walter**
See de la Mare, Walter (John)

**Ramana Maharshi** 1879-1950 **TCLC 84**

**Ramoacn y Cajal, Santiago** 1852-1934 **TCLC**
**93**

**Ramon, Juan**
See Jimenez (Mantecon), Juan Ramon

**Ramos, Graciliano** 1892-1953 **TCLC 32**
See also CA 167; HW 2; LAW; WLIT 1

**Rampersad, Arnold** 1941- **CLC 44**
See also BW 2, 3; CA 133; 127; CANR 81;
DLB 111; INT 133

**Rampling, Anne**
See Rice, Anne
See also GLL 2

**Ramsay, Allan** 1686(?)-1758 **LC 29**
See also DLB 95; RGEL 2

**Ramsay, Jay**
See Campbell, (John) Ramsey

**Ramuz, Charles-Ferdinand** 1878-1947 **TCLC**
**33**
See also CA 165

**Rand, Ayn** 1905-1982 **CLC 3, 30, 44, 79;**
**WLC**
See also AAYA 10; AMWS 4; BPFB 3;
BYA 12; CA 105; 13-16R; CANR 27, 73;
CDALBS; CPW; DA; DA3; DAC; DAM
MST, NOV, POP; DLB 227, 279; MTCW
1, 2; NFS 10, 16; RGAL 4; SFW 4; TUS;
YAW

**Randall, Dudley (Felker)** 1914-2000 **BLC 3;**
**CLC 1, 135**
See also BW 1, 3; CA 189; 25-28R; CANR
23, 82; DAM MULT; DLB 41; PFS 5

**Randall, Robert**
See Silverberg, Robert

**Ranger, Ken**
See Creasey, John

**Rank, Otto** 1884-1939 **TCLC 115**

**Ransom, John Crowe** 1888-1974 **CLC 2, 4, 5,**
**11, 24**
See also AMW; CA 49-52; 5-8R; CANR 6,
34; CDALBS; DA3; DAM POET; DLB
45, 63; EXPP; MTCW 1, 2; RGAL 4;
TUS

**Rao, Raja** 1909- **CLC 25, 56**
See also CA 73-76; CANR 51; CN 7; DAM
NOV; MTCW 1, 2; RGEL 2; RGSF 2

**Raphael, Frederic (Michael)** 1931- **CLC 2,**
**14**
See also CA 1-4R; CANR 1, 86; CN 7;
DLB 14

**Ratcliffe, James P.**
See Mencken, H(enry) L(ouis)

**Rathbone, Julian** 1935- **CLC 41**
See also CA 101; CANR 34, 73

**Rattigan, Terence (Mervyn)** 1911-1977 **CLC**
**7; DC 18**
See also BRWS 7; CA 73-76; 85-88; CBD;
CDBLB 1945-1960; DAM DRAM; DFS
8; DLB 13; IDFW 3, 4; MTCW 1, 2;
RGEL 2

**Ratushinskaya, Irina** 1954- **CLC 54**
See also CA 129; CANR 68; CWW 2

**Raven, Simon (Arthur Noel)** 1927-2001 **CLC**
**14**
See also CA 197; 81-84; CANR 86; CN 7;
DLB 271

**Ravenna, Michael**
See Welty, Eudora (Alice)

**Rawley, Callman** 1903-
See Rakosi, Carl
See also CA 21-24R; CANR 12, 32, 91

**Rawlings, Marjorie Kinnan** 1896-1953 **TCLC**
**4**
See also AAYA 20; AMWS 10; ANW;
BPFB 3; BYA 3; CA 137; 104; CANR 74;
CLR 63; DLB 9, 22, 102; DLBD 17;
JRDA; MAICYA 1, 2; MTCW 2; RGAL
4; SATA 100; WCH; YABC 1; YAW

**Ray, Satyajit** 1921-1992 **CLC 16, 76**
See also CA 137; 114; DAM MULT

**Read, Herbert Edward** 1893-1968 **CLC 4**
See also BRW 6; CA 25-28R; 85-88; DLB
20, 149; PAB; RGEL 2

**Read, Piers Paul** 1941- **CLC 4, 10, 25**
See also CA 21-24R; CANR 38, 86; CN 7;
DLB 14; SATA 21

**Reade, Charles** 1814-1884 **NCLC 2, 74**
See also DLB 21; RGEL 2

**Reade, Hamish**
See Gray, Simon (James Holliday)

**Reading, Peter** 1946- **CLC 47**
See also BRWS 8; CA 103; CANR 46, 96;
CP 7; DLB 40

**Reaney, James** 1926- **CLC 13**
See also CA 41-44R; CAAS 15; CANR 42;
CD 5; CP 7; DAC; DAM MST; DLB 68;
RGEL 2; SATA 43

**Rebreanu, Liviu** 1885-1944 **TCLC 28**
See also CA 165; DLB 220

**Rechy, John (Francisco)** 1934- **CLC 1, 7, 14,**
**18, 107; HLC 2**
See also CA 5-8R; CAAE 195; CAAS 4;
CANR 6, 32, 64; CN 7; DAM MULT;
DLB 122, 278; DLBY 1982; HW 1, 2;
INT CANR-6; RGAL 4

**Redcam, Tom** 1870-1933 **TCLC 25**

**Reddin, Keith CLC 67**
See also CAD

**Redgrove, Peter (William)** 1932- **CLC 6, 41**
See also BRWS 6; CA 1-4R; CANR 3, 39,
77; CP 7; DLB 40

**Redmon, Anne CLC 22**
See Nightingale, Anne Redmon
See also DLBY 1986

**Reed, Eliot**
See Ambler, Eric

**Reed, Ishmael** 1938- **BLC 3; CLC 2, 3, 5, 6,**
**13, 32, 60**
See also AFAW 1, 2; AMWS 10; BPFB 3;
BW 2, 3; CA 21-24R; CANR 25, 48, 74;
CN 7; CP 7; CSW; DA3; DAM MULT;
DLB 2, 5, 33, 169, 227; DLBD 8; MSW;
MTCW 1, 2; PFS 6; RGAL 4; TCWW 2

**Reed, John (Silas)** 1887-1920 **TCLC 9**
See also CA 195; 106; TUS

**Reed, Lou CLC 21**
See Firbank, Louis

**Reese, Lizette Woodworth** 1856-1935 **PC 29**
See also CA 180; DLB 54

**Reeve, Clara** 1729-1807 **NCLC 19**
See also DLB 39; RGEL 2

**Reich, Wilhelm** 1897-1957 **TCLC 57**
See also CA 199

**Reid, Christopher (John)** 1949- **CLC 33**
See also CA 140; CANR 89; CP 7; DLB 40

**Reid, Desmond**
See Moorcock, Michael (John)

**Reid Banks, Lynne** 1929-
See Banks, Lynne Reid
See also CA 1-4R; CANR 6, 22, 38, 87;
CLR 24; CN 7; JRDA; MAICYA 1, 2;
SATA 22, 75, 111; YAW

**Reilly, William K.**
See Creasey, John

**Reiner, Max**
See Caldwell, (Janet Miriam) Taylor
(Holland)

**Reis, Ricardo**
See Pessoa, Fernando (Antonio Nogueira)

**Remarque, Erich Maria** 1898-1970 **CLC 21**
See also AAYA 27; BPFB 3; CA 29-32R;
77-80; CDWLB 2; DA; DA3; DAB;
DAC; DAM MST, NOV; DLB 56; EXPN;
LAIT 3; MTCW 1, 2; NFS 4; RGWL 2, 3

**Remington, Frederic** 1861-1909 **TCLC 89**
See also CA 169; 108; DLB 12, 186, 188;
SATA 41

**Remizov, A.**
See Remizov, Aleksei (Mikhailovich)

**Remizov, A. M.**
See Remizov, Aleksei (Mikhailovich)

**Remizov, Aleksei (Mikhailovich)** 1877-1957
**TCLC 27**
See also CA 133; 125

**Renan, Joseph Ernest** 1823-1892 **NCLC 26**
See also GFL 1789 to the Present

**Renard, Jules(-Pierre)** 1864-1910 **TCLC 17**
See also CA 202; 117; GFL 1789 to the
Present

**Renault, Mary CLC 3, 11, 17**
See Challans, Mary
See also BPFB 3; BYA 2; DLBY 1983;
GLL 1; LAIT 1; MTCW 2; RGEL 2;
RHW

**Rendell, Ruth (Barbara)** 1930- **CLC 28, 48**
See Vine, Barbara
See also BPFB 3; CA 109; CANR 32, 52,
74; CN 7; CPW; DAM POP; DLB 87,
276; INT CANR-32; MSW; MTCW 1, 2

**Renoir, Jean** 1894-1979 **CLC 20**
See also CA 85-88; 129

**Resnais, Alain** 1922- **CLC 16**

**Revard, Carter (Curtis)** 1931- **NNAL**
See also CA 144; CANR 81; PFS 5

**Reverdy, Pierre** 1889-1960 **CLC 53**
See also CA 89-92; 97-100; DLB 258; GFL
1789 to the Present

**Rexroth, Kenneth** 1905-1982 **CLC 1, 2, 6, 11,**
**22, 49, 112; PC 20**
See also BG 3; CA 107; 5-8R; CANR 14,
34, 63; CDALB 1941-1968; DAM POET;
DLB 16, 48, 165, 212; DLBY 1982; INT
CANR-14; MTCW 1, 2; RGAL 4

**Reyes, Alfonso** 1889-1959 **HLCS 2; TCLC 33**
See also CA 131; HW 1; LAW

**Reyes y Basoalto, Ricardo Eliecer Neftali**
See Neruda, Pablo

**Reymont, Wladyslaw (Stanislaw)**
1868(?)-1925 **TCLC 5**
See also CA 104

**Reynolds, Jonathan** 1942- **CLC 6, 38**
See also CA 65-68; CANR 28

**Reynolds, Joshua** 1723-1792 **LC 15**
See also DLB 104

**Reynolds, Michael S(hane)** 1937-2000 **CLC 44**
   See also CA 189; 65-68; CANR 9, 89, 97

**Reznikoff, Charles** 1894-1976 **CLC 9**
   See also CA 61-64; 33-36; CAP 2; DLB 28, 45; WP

**Rezzori (d'Arezzo), Gregor von** 1914-1998 **CLC 25**
   See also CA 167; 136; 122

**Rhine, Richard**
   See Silverstein, Alvin; Silverstein, Virginia B(arbara Opshelor)

**Rhodes, Eugene Manlove** 1869-1934 **TCLC 53**
   See also CA 198; DLB 256

**R'hoone, Lord**
   See Balzac, Honore de

**Rhys, Jean** 1894(?)-1979 **CLC 2, 4, 6, 14, 19, 51, 124; SSC 21**
   See also BRWS 2; CA 85-88; 25-28R; CANR 35, 62; CDBLB 1945-1960; CD-WLB 3; DA3; DAM NOV; DLB 36, 117, 162; DNFS 2; MTCW 1, 2; RGEL 2; RGSF 2; RHW; TEA

**Ribeiro, Darcy** 1922-1997 **CLC 34**
   See also CA 156; 33-36R

**Ribeiro, Joao Ubaldo (Osorio Pimentel)** 1941- **CLC 10, 67**
   See also CA 81-84

**Ribman, Ronald (Burt)** 1932- **CLC 7**
   See also CA 21-24R; CAD; CANR 46, 80; CD 5

**Ricci, Nino** 1959- **CLC 70**
   See also CA 137; CCA 1

**Rice, Anne** 1941- **CLC 41, 128**
   See Rampling, Anne
   See also AAYA 9; AMWS 7; BEST 89:2; BPFB 3; CA 65-68; CANR 12, 36, 53, 74, 100; CN 7; CPW; CSW; DA3; DAM POP; GLL 2; HGG; MTCW 2; SUFW 2; YAW

**Rice, Elmer (Leopold)** 1892-1967 **CLC 7, 49**
   See also CA 25-28R; 21-22; CAP 2; DAM DRAM; DFS 12; DLB 4, 7; MTCW 1, 2; RGAL 4

**Rice, Tim(othy Miles Bindon)** 1944- **CLC 21**
   See also CA 103; CANR 46; DFS 7

**Rich, Adrienne (Cecile)** 1929- **CLC 3, 6, 7, 11, 18, 36, 73, 76, 125; PC 5**
   See also AMWR 2; AMWS 1; CA 9-12R; CANR 20, 53, 74; CDALBS; CP 7; CSW; CWP; DA3; DAM POET; DLB 5, 67; EXPP; FW; MAWW; MTCW 1, 2; PAB; PFS 15; RGAL 4; WP

**Rich, Barbara**
   See Graves, Robert (von Ranke)

**Rich, Robert**
   See Trumbo, Dalton

**Richard, Keith CLC 17**
   See Richards, Keith

**Richards, David Adams** 1950- **CLC 59**
   See also CA 93-96; CANR 60, 110; DAC; DLB 53

**Richards, I(vor) A(rmstrong)** 1893-1979 **CLC 14, 24**
   See also BRWS 2; CA 89-92; 41-44R; CANR 34, 74; DLB 27; MTCW 2; RGEL 2

**Richards, Keith** 1943-
   See Richard, Keith
   See also CA 107; CANR 77

**Richardson, Anne**
   See Roiphe, Anne (Richardson)

**Richardson, Dorothy Miller** 1873-1957 **TCLC 3**
   See also CA 192; 104; DLB 36; FW; RGEL 2

**Richardson (Robertson), Ethel Florence Lindesay** 1870-1946
   See Richardson, Henry Handel
   See also CA 190; 105; DLB 230; RHW

**Richardson, Henry Handel TCLC 4**
   See Richardson (Robertson), Ethel Florence Lindesay
   See also DLB 197; RGEL 2; RGSF 2

**Richardson, John** 1796-1852 **NCLC 55**
   See also CCA 1; DAC; DLB 99

**Richardson, Samuel** 1689-1761 **LC 1, 44; WLC**
   See also BRW 3; CDBLB 1660-1789; DA; DAB; DAC; DAM MST, NOV; DLB 39; RGEL 2; TEA; WLIT 3

**Richardson, Willis** 1889-1977 **HR 3**
   See also BW 1; CA 124; DLB 51; SATA 60

**Richler, Mordecai** 1931-2001 **CLC 3, 5, 9, 13, 18, 46, 70**
   See also AITN 1; CA 201; 65-68; CANR 31, 62, 111; CCA 1; CLR 17; CWRI 5; DAC; DAM MST, NOV; DLB 53; MAI-CYA 1, 2; MTCW 1, 2; RGEL 2; SATA 44, 98; SATA-Brief 27; TWA

**Richter, Conrad (Michael)** 1890-1968 **CLC 30**
   See also AAYA 21; BYA 2; CA 25-28R; 5-8R; CANR 23; DLB 9, 212; LAIT 1; MTCW 1, 2; RGAL 4; SATA 3; TCWW 2; TUS; YAW

**Ricostranza, Tom**
   See Ellis, Trey

**Riddell, Charlotte** 1832-1906 **TCLC 40**
   See Riddell, Mrs. J. H.
   See also CA 165; DLB 156

**Riddell, Mrs. J. H.**
   See Riddell, Charlotte
   See also HGG; SUFW

**Ridge, John Rollin** 1827-1867 **NCLC 82; NNAL**
   See also CA 144; DAM MULT; DLB 175

**Ridgeway, Jason**
   See Marlowe, Stephen

**Ridgway, Keith** 1965- **CLC 119**
   See also CA 172

**Riding, Laura CLC 3, 7**
   See Jackson, Laura (Riding)
   See also RGAL 4

**Riefenstahl, Berta Helene Amalia** 1902-
   See Riefenstahl, Leni
   See also CA 108

**Riefenstahl, Leni CLC 16**
   See Riefenstahl, Berta Helene Amalia

**Riffe, Ernest**
   See Bergman, (Ernst) Ingmar

**Riggs, (Rolla) Lynn** 1899-1954 **NNAL; TCLC 56**
   See also CA 144; DAM MULT; DLB 175

**Riis, Jacob A(ugust)** 1849-1914 **TCLC 80**
   See also CA 168; 113; DLB 23

**Riley, James Whitcomb** 1849-1916 **TCLC 51**
   See also CA 137; 118; DAM POET; MAI-CYA 1, 2; RGAL 4; SATA 17

**Riley, Tex**
   See Creasey, John

**Rilke, Rainer Maria** 1875-1926 **PC 2; TCLC 1, 6, 19**
   See also CA 132; 104; CANR 62, 99; CD-WLB 2; DA3; DAM POET; DLB 81; EW 9; MTCW 1, 2; RGWL 2, 3; TWA; WP

**Rimbaud, (Jean Nicolas) Arthur** 1854-1891 **NCLC 4, 35, 82; PC 3; WLC**
   See also DA; DA3; DAB; DAC; DAM MST, POET; DLB 217; EW 7; GFL 1789 to the Present; RGWL 2, 3; TWA; WP

**Rinehart, Mary Roberts** 1876-1958 **TCLC 52**
   See also BPFB 3; CA 166; 108; RGAL 4; RHW

**Ringmaster, The**
   See Mencken, H(enry) L(ouis)

**Ringwood, Gwen(dolyn Margaret) Pharis** 1910-1984 **CLC 48**
   See also CA 112; 148; DLB 88

**Rio, Michel** 1945(?)- **CLC 43**
   See also CA 201

**Ritsos, Giannes**
   See Ritsos, Yannis

**Ritsos, Yannis** 1909-1990 **CLC 6, 13, 31**
   See also CA 133; 77-80; CANR 39, 61; EW 12; MTCW 1; RGWL 2, 3

**Ritter, Erika** 1948(?)- **CLC 52**
   See also CD 5; CWD

**Rivera, Jose Eustasio** 1889-1928 **TCLC 35**
   See also CA 162; HW 1, 2; LAW

**Rivera, Tomas** 1935-1984 **HLCS 2**
   See also CA 49-52; CANR 32; DLB 82; HW 1; RGAL 4; SSFS 15; TCWW 2; WLIT 1

**Rivers, Conrad Kent** 1933-1968 **CLC 1**
   See also BW 1; CA 85-88; DLB 41

**Rivers, Elfrida**
   See Bradley, Marion Zimmer
   See also GLL 1

**Riverside, John**
   See Heinlein, Robert A(nson)

**Rizal, Jose** 1861-1896 **NCLC 27**

**Roa Bastos, Augusto (Antonio)** 1917- **CLC 45; HLC 2**
   See also CA 131; DAM MULT; DLB 113; HW 1; LAW; RGSF 2; WLIT 1

**Robbe-Grillet, Alain** 1922- **CLC 1, 2, 4, 6, 8, 10, 14, 43, 128**
   See also BPFB 3; CA 9-12R; CANR 33, 65, 115; DLB 83; EW 13; GFL 1789 to the Present; IDFW 3, 4; MTCW 1, 2; RGWL 2, 3; SSFS 15

**Robbins, Harold** 1916-1997 **CLC 5**
   See also BPFB 3; CA 162; 73-76; CANR 26, 54, 112; DA3; DAM NOV; MTCW 1, 2

**Robbins, Thomas Eugene** 1936-
   See Robbins, Tom
   See also CA 81-84; CANR 29, 59, 95; CN 7; CPW; CSW; DA3; DAM NOV, POP; MTCW 1, 2

**Robbins, Tom CLC 9, 32, 64**
   See Robbins, Thomas Eugene
   See also AAYA 32; AMWS 10; BEST 90:3; BPFB 3; DLBY 1980; MTCW 2

**Robbins, Trina** 1938- **CLC 21**
   See also CA 128

**Roberts, Charles G(eorge) D(ouglas)** 1860-1943 **TCLC 8**
   See also CA 188; 105; CLR 33; CWRI 5; DLB 92; RGEL 2; RGSF 2; SATA 88; SATA-Brief 29

**Roberts, Elizabeth Madox** 1886-1941 **TCLC 68**
   See also CA 166; 111; CWRI 5; DLB 9, 54, 102; RGAL 4; RHW; SATA 33; SATA-Brief 27; WCH

**Roberts, Kate** 1891-1985 **CLC 15**
   See also CA 116; 107

**Roberts, Keith (John Kingston)** 1935-2000 **CLC 14**
   See also CA 25-28R; CANR 46; DLB 261; SFW 4

**Roberts, Kenneth (Lewis)** 1885-1957 **TCLC 23**
   See also CA 199; 109; DLB 9; RGAL 4; RHW

**Roberts, Michele (Brigitte)** 1949- **CLC 48**
   See also CA 115; CANR 58; CN 7; DLB 231; FW

**Robertson, Ellis**
   See Ellison, Harlan (Jay); Silverberg, Robert

**Robertson, Thomas William** 1829-1871
  **NCLC 35**
  See Robertson, Tom
  See also DAM DRAM
**Robertson, Tom**
  See Robertson, Thomas William
  See also RGEL 2
**Robeson, Kenneth**
  See Dent, Lester
**Robinson, Edwin Arlington** 1869-1935 **PC 1,
  35; TCLC 5, 101**
  See also AMW; CA 133; 104; CDALB
  1865-1917; DA; DAC; DAM MST,
  POET; DLB 54; EXPP; MTCW 1, 2;
  PAB; PFS 4; RGAL 4; WP
**Robinson, Henry Crabb** 1775-1867 **NCLC 15**
  See also DLB 107
**Robinson, Jill** 1936- **CLC 10**
  See also CA 102; INT 102
**Robinson, Kim Stanley** 1952- **CLC 34**
  See also AAYA 26; CA 126; CANR 113;
  CN 7; SATA 109; SCFW 2; SFW 4
**Robinson, Lloyd**
  See Silverberg, Robert
**Robinson, Marilynne** 1944- **CLC 25**
  See also CA 116; CANR 80; CN 7; DLB
  206
**Robinson, Smokey CLC 21**
  See Robinson, William, Jr.
**Robinson, William, Jr.** 1940-
  See Robinson, Smokey
  See also CA 116
**Robison, Mary** 1949- **CLC 42, 98**
  See also CA 116; 113; CANR 87; CN 7;
  DLB 130; INT 116; RGSF 2
**Rochester**
  See Wilmot, John
  See also RGEL 2
**Rod, Edouard** 1857-1910 **TCLC 52**
**Roddenberry, Eugene Wesley** 1921-1991
  See Roddenberry, Gene
  See also CA 135; 110; CANR 37; SATA 45;
  SATA-Obit 69
**Roddenberry, Gene CLC 17**
  See Roddenberry, Eugene Wesley
  See also AAYA 5; SATA-Obit 69
**Rodgers, Mary** 1931- **CLC 12**
  See also BYA 5; CA 49-52; CANR 8, 55,
  90; CLR 20; CWRI 5; INT CANR-8;
  JRDA; MAICYA 1, 2; SATA 8, 130
**Rodgers, W(illiam) R(obert)** 1909-1969 **CLC
  7**
  See also CA 85-88; DLB 20; RGEL 2
**Rodman, Eric**
  See Silverberg, Robert
**Rodman, Howard** 1920(?)-1985 **CLC 65**
  See also CA 118
**Rodman, Maia**
  See Wojciechowska, Maia (Teresa)
**Rodo, Jose Enrique** 1871(?)-1917 **HLCS 2**
  See also CA 178; HW 2; LAW
**Rodolph, Utto**
  See Ouologuem, Yambo
**Rodriguez, Claudio** 1934-1999 **CLC 10**
  See also CA 188; DLB 134
**Rodriguez, Richard** 1944- **CLC 155; HLC 2**
  See also CA 110; CANR 66, 116; DAM
  MULT; DLB 82, 256; HW 1, 2; LAIT 5;
  NCFS 3; WLIT 1
**Roelvaag, O(le) E(dvart)** 1876-1931
  See Rolvaag, O(le) E(dvart)
  See also CA 171; 117
**Roethke, Theodore (Huebner)** 1908-1963
  **CLC 1, 3, 8, 11, 19, 46, 101; PC 15**
  See also AMW; CA 81-84; CABS 2;
  CDALB 1941-1968; DA3; DAM POET;
  DLB 5, 206; EXPP; MTCW 1, 2; PAB;
  PFS 3; RGAL 4; WP

**Rogers, Carl R(ansom)** 1902-1987 **TCLC 125**
  See also CA 121; 1-4R; CANR 1, 18;
  MTCW 1
**Rogers, Samuel** 1763-1855 **NCLC 69**
  See also DLB 93; RGEL 2
**Rogers, Thomas Hunton** 1927- **CLC 57**
  See also CA 89-92; INT 89-92
**Rogers, Will(iam Penn Adair)** 1879-1935
  **NNAL; TCLC 8, 71**
  See also CA 144; 105; DA3; DAM MULT;
  DLB 11; MTCW 2
**Rogin, Gilbert** 1929- **CLC 18**
  See also CA 65-68; CANR 15
**Rohan, Koda**
  See Koda Shigeyuki
**Rohlfs, Anna Katharine Green**
  See Green, Anna Katharine
**Rohmer, Eric CLC 16**
  See Scherer, Jean-Marie Maurice
**Rohmer, Sax TCLC 28**
  See Ward, Arthur Henry Sarsfield
  See also DLB 70; MSW; SUFW
**Roiphe, Anne (Richardson)** 1935- **CLC 3, 9**
  See also CA 89-92; CANR 45, 73; DLBY
  1980; INT 89-92
**Rojas, Fernando de** 1475-1541 **HLCS 1; LC
  23**
  See also RGWL 2, 3
**Rojas, Gonzalo** 1917- **HLCS 2**
  See also CA 178; HW 2; LAWS 1
**Rolfe, Frederick (William Serafino Austin
  Lewis Mary)** 1860-1913 **TCLC 12**
  See Corvo, Baron
  See also CA 107; DLB 34, 156; RGEL 2
**Rolland, Romain** 1866-1944 **TCLC 23**
  See also CA 197; 118; DLB 65; GFL 1789
  to the Present; RGWL 2, 3
**Rolle, Richard** c. 1300-c. 1349 **CMLC 21**
  See also DLB 146; RGEL 2
**Rolvaag, O(le) E(dvart) TCLC 17**
  See Roelvaag, O(le) E(dvart)
  See also DLB 9, 212; NFS 5; RGAL 4
**Romain Arnaud, Saint**
  See Aragon, Louis
**Romains, Jules** 1885-1972 **CLC 7**
  See also CA 85-88; CANR 34; DLB 65;
  GFL 1789 to the Present; MTCW 1
**Romero, Jose Ruben** 1890-1952 **TCLC 14**
  See also CA 131; 114; HW 1; LAW
**Ronsard, Pierre de** 1524-1585 **LC 6, 54; PC
  11**
  See also EW 2; GFL Beginnings to 1789;
  RGWL 2, 3; TWA
**Rooke, Leon** 1934- **CLC 25, 34**
  See also CA 25-28R; CANR 23, 53; CCA
  1; CPW; DAM POP
**Roosevelt, Franklin Delano** 1882-1945 **TCLC
  93**
  See also CA 173; 116; LAIT 3
**Roosevelt, Theodore** 1858-1919 **TCLC 69**
  See also CA 170; 115; DLB 47, 186, 275
**Roper, William** 1498-1578 **LC 10**
**Roquelaure, A. N.**
  See Rice, Anne
**Rosa, Joao Guimaraes** 1908-1967 **CLC 23;
  HLCS 1**
  See also CA 89-92; DLB 113; WLIT 1
**Rose, Wendy** 1948- **CLC 85; NNAL; PC 13**
  See also CA 53-56; CANR 5, 51; CWP;
  DAM MULT; DLB 175; PFS 13; RGAL
  4; SATA 12
**Rosen, R. D.**
  See Rosen, Richard (Dean)
**Rosen, Richard (Dean)** 1949- **CLC 39**
  See also CA 77-80; CANR 62; CMW 4;
  INT CANR-30

**Rosenberg, Isaac** 1890-1918 **TCLC 12**
  See also BRW 6; CA 188; 107; DLB 20,
  216; PAB; RGEL 2
**Rosenblatt, Joe CLC 15**
  See Rosenblatt, Joseph
**Rosenblatt, Joseph** 1933-
  See Rosenblatt, Joe
  See also CA 89-92; CP 7; INT 89-92
**Rosenfeld, Samuel**
  See Tzara, Tristan
**Rosenstock, Sami**
  See Tzara, Tristan
**Rosenstock, Samuel**
  See Tzara, Tristan
**Rosenthal, M(acha) L(ouis)** 1917-1996 **CLC
  28**
  See also CA 152; 1-4R; CAAS 6; CANR 4,
  51; CP 7; DLB 5; SATA 59
**Ross, Barnaby**
  See Dannay, Frederic
**Ross, Bernard L.**
  See Follett, Ken(neth Martin)
**Ross, J. H.**
  See Lawrence, T(homas) E(dward)
**Ross, John Hume**
  See Lawrence, T(homas) E(dward)
**Ross, Martin** 1862-1915
  See Martin, Violet Florence
  See also DLB 135; GLL 2; RGEL 2; RGSF
  2
**Ross, (James) Sinclair** 1908-1996 **CLC 13;
  SSC 24**
  See also CA 73-76; CANR 81; CN 7; DAC;
  DAM MST; DLB 88; RGEL 2; RGSF 2;
  TCWW 2
**Rossetti, Christina (Georgina)** 1830-1894
  **NCLC 2, 50, 66; PC 7; WLC**
  See also BRW 5; BYA 4; DA; DA3; DAB;
  DAC; DAM MST, POET; DLB 35, 163,
  240; EXPP; MAICYA 1, 2; PFS 10, 14;
  RGEL 2; SATA 20; TEA; WCH
**Rossetti, Dante Gabriel** 1828-1882 **NCLC 4,
  77; PC 44; WLC**
  See also BRW 5; CDBLB 1832-1890; DA;
  DAB; DAC; DAM MST, POET; DLB 35;
  EXPP; RGEL 2; TEA
**Rossi, Cristina Peri**
  See Peri Rossi, Cristina
**Rossi, Jean Baptiste** 1931-
  See Japrisot, Sebastien
  See also CA 201
**Rossner, Judith (Perelman)** 1935- **CLC 6, 9,
  29**
  See also AITN 2; BEST 90:3; BPFB 3; CA
  17-20R; CANR 18, 51, 73; CN 7; DLB 6;
  INT CANR-18; MTCW 1, 2
**Rostand, Edmond (Eugene Alexis)**
  1868-1918 **DC 10; TCLC 6, 37**
  See also CA 126; 104; DA; DA3; DAB;
  DAC; DAM DRAM, MST; DFS 1; DLB
  192; LAIT 1; MTCW 1; RGWL 2, 3;
  TWA
**Roth, Henry** 1906-1995 **CLC 2, 6, 11, 104**
  See also AMWS 9; CA 149; 11-12; CANR
  38, 63; CAP 1; CN 7; DA3; DLB 28;
  MTCW 1, 2; RGAL 4
**Roth, (Moses) Joseph** 1894-1939 **TCLC 33**
  See also CA 160; DLB 85; RGWL 2, 3
**Roth, Philip (Milton)** 1933- **CLC 1, 2, 3, 4, 6,
  9, 15, 22, 31, 47, 66, 86, 119; SSC 26;
  WLC**
  See also AMWR 2; AMWS 3; BEST 90:3;
  BPFB 3; CA 1-4R; CANR 1, 22, 36, 55,
  89; CDALB 1968-1988; CN 7; CPW 1;
  DA; DA3; DAB; DAC; DAM MST, NOV,
  POP; DLB 2, 28, 173; DLBY 1982;
  MTCW 1, 2; RGAL 4; RGSF 2; SSFS 12;
  TUS

**Rothenberg, Jerome** 1931- **CLC 6, 57**
    See also CA 45-48; CANR 1, 106; CP 7;
    DLB 5, 193
**Rotter, Pat** ed. **CLC 65**
**Roumain, Jacques (Jean Baptiste)** 1907-1944
    **BLC 3; TCLC 19**
    See also BW 1; CA 125; 117; DAM MULT
**Rourke, Constance Mayfield** 1885-1941
    **TCLC 12**
    See also CA 200; 107; YABC 1
**Rousseau, Jean-Baptiste** 1671-1741 **LC 9**
**Rousseau, Jean-Jacques** 1712-1778 **LC 14,
    36; WLC**
    See also DA; DA3; DAB; DAC; DAM
    MST; EW 4; GFL Beginnings to 1789;
    RGWL 2, 3; TWA
**Roussel, Raymond** 1877-1933 **TCLC 20**
    See also CA 201; 117; GFL 1789 to the
    Present
**Rovit, Earl (Herbert)** 1927- **CLC 7**
    See also CA 5-8R; CANR 12
**Rowe, Elizabeth Singer** 1674-1737 **LC 44**
    See also DLB 39, 95
**Rowe, Nicholas** 1674-1718 **LC 8**
    See also DLB 84; RGEL 2
**Rowlandson, Mary** 1637(?)-1678 **LC 66**
    See also DLB 24, 200; RGAL 4
**Rowley, Ames Dorrance**
    See Lovecraft, H(oward) P(hillips)
**Rowling, J(oanne) K(athleen)** 1965- **CLC 137**
    See also AAYA 34; BYA 13, 14; CA 173;
    CLR 66, 80; MAICYA 2; SATA 109;
    SUFW 2
**Rowson, Susanna Haswell** 1762(?)-1824
    **NCLC 5, 69**
    See also DLB 37, 200; RGAL 4
**Roy, Arundhati** 1960(?)- **CLC 109**
    See also CA 163; CANR 90; DLBY 1997
**Roy, Gabrielle** 1909-1983 **CLC 10, 14**
    See also CA 110; 53-56; CANR 5, 61; CCA
    1; DAB; DAC; DAM MST; DLB 68;
    MTCW 1; RGWL 2, 3; SATA 104
**Royko, Mike** 1932-1997 **CLC 109**
    See also CA 157; 89-92; CANR 26, 111;
    CPW
**Rozanov, Vassili** 1856-1919 **TCLC 104**
**Rozewicz, Tadeusz** 1921- **CLC 9, 23, 139**
    See also CA 108; CANR 36, 66; CWW 2;
    DA3; DAM POET; DLB 232; MTCW 1,
    2; RGWL 3
**Ruark, Gibbons** 1941- **CLC 3**
    See also CA 33-36R; CAAS 23; CANR 14,
    31, 57; DLB 120
**Rubens, Bernice (Ruth)** 1923- **CLC 19, 31**
    See also CA 25-28R; CANR 33, 65; CN 7;
    DLB 14, 207; MTCW 1
**Rubin, Harold**
    See Robbins, Harold
**Rudkin, (James) David** 1936- **CLC 14**
    See also CA 89-92; CBD; CD 5; DLB 13
**Rudnik, Raphael** 1933- **CLC 7**
    See also CA 29-32R
**Ruffian, M.**
    See Hasek, Jaroslav (Matej Frantisek)
**Ruiz, Jose Martinez CLC 11**
    See Martinez Ruiz, Jose
**Rukeyser, Muriel** 1913-1980 **CLC 6, 10, 15,
    27; PC 12**
    See also AMWS 6; CA 93-96; 5-8R; CANR
    26, 60; DA3; DAM POET; DLB 48; FW;
    GLL 2; MTCW 1, 2; PFS 10; RGAL 4;
    SATA-Obit 22
**Rule, Jane (Vance)** 1931- **CLC 27**
    See also CA 25-28R; CAAS 18; CANR 12,
    87; CN 7; DLB 60; FW
**Rulfo, Juan** 1918-1986 **CLC 8, 80; HLC 2;
    SSC 25**
    See also CA 118; 85-88; CANR 26; CD-

WLB 3; DAM MULT; DLB 113; HW 1,
2; LAW; MTCW 1, 2; RGSF 2; RGWL 2,
3; WLIT 1
**Rumi, Jalal al-Din** 1207-1273 **CMLC 20; PC
45**
    See also RGWL 2, 3; WP
**Runeberg, Johan** 1804-1877 **NCLC 41**
**Runyon, (Alfred) Damon** 1884(?)-1946 **TCLC
10**
    See also CA 165; 107; DLB 11, 86, 171;
    MTCW 2; RGAL 4
**Rush, Norman** 1933- **CLC 44**
    See also CA 126; 121; INT 126
**Rushdie, (Ahmed) Salman** 1947- **CLC 23, 31,
    55, 100; WLCS**
    See also BEST 89:3; BPFB 3; BRWS 4;
    CA 111; 108; CANR 33, 56, 108; CN 7;
    CPW 1; DA3; DAB; DAC; DAM MST,
    NOV, POP; DLB 194; FANT; INT CA-
    111; LMFS 2; MTCW 1, 2; RGEL 2;
    RGSF 2; TEA; WLIT 4
**Rushforth, Peter (Scott)** 1945- **CLC 19**
    See also CA 101
**Ruskin, John** 1819-1900 **TCLC 63**
    See also BRW 5; BYA 5; CA 129; 114; CD-
    BLB 1832-1890; DLB 55, 163, 190;
    RGEL 2; SATA 24; TEA; WCH
**Russ, Joanna** 1937- **CLC 15**
    See also BPFB 3; CA 5-28R; CANR 11,
    31, 65; CN 7; DLB 8; FW; GLL 1;
    MTCW 1; SCFW 2; SFW 4
**Russ, Richard Patrick**
    See O'Brian, Patrick
**Russell, George William** 1867-1935
    See A.E.; Baker, Jean H.
    See also BRWS 8; CA 153; 104; CDBLB
    1890-1914; DAM POET; RGEL 2
**Russell, Jeffrey Burton** 1934- **CLC 70**
    See also CA 25-28R; CANR 11, 28, 52
**Russell, (Henry) Ken(neth Alfred)** 1927- **CLC
16**
    See also CA 105
**Russell, William Martin** 1947-
    See Russell, Willy
    See also CA 164; CANR 107
**Russell, Willy CLC 60**
    See Russell, William Martin
    See also CBD; CD 5; DLB 233
**Rutherford, Mark TCLC 25**
    See White, William Hale
    See also DLB 18; RGEL 2
**Ruyslinck, Ward CLC 14**
    See Belser, Reimond Karel Maria de
**Ryan, Cornelius (John)** 1920-1974 **CLC 7**
    See also CA 53-56; 69-72; CANR 38
**Ryan, Michael** 1946- **CLC 65**
    See also CA 49-52; CANR 109; DLBY
    1982
**Ryan, Tim**
    See Dent, Lester
**Rybakov, Anatoli (Naumovich)** 1911-1998
    **CLC 23, 53**
    See also CA 172; 135; 126; SATA 79;
    SATA-Obit 108
**Ryder, Jonathan**
    See Ludlum, Robert
**Ryga, George** 1932-1987 **CLC 14**
    See also CA 124; 101; CANR 43, 90; CCA
    1; DAC; DAM MST; DLB 60
**S. H.**
    See Hartmann, Sadakichi
**S. S.**
    See Sassoon, Siegfried (Lorraine)
**Saba, Umberto** 1883-1957 **TCLC 33**
    See also CA 144; CANR 79; DLB 114;
    RGWL 2, 3
**Sabatini, Rafael** 1875-1950 **TCLC 47**
    See also BPFB 3; CA 162; RHW

**Sabato, Ernesto (R.)** 1911- **CLC 10, 23; HLC
2**
    See also CA 97-100; CANR 32, 65; CD-
    WLB 3; DAM MULT; DLB 145; HW 1,
    2; LAW; MTCW 1, 2
**Sa-Carniero, Mario de** 1890-1916 **TCLC 83**
**Sacastru, Martin**
    See Bioy Casares, Adolfo
    See also CWW 2
**Sacher-Masoch, Leopold von** 1836(?)-1895
    **NCLC 31**
**Sachs, Marilyn (Stickle)** 1927- **CLC 35**
    See also AAYA 2; BYA 6; CA 17-20R;
    CANR 13, 47; CLR 2; JRDA; MAICYA
    1, 2; SAAS 2; SATA 3, 68; SATA-Essay
    110; WYA; YAW
**Sachs, Nelly** 1891-1970 **CLC 14, 98**
    See also CA 25-28R; 17-18; CANR 87;
    CAP 2; MTCW 2; RGWL 2, 3
**Sackler, Howard (Oliver)** 1929-1982 **CLC 14**
    See also CA 108; 61-64; CAD; CANR 30;
    DFS 15; DLB 7
**Sacks, Oliver (Wolf)** 1933- **CLC 67**
    See also CA 53-56; CANR 28, 50, 76;
    CPW; DA3; INT CANR-28; MTCW 1, 2
**Sadakichi**
    See Hartmann, Sadakichi
**Sade, Donatien Alphonse Francois**
    1740-1814 **NCLC 3, 47**
    See also EW 4; GFL Beginnings to 1789;
    RGWL 2, 3
**Sade, Marquis de**
    See Sade, Donatien Alphonse Francois
**Sadoff, Ira** 1945- **CLC 9**
    See also CA 53-56; CANR 5, 21, 109; DLB
    120
**Saetone**
    See Camus, Albert
**Safire, William** 1929- **CLC 10**
    See also CA 17-20R; CANR 31, 54, 91
**Sagan, Carl (Edward)** 1934-1996 **CLC 30,
    112**
    See also AAYA 2; CA 155; 25-28R; CANR
    11, 36, 74; CPW; DA3; MTCW 1, 2;
    SATA 58; SATA-Obit 94
**Sagan, Francoise CLC 3, 6, 9, 17, 36**
    See Quoirez, Francoise
    See also CWW 2; DLB 83; GFL 1789 to
    the Present; MTCW 2
**Sahgal, Nayantara (Pandit)** 1927- **CLC 41**
    See also CA 9-12R; CANR 11, 88; CN 7
**Said, Edward W.** 1935- **CLC 123**
    See also CA 21-24R; CANR 45, 74, 107;
    DLB 67; MTCW 2
**Saint, H(arry) F.** 1941- **CLC 50**
    See also CA 127
**St. Aubin de Teran, Lisa** 1953-
    See Teran, Lisa St. Aubin de
    See also CA 126; 118; CN 7; INT 126
**Saint Birgitta of Sweden** c. 1303-1373 **CMLC
24**
**Sainte-Beuve, Charles Augustin** 1804-1869
    **NCLC 5**
    See also DLB 217; EW 6; GFL 1789 to the
    Present
**Saint-Exupery, Antoine (Jean Baptiste
    Marie Roger) de** 1900-1944 **TCLC 2,
    56; WLC**
    See also BPFB 3; BYA 3; CA 132; 108;
    CLR 10; DA3; DAM NOV; DLB 72; EW
    12; GFL 1789 to the Present; LAIT 3;
    MAICYA 1, 2; MTCW 1, 2; RGWL 2, 3;
    SATA 20; TWA
**St. John, David**
    See Hunt, E(verette) Howard, (Jr.)
**St. John, J. Hector**
    See Crevecoeur, Michel Guillaume Jean de

DAM POP; DLB 10, 36, 77, 100; MSW; MTCW 1, 2; RGEL 2; SSFS 12; TEA

**Sayers, Valerie** 1952- **CLC 50, 122**
See also CA 134; CANR 61; CSW

**Sayles, John (Thomas)** 1950- **CLC 7, 10, 14**
See also CA 57-60; CANR 41, 84; DLB 44

**Scammell, Michael** 1935- **CLC 34**
See also CA 156

**Scannell, Vernon** 1922- **CLC 49**
See also CA 5-8R; CANR 8, 24, 57; CP 7; CWRI 5; DLB 27; SATA 59

**Scarlett, Susan**
See Streatfeild, (Mary) Noel

**Scarron** 1847-1910
See Mikszath, Kalman

**Schaeffer, Susan Fromberg** 1941- **CLC 6, 11, 22**
See also CA 49-52; CANR 18, 65; CN 7; DLB 28; MTCW 1, 2; SATA 22

**Schama, Simon (Michael)** 1945- **CLC 150**
See also BEST 89:4; CA 105; CANR 39, 91

**Schary, Jill**
See Robinson, Jill

**Schell, Jonathan** 1943- **CLC 35**
See also CA 73-76; CANR 12, 117

**Schelling, Friedrich Wilhelm Joseph von** 1775-1854 **NCLC 30**
See also DLB 90

**Scherer, Jean-Marie Maurice** 1920-
See Rohmer, Eric
See also CA 110

**Schevill, James (Erwin)** 1920- **CLC 7**
See also CA 5-8R; CAAS 12; CAD; CD 5

**Schiller, Friedrich von** 1759-1805 **DC 12; NCLC 39, 69**
See also CDWLB 2; DAM DRAM; DLB 94; EW 5; RGWL 2, 3; TWA

**Schisgal, Murray (Joseph)** 1926- **CLC 6**
See also CA 21-24R; CAD; CANR 48, 86; CD 5

**Schlee, Ann** 1934- **CLC 35**
See also CA 101; CANR 29, 88; SATA 44; SATA-Brief 36

**Schlegel, August Wilhelm von** 1767-1845 **NCLC 15**
See also DLB 94; RGWL 2, 3

**Schlegel, Friedrich** 1772-1829 **NCLC 45**
See also DLB 90; EW 5; RGWL 2, 3; TWA

**Schlegel, Johann Elias (von)** 1719(?)-1749 **LC 5**

**Schleiermacher, Friedrich** 1768-1834 **NCLC 107**
See also DLB 90

**Schlesinger, Arthur M(eier), Jr.** 1917- **CLC 84**
See also AITN 1; CA 1-4R; CANR 1, 28, 58, 105; DLB 17; INT CANR-28; MTCW 1, 2; SATA 61

**Schmidt, Arno (Otto)** 1914-1979 **CLC 56**
See also CA 109; 128; DLB 69

**Schmitz, Aron Hector** 1861-1928
See Svevo, Italo
See also CA 122; 104; MTCW 1

**Schnackenberg, Gjertrud (Cecelia)** 1953- **CLC 40; PC 45**
See also CA 116; CANR 100; CP 7; CWP; DLB 120; PFS 13

**Schneider, Leonard Alfred** 1925-1966
See Bruce, Lenny
See also CA 89-92

**Schnitzler, Arthur** 1862-1931 **DC 17; SSC 15; TCLC 4**
See also CA 104; CDWLB 2; DLB 81, 118; EW 8; RGSF 2; RGWL 2, 3

**Schoenberg, Arnold Franz Walter** 1874-1951 **TCLC 75**
See also CA 188; 109

**Schonberg, Arnold**
See Schoenberg, Arnold Franz Walter

**Schopenhauer, Arthur** 1788-1860 **NCLC 51**
See also DLB 90; EW 5

**Schor, Sandra (M.)** 1932(?)-1990 **CLC 65**
See also CA 132

**Schorer, Mark** 1908-1977 **CLC 9**
See also CA 73-76; 5-8R; CANR 7; DLB 103

**Schrader, Paul (Joseph)** 1946- **CLC 26**
See also CA 37-40R; CANR 41; DLB 44

**Schreber, Daniel** 1842-1911 **TCLC 123**

**Schreiner, Olive (Emilie Albertina)** 1855-1920 **TCLC 9**
See also AFW; BRWS 2; CA 154; 105; DLB 18, 156, 190, 225; FW; RGEL 2; TWA; WLIT 2

**Schulberg, Budd (Wilson)** 1914- **CLC 7, 48**
See also BPFB 3; CA 25-28R; CANR 19, 87; CN 7; DLB 6, 26, 28; DLBY 1981, 2001

**Schulman, Arnold**
See Trumbo, Dalton

**Schulz, Bruno** 1892-1942 **SSC 13; TCLC 5, 51**
See also CA 123; 115; CANR 86; CDWLB 4; DLB 215; MTCW 2; RGSF 2; RGWL 2, 3

**Schulz, Charles M(onroe)** 1922-2000 **CLC 12**
See also AAYA 39; CA 187; 9-12R; CANR 6; INT CANR-6; SATA 10; SATA-Obit 118

**Schumacher, E(rnst) F(riedrich)** 1911-1977 **CLC 80**
See also CA 73-76; 81-84; CANR 34, 85

**Schuyler, George Samuel** 1895-1977 **HR 3**
See also BW 2; CA 73-76; 81-84; CANR 42; DLB 29, 51

**Schuyler, James Marcus** 1923-1991 **CLC 5, 23**
See also CA 134; 101; DAM POET; DLB 5, 169; INT 101; WP

**Schwartz, Delmore (David)** 1913-1966 **CLC 2, 4, 10, 45, 87; PC 8**
See also AMWS 2; CA 25-28R; 17-18; CANR 35; CAP 2; DLB 28, 48; MTCW 1, 2; PAB; RGAL 4; TUS

**Schwartz, Ernst**
See Ozu, Yasujiro

**Schwartz, John Burnham** 1965- **CLC 59**
See also CA 132; CANR 116

**Schwartz, Lynne Sharon** 1939- **CLC 31**
See also CA 103; CANR 44, 89; DLB 218; MTCW 2

**Schwartz, Muriel A.**
See Eliot, T(homas) S(tearns)

**Schwarz-Bart, Andre** 1928- **CLC 2, 4**
See also CA 89-92; CANR 109

**Schwarz-Bart, Simone** 1938- **BLCS; CLC 7**
See also BW 2; CA 97-100; CANR 117

**Schwerner, Armand** 1927-1999 **PC 42**
See also CA 179; 9-12R; CANR 50, 85; CP 7; DLB 165

**Schwitters, Kurt (Hermann Edward Karl Julius)** 1887-1948 **TCLC 95**
See also CA 158

**Schwob, Marcel (Mayer Andre)** 1867-1905 **TCLC 20**
See also CA 168; 117; DLB 123; GFL 1789 to the Present

**Sciascia, Leonardo** 1921-1989 **CLC 8, 9, 41**
See also CA 130; 85-88; CANR 35; DLB 177; MTCW 1; RGWL 2, 3

**Scoppettone, Sandra** 1936- **CLC 26**
See Early, Jack
See also AAYA 11; BYA 8; CA 5-8R; CANR 41, 73; GLL 1; MAICYA 2; MAICYAS 1; SATA 9, 92; WYA; YAW

**Scorsese, Martin** 1942- **CLC 20, 89**
See also AAYA 38; CA 114; 110; CANR 46, 85

**Scotland, Jay**
See Jakes, John (William)

**Scott, Duncan Campbell** 1862-1947 **TCLC 6**
See also CA 153; 104; DAC; DLB 92; RGEL 2

**Scott, Evelyn** 1893-1963 **CLC 43**
See also CA 112; 104; CANR 64; DLB 9, 48; RHW

**Scott, F(rancis) R(eginald)** 1899-1985 **CLC 22**
See also CA 114; 101; CANR 87; DLB 88; INT CA-101; RGEL 2

**Scott, Frank**
See Scott, F(rancis) R(eginald)

**Scott, Joan CLC 65**

**Scott, Joanna** 1960- **CLC 50**
See also CA 126; CANR 53, 92

**Scott, Paul (Mark)** 1920-1978 **CLC 9, 60**
See also BRWS 1; CA 77-80; 81-84; CANR 33; DLB 14, 207; MTCW 1; RGEL 2; RHW

**Scott, Sarah** 1723-1795 **LC 44**
See also DLB 39

**Scott, Sir Walter** 1771-1832 **NCLC 15, 69, 110; PC 13; SSC 32; WLC**
See also AAYA 22; BRW 4; BYA 2; CD-BLB 1789-1832; DA; DAB; DAC; DAM MST, NOV, POET; DLB 93, 107, 116, 144, 159; HGG; LAIT 1; RGEL 2; RGSF 2; SSFS 10; SUFW 1; TEA; WLIT 3; YABC 2

**Scribe, (Augustin) Eugene** 1791-1861 **DC 5; NCLC 16**
See also DAM DRAM; DLB 192; GFL 1789 to the Present; RGWL 2, 3

**Scrum, R.**
See Crumb, R(obert)

**Scudery, Georges de** 1601-1667 **LC 75**
See also GFL Beginnings to 1789

**Scudery, Madeleine de** 1607-1701 **LC 2, 58**
See also DLB 268; GFL Beginnings to 1789

**Scum**
See Crumb, R(obert)

**Scumbag, Little Bobby**
See Crumb, R(obert)

**Seabrook, John**
See Hubbard, L(afayette) Ron(ald)

**Sealy, I(rwin) Allan** 1951- **CLC 55**
See also CA 136; CN 7

**Search, Alexander**
See Pessoa, Fernando (Antonio Nogueira)

**Sebastian, Lee**
See Silverberg, Robert

**Sebastian Owl**
See Thompson, Hunter S(tockton)

**Sebestyen, Igen**
See Sebestyen, Ouida

**Sebestyen, Ouida** 1924- **CLC 30**
See also AAYA 8; BYA 7; CA 107; CANR 40, 114; CLR 17; JRDA; MAICYA 1, 2; SAAS 10; SATA 39; WYA; YAW

**Secundus, H. Scriblerus**
See Fielding, Henry

**Sedges, John**
See Buck, Pearl S(ydenstricker)

**Sedgwick, Catharine Maria** 1789-1867 **NCLC 19, 98**
See also DLB 1, 74, 183, 239, 243, 254; RGAL 4

**Seelye, John (Douglas)** 1931- **CLC 7**
See also CA 97-100; CANR 70; INT 97-100; TCWW 2

**Seferiades, Giorgos Stylianou** 1900-1971
See Seferis, George
See also CA 33-36R; 5-8R; CANR 5, 36; MTCW 1

**Shelley, Percy Bysshe** 1792-1822 **NCLC 18, 93; PC 14; WLC**
See also BRW 4; BRWR 1; CDBLB 1789-1832; DA; DA3; DAB; DAC; DAM MST, POET; DLB 96, 110, 158; EXPP; PAB; PFS 2; RGEL 2; TEA; WLIT 3; WP

**Shepard, Jim** 1956- **CLC 36**
See also CA 137; CANR 59, 104; SATA 90

**Shepard, Lucius** 1947- **CLC 34**
See also CA 141; 128; CANR 81; HGG; SCFW 2; SFW 4; SUFW 2

**Shepard, Sam** 1943- **CLC 4, 6, 17, 34, 41, 44, 169; DC 5**
See also AAYA 1; AMWS 3; CA 69-72; CABS 3; CAD; CANR 22; CD 5; DA3; DAM DRAM; DFS 3, 6, 7, 14; DLB 7, 212; IDFW 3, 4; MTCW 1, 2; RGAL 4

**Shepherd, Michael**
See Ludlum, Robert

**Sherburne, Zoa (Lillian Morin)** 1912-1995 **CLC 30**
See also AAYA 13; CA 176; 1-4R; CANR 3, 37; MAICYA 1, 2; SAAS 18; SATA 3; YAW

**Sheridan, Frances** 1724-1766 **LC 7**
See also DLB 39, 84

**Sheridan, Richard Brinsley** 1751-1816 **DC 1; NCLC 5, 91; WLC**
See also BRW 3; CDBLB 1660-1789; DA; DAB; DAC; DAM DRAM, MST; DFS 15; DLB 89; WLIT 3

**Sherman, Jonathan Marc CLC 55**

**Sherman, Martin** 1941(?)- **CLC 19**
See also CA 123; 116; CAD; CANR 86; CD 5; DLB 228; GLL 1; IDTP

**Sherwin, Judith Johnson**
See Johnson, Judith (Emlyn)
See also CANR 85; CP 7; CWP

**Sherwood, Frances** 1940- **CLC 81**
See also CA 146

**Sherwood, Robert E(mmet)** 1896-1955 **TCLC 3**
See also CA 153; 104; CANR 86; DAM DRAM; DFS 17; DLB 7, 26, 249; IDFW 3, 4; RGAL 4

**Shestov, Lev** 1866-1938 **TCLC 56**

**Shevchenko, Taras** 1814-1861 **NCLC 54**

**Shiel, M(atthew) P(hipps)** 1865-1947 **TCLC 8**
See Holmes, Gordon
See also CA 160; 106; DLB 153; HGG; MTCW 2; SFW 4; SUFW

**Shields, Carol** 1935- **CLC 91, 113**
See also AMWS 7; CA 81-84; CANR 51, 74, 98; CCA 1; CN 7; CPW; DA3; DAC; MTCW 2

**Shields, David** 1956- **CLC 97**
See also CA 124; CANR 48, 99, 112

**Shiga, Naoya** 1883-1971 **CLC 33; SSC 23**
See Shiga Naoya
See also CA 33-36R; 101; MJW; RGWL 3

**Shiga Naoya**
See Shiga, Naoya
See also DLB 180; RGWL 3

**Shilts, Randy** 1951-1994 **CLC 85**
See also AAYA 19; CA 144; 127; 115; CANR 45; DA3; GLL 1; INT 127; MTCW 2

**Shimazaki, Haruki** 1872-1943
See Shimazaki Toson
See also CA 134; 105; CANR 84; RGWL 3

**Shimazaki Toson TCLC 5**
See Shimazaki, Haruki
See also DLB 180

**Sholokhov, Mikhail (Aleksandrovich)** 1905-1984 **CLC 7, 15**
See also CA 112; 101; DLB 272; MTCW 1, 2; RGWL 2, 3; SATA-Obit 36

**Shone, Patric**
See Hanley, James

**Showalter, Elaine** 1941- **CLC 169**
See also CA 57-60; CANR 58, 106; DLB 67; FW; GLL 2

**Shreve, Susan Richards** 1939- **CLC 23**
See also CA 49-52; CAAS 5; CANR 5, 38, 69, 100; MAICYA 1, 2; SATA 46, 95; SATA-Brief 41

**Shue, Larry** 1946-1985 **CLC 52**
See also CA 117; 145; DAM DRAM; DFS 7

**Shu-Jen, Chou** 1881-1936
See Lu Hsun
See also CA 104

**Shulman, Alix Kates** 1932- **CLC 2, 10**
See also CA 29-32R; CANR 43; FW; SATA 7

**Shusaku, Endo**
See Endo, Shusaku

**Shuster, Joe** 1914-1992 **CLC 21**

**Shute, Nevil CLC 30**
See Norway, Nevil Shute
See also BPFB 3; DLB 255; NFS 9; RHW; SFW 4

**Shuttle, Penelope (Diane)** 1947- **CLC 7**
See also CA 93-96; CANR 39, 84, 92, 108; CP 7; CWP; DLB 14, 40

**Sidhwa, Bapsy (N.)** 1938- **CLC 168**
See also CA 108; CANR 25, 57; CN 7; FW

**Sidney, Mary** 1561-1621 **LC 19, 39**
See Sidney Herbert, Mary

**Sidney, Sir Philip** 1554-1586 **LC 19, 39; PC 32**
See also BRW 1; BRWR 2; CDBLB Before 1660; DA; DA3; DAB; DAC; DAM MST, POET; DLB 167; EXPP; PAB; RGEL 2; TEA; WP

**Sidney Herbert, Mary**
See Sidney, Mary
See also DLB 167

**Siegel, Jerome** 1914-1996 **CLC 21**
See also CA 151; 169; 116

**Siegel, Jerry**
See Siegel, Jerome

**Sienkiewicz, Henryk (Adam Alexander Pius)** 1846-1916 **TCLC 3**
See also CA 134; 104; CANR 84; RGSF 2; RGWL 2, 3

**Sierra, Gregorio Martinez**
See Martinez Sierra, Gregorio

**Sierra, Maria (de la O'LeJarraga) Martinez**
See Martinez Sierra, Maria (de la O'LeJarraga)

**Sigal, Clancy** 1926- **CLC 7**
See also CA 1-4R; CANR 85; CN 7

**Sigourney, Lydia H.**
See Sigourney, Lydia Howard (Huntley)
See also DLB 73, 183

**Sigourney, Lydia Howard (Huntley)** 1791-1865 **NCLC 21, 87**
See Sigourney, Lydia H.; Sigourney, Lydia Huntley
See also DLB 1

**Sigourney, Lydia Huntley**
See Sigourney, Lydia Howard (Huntley)
See also DLB 42, 239, 243

**Siguenza y Gongora, Carlos de** 1645-1700 **HLCS 2; LC 8**
See also LAW

**Sigurjonsson, Johann** 1880-1919 **TCLC 27**
See also CA 170

**Sikelianos, Angelos** 1884-1951 **PC 29; TCLC 39**
See also RGWL 2, 3

**Silkin, Jon** 1930-1997 **CLC 2, 6, 43**
See also CA 5-8R; CAAS 5; CANR 89; CP 7; DLB 27

**Silko, Leslie (Marmon)** 1948- **CLC 23, 74, 114; NNAL; SSC 37; WLCS**
See also AAYA 14; AMWS 4; ANW; BYA 12; CA 122; 115; CANR 45, 65; CN 7; CP 7; CPW 1; CWP; DA; DA3; DAC; DAM MST, MULT, POP; DLB 143, 175, 256, 275; EXPP; EXPS; LAIT 4; MTCW 2; NFS 4; PFS 9, 16; RGAL 4; RGSF 2; SSFS 4, 8, 10, 11

**Sillanpaa, Frans Eemil** 1888-1964 **CLC 19**
See also CA 93-96; 129; MTCW 1

**Sillitoe, Alan** 1928- **CLC 1, 3, 6, 10, 19, 57, 148**
See also AITN 1; BRWS 5; CA 9-12R; CAAE 191; CAAS 2; CANR 8, 26, 55; CDBLB 1960 to Present; CN 7; DLB 14, 139; MTCW 1, 2; RGEL 2; RGSF 2; SATA 61

**Silone, Ignazio** 1900-1978 **CLC 4**
See also CA 81-84; 25-28; CANR 34; CAP 2; DLB 264; EW 12; MTCW 1; RGSF 2; RGWL 2, 3

**Silone, Ignazione**
See Silone, Ignazio

**Silva, Jose Asuncion**
See da Silva, Antonio Jose
See also LAW

**Silver, Joan Micklin** 1935- **CLC 20**
See also CA 121; 114; INT 121

**Silver, Nicholas**
See Faust, Frederick (Schiller)
See also TCWW 2

**Silverberg, Robert** 1935- **CLC 7, 140**
See also AAYA 24; BPFB 3; BYA 7, 9; CA 1-4R, 186; CAAE 186; CAAS 3; CANR 1, 20, 36, 85; CLR 59; CN 7; CPW; DAM POP; DLB 8; INT CANR-20; MAICYA 1, 2; MTCW 1, 2; SATA 13, 91; SATA-Essay 104; SCFW 2; SFW 4; SUFW 2

**Silverstein, Alvin** 1933- **CLC 17**
See also CA 49-52; CANR 2; CLR 25; JRDA; MAICYA 1, 2; SATA 8, 69, 124

**Silverstein, Virginia B(arbara Opshelor)** 1937- **CLC 17**
See also CA 49-52; CANR 2; CLR 25; JRDA; MAICYA 1, 2; SATA 8, 69, 124

**Sim, Georges**
See Simenon, Georges (Jacques Christian)

**Simak, Clifford D(onald)** 1904-1988 **CLC 1, 55**
See also CA 125; 1-4R; CANR 1, 35; DLB 8; MTCW 1; SATA-Obit 56; SFW 4

**Simenon, Georges (Jacques Christian)** 1903-1989 **CLC 1, 2, 3, 8, 18, 47**
See also BPFB 3; CA 129; 85-88; CANR 35; CMW 4; DA3; DAM POP; DLB 72; DLBY 1989; EW 12; GFL 1789 to the Present; MSW; MTCW 1, 2; RGWL 2, 3

**Simic, Charles** 1938- **CLC 6, 9, 22, 49, 68, 130**
See also AMWS 8; CA 29-32R; CAAS 4; CANR 12, 33, 52, 61, 96; CP 7; DA3; DAM POET; DLB 105; MTCW 2; PFS 7; RGAL 4; WP

**Simmel, Georg** 1858-1918 **TCLC 64**
See also CA 157

**Simmons, Charles (Paul)** 1924- **CLC 57**
See also CA 89-92; INT 89-92

**Simmons, Dan** 1948- **CLC 44**
See also AAYA 16; CA 138; CANR 53, 81; CPW; DAM POP; HGG; SUFW 2

**Simmons, James (Stewart Alexander)** 1933- **CLC 43**
See also CA 105; CAAS 21; CP 7; DLB 40

**Simms, William Gilmore** 1806-1870 **NCLC 3**
See also DLB 3, 30, 59, 73, 248, 254; RGAL 4

**Simon, Carly** 1945- **CLC 26**
See also CA 105

**Simon, Claude (Henri Eugene)** 1913-1984
**CLC 4, 9, 15, 39**
See also CA 89-92; CANR 33, 117; DAM
NOV; DLB 83; EW 13; GFL 1789 to the
Present; MTCW 1

**Simon, Myles**
See Follett, Ken(neth Martin)

**Simon, (Marvin) Neil** 1927- **CLC 6, 11, 31,
39, 70; DC 14**
See also AAYA 32; AITN 1; AMWS 4; CA
21-24R; CANR 26, 54, 87; CD 5; DA3;
DAM DRAM; DFS 2, 6, 12; DLB 7, 266;
LAIT 4; MTCW 1, 2; RGAL 4; TUS

**Simon, Paul (Frederick)** 1941(?)- **CLC 17**
See also CA 153; 116

**Simonon, Paul** 1956(?)- **CLC 30**

**Simonson, Rick ed. CLC 70**

**Simpson, Harriette**
See Arnow, Harriette (Louisa) Simpson

**Simpson, Louis (Aston Marantz)** 1923- **CLC
4, 7, 9, 32, 149**
See also AMWS 9; CA 1-4R; CAAS 4;
CANR 1, 61; CP 7; DAM POET; DLB 5;
MTCW 1, 2; PFS 7, 11, 14; RGAL 4

**Simpson, Mona (Elizabeth)** 1957- **CLC 44,
146**
See also CA 135; 122; CANR 68, 103; CN
7

**Simpson, N(orman) F(rederick)** 1919- **CLC
29**
See also CA 13-16R; CBD; DLB 13; RGEL
2

**Sinclair, Andrew (Annandale)** 1935- **CLC 2,
14**
See also CA 9-12R; CAAS 5; CANR 14,
38, 91; CN 7; DLB 14; FANT; MTCW 1

**Sinclair, Emil**
See Hesse, Hermann

**Sinclair, Iain** 1943- **CLC 76**
See also CA 132; CANR 81; CP 7; HGG

**Sinclair, Iain MacGregor**
See Sinclair, Iain

**Sinclair, Irene**
See Griffith, D(avid Lewelyn) W(ark)

**Sinclair, Mary Amelia St. Clair** 1865(?)-1946
See Sinclair, May
See also CA 104; HGG; RHW

**Sinclair, May TCLC 3, 11**
See Sinclair, Mary Amelia St. Clair
See also CA 166; DLB 36, 135; RGEL 2;
SUFW

**Sinclair, Roy**
See Griffith, D(avid Lewelyn) W(ark)

**Sinclair, Upton (Beall)** 1878-1968 **CLC 1, 11,
15, 63; WLC**
See also AMWS 5; BPFB 3; BYA 2; CA
25-28R; 5-8R; CANR 7; CDALB 1929-
1941; DA; DA3; DAB; DAC; DAM MST,
NOV; DLB 9; INT CANR-7; LAIT 3;
MTCW 1, 2; NFS 6; RGAL 4; SATA 9;
TUS; YAW

**Singe, (Edmund) J(ohn) M(illington)**
1871-1909 **WLC**

**Singer, Isaac**
See Singer, Isaac Bashevis

**Singer, Isaac Bashevis** 1904-1991 **CLC 1, 3,
6, 9, 11, 15, 23, 38, 69, 111; SSC 3, 53;
WLC**
See also AAYA 32; AITN 1, 2; AMW;
AMWR 2; BPFB 3; BYA 1, 4; CA 134;
1-4R; CANR 1, 39, 106; CDALB 1941-
1968; CLR 1; CWRI 5; DA; DA3; DAB;
DAC; DAM MST, NOV; DLB 6, 28, 52,
278; DLBY 1991; EXPS; HGG; JRDA;
LAIT 3; MAICYA 1, 2; MTCW 1, 2;
RGAL 4; RGSF 2; SATA 3, 27; SATA-
Obit 68; SSFS 2, 12, 16; TUS; TWA

**Singer, Israel Joshua** 1893-1944 **TCLC 33**
See also CA 169

**Singh, Khushwant** 1915- **CLC 11**
See also CA 9-12R; CAAS 9; CANR 6, 84;
CN 7; RGEL 2

**Singleton, Ann**
See Benedict, Ruth (Fulton)

**Singleton, John** 1968(?)- **CLC 156**
See also BW 2, 3; CA 138; CANR 67, 82;
DAM MULT

**Sinjohn, John**
See Galsworthy, John

**Sinyavsky, Andrei (Donatevich)** 1925-1997
**CLC 8**
See Tertz, Abram
See also CA 159; 85-88

**Sirin, V.**
See Nabokov, Vladimir (Vladimirovich)

**Sissman, L(ouis) E(dward)** 1928-1976 **CLC
9, 18**
See also CA 65-68; 21-24R; CANR 13;
DLB 5

**Sisson, C(harles) H(ubert)** 1914- **CLC 8**
See also CA 1-4R; CAAS 3; CANR 3, 48,
84; CP 7; DLB 27

**Sitting Bull** 1831(?)-1890 **NNAL**
See also DA3; DAM MULT

**Sitwell, Dame Edith** 1887-1964 **CLC 2, 9, 67;
PC 3**
See also BRW 7; CA 9-12R; CANR 35;
CDBLB 1945-1960; DAM POET; DLB
20; MTCW 1, 2; RGEL 2; TEA

**Siwaarmill, H. P.**
See Sharp, William

**Sjoewall, Maj** 1935- **CLC 7**
See Sjowall, Maj
See also CA 65-68; CANR 73

**Sjowall, Maj**
See Sjoewall, Maj
See also BPFB 3; CMW 4; MSW

**Skelton, John** 1460(?)-1529 **LC 71; PC 25**
See also BRW 1; DLB 136; RGEL 2

**Skelton, Robin** 1925-1997 **CLC 13**
See Zuk, Georges
See also AITN 2; CA 160; 5-8R; CAAS 5;
CANR 28, 89; CCA 1; CP 7; DLB 27, 53

**Skolimowski, Jerzy** 1938- **CLC 20**
See also CA 128

**Skram, Amalie (Bertha)** 1847-1905 **TCLC 25**
See also CA 165

**Skvorecky, Josef (Vaclav)** 1924- **CLC 15, 39,
69, 152**
See also CA 61-64; CAAS 1; CANR 10,
34, 63, 108; CDWLB 4; DA3; DAC;
DAM NOV; DLB 232; MTCW 1, 2

**Slade, Bernard CLC 11, 46**
See Newbound, Bernard Slade
See also CAAS 9; CCA 1; DLB 53

**Slaughter, Carolyn** 1946- **CLC 56**
See also CA 85-88; CANR 85; CN 7

**Slaughter, Frank G(ill)** 1908-2001 **CLC 29**
See also AITN 2; CA 197; 5-8R; CANR 5,
85; INT CANR-5; RHW

**Slavitt, David R(ytman)** 1935- **CLC 5, 14**
See also CA 21-24R; CAAS 3; CANR 41,
83; CP 7; DLB 5, 6

**Slesinger, Tess** 1905-1945 **TCLC 10**
See also CA 199; 107; DLB 102

**Slessor, Kenneth** 1901-1971 **CLC 14**
See also CA 89-92; 102; DLB 260; RGEL
2

**Slowacki, Juliusz** 1809-1849 **NCLC 15**
See also RGWL 3

**Smart, Christopher** 1722-1771 **LC 3; PC 13**
See also DAM POET; DLB 109; RGEL 2

**Smart, Elizabeth** 1913-1986 **CLC 54**
See also CA 118; 81-84; DLB 88

**Smiley, Jane (Graves)** 1949- **CLC 53, 76, 144**
See also AMWS 6; BPFB 3; CA 104;
CANR 30, 50, 74, 96; CN 7; CPW 1;
DA3; DAM POP; DLB 227, 234; INT
CANR-30

**Smith, A(rthur) J(ames) M(arshall)**
1902-1980 **CLC 15**
See also CA 102; 1-4R; CANR 4; DAC;
DLB 88; RGEL 2

**Smith, Adam** 1723(?)-1790 **LC 36**
See also DLB 104, 252; RGEL 2

**Smith, Alexander** 1829-1867 **NCLC 59**
See also DLB 32, 55

**Smith, Anna Deavere** 1950- **CLC 86**
See also CA 133; CANR 103; CD 5; DFS 2

**Smith, Betty (Wehner)** 1904-1972 **CLC 19**
See also BPFB 3; BYA 3; CA 33-36R;
5-8R; DLBY 1982; LAIT 3; RGAL 4;
SATA 6

**Smith, Charlotte (Turner)** 1749-1806 **NCLC
23, 115**
See also DLB 39, 109; RGEL 2; TEA

**Smith, Clark Ashton** 1893-1961 **CLC 43**
See also CA 143; CANR 81; FANT; HGG;
MTCW 2; SCFW 2; SFW 4; SUFW

**Smith, Dave CLC 22, 42**
See Smith, David (Jeddie)
See also CAAS 7; DLB 5

**Smith, David (Jeddie)** 1942-
See Smith, Dave
See also CA 49-52; CANR 1, 59; CP 7;
CSW; DAM POET

**Smith, Florence Margaret** 1902-1971
See Smith, Stevie
See also CA 29-32R; 17-18; CANR 35;
CAP 2; DAM POET; MTCW 1, 2; TEA

**Smith, Iain Crichton** 1928-1998 **CLC 64**
See also CA 171; 21-24R; CN 7; CP 7; DLB
40, 139; RGSF 2

**Smith, John** 1580(?)-1631 **LC 9**
See also DLB 24, 30; TUS

**Smith, Johnston**
See Crane, Stephen (Townley)

**Smith, Joseph, Jr.** 1805-1844 **NCLC 53**

**Smith, Lee** 1944- **CLC 25, 73**
See also CA 119; 114; CANR 46; CSW;
DLB 143; DLBY 1983; INT CA-119;
RGAL 4

**Smith, Martin**
See Smith, Martin Cruz

**Smith, Martin Cruz** 1942- **CLC 25; NNAL**
See also BEST 89:4; BPFB 3; CA 85-88;
CANR 6, 23, 43, 65; CMW 4; CPW;
DAM MULT, POP; HGG; INT CANR-
23; MTCW 2; RGAL 4

**Smith, Patti** 1946- **CLC 12**
See also CA 93-96; CANR 63

**Smith, Pauline (Urmson)** 1882-1959 **TCLC
25**
See also DLB 225

**Smith, Rosamond**
See Oates, Joyce Carol

**Smith, Sheila Kaye**
See Kaye-Smith, Sheila

**Smith, Stevie CLC 3, 8, 25, 44; PC 12**
See Smith, Florence Margaret
See also BRWS 2; DLB 20; MTCW 2;
PAB; PFS 3; RGEL 2

**Smith, Wilbur (Addison)** 1933- **CLC 33**
See also CA 13-16R; CANR 7, 46, 66;
CPW; MTCW 1, 2

**Smith, William Jay** 1918- **CLC 6**
See also CA 5-8R; CANR 44, 106; CP 7;
CSW; CWRI 5; DLB 5; MAICYA 1, 2;
SAAS 22; SATA 2, 68

**Smith, Woodrow Wilson**
See Kuttner, Henry

**Smith, Zadie** 1976- **CLC 158**
See also CA 193

**Spoto, Donald** 1941- **CLC 39**
See also CA 65-68; CANR 11, 57, 93
**Springsteen, Bruce (F.)** 1949- **CLC 17**
See also CA 111
**Spurling, Hilary** 1940- **CLC 34**
See also CA 104; CANR 25, 52, 94
**Spyker, John Howland**
See Elman, Richard (Martin)
**Squires, (James) Radcliffe** 1917-1993 **CLC 51**
See also CA 140; 1-4R; CANR 6, 21
**Srivastava, Dhanpat Rai** 1880(?)-1936
See Premchand
See also CA 197; 118
**Stacy, Donald**
See Pohl, Frederik
**Stael**
See Stael-Holstein, Anne Louise Germaine Necker
See also EW 5; RGWL 2, 3
**Stael, Germaine de**
See Stael-Holstein, Anne Louise Germaine Necker
See also DLB 119, 192; FW; GFL 1789 to the Present; TWA
**Stael-Holstein, Anne Louise Germaine Necker** 1766-1817 **NCLC 3, 91**
See Stael; Stael, Germaine de
**Stafford, Jean** 1915-1979 **CLC 4, 7, 19, 68; SSC 26**
See also CA 85-88; 1-4R; CANR 3, 65; DLB 2, 173; MTCW 1, 2; RGAL 4; RGSF 2; SATA-Obit 22; TCWW 2; TUS
**Stafford, William (Edgar)** 1914-1993 **CLC 4, 7, 29**
See also AMWS 11; CA 142; 5-8R; CAAS 3; CANR 5, 22; DAM POET; DLB 5, 206; EXPP; INT CANR-22; PFS 2, 8, 16; RGAL 4; WP
**Stagnelius, Eric Johan** 1793-1823 **NCLC 61**
**Staines, Trevor**
See Brunner, John (Kilian Houston)
**Stairs, Gordon**
See Austin, Mary (Hunter)
See also TCWW 2
**Stalin, Joseph** 1879-1953 **TCLC 92**
**Stampa, Gaspara** c. 1524-1554 **PC 43**
See also RGWL 2, 3
**Stampflinger, K. A.**
See Benjamin, Walter
**Stancykowna**
See Szymborska, Wislawa
**Standing Bear, Luther** 1868(?)-1939(?) **NNAL**
See also CA 144; 113; DAM MULT
**Stannard, Martin** 1947- **CLC 44**
See also CA 142; DLB 155
**Stanton, Elizabeth Cady** 1815-1902 **TCLC 73**
See also CA 171; DLB 79; FW
**Stanton, Maura** 1946- **CLC 9**
See also CA 89-92; CANR 15; DLB 120
**Stanton, Schuyler**
See Baum, L(yman) Frank
**Stapledon, (William) Olaf** 1886-1950 **TCLC 22**
See also CA 162; 111; DLB 15, 255; SFW 4
**Starbuck, George (Edwin)** 1931-1996 **CLC 53**
See also CA 153; 21-24R; CANR 23; DAM POET
**Stark, Richard**
See Westlake, Donald E(dwin)
**Staunton, Schuyler**
See Baum, L(yman) Frank

**Stead, Christina (Ellen)** 1902-1983 **CLC 2, 5, 8, 32, 80**
See also BRWS 4; CA 109; 13-16R; CANR 33, 40; DLB 260; FW; MTCW 1, 2; RGEL 2; RGSF 2
**Stead, William Thomas** 1849-1912 **TCLC 48**
See also CA 167
**Stebnitsky, M.**
See Leskov, Nikolai (Semyonovich)
**Steele, Sir Richard** 1672-1729 **LC 18**
See also BRW 3; CDBLB 1660-1789; DLB 84, 101; RGEL 2; WLIT 3
**Steele, Timothy (Reid)** 1948- **CLC 45**
See also CA 93-96; CANR 16, 50, 92; CP 7; DLB 120
**Steffens, (Joseph) Lincoln** 1866-1936 **TCLC 20**
See also CA 198; 117
**Stegner, Wallace (Earle)** 1909-1993 **CLC 9, 49, 81; SSC 27**
See also AITN 1; AMWS 4; ANW; BEST 90:3; BPFB 3; CA 141; 1-4R; CAAS 9; CANR 1, 21, 46; DAM NOV; DLB 9, 206, 275; DLBY 1993; MTCW 1, 2; RGAL 4; TCWW 2; TUS
**Stein, Gertrude** 1874-1946 **DC 19; PC 18; SSC 42; TCLC 1, 6, 28, 48; WLC**
See also AMW; CA 132; 104; CANR 108; CDALB 1917-1929; DA; DA3; DAB; DAC; DAM MST, NOV, POET; DLB 4, 54, 86, 228; DLBD 15; EXPS; GLL 1; MAWW; MTCW 1, 2; NCFS 4; RGAL 4; RGSF 2; SSFS 5; TUS; WP
**Steinbeck, John (Ernst)** 1902-1968 **CLC 1, 5, 9, 13, 21, 34, 45, 75, 124; SSC 11, 37; WLC**
See also AAYA 12; AMW; BPFB 3; BYA 2, 3, 13; CA 25-28R; 1-4R; CANR 1, 35; CDALB 1929-1941; DA; DA3; DAB; DAC; DAM DRAM, MST, NOV; DLB 7, 9, 212, 275; DLBD 2; EXPS; LAIT 3; MTCW 1, 2; NFS 17; RGAL 4; RGSF 2; RHW; SATA 9; SSFS 3, 6; TCWW 2; TUS; WYA; YAW
**Steinem, Gloria** 1934- **CLC 63**
See also CA 53-56; CANR 28, 51; DLB 246; FW; MTCW 1, 2
**Steiner, George** 1929- **CLC 24**
See also CA 73-76; CANR 31, 67, 108; DAM NOV; DLB 67; MTCW 1, 2; SATA 62
**Steiner, K. Leslie**
See Delany, Samuel R(ay), Jr.
**Steiner, Rudolf** 1861-1925 **TCLC 13**
See also CA 107
**Stendhal** 1783-1842 **NCLC 23, 46; SSC 27; WLC**
See also DA; DA3; DAB; DAC; DAM MST, NOV; DLB 119; EW 5; GFL 1789 to the Present; RGWL 2, 3; TWA
**Stephen, Adeline Virginia**
See Woolf, (Adeline) Virginia
**Stephen, Sir Leslie** 1832-1904 **TCLC 23**
See also BRW 5; CA 123; DLB 57, 144, 190
**Stephen, Sir Leslie**
See Stephen, Sir Leslie
**Stephen, Virginia**
See Woolf, (Adeline) Virginia
**Stephens, James** 1882(?)-1950 **SSC 50; TCLC 4**
See also CA 192; 104; DLB 19, 153, 162; FANT; RGEL 2; SUFW
**Stephens, Reed**
See Donaldson, Stephen R(eeder)
**Steptoe, Lydia**
See Barnes, Djuna
See also GLL 1

**Sterchi, Beat** 1949- **CLC 65**
See also CA 203
**Sterling, Brett**
See Bradbury, Ray (Douglas); Hamilton, Edmond
**Sterling, Bruce** 1954- **CLC 72**
See also CA 119; CANR 44; SCFW 2; SFW 4
**Sterling, George** 1869-1926 **TCLC 20**
See also CA 165; 117; DLB 54
**Stern, Gerald** 1925- **CLC 40, 100**
See also AMWS 9; CA 81-84; CANR 28, 94; CP 7; DLB 105; RGAL 4
**Stern, Richard (Gustave)** 1928- **CLC 4, 39**
See also CA 1-4R; CANR 1, 25, 52; CN 7; DLB 218; DLBY 1987; INT CANR-25
**Sternberg, Josef von** 1894-1969 **CLC 20**
See also CA 81-84
**Sterne, Laurence** 1713-1768 **LC 2, 48; WLC**
See also BRW 3; BRWC 1; CDBLB 1660-1789; DA; DAB; DAC; DAM MST, NOV; DLB 39; RGEL 2; TEA
**Sternheim, (William Adolf) Carl** 1878-1942 **TCLC 8**
See also CA 193; 105; DLB 56, 118; RGWL 2, 3
**Stevens, Mark** 1951- **CLC 34**
See also CA 122
**Stevens, Wallace** 1879-1955 **PC 6; TCLC 3, 12, 45; WLC**
See also AMW; AMWR 1; CA 124; 104; CDALB 1929-1941; DA; DA3; DAB; DAC; DAM MST, POET; DLB 54; EXPP; MTCW 1, 2; PAB; PFS 13, 16; RGAL 4; TUS; WP
**Stevenson, Anne (Katharine)** 1933- **CLC 7, 33**
See also BRWS 6; CA 17-20R; CAAS 9; CANR 9, 33; CP 7; CWP; DLB 40; MTCW 1; RHW
**Stevenson, Robert Louis (Balfour)** 1850-1894 **NCLC 5, 14, 63; SSC 11, 51; WLC**
See also AAYA 24; BPFB 3; BRW 5; BRWC 1; BRWR 1; BYA 1, 2, 4, 13; CDBLB 1890-1914; CLR 10, 11; DA; DA3; DAB; DAC; DAM MST, NOV; DLB 18, 57, 141, 156, 174; DLBD 13; HGG; JRDA; LAIT 1, 3; MAICYA 1, 2; NFS 11; RGEL 2; RGSF 2; SATA 100; SUFW; TEA; WCH; WLIT 4; WYA; YABC 2; YAW
**Stewart, J(ohn) I(nnes) M(ackintosh)** 1906-1994 **CLC 7, 14, 32**
See Innes, Michael
See also CA 147; 85-88; CAAS 3; CANR 47; CMW 4; MTCW 1, 2
**Stewart, Mary (Florence Elinor)** 1916- **CLC 7, 35, 117**
See also AAYA 29; BPFB 3; CA 1-4R; CANR 1, 59; CMW 4; CPW; DAB; FANT; RHW; SATA 12; YAW
**Stewart, Mary Rainbow**
See Stewart, Mary (Florence Elinor)
**Stifle, June**
See Campbell, Maria
**Stifter, Adalbert** 1805-1868 **NCLC 41; SSC 28**
See also CDWLB 2; DLB 133; RGSF 2; RGWL 2, 3
**Still, James** 1906-2001 **CLC 49**
See also CA 195; 65-68; CAAS 17; CANR 10, 26; CSW; DLB 9; DLBY 01; SATA 29; SATA-Obit 127
**Sting** 1951-
See Sumner, Gordon Matthew
See also CA 167

**Stirling, Arthur**
  See Sinclair, Upton (Beall)
**Stitt, Milan** 1941- **CLC 29**
  See also CA 69-72
**Stockton, Francis Richard** 1834-1902
  See Stockton, Frank R.
  See also CA 137; 108; MAICYA 1, 2; SATA 44; SFW 4
**Stockton, Frank R. TCLC 47**
  See Stockton, Francis Richard
  See also BYA 4, 13; DLB 42, 74; DLBD 13; EXPS; SATA-Brief 32; SSFS 3; SUFW; WCH
**Stoddard, Charles**
  See Kuttner, Henry
**Stoker, Abraham** 1847-1912
  See Stoker, Bram
  See also CA 150; 105; DA; DA3; DAC; DAM MST, NOV; HGG; SATA 29
**Stoker, Bram TCLC 8; WLC**
  See Stoker, Abraham
  See also AAYA 23; BPFB 3; BRWS 3; BYA 5; CDBLB 1890-1914; DAB; DLB 36, 70, 178; RGEL 2; SUFW; TEA; WLIT 4
**Stolz, Mary (Slattery)** 1920- **CLC 12**
  See also AAYA 8; AITN 1; CA 5-8R; CANR 13, 41, 112; JRDA; MAICYA 1, 2; SAAS 3; SATA 10, 71, 133; YAW
**Stone, Irving** 1903-1989 **CLC 7**
  See also AITN 1; BPFB 3; CA 129; 1-4R; CAAS 3; CANR 1, 23; CPW; DA3; DAM POP; INT CANR-23; MTCW 1, 2; RHW; SATA 3; SATA-Obit 64
**Stone, Oliver (William)** 1946- **CLC 73**
  See also AAYA 15; CA 110; CANR 55
**Stone, Robert (Anthony)** 1937- **CLC 5, 23, 42**
  See also AMWS 5; BPFB 3; CA 85-88; CANR 23, 66, 95; CN 7; DLB 152; INT CANR-23; MTCW 1
**Stone, Zachary**
  See Follett, Ken(neth Martin)
**Stoppard, Tom** 1937- **CLC 1, 3, 4, 5, 8, 15, 29, 34, 63, 91; DC 6; WLC**
  See also BRWC 1; BRWR 2; BRWS 1; CA 81-84; CANR 39, 67; CBD; CD 5; CDBLB 1960 to Present; DA; DA3; DAB; DAC; DAM DRAM, MST; DFS 2, 5, 8, 11, 13, 16; DLB 13, 233; DLBY 1985; MTCW 1, 2; RGEL 2; TEA; WLIT 4
**Storey, David (Malcolm)** 1933- **CLC 2, 4, 5, 8**
  See also BRWS 1; CA 81-84; CANR 36; CBD; CD 5; CN 7; DAM DRAM; DLB 13, 14, 207, 245; MTCW 1; RGEL 2
**Storm, Hyemeyohsts** 1935- **CLC 3; NNAL**
  See also CA 81-84; CANR 45; DAM MULT
**Storm, (Hans) Theodor (Woldsen)** 1817-1888 **NCLC 1; SSC 27**
  See also DLB 129; EW; RGWL 3
**Storm, Theodor** 1817-1888 **SSC 27**
  See also CDWLB 2; RGSF 2; RGWL 2
**Storni, Alfonsina** 1892-1938 **HLC 2; PC 33; TCLC 5**
  See also CA 131; 104; DAM MULT; HW 1; LAW
**Stoughton, William** 1631-1701 **LC 38**
  See also DLB 24
**Stout, Rex (Todhunter)** 1886-1975 **CLC 3**
  See also AITN 2; BPFB 3; CA 61-64; CANR 71; CMW 4; MSW; RGAL 4
**Stow, (Julian) Randolph** 1935- **CLC 23, 48**
  See also CA 13-16R; CANR 33; CN 7; DLB 260; MTCW 1; RGEL 2
**Stowe, Harriet (Elizabeth) Beecher** 1811-1896 **NCLC 3, 50; WLC**
  See also AMWS 1; CDALB 1865-1917; DA; DA3; DAB; DAC; DAM MST, NOV; DLB 1, 12, 42, 74, 189, 239, 243; EXPN;

JRDA; LAIT 2; MAICYA 1, 2; NFS 6; RGAL 4; TUS; YABC 1
**Strabo** c. 64B.C.-c. 25 **CMLC 37**
  See also DLB 176
**Strachey, (Giles) Lytton** 1880-1932 **TCLC 12**
  See also BRWS 2; CA 178; 110; DLB 149; DLBD 10; MTCW 2; NCFS 4
**Strand, Mark** 1934- **CLC 6, 18, 41, 71**
  See also AMWS 4; CA 21-24R; CANR 40, 65, 100; CP 7; DAM POET; DLB 5; PAB; PFS 9; RGAL 4; SATA 41
**Stratton-Porter, Gene(va Grace)** 1863-1924
  See Porter, Gene(va Grace) Stratton
  See also ANW; CA 137; DLB 221; DLBD 14; MAICYA 1, 2; SATA 15
**Straub, Peter (Francis)** 1943- **CLC 28, 107**
  See also BEST 89:1; BPFB 3; CA 85-88; CANR 28, 65, 109; CPW; DAM POP; DLBY 1984; HGG; MTCW 1, 2; SUFW 2
**Strauss, Botho** 1944- **CLC 22**
  See also CA 157; CWW 2; DLB 124
**Streatfeild, (Mary) Noel** 1897(?)-1986 **CLC 21**
  See also CA 120; 81-84; CANR 31; CLR 17, 83; CWRI 5; DLB 160; MAICYA 1, 2; SATA 20; SATA-Obit 48
**Stribling, T(homas) S(igismund)** 1881-1965 **CLC 23**
  See also CA 107; 189; CMW 4; DLB 9; RGAL 4
**Strindberg, (Johan) August** 1849-1912 **DC 18; TCLC 1, 8, 21, 47; WLC**
  See also CA 135; 104; DA; DA3; DAB; DAC; DAM DRAM, MST; DFS 4, 9; DLB 259; EW 7; IDTP; LMFS 2; MTCW 2; RGWL 2, 3; TWA
**Stringer, Arthur** 1874-1950 **TCLC 37**
  See also CA 161; DLB 92
**Stringer, David**
  See Roberts, Keith (John Kingston)
**Stroheim, Erich von** 1885-1957 **TCLC 71**
**Strugatskii, Arkadii (Natanovich)** 1925-1991 **CLC 27**
  See also CA 135; 106; SFW 4
**Strugatskii, Boris (Natanovich)** 1933- **CLC 27**
  See also CA 106; SFW 4
**Strummer, Joe** 1953(?)- **CLC 30**
**Strunk, William, Jr.** 1869-1946 **TCLC 92**
  See also CA 164; 118
**Stryk, Lucien** 1924- **PC 27**
  See also CA 13-16R; CANR 10, 28, 55, 110; CP 7
**Stuart, Don A.**
  See Campbell, John W(ood, Jr.)
**Stuart, Ian**
  See MacLean, Alistair (Stuart)
**Stuart, Jesse (Hilton)** 1906-1984 **CLC 1, 8, 11, 14, 34; SSC 31**
  See also CA 112; 5-8R; CANR 31; DLB 9, 48, 102; DLBY 1984; SATA 2; SATA-Obit 36
**Stubblefield, Sally**
  See Trumbo, Dalton
**Sturgeon, Theodore (Hamilton)** 1918-1985 **CLC 22, 39**
  See Queen, Ellery
  See also BPFB 3; BYA 9, 10; CA 116; 81-84; CANR 32, 103; DLB 8; DLBY 1985; HGG; MTCW 1, 2; SCFW; SFW 4; SUFW
**Sturges, Preston** 1898-1959 **TCLC 48**
  See also CA 149; 114; DLB 26
**Styron, William** 1925- **CLC 1, 3, 5, 11, 15, 60; SSC 25**
  See also AMW; BEST 90:4; BPFB 3; CA 5-8R; CANR 6, 33, 74; CDALB 1968-1988; CN 7; CPW; CSW; DA3; DAM

NOV, POP; DLB 2, 143; DLBY 1980; INT CANR-6; LAIT 2; MTCW 1, 2; NCFS 1; RGAL 4; RHW; TUS
**Su, Chien** 1884-1918
  See Su Man-shu
  See also CA 123
**Suarez Lynch, B.**
  See Bioy Casares, Adolfo; Borges, Jorge Luis
**Suassuna, Ariano Vilar** 1927- **HLCS 1**
  See also CA 178; HW 2; LAW
**Suckert, Kurt Erich**
  See Malaparte, Curzio
**Suckling, Sir John** 1609-1642 **LC 75; PC 30**
  See also BRW 2; DAM POET; DLB 58, 126; EXPP; PAB; RGEL 2
**Suckow, Ruth** 1892-1960 **SSC 18**
  See also CA 113; 193; DLB 9, 102; RGAL 4; TCWW 2
**Sudermann, Hermann** 1857-1928 **TCLC 15**
  See also CA 201; 107; DLB 118
**Sue, Eugene** 1804-1857 **NCLC 1**
  See also DLB 119
**Sueskind, Patrick** 1949- **CLC 44**
  See Suskind, Patrick
**Sukenick, Ronald** 1932- **CLC 3, 4, 6, 48**
  See also CA 25-28R; CAAS 8; CANR 32, 89; CN 7; DLB 173; DLBY 1981
**Suknaski, Andrew** 1942- **CLC 19**
  See also CA 101; CP 7; DLB 53
**Sullivan, Vernon**
  See Vian, Boris
**Sully Prudhomme, Rene-Francois-Armand** 1839-1907 **TCLC 31**
  See also GFL 1789 to the Present
**Su Man-shu TCLC 24**
  See Su, Chien
**Summerforest, Ivy B.**
  See Kirkup, James
**Summers, Andrew James** 1942- **CLC 26**
**Summers, Andy**
  See Summers, Andrew James
**Summers, Hollis (Spurgeon, Jr.)** 1916- **CLC 10**
  See also CA 5-8R; CANR 3; DLB 6
**Summers, (Alphonsus Joseph-Mary Augustus) Montague** 1880-1948 **TCLC 16**
  See also CA 163; 118
**Sumner, Gordon Matthew CLC 26**
  See Police, The; Sting
**Sun Tzu** c. 400B.C.-c. 320B.C. **CMLC 56**
**Surtees, Robert Smith** 1805-1864 **NCLC 14**
  See also DLB 21; RGEL 2
**Susann, Jacqueline** 1921-1974 **CLC 3**
  See also AITN 1; BPFB 3; CA 53-56; 65-68; MTCW 1, 2
**Su Shi**
  See Su Shih
  See also RGWL 2, 3
**Su Shih** 1036-1101 **CMLC 15**
  See Su Shi
**Suskind, Patrick**
  See Sueskind, Patrick
  See also BPFB 3; CA 145; CWW 2
**Sutcliff, Rosemary** 1920-1992 **CLC 26**
  See also AAYA 10; BYA 1, 4; CA 139; 5-8R; CANR 37; CLR 1, 37; CPW; DAB; DAC; DAM MST, POP; JRDA; MAICYA 1, 2; MAICYAS 1; RHW; SATA 6, 44, 78; SATA-Obit 73; WYA; YAW
**Sutro, Alfred** 1863-1933 **TCLC 6**
  See also CA 185; 105; DLB 10; RGEL 2
**Sutton, Henry**
  See Slavitt, David R(ytman)
**Suzuki, D. T.**
  See Suzuki, Daisetz Teitaro

**Suzuki, Daisetz T.**
See Suzuki, Daisetz Teitaro
**Suzuki, Daisetz Teitaro** 1870-1966 **TCLC 109**
See also CA 111; 121; MTCW 1, 2
**Suzuki, Teitaro**
See Suzuki, Daisetz Teitaro
**Svevo, Italo SSC 25; TCLC 2, 35**
See Schmitz, Aron Hector
See also DLB 264; EW 8; RGWL 2, 3
**Swados, Elizabeth (A.)** 1951- **CLC 12**
See also CA 97-100; CANR 49; INT 97-100
**Swados, Harvey** 1920-1972 **CLC 5**
See also CA 37-40R; 5-8R; CANR 6; DLB 2
**Swan, Gladys** 1934- **CLC 69**
See also CA 101; CANR 17, 39
**Swanson, Logan**
See Matheson, Richard (Burton)
**Swarthout, Glendon (Fred)** 1918-1992 **CLC 35**
See also CA 139; 1-4R; CANR 1, 47; LAIT 5; SATA 26; TCWW 2; YAW
**Sweet, Sarah C.**
See Jewett, (Theodora) Sarah Orne
**Swenson, May** 1919-1989 **CLC 4, 14, 61, 106; PC 14**
See also AMWS 4; CA 130; 5-8R; CANR 36, 61; DA; DAB; DAC; DAM MST, POET; DLB 5; EXPP; GLL 2; MTCW 1, 2; PFS 16; SATA 15; WP
**Swift, Augustus**
See Lovecraft, H(oward) P(hillips)
**Swift, Graham (Colin)** 1949- **CLC 41, 88**
See also BRWS 5; CA 122; 117; CANR 46, 71; CN 7; DLB 194; MTCW 2; RGSF 2
**Swift, Jonathan** 1667-1745 **LC 1, 42; PC 9; WLC**
See also AAYA 41; BRW 3; BRWC 1; BRWR 1; BYA 5, 14; CDBLB 1660-1789; CLR 53; DA; DA3; DAB; DAC; DAM MST, NOV, POET; DLB 39, 95, 101; EXPN; LAIT 1; NFS 6; RGEL 2; SATA 19; TEA; WCH; WLIT 3
**Swinburne, Algernon Charles** 1837-1909 **PC 24; TCLC 8, 36; WLC**
See also BRW 5; CA 140; 105; CDBLB 1832-1890; DA; DA3; DAB; DAC; DAM MST, POET; DLB 35, 57; PAB; RGEL 2; TEA
**Swinfen, Ann CLC 34**
See also CA 202
**Swinnerton, Frank Arthur** 1884-1982 **CLC 31**
See also CA 108; DLB 34
**Swithen, John**
See King, Stephen (Edwin)
**Sylvia**
See Ashton-Warner, Sylvia (Constance)
**Symmes, Robert Edward**
See Duncan, Robert (Edward)
**Symonds, John Addington** 1840-1893 **NCLC 34**
See also DLB 57, 144
**Symons, Arthur** 1865-1945 **TCLC 11**
See also CA 189; 107; DLB 19, 57, 149; RGEL 2
**Symons, Julian (Gustave)** 1912-1994 **CLC 2, 14, 32**
See also CA 147; 49-52; CAAS 3; CANR 3, 33, 59; CMW 4; DLB 87, 155; DLBY 1992; MSW; MTCW 1
**Synge, (Edmund) J(ohn) M(illington)** 1871-1909 **DC 2; TCLC 6, 37**
See also BRW 6; BRWR 1; CA 141; 104; CDBLB 1890-1914; DAM DRAM; DLB 10, 19; RGEL 2; TEA; WLIT 4

**Syruc, J.**
See Milosz, Czeslaw
**Szirtes, George** 1948- **CLC 46**
See also CA 109; CANR 27, 61, 117; CP 7
**Szymborska, Wislawa** 1923- **CLC 99; PC 44**
See also CA 154; CANR 91; CDWLB 4; CWP; CWW 2; DA3; DLB 232; DLBY 1996; MTCW 2; PFS 15; RGWL 3
**T. O., Nik**
See Annensky, Innokenty (Fyodorovich)
**Tabori, George** 1914- **CLC 19**
See also CA 49-52; CANR 4, 69; CBD; CD 5; DLB 245
**Tacitus** c. 55-c. 117 **CMLC 56**
See also AW 2; CDWLB 1; DLB 211; RGWL 2, 3
**Tagore, Rabindranath** 1861-1941 **PC 8; SSC 48; TCLC 3, 53**
See also CA 120; 104; DA3; DAM DRAM, POET; MTCW 1, 2; RGEL 2; RGSF 2; RGWL 2, 3; TWA
**Taine, Hippolyte Adolphe** 1828-1893 **NCLC 15**
See also EW 7; GFL 1789 to the Present
**Talayesva, Don C.** 1890-(?) **NNAL**
**Talese, Gay** 1932- **CLC 37**
See also AITN 1; CA 1-4R; CANR 9, 58; DLB 185; INT CANR-9; MTCW 1, 2
**Tallent, Elizabeth (Ann)** 1954- **CLC 45**
See also CA 117; CANR 72; DLB 130
**Tallmountain, Mary** 1918-1997 **NNAL**
See also CA 161; 146; DLB 193
**Tally, Ted** 1952- **CLC 42**
See also CA 124; 120; CAD; CD 5; INT 124
**Talvik, Heiti** 1904-1947 **TCLC 87**
**Tamayo y Baus, Manuel** 1829-1898 **NCLC 1**
**Tammsaare, A(nton) H(ansen)** 1878-1940 **TCLC 27**
See also CA 164; CDWLB 4; DLB 220
**Tam'si, Tchicaya U**
See Tchicaya, Gerald Felix
**Tan, Amy (Ruth)** 1952- **AAL; CLC 59, 120, 151**
See also AAYA 9; AMWS 10; BEST 89:3; BPFB 3; CA 136; CANR 54, 105; CDALBS; CN 7; CPW 1; DA3; DAM MULT, NOV, POP; DLB 173; EXPN; FW; LAIT 3, 5; MTCW 2; NFS 1, 13, 16; RGAL 4; SATA 75; SSFS 9; YAW
**Tandem, Felix**
See Spitteler, Carl (Friedrich Georg)
**Tanizaki, Jun'ichiro** 1886-1965 **CLC 8, 14, 28; SSC 21**
See Tanizaki Jun'ichiro
See also CA 25-28R; 93-96; MJW; MTCW 2; RGSF 2; RGWL 2
**Tanizaki Jun'ichiro**
See Tanizaki, Jun'ichiro
See also DLB 180
**Tanner, William**
See Amis, Kingsley (William)
**Tao Lao**
See Storni, Alfonsina
**Tapahonso, Luci** 1953- **NNAL**
See also CA 145; CANR 72; DLB 175
**Tarantino, Quentin (Jerome)** 1963- **CLC 125**
See also CA 171
**Tarassoff, Lev**
See Troyat, Henri
**Tarbell, Ida M(inerva)** 1857-1944 **TCLC 40**
See also CA 181; 122; DLB 47
**Tarkington, (Newton) Booth** 1869-1946 **TCLC 9**
See also BPFB 3; BYA 3; CA 143; 110; CWRI 5; DLB 9, 102; MTCW 2; RGAL 4; SATA 17
**Tarkovskii, Andrei Arsen'evich**
See Tarkovsky, Andrei (Arsenyevich)

**Tarkovsky, Andrei (Arsenyevich)** 1932-1986 **CLC 75**
See also CA 127
**Tartt, Donna** 1964(?)- **CLC 76**
See also CA 142
**Tasso, Torquato** 1544-1595 **LC 5**
See also EFS 2; EW 2; RGWL 2, 3
**Tate, (John Orley) Allen** 1899-1979 **CLC 2, 4, 6, 9, 11, 14, 24**
See also AMW; CA 85-88; 5-8R; CANR 32, 108; DLB 4, 45, 63; DLBD 17; MTCW 1, 2; RGAL 4; RHW
**Tate, Ellalice**
See Hibbert, Eleanor Alice Burford
**Tate, James (Vincent)** 1943- **CLC 2, 6, 25**
See also CA 21-24R; CANR 29, 57, 114; CP 7; DLB 5, 169; PFS 10, 15; RGAL 4; WP
**Tauler, Johannes** c. 1300-1361 **CMLC 37**
See also DLB 179
**Tavel, Ronald** 1940- **CLC 6**
See also CA 21-24R; CAD; CANR 33; CD 5
**Taviani, Paolo** 1931- **CLC 70**
See also CA 153
**Taylor, Bayard** 1825-1878 **NCLC 89**
See also DLB 3, 189, 250, 254; RGAL 4
**Taylor, C(ecil) P(hilip)** 1929-1981 **CLC 27**
See also CA 105; 25-28R; CANR 47; CBD
**Taylor, Edward** 1642(?)-1729 **LC 11**
See also AMW; DA; DAB; DAC; DAM MST, POET; DLB 24; EXPP; RGAL 4; TUS
**Taylor, Eleanor Ross** 1920- **CLC 5**
See also CA 81-84; CANR 70
**Taylor, Elizabeth** 1932-1975 **CLC 2, 4, 29**
See also CA 13-16R; CANR 9, 70; DLB 139; MTCW 1; RGEL 2; SATA 13
**Taylor, Frederick Winslow** 1856-1915 **TCLC 76**
See also CA 188
**Taylor, Henry (Splawn)** 1942- **CLC 44**
See also CA 33-36R; CAAS 7; CANR 31; CP 7; DLB 5; PFS 10
**Taylor, Kamala (Purnaiya)** 1924-
See Markandaya, Kamala
See also CA 77-80; NFS 13
**Taylor, Mildred D(elois)** 1943- **CLC 21**
See also AAYA 10, 47; BW 1; BYA 3, 8; CA 85-88; CANR 25, 115; CLR 9, 59; CSW; DLB 52; JRDA; LAIT 3; MAICYA 1, 2; SAAS 5; SATA 135; WYA; YAW
**Taylor, Peter (Hillsman)** 1917-1994 **CLC 1, 4, 18, 37, 44, 50, 71; SSC 10**
See also AMWS 5; BPFB 3; CA 147; 13-16R; CANR 9, 50; CSW; DLB 218, 278; DLBY 1981, 1994; EXPS; INT CANR-9; MTCW 1, 2; RGSF 2; SSFS 9; TUS
**Taylor, Robert Lewis** 1912-1998 **CLC 14**
See also CA 170; 1-4R; CANR 3, 64; SATA 10
**Tchekhov, Anton**
See Chekhov, Anton (Pavlovich)
**Tchicaya, Gerald Felix** 1931-1988 **CLC 101**
See also CA 125; 129; CANR 81
**Tchicaya U Tam'si**
See Tchicaya, Gerald Felix
**Teasdale, Sara** 1884-1933 **PC 31; TCLC 4**
See also CA 163; 104; DLB 45; GLL 1; PFS 14; RGAL 4; SATA 32; TUS
**Tecumseh** 1768-1813 **NNAL**
See also DAM MULT
**Tegner, Esaias** 1782-1846 **NCLC 2**
**Teilhard de Chardin, (Marie Joseph) Pierre** 1881-1955 **TCLC 9**
See also CA 105; GFL 1789 to the Present

**Temple, Ann**
See Mortimer, Penelope (Ruth)
**Tennant, Emma (Christina)** 1937- **CLC 13, 52**
See also CA 65-68; CAAS 9; CANR 10, 38, 59, 88; CN 7; DLB 14; SFW 4
**Tenneshaw, S. M.**
See Silverberg, Robert
**Tenney, Tabitha Gilman** 1762-1837 **NCLC 122**
See also DLB 37, 200
**Tennyson, Alfred** 1809-1892 **NCLC 30, 65, 115; PC 6; WLC**
See also BRW 4; CDBLB 1832-1890; DA; DA3; DAB; DAC; DAM MST, POET; DLB 32; EXPP; PAB; PFS 1, 2, 4, 11, 15; RGEL 2; TEA; WLIT 4; WP
**Teran, Lisa St. Aubin de CLC 36**
See St. Aubin de Teran, Lisa
**Terence** c. 184B.C.-c. 159B.C. **CMLC 14; DC 7**
See also AW 1; CDWLB 1; DLB 211; RGWL 2, 3; TWA
**Teresa de Jesus, St.** 1515-1582 **LC 18**
**Terkel, Louis** 1912-
See Terkel, Studs
See also CA 57-60; CANR 18, 45, 67; DA3; MTCW 1, 2
**Terkel, Studs CLC 38**
See Terkel, Louis
See also AAYA 32; AITN 1; MTCW 2; TUS
**Terry, C. V.**
See Slaughter, Frank G(ill)
**Terry, Megan** 1932- **CLC 19; DC 13**
See also CA 77-80; CABS 3; CAD; CANR 43; CD 5; CWD; DLB 7, 249; GLL 2
**Tertullian** c. 155-c. 245 **CMLC 29**
**Tertz, Abram**
See Sinyavsky, Andrei (Donatevich)
See also CWW 2; RGSF 2
**Tesich, Steve** 1943(?)-1996 **CLC 40, 69**
See also CA 152; 105; CAD; DLBY 1983
**Tesla, Nikola** 1856-1943 **TCLC 88**
**Teternikov, Fyodor Kuzmich** 1863-1927
See Sologub, Fyodor
See also CA 104
**Tevis, Walter** 1928-1984 **CLC 42**
See also CA 113; SFW 4
**Tey, Josephine TCLC 14**
See Mackintosh, Elizabeth
See also DLB 77; MSW
**Thackeray, William Makepeace** 1811-1863 **NCLC 5, 14, 22, 43; WLC**
See also BRW 5; CDBLB 1832-1890; DA; DA3; DAB; DAC; DAM MST, NOV; DLB 21, 55, 159, 163; NFS 13; RGEL 2; SATA 23; TEA; WLIT 3
**Thakura, Ravindranatha**
See Tagore, Rabindranath
**Thames, C. H.**
See Marlowe, Stephen
**Tharoor, Shashi** 1956- **CLC 70**
See also CA 141; CANR 91; CN 7
**Thelwell, Michael Miles** 1939- **CLC 22**
See also BW 2; CA 101
**Theobald, Lewis, Jr.**
See Lovecraft, H(oward) P(hillips)
**Theocritus** c. 310B.C.- **CMLC 45**
See also AW 1; DLB 176; RGWL 2, 3
**Theodorescu, Ion N.** 1880-1967
See Arghezi, Tudor
See also CA 116
**Theriault, Yves** 1915-1983 **CLC 79**
See also CA 102; CCA 1; DAC; DAM MST; DLB 88
**Theroux, Alexander (Louis)** 1939- **CLC 2, 25**
See also CA 85-88; CANR 20, 63; CN 7

**Theroux, Paul (Edward)** 1941- **CLC 5, 8, 11, 15, 28, 46**
See also AAYA 28; AMWS 8; BEST 89:4; BPFB 3; CA 33-36R; CANR 20, 45, 74; CDALBS; CN 7; CPW 1; DA3; DAM POP; DLB 2, 218; HGG; MTCW 1, 2; RGAL 4; SATA 44, 109; TUS
**Thesen, Sharon** 1946- **CLC 56**
See also CA 163; CP 7; CWP
**Thespis** fl. 6th cent. B.C.- **CMLC 51**
**Thevenin, Denis**
See Duhamel, Georges
**Thibault, Jacques Anatole Francois** 1844-1924
See France, Anatole
See also CA 127; 106; DA3; DAM NOV; MTCW 1, 2; TWA
**Thiele, Colin (Milton)** 1920- **CLC 17**
See also CA 29-32R; CANR 12, 28, 53, 105; CLR 27; MAICYA 1, 2; SAAS 2; SATA 14, 72, 125; YAW
**Thistlethwaite, Bel**
See Wetherald, Agnes Ethelwyn
**Thomas, Audrey (Callahan)** 1935- **CLC 7, 13, 37, 107; SSC 20**
See also AITN 2; CA 21-24R; CAAS 19; CANR 36, 58; CN 7; DLB 60; MTCW 1; RGSF 2
**Thomas, Augustus** 1857-1934 **TCLC 97**
**Thomas, D(onald) M(ichael)** 1935- **CLC 13, 22, 31, 132**
See also BPFB 3; BRWS 4; CA 61-64; CAAS 11; CANR 17, 45, 75; CDBLB 1960 to Present; CN 7; CP 7; DA3; DLB 40, 207; HGG; INT CANR-17; MTCW 1, 2; SFW 4
**Thomas, Dylan (Marlais)** 1914-1953 **PC 2; SSC 3, 44; TCLC 1, 8, 45, 105; WLC**
See also AAYA 45; BRWS 1; CA 120; 104; CANR 65; CDBLB 1945-1960; DA; DA3; DAB; DAC; DAM DRAM, MST, POET; DLB 13, 20, 139; EXPP; LAIT 3; MTCW 1, 2; PAB; PFS 1, 3, 8; RGEL 2; RGSF 2; SATA 60; TEA; WLIT 4; WP
**Thomas, (Philip) Edward** 1878-1917 **TCLC 10**
See also BRW 6; BRWS 3; CA 153; 106; DAM POET; DLB 19, 98, 156, 216; PAB; RGEL 2
**Thomas, Joyce Carol** 1938- **CLC 35**
See also AAYA 12; BW 2, 3; CA 116; 113; CANR 48, 114; CLR 19; DLB 33; INT CA-116; JRDA; MAICYA 1, 2; MTCW 1, 2; SAAS 7; SATA 40, 78, 123, 137; WYA; YAW
**Thomas, Lewis** 1913-1993 **CLC 35**
See also ANW; CA 143; 85-88; CANR 38, 60; DLB 275; MTCW 1, 2
**Thomas, M. Carey** 1857-1935 **TCLC 89**
See also FW
**Thomas, Paul**
See Mann, (Paul) Thomas
**Thomas, Piri** 1928- **CLC 17; HLCS 2**
See also CA 73-76; HW 1
**Thomas, R(onald) S(tuart)** 1913-2000 **CLC 6, 13, 48**
See also CA 189; 89-92; CAAS 4; CANR 30; CDBLB 1960 to Present; CP 7; DAB; DAM POET; DLB 27; MTCW 1; RGEL 2
**Thomas, Ross (Elmore)** 1926-1995 **CLC 39**
See also CA 150; 33-36R; CANR 22, 63; CMW 4
**Thompson, Francis (Joseph)** 1859-1907 **TCLC 4**
See also BRW 5; CA 189; 104; CDBLB 1890-1914; DLB 19; RGEL 2; TEA
**Thompson, Francis Clegg**
See Mencken, H(enry) L(ouis)

**Thompson, Hunter S(tockton)** 1937(?)- **CLC 9, 17, 40, 104**
See also AAYA 45; BEST 89:1; BPFB 3; CA 17-20R; CANR 23, 46, 74, 77, 111; CPW; CSW; DA3; DAM POP; DLB 185; MTCW 1, 2; TUS
**Thompson, James Myers**
See Thompson, Jim (Myers)
**Thompson, Jim (Myers)** 1906-1977(?) **CLC 69**
See also BPFB 3; CA 140; CMW 4; CPW; DLB 226; MSW
**Thompson, Judith CLC 39**
See also CWD
**Thomson, James** 1700-1748 **LC 16, 29, 40**
See also BRWS 3; DAM POET; DLB 95; RGEL 2
**Thomson, James** 1834-1882 **NCLC 18**
See also DAM POET; DLB 35; RGEL 2
**Thoreau, Henry David** 1817-1862 **NCLC 7, 21, 61; PC 30; WLC**
See also AAYA 42; AMW; ANW; BYA 3; CDALB 1640-1865; DA; DA3; DAB; DAC; DAM MST; DLB 1, 183, 223, 270; LAIT 2; NCFS 3; RGAL 4; TUS
**Thorndike, E. L.**
See Thorndike, Edward L(ee)
**Thorndike, Edward L(ee)** 1874-1949 **TCLC 107**
See also CA 121
**Thornton, Hall**
See Silverberg, Robert
**Thubron, Colin (Gerald Dryden)** 1939- **CLC 163**
See also CA 25-28R; CANR 12, 29, 59, 95; CN 7; DLB 204, 231
**Thucydides** c. 455B.C.-c. 395B.C. **CMLC 17**
See also AW 1; DLB 176; RGWL 2, 3
**Thumboo, Edwin Nadason** 1933- **PC 30**
See also CA 194
**Thurber, James (Grover)** 1894-1961 **CLC 5, 11, 25, 125; SSC 1, 47**
See also AMWS 1; BPFB 3; BYA 5; CA 73-76; CANR 17, 39; CDALB 1929-1941; CWRI 5; DA; DA3; DAB; DAC; DAM DRAM, MST, NOV; DLB 4, 11, 22, 102; EXPS; FANT; LAIT 3; MAICYA 1, 2; MTCW 1, 2; RGAL 4; RGSF 2; SATA 13; SSFS 1, 10; SUFW; TUS
**Thurman, Wallace (Henry)** 1902-1934 **BLC 3; HR 3; TCLC 6**
See also BW 1, 3; CA 124; 104; CANR 81; DAM MULT; DLB 51
**Tibullus** c. 54B.C.-c. 18B.C. **CMLC 36**
See also AW 2; DLB 211; RGWL 2, 3
**Ticheburn, Cheviot**
See Ainsworth, William Harrison
**Tieck, (Johann) Ludwig** 1773-1853 **NCLC 5, 46; SSC 31**
See also CDWLB 2; DLB 90; EW 5; IDTP; RGSF 2; RGWL 2, 3; SUFW
**Tiger, Derry**
See Ellison, Harlan (Jay)
**Tilghman, Christopher** 1948(?)- **CLC 65**
See also CA 159; CSW; DLB 244
**Tillich, Paul (Johannes)** 1886-1965 **CLC 131**
See also CA 25-28R; 5-8R; CANR 33; MTCW 1, 2
**Tillinghast, Richard (Williford)** 1940- **CLC 29**
See also CA 29-32R; CAAS 23; CANR 26, 51, 96; CP 7; CSW
**Timrod, Henry** 1828-1867 **NCLC 25**
See also DLB 3, 248; RGAL 4
**Tindall, Gillian (Elizabeth)** 1938- **CLC 7**
See also CA 21-24R; CANR 11, 65, 107; CN 7

**Tiptree, James, Jr.** CLC 48, 50
See Sheldon, Alice Hastings Bradley
See also DLB 8; SCFW 2; SFW 4

**Tirone Smith, Mary-Ann** 1944- **CLC 39**
See also CA 136; 118; CANR 113

**Tirso de Molina** 1580(?)-1648 **DC 13; HLCS 2; LC 73**
See also RGWL 2, 3

**Titmarsh, Michael Angelo**
See Thackeray, William Makepeace

**Tocqueville, Alexis (Charles Henri Maurice Clerel Comte) de** 1805-1859 **NCLC 7, 63**
See also EW 6; GFL 1789 to the Present; TWA

**Toffler, Alvin** 1928- **CLC 168**
See also CA 13-16R; CANR 15, 46, 67; CPW; DAM POP; MTCW 1, 2

**Toibin, Colm**
See Toibin, Colm
See also DLB 271

**Toibin, Colm** 1955- **CLC 162**
See Toibin, Colm
See also CA 142; CANR 81

**Tolkien, J(ohn) R(onald) R(euel)** 1892-1973 **CLC 1, 2, 3, 8, 12, 38; WLC**
See also AAYA 10; AITN 1; BPFB 3; BRWS 2; CA 45-48; 17-18; CANR 36; CAP 2; CDBLB 1914-1945; CLR 56; CPW 1; CWRI 5; DA; DA3; DAB; DAC; DAM MST, NOV, POP; DLB 15, 160, 255; EFS 2; FANT; JRDA; LAIT 1; MAICYA 1, 2; MTCW 1, 2; NFS 8; RGEL 2; SATA 2, 32, 100; SATA-Obit 24; SFW 4; SUFW; TEA; WCH; WYA; YAW

**Toller, Ernst** 1893-1939 **TCLC 10**
See also CA 186; 107; DLB 124; RGWL 2, 3

**Tolson, M. B.**
See Tolson, Melvin B(eaunorus)

**Tolson, Melvin B(eaunorus)** 1898(?)-1966 **BLC 3; CLC 36, 105**
See also AFAW 1, 2; BW 1, 3; CA 89-92; 124; CANR 80; DAM MULT, POET; DLB 48, 76; RGAL 4

**Tolstoi, Aleksei Nikolaevich**
See Tolstoy, Alexey Nikolaevich

**Tolstoi, Lev**
See Tolstoy, Leo (Nikolaevich)
See also RGSF 2; RGWL 2, 3

**Tolstoy, Aleksei Nikolaevich**
See Tolstoy, Alexey Nikolaevich
See also DLB 272

**Tolstoy, Alexey Nikolaevich** 1882-1945 **TCLC 18**
See Tolstoy, Aleksei Nikolaevich
See also CA 158; 107; SFW 4

**Tolstoy, Leo (Nikolaevich)** 1828-1910 **SSC 9, 30, 45, 54; TCLC 4, 11, 17, 28, 44, 79; WLC**
See Tolstoi, Lev
See also CA 123; 104; DA; DA3; DAB; DAC; DAM MST, NOV; DLB 238; EFS 2; EW 7; EXPS; IDTP; LAIT 2; NFS 10; SATA 26; SSFS 5; TWA

**Tolstoy, Count Leo**
See Tolstoy, Leo (Nikolaevich)

**Tomalin, Claire** 1933- **CLC 166**
See also CA 89-92; CANR 52, 88; DLB 155

**Tomasi di Lampedusa, Giuseppe** 1896-1957
See Lampedusa, Giuseppe (Tomasi) di
See also CA 111; DLB 177

**Tomlin, Lily** CLC 17
See Tomlin, Mary Jean

**Tomlin, Mary Jean** 1939(?)-
See Tomlin, Lily
See also CA 117

**Tomline, F. Latour**
See Gilbert, W(illiam) S(chwenck)

**Tomlinson, (Alfred) Charles** 1927- **CLC 2, 4, 6, 13, 45; PC 17**
See also CA 5-8R; CANR 33; CP 7; DAM POET; DLB 40

**Tomlinson, H(enry) M(ajor)** 1873-1958 **TCLC 71**
See also CA 161; 118; DLB 36, 100, 195

**Tonson, Jacob** fl. 1655(?)-1736 **LC 86**
See also DLB 170

**Toole, John Kennedy** 1937-1969 **CLC 19, 64**
See also BPFB 3; CA 104; DLBY 1981; MTCW 2

**Toomer, Eugene**
See Toomer, Jean

**Toomer, Eugene Pinchback**
See Toomer, Jean

**Toomer, Jean** 1892-1967 **BLC 3; CLC 1, 4, 13, 22; HR 3; PC 7; SSC 1, 45; WLCS**
See also AFAW 1, 2; AMWS 3, 9; BW 1; CA 85-88; CDALB 1917-1929; DA3; DAM MULT; DLB 45, 51; EXPP; EXPS; LMFS 2; MTCW 1, 2; NFS 11; RGAL 4; RGSF 2; SSFS 5

**Toomer, Nathan Jean**
See Toomer, Jean

**Toomer, Nathan Pinchback**
See Toomer, Jean

**Torley, Luke**
See Blish, James (Benjamin)

**Tornimparte, Alessandra**
See Ginzburg, Natalia

**Torre, Raoul della**
See Mencken, H(enry) L(ouis)

**Torrence, Ridgely** 1874-1950 **TCLC 97**
See also DLB 54, 249

**Torrey, E(dwin) Fuller** 1937- **CLC 34**
See also CA 119; CANR 71

**Torsvan, Ben Traven**
See Traven, B.

**Torsvan, Benno Traven**
See Traven, B.

**Torsvan, Berick Traven**
See Traven, B.

**Torsvan, Berwick Traven**
See Traven, B.

**Torsvan, Bruno Traven**
See Traven, B.

**Torsvan, Traven**
See Traven, B.

**Tourneur, Cyril** 1575(?)-1626 **LC 66**
See also BRW 2; DAM DRAM; DLB 58; RGEL 2

**Tournier, Michel (Edouard)** 1924- **CLC 6, 23, 36, 95**
See also CA 49-52; CANR 3, 36, 74; DLB 83; GFL 1789 to the Present; MTCW 1, 2; SATA 23

**Tournimparte, Alessandra**
See Ginzburg, Natalia

**Towers, Ivar**
See Kornbluth, C(yril) M.

**Towne, Robert (Burton)** 1936(?)- **CLC 87**
See also CA 108; DLB 44; IDFW 3, 4

**Townsend, Sue** CLC 61
See Townsend, Susan Lilian
See also AAYA 28; CA 127; 119; CANR 65, 107; CBD; CD 5; CPW; CWD; DAB; DAC; DAM MST; DLB 271; INT 127; SATA 55, 93; SATA-Brief 48; YAW

**Townsend, Susan Lilian** 1946-
See Townsend, Sue

**Townshend, Pete**
See Townshend, Peter (Dennis Blandford)

**Townshend, Peter (Dennis Blandford)** 1945- **CLC 17, 42**
See also CA 107

**Tozzi, Federigo** 1883-1920 **TCLC 31**
See also CA 160; CANR 110; DLB 264

**Tracy, Don(ald Fiske)** 1905-1970(?)
See Queen, Ellery
See also CA 176; 1-4R; CANR 2

**Trafford, F. G.**
See Riddell, Charlotte

**Traill, Catharine Parr** 1802-1899 **NCLC 31**
See also DLB 99

**Trakl, Georg** 1887-1914 **PC 20; TCLC 5**
See also CA 165; 104; EW 10; LMFS 2; MTCW 2; RGWL 2, 3

**Tranquilli, Secondino**
See Silone, Ignazio

**Transtroemer, Tomas Gosta**
See Transtromer, Tomas (Goesta)

**Transtromer, Tomas**
See Transtromer, Tomas (Goesta)

**Transtromer, Tomas (Goesta)** 1931- **CLC 52, 65**
See also CA 129; 117; CAAS 17; CANR 115; DAM POET; DLB 257

**Transtromer, Tomas Gosta**
See Transtromer, Tomas (Goesta)

**Traven, B.** 1882(?)-1969 **CLC 8, 11**
See also CA 25-28R; 19-20; CAP 2; DLB 9, 56; MTCW 1; RGAL 4

**Trediakovsky, Vasilii Kirillovich** 1703-1769 **LC 68**
See also DLB 150

**Treitel, Jonathan** 1959- **CLC 70**
See also DLB 267

**Trelawny, Edward John** 1792-1881 **NCLC 85**
See also DLB 110, 116, 144

**Tremain, Rose** 1943- **CLC 42**
See also CA 97-100; CANR 44, 95; CN 7; DLB 14, 271; RGSF 2; RHW

**Tremblay, Michel** 1942- **CLC 29, 102**
See also CA 128; 116; CCA 1; CWW 2; DAC; DAM MST; DLB 60; GLL 1; MTCW 1, 2

**Trevanian** CLC 29
See Whitaker, Rod(ney)

**Trevor, Glen**
See Hilton, James

**Trevor, William** CLC 7, 9, 14, 25, 71, 116; **SSC 21, 58**
See Cox, William Trevor
See also BRWS 4; CBD; CD 5; CN 7; DLB 14, 139; MTCW 2; RGEL 2; RGSF 2; SSFS 10

**Trifonov, Iurii (Valentinovich)**
See Trifonov, Yuri (Valentinovich)
See also RGWL 2, 3

**Trifonov, Yuri (Valentinovich)** 1925-1981 **CLC 45**
See Trifonov, Iurii (Valentinovich)
See also CA 103; 126; MTCW 1

**Trilling, Diana (Rubin)** 1905-1996 **CLC 129**
See also CA 154; 5-8R; CANR 10, 46; INT CANR-10; MTCW 1, 2

**Trilling, Lionel** 1905-1975 **CLC 9, 11, 24**
See also AMWS 3; CA 61-64; 9-12R; CANR 10, 105; DLB 28, 63; INT CANR-10; MTCW 1, 2; RGAL 4; TUS

**Trimball, W. H.**
See Mencken, H(enry) L(ouis)

**Tristan**
See Gomez de la Serna, Ramon

**Tristram**
See Housman, A(lfred) E(dward)

**Trogdon, William (Lewis)** 1939-
See Heat-Moon, William Least
See also CA 119; 115; CANR 47, 89; CPW; INT CA-119

**Trollope, Anthony** 1815-1882 **NCLC 6, 33, 101; SSC 28; WLC**
See also BRW 5; CDBLB 1832-1890; DA; DA3; DAB; DAC; DAM MST, NOV; DLB 21, 57, 159; RGEL 2; RGSF 2; SATA 22

**Trollope, Frances** 1779-1863 **NCLC 30**
See also DLB 21, 166

**Trotsky, Leon** 1879-1940 **TCLC 22**
See also CA 167; 118

**Trotter (Cockburn), Catharine** 1679-1749 **LC 8**
See also DLB 84, 252

**Trotter, Wilfred** 1872-1939 **TCLC 97**

**Trout, Kilgore**
See Farmer, Philip Jose

**Trow, George W. S.** 1943- **CLC 52**
See also CA 126; CANR 91

**Troyat, Henri** 1911- **CLC 23**
See also CA 45-48; CANR 2, 33, 67, 117; GFL 1789 to the Present; MTCW 1

**Trudeau, G(arretson) B(eekman)** 1948-
See Trudeau, Garry B.
See also CA 81-84; CANR 31; SATA 35

**Trudeau, Garry B.** **CLC 12**
See Trudeau, G(arretson) B(eekman)
See also AAYA 10; AITN 2

**Truffaut, Francois** 1932-1984 **CLC 20, 101**
See also CA 113; 81-84; CANR 34

**Trumbo, Dalton** 1905-1976 **CLC 19**
See also CA 69-72; 21-24R; CANR 10; DLB 26; IDFW 3, 4; YAW

**Trumbull, John** 1750-1831 **NCLC 30**
See also DLB 31; RGAL 4

**Trundlett, Helen B.**
See Eliot, T(homas) S(tearns)

**Truth, Sojourner** 1797(?)-1883 **NCLC 94**
See also DLB 239; FW; LAIT 2

**Tryon, Thomas** 1926-1991 **CLC 3, 11**
See also AITN 1; BPFB 3; CA 135; 29-32R; CANR 32, 77; CPW; DA3; DAM POP; HGG; MTCW 1

**Tryon, Tom**
See Tryon, Thomas

**Ts'ao Hsueh-ch'in** 1715(?)-1763 **LC 1**

**Tsushima, Shuji** 1909-1948
See Dazai Osamu
See also CA 107

**Tsvetaeva (Efron), Marina (Ivanovna)** 1892-1941 **PC 14; TCLC 7, 35**
See also CA 128; 104; CANR 73; EW 11; MTCW 1, 2; RGWL 2, 3

**Tuck, Lily** 1938- **CLC 70**
See also CA 139; CANR 90

**Tu Fu** 712-770 **PC 9**
See Du Fu
See also DAM MULT; TWA; WP

**Tunis, John R(oberts)** 1889-1975 **CLC 12**
See also BYA 1; CA 61-64; CANR 62; DLB 22, 171; JRDA; MAICYA 1, 2; SATA 37; SATA-Brief 30; YAW

**Tuohy, Frank** **CLC 37**
See Tuohy, John Francis
See also DLB 14, 139

**Tuohy, John Francis** 1925-
See Tuohy, Frank
See also CA 178; 5-8R; CANR 3, 47; CN 7

**Turco, Lewis (Putnam)** 1934- **CLC 11, 63**
See also CA 13-16R; CAAS 22; CANR 24, 51; CP 7; DLBY 1984

**Turgenev, Ivan (Sergeevich)** 1818-1883 **DC 7; NCLC 21, 37, 122; SSC 7, 57; WLC**
See also DA; DAB; DAC; DAM MST, NOV; DFS 6; DLB 238; EW 6; NFS 16; RGSF 2; RGWL 2, 3; TWA

**Turgot, Anne-Robert-Jacques** 1727-1781 **LC 26**

**Turner, Frederick** 1943- **CLC 48**
See also CA 73-76; CAAS 10; CANR 12, 30, 56; DLB 40

**Turton, James**
See Crace, Jim

**Tutu, Desmond M(pilo)** 1931- **BLC 3; CLC 80**
See also BW 1, 3; CA 125; CANR 67, 81; DAM MULT

**Tutuola, Amos** 1920-1997 **BLC 3; CLC 5, 14, 29**
See also AFW; BW 2, 3; CA 159; 9-12R; CANR 27, 66; CDWLB 3; CN 7; DA3; DAM MULT; DLB 125; DNFS 2; MTCW 1, 2; RGEL 2; WLIT 2

**Twain, Mark** **SSC 34; TCLC 6, 12, 19, 36, 48, 59; WLC**
See Clemens, Samuel Langhorne
See also AAYA 20; AMW; AMWC 1; BPFB 3; BYA 2, 3, 11, 14; CLR 58, 60, 66; DLB 11; EXPN; EXPS; FANT; LAIT 2; NFS 1, 6; RGAL 4; RGSF 2; SFW 4; SSFS 1, 7; SUFW; TUS; WCH; WYA; YAW

**Tyler, Anne** 1941- **CLC 7, 11, 18, 28, 44, 59, 103**
See also AAYA 18; AMWS 4; BEST 89:1; BPFB 3; BYA 12; CA 9-12R; CANR 11, 33, 53, 109; CDALBS; CN 7; CPW; CSW; DAM NOV, POP; DLB 6, 143; DLBY 1982; EXPN; MAWW; MTCW 1, 2; NFS 2, 7, 10; RGAL 4; SATA 7, 90; SSFS 17; TUS; YAW

**Tyler, Royall** 1757-1826 **NCLC 3**
See also DLB 37; RGAL 4

**Tynan, Katharine** 1861-1931 **TCLC 3**
See also CA 167; 104; DLB 153, 240; FW

**Tyutchev, Fyodor** 1803-1873 **NCLC 34**

**Tzara, Tristan** 1896-1963 **CLC 47; PC 27**
See also CA 89-92; 153; DAM POET; MTCW 1

**Uchida, Yoshiko** 1921-1992 **AAL**
See also AAYA 16; BYA 2, 3; CA 139; 13-16R; CANR 6, 22, 47, 61; CDALBS; CLR 6, 56; CWRI 5; JRDA; MAICYA 1, 2; MTCW 1, 2; SAAS 1; SATA 1, 53; SATA-Obit 72

**Udall, Nicholas** 1504-1556 **LC 84**
See also DLB 62; RGEL 2

**Uhry, Alfred** 1936- **CLC 55**
See also CA 133; 127; CAD; CANR 112; CD 5; CSW; DA3; DAM DRAM, POP; DFS 15; INT CA-133

**Ulf, Haerved**
See Strindberg, (Johan) August

**Ulf, Harved**
See Strindberg, (Johan) August

**Ulibarri, Sabine R(eyes)** 1919- **CLC 83; HLCS 2**
See also CA 131; CANR 81; DAM MULT; DLB 82; HW 1, 2; RGSF 2

**Unamuno (y Jugo), Miguel de** 1864-1936 **HLC 2; SSC 11; TCLC 2, 9**
See also CA 131; 104; CANR 81; DAM MULT, NOV; DLB 108; EW 8; HW 1, 2; MTCW 1, 2; RGSF 2; RGWL 2, 3; TWA

**Undercliffe, Errol**
See Campbell, (John) Ramsey

**Underwood, Miles**
See Glassco, John

**Undset, Sigrid** 1882-1949 **TCLC 3; WLC**
See also CA 129; 104; DA; DA3; DAB; DAC; DAM MST, NOV; EW 9; FW; MTCW 1, 2; RGWL 2, 3

**Ungaretti, Giuseppe** 1888-1970 **CLC 7, 11, 15**
See also CA 25-28R; 19-20; CAP 2; DLB 114; EW 10; RGWL 2, 3

**Unger, Douglas** 1952- **CLC 34**
See also CA 130; CANR 94

**Unsworth, Barry (Forster)** 1930- **CLC 76, 127**
See also BRWS 7; CA 25-28R; CANR 30, 54; CN 7; DLB 194

**Updike, John (Hoyer)** 1932- **CLC 1, 2, 3, 5, 7, 9, 13, 15, 23, 34, 43, 70, 139; SSC 13, 27; WLC**
See also AAYA 36; AMW; AMWC 1; AMWR 1; BPFB 3; BYA 12; CA 1-4R; CABS 1; CANR 4, 33, 51, 94; CDALB 1968-1988; CN 7; CP 7; CPW 1; DA; DA3; DAB; DAC; DAM MST, NOV; POET, POP; DLB 2, 5, 143, 218, 227; DLBD 3; DLBY 1980, 1982, 1997; EXPP; HGG; MTCW 1, 2; NFS 12; RGAL 4; RGSF 2; SSFS 3; TUS

**Upshaw, Margaret Mitchell**
See Mitchell, Margaret (Munnerlyn)

**Upton, Mark**
See Sanders, Lawrence

**Upward, Allen** 1863-1926 **TCLC 85**
See also CA 187; 117; DLB 36

**Urdang, Constance (Henriette)** 1922-1996 **CLC 47**
See also CA 21-24R; CANR 9, 24; CP 7; CWP

**Uriel, Henry**
See Faust, Frederick (Schiller)

**Uris, Leon (Marcus)** 1924- **CLC 7, 32**
See also AITN 1, 2; BEST 89:2; BPFB 3; CA 1-4R; CANR 1, 40, 65; CN 7; CPW 1; DA3; DAM NOV, POP; MTCW 1, 2; SATA 49

**Urista, Alberto H.** 1947- **HLCS 1; PC 34**
See Alurista
See also CA 45-48, 182; CANR 2, 32; HW 1

**Urmuz**
See Codrescu, Andrei

**Urquhart, Guy**
See McAlmon, Robert (Menzies)

**Urquhart, Jane** 1949- **CLC 90**
See also CA 113; CANR 32, 68, 116; CCA 1; DAC

**Usigli, Rodolfo** 1905-1979 **HLCS 1**
See also CA 131; HW 1; LAW

**Ustinov, Peter (Alexander)** 1921- **CLC 1**
See also AITN 1; CA 13-16R; CANR 25, 51; CBD; CD 5; DLB 13; MTCW 2

**U Tam'si, Gerald Felix Tchicaya**
See Tchicaya, Gerald Felix

**U Tam'si, Tchicaya**
See Tchicaya, Gerald Felix

**Vachss, Andrew (Henry)** 1942- **CLC 106**
See also CA 118; CANR 44, 95; CMW 4

**Vachss, Andrew H.**
See Vachss, Andrew (Henry)

**Vaculik, Ludvik** 1926- **CLC 7**
See also CA 53-56; CANR 72; CWW 2; DLB 232

**Vaihinger, Hans** 1852-1933 **TCLC 71**
See also CA 166; 116

**Valdez, Luis (Miguel)** 1940- **CLC 84; DC 10; HLC 2**
See also CA 101; CAD; CANR 32, 81; CD 5; DAM MULT; DFS 5; DLB 122; HW 1; LAIT 4

**Valenzuela, Luisa** 1938- **CLC 31, 104; HLCS 2; SSC 14**
See also CA 101; CANR 32, 65; CDWLB 3; CWW 2; DAM MULT; DLB 113; FW; HW 1, 2; LAW; RGSF 2; RGWL 3

**Valera y Alcala-Galiano, Juan** 1824-1905 **TCLC 10**
See also CA 106

**Valery, (Ambroise) Paul (Toussaint Jules)** 1871-1945 **PC 9; TCLC 4, 15**
See also CA 122; 104; DA3; DAM POET; DLB 258; EW 8; GFL 1789 to the Present; MTCW 1, 2; RGWL 2, 3; TWA

**Valle-Inclan, Ramon (Maria) del** 1866-1936 **HLC 2; TCLC 5**
See also CA 153; 106; CANR 80; DAM MULT; DLB 134; EW 8; HW 2; RGSF 2; RGWL 2, 3

**Vallejo, Antonio Buero**
See Buero Vallejo, Antonio

**Vallejo, Cesar (Abraham)** 1892-1938 **HLC 2; TCLC 3, 56**
See also CA 153; 105; DAM MULT; HW 1; LAW; RGWL 2, 3

**Valles, Jules** 1832-1885 **NCLC 71**
See also DLB 123; GFL 1789 to the Present

**Vallette, Marguerite Eymery** 1860-1953 **TCLC 67**
See also CA 182; DLB 123, 192

**Valle Y Pena, Ramon del**
See Valle-Inclan, Ramon (Maria) del

**Van Ash, Cay** 1918- **CLC 34**

**Vanbrugh, Sir John** 1664-1726 **LC 21**
See also BRW 2; DAM DRAM; DLB 80; IDTP; RGEL 2

**Van Campen, Karl**
See Campbell, John W(ood, Jr.)

**Vance, Gerald**
See Silverberg, Robert

**Vance, Jack CLC 35**
See Vance, John Holbrook
See also DLB 8; FANT; SCFW 2; SFW 4; SUFW 1, 2

**Vance, John Holbrook** 1916-
See Queen, Ellery; Vance, Jack
See also CA 29-32R; CANR 17, 65; CMW 4; MTCW 1

**Van Den Bogarde, Derek Jules Gaspard Ulric Niven** 1921-1999 **CLC 14**
See Bogarde, Dirk
See also CA 179; 77-80

**Vandenburgh, Jane CLC 59**
See also CA 168

**Vanderhaeghe, Guy** 1951- **CLC 41**
See also BPFB 3; CA 113; CANR 72

**van der Post, Laurens (Jan)** 1906-1996 **CLC 5**
See also AFW; CA 155; 5-8R; CANR 35; CN 7; DLB 204; RGEL 2

**van de Wetering, Janwillem** 1931- **CLC 47**
See also CA 49-52; CANR 4, 62, 90; CMW 4

**Van Dine, S. S. TCLC 23**
See Wright, Willard Huntington
See also MSW

**Van Doren, Carl (Clinton)** 1885-1950 **TCLC 18**
See also CA 168; 111

**Van Doren, Mark** 1894-1972 **CLC 6, 10**
See also CA 37-40R; 1-4R; CANR 3; DLB 45; MTCW 1, 2; RGAL 4

**Van Druten, John (William)** 1901-1957 **TCLC 2**
See also CA 161; 104; DLB 10; RGAL 4

**Van Duyn, Mona (Jane)** 1921- **CLC 3, 7, 63, 116**
See also CA 9-12R; CANR 7, 38, 60, 116; CP 7; CWP; DAM POET; DLB 5

**Van Dyne, Edith**
See Baum, L(yman) Frank

**van Itallie, Jean-Claude** 1936- **CLC 3**
See also CA 45-48; CAAS 2; CAD; CANR 1, 48; CD 5; DLB 7

**Van Loot, Cornelius Obenchain**
See Roberts, Kenneth (Lewis)

**van Ostaijen, Paul** 1896-1928 **TCLC 33**
See also CA 163

**Van Peebles, Melvin** 1932- **CLC 2, 20**
See also BW 2, 3; CA 85-88; CANR 27, 67, 82; DAM MULT

**van Schendel, Arthur(-Francois-Emile)** 1874-1946 **TCLC 56**

**Vansittart, Peter** 1920- **CLC 42**
See also CA 1-4R; CANR 3, 49, 90; CN 7; RHW

**Van Vechten, Carl** 1880-1964 **CLC 33; HR 3**
See also AMWS 2; CA 89-92; 183; DLB 4, 9, 51; RGAL 4

**van Vogt, A(lfred) E(lton)** 1912-2000 **CLC 1**
See also BPFB 3; BYA 13, 14; CA 190; 21-24R; CANR 28; DLB 8, 251; SATA 14; SATA-Obit 124; SCFW; SFW 4

**Vara, Madeleine**
See Jackson, Laura (Riding)

**Varda, Agnes** 1928- **CLC 16**
See also CA 122; 116

**Vargas Llosa, (Jorge) Mario (Pedro)** 1939- **CLC 3, 6, 9, 10, 15, 31, 42, 85; HLC 2**
See Llosa, (Jorge) Mario (Pedro) Vargas
See also BPFB 3; CA 73-76; CANR 18, 32, 42, 67, 116; CDWLB 3; DA; DA3; DAB; DAC; DAM MST, MULT, NOV; DLB 145; DNFS 2; HW 1, 2; LAIT 5; LAW; LAWS 1; MTCW 1, 2; RGWL 2; SSFS 14; TWA; WLIT 1

**Vasiliu, George**
See Bacovia, George

**Vasiliu, Gheorghe**
See Bacovia, George
See also CA 189; 123

**Vassa, Gustavus**
See Equiano, Olaudah

**Vassilikos, Vassilis** 1933- **CLC 4, 8**
See also CA 81-84; CANR 75

**Vaughan, Henry** 1621-1695 **LC 27**
See also BRW 2; DLB 131; PAB; RGEL 2

**Vaughn, Stephanie CLC 62**

**Vazov, Ivan (Minchov)** 1850-1921 **TCLC 25**
See also CA 167; 121; CDWLB 4; DLB 147

**Veblen, Thorstein B(unde)** 1857-1929 **TCLC 31**
See also AMWS 1; CA 165; 115; DLB 246

**Vega, Lope de** 1562-1635 **HLCS 2; LC 23**
See also EW 2; RGWL 2, 3

**Vendler, Helen (Hennessy)** 1933- **CLC 138**
See also CA 41-44R; CANR 25, 72; MTCW 1, 2

**Venison, Alfred**
See Pound, Ezra (Weston Loomis)

**Verdi, Marie de**
See Mencken, H(enry) L(ouis)

**Verdu, Matilde**
See Cela, Camilo Jose

**Verga, Giovanni (Carmelo)** 1840-1922 **SSC 21; TCLC 3**
See also CA 123; 104; CANR 101; EW 7; RGSF 2; RGWL 2, 3

**Vergil** 70B.C.-19B.C. **CMLC 9, 40; PC 12; WLCS**
See Virgil
See also AW 2; DA; DA3; DAB; DAC; DAM MST, POET; EFS 1

**Verhaeren, Emile (Adolphe Gustave)** 1855-1916 **TCLC 12**
See also CA 109; GFL 1789 to the Present

**Verlaine, Paul (Marie)** 1844-1896 **NCLC 2, 51; PC 2, 32**
See also DAM POET; DLB 217; EW 7; GFL 1789 to the Present; RGWL 2, 3; TWA

**Verne, Jules (Gabriel)** 1828-1905 **TCLC 6, 52**
See also AAYA 16; BYA 4; CA 131; 110; DA3; DLB 123; GFL 1789 to the Present; JRDA; LAIT 2; MAICYA 1, 2; RGWL 2, 3; SATA 21; SCFW; SFW 4; TWA; WCH

**Verus, Marcus Annius**
See Aurelius, Marcus

**Very, Jones** 1813-1880 **NCLC 9**
See also DLB 1, 243; RGAL 4

**Vesaas, Tarjei** 1897-1970 **CLC 48**
See also CA 29-32R; 190; EW 11; RGWL 3

**Vialis, Gaston**
See Simenon, Georges (Jacques Christian)

**Vian, Boris** 1920-1959 **TCLC 9**
See also CA 164; 106; CANR 111; DLB 72; GFL 1789 to the Present; MTCW 2; RGWL 2, 3

**Viaud, (Louis Marie) Julien** 1850-1923
See Loti, Pierre
See also CA 107

**Vicar, Henry**
See Felsen, Henry Gregor

**Vicker, Angus**
See Felsen, Henry Gregor

**Vidal, Gore** 1925- **CLC 2, 4, 6, 8, 10, 22, 33, 72, 142**
See Box, Edgar
See also AITN 1; AMWS 4; BEST 90:2; BPFB 3; CA 5-8R; CAD; CANR 13, 45, 65, 100; CD 5; CDALBS; CN 7; CPW; DA3; DAM NOV, POP; DFS 2; DLB 6, 152; INT CANR-13; MTCW 1, 2; RGAL 4; RHW; TUS

**Viereck, Peter (Robert Edwin)** 1916- **CLC 4; PC 27**
See also CA 1-4R; CANR 1, 47; CP 7; DLB 5; PFS 9, 14

**Vigny, Alfred (Victor) de** 1797-1863 **NCLC 7, 102; PC 26**
See also DAM POET; DLB 119, 192, 217; EW 5; GFL 1789 to the Present; RGWL 2, 3

**Vilakazi, Benedict Wallet** 1906-1947 **TCLC 37**
See also CA 168

**Villa, Jose Garcia** 1914-1997 **AAL; PC 22**
See also CA 25-28R; CANR 12; EXPP

**Villarreal, Jose Antonio** 1924- **HLC 2**
See also CA 133; CANR 93; DAM MULT; DLB 82; HW 1; LAIT 4; RGAL 4

**Villaurrutia, Xavier** 1903-1950 **TCLC 80**
See also CA 192; HW 1; LAW

**Villaverde, Cirilo** 1812-1894 **NCLC 121**
See also LAW

**Villehardouin, Geoffroi de** 1150(?)-1218(?) **CMLC 38**

**Villiers de l'Isle Adam, Jean Marie Mathias Philippe Auguste** 1838-1889 **NCLC 3; SSC 14**
See also DLB 123, 192; GFL 1789 to the Present; RGSF 2

**Villon, Francois** 1431-1463(?) **LC 62; PC 13**
See also DLB 208; EW 2; RGWL 2, 3; TWA

**Vine, Barbara CLC 50**
See Rendell, Ruth (Barbara)
See also BEST 90:4

**Vinge, Joan (Carol) D(ennison)** 1948- **CLC 30; SSC 24**
See also AAYA 32; BPFB 3; CA 93-96; CANR 72; SATA 36, 113; SFW 4; YAW

**Viola, Herman J(oseph)** 1938- **CLC 70**
See also CA 61-64; CANR 8, 23, 48, 91; SATA 126

**Violis, G.**
See Simenon, Georges (Jacques Christian)

**Viramontes, Helena Maria** 1954- **HLCS 2**
See also CA 159; DLB 122; HW 2

**Virgil**
See Vergil
See also CDWLB 1; DLB 211; LAIT 1; RGWL 2, 3; WP

**Visconti, Luchino** 1906-1976 **CLC 16**
See also CA 65-68; 81-84; CANR 39

**Vittorini, Elio** 1908-1966 **CLC 6, 9, 14**
See also CA 25-28R; 133; DLB 264; EW 12; RGWL 2, 3

**Walter, Villiam Christian**
　See Andersen, Hans Christian
**Walters, Anna L(ee) 1946- NNAL**
　See also CA 73-76
**Walther von der Vogelweide** c. 1170-1228
　**CMLC 56**
**Walton, Izaak 1593-1683 LC 72**
　See also BRW 2; CDBLB Before 1660;
　DLB 151, 213; RGEL 2
**Wambaugh, Joseph (Aloysius), Jr. 1937- CLC
3, 18**
　See also AITN 1; BEST 89:3; BPFB 3; CA
　33-36R; CANR 42, 65, 115; CMW 4;
　CPW 1; DA3; DAM NOV, POP; DLB 6;
　DLBY 1983; MSW; MTCW 1, 2
**Wang Wei 699(?)-761(?) PC 18**
　See also TWA
**Ward, Arthur Henry Sarsfield 1883-1959**
　See Rohmer, Sax
　See also CA 173; 108; CMW 4; HGG
**Ward, Douglas Turner 1930- CLC 19**
　See also BW 1; CA 81-84; CAD; CANR
　27; CD 5; DLB 7, 38
**Ward, E. D.**
　See Lucas, E(dward) V(errall)
**Ward, Mrs. Humphry 1851-1920**
　See Ward, Mary Augusta
　See also RGEL 2
**Ward, Mary Augusta 1851-1920 TCLC 55**
　See Ward, Mrs. Humphry
　See also DLB 18
**Ward, Peter**
　See Faust, Frederick (Schiller)
**Warhol, Andy 1928(?)-1987 CLC 20**
　See also AAYA 12; BEST 89:4; CA 121;
　89-92; CANR 34
**Warner, Francis (Robert le Plastrier) 1937-
CLC 14**
　See also CA 53-56; CANR 11
**Warner, Marina 1946- CLC 59**
　See also CA 65-68; CANR 21, 55; CN 7;
　DLB 194
**Warner, Rex (Ernest) 1905-1986 CLC 45**
　See also CA 119; 89-92; DLB 15; RGEL 2;
　RHW
**Warner, Susan (Bogert) 1819-1885 NCLC 31**
　See also DLB 3, 42, 239, 250, 254
**Warner, Sylvia (Constance) Ashton**
　See Ashton-Warner, Sylvia (Constance)
**Warner, Sylvia Townsend 1893-1978 CLC 7,
19; SSC 23; TCLC 131**
　See also BRWS 7; CA 77-80; 61-64; CANR
　16, 60, 104; DLB 34, 139; FANT; FW;
　MTCW 1, 2; RGEL 2; RGSF 2; RHW
**Warren, Mercy Otis 1728-1814 NCLC 13**
　See also DLB 31, 200; RGAL 4; TUS
**Warren, Robert Penn 1905-1989 CLC 1, 4,
6, 8, 10, 13, 18, 39, 53, 59; PC 37; SSC
4, 58; WLC**
　See also AITN 1; AMW; BPFB 3; BYA 1;
　CA 129; 13-16R; CANR 10, 47; CDALB
　1968-1988; DA; DA3; DAB; DAC; DAM
　MST, NOV, POET; DLB 2, 48, 152;
　DLBY 1980, 1989; INT CANR-10;
　MTCW 1, 2; NFS 13; RGAL 4; RGSF 2;
　RHW; SATA 46; SATA-Obit 63; SSFS 8;
　TUS
**Warrigal, Jack**
　See Furphy, Joseph
**Warshofsky, Isaac**
　See Singer, Isaac Bashevis
**Warton, Joseph 1722-1800 NCLC 118**
　See also DLB 104, 109; RGEL 2
**Warton, Thomas 1728-1790 LC 15, 82**
　See also DAM POET; DLB 104, 109;
　RGEL 2

**Waruk, Kona**
　See Harris, (Theodore) Wilson
**Warung, Price TCLC 45**
　See Astley, William
　See also DLB 230; RGEL 2
**Warwick, Jarvis**
　See Garner, Hugh
　See also CCA 1
**Washington, Alex**
　See Harris, Mark
**Washington, Booker T(aliaferro) 1856-1915
BLC 3; TCLC 10**
　See also BW 1; CA 125; 114; DA3; DAM
　MULT; LAIT 2; RGAL 4; SATA 28
**Washington, George 1732-1799 LC 25**
　See also DLB 31
**Wassermann, (Karl) Jakob 1873-1934 TCLC
6**
　See also CA 163; 104; DLB 66
**Wasserstein, Wendy 1950- CLC 32, 59, 90;
DC 4**
　See also CA 129; 121; CABS 3; CAD;
　CANR 53, 75; CD 5; CWD; DA3; DAM
　DRAM; DFS 17; DLB 228; FW; INT CA-
　129; MTCW 2; SATA 94
**Waterhouse, Keith (Spencer) 1929- CLC 47**
　See also CA 5-8R; CANR 38, 67, 109;
　CBD; CN 7; DLB 13, 15; MTCW 1, 2
**Waters, Frank (Joseph) 1902-1995 CLC 88**
　See also CA 149; 5-8R; CAAS 13; CANR
　3, 18, 63; DLB 212; DLBY 1986; RGAL
　4; TCWW 2
**Waters, Mary C. CLC 70**
**Waters, Roger 1944- CLC 35**
**Watkins, Frances Ellen**
　See Harper, Frances Ellen Watkins
**Watkins, Gerrold**
　See Malzberg, Barry N(athaniel)
**Watkins, Gloria Jean 1952(?)-**
　See hooks, bell
　See also BW 2; CA 143; CANR 87; MTCW
　2; SATA 115
**Watkins, Paul 1964- CLC 55**
　See also CA 132; CANR 62, 98
**Watkins, Vernon Phillips 1906-1967 CLC 43**
　See also CA 25-28R; 9-10; CAP 1; DLB
　20; RGEL 2
**Watson, Irving S.**
　See Mencken, H(enry) L(ouis)
**Watson, John H.**
　See Farmer, Philip Jose
**Watson, Richard F.**
　See Silverberg, Robert
**Waugh, Auberon (Alexander) 1939-2001
CLC 7**
　See also CA 192; 45-48; CANR 6, 22, 92;
　DLB 14, 194
**Waugh, Evelyn (Arthur St. John) 1903-1966
CLC 1, 3, 8, 13, 19, 27, 44, 107; SSC
41; WLC**
　See also BPFB 3; BRW 7; CA 25-28R; 85-
　88; CANR 22; CDBLB 1914-1945; DA;
　DA3; DAB; DAC; DAM MST, NOV,
　POP; DLB 15, 162, 195; MTCW 1, 2;
　NFS 17; RGEL 2; RGSF 2; TEA; WLIT
　4
**Waugh, Harriet 1944- CLC 6**
　See also CA 85-88; CANR 22
**Ways, C. R.**
　See Blount, Roy (Alton), Jr.
**Waystaff, Simon**
　See Swift, Jonathan
**Webb, Beatrice (Martha Potter) 1858-1943
TCLC 22**
　See also CA 162; 117; DLB 190; FW
**Webb, Charles (Richard) 1939- CLC 7**
　See also CA 25-28R; CANR 114
**Webb, James H(enry), Jr. 1946- CLC 22**
　See also CA 81-84

**Webb, Mary Gladys (Meredith) 1881-1927
TCLC 24**
　See also CA 123; 182; DLB 34; FW
**Webb, Mrs. Sidney**
　See Webb, Beatrice (Martha Potter)
**Webb, Phyllis 1927- CLC 18**
　See also CA 104; CANR 23; CCA 1; CP 7;
　CWP; DLB 53
**Webb, Sidney (James) 1859-1947 TCLC 22**
　See also CA 163; 117; DLB 190
**Webber, Andrew Lloyd CLC 21**
　See Lloyd Webber, Andrew
　See also DFS 7
**Weber, Lenora Mattingly 1895-1971 CLC 12**
　See also CA 29-32R; 19-20; CAP 1; SATA
　2; SATA-Obit 26
**Weber, Max 1864-1920 TCLC 69**
　See also CA 189; 109
**Webster, John 1580(?)-1634(?) DC 2; LC 33,
84; WLC**
　See also BRW 2; CDBLB Before 1660; DA;
　DAB; DAC; DAM DRAM, MST; DFS
　17; DLB 58; IDTP; RGEL 2; WLIT 3
**Webster, Noah 1758-1843 NCLC 30**
　See also DLB 1, 37, 42, 43, 73, 243
**Wedekind, (Benjamin) Frank(lin) 1864-1918
TCLC 7**
　See also CA 153; 104; CDWLB 2; DAM
　DRAM; DLB 118; EW 8; LMFS 2;
　RGWL 2, 3
**Wehr, Demaris CLC 65**
**Weidman, Jerome 1913-1998 CLC 7**
　See also AITN 2; CA 171; 1-4R; CAD;
　CANR 1; DLB 28
**Weil, Simone (Adolphine) 1909-1943 TCLC
23**
　See also CA 159; 117; EW 12; FW; GFL
　1789 to the Present; MTCW 2
**Weininger, Otto 1880-1903 TCLC 84**
**Weinstein, Nathan**
　See West, Nathanael
**Weinstein, Nathan von Wallenstein**
　See West, Nathanael
**Weir, Peter (Lindsay) 1944- CLC 20**
　See also CA 123; 113
**Weiss, Peter (Ulrich) 1916-1982 CLC 3, 15,
51**
　See also CA 106; 45-48; CANR 3; DAM
　DRAM; DFS 3; DLB 69, 124; RGWL 2,
　3
**Weiss, Theodore (Russell) 1916- CLC 3, 8,
14**
　See also CA 9-12R; CAAE 189; CAAS 2;
　CANR 46, 94; CP 7; DLB 5
**Welch, (Maurice) Denton 1915-1948 TCLC
22**
　See also BRWS 8; CA 148; 121; RGEL 2
**Welch, James 1940- CLC 6, 14, 52; NNAL**
　See also CA 85-88; CANR 42, 66, 107; CN
　7; CP 7; CPW; DAM MULT, POP; DLB
　175, 256; RGAL 4; TCWW 2
**Weldon, Fay 1931- CLC 6, 9, 11, 19, 36, 59,
122**
　See also BRWS 4; CA 21-24R; CANR 16,
　46, 63, 97; CDBLB 1960 to Present; CN
　7; CPW; DAM POP; DLB 14, 194; FW;
　HGG; INT CANR-16; MTCW 1, 2; RGEL
　2; RGSF 2
**Wellek, Rene 1903-1995 CLC 28**
　See also CA 150; 5-8R; CAAS 7; CANR 8;
　DLB 63; INT CANR-8
**Weller, Michael 1942- CLC 10, 53**
　See also CA 85-88; CAD; CD 5
**Weller, Paul 1958- CLC 26**
**Wellershoff, Dieter 1925- CLC 46**
　See also CA 89-92; CANR 16, 37
**Welles, (George) Orson 1915-1985 CLC 20,
80**
　See also AAYA 40; CA 117; 93-96

**Wellman, John McDowell** 1945-
See Wellman, Mac
See also CA 166; CD 5
**Wellman, Mac** CLC 65
See Wellman, John McDowell; Wellman, John McDowell
See also CAD; RGAL 4
**Wellman, Manly Wade** 1903-1986 CLC 49
See also CA 118; 1-4R; CANR 6, 16, 44; FANT; SATA 6; SATA-Obit 47; SFW 4; SUFW
**Wells, Carolyn** 1869(?)-1942 TCLC 35
See also CA 185; 113; CMW 4; DLB 11
**Wells, H(erbert) G(eorge)** 1866-1946 SSC 6; TCLC 6, 12, 19, 133; WLC
See also AAYA 18; BPFB 3; BRW 6; CA 121; 110; CDBLB 1914-1945; CLR 64; DA; DA3; DAB; DAC; DAM MST, NOV; DLB 34, 70, 156, 178; EXPS; HGG; LAIT 3; MTCW 1, 2; NFS 17; RGEL 2; RGSF 2; SATA 20; SCFW; SFW 4; SSFS 3; SUFW; TEA; WCH; WLIT 4; YAW
**Wells, Rosemary** 1943- CLC 12
See also AAYA 13; BYA 7, 8; CA 85-88; CANR 48; CLR 16, 69; CWRI 5; MAICYA 1, 2; SAAS 1; SATA 18, 69, 114; YAW
**Wells-Barnett, Ida B(ell)** 1862-1931 TCLC 125
See also CA 182; DLB 23, 221
**Welsh, Irvine** 1958- CLC 144
See also CA 173; DLB 271
**Welty, Eudora (Alice)** 1909-2001 CLC 1, 2, 5, 14, 22, 33, 105; SSC 1, 27, 51; WLC
See also AMW; AMWR 1; BPFB 3; CA 199; 9-12R; CABS 1; CANR 32, 65; CDALB 1941-1968; CN 7; CSW; DA; DA3; DAB; DAC; DAM MST, NOV; DLB 2, 102, 143; DLBD 12; DLBY 1987, 2001; EXPS; HGG; LAIT 3; MAWW; MTCW 1, 2; NFS 13, 15; RGAL 4; RGSF 2; RHW; SSFS 2, 10; TUS
**Wen I-to** 1899-1946 TCLC 28
**Wentworth, Robert**
See Hamilton, Edmond
**Werfel, Franz (Viktor)** 1890-1945 TCLC 8
See also CA 161; 104; DLB 81, 124; RGWL 2, 3
**Wergeland, Henrik Arnold** 1808-1845 NCLC 5
**Wersba, Barbara** 1932- CLC 30
See also AAYA 2, 30; BYA 6, 12, 13; CA 29-32R, 182; CAAE 182; CANR 16, 38; CLR 3, 78; DLB 52; JRDA; MAICYA 1, 2; SAAS 2; SATA 1, 58; SATA-Essay 103; WYA; YAW
**Wertmueller, Lina** 1928- CLC 16
See also CA 97-100; CANR 39, 78
**Wescott, Glenway** 1901-1987 CLC 13; SSC 35
See also CA 121; 13-16R; CANR 23, 70; DLB 4, 9, 102; RGAL 4
**Wesker, Arnold** 1932- CLC 3, 5, 42
See also CA 1-4R; CAAS 7; CANR 1, 33; CBD; CD 5; CDBLB 1960 to Present; DAB; DAM DRAM; DLB 13; MTCW 1; RGEL 2; TEA
**Wesley, John** 1703-1791 LC 88
See also DLB 104
**Wesley, Richard (Errol)** 1945- CLC 7
See also BW 1; CA 57-60; CAD; CANR 27; CD 5; DLB 38
**Wessel, Johan Herman** 1742-1785 LC 7
**West, Anthony (Panther)** 1914-1987 CLC 50
See also CA 124; 45-48; CANR 3, 19; DLB 15
**West, C. P.**
See Wodehouse, P(elham) G(renville)

**West, Cornel (Ronald)** 1953- BLCS; CLC 134
See also CA 144; CANR 91; DLB 246
**West, Delno C(loyde), Jr.** 1936- CLC 70
See also CA 57-60
**West, Dorothy** 1907-1998 HR 3; TCLC 108
See also BW 2; CA 169; 143; DLB 76
**West, (Mary) Jessamyn** 1902-1984 CLC 7, 17
See also CA 112; 9-12R; CANR 27; DLB 6; DLBY 1984; MTCW 1, 2; RGAL 4; RHW; SATA-Obit 37; TCWW 2; TUS; YAW
**West, Morris L(anglo)** 1916-1999 CLC 6, 33
See also BPFB 3; CA 187; 5-8R; CANR 24, 49, 64; CN 7; CPW; MTCW 1, 2
**West, Nathanael** 1903-1940 SSC 16; TCLC 1, 14, 44
See also AMW; AMWR 2; BPFB 3; CA 125; 104; CDALB 1929-1941; DA3; DLB 4, 9, 28; MTCW 1, 2; NFS 16; RGAL 4; TUS
**West, Owen**
See Koontz, Dean R(ay)
**West, Paul** 1930- CLC 7, 14, 96
See also CA 13-16R; CAAS 7; CANR 22, 53, 76, 89; CN 7; DLB 14; INT CANR-22; MTCW 2
**West, Rebecca** 1892-1983 CLC 7, 9, 31, 50
See also BPFB 3; BRWS 3; CA 109; 5-8R; CANR 19; DLB 36; DLBY 1983; FW; MTCW 1, 2; NCFS 4; RGEL 2; TEA
**Westall, Robert (Atkinson)** 1929-1993 CLC 17
See also AAYA 12; BYA 2, 6, 7, 8, 9; CA 141; 69-72; CANR 18, 68; CLR 13; FANT; JRDA; MAICYA 1, 2; MAICYAS 1; SAAS 2; SATA 23, 69; SATA-Obit 75; WYA; YAW
**Westermarck, Edward** 1862-1939 TCLC 87
**Westlake, Donald E(dwin)** 1933- CLC 7, 33
See also BPFB 3; CA 17-20R; CAAS 13; CANR 16, 44, 65, 94; CMW 4; CPW; DAM POP; INT CANR-16; MSW; MTCW 2
**Westmacott, Mary**
See Christie, Agatha (Mary Clarissa)
**Weston, Allen**
See Norton, Andre
**Wetcheek, J. L.**
See Feuchtwanger, Lion
**Wetering, Janwillem van de**
See van de Wetering, Janwillem
**Wetherald, Agnes Ethelwyn** 1857-1940 TCLC 81
See also CA 202; DLB 99
**Wetherell, Elizabeth**
See Warner, Susan (Bogert)
**Whale, James** 1889-1957 TCLC 63
**Whalen, Philip** 1923-2002 CLC 6, 29
See also BG 3; CA 9-12R; CANR 5, 39; CP 7; DLB 16; WP
**Wharton, Edith (Newbold Jones)** 1862-1937 SSC 6; TCLC 3, 9, 27, 53, 129; WLC
See also AAYA 25; AMW; AMWR 1; BPFB 3; CA 132; 104; CDALB 1865-1917; DA; DA3; DAB; DAC; DAM MST, NOV; DLB 4, 9, 12, 78, 189; DLBD 13; EXPS; HGG; LAIT 2, 3; MAWW; MTCW 1, 2; NFS 5, 11, 15; RGAL 4; RGSF 2; RHW; SSFS 6, 7; SUFW; TUS
**Wharton, James**
See Mencken, H(enry) L(ouis)
**Wharton, William (a pseudonym)** CLC 18, 37
See also CA 93-96; DLBY 1980; INT 93-96
**Wheatley (Peters), Phillis** 1753(?)-1784 BLC 3; LC 3, 50; PC 3; WLC
See also AFAW 1, 2; CDALB 1640-1865;

DA; DA3; DAC; DAM MST, MULT, POET; DLB 31, 50; EXPP; PFS 13; RGAL 4
**Wheelock, John Hall** 1886-1978 CLC 14
See also CA 77-80; 13-16R; CANR 14; DLB 45
**White, Babington**
See Braddon, Mary Elizabeth
**White, E(lwyn) B(rooks)** 1899-1985 CLC 10, 34, 39
See also AITN 2; AMWS 1; CA 116; 13-16R; CANR 16, 37; CDALBS; CLR 1, 21; CPW; DA3; DAM POP; DLB 11, 22; FANT; MAICYA 1, 2; MTCW 1, 2; RGAL 4; SATA 2, 29, 100; SATA-Obit 44; TUS
**White, Edmund (Valentine III)** 1940- CLC 27, 110
See also AAYA 7; CA 45-48; CANR 3, 19, 36, 62, 107; CN 7; DA3; DAM POP; DLB 227; MTCW 1, 2
**White, Hayden V.** 1928- CLC 148
See also CA 128; DLB 246
**White, Patrick (Victor Martindale)** 1912-1990 CLC 3, 4, 5, 7, 9, 18, 65, 69; SSC 39
See also BRWS 1; CA 132; 81-84; CANR 43; DLB 260; MTCW 1; RGEL 2; RGSF 2; RHW; TWA
**White, Phyllis Dorothy James** 1920-
See James, P. D.
See also CA 21-24R; CANR 17, 43, 65, 112; CMW 4; CN 7; CPW; DA3; DAM POP; MTCW 1, 2; TEA
**White, T(erence) H(anbury)** 1906-1964 CLC 30
See also AAYA 22; BPFB 3; BYA 4, 5; CA 73-76; CANR 37; DLB 160; FANT; JRDA; LAIT 1; MAICYA 1, 2; RGEL 2; SATA 12; SUFW 1; YAW
**White, Terence de Vere** 1912-1994 CLC 49
See also CA 145; 49-52; CANR 3
**White, Walter**
See White, Walter F(rancis)
**White, Walter F(rancis)** 1893-1955 BLC 3; HR 3; TCLC 15
See also BW 1; CA 124; 115; DAM MULT; DLB 51
**White, William Hale** 1831-1913
See Rutherford, Mark
See also CA 189; 121
**Whitehead, Alfred North** 1861-1947 TCLC 97
See also CA 165; 117; DLB 100, 262
**Whitehead, E(dward) A(nthony)** 1933- CLC 5
See also CA 65-68; CANR 58; CBD; CD 5
**Whitehead, Ted**
See Whitehead, E(dward) A(nthony)
**Whiteman, Roberta J. Hill** 1947- NNAL
See also CA 146
**Whitemore, Hugh (John)** 1936- CLC 37
See also CA 132; CANR 77; CBD; CD 5; INT CA-132
**Whitman, Sarah Helen (Power)** 1803-1878 NCLC 19
See also DLB 1, 243
**Whitman, Walt(er)** 1819-1892 NCLC 4, 31, 81; PC 3; WLC
See also AAYA 42; AMW; AMWR 1; CDALB 1640-1865; DA; DA3; DAB; DAC; DAM MST, POET; DLB 3, 64, 224, 250; EXPP; LAIT 2; PAB; PFS 2, 3, 13; RGAL 4; SATA 20; TUS; WP; WYAS 1
**Whitney, Phyllis A(yame)** 1903- CLC 42
See also AAYA 36; AITN 2; BEST 90:3; CA 1-4R; CANR 3, 25, 38, 60; CLR 59;

**Wilson, Ethel Davis (Bryant)** 1888(?)-1980
  **CLC 13**
    See also CA 102; DAC; DAM POET; DLB
    68; MTCW 1; RGEL 2
**Wilson, Harriet**
    See Wilson, Harriet E. Adams
    See also DLB 239
**Wilson, Harriet E.**
    See Wilson, Harriet E. Adams
    See also DLB 243
**Wilson, Harriet E. Adams** 1827(?)-1863(?)
  **BLC 3; NCLC 78**
    See Wilson, Harriet; Wilson, Harriet E.
    See also DAM MULT; DLB 50
**Wilson, John** 1785-1854 **NCLC 5**
**Wilson, John (Anthony) Burgess** 1917-1993
    See Burgess, Anthony
    See also CA 143; 1-4R; CANR 2, 46; DA3;
    DAC; DAM NOV; MTCW 1, 2; NFS 15;
    TEA
**Wilson, Lanford** 1937- **CLC 7, 14, 36; DC 19**
    See also CA 17-20R; CABS 3; CAD; CANR
    45, 96; CD 5; DAM DRAM; DFS 4, 9,
    12, 16; DLB 7; TUS
**Wilson, Robert M.** 1944- **CLC 7, 9**
    See also CA 49-52; CAD; CANR 2, 41; CD
    5; MTCW 1
**Wilson, Robert McLiam** 1964- **CLC 59**
    See also CA 132; DLB 267
**Wilson, Sloan** 1920- **CLC 32**
    See also CA 1-4R; CANR 1, 44; CN 7
**Wilson, Snoo** 1948- **CLC 33**
    See also CA 69-72; CBD; CD 5
**Wilson, William S(mith)** 1932- **CLC 49**
    See also CA 81-84
**Wilson, (Thomas) Woodrow** 1856-1924
  **TCLC 79**
    See also CA 166; DLB 47
**Wilson and Warnke eds. CLC 65**
**Winchilsea, Anne (Kingsmill) Finch**
    1661-1720
    See Finch, Anne
    See also RGEL 2
**Windham, Basil**
    See Wodehouse, P(elham) G(renville)
**Wingrove, David (John)** 1954- **CLC 68**
    See also CA 133; SFW 4
**Winnemucca, Sarah** 1844-1891 **NCLC 79; NNAL**
    See also DAM MULT; DLB 175; RGAL 4
**Winstanley, Gerrard** 1609-1676 **LC 52**
**Wintergreen, Jane**
    See Duncan, Sara Jeannette
**Winters, Janet Lewis CLC 41**
    See Lewis, Janet
    See also DLBY 1987
**Winters, (Arthur) Yvor** 1900-1968 **CLC 4, 8, 32**
    See also AMWS 2; CA 25-28R; 11-12; CAP
    1; DLB 48; MTCW 1; RGAL 4
**Winterson, Jeanette** 1959- **CLC 64, 158**
    See also BRWS 4; CA 136; CANR 58, 116;
    CN 7; CPW; DA3; DAM POP; DLB 207,
    261; FANT; FW; GLL 1; MTCW 2; RHW
**Winthrop, John** 1588-1649 **LC 31**
    See also DLB 24, 30
**Wirth, Louis** 1897-1952 **TCLC 92**
**Wiseman, Frederick** 1930- **CLC 20**
    See also CA 159
**Wister, Owen** 1860-1938 **TCLC 21**
    See also BPFB 3; CA 162; 108; DLB 9, 78,
    186; RGAL 4; SATA 62; TCWW 2
**Witkacy**
    See Witkiewicz, Stanislaw Ignacy

**Witkiewicz, Stanislaw Ignacy** 1885-1939
  **TCLC 8**
    See also CA 162; 105; CDWLB 4; DLB
    215; EW 10; RGWL 2, 3; SFW 4
**Wittgenstein, Ludwig (Josef Johann)**
    1889-1951 **TCLC 59**
    See also CA 164; 113; DLB 262; MTCW 2
**Wittig, Monique** 1935(?)- **CLC 22**
    See also CA 135; 116; CWW 2; DLB 83;
    FW; GLL 1
**Wittlin, Jozef** 1896-1976 **CLC 25**
    See also CA 65-68; 49-52; CANR 3
**Wodehouse, P(elham) G(renville)** 1881-1975
  **CLC 1, 2, 5, 10, 22; SSC 2; TCLC 108**
    See also AITN 2; BRWS 3; CA 57-60; 45-
    48; CANR 3, 33; CDBLB 1914-1945;
    CPW 1; DA3; DAB; DAC; DAM NOV;
    DLB 34, 162; MTCW 1, 2; RGEL 2;
    RGSF 2; SATA 22; SSFS 10
**Woiwode, L.**
    See Woiwode, Larry (Alfred)
**Woiwode, Larry (Alfred)** 1941- **CLC 6, 10**
    See also CA 73-76; CANR 16, 94; CN 7;
    DLB 6; INT CANR-16
**Wojciechowska, Maia (Teresa)** 1927-2002
  **CLC 26**
    See also AAYA 8, 46; BYA 3; CA 9-12R,
    183; CAAE 183; CANR 4, 41; CLR 1;
    JRDA; MAICYA 1, 2; SAAS 1; SATA 1,
    28, 83; SATA-Essay 104; SATA-Obit 134;
    YAW
**Wojtyla, Karol**
    See John Paul II, Pope
**Wolf, Christa** 1929- **CLC 14, 29, 58, 150**
    See also CA 85-88; CANR 45; CDWLB 2;
    CWW 2; DLB 75; FW; MTCW 1; RGWL
    2, 3; SSFS 14
**Wolf, Naomi** 1962- **CLC 157**
    See also CA 141; CANR 110; FW
**Wolfe, Gene (Rodman)** 1931- **CLC 25**
    See also AAYA 35; CA 57-60; CAAS 9;
    CANR 6, 32, 60; CPW; DAM POP; DLB
    8; FANT; MTCW 2; SATA 118; SCFW 2;
    SFW 4; SUFW 2
**Wolfe, George C.** 1954- **BLCS; CLC 49**
    See also CA 149; CAD; CD 5
**Wolfe, Thomas (Clayton)** 1900-1938 **SSC 33;
  TCLC 4, 13, 29, 61; WLC**
    See also AMW; BPFB 3; CA 132; 104;
    CANR 102; CDALB 1929-1941; DA;
    DA3; DAB; DAC; DAM MST, NOV;
    DLB 9, 102, 229; DLBD 2, 16; DLBY
    1985, 1997; MTCW 1, 2; RGAL 4; TUS
**Wolfe, Thomas Kennerly, Jr.** 1930- **CLC 147**
    See Wolfe, Tom
    See also CA 13-16R; CANR 9, 33, 70, 104;
    DA3; DAM POP; DLB 185; INT
    CANR-9; MTCW 1, 2; TUS
**Wolfe, Tom CLC 1, 2, 9, 15, 35, 51**
    See Wolfe, Thomas Kennerly, Jr.
    See also AAYA 8; AITN 2; AMWS 3; BEST
    89:1; BPFB 3; CN 7; CPW; CSW; DLB
    152; LAIT 5; RGAL 4
**Wolff, Geoffrey (Ansell)** 1937- **CLC 41**
    See also CA 29-32R; CANR 29, 43, 78
**Wolff, Sonia**
    See Levitin, Sonia (Wolff)
**Wolff, Tobias (Jonathan Ansell)** 1945- **CLC 39, 64, 172**
    See also AAYA 16; AMWS 7; BEST 90:2;
    BYA 12; CA 117; 114; CAAS 22; CANR
    54, 76, 96; CN 7; CSW; DA3; DLB 130;
    INT CA-117; MTCW 2; RGAL 4; RGSF
    2; SSFS 4, 11

**Wolfram von Eschenbach** c. 1170-c. 1220
  **CMLC 5**
    See Eschenbach, Wolfram von
    See also CDWLB 2; DLB 138; EW 1;
    RGWL 2
**Wolitzer, Hilma** 1930- **CLC 17**
    See also CA 65-68; CANR 18, 40; INT
    CANR-18; SATA 31; YAW
**Wollstonecraft, Mary** 1759-1797 **LC 5, 50**
    See also BRWS 3; CDBLB 1789-1832;
    DLB 39, 104, 158, 252; FW; LAIT 1;
    RGEL 2; TEA; WLIT 3
**Wonder, Stevie CLC 12**
    See Morris, Steveland Judkins
**Wong, Jade Snow** 1922- **CLC 17**
    See also CA 109; CANR 91; SATA 112
**Woodberry, George Edward** 1855-1930
  **TCLC 73**
    See also CA 165; DLB 71, 103
**Woodcott, Keith**
    See Brunner, John (Kilian Houston)
**Woodruff, Robert W.**
    See Mencken, H(enry) L(ouis)
**Woolf, (Adeline) Virginia** 1882-1941 **SSC 7;
  TCLC 1, 5, 20, 43, 56, 101, 123, 128;
  WLC**
    See also AAYA 44; BPFB 3; BRW 7;
    BRWR 1; CA 130; 104; CANR 64; CD-
    BLB 1914-1945; DA; DA3; DAB; DAC;
    DAM MST, NOV; DLB 36, 100, 162;
    DLBD 10; EXPS; FW; LAIT 3; LMFS 2;
    MTCW 1, 2; NCFS 2; NFS 8, 12; RGEL
    2; RGSF 2; SSFS 4, 12; TEA; WLIT 4
**Woollcott, Alexander (Humphreys)**
    1887-1943 **TCLC 5**
    See also CA 161; 105; DLB 29
**Woolrich, Cornell CLC 77**
    See Hopley-Woolrich, Cornell George
    See also MSW
**Woolson, Constance Fenimore** 1840-1894
  **NCLC 82**
    See also DLB 12, 74, 189, 221; RGAL 4
**Wordsworth, Dorothy** 1771-1855 **NCLC 25**
    See also DLB 107
**Wordsworth, William** 1770-1850 **NCLC 12,
  38, 111; PC 4; WLC**
    See also BRW 4; BRWC 1; CDBLB 1789-
    1832; DA; DA3; DAB; DAC; DAM MST,
    POET; DLB 93, 107; EXPP; PAB; PFS 2;
    RGEL 2; TEA; WLIT 3; WP
**Wotton, Sir Henry** 1568-1639 **LC 68**
    See also DLB 121; RGEL 2
**Wouk, Herman** 1915- **CLC 1, 9, 38**
    See also BPFB 2, 3; CA 5-8R; CANR 6,
    33, 67; CDALBS; CN 7; CPW; DA3;
    DAM NOV, POP; DLBY 1982; INT
    CANR-6; LAIT 4; MTCW 1, 2; NFS 7;
    TUS
**Wright, Charles (Penzel, Jr.)** 1935- **CLC 6,
  13, 28, 119, 146**
    See also AMWS 5; CA 29-32R; CAAS 7;
    CANR 23, 36, 62, 88; CP 7; DLB 165;
    DLBY 1982; MTCW 1, 2; PFS 10
**Wright, Charles Stevenson** 1932- **BLC 3;
  CLC 49**
    See also BW 1; CA 9-12R; CANR 26; CN
    7; DAM MULT, POET; DLB 33
**Wright, Frances** 1795-1852 **NCLC 74**
    See also DLB 73
**Wright, Frank Lloyd** 1867-1959 **TCLC 95**
    See also AAYA 33; CA 174
**Wright, Jack R.**
    See Harris, Mark

**Zhukovsky, Vasily (Andreevich)** 1783-1852
 **NCLC 35**
  See Zhukovsky, Vasilii Andreevich
**Ziegenhagen, Eric CLC 55**
**Zimmer, Jill Schary**
  See Robinson, Jill
**Zimmerman, Robert**
  See Dylan, Bob
**Zindel, Paul** 1936-2003 **CLC 6, 26; DC 5**
  See also AAYA 2, 37; BYA 2, 3, 8, 11, 14;
  CA 73-76; CAD; CANR 31, 65, 108; CD
  5; CDALBS; CLR 3, 45, 85; DA; DA3;
  DAB; DAC; DAM DRAM, MST, NOV;
  DFS 12; DLB 7, 52; JRDA; LAIT 5;
  MAICYA 1, 2; MTCW 1, 2; NFS 14;
  SATA 16, 58, 102; WYA; YAW
**Zinov'Ev, A. A.**
  See Zinoviev, Alexander (Aleksandrovich)

**Zinoviev, Alexander (Aleksandrovich)** 1922-
 **CLC 19**
  See also CA 133; 116; CAAS 10
**Zoilus**
  See Lovecraft, H(oward) P(hillips)
**Zola, Emile (Edouard Charles Antoine)**
  1840-1902 **TCLC 1, 6, 21, 41; WLC**
  See also CA 138; 104; DA; DA3; DAB;
  DAC; DAM MST, NOV; DLB 123; EW
  7; GFL 1789 to the Present; IDTP; LMFS
  2; RGWL 2; TWA
**Zoline, Pamela** 1941- **CLC 62**
  See also CA 161; SFW 4
**Zoroaster** 628(?)B.C.-551(?)B.C. **CMLC 40**
**Zorrilla y Moral, Jose** 1817-1893 **NCLC 6**
**Zoshchenko, Mikhail (Mikhailovich)**
  1895-1958 **SSC 15; TCLC 15**
  See also CA 160; 115; RGSF 2; RGWL 3

**Zuckmayer, Carl** 1896-1977 **CLC 18**
  See also CA 69-72; DLB 56, 124; RGWL
  2, 3
**Zuk, Georges**
  See Skelton, Robin
  See also CCA 1
**Zukofsky, Louis** 1904-1978 **CLC 1, 2, 4, 7,
  11, 18; PC 11**
  See also AMWS 3; CA 77-80; 9-12R;
  CANR 39; DAM POET; DLB 5, 165;
  MTCW 1; RGAL 4
**Zweig, Paul** 1935-1984 **CLC 34, 42**
  See also CA 113; 85-88
**Zweig, Stefan** 1881-1942 **TCLC 17**
  See also CA 170; 112; DLB 81, 118
**Zwingli, Huldreich** 1484-1531 **LC 37**
  See also DLB 179

# *PC* Cumulative Nationality Index

Blok, Alexander (Alexandrovich) **21**
Brodsky, Joseph **9**
Lermontov, Mikhail Yuryevich
Mandelstam, Osip (Emilievich) **14**
Pasternak, Boris (Leonidovich) **6**
Pushkin, Alexander (Sergeyevich) **10**
Tsvetaeva (Efron), Marina (Ivanovna) **14**
Yevtushenko, Yevgeny (Alexandrovich) **40**

## SALVADORAN

Alegria, Claribel **26**
Dalton, Roque **36**

## SCOTTISH

Burns, Robert **6**
Scott, Walter **13**

## SENEGALESE

Senghor, Léopold Sédar **25**

## SINGAPORAN

Thumboo, Edwin Nadason **30**

## SOUTH AFRICAN

Brutus, Dennis **24**

## SPANISH

Castro, Rosalia de **41**
Fuertes, Gloria **27**
García Lorca, Federico **3**
Guillén, Jorge **35**

Jiménez (Mantecón), Juan Ramón **7**

## ST. LUCIAN

Walcott, Derek **46**

## SWEDISH

Ekeloef, (Bengt) Gunnar **23**

## SYRIAN

Gibran, Kahlil **9**

## WELSH

Abse, Dannie **41**
Thomas, Dylan (Marlais) **2**

Nationality Index

Title Index

ISBN 0-7876-6344-1

90000

9 780787 663445

145 -

145 -